THE CAMBRIDGE HISTORY OF
THE SECOND WORLD WAR

The conflict that ended in 1945 is often described as a 'total war', unprecedented in both scale and character. Volume III of *The Cambridge History of the Second World War* adopts a transnational approach to offer a comprehensive and global analysis of the war as an economic, social and cultural event. Across 27 chapters and four key parts, the volume addresses complex themes such as the political economy of industrial war, the social practices of war, the moral economy of war and peace and the repercussions of catastrophic destruction. A team of nearly 30 leading historians together show how entire nations mobilized their economies and populations in the face of unimaginable violence, and how they dealt with the subsequent losses that followed. The volume concludes by considering the lasting impact of the conflict and the memory of war across different cultures of commemoration.

MICHAEL GEYER is Samuel N. Harper Professor of German and European History in the Department of History at the University of Chicago.

ADAM TOOZE is Barton M. Biggs Professor of History at Yale University.

THE CAMBRIDGE HISTORY OF
THE SECOND WORLD WAR

GENERAL EDITOR

EVAN MAWDSLEY, *Honorary Professorial Research Fellow and formerly
Professor of International History at the University of Glasgow.*

The Cambridge History of the Second World War is an authoritative new account of the conflict that unfolded between 1939 and 1945. With contributions from a team of leading historians, the three volumes adopt a transnational approach, to offer a comprehensive, global analysis of the military, political, social, economic and cultural aspects of the war. Volume I provides an operational perspective on the course of the war, examining strategies, military cultures and organisation, and the key campaigns, whilst Volume II reviews the 'politics' of war, the global aspirations of the rival alliances, and the role of diplomacy. Volume III considers the war as an economic, social and cultural event, exploring how entire nations mobilized their economies and populations, and dealt with the catastrophic losses that followed. The volumes conclude by considering the lasting impact of the Second World War and the memory of war across different cultures of commemoration.

VOLUME I
Fighting the War
EDITED BY JOHN FERRIS AND EVAN MAWDSLEY

VOLUME II
Politics and Ideology
EDITED BY RICHARD J. B. BOSWORTH AND JOSEPH A. MAIOLO

VOLUME III
Total War: Economy, Society and Culture
EDITED BY MICHAEL GEYER AND ADAM TOOZE

THE CAMBRIDGE
HISTORY OF
THE SECOND WORLD WAR

*

VOLUME III
Total War: Economy, Society and Culture

*

Edited by
MICHAEL GEYER
and
ADAM TOOZE

CAMBRIDGE
UNIVERSITY PRESS

CAMBRIDGE
UNIVERSITY PRESS

University Printing House, Cambridge CB2 8BS, United Kingdom

Cambridge University Press is part of the University of Cambridge.

It furthers the University's mission by disseminating knowledge in the pursuit of
education, learning and research at the highest international levels of excellence.

www.cambridge.org
Information on this title: www.cambridge.org/9781107039957

First published 2015
Paperback edition first published 2017
Reprinted 2018

Printing in the United Kingdom by TJ International Ltd. Padstow Cornwall

A catalogue record for this publication is available from the British Library

ISBN 978-1-107-03995-7 Hardback
ISBN 978-1-108-40641-3 Paperback

Contents

Contents

vi

Contents

Contents

Illustrations

The colour plates can be found between pages 434 and 435

Figure

Map

Every effort has been made to contact the relevant copyright-holders for the images reproduced in this book. In the event of any error, the publisher will be pleased to make corrections in any reprints or future editions.

Tables

Contributors to volume III

RICHARD BESSEL is Professor of Twentieth-Century History at the University of York.

MONICA BLACK is Associate Professor of History at the University of Tennessee, Knoxville.

MARK PHILIP BRADLEY is Bernadotte E. Schmitt Professor of International History at the University of Chicago.

DOROTHEE BRANTZ is Professor of Urban History and Director of the Center for Metropolitan Studies at the Technical University of Berlin.

CATHRYN CARSON is Associate Professor of History at the University of California, Berkeley.

GEOFFREY COCKS is Professor of History at Albion College, Michigan.

LIZZIE COLLINGHAM is an independent scholar.

DAVID EDGERTON is Hans Rausing Professor of the History of Science and Technology and Professor of Modern British History at King's College London.

DAVID C. ENGERMAN is Ottilie Springer Professor of History at Brandeis University.

JEFFREY FEAR is Professor of International Business History at the University of Glasgow.

SABINE FRÜHSTÜCK is Professor of Modern Japanese Cultural Studies in the Department of East Asian Languages and Cultural Studies at the University of California, Santa Barbara.

MICHAEL GEYER is Samuel N. Harper Professor of German and European History in the Department of History at the University of Chicago.

PETER E. GORDON is Amabel B. James Professor of History, and Faculty Affiliate at the Minda de Gunzburg Center for European Studies at Harvard University.

RÜDIGER HACHTMANN is a Wissenschaftlicher Mitarbeiter at the Zentrum für Zeithistorische Forschung in Potsdam.

JOCHEN HELLBECK is Professor of History at Rutgers University.

GREGG HUFF is Senior Research Fellow at Pembroke College, University of Oxford.

JEREMY K. KESSLER is Associate Professor of Law at Columbia University.

YASMIN KHAN is University Lecturer in British History at the University of Oxford, and a Fellow of Kellogg College.

JIE-HYUN LIM is Professor of History and Director of the Institute for Critical Transnational Studies at Sogang University, Seoul.

JAMIE MARTIN is a doctoral candidate in the Department of History at Harvard University.

MICHAEL MILLER is Professor of History at the University of Miami.

RANA MITTER is Professor of the History and Politics of Modern China at the Institute for Chinese Studies, University of Oxford.

LUCY NOAKES is Reader in History in the School of Humanities at the University of Brighton.

CHRIS PEARSON is Senior Lecturer in Twentieth-Century History in the Department of History at the University of Liverpool.

DEVIN O. PENDAS is Associate Professor of History at Boston College.

STEPHEN PORTER is Assistant Professor of History and Director of the International Human Rights Certificate at the University of Cincinnati.

TIMOTHY B. SMITH is Professor of History at Queen's University in Kingston, Ontario.

ADAM TOOZE is Barton M. Biggs Professor of History at Yale University.

Introduction to volume III

MICHAEL GEYER AND ADAM TOOZE

Substance, scale and scope of peoples' war

The ambition of the third volume of the Cambridge History of the Second World War is to advance a history of the Second World War as an economic, social and cultural event on a global scale. This volume features economy, society and culture as forces in and of war. It puts war-making at its centre; it is unabashedly war-centric. It is global in that it posits the discrete, regional worlds of war as overlapping and interacting fields of force spanning the globe so that actions in one field push against others and histories and memories overlay each other. To the common vectors of globality such as communication and commerce, this volume adds violence. It proposes to think the Second World War as a culminating moment in the forceful, 'energetic transformation of the world'.[1]

The editorial ambitions for this volume stretch the extant empirical work on economy, society and culture and, indeed, have stretched the knowledge and imagination of the editors. But the history of war as an economic, social and cultural event is an ambition worth pushing as far as we are capable, because in contrast to the military or the political and ideological histories of the Second World War there is no narrative frame for the Second World War as a global economic, social and cultural event that we could have accepted, modified or rejected. Whereas the idea of global or, in any case, world-wide war is quite well established in strategic studies, we are only beginning to understand the World Wars as pivotal moments in the process

---

1 Jan Patočka, 'Wars of the Twentieth Century and the Twentieth Century as War', trans. Erazim Kohák, in Jan Patočka, ed., *Heretical Essays in the Philosophy of History* (Chicago, Ill.: Open Court, 1996), pp. 119–37, here p. 124.

of globalization.[2] What we have tried to do is to stake out a field of study; and what we have asked our authors to do is to offer in their respective essays some enticement for such a future history. Hence, this volume in the Cambridge History, unlike the first two, is less a summation of what we know than an invitation to explore what we ought to know and the way we might want to tell the history of a war that was fought by peoples against peoples and engulfed the entire world. We now know a lot more about what ought to be done than when we started out and we hope the volume will have a similar effect for the reader.

The crux of the matter is that the Second World War was a war that engulfed entire peoples – their economies, their societies, their cultures. In the wake of the horrors of the Thirty Years War and the bloodshed of the revolutionary era, both the eighteenth and nineteenth centuries had seen a determined effort to institute a division between 'war and (non-combatant) society'. In the First World War, on the Western Front at least, this distinction had been largely upheld. As Richard Bessel points out in this volume, in the long history of warfare the ratio between civilian and combatant casualties reached an all-time low in the First World War. But in the Second World War that distinction collapsed. The Second World War was a war fought with, for and against peoples; in short, it was a war of peoples. Obviously, there are significant gradations, say, between Leningrad, Essen, Detroit and Calcutta. Like all 'great wars' the Second World War was a composite war. Moreover, there were fundamental differences between the regimes that fought this war. But it was a war of all against all, a war literally with, for and against peoples; that is, a war that encompassed entire societies with their respective economies and cultures not simply as a (passive) 'effect' or impact but as an (active) 'pursuit' or mobilization and that stretched far beyond combatant nations across the entire world. This notion of a war with, for and against peoples picks up and transforms nineteenth-century notions of peoples' war much as it sets itself off from the post-twentieth-century concept of a 'war amongst people'.[3]

---

2 Adam Tooze and Ted Fertik, 'The World Economy and the Great War', *Geschichte und Gesellschaft* 40:2 (2014), 214–38. Charles Bright and Michael Geyer, 'Regimes of World Order: Global Integration and the Production of Difference in Twentieth-Century World History', in Jerry H. Bentley, Renate Bridenthal and Anand A. Yang, eds., *Interactions: Transregional Perspectives on World History* (Honolulu: University of Hawai'i Press, 2005), pp. 202–38.

3 Stig Förster and Jörg Nagler, eds., *On the Road to Total War: The American Civil War and the German Wars of Unification, 1861–1871* (Cambridge University Press, 1997). Rupert Smith, *The Utility of Force: The Art of Warfare in the Modern World* (London and New York: Allen Lane, 2005).

The first two volumes of the Cambridge History amply demonstrate that the Second World War was a high-intensity, battle-centric war. But these two volumes also make clear that it was a war in which entire societies mobilized. What that means in practice is a key subject for debate in the current volume. While governments and state apparatuses managed this process with varying degrees of suasion and compulsion, mobilization had also to take place from the ground up. The war was fought not merely in the name of peoples. Societies and nations did not simply give the war its purpose by defining 'war aims', for which the military then provided the means to be deployed. Populations were not merely a resource to be spent. Both as friends and foes they were a force that all military organizations and all governments reckoned with. Would people support the war? Could women be trusted to mobilize in support of the war effort? Could people be bombed into submission? Would men and women fight to the point of self-destruction? Societies, economies and cultures became an element, a force, in the military pursuit of war to be reckoned with at all times. Peoples threw themselves into the war in comprehensive mobilizations of economy, society and culture and they were targeted and destroyed by the war in military actions such as Scorched Earth or Strategic Bombing. It was a war fought not only for the control of territory, people and resources, but rather for the destruction of political regimes and social utopias. It was a war for distinct and mutually exclusive ideas of social order and, indeed, about the 'right' way to live.

The all-embracing violence of the Second World War has raised disturbing questions about the nature of and the restraints on warfare and violence, which by the beginning of the twentieth century had begun to be seen as key achievements of modern civilization. In turn, this disquiet has shaped the memory and history of the war. For to insist that the Second World War is best understood as a war of peoples against peoples does not imply that all conduct of war is the same. Quite the contrary! The conduct, goals and effects of peoples contending in the war differed radically. If entire peoples became enemies, this did not mean that all enemies were the same. In each case the relationship between the conduct of operations, the goals to be achieved and the actual effects generated was vastly complex. To cite two examples of such apparent incongruities, Nazi Germany paid the farmers of occupied Denmark for their food deliveries, while shooting thousands of Italian villagers in reprisals for guerrilla resistance and starving the urban population of the Soviet Union to death. The USA while it scrupulously sought to define the civil rights of its conscientious objectors and at Bretton Woods carefully prepared the blueprints for a post-war monetary order, set about annihilating the cities of Japan in order to hasten the peace. To come to grips with the incongruities of wars pursued by people against people, we need a history of war that takes seriously economy, society and culture as forces of war. It takes a history that is keenly aware of the 'Dynamism of Total War', but also of the limitations on what on the face of it appears to be unlimited violence.[4] If Clausewitz was impressed by the limits imposed on the dynamics of violence by nature, historians and theorists of twentieth-century wars should rather be impressed by the second nature of human choice – the naturalized world of human institutions – in shaping regimes of violence.

Wars with, for and against peoples encompass economies, societies and cultures as forces of war, but they have their own gradations of intensity; that is, peoples' wars may be usefully described as totalizing, but not as 'total'. The common argument against the notion of total war is that this kind of war is never quite as total as it is made out to be.[5] But this is a rather weak disclaimer for a war in which entire populations became the subject and object of violence. The reason that we prefer the term, war with and against peoples is precisely that it opens the door to a multi-faceted qualification of war, or, more appropriately, the 'war regimes' of individual belligerents. By contrast, the idea of total war allows only for variations of degree. Wars can be distinguished only to the extent that they are more or less total. By stealth, therefore, the concept turns the complex reality of a war that engulfs entire nations into a blunt and implicitly normative concept. However far historians might want to remove the notion of total war from the prescriptive fantasies of Erich Ludendorff, they are still stuck with his optic that makes the subordination of economy, society and culture to the military into the basic yardstick of totality.[6] By contrast, the notion of a war of peoples allows the history of a war that engulfed and enflamed entire nations and peoples to be separated from the militaristic and fascistic imperative of total top-down mobilization.

The notion of a war with, for and against peoples also provides us with the potential for a historical narrative that ranges back to the revolutionizing, nationalizing and imperializing dimension of the first epoch of totalizing and global war, the period of the French Revolution and the Napoleonic Wars,

4 Raymond Aron, *The Century of Total War* (Boston: Beacon Press, 1954), pp. 32–55.
5 Mark E. Neely Jr., 'Was the Civil War a Total War?', *Civil War History* 50:4 (2004), 434–58.
6 Roger Chickering, 'Total War: The Use and Abuse of a Concept', in Manfred Boemeke, Roger Chickering and Stig Förster, eds., *Anticipating Total War: The German and American Experiences, 1871–1914* (Cambridge University Press, 1999), pp. 13–28.

and builds a bridge to the second age of similar struggles in the mid-twentieth century. If Ludendorff stands for 'total war' fantasies of societies absolutely subordinated to the state, we find the contemporary antidote most clearly expressed in Mao Zedong's 'protracted (people's) war'.[7] Again, we should be wary of turning Mao's politics of war, 'protracted people's war', into a normative construct. 'People's war' is not necessarily what people want or what people do, even if they do fight a war that engulfs them all. The stresses and strains in Mao's first base area at Yan'an were all too evident.[8] However, the term alerts us to the recognition that the 'age of extremes' (Eric Hobsbawm) was an age of revolutions that discovered economy, society and culture as dynamic fields of violent energy – *bios*, as the Greeks would call it – that propelled violence.

Understood in this way societies, economies and cultures are not merely frames or resources for war, as a more sedate liberal understanding would have it. They are the energy that makes war as a military and political and ideological project. It was this crucial insight that Clausewitz brought to the modern understanding of war and it is this force that he sought to tame. Without society's energy, war was a mere exercise in statecraft coupled with abstract technical skill. What gave war – in the nineteenth and twentieth centuries – its terrifying historical potency was its engagement with the live forces of society. In turn, the acts of war orchestrated by militaries and directed by political will, rearrange these force fields; they make and remake economies, societies and cultures. Rather than 'impacting' society, the Second World War was a societal project of transformation. If we think of the Second World War in this way, as a clash of radical and, indeed, revolutionary projects, to remake societies, fuelled by mobilizing peoples, we might not only find a more apposite place for a history of extermination and extirpation as part of this war, but also get a more appropriate understanding of what a totalizing war of peoples with, for and against peoples entails and how it can be narrated.

Forays into historiography

Three dimensions stand out that provide an analytic framework for grasping the historical reality of the Second World War as a war of peoples – first, the

---

7 Mao Zedong, *On the Protracted War* (Peking: Foreign Languages Press, 1954).
8 Mark Selden, *China in Revolution: The Yenan Way Revisited* (2nd edn, Amonk, NY: M. E. Sharpe, 1995).

encompassing mobilization for violence; second, the socialization of the risks of death; third, the formation of involuntary communities of friends and enemies.

First, mobilization for war encompasses economy, society and culture. It requires a comprehensive social effort, rather than the 'mere' mobilization of men of a certain age, of specialized industries, and elite interests. Though it is 'total' in the Ludendorffian sense only in exceptional circumstances, the war effort imposed severe privations, varying from the rationing of consumer goods essential to normal standards of living to outright starvation. Peoples are the active subjects of mobilization, though the effort is typically orchestrated by national governments (rather than the military) and entails varying degrees of compulsion. As the essays in this volume make clear, much of the complex dynamism of the Second World War derives from the variety of different modes of mobilization in use: ranging from the revolutionary land redistribution orchestrated by China's communist activists, by way of Japan's slash and burn war financing, to the highly technocratic models of wartime Keynesianism developed in Britain and the USA. The bottom line of a war of peoples is the comprehensive mobilization of society, but each of these mobilizations has its own gradation toward 'absolute war'. Siege societies like the one in Leningrad perhaps come closest to absolute war.

In thinking through what this process of mobilization entails we might well take the image of Rosie the Riveter as an example. It is a selective image of course, one among many such images in the USA and around the world.[9] The image of women partaking in war, directly or indirectly, had become something of a global symbol for the determination to fight. There are intriguing exceptions such as Japan and telling American preferences, say, for a young white, well-nourished female worker over, say an African-American, male or female, or the Soviet and Chinese preference for the fighting female.[10] We also know that for the Rosies no straight road lay ahead from the war toward emancipation and civil rights. Rosie's image and Rosie's real-life experience were two quite different things. But what we are

---

9 Maureen Honey, *Creating Rosie the Riveter: Class, Gender, and Propaganda during World War II* (Amherst: University of Massachusetts Press, 1984). Penny Colman, *Rosie the Riveter: Women Working on the Home Front in World War II* (New York: Crown Publishers, 1995). United States National Park Service, *Rosie the Riveter/WWII Home Front National Historical Park, California* (Washington, DC: US Dept. of the Interior, National Park Service, 2011). Donna B. Knaff, *Beyond Rosie the Riveter: Women of World War II in American Popular Graphic Art* (Lawrence: University Press of Kansas, 2012).

10 Anna Krylova, *Soviet Women in Combat: A History of Violence on the Eastern Front* (Cambridge University Press, 2010).

interested in is Rosie – as riveter, girlfriend or mother – making war possible, and making far-away war possible in no minor way. True, she is an 'icon' that can and should be studied with all the subtlety of a history of images; but as icon she points above all to the war-making power of society. Whatever she may have felt, dreamt or experienced; however much she was part of an elaborate division of labour and, hence, a replaceable cog in the wheel of the wartime economy; and however much she may have had doubts fostered by the culture of her upbringing about reconciling her femininity with men's menial work; she produced the means of massive violence that made war happen. It diminishes her role not to think of her as a force in war.

The second distinguishing feature of a war of peoples is the socialization of the existential risk of injury, violation and privation and the danger of being killed. Entire populations participate in violent action; entire populations suffer the effects of violence, whether as combatants, belligerents, or as non belligerents; entire populations become objects of violence because they are perceived as hostile. War directly or indirectly enrols everyone, although once again the degree of endangerment differs among peoples and within nations. So too do the benefits and privations, as peoples become subjects and objects of violence. The bottom line is that on one hand (civil) economy, society and culture become weaponized and on the other the economy, society and culture of the opponent become targets of violence.

Talk of peoples' war and the socialization of the risk of death raises anxieties. It is commonly asserted that 'total war' or 'peoples' war' must lead to indiscriminate violence, as if violence once released from its institutional moorings in the military spills over uncontrollably and indiscriminately. Liberal states, notably Britain and the USA, hasten to insist that this is 'not what we do', even if their comprehensive ways of war-fighting produced very high levels of 'collateral damage' and provided their opponents with powerful justifications for their own efforts at totalization. Such juxtapositions are always already part of a discourse on what is right and what is wrong in war. Bracketing such distinctions does not make all belligerents equally right or equally wrong, but it suggests that the choice of war to be fought is itself a suitable and, indeed, a crucial subject for enquiry. All the belligerents in the Second World War discriminated in their use of force; however, they discriminated in radically different ways. Life and death were valued very differently. The Nazi war machine fiercely protected its own, while delivering entire populations to death. The Japanese cared little for the lives of the comfort women they enslaved. RAF Bomber Command targeted the urban fabric of Germany. The Americans sought to distinguish more carefully between military and civilian targets. But after the horrific destruction of two Japanese cities, their greatest military-technological triumph, the A-bomb, was subjected to the 'nuclear taboo'.[11] Rather than being a point of anxious line-drawing, the socialization of danger and privation in a war of peoples should be taken as the starting point for a 'moral history' of war that takes the labour of making choices in the pursuit of war – in defining friend and foe – as its crucial subject.[12]

It was the seeming limitlessness of the enrolment of entire societies in war-fighting and the resulting socialization of the dangers of war that required new efforts to specifically demarcate non-combatants and humanitarian zones. Nineteenth-century models of the law of war operated on the basis of a confined military model that posited a civilian world as the stable background of military action, a vision that could still be upheld in many of the arenas of the First World War. By contrast, the all-encompassing socialization of violence from the 1930s onwards required new and urgent efforts to define groups of people, activities, places and objects who would be put *hors de combat*, a legal or customary (moral) hedge that was more often upheld only in the breach. The twentieth century is thus heavily weighted toward national and international legal efforts to regulate and contain war.[13]

Much of this is covered in volume II of the Cambridge History of the Second World War. But it seemed to us that the debate on what is right or wrong in war – and, we might add, which war is right and which one is wrong – extends far beyond strictly military, political and legal discourses. We would submit that this debate is the crucial cultural labour of the Second World War. This labour exceeds the more classic themes of a cultural history of war, the representation of war and the articulation of the war experience.[14] The ramified debate over the rights and wrongs of war and of particular forms of war-making is the necessary corollary to the history of seemingly limitless mobilization and the socialization of risk in wars of peoples. Recognizing this connection between the totalization and problematization of war

11 Nina Tannenwald, 'Stigmatizing the Bomb: Origins of the Nuclear Taboo', *International Security* 29:4 (2005), 5–49.

12 For a similar argument: Michael Bess, *Choices under Fire: Moral Dimensions of World War II* (New York: Alfred A. Knopf, 2006). As a general statement: Didier Fassin, 'Les Economies Morales Revisitées', *Annales. Histoire, sciences sociales* 64:6 (2009), 1237–66.

13 Daniel Marc Segesser, *Recht statt Rache oder Rache durch Recht? Die Ahndung von Kriegsverbrechen in der internationalen fachwissenschaftlichen Debatte 1872–1945* (Paderborn: Schöningh, 2010). The First World War proved to be the turning point. See Isabel V. Hull, *A Scrap of Paper: Breaking and Making International Law in the Great War* (Ithaca: Cornell University Press, 2014).

14 Michael Burleigh, *Moral Combat: A History of World War II* (London: HarperPress, 2010).

also serves as an antidote against a heedless relativization that considers all belligerents in the Second World War as equally guilty, because all of them overstepped the limits on violence imposed by a nineteenth-century 'liberal conscience'.[15]

Third and not least, a war of peoples against peoples creates involuntary communities of friends and enemies. The comprehensive mobilization of societies engenders a communitarization of identities. Thus, the Japanese at large become the enemy, irrespective of what individuals or groups fear or hope and quite irrespective of the way they experience war and articulate their experience. If surrender is the goal of all war, surrender in a war of peoples entails violent subjection. It no longer suffices to destroy armies or occupy capitals in order to ascertain victory and defeat; indeed, it becomes quite uncertain what it takes to defeat an enemy, if the question is how to break the will of peoples. The trepidations of nineteenth-century militaries about permanent war had become twentieth-century reality. It now seemed necessary, in a perverse reversal of the grammar of war, to pound peoples into submission in order to make governments and military leaders yield. This brutal logic was given a further twist by the experience of the First World War. Between the Bolshevik seizure of power in November 1917 and the collapse of the Central powers a year later, internal collapse had been decisive in bringing about the end of the Great War. The bellicist regimes that emerged in the interwar period were bent on hardening themselves specifically against any repetition of that traumatic collapse. As a result, Fascist Italy, Nazi Germany, Imperial Japan and the Soviet Union all raised their internal repressive and persuasive capacities to an extraordinary new pitch. This time there would be no failure of will. Nothing less than the destruction of economy, society and culture would be the prerequisite of victory and defeat

The intensity of the communitarian drive leaves its telltale mark in radical-izing, exclusionary policies. These ranged from surveillance to far more dramatic measures such as harassment, internment, displacement and, some would argue, even genocide and the Holocaust.[16] The latter issue is not to be decided here, not least because it is treated extensively in Volume II,

---

15 Michael Howard, *War and the Liberal Conscience*. George Macaulay Trevelyan Lectures at the University of Cambridge, 1977 (London: Temple Smith, 1978).

16 Annette Becker, 'Captive Civilians', in Jay. M. Winter, ed., *The Cambridge History of the First World War*, vol. III: *Civil Society* (Cambridge University Press, 2013), pp. 257–82. Norman M. Naimark, *Fires of Hatred: Ethnic Cleansing in Twentieth-Century Europe* (Cambridge, Mass.: Harvard University Press, 2001).

where genocidal policies are linked to ideological war, or what German historians call Weltanschauungskrieg. However, we pick up a related thread in Volume III by investigating in some detail the question of limiting war and making peace in an age of total enmity. Indirectly we take on Carl Schmitt, who made the link between enmity and communitarized identity the lynchpin of his defence of German war.[17] Contra Schmitt we maintain that nations do not just vary widely among themselves, but that each case demonstrates the existence of political and, indeed, cultural and moral choice. The totalization of enmity and communitarization of identity are not destiny. In fact, a totalizing war is difficult to sustain – and surely not only because of its privations. By 1945 the dramatic 'overkill' prosecuted by the Allies was deployed not only by states that were vastly superior in material terms but also by societies that were desperate to end the war that they had not chosen, as quickly as possible and by any and all means available.

What impelled this urgency? We can grasp how high the stakes had become in war-making only when we consider that in peoples' war the choices made concerning the conduct of a war shaped entire societies indelibly. There was no return to the status quo ante. That possibility was already foreclosed in the First World War. The omnivorous reconfiguration of society in the mode of war made the Second World War a transformative 'event' in the long history of societies' embattled transformation. If war is not the father of all things, it can be thought of as a 'vanishing mediator', in the manner that Protestantism functions for Max Weber in his famous account of the origins of capitalism.[18] The society that moves out of war is different from the one that entered war. The 'new normal' constituted by the war persists long after the war has receded into memory.

The new reality, the trajectory altered by war opens opportunities and provides new horizons both for victors and vanquished. It is also, of course, defined by the bitter reality of lives unlived and futures destroyed. In both senses, seventy years on from the war, we live still, for worse and for better, among its consequences. Any comparative history of the Second World War will be shaped by the intensity of wartime alliances and enmities and, in the case of Nazi politics, the eliminationist logic of the war. This is the main reason why stepping across the battle lines of the war to engage in comparison is still

17 Carl Schmitt, *Theorie des Partisanen: Zwischenbemerkungen zum Begriff des Politischen* (Berlin: Duncker und Humblot, 1963).
18 Fredric Jameson, 'The Vanishing Mediator: Narrative Structure in Max Weber', *New German Critique* 1 (Winter, 1973), 52–89.

such hard labour. While it is difficult enough systematically to compare French, German and British war experience at the Front and at home for the First World War, any such comparison in the Second World War is fraught. It is not only that the spatial scope needs expansion from the Western (and Eastern) Front to global terrestrial and maritime theatres of war, which all have, chameleon-like, their own respective colour befitting their environment. But even the now common caution that entities to be compared need not be alike does not diminish the far more serious taint of comparison, because one always has to contend with the politics of enmity and alliance that precede the analytics of comparison.[19] This is the case with respect to forces employed in direct confrontation, such as the Wehrmacht and the Red Army, and it is equally true for more distant comparisons, such as the racism of US forces in the Pacific and the German forces in their Russian campaign.[20] Economy, society and culture are not value-free, analytic or innocent aspects of a war culture or war experience. They are part and parcel of national and social projects that shaped the way peoples' wars were fought and the ends to which they were fought. As the inheritors of these projects, whether as winners, losers or bystanders we are implicated. The act of comparison, though analytically necessary, cannot but be contentious.

The future's past

In struggling to come to terms with this vastly complex object we orientate ourselves with regard to three historical literatures, which pertain, roughly speaking, to the three domains of social or societal history, cultural history and economic history. Each of these is in its own way problematic, but all three provide vital pointers to the way in which a history of peoples' war might be written.

If there is any partial history that has taken on the challenge of writing not simply a social history but a comprehensive societal history of the 1930s and 1940s it is the literature on the history of the European Jewry and the Nazi Judeocide. The very act of Nazi extermination first led to a careful

---

19 The East Asian case suggests that this is not entirely a matter of the old opposition between Nazism, Stalinism and Liberalism. For the latter see Michael Geyer and Sheila Fitzpatrick, eds., *Beyond Totalitarianism: Stalinism and Nazism Compared* (Cambridge University Press, 2009). For the former see Tessa Morris-Suzuki, ed., *East Asia beyond the History Wars: Confronting the Ghosts of Violence* (Abingdon and New York: Routledge, 2013).

20 The most daring wager in this regard is John W. Dower, *Cultures of War: Pearl Harbor, Hiroshima, 9–11, Iraq* (New York: W. W. Norton, 2010).

reconstruction of the murderous violence and of its victims, but scholars then moved backward and forward to demonstrate the fate of Jewry as it moved through and beyond the terrible cataclysm. The subject has elicited rich philosophical and religious reflections on the cataclysm of destruction. Scholarship has also moved with massive elaboration over every facet of the history of perpetrators and bystanders, considering every level of motivation and every dimension of society and its institutions. The history of the Holocaust has emerged as the most comprehensive and most encompassing of the many societal histories of the Second World War, and in this it is a model to be emulated.[21]

Then again, there are obvious problems with taking the historiography of European Jewry as a model for the history of the war. For one, it is debatable whether the Nazi politics of extermination is part of a history of war or whether it is mass murder committed under the guise of war.[22] For another, while this history is more than a history of the 'bloodlands', the Holocaust remains a European history that is not easily translated into the global world of the Second Word War.[23] It nevertheless provides a touchstone for how a history of violent social mobilization might be written. This is especially the case if the focus is widened from the Judeocide to the entangled histories of racialized forced labour and the programmes for colonial settlement and mass starvation conceived by the Nazi regime – again a controversial proposition, but certainly a defensible one.[24] This entire complex in turn provides important points of connection and comparison to literatures on the transformational violence and the remaking of both Soviet society, Imperial Japan and Fascist Italy at home and of their colonial possessions.[25] The result

21 Illustrative texts of the richness of this literature include Saul Friedländer, *The Years of Extermination: Nazi Germany and the Jews, 1939–1945* (New York: HarperCollins 2007), Michael Wildt, *Hitler's Volksgemeinschaft and the Dynamics of Racial Exclusion: Violence against Jews in Provincial Germany, 1919–1939* (Oxford: Berghahn, 2012), Christopher Browning, *Ordinary Men: Reserve Police Battalion 101 and the Final Solution in Poland* (New York: HarperCollins, 1992).
22 American Jewish Conference, *Nazi Germany's War against the Jews* (New York: The American Jewish Conference, 1947).
23 Timothy Snyder, *Bloodlands: Europe between Hitler and Stalin* (New York: Basic Books, 2010). Dan Stone, *The Holocaust and Historical Methodology* (New York: Berghahn, 2012).
24 In exemplary fashion for Belorussia, Christian Gerlach, *Kalkulierte Morde. Die deutsche Wirtschafts-und Vernichtungspolitik in Weissrussland 1941 bis 1944* (Hamburg: Hamburger Edition, 2000). And Militärgeschichtliches Forschungsamt, *Das Deutsche Reich und der Zweite Weltkrieg. Beiträge zur Militär-und Kriegsgeschichte* (10 vols., Stuttgart: Deutsche Verlags-Anstalt, 1979–2008), especially vols. v, ix and x. *Germany and the Second World War* (Oxford and New York: Clarendon Press, 1990–).
25 Exemplary is Louise Young, *Japan's Total Empire: Manchuria and the Culture of Wartime Imperialism* (Berkeley: University of California Press, 1998).

is to graphically demonstrate how war overwhelms and eats up society. This was the experience not only of Germany, but of all combatant societies that were literally torn into pieces by war – the Soviet Union, Poland, Yugoslavia, China and Japan fall into this category. The 'extremely violent' arenas of the Second World War have all produced literatures in which the lines between social, cultural, political and economic history and the history of diplomacy have been productively bridged. There have been few areas where the contrasting perspectives of history from above and below have been more self-consciously reflected upon, few areas where questions of memory and the politics of history have been more exhaustively and creatively explored. Despite the enormous sensitivities involved in approaching these fields of death and destruction they must be an essential touchstone for any history of war with and against peoples.

A second important point of historiographical reference for thinking through the history of the Second World War must be the enormous and fertile literature on the First World War.[26] In recent decades, the pre-eminent avenue of research on the First World War has been cultural history. The concept of 'culture de guerre' has enabled historians of the Great War to make tremendous strides in diminishing the distance between war and home fronts. Given that societal mobilization cut so much deeper and the endangerment of entire societies was so much more pervasive, one might expect the historical literature of the Second World War to be 'war culture' on steroids. But caution must be exercised in the translation of such freighted concepts. 'Culture de guerre' was introduced by French historians as a term with which to criticize the idea of a stark juxtaposition between official ideology and a victimized disillusioned population that tended to be presumed by critical, pacifist accounts of the First World War. By contrast, the concept of 'culture de guerre' stressed the active and bellicose self-mobilization of the French Third Republic during the First World War. For it to be transplanted to the 1930s and 1940s one would need to rethink the entire problematic, bearing in mind that the politics of Second World War, nowhere more so than in France, were in fact shaped by the disillusionment and pacifist backlash caused by the broken promises and 'empty' propaganda of the Great War. As a result, war cultures in the Second World War were distinctly more programmatic and were more keenly organized, and more vigorous in their determination to deliver

---

26 Winter, ed., *The Cambridge History of the First World War.*

real benefits and results. This was as true of Hitler's Germany as it was of the war effort of New Deal America.[27]

Perhaps not surprisingly, in the wake of the propaganda-saturated war and McCarthyism, the early histories of the Second World War tended to take ideology lightly. But since the 1970s the pendulum has swung decisively in the opposite direction. Ideology returned. We have learned to take Hitler, Mussolini, Stalin and their contemporaries deadly seriously. Their ideas had the force that they did because an entire generation of technocratic officials, what Michael Wildt has dubbed the 'unconditional generation', stood ready to put them into action with terrifying literal mindedness.[28] Among the main combatants, the distinctions between official propaganda and spontaneous war culture, which structure the discussions of the First World War, largely collapsed. Evidence from the everyday life of both the home front and the front line suggests how deeply the rhetoric of dictatorial regimes of the 1930s saturated the minds of those who bore the brunt of the fighting. Likewise on the Anglo-American side, the Atlantic Charter may have started less as a programme and more as a motivational idea (see Volume II on this entire matter), but over the course of the war it developed programmatic 'feet' and permeated policy and politics. The promises of the Beveridge report achieved a circulation far beyond that to be expected of a technical report. It is a measure of the thoroughgoing ideological structuration of the Second World War, by comparison with the First World War, that as the war went on the space for politicized pacifism shrank to virtually nothing, even in the Western states that accommodated conscientious objectors.

By contrast with the preponderance of cultural history literature on the First World War, if there is one area in which the literature on the Second World War might be said to be squarely 'ahead' of the literature on its predecessor, it is the field of economic history with its various sub-fields, including financial history, the history of economics and economic planning, industrial and agrarian history and business history. Not only are studies in these areas vastly more abundant for the period of the 1930s and 1940s than they are for 1914–18, but they are necessarily situated within a longer trajectory that begins with the recovery from the Great Depression and the unprecedented armaments efforts of the 1930s. Recent literatures on forced

---

27 James T. Sparrow, *Warfare State: World War II Americans and the Age of Big Government* (Oxford University Press, 2011).
28 Michael Wildt, *Generation des Unbedingten. Das Führungskorps des Reichssicherheitshauptamtes* (Hamburg: Hamburger Edition, 2002).

labour culminating in 'destruction through labour', on expropriation, on Aryanization and on projects of colonial settlement have all contributed to this fertile enquiry into the intersection between productivity and violence. But a pattern was set already in the 1960s with pioneering works on military-economic strategy, notably by Alan Milward. His early study of the Nazi war effort segued with his histories of occupied France and Norway, the first global synthesis of the economic history of the war and later studies of European reconstruction in the age of the Marshall Plan and the European rescue of the nation state.[29] With his idea of a 'strategic synthesis' Milward offered a highly rationalistic and yet holistic and compelling image of the imbrication of military and economic strategy.[30] This strategic synthesis was later elaborated upon by authors such as Tim Mason and Gabriel Kolko to form a truly embracing societal concept of war.[31] However problematic their class-bound approach to the political economy of the Second World War may have been, it created a capacious frame within which the history of war-making could be thought of as a socio-economic process, leading from the stresses of rearmament, to the violence of the war and occupation. Crucially, this is now beginning to be extended beyond the artificial dividing line of 1945 into the so-called 'post-war' period.[32] In the age of the Cold War, the logic of armaments and the threat of total destruction continued to be decisive in an era all too often characterized in terms of the 'democratic welfare state'.

Economic history is important not only for establishing a robust sense of the war as social and economic process. Also, given the interconnections forged by the economic development of the nineteenth century and reinforced by the arms race, economic histories of the war are necessarily interwoven, international histories. The USA, as the arsenal of the Western alliance, was fed, for instance, by an aluminium industry laid out across a

29 Alan S. Milward *The German Economy at War* (London: Athlone Press, 1965), *The New Order and the French Economy* (Oxford: Clarendon Press, 1970), *The Fascist Economy in Norway* (Oxford University Press, 1972), *The Reconstruction of Western Europe, 1945–1951* (London: Methuen, 1984), *The European Rescue of the Nation State* (London: Routledge, 1992). The sharp break between the works on the period before and after 1945 remains telling.
30 Alan S. Milward, *War, Economy and Society, 1939–1945* (London: Allen Lane, 1977).
31 Timothy W. Mason and Jane Caplan, *Nazism, Fascism and the Working Class* (Cambridge University Press, 1995). G. Kolko, *Century of War: Politics, Conflict and Society since 1914* (New York: The New Press, 1995).
32 David Edgerton, *Warfare State: Britain, 1920–1970* (Cambridge University Press, 2005) anticipated for Germany by Michael Geyer, *Deutsche Rüstungspolitik, 1860–1980* (Frankfurt: Suhrkamp, 1984).

sprawling global geography. Labour mobilization was both a quintessential national project of peoples' war and an enterprise of continental and indeed global scale, reaching, one last time, across the full expanse of the British and French empires. Economic history resoundingly confirms the older observation of strategic histories written by the likes of Andreas Hillgruber and Richard Overy.[33] Simply put, the war was won by those powers that were capable of waging war as a comprehensive global war. This was true above all for Great Britain (especially in the time of existential need in 1940) and the USA and to a much lesser degree for the Soviet Union, which is why the great military exertions of the Soviet Union did not translate into a commensurate global victory. It is certainly not the case for Germany and Japan as well as Italy. The three nations waged world-wide parallel wars, but were incapable of launching integrated global campaigns. The example is important for our purposes, because it makes clear that we must distinguish the world-wide dimensions of a 'world' war from the global dimensions of the war. In common parlance the two words may be interchangeable, but analytically they are better kept separate. The adjective 'global' distinguishes a distinct military, political, economic, social and cultural enterprise that deliberately and purposively connects parts of the world with the purpose of advancing the war. Globality entails setting up the infrastructure of connecting discrete spaces and actions in the world and linking them together for a common enterprise. Globality is always a second-nature effort of making over the world.

Conceived in these terms it is clear that contrary to what much of the globalization literature asserts, war is an eminently powerful globalizer. Indeed, the war was a singularly powerful promoter across the world of new global networks. However, as the above example shows, it is not just anybody's globalization and it is not simply flows (of people, goods, money, narratives, iconic images) that percolate through the world. It is connections that are deliberately set up and orchestrated to wage and win war as well as to make peace. Indeed, it is, we hope, one of the effects of this volume that we historians come to realize that none of the nations – this includes the most autarkic belligerent, the Soviet Union, on one hand and the most advanced producer, the USA, on the other – was capable of waging war out of its own national capacities. It is not only that alliances had to be forged and war had to be waged with a multiplicity of combatants fighting together.

---

33 Andreas Hillgruber, *Der Zenit des Zweiten Weltkrieges, Juli 1941* (Wiesbaden: Franz Steiner, 1977). Richard J. Overy, *Why the Allies Won* (New York: W. W. Norton, 1995).

Every major war-fighting power had to reach beyond itself in order to persist in the Second World War. Again, if we chose a somewhat more academic language, we could say that the war effort necessarily had to be produced and reproduced transnationally, which, putting it in a more straightforward way, is not more than saying that in order to wage war, nations had to be able to set up (by force if necessary) the commodity circuits (say of bauxite or oil) far beyond their borders that kept the war machinery going. It is this capacity – the capacity to reproduce war effort on a global scale – that makes a world war into a global war.

Encompassing this extraordinarily complex and ramified war is a huge challenge. In our effort to push toward a truly global history of the Second World War of the twentieth century we chose to break as far as possible with national histories and to adopt a thematic approach, challenging ourselves and our contributors to treat their respective theme in as wide-ranging a manner as possible. Sometimes authors chose straight-up international comparison. Sometimes the essays moved in the direction of an entangled transnational history. We may hope that the next major anniversary of the war will see scholarship that goes further than we are able to do here in showing how high-level decision-making, the technologies (of transport and communications) and skills (languages) and the labour of hundreds of millions of ordinary people combined to give the Second World War its second nature as a global war. This would surely take in the areas that we have slighted in this volume – Latin America, Africa and the Near East – and analyse them more clearly than we have been able to do here in their specific relationships of engagement with or isolation from the war. Not least, it might demonstrate the power of narratives and icons – and for that matter of dream-worlds – that swept together the very disparate experiences of this war. Only a global history of the Second World War, and an economic, social and cultural history at that, would reveal how deeply disparate and unequal this war was – and how deeply this global war unsettled the peoples across the world. We have lived with the fallout of the Second World War ever since.

PART I

*

POLITICAL ECONOMY

Introduction to Part I

MICHAEL GEYER AND ADAM TOOZE

The First World War had been won by global economic force.[1] The global superiority of the victorious powers, foremost the USA and Great Britain, was smothering in the aftermath of the war. In the 1930s, it took the brinkmanship of states set on destroying the international system, a veritable revolution in international affairs, to challenge this strategic advantage. Their defiance of global hegemony unleashed a world-wide mobilization quite unlike anything previously seen in the history of the modern state system. There had been an arms race before 1914, but it was dwarfed by the industrial armaments process in the decade between 1931 and 1941 and the totalizing mobilization of belligerent nations between 1941 and 1945. The Second World War was, as Jeffrey Fear puts it in his essay, a 'war of factories' – a theme that is also echoed in the plate section. In the course of the war the practices and institutions of production, finance, research and development, logistics and consumption were all massively reshaped and redirected.

There can be little argument that the Second World War was a key moment in the process of making and remaking the national and international economy. Indeed, a case can be made that the very idea of the national economy as an object of government originated between 1914 and 1945 in an age of totalizing war.[2] Superficially this nationalization of the economy might appear to be counter-posed to globalization, but the more complicated truth is that national mobilization embedded the economies of

---

[1] Adam Tooze and Ted Fertik, 'The World Economy and the Great War', *Geschichte und Gesellschaft* 40:2(2014), 214–38.

[2] Daniel Speich Chassé, *Die Erfindung des Bruttosozialprodukts. Globale Ungleichheit in der Wissensgeschichte der Ökonomie* (Göttingen: Vandenhoeck & Ruprecht, 2013). Philipp Lepenies, *Die Macht der einen Zahl. Eine politische Geschichte des Bruttoinlandsprodukts*, Orig.-Ausg. ed. (Frankfurt am Main: Suhrkamp, 2013). Adam Tooze, *Statistics and the German State, 1900–1945: The Making of Modern Economic Knowledge* (Cambridge University Press, 2001).

even the most self-sufficient and reluctant belligerents like the Soviet Union in the world economy. David Edgerton's essay demonstrates how central the control of resources beyond the nation's border was for the war effort and how the defence of access routes became a key element of war-making. Indeed, the world's economy, its choking points, became targets of war-fighting. As Volume I of the Cambridge History of the Second World War suggests, the role and place of an 'economic strategy' to defeat the enemy was debated controversially among all belligerents. The present volume makes evident that the condition of globality that had acquired such force since the mid-nineteenth century in a process of globalizing marketization continued to unfold but now through the violent and complex dynamic of belligerent mobilization and incorporation across borders. The after-effects of this embedded nationalization of the economy were only undone in the 1970s and 1980s.[3]

It is one of the characteristics of the Second World War that it pitted not simply nation states and their armies, but competing strategies of mobilization against each other. Of course, they did have certain characteristics in common. Thus, one of the dramatic features of totalizing mobilization for war was the shift from generalized media of social circulation such as money, to a specific and direct appropriation of particular materials, people(s) or ideas for highly particular purposes. 'Appropriation' in turn now became a process not simply of extraction (of resources, technologies or ideas), but of deliberate creation, research and development, for the purpose of destruction. How these object-driven mobilizations could be achieved, depended in turn on what instruments and what intelligence was available, the configuration of alliances domestic and international, the moment in the war, and the goals that were being pursued by the combatants. In other words, mobilizations by all belligerents were driven to no small degree by the exigencies of war rather than by some kind of deliberate or planned approach. However, they were neither random nor were they the same. Despite their incidental, improvisational and often chaotic quality, they were shaped by and in turn moulded competing wartime political economies.

A distinctive mode of mobilization employed by the Western powers was a highly formalized, public and contractual model. The outlines of this strategy could already be seen in play in First World War bond finance that

---

3 Niall Ferguson, ed., *The Shock of the Global: The 1970s in Perspective* (Cambridge, Mass.: The Belknap Press of Harvard University Press, 2010).

was taken to an extreme pitch in populist war bond drives.[4] These populist drives were reinforced and expanded after 1939/41 and while no less spectacular, they were now even more encompassing and a lot more coercive. And yet, because the muscular appeal to mass-participation in the war effort was so central, they ended up entrenching a model of bond-owning, democratic capitalism on the one hand and claims to participatory citizenship and a purchase into the largesse of the state on the other.[5] Through these practices of the public, contractual mobilization of entrepreneurs, labourers and consumers, economic liberty came to be a central stake in the war.

A second mode of mobilization is best described as 'systemic', evoking the organized and holistic quality of this approach. We use the term 'systemic' not to designate a higher stage of 'organized' or 'corporate' capitalism, but an alternative political economy, whose medium is the management of flows.[6] In financial terms this was the model of circuit-based, 'internal financing' based on a newly emergent understanding of macroeconomics and the highly developed institutions of national financial systems, but simultaneously on the power of the state to extract monetary contributions or to socialize the cost of inflation. As Tooze and Martin show, these techniques were employed by all sides in the war. In the West, Keynesianism provided the frame for the contractual model. Containing inflationary pressure enabled the war to be managed on the basis of volunteerism and social partnership. In Nazi Germany, the Soviet Union and Japan, systemic management was combined with unprecedented biopolitical coercion, the control of all aspects of human life. This was the terrain of planning – with far-reaching ramifications for the theory and practice of industrial development – discussed by Engerman in a later section, or the modes of labour mobilization surveyed by Hachtmann.

It depends on theoretical proclivities, not to be decided here, whether the systemic strategy must be considered inherently unstable and liable to overreach, or whether it was the brinkmanship of Germany, Japan and Italy and, in a very different way, the desperate catch-up mobilization cum industrialization of the Soviet Union that led them to ever-more radical and dynamically unsustainable modes of mobilization. This strategy is often

---

4 J. Adam Tooze, *The Deluge: The Great War and the Remaking of Global Order, 1916–1931* (London: Penguin, 2014).
5 James T. Sparrow, *Warfare State: World War II Americans and the Age of Big Government* (Oxford University Press, 2011).
6 Robert A. Brady, *Business as a System of Power* (New York: Columbia University Press, 1943).

described as 'totalitarian' due to certain formal qualities of the state's control over the process.[7] But what really matters is something else. Huff's discussion of Japan's rapacious war finance in occupied Asia (much as Hachtmann's and Hellbeck's essays) is a stark illustration of a slash and burn logic of mobilization. It was not plain robbery or extortion, although that existed as well on a scale that is still difficult to fathom.[8] It depended rather more on Japan's ability to tax the holders of currency, who had to be persuaded or coerced into holding the asset to be taxed in the first place. This was a dynamic spiral of a self-consuming mobilization that reached beyond the nation into occupied territories and relentlessly pillaged and eviscerated what Hannah Arendt calls superfluous populations, for whom the naked violence of this scheme of mobilization was up front and centre. This could take the form, as Collingham shows, of the rapacious exaction of food. It might involve, as Khan shows in a later section, the contingent redisposition of populations and spaces on a continental scale. It could also, as Sabine Frühstück describes, be enacted on the body of a woman forced into sexual slavery in a military brothel whose services were paid for with a special type of currency token. What we capture here is mobilization as an act of destruction and ultimately of self-destruction.

A third, grand alternative of mobilization is far more difficult to capture. Beyond the realm of the industrial and urban war, the agrarian history of the war, surveyed by Tooze in 'The War of the Villages' (in the next section), but evident also in Collingham's essay on food, points to a radically different and, indeed, revolutionary model of mobilizing a population for war. This was the 'green', 'red' and 'black' mobilization based on the promise of land redistribution through revolutionary war that had its pivot not in the city but in the countryside. This was mobilization by expropriation and redistribution that made only tactical distinctions between internal and external war. If it is true that the two World Wars were the great levellers of the twentieth century, flattening the wealth and income distributions, as Piketty suggests, this was radically true of the mode of mobilization in revolutionary peasant wars, in which the distinction between the political and social goals

---

7 The idea of a self-destructive dynamic of totalitarianism was introduced by Hannah Arendt, *The Origins of Totalitarianism* (new edn, New York: Harcourt, Brace, and World, 1966 [1951]).

8 While we know a great deal about certain aspects like art theft, land reform or asset redistribution in liberated countries (from Czechoslovakia to Korea), the entire theme of world-wide property redistribution during and in the aftermath of the Second World War is still awaiting its historians.

of war – a more equitable political and economic order dominated by the rural masses – and the military resources deployed to obtain those goals – the mobilized peasantry seizing control of the land and its resources – were blurred in the extreme.[9] In this mode of combined military, political and economic struggle the Maoist and Yugoslav movements would come to serve as a model for revolution throughout the 'Third World' after 1945, with Spain as a dire warning of catastrophic failure.

If the discussion of modes of mobilization summarizes and pinpoints the research of the past century and demonstrates that there are still considerable lacunae to be covered, the last three essays of the section on political economy point into the future. Michael Miller's essay on 'Transportation', sketches the outlines of what must become the systematic study of sea, land and air transport and its major hubs as well as of communication and communication networks – in short the study of the (embattled) infrastructure of war as it stretches across the globe. Whether we chose a war-centric, a civil society or a market approach to make sense of the global condition of the twentieth century, the 1940s clearly emerge as a pivot of infrastructure-globalization. In turn, this departure will highlight the strategic role of the battle over control in all three oceans – the Atlantic, the Indian and the Pacific – and not least help to decide the geopolitical debate between Mahan and Mackinder, over the future of land- vs. sea-power, that started off the century.

Equally important are the technological shifts tracked by Cathryn Carson over the transwar period from the 1930s to the 1950s. As the wartime struggle unfolded, the logic of mobilization and immobilization triggered a series of vaulting moves by both sides that had the effect of hugely enhancing the combatants' range of vision and reach and, above all, destructive power. If the U-boats tried to cut the transatlantic supply lines, the key to defeating the U-boats were the invisible beams of sonar and unprecedented long-range air power. Radar would find the bombers in the dark night sky. And when conventional air defences failed, the answer to crushing Allied air superiority would be the jet, the cruise missile and ballistic missile. In military terms these latter developments proved to be inconsequential in the context of the Second World War. By contrast, the development of the atomic bomb had an immediate, if still debated impact. Of course, the military use of nuclear

---

9 Thomas Piketty, *Capital in the Twenty-First Century*, trans. Arthur Goldhammer (Cambridge, Mass.: The Belknap Press of Harvard University Press, 2014). Eric R. Wolf, *Peasant Wars of the Twentieth Century* (New York: Harper & Row, 1969).

weapons as an instrument of war was rejected after 1945 into the present. Still, what gives these wartime technologies their world historical significance was the way in which over the decades that followed they would alter humanity's relationship to the planet.[10]

Taken together, the human appropriation of resources in the Second World War was quite unprecedented and Pearson in his essay challenges us to think about the implications of this drama for humanity's natural environment. He thus points us toward the question that must surely be front and centre at the beginning of the twenty-first century: where is the world historic event of the Second World War to be located in relation to the great rupture of the Anthropocene, the age of the preponderant human impact over the Earth's ecosystem? It is commonplace for environmental historians – ecological research uses a much more extensive time frame reaching back to the rise of agriculture in the Neolithic Revolution – to demarcate the advent first of the industrial revolution and second of ultra-rapid economic growth after 1945, thus unselfconsciously aligning the Anthropocene with the 'post-war'. It is time to rethink this shorthand and to take 1937/41 as a more compelling starting point. Even the ecological research on the Anthropocene would do well to consider the dramatic armaments-fuelled recovery from the Great Depression as a critical threshold in the grand transformation that made our world today. War did not make the Anthropocene, but it made a crucial difference.

---

10 Günther Anders, *Die Antiquiertheit des Menschen* (Munich: C. H. Beck, 2002).

The economics of the war with Nazi Germany

ADAM TOOZE AND JAMIE MARTIN

The entanglement between war and economics revealed by the First World War was to become one of the defining features of the first half of the twentieth century. Never before had war been so resource-intensive, never before were economies so self-consciously reorganized around the needs of war. The war economies of the First World War were novel and unanticipated improvisations, experiments in organization. In 1914 the sense of a break was dramatic and shocking, but it had the virtue of clarity. There had been peace and then there was war. After the First World War the victorious powers struggled to restore the clarity of this boundary between war and peace. The new self-conscious ideology of peacefulness that was such a characteristic feature of international relations in the 1920s had its counterpart in the effort to restore the international economy.[1] The relationship between economic restoration and pacification was reciprocal. Curbing arms expenditure and restoring the 'knave proof' discipline of the international gold standard were conjoined aims. Perhaps this nexus was best exemplified by the British 'ten year rule' adopted in 1919. To create the conditions necessary for fiscal consolidation and a return to the gold standard, this mandated that military budgeting should proceed on the assumption that no major war should be expected within ten years. In 1928 Churchill had it made self-perpetuating.

Generalized across the international system in the 1920s, the manipulation of these relationships between finance and strategy was one of the most potent weapons in the arsenal of the liberal powers. But acknowledging this connection also implied a new and terrifying vulnerability. A breakdown in the security system would involve a rupture in the balance of the

---

1 A. Iriye, ed., *The Cambridge History of American Foreign Relations*, vol. III: *The Globalizing of America, 1913–1945* (Cambridge University Press, 1993). Adam Tooze, *The Deluge: The Great War and the Remaking of the Global Order* (London: Allen Lane, 2014).

international economy. Conversely, a rupture in the international economy would most likely have security implications. The hypothetical of total war changed the nature of peacetime economic government and the meaning of the response to the crisis. The restoration of the 1920s was always incomplete and fragile and the shocking collapse of the Great Depression was just such a destabilizing crisis. Not only was it the worst on record, but it immediately reopened the floodgates to the models of national economic mobilization that had emerged from the First World War. National economic recovery programmes all too easily shaded over into rhetorical and then real rearmament. Given the implosion of the world economy, consolidated national economies anchoring regional blocs emerged after 1929 as the de facto norm. It was all too easy to imagine these trading blocs as antagonist strategic platforms. As a result, by 1939, quite unlike in 1914, all the major powers had been living for the best part of a decade under the shadow of war. Not that 'business as usual' was immediately abandoned. But the very fact that that term had such attractive resonance pointed to the shadow of its alternative, total war. This essay will explore how the major powers of Europe and the USA confronted this challenge, how they mobilized their economies when war came in 1939, and how at the end of the Second World War they once again wrestled with the problem of how to restore economic peace. Viewed in terms of strictly economic metrics it is conventional to draw a sharp line in 1945 separating the troubled interwar era from the 'post-war' era of triumphant growth. In terms of economic success the difference is undeniable. But the moniker of 'post-war' is seriously misleading when applied to the 1950s, a period of intense military confrontation in the early Cold War and violent decolonization struggles. Alongside the famous welfare state initiatives of the 1940s, the warfare states that had first taken shape in the First World War were more entrenched than ever.[2] Recognizing this casts new light on the nature of the 'post-war' international economic order.

The breakdown of order

The last hurrah of the effort to institutionalize peace after the First World War came at the Naval Arms Control Conference in London in 1930. Under the sign of the new ideology of peace enshrined in the Kellogg-Briand pact and its renunciation of war, the USA, Britain and Japan, with France making a

---

2 D. Edgerton, *Warfare State: Britain, 1920–1970* (Cambridge University Press, 2005).

reluctant fourth, reaffirmed their commitment to arms limitation. They did so within months of having ratified the latest of the post-war debt deals capped by the Young Plan for German reparations. At the same time, loyally following the dictates of the gold standard they reacted to the hiking of US interest rates and the implosion of Wall Street by setting in motion a world-wide deflation. Arms control was part of a piece with fiscal austerity and monetary deflation. In an unprecedented global radio broadcast to celebrate the conclusion of the London naval agreement, President Hoover and Prime Ministers MacDonald and Hamaguchi took turns to hail a new era of internationalism, financial stability and military retrenchment. What they did not appreciate was the damage which the financial and economic crisis unleashed by coordinated global deflation would do to their vision of global pacification.

The unhinging of the world order set in motion by the Depression became manifest on the weekend of 18–20 September 1931 when rogue nationalists in Japan's army unleashed the annexation of Manchuria with the Mukden incident, and the government of Great Britain declared its departure from the gold standard. It was followed by the rest of the Empire and all of its smaller trading partners, as well as Japan. At first this was viewed as a temporary expedient. The USA, France and Italy remained on gold. In the summer of 1931 Germany had been forced to adopt exchange controls to contain the crisis in its banking sector and the wasting of its foreign reserves, while retaining the official parity of the Reichsmark. A major global confer-ence was scheduled for London in the summer of 1933 to discuss the restoration of the world economy. But over the winter of 1932–33 another wave of bank failures swept across the USA and Franklin D. Roosevelt (FDR) in his first hundred days chose to prioritize national recovery. Adopting a beggar-thy-neighbour approach he allowed an unchecked 30 per cent devalu-ation of the dollar, the first step in a comprehensive retreat from inter-national engagement that marked the early years of the New Deal. The British and French protested, but with little real credibility. After all it had been Britain that pulled the plug on the gold standard. And in 1932 it was Britain that in a spectacular historical reversal led the Empire in the creation of a tariff bloc.

With the dollar plunging and the London Economic Conference offering an embarrassing display of the weakness of liberalism, Fascist Italy, Hitler's new government in Germany and the ultra-imperialists in Japan all openly proclaimed their nationalist contempt for the international order. The status quo powers seemed to have no answer. Not only was the world economy in tatters, but the nationalist alternative seemed to be working. By 1935, world trade had not yet returned to 1929 levels, but recovery was well under way notably in those states that had abandoned the gold standard. Devaluing states gained export competitiveness and diverted domestic demand away from more expensive imports. Most importantly, liberation from the gold standard's disciplinary rules allowed them to employ a suite of new expansionary monetary and fiscal techniques.[3] By contrast, the few countries that clung to the gold standard after 1933 – the so-called 'gold bloc' consisting of Belgium, the Netherlands, Poland, Czechoslovakia, Switzerland and France – continued to suffer from weakening balance of payments, anaemic industrial production, high unemployment and worsening fiscal deficits. France, the richest member of the 'gold bloc' led the way, doggedly maintaining a deflationary stance, even as the country sank deeper into recession and political turmoil.[4]

France's financial impasse was not separable from its increasingly alarming security situation. In East Asia the confrontation of Russian and Japanese interests in Manchuria and northern China had raised tensions since the late 1920s, culminating in the occupation of Manchuria in 1931. In October 1935 Mussolini launched his attack on Abyssinia. France and Britain might have been able to isolate East Asia and the Mediterranean as regional threats, but for the simultaneous upheaval in Germany. It was Hitler's increasingly overt challenge to the security order in Western and Eastern Europe that forced Britain and France to respond, creating a truly continental crisis.

In its early months Hitler's government had conformed assiduously to the ideology of peace that was such a marked feature of international relations in the 1920s. Civilian work-creation and national rehabilitation were to the fore. The Third Reich would not openly announce its remilitarization until March 1935. But behind the scenes plans for a massive military buildup had been in place since the earliest days of the regime. In June 1933, Schacht, Göring and Blomberg had agreed on an eight-year plan of rearmament to be financed by the Metallforschungsgesellschaft, an off-the-books front company underwritten by the Reichsbank. Already by 1935, however, military spending was running far ahead of target and in 1936 it would reach 11 per cent of total national income. This figure was historically unprecedented in a peacetime

---

3 Barry Eichengreen, *Golden Fetters: The Gold Standard and the Great Depression, 1919–1939* (Oxford University Press, 1992), p. 367.
4 See Kenneth Mouré, *Managing the Franc Poincaré: Economic Understanding and Political Constraint in French Monetary Policy, 1928–1936* (Cambridge University Press, 1991).

capitalist state.[5] On the eve of the First World War in 1914, by contrast, the military spending of all the major European powers had hovered between 3 and 4 per cent of GDP.[6] Nor was Nazi Germany alone. The Soviet Red Army was undergoing dramatic modernization. Italy's attack on Abyssinia pushed its military burden over 12 per cent. When Japan attacked China in 1937 and it began a phase of semi-mobilization for war, military spending would surge to over 20 per cent of GDP.

How was such a drastic reallocation of resources possible? In Stalin's Soviet Union the answer was consistent and radical. The entire economy was restructured around collectivized agriculture and a rapidly expanding, state-controlled industrial complex. Civilian consumption was squeezed to the point of provoking a dreadful famine in the countryside. Meanwhile, the share of armaments in industrial production rose from 2.6 per cent in 1930, to 5.7 in 1932, 10 per cent in 1937 and 20 per cent by 1940. Though there was a lull in 1937 as the Communist Party was convulsed by the purges, after 1938 35–40 per cent of all steel produced in the Soviet Union was directed to the armaments sector. Production of aircraft and artillery surged. The regime advertised itself as bringing tractors to the countryside. But no less remarkable was its achievement in creating a world-beating capacity for the design and production of armoured vehicles, that already in 1936, while the Soviet Union was at peace, was turning out 5,000 tanks per year. From its inception in the 'war scare' of 1926, Stalin's regime lived under the shadow of war.

Though bent on remilitarization and international confrontation, Nazi Germany was not a socially revolutionary regime. Seizures and state ownership were limited on an ad hoc basis to particular troublesome or strategic industries, notably aircraft (Junkers) and steel (Reichswerke Hermann Göring). The key was to use state expenditure to mobilize and redirect the huge capacity left idle by the Great Depression. Already in December 1933 all new allocations of money for the work-creation schemes of the Reich were frozen. Thereafter, the civilian economy was consistently put in second place. Apart from the allocation of spending, the other main means of redirecting the German economy were the currency controls put in place during the crisis of 1931. These gave the Reichsbank full control over all imports. In 1934 they were consolidated by Hjalmar Schacht, Hitler's central

5 Adam Tooze, 'The Economic History of the Nazi Regime', in Jane Caplan, ed., *Nazi Germany* (Oxford University Press, 2008), pp. 180–1.
6 Richard Overy and Andrew Wheatcroft, *The Road to War: The Origins of World War II* (Harmondsworth: Penguin, 1999), p. 58.

banker, into the New Plan. Contrary to the idea that Hitler instigated a Keynesian recovery, everything possible was done to prevent surging government spending and industrial employment spilling over into increased consumption. Sectors such as textiles and food production were throttled back, while chemicals and engineering boomed. Meanwhile, Hitler declared a general price stop in 1936. And the destruction of the labour movement held down wage growth. But how was Germany to pay for the imported raw materials its booming heavy industry consumed? Much was made at the time of Schacht's efforts to redirect German trade toward its 'informal Empire' in Southeastern Europe. But Yugoslavia, Romania and Bulgaria were a poor substitute for the global trading network Germany had built up since the nineteenth century. In global markets the failure to devalue the Reichsmark left German exports grossly uncompetitive. So from 1935 Schacht resorted to an elaborate export subsidy scheme to boost hard currency earnings, paid for by a compulsory levy on those profiting from the domestic boom.

Market liberals would of course object that such systems were grossly inefficient. The modern neoliberalism of Friedrich Hayek originated in a critique of the planned economies of the 1930s. But the instruments of state control employed by regimes such as Hitler's were themselves the product of the crisis of the market economy. Furthermore, even if there were inevitable inefficiencies, the recovery taking place from the early 1930s onwards was undeniable, as was the fact that the managers of the planned economies developed their own particular skill set. Soviet factory managers and construction engineers became expert at the 'storming' investment surges that drove Stalin's Five-Year Plans. Meanwhile, in the Third Reich officials perfected the delicate balancing of limited stocks of hard currency. But above all, for all their inefficiencies, systems of central planning enabled states to make periodic strategic decisions. Stalin set his economy on a forced march toward industrialization. Hitler's first move in 1933 was to suspend payment on Germany's international debts and to prioritize rearmament, using the foreign exchange controls to prevent any currency panic. The question over the winter of 1935–36 was whither the Nazi economy? On the answer to this question would hang Europe's economic and political future. With full employment rapidly approaching and the remobilization of the German armed forces now publicly declared there were those around Hjalmar Schacht arguing for a strategy of moderation. Meanwhile, the army and Hermann Göring and the Luftwaffe were pushing for a further acceleration of armaments. For Germany's neighbours this debate had ominous implications. How would they respond?

Arms race

Facing not only Germany but the naval threats posed by Mussolini and Imperial Japan, it was clear by 1936 that Britain would have to accelerate rearmament. London's successful management of the dirty float of sterling since 1931 had enabled substantial recovery driven by the expanding consumption of a burgeoning middle class and increasingly affluent workers. For both financial and strategic reasons, the British preferred to pursue a strategy of highly concentrated rearmament that built very substantial military-industrial capacity above all in aircraft, while permitting 'business as usual' to continue as far as possible. The two most important elements of this strategy were the large investment in the radar defensive chain and the construction of a substantial shadow production capacity for key aircraft. This expansion in industrial capacity had begun as early as 1935, with the construction of new ordnance and armament facilities and specialized factories – managed by automobile companies, although owned by the state – producing aircraft and aero-engines.[7] By 1940, Britain was making more aircraft than any other state.[8] Chamberlain's policy of Appeasement was thus a strategy that balanced the priorities of home defence, imperial security and domestic political economy. Pivotal to this was a diplomatic effort to contain Hitler while simultaneously pursuing targeted, though still ambitious, programmes of rearmament at home.

France's options were less attractive. In the aftermath of the First World War the weakness of the French franc had been seared into the nation's consciousness as a symbol of national enfeeblement. After 1924 it had seemed as though the Republic, despite having defeated Germany, might slide, like Italy, toward financial chaos and political extremism. Poincaré's stabilization campaign in 1926 had rallied the Republican forces and given the Bank of France the biggest gold reserves in Europe. And France had clung to that position through the Depression. But the deflation that this necessitated hobbled any effort at rearmament and helped to paralyze France in strategic terms. When Mussolini invaded Abyssinia and Hitler remilitarized the Rhineland in the spring of 1936, France was in no position to react. While Britain began investing in its air defences, France and its continental allies were in a more exposed position. In 1936 both Czechoslovakia and Romania

---

7 David Edgerton, *Britain's War Machine: Weapons, Resources, and Experts in the Second World War* (London: Allen Lane, 2011), p. 200.
8 Edgerton, *Warfare State*, p. 74.

dramatically accelerated military spending. In April 1936 Poland, the last member of the gold bloc in Eastern Europe, initiated large-scale rearmament. To ensure that this did not provoke a currency crisis Warsaw imposed exchange controls, further exposing France's isolation.

In 1936 the turn toward a broad-based Popular Front strategy initiated by the Comintern in Moscow changed the political complexion of Europe. In Sweden and Spain the possibility came into view of progressive coalitions with communist support taking power. In France, in May 1936 Léon Blum's alliance of left parties won office, campaigning on an economic programme of work-creation and social insurance policies modelled on the American New Deal.[9] From the summer of 1936 amidst a dramatic wave of strikes, the Blum government would begin implementing a thoroughgoing programme of domestic reform, including most notably paid vacations and the eight-hour week. This expansive economic policy would put huge pressure on France's precarious gold peg. As the socialists took office, French conservatives feared that Blum might try to accommodate the need for both defence and social policy spending by adopting his own version of Schachtianism, a planned economy based on exchange controls. It was this threat that finally broke the deadlock in French policy and opened the door to the obvious alternative, which was a devaluation of the franc. To devalue the franc in an aggressive beggar-thy-neighbour fashion as FDR had done the dollar in 1933 might maximize France's competitive advantage but it risked a speculative crisis and by alienating Britain and the USA it would only worsen France's security situation. Instead, with the Spanish Civil War raging in the background, Blum initiated a coordinated devaluation in cooperation with Britain and the USA in an informal arrangement known as the Tripartite Agreement.[10] This agreement was more a set of declarations of support for currency stability and of democratic solidarity than any kind of formal partnership, but it represented a milestone in international economic cooperation. It was the first international economic agreement negotiated by Treasury officials and not private central bankers, prefiguring post-war financial diplomacy.[11]

The impact of the French devaluation was to further increase competitive pressure on the rest of the European economies. Italy's waning reserves had

---

9 Philip Nord, *France's New Deal: From the Thirties to the Postwar Era* (Princeton University Press, 2012).

10 Charles Kindleberger, *The World in Depression, 1929–1939* (Berkeley: University of California Press, 1986), pp. 255–61.

11 Patricia Clavin, *The Failure of Economic Diplomacy: Britain, Germany, France and the United States, 1931–36* (Basingstoke: Macmillan, 1996), p. 189.

forced Mussolini to introduce exchange controls in 1934. And with the Italian economy stretched hard by the expenses of his African campaigns he decided to relieve pressure on the lira by nationalizing the Italian central bank and carrying out a de facto 40 per cent devaluation in October 1936. Increasingly, the regime resorted to both differentiated exchange rates and artificially controlled prices to contain the pressures within its domestic economy and manage the balance of payments. Tourists were offered super-attractive exchange rates. Exporters were incentivized through premia paid in lira. Italian consumers of food and raw materials, for their part, found themselves paying one-third more than world market prices. Meanwhile, new investment was channelled into autarchy and armaments-related projects by IRI and IMI, the two agencies formed at the height of the crisis in 1931 to bail out the ailing Italian banking system.

The crucial question in 1936 was which path Germany would choose at this turning point in the world recovery. As the strategic debate within the regime intensified, Reichsbank President Schacht led a cluster of interests calling for Germany's re-entry into a multilateral system of trade. This path had significant support among the German business elite, who chafed at the onerous controls on currency and exchange. At the Reichsbank there was perpetual anxiety about the low level of German currency reserves that were rarely enough to cover more than a few months of essential imports. In August 1936, Schacht travelled to Paris in what appears to have been an attempt to negotiate the devaluation of the Reichsmark in coordination with the emerging Tripartite Agreement.[12] Perhaps Germany's worsening financial situation would offer an opportunity for a European settlement, in which financial and colonial concessions could be bartered against a freeze in German armaments.[13] But this was to misjudge Hitler's intentions. Faced with a choice between Schacht's rebalancing proposal and the calls from Göring and the army to accelerate spending, Hitler decided definitively in favour of the latter. In his 'Four-Year Plan' memorandum, Hitler declared that Germany must be ready for war within four years. Göring was placed in charge of a central office charged with ensuring self-sufficiency by means of investment in the synthetic production of rubber, iron ore, petrol, textiles and industrial fats.[14]

12 Adam Tooze, *The Wages of Destruction: The Making and Breaking of the Nazi Economy* (London: Allen Lane, 2006), p. 223.

13 Zara Steiner, *The Triumph of the Dark: European International History, 1933–1939* (Oxford University Press, 2011), pp. 258–9.

14 Tooze, *Wages of Destruction*, pp. 203–24.

In September 1936, France responded in kind. The Blum government approved a 14 billion franc programme of rearmament – the largest in France's history. Even with the devaluation taking effect, this strained France's financial situation.[15] In February 1937, Blum announced a 'pause' of the Popular Front's social insurance and work-creation policies.[16] But even these cutbacks in non-military spending were insufficient to convince the fiscally orthodox Ministry of Finance to devote enough resources to put French rearmament on pace with the German.[17] In the course of 1937 the instability of the franc and continued domestic struggles put paid to the Popular Front experiment.

But even in Germany political will alone was not enough to underwrite rearmament. Having opted against devaluation in 1937 the Third Reich found itself having to introduce comprehensive rationing of iron, steel and non-ferrous metals to cope with the shortfall in foreign exchange and to redirect production toward exports. Around Schacht and his cohorts, the hope that the Third Reich might be directed back toward a path of fiscal conservatism revived. In early 1938 the off-the-books financing mechanisms were wound up. An attempt was made to shift to a more conventional mode of financing using bonds. After a series of smaller trial runs, 5.5 billion Reichsmarks were issued in 1938, far more debt than the Reich had ever previously sold in peacetime. But once more this consolidation was undone by the aggression of Hitler's foreign policy which now reached out for Germany's neighbours to the east: first Austria and then the Sudetenland. The resulting war scare had the effect of precipitating a further shocking acceleration of both immediate spending and medium-term armaments planning. In Nazi Germany by 1938, even though it was nominally at peace, military spending was surging to 17 per cent of national income and beyond.[18]

At this level of spending, with Germany at full employment the problem that British economists would later dub the 'inflationary gap' became acute. The question of state finance was no longer a technical matter for the Finance Ministry but was manifestly intertwined with every other area of social and economic life. The government's borrowing requirement was so large

---

15 Steiner, *Triumph of the Dark*, p. 275.
16 Robert Frankenstein, *Le Prix du Réarmement Français, 1935–1939* (Paris: Publications de la Sorbonne, 1982), p. 82.
17 L. D. Schwarz, 'Searching for Recovery: Unbalanced Budgets, Deflation and Rearmament in France during the 1930s', in W. R. Garside, ed., *Capitalism in Crisis: International Responses to the Great Depression* (New York: St. Martin's Press, 1993), pp. 96–113.
18 Mark Harrison, 'Resource Mobilization for World War II: The USA, UK, USSR and Germany, 1938–1945', *Economic History Review* 41:2 (1988), 171–92 (p. 184).

that it was on a par with the total flow of private business investment. Both government spending and investment had to be financed from the same common pool of 'social saving' – the portion of national income that remained after consumption by households and regular government spending. Whatever the channel through which these funds were tapped, whether it was through savings accounts, retained corporate profits, taxation, the stock market, the bond market or over-the-counter investments by insurance or pension funds, the trade-off could not be escaped – private investment and military spending came out of the same pool. The basic problem of economic government was how to balance these competing claims on national resources. From 1936 onwards Germany's advanced government statistical service and economic advisory staffs had been compiling more and more sophisticated estimates of this all-important balance.[19] But unlike in Britain and the USA there was no space for open controversy about national economic policy in the Third Reich and their inside influence on government was limited. At the highest level, on the part of Hitler and his intimate circle it was far from obvious that there was any interest in achieving a balance. When in January 1939 Hjalmar Schacht tried to rally the Reichsbank directorate against the excessive demands on the economy, they were forcibly retired. Decision-making processes in the Third Reich were famously incoherent. But there was no mistaking the direction of Hitler's restless, dynamic drive to international confrontation. It was the struggle to square that aggression with the available resources that resulted in incoherence, not the other way around. In 1938 to make room for further arms spending private share issues and mortgage lending were drastically curtailed, but that was not enough to save the last bond issue of the year that was an embarrassing flop. As Germany's foreign exchange reserves depleted, in early 1939 there was no option but to shift steel rations away from military orders toward exports. To take pressure off the capital markets, a novel financing scheme was introduced under which government suppliers were paid not in cash but in tax credits, but the resulting cash flow squeeze drove contractors to borrow on overdraft from their banks. The force of the macroeconomic constraint could not be escaped through better organization. The root cause of the imbalance was strategic not technical and Hitler showed no desire to de-escalate the international situation; first he gave top priority to German naval expansion, then he occupied Prague and set course for confrontation over Poland.

19 Adam J. Tooze, *Statistics and the German State, 1900–1945: The Making of Modern Economic Knowledge* (Cambridge University Press, 2001).

In Britain and France economic observers followed what they could make out of the drama in Nazi Germany with bated breath. Was an economic crisis driving Hitler to war? Might economic concessions open the door to negotiations? Was the regime fully in control? What was clear was that Germany's hugely increased armaments effort in 1938 demanded an escalation of their own efforts. After the Anschluss, the British Cabinet approved a dramatic acceleration of air rearmament, calling for the production of up to 12,000 new aircraft over the following two years.[20] Worries about the interference of rearmament with 'business as usual' were put aside, although care was still taken not to stray too far from economic orthodoxy: the Treasury repeatedly rejected plans for economic planning mechanisms to coordinate the expanded military production, and the Bank of England's calls for exchange controls to protect sterling from the financial pressures of rearmament also fell on deaf ears. But Hitler was forcing the pace. The Prague coup of March 1939 led to a doubling of the size of the territorial army, the introduction of conscription, and the establishment of a peacetime supply ministry to plan and coordinate rearmament and cooperation between labour and industry on industrial production. By the eve of the war in 1939, Chamberlain's conservative government had been forced to countenance an unprecedented array of interventionist measures.[21]

The French were more unwavering in their commitment to the orthodoxies of economic liberalism. In 1938, the Senate roundly rejected Blum's suggestion that exchange controls accompany his new proposal for rearmament, a defeat that led to the fall of what was left of the Popular Front government. Blum's successor, the right-wing Édouard Deladier, called for the doubling of France's defence spending in April, but his Minister of Finance, Paul Reynaud, rejected any means of financing it that were not in line with the strict principles of fiscal moderation and laissez-faire. In the face of a general strike that broke out in November 1938, Reynaud insisted that rearmament be accompanied by cutbacks in all non-military and social spending, shifting the burden onto the backs of labour. Reynaud hoped that rearmament could be financed through the revenue of savings bonds. As long as confidence in the French economy could be maintained, the willingness of French savers to support the state would allow rearmament without

---

20 G. C. Peden, *British Rearmament and the Treasury, 1932–1939* (Edinburgh University Press, 1979), p. 156.
21 Talbot Imlay, *Facing the Second World War: Strategy, Politics, and Economics in Britain and France, 1938–1940* (Oxford University Press, 2003), pp. 299–354.

inflation. But, as in Germany, even if the domestic balance could be preserved, the foreign account posed a constant challenge. How was France with its national economy devoted increasingly to armaments to pay for imports, above all of American aircraft? By the summer of 1939, with armaments spending surging ahead of revenue, the French state was without a coherent strategy: it had neither the money to pay for, nor the institutional mechanisms to coordinate, the industrial production needed to fight and win the coming European war.[22]

By 1939 as war approached the macroeconomic balance of the major combatants was quite unlike that in 1914. The conventions of the regular international economy had long ago been abandoned. Germany, Japan, Italy, France, Britain and the Soviet Union were unbalanced by government spending to a degree never seen before in peacetime. The one exception was the USA, where military spending was less than 2 per cent of GDP and the economy was still struggling to recover from the double-dip recession that struck in 1937. When war finally began in September 1939 there was on all sides a wave of recrimination about inadequate preparation. Even in Nazi Germany there were those who believed that more could have been done. And they were, of course, right. But rather than appropriating these contemporary arguments as our own, if we view the 1930s in longer-term perspective what we should not underestimate is the novelty and drama of the situation created by the collapse of the first effort at comprehensive political and economic stabilization in the wake of total war. Not only did the governments of the world face the immediate problem of recovery from the Great Depression, but they had to square that demand with the hypothetical of a total war, the scale of which was only gradually becoming clear even to those who were bent on unleashing it. That the result was a series of makeshift and more or less unbalanced improvisations can hardly be surprising. The financial effort involved and the industrial, technological and strategic uncertainties that had to be balanced posed huge new problems for modern government.

War mobilization

The outbreak of the war over Poland in September 1939 at least had the effect of clarifying strategic positions. Britain and France were preparing for an attritional, economic war. Unlike in 1914 they did not count on the offensive.

22 Imlay, *Facing the Second World War*, pp. 255–98.

They instituted a blockade, moderately accelerated their military spending and made plans for large-scale procurement from the USA enabled by the cash-and-carry provisions that passed Congress in November 1939. Stalin and Mussolini were playing a waiting game. Stalin used the time he believed that he had bought through the Molotov–Ribbentrop pact to accelerate arms spending. Mussolini did not. In 1940 Italian military spending at 12 per cent of GDP was barely higher than it had been in 1937 during the Ethiopian war.

There were those in the Nazi regime who wanted to play a long game. Economics Minister Funk and the chief military-economic planner of the Wehrmacht General Thomas were in this camp. But Hitler dismissed their view as quixotic. It might be comforting to prepare plans that would stretch Germany's raw materials out over a three-year war. But Germany could not profit from such a conflict. It would play into the hands of its enemies who had far greater access to world markets. The Wehrmacht needed to achieve a major breakthrough to change the terms of the war as soon as possible. Awed by Germany's spectacular successes in the early war years, post-war analysts jumped to the conclusion that Hitler's reasoning was part of a well worked-out Blitzkrieg strategy in which everything from weapons procurement, to the economics of armaments planning and diplomacy was geared toward facilitating Hitler's salami-slicing aggression. In fact, there is no evidence that any such grand strategy existed. Even at the end of 1939 no one anticipated Germany's lightning battlefield victories in 1940 and 1941. Hitler's insistence on immediate action in 1939 was not the result of a brilliant grand strategy or a peculiar gift for military prophecy. It was rather the necessary and rather desperate conclusion to draw from the situation created by Hitler's aggression and the decision by Britain and France to stand and fight.

In a long-term race for further economic mobilization Germany had little to gain. Its economy unlike that of virtually all the other combatants' was already at overfull employment in 1939 so it had least scope to mobilize additional labour. Civilian consumption and investment had never been the main priority in Hitler's economic miracle, so there was less cushion there too. When war broke out Minister of Economic Affairs Funk proposed large tax increases. But since the German population was already very heavily taxed by international standards, Hitler deemed this politically inopportune. Instead, rationing and the redirection of production were used to curtail consumption. It was from the bulging accounts of the savings banks that the government helped itself to the funds it needed. Certainly, there was no lack of mobilization. Already in the first months of the war the German military burden surged toward 40 per cent of GDP, putting all the other powers to shame. But to talk of a long-term German economic strategy in 1939 would be to miss the point. In the first year of the war Hitler was going for broke and to the amazement of the world, the gamble paid off.

Germany's lightning victories in Western Europe in the spring of 1940 suddenly shifted the balance and inverted the time horizons of the combatants. France became the object of German pillage and occupation. Its economy was thrown from a mobilization footing into disorder and stagnation. By 1943, even before fighting resumed on French soil, output had plunged to less than 70 per cent of its pre-war level. To take advantage of France's defeat, Italy opportunistically joined the war and doubled its military spending as a share of GDP by 1941 to a modest 23 per cent. Germany's posture shifted from gambling on a quick victory in France to hoping that that victory would force Britain to surrender. It did not. Germany's victories forced the British Empire to reconfigure its long-range war strategy to reflect the changed circumstances. Britain was far more vulnerable to attack both by air and by sea than ever before. But contrary to Churchillian rhetoric, Britain was never alone. The loss of its military and economic allies in Europe led it to draw more than ever on the Empire and the USA. The basic direction of British armaments strategy directed toward aerial and naval warfare remained in place, but the stresses to which Britain was subject revealed themselves in the macroeconomic balances. The budget deficit exploded from £108 million to £2.9 billion in 1942. Taxes were hiked sharply. By 1941 British military spending as a share of GDP had surged ahead of even that of Germany. During this early phase of the war, the UK was the most mobilized war economy in the world.

Early in the war Britain benefited from the fact that in 1939 the UK workforce was still underemployed. Women, most notably, were far easier to mobilize in Britain than in Germany because the rate of employment among women had been so much lower in 1939. By the end of 1941 British GDP was 21 per cent greater than in 1938. But as government spending surged it was clear that draconian measures could not be avoided. In its desperate experiment in macroeconomic imbalance, Britain mobilized the best available economic expertise. In the crisis summer of 1940 John Maynard Keynes was drafted into the Treasury, where he and his team diagnosed the same problem their German counterparts had faced two years earlier, what Keynes had dubbed an 'inflationary gap'. As the war effort hit high gear, the government's demands exceeded the total pool of social savings. In early 1941 relative to total government spending of £3.7 billion they found

£500 million that could not be covered. Unlike in Germany in the late 1930s the British experts had an attentive audience. The stringent budget presented to Parliament in the spring of 1941 was explicitly based on Keynesian macroeconomic methods and the modern national income statistics. The inflationary pressure that had been building up sharply between 1939 and 1941 began to be curtailed.[23] For many, the 1941 budget seemed to herald a new dawn for the rational management of the national economy. 'It is on the assumption of this wider responsibility,' wrote the economist Nicholas Kaldor in summer 1941, 'that our best hope lies for the post-war world'.[24]

And Britain's war effort was emphatically global. In 1940 the trade deficit gaped to 9.5 per cent of GDP. Over the war as a whole Britain benefited from a net inflow on current account of £10 billion. Of this £1.1 billion came from the sale of British investments abroad; £3.5 billion was made up of new borrowing, of which £2.7 billion was contributed by the Empire's Sterling Area, the majority from India, Burma and the Middle East. But the imperial loans were dwarfed by funds provided by the USA, which ran to £5.4 billion.

Churchill described the Lend-Lease Law that FDR signed into effect on 11 March 1941 as the 'least sordid act in history'. In Berlin it was taken as tantamount to an American declaration of war. In fact, the peculiar structure of Lend-Lease was the direct result of earlier unhappy experiences in Anglo-American war finance. In the First World War Britain and France had relied first on private loans and then on Liberty Loans to fuel their struggle against the Central powers. By 1933, after the failure of inter-allied debt diplomacy they were officially declared in default. Congress could not therefore approve new loans, but resorted instead to the fiction of Lend-Lease. America's aid appeared denominated as dollars in the accounts of the US federal government, but the arms, raw materials and food were provided to its Allies in kind and did not therefore appear in their regular national accounts as obligations to the USA. Nevertheless, the relief provided was enormous. By early 1941 the sum total of Britain's foreign currency reserves not already committed to overseas orders amounted to less than $2 billion, sufficient to cover no more than a few months of procurement. By the end of the war, according to US accounts, Lend-Lease would funnel over $50 billion into the

---

Allied war effort, of which $31 billion were directed to Britain. Britain's allocation of American largesse was greater than Germany's total domestic war effort in 1942. Supplies to its Allies would make up no less than 17 per cent of the US war effort.

Where did this vast flow of resources come from? In 1939 the US economy was still at a low ebb. When FDR launched his momentous plans for the peacetime draft, a two-ocean navy and a world-conquering 65,000 plane air-fleet in May 1940, the American economy was still operating at less than 80 per cent of capacity.[25] From 1939 onwards the US economy began to surge under the impact of British and French military orders, the domestic industrial investment these unleashed and increased federal government spending. In 1941 real US GNP rose 16 per cent. More remarkably, in 1942 and 1943, when unemployment among American men had fallen to zero, growth continued at 13 per cent. Between 1938 and 1944 US GDP increased by 87 per cent. Efficiency gains due to mass production of war equipment contributed about a quarter of this output growth. In this respect the USA was similar to the other combatants. The truly distinctive feature of the US war economy was labour mobilization, which accounted for three-quarters of the production surge. Between 1940 and 1943 11.25 million men and women joined or rejoined the American labour force, more than the total industrial workforce of Germany. An even bigger contribution was made by the lengthening of working hours which rose from an exceptionally low level of 35.6 per week in US manufacturing in 1938 to 45.2 in 1944. Despite the images of American industrial might dramatized by Ford's famous B-17 production line, new investment played a surprisingly small role in the US war effort. The US federal government spent lavishly on war factories. Net government investment between 1942 and 1945 ran to a massive $99.4 billion. Gigantic synthetic rubber, aluminium and aircraft industries were built from scratch. But over the same period private investment was so drastically curtailed that it fell below depreciation, reducing the private capital stock by $6.2 billion. Combined with the dramatic growth in output, this concerted reallocation of resources enabled the USA both to mount a gigantic war effort and to increase the private standard of consumption relative to 1939, while providing a huge flow of resources to its Allies.

There was anxiety, of course, about over-taxing even America's abundant resources. In the First World War the USA had seen its prices rise by 120 per

25 Byrd L. Jones, 'The Role of Keynesians in Wartime Policy and Postwar Planning, 1940–1946', *American Economic Review* 62:2 (1972), 125–33 (p. 127).

cent between 1913 and 1920, less than the European combatants but enough to unleash an unprecedented wave of labour unrest.[26] But the role of Keynesians in the USA in the early phase of the Second World War was not to argue for compulsory saving, as their master was doing in the UK, but to warn against higher taxation, which might retard the long-awaited recovery.[27] Provided the USA reorganized its tax system, as the Harvard Keynesian Alvin Hansen wrote in 1941, the war boom promised to generate 'enormous revenues'.[28] No change brought by the war to American society was more profound than that in its tax system. The First World War had laid the foundations of America's modern fiscal apparatus. The number of Americans filing income tax returns leapt from 350,000 in 1914 to 5 million by 1918. But it was in the Second World War that filing federal income tax became a truly national experience. Between 1939 and 1943 the numbers filing with the Internal Revenue Service (IRS) increased from 7.5 million to 45 million. In total between 1942 and 1945, 47 per cent of US spending was covered by taxes, 27 per cent from borrowing and the rest through money creation. Though this meant that the money supply doubled, highly effective price regulations were enough to hold inflation in check for the duration of the war at least.

Economics of occupied Europe

For Hitler and the SS the announcement of Lend-Lease in the spring of 1941 was confirmation that London and Washington were firmly in the grips of the world Jewish conspiracy. As in the First World War, whether war was declared or not, Germany's real antagonist was the economic might of the USA. When Hitler's victory over France had the effect not of forcing Britain to surrender, but of bonding London and Washington more closely together, this drove the Third Reich toward a two-pronged response. In military-industrial terms, it responded by ploughing further investment into raw material autarchy and preparations for a large-scale air war. The synthetic chemicals complex at Auschwitz, the largest single industrial investment project of the Third Reich designed to produce rubber and air fuel, was a pillar of this new strategy. At the same time, the invasion of the Soviet Union,

---

26 Earl J. Hamilton, 'The Role of War in Modern Inflation', *Journal of Economic History* 37:1 (1977), 13–19 (p. 170).

27 Donald Winch, *Economics and Policy: A Historical Survey* (New York: Walker and Co, 1969), pp. 263–4, 274–7.

28 Alvin Hansen, 'Deficit Financing and Inflation Potentialities', *Review of Economics and Statistics* 23:1 (1941), 1–7.

expected to take no more than one campaigning season, was conceived as a way of securing for Germany the oil, grain, alloy metals and slave labour that it would need to pursue an intercontinental war. It was in the autumn of 1941, therefore, as the resistance of the Red Army broke the onrush of the BABAROSSA offensive that the strategic dilemma of German war planning became fully apparent. If it could not win quickly in the east, the Third Reich faced a two-front war of epic proportions. In the west the Germans faced the British and American economies whose combined output in 1942 was four times larger than that of the Reich. In the east, the Soviet Union had a population at least twice that of the Reich and an economy that matched Germany's, commanded by the most radical mobilization regime the world had ever seen.

The performance of the Soviet war economy was one of the true surprises of the Second World War. In the First World War poverty and underdevelopment had undermined the tsarist war effort and brought Russia to collapse by 1917. In October 1941 Stalin's regime was shaken by the onslaught of the Wehrmacht and came close to breaking point. But Moscow rallied and, sustained by the capital investment, organization and coercive capacity stamped out of the ground since 1928, it performed the most remarkable mobilization of any of the combatants. Despite suffering a fall in output of at least 35 per cent as a result of the German invasion, defence production in 1942 was 3.7 times that of 1940. There were huge gains in productivity in the Soviet armaments factories, which achieved the most remarkable performance of any of the combatants, under extremely adverse circumstances. Since the onset of forced industrialization in 1928 Soviet engineers and factory managers had become inured to the stresses of 'storming growth' and imperative production targets. After 1941 the triumph of the Soviet war economy lay in its success in surviving one crisis after another. Among the major European combatants no other population suffered such hardship. In 1942 the year in which the Red Army stopped the onslaught of the Wehrmacht, civilian consumption was reduced to less than 40 per cent of Soviet GDP. Inessential spending of all kinds was slashed to the bone. To contain inflationary pressures, taxes were increased dramatically. But the prices of what little food and clothing could be bought through regular retail channels tripled. The urban population that did not enjoy high priority in ration allocations was reduced to the level of starvation. In the cities mortality sky-rocketed. In a desperate bid to hold Stalin in the war against Germany, Lend-Lease was extended to the Soviets in October 1941 and by the end of the war the Soviet Union would receive US$11.3 billion in funds. But the pipeline of foreign aid took time to build up. In 1942, the year of Stalingrad, Soviet net imports amounted to only 5 per cent of GDP. Where Lend-Lease played a crucial role was not in the early defensive battles, but in helping to sustain the monumental series of counter-offensives that took the Red Army to Berlin. For the last two years of the war 10 per cent of Soviet GDP was being provided through foreign aid, amounting to as much as one-fifth of the total Soviet war effort.

On the German side, as the Blitzkrieg invasion of the Soviet Union unravelled, Fritz Todt, who had headed Hitler's Ministry of Munitions since early 1940, argued that Hitler must escape the vice of a two-front war by opening peace talks with Stalin. But when Todt was killed in a mysterious plane crash in February 1942, this call for diplomacy lost its most powerful exponent. He was replaced by a coalition of loyalists wholly committed to the Nazi war effort. The front man for this new team was Albert Speer, Todt's charismatic replacement as Munitions Minister. The SS man Herbert Backe, State Secretary in the Agricultural Ministry, took charge of mobilizing the food economy of Europe. Gauleiter Fritz Sauckel organized the press gangs that would bring foreign labour to Germany. Heinrich Himmler's SS would act as enforcers. And Göring provided the necessary figurehead. Goebbels set up a special section in the Propaganda Ministry to publicize the triumphs of the armaments miracle, which duly followed as labour and raw materials were pumped into the armaments factories built since the mid-1930s and Germany benefited like the other combatants from the efficiencies of mass production. Against the odds, this combination would sustain the German war economy down to the winter of 1944–45. The Wehrmacht would run out of room before it ran out of material. There would be no repeat of the collapse of November 1918. They could in no way alter the outcome. But the inferno in which Hitler choreographed his regime's downfall would not burn out for lack of fuel.

Like the British and Soviet war efforts, the Axis war effort was a multi-national affair. In Italy, after a long lull between 1936 and 1940 armaments expenditure surged, largely at the expense of private investment. But Italy like the rest of occupied Europe was hobbled by chronic shortages of oil, food and essential raw materials. From 1942, real mobilization gave way to inflation and disorganization. In the summer of 1943, in the weeks before the collapse of Mussolini's regime, the black-market price of bread in Rome was eight times the price of the official ration. Rice fetched ten times the official price. And by 1943 the disintegration of the Fascist regime was symptomatic of dislocation making itself felt across the entire economy of occupied Europe.

In 1940 in the flush of its Blitzkrieg victories, German Economics Minister Funk had talked in bold terms about a new European currency system. When asked to comment, Keynes remarked that it was best that he did not reply because he objected to nothing in Funk's proposal, other than that Germany stood at its centre. As it turned out, the fact that it was Nazi Germany that stood at the centre did indeed make all the difference. From 1940 onwards the clearing accounts of the Reichsbank became the basis for a massive system of exploitation. This did not burden all of Europe equally. Allies such as Romania and Italy, Finland, Croatia and Bulgaria all benefited from net imports from Germany even after the turning point on the Eastern Front. So too did favoured occupied territories such as Norway. Even the rump of Poland, the General Government, which was a major staging area for the Wehrmacht's war with Russia, imported, according to the official statistics, more from Germany than it delivered. By contrast, Denmark, the Netherlands, France, Belgium and even Serbia and Greece found themselves on the end of highly one-sided trading relationships, making deliveries for Germany and paying for the Wehrmacht occupation in exchange for Reichsbank credits that were never redeemed.

Overall, France made the largest contribution to the German war effort. In 1943–44 French payments to Germany may have risen to as much as 55 per cent of French GDP. In material terms the impact on the French population was dramatic. In the cities of France the meat and fat rations in 1943 were half what they had been in the first year of the war and less than 20 per cent of pre-war consumption. Even bread consumption was cut by 30 per cent. In Belgium the miners digging coal for Germany went hungry. With the official ration providing at most 1,500 calories per day, for city dwellers there was no alternative but recourse to the dangerous and exorbitant black market which by 1943 perhaps accounted for 20 per cent of French GDP. France and Belgium were rich societies with deep reserves of wealth. In a poor and import-dependent society the combined impact of the Allied blockade and the Axis invasion was disastrous. The worst-case scenario was Greece, where output collapsed by 70 per cent in 1941 and 1942, the Axis armies took what they needed from the land and prices sky-rocketed. As a result, as many as 360,000 people starved to death in Athens–Piraeus and across the Greek islands. Perhaps as many as one in twenty of the Greek population perished in the famine.

The overall contribution of the occupied territories to the German war effort was not comparable in quality to what the USA could supply to Britain. Oil, steel and non-ferrous metals remained desperately short. But in quantitative terms the contribution of the occupied territories was very large. As in the case of Lend-Lease, the sheer scale and multi-facetedness of wartime economic integration defied regular national accounting. There is a bitter historic irony in the fact that our modern techniques of national income accounting reached a new pitch of refinement at the moment that slave labour returned to some of the most advanced economies of the world. But, according to the latest calculations, France alone may have contributed one-sixth of the Reich's war expenditure between 1940 and 1944. In 1943 as the German military effort surged to 60 per cent of domestic income, a quarter of the Reich's military budget was covered by the occupied territories, by means of a current account deficit amounting to 16 per cent of German GDP. However, even at the height of the Nazi exploitation of Europe, the majority of the Third Reich's war effort was covered out of Germany's own resources. A large part came in through taxes, the revenues of which doubled between 1938 and 1943, as wartime earnings and profits surged. On top of that, out of the Reich's expenditure in 1943 of 153 billion Reichsmarks, 87 billion were funded through borrowing, equivalent to almost all the Reich's spending on the Wehrmacht. The vast majority of this debt was placed directly with Germany's financial institutions. These then took in deposits from savers which were recycled to the state. Much has been made of the fact that this system of 'silent financing' did not involve the popular war bond drives familiar from the First World War. It has been alleged that Hitler's regime shrank from a financial referendum. But, in fact, all of the combatants relied in varying degrees on such indirect fund-raising mechanisms. In Britain the large wartime surpluses of the health and unemployment insurance funds were credited to the account of the National Debt Commissioner. In the USA, the banking system, savings banks and insurance funds provided more than enough funds to cover the cost of Lend-Lease. Though its mechanism of financing may have done without fanfare, Hitler's regime made no secret of the crucial role that savings played in the mobilization of the war economy. At every turn, the Volksgenossen were loudly called upon to save for victory. Thanks to rationing and the effective suppression of the black market their options were, in any case, limited. Rather than thinking of institutional funding as a flight from 'democratic' bond financing, it seems more appropriate to think of 'silent financing' as an organizational expression of the new macroeconomic approach to public finance that Keynes and others had been calling for since 1939. So long as the circuit of wages, savings, borrowing and government expenditure was maintained, the flow of funds provided the indispensable frame for Germany's hybrid war economy, half way between a terroristic Stalinist dictatorship and a profit-driven market economy. It was after the summer of 1944, when the prospect of imminent defeat became too obvious to ignore, that in Germany too the financial foundation of the war economy began to disintegrate. As the money supply bloated and price incentives lost their meaning, outright coercion became increasingly essential to maintain production.

Across Europe, Hitler's war bequeathed a monetary and financial disaster. In the chaotic two-year period following Mussolini's overthrow, Italy's price level soared by a factor of fifteen. As France was consumed by something akin to civil war, in 1944 its price level doubled. Plans to cement liberation with an austere anti-inflationary policy were abandoned in favour of monetizing government spending. This had the effect between 1944 and 1950 of reducing France's public debt as a share of GDP from 181 to 51 per cent. To undo the financial effects of German occupation as quickly as possible Belgium, Denmark and Norway, as well as Poland, Czechoslovakia and Yugoslavia, carried out wholesale currency reforms, backed up by draconian taxes on wartime profiteers. Austria introduced a new national currency in November 1945. Meanwhile, in post-war Germany, the Reichsmark remained in circulation and Hitler's price stop decree of 1936 continued to be effectively enforced. This worked remarkably well in holding back a vast monetary overhang, which by 1947 was estimated at ten times the volume of money in circulation in 1936. Perhaps half of this surplus purchasing power spilled over into a restricted, but spectacularly expensive black market, where items such as butter, sugar and stockings went for 100 times official prices. Transactions between German civilians and the soldiers of the occupying forces were commonly denominated in cigarettes. Meanwhile, the bulk of economic life was reduced to a rudimentary level of rationing and barter. The Nazi occupation of Europe had at least maintained a division of labour from which many farmers and businessmen in occupied Europe had benefited handsomely. The question that inescapably posed itself with the end of the war was how Germany and Europe could be reconstructed and reinserted into a wider international economic order.

A new order?

In August 1941 in the Atlantic Charter, Churchill and Roosevelt had committed themselves to a return to a system of multilateral trade combined with guarantees for social security and labour protections at the national level.[29]

---

29 Elizabeth Borgwardt, *A New Deal for the World: America's Vision for Human Rights* (Cambridge, Mass.: The Belknap Press of Harvard University Press, 2005), pp. 42–5.

Such liberal sentiments were easy to agree on. The difficult work of post-war economic planning had begun in a much more conflictual way over the demands of Article VII of the 1940 Lend-Lease Agreement, which specified that Britain's receipt of American aid was contingent upon its commitment to non-discrimination in post-war trade – in other words, to the removal of the system of imperial preference it had erected at the 1932 Ottawa Conference. Under influence of the free trade Secretary of State Cordell Hull, the USA targeted the economic blocs created by the British as well as the Germans and Japanese in the 1930s as one of the primary causes of the outbreak of the war and the first set of obstacles to be removed in reshaping post-war international order according to American globalist designs.[30] For the British, on the other hand, the commonwealth system of trade restrictions and currency controls, even if it was tarred with the brush of Schachtianism, seemed to offer the surest means of coping with what promised to be its catastrophic post-war balance of payments deficits, particularly if the US economy went into downturn after the war, as many feared, and transmitted the deflationary effects of its recession abroad. British imperialists and conservatives feared that abolishing imperial preference would threaten the political survival of the Empire, while the left worried it would make the pursuit of full employment and post-war social insurance schemes impossible.[31] In December 1942 the publication of William Beveridge's scheme for comprehensive post-war social security had attracted attention across Europe and spurred on a flurry of economic and social planning.[32] With the publication of the White Paper on Employment Policy in 1944, Britain's wartime coalition had officially committed itself to guaranteeing post-war employment.[33] How were such far-reaching promises of domestic activism to be reconciled with the constraints of a liberal international order?

In August 1941, in an effort to seize the initiative, Keynes had begun working on a plan to guarantee that the British re-entry into a multilateral

---

30 G. John Ikenberry, 'Creating Yesterday's New World Order: Keynesian "New Thinking" and the Anglo-American Postwar Settlement', in Judith Goldstein and Robert O. Keohane, eds., *Ideas and Foreign Policy: Beliefs, Institutions, and Political Change* (Ithaca: Cornell University Press, 1993), pp. 57–86 (pp. 63–6).
31 Richard N. Gardner, 'Sterling–Dollar Diplomacy in Current Perspective', *International Affairs* 62:1 (1985), 21–33 (p. 23). Alfred E. Eckes, *A Search for Solvency: Bretton Woods and the International Monetary System, 1941–1971* (Austin: University of Texas Press, 1975), p. 51.
32 Paul Addison, *The Road to 1945: British Politics and the Second World War* (London: Quartet, 1977), p. 171.
33 Jim Tomlinson, 'Why Was There Never a "Keynesian Revolution" in Economic Policy?', *Economy and Society* 10:1 (1981), 72–87.

system would be as little damaging to its post-war position as possible. His original designs called for the creation of an International Clearing Union that would settle payments by means of a new international currency called bancor. Rather than facing the merciless discipline of the financial markets, member states would have access to overdraft facilities in a new international bank, which they could use to cushion any necessary adjustment in their balance of payments. This system would accommodate Britain's status as international debtor, as it would force creditor countries, like the USA, to make their surplus available to countries in deficit. Keynes envisioned a system of quasi-automatic rules requiring adjustment by surplus as well as deficit economies, thus replicating by organizational means the self-equilibrating powers once attributed to a certain idealized vision of the gold standard.

In late 1941 officials in the USA began work on their own schemes for an international monetary system, one better reflecting the dominant position of the USA as the world's dominant creditor. Responsibility for post-war economic planning had moved from the State Department into the hands of a group of Keynesian-minded economists around Harry Dexter White in Henry Morgenthau's Treasury. Perhaps not surprisingly, the Americans showed little interest in a synthetic global currency. Instead, in April 1942, White's team proposed the creation of an International Stabilization Fund, which would provide financial assistance to member states experiencing temporary balance of payments difficulties, and a Reconstruction Bank, for post-war relief and redevelopment. Membership in the Fund would require states to remove exchange controls, lower tariffs, and relinquish sovereignty over adjusting their exchange rates without supranational approval.[34] With funds of $5 billion subscribed by its members, White's Stabilization Fund would have broad discretionary powers to determine which deficit countries were eligible for its financial assistance. Crucially, this would give the USA, as the largest contributor to the Fund, the right to exercise oversight over all its members and to have the final say in who received assistance.[35] Unlike in Keynes's project, no requirements were placed on the surplus members of the system to address the inadequate level of domestic demand that was the necessary concomitant of their export surplus.

---

34 Eckes, *A Search for Solvency*, p. 48.
35 Harold James, *International Monetary Cooperation since Bretton Woods* (Oxford University Press, 1996), p. 41.

While the plans of Keynes and White differed on the roles to be played by their proposed international institutions, both the British and the American negotiators shared a broad understanding of what 'the economic lessons of the 1930s' called for. While British and American experts agreed on the need to return to a system of fixed exchange rates and to remove exchange controls and clearing arrangements as quickly as possible, they also envisioned a system that gave states greater latitude to intervene in their national economies than had been possible under the gold standard. Given the speculative attacks which had undone the global financial system in the early 1930s there could be no return to the world of before 1914 when capital had moved without restrictions. Nor should maladjusted parities force damaging deflations. Better to adjust the par value of currencies in a coordinated fashion, on the lines of the Tripartite Agreement with France in 1936, thus enabling stimulative and full employment policies to be maintained even in the face of external pressure. In this way, the tools of national economic governance, which had been used to underpin aggressive rivalry in the 1930s, would be reconciled with the disciplined cooperation of a restored international economy.[36]

Negotiations over the Keynes and White plans began in the summer of 1942, and a compromise on monetary matters, unlike on the politically explosive issue of trade, was achieved relatively quickly. In September 1943, Keynes dropped his idea of the Clearing Union and by April 1944 the British had accepted a modified version of the original White Plan with a larger stabilization fund.[37] A conference to finalize the details of the Keynes–White plans was organized for July 1944, just three weeks after the D-Day invasion, at the Bretton Woods resort in New Hampshire, to which representatives from forty-four non-Axis countries were invited. While a lot of time was spent in arguing over IMF quotas and the topic of trade barriers was avoided for fear of producing an immediate deadlock, the conference was decisive in another respect. During the proceedings, it became clear that as the war had taken such a disastrous toll on the stability of all the other major world economies, the US dollar alone would play the key role at the heart of the new monetary system. Fixed to gold at $35 an ounce, the US dollar would become the world's de facto currency of reserve, with the value of all other currencies pegged at adjustable rates.

---

36 John Ruggie, 'International Regimes, Transactions, and Change: Embedded Liberalism in the Postwar Economic Order', *International Organization* 36:2 (1982), 379–415.
37 Eckes, *A Search for Solvency*, p. 105.

While the Bretton Woods Conference itself was hailed as a success, in the face of the ruined state of the European and Asian economies it did not by itself guarantee an immediate return to the multilateral world economic system that US planners had envisaged. For economies in the state of Italy or France any immediate return to full-blown international competition was unthinkable. As the war ended, a high stakes struggle began in which questions of grand strategy, financial and economic reconstruction were inextricably intertwined. Already in December 1945, the Soviets, with whom Harry Dexter White had carried on surreptitious negotiations, indicated that they would refuse to join the Bretton Woods institutions, in one of the first moves that suggested the wartime alliance would not long outlast the peace.[38] And even among the capitalist powers, the wartime visions of the post-war order proved bitterly divisive. Planning for the creation of an International Trade Organization (ITO) began in earnest only in December 1945, by which point the wartime enthusiasm for internationalist experimentation had already mostly faded.[39] The Charter for the ITO laboriously agreed upon at Havana in March 1948 was promptly voted down by the US Congress, leading to the opening of a new round of conferences, known optimistically as the General Agreement on Tariffs and Trade (GATT).[40] Tariffs, however, were a secondary consideration if countries lacked the currency to make imports. And after 1945 one problem dominated all others – the world-wide shortage of dollars.

In 1945 the booming US economy was responsible for a record share of 60 per cent of all manufacturing world-wide. The dollar gap thus came to stand as the main obstacle to reconstruction. The situation was particularly manifest in the British case, which emerged from the war as America's major ally and as the second largest economy in the world, but also as America's largest debtor, owing $12 billion to the USA, in addition to 3.7 billion in sterling balances, valued at between $12 and $16 billion depending on the exchange rate, to the Empire and other creditors. The UK thus became the crash test dummy for the new economic order.[41] In 1946, the USA agreed on a loan of $3.75 billion to Britain, on the condition that London move to the full implementation of the Bretton Woods model of fixed, but fully convertible

---

38 James, *International Monetary Cooperation*, pp. 68–71.
39 Ibid., pp. 62–3.
40 Richard Toye, 'Developing Multilateralism: The Havana Charter and the Fight for the International Trade Organization, 1947–1948', *International History Review* 25:2 (2003), 282–305.
41 Eckes, *A Search for Solvency*, p. 280.

currencies in June 1947. As the other signatories to Bretton Woods looked on and its reserves rapidly drained away, Britain suffered a currency crisis so severe that within only six weeks it had to abandon convertibility and retreat to wartime exchange controls. Clearly any implementation of the wartime designs would have to wait. This debacle gave new impetus to the joint-European investment programme announced by Secretary of State George Marshall, which promised as much as $16 billion in investment to raise European productivity so that it could hold its own in trade with the USA. But not only was this a tall order in economic terms, it was a red flag to the Soviet Union. After Bretton Woods in 1944, the offer of Marshall aid to the countries occupied by the Red Army in 1947, followed in June 1948 by the introduction of the new currency the Deutschmark in the British and American zones would mark crucial moments in the escalation of the Cold War. Rather than unifying the world, the Anglo-American post-war architecture would come to mark the front line in a confrontation in which armed blocs defined by their economic systems as much as their politics would divide the world between them.

After the Second World War the idea of restoring something like a true state of peace as the foundation for a reconstructed world economy slipped away even more quickly and radically than it had done after the First World War. Within only five years of the end of the war, the communist invasion of South Korea turned the Cold War into a major shooting war that required a dramatic remobilization of both the US and British economies and unleashed a tidal wave of inflation in global commodity markets. The Marshall Plan was supposed to culminate in 1952 with restoration of competitiveness such that Europe could make good on the institutional design of Bretton Woods. The Korean War and the entanglement of the French and British in wars of decolonization set that back to 1958. Nor was this merely an adjustment in timeline. What NATO believed itself to be facing after 1950 was the imminent possibility of all-out Soviet assault. The hypothetical of total war, which had overshadowed the 1930s, returned with a vengeance. In the early 1950s defence spending in Britain and France exceeded 10 per cent. In the USA it peaked in 1953 at 15 per cent of GDP. These figures were high even by the standards of the 1930s arms race. They were triple the figures that had been normal among European powers before 1914 and ten times what the US federal government had been in the habit of spending on defence up to 1940. What we should be asking about the organization of the capitalist world after the Second World War is not how war was left behind, but how, unlike in the 1930s, a prolonged state of high mobilization was made sustainable. On the weaker members of the Western coalition, above all France and to a lesser extent Britain, this took its toll. As in the 1930s high military spending was combined after 1950 with very rapid economic growth. But this time, despite the lop-sided quality of this growth boom and despite the fact that Germany's economy was roaring ahead, Europe's reconstruction was contained within a set of international economic, financial and security institutions. These were unprecedented in the sophistication with which they interlinked military, diplomatic, economic, financial and social concerns. But above all, unlike in the interwar era, they were securely founded on both sides of the Atlantic.

2

Finance for war in Asia and its aftermath

GREGG HUFF

For Japan and China, finance for war in Asia and its repercussions stretched over fourteen years from 1937 to 1950, involved thirteen major monetary regimes, yielded more than a fair share of exploitation, and in China led to dramatic collapse. Issues of war finance engaged Japan, republican or nationalist China and the Chinese Communists throughout all fourteen years, and for the Japanese also included Southeast Asia between 1941 and 1945. By May 1942, Japan controlled that region's six main countries of Burma, Thailand (Siam), Malaya (including Singapore), Indonesia (Netherlands India), Indochina and the Philippines.[1]

War can be financed by selling bonds to the public, through taxation, and by printing money. As well as printing money in the literal sense of currency rolling off presses this last includes indirect creation of money in the form of bank deposits, matched by holdings of bonds in the banks' balance sheets. Indirect money was, however, unimportant in Asia except to some extent in Japan. The main aim of this chapter is to analyse choices of war finance in Asia and to show how these depended on institutional capability, political will and the ability of government to innovate and adapt fiscal and monetary arrangements in response to the need for increased finance to pay for war. I argue that war-enforced economic and administrative constraints typically forced governments to obtain a high proportion of war finance from printing money. It is, Keynes remarked, what governments and military administrations do to

1 Thanks go to the editors and to Richard DuBoff, Campbell Leith, Shinobu Majima, Tetsuju Okazaki and Xun Yan for many helpful comments and suggestions. I owe a particular debt of gratitude to Andrew Bain and Hugh Rockoff who commented extensively on the chapter and whose detailed comments and suggestions fundamentally shaped it. Shingo Kakino provided outstanding research assistance. Support and funding from ESRC grant (RES-062-23-1392) made this chapter possible and is gratefully acknowledged.

finance themselves if no other methods exist.[2] Although that was not wholly true in Asia, governments sometimes persisted with promiscuous monetary creation as the apparently easy financial option.

Overwhelmingly, one or other of the three methods of finance was used to pay for war in Asia and this chapter deals only with them. However, finance by no means exhausts the ways in which governments obtain resources. These include labour extraction, compulsory, uncompensated deliveries, price controls, a shift to war expenditure at the expense of non-war spending, and direct confiscation.[3] Asia has numerous examples of all these types of resource mobilization. The most egregious in Southeast Asia was the use of forced labour and materials taken from elsewhere in the region to build the Siam–Burma railway. Nationalist China drafted millions of soldiers and, to help feed them, began in July 1942 the compulsory purchase of foodstuffs which a year later turned into 'compulsory borrowing'. Japan paid for the war partly by price controls, by a savage shift of resources away from consumption in favour of military expenditure, and by drafting large numbers of workers including, eventually, school children. All of the combatants in China seized goods, food and property.

Money, like any commodity, can be taxed, and governments can finance themselves, perhaps even chiefly, through monetary expansion and therefore seigniorage, defined as the revenue that governments obtain from their right to issue money and the difference between the cost of printing money and what it will buy. Heavy reliance on printing money to finance war is, however, almost certain to cause high inflation and, moreover, create the danger that inflation may quickly spiral out of control. Hyperinflation is a term often used loosely to denote price rises of possibly no more than 150 per cent or 200 per cent a year. In this chapter, hyperinflation is defined using the commonly accepted Philip Cagan criterion of price increases of 50 per cent a month for three consecutive months and the Carmen Reinhart–Kenneth Rogoff requirement of inflation of 40 per cent per month. When inflation breaches even a much lower level than the Reinhart–Rogoff threshold it

---

2 J. M. Keynes, *A Tract on Monetary Reform* in *The Collected Writings of John Maynard Keynes* (30 vols., London: Macmillan for the Royal Economic Society, 1971), vol. iv, p. 37.
3 Hugh Rockoff, *Until It's Over, Over There: The US Economy in World War II.* NBER Working Paper 10580 (Cambridge, Mass.: National Bureau of Economic Research 2004), pp. 7–8 and *America's Economic Way of War: War and the US Economy from the Spanish-American War to the Persian Gulf War* (Cambridge University Press, 2012), pp. 4–5, 16–17, 24–5.

becomes, as they emphasize, 'pernicious'. Unless soon corrected, hyperinflation will almost certainly accelerate and destroy seigniorage as a means of finance.[4]

The effective taxation of money, and so seigniorage as a revenue source, relies on the public being willing to hold currency issued by the government. That, in turn, depends partly on avoiding too much inflation. In time, if prices continuously increase, people demand less money because its real value falls and the cost of holding currency rises or, to say the same thing, the demand curve for money slopes downwards. Barter may begin to substitute for a money economy or even supplant it. And yet, as this chapter shows, money is not that easily replaced. Even when high inflation has destroyed the motive for holding money as a store of value to purchase goods at a later date, it is still likely to be held for transactional reasons of everyday purchases and payments. Moreover, war finance in Asia demonstrates that governments can effectively coerce the public into holding state-issued money.

So long as people hold money, inflation acts as a form of tax on it. Money is the tax base and inflation the rate of taxation. A main argument of this chapter is that long periods of war and occupation in Asia could be financed by printing money because the demand for it held up sufficiently well that hyperinflation was largely avoided and confidence in money was not entirely destroyed. The dependence on finance through monetary creation, and for the most part the success of this technique, gave the financing of war in Asia between 1937 and 1945 a discernible unity.

Finance for war, although highly unlikely to dissuade great powers like Japan and China from conflict, can be so managed that it seriously harms the war effort and, furthermore, gives rise to major post-war difficulties. Poorly managed finance, through generating high inflation, can create confusion or possibly panic; public resentment is likely to arise if war finance creates an unfair distribution of the burden of financing war. When panic or public disillusionment spread, they undermine national morale and greatly harm the war effort. There is, observed Keynes, who claimed to borrow the point from Lenin, 'no subtler, no surer means of overturning the existing basis of society than to debauch the currency'.[5]

---

4 Philip Cagan, 'The Monetary Dynamics of Hyperinflation', in Milton Friedman, ed., *Studies in the Quantity Theory of Money* (University of Chicago Press, 1956), pp. 25–117 (p. 25); Carmen M. Reinhart and Kenneth S. Rogoff, *This Time is Different: Eight Centuries of Financial Folly* (Princeton University Press, 2009), pp. 4–5.

5 J. M. Keynes, *The Economic Consequences of the Peace* in *The Collected Writings of John Maynard Keynes*, vol. II, p. 149.

After the Japanese surrender on 15 August 1945, a new set of economic and social problems associated with wartime finance assumed prominence. An early post-war issue was that a monetary overhang of large quantities of money printed during the war threatened financial stability and high inflation. The chapter demonstrates that the overhang of a swollen wartime money supply may be dealt with in three ways. One is to repudiate the wartime currency. In occupied areas, this has the attraction of a natural reluctance to assume responsibility for money inherited from a former enemy's wartime finance, even though de-monetization disenfranchises large numbers of ordinary people and creates fundamental post-war economic problems. A second is to absorb wartime money but possibly try to counter inflationary forces with macroeconomic stabilization measures. The third is simply to ignore monetary overhang, the inflation effects of which are much compounded if government then relies on finance through ever greater monetary creation. Asia provides examples of all these possibilities and their consequences.

The proximate post-war aftermath of wartime finance in Asia lasted well beyond the problem of dealing with monetary overhang. It extended in China to the June 1949 surrender by the Chinese nationalist commander, General Tu Yu-ming, to Communist forces, by which time President Chiang Kai-shek had already resigned and fled to Taiwan with his government's remaining gold reserves (some three million ounces, equal to $207 million at the 1945 free market price in China); it included the post-war collapse of the Japanese economy and its stabilization by 1950; and it encompassed the achievement, also around 1950, of something like economic normalization in Malaya, the Philippines, Thailand and, to a lesser extent, Burma, though not in Indonesia or Vietnam in Indochina where conflict and revolutionary movements, often reliant on financing themselves through printing money, dominated.

Japan: financing war at home

Japan, although its mobilization for war was badly managed and often poorly executed, never had any difficulty in financing war, starting with the so-called Peking Incident in 1937 and continuing until the Pacific War ended in 1945.[6] Finance for both the Sino-Japanese and the Pacific War was at the expense of much higher inflation than for other major combatants, drastic cuts in civilian

---

6 Jerome B. Cohen, *Japan's Postwar Economy* (Bloomington: Indiana University Press, 1960), p. 84. On the problems of Japanese war mobilization, see Richard Rice, 'Economic Mobilization in Wartime Japan: Business, Bureaucracy, and Military in Conflict', *Journal of Asian Studies* 38:4 (1979), 689–94.

Table 2.1 *Japan war expenditure, 1940–1944*

Gross national product (1934–36 yen m)	20,628	20,908	20,820	21,085	20,113
Percent of gross national product					
Total government expenditure	20.1	25.1	32.5	39.9	48.9
Central government expenditure	15.1	19.9	28.6	35.9	45.0
Central government war expenditure	11.8	16.4	24.4	32.2	41.0
Pay, travel, subsistence	3.0	3.7	4.4	5.1	6.9
Munitions industries	6.8	8.7	12.1	19.1	24.7
Other	2.0	4.0	7.6	7.8	9.3
Private capital formation	12.8	10.4	8.9	10.4	13.0
Consumer expenditures	67.1	64.5	58.6	49.7	38.1
(War expenditure abroad)	2.5	5.5	6.2	7.5	14.4

Notes: Percentages are approximate. They derive from the United States Strategic Bombing Survey which gives different GDP figures than in the table. Figures in the table are from Ohkawa and Shinohara.

Sources: United States Strategic Bombing Survey, *The Effects of Strategic Bombing on Japan's War Economy* (Washington, DC: Overall Economic Effects Division, United States Strategic Bombing Survey, 1946), p. 15; Kazushi Ohkawa and Miyohei Shinohara with Larry Meissner, *Patterns of Japanese Economic Development: A Quantitative Appraisal* (New Haven: Yale University Press, 1979), pp. 259–60.

consumption, and considerable repressed inflation. Remarkably, though, eight years of war were financed without more than high inflation. That was achieved through a combination of strong Japanese government direction, a corporate and financial sector responsive to this lead and underwritten by state guarantees, and a compliant public.

Military spending, having already risen sharply between 1931 and 1936, further gained pace after the 1937 outbreak of the China war. Central government expenditure, largely a reflection of military spending, expanded swiftly during the Pacific War. It was still around a fifth of GDP in 1940, but by 1944 reached roughly half of national income. Since GDP declined somewhat after 1939 and then stagnated from 1940 to 1944, the shift to a war economy was at the expense of consumer expenditure, which fell from about two-thirds of GDP in 1940 to two-fifths by 1944 (Table 2.1).

Official statistics indicate falls in real per capita household consumption expenditure of over two-fifths between 1937 and 1944 and almost a third from 1940 to 1944.[7] An even more savage contraction is suggested by data showing

7 Keizai Kikakucho, ed., *Kokumin Shotoku Hakusho* (White Paper on National Income), 1963 fiscal year issue (Tokyo: Printing Bureau of the Ministry of Finance, 1965), pp. 164–5.

Table 2.2 *Japan government debt and finance, 1932–1944*

	1932–36	1937–41	1942–44	1932–44
Increase in debt (Y bn)				
Central government	4.3	30.4	110.2	144.9
Total government	5.4	30.9	111.0	147.3
Rate of debt increase per year	9.3	25.2	50.5	24.0
Debt increase as % of national product	7.0	18.4	57.6	33.6
Distribution of central government debt increase	32	36	29	30
Banking system	38	44	50	47
Other financial institutions	30	20	21	23
Others				

Note: Local government accounts for the difference between total government and central government.

Source: Goldsmith, *Financial Development*, p. 127.

that in 1944 defence expenditure accounted for 76 per cent of GDP. That percentage does not, however, measure a corresponding cut in living standards: it includes as part of military government spending items such as subsidies, pensions and expenditure for military government bonds. A substantial part of these outlays went to individuals and was spent on consumption.[8] Nevertheless, civilian living standards dropped precipitately. Evidence of this includes a reduction in average daily calorie intake from an estimated 2,250 in 1940 to 1,800 by 1944; a decrease in the net supply of cotton cloth from 2,184 million square yards in 1937 to 51 million square yards; and a similar decline in the availability of woollens. Few, if any, additional supplies of silk or synthetic fibre compensated for the lack of cottons and wool.[9]

Beginning with the China war, increased military spending led to a ballooning government deficit financed chiefly through the Bank of Japan and other financial institutions. Government debt, shown in Table 2.2, rose rapidly during the Sino-Japanese War and even more swiftly from 1942 to

8 Akira Hara, 'Japan: Guns before Rice', in Mark Harrison, ed., *The Economics of World War II: Six Great Powers in International Comparison* (Cambridge University Press, 1998), pp. 224–67 (p. 257).
9 United States Strategic Bombing Survey [hereafter USSBS], *The Effects of Strategic Bombing on Japan's War Economy* (Washington, DC: Overall Economic Effects Division, USSBS, 1946), pp. 32–3.

1944. The increase in debt, equal to about a sixth of national income between 1937 and 1941, reached some three-fifths in 1942 to 1944.[10]

Neither taxes nor the sale of bonds to the public financed much of wartime government debt. In April 1940, Japan enacted, as the Tax Reform Law, a revised tax system which had personal income tax as its nucleus and the system's main income generator. But despite this, and although the public faced a host of consumption and indirect taxes, Japan made no serious attempt to adapt the tax system to provide a large share of war finance.[11] The taxation of income applied to individuals but not corporations and even here wartime inflation eroded the tax take. Japan did not, unlike, for example, the USA, try to create widespread bond ownership among its citizens.[12]

Government debt was financed chiefly through an 'internal financing circuit' which relied on thrift institutions (savings banks, post office saving system, trust accounts, urban and rural credit cooperatives) and commercial banks.[13] Table 2.2 shows that between 1932 and 1944 thrifts took 47 per cent of government debt. The government distributed a further 30 per cent of debt to banks.

Individual saving, organized through neighbourhood associations, was compulsory in all but name. The government prescribed rates of saving according to an individual's income and people were expected to compete with one another in saving. Permission to withdraw savings had to be obtained from the head of the neighbourhood association and reasons for requesting a withdrawal explained to him in detail.[14] The thrifts, swamped with personal savings, were directed to put these funds at the government's disposal by holding bonds. A large part of government debt was therefore financed in a not immediately inflationary way.[15]

Bond quotas were allocated to the various banks by the government. Quota size was based on the government's need to sell bonds which, in turn, depended on required war finance. The government used large subsidies to

---

10 Raymond W. Goldsmith, *The Financial Development of Japan, 1868–1977* (Princeton University Press, 1983), pp. 127–8.

11 Henry Shavell, 'Postwar Taxation in Japan', *Journal of Political Economy* 56:2 (1948), 124–37 (p. 125).

12 Jerome B. Cohen, *Japan's Economy in War and Reconstruction* (Minneapolis: University of Minnesota Press, 1949), p. 85.

13 Ibid., p. 85.

14 United States Office of Strategic Services, Research and Analysis Branch, *Control of Inflation in Japan*, R&A 2451 (Washington, DC, 1 October 1945), pp. vi, 18–19; Sheldon Garon, 'Luxury is the Enemy: Mobilizing Saving and Popularizing Thrift in Wartime Japan', *Journal of Japanese Studies* 26:1 (2000), 41–78 (pp. 55–9).

15 Goldsmith, *Financial Development*, p. 128.

stimulate war production and oversaw bank lending to munitions industries, at first by approving the outcome of negotiations between the banks and industries but later simply by telling the banks how much and to whom to lend.[16] Banks could continue to buy government bonds because a high proportion of income generated by war production found its way back to them as deposits and closed this component of Japan's internal financing circuit.

Between 1941 and 1945, currency in circulation increased more than sevenfold and bank deposits almost trebled but wholesale prices, according to the official index, less than doubled. In reality, prices increased substantially more than this. Table 2.3 suggests that by 1944 actual wholesale prices were some 43 per cent above the official index. However, that, too, probably understates price rises, since by 1943 black market prices for main consumer goods were far above official prices and by mid-1945 often ten to 100 times higher. Rice prices on the black market rose from six times more than the official price in December 1943 to 28 times in mid-1944. By November 1944, they were 44 times higher than official prices and this increased to 70 times in July 1945.[17] Nevertheless, during the eight years of war, rigid price and financial controls operated sufficiently effectively to leave post-war Japan with considerable repressed inflation.[18]

Japan's internal financing mechanism 'succeeded rather well' until mid-1944. Subsequently, however, bond absorption by financial institutions could not match sharply increased war expenditure; government finance had to rely heavily on money printed by the Bank of Japan.[19] That continued after 1945 and, as discussed below, inflation surged.

China: nationalist, Japanese-occupied and communist

Monetary regimes

Between 1937 and 1949, China, as Map 2.1 shows, had six main monetary regimes: nationalist Chinese currency; four different Japanese occupation currencies, each with its own so-called puppet bank; and, as the sixth, various communist currencies. Additionally, Japanese forces introduced military yen

---

16 Cohen, *Japan's Economy*, pp. 85–6; Juro Teranishi, 'The Main Bank System', in Tetsuji Okazaki and Masahiro Okuno-Fujiwara, eds., *The Japanese Economic System and its Historical Origins* (Oxford University Press, 1999), pp. 63–96 (pp. 75–9).
17 USSBS, *Effects*, p. 225.
18 Cohen, *Japan's Postwar Economy*, p. 84.
19 Ibid., p. 89.

Table 2.3 *Japan money supply and prices, 1934/36–1945*

	Money in circulation		Wholesale prices (official) 1934/36 = 1	Wholesale prices (actual) 1936 = 1	Ratio of free (black market) to official prices
	Currency Y million	Bank deposits Y million			
1934/ 36	2,330	4,579			
1937	3,155	5,855	1.3	1.2	
1938	3,478	7,293	1.3	1.3	
1939	4,654	10,484	1.5	1.5	
1940	6,000	13,157	1.6	1.7	
1941	7,827	15,972	1.8	1.8	
1942	9,274	20,254	1.9	2.4	
1943	13,099	23,137	2.0	2.7	
1944	22,856	31,801	2.3	3.3	
1945	56,658	46,180	3.5		29.7

Note: The deposit figure for 1945 reflects the expansion of deposits of the Yokohama Specie Bank in China. See Cohen, *Japan's Economy*, pp. 90, 96–7. For 1945 the ratio of free to official prices refers to December.

Sources: Money supply: Goldsmith, *Financial Development*, p. 112; Wholesale and Tokyo prices: Bank of Japan, *Hundred-Year Statistics of the Japanese Economy* (Tokyo, 1966), p. 77; Actual wholesale prices: Cohen, *Japan's Economy*, p. 97; Ratio free to official prices: Mitsuhiro Fukao, Masao Oumi and Kimihiro Etoh, 'Japan's Experience in the Immediate Postwar Period: Moving Toward a Single Exchange Rate and Denationalization of Trade', in Juro Teranishi and Yutaka Kosai, eds., *The Japanese Experience of Economic Reforms* (Basingstoke: Macmillan, 1993), p. 110.

(*gunpyo*). Distrustful of civilian administrators and anxious to have its own spending power, the Japanese military printed this scrip (unbacked military notes, literally campaign money given to invading forces) in substantial quantities.[20]

Deflation forced on China by the USA's silver repurchase programme in the 1930s caused it to abandon the silver standard in November 1935. After that, the nationalists issued the fabi (meaning legal tender) as their standard

20 Okinori Kaya, 'Money and Banking', *Oriental Economist* (March 1943), 131–2; Richard A. Banyai, *Money and Banking in China and Southeast Asia during the Japanese Military Occupation 1937–1945* (Taipei: Tai Wan Enterprises, 1974), pp. 47–55.

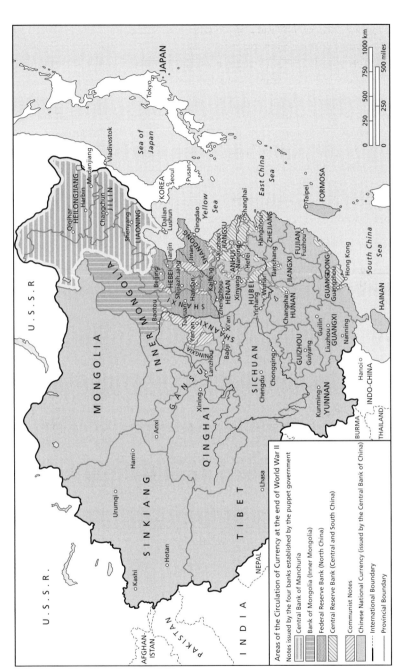

2.1 China monetary areas, 1945

paper money. It gave way to the gold yuan note in August 1948, followed by the silver yuan note in July 1949.

Rather than take over existing banks, the Japanese preference in China, and also Southeast Asia, was to establish new ones to ensure total control. Occupation resulted in four different banks to issue currencies for each of four main occupied regions. The Central Bank of Manchou, established soon after Japanese occupation, functioned as Manchuria's sole bank of issue between 1933 and 1945. Manchurian currency, integrated into the yen bloc and redeemable at par in Japanese yen, had a similar stability to the yen for most of the war. After it, however, the invasion of Manchuria by Russia, which introduced large quantities of military scrip, and China's civil war brought economic chaos. Beginning in 1937, the Mengcheng Bank (Bank of Mongolia) became the monopoly currency issuer in two Inner Mongolian provinces. From 1938 to 1945 in North China, the Japanese-initiated Federal Reserve Bank (FRB) circulated its own currency, as in South and Central China did the Central Reserve Bank (CRB), operative in Nanjing and Shanghai from January 1941.

As well as the six main monetary regimes, several others operated in China. These included some small Japanese-controlled banks with their own currencies and various minor regimes. However, most of China's small monetary regimes were in areas run by the Communists. Between 1930 and 1948, they issued about thirty local currencies, and in 1948 ten different Communist paper currencies still circulated in border regions and 'liberated' areas.[21]

From 1937 onwards, almost all monetary regimes in China relied on inconvertible paper with little or no backing. Exceptions were various commodity standards with at least some backing in real goods operated by the Communists; yen backing for the Manchuria currency; and brief nationalist experiments to try to bolster confidence in their currency by allowing limited convertibility into precious metals. All China's monetary regimes were strongly regional until after August 1945, and among them rates of note and price increase differed greatly.

Nationalist-controlled China

In 1937, republican China was ill-prepared for war. The nationalists had, despite warnings, made little progress in developing the necessary industrial base. Nor was agreement between the nationalists and Communists to forge

---

21 Colin D. Campbell and Gordon C. Tullock, 'Hyperinflation in China, 1937–49', *Journal of Political Economy* 62:3 (1954), 236–45 (p. 236).

Table 2.4 *Nationalist China cash budgetary and military expenditure, 1937–1945 (millions of CNC$)*

	Cash budgetary expenditure	Military expenditure	Military as % of cash budgetary expenditure
1937–38	2,103	1,388	66.0
1938 (2nd half)	1,181	699	59.2
1939	3,063	1,600	52.2
1940	5,245	3,911	74.6
1941	10,892	6,616	60.7
1942	26,602	15,216	57.2
1943	63,352	42,944	67.8
1944	182,832	131,080	71.7
1945	1,266,438	1,075,367	84.9

Notes: The picture of military expenditure is approximate. It excludes outlay for communications, economic development and subsidies to provincial and local governments and all these were mainly for war ends. However, emergency expenditures are included as military and probably contained some non-military components.
Source: Young, *China's Wartime Finance*, p. 16.

a politically united war front reached until after fighting with Japan began. Soon after this, the nationalists organized administrative bodies, overseen by their leader Chiang Kai-shek, to press forward the war effort, but within five months this 'administration of the wartime state was in utter chaos'.[22] Nevertheless, China had somehow to try to finance the mobilization and equipment of a military capable of opposing, or at least slowing, vastly superior Japanese forces.

Between 1937 and 1945, increased military spending caused nationalist Chinese government expenditure to balloon. Table 2.4 shows that military expenditure normally accounted for from three-fifths to two-thirds of government outlays. Even this probably understates military expenditure.

At the outset of the war, printing money was the only realistic internal means for the nationalists to generate much of the required war finance, given the regime's obvious administrative and institutional weakness; and given Japan's occupation of seven of twenty-two mainland Chinese provinces

22 Lloyd E. Eastman, 'Nationalist China during the Sino-Japanese War 1937–1945', in John K. Fairbank and Albert Feuerwerker, eds., *The Cambridge History of China*, vol. XIII, part 2: *Republican China, 1912–1949* (Cambridge University Press, 1986), pp. 547–608 (p. 559).

including the main industrial areas, with consequent declines for the nationalists in the output and availability of many goods. Pre-1937 fiscal arrangements had relied primarily on customs revenue, which was now no longer available because Japan soon occupied strategic coastal areas and ports. The other two main revenue sources of taxes on salt and commodities also dried up. Nor, despite some attempts, could private or corporate saving take up much of the slack.[23] China lacked a tradition of bond sales and, from 1938, risk, high inflation, and low fixed interest rates made bonds unattractive.

The nationalist government nevertheless continued to eschew any real effort to pay for the war by any financial method other than through printing money. Beginning in 1939, note issue typically increased at well over 100 per cent a year and money creation amounted to between 66 per cent and 78 per cent of government expenditure (Table 2.5). In 1944, China's Finance Minister H. H. Kung justified the reliance on money creation as the obvious solution: 'When Japan invaded China in 1937, China's monetary system was prepared for the emergency ... The new system [of paper money] enabled the government to rely on the increase of bank credit as a means of emergency war finance.'[24]

Monetary expansion on the scale practised by China could only result in high inflation. Inflation was exacerbated by output declines in a number of commodities, difficulties in obtaining usual imports due to Japanese control of coastal areas, large refugee inflows, and seriously inadequate transport. Numerous price control schemes were ineffective. Poor transport caused large regional price variations, but in 1939 and 1940 average retail price rises in nationalist China exceeded 100 per cent annually. Between 1941 and 1944, the increase escalated to approximately 240 per cent a year, consistent with average price rises of about 10 per cent a month in each of these years and an overall increase in prices of more than 3,700 per cent. Beginning late in 1944, inflation further accelerated and a price rise of 250 per cent during the eight months of 1945 threatened Cagan-type hyperinflation (Table 2.6). However, after Japan's August surrender prices fell sharply amid optimism that something like normality would now be established.

As inflation increased, the volume of nationalist paper money greatly expanded, since the government insisted on printing notes in the same, historically low, denominations. Most of the notes were printed in the USA

---

23 William C. Kirby, 'The Chinese War Economy', in James C. Hsiung and Steven I. Levine, eds., *China's Bitter Victory: The War with Japan 1937–1945* (Armonk, NY: M. E. Sharpe, 1992), pp. 185–212 (p. 193).

24 H. H. Kung, 'China's Financial Problems', *Foreign Affairs* 23:1 (1944), 222–32 (pp. 222–3).

Table 2.5 *Nationalist China government expenditure, revenue, deficit covered by borrowing and increase in note issue, 1936–1945*

	Expenditure	Revenue (non-borrowed)	Deficit covered by borrowing	Increase in note issue
(a) Millions of CNC$				
1936–37	1,167	870	297	
1937–38	2,091	559	1,532	320
1938 (2nd half)	1,169	297	872	578
1939	2,797	715	2,082	1,982
1940	5,288	1,317	3,970	3,580
1941	10,003	914	9,090	7,266
1942	24,511	4,592	19,919	19,227
1943	58,816	15,882	42,934	41,019
1944	171,690	35,609	136,081	114,082
1945	1,215,089	150,061	1,065,028	842,471

	Non-borrowed revenue as % of expenditure	Deficit covered by borrowing as a % of expenditure	Increase in note issue as % of expenditure	% increase in note issue
(b) Percentages				
1936–37	74.6	25.4		
1937–38	26.7	75.9	15.8	
1938 (2nd half)	25.4	74.6	49.4	
1939	25.6	74.4	70.9	
1940	24.9	75.1	67.7	80.6
1941	9.1	90.9	72.6	103.0
1942	18.7	81.3	78.4	164.6
1943	27.0	73.0	69.7	113.3
1944	20.7	79.3	66.4	178.1
1945	12.3	87.7	69.3	638.5

Notes: 1. Until 1939 data are for fiscal years ending 30 June and thereafter for calendar years. 2. Data for 1945 are for the whole year and cannot be broken down to show the period ending 15 August. 3. Note issue is for government banks. Data for note issue in Chang, *Inflationary Spiral*, pp. 374, 376 differ slightly from above figures.
Source: Young, *China's Wartime Finance*, pp. 12, 162.

Table 2.6 *Nationalist, Japanese-occupied and Communist China prices, 1937–1945 (Jan.–June 1937 = 1)*

	Avg. retail market in nationalist China	(Tianjin)	(Beijing)	(Shanghai)	(Yan an)
(a) Price indexes					
1937	1.00	1.00	1.00	1.00	1.00
1938	1.45	1.29			1.43
1939	3.23	2.47		3.18	2.37
1940	7.24	3.48		5.23	5.00
1941	19.8		5.84	15.6	22.0
1942	66.2		11.7	44.7	99.0
1943	228		33.5	214	1,199
1944	755		351	2,490	5,647
1945 Aug.	2,647		3,791	85,200	
1945 Dec.	1,799		1,460	54,200	
(b) Annual percentage price increases					
1937					
1938	45.0	29.0			43.0
1939	122.8	91.5			65.7
1940	124.1	40.9		64.5	111.0
1941	173.5	100.0		198.3	340.0
1942	234.3		100.3	186.5	350.0
1943	244.4		186.3	378.7	1,111.1
1944	231.1		947.8	1,063.6	371.0
1945	138.3		316.0	2,076.7	

Sources: Young, *China's Wartime Finance*, pp. 152, 349; Schran, *Guerrilla Economy*, p. 184.

and had to be flown over the Hump (the Himalayas) to reach nationalist territory. Between 1943 and 1945, the weight of airlifted notes averaged about 150 tons monthly. By this latter part of the Pacific War, large purchases might require a briefcase or even a suitcase full of notes. Banks made up bundles of notes in denominations of 20, 50 or 100 Chinese dollars; these were commonly taken at value without counting.[25]

25 Arthur N. Young, *China's Wartime Finance and Inflation, 1937–1945* (Cambridge, Mass.: Harvard University Press, 1965), pp. 159–61 and 321.

The nationalist government also insisted on a fixed fabi exchange rate. That enabled China, and Chinese officials, to siphon off large amounts of US dollar foreign exchange and substantially contributed to undermining American support for China. Although by December 1944 just 0.1753 of a US cent was needed to buy a fabi in the readily available black market, the USA still had to pay the official rate of five cents, 28.5 times as much. By June 1945, overpayment for fabi had risen to 85.3 times the market rate.[26] General Joseph Stillwell reflected widespread American infuriation over fabi overvaluation when observing, as early as February 1944, that 'If this keeps up, they will pay us all they owe us with a basket of oranges'.[27] Particularly destructive to support for China in the USA was the filtering back of stories of the endemic government corruption and a blatantly unfair share out of the burdens of war and war finance to the detriment of ordinary Chinese. From 1938 onwards, people with influential (political) connections enriched themselves by black market currency arbitrage between the dollar and fabi. Many of these individuals built up asset holdings abroad and left nationalist China before its eventual collapse.[28]

Remarkably, however, in light of nationalist China's sustained, quite high inflation, price rises did not accelerate out of control. 'Inflation', as the historian of China's war finance emphasized, 'did not become hyperinflation in 1937–1945 [so that China] was able to use inflationary finance to meet a large part of the government's needs all through the war, and thereafter until 1947 before hyperinflation set in'.[29] China avoided hyperinflation and could finance the Sino-Japanese and Pacific Wars chiefly through monetary expansion because the demand for money, despite obviously high inflation, did not collapse. To be sure, real balances (the nominal value of money divided by the price level and so adjusted for inflation) fell considerably, indicative of the growing unwillingness of people to hold money (Figure 2.1). A consequent erosion of the (money) tax base from which the government could generate finance from seigniorage almost certainly caused this revenue to decline. To try to make up for falling seigniorage, the government had to print ever greater quantities of money. That was at the cost of increasing to very high

26 For market and official exchange rates, see John G. Greenwood and Christopher J. R. Wood, 'The Chinese Hyperinflation. Part 2: The Crisis of Hyperinflation', *Asian Monetary Monitor* 1:2 (1977), 32–45 (p. 42).

27 Quoted in Young, *China's Wartime Finance*, p. 280.

28 Arthur N. Young, *China and the Helping Hand, 1937–1945* (Cambridge, Mass.: Harvard University Press, 1965), p. 258 and *China's Wartime Finance*, p. 238.

29 Young, *China's Wartime Finance*, pp. 309–10.

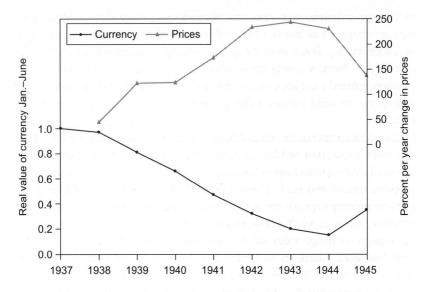

2.1 Nationalist China real value of currency and rate of change in prices, 1937–1945

percentages inflation as a tax and, since money was widely held by the public, levying this taxation on a large number of poor people.

How was hyperinflationary collapse avoided and why did the Chinese continue to hold money to the extent they did when its value was being comprehensively debauched? Inflation judged by the public as 'not too high' and so 'acceptable' would help to sustain seigniorage. So-called money illusion (mistaking nominal for real (inflation-adjusted) values) may also be a part of persuading (or fooling) people into holding government-issued currency. There was, however, more than public acceptance or financial unawareness to the story in China.

A reason for the continued holding of money was its use as a medium of exchange and so retention of transactional benefits. Money was needed to pay taxes and in other dealings with the government as well as to make everyday purchases. Indeed, even throughout China's post-1947 hyperinflation the fabi and its successors, although eschewed as a unit of account and store of value, still functioned as the principal medium of exchange.[30] While China's high proportion of peasant agriculturalists made it easier

30 Campbell and Tullock, 'Hyperinflation in China', pp. 241–4.

to survive inflation, this also contributed to holding down inflation by supporting money demand. Under inflationary conditions, Keynes observed, as 'more money flows into the pockets of the peasants, it tends to stick there'.[31] In China, a strong rural tendency to hoard the fabi, despite high inflation, existed until about 1940, although it is unclear how far this peasant willingness to hold money subsequently persisted and therefore curbed inflation.[32]

US military expenditure contributed to Chinese inflation by increasing the demand for materials and labour, but this was probably more than counterbalanced by American help in financing the war through sending equipment, supplies, money and gold. These inflows significantly reduced the need for Chinese military expenditure with a consequent reduction in money creation to finance the war. Additionally, financial aid from the USA helped to support the foreign exchange value of the fabi and so somewhat limited inflation. American gold shipments to China, like Allied gold consignments to India and various Middle Eastern countries, were partly intended to try to keep down the money supply and dampen inflation by soaking up excess purchasing power. Probably more important in China than any reduction in inflation through an absorption of purchasing power was that confidence in the fabi may have been fostered by gold, shipped by the USA and sold on behalf of and by China's Central Bank.[33] That would have prevented as great a flight from the fabi as would otherwise have occurred, and so helped to restrict inflation.

Gold was successfully used elsewhere during the Second World War to manipulate expectations about the currency. In Greece, Nazi Germany's release of gold at intervals 'sufficed periodically to restore enough short-run public confidence in the drachma to maintain the seigniorage maximisation policy'.[34] In a similar way, it could be, as China's Finance Minister H. H. Kung claimed, that American gold shipments engendered confidence in China's currency. At the end of December 1944, Kung telegraphed US Treasury Secretary Henry Morgenthau that 'the recent gold shipment is one of the outstanding factors contributing to the strengthening of fapi

---

31 Keynes, *Tract on Monetary Reform*, p. 66.
32 Kung, 'China's Financial Problems', p. 229; Chang Kia-Ngau, *The Inflationary Spiral: The Experience of China, 1939–1950* (New York: John Wiley & Sons, 1958), pp. 31–2; Eastman, 'Nationalist China', p. 586.
33 Young, *Helping Hand*, p. 317.
34 Michael Palairet, *The Four Ends of the Greek Hyperinflation of 1941–1946* (Copenhagen: Museum Tusculanum Press, 2000), p. 102.

[now known as the fabi], because people believe that the arrival of gold has increased the much needed reserve of our currency'.[35]

By later 1944, American support for China faltered and foot-dragging on gold shipments to the nationalists became apparent; Treasury Secretary Morgenthau regarded these as like 'putting money down a rat-hole'.[36] Arthur Young maintained that a continued willingness of the USA to supply gold to China might have altered its wartime and post-1945 inflation experiences and so the Republic's entire history:

> Certainly the withholding of gold from China aggravated the inflation, with all the grave consequences that followed during and after the war. To say how much that action aggravated inflation would be speculation. But those who held back gold, despite China's pleas and in violation of a clear American commitment, must bear part of the responsibility for later tragic events.[37]

Evidence for gold's importance exists: during the fourteen months between the September 1943 announcement of gold shipments and October 1944, by which time gold sales had effectively exhausted the Central Bank's stock of gold, monthly inflation averaged 9.0 per cent. That compares with averages of 12.1 per cent in the preceding fourteen months and 17.9 per cent in the subsequent nine months leading up to the Japanese surrender.[38] Good harvests in the autumn of 1943 may, however, have played a part in holding down price rises. Robert Brandfon disputes Young's argument on the grounds that more gold shipments would not have restricted inflation by soaking up purchasing power.[39] He does not, however, test for causation a correlation between lower inflation and gold shipments, or explore the possible effect of these on boosting confidence in the fabi.

Milton Friedman has hypothesized that if the USA had not undertaken its silver purchase programme, China might not have had to abandon the silver standard as soon as it did. Although hyperinflation would ultimately have happened, it might have taken longer to unfold and so given nationalist China a somewhat better chance of avoiding catastrophic collapse and

---

35 Quoted in Young, *China's Wartime Finance*, p. 284, and see also Shun-Hsin Chou, *The Chinese Inflation, 1937–1949* (New York: Columbia University Press, 1963), pp. 224–32.

36 Hebert Feis, *The China Triangle: The American Effort in China from Pearl Harbor to the Marshall Mission* (Princeton University Press, 1953), p. 301.

37 Young, *China's Wartime Finance*, p. 298 and *Helping Hand*, p. 338.

38 Young, *China's Wartime Finance*, pp. 284–6, 349, 369.

39 Robert Leon Brandfon, 'The Young Thesis, the Loss of China, and United States Gold Policy', *International History Review* 9:2 (1987), 227–49.

Communist takeover.[40] Friedman's argument is cautiously formulated and, like Young's, necessarily counterfactual. But both arguments are provocative and point to the far-reaching historical impact that war finance may have.

Japanese-occupied China

In China and, as discussed later, also in Southeast Asia, the financial techniques Japan adopted to finance occupation avoided any real payment. Japan firmly adhered to the first financial principle of occupation: that the occupied country should bear the cost of being occupied.[41] Japan had only a limited range of options available to finance its occupation of China. Neither bond sales nor taxation offered much scope to raise funds; finance was necessarily chiefly through printing money. That, however, largely sufficed and through eight years of Asian war the 'Japanese have, perhaps, been the most successful of all nations in the issuance of military currency – successful in the sense of gaining the most per unit of effort spent upon the currency issued'.[42]

Beginning in 1938, Japan isolated the Home Islands from money supply and inflation in occupied areas by issuing currency, the so-called 'puppet' notes, which could not be used outside occupied territories.[43] Monetary expansion by the four principal banks set up by Japan and the inflation histories of their associated regions differed considerably (Tables 2.6 and 2.7). While the Manchou Central Bank was relatively restrained in its currency issue, the Federal Reserve Bank and the Central Reserve Bank were not. After 1943, as the war turned against Japan and confidence in occupation monies wavered, finance through money creation required an increasing volume of notes. In consequence, Japanese issue of currency gained considerable momentum and while at first inflation in nationalist China had generally outdistanced that in Japanese-occupied regions, beginning in 1944 this ranking sharply reversed. Inflation was particularly high in Shanghai, where between December 1944 and August 1945 monthly price increases averaged well over 40 per cent.

40 Milton Friedman, 'Franklin D. Roosevelt, Silver, and China', *Journal of Political Economy* 100:1 (1992), 62–83; Milton Friedman and Anna Jacobson Schwartz, *A Monetary History of the United States, 1867–1960* (Princeton University Press, 1963), pp. 489–91.
41 Richard A. Lester, 'Review of Bloc and Hoselitz, *Economics of Military Occupation*', *American Economic Review* 34:2, part 1 (1944), 395–6.
42 Richard A. Lester, *International Aspects of Wartime Monetary Experience* (Princeton: International Finance Section, Department of Economics, 1944), p. 3.
43 Lincoln Li, *The Japanese Army in North China, 1937–1941: Problems of Political and Economic Control* (Tokyo: Oxford University Press, 1975), pp. 138–40; Henry Simon Bloc and Bert F. Hoselitz, *Economics of Military Occupation: Selected Problems* (revised edn, University of Chicago Press, 1944), pp. 8, 20.

Table 2.7 *China: Japanese and puppet note issues, 1937–1945*

(a) Millions

	Manchukuo Central Bank (yen)	Federal Reserve Bank (FRB$)	Central Reserve Bank (CRB$)	China Incident Military Notes (MY)	Mengcheng Bank (yen)
1937	307			1.4	13
1938	426	162		36	36
1939	624	458		151	60
1940	947	715		248	63
1941	1,201	964	237	244	114
1942	1,670	1,581	3,477	381	143
1943	3,011	3,762	19,150	407	379
1944	5,877	15,841	139,699	671	1,058
Aug. 1945	8,158	83,506	2,697,231	1,516	2,799

(b) Percentage increase

	Manchukuo Central Bank (yen)	Federal Reserve Bank (FRB$)	Central Reserve Bank (CRB$)	China Incident Military Notes (MY)	Mengcheng Bank (yen)
1937					
1938	38.8			2,471.4	176.9
1939	46.5	182.7		319.4	66.7
1940	51.8	56.1		64.2	5.0
1941	26.8	34.8		1.6	81.0
1942	39.1	64.0	1,367.1	56.1	25.4
1943	80.3	138.0	450.8	6.8	165.0
1944	95.2	321.1	629.5	64.9	179.2
Aug. 1945	38.8	427.2	1,830.7	125.9	164.6

Note: For 1945 yen notes are for 31 July and other 1945 figures are for 31 August.
Source: Young, *China's Wartime Finance*, p. 366.

For the most part, however, Japan, like nationalist China, probably succeeded in financing the war chiefly by printing money.[44] If so, much of the cost of war finance would have fallen, as in nationalist China, on the mass of

44 Li, *Japanese Army*, p. 55.

population in the form of a high and escalating inflation tax. Any and everyone who held money paid it.

Key to successful Japanese war finance in occupied China was that, despite high inflation, the demand for money apparently held up well for much of the war. Again, as for nationalist areas, one asks why? Similar transactional motives to those indicated above for China applied in Japanese-occupied areas. Japan actively promoted the adoption of its occupation currencies by requiring their use to pay for government services, by displacing Chinese national money through systematic, progressive depreciation of its exchange value, and, before long, by outlawing the fabi's use altogether. After declaring Chinese national currency no longer legal tender in early 1938, Japan enforced this with compelling sanctions: 'all circulation of Chinese national currency was prohibited in certain specified areas and any person bearing or using such outlawed currency in those areas was subject to punishment, often death'.[45] Like the Japanese, the nationalists and Communists outlawed the use or possession of any currency other than their own.[46]

Communist-controlled China

Heeding Mao's 1934 stricture of 'extreme caution' in printing bank notes, between 1930 and 1934 Communist armies issued silver coins bearing the hammer and sickle insignia.[47] However, after China left the silver standard the Communists began the issue of paper through a dozen or more banks (Figure 2.1).[48] The Communists managed fiscal systems with varying degrees of success, but deficit finance appears to have been the rule and in some areas was extreme. Communist finance relied significantly on trade with Japanese- and nationalist-run regions to gain 'foreign exchange' and also goods that could be acquired only expensively, if at all, through import substitution. Finance also depended partly on obtaining fabi through seizure.[49] In poor regions, the likelihood of smaller supplies of fabi to seize together with less economic surplus to tax helps to explain usually greater deficit finance in these areas. The biggest fiscal deficits seem generally to have been in border regions. Since people in these apparently tended not to hold paper money,

45 Lester, *International Aspects*, p. 4; Young, *Helping Hand*, p. 67.
46 Campbell and Tullock, 'Hyperinflation in China', p. 236.
47 Peter Schran, *Guerrilla Economy: The Development of the Shensi-Kansu-Ninghsia Border Region, 1937–1945* (Albany: State University of New York Press, 1976), p. 58; Young, *China's Wartime Finance*, p. 58.
48 Young, *China's Wartime Finance*, p. 186.
49 Edgar Snow, *Red Star over China* (London: Victor Gollancz, 1973), pp. 230–1.

perhaps reflecting a high element of barter in daily transactions, inflation was higher than if the propensity to hold currency had been greater.[50]

The inflation history of Communist-controlled China is far from complete. Some regions, like Shanxi-Chaha'er-Hebei (Shanshi-Chahar-Hopei), were relatively successful in restricting inflation, but many Communist areas had much higher price rises than their nationalist counterparts.[51] While the success of Shandong's successful 'fiscal-military' state derived partly from revenue obtained from a salt monopoly, restraint in monetary expansion must have been important.[52] The highest inflation in Communist areas was in the Shaanxi-Gansu-Ningxia (Shensi-Kansu-Ningsia) border region and far above the nationalist average (Table 2.7).[53]

The Communists used high inflation in nationalist areas as a propaganda tool both before and after 1945, and were anxious to avoid something similar happening to themselves. Partly to instil confidence and forestall this possibility, the Communists often expressed their currencies as equivalent to a commodity or basket of commodities and claimed that they were backed accordingly. It seems doubtful, however, that Communist monies were usually, or even more than rarely if at all, fully backed. In northern Jiangsu (Kiangsu) province, the government promised that one catty of wheat would be given in exchange for a dollar, but serious commodity shortages apparently made that material assurance merely a deception.[54] Accounts kept in units of a commodity, for example millet, and its use for the payment of taxes and wages were introduced to separate these payments from currency fluctuations, but had the disadvantage of being subject to fluctuations in the commodity itself.[55]

During the post-1945 hyperinflation, the Communists introduced a 'parity unit' for bank deposits based on several commodities to protect against inflation. In Shanghai, the commodity basket consisted of 1.72 pounds of medium-grade rice, a foot of twelve pound 'dragon head' cloth, an ounce of peanut oil and 1.33 pounds of coal briquettes. The monetary value of this

---

50 Schran, *Guerrilla Economy*, p. 201.
51 Young, *China's Wartime Finance*, p. 187; Michel Lindsay, 'The Taxation System in the Shansi-Chama-Hopei Border Region', *China Quarterly* 42 (1970), 1–15 (p. 4).
52 Sherman Xiaogang Lai, *A Springboard to Victory: Shandong Province and Chinese Communist Military and Financial Strength, 1937–1945* (Leiden: Brill, 2011).
53 Young, *China's Wartime Finance*, p. 188; Schran, *Guerrilla Economy*, p. 200.
54 Young, *China's Wartime Finance*, pp. 187–8.
55 Lyman Van Slice, 'The Chinese Communist Movement during the Sino-Japanese War 1937–1945', in Fairbank and Feuerwerker, eds., *The Cambridge History of China*, vol. XIII, part 2: *Republican China*, pp. 609–722 (p. 656).

parity unit was the sum of the current prices of its commodity constituents. However, the realization of their money equivalent, with which the commodities could actually be bought, was never adequately tested because bank accounts were often blocked.[56]

Financing occupation in Southeast Asia

In Southeast Asia, Japan used occupation costs (expenses incurred by the occupying country but paid by the occupied), military scrip and bilateral clearing arrangements to finance occupation and pay for the goods it sent home. There was, at best, minimal institutional scope for financing occupation except through money creation, which accounted for the great bulk of Japanese finance. Neither the Thai and Indochinese governments nor Japanese military administrations could borrow abroad. Only very limited quantities of bonds could be sold to Southeast Asia's banks or through its stock markets. European banks dominated in pre-war Southeast Asia but the Japanese liquidated most of these, while stock markets in the region were either minuscule or non-existent.

Once cut off from global, chiefly Western, markets, Southeast Asia's economies collapsed and so too did their tax bases. To try to obtain finance, Japanese administrators initiated savings campaigns and introduced new taxes. Taxation efforts included 'voluntary' gifts from Chinese businessmen, lotteries, and taxes on gambling, amusement parks, cockpits, bicycles and hand carts. Prostitutes were taxed and efforts to generate revenue from the great wartime upsurge in prostitution included taxing dance hostesses (taxi dancers), female visitors to dance halls, waitresses, restaurants and coffee shops. But taxes, like saving, raised only small amounts of finance.

Monetary creation in Southeast Asia proceeded along two routes. In Malaya, Indonesia, the Philippines and Burma, all administered by military governments, the Japanese transferred resources to themselves simply by printing as military scrip the required amount of currency. Scrip – legal tender only in the country for which it was printed – was, as before the war, denominated in rupees, dollars, guilders and pesos for Burma, Malaya, Indonesia and the Philippines respectively but carried new, 'appropriate' pictures – banana plants for Malaya and Indonesia, pagodas for Burma. Occupation currencies attracted derisive names: 'banana money' in Malaya and Indonesia, 'Mickey Mouse money' in the Philippines.

56 Campbell and Tullock, 'Hyperinflation in China', p. 243.

In Thailand and Indochina, pre-war administrations of a Thai government and the French colonial regime remained in place. Japan exercised control through these governments and used baht (Thailand) and piastres (Indochina) to buy goods it exported and to meet local military and administrative (occupation) costs. The continuance of pre-war currencies made acquiring money more complicated for Japan than in the militarily administered countries, but not overly so. First, the Yokohama Specie Bank credited at the Bank of Japan in Tokyo the accounts of the Bank of Siam or Banque de l'Indochine with the yen equivalent of baht or piastres to be given to Japan. These Southeast Asian 'central banks' then credited the Yokohama Specie Bank in Bangkok or Saigon with local currency for military use. Yen credited to Thailand and Indochina were 'special' which, in reality, meant merely paper credits. As part of bilateral clearing arrangements, special yen nominally offset exports of goods to Japan, including large amounts or rice, but they could not be spent in Japan or used to purchase imports from Japan.

By 1944, systematic Allied destruction of the Japanese merchant marine almost entirely prevented Japan from transporting even essential war materials like oil and rice. Even so, Japan, by exchanging unbacked paper money for Southeast Asian real resources, achieved substantial levels of exploitation in Southeast Asia. Transfers to Japan, when valued at pre-war (1937) exchange rates rather than arbitrary Japanese wartime-imposed rates, reached as much as a third of Indochinese GDP. They were as high as 11 per cent of Thai national income and over a fifth of Indonesian GDP.[57]

In Malaya, the Philippines and Indonesia, price rises far outdistanced monetary expansion and have often been described as hyperinflation. However, by either the Cagan or Reinhart–Rogoff criteria, hyperinflation was not typical until quite late in the war and even then, it did not persist for the three consecutive months specified by Cagan. Five main reasons explain the willingness of Southeast Asians to hold money despite obviously quite high inflation. Taken together, they helped Japan to protect seigniorage by maintaining a (money) tax base and so avoiding the need to issue as much new money as would have been required if the demand for money had been less and therefore the rise in prices greater. First, in Southeast Asia, as in China, the Japanese backed currencies in Southeast Asia with effective coercion. After the first year of occupation, the mere possession of pre-war currencies was deemed criminal and punishable with arrest, often torture, or even

---

57 Gregg Huff and Shinobu Majima, 'Financing Japan's World War II Occupation of Southeast Asia', *Journal of Economic History*, 73, 4 (2013), 937–77 (pp. 942–3).

death.[58] Second, for Southeast Asians, prevented from communicating with the outside world, good substitutes for Japanese-approved money (scrip, Thai baht or Indochinese piastres) did not exist. Third, Southeast Asia's highly specialized economies and country, or often regional, Japanese-enforced autarky combined to restrict the scope for barter as a substitute for money and so increased the latter's transactional benefits. Some economies specialized in rubber, tin or sugar which had little or no barter demand, while in regions specialized in rice its abundance limited barter value. Fourth, money retained its usefulness as a unit of account and medium of exchange. Rationed items, including food and clothing, had to be bought with Japanese-approved money and it had to be used to pay taxes. Furthermore, the Japanese employed large numbers of Southeast Asians and they were paid partly or entirely in scrip, baht or piastres. Finally, although confidence in scrip fell because the Allies announced that it would become worthless after Japan surrendered, not all Southeast Asians believed this propaganda.

Transactional reasons to hold money applied throughout Southeast Asia, but perceptions within the region diverged on the usefulness of money as a store of value available to command goods at a later date. In Malaya, Indonesia and the Philippines, reluctance to hold money as a store of value grew as the war continued. Axis reversals especially eroded scrip as a store of value. In Malaya, 'Every time there was an Axis defeat, particularly Japanese defeats, prices of goods jumped up. Every Allied victory . . . and every visit of B-29s over Malaya, caused spurts of prices in foodstuffs. Saipan, Iwo Jima, Manila, Rangoon, and Okinawa were inflation spring-boards'.[59] In the Philippines, prices rose each time air raid precautions and defence drills were held in Manila.[60]

By contrast, in Thailand and Indochina, the willingness to hold money as a store of value was impressively high. That allowed Japan to acquire real

---

58 'Zairai Tsuka Kaishu Mondai Nitsuite' (Withdrawal of Local Money from Circulation) (by Higuchi Goro), Singapore, Dec. 1943, p. 17, Japan, National Institute for Defense Studies, Military Archives Collection, Nansei Gunsei – 17, Southern Area Military Administration, So Cho Shi 23; C. D. Adhearne, 'The Malayan Currency Problem No. 2', p. 1, United Kingdom, National Archives, Kew [hereafter NA], CO852/510/24; Telegram BMA to SACSEA, Nov. 1945, NA, WO203/390; 'Economic Conditions in the Philippines', 13 Oct. 1942, p. 7, United States, National Archives and Records Administration, 226 16 208.

59 Chin Kee Onn, *Malaya Upside Down* (Singapore: Jitts & Co., 1946), p. 45.

60 Ricardo T. Jose, 'The Rice Shortage and Countermeasures during the Japanese Occupation', in Ikehata Setsuho and Ricardo Trota Jose, eds., *The Philippines under Japanese Occupation* (Manila: Manila University Press, 1999), p. 211.

resources without nearly as much need to print money as elsewhere in Southeast Asia, and so also have much less inflation than in other countries in the region. Holdings of money in Thailand and Indochina rose at about the same rate as prices, or, in other words, real balances remained more or less constant. High real balances in Thailand, Indochina and, for part of the war, in Burma are explained mainly by the dominance in all three economies of numerous small peasant rice growers. Like their counterparts in China, they displayed a tendency to hoard money, even in the face of inflation. Only 20–25 per cent of notes in circulation in Thailand were in Bangkok; 'The rest are in the provinces, where they largely disappear into farmers' hoards: and the demand of the provinces for fresh supplies of notes is a never ceasing one'.[61] In Burma, villagers in rice-producing districts insisted on payment in Japanese currency: 'They thought it was better than British and enjoyed the feeling of wealth which they got by carrying away large wads of brand new Jap notes.'[62]

Post-war finance

Inflation, crisis and solutions in Japan

High inflation was almost unavoidable in post-war Japan because of years of price controls to stifle inflation, because of substantial pent-up consumer demand, and because of a large monetary overhang created by the Bank of Japan's printing of notes, beginning in mid-1944, to finance the war. An inflationary challenge was all the greater due to the need for extensive economic reconstruction which required high government spending and would be difficult, if not impossible, to finance in a non-inflationary way. Japan's tax system remained incapable of offsetting more than a small share of government reconstruction expenditure.[63] Nor did personal saving offer a promising option due to the wartime cut in living standards; if the war had continued mass starvation would have been likely by the autumn of 1945.[64]

---

61 Thailand, *Report of the Financial Adviser Covering the Years 1941 to 1950* (Bangkok, 1951), p. 55.

62 A. K. Potter, 'Currency Policy, Burma', 31 May 1945, United Kingdom, India Office Records [hereafter IOR], M4/306.

63 Shavell, 'Postwar Taxation', pp. 125–6, 130.

64 B. F. Johnson, *Japanese Food Management in World War II* (Stanford University Press, 1953), pp. 140, 149; Cohen, *Japan's Economy*, p. 386; Juro Teranishi, 'Inflation Stabilization with Growth: The Japanese Experience, 1945–1950', in Juro Teranishi and Yutaka Kosai, eds., *The Japanese Experience of Economic Reform* (Basingstoke: Macmillan, 1993), pp. 61–85 (p. 64).

The government had underwritten 'practically every element of risk incident to private enterprise associated with the war' and, with debts twice the aggregate capital and surplus reserves of all corporations in Japan, could not look to Japanese industry for finance. Debt was overcome by, in effect, near total repudiation through a war indemnity tax heavily concentrated on war and munitions industries and the larger financial institutions. The tax, a confiscatory 100 per cent at source, helps to explain a 'non-existent' market for government bonds.[65]

By March 1946, Japan had enacted numerous measures to counter monetary overhang and stabilize the economy. These included requiring the deposit of notes of over ten yen (and subsequently five yen) for redeposit with the Bank of Japan, price and wage controls and freezing deposits. Controls were, however, poorly implemented and whatever effect they might have had was soon swamped by continued government deficit financing.[66] Between 1945 and 1946, the currency component of money supply increased by 67 per cent and the next year rose a further 134 per cent (Table 2.8).

Government economic reconstruction employed a variant of the 'big push' model implemented with government deficit finance and monetized through the Bank of Japan. The post-war Japanese 'big push', proposed by Arisawa Hiromi of Tokyo University and working through the supply side of the economy, emphasized the complementarities and linkages of heavy and chemical industries. Materials, capital injections and subsidies were, for example, concentrated in the coal industry and its output used to produce steel. Greater steel output was, in turn, channelled into increasing coal production and as an input to other, targeted industries. In directing supply in the economy, the government set priorities for materials to go to key industries.[67]

Funds for rebuilding Japan's industrial base were distributed through the Reconstruction Finance Corporation, established in October 1946 and operative in January 1947. The bulk of finance for the Corporation came directly

---

65 Shavell, 'Postwar Taxation', pp. 133–4.
66 Cohen, *Japan's Economy*, pp. 417–18, 454–6.
67 Yutaka Kosai, 'The Postwar Japanese Economy, 1945–1973', in Kozo Yamamura, ed., *The Economic Emergence of Modern Japan* (Cambridge University Press, 1997), pp. 159–202 (pp. 165–6); Masahiro Kuroda, 'Price and Goods Control in the Japanese Postwar Inflationary Period', in Teranishi and Kosai, eds., *The Japanese Experience of Economic Reforms*, pp. 39, 51–6; Mark Metzler, *Capital as Will and Imagination: Schumpeter's Guide to the Postwar Japanese Miracle* (Ithaca: Cornell University Press, 2013), pp. 89–92. For a recent reworking of the 'big push' theory, see Kevin M. Murphey, Andrei Shleifer and Robert W. Vishny, 'Industrialization and the Big Push', *Journal of Political Economy* 97:5 (1989), 1003–26.

Table 2.8 *Japan money supply and prices, 1945–1953*

	Currency 1945 = 1	Bank deposits 1945 = 1	Wholesale prices (official) 1945 = 1	Tokyo retail prices (official) 1945 = 1	Ratio of free (black market) to official prices
(a) Index					
1945	1.0	1.0	1.0	1.0	29.7
1946	1.67	0.36	4.65	6.10	8.3
1947	3.90	0.66	13.76	16.45	5.1
1948	5.58	0.79	36.51	48.26	2.9
1949	6.32	1.59	59.61	78.52	1.8
1950	7.51	2.31	70.45	77.13	1.3
1951	9.01	3.22	97.77	99.84	1.1
1952	10.26	4.54	99.69	96.94	
1953	11.36	5.28	100.37	100.32	
(b) % change	Currency	Bank deposits	Wholesale prices (official)	Tokyo retail prices (official)	
1946	67.5	-64.0	365.3	509.7	
1947	132.9	82.1	195.7	169.8	
1948	43.0	20.7	165.4	193.3	
1949	13.3	101.3	63.3	62.7	
1950	18.9	44.8	18.2	-1.8	
1951	19.9	39.7	38.8	29.4	
1952	13.8	41.0	2.0	-2.9	
1953	10.8	16.2	0.7	3.5	

Note: For 1945 the ratio of free to official prices refers to December, for 1946 to September to December, and for 1951 to January to April.
Sources: Currency and bank deposits: Goldsmith, *Financial Development*, p. 136. Wholesale and Tokyo prices: Bank of Japan, *Hundred-Year Statistics*, pp. 77, 80; Ratio free to official prices: Fukao, Oumi and Etoh, 'Japan's Experience', p. 110.

from the Bank of Japan; it supplied almost four-fifths of the Reconstruction Bank's funds through purchases of securities, chiefly debentures and loans.[68]

68 Cohen, *Japan's Economy*, pp. 449, 446, 466; Goldsmith, *Financial Development*, p. 141; Juro Teranishi, 'Financial Sector Reform after the War', in Teranishi and Kosai, eds., *The Japanese Experience of Economic Reforms*, p. 170.

State support for the Reconstruction Bank was paralleled by the rise in government debt and, to finance debt, large increases in money supply. In 1945, the Bank of Japan had made less than a quarter of its resources available to the government, but by 1948 the proportion was over four-fifths.[69]

Between 1945 and 1949, the quantity of currency rose a little over six times but circulation velocity gained traction and prices increased by something over sixty times. Like its wartime counterpart, post-1945 Japanese price history suffers from a lack of clarity: official figures greatly understate inflation, although seemingly not in any consistent way. The sixty-fold rise shown by the official statistics for 1945 to 1949 compares with an increase of seventy-eight times for 'actual' wholesale prices. Between 1946 and 1949, black market prices were from three to eight times above official prices (Table 2.8). However, both official and actual wholesale indexes indicate that, except for 1946, price rises between 1945 and 1949 fell well short of Cagan-type hyperinflation (Table 2.8). Even so, the Japanese experience has been described as hyperinflation: 'that term should be applicable to . . . an almost 80-fold increase, or nearly 200 per-cent a year, in reported consumer prices'.[70] Whatever the terminology, ordin-ary Japanese suffered greatly from escalating prices, as well as desperate shortages of basic foodstuffs and consumer goods.[71]

Orthodox stabilization measures abruptly halted high Japanese inflation, if at the expense of severe economic contraction and high unemployment. In February 1949, the USA, as the occupying power, dispatched Joseph Dodge to Japan to implement economic stabilization. Dodge, who had previously formulated post-war reconstruction plans for Germany, instigated extreme fiscal austerity and associated policies, popularly known as the Dodge Line. It aimed to create a budget surplus (in fact achieved in 1950) and eliminate the need for monetary expansion to finance government deficits. The Dodge mission, and another in 1950 led by Carl Shoup, resulted in the dissolution of the Reconstruction Finance Bank.[72]

High rates of output growth and a substantial increase in gross capital formation accompanied Japan's post-war inflation. The 'great Japanese

69 Goldsmith, *Financial Development*, p. 140; Hiroshi Yoshikawa and Tetsuji Okazaki, 'Postwar Hyper-inflation and the Dodge Plan: An Overview', in Teranishi and Kosai, eds., *The Japanese Experience of Economic Reforms*, pp. 93–4.
70 Goldsmith, *Financial Development*, p. 133.
71 See, for example, John Dower, *Embracing Defeat: Japan in the Aftermath of World War II* (New York: W. W. Norton, 2000), pp. 87–120.
72 For discussion of the Shoup mission and early post-war Japan, see W. Elliot Brownlee, Eisaku Ide and Yasunori Fukagai, eds., *The Political Economy of Transitional Tax Reform: The Shoup Mission to Japan in Historical Perspective* (Cambridge University Press, 2013).

inflation' of 1945 to 1949, Raymond Goldsmith concludes, apparently did not seriously interfere with recovery from the physical damage and disruption of the Second World War.[73] Mark Metzler goes further than this and views the debt-financed 'big push' as fundamental to swift post-war recovery.[74] In 1952, Japanese GDP reached its 1937 level and then grew rapidly for over three more decades.

Southeast Asia: monetary overhang and political change

Throughout Southeast Asia, swift monetary expansion during the Second World War created a potentially serious problem of rapid post-war inflation. Much of the region avoided this problem of 'monetary overhang' by simply repudiating wartime currencies. Where that happened it was justified by the currencies having been issued by the Japanese.

Indochina and Indonesia were the two striking exceptions to the avoidance of monetary overhang. Between 1945 and 1949, inflation surged in Indochina but it is unclear how much of this was due to an overlarge inherited wartime money supply; how much was caused by the Democratic Republic of Vietnam's printing of currency as the main way to finance its new government in the north; how much was the result of French financial needs to pay for government in the south; and how much was attributable to the first phase of the Indochinese revolution.

The Dutch returned to Indonesia militarily too weak in Java and Sumatra to dominate. Indonesian republican forces held sway except in six large cities and part of a seventh controlled by the Dutch. The sole options available to Dutch administrators were to retain the Japanese military to keep order and to make Japanese scrip the official tender of the government. Moreover, the Dutch put into circulation, as the only way to finance their urban administrations, a large amount of captured Japanese scrip and further authorized the Japanese to print yet more scrip to pay for supplies requisitioned from them. Indonesian republicans also used scrip, which was widely recognized and accepted in the countryside. When on 6 March 1946 the Dutch, and then on 31 October 1946 Indonesian republicans, finally issued their own currencies, these further added to Indonesia's grossly overlarge stock of money and stoked already high inflation.[75]

---

73 Goldsmith, *Financial Development*, p. 133; Teranishi, 'Inflation Stabilization', p. 67.
74 Metzler, *Capital*, pp. 82–108.
75 Robert Cribb, 'Political Dimensions of the Currency Question 1945–1947', *Indonesia* 31 (1981), 113–36.

Elsewhere in Southeast Asia, post-war administrations sidestepped monetary overhang. Thailand wrote off its yen credits although still inheriting the volume of currency that they had backed. Beginning in 1947, the Thai government set up an amortization fund for surplus, wartime currency but this was of limited use since notes were mainly in peasant hoards and so impossible to amortize. Peasant physical currency holdings were, however, thought to result in much 'automatic amortization' from loss, mutilation and destruction.[76] The Philippines and Malaya both demonetized Japanese currency.[77] Nor was it accorded post-war value in Burma. Demonetization exchanged the challenge of monetary overhang for that of how to restart a monetary economy. The Philippines faced a 'monetary crisis' until currency could be issued and put into circulation.[78] In Singapore, the Straits dollar was reintroduced as quickly as possible but before that barter partially substituted for a monetary economy and cigarettes served as a form of money. Although they 'could buy almost anything', few people except the British military had any cigarettes.[79]

The sudden lack of money in Burma created considerable disruption. Because peasants in the rice-growing districts had relied on Japanese notes, they had no British Burma currency. The British solution to restarting a monetary economy was to extend interest-free loans to peasant cultivators in small coins likely to be spent – 24 rupees (US$7.23) for those working one yoke of oxen and 36 rupees for more than a yoke.[80]

Nationalist China: post-war hyperinflation and political eclipse

After the August 1945 Japanese surrender, Central Reserve Bank notes continued to circulate in South and Central China as the only available currency, but within four months China had organized the redemption of these notes and Federal Reserve Bank currency. In both Central and Federal Reserve Bank areas, nationalists' redemption policy set exchange rates for occupation currency at such an unfavourable level that it was spent as quickly as possible and promoted inflation. Unfavourable rates caused many

76 Thailand, *Report 1941–1950*, pp. 54–5.
77 'P.I. Currency is Stabilized on 2–1 Base', *Shanghai Evening Post*, 5 January 1945.
78 Toribio Teodoro, 'Philippine Manufacturing Industries', 12 July 1945, p. 5, University of the Philippines, Diliman, Manuel A. Roxas Papers, box 39.
79 O. W. Gilmour, *With Freedom to Singapore* (London: Ernest Benn, 1950), pp. 103–4.
80 'Currency in Burma', 17 Sept. 1945, IOR, M4/306; 'Currency Problems in Burma', *The Times*, 24 May 1945; Marilyn Longmuir, *The Money Trail: Burmese Currencies in Crisis* (Dekalb, Ill.: Southeast Asia Publications, 2002), pp. 96–101.

Table 2.9 *China government expenditure, revenue and deficit, 1945–1948 (CNC$ billions)*

	Expenditure	Revenue	Deficit	Increase in note issue	Land tax
1945	2,348.1	1,241.4	1,106.7		188.6
1946	7,574.8	2,877.0	4,697.8	2,694.2	624.7
1947	43,393.9	14,064.4	29,329.5	29,462.4	3,015.9
1948	655,471.1	220,905.5	434,565.6	341,573.7	

	Deficit as % of expenditure	Increase in note issue as % of deficit	% increase in note issue	Land tax as % of deficit
1945	47.1			17.0
1946	62.0	57.4		13.3
1947	67.6	100.5	993.5	10.3
1948	66.3	78.6	1,059.4	

Notes: 1. Increase in note issue is calculated as the difference in note issue outstanding for successive years. 2. Land tax is its estimated money value and is for the years 1945–46, 1946–47 and 1947–48.
Source: Chang, *Inflationary Spiral*, p. 71.

to view the nationalists as exploiters; the Communists capitalized heavily on this public dissatisfaction.[81]

The inflationary repercussions of monetary overhang, although considerable, soon faded compared to those of large and increasing government expenditure. At least 80 per cent of this was for military outlays.[82] Once again, the government financed itself chiefly through monetary expansion: note issue between 1946 and 1948 equalled 87.9 per cent of the government deficit and inevitably led to high inflation (Table 2.9). Extreme economic dislocation and transport shortages attributable to eight years of war now aggravated inflation even more than between 1937 and 1945. About half of railway locomotives, a third of freight wagons and 40 per cent of passenger carriages were destroyed during the Sino-Japanese War. In mid-1946, water freight traffic inland from Shanghai still remained severely restricted.[83] Civil

81 Young, *China's Wartime Finance*, p. 182 and *Helping Hand*, p. 386; Greenwood and Wood, 'Chinese Hyperinflation', p. 37.
82 Andrew Chung Huang, 'The Inflation in China', *Quarterly Journal of Economics* 62:4 (1948), 562–75 (p. 571).
83 Huang, 'Inflation in China', p. 570.

Table 2.10 *Shanghai wholesale prices, 1946–1949*

		Jan. 1946 = 1	% change in prices
1946	Jan.	1	
	June	2	135.9
	Dec.	4	80.2
1947	March	9	103.4
	June	18	109.6
	Sept.	29	59.5
	Dec.	63	117.1
1948	March	203	223.7
	June	1,233	506.8
	July	1,795	45.5
	Aug.	3,486	94.3
	Sept.	3,686	5.7
	Oct.	4,124	11.9
	Nov.	47,589	1,053.9
	Dec.	67,062	40.9
1949	Jan.	240,954	259.3
	Feb.	1,680,217	597.3
	March	7,584,817	351.4
	April	392,171,830	5,070.5

Notes: 1. For an index with Jan. June 1937 = 1, the price index in January 1946 was 1,603.2. 2. The index in the table is linked at August 1948 using data for 19 August and for all of August for the continuing (gold yuan) series for August 1948 to April 1949. Because the earlier series (1946 to August 1948) ends on 19 August it omits inflation for the remainder of August and the index in this table may somewhat understate inflation.
Source: Chang, *Inflationary Spiral*, pp. 79, 371–2.

war with the Communists, from late 1947, added to economic pressure as well as to the need for yet further war finance.

In response to mounting inflation, and beginning in 1948 with the onset of hyperinflation as defined by Cagan (Table 2.10), the government made numerous attempts to control prices. These were generally brief and, even when brutally backed up by the secret police, always ineffective.[84] Often, control measures did not operate beyond the Shanghai city limits where

---

84 Chang, *Inflationary Spiral*, p. 80.

Table 2.11 *China and world hyperinflations, 1914–1953 (Ratios of indexes at end to beginning of inflation)*

	Inflation period	Price index	Note issue index
China	Sept. 1945–May 1949	105 × 10^9	302 × 10^6
	July 1937–April 1949	151.73 × 10^12	1.62 × 10^12
Germany	1914–1923	1.26 × 10^12	157 × 10^9
Greece	1939–Nov. 1944	0.21 × 10^12	0.77 × 10^9
		21.55 × 10^12	18.21 × 10^12
Hungary	July 1945–July 1946	399,620 × 10^24	22.60 × 10^15

Note: In the table, 10^6 represents 1 million, 10^9 one billion, 10^12 one trillion, 10^15 one quadrillion, and 10^24 one septillion. For example, between September 1945 and May 1949, note issue in China rose by 302 million and prices by 105 billion while from July 1937 to April 1949 prices in China increased by 151 trillion 730 billion. For July 1937 to April 1949 the ratio of Chinese note issue allows for the conversion of Central Reserve Bank notes into fabi at 200 to one fabi (yuan). This greatly overvalued the fabi. See Young, *China's Wartime Finance*, p. 182.

Sources: Teh-wei Hu, 'Hyperinflaion and the Dynamics of the Demand for Money in China, 1945–1949', *Journal of Political Economy* 79:1 (1971), 186–95 (p. 187); Chou, *Chinese Inflation*, p. 261.

General Chiang had his headquarters.[85] As hyperinflation spiralled out of control, the government sought, in August 1948, to give some credibility to the currency by replacing the fabi with the gold yuan note and, a year later, superseding this with the silver yuan. Small gold, and later silver, sales were undertaken to signal backing for the currency and as anti-inflationary measures. Unlike during the early part of the Pacific War, however, America no longer looked like China's guarantor, and the time had passed when selling some of the government's limited stocks of specie might encourage confidence. Escalating inflation seems to have been fully anticipated; the public dismissed the likelihood of successful government reform programmes almost as soon as they were announced. In October 1948, a Central Bank offer to convert gold yuan notes into gold resulted in some 60,000 people trying to collect conversion applications and a riot in which dozens of people were killed or injured.[86] By May 1949, prices were 105 billion times their level in September 1945 and had increased at an average rate of 78 per cent a month (Table 2.11).

85 Chou, *Chinese Inflation*, p. 26.
86 Chang, *Inflationary Spiral*, pp. 80–3.

The choices in war finance made by nationalist leaders and a clearly unequal share-out of the war's financial burden undermined support for the government.[87] Toward the latter part of the civil war, it became questionable whether or not the government remained morally sustainable.[88] If it did not, that was partly due its war finance policies. Certainly, these left the nationalist government no longer financially viable. By December 1948, hyperinflation had reduced annual government income to effectively zero.[89]

Historians, for example Lloyd Eastman, often conclude that 'of the many causes [of the debility of the nationalist government] inflation was the most potent'.[90] That is undeniable in the sense that hyperinflation destroyed seigniorage, long the main source of revenue for the government, and left it bankrupt. Perhaps more accurately, however, hyperinflation was a very visible symptom of institutional failure: the political incapacity of a monumentally corrupt, poorly managed and financially inept government. It was unable, over a period of twelve years, to institute policies to control inflation. After the nationalist surrender in June 1949, the Communists soon ended hyperinflation, like Japan in 1949, through orthodox stabilization measures. They cut expenditure, refused to print large quantities of money, established effective taxation, and imposed compulsory saving on the public.

The ranking of China's among the world's great hyperinflations depends on the period taken into account (Table 2.11). If Chinese hyperinflation is regarded as starting in 1937, it stands in magnitude second only to post-Second World War Hungary and is the most lengthy of all hyperinflations. Often, however, hyperinflation, as defined by Cagan or Reinhart–Rogoff, spans only a relatively brief period. In China, hyperinflation did not start until 1948 and at some point before that could conceivably have been avoided. A dating of hyperinflation from a starting point of August 1945, or possibly early 1946, to May 1949 places China only mid-table in world hyperinflations, although this still makes China's a long-lasting inflation, since it includes the 1945 to 1947 run-up to the total loss of control over prices.

---

87 Suzanne Pepper, 'The KMT-CCP Conflict 1945–1949', in Fairbank and Feuerwerker, eds., *The Cambridge History of China*, vol. XIII, part 2: *Republican China*, pp. 723–88 (p. 745).

88 Cf. Conrad Brandt, Benjamin Schwartz and John K. Fairbank, *A Documentary History of Chinese Communism* (London: Allen & Unwin, 1952), pp. 19–20.

89 Chou, *Chinese Inflation*, p. 270. Chou calculated that government incomes and expenditures were one-1272.4 millionth and one-5245.5 millionth as large as in 1936–37.

90 Eastman, 'Nationalist China', p. 584.

Conclusion

Almost the first question that follows a decision to go to war, Hugh Rockoff points out, is how to pay for the war.[91] This chapter has explored how during the Second World War the nationalist Chinese, the Chinese Communists and the Japanese – at home, in China and in Southeast Asia – answered this question. Often the answer was a heavy reliance on printing money and associated seigniorage. Only Japan, at home, could fashion a different response and, until 1944, finance war without depending chiefly on money creation. Strong institutions and a government in full control of the financial system and able to bend the population to its will enabled a large share of war finance to come from bond absorption and 'voluntary' saving.

Early in the Sino-Japanese War, nationalist China had to rely substantially on printing money because it had been pushed back into less productive Chinese regions and was cut off from coastal access. Even after 1945, however, the Chiang Kai-shek government made no determined effort to develop an effective tax system and stuck instead to the easy option of a near-total dependence on printing money. A failure to move toward sustainable economic policies reflected institutional weakness, endemic corruption and a leadership apparently willing to believe that finance through money creation could go on indefinitely.[92]

Elsewhere in Asia the printing press dominated. Administratively, Japan was badly stretched in trying to occupy not just much of China but, by early 1942, also the 1.7 million square miles of Southeast Asia. The magnitude of Japanese ambitions in foreign lands left little option other than finance by issuing a variety of occupation currencies. Printing money afforded an administratively low-cost way to enforce taxation and finance war and, furthermore, could be done without apparently even levying taxes.

A striking aspect of Asian war finance was that the several regimes which sought to finance war and occupation principally through monetary expansion largely succeeded in doing so. Monetary creation could successfully finance war because the demand for paper money held up well – and certainly much better than might have been expected – despite high and continuous inflation. One reason for the maintenance of a demand for money was its continued usefulness as a medium of exchange. Rather than turning chiefly to barter in

91 Hugh Rockoff, *America's Economic Way of War: War and the US Economy from the Spanish–American War to the Persian Gulf War* (Cambridge University Press, 2012), pp. 16, 317.
92 Young, *China's Wartime Finance*, pp. 316–17.

response to high inflation, Asians still found money useful for everyday transactions. The second reason was that in China for, at the least, much of the Sino-Japanese War and in rural Burma and Thailand throughout the Pacific War, peasants hoarded money as a store of value.

A third, and outside peasant areas crucial, explanation for why money was held was that legal requirements to use government currency were backed up with effective, if drastic, enforcement mechanisms. Although extreme, this inducement to hold government-approved money was not without historical precedent. During the Terror, Revolutionary France employed similar tactics to those used by the Japanese to boost demand for the assignat. It has been described as a 'guillotine-backed currency', which is to say one underpinned by the sanction of execution. That threat proved sufficient to enable France to finance the war with the German Empire and Austria that began in April 1792 by printing assignats.[93] Japan, in occupied China and Southeast Asia, similarly ensured, through guillotine-like sanctions, that seigniorage could largely finance war. Both Southeast Asia and China had relatively moderate, Latin American-like inflation for much of the war, and quite high inflation, or months of hyperinflation, only near its end, when Japan was clearly defeated and its authority weakened.

Post-war Chinese hyperinflation, along with the Austrian and Hungarian, ranks as one of the great twentieth-century hyperinflations and, since these are essentially a twentieth-century phenomenon associated with printing paper money, also among the world's great hyperinflations. Price rises in Japan after the war are widely referred to as hyperinflation, but, applying the Cagan metric, this looks to have been brief. The chapter shows, however, that in both China and Japan a similar inflationary causal chain operated: inflation had its roots in large government deficits, chiefly financed by printing money, and was exacerbated in its initial phases by sharp falls in output and economic disorganization. But in the ending of high inflation or hyperinflation, nationalist and Japanese experience sharply diverged. Japan avoided disaster; nationalist China, unable to bring hyperinflation under control, did not. Austerity forced on the Japanese by the Dodge and Shoup missions quickly ended excessive inflation. In China, the Communists established institutions and a leadership capable of effecting similarly harsh stabilization policies. These abruptly halted hyperinflation, and thereby provided the economic basis on which to consolidate the Chinese Communist revolution.

---

93 Thomas J. Sargent and François R. Velde, 'Macroeconomic Features of the French Revolution', *Journal of Political Economy* 103:3 (1995), 474–518 (pp. 503–7).

3

War of the factories

JEFFREY FEAR

On 20 August 1939 in the fuzzily demarcated no-man's land between Soviet-Protectorate Mongolia and Japanese-occupied Manchukuo (Manchuria) near Lake Buir Noir one of the most important but largely forgotten battles of the Second World War began with a morning bombardment by 200 Soviet bombers. After months of incursions by Japan's Kwantung Army, Stalin instructed his new commander in the east, Georgy Zhukov, to move over to the offensive. The battle would be a setpiece display of Soviet military-industrial modernity. Against the Japanese the Red Army amassed 581 aircraft, and 498 armoured vehicles, including a few prototypes of what would become the legendary T-34. Over 4,000 trucks moved 50,000 tons of supplies hundreds of miles to the front line; by contrast the Japanese had just 800 trucks in all of Manchuria. By the opening of the battle of Khalkhin Gol, the Soviets outnumbered the Japanese 2:1 in planes, tanks and artillery. After wrong-footing the Japanese with weeks of disinformation operations, two Soviet motorized pincers, covered by smothering tactical air support, swung around the Japanese northern and southern flanks, encircling and destroying the entire Kwantung's 6th Army. Foreshadowing the German Blitzkrieg, the Soviet attack taught the Japanese a humiliating lesson in the backwardness of their own army, which since 1937 had been engaged in a running battle with inferior Chinese forces.[1]

Nomonhan, as the Japanese called it, was only the opening trailer. Six years later, in the spring of 1945 as he prepared the last assault on Berlin, Zhukov would array 7,500 combat aircraft, 14,600 guns, 3,155 tanks and self-propelled guns, and over 1,500 rocket launchers. As the victor in the most intensive land conflict the world had ever seen, the Soviet Union between

---

[1] Stuart D. Goldman, *Nomonhan 1939: The Red Army's Victory that Shaped World War II* (Annapolis: Naval Institute Press, 2012).

1941 and 1945 equipped its forces with over 100,000 tanks, 130,000 aircraft, 800,000 guns and mortars, 1 billion shells and bombs, and 40 billion small arms cartridges.[2] The logistical backbone of the Allied armies was provided by the 3 million trucks and jeeps and 5,600 merchant ships built by the USA, in addition to more than 8,000 naval vessels and a staggering 286,000 aircraft, including tens of thousands of complex heavy bombers.[3]

Creating the lethal productive and innovative capacity in factories and destroying one's enemies' industrial capacities was central to winning the Second World War. From very different industrial bases and starting points, the war transformed how firms and factories operated, pioneering many innovations that have become the norm in the global economy since the 1980s such as contract manufacturing, a reliance on deep networks of subcontractors (outsourcing), a stress on global logistics and supply chains for end-products and raw materials, and 'just-in-time' operations. Complex weapons such as aircraft, tanks and ships, but also trucks, jeeps, artillery pieces, aviation fuel, copper wire and ammunition were the products of complex transnational value and supply chains that often stretched around the globe. Far from being the end of globalization, cross-border flows of goods, services, capital and labour continued to connect and reshape the planet in meaningful ways. The Second World War represented a repurposed, albeit temporary, redirection of the international economy for military and industrial purposes.

Soviet Union

The armoured force that humiliated the Japanese army at Khalkhin Gol in August 1939 was the product of a programme of forced Soviet industrialization in which economic development and militarization were coterminous. It is barely an exaggeration to say that the Soviet Union never 'converted' to war production, because industrializing to produce armaments was a central reason for its (continuing) existence.[4]

---

2 Mark Harrison, 'The Second World War', in R. W. Davies, Mark Harrison and S. G. Wheatcroft, eds., *The Economic Transformation of the Soviet Union, 1913–1945* (Cambridge University Press, 1994), pp. 238–67, figures from pp. 241–2.

3 Arthur Herman, *Freedom's Forge: How American Business Produced Victory in World War II* (New York: Random House, 2012), p. ix. Chris Bellamy, *Absolute War: Soviet Russia in the Second World War* (New York: Alfred A. Knopf, 2007), pp. 440–5.

4 Mark Harrison, 'The Soviet Union: The Defeated Victor', in Mark Harrison, ed., *The Economics of World War II: Six Great Powers in International Comparison* (Cambridge University Press, 1998), pp. 268–301 (p. 271). Mark Harrison, *Soviet Planning in Peace and*

The First Five-Year Plan of 1928 laid out expansive targets for heavy industry and electrification. Although not all targets were achieved, between 1928 and 1932 coal tonnage nearly doubled, electric power generation went up 2.5 times, ten times as many metal-cutting tools were manufactured, and motor vehicle production went up over twenty times. Steel production began to surge after 1932, driven upwards in no small part by the construction of a massive new steel plant at Magnitogorsk. Stamped almost out of the ground, it was sited on top of large reserves of especially pure iron near the Urals, beyond the range of any invader.[5]

The next two Five-Year Plans saw even more impressive gains. By 1940 steel production had risen three times relative to 1932 to 18.3 million tons. Coal production had gone up 2.5 times to 165.9 million tons, electrical generation 3.5 times to 48.3 billion kilowatts/hr, machine tools up 3 times to 58,400, and motor vehicles up 6 times to 199,900 vehicles in 1937. The Soviet Union had made itself into the world's third leading heavy industrial power behind the USA and Germany and its emphasis was emphatically military. In 1938 33–42 per cent of all iron and steel materials and 26 per cent of all industrial production flowed into military production. The armaments industry took over 60 per cent of machine building and metal working production and almost three-quarters of all capital investment in the metals sector. Out of a total manufacturing workforce of 13 million, 3 million were employed in defence production. In propagandistic terms, the world of production was routinely linked to war preparation. Workers were members of 'industrial shock brigades'; planners were 'combat staff'; agricultural labourers were 'recruited' into industry. Millions slaved in the Gulags as conscript labour.[6] The habits of 'storming' with which engineers, factory managers and workers met the targets laid down by the Five-Year Plans would help to make the war economy of the Soviet Union not just more resilient than that of tsarism, but also more resilient than that of any other combatant. It was a brutal achievement of output at the cost of great human misery.

War, 1938–1945 (Cambridge University Press, 1985), pp. 5–41, armament figures below from Table 1-2. Mark Harrison and Paul R. Gregory, *Guns and Rubles: The Defense Industry in the Stalinist State* (New Haven: Yale University Press, 2008). Lennart Samuelson, *Plans for Stalin's War Machine* (Basingstoke: Macmillan, 2000). R. W. Davies, 'Industry', in Davies, Harrison and Wheatcroft, eds., *Economic Transformation*, pp. 131–57.

5 Stephen Kotkin, *Magnetic Mountain: Stalinism as a Civilization* (Berkeley: University of California Press, 1997).

6 R. W. Davies, 'Changing Economic Systems: An Overview', in Davies, Harrison and Wheatcroft, eds., *Economic Transformation*, pp. 1–23.

As the clash with the Japanese made clear, Stalinism built not just new industrial capacity but fundamentally new capabilities. From a near standing start in 1930, by 1940 the Soviets were producing over 10,000 aircraft, just under 3,000 tanks, 15,300 artillery pieces, and 1.46 million rifles per year. And Soviet armaments were not just abundant, key weapons such as the T-34 or KV-1 tank were path-breaking examples of military technology. Soviet artillery was among the best in the world; Katyusha rocket launchers appeared in July 1941. And in the air as well, the heavily armoured ground attack aircraft, Ilyushin Il-2, and extremely manoeuvrable fighter, Yak-1, were a qualitative match for anything available in the West.[7] By the outbreak of the war, the Soviets had developed a war capacity in a few key simple-to-use, highly reliable weapons systems that would prove foundational, *if* the Soviets could manage to survive the onslaught of their opponents and the enormous losses they inflicted.

Japan

The radicalism of Stalin's determination to harness militarization to socio-economic transformation can be contrasted with Japan, which despite its long tradition of state-sponsored industrialization, its colonization of Taiwan, Korea and Manchuria and its relatively high level of military spending took time in the 1930s to develop a large-scale military-industrial programme. Until 1937, military procurement focused on light equipment for a largely labour-intensive, ground-oriented army imbued with a dogmatic sense of the superiority of morale to material. Japan's own economy remained concentrated on labour-intensive, 'light industry' such as in silk or textiles. Dominated by large *zaibatsu* (family-owned conglomerates) such as Mitsui, Mitsubishi and Sumitomo, which desired a largely liberal market order, tensions with the military and reformist bureaucrats that desired a planned economy along Soviet lines resulted in coups and assassinations of corporate executives and business-friendly civilian ministers. The two groups were 'rarely in a state of collaboration'.[8] For the military, Manchuria should transform the material base for the heavy industrial transformation of Japan, but the army and private business formed an 'uneasy partnership', which was

---

7 Bellamy, *Absolute War*, pp. 175–8.
8 On *zaibatsu*–military tensions, see Hironori Sasada, *The Evolution of the Japanese Developmental State: Institutions Locked in by Ideas* (London: Routledge, 2013), esp. 39–117 (quote from p. 119).

closer to a 'non-aggression pact'. State-owned enterprises dominated invest-ment there.[9]

The one area in which Japan developed a truly substantial heavy industrial capacity prior to the 1930s was in naval construction. Since the Washington Naval Conference of 1921, Japan had been recognized as the third naval power behind Britain and USA. Since the turn of the century it had been a technological leader in key areas such as aircraft carriers, as well as anti-aircraft destroyers and highly effective torpedoes. Japan's flagships the *Yamato* and *Musashi* were the largest and most heavily armed battleships ever constructed. By contrast with its ground forces, Japan's navy opted for cutting-edge quality to offset the material superiority of the US and British navies. But despite its high level of military spending and early mobilization Japan never developed the overall productive capacity to replace ships that were sunk. Nor did it have the raw materials or the sources of fuel that would allow it to challenge for overall naval domination.

Where Japan's combination of economic development policy and militar-ism was at its most ambitious was in Manchukuo, which was built on the idea of a 'national defence state'.[10] The construction of the new puppet state after 1931 served as an anti-depression reflationary policy. It also accelerated military expenditure and promised to give Japan a measure of national resource self-sufficiency in the form of the 'Japan–Manchukuo economic bloc'. As Japan's aggression extended across the Pacific Rim this morphed into the 'Greater East Asia Co-Prosperity Sphere'.[11] Whereas Japan's early colonial conquests Taiwan or Korea were seen as sources of food suppliers to the home market, Manchukuo became an imagined ideal Japan, promising a solution to the miseries of capitalism at home. While army planning stressed national autarkic defence needs, private industry desired export promotion and saw a potential new market. Over the course of the 1930s new industrial conglomerates such as Nissan concentrated their activities there and built an impressive array of new industrial facilities. As in the Soviet Union, the industrialization of Manchukuo was linked to military needs. About 5,300 kilometres of railroad track were laid; new railway hub-towns sprang up that

9 Louise Young, *Japan's Total Empire: Manchuria and the Culture of Wartime Imperialism* (Berkeley: University of California Press, 1998), esp. pp. 183–240. Ramon H. Myers and Mark R. Peattie, eds., *The Japanese Colonial Empire, 1895–1945* (Princeton University Press, 1984).

10 Erich Pauer, ed., *Japan's War Economy* (London: Routledge, 1999), p. 2.

11 Ikuhiko Hata, 'Continental Expansion 1905–1941', in Peter Duus, ed., *The Cambridge History of Japan*, vol. VI: *The Twentieth Century* (Cambridge University Press, 1988), pp. 271–314 (pp. 299–302).

linked Manchuria more tightly with Korea; the showcase 'new capital' of Xinjing (Changchun) saw a massive building boom. The 'Asia Express' from Dalian to Xinjing was the highest speed train in the East, the equal of the fastest trains in the West – a potent symbol of Japanese modernization. A total of 1.1 billion yen poured into the region with investors including the Showa Steelworks, Sumitomo Steel Pipe, the Manchuria Arsenal Corporation, Manchuria Chemical Industry Company and the Dowa Automobile Manufacturing Company. Like the Soviet Union, this development was state planned with military and economic goals fused together as one, but private industry was expected to finance and build the new society, creating a frequently uneasy alliance between private capitalist business and the military.[12]

However, the dream of self-sufficiency remained out of reach. Japan remained 90 per cent dependent on imported oil, most of which came from the USA. This was gradually throttled after the invasion of China in 1937 until Japan was struck by the complete embargo of oil in mid-1941. Control of key resources such as rubber, tin and oil in Asia lay not with Japan but with the empires of Britain and the Netherlands. British Malaya produced 40 per cent of the world's natural rubber and 60 per cent of its tin. The Dutch East Indies islands of Borneo, Java and Sumatra had rich oilfields. Japan's war in China and its urgent burst of naval construction after 1937 made it more dependent on imported materials. Paradoxically, the shift to heavy industry and the effort to construct synthetic chemicals capacity made Japan even more reliant on the import of Western technologies to set up the new factories. Throughout the 1930s, Japan ran a persistent and increasingly alarming trade deficit with countries outside the yen bloc that grew from 186 million yen in 1933 to over 1 billion yen by 1941. In pursuit of the army's autarkic dreams, Japan drew down its gold reserves to almost zero.[13]

The floodgates for this unbalanced burst of industrialization and militarization were opened by the assassination in 1936 of the Japanese finance minister who had sought to limit military spending. The army had its Six-Year Plan to build industrial production capacity. The navy added its Third Supplement Plan. Together with the Manchuria Five-Year Development Plan these raised the budget by 40 per cent to shift the Japanese economy in earnest to heavy

---

12 Young, *Japan's Total Empire*. Yûzô Yamamoto, 'Japanese Empire and Colonial Management', in Takafusa Nakamura and Kônosuke Odaka, eds., *The Economic History of Japan, 1600–1990*, vol. III: *Economic History of Japan, 1914–1955: A Dual Structure* (Oxford University Press, 1999), pp. 223–46.

13 Figures from Takafusa Nakamura, 'Depression, Recovery, and War', in Duus, ed., *The Cambridge History of Japan*, vol. VI, pp. 451–93 (Table 9.7, pp. 482–5).

industry. Symbolically, the keel for the super-battleship *Yamato* was laid in 1937. After the Sino-Japanese War started, three further 'control' laws were introduced to mobilize industry for armaments, to limit trading in key commodities, and restrict investment in 'non-urgent and unnecessary goods'. A new Planning Bureau was established to allocate key goods for defence needs and a broad array of mobilization, production, commodity, financial and distribution controls were put in place. There were also major changes in labour and corporate law.[14] By 1939 all wages and prices were subject to a uniform system of controls. By 1941 coal production was 25 per cent over 1937 levels, steel was up by 32 per cent, machinery by 88 per cent and chemicals by 20 per cent. At the same time agricultural production dropped by 5 per cent and the rice harvest was down by 17 per cent. Prior to Pearl Harbor, Japan's planners had already opted for 'guns before rice'.[15] By the end of the war supplies of crucial civilian goods had fallen to starvation levels. A measure of this trade-off is that by the end of the war the military planned to appropriate Japan's entire potato crop to make gasoline despite rampant malnutrition.[16]

Germany

Adolf Hitler's National Socialist regime took office on 30 January 1933 bent on rebuilding Germany for an unprecedented programme of conquest and colonial settlement. In East and West the economic strength of Germany's opponents, their abundant land, their raw materials and industrial capacities hung like a shadow over the ambitions of the Third Reich. Orchestrating the encircling coalition of his enemies Hitler imagined a world Jewish conspiracy. His aim was to build for Germany a 'living space' (*Lebensraum*, a phrase also adopted by the Japanese) that would rival the continental USA and Britain's global empire. To realize this amalgam of strategy and ideology the Third Reich built a military-industrial complex unique in its brutality. It was an industrial economy of extraordinary juxtapositions in which high-tech 'wonder weapons' such as the V-2 ballistic missiles or Me 262 jet fighters

14 More detail in Akira Hara, 'Wartime Controls', in Nakamura and Odaka, eds., *The Economic History of Japan, 1600–1990*, vol. III: *Economic History of Japan*, pp. 247–86.
15 Akira Hara, 'Japan: Guns before Rice', in Harrison, ed., *Six Great Powers*, pp. 224–67.
16 Takafusa Nakamura, 'The Japanese War Economy as a "Planned Economy"', in Pauer, ed., *Japan's War Economy*, pp. 9–22. Nakamura, 'Depression, Recovery, and War', pp. 477–85, figures from Table 9.9, p. 489. Hara, 'Japan: Guns before Rice'. Jerome B. Cohen, *Japan's Economy in War and Reconstruction* (Minneapolis: University of Minnesota Press, 1949), p. 189.

were constructed on the backs of forced or slave labourers, who were used up as 'a kind of raw material expended like fuel'.[17]

Unlike the Soviet Union that built its armament industry from scratch, or Japan that had to redirect its economy away from light industry, Germany's problem was to convert its existing heavy industrial capacities to military production. The savage recession that struck Germany after 1929 conveniently freed circa 50 per cent of industrial capacity for redeployment. Against this backdrop, a huge surge of government armaments expenditure resulted in a massive shift in the priorities of production. In the six years between January 1933 and the autumn of 1938, Hitler's regime was able to raise 'the share of national output going to the military from less than 1 to almost 20 per cent. Never before had national production been redistributed on this scale or with such speed by a capitalist state.' Nor was this simply a matter of shifting existing capacity. Between 1933 and 1939 no less than 60 per cent of all new investment went toward armament or autarchic industries.[18]

The set piece of Nazi military-industrial investment was the Four-Year Plan initiated just after the Berlin Olympics in 1936. Outwardly this was a plan to ease Germany's chronic hard currency shortage with the domestic production of key raw materials. Secretly, it was a directive to prepare Germany for war within four years. Under the command of a light-weight organization headed by Göring, the Four-Year Plan bundled together the various investment programmes that had been set in motion since 1933 in synthetic oil, air fuel, synthetic rubber (Buna), synthetic fibres, domestically sourced iron ore and an expansion of Germany's internal waterways. The synthetic rubber programme in particular involved technological gambles on untried production processes that were of doubtful commercial viability but indispensable from a strategic point of view. The Four-Year Plan placed the

---

17 Michael Thad Allen, *The Business of Genocide: The SS, Slave Labor, and the Concentration Camps* (Chapel Hill: University of North Carolina Press, 2005), pp. 222–32 (p. 230). Mark Mazower, *Hitler's Empire: How the Nazis Ruled Europe* (London: Penguin, 2009). Hein Klemann and Sergei Kudryashov, *Occupied Economies: An Economic History of Nazi-Occupied Europe, 1939–1945* (London: Berg, 2012).

18 Quote from Adam Tooze, *The Wages of Destruction: The Making and Breaking of the Nazi Economy* (London: Allen Lane, 2006), p. 659; Jonas Scherner, 'Nazi Germany's Preparation for War: Evidence from Revised Industrial Investment Series', *European Review of Economic History* 14 (2010), 433–68. Debate about the nature of this recovery in Werner Abelshauser, 'Guns, Butter, and Economic Miracles', in Harrison, ed., *Six Great Powers*, pp. 122–76. For a critique of the 1930s recovery, see Mark Spoerer, 'Demontage eines Mythos? Zu der Kontroverse über das nationalsozialistische Wirtschaftswunder', *Geschichte und Gesellschaft* 31:3 (2005), 415–38 and Christoph Buchheim, 'Die Wirtschaftsentwicklung im Dritten Reich – mehr Desaster als Wunder: Eine Erwiderung auf Werner Abelshauser', *Vierteljahrshefte für Zeitgeschichte* 49 (2001), 653–64.

large chemical company, IG Farben, at the centre of the war effort. Whereas relations between Göring's office and IG Farben were amicable, enabled by the employment of key IG staff within the Four-Year Plan organization, Göring's plans for iron and steel aroused more opposition. In 1937 it took draconian threats against the leaders of German heavy industry, including the mighty Vereinigte Stahlwerke, to overcome their opposition to the development of the ore fields in Salzgitter. When these assets were combined with those acquired following the Anschluss of Austria, the Reichswerke 'Hermann Goering' emerged as one of the largest heavy industrial conglomerates in the world, a sort of gangster corporation that expropriated business assets across Nazi-occupied Europe.[19]

But neither Göring's kleptocratic activities nor Hitler's direct personal engagement in the priorities of the steel rationing system imposed in 1937 could alter Germany's basic dilemma. With military spending surging toward 20 per cent of GNP and Germany's potential enemies accelerating their own rearmament, the spare capacity available in the early 1930s was rapidly depleting. And yet, despite the increasingly obvious scarcities, Hitler decided in 1938 on an all-out armaments effort. In short succession he ordered the construction of the so-called Westwall fortifications, a huge expansion of the air force by five times including an order for 7,000 twin-engine bombers and an acceleration of the army buildup. In January 1939 he followed this with a sudden shift in priorities toward the accelerated naval 'Z' programme. To contain this wave of military demands, the regime imposed wage and price controls, rationing and regulations such as controls on job movement or compulsory work orders affecting over a million workers, but these served only to displace scarcities from one sector to another. Among those sectors that suffered worst were housing investment and the Reichsbahn, which fell behind in basic maintenance. As with Japan, Germany's foreign currency stocks steadily depleted. By early 1939 the situation of the Reichsbank had become so serious that all military priorities gave way to the overriding need to increase exports of industrial goods.

Yet in spite of the considerable industrial capacity of Germany and the impression created by the Wehrmacht's battlefield success early in the war,

19 Discussion is based on Tooze, *Wages of Destruction*, pp. 203–325. On IG Farben, see Peter Hayes, *Industry and Ideology: IG Farben in the Nazi Era* (Cambridge University Press, 2000 [1987]). Richard Overy, 'Heavy Industry in the Third Reich: The Reichswerke Crisis', and 'The Reichswerke "Hermann Göring": A Study in German Economic Imperialism', both in his *War and Economy in the Third Reich* (Oxford: Clarendon Press, 1994), pp. 93–118 and 144–74.

Germany's own military experts took a bleak view of their country's situation in the late 1930s. They did not regard the Third Reich as having a comfortable superiority in modern armaments. We now know that at the outbreak of the war, Germany had no clear military superiority in terms of the production of weaponry. Furthermore, with the prospect of a blockade, as in the First World War, the medium-term outlook was bleak. If Germany could not source grain, oil and rubber from abroad, the longer-term prospects were even worse. The urgency of Nazi aggression, as in Japan, would stem not so much from a sense of superiority as from this pessimistic assessment of their situation.[20]

Great Britain and the British Empire

Thanks to Churchill's dramatic rhetoric, Britain in 1940 is often imagined as standing alone and ill-prepared for war. For years before he took office as wartime leader, Churchill had been a vigorous critic of Appeasement and Britain's failure to deter German aggression. But Churchill's determination to continue the war in 1940 was fired not only by his combative spirit. It was also based on a sober assessment of Britain's substantial technological and industrial power in the two areas that counted most – air and naval warfare. Despite the Prime Minister's rhetoric, Britain never stood alone. Britain fought the war not as an isolated nation state, but as a 'world island' drawing huge strength from its overseas Empire, the largest merchant fleet in the world and its privileged relationship to the USA.[21] This would enable it to withstand both the loss of its Allies in Europe in 1940 and the even more humiliating losses to Japan in Asia in 1942.

In 1939 Britain was by no means unprepared for war.[22] As early as 1935 when Germany began expanding its air force, Britain vowed to keep pace. Despite the reservations of the Treasury, the first factories supported

20 A comparison of GDP and production figures: Mark Harrison, 'The Economics of World War II: An Overview', in Harrison, ed., *Six Great Powers*, pp. 1–42.
21 David Edgerton, *Britain's War Machine: Weapons, Resources, and Experts in the Second World War* (London: Allen Lane, 2011) and David Edgerton, *Warfare State: Britain, 1920–1970* (Cambridge University Press, 2005).
22 G. C. Peden, *Arms, Economics and British Strategy: From Dreadnoughts to Hydrogen Bombs* (Cambridge University Press, 2007), pp. 102–63. Arms production from Harrison, 'Overview', pp. 15–16, Table 1.6. Edgerton, *Britain's War Machine*, pp. 11–85. Neil Forbes, 'Democracy at a Disadvantage? British Rearmament, the Shadow Factory Scheme and the Coming of War 1936–40', *Jahrbuch für Wirtschaftsgeschichte* 2 (2014), forthcoming.

by government grants and loans to expand the air force began to be built in 1936 and rearmament quickened its pace in 1938. The characteristic feature of British armaments planning was the so-called Shadow Scheme, which was directed toward building capacity for airframe and aero-engine production. The state-financed shadow factories were located near the sites of existing mass production factories, mostly in the automotive and engineering sectors, whose management and staff would put them into wartime production. One such factory was Castle Bromwich in the West Midlands run by the Nuffield Organization, which contracted over-ambitiously to deliver 1,000 Spitfires by 1940. Though the output of Spitfires was disappointing, in the hands of Vickers-Armstrong the Castle Bromwich plant would become a key site for the production of Avro Lancaster bombers. Already by 1940 Britain was out-producing Germany in aircraft by a margin of 30 per cent, in 1941 by 60 per cent. After the air raids of 1940 revealed the vulnerability of Coventry, the dispersal of shadow factory production began in earnest.

The Rolls-Royce Merlin aero engine, probably the finest engine of the war, was first manufactured in Derby and then at Crewe and Glasgow. By June 1940, the Merlin engine was also licensed to Ford (in the UK) and Packard (in the USA), which helped to ramp up US production well ahead of Pearl Harbor. Initially, the Rolls-Royce executives did not think American workshops could produce reliable and advanced engines because they would not have the craft and skilled machinists to manufacture the engine properly. For their part, the Americans found that Rolls-Royce drawings were not accurate enough to translate into mass production. Redrafting the design drawings for mass production took nearly a year. After 1939 a division of labour emerged in which Ford, Packard and the UK-based Crewe and Glasgow shadow factories focused on mass production, while the main Rolls-Royce plant produced over 100 different sorts of speciality Merlins. Meanwhile, the continuous development work of Rolls-Royce's engineering department raised the power output of the Merlins fitted to the Spitfire from 1,000 hp to well over 1,500 hp. Whereas before the war Rolls-Royce had produced a few hundred engines per year, at the Glasgow shadow factory, for which the foundations were laid in 1939, peak production would reach 400 engines per week, employing 15,000 mostly unskilled workers. Packard in Detroit would produce 60,000 Merlins, employing around 36,000 employees, one-third of whom were unskilled women workers. Crucially, thanks to early British orders the first Merlin engines came off Packard's assembly lines only weeks after Pearl Harbor in January 1942. By the end of the war, production of

Merlin engines was split into equal thirds between Rolls-Royce and its associated shadow factories, Ford UK and the US producers.[23]

The story of the Merlin is emblematic of the transatlantic networks that characterized British war production. North America was the essential reserve capacity of the British war effort. After Dunkirk British stocks of rifles were replenished from factories in Toronto in Canada, Massachusetts in the USA, Orange in Australia, and Calcutta in India. The Long Branch Arsenal in Canada produced the standard Bren light machine-gun. The Universal Bren Gun Carrier was designed by Vickers, but produced by Ford Motor Company in Britain, Canada and the USA. By the end of the war, production overseas accounted for half of the total. After 1938, production of aircraft (B-24s, Hudson bombers), tanks (Valentine), bomb-sights (Mark XIV), tank radios, artillery pieces and anti-tank guns (57mm 6-pounder) was shifted abroad. Even the P-51 Mustang, a decisive weapon for the American Air Force once it was equipped with the Merlin engine, originated with a British contract. No less emblematic were the rough and ready merchant ships based on British designs that became known as Liberty ships, which first began coming off America's slipways in August 1941. A dynamic West Coast entrepreneur, Henry Kaiser, established his famous Richmond shipyard in the San Francisco Bay area to meet the demand of British orders.[24]

The USA

After Pearl Harbor, the mass production achievements of the American arsenal of democracy were to become legendary. But the ability of American industry to bring mass production on line already by the middle of 1942 was the result of three crucial impulses.

First, between 1938 and 1940 British and French orders pumped hundreds of millions of dollars of war contracts into American factories. The British (and French) acted as a sort of venture capitalist that financed the designs, machine tools or equipment and preparation needed *in advance* of mass production.[25]

23 Peter Botticelli, 'Roll-Royce and the Rise of High-Technology Industry', in Thomas K. McCraw, ed., *Creating Modern Capitalism* (Cambridge, Mass.: Harvard University Press, 1997), pp. 96–129, esp. pp. 113–18. Herman, *Freedom's Forge*, pp. 195–206.

24 Edgerton, *Britain's War Machine*, pp. 59–65, 78–85. Benjamin Coombs, *British Tank Production and the War Economy, 1934–1945* (London: Bloomsbury, 2013), pp. 110–22. Tim Schanetzky, 'Henry J. Kaiser (1882–1967)', in Jeffrey Fear, ed., *Immigrant Entrepreneurship: German–American Business Biographies*, vol. 4 (www.immigrantentrepreneurship. org/entry.php?rec=59).

25 Mark R. Wilson, *Destructive Creation: American Business and the Winning of World War II* (Philadelphia: University of Pennsylvania Press, forthcoming), ch. 2.

In 1938, French and British contracts amounted to about $350 million (worth $5.8 billion in 2012) with $84 million allocated for aircraft engines alone. By mid-1940 Britain and France had 13,000 planes under order, while the US Army and Navy had ordered just 5,000. Most importantly, British and French began ordering B-24 'Liberators' (a name provided by the RAF) in 1939 from Consolidated Aircraft in San Diego. It was to become the most produced heavy bomber of the war with the Ford factory at Willow Run responsible for half of the entire total. The P-51 design for the fighter escorts that in 1944 would accompany them over Germany was developed under a 1940 contract for the British and first flown by the RAF as early as October 1940, but only became a superior, long-range fighter when partnered with the British Merlin Rolls-Royce engine.[26] The workhorse of the US Army, the M4 Sherman tank, went into production in October 1941, but was based on a British contract for over 3,500 medium (M3) tanks in mid-1940 the first of which rolled off the Chrysler line in April 1941. In 1941 about half of all tanks and one-third of all aircraft produced in the USA were shipped to the UK.[27]

Second, particularly in regards to the Navy, the USA itself initiated a sustained period of rearmament already beginning in the 1930s. Three successive Naval Acts of 1934, 1936 and 1938 modernized the US fleet, integrated aircraft development and procurement, and rejuvenated beleaguered shipyards. At the time, half of all naval production took place in government shipyards, but a few key private companies became involved, such as the shipbuilding subsidiaries of Bethlehem and US Steel, Newport News, the Bath Iron Works, New York Shipbuilding Corporation and the Electric Boat Company of Connecticut. The two main carriers at the decisive battle of Midway, the *Enterprise* and *Yorktown*, were ordered in 1934, produced by Newport News, and launched in 1936. They were equipped with newly designed 'Dauntless' dive-bombers from the Douglas Aircraft Company, which began to enter service in mid-1939.

The USA beat back the initial Japanese onslaught with a fleet ordered in the 1930s. But what would give the USA overwhelming superiority in the later stages of the war was the huge rearmament drive launched by Roosevelt in the spring of 1940. The Naval Expansion Act of 1940 placed new orders for a fleet that vastly outclassed any other in the world: 18 new aircraft carriers of various sorts, 7 new battleships, 33 cruisers, 115 destroyers,

---

26 Paul Kennedy, *Engineers of Victory: The Problem Solvers Who Turned the Tide in the Second World War* (New York: Random House, 2013).

27 Herman, *Freedom's Forge*, pp. 86–106. Sherman N. Mullin, 'Robert E. Gross and the Rise of Lockheed: The Creative Tension between Engineering and Finance', in Peter J. Westwick, ed., *Blue Sky Metropolis: The Aerospace Century in Southern California* (Berkeley: University of California Press and San Marino: Huntington Library, 2012), pp. 57–78.

43 submarines and 15,000 aircraft. In May 1940 Roosevelt also commanded the construction of an unprecedented air force. On 29 December 1940 he declared the USA to be the 'Arsenal of Democracy' and after months of sustained campaigning against neutrality in March 1941 pushed the Lend-Lease Act through Congress. Twelve to eighteen months prior to Pearl Harbor the USA was thus putting in place crucial designs, weapons systems and production tools.

As William 'Bill' Knudsen, Chairman of the Office of Production Management (OPM) told Roosevelt: 'Everyone knows that America is the greatest mass producer in the world. [But] Not everyone knows that mass production takes time to get started.' Charles Kettering, founder of Delco and head of research and development at General Motors, also highlighted: 'Mass production is the way to make a lot of something at minimum time per unit, and . . . the American nation has that trick down finer than any other nation on earth . . . The only thing that might spoil the national defense program was that the public didn't know how long you have to work on the make-ready before you can make a lot of anything.'[28] This 'make-ready' period was the crucial phase.

For Chrysler, which built the army-designed M3 (Grant/Lee) and M4 (Sherman) tanks at the famous Detroit Tank Arsenal, the 'make-ready' required 186 pounds of blueprints supplied by the Army's Rock Island Arsenal for 3,500 distinct parts. This meant around 6,000 additional drawings and 75,000 prints sent to prime contractors and their subcontractors. All of the parts required machine tools to be created, some standardized, some specialized. Speciality machines, tools, jigs, lathes, boring, milling, drilling or pressing equipment needed purchasing. For Chrysler's new tank factory, this meant over 8,500 fixtures, machines and jigs. When the M3 was phased out by mid-1942, Chrysler had to redesign everything for the M4. Begun in March 1941, Ford's Willow Run plant with its mile-long assembly line needed some 16,000 tools and 7,000 jigs. Two hundred relatively unknown machine tool makers supplied the key equipment for the US mass production system. Indeed, they even supplied Japan's Mitsubishi and Kawasaki aircraft factories and a considerable portion of equipment for the Soviet Union's industrialization drive. In 1941 their production had doubled relative to 1940 to 185,000 machine tools.[29]

28 Quoted in Maury Klein, *A Call to Arms: Mobilizing America for World War II* (New York: Bloomsbury, 2013), p. 239. Knudsen quote from Herman, *Freedom's Forge*, p. 146.
29 Herman, *Freedom's Forge*, pp. 145–55, 231.

The 'big box' firms such as Ford, Chrysler, General Motors, Studebaker, Packard, Kaiser Shipyards, Boeing, Douglas Aircraft, Consolidated Aircraft, Lockheed Vega (where the real Rosie the Riveter worked) were essentially assembly plants, which means that they were supplied by hundreds of other plants whose parts had to arrive on time, be reliable, and be fitted together. Delays in delivery of machine tools and parts combined with a shortage of skilled workers bedevilled Ford's Willow Run plant, earning it the nickname 'Will it Run?' With their separate chains of subcontractors, prime contractors prepared major sub-assemblies and the government itself often furnished key components such as electronic navigation systems, armaments or engines so that aircraft production represented a significant public–private partnership. All such assembly plants depended upon a vast array of subcontractors, which needed to be webbed together with information, knowledge, blueprints and tight delivery schedules. The B-25 Mitchell and B-24 Liberator had tens of thousands of parts as opposed to an automobile of some 5,000–15,000 parts. In the most complex and innovative bomber project of the war, the B-29 super heavy bomber, the nose segment alone had over 8,000 parts and over 1 million rivets. For the B-29 alone, Boeing coordinated 1,400 subcontractors with the government/military managing their own. Indeed, one historian of the B-29 called the aircraft the most *organizational* airplane ever built' (italics in original).[30] Overall, America's gigantic mass production capacity consisted of 25,000 prime contractors and 120,000 subcontractors organized into a network of distinct regions around such centres as Detroit, Los Angeles or Seattle. The sheer speed of this conversion had its costs. The rate of disabling injuries at work rose by 30 per cent from 1940. Between 1941 and 1945 about 86,000 died in industrial accidents, just under one-quarter of those who died in combat; about 100,000 workers per year suffered permanent partial disabilities, which amounted to roughly a half a million industrial 'casualties' by the end of the war relative to 671,000 soldier casualties; just over 2 million per year suffered temporary disabilities in factories.[31]

30 Jacob Vander Meulen, *Building the B-29* (Washington, DC: Smithsonian Institution Press, 1995). Herman, *Freedom's Forge*, pp. 176–91. Jonathan Zeitlin, 'Flexibility and Mass Production at War: Aircraft Manufacture in Britain, the United States, and Germany 1939–1945', *Technology and Culture* 36:1 (1995), 46–79.

31 Klein, *A Call to Arms*, ch. 11, on accidents, pp. 2, 712. Figures from Andrew E. Kersten, *Labor's Home Front: The American Federation of Labor during World War II* (New York: New York University Press, 2006), pp. 167–8, Tables 6.1–6.3. US military casualties from www.nationalww2museum.org. Charles K. Hyde, *Arsenal of Democracy: The American Automobile Industry in World War II* (Detroit: Wayne State University Press, 2013).

Decisive year in the 'battle of the factories': 1942

The entry of the USA into the war after Pearl Harbor was the decisive turning point when 'economic fundamentals reasserted themselves'.[32] Through Lend-Lease first to Britain, then to the Soviets, the USA had already begun building a crucial production bridge, a sort of giant contract manufacturer for the Allies. But the most dramatic story of 1942 was the resurrection of Soviet war production. This is a story not of foreign aid, but of the resilience of the Stalinist regime. The key story was the 'Great Evacuation' of 1941/42, that is, the remarkable relocation *and* restarting of Soviet production facilities in the Urals. The most 'heroic' aspect of the Soviet Union's experience was not its planning, but its sheer improvisation as thousands of plants were dismantled, shipped east of the Urals and then rebuilt to outproduce the Germans in 1942.

By the end of 1941 the Germans had occupied a territory accounting for 40 per cent of Soviet population as well as 7,500 large-scale factories, 749 heavy- and medium machine building plants, the heart of the metal engineering industry and 61 large-scale power plants. This amounted to around three-quarters of Soviet industrial capacity, one-third of its rail, and 40 per cent of its electricity and pre-invasion population. Of the 382 ammunition plants in the Soviet Union in 1941, 303 had to be evacuated or were destroyed in 1941. Aircraft production dropped from 2,300 a month prior to the invasion to 627 planes by November 1941. Lack of cranes and loading equipment meant that factory equipment had to be manually hauled onto railway cars before the workers themselves climbed aboard. An estimated 1.5 million railcars were loaded and shipped east. Many of the workers rode on top of the equipment in open railcars without tarps for cover; minimal rations were provided at 'evacopoints'. In the second half of 1941 an estimated 2,600 industrial factories were relocated to the Urals, Western Siberia, Central Asia and Kazakhstan along with a workforce of 12 million people in addition to 13 million other refugees.[33]

Even more remarkably, in 1942 Soviet workers reassembled the factories and restored production in the worst conditions imaginable on the open steppes in the middle of a snowy winter with few amenities. Factories restarted

---

32 Harrison, 'Overview', p. 2.
33 Frederick Kagan, 'The Evacuation of Soviet Industry in the Wake of "Barbarossa": A Key to the Soviet Victory', *Journal of Slavic Military Studies* 8:2 (1995), 387–414, see p. 393, figures from p. 401. Richard Overy, *Why the Allies Won* (New York: W. W. Norton, 1995), pp. 182–3.

Table 3.1 *Selected key arms production, major combatants, 1942 (000s, except ships)*

	USSR	Japan	Germany	UK	USA
Rifles	4,049	440	1,370	595	1,542
Machine pistols	1,506	–	232	1,438	651
Machine-guns	356	71	117	284	662
Guns	127	13	41	106	188
Mortars	230	1.5	9.8	29.2	11.0
Tanks/SPG	24.4	1.2	6.2	8.6	27.0
Combat aircraft	21.7	6.3	11.6	17.7	24.9
Major naval vessels/submarines	19	68	244a	239	1,584

Note: [a] Submarines for Germany

Source: Harrison, 'The Economics of World War II: An Overview', Table 1.6.

on open ground in freezing temperatures with strings of electric lights around the machinery. Workers dug out holes in the ground and huddled around open fires. Yet somehow of 1,500 relocated factories, only fifty-five were idle by the spring of 1942. Vast new production centres took shape such as the Stalin Tractor Factory in Chelyabinsk. Originally conceived as one of the tractor plants of the First Five-Year Plan, in 1941 Tankograd became the new home for the Leningrad Kirov works along with six other evacuated plants. Its workforce rocketed to 60,000 turning out 18,000 tanks and 48,500 tank engines.[34]

In 1942 the Soviet Union anchored the Allied war effort in industrial as well as military terms (Table 3.1). Whether at sea, on land or in the air Allied production hugely exceeded that of the Axis in 1942 and in the second half of the year this material preponderance began to make itself decisively felt on the battlefields of the Atlantic, Russia and North Africa.

Some within the German leadership responded to this glaring imbalance with fatalism. Ernst Udet, head of procurement for the Luftwaffe, shot

34 G. A. Kumanev, 'The Soviet Economy and the 1941 Evacuation', in Joseph L. Wieczynski, ed., *Operation Barbarossa: The German Attack on the Soviet Union June 22, 1941* (Salt Lake City: Charles, Schlacks, 1993), pp. 163–93. Harrison, *Soviet Planning in Peace and War*, pp. 109–58, capacity and losses figures from Tables 14–17. Richard Overy, *Russia's War: A History of the Soviet War Effort, 1941–1945* (London: Penguin, 1997), pp. 154–85, 191–8. Bellamy, *Absolute War*, p. 461, Illustration 15.4 has a map of industrial enterprises in the Urals. Mark Harrison, 'Why Didn't the Soviet Economy Collapse in 1942?', in Roger Chickering, Stig Förster and Bernd Greiner, eds., *A World at Total War: Global Conflict and the Politics of Destruction, 1937–1945* (Cambridge University Press, 2005), pp. 137–56. Lennart Samuelson, *Tankograd: The Formation of a Soviet Company Town: Cheliabinsk 1900s–1950s* (Basingstoke: Palgrave Macmillan, 2011), pp. 217–53.

himself. General Friedrich Fromm, director of the army's armament procurement, thought Germany would have to make peace. He would later be executed for his role in the last ditch effort to overthrow Hitler in July 1944. Others set themselves to outdoing America. Despite his doubts about Germany's armaments effort, Fritz Todt, head of the Ministry for Weapons and Munitions, set about streamlining the organization of the war economy in 1942. However, in February 1942 Todt's plane mysteriously exploded in mid-air. Two days later Hitler named Albert Speer as his replacement. He immediately adopted Todt's organization and put a committee of Central Planning at its head.[35]

The role of Speer, the subsequent alleged 'armaments miracle', and the nature of the German war economy has been the subject of considerable controversy. The revised historiography based on new archival evidence and data sources makes clear that Speer's self-stylization as a worker of 'armaments miracles' cannot be upheld. Instead Speer's success rested on generic sources: large-scale investments in the early war years, longer production runs of fewer numbers of weapons, and a concerted reallocation of raw materials and forced labour.[36] Between 1939 and 1943 German industrial capital stock surged from 56 billion RM to 70 billion RM (Table 3.2). As in any modern industrial system it took at least 8–16 months for this new capacity to come online.

By the end of the war, Germany had more machine tools per worker than in the USA in almost all categories of machines. They were manned by forced labour recruited from POWs and press-ganged populations of Eastern and Western Europe. In December 1941, 44 per cent of the workforce at the Daimler-Benz aero engine plant at Genshagen was skilled and mostly German. A year later the share of skilled labour had been slashed to 28 per cent. By October 1944, the Genshagen workforce was 67 per cent foreign and included around 1,000 women from the Ravensbrück concentration camp. Such a shift could be found all across high-priority armaments contractors such as Daimler and MAN. The first order of Panther tanks in May 1942 brought MAN a barracks for 2,000 Russian *Ostarbeiter*. By the end of the war, MAN employed over 8,500 forced

35 Tooze, *Wages of Destruction*, pp. 501–12. On the threat of Willow Run and Ford, see Lutz Budrass, *Flugzeugindustrie und Luftrüstung in Deutschland, 1918–1945* (Düsseldorf: Droste Verlag, 1998), pp. 789–92.

36 Tooze, *Wages of Destruction*, pp. 429–52, 552–89 and Adam Tooze, 'No Room for Miracles: German Industrial Output in World War II Reassessed', *Geschichte und Gesellschaft* 31:3 (2005), 439–64.

Table 3.2 *German industrial investments, 1936–1943 (millions of RM)*

	1936	1937	1938	1939	1940	1941	1942	1943
Total industrial investments	2,650	3,390	4,506	5,422	5,873	6,731	6,884	5,472
(1) Construction investments in industries (of which)	651	851	1,145	1,392	1,628	2,002	2,181	1,834
Armaments	178	215	347	492	855	948	1,046	699
Autarky	263	525	633	633	676	787	828	875
Non-war-related	210	111	165	267	97	267	307	260
(2) Equipment investments in industries (of which)	1,999	2,539	3,361	4,050	4,245	4,729	4,703	3,638
Armaments	324	364	533	717	1,554	1,723	1,902	1,763
Autarky	643	1,286	1,545	1,543	1,578	1,340	1,097	934
Non-war-related	1,032	889	1,283	1,790	1,173	1,666	1,704	1,338

Source: Jonas Scherner, 'Nazi Germany's Preparation for War: Evidence from Revised Industrial Investment Series', *European Review of Economic History* 14 (2010), 433–68, Table A7. Non-war-related investments calculated as a residual of the other two so should be considered only an estimate.

labourers (33 per cent of the workforce); at its Nürnberg tank plant it employed workers from twenty-five different countries.[37]

Paradoxically, the early mobilizers were reorganizing, reprioritizing and retooling in 1942/43, just as Allied mass production was ramping up and was already much larger than the Axis. Faced with the overwhelming material superiority of its enemies, Germany's conversion to a new phase of mass production in the early 1940s was a high stakes gamble. On the one hand, it concentrated production at new facilities on fewer proven types of weapons system, notably the Me 109 or Focke-Wulf 190 fighters, whose designs were

37 Neil Gregor, *Daimler-Benz in the Third Reich* (New Haven: Yale University Press, 1998), pp. 112–32. Budrass, *Flugzeugindustrie*, pp. 825–9, Table 80. Cristiano Andrea Ristuccia and Adam Tooze, 'Machine Tools and Mass Production in the Armaments Boom: Germany and the United States 1929–44', *Economic History Review* 66:4 (2013), 953–74. Johannes Bähr, Ralf Banken and Thomas Flemming, *Die MAN: Eine deutsche Industriegeschichte* (Munich: Beck, 2008), pp. 299–339.

frozen in essential respects. On the other hand, the Luftwaffe gambled on bringing revolutionary designs such as the Me 262 jet fighter into early mass production. Intermediary designs such as the Me 210 medium bomber and the He 177 heavy bomber were abandoned as dead-ends. The result was that while Germany waited for a new generation of wonder weapons to come into production, Albert Speer's production miracle, in fact, consisted of increasingly obsolete designs. Under the impact of Allied bombing, their production accelerated in one gigantic late surge in the first half of 1944 as every last scrap of raw materials and every available foreign worker was pressed into service. The Japanese saw a similar production pattern until the submarine blockade strangled its war economy before its cities went up in flames.[38] During these surges in production there were undeniable economies of scale and learning effects that resulted in a considerable increase in per capita productivity, but these were bought through the ruthless stripping of other sectors of the economy and the sweat, blood and exhaustion of the workforce.

Transformations

The impact of the wartime mass production boom on industry across the world was dramatic. First, the war created new zones of industrial production both in occupied and in colonized areas such as Eastern Silesia around Auschwitz and in Manchuria, but also in existing centres of production. In the heartland of Japan, for instance, the war concentrated investment around the 'Pacific belt' of Osaka-Kobe, Nagoya and Tokyo-Yokohama. Just over 70 per cent of all Japanese aircraft production stemmed from plants within 35 miles of Tokyo, Nagoya and Osaka. Ninety per cent of all propellers stemmed from three factories, two of which were in Osaka. Most engines were sourced in Nakajimi close to Tokyo and Mitsubishi in Nagoya. Nagoya's expansion was compounded by the growth of heavy and chemical industries and the 1936 move of Toyoda Spinning and Weaving, the core of what would later become the Toyota group. Near Nagoya, the city of Yokkaichi boomed due to military contractors such as Fuji Electric, Nippon

---

38 Mark P. Parillo, *The Japanese Merchant Marine in World War II* (Annapolis: Naval Institute Press, 1993). Cohen, *Japan's Economy*, pp. 114–92; on its aircraft industry, pp. 208–33. Masayasu Miyazaki and Osamu Itô, 'Transformation of Industries in the War Years', in Nakamura and Odaka, eds., *The Economic History of Japan, 1600–1990*, vol. III: *Economic History of Japan*, pp. 287–332 (pp. 287–97).

Sheet Glass and Daikyo Oil. Altogether the war created a new heavy industrial region around Tokyo-Yokohama that remained after the war.[39]

On the other side of the Pacific, the armaments boom saw the industrialization of the American West, particularly California. Government spending for armaments transformed the region with southern California and Seattle emerging as centres of the American aerospace industry. The Greater Los Angeles area alone produced 10 per cent of all armaments during the Second World War and attracted hundreds of thousands of people, creating severe housing shortages. Scientific research (and émigrés) helped CalTech become a major centre for physics research. Military investment spurred San Diego. Boeing dominated the Pacific Northwest, but plants to build B-29s had been placed in Renton in Washington, Wichita and Omaha in Nebraska, and Marietta in Georgia. Although receiving less federal investment than the west, US strategic planning deliberately dispersed manufacturing plants to southern states, particularly shipbuilding (Norfolk, Charleston, Mobile) and aircraft factories (Birmingham, New Orleans, and outside Atlanta).[40]

Similarly in the Soviet Union, Britain and Germany the demands of the new high tech war partially shifted the centre of industrial production away from nineteenth-century heavy industrial regions. The war permanently shifted a good portion of industrial production behind the Volga. Britain saw less dramatic regional shifts, but the greater London area gained new industries; stronger industrial policies placed dispersed factories in 'Special Areas' of high unemployment such as at Glasgow or Accrington.[41] While the Ruhr remained important, new regions of engineering expertise such as Baden-Württemberg or Bavaria arose. Silesia and the ancient metalworking areas of central and eastern Germany took on a new significance as they lay beyond the range of Allied bombing, at least until 1944. This was also accompanied by a profound sectoral shift. As Lutz Budrass emphasized: 'The mass production of aircraft dragged the electrotechnical, chemical, aluminum, and mechanical engineering industries along with it.' One might

---

39 Association of Japanese Geographers, eds., *Geography of Japan* (Tokyo: Teikoku-Shoin, 1980), pp. 246–98. Cohen, *Japan's Economy*, pp. 208–9.
40 Gerald D. Nash, *The American West Transformed: The Impact of the Second World War* (Bloomington: Indiana University Press, 1985), 10% figure from p. 62. Westwick, ed., *Blue Sky Metropolis*. David Kennedy, *Freedom from Fear: The American People in Depression and War, 1929–1945* (Oxford University Press, 1999). Gregory Hooks, 'Guns and Butter, North and South: The Federal Contribution to Manufacturing Growth 1940–1990', in Philip Scranton, ed., *The Second Wave: Southern Industrialization from the 1940s to the 1970s* (Athens, Ga.: University of Georgia Press, 2001), pp. 255–85.
41 Peter Scott, *Triumph of the South: A Regional Economic History of Early Twentieth Century Britain* (Aldershot: Ashgate, 2007), pp. 253–86.

add the optical and electronics industries. Moreover, the demand for aviation fuel, rubber and nitrates propelled the drive to find synthetic substitutes.[42]

Second, the war transformed business–government relations. Only in the Soviet Union was the war economy a state-owned effort. In all the other combatants it involved a hybrid of private enterprise and enormous government spending that inspired both bold predictions of a new era of managed economies and gloomy obituaries for the free market. Whereas Hayek warned against the *Road to Serfdom*, the American political economist James Burnham, writing in 1942, coined the phrase 'managerial revolution' to describe a common trend across the developed world. For Burnham this was a result of a combination of greater state enterprises combined with the separation of private ownership and managerial control centring on a cult of statistics and planning. Robert McNamara and his 'Whiz Kids', responsible for turning around the Ford Motor Company, personified this new culture in the 1950s. McNamara spent the latter part of the war in the US Army Air Force in its Office of Statistical Control analysing the efficiency of strategic bombing in the Pacific.[43] In Japan wartime control associations segued into highly concentrated post-1945 business associations. Debt-led war financing replaced families with banks in the centre of Japan's big business conglomerates (Mitsui, Mitsubishi or Sumitomo), which dispersed ownership and substituted equity with debt. Such main banks played an important role in rebuilding these networked firms after 1945.[44]

The transformation of business–government relations utterly transformed the organization of the American war economy. In the First World War the American government financed just 10 per cent of war capacity with armaments production being heavily concentrated in a few key arsenals. The far larger mobilization and heightened technological innovation of the Second World War involved huge risks. So US government financed over two-thirds of all the new armaments plants and owned roughly 25 per cent of all capital assets

---

42 Budrass, *Flugzeugindustrie*, p. 889.

43 James Burnham, *The Managerial Revolution or What is Happening in the World Now* (London: Putnam, 1942). John A. Byrne, *The Whiz Kids: The Founding Fathers of American Business – and the Legacy They Left Us* (New York: Doubleday, 1993).

44 Ito Osamu, 'The Transformation of the Japanese Economy', in Pauer, ed., *Japan's War Economy*, pp. 171–87 and Okazaki Tetsuji, 'Wartime Financial Reforms and the Transformation of the Japanese Financial System', in Pauer, ed., *Japan's War Economy*, pp. 144–70. Miyazaki and Itô, 'Transformation of Industries', pp. 306–14. Hara, 'Wartime Controls', pp. 267–85.

in manufacturing by 1945.[45] These so-called 'government-owned, contractor-operated' or GOCO plants accounted for the vast majority of wartime investment. Though many of these plants were later sold to their private operators, the tight ties of the military–industrial complex remained through the Cold War. To take just one example among many, except between 1945 and 1952 when the army managed it, Chrysler operated the Detroit tank arsenal between 1942 and 1982. It was then taken over by General Dynamics and turned out the latest generation of M1 Abrams battletanks until it was closed in 1996.[46]

It might seem that Great Britain's post-war political economy contrasted with that of America. To flank its ambitious welfare schemes, the Labour government that took office in 1945 made good on long-standing socialist calls for nationalization of basic industries. By 1950 one-fifth of the British economy had been nationalized including aviation, coal, iron and steel, railways, electricity and gas, and the Bank of England. But, if we focus on the hard core of the British warfare state, on firms such as Vickers and Rolls-Royce, then the similarities rather than the differences between Britain and the USA are more striking. In Britain as in the USA, the armaments burst of the 1930s and 1940s laid the foundations for a military–industrial complex that continued into the Cold War, shaping the British economy down to the late 1960s.

Third, the huge productive effort of the Second World War left a substantial material and organizational legacy even in the badly bombed industrial centres of Germany and Japan. In West Germany, thanks to the 1938–43 investment boom (see Table 3.2), industrial capacity was roughly 20 per cent higher in 1948 than ten years earlier. Machine tools did not suffer the same damage as buildings or transportation. However, even more important than industrial capacity, which might represent outmoded technology, was the development of new technical and organizational capabilities, embodied in people, knowledge and processes. In the post-war period technological change and productivity improvements would be the biggest drivers of unprecedented economic growth. This involved a broad-based extension of business enterprise and human capital. As discussed above, working with large firms demanded close tolerances, working-to-design, and delivery

45 Figures from Gerald T. White, *Billions for Defense: Government Financing by the Defense Plant Corporation during World War II* (University of Alabama Press, 1980), p. 2. Wilson, *Destructive Creation*.
46 Harold G. Vatter, 'The War's Consequences' and 'The Inheritance of the Preceding Decades', in Harold G. Vatter and John F. Walker, eds., *History of the U.S. Economy since World War II* (Armonk: M. E. Sharpe, 1996), chs. 1 and 2.

schedules that upgraded skills and transferred knowledge to smaller firms. Japanese historiography is exemplary in highlighting the importance of small and mid-size firms and the widespread use of subcontractors, which became a mainstay of its post-war economy. During the war a boom in new, smaller owner-operated firms in manufacturing occurred.

From the war emerged the hierarchical and unequal, but highly effective model of Japan's flexible 'dual structure' in which smaller firms paying lower wages buffered market volatility to the benefit of centre firms, which developed long-term employment relations and more stable profit rates. The armaments boom extended this model to the heavy industrial core. New sources of power such as electricity and gasoline-powered motors helped to decentralize production to thousands of small workshops. Whereas many firms in Japan had previously worked for themselves for local or regional contracts, they were through the war integrated into the top-tier and top quality production networks of the prime contractors. 'Clustered control' of this type led to a tremendous concentration of networked manufacturing capacity in the Osaka-Nagoya and Tokyo-Yokohama region. Toyota's famous network of subcontractors began during the war.[47]

A similar story can be found in the other great industrial success story of the post-war period, Germany. Here too subcontracting was the key to the mobilization of a heterogeneous, broad-based manufacturing network of small to mid-size businesses (*Mittelstand*), which happened to be naturally dispersed in many smaller towns. A major war producer such as Messerschmitt, for instance, was less a single firm than a web of over 3–4 tiers of over 130 firms, which were direct or indirect subcontractors. Of roughly 150 firms classified as armament firms in 1944 in the area around Augsburg with Messerschmitt or MAN as lead companies, 45 per cent of them employed less than 100 workers. This dense undergrowth of Mittelstand firms has contributed enormously to German industrial success to the present day. For example many of the prime suppliers of components for the Junker 88 programme would find themselves ten years later as suppliers to West Germany's booming automobile industry in the 1950s.[48]

---

47 Miyazaki and Itô, 'Transformation of Industries', pp. 320–6. Tetsuji Okazaki, 'The Supplier Network and Aircraft Production in Wartime Japan', *Economic History Review* 64:3 (2011), 973–94. Toshihiro Nishiguchi, *Strategic Industrial Sourcing: The Japanese Advantage* (Oxford University Press, 1994), pp. 1–49, esp. pp. 35–44. Takafusa Nakamura, 'The Age of Turbulence, 1937–54', in Nakamura and Odaka, eds., *The Economic History of Japan*, vol. III, pp. 55–110 (pp. 82–5).

48 Jonas Scherner, Jochen Streb and Stephanie Tilly, 'Supplier Networks in the German Aircraft Industry during World War II and their Long-term Effects on West

Only after the war did Japan and Germany emerge as the automotive powerhouses that they remain today.

Fourth, while many have spoken about the war as interrupting globalization, the weapons of war often embodied long, global supply chains. Industrial manufacturing depended upon the supply of key raw materials, which politicized government–business relations across countries such as between the USA and Latin America.

Copper became a strategic good. By the end of the war, American Lend-Lease aid to the Soviet Union provided around 1 million miles of telephone wire. A B-29 needed miles of wire to control both its innovative, electrically driven remote control turrets with coordinating computers and its wing flaps. Brass for small arm shell casings contained copper. American mining companies (Anaconda – perhaps an appropriate name) had long dominated the copper sector in Chile, but Chile was a main source of globally traded copper and was neutral with good relations to Germany. US copper procurement generated intense intergovernmental tension between Chile and the USA, culminating in severe post-war political protests in Chile.

Chile was also a major supplier of nitrates. During the First World War, the Haber-Bosch process enabled the European combatants to produce ammonia as the foundational ingredient both for fertilizer production and nitroglycerine, or TNT. Only the USA remained a major consumer of Chilean natural nitrate. During the Second World War, while the USA imported nitrates from Chile, it doubled its capacity of synthetic nitrogen plants. Wartime demand for both copper and nitrates distorted the Chilean economy, but those synthetic plants shifted to fertilizer production after the war, which phased out US demand for Chilean nitrate imports.[49]

Aluminium became one of the key strategic commodities of the twentieth century with the 1930s shift to aluminium for aircraft, a symbol of 'metallic modernity'. For aluminium production, the key mineral is bauxite, which

Germany's Automobile Industry during the "Wirtschaftswunder"', *Business History* (online Jan. 2014), pp. 1–25. Stefan Gründer, *Geplantes 'Wirtschaftswunder': Industrie-und Strukturpolitik in Bayern* (Munich: Oldenbourg, 2009), esp. pp. 44–66. Jeffrey Fear, 'Die Rüstungsindustrie im Gau Schwaben 1939–1945', *Vierteljahrshefte für Zeitgeschichte* 35 (1987), 193–216. Michael Geyer, 'Zum Einfluss der nationalsozialistischen Rüstungspolitik auf das Ruhrgebiet', *Rheinische Vierteljahrsblätter* 45 (1981), 201–64.

49 Graeme S. Mount, 'Chile: An Effort at Neutrality', in Thomas M. Leonard and John F. Bratzel, eds., *Latin America during World War II* (Lanham, Md.: Rowman & Littlefield, 2007), pp. 162–82; also Joseph Smith, 'Benefits of Cooperation', in Leonard and Bratzel, eds., *Latin America during World War II*, pp. 144–61. Samuel van Valkenburg, *America at War: A Geographical Analysis* (New York: Prentice-Hall, 1943), pp. 150–99. Mirko Lamer, *The World Fertilizer Economy* (Stanford University Press, 1957), pp. 454–63.

requires an immense amount of processing. Electricity consumption alone made it a highly capital-intensive industry requiring vast amounts of cheap, usually water, power. Manufacturing alumina, an intermediate product, usually took place on the site of bauxite mines, but smelting aluminium took place near sites of cheap electricity generation such as at Shawinigan Falls, Canada or at the fjords of Norway. Thus the mining of bauxite and the smelting of alumina usually occurred in two different areas of the world; the expense and complexity made it one of the most vertically integrated, yet spatially dispersed industries in the world.

A global scramble to control bauxite mines by big multinationals propelled bauxite mining and aluminium production through foreign direct investment in the interwar period. Huge deposits were discovered in British Guyana, Dutch Guiana (Suriname), and French Guiana. Alcoa swiftly gained dominant rights in the British and Dutch territories and opened an aluminium refinery as a Canadian subsidiary (Alcan). In the early 1930s, the British government negotiated rights that Alcan/Canada supply aluminium in case of war. Indeed, during the war Canada supplied 60 per cent of British wartime supply of aluminium, often with sourced bauxite from Guyana. The British Aluminium Company (BACo) had gained the rights to develop bauxite mines in Ghana already in 1933, but did not begin mining in earnest until the Ministry of Aircraft ordered it to begin in December 1940. During the 1940s, bauxite was discovered in Jamaica, which became the main source of bauxite for American firms, particularly Kaiser Aluminum and Reynolds Metals, which broke Alcoa's aluminium monopoly. In 1942, Alcan established a bauxite trading post inside a new US naval base in Trinidad, a striking symbol of the military–industrial complex created by the Second World War. After the war Alcoa further expanded into Suriname. Thus, the wartime demand for aluminium rerouted trade connections between the Caribbean, Canada and the USA, as well as Britain and Ghana.

Without rich bauxite mines at home, both the Germans and Japanese were at a huge comparative disadvantage. Both still developed substantial smelting capacity. Germany's Vereinigte Aluminium Werke (VAW) opened up links to Hungarian bauxite mines and built the largest aluminium smelting plants in the world. The Japanese too founded aluminium smelters in the 1930s, but had no domestic bauxite deposits and were initially blocked from the mining rights in Dutch and British territories. Eventually, a public–private partnership with the Japanese navy and three *zaibatsu* (Furukawa, Mitsubishi and Mitsui) developed an alumina refinery in Taiwan and contracted bauxite supplies on the Bintan Island just south of Singapore with the Dutch.[50] Exports to Japan began in 1935; ANTAM of Indonesia still exports to Japan and China today from Bintan.

Conclusion: militarized globalization

The war of the factories was essential to the outcome of the war. The Second World War raised the bar in both the scale of production and complexity of the products manufactured, which reshaped production and logistical processes both nationally and internationally with immense consequences for the post-war period. It involved a comprehensive effort at state mobilization and financing, permanently redefining the role of the state in capitalist economies. It also involved a broad-based form of mobilization within corporate capitalism that moved well beyond military arsenals or top-tier firms to include a broad base of small to mid-size firms in new regions, which led to an upgrading of skills and the formation of ramified organizations – a managerial revolution. A new sort of networked firm was born that was really a cluster of firms around a lead producer or designer.[51]

Furthermore, producing such weapons constructed what might be described as a transnational production system that stretched beyond the bounds of the nation state and was no longer based on a simple division of labour between the producers of raw materials and their processes, but revolved around the complex exchange of technologies, knowledge and productive tasks within the core of advanced industrial capitalism and reintegrated the so-called periphery in novel ways. This was not the end of globalization, but a repurposed form of international industrial organization coordinated by national governments for military ends. The USA and UK especially, mobilized their connections in the global economy against the Axis, while Germany and Japan evinced a form of imperialist regionalism – a violent attempt to assert themselves as global powers by means of 'mutant globalizations based on ideology or coercion'.[52] The building of Me 262s or V-2 rockets on the backs of foreign slave labourers was the most grotesque case in point.

50 Robin S. Gendron, Mats Inqulstad and Espen Storli, eds., *Aluminum Ore: The Political Economy of the Global Bauxite Industry* (Vancouver: University of British Columbia Press, 2013), chs. 1–3. Mimi Sheller, *Aluminum Dreams: The Making of Light Modernity* (Cambridge, Mass.: MIT Press, 2014).

51 Appearing in the 1920s, the war accelerated its adoption; see Michael Schwartz, 'Markets, Networks, and the Rise of Chrysler in Old Detroit 1920–1940', *Enterprise and Society* 1:1 (March 2000), 63–99.

52 Quoted in Geoffrey Jones, *Entrepreneurship and Multinationals: Global Business and the Making of the Modern World* (Cheltenham: Edward Elgar, 2013), p. 6.

If one accepts the default definition of globalization as an increase in cross-border flows of goods and services, capital and labour, then the mobilization for war initiated a sort of militarized, non-market globalization process that remarkably bears many of the hallmarks of the post-1980s second wave of globalization: outsourcing, contract manufacturing, the stress on logistics and transport, speed in production, and extended value chains.[53] The statistical volumes of trade, capital or labour flows are indeed trenchant indicators of globalization, but qualitative alterations in the organization of production, the exchange of knowledge, relationships between producers, subcontractors and suppliers were also highly significant, many of which started during the Second World War and had a significant impact on the post-war period. The Merlin engines 'Designed in Derby, Assembled in America' that powered the Allied bomber fleets and their escorts, or the thousands of Katyusha rocket launchers sitting on Studebaker trucks that hurled their firepower against Berlin in the spring of 1945 might best symbolize this new global military–industrial division of labour.

53 Richard M. Leighton and Robert W. Coakley, *Global Logistics and Strategy, 1940–1943* (Washington, DC: US Government Printing Office, 1995).

4

Controlling resources

Coal, iron ore and oil in the Second World War

DAVID EDGERTON

To a degree not evident in most histories of the war, its great generalissimos engaged directly, routinely and expertly with the material, the quantitative and the economic. It was clear to Churchill, Stalin, Hitler and Roosevelt that success in modern war required control of key resources, to be acquired for oneself and denied to the enemy. Hitler is well known to have been interested in raw materials, especially oil, though there is a tendency to see his interventions as ignorant.[1] But he was hardly unique in an age when the economy was thought of in very material ways; where elites knew where the world's major resources came from, what they were used for, who owned them, and how they might or might not be substituted for. While the coal of the Ruhr or the oil of Ploieşti or the iron ore of Lapland did not stir the imagination as did the silver of Potosí or the mercury of Almadén in the early modern period, they were nevertheless known to educated men of affairs of the mid-twentieth century. This chapter is thus in part an exercise in making familiar again what was once obvious to all people seriously concerned with war and statecraft. It was also familiar in some respects to the general public. Wartime propaganda films repeatedly told of the centrality of the material to modern war, from newsreels reporting events to films encouraging the salvage of waste materials. It is not a complicated story, but it is now unfamiliar.

That raw material supply would be a feature of a future war was obvious from the First World War, and from the international politics of the interwar

---

[1] There is no systematic study, to my knowledge, of Hitler's economic thought, but by far the richest account is Adam Tooze, *The Wages of Destruction: The Making and Breaking of the Nazi Economy* (London: Allen Lane, 2006), whose central argument is that Hitler and the Nazis pursued a reckless policy, but one which was demanded by the nature of their challenge to the world order.

years.[2] In the Great War coal was in short supply all over Europe as trade patterns changed, production fell and transport problems developed. Everywhere state involvement in the industry followed. The effects were widely felt – even the lights of Lisbon were dimmed by a lack of British coal for the gas and electricity works. Oil became a huge factor in the war, with Allied bodies controlling the flow to Europe from the Americas, the Middle East and the Far East – Royal Dutch/Shell and Standard Oil of New Jersey emerging as critical agents. Active steps were taken to deprive the Central powers of oil; anticipating the fall of Romania in 1916 British agents destroyed much of the oilfields and the refineries; they were to take over Baku in the summer of 1918 to deny that even more important source of supply to Germany.[3] Such issues did not disappear in the interwar years: raw materials were the stuff of international tension, compounding and compounded by economic instability. New economic boundaries cut across established interlinkages of raw materials – Lorraine iron ore and Ruhr coal now needed to cross borders, as did Silesian coal; they were now the subject of international politics. In the 1930s Britain, for example, made bilateral deals whereby British coal was exchanged for Nordic timber. Rubber caused problems between Britain, which controlled most of the production, and the USA, the world's greatest user: a British price-control scheme collapsed in 1928.[4] In 1934 all the major colonial producers – Britain, the Netherlands and France – formed a cartel, to which US companies responded in various ways including developing new plantations in Brazil, Liberia and the Philippines. Oil also involved great power rivalries – the US companies got only a very small share of Middle East oil, where operations were dominated by the British. In Mexico and Venezuela Royal Dutch/Shell was a very big player, as it was in the Dutch East Indies. Following the Russian revolution supplies from Baku were never allowed back into the world market on a substantial scale; a similar fate befell Mexico's production following the government's expropriation of Royal Dutch/Shell's subsidiary, Mexican Eagle, and the smaller US operations in 1938. The British broke off diplomatic relations and the USA and Britain boycotted Mexican oil, which found a new outlet in Nazi Germany. Furthermore the significance and

2 W. G. Jensen, 'The Importance of Energy in the First and Second World Wars', *The Historical Journal* 11 (1968), 538–54; Simon Ball, 'The German Octopus: The British Metal Corporation and the Next War, 1914–1939', *Enterprise & Society* 5 (2004), 451–89.
3 Daniel Yergin, *The Prize: The Epic Quest for Oil, Money, and Power* (New York: Free Press, 1990).
4 See two great novels on these themes: Ilya Ehrenberg, *Life of the Automobile* (London: Serpent's Tail, 1999) [1929]) and Madelon H. Lulofs, *Rubber* (Singapore: Oxford University Press, 1988) [1931]).

the possibilities of synthetic substitutes had become well known during the war, and were promoted in the interwar years: Germany developed synthetic petrol, nitrate and rubber processes; synthetic rubber was a promising possibility for US tyre companies combating British attempts to corner the world market in the 1920s.

It is a still common, and still justified, complaint that histories of war are too often written without taking material questions into account. A less common but perhaps more significant point is that many accounts are undergirded by dubious accounts of the material. One common assumption is that the material is a constant background feature, ultimately determining the fate of nations but essentially unchanging. A powerful example in the British and American literature is the long grip of nationalist declinist accounts which emphasized British material and materiel weakness by comparison with inflated German strength in both. As this essay will show, the material could change radically and very quickly. For example, only in the case of the USSR did invasion not yield raw materials at essentially pre-war production levels; here (essentially in the Ukraine) a scorched earth policy of astonishing severity and consistency was applied. This is not to say that elsewhere conquest was worthwhile, for getting production was one thing, transporting the product quite another. Changed patterns of trade and production of key materials were, as we shall see, central to the history of the war. It will also become clear that long-standing differences in income per head were important in allowing adaptation to such changes, and imposing unwelcome changes on enemies. We need material histories of events not merely of the *longue durée*.[5]

A fresh material history of the Second World War can throw into relief neglected questions of meaning and understanding of the nature of modern war (by both actors and historians), and of the basis of military power. In older treatments and tabulations of the material side of war, two sets of numbers stand out: first, the comparative production of various weapons (in numbers produced), and second, measures of control of certain raw materials (as proportions). The idea of 'strategic materials', a commonplace from the late 1930s, was typically expressed as a list of around ten to twenty such materials, indicating what proportion was home/imperially produced; such tabulations remain at the centre of discussion of raw materials and war.[6] They embody

5 Tooze, *Wages of Destruction*.
6 For uses of such tables see for example, John Ellis, *The World War II Databook* (London: Aurum, 1993), pp. 273–96, and I. C. B. Dear and M. R. D. Foot, eds., *The Oxford Companion to World War II* (Oxford University Press, 1995), pp. 931, 1063.

very particular assumptions. First, by emphasizing shares controlled they fail to distinguish between very different quantitative requirements, between hundreds of millions of tons of coal and thousands of tons of some metal ores, for example. Second, by focusing on nation and empires they over-stress the significance of political boundaries – national and imperial – as indicators of control, underplaying distance, wealth and power of many other kinds. In war as in peace economic national and imperial boundaries were not necessarily fundamental and of course borders changed radically in the war, even though this is not always reflected in maps found in textbooks. Third, they assert the strategic significance of particular materials, and thereby ignore alternatives, both in terms of source of supply, and indeed different kinds of materials being used for the same ends. They also neglect the role of firms, the leaders of which would often have been known to political leaders. For the suppliers of raw materials were, excepting the case of the Soviet Union, generally private firms   it was not till after the war that many countries nationalized coal-mining for example. Firms, their nationality, the politics of their leaders, could sometimes raise serious strategic questions. Oil companies were generally nationally focused, even if they did not necessarily operate in imperial territories (thus Anglo-Iranian, a state-owned British firm operated in formally independent Iran). The Anglo-Dutch/Shell companies produced in the Dutch not the British Empire, and elsewhere, but before the war, the politics of its head, Sir Henry Deterding, were not necessarily pro-British. Furthermore there were important international links between firms which would attract suspicion later – for example patent agreements covering synthetic oil and rubber between IG Farben and British and US chemical and oil companies. These are areas crying out for more research.[7]

In this chapter I focus on the three great raw materials of the twentieth century: coal, in a class of its own, and iron ore and oil (more strictly, petroleum and its derivatives). The only other materials in the same quantitative class as oil and iron ore were building materials, including timber and cement, and the three great grains of the world – wheat, rice and maize. There were close connections between coal and iron ore, and some between coal and oil. Blast furnaces for making iron combined iron ore with coke derived from coal, and making iron into steel required more still, such that, for example, around 20 per cent of German coal production went to iron and steel production. Generally speaking steel production needed more coal than iron

---

7 Ball, 'German Octopus'; Scott Newton, *The Profits of Peace: The Political Economy of Anglo-German Appeasement* (Oxford University Press, 1996).

ore, and more coal was consumed than steel produced. Coal was also used to make petrol and other fuels, though the conversion ratio was poor – about one-tenth of wartime German coal output was used for this. I will make some reference to less used but in some respects better-known materials – rubber and the ores of tungsten, manganese, chrome and aluminium (bauxite).

My discussion is based on physical quantities.[8] These present problems. First, quantity ignores the huge variation in the economic value and cost of different materials (for example, copper, aluminium and tin cost ten, twenty, fifty times more than pig iron). Second, quantities efface the fact that coal, petroleum and iron ore were far from uniform – they came in various forms, of very different purities, calorific value, ease of access and so on. For example, anthracite had a much greater energy content per ton than lignite (brown coal), and the iron ore of Lapland had a much greater iron content than that of Lorraine. Third, small quantities could have huge effects – for example, it was hardly possible to have an engineering industry without cutting tools incorporating tungsten, or to make good iron and steel without a measure of manganese ore, or to have steel cans for food without a vital thin layer of tin. But quantity was a decisive parameter for these materials both in that war-fighting demanded quantity, and because the quantities determined the level of transportation needed, which was, as we will see, a crucial issue.

Coal, iron ore and petroleum

Coal was the main energy source of industrialized societies, the key fuel for transport on land and sea, industry, electricity and gas generation, the making of iron and steel, and domestic heating. In 1940 world production of coal was around 1.7 billion tons. It was dug out of the ground only in particular localities – for example in parts of the USA, a number of European regions, and parts of Japan and northwestern China and Manchuria. Petroleum, produced at around 300m tons per annum, otherwise known as crude oil, was distributed in a very different way. Europe was a marginal producer, the Americas being dominant, with the USSR second. Iron ore, produced at around 200m tons per annum, was widely distributed, but high-quality ores

---

8 I will refer throughout to tons. I have generally rounded measurements which appear in the initial sources usually as long tons, but sometimes as short tons or metric tonnes. It should be noted that many oil industry statistics measure quantities in barrels, a measure of volume. A rough average conversion factor is seven barrels per ton.

were concentrated in very particular places, some small enough for a single mine. As in the case of coal, Europe and its environs rivalled the USA in output. These sources of supply do not indicate where materials *had* to be got from, only where they were got from. Not all sources known today were known during the war, much less exploited. What are today major sources of supply were often (though certainly not always) minor or non-existent sources of supply (for example Middle East oil, or Brazilian or Australian iron ore), and places then major are now minor (for example, the British coalfields). But even over short time scales, relative exploitation of different sources could change quite dramatically.

There were good economic reasons for consuming bulky and cheap raw materials (as coal, iron ore and crude oil all were) close to centres of production, but all typically travelled long distances. Coal was a nearly universally available fuel. More coal probably moved by sea (typically in coal-powered ships) between countries than the quantity of oil so shipped. Seaborne trade in coal was by no means all international: Japanese coal went to its destination in Japan by ship, as did much British coal. The great majority of the world's oil products travelled by sea or water – tankers sailed from the Gulf of Mexico to the great centres of population of the east coast of the USA; within the USSR oil travelled in ships across the Black Sea, and across the Caspian, and up the Volga by barge; and of course most of the output of the Caribbean, the Middle East and the East Indies travelled great distances by sea. Oil pipelines were as yet poorly developed, but the war would give them a boost, though railways remained a major means of transporting oil too. Iron ore also travelled long distances by sea and train. These materials represented very high proportions of total freight. The railway systems of the world can usefully be thought of as coal-powered coal pipelines.[9] For over one hundred years more than half the freight on British railways was coal, which could be handled at thousands of stations; for decades it was Britain's largest export in bulk, and was visible not just on railways and in docks, but on every street.[10] During the war the quantity of oil products entering British ports was about the same as the total of all food, raw materials and manufactures. Some one-third of freight on German railways consisted of coal and about one-quarter of Soviet rail freight.

---

9 Tooze, *Wages of Destruction*, pp. 342–3 for an overview of the significance of coal.
10 See Timothy Mitchell, *Carbon Democracy: Political Power in the Age of Oil* (London: Verso, 2013), though as implied above, in the period we are concerned with the differences between coal and oil production and transportation are nowhere near as great as he suggests, or as they were to become.

The history of the control of raw materials in wartime is as much a history of the control of transport, as of production. The scale of transportation of all these materials, and their location in very specific parts of nation states, indicates that we should not conflate availability of a raw material with national production. Furthermore in wartime, borders, both political and economic, changed often very radically. The war was not fought by autarkic nations, but by much larger entities, such as the remarkably self-sufficient Japanese Greater East Asia Co-Prosperity Sphere and the vast zone of German occupation in Europe incorporating what had been major independent economies now in effect trading with each other more than before, forming a 'European war economy'. The USSR was broadly self-sufficient even after losing some of its most productive territories, but there were major shifts in where in that vast territory raw materials came from. Britain was not in material terms just the British Isles, nor indeed just the Empire, but part of a global Anglo-American system which dominated the seas of the world (Table 4.1).

Raw materials and strategy

The economic blocs which were at war in the 1940s were created by force and were not the same as those that arose in the interwar years. But they were in part at least a response to economic developments of the 1930s. The 1930s saw a great strengthening of autarkic tendencies in the world economy. There were many reasons for it. The most important was the economic crisis after 1929 which saw extraordinary movements in trade, prices and output. Collapsing demand and prices on world markets led to states acting to maintain internal prices and employment and to save foreign exchange by restricting imports. Autarky was not an alternative to a smoothly functioning international economy, but rather a response to a highly unstable system that was undermining the welfare of peoples. Nor was it confined to fascist nations. The USA imposed the high Smoot-Hawley tariff in 1930 and set off a series of moves which massively reduced the value and volume of, for example, transatlantic trade. Tariffs and quotas also provided an opportunity to those who already wanted to promote national or imperial trade over international trade. Thus Britain, the world's greatest importer, broadly free-trading, moved to a comprehensive national system of protection with imperial preference, leading to a definite imperialization of British trade in the 1930s.

Economic nationalism was a powerful, and for many, progressive force, even if for liberals it went along with a danger of militarism. The connections

Table 4.1 Production, exports and imports of coal, iron ore and petroleum, 1937 (millions of tons)

	Poland	France	UK	Germany	Japan	USA	USSR	China	Other major
Population millions	34	40	45	65	71+73 (Taiwan, Korea and Manchuria)	132	170	500	n/a
Coal production**	36	ca. 37	234	182	37* Manchuria 15	395	78*	12	None
Coal exports** incl. bunker	10	–	47	38	Manchuria 4	12	–	–	None
Coal imports	–	21	–	4.5	4.3	–	–	–	Italy 11 Canada 9 Netherlands 8 Sweden 6 Belgium 6 Denmark 4 Argentina 3 Australia 3
Iron ore production (total ore)	1	37	14	8	0.7 Korea and Manchuria 2	74	27*	n/a	Sweden 15, Luxem 8, Algeria 2.8 Sp Morr 1.4
Iron ore imports	0.5	–	7	20	3.7*	2.4	–	–	None
Iron ore exports	–	19	–	–	Korea 1m	–	–	1.3*	Sweden 14 Algeria 2.5 Belg/Lux 2.2 Chile 1.5 Sp Mo 1.2 US 1.2

Table 4.1 (cont.)

	Poland	France	UK	Germany	Japan	USA	USSR	China	Other major
Crude oil production	–	–	–	–	–	173	27	–	Norway 1 Tunis 1
Oil imports Crude, motor, fuel and gas oil only	n/a	7	10	3	4*	8 (but net exporter)	–	0.4	Venezuela 27, Iran 10, Romania 7, NEI 7, Mexico 7, Iraq 4, NWI 22m, Canada 6 Then follow at over 1m Malaya, Australia, Argentina, Italy, and under 1m India, South Africa, Spain, Sweden, Brazil, Netherlands, Belgium

* Data for 1936.

** Excludes both anthracite and lignite. The two largest figures in each category are highlighted.

Note: German coal production is underreported as it exploited large reserves of lignite (brown coal) which was much less calorific than bituminous coal. Taking this into account German coal production was similar to British. There was a significant difference between British and French oil imports – the French imported large amounts of crude for home refining while British imports were mostly of more valuable finished products.

Source: Imperial Institute, *The Mineral Industry of the British Empire and Foreign Countries, Statistical Summary (Production, Imports and Exports) 1935–1937* (London: HMSO, 1938).

between militarism and economic nationalism are in fact quite complex. The USA and the USSR were the only nearly autarkic powers, yet the scale of armaments manufacture in the 1930s was very different in each. For Nazi Germany the die was cast by Hitler in 1936: conquest not trade was the future, rearmament and local substitutes the (expensive) means of achieving this.[11] The Japanese likewise conquered, not least in China. The Guomindang government of nationalist China wanted self-sufficiency to better fight the Japanese.[12] The British and French were confident in their ability to dominate without national or even imperial self-sufficiency. Great Britain, easily the least self-sufficient, was hardly pacifist; its reliance on imports from overseas implied powerful armed forces to secure those supplies. What the relationship between militarism and economic nationalism was and would be was not a matter of economic geography but of scale and wealth and politics. The options open to rich countries were different from those open to the poor.

Broadly speaking the search for autarky was a costly strategy of the relatively poor. Germany pursued an ambitious project of using coal and chemistry to put into production new and improved processes for making synthetic petrol, rubber and fibres (it also set up a German whaling industry for the first time). Germany's problem was not that it did not have oil, or rubber, or cotton, rather it was that it did not have the ability to import (or export) in the face of an opponent. Germany could and did use force to acquire resources, but in doing so made itself vulnerable, not least to economic sanctions, for it never succeeded in becoming wholly self-sufficient. Indeed, in 1939 Britain and France did impose a blockade, which was only partially bypassed by the economic pact with the USSR through which Germany accessed Soviet oil and grain and ores for the first time since 1933. Germany's conquests of 1940 did not alleviate its raw material problem, but rather added to it, for it conquered territories which had been net importers of coal and of oil.[13] It did, however, benefit from the accession of Romania to the Axis in November 1940. But Germany's resources were not enough for a global war against Britain (and as was likely the USA), and for this reason Hitler took the gamble of an eastern Blitzkrieg in June 1941 – to acquire the huge coal and iron ore (and grain) resources of the Ukraine and the petroleum and refineries of Baku. This was possible only if a quick

---

11 Tooze, *Wages of Destruction*, pp. 214–30.
12 Margherita Zanasi, *Saving the Nation: Economic Modernity in Republican China* (University of Chicago Press, 2006).
13 Tooze, *Wages of Destruction*, p. 425.

victory was assured.[14] Germany got practically no coal, iron ore or oil from
the USSR. With a still-functioning Soviet state, one prepared to take the most
extreme measures, even a quick conquest did not pay. This was a unique
case, though perhaps insufficiently appreciated as such, for all the other
conquests of Germany and Japan paid, though never enough. The consequences were great: Germany remained boxed in to a war-economic space
which could not sustain an intercontinental war. Italy too pursued, from the
1920s, a policy of autarky, successful in wheat, and from the 1930s a policy of
conquest. Had oil sanctions been imposed against it in 1935/36 it would have
failed in its ambitions.[15] From 1940 it was to depend on German coal, and on
German oil, both in very short supply.

The Japanese home islands were a long way from self-sufficiency, but this
is not the relevant criterion, for Japan had important resources in its imperial
territories, Formosa, Korea and Manchuria, and its more recent conquests.
From 1937 it acquired important supplies of coal and iron ore. Furthermore,
unlike Germany after 1939 it continued to trade on world markets, stockpiling key resources. From 1940, in the wake of its takeover of French Indochina, an important source of rubber, it had had progressive economic
sanctions imposed upon it; by mid-1941 it was cut off. Now Japan launched
a fresh war for resources, in which its central aim, in which it succeeded, was
to obtain oil. This required the neutralization of both the US and British
forces based in their imperial territories of the Philippines and Malaya, places
which had been significant exporters of iron ore to Japan. The new Japanese
empire, the Greater East Asia Co-Prosperity Sphere, achieved broad self-
sufficiency, certainly in oil, coal and iron ore, as well as bauxite, and was
indeed to deprive the USA of most of its rubber and tin. This was a
remarkable achievement, but its 'Achilles' heel' as the expression has it,
was the need to ship materials over vast distances without the sort of naval
power that could defeat the US Navy. Further, the Japanese economic area
was very poor – the levels of raw material consumption even in Japan were a
fraction of those of Germany, let alone Britain or the USA.

For a rich country like Britain, strategies of conquest and self-sufficiency
were perfectly possible but not generally resorted to. Britain was the largest
importer in the world and imported more from outside than from inside the
Empire, most especially in raw materials. In its dependence on imports the

---

14 Ibid., pp. 429–60.
15 Cristiano Andrea Ristuccia, 'The 1935 Sanctions against Italy: Would Coal and Oil Have
Made a Difference?', *European Review of Economic History* 4 (2000), 85–110.

British position was far worse than the German, and comparable to that of Japanese home islands in 1940. From a nationalist perspective this dependence was seen as a profound weakness, but from the perspective of the attenuated but still strong economic internationalism of the British elite, imports were a source of strength. Britain could exploit cheap supplies of raw materials (and food) from abroad and impose costly autarky on its enemies, both by the use of sea power.[16] This is not to say that Britain did not sometimes engage in conquest to secure raw materials, for example in its seizure of Iraq in 1941, and its move into southern Iran the same year, or develop imperial oil resources especially (as in Trinidad), but these were not core strategies.

Offensive, economic warfare was. Britain and France, and then the USA, put a great deal of faith in it. The British and French Allies were quick to impose general sanctions on Germany in 1939, and proposed two main offensives. Neither was in fact directed against Germany itself, but against supplies of raw materials from neutrals: Swedish iron ore and Soviet oil. This meant attacking the iron ore mines of Lapland via Norway and the oilfields and refineries of Baku via airbases in Syria. Preliminary action was taken in the first case which led to the German invasion of Norway in April 1940, just prior to the conquest of the Netherlands, Belgium and France. Its failure brought down the British government. The Allies thought better of the Baku plan.[17]

The sweeping German victories of April–June 1940 faced Britain with a very difficult situation. Its options have been interpreted as either fighting on 'alone' and nationally, though with the help of the USA, or making a deal with Hitler and living as an offshore imperial island remaining unconnected to a Nazi continent. In fact neither describes the dangers or the possibilities Britain faced. A status quo pact with Hitler implied not imperial isolation but trade with and through Axis Europe on a very large scale. German land conquests gave Germany control of vital Nordic timber and Swedish iron ore, and the defeat of France and the entry of Italy into the war gave the Axis control of the Mediterranean and thus of Algerian iron ore, and easy access to oil products from the British refineries in Abadan and Haifa. On the other hand, fighting on was possible not because Britain could find new strength

16 David Edgerton, *Britain's War Machine: Weapons, Resources and Experts in the Second World War* (London: Allen Lane, 2011).

17 Talbot C. Imlay, *Facing the Second World War: Strategy, Politics, and Economics in Britain and France, 1938–1940* (Oxford University Press, 2003).

from turning inward (as much historiography used to imply) but because it could remain turned outward, but in new ways. Britain not only did not feel itself to be alone, but was not alone. It was able to reorient its raw material supplies westwards, from Europe and the Middle East to the Americas (similar considerations apply to food, though here the critical connections to the southern hemisphere remained unaffected). It acquired allies, some of which provided it with much-needed additional shipping, notably but not only the large Norwegian fleet of both cargo ships and tankers. The volume of Britain's imports fell but the value did not: the cheap and bulky was replaced with the refined, concentrated and expensive. Thus, as iron ore imports fell, steel imports and manufactured imports increased. Oil imports surged, but came increasingly from the USA.

Resources flowed, though not without difficulty and expense. The USA and Britain, with the USA leading, established a new world war economy controlled from Washington (incorporating the Belgian and parts of the Dutch and French empires). One of the agencies set up in early 1942 to do this was the Combined Raw Materials Board. The USA itself was at the centre of the productive effort raising its output of coal, iron and oil very dramatically: by the middle of the war the USA was producing half the world's coal and iron ore and nearly two-thirds of its oil. Its allies in the United Nations controlled more than half of the rest. The capacity of the Axis to interfere in the production or movement of materials by the United Nations was in fact very limited. German submarines were no match for Anglo-American naval and merchant shipping, or the productive forces of the alliance.[18] There was no serious bombing of industrial facilities in Britain after early 1941; the U-boat threat was held at bay from 1941 until its defeat in May 1943.

By contrast the United Nations (as the Allies styled themselves from January 1942) were able to interfere with the supply of raw materials to the Axis. And they did so to dramatic effect from the beginning of large-scale Anglo-American operations in 1944 (a year which saw an upsurge in activity on sea and in the air as well as on land). Japanese, German and Italian shipping were wiped off the seas. Attacks on internal rail transport in Europe and on synthetic oil plants led to dramatic drops in coal and oil product output. The few neutrals were more than ever susceptible to pressure to diminish supplies of iron ore (Sweden), tungsten ore (Spain and Portugal)

18 Edgerton, *Britain's War Machine*.

and chrome ore (Turkey). Without coal and iron ore Japanese steel plants could not work; aircraft plants, if still working, were producing aircraft which could not fly for lack of fuel, for it could not be brought in to Japan. The destruction of transport made a mockery of the overall self-sufficiency of the still standing Japanese empire, and indeed that of the German empire too. For, surprising as it may seem, Germany still controlled the bulk of its war economy at the beginning of 1945, and with the exception of the Philippines, all the economically significant Japanese acquisitions of the war were still in Japanese hands at the end of the war.

Coal

Coal was the key energy source of all the belligerent powers, even the major oil producers. But not everyone had coal. The USA, USSR, Britain and Germany certainly did, but Japan, France and Italy relied on imports, in all cases greater than their imports of oil. The war in Europe had a profound influence on the pattern of coal movement. The first consequence of the war was that in 1939 Poland and Germany ceased to export to the largest importer – France; Britain, the world's largest exporter, increased its exports to France to compensate. In 1940 Britain was forced or wanted to cease supply to France, Italy, Egypt and other European markets, which was fortunate, as output of its mines also fell as labour was drafted. While Britain was out of the European coal economy, the German-controlled Continent had to make up for British coal supplies: Italy now needed around 10m tons per annum from Germany, which now had to go by rail rather than by sea; further millions had to go to the Nordic countries. France would have to go without. Thus the consumption of coal in continental Europe probably fell as a result of the British blockade.

Germany maintained, for most of the war, the output of most of the Western and Central European coal-mines. The German Reich annexed territories on its borders with rich coal seams – eastern Upper Silesia (where a new industrial centre was built in Auschwitz), Luxembourg and Alsace-Lorraine: much of it had been in the Reich up to 1919. The amount of coal mined overall increased, with all the increase coming from Silesia (which included the former Polish coalfields). Expressed in terms of bituminous coal equivalent, German production in million metric tons was 240m tons in 1940–41 from the pre-war German territories, another 76 million came from annexed territories (Alsace-Lorraine, Czechoslovakia, Austria and Upper Silesia), giving a total of 315m tons. The equivalent total for 1943–44 was 348m tons. A further 87m tons came from production in occupied but not annexed territories, which remained roughly constant into 1943.[19] Germany's per capita output of coal was high, but well under Britain's. And German coal had to go further than British coal, for it was at the base of many more industrial processes. One such was the making of chemicals, and bulk products like synthetic petrol, diesel and rubber. In terms of quantities, synthetic fuels were by far the most important – Germany produced half its liquid fuels from coal, mainly by the hydrogenation process. Many tons of coal were needed to produce a ton of aviation spirit or diesel for submarines, such that perhaps 20 million tons of coal were turned into oil per annum, about half the quantity needed for iron production.

Germany had hoped for a large net increase in coal availability. The Donbass (or Don Basin) in the Ukraine – capital Stalino – supplied more than half of the USSR's coal, producing as much as the whole of Silesia, or half the Ruhr, around 80m tons. It was captured in 1941 but in stark contrast to the cases of all the other coalfields the Nazis (or Japanese) took over, a serious scorched earth programme was in place, and the Ukraine, unlike equivalent parts of Poland, Belgium, France or northern China, ceased to be an industrial centre. Coal production was negligible even after the sending in of 2,000 German miners with tens of thousands of prisoners of war.[20] At some points Germany had to export coal to the Ukraine.

The USSR never made up the loss but it made dramatic efforts to do so, developing Siberian fields first exploited before the war – the Kuznets Basin (Kumbass) and the Karaganda Basin – which supplied the emergent industrial areas east of the Urals, like the giant steelworks at Magnitogorsk and the tank factories of Chelyabinsk (Tankograd, or Tank City). In Vorkuta (Pechora Basin), part of the Gulag system and north of the Arctic Circle, there was one mine at the beginning of the war, and sixteen by the end.

The Japanese home islands needed large imports of coal which mostly came from the Empire. The coal output of the Japanese empire (94 million tons) was half that of Britain; in 1940 output in Japan proper was around 60 per cent of the imperial total. Coal had to be transported by sea, not only from China and Manchuria, but from the coal-mining areas of Japan to the

19 Charles Webster and Noble Frankland, *Strategic Air Offensive Against Germany*, vol. IV: *Annexes and Appendices* (London: HMSO, 1961), p. 490.
20 Bernhard R. Kroener, Rolf-Dieter Muller and Hans Umbreit, *Germany and the Second World War: Organization and Mobilization of the German Sphere of Power*, vol. v, Part 2: *Wartime Administration, Economy, and Manpower Resources 1942–1944/5* (Oxford University Press, 2003), p. 217.

areas of use – which became increasingly difficult.[21] During the war, Japan took over, geographically and financially, nearly the whole of the Chinese coal industry where output peaked in 1942 at 66m tonnes.[22] Yet from 1940 mainland Japan would see falls in both domestic production and imports, with a collapse toward the end, such that it could use only about half the total (increasing) capacity to produce iron and steel.[23] German coal production suffered the same fate: it halved between September and December 1944, due to the interruption of rail transport.[24]

There was one common feature to all coal production during the war, and that was shortages of labour. There were somewhere approaching 3 million coal-miners in the belligerent powers, usually men who could be employed in the armed forces, and they tended to leave or be recruited. If miners represented the proletariat of the world, it was clear that overall the workers' wartime experience was one of radically decreasing welfare, working conditions and productivity, the USA excepted, and Britain largely so. With the great and significant exception of the USA the result was not only the use of forced labour, but also declining productivity. The USA saw a decrease in the coal-mining workforce, but by the end of the war it was producing 200m more tons of coal than before the war, its wartime increment equal to British production at the end of the war. It ended up producing three times as much coal as Britain. In 1944 620 million tons of coal were produced by 393,000 miners, some 1,500 tons per miner per annum. Productivity had increased rapidly, with longer working weeks and hours, more mechanization and some increase in open cast mining.[25] The contrast with Japan was striking. By 1944 there were 353,574 men in the mines, and 70,577 women, a proportion not seen since the 1920s, an overall increase over pre-war of around 100,000, mostly forcibly recruited in Korea.[26] However, productivity more than

21 Akira Hara, 'Japan: Guns before Rice', in Mark Harrison, ed., *The Economics of World War II: Six Great Powers in International Comparison* (Cambridge University Press, 1998), pp. 224–67 (p. 231).

22 Elspeth Thomson, *The Chinese Coal Industry: An Economic History* (London: Taylor & Francis, 2004).

23 Muzaffer Erselcuk, 'Iron and Steel Industry in Japan', *Economic Geography* 23 (1947), 105–29; USSBS, *Coal and Metals in Japan's War Economy* (vol. 36, 1947) (https://archive.org/stream/coalsmetalsinjap36unit#page/88/mode/2up).

24 Webster and Frankland, *Strategic Air Offensive*, vol. IV: *Annexes and Appendices*, p. 506.

25 Leo Fishman and Betty G. Fishman, 'Bituminous Coal Production during World War II', *Southern Economic Journal* 18 (1952), 391–6.

26 Sachiko Sone, 'Japanese Coal Mining: Women Discovered', in Kuntala Lahiri-Dutt and Martha Macintyre, eds., *Women Miners in Developing Countries: Pit Women and Others* (Aldershot: Ashgate, 2006), pp. 51–71.

halved, and thus output fell, partly because miners were so badly fed by the end of the war. Toward the end of the war, with about the same number of miners, the USA produced ten times more coal.

Germany also used large numbers of forced labourers, productivity fell and food was an issue here too. In Silesia in 1942 one coal complex started a system of 'performance feeding' of forced labourers who now got rations on the basis of production; the system was to spread to all forced labour workers as from the end of 1943.[27] The Soviet Union had Gulag-operated coal-mines in the north and used many forced labourers in the expanding Karaganda and Kuznets fields east of the Urals.

In Britain the number of miners, the output of coal, and the productivity of work would all decrease during the war, but although coal was short by British standards, it never became a constraint.[28] In Britain from 1943, one in ten conscripts was sent into the mines, a total of 21,800 young men; more than 8,000 appealed overwhelmingly unsuccessfully against this, showing just how unpopular the mines were, even at normal mining wages.[29] Britain (like Germany) had twice the number of miners the USA did, and produced one-third the amount of coal (about 300 tons per miner per annum).

Iron ore

During the war, iron ore (expressed as a quantity of ore) was produced at the rate of roughly 200m tons per annum, with US production surging from around a quarter to one-half. In terms of labour it was efficiently produced – some 1,000 tons per worker per annum in Britain, and more than twice that in the USA.[30] The great bulk of the vast output of the USA came from seams around Lake Superior. Lorraine was the second largest source, and in the interwar years France was the largest exporter in the world. French Algeria had an important mine at Ouenza, which with others supplied not France but other European producers. The main centre in the western USSR was in the Ukraine, in Krivoy Rog. Magnitogorsk, the 'magnetic mountain' of iron ore, was in the Urals. Of the important iron and steel producers only the USSR

27 Tooze, *Wages of Destruction*, pp. 530–1.
28 W. K. Hancock and M. M. Gowing, *British War Economy* (London: HMSO, 1949), pp. 467–79.
29 H. M. D. Parker, *Manpower: A Study of Wartime Policy and Administration* (London: HMSO, 1957), pp. 252–5.
30 L. Rostas, *Comparative Productivity in British and American Industry* (Cambridge University Press, 1948), p. 232.

and the USA were self-sufficient in high-grade ore. Japan, Britain and Germany depended on large scale imports pre-war. Germany imported from France (including Alsace-Lorraine, which it had lost in 1919, and had been its major source before 1914), Sweden and elsewhere. Britain imported from Sweden, French North Africa, Newfoundland, Spain and Sierra Leone, and Japan from Manchuria, North China, Malaya and the Philippines. Sweden, after France the most important exporter by far, produced most of its ore from two sites, Kiruna and Gällivare in Swedish Lapland, connected by the same railway line to both Swedish and Norwegian ports.

The most important immediate impact of the war was that Germany could no longer import ore from France, or from Spain or North Africa. It became increasingly dependent on Swedish ore, in terms of bulk, Germany's biggest import by far. One could easily imagine that cutting off the Swedish ore would halve Germany's steel production, and thus destroy its capacity to wage war. One of Britain's first offensive actions in 1940 was the mining of (neutral) Norwegian waters to prevent the winter passage of Swedish iron ore to Germany, and a move to take the Swedish ore mines via Narvik.[31] In response Germany invaded Norway, and was indeed able to secure Swedish ore till the end of the war. In any case from 1940 it was able to get ore once more from a re-annexed Alsace-Lorraine, and indeed from French Lorraine. A little came, briefly, from the USSR. Already in the 1930s the Nazis were urging the exploitation of domestic iron ore, and by 1939 a large modern steelworks using local ores was in production: it was built under strong pressure from Göring and Hitler, and against the wishes of much of the steel industry, who were concerned about over-capacity and the use of low-grade ores.[32] The Nazis captured the huge Krivoy Rog iron ore deposits and mines of the Ukraine in 1941. As in the case of the coal-mines of the Ukraine, and the iron and steelworks, they were put out of commission; only 300,000 tons were produced by the end of 1942.[33] (The Soviet Union was fortunate in having iron ore deposits beyond the Urals and built a new steel industry there, the most famous case being the new steelworks at Magnitogorsk.[34])

The British expectation that Germany could not cope without Swedish ore, so superficially attractive, was probably mistaken, though it did have

---

31 Christian Leitz, *Nazi Germany and Neutral Europe during the Second World War* (Manchester University Press, 2000); Imlay, *Facing the Second World War*.
32 Tooze, *Wages of Destruction*, pp. 234–9.
33 Alan S. Milward, *War, Economy and Society, 1939–1945* (London: Allen Lane, 1977), p. 149.
34 Stephen Kotkin, *Magnetic Mountain: Stalinism as a Civilization* (Berkeley: University of California Press, 1996).

such supplies until near the very end of the war. Ironically enough it was Britain and not Germany which was cut off from Swedish ore, in 1940, and it coped. In fact Britain suffered a drastic loss of iron ore – for in addition to the Swedish ore it lost access to Algerian supplies also. Like Germany it increased the proportion of domestic ores. Yet it still had overseas supplies, from Sierra Leone and Newfoundland, but crucially was able to increase imports not of ore, but of steel and of steel products, above all from the USA.

Japan proper was even less well endowed with iron ore than Britain and its main suppliers in 1940 were Malaya and the Philippines, then parts of the British and American Empires. But it also had major sources in Manchuria and Korea, indeed pig iron and steel were produced there.[35] Manchuria and Korea accounted for 32 per cent of imperial pig iron production; it came from four large works, two in Manchuria, and two in Korea.[36] By 1942 it had control of Malaya and the Philippines as well, but supplies of ore from here were replaced with Chinese sources, including Hainan island.[37] The problem for Japan in iron ore, as in coal, was not controlling sites of production, but transporting the ore (or its products). Indeed large numbers of specialized iron ore carriers were built. From 1944 especially imports of ore and thus output of steel collapsed; the Americans even interfered with ore flowing down the Yangzi River. An additional problem was that most of Japan's ore was low grade and required additional coke to reduce; large amounts of scrap iron had been used pre-war, but this was one of the crucial imports that were embargoed by the USA from 1940.

Oil

Global production of crude at around 300m tons in 1940 was higher than, but comparable to that of iron ore. Production was concentrated in the Americas.[38] The great oil well concentrations were in the Gulf of Mexico (both in the USA and Mexico), in California, and Lake Maracaibo in Venezuela (which shipped its crude to the Dutch West Indies). The whole Eurasian landmass, together with the Dutch East Indies, only produced as much as the

35 Muzaffer Erselcuk, 'Iron and Steel Industry in Japan', *Economic Geography* 23:2 (1947), 105–29.

36 Kazuo Hori, 'Colonial Economy under Japanese Imperialism: Comparison with the Case of India', *International Journal of South Asian Studies* 4 (2011), 40.

37 USSBS, *The War against Japanese Transportation, 1941–1945* (vol. 54) (https://archive.org/stream/waragainstjapane54unit#page/20/mode/2up).

38 John W. Frey and H. Chandler Ide, eds., *A History of the Petroleum Administration for War, 1941–1945* (Honolulu: University of Hawai'i Press, 2005 [1946]), p. 172.

Caribbean producers and Mexico.[39] Baku in the USSR was overwhelmingly the most important production centre outside the Americas, and was comparable to the Venezuela/Dutch West Indies complex. Baku was the most northerly and by far the most important field in the Middle East. The Ploieşti oilfields and associated refineries in Romania, Abadan in Iran, Pelambang in Sumatra, and Kirkuk-Mosul in Iraq were other significant but smaller centres of production. These places refined the petroleum too – excepting the case of France, and parts of the USA – and it was only after the war that large refineries were built close to centres of consumption of petrol rather than the production of crude. Thus the oil-tankers on the world's seas typically transported not crude but petrol, aviation spirit, fuel oil and diesel. Tankers plied long routes. The oilfields closest to Britain were the Ploieşti ones, at 2,000 miles the same distance as Berlin from Baku, or New York from the oilfields of the Gulf of Mexico. The closest major oil centre to Japan was in the Dutch East Indies, a distance equivalent to London–New York or London–Sierra Leone, say 3,500 miles. Thus every belligerent relied on long-distance supply, only the USA and USSR from within their own borders. Germany was better placed than most in that it was close to Romania.

Although we think of oil as a very capital-intensive industry, it in fact employed a very large workforce, both in the oilfields and in the refineries. In terms of tonnage of usable products, output per worker was similar to that of the coal industry. Thus there were around 250,000 oil workers in the USA in the late 1930s (mostly in the oilfields) producing about 1,000 tons each on average.[40] In Iran the Anglo-Iranian company employed 50,000 and produced 10m tons per annum in the late 1930s, comparable to the coal output of the same number of British coal-miners.[41] The huge Aruba refinery produced around 15m tons with 10,000 workers. The Venezuelan oilfields (which shipped their crude to Aruba and Curaçao) employed about 20,000 workers in Venezuela itself.[42] Baku had many tens of thousands of oil workers.

Crude oil was not, however, the only possible source of the products known as fuel oil (for ships), gas oil (diesel), motor spirit (petrol) or aviation spirit (avgas). They could be made from coal distillation, and various

39 Ibid., pp. 257–9.
40 For 1937, 150,000 in production (including gas), 83,000 in refineries and 20,000 in pipelines. United States Bureau of Labor Statistics, *Handbook of Labor Statistics, 1941 edition* (Washington, DC: US Government Printing Office, 1942), vol. I, pp. 828–33.
41 J. H. Bamberg, *The History of the British Petroleum Company*, vol. II: *The Anglo-Iranian Years, 1928–1954* (Cambridge University Press, 1994), pp. 81, 121.
42 Edwin Lieuwen, *Petroleum in Venezuela: A History* (Berkeley: University of California Press, 1957), p. 87.

chemical treatments of coal. Such processes were developed in many countries, but above all in Germany, where work started on this before the Great War. Synthetic petrol production was given a very great push by the Four-Year Plan programme of 1936, giving Germany a highly significant domestic source for nearly all its wartime aviation spirit, much of its petrol, and a considerable proportion of its diesel. At peak Germany was making some 7m tons of oil products, one-half derived from coal. Britain and Japan had smaller programmes of synthetic oil production.

Germany did get oil products derived from crude oil, even though cut off from the big suppliers from 1939. Romania was neutral until November 1940, but its Ploieşti field and refineries had supplied Germany and would continue to do so until the summer of 1944.[43] Germany thus had the largest European petroleum centre. It had its eyes on by far the greatest centre in all of Eurasia, Baku. Baku produced around 30m tons, three or four times more than peak German consumption. Whereas access to Soviet coal and iron ore would have given Germany a significant boost, control of Baku could *potentially* be transformational. In 1942 Baku became the central military objective for the Nazis, with an additional benefit that advances toward it would push back Soviet airbases out of range of Ploieşti.[44] In fact, even a fully operating Baku under Nazi control would have had difficulty getting its product out – navigation across the Black Sea (there was a pipeline to it) and the Mediterranean was not secure, there was lack of capacity on the Danube, and overland routes could only transport small quantities.[45] Similarly, even if they had captured the much smaller Abadan and the Iraqi fields undamaged, they would have been of relatively little use to the Germans, as they could not transport the product by sea, land facilities barely existed, and the impact on Allied production would have been minimal.[46] In the event, the Germans reached only Grozny, hundreds of miles from Baku. The Soviets had destroyed the refinery at Krasnador, and the refineries and oil wells in Maikop from which the Germans would get tiny output. In fact, the Soviets

43 Jan Luiten van Zanden, Joost Jonker, Stephen Howarth and Keetie Sluyterman, *A History of Royal Dutch Shell*, vol. II: *Powering the Hydrocarbon Revolution, 1939–1973* (Oxford University Press, 2007), p. 69.
44 Joel Hayward, 'Hitler's Quest for Oil: The Impact of Economic Considerations on Military Strategy, 1941–42', *Journal of Strategic Studies* 18 (1995), 94–135. Joel Hayward, *Stopped at Stalingrad: The Luftwaffe and Hitler's Defeat in the East, 1942–1943* (Lawrence: University Press of Kansas, 1998), p. 20.
45 Hayward, *Stopped at Stalingrad*, p. 21.
46 Klaus Schmider, 'The Mediterranean in 1940–1941: Crossroads of Lost Opportunities?', *War & Society* 15 (1997), 19–41.

temporarily evacuated Baku, sending workers and equipment north to create a 'second Baku', and sealed many wells, and readied the site for complete destruction. As a result of these measures Baku production fell. It would surely have not fallen intact into German hands. The best Germany could hope for was to deprive the Soviet Union of oil. All it managed to achieve was to reduce production and force the building of new transport links from Baku to replace captured railway lines and the Volga River route, blocked at Stalingrad.

By contrast, Japan was brilliantly successful in acquiring a major source of supply by conquest. Before 1940 Japan relied mainly on the USA for its oil. The Japanese were able to wage war against China from 1937 with such supplies and built up significant stockpiles. But from 1940 the Americans, the British and the Dutch imposed increasing economic sanctions on Japan, including measures to prevent stockpiling and imports of high-grade oil products, notably aviation spirit. In the summer of 1941 came a complete oil embargo on Japan, part of a general economic war against Japan. The Japanese response was an exceedingly rapid advance directed at the Dutch East Indies, which were captured in early 1942, and which could in principle supply Japan's needs. Royal Dutch/Shell had detailed plans and routine training to disable all plants for six months. It successfully destroyed Balik Papan (Borneo) but the greatest refinery, Pladju (Pelambang, Sumatra), was captured by parachute troops before it could be destroyed.[47] The other large refinery was nearby, and was run by Standard Oil/Socony-Vacuum (Stanvac). The Japanese restored 75 per cent of Dutch East Indies crude production by 1943, and refinery output to 40 per cent, about their pre-war imports. The problem was that Japan was, toward the end of the war, to lose its tankers, mainly to US submarines. As a result the Japanese resorted to using oil residues, shale oil, oil from coal (on a very small scale), and what would now be called biofuels. Diesel fuels were made from coconut, copra, soy bean and pine-root oil. Ethanol for aviation fuel was made from sweet potatoes, cane sugar and molasses and other sources. At the end of the war, though this is perhaps apocryphal, the gigantic battleship *Yamato* was burning soybean oil. Aviation spirit was also made by cracking pine root oil. These were desperate, hugely expensive measures. It was hardly necessary for British carrier-borne aircraft to attack first the Shell Pladju refinery and then the nearby Stanvac plant, in January 1945.

47 Van Zanden et al., *A History of Royal Dutch Shell*, vol. ii, pp. 65–6.

Britain pursued a very different policy from Germany. Its imperial supplies were limited to Trinidad and Burma, and it created only a small hydrogenation programme. It would rely on extra-imperial sources where its companies had oil concessions and refineries. Most of its supplies came, at first, from Venezuela/Dutch West Indies, and Iran and Iraq. But in 1940/41 the position changed radically, and the British Isles were now supplied mainly from the USA, essentially to save on shipping, both because the Mediterranean was closed and because the USA was closer than Curaçao (Shell) or Aruba (Standard Oil) or Point-a-Pierre (Trinidad Leaseholds). Britain, and the British Empire, now fitted into a global supply system for oil products dominated by US supplies and US investments, including in British refineries. But for operations in the East and Mediterranean, and for supplying the Eastern Empire, Britain relied on facilities in what was coming to be called the Middle East. In 1941 British forces invaded Iraq and divided Iran into spheres of interest with the USSR. In 1942 the British reckoned Abadan strategically more important than Egypt because of the huge refinery and oilfield there.[48] Abadan was the main supply centre for British imperial forces in the Middle East and India and points east (the fields and refineries of Burma were effectively destroyed by the British, and the Dutch East Indies had been lost); Abadan was expanded to supply 100 octane aviation spirit to the USSR by pipeline and railway, with US finance and US made equipment. Such was the quantity of US and Caribbean production that the loss of the Dutch East Indies and of Burma was hardly felt, nor was the loss of direct access via the Mediterranean to Middle East oil. Imports into Britain at the end of the war reached 20m tons, double the pre-war level and nearly three times peak German output. This figure does not include the huge quantities which went direct to British forces overseas, or to the British Empire as a whole, from the USA, or indeed from the Middle East. For example some 5m tons went to Northwest Europe from D-Day to the end of the war. Despite the claims made about the PLUTO undersea pipelines built by the British, well over 90 per cent went by tanker, and most of that never touched Britain, and was not accounted for in British imports.

The Germans and the Japanese were very successful in that for most of the war they were able to get oil products, securely so, on a greater scale than pre-war. They were able to mount very significant operations on land, sea and air. Nevertheless they had very low oil usage compared to Britain as well

---

48 Schmider, 'The Mediterranean', p. 31.

as to the USA. The upshot was that the Allied armies were fully motorized, requiring vast tonnages of petrol and lubricants to keep them going – tanks, lorries, jeeps and motorcycles were everywhere, as were aircraft. Warships could steam at will. By contrast, the German and Japanese armies were horse- and human-powered, reflecting enormous disparities not only in fuel, but in other materials too. These differences were radically increased toward the end of the war as vast Allied forces went into action, and the Axis powers were deprived of more and more oil products. The Germans did interfere with United Nations supply to some extent. They sunk tankers in the Atlantic; they sunk barges taking crude from Lake Maracaibo to the Antilles, and even attacked one of the refineries by submarine. But the USA could and did respond by building around 500 standard T2 tankers alongside the better-known general cargo Liberty ships, and by reducing exposure at sea by transferring oil products from ships to internal US railways, and to new pipelines which took crude and products from the Gulf of Mexico for consumption in the northeast, and for transfer to Britain and elsewhere. By sharp contrast, as we have seen, the Japanese were unable to move their oil from 1944. By 1944 Germany had lost Romanian supplies, and their synthetic oil plants were under sustained and successful attack, in contrast to unsuccessful British raids in 1940/41 and US raids on Ploieşti in 1943. The upshot was that at the end of the war there were spectacular differences between the belligerents. In November 1944 just one large USAAF bomber raid on Germany attacking synthetic oil plants, used more than 34,000 barrels of aviation spirit; in that month total Luftwaffe consumption was down to 12,500 a day.[49] In the summer of 1944 the US Fifth Fleet in the Pacific used 93,000 barrels of various fuels and lubricants, excluding aviation spirit, every day. This compared with total Japanese consumption, military and civilian, in all theatres, at 103,000 barrels per day.[50]

Other raw materials

While the German advances in the war did deprive the Allies of valuable resources of coal (in the Soviet Union) and iron ore in many places, they did not deprive them of resources unobtainable elsewhere. By contrast, Japan captured the great bulk of world rubber production, and more than half of

49 Robert Goralski and Russell Freeburg, *Oil and War: How the Deadly Struggle for Fuel in WWII meant Victory or Defeat* (New York: William Morrow, 1987), p. 283.
50 Ibid., p. 317.

world tin. In both cases the USA had been the major customer, though the supplying territory was mainly British. But they were costs the USA could bear. The USA very quickly created a synthetic rubber and by the end of the war produced more than had previously been imported, and was producing seven times more than the German wartime peak.[51] In the case of tin, nearly half the world supply was smelted by British-owned firms in Penang and Singapore; and easily the largest single market was the USA which consumed half the world's tin. Britain was primarily supplied from British smelters, which drew on Britain and Bolivia for ore.[52] The USA responded by building its first smelter, to process Bolivian ore. In other products too replacements were found: the insecticide pyrethrum, for which Japan itself was the main supplier, now came from Kenya and was supplemented by new synthetic insecticides, notably DDT. Quinine was replaced by synthetic anti-malarials, notably mepacrine.

There were some materials which Germany found very difficult to source within its own expanded borders. One was manganese ore, needed in steel production. This was one of the large items imported from the USSR during the pact. The Germans seized Nikopol in Ukraine which was a major source, and were desperate to keep hold of it, just as they were later to retain manganese and other mineral resources from the Balkans and Finland. For Hitler the ores were vital reasons to hold territory, for others this posture was a measure of the desperate position of the Reich: not to defend these resources, which were likely to be lost, was in effect to admit the war was over, since without them Germany would lose the war.[53] Germany also resorted to desperate attempts to produce new weapons which minimized the use of scarce resources. The jet engine is a surprising but striking case – it economized on high quality steel and nickel and chrome, on skilled labour, and also used cheap fuel rather than expensive aviation spirit. But the benefit was negligible and the costs very high.[54] Germany also economized on

---

51 Peter J. T. Morris, *The American Synthetic Rubber Research Program* (Philadelphia: University of Pennsylvania Press, 1989); William G. Clarence-Smith, 'The Battle for Rubber in the Second World War: Cooperation and Resistance', in Jonathan Curry-Machado, ed., *Global Histories, Imperial Commodities, Local Interactions* (Basingstoke: Palgrave Macmillan, 2013), pp. 204–23; Jochen Streb, 'Can Politicians Speed Up Long-Term Technological Change? Some Insights from a Comparison of the German and US-American Synthetic Rubber Programs Before, During and After World War II', *Essays in Economic and Business History* 21 (2003), S33–49.
52 Klaus Knorr, *Tin under Control* (Stanford: Food Research Institute, Stanford University, 1945).
53 Kroener et al., *Germany and the Second World War*, vol. v, Part 2: *Wartime Administration, Economy, and Manpower Resources*, pp. 465–7.
54 Hermione Giffard, 'Engines of Desperation: Jet Engines, Production and New Weapons in the Third Reich', *Journal of Contemporary History* 48 (2013), 821–44.

tungsten by mass use of long-lasting tungsten carbide tools rather than tungsten steel tools.[55] Here a complex set of raw material policies operated with neutrals. For example, the British and Americans had total control over Spanish oil imports – they imposed embargoes to various degrees not (as they could have) to bring down Franco, but to reduce his exports of tungsten to Germany; the USA wanted to force them to nothing, but Britain, conscious of its investments, went for a deal.[56] As the war went against Germany so the neutrals were more successfully pressured to reduce supplies of tungsten ore from Spain and Portugal, and chrome ore from Turkey. Similarly, flows of Swedish iron ore and ball-bearings fell.[57]

Conclusion

In examining the effect of the atomic bomb on Japan, the USSBS commented that 'Japan's economy was in large measure being destroyed twice over, once by cutting off of imports, and secondly by air attack.'[58] Germany too was, in the last year of the war, defeated many times over. This is not to say that victory for the Allies was inevitable or indeed easy, but when it came it was overwhelming and self-reinforcing. Material defeat came not with the loss of one key raw material, or this or that indispensable metal, but through multiple, interconnected losses. There was no one clinical 'knock-out blow', nor even a war of attrition, but rather overkill. This last phase of the war, spectacularly different from earlier phases, not only brought to bear the material superiority of the United Nations, but also led to this very superiority being increased by military action. Earlier Axis success had been greater than material power might imply, which doubly makes the point that it is not an independent, only slowly changing variable, but one that could change radically. The material history of the war was not a key background element, but was something which shaped events and was shaped by events.

This is perhaps most clear in the case of oil, and perhaps for that reason the story of oil in the war is often alluded to. Indeed it is tempting to say that the

---

55 Hermione Giffard, 'A Hard Sell: Disparities in the Inter-War Adoption of Tungsten Carbide Cutting Tools in Germany, the United States and Britain', forthcoming.

56 Leonard Caruana and Hugh Rockoff, 'A Wolfram in Sheep's Clothing: Economic Warfare in Spain, 1940–1944', *Journal of Economic History* 63 (2003), 100–26.

57 Leitz, *Nazi Germany and Neutral Europe*; R. N. Wylie, *Britain, Switzerland and the Second World War* (Oxford University Press, 2003); R. N. Wylie, ed., *European Neutrals and Non-Belligerents during the Second World War* (Cambridge University Press, 2001).

58 USSBS, *Summary Report (Pacific War)* (Washington, DC: United States Government Printing Office, 1946).

war was won by those who had oil, and lost by those who did not. There is something in this, but not too much, as those who had oil also had coal in superior quantities – indeed they had superiority in nearly everything. Furthermore both Germany and Japan had secure, though low, oil supplies – the key point is they were actively deprived of those supplies by Allied action only at the end of the war. They lost the capacity to move coal too. And it was coal that was the central raw material of the war, the most mined, the most moved, the most used material by every belligerent. And what was really telling here was what the ground would yield, and what labour could be deployed and how efficiently it could work. Here the USA had a crushing double advantage, an extreme though important case of a vital general phenomenon.[59]

59 I am most grateful for assistance of many kinds to Adam Tooze, Anand Toprani, Takeshi Sakade, Kazou Hori and Hsien-Hao Fu.

5

The human fuel

Food as global commodity and local scarcity

LIZZIE COLLINGHAM

Food has always been a weapon of war. The Second World War was no exception. Indeed, the impact of the conflict on food supplies was as deadly in its effect on the world population as military action. While the war caused some 19.5 million military deaths, at least 20 million people died as a result of starvation, malnutrition and its associated diseases.[1]

In August 1940, the British imposed a blockade on all goods, including food, entering occupied continental Europe. By the end of 1942 Japan had imposed a blockade on nationalist China. US submarines attacked Japanese shipping lines while German U-boats patrolled the Atlantic. Civilian food supplies had to compete with coal and fuel, steel, phosphates for explosives, military supplies and troops, for limited shipping space. Starvation was used as a targeted means of extermination by both Germany and Japan and both Axis and Allied powers inflicted famine and malnutrition on vulnerable populations.

Countries with modern agricultural sectors fared better than those with peasant-based agrarian economies. The more developed the agricultural sector the more room it had to readjust and weather the impact of war. Small-scale farmers were more difficult for a government to control and tended to reduce production and withdraw into self-sufficiency. Peasants were vulnerable to the effects of wartime inflation which undermined the purchasing power of the poor and created the conditions for famine.

In all the combatant countries agriculture struggled to win the internal competition for resources. Military conscription combined with the draw of higher paid work opportunities drained workers from the farms in Allied and Axis countries alike. Mechanization in order to compensate was difficult because the production of agricultural machinery declined precipitously as

---

1 John Ellis, *The World War II Databook: The Essential Facts and Figures for All the Combatants* (London: Aurum Press, 1993), pp. 253–4.

industrial plants switched to making tanks and arms. Fuel shortages and a lack of spare parts often prevented the proper use of those machines that were available. The military demand for oxen and horses meant that even draught animals were in short supply. The fertilizer industry lost the competition with the munitions industry for limited supplies of nitrogen and phosphorous and the lack of fertilizer meant that farmers struggled to increase yields.[2]

Agriculture needed to raise rather than simply maintain its production levels. Each nation's food requirements rose as the working day lengthened and more of the population moved into physically demanding heavy industries and the military. Rising wages meant that demand for food increased, especially for meat and milk products. Securing the food supply preoccupied all the governments drawn into the conflict as every sector of the war economy – military capability, industrial productivity and civilian morale – was reliant on it.

In the interwar years the issue of food security played a surprisingly important part in propelling both Germany and Japan toward aggression. The need to secure a food supply played into the hands of those espousing aggressive, expansionist policies. Rather than engaging with the global food market, both countries chose to look to their militaries to appropriate enough land to reverse rural decline and secure the nations' food supply. Empire was seen as a means of making 'peace with modernity' by transforming those groups which had been destabilized by the process of modernization, into a positive force for progress. In this way the desire for a secure food supply was transformed into a powerful motivating force for conflict.[3]

Post-1918 Germany was in a difficult position with regard to its food supply. Food and fodder made up half of the country's imports and this, as well as reparations payments, left too little to buy the large quantities of raw materials needed in order to regenerate industry.[4] Prominent agronomists debated the course that the country should take in order to feed the workers

2 Joachim Lehmann, 'Agrarpolitik und Landwirtschaft in Deutschland 1939 bis 1945', in Bernd Martin and Alan S. Milward, eds., *Agriculture and Food Supply in the Second World War. Landwirtschaft und Versorgung im Zweiten Weltkrieg* (Ostfildern: Scripta Mercaturae Verlag, 1985), pp. 29–49 (pp. 39–40); Arnulf Huegel, *Kriegsernährungswirtschaft Deutschlands während des Ersten und Zweiten Weltkrieges im Vergleich* (Konstanz: Hartung-Gorre Verlag, 2003), pp. 300–2.

3 Louise Young, *Japan's Total Empire: Manchuria and the Culture of Imperialism* (Berkeley: University of California Press, 1998), pp. 309, 351; Yamamuro Shin'ichi, *Manchuria under Japanese Dominion* (Philadelphia: University of Pennsylvania Press, 2006), pp. 268–9.

4 John E. Farquharson, 'The Agrarian Policy of National Socialist Germany', in Robert G. Moeller, ed., *Peasants and Lords in Modern Germany* (London: Allen & Unwin, 1986), pp. 233–59 (p. 233).

with the white bread, butter and pork which they desired. The liberal option would have been to follow Britain's example and down-scale Germany's woefully large, inefficient and indebted agricultural sector and channel the surplus workers into industry where they would produce the manufactured goods which could then be exchanged for cheap food imports. Conservatives opposed integration into the world economy and favoured agricultural protectionism and the goal of food self-sufficiency or autarky which would allow Germany to withdraw from the international food market.[5] This debate transformed food preferences into a political statement. Conservative housewives' associations called on women to support the German farmer by serving their families rye bread rather than crusty white rolls made from imported wheat and home-grown apples rather than bananas and oranges.[6]

After 1933 agricultural reform may have been a low priority for many in the National Socialist leadership as they focused on preparing for war. But it is a mistake, which many historians have made, to conclude that issues of agriculture, farming and food supply were of little importance in determining wider National Socialist policy.[7] Adam Tooze makes the point that, 'as hard as it may be for us to credit, agrarian ideology is crucial if we are to understand, not the archaism of Hitler's regime, but its extraordinary militancy'.[8] Many leading National Socialists were scarred by their experience of the First World War. They were convinced that starvation had contributed to the nation's defeat in 1918 and, moreover, they had observed how a hungry and defeated Germany had been vulnerable to communist revolution.[9] The regime's attempts to achieve food autarky were only moderately successful. Germany continued to rely on large fodder imports for its domestic meat production.[10] The NSDAP's protectionist agricultural policies also caused food prices to rise.

5 Martin Kutz, 'Kriegserfahrung und Kriegsvorbereitung. Die agrarwirtschaftliche Vorbereitung des Zweiten Weltkrieges in Deutschland vor dem Hintergrund der Weltkrieg I – Erfahrung', *Zeitschrift für Agrargeschichte und Agrarsoziologie* 32 (1984), 59–82, 135–4 (pp. 73–4).
6 Nancy R. Reagin, *Sweeping the German Nation: Domesticity and National Identity in Germany, 1870–1945* (Cambridge University Press, 2007), pp. 93–9; Uwe Spiekermann, 'Brown Bread for Victory: German and British Wholemeal Politics in the Inter-War Period', in Frank Trentmann and Flemming Just, eds., *Food and Conflict in Europe in the Age of the Two World Wars* (Basingstoke: Palgrave Macmillan, 2006), pp. 143–71 (p. 148).
7 Gustavo Corni, *Hitler and the Peasants: Agrarian Policy of the Third Reich, 1930–1939* (Oxford: Berg, 1990), pp. xv–xvi.
8 Adam Tooze, *The Wages of Destruction: The Making and Breaking of the Nazi Economy* (London: Allen Lane, 2006), p. 180.
9 Ian Kershaw, *Hitler, 1889–1936: Hubris* (London: Allen Lane, 1998), pp. 97, 109.
10 Richard Perren, *Taste, Trade and Technology: The Development of the International Meat Industry since 1840* (Aldershot: Ashgate, 2006), pp. 96, 98.

Hitler was plagued by fear of the social unrest expensive and scarce food might cause.[11] In 1936 he demanded that food prices should be brought under control; in 1937 he worried about the quantity of food imports the country needed; in 1938 he gave a speech in which he warned that unless the problem of food shortages could be solved the regime would face a crisis. Again in February 1939, he told a meeting of troop commanders that the food question was the most urgent problem facing Germany.[12]

The National Socialist solution was the conquest of *Lebensraum*. In his unpublished 'Second Book' (1928) Hitler formulated the argument that Germany needed its own version of the American West.[13] In 1932 Heinrich Himmler and Walther Darré were already planning a large eastern empire with agricultural estates run by an aristocracy of SS members and worked by enslaved former inhabitants.[14] In 1936 the Reichsnährstand (Reich Food Corporation), created by the regime to reform agriculture, confirmed the need for expansion, calculating that in order to achieve food self-sufficiency while maintaining the current standard of living, Germany needed another 7–8 million hectares of farmland.[15] *Lebensraum* would ensure that all Germans were well fed while making Germany immune to blockade and capable of challenging British and American hegemony. There should be no doubt that the desire to secure the German food supply was a key motive for German aggression toward Poland and the Soviet Union.

In the winter of 1940 Germany had reached an impasse. Having successfully employed Blitzkrieg in Poland and Western Europe, the war had stalled over Britain. The Sicherheitsdienst, nutritionists working for the Institute of the Physiology of Work and Leonardo Conti at the Ministry of Health, all argued that the present rations were inadequate to sustain war production and that Germany was building toward a food crisis.[16] It is not an exaggeration to say

---

11 Farquharson, 'Agrarian Policy', pp. 244–5.
12 Corni, *Hitler and the Peasants*, p. 249; Rolf-Dieter Müller, 'Die Mobilisierung der deutschen Wirtschaft für Hitlers Kriegführung', in Bernhard R. Kroener, Rolf-Dieter Müller and Hans Umbreit, eds., *Das Deutsche Reich und der Zweite Weltkrieg*, vol. v, Part 1: *Organisation und Mobilisierung des deutschen Machtbereichs. Kriegsverwaltung, Wirtschaft und Personelle Resourcen 1939–1941* (Stuttgart: Deutsche Verlags-Anstalt, 1988), pp. 347–689 (p. 397).
13 Tooze, *Wages of Destruction*, p. 658; Gustavo Corni and Horst Gies, *Brot, Butter, Kanonen. Die Ernährungswirtschaft in Deutschland unter der Diktatur Hitlers* (Berlin: Akademie Verlag, 1997), p. 19.
14 Corni, *Hitler and the Peasants*, pp. 27–8.
15 Tooze, *Wages of Destruction*, p. 197.
16 Müller, 'Die Mobilisierung der deutschen Wirtschaft', p. 402; Alexander Neumann, 'Nutritional Physiology in the Third Reich 1933–45', in Wolfgang Uwe Eckart, ed.,

that food paranoia developed among the National Socialist leadership. In January 1941 Herbert Backe, the representative for agriculture in Göring's office for the Four-Year Plan, submitted an extremely negative annual report on the food situation. He also suggested a solution.

Hitler had now turned his attention toward the Soviet Union, hoping that if victory could be achieved in the east in two or three months and before the USA was drawn into the conflict, Britain would be left isolated and more willing to capitulate.[17] In meetings with Göring and Hitler, Backe supplied additional grounds for an attack. He saw the agricultural riches of the east not just as the eventual spoils of war but as the means to solve the current food shortage. He argued that food from the fertile central area of Russia and the Ukraine could be diverted away from Soviet cities and onto the plates of the Wehrmacht instead. The memorandum from 2 May 1941, outlining Backe's Hunger Plan, acknowledged that 'unbelievable hunger' would rule in northern Russia where the industrial areas would 'die out, so to speak', but stated that any sympathy for the starving Soviets would be misplaced as, 'the war can only be continued if the *entire* Wehrmacht is fed from Russia in the third year of the war'.[18]

As soon as the attack on the Soviet Union began in June 1941 the Plan was implemented. No provision was made to introduce rationing in the occupied Soviet cities and road blocks were set up around major cities to prevent peasants taking produce into the markets. The siege of Leningrad, where 1 million died of starvation, the blockades of the Ukrainian cities of Kiev and Kharkov, which accounted for at least another 200,000 deaths from starvation, were not incidental consequences of war but the result of this deliberate strategy.[19]

The General Plan for the East emerged from Himmler's office of the Reich Commissioner for the Strengthening of the German Race. Teams of agrarian experts worked on the detail of how to transform the east into a rural

    Man, Medicine and the State: The Human Body as an Object of Government (Stuttgart: Franz Steiner Verlag, 2006), pp. 49–60 (p. 55).

17 Alex J. Kay, *Exploitation, Resettlement, Mass Murder: Political and Economic Planning for German Occupation Policy in the Soviet Union, 1940–1941* (Oxford: Berghahn Books, 2006), p. 145.

18 William Moskoff, *The Bread of Affliction: The Food Supply in the USSR during World War II* (Cambridge University Press, 1990), p. 42; Christian Gerlach, *Krieg, Ernährung, Völkermord. Forschungen zur deutschen Vernichtungspolitik im Zweiten Weltkrieg* (Hamburg: Hamburger Edition, 1998), pp. 46, 49.

19 Horst Boog, Joachim Hoffmann, Ernst Kluk, Rolf-Dieter Müller and Gerd Ueberschär, *Der Angriff auf die Sowjetunion* (Stuttgart: Deutsche Verlags-Anstalt, 1983), pp. 1010–13; A Citizen of Kharkiv, 'Lest We Forget: Hunger in Kharkiv in the Winter 1941–1942', *Ukrainian Quarterly* 4:1 (1948), 72–9 (pp. 74–6).

empire. A mass migration of Germans was expected, who would live in idyllic German towns and villages.[20] The documents spoke euphemistically of 'resettlement', 'evacuation' and 'Germanization' of the indigenous population. In fact, it was planned that while 14 million would remain in the area as slaves, the rest, calculated at 70 million in December 1942, would be deported to labour camps further east where most were expected to work themselves to death.[21] Once the regime acquired a taste for mass annihilation there was some discussion about whether it would be simpler just to execute them. Hitler likened the fate of the Slavs to that of America's 'Red Indians'.[22]

The full extent of the agrarian radicalism of the Nazis is rarely fully appreciated because many of the crimes they planned to perpetrate remained on paper. Between 1939 and 1942 hundreds of thousands of Polish farmers, many of them Jewish, were evicted in order to make way for ethnic Germans. A few were sent to the Reich as forced labourers, others to concentration camps and at least 18,000 to the extermination camps at Majdanek and Auschwitz.[23] But only fragments of the General Plan for the East were ever realized. Nevertheless, there should be no doubt that, if the Germans had succeeded in defeating the Soviet Union, they would have conducted a far more extensive and terrible genocide in the name of agricultural reform than that which they were able to carry out under the limitations of occupation while they were still fighting the war.[24]

The issue of securing the nation's food supply was as incendiary in 1930s Japan as it was in National Socialist Germany. Japan's ailing agricultural sector was unable to produce enough food to feed the expanding urban population who were demanding more rice as their incomes rose.[25] Imports

20 Gert Grönung, 'Die "Allgemeine Anordnung Nr. 20/VI/42" – Über die Gestaltung der Landwirtschaft in den eingegliederten Ostgebieten', in Mechtild Rössler, Sabine Schleiermacher and Cordula Tollmien, eds., Der 'Generalplan Ost'. Hauptlinien der nationalsozialistischen Planungs- und Vernichtungspolitik (Berlin: Akademie Verlag, 1993), pp. 131–5 (pp. 132–4).

21 Karl Heinz Roth, '"Generalplan Ost" – "Gesamtplan Ost". Forschungsstand, Quellenprobleme, neue Ergebnisse', in Rössler et al., eds., Der 'Generalplan Ost', pp. 25–95 (p. 41).

22 Tooze, Wages of Destruction, pp. 467–8, 492.

23 Czeslaw Madajzyk, 'Vom "Generalplan Ost" zum "Generalsiedlungsplan"', in Rössler et al., eds., Der 'Generalplan Ost', pp. 12–17 (p. 16); Roth, '"Generalplan Ost"', pp. 33–4; Elizabeth Harvey, Women and the Nazi East: Agents and Witnesses of Germanization (London: Yale University Press, 2003), p. 240.

24 Bruno Wasser, 'Die "Germanisierung" im Distrikt Lublin als Generalprobe und erste Realisierungsphase des "Generalplans Ost"', in Rössler et al., eds., Der 'Generalplan Ost', pp. 271–93 (pp. 288–90).

25 Peter Duus, 'Introduction – Japan's Wartime Empire: Problems and Issues', in Peter Duus, Ramon H. Myers and Mark R. Peattie, eds., The Japanese Wartime Empire,

of rice from Taiwan and Korea worsened Japan's agricultural crisis by depressing domestic farming incomes and the world-wide fall in food prices caused by the Great Depression pushed the countryside deep into debt.[26] In 1934 the northern provinces were struck by famine.[27] Industrial unemployment added to the sense of crisis. Right-wing groups were convinced of the need for greater independence from Western capitalism. On the night of 18 September 1931 two young officers took the matter of acquiring an empire into their own hands and planted a bomb on the Japanese-owned stretch of railway, which they claimed was the work of bandits sponsored by the Chinese regional government. This led to the Japanese occupation of Manchuria, which the army saw as a rich source of gold, coal, cotton, livestock and soya beans.[28]

In 1937 the Ministry of Agriculture set about solving Japan's agrarian crisis with the Plan for the Settlement of One Million Households over Twenty Years. One million poor tenant farmers were to be sent to cultivate Manchuria, allowing for the consolidation of farms in Japan. Although the plan did not envisage the wholesale extermination of the indigenous population, the implementation was brutal. An official who organized forcible land purchases described how, 'we trampled underfoot the wishes of farmers . . . and, choking off their entreaties full of lamentations and kneeling, forced them to sell [their land]. . . . we would be leaving them to a future of calamity, and I felt that we had committed a crime by our actions.' The Chinese twisted the name of the colonial office (*kaituoju*) and renamed it the 'office of murders' (*kaidaoju*).[29]

By this time Prince Konoe Fumimaro was Prime Minister, with Hirota Koki as his foreign minister. Both men were profoundly opposed to free trade and industrialization, and aggressive advocates of imperialism. They took Japan down an isolationist path which made war with the West ever more likely.[30] A skirmish between Japanese and Chinese troops in the small

1931–1945 (Princeton University Press, 1996), p. xv; B. F. Johnston with Mosaburo Hosoda and Yoshio Kusumi, *Japanese Food Management in World War II* (Stanford University Press, 1953), p. 76.

26 Kerry Smith, *A Time of Crisis: Japan, the Great Depression and Rural Revitalization* (Cambridge, Mass.: Harvard University Press, 2001), pp. 59, 64.

27 Mikiso Hane, *Peasants, Rebels and Outcastes: The Underside of Modern Japan* (New York: Pantheon Books, 1982), pp. 134–5; Young, *Japan's Total Empire*, p. 324.

28 Kershaw, *Fateful Choices*, p. 94; Louise Young, 'Imagined Empire: The Cultural Construction of Manchukuo', in Duus et al., eds., *The Japanese Wartime Empire*, pp. 71–96 (p. 77).

29 Shin'ichi, *Manchuria Under Japanese Dominion*, p. 203.

30 Akira Iriye, *The Origins of the Second World War in Asia and the Pacific* (London: Longman, 1987), pp. 38–9.

town of Wanping in July 1937 escalated the Japanese occupation of Manchuria into full-scale war with nationalist China. Japan's war in China placed them in opposition to America, Britain and the Netherlands, whose interests were bound up with the success of the nationalists.[31] The sensible course of action would have been to placate the USA with a peace deal in China. But as the Wehrmacht stormed across Western Europe in the spring and summer of 1940, the weakness of the European colonial powers encouraged the Japanese Chiefs of Staff to think that they could take over the entire Southeast Asian treasure house of resources.[32] The military command felt that this was their chance to establish Japan's claim as a great power in East Asia. When they authorized the attack on Pearl Harbor on 7 December 1941 Japan's leaders knew they were entering a war they could not hope to win but the military commanders were convinced that a 'decisive battle' would bring America to the negotiating table. Unfortunately, they misjudged the fact that once at war the USA was not likely to accept anything less than complete surrender.[33]

If the German and Japanese agricultural empires failed to live up to the new settlers' expectations (who found themselves living in primitive conditions subject to repeated attack by partisans), they were an even greater disappointment to their rulers.[34] Throughout the summer of 1941 the National Socialists were frustrated by the small amount of food the army was extracting from the occupied areas. As fear of a food crisis at home grew, the pressure to squeeze more food out of the occupied territories increased, and was repeatedly used to justify one act of atrocity after another. By September it was clear that the conflict would drag on over the winter and Backe inflamed the situation by reiterating that the Wehrmacht must take more food out of the occupied Soviet areas or rations within Germany would have to be reduced. He was adamant that he would not supply the Wehrmacht with grain and meat from German farms.[35]

Rather than waste precious food resources, the decision was taken to allow the large number of Soviet prisoners of war to starve to death. By February 1942, 60 per cent of the 3.35 million Soviet prisoners were dead.[36]

---

31 Kershaw, *Fateful Choices*, p. 333.
32 Duus, 'Introduction', p. xvii; Iriye, *Origins*, p. 171.
33 Kershaw, *Fateful Choices*, p. 127.
34 Czeslaw Luczak, 'Landwirtschaft und Ernährung in Polen während der deutschen Besatzungszeit 1939–1945', in Martin and Milward, eds., *Agriculture and Food Supply*, pp. 117–27 (p. 120); Tooze, *Wages of Destruction*, p. 464; Harvey, *Women and the Nazi East*, pp. 270, 446; Young, *Japan's Total Empire*, p. 404.
35 Gerlach, *Krieg, Ernährung, Völkermord*, p. 38.
36 Boog et al., *Der Angriff*, p. 1019.

Military commanders and quartermasters were also calling for the removal of 'useless eaters' from the Soviet civilian food chain. In the late summer of 1941 the SS and the police began to systematically murder *all* Soviet Jews rather than just adult men.[37] Frequently, the reason given was that it would ease the food situation. In August the quartermaster-general reported that the annihilation of the Jews in central Lithuania would alleviate the food supply problems for Army Group North. In Kiev the German authorities claimed that a systematic massacre of Jews on 29 and 30 September had improved the food and housing conditions for the rest of the civilian population. By the end of 1941, 800,000 Soviet Jews had been murdered.[38]

The massacre of the Soviet Jews, the death of millions of Soviet prisoners of war and the agonies of the inhabitants of the blockaded Soviet cities did nothing to alleviate the food crisis which developed on the Eastern Front that winter. In the exceptionally bitter cold, German troops shivered in inadequate clothing and went hungry as food supplies struggled to reach them through a quagmire of mud, rutted roads and snow.[39] The flawed logic of the Hunger Plan began to manifest itself. In Belorussia livestock rearing was expected to die out as feed imports stopped. This was all very well as long as front-line troops were not relying on local meat supplies.[40] The indiscriminate plunder of the soldiers made matters worse. The devastation was at its worst closest to the front line but a desolate area known as the *Kahlfrass* (defoliated) zone, in which the villages had been stripped of food, stretched back hundreds of kilometres.[41]

In the Reich the food supply was a source of anxiety. Food shortages became commonplace in German cities over the winter of 1941/42. Potatoes periodically disappeared from the shops and fruit and vegetables were rarities. Nutritionists were concerned that industrial workers were losing weight. Miners in the Ruhr area were thought to have lost up to 6 kilograms.[42] In the spring Backe had to break into the grain reserves in order to

---

37 Gerlach, *Krieg, Ernährung, Völkermord*, pp. 26–7.
38 Ibid., pp. 72, 68.
39 Omer Bartov, *The Eastern Front, 1941–45: German Troops and the Barbarisation of Warfare* (London: Macmillan, 1985), pp. 24–5.
40 Christian Gerlach, *Kalkulierte Morde. Die deutsche Wirtschafts-und Vernichtungspolitik in Weissrussland 1941 bis 1944* (Hamburg: Hamburger Edition, 2000), p. 49.
41 Gerlach, *Krieg, Ernährung, Völkermord*, p. 70.
42 Rolf-Dieter Müller, 'Albert Speer und die Rüstungspolitik im totalen Krieg', in Kroener, Müller and Umbreit, eds., *Das Deutsche Reich und der Zweite Weltkrieg*, vol. v, Part 1: *Organisation und Mobilisierung des deutschen Machtbereichs*, pp. 275–776 (p. 486); Corni and Gies, *Brot, Butter, Kanonen*, p. 562.

meet the bread ration. Increasing numbers of forced workers were being brought in from the east to meet the labour needs of industry and agriculture but they also raised the national grain requirement by about 2 million tons. The Sicherheitsdienst warned that the workers and urban population were in a mood reminiscent of 1918, pessimistic about the outcome of the war and critical of the regime.[43] In August, Backe informed Göring that he would be unable to raise the ration in the autumn to help people through the winter. Göring responded by gathering together the heads of the occupied territories and demanding that they release their stocks of food with no regard for the consequences for the indigenous population.

The National Socialists regarded occupied Europe as a source of plunder. Besides the large quantities of food requisitioned by the occupation governments, Hitler attempted to tap into the surplus food on the black markets by ordaining in April 1942 that soldiers on leave could bring back food parcels or, as they became known, *Führerpakete*. Maranja Mellin watched with wonder as dried beans, liver sausage, carrots in meat sauce, pears, almonds, cinnamon and pepper emerged from her father's parcel from Paris. Another young girl speculated that if everyone was bringing home the same 'mountains of booty' as her father there can be 'nothing left in France'.[44] There was certainly very little left in Greece, which the occupying forces stripped of currants and olive oil, fresh fruit and vegetables, much of which left the ports destined for Libya to feed the troops stationed in North Africa. Raging inflation prevented ordinary Greek civilians from accessing what little food was available in the shops or on the black market. The deprivation was so great that an exception was made to the Allied blockade of occupied Europe in order to allow food aid into Greece. Nevertheless, by the end of the war half a million Greeks, 14 per cent of the population, had lost their lives to starvation.[45] Göring's August demands required further demoralizing ration cuts in France and made unfeasible demands on the already starving Poles in the General Government.[46] 'It makes no difference to me in this connection

43 Tooze, *Wages of Destruction*, p. 563.
44 Margarete Dörr, 'Wer die Zeit nicht miterlebt hat ...' *Frauenerfahrungen im Zweiten Weltkrieg und in den Jahren danach* (3 vols., Frankfurt: Campus Verlag, 1998), vol. I, pp. 20–1.
45 Maggie Black, *A Cause for Our Times: Oxfam, the First Fifty Years* (Oxford: Oxfam, 1992), pp. 6–8; Mark Mazower, *Inside Hitler's Greece: The Experience of Occupation, 1941–44* (London: Yale University Press, 1993), p. 27; Polymeris Voglis, 'Surviving Hunger: Life in the Cities and Countryside during the Occupation', in Robert Gildea, Olivier Wieviorka and Anette Warring, eds., *Surviving Hitler and Mussolini: Daily Life in Occupied Europe* (Oxford: Berg, 2006), pp. 16–41 (pp. 23, 36–7).
46 Tooze, *Wages of Destruction*, p. 547.

if you say that your people will starve,' he ranted. 'Let them do so, as long as no German collapses from hunger.'[47]

At the same meeting it appears that the fate of the surviving Jews in the occupied territories was discussed but the minutes of what was said have been removed. Göring almost certainly urged the speeding up of the Holocaust. In the General Government, where it was argued that the removal of the Jews would stamp out the black market, the transports to the extermination camps increased after the August meeting. In the following ten weeks 750,000 Jews were killed in Belzec and Treblinka.[48]After returning to the Ukraine from the meeting, Erich Koch explicitly informed his officials, 'the food situation in Germany is serious . . . The raising of the bread ration is a political necessity, in order to drive the war on to victory. The missing amounts of grain must be obtained from the Ukraine . . . The feeding of the civilian population is irrelevant in view of this situation.'[49] The regional commissars were instructed to accelerate the Jewish extermination and given five weeks to complete the process. By the end of October at least a quarter of a million Ukrainian Jews had been shot.[50] The blockade of the major cities was tightened while an intensive food confiscation campaign was begun in the villages. The killing of the Jews did nothing to dampen down the black market. Only an exceptionally good harvest that summer allowed the General Government to supply Germany with more than half the rye, oats and potatoes and more than a quarter of the barley which was eaten in Germany that year.[51] The supplies of grain, meat and fat extracted from the Soviet Union also increased, from 3.5 million tons to 8.78 million tons. Although most of this was eaten on the spot by the Wehrmacht, large transports of food were sent to the Reich from the Ukraine in the autumn of 1942.[52] Goebbels announced with satisfaction that Germany was 'digesting' the occupied territories.[53]

Over 7 million tons of Soviet grain, 17 million cattle, 20 million pigs, 27 million sheep and goats, and more than 100 million domestic fowl disappeared into the stomachs of the German soldiers and administrators.[54] But

---

47 Ibid.
48 Gerlach, *Krieg, Ernährung, Völkermord*, pp. 220, 231–2.
49 Ibid., p. 241.
50 Ibid., pp. 244–5.
51 Ibid., p. 246. Luczak gives different figures for potatoes: 500,200 tons of potatoes; 50.9 per cent of rye, 28 per cent of barley, 65.6 per cent of oats and 51.8 per cent of potatoes. Luczak, 'Landwirtschaft und Ernährung', pp. 126–7.
52 Corni and Gies, *Brot, Butter, Kanonen*, p. 564.
53 Tooze, *Wages of Destruction*, p. 548.
54 Moskoff, *Bread of Affliction*, p. 48.

the Germans never succeeded in their aim of feeding the entire Wehrmacht on eastern plunder. The backward nature of Soviet agriculture; the loss of agricultural labour, machines, animals and fertilizer; the disruption caused by the continued fighting; the contradictions of the German agricultural policy which demanded draconian collection quotas without price incentives; the growth of the black market and the Soviet peasants' ability to hide food stores from the German farm administrators, all combined to frustrate German hopes.

Backe's insistence on looking to the relatively backward Ukraine as the Reich's bread basket revealed just how little he understood the economics of agriculture and food supply. The more modern, flexible agricultural sectors of Belgium, Holland and Denmark were far better able to restructure and adapt to the pressures of wartime. Denmark, Holland and France actually contributed more food to wartime Germany than the occupied Soviet Union. If the official figures for the amounts of food requisitioned by the occupying forces are counted together with the amounts exported to Germany, then Denmark, Holland and France collectively contributed 21.4 million tons of grain-equivalent, in comparison to the 14.7 million tons provided by the occupied Soviet Union.[55] However, Western European agricultural spoils would probably have been far greater if Göring had not insisted on implementing ruthless requisitioning policies which simply treated the occupied countries as short-term sources of plunder. The case of Denmark demonstrates that price incentives were far more effective in encouraging farmers to maintain productivity. As Danes were regarded as fellow Aryans, the government was subject to far less interference by the occupying forces. The Danish agricultural authorities suppressed the black market by limiting rationing to butter and meat and incentivizing farmers to produce milk, pork and bacon which were in demand in Germany. The fact that Denmark was able to export 200,000 tons of butter to the Reich between 1940 and 1943, in comparison to a paltry 49,000 tons of butter from France, demonstrated that a more lenient occupational strategy reaped greater rewards.[56]

Japan's empire was equally disappointing as a means of securing the nation's food supply. By mid-1942 the Japanese were the masters of Southeast

---

55 Karl Brandt in collaboration with Otto Schiller and Franz Ahlgrimm, *Management of Agriculture and Food in the German-Occupied and Other Areas of Fortress Europe: A Study in Military Government* (Stanford University Press, 1953), pp. 611–12.
56 Mogens R. Nissen, 'Danish Food Production in the German War Economy', in Trentmann and Just, eds., *Food and Conflict in Europe*, pp. 172–92 (pp. 173–7, 185).

Asia, which had produced 67 per cent of the rice entering pre-war world trade.[57] This should have been the answer to Japan's rice shortage problems. However, due to chaotic mismanagement rather than a malicious, premeditated policy, the Southeast Asian rice industry disintegrated.[58] A decisive blow to trade was the massacre of Malayan Chinese in February and March 1942. This was probably not the result of a genocidal policy of extermination but of an uncontrolled killing spree instigated by the *Kempeitai* (Japanese military police) and the ordinary troops.[59] It reinforced the collapse of the region's commercial networks which were already severely strained by the loss of labour to Japanese war-related projects, the breakdown of irrigation works and rice mills and the disarray of the transport system, which cut deficit areas off from areas of surplus rice production.[60] The Japanese tried to make a virtue out of the disintegration of the inter-regional food trade and introduced the catastrophic policy of 'regional autarky', banning the movement of commodities (including rice) across national and regional borders from mid-1943.[61]

Despite a vigorously promoted 'Grow More Food Campaign' the region suffered from severe food shortages as the peasants followed the pattern of disillusioned farmers the world over, and reduced their cultivation to subsistence levels.[62] The inhabitants of Singapore were reduced to living on rubbery tapioca which provided calories but little nutrition.[63] In Malaya the malnourished population was afflicted by tropical ulcers, malaria and beri-beri, while tuberculosis claimed thousands.[64] By 1946 the death rate in

---

57 Paul H. Kratoska, 'The Impact of the Second World War on Commercial Rice Production in Mainland South-East Asia', in Paul H. Kratoska, ed., *Food Supplies and the Japanese Occupation in South-East Asia* (Basingstoke: Macmillan, 1998), p. 9.

58 Mark R. Peattie, 'Nanshin: The "Southward Advance", 1931–1941, as a Prelude to the Japanese Occupation of Southeast Asia', in Duus et al., eds., *The Japanese Wartime Empire*, pp. 189–242 (pp. 239–40).

59 Cheah Boon Kheng, 'Memory as History and Moral Judgement: Oral and Written Accounts of the Japanese Occupation of Malaya', in P. Lim Pui Huen and Diana Wong, eds., *War and Memory in Malaysia and Singapore* (Singapore: Institute of Southeast Asia Studies, 2000), pp. 23–42 (pp. 32–3); Yoji Akashi, 'Japanese Policy towards the Malayan Chinese, 1941–45', *Journal of Southeast Asian Studies* 1:2 (1970), 61–89 (pp. 66–7).

60 Kratoska, 'The Impact of the Second World War', p. 18.

61 Aiko Kurasawa, 'Transportation and Rice Distribution in South-East Asia during the Second World War', in Kratoska, ed., *Food Supplies and the Japanese Occupation*, pp. 32–67 (p. 33).

62 Abu Talib Ahmad, 'The Malay Community and Memory of the Japanese Occupation', in Huen and Wong, eds., *War and Memory*, pp. 45–89 (p. 62).

63 Paul H. Kratoska, *The Japanese Occupation of Malaya: A Social and Economic History* (London: Hurst, 1998), p. 255.

64 Chin Kee Onn, *Malaya Upside Down* (Singapore, Federal Publications, 1976), pp. 176–7.

Malaya had doubled.[65] Upper Burma and Tonkin in what is now northern Vietnam were cut off from their usual supplementary rice supplies.[66] In Tonkin the problem was exacerbated by the reallocation of land from rice to jute and hemp, imposed by the Japanese army who needed more of these raw materials for making rope and sacks.[67] Unreasonable government levies to supply the Japanese military were made worse when the army began to go out into the villages to directly requisition rice.[68] Both areas were afflicted by famine. It is unclear how many died in Burma. The Japanese authorities made no attempt to gather accurate figures for the number of deaths. It has been estimated that between 1 and 2 million Vietnamese died.[69] For many villages in North Vietnam the famine killed more people than the Vietnam War.[70]

Grotesquely, in March 1945 the Japanese were in possession of 500,000 tons of rice, in store in the south of Vietnam. This was supposed to be shipped to hungry Japanese troops in the Pacific and civilians in Japan.[71] But the highly effective American blockade of Japanese shipping made it almost impossible to transport these supplies. By October, 30,000 tons of the stores had rotted and were no longer fit for consumption.[72] When in November 1945 Chinese nationalist troops were brought in to disarm the Japanese troops, they ransacked the area and transported as much food as possible over the border into China.[73]

Japanese soldiers, waiting for supplies, would have been extremely glad of the Vietnamese rice. The American blockade had a devastating impact on the Imperial Army's troops scattered across the Pacific islands. Although food was not decisive in determining the outcome of the Pacific War, it certainly played an important role in victory and defeat in this arena. American abundance was stunning when contrasted with the poverty of their Japanese opponents.

---

65 Paul H. Kratoska, 'Malayan Food Shortages and the Kedah Rice Industry during the Japanese Occupation', in Kratoska, ed., *Food Supplies and the Japanese Occupation*, pp. 101–34 (p. 109).
66 James Scott, 'An Approach to the Problems of Food Supply in Southeast Asia during World War Two', in Martin and Milward, eds., *Agriculture and Food Supply*, pp. 269–96 (p. 280).
67 Bui Minh Dung, 'Japan's Role in the Vietnamese Starvation of 1944–45', *Modern Asian Studies* 29:3 (1995), 573–618 (p. 591).
68 Ibid., p. 607.   69 Ibid., p. 576.
70 Motoo Furuta, 'A Survey of Village Conditions during the 1945 Famine in Vietnam', in Kratoska, ed., *Food Supplies and the Japanese Occupation*, pp. 208–37 (p. 237).
71 Dung, 'Japan's Role in the Vietnamese Starvation', pp. 613–14.
72 Kratoska, 'The Impact of the Second World War', p. 24.
73 Nguyên Thê Anh, 'Japanese Food Policies and the 1945 Great Famine in Indochina', in Kratoska, ed., *Food Supplies and the Japanese Occupation*, pp. 208–26 (p. 223).

The war had pulled American agriculture out of the Depression. America's plentiful resources meant that it was able to continue producing farm machinery and fertilizers. In fact the agricultural revolution of the 1930s was accelerated by the war and transformed farming into an industry.[74] Consequently, the USA was able to meet with ease the food requirements of its 11.5 million servicemen, while rationing had the least impact on the structure and content of civilian meals than in any other country. American soldiers and civilians alike consumed significantly more and better food than their Allies or their enemies. Stan Tutt, an Australian soldier based on New Guinea, felt like a second-class citizen in comparison with the Americans who had a mosquito-proof recreation hut, regular deliveries of mail and oranges, a vegetable garden and meat every day. The difference was brought home to Stan one morning as he unloaded trucks, tantalized by the aroma of bacon and eggs frying in the American camp across the road. 'We [had] not eaten a fresh egg since coming to New Guinea,' he commented sourly.[75]

Conversely, by the spring of 1943 the Americans had succeeded in disrupting the flow of food to Japanese troops. The Japanese high command responded by calling on their soldier to become self-sufficient. On Bougainville they were told, 'The regiment will confidently complete its mission even if its supply line is cut in the rear by bravely establishing a self-supporting status in the present location.'[76] Throughout the Pacific, Japanese units began to lead semi-agrarian, semi-military existences.[77] They also began to starve. Surveying the famished survivors from Guadalcanal, Lieutenant-General Imamura was moved to tears by men, 'thin as thread, their faces ... blistered in blue'. In the face of starvation the Japanese fighting spirit (*bushido*) was of little use.[78] Japanese commanders' faith in *bushido* was not, however, entirely misplaced. The majority of Japanese troops chose to starve to death rather than surrender. Estimates suggest that 60 per cent (more than 1 million) of the total 1.74 million Japanese military deaths between 1941 and

---

74 Joachim Bengelsdorf, *Die Landwirtschaft der Vereinigten Staaten von Amerika im Zweiten Weltkrieg* (St Katharinen: Scripta Mercaturae Verlag, 1997), p. 109.
75 Cited by E. Daniel Potts and Annette Potts, *Yanks Down Under, 1941–45: The American Impact on Australia* (Oxford University Press, 1985), pp. 289–90.
76 Japanese Pamphlet no. 27, 30 December 1943, Air Dept. Wellington, New Zealand, Australian War Memorial [hereafter AWM] 54 423/5/22.
77 'Ration Supply and Ration Scale of Japanese Land Forces in SWPA', 6 February 1944, AWM 55 12/47 (69), p. 8.
78 Hiotoshi Imamura, 'Extracts from the Tenor of my Life', National Library of Australia, mfm PMB 569, III, p. 151.

1945 were caused by starvation and diseases associated with malnutrition.[79] By failing to provision their troops the Japanese high command displayed a criminal contempt for their troops while handing the Allies an excruciatingly effective weapon. As the US fleet moved through the Pacific it captured only those islands of strategic interest. The remaining Japanese garrisons were left to 'wither on the vine'.[80]

The American blockade combined with bombardment also had a devastating impact on the home islands. By the summer of 1945 the rail and sea connection between the main islands had been destroyed. Extensive minefields around Japan's shores prevented the import of Manchurian soya beans and millet across the Sea of Japan.[81] The government reduced the staple rice ration by 10 per cent and substituted it with sweet potatoes and soya beans. The level of salt in the urban population's diet was close to the minimum for survival.[82] The Japanese were not yet dying of starvation in large numbers but they were clearly defeated. The urban population was steadily losing weight and around a quarter of townspeople were suffering from malnutrition.[83] American analysts later debated whether starvation would have sparked a revolution or persuaded the government to surrender. But even in July 1945, the militarists in the government had no intention of surrendering. Instead they began arming schoolboys with bamboo spears in preparation for the decisive battle on the mainland.[84] Rather than choosing the slow and painful option of continued blockade, or the potentially extremely bloody option of an invasion, the US president chose to drop the atom bomb on Hiroshima on 6 August. But it was not until the Soviets invaded Manchuria two days later and a second bomb was dropped on Nagasaki on 9 August that the shock was great enough for the emperor to defy the hotheads in his government and announce Japan's surrender on 15 August 1945.[85]

79 Akira Fujiwara, *Uejini shita eireitachi* (Tokyo: Aoki Shoten, 2001), pp. 135–8. I am grateful to Katarzyna Cwiertka for translating his data.

80 John Keegan, *The Second World War* (London: Hutchinson, 1989) p. 303.

81 Richard Frank, *Downfall: The End of the Imperial Japanese Empire* (New York: Random House, 1999), p. 149; Mark P. Parillo, *The Japanese Merchant Marine in World War II* (Annapolis: Naval Institute Press, 1993), p. 204.

82 Erich Pauer, 'Neighbourhood Associations and Food Distribution in Japanese Cities in World War II', in Martin and Milward, eds., *Agriculture and Food Supply*, pp. 219–41 (p. 227); Johnston, *Japanese Food Management*, pp. 147–50.

83 John W. Dower, *Embracing Defeat: Japan in the Aftermath of World War II* (New York: W. W. Norton, 2000), p. 92.

84 Frank, *Downfall*, pp. 188–9; Kappa Senoh, *A Boy Called H: A Childhood in Wartime Japan* (Tokyo: Kodansha International, 1997), p. 395.

85 Robert P. Newman, *Truman and the Hiroshima Cult* (East Lansing: Michigan State University Press, 1995), p. 105; Frank, *Downfall*, pp. 271–2, 287.

Britain in 1939 appeared equally vulnerable to blockade. In peacetime Britain relied on ten to fifteen ships arriving in its ports each day, bringing in 22 million tons of food a year.[86] Throughout the Empire an intensive network of 'cross-trade' carried tea from India to Australia, beef cattle from Madagascar to sugar-producing Mauritius, cocoa beans from West Africa to America. Burmese rice was a staple food in India and Ceylon, Fiji, the Gambia, Kenya, Mauritius, South Africa and Zanzibar. German U-boats in the Atlantic, the loss of Burma to the Japanese in 1942 and a world-wide shortage of shipping space, threw the international food trade into disarray. The Allies responded by setting up the Combined Food Board which was responsible for coordinating the agricultural output and food trade of more than half of the world's population.[87] Its decisions were contingent on those of the Combined Shipping Adjustments Board.[88] The war waged at sea was mirrored in the meeting rooms of the Combined Boards where British, Canadian and American officials battled for access to shipping space.

The efforts of Britain's farmers were impressive. Before the war virtually all of Britain's bread wheat was imported. By 1943 the ploughing-up of pasture land meant that farmers were producing half the nation's bread grain.[89] But the reorganization of British agriculture only extended the number of days a year when the island could feed itself from 120 to 160.[90] The achievement of the ploughing-up campaign was that it allowed the government to prioritize the import of condensed high-energy foods, such as meat and dairy products, rather than bulky wheat and fodder. Britain continued to rely heavily on its imperial trading network. Indeed, the fact that Britain was able to draw on the resources of a wide variety of countries with more productive agricultural systems was the strength of the British food policy.[91]

---

86 R. L. Adams, *Farm Problems in Meeting Food Needs* (Berkeley: University of California Press, 1942), p. 12.
87 Eric Roll, *The Combined Food Board: A Study in Wartime International Planning* (Stanford University Press, 1956), p. 47.
88 Alan S. Milward, *War, Economy and Society, 1939–1945* (London: Allen Lane, 1977), p. 278.
89 John Martin, 'The Structural Transformation of British Agriculture: The Resurgence of Progressive High-Input Arable Farming', in Brian Short, Charles Watkins and John Martin, eds., *The Front Line of Freedom: British Farming in the Second World War* (Exeter: British Agricultural History Society, 2006), pp. 16–35 (p. 34).
90 Alan F. Wilt, *Food for War: Agriculture and Rearmament in Britain before the Second World War* (Oxford University Press, 2001), p. 224.
91 Roy Fraser Holland, 'Mobilization, Rejuvenation and Liquidation: Colonialism and Global War', in Loyd E. Lee, ed., *World War II: Crucible of the Contemporary World – Commentary and Readings* (London: M. E. Sharpe, 1991), pp. 159–90 (p. 169).

The USA provided Britain with dried egg, condensed milk, Spam and frozen meat. Wrangling in Washington over how much meat America should send Britain turned out to be more of a threat to the meat supply than the U-boats. Even at the height of the U-boat blockade in 1942 only about 9 per cent of all food shipments to Britain were sunk.[92] When from April to September 1942 the Ministry of Food was forced to break into their reserves of canned corned beef, this was due to the fact that the Americans were sending Britain far less than the promised 40,000 tons of frozen meat a month, rather than to the sinking of ships; 40,000 tons represented only 2 per cent of American monthly meat consumption but 10 per cent of the British monthly meat ration. By January 1943, even though American meat production was at a record high, the USA was only delivering half of what it had pledged.[93]

Competition for American red meat was intense. Apart from British demands, in November 1941 the USA began sending the Soviet Union 500,000 tons per month of concentrated, high-calorie food; US servicemen each consumed 234 pounds of meat per year; while civilians ate a substantial 140 pounds per head and still complained that there was too little high-grade meat available at the butcher's.[94] British supplies were being drained by the added demands of the military campaign in northern Africa. In March 1943 the Ministry of Food warned the War Cabinet that Britain was consuming three-quarters of a million tons more goods than it was importing. They claimed that at this rate food reserves would run out within two months.[95] The Americans were suspicious of such claims, certain that British meat stocks were more than adequate. The British had made over-inflated demands on the American supply over the winter of 1940/41 and American officials were aware that a tendency to overestimate stock requirements was built into British calculations.[96] The issue was only resolved when meat rationing was introduced in the USA in March 1943 and Harry Hopkins, the chief administrator of Lend-Lease, intervened to secure a level of meat exports which satisfied British administrators.[97]

92 John Costello and Terry Hughes, *The Battle of the Atlantic: The Epic Story of Britain's Wartime Fight for Survival* (London: Fontana, 1980), p. 230.
93 Kevin Smith, *Conflict over Convoys: Anglo-American Logistics Diplomacy in the Second World War* (Cambridge University Press, 1996), pp. 187–8.
94 Amy Bentley, *Eating For Victory: Food Rationing and the Politics of Domesticity* (Chicago: University of Illinois Press, 1998), pp. 61, 93–4.
95 George W. Baer, *One Hundred Years of Sea Power: The US Navy, 1890–1990* (Stanford University Press, 1996), p. 201.
96 R. J. Hammond, *Food and Agriculture in Britain, 1939–45: Aspects of Wartime Control* (Stanford University Press, 1954), pp. 186–7.
97 Smith, *Conflict over Convoys*, p. 190.

Meanwhile the Dominions restructured their agricultural sectors in order to supply Britain with food. Canada switched from arable to livestock farming and became Britain's chief supplier of bacon.[98] New Zealand switched from making butter to producing cheese and then back to butter in response to the loss of Britain's vegetable oil supply in Southeast Asia.[99] Australia was transformed into a vast food-processing plant for the US Army. Indeed, it 'supplied more food per head of population to the Allied larder than did any other country'.[100] Forty per cent of Britain's wartime meat requirements came from Argentina.[101] West African women and children cracked open millions of palm fruits to produce more than 400,000 tons of palm kernels from which was manufactured the weekly ration of 3 ounces of margarine.[102] Although Britain reduced the weight of its food imports by half it still managed to import 56 per cent of the calories consumed by Britain's wartime population. Taste, however, was sacrificed for energy. On her way through wartime London, one of Elizabeth Jane Howard's protagonists ate a typical meal: 'two grey sausages encased in what felt like mackintosh, a scoop of a paler grey mashed potato and carrots. Her glass of water tasted strongly of chlorine.'[103] Hard, yet watery scrambled eggs made from egg powder, soapy processed cheese from a tube, bright yellow margarine, and grey, lumpy mince – foods like these made up the unpalatable and monotonous English wartime menu.

The British government went to great lengths (price controls, subsidies and rationing) to protect its citizens from wartime inflation. The same cannot be said for its colonial administrations with the exception of the Middle East Supply Centre (MESC). The MESC managed to hold uncontrolled hoarding and runaway inflation in check. Indeed, infant mortality declined in the region during the war, which is usually an indicator of satisfactory nutrition.[104] But

---

98 G. E. Britnell and V. C. Voake, *Canadian Agriculture in War and Peace, 1935–50* (Stanford University Press, 1962), pp. 248, 268.

99 J. V. T. Baker, *The New Zealand People at War: War Economy* (Wellington: Historical Publications Department of Internal Affairs, 1965), p. 201.

100 D. P. Mellor, *The Role of Science and Industry: Australia in the War of 1939–1945*, series 4, vol. v (Canberra: AWM, 1958), pp. 609–10.

101 Ashley Jackson, *The British Empire and the Second World War* (London: Hambledon Continuum, 2006), p. 94.

102 Viscount Swinton, *I Remember* (London: Hutchinson & Co., n.d.), p. 206.

103 Elizabeth Jane Howard, *Confusion* (London: Pan Books, 1993), p. 210. One of the best places to find vivid descriptions of ghastly English wartime meals are the Cazalet chronicles.

104 E. M. H. Lloyd, *Food and Inflation in the Middle East, 1940–1945* (Stanford University Press, 1956), pp. 327–9.

in most parts of the Empire rationing was not imposed on food systems that were considered beyond full colonial control. The result was that the poor, who bought their food on a daily basis, were faced by inexorable price rises which eventually robbed them of their entitlement to food.[105] In many parts of Africa, villagers resorted to eating seed nuts, roots and berries.[106] Famine struck northern Nigeria and Tanganyika in 1942.

Despite the fact that India was an important military base, the government made lamentably little effort to maintain economic stability within the colony. A combination of incompetence and complacency allowed a nation-wide food shortage to develop. In Bengal, food shortages led to spiralling inflation which deprived the poor of their capacity to buy what little food was available. A terrible famine ensued which killed at least 1.5 million Bengalis between 1943 and 1944. Smallpox, cholera and malaria killed a further 1.5 million already weakened by famine.[107] In the words of Leo Amery, Secretary of State for India, this failure on the part of the colonial government was 'the worst blow we have had to our name as an Empire in our lifetime'.[108]

It was only with the appointment of Viscount Wavell as Viceroy in September 1943 that decisive steps were taken to remedy the situation. But the British government refused Wavell's request for relief food shipments for India. The fighting in North Africa diverted thousands of tons of shipping from civilian to military supply; more ships were allocated to the buildup of American troops in Britain. Churchill prioritized the needs of the military, followed by British civilians. The amount of shipping travelling to the Indian Ocean was cut by 60 per cent.[109] This freed up enough ships to augment imports (much of it Argentinian meat) to the British Isles by about 2 million tons.[110] The success of the British government in sheltering its own civilians from the worst consequences of the disruption of world trade came at a cost elsewhere in the Empire. The food stores of the sugar-producing island of Mauritius were virtually exhausted by March 1943. They limped through

---

105 Amartya Sen, *Poverty and Famines: An Essay on Entitlement and Deprivation* (Oxford: Clarendon Press, 1981), pp. 155–6.

106 Ashley Jackson, *Botswana, 1939–1945: An African Country at War* (Oxford: Clarendon Press, 1999), p. 156.

107 Paul R. Greenough, *Prosperity and Misery in Modern Bengal: The Famine of 1943–1944* (Oxford University Press, 1982), p. 140.

108 Alex von Tunzelmann, *Indian Summer: The Secret History of the End of Empire* (London: Simon & Schuster, 2007), p. 391.

109 Tunzelmann, *Indian Summer*, p. 138.

110 Smith, *Conflict over Convoys*, p. 156.

with mercy deliveries of wheat and manioc starch but throughout the entire war the island never received a cargo of pulses, the main source of protein in the local diet. In contrast to the British who ended the war generally physically healthier, by 1945 the Mauritians were severely malnourished.[111] Churchill was adamant that the restriction on Indian Ocean shipping would not be lifted in order to send food aid to India. A government committee decided that the risk of civilian hunger in India was a lesser evil than jeopardizing British civilian supplies or military supplies for the Indian army. It was not until Wavell appealed directly to Asian military commanders to take a cut in supplies that he was able to get the Cabinet to agree to a shipment of 200,000 tons of grain for Indian civilians.[112] The plight of the Bengal famine victims placed a question mark over the sincerity of the Allies' claim that they were fighting to bring freedom from want – let alone justice, fairness and tolerance – to the world.[113] Although Britain did not set out with the explicit intention of exporting wartime hunger to the Empire, this is, in fact, what happened.

The Soviet Union and nationalist China, rather than exporting hunger, displaced it internally onto the peasantry. The level of hunger in the Soviet Union made a mockery of the argument, propounded by the pre-war British and German governments, that an adequate food supply was a cornerstone of success in the circumstances of total war. In the European theatre it was the population who survived on the least food who did the most to defeat Germany. Even after the Allied invasion of France the majority of the Werhrmacht's fighting capacity was concentrated on the Eastern Front. The Red Army was responsible for 80 per cent of Germany's total battle casualties.[114] For every Briton or American that died as a result of the war, eighty-five Soviet citizens lost their lives.[115]

The weakest part of the Soviet wartime edifice was undoubtedly agriculture. With the nation's best agricultural land lost to the Germans, it was not a question of carefully balancing production to favour bread grains and

---

111 *The Production of Food Crops in Mauritius during the War* (Port Louis, Mauritius: J. Eliel Felix, Acting Government Printer, 1947).

112 Johannes H. Voigt, *India in the Second World War* (London: Arnold-Heinemann, 1987), pp. 207–8.

113 Sunil Siddharth Amrith, 'The United Nations and Public Health in Asia, c.1940–1960', PhD dissertation, University of Cambridge, 2004, pp. 62–3.

114 Richard Overy, *Russia's War* (London: Penguin, 1998), p. 327; Max Hastings, *Das Reich: The March of the 2nd Panzer Division through France, June 1944* (London: Pan Books, 2009), pp. 2–3.

115 John Barber and Mark Harrison, *The Soviet Home Front, 1941–1945: A Social and Economic History of the USSR in World War II* (London: Longman, 1991), p. ix.

maintain a minimum level of fats, fodder and meat, but a desperate struggle to cultivate as much of anything as possible. Collectivization served the government well in that it meant that it was able to extract every grain of food from the farms. The peasantry survived on the potatoes cultivated in their private plots.[116] If they had been able to retreat into self-sufficiency the situation in the cities would have become untenable. But ruthless procurement quotas pushed the countryside into a vicious cycle of over-extraction and falling productivity. The grain harvest of 95.6 million tons in 1940 fell to 26.7 million in 1942.[117] The Soviet Union struggled to feed its vast army, and American Lend-Lease food was crucial to feeding the military from 1943. Lend-Lease freed up domestic food supplies for civilians but Irene Rush, an Australian teacher trapped in wartime Moscow, recalled how she and her friends resorted to eating throat pastilles and, for want of cooking oil, fried their food in Vaseline.[118] Acquiring the meagre food rations could take hours. At Andrei Sakharov's cartridge factory in Ulyanovsk a worker might come off the night shift at 8.00 a.m. and then have to stand in the 'silent, unyielding queue' until the middle of the afternoon before he received his bread ration.[119] Even on the industrial assembly lines, men and women collapsed and died as a result of starvation.[120] The communist regime was forced to resort to the free market in order to feed its people. In the towns and cities the peasant farm market was the *only* source of fresh vegetables and dairy products.[121]

Lack of food came close to collapsing the economy and the war effort, but it did not break Soviet morale. The people stayed on the assembly lines and continued to yoke themselves to their ploughs despite appalling hardship. Fear may have ruled in Stalin's Russia but the Soviets' determination was also derived from the knowledge that German victory would bring about the annihilation of their homes and families. Under certain conditions, the Soviets demonstrated that hunger, malnutrition and deaths from starvation do not necessarily prevent a nation from fighting, and indeed winning, a total war.

The country worst hit by starvation was China. Chiang Kai-shek assumed that because China was an agricultural country it would withstand the strains

---

116 Barber and Harrison, *The Soviet Home Front*, pp. 85–6.
117 Walter S. Dunn, *The Soviet Economy and the Red Army, 1930–1945* (Westport, Conn.: Praeger, 1995), p. 43.
118 Irene Rush, *Memoir* (National Library of Australia, Canberra, MS8316), pp. 177–9.
119 Andrei Sakharov, *Memoirs* (London: Hutchinson, 1990), p. 53.
120 Moskoff, *Bread of Affliction*, p. 37.
121 Barber and Harrison, *The Soviet Home Front*, pp. 83–4.

of war better than an industrialized one.[122] He could not have been more wrong. It was those agrarian nations whose peasant populations lived on the margins of subsistence which were most vulnerable to the disruptions of war. American journalists Theodore White and Annalee Jacoby described the Chinese peasant as a gardener rather than a farmer.[123] On this fragile foundation rested nationalist China's entire war effort. During the first three years of war the nationalists coped relatively well. They managed to suppress inflation and to boost agricultural productivity and food was quite plentiful.[124] Then, in 1940, the Japanese occupied Yichang, a strategic town which linked the food-producing province of Sichuan to the war zones. They cut the railroad linking Yunnan and rice-producing northern Indochina. They also captured the major ports in Fujian through which flowed food for Guangdong. Free China's international grain imports were brought to a halt. In the south more than two million people were immediately threatened with starvation.[125] At the same time, the rice and wheat harvests were adversely affected by bad weather and a food panic ensued.[126] An inflationary spiral was set in motion which lasted until the nationalists' defeat by the communists in 1949. The purchasing power of white-collar workers in the civil bureaucracy fell to less than 15 per cent of its pre-war level. The government introduced rationing but it did not have sufficient funds to pay for its food requirements. Instead the peasantry were forced to pay their taxes in kind.[127] In this way the civil administration in the cities was fed, but the price was paid in the villages. Cut off from food supplies, the army in the northern war zones was forced to requisition everything from the local peasantry. The army demanded 'food, animal feed, draft animals, wood, coal, clothing, transport equipment, and cooking utensils'. More than a

---

122 Jin Pusen, 'To Feed a Country at War: China's Supply and Consumption of Grain during the War of Resistance', in David P. Barrett and Larry N. Shyu, eds., *China in the Anti-Japanese War, 1937–1945: Politics, Culture and Society* (New York: Peter Lang, 2001), pp. 157–69 (p. 159).

123 Theodore H. White and Annalee Jacoby, *Thunder Out of China* (London: Victor Gollancz, 1947), pp. 30–1.

124 Tsung-han Shen, 'Food Production and Distribution for Civilian and Military Needs in Wartime China, 1937–1945', in Paul Sih, ed., *Nationalist China during the Sino-Japanese War, 1937–1945* (New York: Exposition Press, 1977) pp. 167–93 (p. 176).

125 Hans J. van de Ven, *War and Nationalism in China, 1925–1945* (London: Routledge Curzon, 2003), pp. 260, 268.

126 Ibid., p. 269.

127 Lloyd E. Eastman, 'Nationalist China during the Sino-Japanese War, 1937–1945', in Lloyd E. Eastman, Jerome Ch'en, Suzanne Pepper and Lyman P. van Slyke, *The Nationalist Era in China, 1927–1949* (Cambridge University Press, 1991), pp. 115–76 (pp. 154–7).

million farmers were conscripted to build roads, dig anti-tank trenches and construct dykes along the banks of the Yellow River. The peasants were not paid and were expected to provide their own food.[128] Agricultural production, which was already under an immense strain due to the drafting of able-bodied men into the army, began to collapse.

In 1942 Henan was assailed by drought followed by frost and hail and, finally, a plague of locusts. The harvest fell by three-quarters and all of it was requisitioned by the army.[129] 'Peasants who were eating elm bark and dried leaves had to haul their last sack of seed grain to the tax collector's office,' commented White, who visited the province in March 1943. He estimated that about 5 million people were dead or dying.[130] In Guangdong, army requisitioning created a famine in which 1.5 million peasants died. Large amounts of the requisitioned rice were smuggled across the front line and sold to the Japanese. Famine was imposed on the peasantry in the name of feeding the military but the troops were also famished. They turned on their own people, plundering and murdering as they searched for food and valuables.[131] They paid for their behaviour when the Japanese launched a new offensive in the spring of 1944. Nationalist China's best divisions were away in Burma fighting for the British whose priority was to retake Rangoon. As the overwhelmed nationalist army retreated, as many as 50,000 of the soldiers were disarmed, and one-fifth of these murdered, by the peasantry.[132]

In order to withstand the strains of the Second World War a nation ideally required a large and well-equipped army which could be fed with a steady stream of food, medicines and arms. It therefore needed a strong industrial base which could produce these supplies and a logistical apparatus to deliver them to the front. A flexible capitalized agricultural sector which could adapt to wartime difficulties and still produce increased quantities of nutritious food was an enormous advantage. On the home front, a nation required a robust civilian economy, an efficient administration and a reasonably united population. Moreover, the government needed the money to finance the war effort. Nationalist China lacked virtually all of these things.[133] Two million nationalist soldiers died in the war against Japan and 15 million civilians,

---

128 Ibid., pp. 173–4.
129 Lloyd E. Eastman, *Seeds of Destruction: Nationalist China in War and Revolution, 1937–1949* (Stanford University Press, 1984), p. 68.
130 White and Jacoby, *Thunder Out of China*, pp. 166–7.
131 R. J. Rummel, *China's Bloody Century: Genocide and Mass Murder since 1900* (London: Transaction Publishers, 2007), pp. 113–16.
132 Eastman, 'Nationalist China', p. 174.
133 Ven, *War and Nationalism*, p. 295.

85 per cent of whom were peasants, virtually all of them the victims of deprivation and starvation.[134] The suffering of nationalist China's civilians underlines the importance of food in wartime. In 1945 the US War Food Administration stated that food 'is a weapon of war. As such, it ranks with ships, airplanes, tanks and guns. Food, particularly American food, has been especially crucial in the present war, because it has been essential to the fighting efficiency of our allies as well as our own military forces, and has been required to maintain colossal industrial productivity here and in other allied countries. Modern war demands enormous food production.'[135]

134 Bradley F. Smith, *The War's Long Shadow: The Second World War and its Aftermath – China, Russia, Britain, America* (London: André Deutsch, 1986), p. 48.
135 Bengelsdorf, *Die Landwirtschaft der Vereinigten Staaten*, p. 301.

6

Sea transport

MICHAEL MILLER

In one of the very large volumes the US Army produced after the Second World War to describe the role of transportation, supply, and logistics corps in that conflict, the authors noted that 'American soldiers were called upon to perform transportation jobs under every conceivable operating condition and on every continent but Antarctica.'[1] Their presence in American and British port cities, but also in Persian Gulf harbours, along the Brahmaputra River to the upper reaches of Assam, across French North Africa, or throughout the archipelagos of the Southern and Central Pacific underscores the essential feature of this war and transport's contribution to it: global engagement made possible by carriage of great numbers of men and enormous volumes of cargo to nearly every corner of the world.

This was not the first truly global war where mastery of transport was pivotal. Much of what occurred between 1939 and 1945 had been rehearsed in the First World War. Then Allied victory had come from the ability to mobilize and move the world's resources, material and human, across the seas while denying these to the enemy. But the task in the Second World War was immensely complicated by the scale, weaponry and initial consequences of that conflict. Dispersal of major battle theatres to the Middle East, the Indian Ocean and the Pacific stretched shipping demands far beyond the once daunting challenges of the 1914–18 experience. In the Second World War it was incumbent on the maritime powers not only to sustain civilian supply and industrial production at their home bases but to convey, simultaneously, massive armies and their equipment to distant reaches of the planet. All this had to be accomplished against a submarine threat whose range and lethality were substantially greater than in the first global encounter. Aerial bombing of

---

1 Joseph Bykofsky and Harold Larson, *The Transportation Corps: Operations Overseas* (Washington, DC: Center of Military History, United States Army, 1954), p. 6.

ships and home ports intensified vulnerability at sea or at the critical point of discharge and transit. German conquest of Europe and its drive deep into Russia equally scrambled earlier estimations. In the First World War, the Allies had relied heavily on neutral merchant fleets to supplement their own, but these now potentially fell within the German orbit. France, one of the great victors of the First World War and possessor of the Allies' second largest merchant fleet before American entry, was this time a German base for submarines and surface raiders, a nearer home port for blockade runners, a departure point for trans-Mediterranean supply to Axis forces in North Africa, a repository of shipping for all sides to plunder, and consequently a reminder that in this war the history of transport was not solely an Allied matter. In the Pacific and Indian Ocean theatres the terms of engagement were in fact reversed: Allied submarines and air forces sought to deny Japanese access to the sea lanes they initially controlled.

The dynamic between strategy and transport was also re-contoured by the scale and initial outcome of the battle for France. In the First World War the strategic balance with shipping reduced to dominance of the sea lanes to control world supplies and to starve out the enemy through interdiction. A comparable approach, when pursued again, would be far less effective against a German-occupied continent. The interplay between strategic planning and overseas logistics was therefore considerably more complex and ever-evolving than it had been earlier. Strategy determined shipping problems, but shipping problems also determined strategy, because ships allocated to one theatre translated into men and equipment denied to another. Faced by the prospect of a two-theatre war, the decision to adopt a Europe-first posture was at least in part a consequence of shorter and more efficient lines of communication across the North Atlantic.[2] Shortages in tonnage and escorts put plans for a cross-Channel invasion in 1942 on hold and prompted the invasion of North Africa, whose consumption of shipping resources delayed still further the buildup in Britain.[3] All the ambitious commitments undertaken at the Casablanca Conference in January 1943 had to be rethought once the supply of troop, cargo, and escort ships was calculated into the equation.[4] Strategic choices were especially hostage to the availability of landing craft and other

2 Ibid., p. 8; Chester Wardlow, *The Transportation Corps: Responsibilities, Organization, and Operations* (Washington, DC: Office of the Chief of Military History, 1951), p. 3.
3 Richard M. Leighton and Robert W. Coakley, *Global Logistics and Strategy, 1940–1943* (Washington, DC: Center of Military History, 1955), pp. 357–60, 374–5, 719.
4 C. B. A. Behrens, *Merchant Shipping and the Demands of War* (London: HMSO, 1955), pp. 328–35.

forms of assault ships.[5] By the same token, the prospect of disrupting Axis supply lines to North Africa explained British commitment to Malta, despite the murderous run through the Mediterranean.[6]

This chapter on seaborne transport in the Second World War will therefore pursue four thematic lines of development. First, in accordance with the scope of the conflict, it will place the history of transport on a global and often globally interlocked scale. Second, to capture the distinctive challenges of the Second World War, it will compare the two world war experiences. Third, while the story of the maritime Allied nations will dominate, it will comprehend Axis cross-sea traffic. Finally, it will place the experience of the war within a broader temporal perspective which looks back to pre-war maritime infrastructures of knowledge, expertise, networks and installations and forward to the post-war maritime consequences of five years of global war at sea. Throughout, the focus will be on overseas transport logistics. Movement of troops or equipment or supplies overland by railroads or waterways or trucks or packhorses will enter into this narrative only as a precondition or extension of transoceanic carriage. That limiting factor will be offset, however, by the inclusion of nearly all theatres of combat into this history.

Two matters cloud any discussion of global transport in the Second World War. One is the ultimate victory of the Allies. The other is the cornucopia of statistics trumpeted in nearly all the histories of that triumph: 55,312,000 deadweight tons of ships constructed in American shipyards, 7,639,491 individuals and 132,000,000 freight tons deployed overseas by the US Army between December 1941 and December 1945, or the growth of the British Transportation Service from a mere 500 in 1939 to a force of 146,000 at its peak point.[7] The first presumes inexorability, the second the sheer conquering power of resources. Neither captures the depth or the extraordinary range of the challenges that faced Allied forces as they waged war across the globe. Nor do they capture the learning experience that preceded the crushing victories of 1945. Nor do they include the transport history of all the combatants. The breathtaking numbers are significant and it is useful to rattle them off at the beginning as a reminder of just how vast the

5 Robert Coakley and Richard M. Leighton, *Global Logistics and Strategy 1943–1945* (Washington, DC: Office of the Chief of Military History, 1968), pp. 6, 806–8.
6 S. W. Roskill, *The War at Sea, 1939–1945* (London: HMSO, 1954), vol. i, pp. 305, 524.
7 Ibid., p. 153; Chester Wardlow, *The Transportation Corps: Movements, Training, and Supply* (Washington, DC: Center of Military History, 1956), pp. 86, 327; R. Micklem, *The Second World War, 1939–1945. Army: Transportation* (London: War Office, 1950), p. viii.

accomplishment was. But two case histories – Allied transport victory via the Persian corridor and Japanese transport defeat in eastern waters – might take us closer to what had to be done.

Among the heaviest diversions of Allied ships from home supply or transport of troops and equipment abroad was the scraping together of aid convoys to Russia. Three routes prevailed. The transpacific passage to Vladivostok benefited from the absence of war between the USSR and Japan, but only so far as non-military equipment was shipped. The Arctic and White Sea route was the most direct, but only partially ice-free. It was also deadly, because German air and naval bases in Norway provided the means to seek out and massacre British ships. The gold standard for disaster in the war became convoy PQ 17 in the summer of 1942 when only eleven of thirty-six merchant ships made it through. PQ 18, which sailed in September, lost thirteen of its forty vessels. Such unsustainable losses coupled to a scarcity of escorts at a time when the invasion of North Africa was sucking up much of the available shipping led the British to all but suspend Arctic operations. Fewer than fifty ships made the run in 1943. What had hitherto been a rather minor aid route, through the Persian Gulf and Iran to southern Russia, now assumed paramount importance.[8]

The Persian Corridor, as this route became known, was to sum up a very large share of the transport burdens in the Second World War, as well as how they were solved. Its origins emerged from the global scale and commitments of this war, mass murder on the sea lanes, and the basic conundrum of a conflict where, no matter how many replacement ships were built, one theatre's pressing needs was another theatre's deprivation. It also caught another logistical nightmare: how to turn around ships effectively for multiple passages of limited tonnage when distances stretched halfway around the world and the receiving ports were designed for lazier days. Persia was thousands of sea miles from either Britain or America, and closure of the Suez Canal route added thousands of sea miles more. Of available ports in the Gulf, only Basra-Margil afforded the means for sizeable turnover, and much of the cargo discharged through its harbour went to supply British forces in Iraq. Bandar Shahpur, the Iranian port joined to the Trans-Persian Railway, was estimated to be able to move somewhere between 400 and 800 tons a day, a trickle where a flow was required. Khorramshahr, on the Karun

---

8 Bykofsky and Larson, *Operations*, p. 377; S. W. Roskill, *The War at Sea, 1939–1945* (London: HMSO, 1956), vol. II, pp. 134–43, 279–88, 299; Behrens, *Merchant Shipping*, pp. 254–5.

River and thus a staging point for inland water transport, was 120 kilometres from its closest railroad connection and, in 1942, amounted to 'little more than an anchorage'. Without the Trans-Persian Railway the Persian Corridor made little sense, but this line, 1,386 kilometres from the Caspian Sea, was single track and ran through deserts and mountains where water was sufficient for perhaps two trains a day. Most of its freight cars lacked brakes, its locomotives were without headlights, and neither were available in sufficient numbers. If Bandar Shahpur's capacity was at most 800 tons daily, the railroad's was perhaps 200, together a perfect prescription, as heavy traffic began to sail in, for severe congestion. Whereas turnaround shipping time for US ships sailing to Britain and back in 1943 through early 1944 averaged 69.4 days, the comparable figure for the Persian Gulf was 241.7 days, scaled down to a still crippling 157.2 days once passage through the Mediterranean and Suez reopened. Tapped as a major strategic conduit for surviving the war, the Persian Corridor would tie up scarce shipping for very long periods and require that the first wave of ships bring in the necessary material – locomotives and rolling stock, construction equipment for port and rail expansion, managing personnel – to expand capacity before there was any prospect of fulfilling aid goals to the Soviets.[9] These rudimentary and constricting conditions would recur across multiple fronts in this kind of war, especially when an entire theatre of operations opened along the remote archipelagos of the South Pacific.

Over time the British, and then the Americans who largely relieved them in Persia by March 1943, met and surpassed the commitments made to their ally. By October 1943, 200,000 tons of cargo a month were pouring through to Russia and over 5 million tons had been transported by VE Day. How this occurred reprised other, problem-solving patterns in the transportation history of the Second World War. Port and shipping experts were brought in to assess, recommend and take charge. To move cargo up the Karun or the Tigris to railheads, Britain's Inland Water Transport leaned on pre-existing riverboat investments in knowledge, material and workshops and then expanded these considerably; perhaps a quarter of Soviet aid through the Gulf moved by this track. Sophisticated operational logistics were introduced to coordinate, schedule and route traffic flows through the ports and

---

9 Micklem, *Transportation*, pp. 73–93; Bykofsky and Larson, *Operations*, pp. 375–82 (quoted p. 379), pp. 387–403, 406–11; R. S. MacTier to B. Sanderson, 6 December 1942. The National Archives UK (TNA), Ministry of War Transport/ Port and Transit (MT 63)/ 338; Wardlow, *Responsibilities*, p. 280.

upcountry. To add the necessary transport capacity, the Allies built out harbour installations and shipped in locomotives, rolling stock, river craft and trucks. The mere 'anchorage' at Khorramshahr, by 1944, was unloading close to 200,000 tons a month. Much of this repeated the First World War experience when maritime expertise and infrastructure had been mobilized and when a comparable port expansion had been rushed through at Basra. But the scale of the challenge – constructing massive supply routes to major fronts, not sideshows, on the far side of the world in the coarsest of conditions – as well as the combination of vast commitments, initial snafus and delays, and then extraordinary, winning performance captured the signature dimension to transport in the Second World War.[10]

The destruction of the Japanese merchant marine in the Second World War caught in stark relief the other face to transportation history in this global battle: what befell powerful combatants when control of sea lanes was lost and lines of communication were severed. By the start of the war Japan possessed one of the largest merchant fleets in the world and could put on the open seas some 6 million plus tons of shipping at the time of the attack on Pearl Harbor. That investment reflected the voluminous daily flows of food and raw materials from abroad that were required to feed the Japanese nation and sustain its industrial production. Japan, like Great Britain, lived or died by the sea.[11]

Naval war with the USA tested that maxim to its limit. Japan's vulnerability in the war was threefold. First, the rapid conquest of Southeast Asia in the opening months of 1942 had brought the oil, metal and organic bounty of this resource-rich region within Japan's orbit, but only to the extent that Japan could defend extended sea lanes wrapping around the South China Sea and into the Indian Ocean. Supply of armies on the Chinese mainland, in the Philippines, the East Indies, Malaya and Burma, and scattered in garrisons over countless islands, simply magnified the demands on shipping and its defence. Second, despite a very large merchant fleet, and home shipyards, tonnage was never sufficient for an island empire's transportation needs.

---

10 Bykofsky and Larson, *Operations*, pp. 378, 389, 394, 399, 397, 408–10; Micklem, *Transportation*, pp. 74, 85, 92–100; Basra Papers, 11 September 1917, TNA, Ministry of Shipping (MT 25)/14.

11 Keiichiro Nakagawa, 'Japanese Shipping in the Nineteenth and Twentieth Centuries: Strategy and Organization', in Tsunehiko Yui and Keiichiro Nakagawa, eds., *Business History of Shipping: Strategy and Structure* (Tokyo: University of Tokyo Press, 1985), pp. 1–31; USSBS, *The War against Japanese Transportation, 1941–1945* (Washington, DC: United States Strategic Bombing Survey, 1947), pp. 1–2; Mark P. Parillo, *The Japanese Merchant Marine in World War II* (Annapolis: Naval Institute Press, 1993), pp. 33–5, 38.

Even before Pearl Harbor Japanese freighters were being withdrawn from western imperial harbours to service military requirements in China.[12] Total war footing and requisitions by the Japanese army and navy left a bare minimum of ships to cover home islands supply.[13] Third, the US Navy possessed the determination and the means to shut down shipping lanes and annihilate Japan's merchant marine. Despite the Allied setbacks that began with Pearl Harbor, American submarines went almost immediately to work, beginning an unrelenting process of strangulation.[14]

There is no story of destruction at sea in this war to compare to the sweeping of Japanese transport from the waters of the East. Ironically, the weapon so feared by the Allies on the North Atlantic became the attack weapon of choice in the Pacific. Submarines accounted for the most 'kills' in the theatre and in certain periods of the war practically picked off Japanese vessels at will, a lethality that crescendoed to 3 million tons of Japanese shipping sunk between September 1943 and December 1944 alone. Still more lethal were carrier strikes. When they occurred, as at Truk in February 1944 where 186,000 tons were blown out of the water, their results were ruinous; only the concentration of naval ships on combat missions limited their full potential. Throughout the campaign, land-based aircraft provided reconnaissance for submarines, blasted ore ships moving down the Yangzi, or struck at sitting-duck ships at sea. 1945 saw B-29 bombers effectively shut down ports and critical straits traffic between Kyushu and Honshu through mine drops by air. After US seizure of Okinawa and Iwo Jima, Japanese transport vessels operated only at their most extreme peril outside the Sea of Japan and Yellow Sea. Over the course of the war, the Allied campaign against Japanese transport destroyed more than 8 million tons of Japanese shipping, although more important than the numbers of ships sent to the bottom of the ocean was the closure of nearly all sea lanes, and even port access, to an island nation that could not live off its own resources.[15]

Confronted with this carnage the Japanese gave priority to the carriage of the most vital raw materials, reallocated sourcing to regions closer and closer

12 I. J. Brugmans, *Van Chinavaart tot Oceaanvaart. De Java-China-Japan Lijn, Koninklijke Java-China-Paketvaart Lijnen, 1902–1952* (Amsterdam: Koninklijke Java-China-Paketvaart Lijnen, 1952), p. 157.

13 USSBS, *War against Japanese Transportation*, p. 2.

14 Ibid., p. 36.

15 Ibid., pp. 2–8, 38, 41, 45, 48–9, 83–8, 94, 102–5; Parillo, *Japanese Merchant Marine*, pp. 143, 197–9, 204–21; W. N. Medlicott, *The Economic Blockade* (London: HMSO, 1959), vol. II, pp. 401–8.

to home, and initiated a crash campaign to build more tankers. For a time, therefore, they were able to prolong the sounding of the death knell. But they were also complicit in their own destruction, for they succeeded in practically none of the measures that proved so decisive on the Atlantic. Only belatedly did they awaken to the need to convoy vulnerable freighters and never marshalled a sufficient escort fleet. Like the USA they attempted to mass-produce standard-sized ships, but resisted substituting welding for riveting and failed to construct either the numbers or the quality of shipping to overcome their colossal losses. In the application of radar, sonar and Huff-Duff technology to detect submarines lurking nearby, they lagged far behind Allied breakthroughs. They introduced state-run shipping controls and enlisted the professional expertise of shipping company personnel, but the refusal of the army and navy to coordinate with civilian command produced extraordinary wastage of carrying space on the high seas.[16]

The failure of the Japanese to sustain their lines of communication presented all the dangers that nearly sank the Allied war effort in Europe as well: that sea lanes would not remain open, that there would never be enough ships, that submarines and planes would produce attrition by sea. Even the one gap in Allied strategy in the East, the failure to attack systematically the Japanese rail system and cripple transportation on Honshu,[17] had its counterpart in the West: the prospect that ports would turn into bottlenecks and squeeze off flows regardless of what triumphs occurred on the oceans. In many ways the story of Japanese transportation collapse in the East was the perfect foil for the story of Allied transportation victory in the West. Writing up *The War against Japanese Transportation* in 1947, the United States Strategic Bombing Survey (USBSS) concluded that 'The war against shipping was perhaps the most decisive single factor in the collapse of the Japanese economy and the logistic support of Japanese military and naval power.'[18] It is now necessary to see why this did not become the case for the Allies on the other side of the world.

The basic fact in the Second World War history of Allied transportation was that there were never enough ships. Despite the 18,000,000 tons of shipping with which the British Empire began the war (approximately

---

16 Parillo, *Japanese Merchant Marine*, pp. 6–9, 15, 97–110, 152–72; USSBS, *War against Japanese Transportation*, pp. 32–3, 48–9, 54–6, 102–5; Medlicott, *Economic Blockade*, vol. II, pp. 404–5.
17 USSBS, *War against Japanese Transportation*, pp. 8–12.
18 Ibid., p. 6.

30 per cent of the world's fleet), the 8,500,000 additional tons of shipping possessed by the USA in 1939, the colossal 60,000,000 tons that came rolling off American and British shipyards, and relentless efforts to scrape up ships from all over the world, there was always a demand for still more ships.[19] The Allies had faced the same gnawing shortage in the First World War. In fact the life-or-death struggle waged on the North Atlantic in 1942 to sustain Britain's lines by sea had been fought twenty-five years earlier in 1917 with no less grim determination. Then as well the submarine danger had been, however, only the most urgent among a wider set of challenges eating away at shipping resources, and so it is necessary to see the problem in all its multiple dimensions.

It must be understood, to begin with, that shipping networks by the beginning of the twentieth century were interlocked into a global system of supply. Broad systemic disruptions which both World Wars imposed could nearly always be offset by the substitution of one source for another but at the cost of a rational distribution of shipping resources by space and time. Thus, in the First World War, when Britain and France had been cut off from much of their supply of beet sugar grown close at hand on the Continent, alternative sources in Java, Mauritius and Cuba had been tapped, but at the expense of assigning ships to very long ocean voyages. The more distant the source of substitute supplies, the more time consumed in deployment of ships on single voyages at sea.

For the First World War the solutions had come through state and inter-Allied centralization and allocation of transport, buying and distribution, and during the crisis year of 1917, through the concentration of ships wherever possible on the shorter North Atlantic run.[20] The former provided a template for rationalization in the Second World War, but preferential restriction to the shortest route was far less an option this time around. The same fundamental requirements – importation of food and war-making materials that Britain could not produce on its own, transporting a massive American army across the Atlantic – remained. But in this global war, ships also had to be found to transport and supply the British Army in the eastern Mediterranean via the extended Cape route (13,000 miles to Suez rather than fewer than 3,000), or a full-scale American theatre in the Pacific. After the German conquest of France, the sea route to London, as long as it remained opened, took ships above and around Scotland, adding days to normal passage

19 Wardlow, *Responsibilities*, pp. 135–6.
20 C. Ernest Fayle, *The War and the Shipping Industry* (London: Humphrey Milford/Oxford University Press, 1927), pp. 279, 331–2.

through the Channel. Space and time were therefore far less easily conquered between 1939 and 1945. By US Army calculations, round-trips from San Francisco to the Southwest Pacific took up 115 days for freighters and 69 days for troop transports.[21] The maths is compelling: a ship that takes 115 days to complete a voyage and return makes only three voyages in a year. Add to this ships sailing to the Persian Gulf and Vladivostok with Lend-Lease aid to Russia, or to South Asia with Lend-Lease for China, as well as ships assigned to carry food to civilian populations in distant theatres of war, and the strain on shipping, regardless of all the tonnage built to replace ships sunk at sea, becomes palpable.

As in the preceding war, the British concentrated broad powers in the hands of a state shipping agency. The Ministry of War Transport (MOWT) as it emerged in 1941 oversaw seaborne requirements and assigned merchant ships to those routes deemed necessary for national interests. Roosevelt replicated this system across the Atlantic with the creation of the War Shipping Administration (WSA). Created to broker between the two was the Combined Shipping Adjustment Board. A rough agreement allocated responsibility for transport in the western hemisphere to the Americans and in the east to the British. By the third year of the war, then, structures were in place to ration Allied shipping and to coordinate its distribution between home needs and global theatres. The operational reality was less felicitous. In America, the WSA assigned ships but the military services controlled them. An Army Transportation Corps which managed troop and supply movements and, like its counterpart, the British Transportation Service, was indispensable to global transport of Allied forces, grew to a staff of 3,100 at headquarters and 180,000 in the field by 1945. It thus presented a powerful parallel centre of authority. Meanwhile, each ally suspected the other of living too high off the hog. The US military viewed British home needs as a diversion of ships from their proper war-fighting mission while British shipping men were convinced that America's call upon ships could be pared back with less luxurious support per fighting man. To complicate matters further, the Allies agreed that the British would concentrate on warship construction, the Americans on carrying power, more signs of close and rationalized cooperation but with the result that the British could argue as equals but, effectively, had to beg. And if a Europe-first policy was agreed by all, de facto emergency assignments to the Pacific in 1942 shrunk the pool available to the rest of the world.

---

21 Behrens, *Merchant Shipping*, pp. 109–10; Leighton and Coakley, *Global Logistics*, p. 725.

What smoothed the waters were two things: Roosevelt's decisive support for the primacy of British home needs and the close working relationship that evolved between representatives of the MOWT and WSA from day-to-day experience of working together on both sides of the Atlantic. Moreover, the British were not without resources upon which the USA was dependent. They held the great pre-war liners, the Queens, but also the French Line's *Ile de France* and the Holland America Line's *Nieuw Amsterdam*, and provided the bulk of troop transport across the Atlantic. The giant Queens were modified to carry as many as 15,000 men per voyage, a great risk but manageable because of their considerable speed. Sailing on their own, they required no escorts, yet another contribution to managing the shipping shortage.[22]

The art of stowage, passed down from sailing days when poorly stored cargo could shift in the hold and capsize a vessel to modern times where stevedores took great pride in their utilization of every nook and cranny, offered comparable space-saving opportunities. In the First World War, prodigious efforts had been made to fill ships down to their load lines while exploiting all interior space. The Second World War and its hypertrophied challenges took these measures several steps further. Cargo was lashed to the decks of ships. Tens of thousands of planes crossed the seas outdoors, especially on false decks constructed above the main decks of tankers. Britain's Military Cargo Branch, beginning with the invasion of North Africa, devised a method to ensure that when the forces hit the beach their weapons would be unloaded from support ships 'in the precise order required by the Force Commander in relation to his plan of action'. This system, known as 'tactical loading', began with plans to scale of every deck, compartment and obstruction of every ship assigned to the invasion fleet. Scale models of vehicles were then prepared to determine which vehicles in which numbers could go in which ships, with the sequence of discharge of vehicles, guns and everything else determining loading strategies.[23]

Command structures over ships or stowage mattered little, however, if ships and goods piled up in ports. For all their vaunted warehouse facilities, the harbour's classic building by the twentieth century was the shed, an open

---

22 Behrens, *Merchant Shipping*, pp. 262, 273–92, 362–73, 442–51; Wardlow, *Movements*, pp. 4–10; Wardlow, *Responsibilities*, pp. 155, 164–5, 220–7; Bykofsky and Larson, *Operations*, pp. 85–8.

23 J. A. Salter, *Allied Shipping Control: An Experiment in International Administration* (Oxford: Clarendon Press, 1921), p. 214; Wardlow, *Movements*, pp. 360–8; 'Resumé of the Operations of Military Cargo Branch', TNA, Ministry of War Transport/Sea Transport (MT 40) 117, p. 16 (quoted).

area covered by a mere roof and walls and designed for the orderly transfer of freight through the port as rapidly as possible. The First World War had indicated what terrible congestion modern warfare could impose on the world's harbours. Warships occupied berths or ate up dry dock space. Ports capable of handling the passing steamer or two were suddenly transformed into shipping junctions. Even great ports like New York buckled under the pressure. In Britain the two greatest bottlenecks had resulted from ship diversion and the rippling effects of slowdowns along the chain of inland transport. Ships in urgent need of repair had put into harbours that lacked either the proper cranes to lift the cargo or the railroad infrastructure to move it out. Purposeful diversion of ships to west coast ports to avoid the submarine-infested London approaches had encountered staggering difficulties. London was a lighterage port that could not be converted overnight to massive rail use. One effort to divert cargoes to Plymouth underscored the futility of feeding the entire London basin via rail deliveries from other ports. Out of 27,000 tons off-loaded, only 7,000 made their way to the capital, and there were railroad backups while they did so. It took approximately three weeks to unload the ships in Plymouth, whereas the job would have been done in seven days in London. Across the board the larger problem had been overworked rail lines that clogged distribution from ports that in turn congested quays and fairways.[24] To conquer space was thus for naught if needed ships just sat in harbours.

None of this eluded the considerable planning for ports that preceded the Second World War, although by the 1930s it was also clear that one had to factor in air power: could west coast harbours and rail and road networks handle wholesale diversion of shipping should air strikes close east coast ports, including London? A Committee of Imperial Defence memorandum from April 1939 identified the problem in its baldest terms:

> the trading habits of the community pass goods from the ports to their destinations through complex but relatively well defined and regulated channels which have been built up to meet the normal demand, and in general the length of the inland haul has been reduced to a minimum. Any alteration of those channels is likely to cause congestion by making a port handle more traffic than it can reasonably manage, or by upsetting normal trading habits in controlling the progress and movement of goods, or by

24 Traffic Diversion Committee, 19 November 1918, TNA, MT 25/6; Final Report of Port Transit Committee 1921, 15 March 1921, TNA, MT 25/62; C. Ernest Fayle, *Seaborne Trade* (New York: Longmans, Green & Co., 1924), vol. III, pp. 164, 334–5.

throwing a sudden and heavy burden upon inland transport. Congestion at any one point has widespread effects and when it once starts it increases in geometric rather than arithmetic progression, and is increasingly difficult to overcome.[25]

In the event, German bombers, mines and torpedo boats did force massive diversions. Liverpool and other west coast ports were also hammered. An eight-day blitz of Liverpool in May 1941 wreaked so much damage and havoc that port working capacity was temporarily cut by 70 per cent. All the problems envisioned by planners came back to haunt them in spades. Liverpool was wracked by rail and road congestion. Last-minute diversions sent ships to ports that lacked the equipment to discharge them. Glasgow's port infrastructure, designed for regional traffic, was overwhelmed by the material diverted to it. Only the failure of the Luftwaffe to sustain its assaults or to paralyze inland transport networks limited the most dire effects to short-term immobilization.[26]

These were just the first of the woes that beset port clearance throughout the war. Again it was the scale of global commitment that threatened to negate all advances in shipping power. Major operations in the eastern Mediterranean buried sleepy ports from Freetown to Suez under ships and cargo. A shipowner sent to sort out the situation found the 'whole of the shipping position in the Middle East . . . in a most ghastly muddle'.[27] Another shipping expert remarked of Suez: 'Forty thousand tons of miscellaneous general cargo lying in an open dump in the desert looks pretty bad. A good deal that went in will never come out and a good deal more will never be identified.'[28] This echoed the confusion that had befallen Haiphong in 1939 where 40,000 tons of cargo were pouring in monthly for China and where the rail system could move out only 8,000. 'There is cargo at present here,' a station master had told two British shipping men, 'which will never leave Haiphong.'[29]

Still worse awaited campaigns in the Pacific. Over the course of the war the USA shipped approximately 35,000,000 tons and 2,000,000 personnel

25 Committee of Imperial Defence, Diversion of Shipping to West Coast Ports, Memorandum by the Minister of Transport, April 1939, TNA, MT 63/94, p. 7.
26 Report of Weir Committee on port and transport difficulties at Liverpool 1940–1941, TNA, MT63/48; Port Emergency Committee, c.1946, Merseyside Maritime Museum, Mersey Docks and Harbour Board, 14/2 vol. II; Behrens, *Merchant Shipping*, pp. 126–42.
27 Charles Hill, Report on the Shipping Position in the Middle East, 1941, TNA, Ministry of War Transport/Private Office Papers (MT 62)/27.
28 E. H. Murrant to B. Sanderson, 10 February 1942, TNA, MT 63/291.
29 G. Findlay Andrew to W. H. Lock, 30 January 1939, School of Oriental and African Studies, John Swire and Sons Ltd Papers JSS II 2/17/Box 53.

across this largest of oceans. Even within the Pacific zone the distances were formidable: 1,100 miles from staging points in Brisbane to New Guinea. In this theatre the word 'port', with few exceptions, was a glorification. Unloading took place by human chains or along jerry-rigged wharfages amidst torrential rains, draining heat, mosquitoes, air attacks and little if anything in the way of inland transport networks. The advance from one archipelago to another converted former attack beaches into logistical staging points, doubling down the obstacles already experienced. Not surprisingly, harbour congestion was endemic throughout the area. Lacking the means to store or move out supplies and equipment, theatre commanders refused to release ships and instead used them as 'floating warehouses'. At one point in 1944, there were 190 ships hijacked in this way at Hollandia and Leyte. Under these conditions, ship turnaround was an oxymoron.[30]

The learning curve on clearing ports was therefore a steep one, but two lessons bequeathed from the First World War eased the ascension. The first was that forceful governmental intervention could break through logjams. Port and Transit Committees, a wartime fabrication, had organized mobile labour reserves, pooled railway cars, and forced companies to clear out sheds. Their legacy, Port Emergency Committees, were ready to go as Britain entered the Second World War. When these faltered before the vastness of the problems, the government went a step further and appointed Regional Directors in early 1941 with full powers over port operations in the leading west coast harbours. By far the most successful of these was Robert Letch, who had been assistant manager at the Port of London Authority. Letch, as Regional Director at Glasgow, and then at Liverpool, wrote the book on how to run a major port under Second World War conditions. His success in speeding up transit flows and breaking port congestion reflected the still more important lesson learned from the previous war: that with mobilization of men experienced in running a global maritime system, nearly any transport mess could be righted. To all the crisis zones of the war – the Middle East, the Persian Corridor, the South Pacific – the British and the Americans sent out port and shipping experts to inspect and correct the worst of harbour chaos.[31]

---

30 Bykofsky and Larson, *Operations*, pp. 429, 443–4 ('floating'), 458–60, 485, 502–5; Wardlow, *Movements*, pp. 101, 328; Leighton and Coakley, *Global Logistics*, p. 390.
31 Behrens, *Merchant Shipping*, pp. 130–7; Traffic Arrangements at Glasgow Docks, 6 March 1939, TNA, MT 63/69; Bykofsky and Larson, *Operations*, pp. 396–7, 427; Michael B. Miller, *Europe and the Maritime World: A Twentieth-Century History* (Cambridge University Press, 2012), pp. 224–5, 285–6.

Over time, therefore, knowledge and sheer resource commitment overcame the worst of obstacles. In the Pacific, big engineering projects – the construction of wharfs and docks – but also nuts and bolts initiatives like the formation of a water relay along the New Guinea coast utilizing commandeered coasters and fishing boats succeeded in moving men and equipment along extended fronts. Beginning with landings in the Marshalls, amphibian trucks ferried in guns and supplies directly from the LSTs (Landing Ship, Tank). Engineers and organizational ingenuity, backed by plenty of transport troop muscle, could produce staggering results. Right after the landings in Saipan most cargo came in via landing craft. Nine months later, this nowhere harbour was offloading close to 400,000 tons a month, the equivalent of a medium-sized Western port before the war. In Britain, a Diversion Room gathered together representatives of the Admiralty, the Ministry of War Transport, supply departments, customs, and the nation's nine major ports to match ships with ports. In the USA, war and civilian agencies, working closely with experienced railroad men, coordinated massive internal traffic flows. Requiring licences to ship, they managed to control the timing and quantity of movements from factories or supply bases to the harbours.[32]

In the West, victory over port incapacitation was wrested fairly early in the war, before the Battle of the North Atlantic reached its peak. That was significant, because, all told, 4,786 Allied merchant ships totalling 21,000,000 tons grt were lost in the Second World War. This was a figure greater than the entire British deepwater merchant marine in 1939. Submarines accounted for nearly 70 per cent of the tonnage sunk. Their prime hunting ground was the North Atlantic, where two-thirds of their take occurred.[33] The Allies had learned from the First World War that only convoys could protect against unbearable losses, although any illusion that this alone could be sufficient the second time around is easily dispelled by reading Nicholas Monsarrat's *The Cruel Sea*.[34] The pivotal battle that took place on this stretch of the world's oceans can be followed in the chapter, 'Global Shipping War', in the first volume of this work. Here, in the context of the basic transportation question confronting the Allies throughout the war – how to find the necessary ships to sustain national survival but also to align capacity with global strategic

32 Bykofsky and Larson, *Operations*, pp. 458–65, 516–23; Behrens, *Merchant Shipping*, pp. 32–3, 141; Wardlow, *Movements*, pp. 15, 100–1, 272, 359.
33 L. L. Von Münching, *De Nederlandse koopvaardijvloot in de tweede wereldorloog. De lotgevallen van Nederlandse koopvaardijschepen en hun bemanning* (Bussum: De Boer Maritiem, 1978), p. 150.
34 Nicolas Monsarrat, *The Cruel Sea* (New York: Alfred A. Knopf, 1951).

objectives – what needs to be remembered is the degree to which both sides of this matter were immensely complicated by German conquest of the European continent.

The furiousness of the Battle of the North Atlantic can be traced in large part to the presence of air and submarine bases along continental coastlines. At the same time, reversals from the First World War – a conquered and ambivalently neutral France, an Axis Italy – cut communication lines through the Mediterranean for much of the first half of the war. Unsustainable losses at sea and the space–time erasure of shipping power on long routes around the Cape were thus two sides of the same lethal coin. An occupied Europe, moreover, added two other dimensions largely unknown in the First World War.

The first was the degree to which Axis shipping sailed in waters denied to the Central powers between 1914 and 1918. In addition to ore transport in northern seas, German and Italian fleets were active in the Mediterranean through the first years of the war while blockade runners sailed around Cape Horn or the Cape of Good Hope with vital rubber and tin cargoes. Smuggling operations meanwhile took advantage of porous routes across the South Atlantic.[35] But the more the Germans used the seas, the more they too tethered strategic initiatives to open sea lanes. British submarines and aircraft subjected Axis cross-Mediterranean transport to the same withering assault the Germans were waging in the Atlantic. This interlocked battle of air and sea hinged on British striking power from Malta which, in turn, hinged on British forward airbases in Libya to protect supply lines to the island. Thus German success in keeping their communication lines open ebbed and flowed with Rommel's see-saw progress on the North African continent. Huge shipping losses occurred in 1941. As the Afrika Korps advanced east and placed Malta in a razor-thin position of survival over the first half of 1942, the shipping lanes cleared to Tripoli. The Allied counter-offensive of November 1942 then relieved the pressure on Malta and provided the air, surface and submarine means to shut Rommel off from sea supply.[36]

As the war wore on, German sea transport's role turned grotesque. Bottled up in the Baltic or along occupied coasts, its principal function by the last months of the war was to provide an escape route for wounded and refugees fleeing the Red Army approaching from the east. There were horrifying incidents, like the sinking of the famed liner, *Cap Arcona*, with 6,000 on board.

---

35 Medlicott, *Economic Blockade*, vol. ii, pp. 166–72, 433.
36 Roskill, *War at Sea*, vol. i, pp. 524–38, vol. ii, pp. 43–72, 340–5, 430–3.

Most of these were concentration camp inmates whom the SS had crammed onto the vessel, very possibly with the intention of scuttling the ship at sea. RAF fighters beat them to the punch, firing and raking the ship and two others packed with the same doomed cargo.[37]

But not all the ships the Allies sank were German or Italian, and this too represented a reversal from the First World War when the Allies had supplemented their merchant fleets with those of non-combatants. After 1940, the potentially vast pool of 'neutral' ships was now to be shared with the conquerors. Sixty-five Dutch ships fell to the invaders. Between 800,000 and 900,000 tons of the Norwegian fleet, if those trapped in Danish and Swedish harbours are also counted, were in German hands or isolated. More Danish, Norwegian and Greek ships languished in French or French colonial harbours. To the Allies' good fortune, the bulk of Norwegian and Dutch ships did come over to their side and went a long way toward narrowing the shipping shortage, particularly in the war's early years before the immense shipbuilding programme was fully under way. Norwegian tankers and dry cargo freighters were immensely valued; over the course of the war 10 per cent of the oil imported into Britain travelled in Norwegian bottoms. British charters of Dutch ships in just the first months following the occupation of the Netherlands totalled approximately 1.5 million tons. The *Nieuw Amsterdam* alone transported several hundreds of thousands of troops by war's end. Dutch KPM vessels provided an outer screen of transport and supply between Australia and New Guinea in the critical months that followed the Japanese invasions. The Dutch brought over as well their famed tug and salvage fleet. Smits's *Zwarte Zee* towed docks from New Orleans to Freetown and across the Channel during the Normandy invasion. It also brought safely into port close to 225,000 tons of rescued shipping, still another contribution to Allied carrying needs.[38]

The fate of France's merchant marine under the hybrid Vichy regime highlights all the strange combinations the Second World War introduced

---

37 Susanne Wiborg and Klaus Wiborg, *1847–1997. Unser Feld ist die Welt. 150 Jahre Hapag-Lloyd* (Hamburg: Hapag-Lloyd AG, 1997), p. 307; Günther Steinweg, *Die Deutsche Handelsflotte im Zweiten Weltkrieg. Aufgaben und Schicksal* (Göttingen: Otto Schwartz, 1954), pp. 54–6.

38 Kaare Petersen, *The Saga of Norwegian Shipping: An Outline of the History, Growth and Development of a Modern Merchant Marine* (Oslo: Dreyers, 1955), pp. 118, 154–6; Münching, *Nederlandse*, pp. 16–17, 178, 132–46, 207; H. Th. Bakker, *De K.P.M. in oorlogstijd. Een overzicht van de verrichtingen van de Koninklijke Paketvaart-Maatschappij en haar personeel gedurende de wereldoorlog, 1939–1945* (Amsterdam: N. V. Koninklijke Paketvaart-Maatschappij, 1950), pp. 150–7, 180–1, 225.

into the disposition of available shipping. Some 3 million tons strong in 1939, this fleet was carved up among the Germans, Japanese, British and Americans until, at a low point in 1943, only 50,000 tons remained under French control. French ships transported North African phosphates for the Germans and Italians and, from the end of 1941, supplies (excluding arms and munitions) to Axis armies in the Western Desert. After the Allied offensive in November 1942, the Germans took most of the remaining fleet. Over 200,000 tons of French shipping were lost in the subsequent Tunisian and Sicilian campaigns. Denied the full complement of French merchant shipping after the armistice, Britain also could cut loose from the heavy commitment of its trampers to the French coal trade. At the same time, hundreds of thousands of tons of French ships sitting in British ports at the time of the armistice were requisitioned for British use. With each progressive conquest or rallying of imperial territories, hundreds of thousands more tons passed into Allied hands.[39] In this case, then, the penury of shipping fell hardest upon the populations of France and its colonies who went hungry and froze, or saw their imports and exports blocked.

Thus the shipping deficit, if never resolved, was substantially eased by inter-Allied cooperation, stowage ingenuity, success at keeping ports open and cleared, augmentation from continental fleets, and a massive construction programme. What mattered as well was knowledge, borrowed from extant maritime expertise but also learned by experience over the course of the war. The North African invasion in 1942 was preceded by extensive quantitative study – how many hatches in the ports could be worked at one time, how many locomotives and rail cars would be needed – but all this came to naught amidst the chaos of actual operations. Improvisation haunted planning and execution throughout. Constant indecision and change, practically to the last minute, made a mockery of any pretence to logistical precision. Much of the equipment shipped to Britain in advance was improperly marked and buried in improvised storage facilities. It had about as much chance of being found as a book mis-shelved in a university library. An already frightfully tight shipping situation was thus made tighter still as replacement supplies had to be shipped in. More shipping space was eaten up by the ridiculously long American wish-lists of essential supplies.

39 Affrètement au Reich des navires français de Méditerranée, July 1943, Service historique de la marine (SHM), TT B10; Etude sur la situation de la flotte commerciale au 1er mai 1944, May 1944, SHM, TT B11; Medlicott, *Economic Blockade*, vol. II, pp. 365–6, 377; Behrens, *Merchant Shipping*, pp. 79–80.

Orderly let alone prompt loading and dispatch of vessels was impossible as new, revised orders poured in. Once ashore at Oran in November 1942, truck shortages, lack of road signs, and selection of dump sites that turned with rain into quagmires, slowed the process of moving out. A month after the landings, Eisenhower could but confess that the record to that point was 'in conflict with all operational and logistical methods laid down in textbooks' and would be condemned 'by all Leavenworth and War College classes for the next twenty-five years'.[40]

The final phase in Europe, from D-Day through VE Day, revealed just how far the learning process had advanced operational skills since this somewhat shambolic performance. The magnitude of the logistical task facing the Allies was vast, despite the short sea crossing: transport of several millions of men, and all their fighting equipment and supplies, plus all their transport vehicles and petrol, and all this initially onto beaches, then through ports destroyed by Allied bombing and German demolitions, and then along an inland infrastructure of railroads, bridges and canals, much of which, especially in the crucial landing and breakout areas, had been subjected to the same pounding from air or ground demolition crews. The possibilities for failure were capacious, and barely skirted. For a week after the landings, embarkation procedures fell into a state of disarray. Inordinately slow turn-around of coasters at the landing fields thwarted plans for an efficient shuttle of equipment across the Channel. There were initially too few truck companies. Still, the greatest breakdowns were less the product of faulty command structures than rapidly changing battle needs, or the unanticipated delays in capturing and opening ports, or because after the breakout from Normandy advancing troops outpaced supply lines.

By the summer of 1944 the leading motif in Allied transport was its mastery of mass manoeuvre. Errors now proved temporary kinks quickly smoothed out. Pre-shipment of equipment to Britain precluded the confusion in supply that had plagued the invasion of North Africa. When, following the landings, US divisions sailed directly across the Atlantic to the Continent, stores were concentrated at Elmira and then dispatched in tandem with troop deployments. Despite slowdowns in moving people and equipment out, and the washing away of the American Mulberry, transport units exceeded expectations in the material they moved onto the beaches. There was also one great stroke of luck: the capture of Antwerp with its

---

40 Bykofsky and Larson, *Operations*, pp. 137–48, 162–6; Leighton and Coakley, *Global Logistics*, pp. 416–55 (Eisenhower cited p. 455).

extraordinary installations still intact. One of the Continent's three greatest ports, and its premier general cargo port, Antwerp, once opened, was ideal for unloading the material shipped over for armies. Endowed with superb rail networks and the Albert Canal, it was excellently positioned for supplying Allied troop movements eastwards to Germany. From a transportation perspective, the final months of the war in Europe thus followed one successful narrative after the other: capture and reconstruction of lines of communication inward, accomplished organization of express services, and the streaming of several millions of men and still more millions of freight tons onto the Continent.[41]

How does the war fit within the history of modern transport and logistics? It has been seen how transport logistics repeated yet surpassed the experience of the First World War, but precedents also reached back to the pre-existent infrastructure upon which wartime improvisations and accomplishments incessantly drew. Replacement shipping was one of the success stories of the Second World War, yet the war could not have been fought without the vast merchant fleets that were available at its start, some tens of millions more tons of ships than in 1914, including a very sizeable tanker fleet constructed since 1918. The great ports of the world were products of generation-to-generation investment, but major expansion in docks and installations had occurred between the wars from Liverpool to Calcutta to render these still greater gateways for troops and material. Lines of communication along global fronts commandeered European imperial riverboat networks dating back to the nineteenth century. When inland fleets were lost, as occurred for the Irrawaddy Flotilla Company in Burma, officers and crews escaped to join the Joint Steamers operations along the Brahmaputra.

Thus equally critical was pre-war investment in knowledge, expertise and organization. Finding ships was one thing. Knowing how to use them in a highly systematized global manner was another. The MOWT not only dispatched port experts to the Clyde or Suez but packed itself with the directors and managers of Britain's merchant steamship lines who had spent their professional careers within organizations that coordinated global transport on a day-to-day basis. Their equivalents could be found in the highly militarized American transport services across the Atlantic. Skill reservoirs ran very deep: a ready-made corps of sea captains and officers, agents, forwarders, brokers and stevedores, and a maritime culture that prided itself

---

41 Micklem, *Transportation*, pp. 142–74; Bykofsky and Larson, *Operations*, pp. 233–80, 302–44; Wardlow, *Movements*, pp. 155–8.

on hands-on training and expertise. In the pre-war maritime world, bottom-up training was the norm. Even those destined to occupy positions at the top had begun with several years of learning the basics. At the war's start, there was a very sizeable body of men who knew cargoes, knew how to load and turn around ships, knew routes, knew harbours, and who had years of experience in troubleshooting or in casually piecing together overseas networks through which the world's peoples and commodities passed in great volumes. The militarized operations of the Second World War, far from putting together a global transport system from scratch, improvised upon a pre-existing one while mobilizing the people who knew how to run it.

The world of shipping, however, could never be quite the same after the Second World War. Most far-reaching were the shock effects of Japanese conquest of Southeast Asia and the beginning of the unravelling of empire. Asian merchant fleets had never disappeared from the seas, not even at the peak of imperial power; but decolonization signalled the beginnings of a more assertive and world-intervening role for non-Western maritime nations. Post-war route structures reflected these trends. By the 1960s Australian exports flowed more toward Japan than Britain. Western shipping lines, expelled from imperial bases, pioneered new cross-trades that departed from earlier Eurocentric world connectedness. Within European shipping circles new hierarchies emerged. The First World War had catapulted Greek shipping to world-wide status. After the Second, Greek entrepreneurs took advantage of bargain basement American tanker and Liberty ship sales to begin their climb to the top of the shipping world.[42]

On the technical side of sea transport it can be said that all three of the great modifications to cargo handling in the second half of the century – palletization, RoRo and containerization – advanced with the war. Infatuated with the prospect of expediting cargo shipments through unit loads, the US military strapped cargo to platforms for deployment in both war theatres. Pallets were utilized in transoceanic carriage, but also as 'skidloads' on sleds to bring in ammunition with the troops as they landed on beaches.[43] The concept of RoRo, or transporting cargo in loaded trucks driven off and on ships, borrowed from the widespread use of landing craft. And if the roots of containerization extended back to the nineteenth century, the lashing of heavily tarred crates to decks to extend carrying capacity in the war

---

42 Gelina Harlaftis, *A History of Greek-Owned Shipping: The Making of an International Tramp Fleet, 1830 to the Present Day* (London: Routledge, 1996), pp. 235–40.

43 Wardlow, *Movements*, pp. 395–6; Bykofsky and Larson, *Operations*, p. 516.

encouraged comparable practice in the years after. Appropriately, the voyage that inaugurated the container age, the sailing of the *Ideal-X* in 1956 with truck bodies fastened to it, occurred upon a war surplus T-2 tanker, the sort of ship to which a spar deck had been outfitted for the carriage of aircraft. In the end, then, the history of transport in the Second World War stood between the routinization of one age of globalization and the coming of a new one.

7

Knowledge economies

Toward a new technological age

CATHRYN CARSON

The Second World War marks the transition to a new mode of warfare, one in which scientific and technical knowledge transformed the fighting of war. That summary statement captures the views of the insiders who built their nations' new systems of research and development (R&D), as well as the public that stood in awe of the war's spectacular weapons. On a closer look, however, the picture is more complicated. The atomic bomb was only the most obvious of the research-driven developments that signalled the entrance into a new scientized world of military might. How is that forward-looking observation to be reconciled with the argument that the Second World War was ultimately decided by other things than pathbreaking weapons systems: raw materials and manpower, production capacity and economic mobilization, and mass deployment of largely standardized weapons?

To make sense of this contrast, we need to look not simply at new science-based weapons that were brought to deployment, but at the R&D systems that guided them into being. These R&D systems were complex social structures uniting human resources, high-tech industrial capacity and organizational connectivity to bring new knowledge to bear on the conduct of war. By the outbreak of the Second World War, these systems had been built up at regional, national and global scales. Their coupling into the machinery of war planning and war-fighting created an interlocking set of mechanisms that became part of the mobilization of national strength. This chapter thus situates wartime science and technology in the context of pre-war efforts to put new knowledge to work across the industrialized world. Exploring both incremental and transformative change in war-fighting technologies, it takes R&D systems as its overarching category. This choice forces it to move continuously across domains that are typically distinguished as basic science, applied science and engineering – categories we have inherited from post-Second World War analysts, who used them to frame the lessons they wanted to take from the war.

Most historical studies have focused on the outputs of national R&D systems and asked what made them succeed or fail. Instead, this chapter highlights the global character of these developments and their disrespect for the temporal end of the war. It explores national innovation systems as individual experiments within a larger landscape of war-relevant R&D. Finally, it insists on the contingency of the war's ending moment. The biggest story of science, technology, and the Second World War is not which new weapons systems were ready by mid-1945. It is how wartime knowledge economies crystallized expectations and relationships that set the terms for an unfolding dynamic of high-technology war.

Building the system

The mobilization of scientists in the Second World War is sometimes thought of as an unusual break, something only a cataclysm on the scale of the war could explain. It is true that the Second World War was fantastically effective in putting researchers to work for military needs. But the R&D systems that were built up by the early twentieth century produced large numbers of scientists, technologists and engineers for whom collaboration with state, military and industry was familiar, desirable, even taken for granted. In nearly all of the great powers, what happened in the war was less a break than an intensification, and in every nation it built on connections that had been made in the past.

An appropriate starting point is the late nineteenth century, when the second industrial revolution unfolded across industrialized Europe and reached into North America, late-tsarist Russia and Meiji-period Japan. Over the space of a few decades, new industries were created around electrotechnology, organic and physical chemistry, advances in metallurgy, pharmaceuticals, precision optics, and other science-related areas. Possible payoffs in industrial competitiveness and patenting made it attractive to engage in research toward inventions, improvements and tuning of processes. As large corporations were consolidated, their resources let them hire technical specialists and invest in laboratories with longer time horizons for financial returns. The great chemical and electrical firms were the standard-bearers of industrial science for decades, as companies such as Bayer, Hoechst, BASF (Badische Anilin- und Soda-Fabrik), DuPont, Siemens, American Telephone & Telegraph and General Electric built up large in-house research teams.

While it was big business and its laboratories that had the leverage to begin shaping R&D systems at scale, similar moves were visible in smaller units inside medium-sized enterprises, research efforts within firms in closer connection to manufacturing, or sector-wide collaborative settings. Infrastructure for testing materials and improving processes and products found homes inside a wide range of heavy industry, including steel and soon the armaments and parts of the automotive sectors.[1]

The personnel for research had to pass through institutions of specialist training. Around this time, engineering training was being scientized as well. In an era in which mass higher education was still decades off, the needs of students heading into technical employment were a pressure point for increasing the prestige and resources of the technical universities and colleges. Up to the First World War and a decade or more past it, students from peripheral countries (e.g. Japan, Russia, the USA) or imperial dominions travelled to the centre for doctoral education, mainly Great Britain, Germany and France. It was on top of this differentiated educational structure that venues for basic science were built out, above all in the universities. Characteristically, the Nobel Prizes, which were first awarded in 1901, were funded from the estate of the Swedish armaments manufacturer and inventor of dynamite Alfred Nobel.[2]

The progress of research increasingly mattered to governments. As states took on testing and regulatory roles for new technologies, they established modern bureaux of standards, such as the German Imperial Physical Technical Institute (founded 1887) and the British National Physical Laboratory (founded 1902). Other offices that might incorporate teams of technical experts included agencies serving agriculture, public health and municipal infrastructure. The technicalization of the civil service was highly contested,

---

1 François Caron, Paul Erker and Wolfram Fischer, *Innovations in the European Economy between the Wars* (Berlin: de Gruyter, 1995); David E. H. Edgerton, ed., *Industrial Research and Innovation in Business* (Cheltenham: Edward Elgar, 1996); Ulrich Marsch, *Zwischen Wissenschaft und Wirtschaft. Industrieforschung in Deutschland und Grossbritannien, 1880–1936* (Paderborn: Schöningh, 2000); Michael Stephen Smith, *The Emergence of Modern Business Enterprise in France, 1800–1930* (Cambridge, Mass.: Harvard University Press, 2006); Naomi R. Lamoreaux, Kenneth L. Sokoloff and Dhanoos Sutthiphisal, 'The Reorganization of Inventive Activity in the United States during the Early Twentieth Century', in Dora L. Costa and Naomi R. Lamoreaux, eds., *Understanding Long-Run Economic Growth* (University of Chicago Press, 2011), pp. 235–74.

2 For examples of national stories, see Roger L. Geiger, *To Advance Knowledge: The Growth of American Research Universities, 1900–1940* (Oxford University Press, 1986); Dominique Pestre, *Physique et physiciens en France, 1918–1940* (Paris: Editions des archives contemporaines, 1984).

and it was a local and regional as much as a national story. In the military forces, scientifically trained officers remained largely outsiders. However, there were spaces within where civil and naval engineering expertise was recognized. Technical competence in ballistics, fire control and munitions had homes inside the services, while industrial fabrication of firearms, artillery pieces, ammunition and explosives created networks of contracting and information exchange.[3]

Even when these systems had internal frictions, connectivity across them was engineered in. Informal recruiting networks and consulting relationships linked firms to professors and educational institutions. Formally, academies of sciences, whose members were the most distinguished scientific researchers, provided regional or national forums. With the exception of the Royal Society in Great Britain, academies often stood under government sponsorship. Disciplinary professional groups could do similar work on a more focused basis. Advisory boards for government organs – for instance, committees consulting on explosives for the French and British ordnance offices – brought academics into military affairs. (Across continental Europe, professors were employees of the state.) Representatives of large industrial firms moved in these circles, too, particularly in domains viewed as important to state power. The linkages were closest among members of social elites.

With local variations, this model settled in widely. In Germany, most tellingly, it took concrete form in the Kaiser Wilhelm Society for the Promotion of the Sciences. When the KWG was founded in 1911, it was meant to advance cutting-edge fundamental research. While it shared common elements with other extra-university institutes, such as the Institut Pasteur in Paris (founded 1887) and the Carnegie Institution in Washington (founded 1902), the KWG stood apart for its ambition and became the paradigm for organizations such as the Japanese Riken (Rikagaku Kenkyujo, Institute of Physical and Chemical Research, founded 1917). In the KWG the elite of German banking and the chairmen of the board of Krupp, Bayer and others joined forces with the highest levels of science and Prussian ministry officials. In the next few years the first Kaiser Wilhelm Institutes opened their doors,

---

3 An effective overview is most readily available for Germany: Alan Beyerchen, 'On the Stimulation of Excellence in Wilhelmian Science', in Jack R. Dukes and Joachim Remak, eds., *Another Germany: A Reconsideration of the Imperial Era* (Boulder: Westview, 1988), pp. 139–68; Margit Szöllösi-Janze, 'Science and Social Space: Transformations in the Institutions of *Wissenschaft* from the Wilhelmine Empire to the Weimar Republic', *Minerva* 43 (2005), 339–60.

including institutes for chemistry, physical chemistry and electrochemistry, biology, labour physiology and coal research. As well-endowed as it was connected, the KWG was a private organization drawing on public funds along with significant individual and corporate donations.[4]

Pointing toward war

The First World War drew these threads together more tightly – or, better, suggested how tightly they might be drawn. Fought with massive material infrastructures, the war drew on products of industrial transformations that were partially integrated into the European arms race: refined munitions, capacities for gun-laying on land and at sea, communications by telephone and wireless telegraphy (radio), the sheer availability of electrical components and motorized equipment. German U-boats opened the door to underwater warfare. The British, French and Americans countered not just with mines, depth charges and torpedoes but also with brand-new sound detection techniques, precursors of sonar that supported the convoy system in keeping the shipping lanes open. The war saw the rapid development of gas warfare in multiple forms (irritants like tear gas, chlorine and phosgene for asphyxiation, mustard gas for its blistering effect). Fritz Haber, director of the Kaiser Wilhelm Institute for Physical Chemistry, put his institute at the German army's disposal for work on poison gases, and by the end of a war that the USA had been late to join, the Chemical Warfare Service had networked American industrial, academic and government chemists to an extent never before seen. Chemical weapons generated widespread revulsion, leading to the Geneva Protocol forbidding their use in 1925, although some commentators asked why death by chemical attack was worse than death by less scientific means. Chemistry also figured into the wartime materials economy. The Haber–Bosch process, discovered during Haber's university career and scaled up by BASF in 1913–16, allowed the fixation of atmospheric nitrogen to produce ammonia that supplied both German munitions factories and crucial agricultural fertilizer. After the war Haber briefly feared indictment for war crimes; within a year he won the Nobel Prize for his ammonia research.[5]

4 Rudolf Vierhaus and Bernhard vom Brocke, *Forschung im Spannungsfeld von Politik und Gesellschaft* (Stuttgart: Deutsche Verlags-Anstalt, 1990).
5 Guy Hartcup, *The War of Invention: Scientific Developments, 1914–18* (London: Brassey's, 1988); Margit Szöllösi-Janze, *Fritz Haber, 1868–1934: Eine Biographie* (Munich: Beck, 1998); Daniel J. Kevles, *The Physicists: A History of a Scientific Community in Modern America* (New York: Alfred A. Knopf, 1977), chs. 8–9.

Besides specific technologies, the First World War brought about other changes. To make the feedback loops tighter and faster, there was urgent experimentation in organizational forms. Well-placed civilian scientists caucused to form organizations to give high-level advice to governments. Among the critical wartime outcomes were a new National Research Council in the USA (a semi-free-standing body) and the Department of Scientific and Industrial Research in Britain. Even with the successes, however, what outside experts often took away was frustration. Critics created a public drumbeat of complaints about the failures of governments and the military to attend to scientific expertise. Big institutional arguments tended to make little headway. However, seemingly smaller choices started other kinds of change. One important pathway was through higher education. Small numbers of military officers in technicized branches found ways to go back to school for more training. These pathways would get somewhat more routinized over the interwar decades. By the 1930s the USA and Germany had programmes supporting officers in intensive advanced studies; the German system of secret dissertations stands out.

A further outcome of the Great War was surging attention to aviation. At the start of the war, sustained powered flight had been possible for scarcely a decade. Aircraft were rushed into war production with rapid technological modifications, serving for strategic bombing, reconnaissance and other uses. In the aftermath, the R&D machinery kicked into high gear. Building on existing foundations where there were any, starting from scratch where there were not, research centres grew up in all the major industrial powers – even Germany, where military aviation was proscribed by the Treaty of Versailles. These aerodynamics facilities became next-generation interfaces among private institutions, education, industry and the state. The questions they addressed ranged from fundamentals of fluid mechanics and airfoil design to materials and propulsion. Like heavy machinery, aircraft were technologically ambivalent between civil and military uses; like some parts of the chemicals sector, their progress relied on continuous developments in new technical knowledge.[6]

The R&D systems that crystallized between the wars were nationally anchored, of course. The European powers all invested in securing their technical capacity; with an increasingly sharp sense of competition, Germany

---

6 Alex Roland, *Model Research: The National Advisory Committee for Aeronautics, 1915–1958* (Washington, DC: NASA, 1985); Helmuth Trischler, *Luft-und Raumfahrtforschung in Deutschland, 1900–1970. Politische Geschichte einer Wissenschaft* (New York: Campus, 1992).

and Great Britain led the way.[7] While military procurement dropped off sharply at the end of the First World War, other nationally oriented projects took up some of the slack. By the end of the 1920s, the Soviet Union would launch a massive programme of accelerated industrialization, as part of which it built up scientific and engineering capacity across a large number of fields. In Japan a political strain of modernization for national strength lent at least rhetorical support to advocates for science. In the USA, interestingly, the linkages were strongest between universities, private research institutions and industry, while federal support for research was limited to scientific bureaux and the National Advisory Committee for Aeronautics. Simultaneously, large corporations with strong technical departments often worked across multiple countries. Even as nationally based industrial groupings came together – the 1920s saw the consolidation of research strongholds such as IG Farben and the Vereinigte Stahlwerke in Germany and Imperial Chemical Industries in Britain – the circulating expertise of industrial personnel in multinational corporations was the counterpart to the international community of professors and students. By the 1920s and 1930s a new wave of scientization hit existing knowledge-based sectors, including vacuum-tube electronics, organic chemistry, synthetic materials and metallurgy. With the Depression only temporarily holding back corporate investment, laboratory-based research also made inroads into new industries such as rubber, photographic chemicals and petroleum refining. Other kinds of information-sharing took place across borders as Japanese experts made extended tours conferring with experts in Germany and the USA, while technical cooperation had helped both the Red Army and the German military back when both were trying to rebuild.

Into the conflict

After the Nazis came to power in 1933, Germany exited the clandestine phase of rearmament. Its across-the-board if sometimes wildly see-sawing mobilization of the industrial economy was carried out through sharp coordination of private resources with government directives. Britain's preparations in the later 1930s concentrated first of all on its navy and expanded domestic

---

7 Strong arguments for the interpenetration of science and military interests between the wars can be found in David Edgerton, *Warfare State: Britain, 1920–1970* (Cambridge University Press, 2006), and Helmut Maier, *Forschung als Waffe. Rüstungsforschung in der Kaiser-Wilhelm-Gesellschaft und das Kaiser-Wilhelm-Institut für Metallforschung, 1900–1945/48* (Göttingen: Wallstein, 2007).

industrial capacity; France invested heavily in tank production and man-power and looked to purchase American planes. Japan's industrial and financial conglomerates benefited from military orders, and the Soviet Union prepared for a war of men and materiel with mass increases in equipment for both air and ground forces. In the USA, national economic strengthening was formally decoupled from war preparations, but its capacity as a resource for other nations was clear. Once the USA entered the conflict, its reserve force of academic and industrial researchers was mobilized as massively as its manufacturing power.

It is hard to identify any part of war-related industry that was not shaped by demands for technical advances. Those demands might not be met – the hopes of military innovators could exceed even nature's capacity to deliver – but the Second World War can be seen as a vast terrain of technical improvements all the way from the laboratory to the manufacturing floor. Monumental efforts for mobilization included the chemical engineering and metallurgical innovation that underwrote ambitions of materials autarky in Germany's Four-Year Plan (1936–40). Synthetic fuel was key to the Third Reich's war planning, since its access to oil was dependent on trade or military conquest. The challenges associated with synthetic fuel were mainly around scaling up coal liquefaction processes. (Germany's number one plentiful resource was coal.) The synthetic rubber called buna derived from the work of macromolecular chemists in Germany in the late 1920s. By the time the war was launched, their processes became the foundation of large-scale production. Both these efforts were driven forward by a partnership between the regime and the chemical giant IG Farben, embodied in the multiplicity of organizational roles held by the IG industrial chemical leader Carl Krauch. On the side of metallurgy, the limited domestic supply of key constituents in aluminium and steel alloys led to intensive research in the laboratories of the metal-based industries and the Kaiser Wilhelm Institute for Metals Research.[8]

This upscaling was not simple in war economies that were stretched to the limits. One key shortage was trained personnel. With the expansion of technical higher education, huge numbers of scientists and engineers were of draft age. Nearly every country's technical organizers struggled with securing exemptions from call-up orders. By war's end, American war laboratories

---

8 Peter Hayes, *Industry and Ideology: IG Farben in the Nazi Era* (Cambridge University Press, 1987); Adam Tooze, *The Wages of Destruction: The Making and Breaking of the Nazi Economy* (London: Allen Lane, 2006); Jonas Scherner, *Die Logik der Industriepolitik im Dritten Reich* (Stuttgart: Steiner, 2008); Maier, *Forschung als Waffe*.

were bringing aboard students before they completed their graduate or undergraduate degrees. The human resources pressure was intensified when ideological reliability was made part of the equation. Stalin's purges had picked off key figures in the USSR's technical leadership, and an unsettling feature of the Soviet R&D landscape was the system of *sharashkas*, or prison laboratories run by the Department of Special Design Bureaux of Beria's NKVD. For its part, Nazi Germany had driven away huge numbers of trained scientists with its attacks on the Jews. While it is impossible to scope out the effects of the brain drain, the roster of Allied war research was filled with émigrés in hugely responsible positions – leading the Theoretical Division at Los Alamos, for instance (Hans Bethe). Among the Western Allies there was less political scrutiny, more trust in a shared sense of purpose. Even in a classified world, hatred of Germany went a long way.

War research stretched across profound organizational divides. Going into the Second World War, R&D systems were only spottily mediated through formal coordinating structures. Connections across government, industry, academia and private research institutions were as often as not made in committees, creating linkages that were often subject-specific and did not necessarily scale. In Great Britain, for instance, where military-oriented research was significantly advanced in the 1930s, mobilization was mainly the work of individuals and departments committing to work on relevant projects, rather than a mass hue and cry about technical war. Coordination was done through personal consultations. Those relatively loose centralizing mechanisms did not prevent key areas from making huge progress by the war's outbreak. By the time the British reached out across the Atlantic in the summer of 1940, when the Tizard Mission brought over key technologies, data and the invitation to collaborate, British military-relevant R&D was significantly advanced relative to its key ally, the USA.

In some combatant nations, wartime centres of power grew up in different organizational sectors, such as the army, the industrial commissariats and the Academy of Sciences in the Soviet Union. The Soviet arrangement was probably partly a conscious strategy to ensure political control, partly a tribute to the spurring power of competitive development. In Germany, beyond the technocratic appeal of reducing duplication and friction, the rhetoric of coordination in single national will was politically potent. When Carl Krauch made his move to dissolve the Kaiser Wilhelm Society in 1941, he proposed reconstituting it in a larger organization named for Reich Marshal Herman Göring, who was (among other things) a key patron of aviation research. In the end, the German system sat in an unstable equilibrium among these players, Todt's and then Speer's Armaments Ministry, the Reich Education Ministry's organizations, the different military research offices, and even the research ambitions of the SS. Whether these conflicts damaged the progress of German wartime research is an open question. Under certain political constellations, projects could be mobilized very effectively in smaller circles, as examples will show. In such cases, success had as much to do with the preexisting base of research capacity, personnel and access to resources, often through personal connections, as with formal authority structures. This meant that calling for coordination at the highest level could be as much a political play as a practical move. When it was used, it was a strategy of mobilizing frustration to stake claims for control. Across all the combatant nations, complaints about military/non-military coordination were in fact endemic to wartime research. Inter-service rivalry was a common theme, too. The case can be made that Japanese researchers, for instance, contributed relatively little to their country's war efforts because Japan lacked a centralizing R&D authority. However, it is also true that there was less to centralize.

One instance does stand out of relatively successful central coordination – despite critiques of friction and compartmentalization all the same. That is the USA. The curious and perhaps decisive feature of American R&D coordination was that it originated in an initiative of academic and industrial, not government researchers. Looking ahead in 1940 to an American entry into the war that they saw as inevitable, a handful of powerful figures in American science came together behind Vannevar Bush, a former engineering dean at MIT, head of the Carnegie Institution and chairman of the National Advisory Committee for Aeronautics. Bush's National Defense Research Committee (NDRC) was set up in summer 1940 when President Roosevelt approved a one-page proposal. Almost immediately, the NDRC was connected via the Tizard Mission to R&D leaders in Britain. Starting from the NDRC's small staff and Bush's excellent skills in working with the military, there emerged an immensely wide-ranging organization, the Office of Scientific Research and Development (OSRD). The OSRD was formed in mid-1941, some months before the USA entered the war. It reported to the president directly and grew into a research agency of a sort the world had never seen, contracting its work out across the American academic and industrial landscape and reaching into nearly every domain of military-relevant R&D.[9]

9 G. Pascal Zachary, *Endless Frontier: Vannevar Bush, Engineer of the American Century* (New York: Free Press, 1997); Kevles, *The Physicists*.

Incremental R&D

War-related research made a difference in two distinct ways. It could take an existing technology to a new level, or it could create a new one *tout court*. Of those two paths, incremental improvement was typically simpler, faster and – technically and politically – safer. It took a system that was known to perform and tried making it better. Even when it had to generate new knowledge to do that, it was clear what the baseline was. It was also potentially easier to implement: rather than changing an entire weapons system and rebuilding a whole production line, it might be enough to improve a component. But incremental improvement did not have to mean marginal payoff. Some technical developments could change a particular correlation of forces entirely. Others were broadly enough deployed that a modest increase in effectiveness had large cumulative consequences. We can see different aspects of incremental R&D with examples from weapons and weapons systems, innovation in chemical and biomedical research, and the large arena of air defence.

Weapons and weapons systems

Artillery and munitions were central to the fighting, and quality and killing power left plenty of room for innovation. One of the most widely deployed incremental technologies of the Second World War was rocket artillery. Rockets rapidly oxidize (burn) chemical propellants to generate gas that is directed backwards through a nozzle, using the thrust created by the exhaust to propel their payloads at high speed. Reactive propulsion had been one of the desiderata of military innovators world-wide since the 1920s, with many technical variants and possible uses. One line of development that showed early promise was the small solid-fuel rocket. Compared to liquid propellants, these could be technologically less finicky, though also in some ways less excitingly cutting-edge. At least as important, they could be built in ways that were conceptually similar to established forms of artillery with their range of options for shells. Rockets' overwhelming benefit was that they were recoilless, which meant that they just needed to be carried and aimed, not fired from a big, heavy gun capable of withstanding significant force.

The Katyusha rocket launcher is illustrative of the war's rocket artillery weapons. It was developed as part of the Soviet rearmament drive in the Reactive Scientific Research Institute within the People's Commissariat for Heavy Industry. Serious development started in the later 1930s and was wrapped up with power struggles over different directions in rocket technology, which mapped unhappily onto deadly denunciations in Stalin's purges. Rocket artillery was not a Soviet invention alone; the German army produced its own Nebelwerfer series, while the Allies all used rockets for assaults in multiple theatres and fit them for firing from planes. But the Katyusha's distinctive success had much to do with its suitability to Soviet needs. When the launcher was field-tested, it was no more accurate or capable of sustaining a higher rate of fire than conventional options; in fact, the opposite was true. The strength was the package. As deployed starting in 1941, the BM-13 multiple rocket launcher had sixteen rockets of 13.2 cm diameter. Without the need to brace against recoil, it could be mounted in a rack on a truck. The Katyusha became a favoured Soviet weapon because it was light, mobile and impressively destructive in barrages, well-tuned to the character of war on the Eastern Front. It was also good for mass production, since it was cheap and called for none of the careful machining that conventional artillery required.[10]

Other solid rocket technologies filled different niches. The US bazooka and the German Panzerfaust were short-range, shoulder-fired weapons that came into use after 1942. By this time, the conceptual innovation was not the rocket propulsion technology, but rather the warhead, which used a distinctive design known as the shaped charge. Shaped-charge weapons took advantage of the fact that a quantity of explosive layered around an appropriately dimensioned lined cavity would focus the blast energy into an extremely narrow, extremely fast jet. If the explosive were detonated the right way, the jet could perforate a significant thickness of armour. The key delivery requirement was that the shaped-charge warhead be accurately projected nose-first. It could not be thrown like a grenade because of the directionality, or fired from a rifle because of the recoil. A kilo of high explosive deployed with a reusable tube for a rocket launcher could be a close-combat weapon against that mechanized monster, the tank.[11]

The shaped-charge phenomenon had been explored in the 1930s, with an eye to more general explosive use as well as armour-piercing weapons. The key players were German Army Ordnance and the Technical Academy of Luftwaffe and a Swiss private inventor who licensed his discoveries to Great Britain and the USA. If the jet phenomenon was to be exploited most effectively, however, it needed to be better understood. High-speed

---

10 Asif A. Siddiqi, *The Red Rockets' Glare: Spaceflight and the Soviet Imagination, 1857–1957* (Cambridge University Press, 2010), chs. 4–5.
11 John E. Burchard, *Rockets, Guns and Targets* (Boston: Little, Brown, 1948), pp. 50–4.

photography, critical to tracking the progress of jets, was significantly advanced during the war by ballistics experts in Germany and in the OSRD's Explosives Research Laboratory. A fluid-dynamical explanation of how the shaped charge worked was laid out in 1943 by two superb mathematicians, G. I. Taylor and Garrett Birkhoff. And plenty of empirical testing was needed to get a grasp of penetration phenomena, which had implications for detonation and timing.[12] The cycle of research and development never in fact ended. Early versions of the bazooka and the Panzerfaust were presented to the public as spectacular successes. But they were not without flaws, leaving the anti-tank infantry role still very dangerous. And the classic counter-measures dynamic meant that each new increment in armour-penetrating weapons was matched by improvements in tank armour. The German Panzerschreck, playing off captured bazookas, was the fullest wartime development of the rocket-launched shaped charge, while the American super-bazooka was not deployed before the end of the war.

Sectoral innovation

Other domain-area improvements mobilized human resources across a wide research front within a sector of technical knowledge. Chemists and chemical engineers were understood to be great R&D assets and well integrated into war planning. In fact, despite the fascination with flashier branches of science, the chemists' pre-Second World War successes arguably made them the leading incremental innovators of the war.[13] Rocket propulsion (described above) called on them centrally. Along with substitute materials and new alloys, chemists put a diversified effort into next-generation explosives. Gas warfare research took up both offensive and defensive needs. Nerve agents such as tabun (1937) and sarin (1939, both discovered by an IG Farben chemist) and soman (1944, in a Kaiser Wilhelm Institute) were secret developments that Germany brought to factory-scale production. Research on protection and counter-measures against chemical agents was common to every combatant nation. Yet although every country stockpiled chemical weapons, and Japanese forces made some use of them, widespread deployment was apparently forestalled by fears of retaliation. The exception, if it can be thought of this way, was Zyklon B, which was an ordinary industrial

---

12 Peter O. K. Krehl, *History of Shock Waves, Explosions and Impact* (Heidelberg: Springer, 2009); Donald R. Kennedy, *History of the Shaped Charge Effect* (Mountain View, Calif.: D. R. Kennedy & Associates, 1983).

13 W. A. Noyes, Jr., ed., *Chemistry* (Boston: Little, Brown, 1948).

chemical originally developed as a pesticide and repurposed for killing a million human beings at the Auschwitz death camp.

If undetectably small deployments leading to indiscriminate mass killing seemed a particularly threatening aspect of chemical warfare, the chemistry of flame-throwers and incendiary bombs struck observers as less fearsome somehow. Flame-throwers were a modest innovation technically, but coming out of the First World War (and interwar rebellions), they needed work on jelling, nozzles and ignition. If flame-thrower R&D served the purpose of killing human beings standing nearby, incendiary bombs were for delivering death from a distance. Tried out in the First World War, relatively simple incendiaries were available at the start of the Second. When used by the German air force in 1939–40, they were quickly seen to be an important component of the strategic bombing arsenal, as the fires they started were considerably more destructive per ton of payload than high explosives. The NDRC/OSRD and Chemical Warfare Service were thus spurred to develop mass-production alternatives of many varieties, which were used to devastating effect in the Allies' strategic bombing campaigns.

Equally, military medicine adapted to new possibilities. Modern methods of blood transfusion proved field-worthy in the Spanish Civil War and were rapidly scaled up in the Second World War. More complex problems on the side of research had to be solved for penicillin production. By the end of the war, however, penicillin, the first antibiotic, was joining the sulfonamides, the miracle drugs of the 1930s, in Allied physicians' arsenal for treating infections. New treatments were de facto explored for burns, epidemics, frostbite, tropical diseases and other medical consequences of how the war was fought. Not all of this experimentation was in the interest of the patient. Researchers in Germany and Japan exploited prisoners of war and concentration camp inmates in horrific human experiments. Whether or not the results had scientific value, they were carried out in part by trained researchers in established research institutions, including both military-controlled and formally civilian institutions such as the Kaiser Wilhelm Society.[14]

It is hard to imagine, finally, that decades of experience with public health and disease would not have become part of wartime R&D. The military

---

14 Carola Sachse, *Die Verbindung nach Auschwitz. Biowissenschaften und Menschenversuche an Kaiser-Wilhelm-Instituten* (Göttingen: Wallstein, 2003); Gerhard Baader, Susan E. Lederer, Morris Low, Florian Schmaltz and Alexander V. Schwerin, 'Pathways to Human Experimentation, 1933–1945: Germany, Japan, and the United States', in Carola Sachse and Mark Walker, eds., *Politics and Science in Wartime* (University of Chicago Press, 2005), pp. 205–31.

possibilities of bacteriological agents had been watched intently by the eventual combatants during the interwar years. Biological warfare, too, was prohibited by the Geneva Protocol of 1925. However, even if it was unclear that pathogens could be used in a practical weapon, defensive needs were a starting point for research. Alongside British wartime work at Porton Down and its American counterpart at Fort Detrick, the largest biological weapons R&D programme was based in Japan, sponsored by the Army Medical College and the Kwantung Army. The experiments conducted by Unit 731 began early, in the 1930s, after Japan occupied territory in Manchuria. This work focused on known pathogens such as typhus, cholera and bubonic plague, which were used in limited deployments in the China theatre but only ineffectively weaponized.[15]

Air defence

Air defence may be the most pointed example of military possibilities opened up by incremental R&D. The Second World War was the conflict in which air forces grew into maturity. The technical glory of aerial warfare went to offensive innovators; aircraft technologies were spectacular, and their designers were celebrated. But the dynamic of defence was arguably more important. And despite broad fascination with counter-air warfare and brave ground-based defenders, here the story was not so much about guns or ammunition. It was about how to get gunners to hit fast-moving targets before they did damage.

The elements of air defence were incubated during the worried interwar years, with Britain leading the way. It took the outbreak of the air war to drive the components forward and build them into a system that transformed the fighting of the war. The most familiar part of the challenge was directing fire accurately – not to the spot where targets were sighted, but where they were going to go. This was a task of calculation and actuation, coupling human operators to assemblages of electrical and mechanical components. The naval fire control needs of the First World War, hitting moving ships from a platform that was itself rolling and pitching, were reframed for the aeroplane in the interwar years. Even when anti-aircraft guns sat stable on land, they had to predict the future position of an object moving in three dimensions, then move heavy equipment into position to fire – and fast.

15 Brian Balmer, *Britain and Biological Warfare: Expert Advice and Science Policy, 1930–65* (Basingstoke: Palgrave Macmillan, 2001); Walter E. Grunden, *Secret Weapons & World War II: Japan in the Shadow of Big Science* (Lawrence: University Press of Kansas, 2005).

Naval anti-aircraft weapons had to meet even higher demands. The mechanical calculators (or computers) that did this work had their analogues in navigation systems and bomb-sights. Viewed abstractly, the problems they tackled were akin to problems in electrical transmission networks and other engineering domains. Improving fire-control systems was a high priority in Britain and the USA in particular, in the latter in part because of the early attention of the NDRC through the person of Vannevar Bush. Over the course of the conflict, advances in fire control redefined the human–machine relationship in ways that continued to transform the experience of war.[16]

Of course, fire control depended on identifying targets. And as targets moved faster and faster, gunners had less time to confirm and react. With air war, early, accurate detection moved high up on the priority list. One huge opening was radio. Through the first decades of the century, there had been considerable progress in working with radio waves, those man-made electromagnetic signals generated using antennas and vacuum tubes that could carry information through empty space. Developed for wireless communications, radio technology was also recognized for an interesting secondary use: an object passing through a radio beam bounced some small part of the waves back. This understanding of the uses of radio echoes was the basis of military-industrial R&D projects in the 1930s in multiple countries, including Great Britain, Germany, the Soviet Union, Japan, France, Italy, the Netherlands, and the USA. The technical challenges around radar – radio detection and ranging, to use the eventually dominant nomenclature – were not small. German early warning devices were ready by 1939 to serve both gun-laying and ground-based guidance of interceptors. The Chain Home system watching Britain's south and east coasts was simple in design and limited technically. However, its integrated operations network was critical for the Royal Air Force in 1940 in the Battle of Britain. For later entrants into the conflict, the situation was different because of the state of the war. Japanese radar development for the navy and the army benefited from contacts with Germany. The USA took major impulses from the British; that partnership will be touched on again below. The character of the Soviet war effort made indigenous development of radar less important than acquiring equipment

---

16 David A. Mindell, *Between Human and Machine: Feedback, Control, and Computing before Cybernetics* (Baltimore: Johns Hopkins University Press, 2002); Chris C. Bissell, 'Forging a New Discipline: Reflections on the Wartime Infrastructure for Research and Development in Feedback Control in the US, the UK, Germany and the USSR', in Ad Maas and Hans Hooijmaijers, eds., *Scientific Research in World War II* (London: Routledge, 2009), pp. 202–12.

through Lend-Lease. (The USSR had made substantial investments in radar in the 1930s, but the purges drove the effort into the ground.)

This first level of radar technology was tackled by electrical engineers worldwide. Where the balance shifted was a second round of innovation starting in 1940. This centred on refining a new kind of vacuum tube that delivered much more powerful signals at shorter wavelengths, allowing for systems with much higher resolution that could be squeezed into significantly smaller devices. Developed in Britain and secretly ferried across the Atlantic on the Tizard Mission of 1940, the cavity magnetron was immediately made the centre of broad-reaching American R&D relying on American industrial electrical engineering strength. The MIT Radiation Laboratory's radar technologies were small enough to be built into aircraft, assisting in bombing and sub-hunting as well as air combat. They were pervasively integrated into mobile fire-control systems, becoming part of the landscape of ground and naval warfare. In the form of the proximity fuse, they were even designed into artillery shells and rockets to optimize their effect by timing their explosion. Under wartime conditions of secrecy, the advances in detection and ranging enabled by the cavity magnetron were essentially confined to the Allied side.[17]

Well beyond anti-aircraft defences, radar's uses reached into multiple branches of war-fighting, from the battle for control of the Atlantic to execution of bombing campaigns to coordinating air-naval assaults. Radar was a key testing ground for the new mathematical and analytical techniques that came to be known as operations research. Calling radar an incremental improvement can seem counter-intuitive. And yet the case shows what an effect such innovations could have. The key insight is the setting: a technologized war of mass deployment of incremental advantage. In radar the net effect of the Allied–Axis differential was to confirm Allied superiority, reinforcing a balance of power deriving from underlying material conditions without requiring war-changing 'wonder weapons'.

Transformative openings

As an R&D strategy, incremental improvement was low-risk. It started from a weapon or system that was already fixed in a niche. When it tried to do better, the outcome might be one among mutiple options – if tank-killing

17 Louis Brown, *A Radar History of World War II* (Bristol: Institute of Physics Publishing, 1999); Robert Buderi, *The Invention that Changed the World* (New York: Simon & Schuster, 1996).

with bazookas was ineffective, anti-aircraft guns could fill in. There could be tough patches along the way, but it was not wholly new territory, with multiple decision points to call the result good enough. And if the effort failed, the investment that had to be written off was manageable. By contrast, the small number of big gambles of Second World War R&D focused on dark spots on the technological map. For jet-propelled aircraft, liquid-fuelled ballistic missiles and explosives based on nuclear fission, anyone could agree that a huge impact was theoretically possible. A rational calculus would weigh the strategic effects of introducing the weapon, the chance the enemy would do it first, the resources that would have to be thrown at the problem, and the time to the end of the war. But rational calculation about the future is an exercise in imagination, and that is even truer in wartime when gaps in the knowledge base leave key factors unclear. Above all, in war, success or failure depends on what military effect can be delivered by what critical moment. Whether a technology is transformative depends on staging and time.

Jet aircraft

Between the World Wars, significant efforts in government and private R&D establishments delivered huge improvements in conventional aircraft propulsion. The upward performance curve of piston engines and propellers relied on intensive engineering of engine components and the new aeronautical research tools of the 1920s and 1930s, such as wind tunnels. Those developments were coupled back into the refinement of aerodynamic theory in a classic and extremely successful feedback loop, while the overall process of incremental improvement in engines was supported by simultaneous evolution in aircraft structures, materials and fuels. As performance improved, however, some of the limits of conventional propulsion came into view. Whether those limits were important or not depended on what aeroplanes were needed to do. At speeds approaching supersonic and at exceptionally high altitudes, conventional engines were going to hit a performance wall. The jet engine was the work of a small number of aero-engine outsiders in Britain and Germany who followed theoretical developments in advanced airfoil research. When new options emerged in compressors and gas turbines by the end of the 1930s, they could be engineered into a potentially radically more powerful aircraft propulsion system, the turbo-jet.

In some sense, the jet engine was a reality by 1939. That was the moment at which impressive demonstrations in both Germany and Britain made its technical feasibility plain. A demonstration engine, however, even a demonstration plane, was not yet a deployable technology. And if the jet was not yet ready for deployment, it was even less of a system that could strong-arm its way into delivering transformative improvements in a highly developed space of alternatives competing for priority. The pace of wartime development that followed was not so much a matter of lack of high-level enthusiasm (though it was often experienced that way by the turbo-jet's advocates) as it was material, resource and engineering constraints that it proved hard to break through in conditions of war. Above all, the loop of testing and refining could barely get started. The long road to jet aircraft only began with the two fighters that reached use by 1944, the Messerschmidt Me 262 and the Gloster Meteor. In fact, the real payoff of the jet engine came once the countries that sat out serious wartime deployment, including the USA and the Soviet Union, joined in launching high-pressure development programmes. In sheer internal terms, the jet engine was transformative in its possibility, but to make it into a transformative package took it past the end of the war.[18]

Ballistic missiles

Long-range rocket propulsion, for its part, was an enthusiast's dream, at the heart of interwar fascination with interplanetary travel. The military interest was never hidden: a rocket that can travel fast and far can come screaming back to earth. If it follows a ballistic trajectory, it requires fuel only for the boost phase and can concentrate its weight in its warhead. After the rocket engine cuts out, the missile follows its predetermined path at supersonic speed, leaving it nearly impossible to defend against. To access those regimes of distance and speed, however, liquid fuel is necessary, and that fact creates serious technical complications. Combining the challenges of a liquid-fuel propulsion system with aerodynamics and guidance, the feasibility of ballistic missiles was an entirely open question through 1930s. The USA, France and Britain had small-scale, relatively uncoordinated efforts; the Soviet Union did more substantial R&D through the mid-1930s but cut it off when real conflict loomed – it was just too long-range to invest in when so much else needed to

---

18 Edward W. Constant II, *The Origins of the Turbojet Revolution* (Baltimore: Johns Hopkins University Press, 1980); Ralf Schabel, *Die Illusion der Wunderwaffen* (Munich: R. Oldenbourg, 1994); Hermione Giffard, 'Engines of Desperation: Jet Engines, Pro-duction and New Weapons in the Third Reich', *Journal of Contemporary History* 48 (2013), 821–44; Mark Harrison, 'A Soviet Quasi-Market for Inventions: Jet Propulsion, 1932–1946', *Research in Economic History* 23 (2005), 1–59; Philip Scranton, 'Turbulence and Redesign: Dynamic Innovation and the Dilemmas of US Military Jet Propulsion Development', *European Management Journal* 25 (2007), 235–48.

be done. Germany, on the other hand, pushed forward within the Army Ordnance Office under Wernher von Braun (PhD in aeronautical engineering, Berlin, 1934). One of these projects became the A4 or, as it was named by Goebbels, the V-2, the second of Nazi Germany's 'vengeance weapons'.

The A4's development is a story of its advocates pushing the envelope on a technology whose promise could only be scoped out as it was actually tried. By the end of the 1930s, rocket patrons in the military had placed their bets. They pushed the case for massive investment of resources by promising a devastating surprise weapon on a war-deciding time-scale. Getting high-level go-ahead, the army and the Luftwaffe partnered to build a secret research and production facility on the Baltic coastline at Peenemünde, where huge rockets could be tested without fear of discovery. As the war was launched and as the project progressed, ever more ambitious visions were floated – incredibly accelerated time-lines, missiles beyond the A4 with the capacity to deliver a payload all the way across the Atlantic. By the war's later years, the dream of a devastating offensive weapon kept the rocket's priority high, even as planning about its deployment modes was left aside. As Armaments Minister, Albert Speer joined forces with the SS in 1943 to move production into a hellish underground complex called Mittelwerk built and manned by concentration camp inmates, who died by the thousands.

By the end of the war, several thousand A4 rockets had been built. They were launched against London and other Allied-held cities starting in the autumn of 1944. Together with Germany's other vengeance weapon, the V-1, a proto-cruise missile, the V-2/A4 was truly terrifying. But given the state of the war and a body count not much larger than the number of missiles, the effect was negligible in the Second World War. The A4's accuracy was limited, and its explosive payload was small because the thermal engineering of the warhead had not got very far. There was no great strategic plan for its use besides surprise and terror. The range of the A4 was about 200 miles. The other weapons that were dreamed of by the rocketeers – the intercontinental ballistic missiles (ICBMs) for which it was a prototype – would not be ready for more than a decade. They were, of course, built on its model.

Nuclear fission

Nuclear weapons are often viewed as the war's crowning scientific achievement. The USA, in collaboration with the British, gambled that a secret army effort codenamed the Manhattan Project (for the Manhattan District of the Army Corps of Engineers) could bring an atomic bomb to fruition in time to be used during the conflict. In a compressed time-frame driven by fears of competing developments in Germany, a laboratory discovery in a frontier area of science was turned into a functioning weapon of a level of destructiveness never previously reached.[19] Nuclear fission was not even discovered until late 1938, the outcome of basic research in nuclear physics and chemistry. Under certain conditions, the nuclei of particular heavy elements, such as uranium, can be split by a subatomic particle called a neutron, releasing a large amount of energy and likely other neutrons as well. The discovery was made in Germany, whose ranks of nuclear scientists had been thinned by Nazi measures against Jews, but which still had significant strengths to show. The findings were quickly published in the open literature, and they set the members of the small community of nuclear scientists into agitation worldwide. Against the backdrop of academic theorizing and experimentation, it seemed that if certain yet-to-be determined conditions obtained, an uncontrolled chain reaction would be possible, opening the door to nuclear explosives far more powerful than those enabled by chemical reactions (such as TNT). Also on the horizon were controlled uses of fission to power massive engines with almost negligible consumption of uranium fuel.

Scientists pushed the issue into view in multiple nations' scientific-military networks. In Germany, consulting relationships between university scientists and government officials brought fission to state attention by late spring 1939. By the autumn, amid the overall mobilization, leading nuclear scientists were reporting to the Army Ordnance Office. In Japan and the Soviet Union similar contacts were made, though without the same urgency of potentially war-deciding prospects. In France, too, scientists were actively tracking developments.[20] In Britain and the USA, partnerships of German émigré scientists and domestic colleagues stirred up attention in government to begin a focused programme of research in the first half of 1940. As the war in Europe churned forward, the next eighteen months delivered results showing that a bomb in principle was feasible. However, it would take large supplies of uranium and a massive and unproven industrial effort to pick out that tiny fraction that was suitable for a nuclear explosive. Possibly easier was controlled power generation in a reactor. Along the way, all the same, it

19 Richard Rhodes, *The Making of the Atomic Bomb* (New York: Simon & Schuster, 1986); Margaret Gowing, *Britain and Atomic Energy, 1939–1945* (New York: St. Martin's Press, 1964).
20 Mark Walker, *German National Socialism and the Quest for Nuclear Power* (Cambridge University Press, 1989); Grunden, *Secret Weapons*; David Holloway, *Stalin and the Bomb: The Soviet Union and Atomic Energy, 1939–1956* (New Haven: Yale University Press, 1994); Spencer R. Weart, *Scientists in Power* (Cambridge, Mass.: Harvard University Press, 1979).

became clear that a running reactor would generate a new element that was soon named plutonium – another potential nuclear explosive, assuming that theory could predict its properties before it was even observed in the lab.

By the time of Pearl Harbor and the Soviet counter-offensive around Moscow, this situation was known in all the nations that had invested in serious scientific research. In Germany, any project to develop a nuclear explosive would take several years, and it would be a huge challenge to execute under conditions of total war. In 1942 Speer confirmed that assessment and continued the project at a prospecting level. Army and civilian scientists in Germany kept it going as a research programme with an eye to long-term development of reactors; there was no advocate for the German nuclear effort with the crazy ambition of the advocates for the A4. In the USA and Britain, by contrast, spare capacity was imaginable, fear of German progress loomed large, and the time horizon for war-changing weapons was longer. Roosevelt authorized the Manhattan Project, and Churchill coordinated the Anglo-Canadian Tube Alloys project with it. What unfolded was a high-end R&D effort that stretched from fundamental nuclear physics to detonators to shock waves, and in the same breath a gargantuan undertaking spread across the North American continent to produce critical masses of fissionable materials. In a big gamble, the Manhattan Project tackled two routes to a bomb simultaneously. On the uranium path, one of several frontrunner methods to pick out the best isotope for a weapon was scaled up to be housed in the largest building on earth. The plutonium path went through building the world's first nuclear reactors, then chemically picking through the radioactive detritus to separate an element that had never existed in isolated form on earth. The US Army Corps of Engineers under Brigadier General Leslie Groves, the all-encompassing materials priorities system, and the strength and reach of the industrial contractors (such as Westinghouse, Stone & Webster and DuPont) were coupled into the network of scientists who had built up the OSRD and their working relationships with colleagues in Britain. The administration of the Los Alamos weapons design laboratory was contracted to the University of California, and its leadership was entrusted to the Berkeley theoretical physicist J. Robert Oppenheimer.[21]

21 Lillian Hoddeson, Paul W. Henriksen, Roger A. Meade and Catherine Westfall, *Critical Assembly: A Technical History of Los Alamos during the Oppenheimer Years, 1943–1945* (Cambridge University Press, 1993); Kai Bird and Martin J. Sherwin, *American Prometheus: The Triumph and Tragedy of J. Robert Oppenheimer* (New York: Alfred A. Knopf, 2005).

In late 1944, intelligence showed there was no threat of a German nuclear weapon. By that time, however, the Manhattan Project had made it past key technical hurdles. With the war in Europe winding toward its end, options for demonstrating the bomb on Germany evaporated. It was the Trinity test of 16 July 1945, secretly staged in the New Mexico desert, that showed that the project would in fact pan out. A sphere of less than 10 kg of plutonium was detonated with the force of an 18,000 ton cache of TNT. The main purpose of Trinity was to test how the plutonium implosion design and the detonation mechanism worked. On 6 August, the USA exploded the first uranium weapon, untested, over the Japanese city of Hiroshima – one bomber, one bomb, 13 kilotons of conventional explosives' equivalent. On 9 August, Nagasaki was the target of a plutonium device that yielded 21 kilotons. The immediate death toll of the two attacks was 100,000. Japan surrendered on 14 August.

Nuclear weapons overshadowed every other wartime scientific-technical development. Their proximity to VJ Day almost guaranteed that effect. But the bomb came very close to being a failure. With a few months' advance in the war, or a few months' delay in the technology, the Manhattan Project would have delivered no weapon at all. In this first pass at development, the hard aspects of making the bomb were managing the explosive process, designing the detonator, and building the entirely new industrial processes that delivered the fissile material. Once those were demonstrated, the way forward was clear; it was a matter of putting the resources in place. That is, there was no great secret around designing nuclear weapons. Thus as soon as Stalin heard of the American proof of concept in mid-summer, he put the Soviet nuclear project on a fast ramp-up. Espionage helped, but it was by no means decisive. And what made the atomic bomb a usable weapon in August 1945 was the simple delivery system – no guidance system, no aerodynamics, just drop it from a plane. In 1945 nuclear weapons were no more mature a technology than jet engines or the V-2. But the surrounding package was simpler. Success in wartime depends on staging and time.

Conclusion

In focusing on a small number of examples, this chapter has skipped past other arenas. Operations research, encryption and code-breaking, sonar, weather prediction, pest control, plant breeding, social science – the experience of fighting the Second World War was broadly shaped by the uses of new knowledge. What mattered as much as the domains where R&D was put to work was the vision and the practice of integrating it. Both vision and practice carried forward into the post-war world. After 1945 scientists were reimagined as the leading figures in a new mode of warfare, continuing hard-earned relationships and ways of getting things done.

That continuity was explicit, obviously, in the victorious powers, where wartime R&D leaders became post-war policy-makers and government advisors. The same was true in more subtle ways. Even if IG Farben's leaders were tried for war crimes in Nuremberg, its chemists were put back to work. Iconically, Wernher von Braun's V-2 team was reassembled in the USA, along with his rockets, becoming the technical core of the American space programme. German specialists ended up in the Soviet Union working on ICBMs or nuclear weapons, while others were welcomed in smaller countries that were looking to upgrade their capacity. Domestically, the global leitmotiv of the post-Second World War decades was massive state investment in scientific and technical training. Researchers were the civilian reserve force for the conflicts of the future, ready to be redeployed as needs should require. It is not an accident that the post-war decades were equally the high-water mark of the idea of pure science. Trained in basic research, scientists could be remobilized on short notice. Along with industrial capacity, human resources were central to planning for scientized war. They allowed R&D systems to spin up new innovations quickly and get them out to deployment to fit the rapid dynamic of measure/counter-measure warfare. Post-Second World War science was an arena of standing reserves.

In this respect, Second World War research crystallized a societal configuration that had been forming since the second industrial revolution. Knowledge and its bearers were understood as the key agents of change in the new social order. The theorists of knowledge economies were looking at post-1945 America, which meant they were observing that setting where the fullest effects of wartime R&D mobilization carried forward into the post-war order.[22]

22 Fritz Machlup, *The Production and Distribution of Knowledge in the United States* (Princeton University Press, 1962), ch. 5; Peter Drucker, *The Age of Discontinuity: Guidelines to Our Changing Society* (New York: Harper & Row, 1969), ch. 12.

8

Environments, states and societies at war

CHRIS PEARSON

In November 1943 John Adams, a British schoolteacher and *Guardian* newspaper country diarist, observed that 'war has invaded our woods. Carts and tractors, woodmen and land girls are busy among rides that echo with the "din of hewing axes, crashing trees".' But Adams did not lament this transformation of his local woodlands, even if 'one is sorry to see the older and bigger trees go'. Instead, he portrayed the felling as a necessary and efficient operation, commenting on how 'each onlooker finds pleasure in a different aspect of the scene – the hum of the circular saw, a sound as nostalgic as that of a threshing machine, a new view suddenly opening up before his eyes, or merely the sense of good work well done'.[1] Whether expressing a patriotic sense of duty or simply indifferent to the fate of the woods' numerous recently planted pines, Adams integrated the felling unproblematically into the British countryside's traditions, as well as its recent cultural history through quoting the poetry of Matthew Arnold. However, the felling of trees during the Second World War was often a far more fraught activity. For the 'invasion' of Adams's local woods was merely one tiny incident in the extensive history of wartime felling.

This chapter outlines various aspects of the war's environmental history through a focus on the relationship between militarized states, societies and environments during this period of totalizing warfare. Much has been written on the intricate and multiple relationships between 'total war', states and societies in the modern age and the concept of 'total war' requires careful handling, especially as there is no consensus on its definition. According to one of its leading scholars, Roger Chickering, the term is all too easily deployed as

---

1 John Adams, 'Invading the Woods', in Martin Wainwright, ed., *The Guardian Book of Wartime Country Diaries* (London: Guardian Books, 2007), 188.

part of a master narrative that leads inevitably to the gas chambers of Auschwitz and the atomic bombing of Japanese cities in 1945.[2] It is also debatable if the state of total war has ever been reached, given that all wars have known restraints and that no war has, as yet, implicated everyone and everything on the planet.[3] Given these concerns, this chapter deploys the term 'totalizing war' which places more emphasis on war's expanding reach as a process than as a destination point.[4]

Beyond acknowledging the importance of terrain during military operations, historians of totalizing war have rarely considered environmental factors. Furthermore, although research into war's environmental history has laid bare the complex environmental dimensions of warfare, few attempts have been made to consider the relationship between the Second World War's environmental history and totalizing war.[5] This chapter argues that paying attention to the environment creates a fuller understanding of totalizing war between 1939 and 1945. It argues that paying attention to the war's environmental history corroborates many aspects of totalizing warfare that historians have identified: the blurring of military and civilian spheres; the important role of technology; and the mass mobilization of resources. But more significantly, the environment made totalizing warfare possible between 1939 and 1945. States, militaries and societies were only able to sustain the conflict through an active and often problematic engagement with the environment.

The Second World War was profoundly environmental. From the deserts of North Africa to the jungles of Burma, and from the fields of France to the steppes of the USSR, soldiers fought in, through and against the environment, seeking to turn topography, vegetation cover and other environmental features to their advantage. But this chapter does not attend to the environmental dimensions of battlefields, nor the environmental destruction wrought by bombs, bullets and other weapons. Instead, it focuses on the

---

2 Roger Chickering, 'Total War: The Use and Abuse of a Concept', in Manfred F. Boemeke, Roger Chickering and Stig Förster, eds., *Anticipating Total War: The German and American Experiences, 1871–1914* (Cambridge University Press, 1999), pp. 13–38.

3 Jeremy Black, *The Age of Total War, 1860–1945* (Westport, Conn. and London: Praeger, 2006), 4.

4 On modern war's 'totalizing logic', see John Horne, 'Introduction: Mobilizing for "Total War", 1914–1918', in John Horne, ed., *State, Society and Mobilization in Europe during the First World War* (Cambridge University Press, 1997), pp. 1–18 (p. 3).

5 Chapter 6 of Edmund P. Russell's *War and Nature: Fighting Humans and Insects with Chemicals from World War I to Silent Spring* (Cambridge University Press, 2001) is an important exception.

relationship between states, societies and the environment away from the battlefield. At a time of totalizing warfare, the boundaries between state and society and civilian and military became blurred. Therefore, wartime societal uses of nature war cannot be analysed separately from governmental and military mobilizations of the environment. Sustaining the conflict required a massive mobilization of natural resources on the home front and modified, to greater and lesser extents, human–animal relations. It also led to the militarization of civilian environments for training purposes. In these ways, totalizing warfare modified the relationship between people and their environments on multiple scales: individual, local, national and global. But numerous individuals, communities and state officials did not always accept the militarization of the environment. Instead, they attempted to limit the war's impact on valued landscapes, celebrated animal species and natural resources.

As the environmental history of the Second World War is still in its infancy, my choice of examples has been somewhat constrained. Nonetheless, this chapter still manages to cover Britain, Fiji, France, the USA, Germany, Finland and Japan, among other countries. Due to space constraints, it focuses on rural rather than urban environments and does not consider food production, which is the focus of another chapter in this volume. Despite these limitations and caveats, the environment emerges as an integral part of the history of totalizing warfare between 1939 and 1945.

War and natural resources

Technology played a key role in the war and the production of planes, tanks and other weaponry necessitated raw materials. The search for, and extraction of, natural resources was therefore a constant feature of the war, even if its intensity varied chronologically and geographically. The example of aluminium production demonstrates how military and technology objectives led to significant state and commercial mobilizations of natural resources, entailing profound environmental modifications. As Allied and Axis powers boosted aircraft production, aluminium become a sought-after commodity. Strategic and other considerations drove Allied governments to source bauxite from Alcan, a Canadian company, which oversaw mining operations in British Guiana. Once extracted from the earth, the bauxite was shipped to Canada where it was smelted in vast complexes powered by hydroelectricity. Factories in Britain, Australia, Canada and the USA then turned the aluminium into parts for planes and ships. This militarized aluminium commodity chain stretched across the globe and created considerable environmental impacts, such as razed forests, polluted rivers and the release of polynuclear aromatic hydrocarbons into the air during the smelting process.[6] The history of aluminium production demonstrates the interconnected character of economic, technological and environmental processes, the blurring of civilian and military spheres, and the global dimensions of the war's environmental history. It also underscores the significant environmental effects of totalizing warfare, even if environmental concerns were of little concern to officials charged with securing the resources needed to sustain the war effort.

Despite the creation of new networks designed to extract key resources from the earth, most, if not all, belligerent nations experienced resources scarcities. Did these scarcities lead to a more sustainable (in today's parlance) use of resources? The British government played a more active role than it had in the First World War, encouraging local authorities to collect reusable materials, such as metals and paper, and creating a salvage department within the Ministry of Supply. When local authorities failed to heed the call with the necessary vigour, the government compelled them to collect salvage from 1941 onwards. Government and voluntary organizations, such as the Women's Voluntary Service (WVS), launched propaganda campaigns to encourage households to salvage. Failing to reuse and recycle was dubbed unpatriotic and an affront to the war effort.[7] Similar efforts occurred elsewhere. Case studies of individual cities, such as Turku in Finland, show how residents took part enthusiastically in salvage and reuse campaigns to support the war effort.[8] William Tsutsui even suggests that 'acute scarcity in wartime Japan could give rise to a kind of environmental consciousness and conservation sensibility born of want'.[9] While research is currently fragmentary, it seems that in certain places war did not become the 'carnival of waste' that some feared.[10]

---

6 Mathew Evenden, 'Aluminium, Commodity Chains, and the Environmental History of the Second World War', *Environmental History* 16 (2011), 69–93.

7 Tim Cooper, 'Challenging the "Refuse Revolution": War, Waste and the Rediscovery of Recycling, 1900–50', *Historical Research* 81 (2007), 710–31 (pp. 716–18, 729).

8 Rauno Lahtinen and Timo Vuorisalo, '"It's war and everyone can do as they please!": An Environmental History of a Finnish City in Wartime', *Environmental History* 9 (2004), 679–700 (p. 691).

9 William M. Tsutsui, 'Landscapes in the Dark Valley: Toward an Environmental History of Wartime Japan', *Environmental History* 8 (2003), 294–311 (p. 304).

10 Henry Baldwin Ward, 'Warfare and Natural Resources', *Science* 92:2544 (1 October 1943), p. 290.

But did scarcity and austerity make war an 'ecological alternative to peace' as Simo Laakkonen has suggested?[11] More research and reflection on how to define and measure the ecological footprints of war and peace would be needed before any definitive answer could be given. But it seems clear that totalizing warfare was hardly 'environmentally friendly'. Civilian consumption of resources may have fallen, except in the USA, but that was because production and consumption were orientated toward the military.[12] Energy resources were also directed toward the war effort. In Britain, coal output decreased from 231 million tons in 1939 to 183 million tons in 1945. But electricity generation actually increased as supplying power to war industries outweighed any savings made from reductions in domestic civilian consumption.[13] Moreover, interest and participation in recycling schemes quickly evaporated after the war,[14] and the intensive methods of resource extraction that were developed during the war led, in part, to increased post-war consumerism, wiping out any environmental gains ushered in by wartime austerity.[15] It is therefore hard to treat the war as an environmental breathing space. The opposite seems more likely, especially when we take into account the wartime over-exploitation of forests.

Mobilizing forest resources

Many iconic images of the Second World War, such as that of the atomic bomb, present the conflict as a modern war marked by human mastery and fear of technology. Yet some of the modern weaponry relied on 'old' resources and technology: the British Royal Air Force's Mosquito plane boasted balsa-plywood fuselage and wings made from Stika spruce and Douglas fir.[16] As the Mosquito plane demonstrates, militaries continued to rely on wood to wage war, as they have done for centuries.[17] Between

11 Simo Laakkonen, 'War: An Ecological Alternative to Peace? Indirect Impacts of World War II on the Finnish Environment', in Richard P. Tucker and Edmund P. Russell, eds., *Natural Enemy, Natural Ally: Toward an Environmental History of Warfare* (Corvallis: Oregon State University Press, 2004), pp. 175–94 (pp. 187–9).

12 Stephen Broadberry and Peter Howlett, 'Blood, Sweat, and Tears: British Mobilization for World War II', in Roger Chickering, Stig Förster, and Bernd Greiner, *A World at Total War: Global Conflict and the Politics of Destruction* (Cambridge University Press, 2005), pp. 157–76 (pp. 158, 162–3).

13 Ibid., pp. 159–63.

14 Cooper, 'Challenging the "Refuse Revolution"', p. 728.

15 Laakkonen, 'War: An Ecological Alternative to Peace', p. 190.

16 Richard Tucker, 'The World Wars and the Globalization of Timber Cutting', in Tucker and Russell, eds., *Natural Enemy, Natural Ally*, pp. 110–41 (p. 126).

17 John R. McNeill, 'Woods and Warfare in World History', *Environmental History* 9 (2004), 388–410.

1939 and 1945 wood was used for a variety of purposes, from building barracks in Fiji to fuelling saunas on Finnish front lines.[18] There was much truth in a French forester's claim in 1942 that war had ushered in the 'age of wood'.[19]

In an era of totalizing warfare, governments and military commanders sought to tighten their control over forest resources. During the 1930s, Nazi Germany put in place plans to secure timber and other forest products, anticipating a repeat of the Allied timber blockade imposed during the First World War. Wood therefore became one of the many resources extracted from Nazi-occupied Europe.[20] Post-war French reports estimated that German occupation forces had purloined over 26 million cubic metres of construction- and industry-grade timber, in addition to the extraction of firewood to keep troops warm.[21]

If Nazi Germany was able to sate its timber needs by reaching beyond national borders, its Axis partner Japan was forced to fall back on its own resources. No longer able to import timber from mainland Asia and North America, Japan still desperately needed wood for its mining industry, rebuilding bombed-out cities and meeting civilian fuel needs. The Japanese government therefore ordered clear-cutting in old growth forests meaning that the war proved disastrous for Japan's forests: 15 per cent (or 14,000 square miles) of Japanese forests were logged between 1941 and 1945. Not only were whole forests razed, but clear-cutting encouraged the spread of pine bark beetles and increased the risk of erosion and landslides.[22] The fate of Japanese forests provides a clear example of the profound environmental repercussions of totalizing warfare. But the over-exploitation of Japanese forests was still not enough to feed the Japanese war machine. After occupying the Philippines in May 1942 Japan exploited its forests. It placed sawmills under the control of the Philippine Lumber Control Union and made all operators sell to holding companies which directed wood to Japanese armed forces.[23]

---

18 Judith A. Bennett, 'War, Emergency and the Environment: Fiji, 1939–1946', *Environment and History* 7 (2001), 255–87 (p. 268); Laakkonen, 'War: An Ecological Alternative to Peace?, p. 179.
19 René Diderjean, 'Il faut reboiser', *Le Bois*, 25 January 1942, p. 1.
20 Tucker, 'World Wars', p. 123.
21 Chris Pearson, *Scarred Landscapes: War and Nature in Vichy France* (Basingstoke: Palgrave Macmillan, 2008), p. 55.
22 Tsutsui, 'Landscapes in the Dark Valley', pp. 299–301.
23 Greg Bankoff, 'Wood for War: The Legacy of Human Conflict on the Forests of the Philippines, 1565–1946', in Charles E. Closmann, ed., *War and the Environment: Military Destruction in the Modern Age* (College Station, Tex.: Texas A&M University Press, 2009), pp. 32–48 (pp. 41–2).

Allied countries also sought to maximize their timber resources. During the 'Phoney War' the French government passed a decree that made owners of forests over 10 hectares declare the future possibilities for timber production and when they would be realized. Efforts to increase forestry production intensified further after the fall of France in June 1940 as the cost of German occupation and restrictions on imports turned wood into a vital resource.[24] British timber supplies, meanwhile, were threatened when its peacetime timber supply route from Scandinavia was cut off after the German invasion of Norway. In response, the Timber Commission increased the rate of felling within Britain and succeeded in increasing production eightfold in comparison with pre-war levels, aided by the arrival of American foresters in 1942.[25] But the felling was not done to everyone's satisfaction. In stark contrast to John Adams, one *Guardian* country diarist complained that the Scouts drafted in by the Home Timber Production Department to remove dead trees engaged in 'indiscriminate hacking and chopping of young silver birches on the slopes of "my" valley'.[26] Even in the midst of totalizing warfare, observers bemoaned the war-induced destruction, as they saw it, of their local environment.

As with aluminium production, wartime timber commodity chains stretched across the globe. Britain drew on the timber resources of its colonies located far away from combat zones. The Forest Departments and logging companies of Nigeria and the Gold Coast stepped up production of mahogany and supplied firewood, charcoal and other forest products. As mahogany supplies became depleted, foresters experimented with new hardwood species and opened up new sites of exploitation.[27] The British appetite for wood also stretched across the Atlantic. A Timber Control official arrived in Vancouver to explore ways of increasing spruce felling along the Pacific coast and logging operations there supplied wood for Mosquito planes.[28]

The USA similarly sought forest products to build barracks, boats, planes and packaging crates. The Lumber Division of the War Production Board therefore sought to boost production and introduced a variety of measures, including working in partnership with private companies, to replant forests in the northwest. Even though the war effort in the USA did not reach the intensity of other countries, the demands of warfare transformed, to an

---

24 Pearson, *Scarred Landscapes*, p. 47.
25 Tucker, 'World Wars', p. 125.
26 'Send for the Scouts', in Wainwright, ed., *Wartime Country Diaries*, p. 186.
27 Tucker, 'World Wars', p. 130.
28 Ibid., p. 126.

extent, the US timber industry, paving the way for modernized mills and industrial tree plantations.[29]

Given the expense and difficulties of transporting wood in wartime, Allied forces stationed abroad secured timber and forest products locally. Timber production in Fiji increased rapidly in 1942 and 1943 to supply Allied troops with construction-grade timber, poles and firewood. The intensity of demand meant that military authorities bypassed the under-resourced Forestry Department to deal directly with suppliers. Production of wood products reached a peak in 1943 with the production of 3,050,000 cubic feet.[30] Similarly, US and New Zealand troops stationed in the Solomon Islands from 1942 onwards felled trees for military base construction, paying little attention to who owned the trees. In New Guinea, meanwhile, the Australian Imperial Force (AIF) requisitioned civilian sawmills. Military reluctance to release accurate felling figures hindered the compensation of civilians, who also lamented that felling of trees denied them nuts, fruits and other foodstuffs. In the end, the Australian government paid compensation to civilians in New Guinea totalling 4 million Australian pounds. However, neither Allied nor Japanese authorities paid compensation to Solomon Islanders.[31] Like the wartime felling, post-war compensation was uneven, meaning that the war's interconnected environmental and social ramifications were distributed unequally across the Pacific.

As militaries and states mobilized forest resources for construction, scientists experimented with using wood as a replacement material. University of Illinois Professor of Zoology Henry Baldwin Ward marvelled at the inventiveness on display: 'new processes of diverse character use wood to replace metals. At the other extreme wood products are woven into garments for winter clothing or of the delicate character of my lady's sheerest stockings.'[32] German chemists, meanwhile, experimented with turning wood into lubricants, textiles and other replacement products.[33] In France wood and wood charcoal were converted into *gazogène* and used to run cars, however imperfectly.[34] Securing wood for *gazogène* cars contributed to the over-exploitation of French forests. Seeking fuel from the forest also depleted woodlands in

29 Ibid., pp. 127–8.
30 Bennett, 'War, Emergency and the Environment', pp. 267–8.
31 Judith A. Bennett, 'Local Resource Use in the Pacific War with Japan: Logging in Western Melanesia', *War and Society* 21 (2003), 83–118.
32 Ward, 'Warfare and Natural Resources', p. 291.
33 Tucker, 'World Wars', p. 123.
34 Pearson, *Scarred Landscapes*, p. 46.

Japan. In an ecologically costly and labour-intensive bid to produce motor fuel from pine root oil, the government ordered Japanese civilians to strip pine forests bare in 1944 and 1945. Despite producing 70,000 barrels of crude a month, barely any of it was used for fuel as scientists had failed to perfect the necessary techniques.[35] The mobilization of wood resources was both inventive and wasteful.

Alongside state exploitation of wood, civilians relied on forests for everyday essentials, such as keeping warm and cooking food.[36] This 'unofficial' use of the forest is poorly documented and was subject to official and 'expert' condemnation. One French forestry journal noted how 'one remains stupefied that nothing has been done to limit the damage caused by a stupid and ferocious deforestation, to the point where the individual has lost all sense of moderation and even children cut, fell, uproot, and destroy anything that comes to hand'.[37] This view echoed long-standing official condemnation of popular forestry practices and overlooked the state-led over-exploitation of forests. In Japan, meanwhile, civilians extracted firewood from the forest, while farmers removed leaves, undergrowth and other organic matter from the forest floor for use as compost for their fields, thereby depleting forest soils and causing greater erosion.[38] And with food often in short supply, civilians sometimes cleared forest areas to grow crops. For instance, the war led to an increase in slash-and-burn swidden agriculture in the Philippines.[39]

The military, state and civilian extraction of forest resources during the Second World War was extensive. The war's totalizing tendencies intensified production and exacerbated forest depletion from France to Fiji. It also exposed hitherto secluded forests to global markets, expanded, to greater or lesser extents, timber industries through the establishment of new mills and forest roads, and led to new understandings of forestry resources and techniques. For instance, Australian forces surveyed, photographed and mapped forested areas in New Guinea to better facilitate their exploitation.[40] The war was therefore a significant moment in twentieth-century forest history. It modified forest ecology on a global scale and resulted in further state and commercial exploitation of forests in the post-war period. For

---

35 Tsutsui, 'Landscapes in the Dark Valley', p. 300.
36 For the case of Turku in Finland, see Lahtinen and Vuorisalo, '"It's war"', p. 691.
37 Quoted in Pearson, *Scarred Landscapes*, pp. 50–1.
38 Tsutsui, 'Landscapes in the Dark Valley', p. 301.
39 Bankoff, 'Wood for War', p. 42.
40 Bennett, Local Resource Use', pp. 99–100.

instance, totalizing warfare intensified the production of timber based on single-species forests. In this and other ways, it left a profound mark on the world's forests.[41]

Mobilizing animals

Animals were, and are, profoundly integrated within 'human' societies.[42] Like forests, therefore, animals form part of the war–environment relationship. Just as the conditions of totalizing war pushed militaries and civilians to draw heavily on forest resources, so too did they lead to extensive human mobilizations of animals.

Despite the mechanized character of totalizing warfare and the importance of planes, tanks and other technologies, armies still relied on animals, especially horses. In 1939 and 1940, France and Germany both deployed horses to support their combat units. Among its horse-borne units, France had three Spahi brigades and five light cavalry divisions, while two-thirds of its artillery units were drawn by horsepower.[43] On the German side, the majority of infantry units still relied on horses for transportation, despite the technologically advanced image of Blitzkrieg tactics. As horses became exhausted during the rapid German advance through France, German units requisitioned French military and civilian horses. Between 22 June and 30 June 1940 the 218th Infantry Division seized 9,000 French horses and by 1 August 1940, 34,000 requisitioned horses had arrived in Germany from Belgium, Holland and France.[44] Germany also mobilized hundreds of thousands of horses on the Eastern Front. In 1941 the Wehrmacht had 625,000 horses under its control for its invasion of the USSR, using them to pull artillery pieces and other materiel.[45] Japanese authorities similarly mobilized hundreds of thousands of horses, treating them as 'live weapons'. They conscripted hundreds of thousands of horses by issuing green slips to horse owners who were then obliged to relinquish their animals.[46]

41 Tucker, 'World Wars', pp. 135–7. See also Pearson, *Scarred Landscapes*, pp. 135–40 for a case study of France.
42 Harriet Ritvo, 'Animal Planet', *Environmental History* 9:2 (2004), 204–221.
43 Jean Doise and Maurice Vaïsse, *Diplomatie et outil militaire, 1871–1991: Politique étrangère de la France* (Paris: Editions du Seuil, 1992 [1987]), p. 723.
44 R. L. DiNardo, *Mechanized Juggernaut or Military Anachronism? Horses and the German Army of World War II* (Mechanicsberg, PA: Stackpole Books, 2008 [1991]), pp. xiv, 28–30.
45 Ibid., p. 57.
46 Mayumi Itoh, *Japanese Wartime Zoo Policy: The Silent Victims of World War II* (New York: Palgrave Macmillan, 2010), p. 29.

Pigeons too were pressed into service as 'feathered messages'. The British Royal Air Force established a Pigeon Section. Some RAF bomber crews carried pigeons, releasing them to fetch help in the event of their plane being downed. Pigeons were also used to liaise with secret agents and resistance groups in France.[47] The British were not the only ones to exploit the possibilities offered by pigeons: by the end of the war the US Army Pigeon Service reportedly boasted 55,000 birds.[48] In these various ways, animals unwittingly helped sustain totalizing warfare between 1939 and 1945, as they had during the First World War.[49]

Armies used animals to wage war. But one of the war's most profound environmental and social legacies came from militaries treating animals as pests as US armed forces led a sustained campaign against malaria-carrying mosquitoes in the Pacific. Initial malaria control measures were weak. Malaria epidemics and depleted fighting power were the result: in the early stages of the war, malaria caused eight to ten times more casualties among US forces than Japanese troops achieved in battle. In 1943 General Douglas MacArthur took matters in hand, ordering the deployment of malaria control units, the use of prophylactic drugs, such as quinine, and better education for troops. The measures paid off and by June 1944 the malaria rate among troops had dropped by 95 per cent. Within the logic of totalizing warfare, US entomologists developed technologies to annihilate lice and mosquitoes. Aerosol-dispersed insecticides and new louse-control powders relied on pyrethrum sourced from chrysanthemum flowers. But naval blockades prevented their importation. The US Army therefore turned to DDT. Despite concerns about its effect on animal and human health, DDT was easy to produce and an effective killer of lice and mosquitoes. In 1943 it helped wipe out typhus in Naples and the *Reader's Digest* hailed the possibility of 'total victory on the insect front'. Aerial DDT spraying was then introduced in the Pacific. The Chemical Warfare Service and civilian entomologists collaborated on new chemicals and dispersal methods, as some called for the total destruction of the USA's human and insect enemies in the Pacific.[50] Totalizing warfare brought together military and civilian scientists and institutions

47 Marion Benedict Cothren, *Pigeon Heroes: Birds of War and Messengers of Peace* (New York: Coward-McCann, 1944), pp. v, 7–8; Dorothea St. Hill Bourne, *They Also Serve* (London: Winchester Publications, 1948), pp. 201–5.
48 Martin Monestier, *Les animaux-soldats: Histoire militaire des animaux des origines à nos jours* (Paris: Le Cherche Midi, 1996), p. 106.
49 Damien Baldin, ed., *La guerre des animaux, 1914–1918* (Peronne: Historial de la Grande Guerre, 2007).
50 Russell, *War and Nature*, pp. 112–64.

to combat human and insect enemies. The war increased human control over nature through technology which then spilled over into peacetime. The use of DDT is one of the war's most profound environmental and social legacies: from the Pacific to Italy, it remade ecosystems and human DNA.[51]

Civilian attempts to control non-human pests on the home front were widespread. Insects and rodents threatened vital national resources, particularly food supplies. Propaganda campaigns in the USA encouraged farmers and the public to kill 'insect saboteurs' (in the words of *Science News Letter*) to maintain food and cotton production.[52] The British government similarly mobilized against rabbits, rats and other rodents that threatened agricultural output. Measures included the Rabbits Order of October 1939 (no. 1493) which empowered County War Agricultural Executive Committees to destroy rabbits deemed to be damaging crops. Scientists joined the fray. The leading light of animal ecology in Britain, C. S. Elton, secured funding from the Agricultural Research Council to allow his Bureau of Animal Population to develop the most effective way of killing rats, rabbits and mice. Rather than piecemeal killing, the Bureau drew on its pre-war research to advocate the total destruction of the targeted pest population over as wide an area as possible. The Bureau recommended that trapping, ferreting and netting should lead the attack against rabbits, followed by gassing to finish off the task. The demands of totalizing warfare also led to new knowledge about Britain's rodents and new policies against them. Having conducted surveys of mouse and rat populations, the Bureau perfected its technique of delivering poisoned bait using a range of experimental methods, including infra-red photography. Elton and others pushed for more effective and closely managed pest control to be extended into peacetime, principally through the Prevention of Damage by Pests Act (1949).[53]

As with DDT, wartime pest control in Britain aimed to use scientific knowledge and new technologies to annihilate whole species with lasting legacies for the post-war period. The range of measures directed against mice and rats also demonstrates that scientists and government officials took rodents' potential threat to the war effort very seriously. Animals were both allies and enemies during the war.

---

51 Marcus Hall, 'World War II and the Axis of Disease: Battling Malaria in Twentieth-Century Italy,' in Closmann, ed., *War and the Environment*, pp. 112–31 (p. 129).
52 Quoted in Russell, *War and Nature*, pp. 110–11.
53 John Sheail, 'Wartime Rodent-Control in England and Wales', in Brian Short, Charles Watkins and John Martin, eds., *The Front Line of Freedom: British Farming in the Second World War* (Exeter: British Agricultural History Society, 2006), pp. 55–66.

Rats and mice threatened food supplies. But other animals provided a valuable source of protein as totalizing war pushed civilians toward animals that were not normally consumed in peacetime. Rabbits occupied an ambiguous position as both pest and foodstuff. In Finland, the consumption of rabbit meat had declined since the First World War. But during the Second World War urban dwellers once again raised rabbits to go into their own pots and to meet black market demand.[54] Across the Atlantic, beef rationing and other meat shortages led to a booming demand for bison meat. For the first time in its history, Custer State Park in South Dakota was unable to fulfil all of its meat orders, leading park authorities to open a new processing plant for bison meat. Bison meat then flooded into New York. After protracted negotiations, Ed Butters from Coldwater, Michigan, succeeded in buying the Pine Ridge herd from the Oglalas Tribal Council. He transported 25,000 pounds of buffalo meat to restaurants in New York in December 1944 alone. A further 20,000 pounds arrived the following month as restaurants, such as the Lexington, served up buffalo stew and steaks.[55] Meanwhile, huge quantities of birds were destroyed in Japan as the Ministry of Agriculture encouraged the Japanese to hunt songbirds to make up for food shortages. Mist-netting and bird-liming officially harvested 7.5 million songbirds a year, although the actual number of birds killed is likely to have been far higher.[56]

Poaching was another way of supplementing wartime diets. With hunting banned by German occupation authorities and food shortages widespread, French civilians poached to supplement their diets. Some Frenchmen recall bagging up to thirty rabbits a day and post-war reports suggest that wartime poaching reduced rabbit and partridge populations.[57] Poaching was primarily a means of survival, but may also have been a form of disobedience against the German occupier and Vichy regime, which had attempted to subsume hunting into its corporatist view of society while repressing poaching.[58] Hunting and poaching became more closely linked with resistance once *maquisards* adopted the language of hunting (they became the hunted) and

---

54 Lahtinen and Vuorisalo, '"It's War"', p. 688.
55 David A. Nesheim, 'Profit, Preservation, and Shifting Definitions of Bison in America', *Environmental History* 17:3 (2012), 560–7.
56 Tsutsui, 'Landscapes in the Dark Valley', p. 302.
57 See François Marcot, 'La forêt sous l'occupation', in Pierre Gresser, André Robert, Claude Royer and François Vion-Delphin, eds., *Les hommes et la forêt en Franche Comté* (Paris: Bonneton, 1990), p. 138.
58 Archives Départementales du Var 1790 W 56, 'Extrait du Journal officiel du 30 juillet 1941: Loi n° 2673 du 28 juin 1941 relative à l'organisation de la chasse'.

poached animals for survival.[59] Poaching therefore furthered political objectives as well as filling stomachs. The extent of poaching in France is hard to
quantify. But it seems clear that it became a survival strategy, as well as a
further demonstration of the war's environmental underpinnings.

Totalizing warfare modified human–animal relations in various other
ways. War disrupted human–animal relations in rural France. Many French
civilians fleeing the German invasion in spring 1940 had no option but to
abandon domestic creatures, including sheep, cows, cats and dogs. Hungry
stray cats and dogs roamed deserted towns and cities searching for food.[60]
Civilians found the sights and sounds of abandoned animals distressing.
Fleeing refugees saw their own fate reflected in that of the abandoned farm
and domestic animals, as dead horses littered the roadsides, unmilked cows
suffered in fields, and pet cats and dogs were left to fend for themselves. As
Andrew Shennan argues, the untended animals 'epitomised the one-
sidedness of the fight [against the German army]; as images of innocent,
vulnerable victims, they reminded the refugees (consciously or uncon-
sciously) of their own helplessness'.[61] Although some soldiers found the
spectacle of abandoned animals disturbing, others feasted off them.[62] In
Japan, meanwhile, government authorities ordered the destruction of
approximately 200 zoo animals, which they portrayed as a threat to public
safety, and ordered pet owners to 'donate' their cats and dogs to provide fur
for military coats.[63] Conversely, some species had a 'good war'. Less fishing
in the Atlantic allowed cod stocks to recover.[64] Similarly, grey wolf populations in the USSR and Europe reportedly rebounded during the war.[65] These
may be isolated examples, but they show the surprising ways in which
totalizing war reconfigured human–animal relations, if only temporarily.

As combat auxiliaries and meat, animals unwittingly helped sustain war
between 1939 and 1945. But as pests and disease carriers, they posed a threat

---

59 Rod Kedward, 'La Résistance et la polyvalence de la chasse', in Jean-Marie Guillon and
Robert Mencherini, eds., *La Résistance et les Européens du Sud* (Paris: L'Harmattan,
1999), pp. 245–55; Jacques Canaud, *Le temps des maquis: De la vie dans les bois à la
reconquête des cités, 1943–1944* (Précy-sous-Thil: Editions de l'Armançon, 2003), p. 99.
60 Martin S. Alexander, 'War and its Bestiality: Animals and Their Fate during the
Fighting in France, 1940', *Rural History* 25 (2014), 101–24.
61 Andrew Shennan, *The Fall of France: 1940* (Harlow: Pearson Education, 2000), p. 8.
62 Alexander, 'War and its Bestiality'.
63 Itoh, *Japanese Wartime Zoo Policy*, p. 30.
64 Mark Kurlansky, *Cod: A Biography of the Fish that Changed the World* (London: Vintage,
1999), pp. 153–8.
65 Susan D. Lanier-Graham, *The Ecology of War: Environmental Impacts of Weaponry and
Warfare* (New York: Walker and Company, 1993), p. 73.

to civilians and soldiers. The relationship between animals and totalizing war was therefore marked by complexities and contradictions. Nonetheless, animals were an important, if often overlooked, aspect of the war.

Wartime environmental militarization

As well as mobilizing animals and natural resources, armies, navies and air forces militarized vast swathes of national territories to train troops and test weapons. This is another often neglected area of the conflict's history. But it is an integral part of its environmental history and yet another instance of totalizing warfare impinging on environments and people's relationships with them. Environmental militarization for training troops and testing weapons affected civilian land uses, such as farming and forestry, as militaries took control of greater expanses of national and overseas territories.

The US military had already opened thirty-two new army and National Guard bases during the First World War. On entering the Second World War it opened even larger bases, driven, in part, by the greater range of weaponry. The array of new installations was diverse but civilian dispossession was a common theme. For instance, military planners set their sights on land in southeastern Indiana, which they described as 'uninhabited'. Sparsely inhabited would have been a better description, as 2,000 inhabitants were moved off their land for the army's establishment of the Jefferson Proving Ground.[66] Although the newly militarized environments were dotted across the USA, including the remote Alaskan islands,[67] many were located in western states where population densities were lower and much of the land was already under federal control (and often next to Native American reservations), allowing it to be militarized more easily.[68] Such sites included the 8,100 hectare chemical weapons plant at Rocky Mountain Arsenal (established in 1942), selected for its size, transport links and inland location which put it safely out of reach of Axis bombers. Financial considerations also came

---

66 David Havlick, 'Militarization, Conservation and US Base Transformations', in Chris Pearson, Peter Coates and Tim Cole, eds., *Militarized Landscapes: From Gettysburg to Salisbury Plain* (London: Continuum, 2010), pp. 113–34 (pp. 114–16).

67 Peter Coates, 'Amchitka, Alaska: Toward the Bio-Biography of an Island', *Environmental History* 1:4 (1996), 20–45 (pp. 29–30).

68 Gregory Hooks and Chad L. Smith, 'The Treadmill of Destruction: National Sacrifice Areas and Native Americans', *American Sociological Review* 69:4 (2004), 558–75 (p. 564). See also David Loomis, *Combat Zoning: Military Land-Use Planning in Nevada* (Reno: University of Nevada Press, 1993), pp. 9–14.

into play: the land was relatively cheap and sparsely populated. Nonetheless, 200 families lost their homes and farming land to the new weapons facility.[69]

But the largest wartime militarized environment in the USA was the White Sands Proving Ground and Fort Bliss complex at 1.2 million hectares.[70] As with conventional and chemical weapons testing sites, it was the sparsely populated and cheap land that drew military planners and nuclear scientists to this area of New Mexico. White Sands played host to the Trinity nuclear bomb test in July 1945, the explosive culmination of the Manhattan Project's brief to develop nuclear weapons. This explosion lit up the sky, eradicated flora and fauna, and generated a radioactive cloud at a rate of 24 kilometres per hour. The cloud scattered radioactive ash across the desert and ranch land, causing blistering and hair loss in 500–600 cows. Monitors also detected radiation in Las Vegas more than 100 miles from the test site.[71] As with subsequent nuclear tests, unpredictable environmental conditions combined with military ignorance and negligence to put humans and environments at risk.[72]

Wartime nuclear environments were not restricted to western states such as Nevada and New Mexico: nuclear waste from the Manhattan Project was stored at a recently militarized site at Model City in New York State. Originally militarized to produce TNT, this site was far smaller and physically very different from desert testing grounds. Some civilians accepted, or at least portrayed, the dispossession of their land as a necessary sacrifice of war. But as was the case elsewhere, the militarization of this corner of New York State had lasting environmental consequences.[73] Nuclear weapons testing and processing were forms of totalizing warfare that spilled out of chronological and geographical boundaries. Even though the army had militarized 22.3 million hectares of national territory by 1945,[74] the environmental and social ramifications of nuclear weapons testing were poorly contained within the militarized environment.

Nuclear scientists may have sought inspiration from walking and relaxing in the natural beauty of the mountains that surrounded the Los Alamos

---

69 Havlick, 'Militarization', p. 116.
70 Ibid., p. 115.
71 Ryan Edgington, 'Fragmented Histories: Science, Environment and Monument Building at the Trinity Site, 1945–1995', in Pearson, Coates and Cole, eds., *Militarized Landscapes*, pp. 189–208 (pp. 190–5).
72 A. Costandina Titus, *Bombs in the Backyard: Atomic Testing and American Politics* (Reno: University of Nevada Press, 2001 [1996]), pp. 11–17.
73 Andrew Jenks, 'Model City USA: The Environmental Cost of Victory in World War II and the Cold War', *Environmental History* 12:3 (2007), 552–77.
74 Havlick, 'Militarization', p. 115.

Manhattan Project site in New Mexico,[75] but their ideas and technologies created lasting environmental and social legacies in the USA, not to mention Nagasaki and Hiroshima, and sparked a political and popular nuclear culture marked by fascination and fear over the human potential to transform and destroy nature and life in all its forms.[76] Scientists opened up other developments in warfare, such as radiological and biological weapons that could target a nation's entire population, industry and agriculture. For retired US Navy Rear Admiral Ellis M. Zacharias writing in 1947, these 'absolute weapons' could wipe out humans and animals on an unprecedented scale. The whole of the world – human and non-human – was now under threat.[77] The plans and projects implemented within the nuclear militarized environments of the western USA during the Second World War seemed, for some, to have sown the seeds for the absolute annihilation of life.

On a smaller scale than their counterparts across the Atlantic, British armed forces militarized swathes of countryside. These included remote sites such as Gruinard Island off the west coast of Scotland where scientists from the Chemical Defence Establishment at Porton Down tested biological weapons on sheep.[78] But the War Office also militarized more populated sites, thereby removing civilians from their homes and land. In 1940 it requisitioned civilian buildings and land on the Epynt in mid-Wales, provoking the fury of Welsh nationalists. One wrote that 'Step by step the Government of England is devouring Wales . . . a foreign government has no right, England no more than Germany, to destroy a nation . . . our farmers must [take a] stand.'[79] Three years later, the War Office demanded the evacuation of Imber village on Salisbury Plain and Tyneham village in Dorset to make way for military training.[80] Militarization was an important vector of change in the British countryside during the Second World War and deserves

75 Mark Fiege, 'The Atomic Scientists, the Sense of Wonder, and the Bomb', *Environmental History* 12:3 (2007), 578–613.
76 Toshihiro Higuchi, 'Atmospheric Nuclear Weapons Testing and the Debate on Risk Knowledge in Cold War America, 1945–1963', in J. R. McNeill and Corinna R. Unger, eds., *Environmental Histories of the Cold War* (Cambridge University Press, 2010), pp. 301–22.
77 Jacob Darwin Hamblin, 'A Global Contamination Zone: Early Cold War Planning for Environmental Warfare', in McNeill and Unger, eds., *Environmental Histories*, pp. 85–114 (pp. 97–9).
78 Ferenc M. Szasz, 'The Impact of World War II on the Land: Gruinard Island, Scotland, and Trinity Site, New Mexico as Case Studies', *Environmental History Review* 19:4 (1995), 15–30.
79 Quoted in Marianna Dudley, *An Environmental History of the UK Defence Estate, 1945 to Present* (London: Bloomsbury, 2012), p. 174.
80 Ibid., pp. 119–20, 139–40.

to take its place alongside the better-known histories of child evacuees, Land Girls and agricultural modernization.[81]

The military's requisition of these lands and its subsequent refusal to return them to civilians after 1945 created tensions in the post-war era. Dispossessed civilians have represented their eviction as an attack on rural traditions, lifestyles and landscapes. Helen Taylor, a former resident of Tyneham, remembered returning to the village and no longer 'hearing the shouts of happy children, the clip-clop of horses' hooves, the voice of men harvesting the fields, or the cries of the auctioneer on the beach selling off the catch of fish. All is quiet and the buildings I describe now live in ruin, and the life I once knew, and the community of which I was once a part, is no more.'[82] The military–civilian disputes at Tyneham, Imber and the Epynt and the drawn-out processes of memorialization that now exist alongside military training are local manifestations of the continuing social costs of environmental militarization during the Second World War.

As well as militarizing land at home, armed forces militarized environments overseas, in countries occupied through invitation or invasion. The establishment of US military bases and other installations across the Pacific Ocean disrupted fragile environments and caused concern among local populations. US military engineers constructed airfield runways out of a readily available local resource: coral. They dredged huge quantities of coral, using 1 million cubic yards to construct a 7,000 feet by 300 feet coral runway in Penrhyn's Motukohiti district in the Cook Islands. This effectively removed an entire islet from civilian use. On Funafuti (Ellice Islands), coral excavation sites became 'fetid swamps', alarming civilians who needed *babai* pits for growing *pulaka* and land for coconuts. To make matters worse, the US government refused to pay compensation in operational zones.[83]

Environmental militarization had an uneven social impact. To accommodate 20,000 US and New Zealand military personnel, the Fijian government requisitioned land from companies, such as the Australian Colonial Sugar Refinery (CSR), native Fijians and Indian cane farmers, compensating for relocation costs and lost crops. Unsurprisingly, the CSR benefited more from the compensation process than semi-literate or illiterate Indian tenant farmers. So too did native Fijian farmers and tenants as the government

---

81 David Matless, *Landscape and Englishness* (London: Reaktion, 1998), pp. 173–200.
82 Quoted in Tim Cole, 'A Picturesque Ruin? Landscapes of Loss at Tyneham and the Epynt', in Pearson, Coates and Cole, eds., *Militarized Landscapes*, pp. 95–110 (p. 98).
83 Judith A. Bennett, *Natives and Exotics: World War II and Environment in the Southern Pacific* (Honolulu: University of Hawai'i Press, 2009), pp. 97–9.

transferred many Indian-owned leases to the Native Lands Trust Board. As well as leading to longer-term changes in land ownership, environmental militarization and the resultant compensation regime profoundly modified Fijians' attitudes toward their land. As Judith A. Bennett argues, 'while reciprocity and compensatory mechanisms were integral to Fijian social relations, the [wartime compensation] law reinforced the notion that everything was a commodity and had a price'.[84]

Fiji's status as a British Crown Colony meant that American and New Zealand armed forces were technically allies. Nonetheless tensions between military authorities and civilians became evident. This picture was repeated elsewhere. Between 1942 and 1945, several hundred thousand personnel of the US 8th Air Force settled in over sixty purpose-built airfields in the East Anglia region of Britain. Militarization challenged cultural representations of the region as unspoilt and pastoral. Some locals resented the environmental changes wrought by militarization, perceiving them as an affront to 'Englishness'. One local farmer wrote to the Home Office to protest against the proposed establishment of a US cemetery on Madingley Hill near Cambridge, arguing that the site 'should be allowed to preserve its typical English character'.[85] Yet some US personnel regretted the impact of militarization on the countryside. One remembered that 'as each new field was invaded by our crushing machines, as each new hedgerow was smashed and uprooted and shattered, as each great oak succumbed before axe and dynamite and bulldozer, we felt a pang. For there is nothing quite as final, quite as levelling, as an aerodrome.'[86] Although such views may have been rarely expressed, they suggest that not all military personnel viewed the environments they transformed in purely instrumental terms.

Environmental militarization also sparked tensions between armed forces and civilians in countries occupied through invasion. For instance, the German army's expansion of the Falaise firing range in Calvados (France) in November 1940 represented a burden for civilian populations. Firing at Falaise meant the evacuation of buildings, the cessation of forestry and farm work, and the abandonment of cultivated land. At a time of food shortages, the removal of fields from civilian use was no small matter: farmers in

---

84 Bennett, 'War, Emergency and the Environment', pp. 258–64, 277–8. Quote on p. 278.
85 Quoted in Sam Edwards, 'Ruins, Relics, and Restoration: The Afterlife of World War Two American Airfields in England, 1945–2005', in Pearson, Coates and Cole, eds., *Militarized Landscapes*, pp. 209–28 (p. 212).
86 Quoted in ibid., p. 211.

Epaney alone lost 225 hectares out of 647 hectares of cultivated land.[87] But following protests from local councils, the Feldkommandant allowed farmers to cultivate their land outside of firing times, although the cultivation of new land was forbidden.[88] There was therefore some room for manoeuvre with military authorities, but not much.

Falaise was just one flashpoint between civilian populations and German military authorities in occupied France. Whether it concerned the establishment of military bases and training grounds, the construction of fortifications, such as the Atlantic Wall, or the flooding of land for defensive purposes, environmental militarization posed numerous problems for civilian populations and authorities.[89]

Environmental militarization was an important facet in the relationship between totalizing warfare and the environment. It sparked tensions between military authorities and civilian populations and between state and society. Moreover, its legacy is still felt today in local places such as Tyneham, and more globally in the continuation of fears over nuclear weapons and fallout.

Wartime nature protection

Totalizing warfare led to the increased exploitation of natural resources, shifts in human–animal relations, and the militarization of vast swathes of national territories. Its environmental impact was profound and far-reaching. But it was not total. Financial, labour and other constraints limited the total mobilization of the environment. For instance, faulty equipment, Allied bombardments, guerrilla attacks and a poorly motivated local workforce hindered Japanese efforts to boost forestry production in the Philippines.[90] Even during a time of totalizing warfare, human power over the environment was not absolute. Wartime nature protection efforts further limited the war's environmental repercussions, even if their overall impact was small.

As well as generating the knowledge that led to the creation of ever more destructive weapons, scientists called for restraints to be placed on the war's

---

87 Archives départementales du Calvados (hereafter ADC) 6 W 1 Préfet de Calvados, 'Champs de tir: Avis très important', 6 December 1940; ADC 6 W 1 'Extrait du registre des délibérations du Conseil municipal (Epaney), Champ de Tir de Falaise', 12 December 1940.

88 ADC 6 W1 Préfet de Calvados to Maire d'Epaney, 31 December 1940.

89 Chris Pearson, *Mobilizing Nature: The Environmental History of War and Militarization in Modern France* (Manchester University Press, 2012), pp. 170–5.

90 Bankoff, 'Wood for War', pp. 41–2.

environmental impact. At a lecture delivered on 13 November 1942 at the annual meeting of the Texas Academy of Science, Henry Baldwin Ward reflected on the relationship between war and natural resources, which he defined as the 'many and varied types of things found in the world about us, the living and non-living materials that nature furnishes in the vast and little understood complex we call the environment'. Although the USA was well-endowed with natural resources, Baldwin argued that the technologies of the 'machine age' and human wastefulness meant that their destruction could be swift: 'totalitarian warfare not only destroys life and scatters the remnants of the people but makes levies on natural resources that provide for their extinction'. Ward recognized that sacrifice must be made in wartime and placed his faith in scientists who would find new and more efficient ways to use resources. But he also argued that the USA needed to win the war without depleting its resources, thereby threatening its future. The nation therefore had to make the conservation of its natural resources 'an absolute essential', by preventing the pollution of its lakes and rivers, among other measures. He called for the conservation of resources as far as war aims allowed. In the longer term, he believed that citizens needed better scientific knowledge and understanding to realize the importance of conserving resources for the future.[91] Ward's lecture was an eloquent expression of wider attempts to protect national parks, nature reserves and ecologically important animal species from totalizing warfare as government officials, scientists and nature protection bodies continued their pre-war efforts to preserve and protect nature in the midst of totalizing warfare.

Officials at the US Fish and Wildlife Service (FWS) tried to save wildfowl from the impact of increased wartime rice farming in California's Sacramento valley.[92] Across the Atlantic, the Société nationale d'acclimatation de France (SNAF) battled to save its nature reserve in the Camargue against the threats of aerial bombing, intensive agriculture and military-induced flooding, while foresters tried to protect France's forests from the worst effects of civilian and military over-exploitation.[93] In Nazi Germany, the Federal Agency for Water and Air Quality continued to combat industrial air pollution and nature

---

91 Ward, 'Warfare and Natural Resources', pp. 289–92.
92 Robert Wilson, 'Birds on the Home Front: Wildlife Conservation in the Western United States during World War II', in Closmann, *War and the Environment*, pp. 132–49 (pp. 137–9).
93 Chris Pearson, 'A "Watery Desert" in Vichy France: The Environmental History of the Camargue Wetlands, 1940–1944', *French Historical Studies* 32 (2009), 479–509; Pearson, *Scarred Landscapes*, pp. 40–67.

conservationists tried to protect culturally and ecologically significant land-scapes from the war economy, emboldened by the 1935 national conservation law which stated that conservation organizations had to approve any project that would change drastically the environment. In one instance, conserva-tionists, joined by tourist associations and the Prussian Minister for Science, protested against a proposed coal-mine near the Porta Westfalica. Despite reduced personnel, the challenges of operating within a war economy and the wider hardships and adversities of war, environmental protection remained a concern in the Third Reich up until the last few months of the war.[94]

To mobilize support, preservationists turned nature protection into a patriotic activity. The British Royal Society for the Protection of Birds promoted birds as patriotic allies in the fight against insects and other pests without which 'there would not be left a scrap of green stuff on these Islands'. Protecting birds went hand-in-hand with protecting agriculture and the RSPCA branded nesters as 'fifth columnists'.[95] The RSPCA's inter-vention underscores how wartime conditions provided a new opportunity to further long-standing institutional objectives and led it to oppose govern-ment policy (such as the call to destroy wood pigeon nests and eggs[96]). The SNAF similarly elevated nature protection to an act of patriotic duty: it would secure France's most important natural sites for the country's future benefit, thereby contributing 'to the restoration of our most beautiful and dear nation'.[97]

How successful were these wartime nature protection efforts? Preserva-tionists notched up some small victories. The FWS managed to create some new refuges in 1944 and 1945; French foresters extracted some concessions from German military authorities; the SNAF succeeded in having its Camar-gue reserve classified as a site of 'artistic, historic, scientific, legendary or picturesque character'; and German preservationists managed to stall the project to dam and divert the Wutach Gorge River in southwest Germany. These were small and marginal events in the war's history. Nonetheless they demonstrate that war economies and totalizing warfare were never 'total'. Furthermore, wartime conditions also ushered in some new ideas and practices in nature protection. FWS officials started to use DDT as an

---

94 Frank Uekötter, *The Green and the Brown: A History of Conservation in Nazi Germany* (Cambridge University Press, 2006), pp, 94, 100.

95 Alan S. Dobson, *The War Effort of the Birds* (London: Royal Society for the Protection of Birds, n.d.), pp. 1–3.

96 Sheail, 'Wartime Rodent-Control', p. 57.

97 Pearson, *Scarred Landscapes*, p. 82.

insecticide on its refuges after 1945.[98] Across the Atlantic, British officials began planning for post-war nature conservation. The Scott Committee's report of 1942 supported the creation of national parks and the greater protection of nature reserves and other naturally significant sites, while ecologists promoted a more scientifically informed management of nature reserves, despite diverging ideas and conflicts of interest, through such publications as the British Ecological Society's 1944 report *Nature Conservation and Nature Reserves*. As John Sheail argues, 'they ensured that nature conservation and nature reserves had a place in the evolving programme for post-war reconstruction'.[99]

But to portray these individuals and groups as heroic defenders of nature against the horrors of industrialized modern warfare would be to misrepresent them. Ward's aim was emphatically not to save nature for nature's sake. He argued that 'conservation must be defined in terms of *human use* and that is in values for present and future needs of man'.[100] French foresters' main concern was to preserve their control and, as they saw it, rational management of France's forestry resources.[101] German nature protection efforts, meanwhile, can be explained by bureaucratic procedures and routine: 'normal environmental protection, or an attempt at such, during abnormal times',[102] or officials' desire to make themselves seem indispensable to avoid being sent to the Eastern Front (they were aided by the fact that the Nazi regime believed that nature protection was a popular issue[103]). Human interests dictated the scope of wartime nature protection.

Conclusion

Although the Second World War did not produce an image of environmental destruction as striking as the 'lunar' landscapes of the Western Front, the environment mattered between 1939 and 1945. Totalizing warfare was sustained through an extensive mobilization of natural resources, such as forests. It disrupted human–animal relations and led to the creation of new militarized environments on the home front, stoking, in places, military–civilian tensions.

---

98 Wilson, 'Birds on the Home Front', p. 143.
99 John Sheail, 'War and the Development of Nature Conservation in Britain', *Journal of Environmental Management* 44 (1995), 267–83. Quote on p. 280.
100 Ward, 'Warfare and Natural Resources', p. 290. Emphasis in original.
101 Pearson, *Scarred Landscapes*, p. 44.
102 Frank Uekötter, 'Total War? Administering Germany's Environment in Two World Wars', in Closmann, ed., *War and the Environment*, pp. 92–111(p. 106).
103 Ibid., pp. 103–6.

But although the environmental ramifications of totalizing warfare were far-reaching, they were never total due to limits on resource extraction and the small yet significant continuation of nature protection activities throughout the war. The Second World War was profoundly environmental as conflict transformed environments and human relationships with them.

Although more research in this area is needed, totalizing warfare's environmental impact formed part of the social experience of the war. Whether recruited into timber-cutting teams, dispossessed from their homes and land to make way for military training, forced to abandon pets and livestock, or concerned about the impact of war on valued local landscapes, experiences of the wartime environment were diverse and at times distressing. But bar ruined villages and homes, such as those found at Tyneham, or isolated memorials, such as the one dedicated to the Trinity test at White Sands Missile Range, the environmental dimensions of the Second World War are rarely visible in the contemporary landscape. Forests have regrown, animal stocks rebuilt, and polluted sites cleaned up (in 1988 the UK Ministry of Defence declared that Gruinard Island was free from anthrax, although some doubts about the island's safety remained[104]). But the entangled environmental and social legacies of totalizing warfare reverberated throughout the post-war era, as seen in tensions over the ongoing militarization of certain environments, such as Imber and Tyneham, the expansion of global forestry markets, widespread concerns over DDT, and the cultural and physical fallout from nuclear weapons testing. In these various ways, the complex and intimate relationship between totalizing war and the environment did not end in 1945.

104 Szasz, 'Impact of World War II', pp. 22–3.

PART II

*

THE SOCIAL PRACTICE OF PEOPLES'
WAR, 1939–1945

Introduction to Part II

MICHAEL GEYER AND ADAM TOOZE

What does it take to mobilize entire societies for war? What effect do these mobilizations have? And what might be their significance in a history of modern war or, for that matter, in the history of twentieth-century society? If answers to these questions are hard to find, it is not for a lack of studies. If the battlefields of trench warfare were an alien world for the observers of the First World War, it is 'war society' that appears confounding in the Second World War. And rightly so, because everyday practices of social life, even when and where actual physical violence was remote, were shaped by the destructive potency of war. If the political economy of war suspended and fragmented the mediation of money, the social economy of war was fractured and rearranged by the expenditure of violent destruction and the sheer, social energy it took to generate it. Such expenditure came in many and diverse tokens – call-ups, war work, invalidity, death notices, deportations, flights, hatreds, anxieties and so many more. They affected individuals, groups, populations, localities radically differently; the ways of thinking, talking, listening and envisioning suggests a tremendous variety of apperceptions, so much so that any generalization becomes highly suspect. And yet, taken together they amount to a veritable 'anthropological shock' in the face of the social and emotional expenditure of violent energies that was everywhere the common medium of exchange in peoples' war.[1]

As historians have been working up the social economy of war, they were fazed by a puzzle that they took on rather more reluctantly. It appeared that the Second World War was a crucial moment in a longer transition of local

---

[1] A good example is the work of Joanna Bourke. See Joanna Bourke, *Dismembering the Male: Men's Bodies, Britain and the Great War* (London: Reaktion, 1996), *The Second World War: A People's History* (Oxford University Press, 2001) and *Fear: A Cultural History* (London: Virago, 2006).

and global society.[2] While more tentative than the social history of the Second World War, there are some tantalizing propositions in this regard. Already in the 1960s, Geoffrey Barraclough had pointed out that the 1930s and 1940s stood at the cusp of a demographic revolution in which the global expansion of 'white', Western populations gave way to the dramatic expansion and spread of Asian and African populations.[3] More recently, Adam McKeown pointed to the same two decades when discussing the transformation of global migration.[4] Histories of urbanization are more tentative, but they come to similar conclusion. The 1930s and the 1940s are the tipping point in a global transition from rural to urban life.[5] And there are select studies that suggest that in this context subjectivities and sensibilities changed as well – and not just in Hollywood, but in Russia, China and India and perhaps most dramatically and expressively in Africa and South America.[6] If 1941 is the 'zenith of the Second World War', as the military historian Andreas Hillgruber put it, these studies intimate that the war is the pivot of the reorientation of twentieth-century global society.[7]

Social historians do not easily bend to these kinds of grand narratives. Rather than focusing on the grand vistas of global societal transformation, they concentrate on the terrifying potency of societies, entire peoples, fighting war. They find the grand vistas of transformations and flows too airy.[8] We rather side with the social historians in this volume and single-mindedly focus on the question of society's expenditure on war. The purpose is to demonstrate the extraordinary energies of a people's war. As to the grand narratives of social transformation it must suffice to say that, if indeed the 1930s and 1940s prove to be the pivot of the twentieth century, it would

---

2 The most recent effort in this vein actually focuses on the First World War. David Reynolds, *The Long Shadow: The Legacies of the Great War in the Twentieth Century* (New York: W. W. Norton, 2014).

3 Geoffrey Barraclough, *An Introduction to Contemporary History* (Harmondsworth: Penguin, 1967).

4 Adam McKeown, 'Global Migration, 1846–1940', *Journal of World History* 15:2 (2004), 155–89.

5 Frederick Cooper, *Struggle for the City: Migrant Labor, Capital, and the State in Urban Africa* (Beverly Hills, Calif.: Sage, 1983).

6 Pankaj Mishra, *Temptations of the West: How to Be Modern in India, Pakistan, Tibet, and Beyond* (New York: Farrar, Straus & Giroux, 2006).

7 Andreas Hillgruber, *Der Zenit des Zweiten Weltkrieges, Juli 1941* (Wiesbaden: Franz Steiner, 1977).

8 David A. Bell, 'This Is What Happens When Historians Overuse the Idea of Networks', *New Republic*, 25 October 2013. The review refers to Emily S. Rosenberg, ed., *A World Connecting, 1870–1945* (Cambridge, Mass.: The Belknap Press of Harvard University Press, 2012).

follow that our world is indelibly inscribed by the extreme violence that brought it about. However, in order to demonstrate the latter, we had better turn to the 'shock of violence' (Richard Bessel) first.

This enterprise must begin with the reorientation of the geographic imagination of violence. Strategic and demographic flashpoints of violence do not exactly overlap and, indeed, may even be at variance in the Second World War as Richard Bessel and Yasmin Khan show in their respective essays, focusing on mass death and mass injury on the one hand and on mass displacement on the other. Both stretch the temporal arch of violence backwards and forwards from the late 1930s into the late 1940s and thus reinforce from a wider social and demographic angle the more extended notion of the Second World War that political-military historians have also come to underwrite. As Bessel's and Khan's essays vividly describe, the struggle over the 'world island' (Halford Mackinder) with its European face in Russia and its Asian one in China was the most deleterious conflict of the Second World War. While it is true that some smaller nations like Serbia/ Yugoslavia or Greece may have been hit as hard, if not harder than these very large and populous composite nations, the crucial point is that the violent demographics of the war point away from its geostrategic choke points. Thus, while the European war was lost in Russia at huge demographic cost, it was won in the Atlantic by the maritime powers and their industrial and scientific capacities and while the war in China was fierce and unremitting to a degree that is commonly underestimated, the war against Japan was won in the Pacific. The discrepancy between violent demographics and geostrategy has haunted the Second World War ever since. It was in the extraordinary struggles in Russia and China that the future of the Eurasian Empire was decided. In the First World War the Ottoman Empire and Austria-Hungary collapsed into fragmentation and national partition. But despite internal turmoil stretching back to 1905/11 Russia and China did not break. In India, the mayhem of the violent partition of the North was part of a social struggle that enveloped and ran through the geopolitical confrontation of the Second World War.

Not least, this line of thinking would also help us bring to bear another insight of both Bessel and Khan. With the number of non-combatant deaths far outstripping the number of military casualties world-wide, most dramatically in Eurasia, it would seem advisable to think of the war against non-combatant populations as a distinct feature in a peoples' war rather than as one of the unfortunate side-effects of war. But, perhaps, even this is too conventional, because what we have to face is a wider societal war with its distinct causes across the Eurasian continent, its own characteristics as a violent conflict, and its multiple sites of intersections with the Great War. The 'bloodlands' are but one such site.[9] Much as recent studies of the Cold War have highlighted the proliferation of hot wars, the mass deaths of non-combatants point to another, societal war, whose violent geographies emerged first in the 1920s and whose place in the 'age of extremes' is yet fully to be appreciated.[10]

The last essay in this section on the social practices of people's war, Adam Tooze's discussion of rural mobilization, will return to the issue of violent geographies because rural societies stand at the intersection of the geopolitical and geosocial wars that make up the violent geographies of the Second World War. However, it was the geopolitical war that decided the outcome of the Second World War and in that war the Allies' capacity to mobilize ultimately trumped the cunning of military operation that had given the aggressor nations an initial edge. If everywhere mobilization was 'total', the discrepancies between mobilization efforts are all the more noteworthy. As Jochen Hellbeck describes it, there was a divergence between the mobilization efforts not only of the Axis and the Allies, but between the European allies, Great Britain and the Soviet Union. In his reading, it was morale that was the crucial issue, but morale not as some kind of high of emotional engagement in war by an otherwise passive population, but morale as self-mobilization, mediated to be sure by propaganda, in an existential war that everyone experienced as a war of survival. If Hellbeck emphasizes the power of subjective mobilization of society at large, Rüdiger Hachtmann points to the power of institutions and regimes in reordering class, gender and ethnic relations.

We deal here with mobilization of human labour power for war in the most direct sense as coercive and indeed violent practices of reallocating bodies and space. Whether as subjective experience or as institutional practice, coercion and violence were ever-present, and nowhere were they more in the open than in Japanese and German occupied territories. This extended as Frühstück shows in her horrifying piece on sexuality and sexual violence in the next section to the most intimate spheres of men's and women's bodies. In an immense one-way mobilization of gender hierarchies prevailing across the world, in the course of the war millions of women were trafficked

9 Timothy Snyder, *Bloodlands: Europe between Hitler and Stalin* (New York: Basic Books, 2010).
10 Melvyn P. Leffler and Odd Arne Westad, eds., *The Cambridge History of the Cold War* (3 vols., Cambridge University Press, 2010).

and coerced, above all by the Axis powers, but also by the Soviet army in its invasion of Germany in 1945. But egregious as this violent traffic is, it is but an element in the mobilization of bodies for work that Hachtmann and Hellbeck dissect with great care. Labour is the currency with which wartime mobilization was paid that ultimately decided the outcome of the war. In a decisive twist Geoffrey Cocks then reminds us in his essay – focused in an exemplary fashion on Germany – that this expenditure of war should be taken literally, because it can only be fully understood in a social economy of war. In a chilling aperçu he suggests that in thinking war, we should talk as much of immobilization – by way of mass death, but also mass murder – as we talk of mobilization. By means of this eye-opening literalism, he sets up a frame within which mobilization for violent ends can be connected to its consequences, namely immobilization through mass death. Mobilization reaches its hard limit in the destruction it generates. This is war understood as an energetic social field.

A more overtly political account of the war as social practice is the focus of Tooze's concluding sketch of a transnational agrarian history of the war. He returns to some of the flashpoints of violence and dislocation in the Second World War that Khan and Bessel had identified. As in the First World War, but now on a global scale, it is rural society that bore the brunt of the war. Rural societies also proved to be extraordinarily radical and at the same time the site of extreme violence, as the case of Serbia/Yugoslavia and of China suggests. What emerge starkly in this context are the political questions posed by the totalizing force of people's war. There was, it seemed, a natural affinity between strategies of totalizing mobilization and radical revolutionary politics. For the Maoist peasant guerrillas, Soviet communists and Tito's partisans it was relatively straightforward to think of war as a transformative process, including if necessary the selective reappropriation of invented traditions, as in the Soviet case. Hitler's and Hirohito's regimes were regimes of plunder, pillage and wastage of predominantly agricultural societies in an invented tradition of colonialism and imperial population settlement.

By contrast with such revolutionary strategies of war, the war efforts of the Western Allies, exemplified by Britain, were riven by tensions. So that everything could stay the same, how much did everything have to change? In part what the USA and Britain were struggling for in their mobilization for victory was a political regime that would enable them to manage this profound tension. What they kicked off is a struggle for citizenship and rights, which is where the questions of mobilization blend into those posed in the section on the moral economies of people's wars.

9

Death and survival in the Second World War

RICHARD BESSEL

War is about death, and the Second World War left behind more dead than any other war in human history. Estimates of the number of dead, military and civilian, caused by the war vary, and it is not always clear the extent to which civilian deaths (for example, those due to malnutrition) can be attributed to the war. However, the total probably is in the region of 60 million people, with the great majority of the casualties, both military and civilian, on the Allied side – in large measure of the populations of the USSR and China. (The population of the USSR suffered nearly half of all the dead of the Second World War!) What is more, unlike during the First World War, deaths of civilians during the Second substantially exceeded military deaths – a consequence of bombing, war-related famine and, especially, deliberate campaigns of mass murder. Millions of people lost their lives not as a consequence of military campaigns with military objectives, but as a result of actions the fundamental aim of which was just to kill civilians. Combatants and non-combatants alike were confronted with death on an unprecedented scale. Never before had so many people died violent, unnatural deaths in so short a space of time, and over such a wide geographical space.

Yet, that is only part of the story. While the tens of millions died as a result of the Second World War, most people in the combatant countries – both civilian and military – survived. After the war was over they then had to remake their lives in a world that had been permeated by violent and public death; they had somehow to build what may be described as life after death.

Great expectations

People tend to imagine the future through the lens of the past. Expectations of death in a Second World War were, understandably enough, shaped by the experiences and understandings of the First, at least in Europe. On the eve of the Second World War, fears of mass death were widespread – fears of a repetition of the mass slaughter of the Great War coupled with fears of the effects of aerial bombing. Eric Hobsbawm observed, not long before his death: 'A great many Europeans had the experience of Armageddon in the Great War. The fear of another and very likely more terrible war was all the more real because the Great War had given Europe a set of unprecedented and fear-inducing symbols: the aerial bomb, the tank, the gas mask.'[1] Such anxieties were not limited to the British and the French. Germans too expressed fear of a coming war (for example in May 1935, when the reintroduction of conscription provoked anxiety that war was likely in the near future).[2] The memory of the gas attacks on the Western Front during the 1914–18 conflict, and the conviction that the bomber would always get through and therefore that death from the air would be part and parcel of the war of the future, framed expectations of mass death in what increasingly was regarded as the inevitable next war.

Of course, this is a rather Western European perspective. In Asia war had been raging well before the German attack on Poland in 1939, with Japan having invaded China proper in July 1937; and in Asia the First World War had not provided a shock of mass death as it had in Europe. Yet even in Europe things did not exactly unfold in the ways that people had feared. Many of the anxieties that had been so deeply felt in Britain and France on the eve of the Second World War were not fully realized there – and at least in Britain the anticipation aroused greater fear than the actual danger[3] – while many of the greatest threats to life that materialized during the Second World War were beyond people's imagination before the conflict began. The bombing campaigns, particularly during the second half of the war – campaigns that culminated in the firestorms created in Hamburg and Tokyo and in the atomic bombing of Hiroshima and Nagasaki – were of a scale that had not been technologically possible before 1939, and inhibitions about attacking civilian targets crumbled as the war progressed and the intensity

---

1 Eric Hobsbawm, 'C (for Crisis)', *London Review of Books* 31:15 (6 August 2009), pp. 12–13 (review of Richard Overy, *The Morbid Age: Britain between the Wars* (London: Allen Lane, 2009)) (www.lrb.co.uk/v31/n15/eric-hobsbawm/c-for-crisis).

2 This emerges clearly from the SOPADE 'Deutschland-Bericht' for May 1935, where one informant (from Bavaria) noted that 'All groups and strata, fascists and anti-fascists, are united in the conviction that war is unavoidable.' Another noted that 'almost everyone expects war, and all fear it'. See *Deutschland-Berichte der Sozialdemokratischen Partei Deutschlands (Sopade) 1934–1940* (Salzhausen and Frankfurt am Main: Verlag Petra Nettelbeck, 1980), vol. II (1935), pp. 527–34 (quotations from pp. 530, 531).

3 Joanna Bourke, 'Fear and Anxiety: Writing about Emotion in Modern History', *History Workshop Journal* 55 (Spring 2003), 111–33 (p. 114).

of the bombing increased. Even more shocking, and resulting in many times more deaths, were the campaigns of deliberate mass murder that gave the world a new vocabulary: genocide and Auschwitz. In order to imagine what was to come during the Second World War, contemporaries perhaps should have paid closer attention to what had occurred in Eastern Europe and in Armenia during and immediately after the First.[4]

Death in war

In Europe the Second World War is regarded as having begun with the German invasion of Poland in September 1939. However, by the time war had broken out in Europe, the Japanese and Chinese already had been fighting for more than two years, and huge numbers of people already had met their deaths as a result; indeed, the majority of Chinese military casualties in the war occurred during the period 1937–40.[5] Just in the battle for Shanghai in late 1937 some 270,000 Chinese soldiers were killed and wounded (while the Japanese suffered about 40,000 casualties), and thousands of Chinese civilians were killed as well. While the precise number of those who perished as a result of the Sino-Japanese War between July 1937 and August 1945 probably never will be known, estimates of the total of Chinese dead from that conflict range from something in excess of 10 million (over 3 million of whom were Chinese soldiers) to roughly 20 million.[6] By whatever count, the numbers of Chinese civilians who died in the war with Japan far exceeded those of Chinese military casualties, and together they exceeded the total numbers of German and Japanese war dead put together. Chinese cities in nationalist-held areas were bombed repeatedly by the Japanese; the worst affected, Chongqing, was bombed 268 times during 1939–41, causing the deaths of many thousands of people (including 4,400 in just two days of bombing in May 1939).[7] What is

4 See Donald Bloxham, *The Great Game of Genocide: Imperialism, Nationalism, and the Destruction of the Ottoman Armenians* (Oxford University Press, 2005); Peter Gatrell, *A Whole Empire Walking: Refugees in Russia during World War I* (Bloomington: Indiana University Press, 1999).
5 Lloyd E. Eastman, 'Nationalist China during the Sino-Japanese War, 1939–1945', in John K. Fairbank and Albert Feuerwerker, eds., *The Cambridge History of China*, vol. XIII, part 2: *Republican China, 1912–1949* (Cambridge University Press, 1986), pp. 547–608 (p. 569).
6 Eastman, 'Nationalist China', p. 547, n. 1: Eastman notes that 'precise and reliable figures do not exist', and then provides a range of figures for Chinese deaths in the war: among these are an official nationalist account giving a total of 3,311,419 military and over 8,420,000 non-combat 'casualties', and another estimate that he regards as 'credible' – that of Ho Ping-ti, *Studies on the Population of China, 1368–1953* – of 15–20 million deaths.
7 Eastman, 'Nationalist China', p. 567.

more, the Chinese became the objects of what can only be described as massacres carried out by Japanese forces, most notoriously (and in Chinese collective memory most prominently) in what has become known as the 'Rape of Nanjing' during the weeks that followed the Japanese capture of the former capital of the Republic of China in December 1937.[8] For eight years, the Chinese population suffered at the hands of the Japanese occupiers, and when the Japanese finally were defeated in 1945 they left behind a landscape of physical and human devastation. In Guilin, the provincial capital of Guangxi Province (where roughly 1 million people were killed and wounded during the course of the war), it was said that 'the Japanese burnt everything in Guilin – everything, that is, except the flies'.[9]

It was not only the Japanese who caused huge numbers of Chinese deaths: the Chinese armed forces themselves caused the deaths of hundreds of thousands of their countrymen. In June 1938, in order to halt a Japanese military advance near Kaifeng, the Chinese broke open dikes along the Yellow River; in doing so they succeeded not only in stalling the invaders' progress for months but also in causing the death by drowning of what may have been between 325,000 and 440,000 Chinese.[10] What is more, an enormous number of the Chinese soldiers who died had lost their lives not fighting the Japanese but as a result of the terrible conditions that conscripts had had to endure on the long marches to their units after they had been drafted; according to one rough estimate 'the total number of such recruits who perished en route during the eight years of war was probably well in excess of one million'; others literally starved to death due to the inadequate amounts of food supplied to the conscripts, combined with diseases such as dysentery. Not surprisingly, the terrible conditions were a spur to desertion. Lloyd Eastman has noted of the Chinese army that 'official statistics lead to the conclusion that over eight million men, about one of every two soldiers,

8 See the account in IMTFE [International Military Tribunal Far East] *Judgment* (English translation), Chapter VIII, 'Conventional War Crimes (Atrocities), 1010–1018'. According to the IMTFE Judgment: 'Estimates made at a later date indicate that the total number of civilians and prisoners of war murdered in Nanking and its vicinity during the first six weeks of the Japanese occupation was over 200,000' (f. 1014) (www. ibiblio.org/hyperwar/PTO/IMTFE/IMTFE-8.html). The 200,000 figure is a considerable overestimate; a more sober calculation is that offered by Lloyd Eastman, that 'during seven weeks of savagery, at least 42,000 Chinese were murdered in cold blood, many of them buried alive or set afire with kerosene' and that 'about 20,000 women were raped'. See Eastman, 'Nationalist China', p. 552.
9 Graham Hutchings, 'A Province at War: Guangxi during the Sino-Japanese Conflict, 1937–45', *The China Quarterly* 108 (1986), 652–79 (p. 676).
10 Other estimates are much lower. See Eastman, 'Nationalist China', p. 555.

were unaccounted for and presumably either had deserted or died from other than battle-related causes'.[11] And of the more than 40,000 Chinese sent to work in Japan, about 1,000 died while on board ship to Japan and another 6,000 died while working there in poor conditions.[12]

Although the Chinese comprised the lion's share of those who died as a consequence of Japanese military expansion, they were far from the only ones. Perhaps as many as 100,000 Filipinos (almost all of them civilians) were slaughtered in an orgy of violence and destruction committed by Japanese troops as the Americans were poised to take Manila in late February and the first few days of March 1945. In Vietnam the last year of Japanese occupation, 1944–45, was a time of terrible famine, exacerbated by Japanese policies aimed at feeding Japanese troops first and foremost, famine that claimed the lives of between 1 and 2 million people.[13] Although their country (which had been annexed by Japan in 1910) did not become a site of military confrontation during the Second World War, many thousands of Koreans also were among the war's casualties: millions of Koreans were conscripted to work for the Japanese, either in Korea or, in the case of some 670,000 of them, in Japan itself, and thousands of those sent to work in Japan died in the bombing there during the last year of the war. (It has been estimated that over 10,000 of those who died in the atomic bombings in August 1945 were Korean workers.)[14] Of the Koreans brought to Japan to work, an estimated '60,000 or more' perished.[15] The total number of Korean civilians who died as a result of Japanese labour policies may number in the hundreds of thousands.[16]

Although it is impossible to document the total numbers precisely, it is clear that large numbers of Malayans and Indonesians also died as a consequence of Japanese invasion and occupation between 1942 and 1945. Roughly

---

11 Eastman, 'Nationalist China', pp. 573–5. Quotation from p. 575.

12 Saburō Ienaga, *Japan's Last War: World War II and the Japanese, 1931–1945* (Oxford: Basil Blackwell, 1978), pp. 168–9.

13 See Bùi Minh Dũng, 'Japan's Role in the Vietnamese Starvation of 1944–45', *Modern Asian Studies* 29:3 (1995), 573–618. John Dower notes that 'over a million Vietnamese died in Tonkin and Annam' in the starvation of 1945. See John W. Dower, *War without Mercy: Race and Power in the Pacific War* (New York: Pantheon, 1986), p. 297.

14 Dower, *War without Mercy*, p. 47, notes that 'over 10,000 . . . probably were killed in the atomic bombings of Hiroshima and Nagasaki'.

15 Dower, *War without Mercy*, p. 47. See also Rudolph J. Rummel, *Statistics of Democide: Genocide and Mass Murder since 1900* (Münster: LIT Verlag, 1998), p. 33 (Chapter 3: 'Japan's Savage Military') (http://books.google.co.uk/books?id=LFDWp7O9_dIC&pg=PA30&source=gbs_toc_r&cad=4#v=onepage&q&f=false).

16 Rudolph Rummel offers a very speculative estimate of '270,000 to 810,000' Korean labourers who died. See Rummel, *Statistics of Democide*, p. 33.

one-third of the 75,000 Malayans set to work on the Burma–Siam railway (the 'railroad of death') died, and in Malaya thousands of Chinese residents were killed by the Japanese during the occupation.[17] The number of dead among Indonesians (many of whom also were compelled to build the 'railroad of death') was many times higher: the United Nations subsequently claimed 300,000 deaths among Indonesians forced to work for the Japanese, and when longer-term effects of ill treatment are taken into consideration the number is even higher: in 1947 the United Nations Working Group for Asia and the Far East came to the conclusion that 'the total number who were killed by the Japanese, or who died from hunger, disease and lack of medical attention is estimated at 3,000,000 for Java alone, and 1,000,000 for the Outer Islands'.[18] In addition, it has been estimated that roughly 30,000 of the 130,000 Europeans interned by the Japanese in Indonesia did not survive their detention in the prison camps.

Civilian inhabitants on the island of Singapore also fell victim to Japanese atrocity. In the Sook Ching ('purification through purge') Massacre, between 18 February (three days after the British had capitulated) and 4 March 1942 the Kempeitai (Japanese military police) proceeded to eliminate Singapore residents of Chinese extraction suspected of harbouring anti-Japanese sentiments: Chinese men aged between 18 and 50 were processed through screening centres, and those in categories assumed to be hostile to the Japanese (in some cases having tattoos was sufficient!) were shot or bayoneted. Estimates of the numbers killed range from about 5,000 (the Japanese figure) to over 50,000 (as is assumed in Singapore).[19]

17 Dower, *War without Mercy*, p. 296.
18 Quoted in ibid.
19 In a recent interview, Lee Kuon Yew, the father of modern Singapore and who as an 18-year-old almost was included among the victims of the Massacre, reflected:

> So I was Chinese male, tall and they were going for people like me because this was the centre for the collection of ethnic Chinese donations to Chungking to fight the Japanese. So when they came in, they were out to punish us. So they slaughtered 50,000, well the numbers estimate go up to about 90,000 but I think verifiable numbers would be about 50,000. And just randomly but for a stroke of fortune, I would have been one of them.

Interview of Lee Kuon Yew with Mark Jacobson, *National Geographic Magazine*, 9 March 2009 (www.news.gov.sg/public/sgpc/en/media_releases/agencies/pmo/transcript/T-20091228-1). See also Hayashi Hirofumi, 'The Battle of Singapore, the Massacre of Chinese and Understanding of the Issue in Postwar Japan', *The Asia-Pacific Journal: Japan Focus* (http://japanfocus.org/-Hayashi-Hirofumi/3187); C. M. Turnbull, *A History of Singapore: 1819–1988* (2nd edn, Oxford University Press, 1989), pp. 190–1; Yoji Akashi, 'Japanese Policy towards the Malayan Chinese, 1941–1945', *Journal of Southeast Asian Studies* 1:2 (September 1970), 61–89.

After China, the Asian nation that suffered the greatest number of war deaths was Japan: when deaths among Japanese prisoners of war are added to casualties as a direct result of conflict, Japan lost well over 2 million military personnel. Japanese government figures list military deaths during 1937–45 as 1,740,955, the vast majority of whom died between 1941 and 1945 (with the largest numbers killed in combat with American forces); in addition, at least 300,000 of the 1.3 million Japanese soldiers and civilians who surrendered to Soviet forces in August 1945 remained unaccounted for and presumably died in Soviet captivity after the surrender in Manchuria, Korea and the USSR.[20] The precise number of Japanese civilian deaths is less clear, but lies somewhere between 500,000 and a million, depending upon whether or not one includes post-war deaths of people who were injured in the atomic bombings of Hiroshima and Nagasaki or who succumbed due to the dreadful conditions and food shortages in Japan during the early post-war years. Altogether, at least 2.7 million Japanese, soldiers and civilians died as a result of the war.[21] This amounted to between 3 and 4 per cent of the 1941 Japanese population of 74 million.

While the numbers of people who died in Asia as a consequence of the Second World War were enormous, it was in Europe that war-related deaths were the highest, in both relative and absolute terms. It was European countries that lost the largest numbers of people: the USSR among the Allied powers, Germany among the Axis powers, and Poland among those countries that were conquered and occupied. In absolute terms, the greatest losses, both military and civilian, were those suffered by the population of the Soviet Union: of the roughly 60 million dead that can be attributed to the Second World War, nearly half – probably in the region of 27–28 million – were from the USSR.[22] On the Axis side, nearly two-thirds of the military dead were German, approximately 5.3 million (a figure that includes Austrians and ethnic Germans from annexed territories, from other countries – e.g. in Eastern and Southern Europe and from Alsace-Lorraine – as well as Germans from within the 1937 borders of the Reich).[23] The comparative figures for civilian dead are

20 Dower, *War without Mercy*, pp. 297, 299.
21 John W. Dower, *Embracing Defeat: Japan in the Wake of World War II* (New York: W. W. Norton, 2000), p. 45.
22 Catherine Merridale, 'Death and Memory in Modern Russia', *History Workshop Journal* 42 (1996), 1–18 (p. 6). Some estimates inflate the figure further, to 37 or 40 million. Initial Soviet estimates, however, were in the order of 7 million, in an effort to minimize public knowledge of the damage that had been done.
23 Rüdiger Overmans, *Deutsche militärische Verluste im Zweiten Weltkrieg* (Munich: R. Oldenbourg, 1999), p. 228.

even more unbalanced, due in large measure to the campaigns of genocide and the atrocities committed by German and Japanese occupation forces. Indeed, what may be termed loosely as 'Allied civilians' comprised roughly 58 per cent of all casualties of the Second World War.[24] Of course, the Allied bombing campaigns against Japan and Germany caused hundreds of thousands of civilian deaths. Estimates of German dead as a consequence of the Allied bombing campaigns alone range between 635,000 (for the German Reich within the borders of 1942 – i.e. including Austria, the Sudetenland, annexed Polish territories, etc. – and including refugees killed in the bombing), according to the *Statistisches Bundesamt*, and more recent estimates of about 380,000.[25] In addition both Italy and occupied France were bombed heavily by Allied air forces, causing over 54,000 civilian deaths in France and roughly 80,000 in Italy. Nevertheless, over fourteen times as many 'Allied civilians' as 'Axis civilians' were killed as a consequence of the Second World War.

In Europe the scale of war-related death initially was relatively low, relative at least to the fears that had been so pervasive before war broke out and relative to what soon was to follow. German military losses in 1939 were about 19,000 (15,000 of whom died in September, when the Wehrmacht invaded Poland) and about 83,000 in 1940 (50,000 of whom died in May and June, when the Low Countries and France were invaded).[26] Polish military losses during the 1939 campaign, at roughly 60,000 dead and 140,000 wounded,[27] were considerably higher than the German, but when compared with the scale of death during the next five years these totals appear rather small. Yet the relatively low combat casualties in the early campaigns deceive. The outbreak of war in September 1939 was accompanied almost from the outset by mass murder: within weeks of the German invasion SS units were carrying out massacres of civilians in Poland. The first complete extermination of a Jewish community during the Second World War took place in Ostrów Mazowiecka, a Polish district town to

---

24 Figures taken from www.worldwar2-database.blogspot.co.uk/2010/10/world-war-ii-casualties.html
25 Dietmar Süss, *Tod aus der Luft. Kriegsgesellschaft und Luftkrieg in Deutschland und England* (Munich: Siedler, 2011), pp. 14–15. See also Tony Joel, 'The Dresden Firebombing: Memory and the Politics of Commemorating Destruction' (MS), p. 38, who cites the figure given by the German Federal Office for Statistics (Bundesamt für Statistik) in Wiesbaden of roughly 593,000 German civilians killed as a result of bombing. Another 900,000 were injured.
26 Overmans, *Deutsche militärische Verluste im Zweiten Weltkrieg*, pp. 238–9.
27 Norman Davies, *God's Playground: A History of Poland*, vol. II: *1795 to the Present* (Oxford University Press, 1981), p. 439.

the northeast of Warsaw (and near the demarcation line established with the USSR, to which the majority of the town's Jews had fled) on 11 November 1939, when 364 people were killed – 156 men and 208 women and children.[28] After the Polish military campaign ended, Jews who attempted to cross the demarcation line with Soviet-occupied Poland were shot; German 'self-defence' (*Selbstschutz*) organizations, under the command of police *Einsatzgruppen*, murdered between 20,000 and 30,000 Poles; and from October 1939 onwards, mass shootings of Poles and Jews became common.

That was just the beginning. In 1941 and 1942 the majority of the Jews in German-occupied Europe were murdered. This is not the place to offer an account of the systematic campaign to wipe out Europe's Jewish population – an unparalleled crime that has generated a vast literature. However, three aspects of this crime should be underscored in the context of this chapter. First, the mass murder took place overwhelmingly in Eastern, not Western Europe. That the killing occurred largely in Eastern Europe not only reflected settlement patterns of the overwhelming majority of European Jews but also that it unfolded within the context of a 'war of annihilation' in the east that contributed greatly to the erosion of normative constraints. It was in the east that the extermination camps and the major killing fields were located, and most of the victims who had lived in Western Europe (e.g. in France, Belgium, the Netherlands and in Germany itself) were deported to Eastern Europe where they were murdered (e.g. in the Baltic countries, Poland, Ukraine, Belarus). The first German-occupied countries to be declared 'free of Jews' were Estonia and then Serbia, where the Wehrmacht was directly involved in the mass murder campaign and where the head of the military administration in Serbia, SS-Gruppenführer Harald Turner, could report with satisfaction in August 1942 that the 'Jewish question, just like the gypsy question, [is] completely liquidated'.[29]

Second, although the dominant image of the mass murder of the Jewish population in German-occupied Europe is of the industrialized killing of the

---

28 Klaus-Michael Mallmann, "'... Missgeburten, die nicht auf diese Welt gehören". Die deutsche Ordnungspolizei in Polen', in Klaus-Michael Mallmann and Bogdan Musial, eds., *Genesis des Genozids. Polen 1939–1941* (Darmstadt: Wissenschaftliche Buchgesellschaft, 2004), pp. 71–89 (pp. 78–9); Dieter Pohl, *Die Herrschaft der Wehrmacht. Deutsche Militärverwaltung und einheimische Bevölkerung in der Sowjetunion 1941–1944* (Munich: R. Oldenbourg, 2008), p. 256; Arija Margolis, 'The Town and Vicinity, Raped and Robbed', in Arye Margolis, ed., *Memorial Book of the Community of Ostrów Mazowiecka* (translation of *Sefer ha-zikaron le-kehilat Ostrov-Mazovyetsk*, published in Tel Aviv, 1960), pp. 412–13 (www.jewishgen.orp/Yizkor/ostrow/ost409html).

29 Quoted in Walter Manoschek, *'Serbien ist Judenfrei'. Militärische Besatzungspolitik und Judenvernichtung in Serbien 1941/42* (Munich: R. Oldenbourg, 1993), p. 195.

gas chambers, the majority of those murdered in fact were shot in numerous actions carried out by *Einsatzgruppen*, police units and Eastern European auxiliaries, where typically the Jewish inhabitants of towns and villages were rounded up and marched to killing sites where they were shot and dumped in mass graves. Thus the sites of mass murder were not at all limited to the death camps, but are numbered in their thousands across the blood-soaked landscapes of Eastern Europe.

Third, the perpetrators were by no means only Germans. Many of those who did the shooting actively participated in deadly pogroms in German-occupied Europe, guarded the camps, and operated the machinery of mass death were from the populations of the occupied countries. Anti-Semitic prejudice, hostility to Bolshevism (with which Jews had been identified) and opportunism combined to draw thousands of accomplices into the murder campaigns, and without their collaboration it would have been difficult for the Germans to have been so successful in their awful endeavour.

That the epicentre of the German mass murder campaigns lay in Eastern Europe paralleled the fact that by far the greatest number of the military deaths of Europe's Second World War occurred in the east. The 'war of annihilation' launched by Germany against the USSR in June 1941 led to unparalleled loss of life, provided the context for the mass murder campaigns of the German *Einsatzgruppen* (special 'task forces' of the SS Security Police that operated in occupied territories of the USSR behind the advancing Wehrmacht in 1941 and 1942 and were responsible for the deaths of about 2.2 million people, mostly Jews),[30] and saw some of the most extensive and bloody battles ever fought in the history of warfare. Given the scale of the armies involved and the uncompromising ideological drive behind the military confrontation, it is hardly surprising that, of all the fighting fronts of the Second World War, it was where the forces of Germany and the Soviet Union confronted one another from June 1941 to May 1945 that the greatest numbers of dead were left behind. The totals are enormous. Altogether, the Soviet armed forces lost something in the vicinity of 10 million military personnel – the highest number of military losses suffered by any participant in the Second World War. Among German forces, more than half (nearly 52 per cent) of the 5.3 million military dead lost their lives in the east; over and above this, another roughly 23 per cent died in the fighting during the

---

30 For the estimate of 2.2 million victims, see Helmut Krausnick and Hans-Heinrich Wilhelm, *Die Truppe des Weltanschauungskrieges. Die Einsatzgruppen der Sicherheitspolizei und des SD 1938–1942* (Stuttgart: Deutsche Verlags-Anstalt, 1981), pp. 621–2.

last months of the war of whom about two-thirds fell in combat against the Red Army.[31] These figures surpass even the huge numbers of dead that resulted from the Japanese invasion of China.

Elsewhere, on the Allied side the losses suffered by both the UK and the USA – roughly 450,000 altogether (i.e. both military and civilian) in the case of the UK, and about 405,000 in the case of the USA – were substantial, but seem small in comparison with the enormous losses suffered by the USSR, China and Poland (or, on the Axis side, by Germany and Japan). (Italy occupied a peculiar middle position, having lost roughly 200,000 servicemen as an Axis power and another 100,000 soldiers and partisans fighting on the Allied side.)[32] Williamson Murray and Allan Millett have observed that, 'of all the military establishments that fought World War II, the Red Army was the most dangerous in which to serve, the American armed forces the least. The Wehrmacht occupied the second deadliest position.'[33]

The deaths of citizens of the UK and the USA differed from those among the populations of other major powers not only in that they were smaller (comprising slightly less than 1 per cent of the total population in the case of the UK and less than a third of 1 per cent in the case of the USA). They also differed in that they were overwhelmingly military: over 85 per cent of UK casualties were military (the remaining 67,000 dead largely were victims of the German bombing campaigns), and almost all of the American war dead were members of the armed forces. Consequently, the ways in which the Second World War and the dead of that war have been regarded in the UK and the USA have been rather different than the ways they are remembered elsewhere. The American 'greatest generation', the generation that fought in the Second World War, were soldiers!

Not all military casualties met their deaths on the battlefield or as a direct consequence of combat. Millions died in captivity. Exact figures do not exist, but it has been estimated that altogether roughly 35 million soldiers were taken prisoner during the Second World War and that of these about 5 million died while in captivity.[34] The largest number of these deaths were among the roughly 5.7 million Soviet soldiers captured by the Germans, of

---

31 Overmans, *Deutsche militärische Verluste im Zweiten Weltkrieg*, pp. 264–5.

32 www.worldwar2-database.blogspot.co.uk/2010/10/world-war-ii-casualties.html; Williamson Murray and Allan R. Millett, *A War to Be Won: Fighting the Second World War* (Cambridge, Mass.: Harvard University Press, 2000), p. 558.

33 Murray and Millett, *A War to Be Won*, p. 558.

34 See S. P. MacKenzie, 'The Treatment of Prisoners in World War II', *Journal of Modern History* 66:3 (1994), 487–520 (p. 487).

whom up to 3.3 million died as a result of neglect, deliberate ill-treatment and murderous conduct by their captors. Insufficient food, poor sanitary facilities and lack of medical care led to typhus epidemics in the camps; prisoners unable to work – and this included the wounded – were given rations that in effect condemned them to slow death by starvation; and by September 1941 in some cases mortality rates reached 1 per cent per day.[35] Those captured in the early months after Nazi Germany invaded the USSR in June 1941 had very little chance of surviving the war; by February 1942, according to an official in the German Labour Ministry, of the 3.9 million Soviet soldiers captured thus far only 1.1 million still were alive.

German soldiers who landed in Soviet captivity, the great majority of whom were taken prisoner during the Red Army's offensives during the final months of the war, had rather better chances of survival than did the Soviet soldiers who had been taken prisoner by the Wehrmacht earlier in the war. Nevertheless, the survival chances of those taken prisoner during the final phases of the conflict were not good, and altogether roughly a third of the prisoners taken by the Red Army – at least 1 million out of a total of 3,150,000 – perished.[36] German prisoners who found themselves in captivity in the West after the war were considerably more fortunate than those captured by the Red Army, but many thousands died while in the hands of the Western Allies as well. Although claims about an alleged deliberate 'death camp' policy on the part of the Supreme Headquarters Allied Expeditionary Force (SHAEF) with regard to Wehrmacht prisoners are not supported by evidence, conditions were often poor in the makeshift British and American camps and not all the millions of men who were deposited in them survived. The Americans and British may have been guilty of neglect, but not of deliberate killing.[37] More serious charges might be levelled at the

---

35 Christian Streit, *Keine Kameraden. Die Wehrmacht und die sowjetischen Kriegsgefangenen 1941–1945* (3rd edn, Bonn: Dietz, 1991), pp. 128–37, 244–9; Christian Streit, 'The German Army and the Policies of Genocide', in Gerhard Hirschfeld, ed., *The Policies of Genocide: Jews and Soviet Prisoners of War in Nazi Germany* (London: Allen & Unwin, 1986), pp. 1–14 (pp. 9–10).

36 MacKenzie, 'Treatment of Prisoners', p. 511. The Soviet prisoner-of-war administration officially recorded 2,388,443 German soldiers taken prisoner during the 'Great Patriotic War', but the actual number is almost certainly considerably higher. See Andreas Hilger, 'Deutsche Kriegsgefangene im Wiederaufbau der Sowjetunion. Arbeitsorganisation und -leistung im Licht deutscher und russischer Quellen', in Rüdiger Overmans, ed., *In der Hand des Feindes. Kriegsgefangenschaft von der Antike bis zum Zweiten Weltkrieg* (Cologne: Weimar and Vienna, Böhlau, 1999), pp. 441–60 (p. 444).

37 Richard Bessel, *Germany 1945: From War to Peace* (London: Simon & Schuster, 2009), pp. 200–2.

French, who used German prisoners to clear mines along the Atlantic coast, which led to thousands being injured or killed.[38]

In the Far East as well many soldiers who had been taken prisoner died while in captivity – if indeed they made it that far. (In Nanjing, all captured Chinese soldiers were executed. One Japanese officer, Sasaki Toichi, wrote that before his troops entered Nanjing, 'Prisoners surrendered in droves, several thousand in all. Our enraged troops ignored superior orders and slaughtered one bunch after another. We had suffered heavy casualties in the bitter ten-day fighting. Many of our men had lost good friends. The unit hated the Chinese and there was a feeling of wanting to kill every one of the bastards.')[39] Conditions in Japanese prisoner-of-war camps were notoriously bad. Inadequate food and medical provision, disease and extreme brutality on the part of camp guards – often an expression of the contempt that the Japanese felt for enemy soldiers who surrendered – resulted in high mortality rates: 24.8 per cent of British prisoners and 41.6 per cent of American prisoners died in Japanese hands. On the other side, of the 594,000 Japanese soldiers taken prisoner by Soviet forces during the last days of the war, more than half were unaccounted for as of the 1970s.[40]

Prisoners of war who starved while in captivity comprised only a minority of the people who died for lack of food during the Second World War. The conflict disrupted trading patterns and transport links, caused steep rises in food prices, destroyed food-producing areas, led to the diversion of food resources from civilian populations to the military, and saw the deliberate use of starvation as a weapon of war. Famine was not just a fortuitous act of nature; in some instances it was engineered deliberately – 'war by another means' – and employed to kill large numbers of people.[41] Probably the most terrible man-made famine was that caused by the German blockade of Leningrad – one of the longest and almost certainly the most deadly siege in recorded history. From 8 September 1941 until 27 January 1944, the city largely was cut off from supply. Cannibalism became widespread and social norms disintegrated as Leningraders were confronted with terrible choices – such as that faced by a mother who in November 1941 'suffocated her

---

38 MacKenzie, 'Treatment of Prisoners', p. 503. According to MacKenzie 'even the most conservative estimates put the death toll in French camps alone at over 16,500 in 1945'.
39 MacKenzie, 'Treatment of Prisoners', p. 513. Quotation from Saburō Ienaga, *The Pacific War: World War II and the Japanese, 1931–1945* (Oxford: Basil Blackwell, 1979), p. 186.
40 MacKenzie, 'Treatment of Prisoners', pp. 515–18.
41 Cormac Ó Gráda, *Famine: A Short History* (Princeton University Press, 2009), p. 229.

6-week-old daughter in order to feed her other children'.[42] Altogether, at least 700,000 people, and perhaps as many as 1 million, perished in Leningrad during the siege – 653,000 during the first eleven months – as a result of the Germans' 'racially motivated starvation policy'.[43] Leningrad was not the only city in the occupied territories of the Soviet Union that was subjected to a deliberate policy of starvation; the Ukrainian capital of Kiev too suffered famine engineered by the German occupiers, leading to many thousands of deaths.[44]

The early 1940s generally were a time of famine: in Greece between 1941 and 1943 (where according to Red Cross estimates roughly a quarter of a million people died either directly or indirectly as a consequence of famine),[45] in the Netherlands during the Dutch 'hunger winter' of 1944–45, in East Africa, in Vietnam (Tonkin), in China (Honan), and, perhaps worst of all, in Bengal, in British India, in 1943.[46] It has been estimated that 7.5 million people died of starvation and related diseases in China, India and Vietnam during the second half of the Second World War.[47] Excess mortality due to famine in Bengal alone probably was more than 3 million,[48] in what was described by Archibald Wavell, who had been appointed Governor General

---

42 Nadezhda Cherepenina, 'Assessing the Scale of Famine and Death in the Besieged City', in John Barber and Andrei Dzeniskevich, eds., *Life and Death in Besieged Leningrad, 1941–44* (Basingstoke: Palgrave Macmillan, 2005), pp. 28–70 (p. 38).

43 Jörg Ganzenmüller, *Das belagerte Leningrad 1941 bis 1944. Die Stadt in den Strategien von Angreifern und Verteidigern* (Paderborn: Schöningh, 2005), p. 20; Cherepenina, 'Assessing the Scale of Famine and Death', p. 64; Ganzenmüller speaks of 'around one million dead' of the Leningrad population (p. 1). See also David M. Glantz, *The Battle for Leningrad, 1941–1944* (Lawrence: University Press of Kansas, 2002), p. 547; Johannes Hürter, 'Die Wehrmacht vor Leningrad. Krieg und Besatzungspolitik der 18. Armee im Herbst und Winter 1941/42', *Vierteljahrshefte für Zeitgeschichte* 49 (2001), 377–440; Gerhart Hass, 'Leben, Sterben und Überleben im belagerten Leningrad (1941–1944)', *Zeitschrift für Geschichtswissenschaft* 50:12 (2002), 1080–98.

44 Karel C. Berkhoff, *Harvest of Despair: Life and Death in Ukraine under Nazi Rule* (Cambridge, Mass.: Harvard University Press, 2004), pp. 164–86.

45 Mark Mazower, *Inside Hitler's Greece: The Experience of Occupation, 1941–44* (New Haven: Yale University Press, 1993), p. 41; Violetta Hionidou, *Famine and Death in Occupied Greece, 1914–1944* (Cambridge University Press, 2006), p. 158.

46 See Paul Greenough, *Prosperity and Misery in Modern Bengal: The Famine of 1943–1944* (Oxford University Press, 1982).

47 Lance Brennan, 'Government Famine Relief in Bengal, 1943', *Journal of Asian Studies* 43:3 (1988), 541–66 (p. 541).

48 Sugata Bose, 'Starvation amidst Plenty: The Making of Famine in Bengal, Honan and Tonkin, 1942–45', *Modern Asian Studies* 24:4 (1990), 699–727 (p. 702). Amartya Sen, *Poverty and Famines: An Essay on Entitlement and Deprivation* (Oxford: Clarendon Press, 1981), pp. 196–202, estimates the total dead at 2.7–3.0 million; Greenough, *Prosperity and Misery in Modern Bengal*, pp. 299–309, gives a higher figure of 3.5–3.8 million; Ó Gráda, *Famine*, pp. 159–94.

and Viceroy of India in 1943, as 'one of the greatest disasters that has befallen any people under British rule'.[49]

Death from hunger is, obviously, closely related to death from disease, not least because the widespread malnutrition that accompanied the Second World War left those affected more susceptible to disease. While, as Clara Councell (then a junior statistician with the US Public Health Service) observed in early 1941, 'it is only in comparatively recent wars that more men have been lost from military action than from disease',[50] the numbers of deaths due to disease during the Second World War nevertheless were considerable. The great scourge was typhus. Of the nearly 160,000 Germans who died at Stalingrad between November 1942 and February 1943, an estimated 110,000 fell victim not directly to military action but to disease – in particular typhus – and to hunger.[51] In the winter of 1941–42 there were catastrophic outbreaks of typhus in Russia and Poland; between November 1943 and March 1944 Naples witnessed a typhus epidemic (brought into the city by soldiers coming back from Tunisia and Ukraine); and typhus became rampant in German concentration camps during the last months of the conflict (when conditions deteriorated calamitously as provisioning broke down while the numbers of prisoners greatly increased – most notably in Bergen-Belsen, where some 17,000 prisoners, among them Anne Frank, succumbed to the disease in March 1945) and then surfaced in various places in Germany outside the camps.[52] In Asia large numbers of Japanese soldiers were suffering from illness or injury at the end of the war, and more than 81,000 died as a result before they could return to Japan.[53]

Death due to disease was not just unfortunate collateral damage of war, but also arose from deliberate attempts to infect people, whether through medical experiments or as a weapon of war. During the war in China, the Japanese engaged in experiments with biological and chemical warfare: prisoners were injected with lethal infectious diseases and poisons; rats carrying plague-infested fleas were released into fields; plague-infested materials were dropped by air

49 Quoted in Ó Gráda, *Famine*, p. 189.
50 Clara E. Councell, 'War and Infectious Disease', *Public Health Reports* (1896–1970), 56:12 (21 March 1941), p. 547.
51 Friedrich Hansen, *Biologische Kriegsführung im Dritten Reich* (Frankfurt am Main and New York: Campus Verlag, 1993), p. 115.
52 Paul Julian Weindling, *Epidemics and Genocide in Eastern Europe, 1890–1945* (Oxford University Press, 2000), pp. 255, 271, 298, 393–9. On Belsen, see also H. Lavsky, 'The Day After: Bergen-Belsen from Concentration Camp to the Centre of Jewish Survivors in Germany', *German History* 11(1993), 36–59. On Naples, see Hansen, *Biologische Kriegsführung im Dritten Reich*, p. 110.
53 Dower, *War without Mercy*, p. 298.

over Chinese communities; flasks filled with plague bacteria were lowered into wells and reservoirs and plague-infested fleas were spread over rice and wheat fields, with predictable results. The Japanese also spread anthrax and typhoid, and contaminated water sources in Chekiang province, leading to the deaths of many thousands of Chinese as epidemics took their toll in the region in 1942 and 1943.[54] Nor was Europe untouched by biological warfare, as German forces attempted to precipitate a malaria epidemic in Italy.[55] Their attempt to halt the Allied advance up the Italian peninsula in the autumn of 1943 by flooding the marshes south of Rome and then introducing the larvae of malaria-producing mosquitoes, did not much affect American or British soldiers (who had been given anti-malarial drugs); however, it did affect the Italian civilian population, thousands of whom contracted malaria in 1944 as a result.

Finally, this catalogue of death during the Second World War should not overlook suicide. Among both Germans and Japanese, military collapse in 1945 was accompanied by thousands of people choosing to end their lives (and often the lives of family members as well) rather than face life after defeat. In Germany, the wave of suicides that accompanied defeat was not limited to the erstwhile political leadership, military commanders and func-tionaries (altogether 8 of 41 *Gauleiter*, 7 of 47 higher SS and police leaders, 53 of 554 army generals, 14 of 98 Luftwaffe generals and 11 of 53 admirals killed themselves); it also extended to thousands of less prominent people who took their own lives as Allied forces arrived.[56] In Berlin 3,881 people were recorded as having killed themselves in April 1945 and another 977 in May;[57] in the Pomeranian town of Demmin roughly 5 per cent of the entire population killed themselves in 1945;[58] and in the Sudetenland, where

---

54 Sheldon H. Harris, *Factories of Death: Japanese Biological Warfare 1932–45 and the American Cover-Up* (London and New York: Routledge, 1994), pp. 78–9, 111.

55 Frank Snowden, *The Conquest of Malaria: Italy, 1900–1962* (New Haven: Yale University Press, 2005), p. 186.

56 Klaus-Dietmar Henke, *Die amerikanische Besetzung Deutschlands* (Munich: R. Olden-bourg, 1995), pp. 964–5; Christian Goeschel, 'Suicide at the End of the Third Reich', *Journal of Contemporary History* 41:1 (2006), 153–73 (p. 155); Christian Goeschel, *Suicide in Nazi Germany* (Oxford University Press, 2009), pp. 149–66. See also Richard Bessel, 'Hatred after War: Emotion and the Postwar History of East Germany', *History & Memory* 17:1/2 (2005), 195–216 (pp. 199–203).

57 Goeschel, 'Suicide at the End of the Third Reich', p. 162; Goeschel, *Suicide in Nazi Germany*, p. 160.

58 Mecklenburgisches Landeshauptarchiv Schwerin, Kreistag/Rat des Kreises Demmin, No. 46, ff. 62–4: [Der Landrat] des Kreises Demmin to the Präsident des Landes Mecklenburg-Vorpommern, Abteilung Innere Verwaltung, 'Tätigkeitsbericht', [Dem-min], 21 November 1945. See also Ursula Baumann, *Vom Recht auf den eigenen Tod. Die Geschichte des Suizids vom 18. bis zum 20. Jahrhundert* (Weimar: Böhlau, 2001), pp. 376–8.

Germans faced extreme violence and expulsion after the war, 'whole families would dress up in their Sunday best, surrounded by flowers, crosses, and family albums, and then kill themselves by hanging or poison'.[59] In the Pacific, suicide was even more prominent, as Japanese civilians and soldiers alike were instructed to end their lives rather than surrender. As American forces moved island-by-island across the Pacific toward Japan during 1944 and 1945, many Japanese civilians took their own lives and those of their families, sometimes by using hand grenades distributed for the purpose by Japanese military forces. Probably the most terrible wave of suicides was what took place on Okinawa when the Americans invaded: Japanese military commanders ordered the civilian population to kill themselves rather than submit to the enemy, and by the time the battle for the island was over, some 95,000 Japanese civilians were dead – some due to enemy fire, some killed by Japanese soldiers, friends and family members, and some by their own hand.[60] It was a terrible end to a terrible war.

Death and demography: demographic consequences of mass death in the Second World War

The premature, often violent deaths of roughly 60 million people affected the populations and population structures of many countries for decades after 1945. It scarcely could have been otherwise. This was most apparent in the countries that had suffered the greatest losses. Poland, which had contained a multi-ethnic population of approximately 35 million people when invaded in 1939, held only about 24 million (overwhelmingly Polish) people within its (new) borders after the war ended in 1945. This was the consequence of three things: the shifting of the country westwards (with the result that post-war Poland was 20 per cent smaller than pre-war Poland had been); the deaths due to harsh occupation policies and war-related hardship of something in the region of 2.5 million people; and the mass murder of the Jews, of which Poland was the epicentre and in the course of which 90 per cent of Poland's pre-war Jewish population of about 3 million were killed. Thus the Poland that emerged from the war was very different from the Poland that had been invaded in September 1939.

59 Norman M. Naimark, *Fires of Hatred: Ethnic Cleansing in Twentieth-Century Europe* (Cambridge, Mass.: Harvard University Press, 2001), p. 117.
60 Ienaga, *Japan's Last War*, pp. 198–9; Dower, *War without Mercy*, p. 45.

Germany also emerged from the war a very different place. The loss of roughly 6 million people and the uprooting of about 12 million Germans from their homes east of the Oder–Neisse border, the Sudetenland, and elsewhere across Eastern and Southeastern Europe – had profound effects upon the composition of the German population. In particular, the deaths of so many soldiers (combined with the fact that so many of the survivors were prisoners of war when the war ended) meant that women vastly outnumbered men in post-war Germany (leaving occupation troops out of the equation, of course): in the 'Province of Saxony' (i.e. Saxony-Anhalt, in the Soviet Occupation Zone), for example, at the end of 1945 there were twice as many women as men between the ages of 30 and 40 and three times as many between the ages of 20 and 30.[61] In Japan the 'demography of death' left a similar pattern: whereas in 1940 men outnumbered women between the ages of 20 and 29, in 1947 there were over a million more women than men aged between 20 and 29.[62] In the European portions of the USSR the male–female imbalance probably was even greater. One indication of the extent and effect of the wartime losses is that of the Soviet cohort of males born in 1906 and still alive in 1941 (when the cohort was drafted), nearly a third died in the war.[63] Whereas among Russian women born in 1910 only about 4 per cent were widowed at age 30 (i.e. in 1940), among the cohort born only five years later the comparable figure was 30 per cent (i.e. in 1945).[64] Such population patterns meant that millions of women were unable to find male partners in the post-war world, and either had to raise their children on their own or never had the opportunity to establish their own family; and it meant that millions of children, born in the late 1930s and early 1940s, grew up without fathers (many never having known their fathers at all) – something that affected them for the rest of their lives.[65]

---

61 Bundesarchiv Berlin, DO-I-7, f. 58: Statistisches Landesamt an die Abteilung Polizei, Halle/Saale, 8 October 1946.

62 Dower, *Embracing Defeat*, p. 107.

63 Sheila Fitzpatrick, 'War and Society in Soviet Context: Soviet Labor before, during, and after World War II', *International Labor and Working-Class History* 35 (1989), 37–52 (p. 45).

64 See, for example, trends in the USSR as tabulated by Sergei Scherbov and Harrie van Vianen, 'Marriage and Fertility in Russia of Women Born between 1900 and 1960: A Cohort Analysis', *European Journal of Population / Revue Européenne de Démographie* 17 (2001), 281–94 (p. 287).

65 See, for example, Hermann Schulz, Hartmut Radebold and Jürgen Reulecke, *Söhne ohne Väter. Erfahrungen der Kriegsgeneration* (Berlin: Links, 2004); Barbara Stambolis, *Töchter ohne Väter. Frauen der Kriegsgeneration und ihre lebenslange Sehnsucht* (Stuttgart: Klett-Cotta, 2012); Lu Seegers, 'Vaterlose Kriegskinder in der DDR und Polen', in Jürgen Reulecke, Reinhard Schmook and Jacek Jeremicz, eds., *Kriegskinder in*

Nevertheless, for all the physical and psychological effects that wartime losses had on the cohorts of people born during the first half of the twentieth century, it is at least debatable whether the Second World War significantly affected longer-term demographic trends, in particular the longer-term trend toward declining fertility.[66] For example, according to one examination of women in wartime Japan, 'the overall pattern of the 1940s, regardless of the fluctuations early in the decade, was a continuation of the slightly downward trend evident since World War I'.[67] What is not debatable, however, is that the populations of many countries that suffered significant wartime losses were lower and remained substantially lower after the war than they otherwise would have been – a reflection not just of the wartime losses themselves but also of the deficit of births (i.e. of births that otherwise would have occurred) that the war caused.[68] While underlying demographic patterns probably were not really affected, overall population levels certainly were.

Life after death

Although the Second World War left behind more dead than has any other conflict in human history, the great majority of those who experienced the war survived. Tens of millions of people had lost parents, children, husbands, wives, friends, and would have to live with their loss until they themselves died. Many spent years in uncertainty, not knowing whether the missing were alive or dead, still languishing somewhere in prison camps or having died without their bodies being recovered or identified. For many survivors, the early post-war years were dominated by the search for loved

Ostdeutschland und Polen = Dzieci wojny w Niemczech Wschodnich i w Polsce (Berlin: Verlag für Berlin-Brandenburg, 2008), pp. 72–81; Barbara Stambolis, Leben mit und in der Geschichte. Deutsche Historiker Jahrgang 1943 (Essen: Klartext, 2010), pp. 47–60; Lu Seegers and Jürgen Reulecke, eds., Die 'Generation der Kriegskinder'. Historische Hintergründe und Deutungen (Giessen: Psychosozial-Verlag, 2009).

66 See, for example, trends in the USSR as tabulated by Scherbov and van Vianen, 'Marriage and Fertility in Russia', p. 284.

67 Thomas R. H. Havens, 'Women and War in Japan, 1937–1945', American Historical Review 80:4 (1975), 913–34 (p. 930).

68 For example, it has been estimated for Ukraine that the Second World War and Soviet repression during the 1940s led to a deficit of 4.1 million births as well as a 'loss of 7.4 million due to exceptional mortality'. See Jacques Vallin, France Meslé, Serguei Adamets and Serhii Pyrozhkov, 'A New Estimate of Ukrainian Population Losses during the Crises of the 1930s and 1940s', Population Studies 56:3 (2002), 249–64 (p. 263).

ones whose fate remained unknown.[69] Many more survived with injuries –
physical and psychological – that they would have to bear for the rest of
their lives. (However, the proportion who survived their injuries varied
from region to region, depending to a considerable degree on the available
medical care. While medical provision was relatively good for the Western
armies, meaning that their soldiers had a reasonable chance of surviving
their wounds, this was not necessarily the case elsewhere: chances of
survival were particularly poor in China, where a stomach wound or the
loss of a limb meant almost certain death; consequently, 'few cripples were
seen in wartime China'.)[70]

Memories of the war, and of the war dead, thus formed an important part
of the cultures of the post-war world. The history of the post-war world is a
history of life after death.[71] The death and destruction brought about by the
Second World War were not just evoked in textbooks and commemorative
monuments but also remained present in the consciousness of those who had
experienced the conflict, and the commemoration of death in the Second World
War has remained an important part of the public cultures of the post-war
world and of the post-post-war world. Yet not all war deaths are the same,
and commemorating the deaths of civilians is not the same as commemorating the deaths of soldiers. In the USA, where almost all of the dead of the
Second World War had been members of the armed forces, Americans are
accustomed to describing the cohort who came of age during the Great
Depression of the 1930s and then fought in the Second World War, using the
resonant phrase of the television newscaster Tom Brokaw, as 'the greatest
generation'.[72] Theirs was the generation that fought 'the good war',[73] the
great crusade that would achieve (as Franklin Roosevelt put it in his public

---

69 On this subject, for post-war Germany, see Neil Gregor, '"Is He Alive or Long Since
Dead?" Loss, Absence and Remembrance in Nuremberg, 1945–1956', *German History*
21:2 (2003), 183–203. On the problem in post-war Japan, see Dower, *Embracing Defeat*,
pp. 48–58.

70 Eastman, 'Nationalist China', p. 575.

71 On this theme in Europe, see Richard Bessel and Dirk Schumann, eds., *Life after Death:
Approaches to a Cultural and Social History of Europe during the 1940s and 1950s* (Cambridge
University Press, 2003).

72 Tom Brokaw, *The Greatest Generation* (London: Pimlico, 2002). During the NBC's
television coverage of the ceremonies at the 50th anniversary in 1994 of the D-Day
landings in Normandy, Brokaw stated: 'I think this is the greatest generation any
society has ever produced.' He also spoke at the dedication ceremony for the National
World War II Memorial in Washington in May 2004.

73 Studs Terkel, '*The Good War*': *An Oral History of World War Two* (New York: The New
Press, 1984).

prayer on D-Day) 'a peace that will let all of men live in freedom',[74] and that 'saved the world'.[75] It is the dead of this 'greatest generation' who are commemorated in the USA, most notably with the National World War II Memorial in Washington, DC opened to the public in April 2004. Yet, perhaps strangely for a nation that suffered almost no civilian casualties during the Second World War, the most substantial structure in the American capitol dedicated to the memory of the dead of the Second World War is one whose subject is civilian victims (who were not American citizens): the United States Holocaust Memorial Museum (USHMM), dedicated in 1993 and created 'as a permanent living memorial to the victims'.[76] Central to its mission is to keep alive the memory of the dead, something paralleled by numerous other, smaller memorial museums and commemorative monuments that have been established across the USA and elsewhere, far away from where the killing actually took place.

The same may be said of Yad Vashem (meaning 'everlasting name'), established in 1953 as 'the world center for documentation, research, education and commemoration of the Holocaust' and as 'the Jewish people's living memorial to the Holocaust'.[77] This is Israel's official memorial site for the victims of the campaign to murder the Jews of Europe. Nearby, in Israel's National Military and Police Cemetery in Mount Herzl in Jerusalem, among the graves of Israeli soldiers who have died in wars with the Arabs, are monuments in honour of 'the 200,000 Jewish soldiers who fell in the ranks of the Red Army during the Second World War',[78] and the smaller number of those who died fighting in the Polish army. Heroes and victims of the Second

---

74 Quoted in Paul Fussell, *Wartime: Understanding and Behavior in the Second World War* (Oxford University Press, 1989), p. 167. For the full text of Roosevelt's prayer, see Franklin D. Roosevelt, 'Prayer on D-Day', 6 June 1944: online at Gerhard Peters and John T. Woolley, eds., *The American Presidency Project* (www.presidency.ucsb.edu/ws/?pid=16515).

75 Thus David Jobes, Professor of Psychology at The Catholic University of America in Washington, DC and a clinician at the Washington Psychological Center, quoted in the *Washington Post*, 4 June 2013 (www.washingtonpost.com/local/baby-boomers-are-killing-themselves-at-an-alarming-rate-begging-question-why/2013/06/03/d98acc7a-c4if-11e2-8c3b-0b5e9247e8ca_story_1.html).

76 See www.ushmm.org/remember/days-of-remembrance. The stated mission of the USHMM is: 'to advance and disseminate knowledge about this unprecedented tragedy; to preserve the memory of those who suffered; and to encourage its visitors to reflect upon the moral and spiritual questions raised by the events of the Holocaust as well as their own responsibilities as citizens of a democracy' (www.ushmm.org/information/about-the-museum/mission-statement).

77 www.yadvashem.org/yv/en/about/index.asp.

78 Tom Segev, *The Seventh Million: The Israelis and the Holocaust* (New York: Hill & Wang, 1993), p. 421.

World War, commemorated far from the sites where their deaths occurred, were each important for the construction of the identity of the post-war State of Israel: what happened in German-occupied Europe led to its establishment, and its existence was regarded as a guarantee to prevent a recurrence.[79]

Of course, commemorative sites that served to confirm national or state identity also were developed where the fighting and killing occurred. Perhaps the most striking, and certainly the largest, were monuments erected by the Soviet Union – most notably the gigantic 82 metre tall Motherland Statue ('The Motherland Calls!') at the Mamayev Kurgan overlooking Volgograd and commemorating the Soviet heroes of the Battle of Stalingrad, as well as the huge Soviet memorial in Berlin's Treptow Park dedicated to the 80,000 Red Army soldiers who lost their lives in the Battle for Berlin in the spring of 1945. Across the post-war world commemorative sites were prepared, monuments erected and ceremonies conducted to remember the dead – soldiers who fell in battle, civilians who died in the bombings, victims of atrocities and campaigns of mass murder. Some – as, for example, the memorial site at the Bikernieki Forest on the outskirts of the Latvian capital of Riga – delineate the actual sites of mass murder; some – as, for example, the monument in Singapore's Chinatown to the victims of the Sook Ching Massacre, commemorate victims from a local community who were murdered nearby; some – such as the national monument facing the royal palace in the Dam Square in Amsterdam – commemorate resistance; some – such as the Yasukuni Shrine in Tokyo, commemorating the Japanese who died in the service of Japan at war – remain the subject of controversy; some – most prominently, Germany's Memorial to the Murdered Jews of Europe in the centre of Berlin – stand as a stark reminder of crimes against humanity; some – as for example, the Peace Memorial Park in Hiroshima – commemorate those who died in the bombings; some – perhaps most notably the preserved ruins of Oradour-sur-Glane – stand as silent witness to a community destroyed; and across the world there are cemeteries that contain the remains of tens of thousands of soldiers who fell in battle. After 1945, the landscapes of death in the Second World War gave way to landscapes of commemoration of the dead of the Second World War.

Public commemoration of the dead of the Second World War, whether this meant glorifying heroes or sanctifying victims, coexisted with private memories of the dead. Survivors would remain haunted for decades by the scenes of death they had witnessed – such as the Berliner who, in the late

---

79 Ibid., p. 444.

1970s, spoke of what he had seen after the Reich capitol was bombed on 3 February 1945: 'Burnt, shrunken corpses lay in the streets. [. . .] There stood streetcars ablaze, still full of people who could not get out. In front of the orphanage in the Alte Jakobstrasse piles of burned corpses of babies lay on the street.'[80] For millions of people, the site of memory of death in the Second World War was not a public monument but perhaps a faded photograph on the mantelpiece, or a grave on which flowers were placed. The legacy of war was present not just in public monuments but also in private sorrow. The number of families, of survivors, who had lost relatives, lovers and friends, was in the tens of millions, and the losses caused by the Second World War would be with them for the rest of their lives. The extent of private grief may be judged by the fact that in Germany after the war, half the population had lost at least one family member.[81] In the European portions of the USSR the proportion probably was even greater. Survival did not mean escape from the shadow of death.

At their core, death and memories of the dead are about loss and absence. And in many cases that absence is extreme. Millions of those killed during the Second World War effectively disappeared. Their families were wiped out, their communities obliterated, their lives erased as if they had never been. Omer Bartov has written of the landscapes of Eastern Europe, of the great killing fields of the Second World War, of 'sites of nonmemory' where 'one finds today innumerable sites from which vast chunks of history have been completely erased'.[82] Where there are no survivors, there is no direct memory. Death, mass death, may leave sites of memory and sites of mourning behind, but also can obliterate memory.

Conclusion

What general conclusions can be drawn from a discussion of the dead of the Second World War? First, unlike during the First World War, during the Second World War the majority of the dead were civilians, not soldiers. In this it is the First World War, not the Second, that was an exception. The Second

---

80 Jochen Köhler, *Klettern in der Grossstadt. Geschichten vom Überleben zwischen, 1933–1945* (Berlin: Wagenbach, 1981), pp. 193–4.

81 Bessel, *Germany 1945*, pp. 385–6.

82 Omer Bartov, 'Eastern Europe as the Site of Genocide', *Journal of Modern History* 80:3 (2008), 557–93 (p. 557). See also Omer Bartov, *Erased: Vanishing Traces of Jewish Galicia in Present-Day Ukraine* (Princeton University Press, 2007).

World War was not exceptional due to the high proportion of the dead who were civilians (a consequence partly, but far from wholly, of the campaigns of mass murder in German-occupied Europe), but rather to the huge *total number* of people killed. Nothing like that had happened ever before in human history. Second, the overwhelming majority of the dead – some 85 per cent altogether – were on the Allied side. The countries which lost the largest numbers of people were the USSR and China (whose armed forces together suffered almost 90 per cent of all Allied military deaths), and the German-directed campaigns of mass murder were conducted largely against the populations of Allied countries (e.g. Poland – which of all countries consequently lost probably the highest proportion of its population – the Baltic countries, Yugoslavia, the USSR). This is to say that, overall, the Axis was better at killing their real and imagined enemies than were the Allies (although the Americans, through their overwhelming firepower, inflicted many more casualties on their enemies than their enemies did on them). Third, the majority of the deaths that occurred as a consequence of the Second World War took place in Europe. This was true no less for the Axis than for the Allies: nearly two-thirds of the military dead of Axis forces were of those in the German armed forces. This is to say that the greatest killing fields of the Second World War were in Europe. Finally, in terms of the military casualties (as opposed to the German campaigns of racist mass murder, which reached their peak between 1941 and 1944), the most deadly period of the Second World War was its final year. This was true no less in the Pacific War than in the European War. In the Pacific, according to John Dower, 'by any count, late summer 1944 to late summer 1945 was the killing year', not just for the Japanese, 'who were thrown by their desperate generals and admirals into one hopeless confrontation after another', but also for the Americans, whose losses during this period comprised over half of all American casualties in the Pacific.[83] In Europe the intensity of the fighting during the last months of war may be gauged from the fact that well over half of all German military deaths occurred between June 1944 and May 1945, and that more German soldiers died in the first four months of 1945 than in 1939, 1940, 1941 and 1942 put together.[84] Added to this, the bombing campaigns against both Germany and Japan reached their peak during the final phases of the war, when the Germans and Japanese were largely powerless to prevent Allied bombers from operating at will.

83 Dower, *War without Mercy*, pp. 238–9.
84 Overmans, *Deutsche militärische Verluste im Zweiten Weltkrieg*, pp. 238–9.

When the Second World War ended formally in 1945, large parts of a wartorn world were characterized by what one historian of wartime Germany referred to as the 'omnipresence of death'.[85] As never before, death had become part of everyday life.[86] Never before in human history had so many people died a violent, premature death in so short a period. And never before had so many survivors been left with the ruins of lives in the wake of mass death. This left scarred societies, communities, families and individuals. It would take at least a generation before the scars could begin to heal.

85 Bernd-A. Rusinek, *Gesellschaft in der Katastrophe. Terror, Illegalität, Widerstand – Köln 1944/45* (Essen: Klartext Verlag, 1989), p. 115.
86 For Germany, see Richard Bessel, 'The Shadow of Death in Germany at the End of the Second World War', in Alon Confino, Paul Betts and Dirk Schumann, eds., *Between Mass Death and Individual Loss: The Place of the Dead in Twentieth-Century Germany* (Cambridge University Press, 2008), pp. 51–68.

10

Wars of displacement

Exile and uprooting in the 1940s

YASMIN KHAN

People move at times of war. Violence and the threat of violence cause people to move. Civilians try to escape attack, flee to hinterlands, are persecuted and uprooted or are driven to move in order to avoid economic destitution. This has always been the case through history. But the sheer scale of population displacement during the 1940s was something distinctive and epic. Displacement and the threat of uprooting from old homelands became, for many, the norm rather than the exception. In Europe, some 30 million were on the move, in China 90 million fled from the effects of war. Whole regions became completely repopulated. The role of the state as arbiter and executioner of these plans was unprecedented. It was the intention of Hitler – but not only Hitler – to mastermind a new ethnographic landscape. In many places, from Poland to Pakistan, states and especially their borderlands were engineered or re-engineered to fit with ideas of national homogeneity. This happened over a *longue durée* – and is part of the longer history of the twentieth century's ethnic conflict and creation of nation states, which began with the breaking up of the Ottoman Empire after the First World War and has had legacies in the recent past, most notably in the Balkan Wars. The sheer magnitude of the movement astonished even those who had anticipated some movement. Refugee upheavals interlink with the history of ethnic cleansing and genocide, post-war reconstruction in the wake of global war and the emergence of internationalist ideas about development and international responsibilities toward refugees.

The global 'exchange of population'

People were simply on the move everywhere in the 1940s, trying to find a place of safety far away from violence, trying to find a secure way of life for their families. It's difficult to grasp the dimensions of this phenomenon.

Displacement was internal and cross-border, it was forced and unforced, and it was long- and short-term. It encompassed all the technical and legal categories of people who had moved – 'refugees', 'displaced persons', 'the stateless', 'expellees' and 'evacuees', as well as a great many more who never fell under these systems of categorization or control, who escaped under the radar of state oversight. It was also part of a wider story of death and dislocation during wartime; the long-distance separations of families who did not see their fighting men for many years on end, or the absences which occurred for even settled people who did not move, but lost neighbours or saw their communities completely ravished by the high mortality rates of the 1940s. At the end of the war, released prisoners of war, deserters, war criminals, camp followers and demobilized soldiers all roamed over large parts of Europe and beyond, leaving broken or occupied homesteads, often keeping few or no possessions, bereft of private property. Desperate people trailing across borders, sometimes with handcarts or small sacks, at least 11 million official displaced persons (DPs) in Europe alone, completely uncertain of their futures.

The word 'refugee' does not do justice to the scale or scope of the problem. The label 'refugee' can obfuscate as well as illuminate. Sometimes people moved numerous times, only to find their way back to their old homelands. Displacement during the Second World War is best imagined expansively, as something widespread and often open-ended. The 1940s were a time of turmoil and of *potential* uprooting, whether you were a shopkeeper in London or a Ukrainian peasant. Mothers put their children on trains to send them to a place of safety with great fortitude. Exile was part of the cost of war, even when this separation was temporary. And the losses and absences of war overshadowed life for those in places where peoples and whole communities had been eradicated.

This was also a global problem. Europe's experience, although extreme, was far from unique. Stories of wartime displacement from across the globe have much in common, despite the inevitable particularisms and differences, and the differing degrees of proximity to genocidal violence. The years from 1936 to 1950 saw more of the world's population trudging from their place of origin (forcibly or sometimes voluntarily) than ever before in recorded history. The majority of these people lived outside Europe; in Asia, Southeast Asia and the Middle East. Numerically, the single greatest case of wartime population movement took place in China, where some 90 million are estimated to have moved because of the war from central and eastern China into the remote interior. Some – the Jews above all – experienced death camps and attempted eradication through genocide and this is inextricably linked to their experience of exile. Others were less severely touched by violence, but nearly everywhere targeted killing and brutal acts of ethnic cleansing went hand-in-glove with displacement. Many millions of refugees also succumbed to disease or starvation. Wartime displacement changed the global map and shaped the war's aftermath; it transformed the make-up of national populations, influenced the creation of new states and shaped political ideas about the post-war world.

Although much of the current literature on the subject focuses on Europe's experience, European and Asian experiences were intimately interconnected; expulsions and deportations in Europe did not stop at Europe's borders; Poles and Jews were resettled as far away as Mexico and India, often making gruelling journeys through Iran and Central Asia. Nearly 20,000 European Jews took shelter in Shanghai. Some of these Asian stories have barely been integrated into histories of the 'world' war and are often overshadowed by the more comprehensively documented European cases. Everywhere, insecurity about where one would find a safe place in the world abounded and people longed for a permanent place to call home. The displaced rarely made straightforward journeys from A to B but saw the 1940s as a painful chain of disruption, during which time they might make multiple journeys and impossible choices. As the Jewish writer and exile who had made it to the Shanghai ghetto, Yehoshua Rapoport, wrote in his diary in July 1943, 'There is so much insecurity about whether I am on the right list. What security can there be if it is up to human beings to decide? . . . The feeling of insecurity alone is the greatest anguish. Others laugh at my insecurity but I remember Vilna where I was not given an opportunity to go to America or Palestine, I was forgotten.'[1]

Displacement in the 1940s was generated by wartime violence; but was sometimes more tenuously connected directly to conflict. Numerous waves of people moved without any external prompting and without the direction of the state, for instance, the millions who moved from the Low Countries and northern France into southern France as the Nazis pushed forward in the early months of the war. Panic about the treatment of civilians by conquering armies or the fear of being caught up in shooting or bombing triggered spontaneous departures of whole communities.

The ripples of the war radiated out far beyond the epicentres of battle. Blurring the years before and after 1945, the lives of the uprooted were

---

1 Irene Eber, ed., *Voices from Shanghai: Jewish Exiles in Wartime China* (University of Chicago Press, 2008), p. 93.

determined by decolonization and the continued breakup of the old world of land empires into discrete national blocs and, conversely, the consolidation of the post-war USSR. 1945 was not a punctuation point or 'year zero' and the problems of human dislocation intensified after the end of the war. Because of the war, the 'refugee' became a newly identified type of person, identified on the international stage and prioritized in the early days of the UN and in the Geneva Convention of 1951.

Mapping the sheer density and flows of population movement can only ever be partially accurate. There have been surprisingly few attempts to convincingly verify the numbers of people who were uprooted by wartime.[2] Numbers remain highly contested, sometimes for ongoing political reasons. Some people moved several times or only moved internally within the same state or country. At a time of such flux, censuses, when they existed, were old and inaccurate; headcounts may have been exaggerated, particularly when there were competing claims for state resources. Figures could be used to justify claims for post-war aid or other assistance. Anecdotal evidence is often more readily available than hard statistics. As two observers in China wrote in 1946:

> Certainly the long files of gaunt people who moved west across the roads and mountains must have presented a sight unmatched since the days of the nomad hordes; yet no record tells us how many made the trek, where they come from, where they settle anew.[3]

The chronological starting point for the war, and for the beginnings of associated refugee flight can be rolled back much before 1939. Some half a million Spanish republican refugees sought sanctuary in France after their defeat in the Civil War. This was an ominous harbinger of what was to follow in Europe. In particular, the undifferentiated mix of civilians and combatants, the ambivalent and often hostile reception in the 'host' country and the long, protracted and difficult process of settlement, all became themes for other refugees in other parts of the world in the 1940s. Until recently, much of the experience of those refugees, who survived the trek over the Pyrenees mountains only to find themselves held captive in rudimentary camps in

---

2 See introduction to Mark Mazower, Jessica Reinisch and David Feldman eds., *Postwar Reconstruction in Europe: International Perspectives, 1945–1949* (Oxford University Press, 2011). One helpful overview is Robin Cohen, ed., *The Cambridge Survey of World Migration* (Cambridge University Press, 1995).

3 Quoted in Stephen R. Mackinnon, *Wuhan, 1938: War, Refugees and the Making of Modern China* (Berkeley: University of California Press, 2008), p. 44.

southern France, has only been available in French and Spanish. Like so many of the refugee experiences, the historiography is starting to deepen and to be integrated into comparative approaches.[4]

In China in the face of the lightning Japanese attacks of 1937, and especially after the massacres at Nanjing in December 1937, a great exodus had begun. Millions moved south and eastward from the battle-zones of the war in these early years. Some twenty-one provinces suffered Japanese attacks and saw refugee flight as a result. Percentages of the population estimated to be made up of refugees by the end of the war are telling; in Wuhan, 43.5 per cent, in Hunan 42.7 per cent, in Jiangsu, 34.8 per cent.[5] Intellectuals, poets and artists jostled for space with peasants and workers. By the end of the war, after the Japanese defeat, refugees from northern Jiangsu were also fleeing the consequences of civil war, the homeless among them in Shanghai taking shelter in coffin storage buildings and burial grounds, sometimes removing corpses to make way for the living.

Jews began escaping Germany in the 1930s, and between 1933 and 1939 some 90,000 German and Austrian Jews fled to other neighbouring countries. Emigration was technically possible until November 1941 (when it was restricted by the Reich). It became much more challenging under wartime conditions and in the face of the ambivalence or outright hostility of potential host countries including the UK and USA – the visa restrictions placed by the USA on Jewish emigration until 1944 for instance, resulting in the return of some Jews who had even reached the eastern coast of the USA in the ship the *St Louis* in the weeks before the war began. Some Latin American countries such as Bolivia remained relatively open to Jewish emigration in the early years of the war. Other Jews found shelter in Italian-occupied areas or in Switzerland, Spain and Portugal; Norwegian and Danish Jews found some sanctuary in Sweden. Many made long, multi-stage journeys to find safety, forging a path down through the Balkans or Turkey and onwards – against British restrictions – to Palestine. In the early years of the war, some Polish Jewish refugees fled east via Moscow and the Trans-Siberian Railway and spent many months in Japan or China. In the face of British resistance to Jewish emigration to the Middle East, thousands of Jewish displaced did enter Palestine, although they risked interception and internment in Cyprus. By the end of the war, there were at least 250,000 Jewish survivors in Western

---

4 Scott Soo, *The Routes to Exile: France and the Spanish Civil War Refugees, 1939–2009* (Manchester University Press, 2013).
5 Mackinnon, *Wuhan, 1938*, p. 48.

European camps and the survivors of Eastern Europe's Jewish communities had been almost entirely uprooted.

In the east, particularly in Poland, territories had been completely re-engineered so that minorities – squeezed by the Germans on one side and by the USSR on the other – were either shipped to Gulags, conscripted into armies or work-parties or forced to flee. Some 7 million had been expelled, resettled or forcibly reordered according to national and racial hierarchies. As late as 1948, 850,000 displaced people still lived in Europe's refugee camps – among them Poles, Czechs, Latvians, Lithuanians, Estonians and Ukrainians. These bloodlands of Europe saw the most extensive and comprehensive kinds of uprooting and the thinning out of minority populations, the end of multicultural cities where different languages could be heard on the streets and where different communities had lived alongside each other. Churches and synagogues stood derelict, street names and place names had changed overnight.

The forcible use of labourers to carry out work in agriculture, quarries, mines, armaments factories and other industrial war production was another distinctive facet of the Nazi state which also involved the savage relocation of people by force across long distances. Millions of Soviet citizens were shipped out to the Reich's industrial centres of production and grafted in Germany, Austria and Bohemia-Moravia for state and private concerns, with no pay and living at levels of bare subsistence. Many of these labourers would become wartime casualties 'annihilated by work' but others would survive the war only to find themselves stranded in contested territories or eventually returning to Russia. By 1944, as the Reich became increasingly desperate for labour, forced workers came from ever further afield and included teenage girls and boys from across the German-occupied territories. Official figures showed 7.6 million foreign civilians and prisoners of war working in 1944; over a quarter of all the workers registered in the German economy.[6]

But beyond these bloodlands of Europe, there was the fallout from war on a global scale, often less calculated in its bloodiness than in the darkest heart of Europe but also violently disruptive for many civilian populations. In the British Empire in the East, as territories fell to the Japanese, long-settled migrant groups became refugees fleeing 'home'. Shocked by the rapid advance of Japan into Burma in 1942 and scared of aerial bombardment, 140,000 Indians made the horrendous mountainous trek out of Burma,

6 Ulrich Herbert, 'Forced Laborers in the Third Reich: An Overview', *International Labor and Working-Class History* 58 (Fall, 2000), 192–218.

trudging through mud waist-high in monsoon rains, with perhaps 40,000 dying along the way of starvation, exhaustion and disease. Rumoured preferential treatment of European refugees in this case was damaging to Great Britain's imperial status. Many thousands of Sri Lankans, Malayans, Indians and others in Southeast Asia fled inland to avoid Japanese incursions – at one point nearly the entire city of Madras was evacuated for instance, undermining British imperial power in the process.

In areas where the Japanese did take control, the forced movement of workers mirrored some of the displacements to work camps in Europe. The forcible shifting of labour for war work was a distinctive aspect of the Nazi state which shaped the demography of Europe in the war's aftermath. But the harnessing of forced labour also occurred in other parts of the world. The 62,000 Allied prisoners of war who worked on the Thailand–Burma railway have voiced their story. But they worked alongside 200,000 Asian workers from Thailand, Burma, Malaya, Indochina and Indonesia. Many belonged to families of wage-seeking migrants to Southeast Asia and initially volunteered to work of their own free will, but soon many were also swept up by the coercive powers of the Japanese military, unable to leave and half-starved.[7] On the other side of the Bay of Bengal, the war-related famine in Bengal which killed some 3 million people also brought extensive population movement to the region as the starving drifted out of their empty villages and converged on the city, some of them ending up in camps.

Internally, the inflated wages of the wartime economy in Allied zones pulled villagers across North Africa, the Middle East and South Asia into rapidly expanding cities to work in industrial production which underpinned the war effort. The American population was similarly restructured. Industrial production and higher wages in northern and western cities, from Detroit and New York to Philadelphia and Chicago, magnetically drew African-American workers northward, away from southern agriculture. This left lasting political, economic and social legacies for the USA. Unlike elsewhere in the world, much of this movement was permanent. By the end of the war the majority of black Americans lived in cities for the first time.

The rapid building of aerodromes, ports and roads and the new opportunities for work in mines, sucked in new wage labourers from around the British Empire. Slums developed in scale around the edges of many imperial cities, to remain in perpetuity. In South Africa, there were restrictions placed

---

7 Sunil Amrith, *Crossing the Bay of Bengal: The Furies of Nature and the Fortunes of Migrants* (Cambridge, Mass.: Harvard University Press, 2013), pp. 181–212.

on urban migration to no avail. Workers sometimes found themselves cut off from their places of origin once the Axis advanced. Six thousand Ethiopian refugees who had found safety in Kenya or Sudan, for instance, were recruited into Allied battalions that fought in North Africa.[8] Seasonal or casual migrations often became permanent or left people living in new and precarious ways as food shortages and wartime inflation began to escalate. Soldiers recruited into forces such as the Indian army often never returned home, beginning a long chain migration, sometimes back to the post-war industrial cities of Britain. The literature on these imperial displacements during the war is emerging tentatively. As Pamela Ballinger has argued, more expansive interpretations of who constituted a displaced person are relevant if we think about these population movements in their most diverse forms and allow for those who fall outside the usual categories and legal classifications to be subject to historical scrutiny.[9] Asian or African colonial subjects who suffered displacement during the war are no less relevant to the subject, even when lack of state memorialization has meant that the war has often been forgotten or hidden in national narratives.

The continuums of ethnic violence and displacement ran over the convenient end date of 1945. Displacement was in fact a newly intensified problem, traversing VE and VJ Day, as camps were liberated, the displaced tried to find their way back home, or murderous events were avenged. Social upheaval was unleashed on an unprecedented scale and would last for several more years. The tables were turned on the aggressors. Attacks continued against minority groups; but now ethnic Germans became victims. Stranded in hostile terrain or expelled as ethnic contaminants, the vengeful expulsion of Germans in the aftermath of war was one of Europe's most staggering refugee movements. Nearly everywhere, the project was for ethno-homogenization and the achievement of ethno-territorial configuration in a way that would protect borders, secure populations and exile fifth columnists or threats to the state. Indeed, the sweep of expulsions and population dislocation *after* the war – although not comparable with the Holocaust in terms of violence in any way – exceeded wartime figures as 12–13 million Germans lost their homes.

'Wild expulsions' of Germans, controlled mainly by the police, militias and petty officials in Czechoslovakia, Poland and eastern regions of Europe started

---

8 David Killingray, *Fighting for Britain: African Soldiers in the Second World War* (Woodbridge: Boydell & Brewer, 2012), p. 58.

9 Pamela Ballinger, 'Entangled or "Extruded" Histories? Displacement, National Refugees, and Repatriation after the Second World War', *Journal of Refugee Studies* 25:3 (2012), 366–86.

immediately that the German defeat was declared and included vengeful killings, property confiscation, sexual attacks and indiscriminate expulsion of millions of Germans – often irrespective of political allegiance or wartime conduct. Some Germans wanted to head west in any case, to flee Soviet forces or reprisals – perhaps one-tenth of the German refugees left of their own will. But many others, particularly in areas of dense German population concentration, like the Sudetenland, along the Bohemian and Moravian frontiers, had marching orders to gather their portable things and leave within short notice or risked lynching. This line was formalized as policy when the USA, USSR and UK agreed at Potsdam in July 1945 that the transfer of populations of Germans from Poland, Czechoslovakia and Hungary should be facilitated by the victorious powers themselves, although the agreement looked optimistically for this to be conducted in 'an orderly and humane manner'.[10] In reality, again, the plans on maps sat uneasily with post-war disorder. Sheer logistical challenges, elements of brutality and cruelty, lawlessness and problems of food availability confronted the expellees and the agencies overseeing their evacuation. Whenever panic or fear of violence predominated, there was a tendency for voluntary flight and organized expulsions to blend into one another.

Refugees had always faced discrimination depending on whether they were strong and fit, whether they could be employed as labour, whether they had useful skills. Soviets and Allies blamed each other for dumping 'unwanted' expellees illicitly across the border. In the Soviet occupied zones deportation eastward for ethnic Germans, as for Poles, could lead to the Siberian Gulag. In confusion, some Germans were also trying to move eastward, against the flow of Germans being expelled west. As Gunter Lange, a 12-year-old boy at the time recalled near the city of Gorlitz, he encountered, 'thousands of refugees' trying to return to their homes in the east, 'They did not believe that we had to leave there. They could not understand that there was not going to be a return home.'[11] The expellees in the convoys coming from the recovered territories of Poland to the British zone included a high proportion of elderly, women and children, who often needed immediate hospitalization and showed signs of epidemic disease, hunger or maltreatment.

The end of the war and the retraction of European imperial power also shaped the global refugee problem. No longer able to economically sustain the Indian Raj because of the transformations of wartime and in debt to the

10 R. M. Douglas, *Orderly and Humane: The Expulsion of the Germans after the Second World War* (New Haven: Yale University Press, 2012).
11 Ibid., p. 103.

Indian exchequer, the British scrambled from South Asia. The exchange of populations in South Asia which accompanied the division of India and the creation of Pakistan in 1947 saw the 'exchange of population' in Punjab where some 10 million Sikhs, Hindus and Muslims were combed out into ethnically homogeneous states, amid callous violence. The hardening of identities around religious affiliation and the British desire to hurriedly secure a constitutional settlement for the region had a disastrous human fallout. Villagers fled their ancestral villages overnight and crossed the new border by train, bullock cart and on foot. This was not always welcome: as Joginder, a child in 1947, recalled, 'as soon as the Muslims left the others started coming . . . they took away everything, loaded them on bullock cars, and even took away the cattle . . . we felt very sad, we were completely heart broken, we'd been with them for generations, the elder people in our community were extremely sad, we still talk about them.'[12] Other minorities, such as the hybrid Anglo-Indians, no longer felt secure in a rapidly nationalizing environment and sought (but did not always acquire) sanctuary in the UK.

In Palestine in 1948, some 750,000 Palestinians were displaced and left their lands and towns in the midst of war. As the historian Avi Shlaim has put it, the dominant question and one tied inevitably to current political stalemate in the region is 'Did they leave or were they pushed out?'[13] In these debates over the Palestinian flight, the question of Israeli intentions and plans has loomed larger than in most other comparable episodes of ethnic flight. Much discussion has turned on Israeli military or civil responsibility for the creation of the Palestinian refugees. And historical positions have been revised repeatedly in the light of contemporary events. Among Palestinians, the *nakba* is remembered as a trauma and is a consistent referent point for collective memory and action. The Palestinian refugee question is exceptional in a number of ways – the added layers of geopolitics, the war of 1948, the role of the British, the UN and the other Arab states and the creation of the new State of Israel in 1948 in the aftermath of the Holocaust.

But the story is also an eerily familiar one. As elsewhere in times of war, Palestinians fled to stay with relatives, the wealthy tried to remove their assets and others were forced to flee because of economic destitution or lack of water. Memories turned on small details of land or landmarks left behind,

---

12 Cited in Yasmin Khan, *The Great Partition: The Making of India and Pakistan* (New Haven: Yale University Press, 2007), p. 140.
13 Avi Shlaim, 'The Debate about 1948', *International Journal of Middle East Studies* 27:3 (1995), 287–304.

of old ways of life. The tale of flight, and the threshold between life in one place and another is continually reiterated. Others recall being calculatedly and purposefully driven out by Zionist forces as part of strategic assaults on designated villages. The weight of evidence behind centralized planning and action versus spontaneous movement has been thrashed out by historians, with evidence for both centralized and planned removal of Palestinians by the leadership, cut across with countervailing attempts by other Israelis to prevent the acts of targeted violence.

But who was a legitimate Israeli or Palestinian, German or Czech? Ascertaining identity, and who was a legitimate citizen of a state was often an imprecise science. Proving identity during and in the aftermath of war – when people had often lost papers and documents – could be problematic. A man named Joschkowitz was not untypical. He had been born in Germany to Jewish parents and described himself as 'a victim of Nazi and anti-Semitic persecution'. He had fled Germany and stayed temporarily in France, England, Egypt and Iraq before finding himself in India, where he was interned as a 'German' prisoner of war at Dehra Dun. He appealed with desperation for release. 'Several times I have tried to explain to the Authorities the paradox of my position but I don't know why, without result.'[14] Verification processes for Germans who wanted to stay in Poland involved qualifications based on pre-war residency and declarations of loyalty to the state. Officials carried out checks and investigations in DP camps to find German war criminals disguised as displaced persons. Some Upper Silesians with Polish or German citizenship refused these labels and wanted to be identified only as Silesians. How to deal with those who had no desire to be repatriated, such as hundreds of thousands of Latvians and Lithuanians who had fought against the Soviets, but had often been coerced into German armed forces or work parties? Some groups evaded the DP camps, fearing (sometimes rightly) that they would be forcibly taken back to Soviet-ruled territory. Elsewhere, similar complexities occurred. In Southeast Asia, 'Indian' labourers who had worked in Malaya for generations had no desire to be repatriated to the subcontinent. Muslim families in North India struggled to maintain links to kin across the new border to Pakistan, and had to prove that they were not 'Pakistani' as the bilateral relationship deteriorated in the subcontinent. Mixed marriages, linguistic hybridity and multiple displacements created headaches for the state bureaucrats who aspired to create simplified ethnic blocs in the face of human diversity.

---

14 National Archives and Records Administration, Washington DC, File 820.08 Box 143. Letter from A. Joschkowitz to the American consulate in India, 11 January 1944.

Over the long term there were deliberate policies of cultural exclusion; for instance the pulping of German books in Czechoslovakia and the removal of German inscriptions, although German language could still be heard occasionally on the streets in the later 1940s. Many Poles repatriated to their homeland and handed larger farms in the regained territories after the war found the new experience as settlers far from straightforward – seeing the new landscapes as 'strange and forbidding', disturbed by the signs of hurried expulsions from the new homes they came to occupy: sometimes the remnants of unfinished meals still lay on the kitchen tables.[15] Once again, the neat plans for ethnic reordering clashed with human realities on the ground. The imagination of the process and its actual implementation were very often at odds. Everywhere, human complexity was not so easily accommodated within the new post-war borders. Humanity is more nuanced and difficult to shape through bureaucratic process than many politicians have imagined.

Rehoused in their new 'homelands', local people rarely welcomed the displaced unconditionally or with open arms. Sometimes they seemed to threaten the economic status quo, to risk bringing filth, overcrowding or squalor. Others feared ideological subversion or that the refugees had carried with them new or dangerous ideas. In the USSR, the state put under surveillance several million Soviet citizens who had been Nazi captives, as slave labourers or prisoners or war. For the Soviet state, post-war returnees who had lived under Nazi occupation became suspect, viewed as a threat to the state's order and political dogma. Soviet returnees faced 'filtration policies', using individual questionnaires and interrogation to root out suspected subversives. Elsewhere, refugees faced more mundane discrimination – shut out of labour markets, squeezed into barely habitable accommodation, blamed for other social ills.

The achievement of ethnic homogeneity was the implicit or explicit goal for politicians in a number of countries established or reconfigured after the war – from Poland to Pakistan and Israel. Yet the aspiration was often fraught with economic and social complexities because of the differences *between* people of the same faith or ethnicity or because of the gaps left behind when others left or were expelled. There could be an unforeseen cost to the newly configured state when previous inhabitants took their labour and skills with

---

15 Catherine Gousseff, 'Evacuation versus Repatriation: The Polish-Ukrainian Population Exchange, 1944–6', in Jessica Reinisch and Elizabeth White, eds., *The Disentanglement of Populations: Migration, Expulsion and Displacement in Post-War Europe, 1944–9* (Basingstoke: Palgrave Macmillan, 2011), pp. 91–115.

them. Reorganizing the Polish borderlands created economic confusion and met with some local resistance. Sympathetic locals could feel pragmatic ambivalence about the expulsions. In post-war Poland, many German and Silesian workers, such as miners, were held back during the expulsions, even those who wished to move to Germany. In Pakistan, attempts were made to retain Hindu and Parsi businessmen and bankers as their departure undermined the economic foundations of the state. Among Israelis, a number of trade unionists, town dignitaries and leaders stood opposed to the more radical plans for the expulsion of Palestinians.

Everywhere, though, into the late 1940s the idea of 'exchange of population' remained in the ascendancy, and achieved the approval of politicians of all political hues. This was part of an early twentieth-century legacy, dating back to the First World War and in particular, the Treaty of Lausanne of 1923 in which the exchange of Muslims from Greece and Orthodox Christians from Anatolia was formally agreed. The tone was set in the 1920s by this decisive watershed: the first internationally ratified exchange of population. International actors could legitimately, and in concert, organize, oversee and approve exchange of population as a remedy to more complex problems of minorities in socially diverse but ailing empires. Support for this idea as a panacea for the problems of ethnic conflict strengthened rather than weakened over the 1920s and 1930s. The idea of 'exchange of population' was cited in regard to the German expellees in the Potsdam Treaty, it was used as the formal basis of the population transfers across the South Asian Punjab and it informed thinking in Poland, Czechoslovakia, Ukraine and Hungary. On the Arab–Israeli question, there were a number of prominent British, American, Zionist and Arab leaders who all contemplated and favoured to some extent the idea of exchange of population. Displacement of peoples in order to prioritize ethnically homogeneous spaces was, at the time, for many entirely logical. At its worst it was a mass death sentence: Stalin used mass deportations on an unthinkable scale, violently uprooting millions of Poles from the Soviet borderlands and shipping non-Slavs from the Caucuses, from the Baltic states and the Crimea to Siberia and Central Asia in the 1940s. When asked about his plans for the Sudeten Germans Stalin told Czechoslovakia's Prime Minister in 1945, to 'Drive them Out'.[16] But

---

16 Matthew Frank, 'Reconstructing the Nation-State: Population Transfer in Central and Eastern Europe, 1944–8', in Reinisch and White, eds., *Disentanglement of Populations*, pp. 27–48 (p. 32). See also Matthew Frank, *Expelling the Germans: British Opinion and Post-1945 Population Transfer in Context* (Oxford University Press, 2008).

among the Allied powers, there was also a growing (if less murderous) consensus that exchanging people was a legitimate way to resolve ethnic conflicts.

The problems of allocating culpability, of segregating state-directed cleansing from more spontaneous departures of people affected by fear is something that all historians of refugee movements have to grapple with. The project of writing plausible, archival-supported histories of these displacements has been contentious and depends on the availability of sources and the political context. Official discourses often present sanitized and palatable histories of a state's origin. In many places, the political repercussions continue to echo today: for instance the Czech government's equivocation about property rights for Germans; or the tendency of Indians and Pakistanis to blame each other for the refugee movements of 1947; or the conflicting historical interpretations between China and Japan of the Nanjing massacre.

Refugee camps and rehabilitation

Faced with this epic crisis in Europe and in Asia, the emergent international community attempted to try and provide a coordinated response. It was an impressive effort in many ways. The response to the refugees involved the assistance of intergovernmental, governmental and voluntary groups. The international relief organizations operated on a giant and pan-national scale. They attempted to map out the whereabouts of the displaced, established camps, helped to distribute food aid, relocated or repatriated refugees, and tried to reunite families and to ease the threat of epidemic. From 1943 to 1948 and involving forty-four participating nations, the United Nations Relief and Rehabilitation Agency (UNRRA) foreshadowed the United Nations as a unique act of international coordination, employing over 12,000 people from around the world and spending nearly $4 billion. UNRRA has been celebrated for this pioneering internationalism. Nonetheless, the reach of the organization had ideological and geographical limits. German displaced people did not qualify for UNRRA aid or support and did not acquire the status of 'displaced person'; 330,000 DPs were screened in UNRRA camps and over 10 per cent had their claims for help rejected.[17] Internationalism in relief could mean very different things and national differences and cultural relativisms inevitably

17 Daniel Cohen, *In War's Wake: Europe's Displaced Persons in the Postwar Order* (Oxford University Press, 2011), p. 40.

shaped the work of relief workers. American dominance of the organization and the outlook of the four great powers conflicted with the work of relief workers on the ground who wanted to champion their own camps or countries. In tandem, the classificatory regimes designating who was legally and technically a refugee also evolved in terms of who could be included as a legitimate recipient of aid and who would be disqualified.

UNRRA was not Eurocentric. Aid did reach other continents: UNRRA workers in China oversaw deliveries worth $500 million from 1946 to 1947 – the largest single country recipient of aid – amidst complaints of corruption and waste. But other Asians and Africans displaced by war and its aftermath remained untouched by the organization and well beyond its scope or reach. The majority of UNRRA's work focused on the displaced in Eastern Europe and the work of the organization was cut short as the focus of America shifted westward and Cold War priorities under the Marshall Plan began to dominate decisions about post-war spending.[18] The winding up of UNRRA took place before the mass displacements in South Asia, where refugees relied almost entirely on aid from the nascent nation states of India and Pakistan or from small local charities.

A separate UN agency was established in 1949 for Palestinian refugees. Smaller relief, religious and charity organizations filled the gaps in many locations and offered parallel and alternative systems of support with varying degrees of success. The Quaker Friends Relief Service and Friends Ambulance Unit made significant interventions in the Middle East, China and India as well as in Europe, for instance providing services to refugees in Gaza before the UN was present. Other groups dating back to the First World War included Save the Children and Zemgor, while new organizations emerged for the first time such as the Lutheran World Federation and the World Council of Churches. In 1949, the World Council of Churches assessed that religious charities in Germany 'had provided more material aid to the expellees than all the other agencies, domestic and foreign, put together'.[19]

In the mid-twentieth century the refugee became the object of a number of interventions by technically skilled and professionalized groups; doctors, social workers and psychologists examined them, camps became testing grounds for the schemes of engineers and development professionals. Refugees, travelling

---

18 Jessica Reinisch, 'Auntie UNRRA at the Crossroads', *Past & Present* 218, Supplement 8 (2013), 70–97, and 'Internationalism in Relief: The Birth (and Death) of UNRRA', *Past & Present* 210, Supplement 6 (2011), 258–89.
19 Douglas, *Orderly and Humane*, p. 297.

in cramped unsanitary conditions or housed in crowded camps, often suffered from epidemics and the fear of typhus, cholera, flu and other diseases was common. The use of inoculation saved unknown numbers of lives. Some of these schemes and plans bore fruit; a number of the uprooted learned new skills in DP camps that served them for new lives in the host country; for instance vehicle repair, handicrafts or other cottage industries.

Yet the refugee could also be looked upon condescendingly as a charitable victim. The politicians and technocrats feared too much dependency upon the state, and there was much discussion of the risk of apathy and neurosis among the refugees. Politicians and public figures from Lady Mountbatten to Madame Chiang Kai-shek harnessed their fame to publicize the public health cause and were much photographed in refugee camps. The camps also provided an opportunity for middle-class experts to develop their own expertise as international development specialists or to move into charitable and aid work; for instance, a number of middle-class women in Asia who worked in refugee camps became prominent advocates for the rights of displaced women and children. There are striking similarities between women such as Shi Liang, a social activist who publicized the plight of refugees in China, and women like Anis Kidwai or Mridula Sarabhai who worked with relief organizations in Delhi and Punjab.

Interventions could also be intrusive and insensitive, problematizing the displaced as an unsanitary and contaminated individual, and in the worst instances, pathologizing the refugee in a way that grossly exaggerated the risk to public health. Intrusive delousing, disinfection, and the use of isolation could add to the stigma surrounding refugees and encourage segregation from the host populations. DDT powder was used liberally, described by the camp workers as 'dusting' the refugees. As one UNRRA nurse stationed in Halle, Germany wrote in 1945:

> It continues to amaze me that more of them are not ill; for they were living under terrific sanitary conditions. We are still cleaning up some of the worst camps. There have been only two cases of typhus since we came, a few diphtheria, some dysentery, and so far no typhoid. VD is high; tomorrow we are starting to examine the people in every camp.[20]

The segregation of those with TB from the rest of their family members, including children, caused much heartache and difficulty. Indeed, the care of

---

20 Ann Matthews, an American nurse in Halle, Germany, writing in the *American Journal of Nursing* 45:9 (September 1945), p. 751.

children could involve the forcible separation from parents considered by authorities to be too sick, mentally unstable or unsuitable to care for their own children, even when those families had managed to stay united through great perseverance during wartime conditions. An American worker with children in the British Zone recalled:

> I remember the Dakus family – two boys and two girls. Their father was dead and their mother seriously ill with tuberculosis. They were all fine children and it was difficult for the mother to give them up. They wanted to stay together and, after many months of negotiations, we found homes for all of them in a new country.[21]

In a world stripped of the young and able-bodied, fit young male workers found it easier to acquire new homes. But the appearance of neutrality was necessarily undercut by labour shortages and the different labour requirements of the victorious powers. Labour contractors from Britain and as far afield as New Zealand and Australia combed the DP camps for potential sources of labour in the Allied occupied zones, establishing clear hierarchies in the types of refugee that they would prefer to select.[22] The Russians were accused by some DP workers in the Allied zones of holding back young able-bodied men and sending across women and the elderly and causing the separation of families. Some labour contractors besieged DPs immediately they disembarked from crowded and often dangerous rail journeys.

The final years of the war saw a world-wide engagement with the idea of 'development' and an optimistic belief in the ability to solve human crises on epic scales by the organized and efficient deployment of scientific methods. At its most sweeping, this could result in a heavy-handed and even brutal form of 'relief'. In reality, discrepancies and differential treatment of refugees often turned on mundane differences of class or the innate prejudices of those who decided their fate.

Life as a refugee

Despite the commonalities between the displaced in vastly different parts of the world, paradoxically, the one thing that refugees wanted was to be identified as individuals with their own desires, histories and needs. This

---

21 Helen French, 'Displaced Children in Germany', *American Journal of Nursing* 52:12 (1952), 1471–4.
22 Wendy Webster, 'Transnational Journeys and Domestic Histories', *Journal of Social History* 39:3 (2006), 651–66.

was not one passive or united group of victims and many used canny ingenuity in order to find their way through hostile terrain, living off plants and surviving freezing cold conditions, trudging on foot for hundreds of miles, adopting disguises and subterfuge to survive. Sharply variegated by their own wealth and connections, those who could pull strings, manipulate bureaucratic systems or find a way to negotiate and use their assets would do so. Access to information and the ability to negotiate the demands for paperwork was crucial; as Ravinder Kaur has put it, the ability to break 'the codes that the state had invented'.[23] In some locations, survival might mean engaging in prostitution, blackmail or entering the black market economy. Those who could negotiate the black market economy were also more likely to survive, while there were also unpleasant scrambles to appropriate and sell goods belonging to minorities who had been driven out.

Just as there was no standard type of refugee, there was no standard type of refugee accommodation. People were housed in barracks, prisoner of war and detention camps, prisons and schools. Others found space in bombed-out basements or cellars, sheds and derelict buildings. In some places, overcrowding resulted in requisitioning, and families would be forced by the state to share rooms, cooking and toilet facilities with the displaced, exacerbating tensions with the local inhabitants. Some of the Nazi concentration camps were repurposed immediately at the end of the war to house German expellees. Within the official camps run by UNRRA and other organizations, thousands lived side by side for months at a time. Some became adept at exploiting others in their access to food, resources or space. The anxieties of parents weighed on them and there were often concerns about the sexual licence available to teens and young people, removed from usual social mores and strictures. People weighed up the question of where to go next. Some stayed very close to the original camp; the camp at Dachau in Bavaria for instance was used for German expellees at the end of the war, and a community of displaced Germans occupied new homes which were built in close proximity. Other prisoners of war, released from the reoccupied lands in East Asia, ventured to new shores, in New Zealand, Canada and Australia.

Political activism in refugee camps was common although the forms that this took varied. Sometimes refugees protested against their own conditions. In August 1948, 72,000 Bavarian camp dwellers went on hunger strike for

---

23 Ravinder Kaur, 'Planning Urban Chaos: State and Refugees in Post-Partition Delhi', in E. Hust and M. Mann, eds., *Urbanization and Governance in India* (Delhi: Manohar, 2005), pp. 229–50 (p. 235).

better food and conditions. Political activism could permeate a camp. In Shanghai, Chinese refugees from the Sino-Japanese War became radicalized by the Chinese Communist Party (CCP) – militants sought out individuals to recruit into special cells, fostered patriotism and anti-Japanese feeling and recruited them into guerrilla units.[24] In South Asia, religious activists from groups like the Hindu Mahasabha and the Jamaat Islami took the opportunity to do social work with refugees who felt they had been failed by the state, and consolidated their constituencies in the process. The camps provided space for radicalization and for shared grievances to be articulated – and activism and protests for greater refugee rights were common. They also provided a testing-ground for leadership and for youth activism – for instance, for Baltic nationalists in exile – although differences between refugees often surfaced quickly, undercutting any automatic solidarities.

The displaced often worked two or three jobs, taking work where they could; skilled workers taking manual labouring work on docks or mines, and trying to quickly accumulate a little capital as soon as possible. Access to unions could be restricted by the 'locals' and in other places refugees struggled with language and foreign qualifications in order to resume their former professions:

> The group I travelled with, containing two doctors, a veterinarian, several lawyers and other professional people, were given a reception address by the camp commandant in which it was stated that it was no use their showing diplomas to employers, etc., because everyone (in Australia) knew that they had been bought on the black market in Europe.[25]

The miseries of some refugee experiences left lifelong scars. The experience of not only displacement but also of genocide and ethnic cleansing could mar lives irreparably. The recovery from this trauma was dependent not only on the individual but on their avenues for social and political expression. Vida Rosenberg, a Slovene in exile in Austria in 1945, recalled,

> So many people were in the same position that the shock was lessened, we shared each other's burdens and I went to Mass every day which was an enormous support. I was able to verbalise my fears. Blind trust protected us and the prayers with the priests helped us.[26]

---

24 Patricia Stranahan, 'Radicalization of Refugees: Communist Party Activity in Wartime Shanghai's Displaced Persons Camps', *Modern China* 26:2 (2000), 166–93.
25 Helen Murphy, 'The Assimilation of Refugee Immigrants in Australia', *Population Studies* 5:3 (1952), 179–206.
26 John Corsellis and Marcus Ferrar, *Slovenia 1945: Memories of Death and Survival after World War II* (London and New York: I. B. Tauris, 2005), p. 40.

Faith, art, education or entrepreneurship could be routes to healing. Lithuanian refugees in Germany had managed to establish their own educational
organizations and a university in Hamburg attended by hundreds of students
by the late 1940s. Each 'refugee', so often an object of sympathy or pity, was
also an individual person with their own ways of making sense of the events
they had lived through and their own capacity for adaptation and adoption.
As one wrote, 'the only way to protect yourself from this world and to find a
way toward oneself is to create a personal "mythology"'.[27]

For some, new and unimaginable opportunities opened up that only
became clear over time. In West Germany, expellees who had moved as
post-war exiles from the East, profited from the mid-century economic boom
and were relieved as the Cold War continued that they had been fated to find
themselves on the Western side of the Berlin Wall. In cities like New Delhi,
enterprising Punjabi refugees turned small plots of government-granted land
into lucrative businesses. In China, some displaced peasants became industrial workers, earning unexpectedly high wages during the war as the Wuhan
economy and the armament trade burgeoned.

Elsewhere, many displaced developed full lives in new landscapes, including cosmopolitan exchanges – inter-marrying, learning new languages,
adapting and integrating, and educating their children in multiple cultural
contexts. Exile could deliver forms of freedom and opportunity entirely
compatible with nostalgia for a half-remembered earlier world. Some inevitably adapted better than others. 'What life would have been like otherwise'
could only ever be posed as a historical counterfactual, especially once new
borders had become sealed. The life stories of many of the displaced testify
to human beings' remarkable capacity for adjustment.

Conversely, the contemporary political situation and the subsequent life
histories of refugees determined many memories of exile. The continued
existence of minorities and the separation of kinship groups remaining in the
'motherland' could also add to the complications of beginning life anew. As
late as 1960 there were still 150,000 DPs living in camps and other temporary
settlements in Germany, Austria and Italy.[28] Historical traumas could be
renewed or calcified by ongoing conflict in the present. The 'canonization' of
certain memories and the return to certain shared tropes among the victims

27 From the diary of Alfonsas Nyka-Niliinas, cited in Tomas Balkelis, 'Living in the DP
   Camp: Lithuanian Refugees in the West, 1944–1954', in Peter Gatrell and Nick Baron,
   eds., *Warlands: Population Resettlement and State Reconstruction in the Soviet-East European Borderlands, 1945–50* (Basingstoke: Palgrave Macmillan, 2009), p. 41.
28 Gatrell and Baron, eds., *Warlands*, p. 17.

of expulsion – and their use for modern political ends – have occurred in many regions of the world, often intensifying at moments of renewed conflict.

Some refugee camps became transformed over time into legitimate settlements. In many places of the world, from New York to Lahore, it is not unusual to see street names, shop signs or other markers which refer to a long-remembered village which can never be revisited.

Conclusion

The cost to civilians of wartime dislocation becomes almost impossible to contemplate in the aggregate. The war's effect on civilians crashed through the neat dates of 1939–45. The uprooting of so many people was not incidental to the war or a civilian by-product of military campaigns but rooted deeply in European ideologies of nationalism and nation state creation in the 1940s. Yet this was not solely a Nazi project and also transcended the borders of Europe. The astonishing fact is the level of consensus about exchange of population as a policy of last resort. This world being made anew was for some the logical and sensible result of the ending of the great European multi-ethnic empires. The idea of 'exchanging population' as a way to resolve conflict also spilled into Asia and the Middle East where the disintegration of the British Empire was reproducing some of these logics, and where nationalists equally sought to purify and re-engineer their lands as homogeneous spaces. The gulf between these fantasies and the real lives of the displaced has been the subject of an expanding and rich historiography. The lives of the displaced reveal both the deep commonalities and particular subjectivities of the 1940s, and help us to grasp the foundations of much of modern political international relations. Above all, the stories of refugees represent the human face of war, the porous boundaries between people and the places that they call home. Underpinning much of the refugee experience is the elusive notion of 'home' and what it means to people. The stories remind us of the innate ambiguities that surrounded many wartime decisions and the way that human beings in all their manifold complexities often resisted simplistic labelling or categorization by ideology, doctrine or nationality. The uprooted in all their myriad guises deserve a central place in the history of the 1940s.

The war of the cities

Industrial labouring forces

RÜDIGER HACHTMANN

With the commencement of the Second World War, the mobilization and organization of industrial labour forces was the greatest challenge confronted by all participating nations. This was an economic, social, and above all political challenge. Economically, the fullest possible mobilization of all available labour resources was essential for nations to have any realistic prospect of military victory or for those nations attacked to survive. With its seemingly unlimited human and material resources, the USA constituted the exception to the rule. The Axis powers (Germany, Italy and Japan), having risen to power at the expense of left-oriented labour movements, faced the greatest challenge. So how did the primary belligerents – the USA, Great Britain, the Soviet Union, Germany, Italy and Japan – mobilize their labour forces in the service of the war economy?

This chapter[1] begins by outlining the changes made to the labour systems in the six nations identified above. It then examines the establishment of new workers' organizations and the altered status of unions in the Western democracies and in the Soviet Union. Since changes in the three Axis powers were the most pronounced, the chapter pays particular attention to Germany, Italy and Japan. It explores to what extent concepts were transferred between states and who served as the model for whom. The essay then turns to the mobilization of previously untapped labour sources, addressing how it changed the industrial workforce's composition and daily life in the workplace; in this context, the essay highlights the mobilization of female workers and foreign labourers in Germany and Japan.

---

1 I would like to thank Kiran Klaus Patel, Michael Geyer and Adam Tooze for their comments and encouragement.

Labour systems

Beginning in the mid-1930s, the USA and Great Britain pursued diametrically different approaches to labour than that of the Third Reich. On 16 June 1933, less than one hundred days after taking office, Roosevelt pushed through Congress the National Industrial Recovery Act (NIRA). Title 1 of the NIRA suspended anti-trust regulations; however, it also guaranteed employees' right to belong to unions and for those unions to bargain collectively on their behalf. The National Labor Relations Act of 5 July 1935 strengthened this right and forbade employers from discriminating against workers on the basis of union activities or membership. The law also established the National Labor Relations Board, which further strengthened unions through its mediation of labour–management disputes. Even after the Second World War began, American workers' collective bargaining rights expanded. In March 1941, the National Defense Mediation Board (NDMB) was established; it was based on the 1918 National War Labor Board (NWLB), created to prevent conflicts in the First World War armaments industry. Additionally on 11 April 1941, Roosevelt established the Office of Price Administration and Civilian Supply and on 25 June 1941 the Committee on Fair Labor Practices. The Committee combated discrimination on the basis of race, skin colour and national origin. After the USA's official entry into the war, both mobilization efforts and labour market restrictions remained comparatively moderate in accord with agreements reached with key union representatives. The establishment of the War Manpower Commission on 18 April 1942 and the Office of War Mobilization on 27 May 1943 introduced no significant policy changes.[2]

The British government also worked closely with trade unions and the Labour Party, as it had done during the First World War. However, unlike the First World War when the integration of trade unions into the war economy had been impromptu and tentative, in the Second World War unions were actively integrated from the outset. On 10 May 1940, Ernest Bevin, Chairman of the Transport and General Workers' Union, was appointed to the influential post of Minister for Labour and National Service. From October 1940, Bevin also belonged to the War Cabinet. Given Nazi aerial bombardments of Coventry and other British cities, it is unsurprising that Bevin and his fellow ministers instituted more stringent regulations than

---

2 See Alan L. Gropman, *Mobilizing US Industry in World War II: Myth and Reality* (Washington, DC: Institute for National Strategic Studies, Defense University, 1996), pp. 38–55, 83–93, 107.

their American counterparts. The Control of Employment Act of 21 September 1939 forbade British employers from poaching skilled workers from other British companies. One year later, the Emergency Powers (Defence) Act expanded the enforcement powers of the Ministry of Labour and National Service. On 18 July 1940, Order 1305 prohibited strikes and lockouts. The National Service Act of 18 December 1941 made all men and women liable for national service with the exception of mothers with children under 14 and married women living apart from their husbands.[3]

While in the USA and Great Britain the goal was the voluntary cooperation of unions, Hitler's regime opted for the complete and immediate destruction of organized labour – in contrast even to Fascist Italy, where trade unions as well as the Socialist and Communist parties were slowly forced underground between 1921 and 1924/25. When compared with Italy, the speed and brutality of Nazi actions reflected factors besides the regime's fear of a socialist revolution similar to 1918/19. Germany was more industrialized than Italy and its unions much larger and politically engaged; however, they also were politically divided. Thus, on 2 May 1933, the Nazis quickly crushed them, occupying union headquarters, arresting union functionaries, and confiscating union assets.

Overnight, the previous system of labour, characterized by workers' councils and collective bargaining between employers and union representatives, ceased to exist. On 19 May 1933, the National Socialist (NS) regime established Trustees of Labour (*Treuhänder der Arbeit*), which introduced the lowest wage rates since the Great Depression. Trustees could authorize companies to undercut wage contracts in the interest of rearmament. With the creation of the National Labour Regulation Law (*Gesetz zur Ordnung der nationalen Arbeit*, AOG), the temporary powers given to Trustees became permanent. Bellicose in orientation, the AOG disenfranchised the industrial workforce to a much greater extent than its Italian counterpart – *Carta del Lavoro* (23 April 1927).[4] Under the AOG, the First World War front community idealized by leading Nazis became the model for the factory community (*Betriebsgemeinschaft*). The newly introduced terms, *Betriebsführer* and *Gefolgschaft*, linguistically signalled a kind of re-feudalization of the workplace. The employer as *Betriebsführer* became 'Lord of the household', who

---

3 See Chris Wrigley, *British Trade Unions since 1933* (Cambridge University Press, 2002), p. 13; Johannes Paulmann, *Staat und Arbeitsmarkt in Grossbritannien. Krise, Weltkrieg, Wiederaufbau* (Göttingen: Vandenhoeck & Ruprecht, 1993), pp. 244–9.

4 For a detailed account, see Andreas Kranig, *Lockung und Zwang. Zur Arbeitsverfassung im Dritten Reich* (Stuttgart: Deutsche Verlagsanstalt, 1983).

concomitantly safeguarded the *Volksgemeinschaft*, i.e. the Nazi regime's political aims. The new Trustee Councils did not reduce the autocratic powers of management; rather they promoted the company's welfare. In this arrangement workers had no rights.

In 1934, the Nazis introduced greater restrictions on the workers' right to change jobs, and in February 1935 they made workbooks mandatory; both measures aimed at war readiness. These preparatory measures culminated on 22 June 1938 with the introduction of compulsory service and its expansion on 13 February 1939. Thus, the War Economy Ordinance (*Kriegswirtschaftsverordnung*) of 4 September 1939 marked only the continued integration of the German worker into the war economy. On 21 March 1942, the Trustees of Labour and regional labour offices were made direct instruments of the General Plenipotentiary for the Use of Labour, and on 27 July 1943, they were merged with the Gauleiter bureau.

The Soviets embarked on a comparable long-term regimen aimed at controlling work discipline and the labour market. According to the Labour Discipline Law of 15 November 1932, a worker could be dismissed and lose entitlement to food rationing cards, if absent a single day from work without authorization. In December 1938, the Soviets introduced workbooks and began more stringently enforcing the 1932 Labour Discipline Law. On 26 June 1940, one day after France's surrender, the Soviets made it punishable by up to four months' imprisonment for workers to leave their place of employ without employer permission. The following year 3.2 million workers were disciplined and 633,000 sentenced to prison or detention camp.[5] On 26 December 1941, Soviet authorities made unauthorized departure from the workplace an act of 'desertion' punishable by up to eight years in a labour camp. Shortly after the Germans invaded the Soviet Union, Stalin established the Committee for Distribution of Labour. Central and regional authorities could assign workers and staff to jobs, which they had no right to refuse. While the Nazis consistently enforced similar restrictions, implementation in the Soviet case displayed no corresponding consistency. As Russian historian Sheila Fitzpatrick explained, the system 'was a lot less organized than the name suggests'.[6]

---

5 See Andrei Sokolov, 'Forced Labor in Soviet Industry: The End of the 1930s', in Paul Gregory and Valery Lazarev, eds., *The Economics of Forced Labor: The Soviet Gulag* (Stanford: Hoover Institution, 2003), pp. 23–42 (p. 28); Martin Kragh, 'Stalinist Labour Coercion during World War II: An Economic Approach', *Europe–Asia Studies* 63 (2011), 1253–73.

6 Sheila Fitzpatrick, 'War and Society in Soviet Context: Soviet Labor, before, during, and after World War II', *International Labor and Working Class History* 35 (Spring 1989), 37–52 (p. 41).

Workers' organizations

Workers' organizations also took on distinct forms and fulfilled different roles in the six primary belligerents. In the USA and Great Britain, unions received widespread public recognition for their voluntary participation and active collaboration in the war economy, leading to increased membership. This was particularly true in the USA, where the level of union organization was traditionally low (Table 11.1). While in the 1920s Soviet trade unions still had some room to manoeuvre, in the 1930s, the state took complete control. In Fascist Italy, trade unions, organized according to sector, were integrated into a corporatist system, which offered industrial workers no room for articulating their interests.

However, the NS regime pursued the systematic elimination of autonomous special interest groups the most rigorously. On 10 May 1933, a few days after crushing the unions, the NS regime established the German Labour Front (*Deutsche Arbeitsfront*, DAF). Its leader was Robert Ley, an outspoken union opponent, one of Hitler's confidants, and Reich organizational leader (*Reichsorganisationsleiter*). The DAF, under Ley's leadership, bore no resemblance

Table 11.1 *Trade unions and other labour organizations, 1935–1945 (as % of civilian employees)*

	1935	1939/40	1942	1945
UK (Trade Unions)				
Members (in m)	4.8	6.5	?	7.7
Share %	25%	33%	?	39%
USA (Trade Unions)				
Members (in m)	3.6	6.8	9.8	12.1
Share %	9%	15%	18%	23%
Japan (Sanpô)				
Members (in m)	–	3.5	?	6.4
Share %	–	40%	?	80%
Germany (Deutsche Arbeitsfront)				
Members (in m)	15.3	22.1	25.1	25.0
Share %	67%	99%	100%	100%

Sources: Chris Wrigley, *British Trade Unions since 1933* (Cambridge University Press, 2002); Leo Troy, *Trade Union Membership, 1897–1962* (New York: NBER, 1965); Rüdiger Hachtmann, ed., *Ein Koloss auf tönernen Füßen. Das Gutachten des Wirtschaftsprüfers Karl Eicke über die Deutsche Arbeitsfront vom 31. Juli 1936* (Munich: Oldenbourg, 2006).

to a union. Ley coined the phrase 'soldiers of labour' (*Soldaten der Arbeit*), deliberately linking workers with modern, quasi-industrialized warfare; by autumn 1933, it was a household phrase.

The passage of the AOG on 20 January 1934 did not signal a partial defeat of the DAF, as earlier research has suggested. The AOG provided new labour organizations with no rights comparable to those formerly enjoyed by unions. In fact, DAF leaders played a critical role in formulating the AOG,[7] ensuring that the new organization did not emulate the despised unions. On 24 October 1934, Hitler signed an ordinance, formulated by Ley, defining the DAF's goal as being 'the formation of an authentic German *Volksgemeinschaft* and *Leistungsgemeinschaft*'. To this end, the DAF was supposed to ensure that every German worker developed 'the spiritual and corporal make-up that enables him to achieve the highest level of performance and thus guarantees the greatest benefit for the *Volksgemeinschaft*'.[8]

Although DAF membership did not become mandatory until November 1939, from its inception, few workers escaped its coercive tactics. By 1942, it had 25 million members. However, intimidation, coercion and terror alone could not produce the desired *Volks- und Leistungsgemeinschaft*. Thus, the DAF also attempted to win over the workforce through various incentives, including the Strength through Joy association (*Kraft durch Freude*, KdF). Created on 27 November 1933, the KdF sponsored mass tourism and other leisure activities. It was modelled on the Italian Opera Nazionale Dopolavoro (OND) created in April 1925, which in turn was based on contemporary American prototypes. Led by Marion Giani, a former director of Westinghouse in Italy, nearly 40 per cent of Italian workers belonged to the OND by 1939.[9] However, the KdF soon offered more activities than either the OND or the British Workers Travel Union.

From its inception the KdF's *raison d'être* was war. On 14 November 1933, Hitler issued a special directive explaining why every German worker needed vacation time: 'I want a *Volk* with strong nerves, since only a *Volk* that keeps its nerve can make truly great policy.' What Hitler implied, Ley made explicit shortly thereafter: 'We lost the [First World] War, because we

---

7 See Rüdiger Hachtmann, 'Arbeit und Arbeitsfront: Ideologie und Praxis', in Michael Wildt and Marc Buggeln, eds., *Arbeit und Nationalsozialismus* (Göttingen: Wallstein, forthcoming).

8 Quoted in Reichsorganisationsleiter der NSDAP, ed., *Organisationsbuch der NSDAP* (7th edn, Munich: Zentralverlag der NSDAP, 1943).

9 For a detailed study, see Daniela Liebscher, *Freude und Arbeit. Zur internationalen Freizeit- und Sozialpolitik des faschistischen Italien und des NS-Regimes* (Cologne: SH-Verlag, 2009).

lost our nerves.' Consequently for the coming war, 'the Führer' wanted the 'nerves of the people to remain healthy and strong'.[10] KdF activities, the countless 'people's products' manufactured by DAF corporate affiliates, and national competitions rewarding job performance turned the DAF into a 'people's service provider' (volksgemeinschaftlichen Dienstleister).[11]

The AOG's communal orientation and the DAF's organizational structure in particular resonated in Japan, where the government favoured destroying the labour movement and restructuring the Japanese system of labour based on the Nazi model.[12] The affinity of Japanese 'modernizers' and social technocrats for the German model was not new. Even before 1933, the concept of 'factory community', promoted by influential German labour experts, such as Ernst Nicklich, impressed Japanese experts and apparently had been applied by Japanese businesses.[13] After the Nazi seizure of power, Japanese experts, in particular Minami Iwao, studied the Nazi labour system. Since the mid-1930s Minami had been in charge of labour management at Japanese Electric and in the summer of 1934 along with other Japanese experts, he made an extended trip to Germany to study the AOG and other elements of the new German labour system.

When the Hirota cabinet assumed power in late February 1936, the balance of power in Japan shifted to the political right, catalyzing the militarization of Japanese society. In search of a new concept of modernization, the Hirota cabinet turned to Minami, seeking his advice for reorganizing the Japanese labour system and more specifically creating a Japanese-style DAF.[14] Minami's plans envisaged Labour Inspector Bureaux, responsible for wage rates, working conditions, the (coercive) mediation of labour–management conflicts,

---

10 Quoted in Hasso Spode, 'Arbeiterurlaub im Dritten Reich', in Carola Sachse, Tilla Siegel, Hasso Spode and Wolfgang Spohn, eds., *Angst, Belohnung, Zucht und Ordnung. Herrschaftsmechanismen im Nationalsozialismus* (Opladen: Westdeutscher Verlag, 1982), pp. 275–328 (p. 290).

11 On DAF's economic empire, see Rüdiger Hachtmann, *Das Wirtschaftsimperium der Deutschen Arbeitsfront* (Göttingen: Wallstein, 2012); on DAF's other activities, see Ronald Smelser, *Robert Ley: Hitler's Labor Front Leader* (New York: Berg, 1988).

12 Sheldon Garon, *The State and Labor in Modern Japan* (Berkeley: University of California Press, 1987), p. 212.

13 Gertraude Krell, *Vergemeinschaftende Personalpolitik. Normative Personallehren, Werksgemeinschaft, NS-Betriebsgemeinschaft, Betriebliche Partnerschaft, Japan, Unternehmenskultur* (Munich: R. Hampp, 1994), pp. 208–25.

14 On the Japanese labour system's reorganization, see Garon, *State and Labor*, pp. 212–26; Stephen S. Lange, *Organized Workers and Social Politics in Interwar Japan* (Cambridge University Press, 1981), pp. 211–30. On the National Socialist labour model's influence on Japanese experts, see Janis Mimura, *Planning for Empire: Reform Bureaucrats and the Japanese Wartime State* (Ithaca: Cornell University Press, 2011), pp. 162–3.

as well as disciplining employees and employers for behaviours deemed harmful to the community. The plan also called for dissolving collective labour contracts and weakening organized labour. After 1937, Minami's plan slowly became the foundation of the Japanese labour system.

In keeping with the AOG model, Japanese experts wanted to create 'trust councils' in factories, which would overcome the 'class struggle' and secure the 'loyal' subordination of workers to employers. Inspired by Minami's plans, on 24 August 1938, the Welfare and Home Ministry instructed regional administrations to initiate and support the creation of 'industrial patriotic units' (*Sanyo Hokokukai*) at the plant level. By the end of 1939, there were approximately 20,000 Industrial Patriotic Associations based on the DAF's factory community. The 'discussion councils' of Japanese factory communities met the same fate as the German 'trust councils' they imitated, becoming irrelevant by the late 1930s at the latest. Most Japanese companies failed to establish discussion councils until war's end, and where they did exist, they remained non-binding forums.[15]

While the Industrial Patriotic Movement did not alter the position of capital and management, it did have an impact on organized labour. In August 1938, the Japanese government abandoned its pre-1936 strategy of supporting workers' associations, including unions. The new policy left no space for the Japanese Federation of Labour (*Sodomei*) – the social democratic umbrella organization for unions. In October 1937, the Welfare and Home Ministry renounced the class struggle for 'patriotic' reasons until hostilities with China ceased. In the final quarter of 1938, Sodomei was further weakened, when its four largest unions, comprising 40 per cent of its total membership, pulled out. Among them was the steelworkers' union, whose chair after a trip to Nazi Germany became 'strangely ecstatic about the position of labor under Nazi rule'.[16] The historian Sheldon Garon noted the 'suicidal impulses' of social democratic union leaders, who wanted to maintain their influence within the proclaimed new order.[17]

On 8 July 1940, Sodomei dissolved itself; the Industrial Association for Serving the Nation (*Sangyo Hokokukai* or *Sanpo*) – the new plant-based, mass organization for workers – absorbed its members. The parallels to German events of 2 May 1933 – when the social democratic Federation of German

---

15 Andrew Gordon, *The Evolution of Labor Relations in Japan, 1853–1955* (Cambridge, Mass.: Harvard University Press, 1988), pp. 299–326.

16 Garon, *State and Labor*, p. 219.

17 Ibid., p. 220.

Trade Unions (ADGB) expressed its support for the Nazi 'German people's community' – are obvious. And just as the ADGB's capitulation did not satisfy the Nazis, Sodomei's voluntary coordination of labour with regime goals did not satisfy the Japanese authorities.

While Sanpo was modelled on the DAF and early historical studies characterized it as the 'Japanese Labour Front', the two were not identical.[18] Despite numerous parallels, such as both organizations' involvement in developing a new social security system,[19] the very distinct national contexts resulted in significant differences in implementation. In 1940, Sanpo had an estimated 3.5 million members, reaching 6.4 million by the beginning of 1945, a clear majority of industrial workers; however, it was much smaller than the DAF (Table 11.1). A second difference was that Sanpo, like nineteenth-century German industries, utilized the family as the organizing principle for the factory community. In contrast, the DAF envisioned uniting capital, management and labour in factory communities modelled on the idealized First World War front community. To this end, DAF officials introduced plant roll calls and other activities imitating military life. But the most significant distinction was that the DAF had more political weight within National Socialism than Sanpo had in Japan. While Sanpo remained subordinate to the Labour and Home Ministry, in 1938 the DAF leadership seized numerous competencies from rival agencies. Since 1934 it had answered only to Hitler; additionally the DAF had significant authority over housing and resettlement policy.[20] On 15 November 1940, the head of the DAF, Robert Ley, became Reich Commissar for Social Housing, and on 23 October 1942 he was named Reich Housing Commissar. From 7 May 1942, the DAF supervised all conscripted foreigners working for German industries.

Mobilizing women

In all six nations, workers' associations confronted fundamental changes in the industrial workforce's infrastructure. Rearmament and the commencement

18 See, for example, Peter Rindl, *Die gehorsamen Rebellen. Arbeiter in Japan* (Vienna: Europa-Verlag, 1968), pp. 120–30.

19 See Lange, *Organized Workers*, p. 230; on the DAF and its concept, see Marie Luise Recker, *Nationalsozialistische Sozialpolitik im Zweiten Weltkrieg* (Munich: Oldenbourg, 1985), pp. 82–154.

20 See Hachtmann, *Wirtschaftsimperium*, pp. 425–98; Marie Luise Recker, 'Der Reichskommissar für den sozialen Wohnungsbau. Zu Aufbau, Stellung und Arbeitsweise einer führerunmittelbaren Sonderbehörde', in Dieter Rebentisch and Karl Teppe, eds., *Verwaltung contra Menschenführung im Staat Hitlers* (Göttingen: Wallstein, 1986), pp. 333–50.

of hostilities eliminated any residual unemployment caused by the Great Depression. In fact, all six nations experienced a labour shortage, brought on by the insatiable need of their respective armies for soldiers. As a result, all six began mobilizing women – including many who never previously worked in industry.

In Great Britain, the total percentage of women in the industrial workforce increased from one-quarter to almost one-third between 1939 and 1943 – thus slightly exceeding German totals. In fact, between 1933 and 1935, the total percentage of German women in the workforce decreased.[21] However, the percentage of German women working in industry did not. Thus, neither the feminine ideal promoted by National Socialists nor the campaign against married women in the workforce, which predated Hitler's seizure of power, can explain the overall decline in female labourers. Instead, its cause was the Nazis' systematic development of the armaments industry at the expense of the consumer goods industry, where traditionally a high percentage of German women worked. In contrast, male employees dominated the armaments industry, and for that matter the manufacturing industry. However, by 1936, Germany's growing labour shortage forced diehard Nazis to accept women's employment in manufacturing, fundamentally changing the industrial workforce's composition. Thereafter, women's employment in all industries increased dramatically until 1942, when it stabilized at a relatively high level.

In the USA, the total percentage of women in the workforce also increased, reaching nearly 30 per cent by 1942. This increase was due in no small part to propaganda efforts by the Office of War Information, which created the iconic Rosie the Riveter to recruit women for the arms industry.[22] Soviet propaganda offered similar iconic representations of women workers; and women's employment increased even more dramatically than in the USA.[23] While in the 1920s, women constituted only 20 per cent of the workforce, by 1940 they made up 40 per cent. Four years later, women represented almost 60 per cent of the Soviet workforce (Table 11.2), far more than in any other belligerent nation. In Japan and Italy, the percentage

---

21 On women's employment in Germany, see Rüdiger Hachtmann, 'Arbeitsmarkt und Arbeitszeit in der Deutschen Industrie, 1929–1939', *Archiv für Sozialgeschichte* 27 (1987), 177–227 (pp. 200–1); Rüdiger Hachtmann, 'Industriearbeiterinnen in der deutschen Kriegswirtschaft', *Geschichte und Gesellschaft* 19 (1993), 332–66.

22 See Donna B. Knaff, *Beyond Rosie the Riveter: Women in World War II in American Popular Graphic Art* (Lawrence: University Press of Kansas, 2012).

23 Manfred Hildermeier, *Geschichte der Sowjetunion, 1917–1991. Entstehung und Niedergang des ersten sozialistischen Staates* (Munich: Beck, 1998), p. 647.

Table 11.2 *Share of women employees as percentage of workforce in the most important branches of German industry, 1933–1945, including female foreign labour (in %) (a)*

	1933	1936	1939 (b)	1940	1941	1942	1943	1944
Iron, steel and non-ferrous metals	2.9	3.1	6.0	9.4	7.7	9.4	15.0	18.7
Vehicles	8.4	5.4	6.3	?	?	?	24.0	24.7
Raw material processing (c)	21.0	19.2	21.4	22.5	23.5	25.6	30.5	31.6
Metalware	40.1	41.5	40.6	43.5	43.0	44.7	48.1	49.5
Chemicals industry	21.2	20.1	20.5	33.6	33.1	34.5	36.6	37.8
Electrical engineering	37.0	37.0	39.9	36.3	32.7	38.2	42.9	44.3
Fine-mechanical and optical	31.0	27.7	30.0	31.1	34.6	38.9	43.3	45.1
Non-metallic minerals	7.6	6.7	9.1	6.7	6.8	7.9	10.8	12.3
Textiles industry	56.4	55.7	57.9	60.5	61.4	62.2	63.8	62.7
Clothing and footwear	68.2	68.6	70.0	78.7	80.4	80.1	83.1	82.0
Food and drink industry	38.6	41.1	45.0	47.9	47.6	47.4	48.7	48.9
Industry overall (%) (d)	29.3	24.7	26.8	26.8	26.9	28.1	31.3	31.2
For comparison: Share of female labour in total US workforce								
	?	?	?	25.2	25.4	26.7	29.1	29.1
For comparison: Share of female labour in total UK workforce								
	?	?	25.8	26.9	28.6	31.4	32.5	32.3

(a) 'Altreich' (pre-war German territory). From 1939 with Austria and Sudetenland
(b) 1. Half 1939. From 1940: 31 May
(c) And related branches (including iron, steel and metalware)
(d) Until 1939: only German women
Sources: Statistische Jahrbuch für das Deutsche Reich 1939/40; 'Kriegswirtschaftliche Kräftebilanz der deutschen Industrie', from Rolf Wagenführ, *Die deutsche Industrie im Kriege 1939–194* (Berlin 1954); Hugh Rockoff, 'The United States: Ploughshares to Swords', in Mark Harrison, ed., *The Economics of World War II: Six Great Powers in International Comparison* (Cambridge University Press, 1998); Stephen Broadberry and Peter Howlett, 'The United Kingdom: Victory At All Costs', in Harrison, ed., *The Economics of World War II: Six Great Powers in International Comparison.*

of female workers also grew, albeit statistical data for these nations are scant.[24] Increasingly more jobs were open to women.

24 For details on female employment in Japan, see Koji Taira, 'Economic Development and Labor Market in Japan, 1905–1955', in Peter Duus, ed., *The Cambridge History of Japan*, vol. VI: *The Twentieth Century* (Cambridge University Press, 1988), pp. 606–53

The number of women permanently employed in the workfoce also increased. In the USA, 75 per cent of female industrial workers employed during the war were married. In Great Britain, the share of married women increased dramatically – from 16 per cent in 1931 to 43 per cent in 1943.[25] In Germany, this trend had developed by 1936.[26] Moreover, statistics indicated that the percentage of older women in the female workforce also was increasing. In the USA, more than half of all women in the workforce during the war were over 35. In Germany, the pre-war trend of permanent female employment accelerated. Another indicator of permanent female employment was the growing number of women belonging to unions.[27] In Great Britain, the number doubled from 14.7 per cent in 1938 to 29.5 per cent in 1943.[28] To facilitate the employment of mothers, nurseries and kindergartens were established and expanded in all belligerent nations. Of course, women continued to receive lower wages for performing the same work as men.

In all belligerents, traditional gender roles and gender inequality persisted. The war was viewed as an exceptional situation, and women were expected to return to the domestic sphere with its end. In the Third Reich, this view of women also had racist and eugenic dimensions. For example, on 17 May 1942, the NS regime made maternity leave available to German women in occupations not covered under the existing law. To safeguard German women's fecundity, the DAF and other party and government offices pressed for half-day shifts and other forms of part-time work; employers willingly complied since the provision facilitated employee retention in a tight labour market. Meanwhile in Britain the number of women who worked part-time tripled from roughly 300,000 in mid-1942 to approximately 900,000 in mid-1944.[29] Although Germany experienced a similar phenomenon, for the reasons outlined above, the trend was less pronounced (Table 11.3).

(pp. 620–1); on Italy, see Toby Abse, 'Italy', in Jeremy Noakes, ed., *The Civilian in War: The Home Front in Europe, Japan and the USA in World War II* (University of Exeter Press, 1992), pp. 104–25 (p. 107),

25 Peter Dewey, *War and Progress: Britain, 1914–1945* (London: Longman, 1997), p. 64.

26 On marriage as a problematic indicator of permanent employment, see Selina Todd, *Young Women, Work, and Family in England, 1918–1950* (Oxford University Press, 2005), p. 51.

27 On German female industrial workers, see Hachtmann, 'Industriearbeiterinnen in der deutschen Kriegswirtschaft', pp. 334–8 and 362–3.

28 Andrew Thorpe, *Britain in the Era of the Two World Wars, 1914–1945* (London: Longman, 1994), 64.

29 See Paulmann, *Arbeitsmarkt in Grossbritannien*, p. 226, n. 2 and p. 447; Peter Howlett, 'The War-Time Economy, 1939–1945', in Roderick Floud and Paul Johnson, eds., *The Cambridge History of Modern Britain*, vol. III: *Structural Change and Growth, 1939–2000* (Cambridge University Press, 2004), pp. 1–26 (p. 6).

Table 11.3 *Weekly worktime in German industry, 1929–1945 (hours per work, German workers only, 'Altreich')*

	1929	1933	1935	1939 March	1939 Sept.	1940 March	1940 Sept.	1941 March	1941 Sept.	1942 March	1942 Sept.	1943 March	1943 Sept.	1944 March
Capital goods industry:														
All workers	46.3	43.0	45.9	48.2	48.8	48.5	49.9	49.9	50.3	49.6	49.5	49.9	48.9	49.2
Male skilled	–	–	–	50.2	50.7	50.7	52.4	52.3	52.8	52.2	52.0	52.8	51.6	51.9
Male unskilled	–	–	–	49.5	50.9	49.7	52.6	51.4	52.3	50.4	51.2	51.3	50.8	50.9
Female skilled	–	–	–	47.2	46.2	46.7	47.9	47.2	46.1	45.1	43.8	43.8	42.3	41.5
(a)														
Female unskilled	–	–	–	46.8	45.7	43.9	44.7	44.8	44.5	43.6	42.9	42.1	39.0	39.0
Consumer goods industry:														
All workers	45.7	42.9	42.6	45.9	43.5	43.8	45.9	45.8	45.9	45.0	44.8	45.3	43.1	43.3
Male skilled	–	–	–	48.1	46.6	46.9	49.4	49.7	50.0	49.2	49.5	50.5	49.5	49.6
Male unskilled	–	–	–	47.9	47.9	47.5	49.2	49.2	49.4	48.8	49.2	49.4	48.6	48.7
Female skilled[a]	–	–	–	46.5	42.5	43.1	45.3	44.8	44.7	43.8	42.9	43.5	40.2	40.4
Female unskill.	–	–	–	46.8	43.7	44.3	45.0	44.4	44.1	43.2	42.5	42.0	39.2	39.3

[a] Skilled and semi-skilled female labour.

Source: United States Strategic Bombing Survey, *The Effects of Strategic Bombing on the German War Economy* (Washington, DC, 1945, S. 215).

Table 11.4 *Share of civilian foreign workers and POWs in workforce of important branches of German industry, 1942–1944*

	1942	1943	1944
Construction	47.0	50.0	52.1
Non-ferrous metals	17.4	31.0	37.6
Iron and steel	15.4	28.7	33.0
Mining	14.0	25.0	32.8
Mechanical engineering	15.1	29.4	32.0
Chemicals	15.4	26.3	30.2
Electrical engineering. fine-mechanical and optical	13.9	19.3	23.5
Textiles	7.1	12.3	13.0
Industry and crafts total	**14.8**	**25.0**	**28.8**
Agriculture	53.0	58.1	51.4

Source: Ulrich Herbert, *Fremdarbeiter. Politik und Praxis des 'Ausländer-Einsatzes' in der Kriegswirtschaft des 'Dritten Reiches'* (Berlin: Dietz, 1985), p. 229.

Mobilizing foreigners, POWs and concentration camp prisoners

A special case concerns industries in the Old Reich (pre-war German territory) that employed foreign workers. Especially after 1942, industries in the Old Reich depended on foreign labour.[30] At the end of September 1944, almost 6 million foreign workers were working in the Old Reich. And in total 8.4 million foreigners worked in Old Reich industries during the war. In agriculture and construction, they constituted roughly half the workforce; in armaments and other heavy industry, they represented one-third of the workforce by 1944 (Table 11.4). The massive use of foreigners in industry allowed the regime to transfer increasing numbers of German workers to the front, thereby prolonging the war.

---

30 On foreign workers' diverse ethnic backgrounds, see, for example, Mark Spoerer, *Zwangsarbeit unter dem Hakenkreuz. Ausländische Zivilarbieter, Kriegsgefangene und Häftlinge im Deutschen Reich und im besetzten Europa, 1939–1945* (Stuttgart: Deutsche Verlags-Anstalt, 2001). On POWs as labourers, see, for example, Gerhard Schreiber, *Die italienischen Militärinternierten im deutschen Machtbereich, 1943–1945* (Munich: Oldenbourg, 1990); Rolf Keller, *Sowjetische Kriegsgefangene im Deutschen Reich 1941/42. Behandlung und Arbeitseinsatz zwischen Vernichtungspolitik und kriegswirtschaftlichen Erfordernissen* (Göttingen: Wallstein, 2011). On KZ prisoners as labourers, see Marc Buggeln, *Arbeit & Gewalt: Die Aussenlagersysteme des KZ Neuengamme* (Göttingen: Wallstein, 2009).

Table 11.5 *Foreign civilian workers and POWs employed in German industry by nationality, August 1944 (in %)*

Nationality	Civilian workers	POW	Total
Belgian	3.6	2.6	3.3
French	11.4	31.1	16.5
Italian	2.8	22.1	7.7
Netherlands	4.7	–	3.5
Soviet	37.7	32.7	36.0
Polish	29.0	1.5	22.2
Czech 'Protectorate'	4.9	–	3.7
Other	5.9	10.0	7.1
Total (%)	100.0	100.0	100.0
Total workers	**5.721.883**	**1.930.087**	**7.615.970**

Source: Ulrich Herbert, *Fremdarbeiter. Politik und Praxis des 'Ausländer-Ein*satzes' *in der Kriegswirtschaft des 'Dritten Reiches'* (Berlin: Dietz, 1985), p. 271.

Nazi racial ideology created a hierarchy of slavery that by 1942 at the latest dictated daily life in many German industries. At the bottom of this hierarchy were the Jews; for them, work postponed death only by a few months.[31] Eastern European workers from occupied Soviet territories (Table 11.5) occupied the next rung in the Nazi hierarchy. They and the Poles were treated brutally.

The Nazis treated workers from Central and Western Europe better (especially ethnic Danes, Belgians and Dutch), since according to Nazi racial ideology, they shared a common racial heritage. However, Nazi racial hierarchies were not fixed. When Mussolini's regime collapsed in July 1943, the estimated 120,000 Italian guest workers in Germany lost their privileged status as citizens of a friendly regime (a status also held by Slovakian and Hungarian workers). Suddenly, Italians found themselves at the bottom of the Nazi racial hierarchy; particularly the more than half million Italian soldiers in Northern and Central Europe, whom the German army labelled 'traitors' and deported to Germany, where they worked under particularly brutal conditions.

The Nazi use of the masculine term *Der Ausländerarbeiter* implied a male foreign labour force. In reality, it included many female foreign workers,

31 See Wolf Gruner, *Jewish Forced Labor under the Nazis: Economic Needs and Racial Aims, 1938–1944* (Cambridge University Press in association with the US Memorial Museum, 2006).

who overwhelmingly came from nations occupying the bottom rungs of the Nazi racial hierarchy. For example, 51 per cent of female foreign labourers, mostly young, came from occupied Soviet territories. At first, many of these women came voluntarily, lured by recruiters' promises. However, by autumn 1941, no one believed the promises and German authorities had to utilize extreme coercion to meet labour demand.[32] Still the Eastern European labour supply appeared in danger of drying up. In March 1942, Thuringia's Gauleiter, Fritz Sauckel, was named the General Plenipotentiary for the Use of Labour. Between 1943 and 1945, he intensified recruitment efforts, conscripting an estimated 2.5 million foreign workers for industries in Germany. But German industries had an insatiable need for workers. Of the nearly 3.4 million Soviet prisoners of war captured prior to 1 February 1942, approximately 60 per cent succumbed to starvation or disease in captivity. But after the spring of 1942, the Nazis employed Soviet POWs in German industries.

In mid-1942, the Nazis began mobilizing concentration camp (*Konzentrationslager* – KZ) prisoners as a last resort; in particular they were utilized in aeroplane production. By the end of 1944, an estimated 230,000 of the more than 600,000 KZ prisoners worked in private industries crucial to the war effort. An additional 130,000 KZ prisoners worked under indescribable conditions in the caves and tunnels of Mittelbau-Dora and in other concentration camps. At Mittelbau-Dora, KZ prisoners worked on V-1 and V-2 rockets utilized to bomb British cities. While these rockets killed at least 12,000 British residents, they proved more deadly for the KZ prisoners forced to produce them, killing an estimated 20,000.[33]

Initially, foreign workers' employment in Old Reich industries was controversial within the NS regime because of concerns about racial intermixing. Additionally, after 1940/41 their use in the Old Reich conflicted with the occupation authorities' efforts to place local industry at the service of German armaments production. The Japanese war economy faced a similar dilemma.[34]

---

32 On Nazi recruitment methods, see Christian Gerlach, *Kalkulierte Morde. Die deutsche Wirtschafts- und Vernichtungspolitik in Weissrussland, 1941–1944* (Hamburg: Hamburger Edition, 1999), pp. 466–76; Karten Linne and Florian Dierl, eds., *Arbeitskräfte als Kriegsbeute. Der Fall Ost- und Südosteuropa, 1939–1945* (Berlin: Metropol, 2011).

33 See Cord Pagenstecher and Mark Buggeln, 'Zwangsarbeit', in Michael Wildt and Christoph Kreutzmüller, eds., *Berlin 1933–1945* (Munich: Siedler, 2013), pp. 127–42.

34 Racism also informed Canadian and US war policy; the US government interred 112,000 Japanese-Americans in camps in the western USA and the Canadian government interred 23,000 Japanese-Canadians; neither government employed them in forced labour.

Beginning in 1932, the Japanese systematically developed the infrastructure of the puppet state of Manchukuo/Manchuria, and subsequently established numerous modern, state-controlled industrial complexes for armaments production.[35] As a result, the number of workers in industries other than agriculture increased to 5.5 million by 1945, including 500,000 in construction. Countless Manchurian labourers worked under the Batou system – named for the Batou (coolie boss), who recruited workers and delivered them to employers.[36] Japanese business owners and managers preferred this quasi-feudal system of labour relations, because it supposedly corresponded to the customs of the despised Chinese. In Korea, a Japanese colony since 1910, at least 4.5 million Koreans were forced to work for the Japanese occupation powers; as in Manchukuo, they worked long hours for minuscule wages

Like foreign workers in the Old Reich, the 1.5 million Koreans as well as approximately 60,000 Chinese forced to work for industries in mainland Japan did so under deplorable conditions. However, foreign workers in Japan did not play as crucial a role in industry as they did in Germany. In Japan, they worked primarily in mining (coal, ore), doing mostly heavy manual labour in remote areas. When the Americans dropped the atomic bombs in 1945, at least 20,000 Koreans died in Hiroshima and another 2,000 in Nagasaki;[37] some estimates place Korean casualties much higher.

Between 1939 and 1944, the total percentage of Korean and Chinese workers in the Japanese workforce increased by 6 per cent. Roughly 9 per cent of Korean conscripted labourers died; and the Chinese mortality rate was 17.5 per cent, approximating that of Eastern European workers and Italian military internees conscripted by the Nazis.[38]

In addition to using Koreans and Chinese workers, beginning in early 1942 the Japanese military utilized roughly 130,000 white POWs. These Allied POWs were not employed in industry, but on transport infrastructure, in particular on railroad construction largely in the occupied territories. The high number of white prisoners whom the Japanese used for forced labour of

---

35 On the (relative) modernity of the Manchurian arms industry, see Mimura, *Planning for Empire*, pp. 67–68 and 196.

36 David Tucker, 'Labor Policy and the Construction Industry in Manchukuo: Systems of Recruitment, Management and Control', in Paul H. Kratoska, ed., *Asian Labor in the Wartime Japanese Empire: Unknown Histories* (Armonk, NY: Sharpe, 2005), pp. 21–57 (pp. 27, 29–57).

37 See 'Atomic bombings of Hiroshima and Nagasaki', Wikipedia (http://en.wikipedia.org/wiki/Atomic_bombings_of_Hiroshima_and_Nagasaki).

38 Mark Spoerer, 'Zwangsregimen im Vergleich. Deutschland und Japan im Ersten und Zweiten Weltkrieg', in Hans-Christoph Seidel, ed., *Zwangsarbeit im Europa des 20. Jahrhunderts Bewältigung und vergleichende Aspekte* (Essen: Klartext, 2007), pp. 215–18.

course pales before the almost 1 million POWs forced by 1945 to work for the German war economy, including more than 100,000 captured British soldiers.

The Allied powers also utilized POWs as a cheap source of labour. Of the 141,000 German POWs, held in the USA in September 1943, more than 100,000 were required to work, mostly on farms.[39] At least 30,000 German and Italian POWs worked in Canada, the majority in forestry. Of the half million Italians who surrendered in Africa, some 10,000 had to work on the Indian subcontinent, in Australia, or in Britain's African colonies.[40]

The Commonwealth's significance for Britain's prosecution of the war would be difficult to overestimate. South Africa provided coal and foodstuffs and once the war began, the British established an industrial development corporation dedicated to training technicians and a qualified workforce; as a result, the number of South Africans employed in the arms industry more than tripled between 1941 and 1942, growing from 124,000 to 413,000. The Indian subcontinent served as a primary exporter of agricultural products (even as food shortages in some Indian regions increased) as well as a supplier of textiles and light weaponry. In Australia with its 7 million inhabitants, New Zealand with nearly 2 million and Canada with over 11 million, the industrial sector also expanded, and with that expansion the total percentage of women in the industrial workforce increased. In particular, Canada, with its well-developed shipbuilding, vehicle and aviation industries contributed significantly to Allied war production; Canada produced 14,700 military aircraft, accounting for 22 per cent of the Commonwealth's post-1939 production; the Canadian shipbuilding industry, equally important, employed 126,000 workers.[41]

The Soviet command economy had no access to colonies; however, its Gulag system provided a vast disposable labour force. Estimates of the number imprisoned in the Gulag system range from 200,000 to 1 million.[42] Yet its economic significance for the Russian war economy remains a topic of

---

39 On German prisoners held in the USA, see Antonio Thompson, *Men in German Uniform: POWs in America during World War II* (Knoxville: University of Tennessee Press, 2010), pp. 90 and 130.

40 Ashley Jackson, *British Empire and the Second World War* (London: Hambledon Continuum, 2006), p. 361.

41 Jackson, *British Empire*, pp. 252, 490, 494.

42 For the estimates, see Ralf Stettner, '*Archipel GULag*'. *Stalins Zwangslager – Terrorinstrument und Wirtschaftsgigant – Entstehung, Organisation und Funktion des sowjetischen Lagersystems, 1928–1956* (Paderborn: Schöningh, 1996), pp. 297 and 307–8; Paul Gregory, 'An Introduction to the Economics of the Gulag', in Gregory and Lazarev, eds., *Economics of Forced Labor*, pp. 1–21 (pp. 13 and 17).

debate. That said, the prisoners undoubtedly played an important role in certain Soviet industrial sectors. Gulag prisoners could be deployed in extremely inhospitable regions, and unlike wage labourers without the enticement of premium pay. Gulag labourers worked thirteen-hour days doing heavy labour (plus the trek to the worksite) and were a highly mobile labour force. They could be used as a type of 'industrial reserve army', deployed without consent anywhere in the country and may have been essential in the industrialization of northern and eastern Siberia.[43]

Implementing the American model

In all the principal belligerents, industries pledged maximum output via the introduction of a regime of mass production. Its use also had the advantage of allowing the replacement of skilled workers with unskilled ones. However, the degree to which industries in different nations were prepared for this transition varied. Even before the First World War, Henry Ford introduced the assembly line in his plants; in contrast, European nations were latecomers to mass production, only beginning to introduce the American system of production in the 1920s and 1930s. In addition to Taylorism and Fordism, Charles Bedaux's system of performance rating had achieved relatively widespread use in pre-war French and British companies.[44] In contrast, until the mid-1930s, only a few German companies employed it.[45] Yet, by at least the late 1930s, all the principal belligerents had introduced an American-style system of production and labour management.

Only in the USA did the start of the Second World War fail to mark a sharp departure in the development of industrial labour organization and production technology; instead, American companies perfected the system that was the model for all other states.[46] Henry Ford established an enormous operation for aeroplane production, where every 63 minutes a bomber rolled off the assembly line.[47] In Great Britain, the decisions of business elites

43 Gregory, 'Economics of the Gulag', pp. 4–5.
44 Howard F. Gospel, *Markets, Firms and the Management of Labour in Modern Britain* (Cambridge University Press, 1992), p. 55.
45 Paul Erker, 'Das Bedaux-System. Neue Aspekte der historischen Rationalisierungsforschung', *Zeitschrift für Unternehmensgeschichte* 41:4 (1996), 139–58.
46 On the system's perfection, see Mansel G. Blackford, *The Rise of Modern Business in Great Britain, The United States, and Japan* (Chapel Hill: University of North Carolina Press, 2008), pp. 144–68.
47 Richard Overy, *Why the Allies Won* (New York: W. W. Norton, 1995), pp. 95–100; Vincent Curcio, *Henry Ford* (Oxford University Press, 2013), pp. 252–74.

during the interwar period perpetuated traditional practices that conflicted with unfettered rationalization. Still, the Ford system had appeared there long before the Second World War began. Since the end of the 1920s, continuous flow production, particularly in the automobile industry, had been used in some elements of production. Morris, one of Britain's three largest automobile makers, opened a new plant in 1934, which utilized the assembly line for all operations.[48]

Close wartime economic cooperation between the USA and Great Britain accelerated the modernization of British industry; the establishment of the Anglo-American Council on Productivity (AACP), which sponsored joint missions to the USA by British business owners and workers to study American production methods, institutionalized the modernization drive. The extent to which AACP activities contributed to modernization remains unclear.[49] Fearing a devaluation of their labour, skilled British workers in particular resisted the introduction of Taylorism and Fordism. German and Italian workers also resisted, but there the authoritarian regimes quickly crushed opposition.

Although the modernization of industry in Italy paled in comparison to that in the USA, Fordism had been introduced prior to Mussolini assuming power. In 1923, Agnelli Giovanni, the founder of Fiat and later a strong supporter of Mussolini,[50] introduced the assembly line for some elements of production at the Fiat plant at Lingotto. In May 1939, he opened the Mirafiori Plant, which employed more than 20,000 workers and made maximum use of Ford's system. In the early 1930s, the Italian communist theorist Antonio Gramsci spoke of the 'beginning of a Fordist clarion call' in Italy.[51]

French industry also modernized in the 1920s and 1930s. Like Agnelli, Louis Renault, André Citroën and other French industrialists visited the USA, inspected Ford factories, and subsequently introduced modern production

---

48 Blackford, *Rise of Modern Business*, pp. 153–4, 157–68; Dewey, *War and Progress*, p. 100; Steven Tolliday, 'The Diffusion and Transformation of Fordism: Britain and Japan Compared', in Robert Boyer, ed., *Between Imitation and Innovation: The Transfer and Hybridization of Productive Models in the International Automobile Industry* (Oxford University Press, 1998), pp. 57–96.

49 For a sceptical assessment, see Stephen Broadberry and Peter Howlett, 'The United Kingdom: "Victory At All Costs"', in Mark Harrison, ed., *Economics of World War II: Six Great Powers in International Comparison* (Cambridge University Press, 1998), pp. 43–80 (p. 64).

50 On Agnelli's support for Mussolini and fascism, see Vito Avantario, *Die Agnellis. Die heimlichen Herrscher Italiens* (Frankfurt: Campus, 2002), pp. 67–90.

51 Antonio Gramsci, *Gefängnishefte. Kritische Gesamtausgabe* (Hamburg: Argument Hamburg, 1999), vol. IX, p. 2070.

techniques at home. In the Bohemian region of Czechoslovakia, similar advances in industry were made; consequently when the Nazis occupied the 'remainder of Czech territory' in mid-March 1939, they acquired a relatively modern armaments industry as well as Tomas Bata's modern, multinational shoe manufacturing empire.[52]

In Japan, companies also introduced Fordism in the 1920s, albeit in a modest fashion. At that time, Japanese engineers began extensively studying Taylor's 'scientific' management principle and Ford's model of labour organization. In large part, Japan's positive reception of Fordism can be attributed to Friedrich Gottl-Ottililienfeld's enthusiasm for it. Gottl-Ottililienfeld, a German political scientist and economist who coined the term Fordism in 1924, had significant influence among Japanese economic experts.[53] In addition, between 1925 and 1927, Ford and General Motors established subsidiaries in Japan that employed workers on assembly lines. As a result, many Japanese industrialists, including the founder of Toyota, gained practical knowledge of Fordism. In the early 1930s, the Japanese Ministry for Commerce and Industry established the Industry Rationalization Bureau; the new bureau was based on the German *Reichskuratorium für Wirtschaftlichkeit* (1921), which functioned as a kind of publicity bureau for Fordism and Taylorism.[54] By the late 1930s/early 1940s, a growing number of Japanese industries with state support introduced assembly line production, in most cases based on German prototypes.[55] To accelerate the changeover, Germany sent engineers to Japan during the second half of the war.[56]

The Soviet 'arms miracle' (the non-stop, dramatic increase in arms and munitions production) can be attributed to two developments – a reduction in types of weaponry produced and the standardization of production methods. Both developments favoured the dissemination and refinement

---

52 For path-breaking work on Bata, see Anne Sudrow, *Der Schuh im Nationalsozialismus. Eine Produktgeschichte im deutsch-britisch-amerikanischen Vergleich* (Göttingen: Wallstein, 2010).

53 See Mimura, *Planning for Empire*, pp. 115–16 and 129; on the appeal of Ford's mass production techniques in Japan, see also pp. 26–41.

54 On the RKW as model for rationalizing Japanese industry, see ibid., p. 37.

55 Kazuo Kazuo Wada, 'The Emergence of the "Flow Production" Method in Japan', in Haruhito Shiomi and Kazuo Wada, eds., *Fordism Transformed: The Development of Production Methods in the Automobile Industry* (Oxford University Press, 1995), pp. 13–21; on the introduction of the assembly line in other Japanese industries, see Blackford, *Rise of Modern Business*, p. 166.

56 On the introduction of continuous flow production in Japan and its limits, see Erich Pauer, 'Japan's Technical Mobilization in the Second World War', in Erich Pauer, ed., *Japan's War Economy* (New York: Routledge, 1999), pp. 39–64 (pp. 53–9).

of Ford production methods.[57] In the early 1920s, the Soviet leadership had expressed enthusiasm for Fordism. Lenin's positive reception of Taylorism[58] paved the way for Fordism. The desire to catch up with the West economically together with Soviet scientific fetishism resulted in Fordism's unequivocal acceptance as an achievement that had to be transferred to socialism; thus, the Soviets copied the American example. In 1925, Ford's autobiography *My Life and Work* appeared in Russian translation, going through four editions in seven years; it was read 'with a zeal usually reserved for the study of Lenin'.[59] In the late 1920s, the Soviets imported American know-how, entered joint ventures with American companies (including Ford), and employed several thousand foreign consultants. Stephen Kotkin described a 'veritable "Who's Who" of leading capitalist firms, the originators of the culture of Fordism' that during the 1930s 'advised and aided Stalinist industrialization'.[60] The historian Thomas P. Hughes concluded, 'an emotional cult grew up around the methods and even the person of Ford' in the Soviet Union.[61]

Aside from strict economic motives, Soviet enthusiasm for Fordism and Taylorism emerged from a desire to move beyond bourgeois time management and work discipline and thus complete the brutal, high Stalinist industrialization, which relied on a peasant workforce.[62] The Soviets employed Fordism and Taylorism as a form of 'work pedagogy', aimed at indoctrinating a still undisciplined Russian peasantry – much the same as workhouses and other measures had been used to tame an unruly Western European workforce in the eighteenth and nineteenth centuries.

The use of Fordism as a means of controlling the workforce was even more pronounced in Germany. In the mid-1920s, Ford's production system was enthusiastically received in Germany. In 1922, Ford's autobiography appeared in German translation and was an instant success, selling more copies than in any other developed European nation; in its first year alone, it

---

57 Overy, *Why the Allies Won*, pp. 185–207.
58 See Vladimir Lenin, *Die nächste Aufgaben der Sowjetmacht (1918)*, vol. xxvii of *Lenin, Werke* (Berlin: Dietz Verlag, 1978), pp. 249–50.
59 Thomas P. Hughes, *American Genesis: A Century of Invention and Technological Enthusiasm, 1870–1970* (University of Chicago Press, 2004), pp. 269–70.
60 Stephen Kotkin, *Magnetic Mountain: Stalinism as a Civilization* (Berkeley: University of California Press, 1995), p. 364.
61 Hughes, *American Genesis*, p. 269. On the modified Russian edition of Ford's autobiography, see Davis L. Lewis, *The Public Image of Henry Ford: An American Hero and his Company* (Detroit: Wayne State University Press, 1987).
62 Dietrich Beyrau, 'Sowjetisches Modell. Über Fiktionen zu den Realitäten', in Peter Hübner, Christoph Klessmann and Klaus Tenfelde, eds., *Arbeiter im Staatssozialismus. Ideologischer Anspruch und soziale Wirklichkeit* (Cologne: Böhlau, 2005), pp. 47–70.

went through twenty-nine editions. Against the backdrop of Germany's defeat in the First World War, revolution in 1918/19, and hyperinflation in 1923, many German industrialists viewed the book as 'gospel'[63] and its author as a saviour. German industrialists discussed Ford and Fordism during the Weimar era as the solution to all evils. However, its practical implementation remained limited.[64]

By the mid-1930s, the number of companies utilizing the Ford system increased substantially, due to the mass production of arms, the Nazi appointment of special envoys to key industrial sectors (1938), and the reduction in types of vehicles produced. Countless industries began utilizing Taylor's scientific management approach to analyse their operations. They rationalized production, implemented Fordism, and thus reduced reliance on skilled labour. The assembly line's introduction also imposed strict discipline on unskilled female and male labourers. In 1942, the head manager of an aircraft manufacturing plant concluded: 'For us, it is no longer a question of whether we want to utilize continuous flow production, but how we make it flow even better.'[65]

By then, leading industrial managers had their sights set not only on civilian foreign workers, but also POWs and KZ inmates. But the Gestapo and the SS viewed these latter groups as more prone to resistance and to sabotage. The influential manager and aviation-engineering expert Wilhelm Werner spoke directly to the Auto Union AG (today, Audi) about Fordism as a method of control. Based on multiple extended visits to the USA, Werner developed a reputation as an assembly line expert and was named head of the aero-engine ring in 1941. In mid-October 1943, he explained that engine production still relied heavily on craftsmanship. The result was loss of work time, due among other things to unauthorized breaks and absences from the worksite. This 'unproductive time' increased with the use of foreign workers, unless counter-measures were taken. This required the entire operation to utilize the 'American production' system. In addition to increasing output,

63 See, for example, Waldemar Zimmerman, 'Fords Evangelium von der technisch-sozialen Dienstleistung', *Schmollers Jahrbuch* 48 (1924), 87–119.
64 For an overview, see Rüdiger Hachtmann, 'Fordismus', *Docupedia-Zeitgeschichte* (http://docupedia.de/zg/Fordismus).
65 Quoted in Rainer Fröbe, 'Der Arbeitseinsatz von KZ-Häftlingen und die Perspektive der Industrie, 1943–1945', in Ulrich Herbert, ed., *Europa und der 'Reichseinsatz'. Ausländische Zivilarbeiter, Kriegsgefangene und KZ-Häftlingen in Deutschland, 1938–1945* (Essen: Klartext, 1991), pp. 351–83 (p. 355). On KZ prisoners' use on assembly lines, see Rüdiger Hachtmann, 'Fordism and Unfree Labor: Aspects of the Work Deployment of Concentration Camp Prisoners in German Industry between 1941 and 1944', *International Review of Social History* 55:3 (2010), 485–513.

the American system had the advantage of making it easy to identify malingerers; if one worker walked away, the entire operation came to a standstill. Werner asserted, 'With such a system I can coerce 100 percent work out of foreigners.'[66] Unconcerned about the welfare of foreign workers, employers accelerated the work pace. Thus from the viewpoint of KZ prisoners – and likewise foreign workers and POWs – the assembly lines became 'insatiable Gods fond of human sacrifices'.[67]

In modernizing production based on the American model, the Nazi regime moved beyond Taylorism and Fordism. For example, beginning in mid-1942, the Wage Group Catalogue Iron and Metal (*Lohngruppenkatalog Eisen und Metall*, LKEM) introduced a complex job evaluation process based on Charles Bedaux's model.[68] The LKEM's relative modernity and functionality for differing political systems can be gauged by the fact that until 1960, the vast majority of West German metalworkers remained classified according to LKEM categories, albeit Nazi provisions discriminating against 'foreign labourers' were eliminated in 1945.

Nazi authorities merged social engineering and racist concepts in an increasingly sinister amalgam. DAF concepts and policy offer a striking example. The DAF understood itself as the spearhead of anti-Semitism, and since summer 1933, it pushed for the de-judification (*Entjudung*) of the workforce and of management. Moreover, the DAF prepared workers ideologically for a racially segregated workforce. For example, prior to the war, the Labour Science Institute, the DAF's Brain Trust, explained, 'people from the east or east Baltic as a rule were quite good at assembly line and shop work; in contrast people predominantly from the Nordic or Westphalia [regions] were less suited' for assembly work.[69] To reframe labour–management conflicts as the product of racial differences rather than class struggle, the DAF utilized then state-of-the art labour science and sociological methods first developed in the USA. This was no accident, but had precedents. As Gauleiter of Cologne-Aachen and editor of the anti-Semitic *Westdeutscher Beobachter* in the early 1930s, Ley published articles praising Ford's concepts.[70] Thus, Ford

---

66 Quoted in Fröbe, 'Der Arbeitseinsatz von KZ-Häftlingen', p. 362.

67 Buggeln, *Arbeit & Gewalt*, p. 319.

68 For more detail, see Recker, *Nationalsozialistische Sozialpolitik*, pp. 223–49; Tilla Siegel, *Leistung und Lohn in der nationalsozialistischen Ordnung der Arbeit* (Opladen: Westdeutscher Verlag, 1986), pp. 165–209; Rüdiger Hachtmann, *Industriearbeit im Dritten Reich* (Göttingen: Vandenhoeck & Ruprecht, 1989), pp. 207–23.

69 Arbeitswissenschaftliches Institut der DAF, 'Die Einsatzfähigkeit von Arbeitskräften für Fliessbandarbeiten', in *Jahrbuch* (Berlin 1939), vol. I, 441–52, citation on p. 449.

70 Liebscher, *Freude und Arbeit*, pp. 170–1.

had been an icon of the early Nazi movement, both as anti-Semite[71] and as a modern industrialist whose social concepts promised the general pacification of the working class.[72]

The Nazis found Ford's concept of a modern consumer society equally fascinating. On 30 July 1938, Ford's seventy-fifth birthday, the Nazis awarded him the Grand Cross of the Supreme Order of the German Eagle in recognition of his biography, which promised a crisis-proof infinite loop of mass production and mass consumption. It was the highest honour that the regime could bestow upon a foreigner. But the Nazi vision for a mass consumer society, unlike Ford's, would be racially segregated. By 1939, the distinctive features of this mass consumer society had taken shape in Germany.[73] Yet, despite programmes like the KdF, the Nazis never fully developed a mass consumer society; Fordism ultimately served defence priorities; in short, it was War Fordism.

Axis powers and worker loyalty

While the political loyalty of British and American workers is unsurprising, Soviet workers also remained loyal, despite devastating shortages in supply and Stalin's brutal use of force against Soviet citizenry. This loyalty had various sources – the belief that only Stalin could guarantee victory, Soviet propaganda's appeal to nationalism, and the greater threat of Nazi racial ideology. But why, unlike Italian workers, did German workers remain loyal to the NS regime until almost war's end? German infrastructure, industries and homes had been subject to heavy aerial Allied bombardments since 1943. Similarly, why did Japanese workers remain loyal?

Only by comparing NS Germany with Fascist Italy does a plausible explanation for German loyalty emerge. By the mid-1930s, Italian workers seemingly had made peace with fascism; however, this truce proved temporary. Mussolini never alleviated social inequalities; thus Fascist rhetoric proclaiming

71 Curcio, *Ford*, pp. 144–58.
72 Rüdiger Hachtmann, "'Die Begründer der amerikanischen Technik sind fast lauter schwäbisch-allemannische Menschen'. Nazi-Deutschland, der Blick auf die USA und die 'Amerikanisierung' der industriellen Produktionsstrukturen im 'Dritten Reich'", in Alf Lüdtke, Inge Marssolek and Adelheid von Saldern, eds., *Amerikanisierung. Traum und Alptraum im Deutschland des 20. Jahrhunderts* (Stuttgart: Franz Steiner Verlag 1996), pp. 37–66.
73 On KdF tourism, see Hasso Spado, 'Fordism, "Mass Tourism" and the Third Reich: The "Strength through Joy" Seaside Resort as an Index Fossil', *Journal of Social History* 38 (2004), 127–55.

a united nation could only whitewash the harsh realities of Italian society for so long. Consequently, Italian industrial workers, particularly those residing in the heavily industrialized regions of northern and central Italy, never actively supported the regime; mass strikes in Turin and Milan in 1943 made clear just how fragile Mussolini's popular support was.[74] The strikes broke out prior to the Allied invasion of Sicily, and from the outset were directed against the regime. Rationing instituted in Italy in 1939 as well as Allied aerial attacks claiming at least 64,000 lives turned unhappiness with Fascism into hatred. Increasingly regime opponents openly criticized the Fascist dictatorship.

However, the primary reason that Germans remained loyal and Italians did not can be traced to the very different systems of control utilized by the two regimes. If the Nazi dictatorship and the German population remained closely associated with the *Volksgemeinschaft* despite massive Allied bombing raids, seven elements of NS policy were responsible:

(1) In Germany, the Nazis were more successful in destroying the organized labour movement than the Fascists were in Italy. Moreover, they skilfully utilized terror to enforce worker conformity. While foreign workers were subjected to the most draconian measures, German workers were not exempt from intimidation and disciplinary measures in the workplace. Those who failed to meet Nazi standards could be sent to labour education or even concentration camps; by war's end at least 100,000 German workers had been interned in labour education camps.[75]

(2) The dissolution of trade unions and workers' parties allowed the Nazis to destroy the socialist milieu and proletarian subculture, already weakened by post-1918 tensions between socialists and communists. The DAF became the new community service provider, replacing traditional socialist community organizations. The working-class communities were further weakened by Allied bombings that reduced many traditional working–class neighbourhoods and socialist strongholds to rubble.

---

74 Trieste and environs constituted the exception. As part of the Habsburg Empire until 1918, some workers there resented Slavs, making them vulnerable to Fascism. See Tobias Abse, 'Italian Workers and Italian Fascism', in Richard Bessel, ed., *Fascist Italy and Nazi Germany: Comparisons and Contrasts* (Cambridge University Press, 1996), pp. 40–60 (pp. 42–3). On the March 1943 strikes, see Timothy W. Mason, *Nazism, Fascism, and the Working Class*, ed. Jane Caplan (Cambridge University Press, 1995), pp. 274–94.

75 On labour education camps, see Gabriele Lofti, *KZ der Gestapo. Arbeitserziehungslager im Dritten Reich* (Stuttgart: Deutsche-Verlag-Anstalt, 2000); on Nazi use of terror, see also Ian Kershaw, *The End: Hitler's Germany 1944–45* (New York: Penguin, 2011).

(3) Nazi policy systematically eliminated any space in which workers could articulate independent collective interests. Labour law was reconfigured from the ground up and the DAF reorganized labour so as to isolate workers from one another. In his classic work *Behemoth* (1942), Franz Leopold Neumann, described the DAFs 'complete atomization of the German working class'.[76]

(4) The fact that worker discontent in Germany remained within manageable limits also reflected the dramatic shift from devastating unemployment in the early 1930s to full and even over-employment in the mid-to-late 1930s. Moreover, German women's entry into the workforce in 1936 compensated for the lack of increase in real wages; until 1939, women's paid employment brought a real increase in family income. Additionally, Nazi fears about a repeat of the November Revolution of 1918 meant that the regime was careful to ensure that the German population in the Old Reich and in Austria after its annexation in 1938 was adequately supplied with food staples and other daily necessities.

(5) From 1941, the racial stratification of Old Reich industries also played an important role. German workers, as members of the 'master Aryan race', automatically moved up in the staff hierarchy, making them active participants in Nazi rule whether they wanted to be or not. At the very least, this complicity guaranteed the passive loyalty of the workforce, which also feared victor's vengeance if Germany lost the war. In addition, the threat of long prison sentences or even death for showing solidarity with foreign workers also guaranteed loyalty.

(6) After 1942, the sword of Damocles hung over the heads of German workers, as the Nazis shut down less productive factories and sent freed-up workers to the front. The threat of being sent to the front, particularly the dreaded Eastern Front, intensified competition among male German workers, between male and female German workers, as well as with foreign workers. Needing to demonstrate their 'indispensability', male German workers accepted in silence the extension of the work-week and the intensification of labour.

(7) In addition to the ubiquitous Nazi propaganda, German workers could not avoid the social paternalism of the DAF. Despite the bad reputation of the DAF, the popularity of some of its programmes especially among

---

76 Franz L. Neumann, *Behemoth: Struktur und Praxis des Nationalsozialismus 1933–1944*, ed. Gert Schäfer (Frankfurt am Main: Fischer Taschenbuch-Verlag, 1984), p. 480.

younger workers – e.g. KdF tourism and leisure activities, Beauty of Labour (*Schönheit der Arbeit*) and workplace competitions – dampened discontent with the regime.

While the lack of first-hand accounts means that caution is warranted in assessing the workers' attitudes, it is clear that the Nazis slowly integrated a significant share of the German workforce into the *Volksgemeinschaft*, and that many of these workers became Nazi supporters. In the summer of 1942, Walter Ulbricht, the future leader of the communist German Democratic Republic (GDR), interviewed German POWS in Soviet captivity. He was shocked to discover that Nazi 'social demagogy' had made a strong impression on young German workers. In particular, organized KdF trips, the propaganda about the people's car, the DAF promise of social advancement, and anti-Soviet propaganda had made deep inroads into workers' organizations.[77]

As for the related question of why Germany's ally, Japan, had to be overpowered through massive military strikes that culminated in the dropping of atomic bombs on Nagasaki and Hiroshima, loyalty to the Tenno and the samurai ideal were crucial. These attitudes are in some ways similar to the operation of the Führer principle and the warlike cult of masculinity promoted by the Nazis. However, other factors also played a role. First, unions and workers' parties in industrialized Japan traditionally had been weaker than their German counterparts. The density of Japanese labour organization was well below 10 per cent of the workforce. Moreover, the union leadership's voluntary synchronization with regime aims and the voluntary dissolution of labour organizations demoralized those Japanese workers who sympathized with socialism. In addition, in 1932 the independent socialist milieu in Japan appeared much less developed than in Germany.

Yet, the Japanese worker was by no means as compliant as the military regime suggested. The number of workers' disputes and the absenteeism rate during the war were higher in Japan than in Germany. Nevertheless the Japanese military regime chose not to employ the same degree of terroristic coercion domestically as did the Nazi regime, 'because of the lower social significance of industrial workers'. In addition, the communal ideals cultivated in Japanese factories were modelled on the familial community, not the

---

77 Walter Ulbricht, 'Hinweise zur propagandistischen Auswertung der Erfahrungen aus den Diskussionen mit Kriegsgefangenen, vom 12. Sept. 1942', in *Zur Geschichte der Deutschen Arbeiterbewegung. Aus Reden und Aufsätzen*, vol. II: *1933–1946* (Berlin: Dietz 1966), pp. 160–2.

warfront community, as was the case in Germany.[78] However, like Germany, a sense of racial superiority underpinned the communal orientation and here too it was utilized as a means of overcoming the 'class struggle' and class-specific interests. Finally the social paternalistic instruments of integration designed to pacify the workforce appeared to have had some effect; in contrast to Germany, it was at the plant level that the link remained strongest.

Conclusion

Italian fascism, Nazism and the proto-fascist Japanese regime failed on every front, not just militarily. Moreover that failure cannot be attributed solely to Allied superior economic power.[79] The methods by which these regimes attempted to integrate the workforce politically and organizationally into the state-controlled social system proved successful only under the exceptional circumstances of war, and then only temporarily.

The structural weaknesses of organizations like the DAF and Sanpo did not go unnoticed by leading protagonists in either regime. Japanese industry managers, more in tune with employee attitudes than government officials, observed that Sanpo and the 'discussion councils' had not achieved the level of success that proponents predicted. Even the Japanese Home Ministry noticed that workers remained alienated from institutions created after 1939/40. At the height of the Pacific War, many early supporters of industrial patriotic movements reversed their position, now supporting structural changes to Sanpo so as to give workers' voices more weight. In July 1944, the influential chairman of the Labour Service Council considered creating a position for Sanpo, comparable to what unions had occupied in the early 1930s.[80]

A similar discussion had been initiated even earlier in the Third Reich. In early 1935, influential industrialists expressed sharp criticism of the 'masters of DAF' and the Trustee Boards because they 'had no support inside the plants'. In lieu of DAF representatives and trust councils, they wanted representatives with genuine ties to the workforce. Some industrialists even thought of

---

78 As in Nazi Germany this harmonious community was more ideal than reality, see Gordon, *Labor Relations in Japan*, p. 224.
79 See Adam Tooze, *The Wages of Destruction: The Making and Breaking of the Nazi Economy* (London: Allen Lane, 2006).
80 Garon, *State and Labor in Modern Japan*, p. 226.

establishing regional 'labour committees'; in short they proposed recreating pre-1932 constellations for collective bargaining.[81]

At a conference on 20 June 1940 at which almost all relevant representatives of German industry had been in attendance, the topic was the future of labour relations. Attendees agreed that 'DAF representatives were not taken seriously by shop stewards or rank and file workers and that it had been a mistake when the people with actual experience in social policy matters, i.e. trade union officials and business syndicates, had been thrown out.' They also agreed that state control of labour contracts could only be a temporary solution. On a long-term basis, an authoritarian wage policy, dictated by institutions such as trustee councils, was doomed to failure. In the future, worker representatives and employers should 'work together to solve social problems' without the interference of state institutions.[82] The unstated premises underpinning authoritarian organizations like the DAF ultimately were incompatible with the social structures of a modern industrial society.

In short, industrialists understood that authoritarian regulation of employment contracts and labour law did not safeguard employees' rights and thus in the long run could not prevent class struggle and worker protests. Between 1935 and 1937, the Nazis utilized massive coercion and an expanded spy system to suppress a small wave of strikes.[83] In Japan the number of strikes increased dramatically after 1939.[84] When in 1941 Japanese authorities introduced more restrictions on strikes, the rate of absenteeism climbed steeply. In Italy, the mass strike in northern Italy in the spring of 1943 presaged the collapse of Mussolini's regime.

81 Undated protocol of the meeting, sent as attachment from Ernst Poensgen to Fritz Springorum, 16 March 1936, Archiv de August-Thyssen-Hütte, Vereinigte Stahlwerke, Sozialwirtschaftliche Abteilung 14-01-2/1. On this, see Rüdiger Hachtmann, 'Wiederbelebung von Tarifparteien oder Militarisierung der Arbeit? Kontroversen um die Grundlinien der nationalsozialistischen Tarifpolitik und die "künftige Gestaltung der NS-Arbeitsverfassung" 1936 bis 1944', in Karl-Christian Führer, ed., *Tarifbeziehungen und Tarifpolitik in Deutschland im historischen Wandel* (Bonn: Dietz, 2004), pp. 114–40.

82 Meeting with ministerial secretary Dr Kimmich at the Mannesmann House on 20 June 1940, in Rüdiger Hachtmann, 'Von der Klassenharmonie zum regulierten Klassenkampf: Pläne führender Repräsentanten der deutschen Industrie zur Institutionalisierung authentischer Arbeitnehmervertretungen im Dritten Reich', *Jahrbuch Sozialbewegungen,* vol. I: *Arbeiterbewegung und Faschismus* (Frankfurt am Main: Campus, 1984), pp. 159–83.

83 On the German strikes, 1935–37, see Günter Morsch, 'Streik im "Dritten Reich"', *VfZ* 36 (1988), 649–89.

84 For a detailed account, see Gordon, *Labor Relations in Japan*, pp. 314–22 and 440. See also Garon, *Labor in Modern Japan*, p. 249; Taira, 'Economic Development', p. 634.

The Japanese Sanpo, state unions in Fascist Italy, and the Nazi DAF proved to be paper tigers. Although the DAF nominally acquired additional competencies in 1943/44, the largest National Socialist mass organization was eerily quiet after the autumn of 1942, their social base seemingly gone.[85] As an organizational model, the DAF failed even before Allied military attacks destroyed the regime. It failed, even though the German industrial workforce, like the Japanese, did not strike out against the dictatorship. The model of labour relations used in the USA and Great Britain, which encouraged the voluntary, equitable and active involvement of autonomous trade unions proved superior.

85 Rüdiger Hachtmann, 'Introduction', in *Ein Koloss auf tönernen Füssen: Das Gutachten des Wirtschaftsprüfers Karl Eicke über die Deutsche Arbeitsfront vom 31. Juli 1936* (Munich: Oldenbourg, 2006), pp. 60–1.

12

Battles for morale

An entangled history of total war in Europe, 1939–1945

JOCHEN HELLBECK

By the mid-1930s political and military leaders throughout Europe and the world were preparing for war. They believed that the future war, which some actively sought and others tried to defuse, would be even vaster in scope and destructive power than the recent Great War. That war, German general Erich Ludendorff wrote in 1935, had been the world's first 'total war', in that beyond pitting enemy forces against each other it had mobilized entire populations for the war effort and targeted the 'psyche and the vitality of enemy peoples with the goal of undermining and paralyzing them'. In view of technological advances after 1918, notably radio broadcasting and aeroplanes capable of carrying bombs and propaganda leaflets deep behind enemy lines, the next war would encompass the entire territory of all belligerents and 'immediately touch the life and soul of every single member of the belligerent peoples'.[1] To prevail in this war, Ludendorff implied, state leaders required effective methods of mobilizing all the nation's psychological and moral resources.

Since Ludendorff first popularized the term 'total war', numerous scholars have used it to characterize the Second World War as a new type of war – one that had vaster aims, claimed infinitely more lives, and blurred distinctions between front and rear, soldiers and civilians, combatants and noncombatants. A vast literature exists focusing on how respective regimes mobilized their societies and economies in wartime, how war propaganda machines came into being and home fronts were built, and how soldiers of different nations fought. Yet, perhaps because the mandate of total war is assumed to have shaped belligerent regimes and their populations throughout Europe in equal manner, there are virtually no studies that compare different

---

[1] Erich Ludendorff, *Der totale Krieg* (Munich: Luddendorffs Verlag, 1935), pp. 4–5.

regimes with an eye to different understandings of the meaning of war and different ways of waging it.[2] A single chapter cannot do justice to such a vast subject, and so the aim here is more modest: to sketch out how three regimes mobilized for war – Germany, Great Britain and the Soviet Union.[3]

An ongoing focus of the chapter is morale, both at the individual and aggregate levels, and the mechanisms of its creation or undoing. Over the course of the war, all three regimes came to consider moralization (or morale building) and demoralization as essential to the war effort, and they invested considerable effort in observing and shaping the moods and the conduct of their citizens and of enemy populations. Yet they did so with varying intensity and in different ways. Even the lexicon of morale differed from place to place. In 1940, a British researcher for the Mass-Observation project noted, 'The word "morale" has been used widely by press and Government propaganda to describe the state of the public mind about the war and the principles for which we are fighting.'[4] This appears a good working definition of morale for wartime England, but it applies less well to Germany and the Soviet Union, where other terms were used. German wartime observers often spoke of 'the moods and the conduct' (*Stimmungen und Haltung*) of soldiers and civilians; they sometimes also invoked the 'spiritual unity' (*seelische Geschlossenheit*) of the German people. Soviet surveillance agents assessed the 'moods' (*nastroeniia*) and the 'political-moral state' (*politiko-moral'noe sostoianie*) of soldiers and civilians. These distinct terms, the chapter will show, reflected distinct mobilizing practices that differed in their aims.[5]

The chapter explores the battles for morale waged in Great Britain, the Soviet Union and Germany. Moving from country to country, the discussion becomes increasingly dense as it traces how war cultures became entangled, whether by drawing close to one another, as in the British–Soviet alliance, or by clashing, as in Germany's war against Britain and the Soviet Union. The study reveals a great deal of dialogue, through competition and attempted emulation, as well as underlying currents of confidence and crisis, victory and defeat, that needs to be read alongside the well-known military course of events.

---

2 See accompanying bibliographical essay for a discussion of scholarship on social mobilization during the Second World War.
3 The chapter limits itself to the European theatre of war, as it showcases a particularly rich and sustained dialogue between individual belligerents. It leaves largely unaddressed the war cultures of the USA, Japan and the British Empire.
4 Cited in Dorothy Sheridan, ed., *Wartime Women: An Anthology of Women's Wartime Writing for Mass-Observation 1937–45* (London: Heinemann, 1990), pp. 110–11.
5 See also Ian McLaine, *Ministry of Morale: Home Front Morale and the Ministry of Information in World War II* (London: Allen & Unwin, 1979), pp. 1–8.

Britain at war

When Germany attacked Poland, Britons braced for an intense aerial assault, which for years had been their vision of the total war of the future. On 1 September 1939, British authorities enacted a voluntary mass evacuation of 1.5 million school children, their mothers, and teachers from large cities to safer rural areas. The BBC broadcasted a limited radio programme of essential information, religious solace and light musical fare to provide relief from the frenetic war. The dreaded enemy bombers did not materialize, and the evacuation was called off weeks later.[6] The period from September 1939 through April 1940 came to be known as the Phoney War because of the low level of military engagement between Britain and Germany. Yet, the term does not take into account the intense psychological warfare waged by Germany following Britain's declaration of war. On 18 September 1939, Joseph Goebbels's propaganda ministry launched an English-language news station based in Hamburg. It featured nightly broadcasts aimed at the United Kingdom seeking to weaken British war resolve. The British press ridiculed the broadcasters, some of whom spoke with comically upper-class accents, as 'Lord Haw-Haw'. But these broadcasts drew an estimated 6 million British listeners in 1939 and 1940, partly because they provided details on British military losses, about which the BBC remained silent. 'Lord Haw Haw's' reporting not only detailed military events, it also targeted social, economic and political problems in British life, ranging from Britain's enduring slum system and mass unemployment to the cruel colonial practices of the British Empire. In addressing these themes, the broadcasts celebrated National Socialist achievements, thereby presenting Nazi Germany as a revolutionary order committed to social justice.[7]

Compared with the sophistication of Goebbels's propaganda machine, British efforts to mould public morale in the early phase of the war appeared feeble and quaint. British leaders recognized Nazi Germany's edge in disseminating effective propaganda, yet they hesitated to answer in kind, lest they also appear totalitarian. On 4 September 1939, the government activated the Ministry of Information, which had been planned since 1935.[8] One of the

---

6 Uri Bialer, *The Shadow of the Bomber: The Fear of Air Attack and British Politics, 1932–1939* (London: Royal Historical Society, 1989); Siân Nicholas, *The Echo of War: Home Front Propaganda and the Wartime BBC, 1939–1945* (Manchester University Press, 1996), pp. 29–33.

7 Martin A. Doherty, *Nazi Wireless Propaganda: Lord Haw-Haw and British Public Opinion* (Edinburgh University Press, 2000), pp. 48–52.

8 McLaine, *Ministry of Morale*, p. 12.

ministry's first measures was to distribute a poster, which its planners conceived as a 'war-cry' that would rally the British public behind the war effort and put everyone in an 'offensive mood at once'. The poster featured an emblem of the British crown, and underneath it the words: 'YOUR COURAGE, YOUR CHEERFULNESS, YOUR RESOLUTION WILL BRING US VICTORY.' By many accounts the poster failed in its objective. Mass-Observation (M-O), an independent polling agency founded in 1937, reported that ordinary Britons read the slogan cynically, as sacrifices to be made by the many for the few.[9] Internal government documents from the first months of the war spoke of a sense of moral uncertainty, which turned into full-fledged political crisis when on 10 May 1940 Germany invaded the Netherlands, Belgium and France. Prime Minister Chamberlain, whose complacent style of government provoked growing exasperation, resigned that day, replaced by the war-minded Winston Churchill. Later in May, the Ministry of Information foresaw a rise in 'fear, confusion, suspicion, class-feeling, and defeatism' among the British population and recommended changes in BBC programming (a public, yet not state-controlled entity). Since the first days of the war, the BBC had been under fire for its inadequate broadcasting. Specifically, the ministry suggested that the BBC tone down its 'cultured voice' and bring in speakers from the political left or the working class. Clearly Germany's harping on British social inequalities was on the minds of British government officials, who conceded the 'revolutionary' quality of the Nazi order and were under pressure to develop a firm response, in both military and social terms.[10]

These recommendations led to the creation of two new BBC broadcasts, 'Postscripts' (targeting domestic audiences), and 'Britain Speaks' (aimed at US listeners). Both featured the dramatist, social critic and war veteran J. B. Priestley. Priestley aired the first 'Postscript' on 5 June, two days after the evacuation of the British Expeditionary Force from Dunkirk and one day after Churchill's address to the House of Commons, where he proclaimed, 'We shall not flag nor fail. We shall go on to the end. We shall fight on the beaches, we shall fight on the landing grounds ... we shall never surrender.' With his sonorous rhetoric and determination to fight to the end Churchill enthralled British audiences. Priestley's broadcast also signalled resolve, but

---

9 Ibid., p. 31.
10 Ibid., pp. 101–3; Peter Buitenhuis, 'J. B. Priestley: The BBC's Star Propagandist in WWII', *English Studies in Canada* 26:4 (2000), 445–72 (p. 446); Nicholas, *Echo of War*, pp. 56–61.

unlike Churchill he utilized a low-key style of propaganda, describing the Dunkirk evacuation as a typical English story of initial blunders and miscalculations that 'ended as an epic of gallantry'. He contrasted a humane and decidedly rural image of England with the German military machine, which albeit awe-inspiring was soulless and therefore incapable of creating the 'poetry of action which distinguishes war from mass murder'.[11]

Churchill and Priestley's patriotic appeals provided templates through which ordinary Britons came to experience their wartime lives. The Battle of Britain and the London Blitz propelled scores of British citizens to keep diaries in order to record history in the making and their roles as active participants in it. In so doing, they wrote themselves into a story of British endurance, which in different ways Churchill and Priestley had in large measure prefigured.[12] Vere Hodgson, a London social worker, recorded her first diary entry on 25 June 1940, documenting the first London air raid the night before.[13] Hodgson kept her chronicle not just for herself, but also for her cousin who was working as an education officer in Rhodesia and to whom she sent the journal in instalments. In this way, her diary functioned as a personal record of daily trials, as morale-boosting war propaganda, and as a collective test of the British character. On 30 June, in response to a radio speech by Chamberlain with 'the same old stuff about our wonderful advantages', she noted: 'We *don't know* of what we are really made. We may be quite soft. We have not been tried.'[14] Throughout the latter half of 1940, Hodgson moulded herself in Churchill's image of fierce resilience.

11 Buitenhuis, 'J. B. Priestley', pp. 447–8; Nicholas, *Echo of War*, p. 59.
12 In issuing a flood of gripping reports on the German bombing raids on British cities, M-O played a sizeable role in the creation of the myth of the Blitz. The organization was having a 'field day', a wartime observer wrote (H. D. Willcock, 'Mass-Observation', *American Journal of Sociology* 48:4 (1943), 445–56 (p. 452)). In fact, the founders of M-O had initiated their documentary project driven by fear that ordinary Britons might not be up to the task. James Hinton, *The Mass Observers: A History, 1937–1949* (Oxford University Press, 2013); Angus Calder, *The Myth of the Blitz* (London: Pimlico, Kindle edition, Kindle Locations 2614–18. Diaries of the Blitz are legion; see, among others, Angus Calder and Dorothy Sheridan, eds., *Speak for Yourself: A Mass-Observation Anthology, 1937–49* (London: Jonathan Cape, 1984); Dorothy Sheridan, ed., *Wartime Women: An Anthology of Women's Wartime Writing for Mass-Observation, 1937–45* (London: Heinemann, 1990); Simon Garfield, *We Are at War: The Remarkable Diaries of Five Ordinary People in Extraordinary Times* (London: Ebury Press, 2005); Simon Garfield, *Private Battles: Our Intimate Diaries – How the War Almost Defeated Us* (London: Ebury Press, 2006). James Hinton, *Nine Wartime Lives: Mass-Observation and the Making of the Modern Self* (Oxford University Press, 2010).
13 Vere Hodgson, *Few Eggs and No Oranges: A Diary Showing How Unimportant People in London and Birmingham Lived through the War Years, 1940–1945* (London: D. Dobson, 1976), p. 29.
14 Ibid. Note emphasis appears in the original.

'Our Prime Minister is really the greatest man we have ever produced in all our long history', she noted after hearing a 'thrilling' speech by Churchill in December 1940. 'We have never been so near defeat as we were in June, nor so near invasion on our actual soil. It was just touch and go – and he saved us.'[15]

Churchill's government invested massively in arms production and curtailed the production of consumer goods unrelated to the war effort. Still in early 1940, Britain had over 1 million unemployed, astonishing for a nation supposedly at total war. But by March 1941 the expanding war industry necessitated the registration of British women aged eighteen to sixty for war-related labour. This was followed by the conscription of unmarried women aged twenty to thirty in December 1941; the age bracket was extended later. Also in December 1941, all men aged eighteen to fifty were conscripted for the armed forces or the war industry.[16]

While in autumn 1939 government officials beseeched the press to avoid the term 'home front', fearing a backlash from an appeal to arms,[17] a year later they celebrated the sturdiness of the British home front. British wartime culture represented this front through the efforts of maternal, self-sacrificing women.[18] Practising understatement and joking about indescribable conditions, women exhibited some of the same traits that defined the British male soldier of the Great War.[19] The myth of 'Tommy of the Trenches' was now refigured as a female citizen on the home front. Significantly, this myth did not attach itself to Second World War British soldiers, whose fighting spirit received far more critical assessments. The serial defeats suffered by the British Army through 1942 led government leaders to suspect that the pacifist culture of the past twenty years – specifically the prolific writings of British veterans of the Great War calling into question heroic ideals and describing their generation as lost – had corrupted contemporary British soldiers. As late as December 1943 a Director of Military Training lamented:

---

15 Ibid., p. 93; for comments on Priestley and his 'Postscript', see pp. 97 and 135.
16 James Ciment and Thaddeus Russell, eds., *The Home Front Encyclopedia: United States, Britain, and Canada in World Wars I and II* (Santa Barbara: ABC-Clio, 2007), pp. 948–51, 1066; Doherty, *Nazi Wireless Propaganda*, p. 51.
17 McLaine, *Ministry of Morale*, p. 49.
18 Sonya Rose, *Which People's War? National Identity and Citizenship in Wartime Britain, 1939–1945* (Oxford University Press, 2004), pp. 107–50; Susan R. Grayzel, '"Fighting for the Idea of Home Life": Mrs Miniver and Anglo-American Representations of Domestic Morale', in Philippa Levine and Susan R. Grayzel, eds., *Gender, Labour, War and Empire: Essays on Modern Britain* (New York: Palgrave Macmillan, 2009), pp. 139–56.
19 Calder, *Myth of the Blitz*, Kindle Locations 513–31.

The army can achieve nothing if the young soldier has been brought up from the cradle ... to look upon wars and battle as beyond human endurance and something not to be even contemplated ... And this is the way we did in fact bring up our present fighting men between the last war and the present one. Books, literature, cinemas, plays, education, and propaganda were all turned to this end.[20]

Other factors help explain why British soldiers fought less ferociously than their German adversaries, or for that matter, Red Army soldiers. The British Army had abolished the death penalty; it also employed numerous psychiatrists who recorded high incidences of psychic breakdown among servicemen. Neither the German nor the Soviet armed forces utilized psychiatrists, not recognizing war trauma as a valid affliction. Military censorship in the British military was also less rigid than in the other two regimes. While military censors acknowledged the deleterious influence of corresponding with wives and girlfriends, who urged their partners to overstay home leaves or refuse overseas postings, they felt that they could do little to counter these demoralizing efforts.[21] In 1941, the War Office concluded that the German soldier's high level of morale largely was based upon 'a set of convictions that have been seared into his mind by unscrupulous and skilful propaganda'. British unit commanders were instructed to lecture their men on the issues for which they fought. Yet after listening to a lecture, one soldier concluded that 'getting the English worked up enough to defend democracy was an uphill task, as the average soldier appeared to have only three basic interests: football, beer and crumpet'.[22]

The Army's poor performance affected civilian morale in Britain, especially after the 'exhilaration of standing alone' against Hitler passed.[23] In June 1942, Vere Hodgson noted the 'humiliating' news of Tobruk falling to the

---

20 David French, *Raising Churchill's Army: The British Army and the War against Germany, 1919–1945* (Oxford University Press, 2000), Epub edition, 14 and 21. On Britain's lost generation, see Robert Wohl, *The Generation of 1914* (Cambridge, Mass.: Harvard University Press, 1979), ch. 3, esp. p. 112.

21 Margaretta Jolly, 'Briefe, Moral und Geschlecht. Britische und amerikanische Analysen von Briefen aus dem Zweiten Weltkrieg', in Detlef Vogel and Wolfram Wette, eds., *Andere Helme – andere Menschen? Heimaterfahrung und Frontalltag im Zweiten Weltkrieg: Ein Internationaler Verglech* (Essen: Klartext, 1995), pp. 173–204; Angela Schwarz, '"Mit dem grösstmöglichen Anstand weitermachen": Briefe britischer Kriegsteilnehmer und ihrer Angehörigen im Zweiten Weltkrieg', in Vogel and Wette, eds., *Andere Helme – andere Menschen?*, pp. 205–36.

22 French, *Raising Churchill's Army*, p. 73.

23 Gerhard L. Weinberg, *A World at Arms: A Global History of World War II* (Cambridge University Press, 1995), p. 489.

Germans, adding, 'so discouraging to the Russians who are still holding out in Sebastopol'. This comment was no afterthought. Ever since Germany attacked the Soviet Union, Hodgson had admired the resistance put up by Red Army soldiers and Soviet civilians: 'The Russians seem to have guts which the Latins have not.' While the war in the Pacific brought only bad news for Great Britain in 1941 and early 1942, Hodgson drew comfort from reports about the 'indefatigable Russians'.[24] For her and many other Britons, Soviet soldiers and civilians became a moral gold standard in terms of their dedication to the war effort.

Churchill and other government leaders grew alarmed when popular sympathy for the Soviet Union surged after June 1941. They worried that positive reporting on the Soviet ally, in conjunction with the public's habituation to wartime state control, would make communism appear an efficient and superior social and political system.[25] Consequently, the Ministry of Information began stressing that the Soviet Union (always referred to as 'Russia') was essentially a patriotic, nationalist country uninterested in fostering world revolution.[26] Additionally, the ministry sought to reduce communist publicity on the Soviet Union. It took over the 'Anglo-Russian weeks' initiated by the political left. In conjunction with the Soviet embassy, it arranged exhibitions on themes deemed politically safe, such as agriculture, youth and womanhood in Russia.[27] The ministry also used the Russian theme for mobilization purposes. A 1941 poster asking British women to do war work drew on socialist realism and featured what looked like a Soviet female worker. As cultural ideal, the Soviet woman impressed Britons. In her diary, Hodgson extolled the 'really formidable' feats of 'Russian women'.[28]

Popular British enthusiasm for Soviet Russia reached new heights during the Battle of Stalingrad. 'For some people in Britain, Stalingrad seems to be their own native town', the Ministry of Information reported.[29] Vere Hodgson represented a case in point, writing in October 1942: 'We have sent a convoy of stuff, and only hope some of it will arrive and help the people.' Upon hearing of the German defeat at Stalingrad, Hodgson noted, 'Find

24 Hodgson, *Few Eggs and No Oranges*, pp. 151, 168, 199–200 and 214.
25 Mikhail N. Narinsky and Lydia V. Pozdeeva, 'Mutual Perceptions, Images, Ideals, and Illusions', in David Reynolds, Warren F. Kimball and A. O. Chubarian, eds., *Allies at War: The Soviet, American, and British Experience, 1939–1945* (New York: St. Martin's Press, 1994), pp. 307–32; McLaine, *Ministry of Morale*, p. 199.
26 McLaine, *Ministry of Morale*, p. 198.
27 Ibid., p. 202.
28 Hodgson, *Few Eggs and No Oranges*, p. 223.
29 Narinsky and Pozdeeva, 'Mutual Perceptions', p. 316; Nicholas, *Echo of War*, p. 170.

myself getting far too pleased.' The moral infusion provided by the performance of Britain's war ally was palpable.[30] A poll conducted in March and April 1943 revealed widespread British awareness of the superiority of the Soviet military effort as compared to the British military effort.[31]

Total mobilization taxed the morale of British workers, especially in the absence of British military victories. Fearing increased social friction that would destabilize the 'home front', the government chose a unique response, when compared with the German and Soviet wartime regimes. It began announcing post-war changes. For example, the Beveridge report, published on 1 December 1942, proposed introducing comprehensive social security for Britons after war's end. Conservatives criticized the report for its 'totalitarian' tendencies. This criticism was accurate insofar as the report originated from government anxieties about Nazi Germany's revolutionary appeal and popular sympathy for the Soviet Union.[32] But the public embraced the report as a token of recognition that Britons from all classes shared in the great crusade against Hitler.[33] Concomitantly, M-O reported that most Britons did not see their system of government becoming like the Soviet system.[34] Vere Hodgson recorded in her diary: 'It was said the Russians have altered their people by their system of government. This may be so . . . But what do the Russians do with the malingerers and the lazy? . . . This is a free country and the difficulty is to help the deserving while discouraging the unworthy. Utopias here seem to break down.'[35] Her conclusion seemingly included a tinge of regret.

'Strategic bombing' campaigns targeting large German cities were another measure adopted by British leaders to counter the post-Blitz dip in British morale. It was no coincidence that air raids began in spring 1942, when the British Army suffered defeats in Africa and in the Pacific.[36] The campaign's stated aim was to destroy German morale.[37] Yet morale bombing, with its indiscriminate targeting of industrial and residential areas, failed to shatter

---

30 Hodgson, *Few Eggs and No Oranges*, pp. 263 and 293.
31 Narinsky and Pozdeeva, 'Mutual Perceptions', p. 316.
32 Ciment and Russell, eds., *Home Front Encyclopedia*, pp. 780–2.
33 Robert Mackay, *Half the Battle: Civilian Morale in Britain during the Second World War* (Manchester University Press, 2002), pp. 231–9; see also Hodgson, *Few Eggs and No Oranges*, p. 298.
34 Narinsky and Pozdeeva, 'Mutual Perceptions', pp. 315–16.
35 Hodgson, *Few Eggs and No Oranges*, p. 298.
36 Andrew Thorpe, 'Britain', in Jeremy Noakes, ed., *The Civilian in War: The Home Front in Europe, Japan and the USA* (University of Exeter Press, 1992), pp. 14–34 (p. 16).
37 Phillip S. Meilinger, 'Trenchard and "Morale Bombing": The Evolution of Royal Air Force Doctrine before World War II', *Journal of Military History* 60:2 (1996), 243–70.

the Germans' will to fight. On the contrary, the constant aerial threat strengthened their collective resolve; like Londoners during the Blitz, residents of Cologne or Hamburg experienced a heightened sense of *Volksgemeinschaft*, as a consequence of their shared suffering.[38]

During the bombing campaign, the British government largely abstained from inciting public hatred toward Germans, as it had done during the First World War. Yet many wartime publications and lectures showed the Germans as militaristic and barbaric. The Ministry of Information recognized hatred's moral force and argued for the necessity of films that 'emphasize wherever possible the wickedness and evil perpetrated in the occupied countries'.[39] Indeed, a whole series of British films, produced during the war, exposed the brutality of the Nazi occupation regime in France, Belgium, the Netherlands and Norway.[40] (Absent from this series were films on Eastern European countries where Nazi occupation reached an entirely different register of brutality.) Moral outrage at the Germans thus constituted an important factor in rallying Britons behind the war effort, in rousing them to fight a just war.[41] As early as November 1941, Vere Hodgson commented on a BBC recording, 'Nazi cruelty in a Concentration Camp' – a recording that 'made our blood run cold ... This after 2000 years of Christian teaching.'[42]

The Soviet Union at war

The German invasion on 22 June 1941 dealt the Soviet Union a devastating blow. The attack surprised the Red Army, and German mechanized troops advanced deep into Soviet territory. By early September Leningrad was cut off by land, and later that month the Germans captured Kiev. The Red Army lost more than 3 million soldiers by the end of 1941 – either killed or

---

38 Jeremy Noakes, 'Germany', in Noakes, ed., *Civilian in War*, pp. 35–61 (pp. 55–6); Susanne zur Nieden, 'Umsonst geopfert? Zur Verarbeitung der Ereignisse in Stalingrad in biographischen Zeugnissen', *Krieg und Literatur/War and Literature* 5:10 (1993), 33–46 (p. 42).

39 Richard Overy, *Why the Allies Won* (New York: W. W. Norton, 1995), 288; Anthony Aldgate and Jeffrey Richards, *Britain Can Take It: The British Cinema in the Second World War* (Oxford: Blackwell, 1986), p. 133.

40 Anthony Rhodes, *Propaganda: The Art of Persuasion: World War II* (New York: Chelsea House Publishers, 1976), p. 158.

41 Overy, *Why the Allies Won*, pp. 22–3.

42 Hodgson, *Few Eggs and No Oranges*, pp. 193, 467 and 469; Nicholas, *Echo of War*, pp. 158–60.

captured.[43] By 1942, one-third of the Soviet pre-war population lived under German occupation. Compared to 1940, Soviet clothing production had fallen by half, and the production of agriculture and food processing by three-fifths. This meant that most Soviet citizens lived at barely subsistence level during the war, even as the regime demanded up to fifteen-hour workdays. The Second World War's impact on Soviet living standards was 'unparalleled and it far exceeded that felt in the other major countries involved'.[44] How did the Soviet state survive the crippling attack and garner popular participation in the war effort?

One answer lies in the thousands of Soviet citizens who upon hearing war had broken out – Sunday, 22 June 1941 – spontaneously went to their factories or offices to pledge loyalty to the government. Reservists reported for military service, alongside crowds of volunteers exempted from military service on grounds of age, gender or occupation. In Leningrad alone 100,000 volunteers reported to the city's military commissariats by the afternoon of 23 June; the number rose to 212,000 by week's end.[45] For more than a decade, the Soviet state had practised a military-style industrialization campaign, dispatching 'shock workers' to the 'labour front'. Using these established channels, regime officials after 22 June reflexively ordered even larger armies of workers to dig trenches and build barricades. One million Leningraders, more than one-third of the working-age population, worked on defence line construction in July and August 1941. From war's outset, such actions were underwritten by labour laws that enlisted all able-bodied men (aged eighteen to forty-five) and women (aged eighteen to forty) for work and punished avoidance of the labour draft as a severe criminal offence.[46]

The regime entered the war invoking other pre-war values as well, notably the call for ordinary Soviet citizens to excel heroically, whether in industrial production during the 1930s or now at the military front. The communist ideal of political consciousness flowed from the assumption that Soviet citizens would work and fight with redoubled effort if they realized the wider political and moral stakes of the war. Scores of writers, artists and propagandists contributed to this political-moral education campaign; their

---

43 Evan Mawdsley, *Thunder in the East: The Nazi-Soviet War, 1941–1945* (London: Hodder Arnold, 2005), p. 86.
44 John Barber and Mark Harrison, *The Soviet Home Front, 1941–1945: A Social and Economic History of the USSR in World War II* (London: Longman, 1991), pp. 77–8. The situation had improved only marginally by 1944.
45 Ibid., p. 60.
46 Ibid., p. 63.

works reached wide Soviet audiences and proved influential, because they matched ordinary people's wartime observations. This complex dynamic of mobilization and self-mobilization makes it difficult to speak of the wartime Stalinist regime and Soviet society as two distinct entities; nevertheless, the structuring role of communist regime policies remains clear.

Until June 1941, Stalin staked his policies on avoiding war. By many accounts the German invasion robbed him of his breath. But Stalin rebounded and his 3 July 1941 radio address proved radical and timely. The Soviet leader laid out the exceptional stakes of the conflict: 'The issue is one of life and death for the Soviet state, for the peoples of the USSR; the issue is whether the peoples of the Soviet Union shall remain free or fall into slavery.' He then summoned all to fight a total war: 'All our work must be immediately reconstructed on a war footing, everything must be subordinated to the interests of the front.' Stalin was the first statesman during the Second World War to make such a drastic call.[47] He did not use the term 'total war', presumably because the quarter-century-long tradition of mobilizing the population in military style rendered it redundant. In conceptualizing the Soviet war effort spatially and in terms of the distribution of tasks, Soviet media spoke of the 'front' and the 'rear', again underscoring the military saturation of the civilian sector. Such terms made a neologism such as 'the home front' unnecessary.

In his address, Stalin spoke to his 'brothers and sisters', departing from his pre-war paternalism. He called the war a 'Patriotic war' and appealed for the defence of the 'Motherland'. Thanks also to these novel concepts, Stalin became a focal point for popular patriotism; his will to victory and display of firmness, as illustrated in a speech on Moscow's Red Square on 7 November 1941 within range of German artillery fire, had an effect on Soviet audiences like that of Churchill on the British population.[48] Throughout the war, many Red Army soldiers went into combat shouting 'For the Motherland, for Stalin!' – words expressing how well Soviet communist values had blended with the new patriotic idiom.

---

47 Following Khrushchev's 1956 indictment of Stalin, many historians began referencing Stalin's 3 July speech to underscore how long it took him to digest the shock of the German attack. What gets lost in this view is how quickly and resolutely the country was put on a total war footing.

48 Barber and Harrison, *Soviet Home Front*, p. 72. In the wake of the 7 November speech a group of Moscow historians interviewed Soviet soldiers and civilians about how the speech had affected them. Some of the responses were published in L. M. Zak, *My slyshali Stalina, 6–7 noiabria 1941 goda* (Moscow: Ogiz, 1942).

To preserve public morale, the Soviet government went to exceptional lengths, when compared with Great Britain and Nazi Germany, to control the dissemination of news. On 25 June 1941, the government decreed that Soviet citizens must turn in their radio receivers to local authorities. The previous day, the Sovinformburo news agency broadcasting military bulletins to the nation was established.[49] Sovinformburo's early reports gave no indication of the enormous losses experienced by the Red Army. Consequently, many Soviets read official communiqués with considerable scepticism: 'We leafed through a series of the Front newspaper', the writer Vasily Grossman noted in his diary in August 1941: 'I came across the following phrase in a leading article: "The much-battered enemy continued his cowardly advance".'[50] Grossman's 1941 diary describes the panic in Soviet cities as the Germans approached and the drunken stupor of local officials. These scenes obviously could not be included in Grossman's wartime publications, which were to be optimistic and inspirational. Indeed, Grossman risked charges of defeatism had his diary fallen into the wrong hands. As Stalin declared in his 3 July speech, 'all disorganizers of the rear . . . panic-mongers and rumor-mongers' were to be court-martialled.[51] No other state during the Second World War dealt as harshly with defeatism as the Soviet Union. Even Nazi Germany did not adopt tough anti-defeatist sanctions until much later in the war.

Only two options existed for Soviet citizens during the war: hero or coward. 'Be a hero!' read the caption of a photo-poster mass-produced on 30 June 1941. Supposedly the words were those of a Russian mother as she bade farewell to her son, a uniformed Red Army soldier. His posture and gaze spoke confidence and strength. The same motif and words were reproduced on a 30-kopeck stamp, issued in August 1941.[52] The heroic injunction – ingrained in Soviet culture since the Civil War – reappeared in scores of letters from family members to Red Army soldiers.

---

49 Sovinformburo also acted as the Soviet Union's foreign news agency; between 1941 and 1945, it fed British media with hundreds of reports, many of them devoted to the heroism of Red Army soldiers and Soviet civilians. The British hunger for information about the Soviet Union was so great that on 1 December 1942 (just after the Soviet counter-offensive at Stalingrad) a separate 'British division' was created within Sovinformburo. L. V. Pozdeeva, 'Sovetskaia propaganda na Angliiu v 1941–1945 godakh', *Voprosy istorii* 7 (1998), p. 66.
50 Antony Beevor and Luba Vinogradova, eds., *A Writer at War: Vasily Grossman with the Red Army, 1941–1945* (New York: Pantheon Books, 2005), p. 11.
51 Barber and Harrison, *Soviet Home Front*, p. 66.
52 A. Skrylev, 'Kak sozdavalas' marka "Bud" geroem!', *Filateliia SSSR* 5 (1975), 18–20.

While the appeal to be heroic chiefly targeted Red Army soldiers, its character was universal. In his 3 July speech, Stalin called upon Soviet workers to form people's militias to 'defend their freedom, their honor, and their motherland with their exposed breast'. Close to 4 million people joined militias by August 1941. Poorly armed and grossly undertrained, the auxiliary units were quickly wiped out. When the front reached large cities, Stalin expressly forbade many residents from evacuating; they were to turn their cities into fortresses and fight with whatever means possible: 'War is merciless, and it will bring defeat in the first instance to those who show weakness and vacillation.'[53] The heroic standard imposed by Stalin proved extremely costly in human lives, but it also functioned as a cultural norm with mobilizing powers. At least 700,000 civilians died during the siege of Leningrad, and a more foresightful evacuation effort by the government might have saved many lives. Nonetheless, many trapped Leningraders came to regard themselves as actors on a historical stage. In conversation with communist leaders, they created a heroic myth of the blockade – comparable to the British myth of the Blitz – that held intense personal meaning.[54] In total, 11 million medals were issued to Red Army soldiers over the course of the war, suggesting how the policy of fostering heroism and inculcating soldierly pride was transmitted to society as a whole.[55]

Far from receding, communist 'political enlightenment' campaigns increased in scope and intensity after the war began. The party and its youth organization maintained cells in virtually every factory, farm or office. There, they organized lectures and raised funds for the war effort.[56] In view of the expanding industrial workforce and its increasingly female composition, Bolshevik propaganda reached a significantly larger part of the population than before the war. Particularly within the ranks of the Red Army, the Communist Party built a formidable presence during the war. Commissars and politruks, Komsomol secretaries and agitators worked in military units down to the company level. They lectured Red Army soldiers about the war's significance and their role in it. Party membership in the Soviet armed forces soared from 654,000 soldiers in 1941 to 2,984,750 in 1945, at which time more than every fourth serviceman or woman was a party member. Membership in the Komsomol tripled between 1941 and 1945, and by war's end

---

53 Barber and Harrison, *Soviet Home Front*, p. 67.
54 See Lisa A. Kirschenbaum, *The Legacy of the Siege of Leningrad, 1941–1995: Myth, Memories, and Monuments* (Cambridge University Press, 2006).
55 This number does not include decorations awarded to civilian workers.
56 Barber and Harrison, *Soviet Home Front*, p. 69.

more than 20 per cent of Red Army soldiers were Komsomol members. If one adds the number of Party and Komsomol members, a picture of a strongly Communist army emerges.[57]

To facilitate the influx of so many new members, the party simplified its admission criteria.[58] Under the conditions of war, a successful candidate had to prove that he had killed enemy soldiers or destroyed German tanks or planes. The army distributed so-called 'retribution accounts', on which soldiers noted their enemy kill numbers. Soldiers with empty accounts need not apply. In contrast, a renowned sniper, like Vasily Zaytsev, was immediately enlisted. 'I thought,' said Zaytsev in a 1943 interview, 'how can I enter the Party? I don't even know the programme. I read the programme and wrote an application directly in the trenches. Two days later the Party commission invited me to a talk. Back then I had already shot 60 Germans, I had decorations.'[59] Soldiers who were party members were considered the most reliable soldiers and as such were stationed among less reliable troops as leaders by example.[60]

At Communist Party and Komsomol meetings, it was made clear that the death of a communist soldier was no occasion to shed tears, but to ponder a life fulfilled.[61] On the other side of the front line, German soldiers were often perplexed about the apparent calm with which Soviet commissars, soldiers and civilians met death. From the German perspective, this indicated a racially foreign trait, a subhuman, underdeveloped will to live.[62]

The hundreds of Soviet writers who enlisted in the Red Army as war correspondents played a significant role in creating and disseminating wartime behavioural norms.[63] Among the most popular Soviet war correspondents was Vasily Grossman, who wrote for the army paper *Red Star*. Soldiers liked Grossman's features highlighting ordinary soldiers' everyday heroism,

57 Timothy J. Colton, *Commissars, Commanders and Civilian Authority: The Structure of Soviet Military Politics* (Cambridge, Mass.: Harvard University Press, 1979), pp. 16–17 and 21. This increase in communist membership within the army made the office of the Commissar redundant. In October 1942, it was abolished.

58 It lowered the probationary period and dispensed with the pre-war requirement of recommendations by long-standing party members.

59 Jochen Hellbeck, *Stalingrad: The City that Defeated the Third Reich* (New York: Public Affairs, 2015), p. 35.

60 Ibid.

61 Ibid.

62 See, for example, the case of Helmut Hartmann cited below, p. 352.

63 More than 1,000 members of the Soviet Writers' Union went to the front; about 400 died there. *Muzy v shineliakh. Sovetskaia intelligentsiia v gody Velikoi Otechestvennoi voiny. Dokumenty, teksty, vospominaniia* (Moscow: ROSSPEN, 2006), p. 9.

because they saw themselves in his stories. Ilya Ehrenburg was the most prolific Soviet war correspondent with over 1,500 articles, columns and editorials published over four years. Ehrenburg based many of his writings on German letters and diaries, intercepted by Soviet intelligence or taken from German POWs and dead soldiers. He presented excerpts from these documents to showcase the moral depravity of the enemy.[64]

Like Churchill and Priestley in Great Britain, Ehrenburg and other correspondents provided scripts for how millions of Soviets experienced the war and their role in it. They provided templates about the war's meaning and purpose, which Red Army soldiers readily assimilated. Interviewed in 1943, Vasily Zaytsev described how witnessing German war crimes motivated him to fight: 'One sees the young girls, the children, who hang from the trees in the park', he said, adding that 'this has a tremendous impact'. At one level, Zaytsev related his personal experiences; however, the contours of his experience had been pre-established by Ehrenburg, who described scenes of German atrocities in many of his editorials, precisely to incite hatred.

Mobilization in the wartime Red Army was underwritten by draconian sanctions, much harsher than those in the Wehrmacht and the British Army. Between 135,000 and 157,000 Red Army soldiers reportedly were executed during the Great Patriotic War for self-mutilation or other grave crimes, compared with between 13,000 and 15,000 executions in the Wehrmacht and none in the British Army.[65] Since the Civil War, Red Army leaders had employed coercive methods to restore discipline and assert authority. These measures included blocking detachments – dragnets of reliable troops stationed behind the front line to apprehend deserters, send them back to the front, dispatch them to penal units, or have them court-martialled if they lacked the right fighting spirit. Stalin's Order 227 from July 1942 reintroduced blocking detachments and penal units. The order identified the Red Army's 'main deficiency' as a 'lack of order and discipline in the companies, battalions, divisions, in tank units and air squadrons'. Instead of referencing the

---

64 Il'ia Erenburg, *Voina, 1941–1945*, ed. B. Ia. Frezinskii (Moscow: Olimp, 2004).
65 G. F. Krivosheev, ed., *Rossiia i SSSR v voinakh XX veka: Poteri vooruzhennykh sil: statisticheskoe issledovanie* (Moscow: OLMA-Press, 2001), p. 246; Vladimir Naumow and Leonid Reschin, 'Repressionen gegen sowjetische Kriegsgefangene und zivile Repatrianten in der UdSSR 1941 bis 1956', in Klaus-Dieter Müller, Konstantin Nikischkin and Günther Wagenlehner, eds., *Die Tragödie der Gefangenschaft in Deutschland und in der Sowjetunion, 1941–1956* (Cologne: Böhlau, 1998), pp. 335–64 (p. 339); Manfred Messerschmidt, 'German Military Law in the Second World War', in Wilhelm Deist, ed., *The German Military in the Age of Total War* (Dover, NH: Berg Publishers, 1985), pp. 323–35; David French, 'Discipline and the Death Penalty in the British Army in the Second World War', *Journal of Contemporary History* 33 (1998), 531–45.

Red Army tradition of enforcing discipline, Stalin's order claimed that the Germans had resorted first to blocking detachments and penal units. It called upon the Red Army to emulate the enemy.[66] Many Soviet leaders regarded German military discipline as exemplary and found the Red Army seriously wanting in this respect.

Yet Stalin's military orders aimed beyond iron discipline; they utilized a moral register to speak to recruits, urging them to fight like heroes and threatening to shoot as 'traitors' those found 'unreliable, fainthearted, and cowardly' (Order 270 of August 1941). Order 277 shamed commanders of units who retreated, because their actions caused defenceless Soviet citizens, who used to 'love and respect the Red Army, to fall under the yoke of the German oppressors'. The same order also extended a promise to soldiers dispatched to penal units: they would be rehabilitated if they 'redeemed with their own blood their crimes before the Motherland'. Gulag inmates (albeit only those arrested for non-political offences) who volunteered to fight were released from labour camps. More than a million answered this call.[67] Soviet wartime penal culture, thus, served a redemptive purpose, in stark contrast to the German military that foresaw no possibility of redemption and often locked away penal recruits rather than using them for combat.[68]

On 7 November 1942, the anniversary of the October Revolution, Stalin addressed the nation, announcing that 'the day is not far when the enemy will experience new powerful blows by the Red Army. There will be reason to celebrate on our streets!' It was an oblique reference to the Stalingrad offensive to be launched on 19 November 1942. While the German media fell into prolonged silence on the subject of Stalingrad after the encirclement of its troops, elsewhere around the world, newspapers followed the campaign with enormous interest and enthusiasm for the Soviets. Soviet newspapers regularly featured international press clippings to convey the battle's global dimension. For example, *Pravda* cited the *British Daily Herald*: 'The operation was worked out with Stalinist genius, and it was made possible by the successful defence of Stalingrad.' Political officers at Stalingrad also made sure that soldiers understood the world historical significance of their fighting.[69] In

---

66 The claim was false; the Wehrmacht did not employ blocking detachments, and its penal units served purposes other than those imputed by Stalin. See Alex Statiev, 'Penal Units in the Red Army', *Europe-Asia Studies* 62:5 (July 2010), 721–47 (p. 744).

67 Steven Barnes, 'All for the Front, All for Victory! The Mobilization of Forced Labor in the Soviet Union during World War Two', *International Labor and Working-Class History* 58 (2000), 239–60.

68 See Statiev, 'Penal Units in the Red Army'.

69 *Pravda*, 28 November 1942; Hellbeck, *Stalingrad*, pp. 45–6.

September 1942, Vasily Grossman already opined that the world's fate was being decided at Stalingrad.[70] His words were virtually indistinguishable from those of a Canadian paper reporting in late October 1942: 'Stalingrad is fighting not only for the future of the Soviet people but also for the future of all humankind.'[71]

As the first significant victory since December 1941, Stalingrad marked a turning point for the Red Army. In July 1942, Stalin shamed his troops; in February 1943, he saluted his 'army of cadres'. Red Army commanders took pride in beating the Sixth German Army, which they knew to be an elite formation of 'pure-blooded Aryans'. Soviet soldiers also emphasized pride when discussing the shoulder pieces, reintroduced by the Red Army in late January 1943. They argued that the Red Army should adopt the military fashion of other European armies whose recognition it sought.[72] Galina Dokutovich, a navigator in an all-female night bomber regiment, even expressed pride in the derogatory name the Germans assigned her –'night witch'. She noted in her diary on 30 January 1943: 'They call us "immortal Jews" ... that we receive special injections that make us lose half of our femininity. That we are partly women, partly men, that we sleep during the day and throw bombs at night ... How interesting! Interesting because the Germans respect us as an opponent.'[73] In his diary, Soviet writer Vsevolod Vishnevsky observed with satisfaction that Soviet war culture set the standard for Soviet Allies and enemies alike: 'Roosevelt is instructing American cities to study the experience of the defence of Moscow, Leningrad, and Stalingrad. The English Parliament is discussing the Beveridge report, relying on Moscow's experience. Goebbels is calling on the Germans to fight, following Moscow's example.'[74]

Vishnevsky and many other Soviet wartime observers viewed their new Western Allies with ambivalence. After June 1941, the Soviet government stopped reviling 'British imperialism', and began supporting Moscow

---

70 Vasilii S. Grossman, 'Stalingradskaia bitva' (20 September 1942), in V. Grossman, *Gody voiny* (Moscow: Pravda, 1989), p. 29.

71 *Pravda*, 27 October 1942.

72 *Stalingradskaia epopeia: Vpervye publikuemye dokumenty, rassekrechennye FSB RF: Vospominaniia fel'dmarshala Pauliusa; Dnevniki i pis'ma soldat RKKA i vermakhta: Agenturnye doneseniia; Protokoly doprosov; Dokladnye zapiski osobykh otdelov frontov i armii* (Moscow: Zvonnitsa-MG 2000), pp. 366–9; Hellbeck, *Stalingrad*, p. 431.

73 Beate Fieseler, 'Der Krieg der Frauen. Die ungeschriebene Geschichte', in Deutsch-Russisches Museum Berlin-Karlshorst, ed., *Mascha und Nina und Katjuscha: Frauen in der Roten Armee, 1941–1945* (Berlin: Christoph Links Verlag, 2002), p. 63.

74 Vsevolod Vishnevsky, *Leningrad: Dnevniki voennykh let* (Moscow: Voenizdat, 2002), pp. 57–8.

showings of English and American films. They also supported the production of a Soviet film about Moscow and London under German bombardment, which was shown in both countries.[75] But pro-English sentiments contended with lingering and mounting distrust toward the Western Allies, particularly when the Second Front in Europe, promised since 1942, failed to materialize. In March 1943 Ehrenburg published a bitter column in which he described his visit with Soviet tankmen at the front. One of them was preparing supper: 'Taking an American can of sausages, he said: "Let's open the Second Front." I laughed, but [his] eyes were sad.'[76] NKVD surveillance reports from spring 1943 confirmed that many Red Army soldiers had negative attitudes toward the Western Allies.[77] D-Day changed this sentiment briefly, but by the second half of 1944, Soviet reporting on the Western Front receded, and proposals for a British film festival in the Soviet Union, in response to a Soviet festival in Great Britain, fell on deaf ears.[78]

The reversal reflected a fear of ideological contamination, not unlike British leaders' fear of popular Sovietophilia. It drove Soviet policy in the last stages of the war, just as the Red Army crossed into 'bourgeois' states. In October 1944, on the eve of the invasion of East Prussia, the Communist Party intensified 'ideological-political education' among Red Army soldiers, who appeared insufficiently 'tempered' in 'party political' terms. Party membership, expanded since 1941, was tightened at war's end, as party leaders launched a series of internal purges.[79] Some of the harshest sanctions awaited Soviet forced labourers in Germany who expectantly awaited liberation by 'their' Red Army. But rather than being celebrated as martyrs, the survivors were considered contaminated through their contacts with the enemy and submitted to further trials. As part of their repatriation, they had to pass through NKVD filtration camps on the Soviet border where each former POW or *Ostarbeiter* was interrogated at length. Nearly all male repatriates, at least 4.27 million, were sent to forced labour camps. The remaining repatriates had to register with the local police, viewed as potential enemies of the people.[80] For the rest of their lives they remained excluded from the Soviet heroic tale of the Great Patriotic War.

---

75 Narinsky and Pozdeeva, 'Mutual Perceptions', p. 309; Pozdeeva, 'Sovetskaia propaganda na Angliiu', p. 71.
76 Narinsky and Pozdeeva, 'Mutual Perceptions', p. 311.
77 *Stalingradskaia epopeia*, pp. 372–6.
78 Pozdeeva, 'Sovetskaia propaganda na Angliiu', p. 72.
79 *Ideologicheskaia rabota KPSS na fronte: 1941–1945 gg.* (Moscow: Voennoe izd-vo 1960), pp. 253–4.
80 Naumow and Reschin, 'Repressionen gegen sowjetische Kriegsgefangene', pp. 350–1.

Germany at war

Germany attacked the Soviet Union with a force 3.2 million strong, its largest mobilization to date. The vast majority of German soldiers in the Second World War fought on the Eastern Front and died there in especially high numbers. Between July 1941 and May 1944 the mortality rate in the east, in relation to Germany's overall war effort, regularly exceeded 90 per cent; by December 1944 it still stood at 77 per cent.[81] These stark numbers are not only relevant from a military historical standpoint; they also suggest in at least two ways the towering role the war against the Soviet Union played in making and unmaking German morale. First, Hitler launched the war with German morale in mind. The conquered territories would provide food for the German people. Nazi leaders believed that Germans would only support a prolonged war if they suffered less deprivation than in the previous war. Thus popular attitudes toward the war largely depended on how well eastern colonies could be exploited for the German Reich.

Second, in confronting the Soviet Union, the Nazis engaged not only Europe's largest and most populous state, but also a government that virtually placed its entire society on a total war footing from the war's inception. Inevitably, the Soviet system of total political mobilization thrust itself onto German politics and the military. Some Germans advocated emulating the Soviet style of war in order to improve popular morale, but others rejected the Soviet example as incompatible with Germany's racial nature. Instead, Germans placed the burden of total war on alien slave workers so that it could fight the formidable enemy in the east.

Germany's military successes in 1939 and 1940 captivated millions in the Reich, who followed the war in large part through the government newsreel, the *Wochenschau*. Many people went to movie theatres specifically to watch the weekly newsreel.[82] The features were up to forty minutes long, but were entertaining, relating German victories through a new cinematic style that used a multitude of cameras, emphasized images and music over text, and proceeded in a pulsating, exuberant style. Film-makers and critics across the globe noted the innovative artistry of the Nazi newsreel and its ability to 'undermine the moral resistance' of populations in neutral

---

81 Rüdiger Overmans, 'Menschenverluste der Wehrmacht an der "Ostfront"', p. 13 (www.dokst.de/main/sites/default/files/dateien/texte/Overmans.pdf).
82 David Welch, *Propaganda and the German Cinema, 1933–1945* (Oxford University Press, 2001), p. 167.

European countries.[83] Since its 1933 inception, Joseph Goebbels's Ministry of Public Enlightenment and Propaganda aggressively used film and other visual media to advance the Nazi racial agenda and to prepare Germans mentally for war.[84] Goebbels personally supervised Nazi newsreel production; he applauded its use of technique to highlight visually Germans' racial superiority over their enemies in the east and carefully analysed each production in his diary. The Security Service also prominently featured German responses to the *Wochenschau* in its reports on the population's moods, which it produced daily after the outbreak of war. By May 1940 their frequency was lowered to twice a week.[85]

While German news reporting emphasized the connections between front and homeland, the latter invariably played a supporting role. The virile front soldier stood at the centre of Nazi wartime propaganda, his image intended to inspire. Germans in the Reich who corresponded with front soldiers were instructed to collect soldiers' letters and treasure them as evidence of Germany's racial regeneration.[86] At the front, propaganda officers reminded soldiers of their responsibilities as correspondents. They likened war letters travelling to Germany to a stream of healthy blood strengthening the German people's community: 'In his letters and during leave time, the soldier is to act like a blood donor, restoring the belief and willpower of his relations.'[87] Only rarely did Nazi propagandists celebrate the German 'home front' during the early stages of the war, evidently for fear of invoking the dreaded spectre of total war. More often they appealed to civilians to be mindful of the deprivations suffered by soldiers at the front before complaining about hardships at home. In their diaries, some Germans identified with the plight of soldiers at the front, while others prioritized worries about their daily life. But both groups lacked a conception of

83 Siegfried Kracauer, 'The Conquest of Europe on the Screen: The Nazi Newsreel, 1939–1940', *Social Research* 10:3 (1943), 337–57 (p. 338).

84 Welch, *Propaganda and the German Cinema*, p. 92.

85 The Security Service (*Sicherheitsdienst*, or SD) was created as a division of Heinrich Himmler's SS, the military police organization most concerned with the Nazi project of racial purification. Beginning in 1935 it monitored how Germans responded to the new regime's policies. For details, see Heinz Boberach, ed., *Meldungen aus dem Reich. Die geheimen Lageberichte des Sicherheitsdienstes der SS 1938–1945* (17 vols., Herrsching: Pawlak, 1984), vol. I, pp. 11–22.

86 German stationery stores sold special folders that bore the inscription, 'Feldpostbriefe, die die Heimat erreichten', and contained an instruction sheet, signed by a Professor Brechenmacher (author's private archive).

87 Ortwin Buchbender and Reinhold Sterz, *Das andere Gesicht des Krieges. Deutsche Feldpostbriefe, 1939–1945* (Munich: Beck, 1982), pp. 26–7.

themselves as historical subjects, as was the case with Londoners during the Blitz and Leningraders during the siege.[88]

In invading the Soviet Union, Germany confidently expected a Blitzkrieg victory sparing the bulk of its population from an all-out war effort. This approach initially worked; the Security Service reported that Germans exuberantly followed the swift advance of Wehrmacht motorized units. Some bet not on the outcome of the war, which everyone believed preordained, but on the exact date of Soviet defeat.[89] In July 1941, Germans attended *Wochenschau* screenings in record numbers, and movie theatres across Germany added special screenings to accommodate the throng of viewers.[90] Goebbels ecstatically commented on the aesthetic power of these newsreels that showed endless rows of POWs being marched off by German guards.[91] Track (panning) shots emphasizing the human masses were alternated with close-up portraits of captured soldiers' faces, so as to underscore the enemy's racial difference. German viewers were impressed, and they drew radical conclusions, in line with those desired by Nazi propagandists:

> In connection with the images in which the prisoners are seen, often thoughts were voiced concerning the food policy burden posed by prisoners for Germany. Above all, they were strongly interested in the fate of the sometimes shown female gunners, who in the opinion of many members of the Volk it was impossible to see as POWs and repeatedly one heard the wish that such types not be allowed to live.[92]

More than in the earlier phases of the war, these images heightened German viewers' racial consciousness, reinforcing their sense of the war as a profound and necessary ideological conflict. But the pictures also invited other questions: Could German troops contend with the captured human masses? Could they manage Russia's vast space? These questions persisted as the war wore on and Wehrmacht reports kept mentioning fierce battles that eventually stalled the German advance. As hopes for an immediate rout failed to materialize, many Germans seemingly lost interest in the war. With some concern, an Oldenburg schoolteacher noted that his sports comrades bracketed the 'huge battle of extermination at the Eastern Front' out of their

---

88 See Lore Walb, *Ich, die Alte – ich, die Junge. Konfrontation mit meinem Tagebüchern, 1933–1945* (Berlin: Aufbau-Verlag, 1997).
89 Boberach, ed., *Meldungen aus dem Reich*, vol. VII, p. 2440.
90 Ibid., pp. 2563–4.
91 Bianca Pietrow-Ennker, 'Die Sowjetunion in der Propaganda des Dritten Reiches', *Militärgeschichtliche Mitteilungen* 46 (1989), 79–120 (pp. 112–13).
92 Boberach, ed., *Meldungen aus dem Reich*, vol. VII, p. 2564.

conversations, preferring to talk about business affairs. Meanwhile, 'the total number of Soviet prisoners taken since the beginning of the campaign in the East has already surpassed three million'.[93]

Wehrmacht losses were also enormous, prompting acute reactions from fallen soldiers' families. During the first three months of the eastern campaign 185,000 German soldiers died, almost twice as many as during the first twenty-one months of the war.[94] Among them was a cousin of Lore Walb, a student of German literature in Heidelberg: 'Again we are short by one more young life. A human being who was valuable enough to have children. Even if we annihilate the Russians, these subhuman creatures, a horror for all people of culture (just watch the *Wochenschau*!), we, too, will ultimately bleed to death in this struggle!'[95] A profound biological pessimism colours this entry, a sense that Germany risked self-annihilation in trying to save *Kultureuropa*. Compare Walb's despair over her cousin's death with Soviet optimism, where every dead hero was assured a place in the pantheon of history.

Beginning in autumn 1941, the depleted soldierly ranks were being filled with industrial workers previously exempted from the draft. Hundreds of thousands of positions in the expanding war industry needed filling, and Hitler repeatedly called on non-working German women to volunteer for war-related tasks. But, as the SD noted dryly, most housewives would not work for the state unless ordered.[96] It was indeed difficult to convince German women to do men's work as long as the regime railed against 'denatured' Soviet women who fought alongside male Red Army soldiers. Germany's economic pressures were instead shifted onto slave workers from Eastern Europe. According to Russian archives, 1.2 million Soviet civilians were deported to Germany in the autumn of 1941; their number would rise to 4.8 million (among them more than 2 million women and 676,000 children under the age of sixteen). By summer 1944, 7.6 million foreign workers were officially reported as working in the Reich – about one-quarter of all registered workers in the German economy.[97] Millions of other Soviet citizens were forced to labour in coal-mines, factories and collective farms in Ukraine, Belorussia and Russia.

---

93 Hans-Peter Klausch, ed., *Oldenburg im Zweiten Weltkrieg: Das Kriegstagebuch des Mittelschullehrers Rudolf Tjaden* (Oldenburg: Isensee, 2010), p. 90; for the complete entry, see the diary typescripte in Staatsarchiv Oldenburg (Best. 297E No. 58), entry for 14 October 1941. The number of 'more than three million Soviet POWs' captured in the summer and autumn of 1941 still circulates in historical scholarship today, but it is probably exaggerated; see Mawdsley, *Thunder in the East*, p. 86.
94 Mawdsley, *Thunder in the East*, p. 85.
95 Walb, *Ich, die Alte – ich, die Junge*, p. 228 (entry for 8 September 1941).
96 Boberach, ed., *Meldungen aus dem Reich*, vol. VII, p. 2348.
97 Naumow and Reschin, 'Repressionen gegen sowjetische Kriegsgefangene', p. 337.

The fierce resistance in the east forced the German invaders to revise their image of the Soviet people. Hitler and his generals entered the war believing political commissars, working through indoctrination and brute force, were the backbone of the Soviet system. Their execution would bring the collapse of the Soviet armed forces. On 9 August 1941, gunner Helmut Hartmann wrote to a friend in Germany, describing the executions: 'For a week, it was, for example, common that every morning at breakfast we had to shoot some political commissars. An incredibly callous people. They calmly dug their grave, stood before it, and mostly fell into it well, so that we only had to put the dirt on.'[98] But the executions did nothing to diminish their opponent's determination. On the contrary, the utter ruthlessness of Wehrmacht soldiers in all likelihood reinforced Red Army soldiers' determination to fight to the last man, which in turn fed the spiral of brutalization on the Eastern Front.[99]

Since winter 1941 the Soviet's 'fanatical' fighting style became a stock phrase in German war reporting, and Nazi officials began worrying that Germans might begin unduly heroizing the Red Army soldier.[100] The regime continued insisting on the enemy's subhuman features, finding a racial explanation for his fighting strength. Reporting from Stalingrad in October 1942, an SS newspaper conceded that the Soviet soldier 'fights at times even though it is no longer humanly possible for him to fight'. The newspaper added that if French or British troops were defending Stalingrad, it would already be in German hands. Racial biology explained this difference. Soviet soldiers hailed from a 'primitive and dull human stock', this rendered them unable to 'grasp the purpose of life and to cherish life'. Hence, they fought with contempt for death that was foreign to culturally developed Europeans. The report concluded by raising the spectre of Europe succumbing to the 'power of unchained inferiority', and it underscored the fateful role of the Battle of Stalingrad.[101]

Reports about bitter fighting in Stalingrad demoralized German audiences. Already in September 1942, Lore Walb confessed to having lost faith in German victory: 'I can no longer believe in a glorious victory. At best a

98 Deutsches Tagebucharchiv (Emmendingen), Sign. 1614 (Helmut Hartmann to Konrad Henkel).
99 Mark Edele and Michael Geyer, 'States of Exception: The Nazi-Soviet War as a System of Violence, 1939–1945', in Michael Geyer and Sheila Fitzpatrick, eds., *Beyond Totalitarianism: Stalinism and Nazism Compared* (Cambridge University Press, 2009), pp. 345–95 (esp. p. 359).
100 Boberach, ed., *Meldungen aus dem Reich*, vol. XI, pp. 3987–8 and 4084–6.
101 *Das Schwarze Korps*, 28 October 1942.

compromise peace. I do not yet think the worst – therein at least a remnant of the old optimism remains. Gisela, on the other hand, sees black, only black.'[102] To Goebbels, who eagerly read the Security Service reports on Germans' deteriorating moods in the autumn and winter of 1942, the mounting military crisis at Stalingrad offered an opportunity to catalyze Germans' total mobilization – something that Goebbels had sought for some time. In ways resembling Churchill in June 1940 and Stalin in July 1941, Goebbels embraced dire realism as a mobilizing device. In an address delivered at the Berlin Sports Palace just two weeks after the Sixth Army's defeat, Goebbels began by detailing to a carefully selected audience of 14,000 listeners the full magnitude of the threat. He then posed ten rhetorical questions. The fourth question went to the heart of the speech: 'Englanders claim that the German people resist the regime's total war measures. They do not want total war, but capitulation. I ask you: Do you want total war? Do you want it, if necessary, even more total and more radical than we can imagine today?' More than 200 times, hysterical applause, wild shouts and choruses interrupted him. Presented as an 'imposing demonstration of the German people's will to fight to the end', the speech was broadcast live to millions, printed in the daily papers the following morning, and broadcast again the following Sunday.[103]

In his address Goebbels invoked 'our enemies who are listening to us over their radio'. Curiously, he mentioned only one enemy by name – 'the Englanders'. The Soviet Union, the adversary against which Germany's total war effort was directed in the first place, went unmentioned, presumably because Goebbels felt it below Germans to converse with 'subhumans'. Goebbels also did not mention that the German design of total war resembled the Soviet war effort. The Nazis called up all non-working German women for work in war-related industries and stopped the production of consumer goods unrelated to the war. The regime appealed to voluntarism as a principal source of mobilization. In Goebbels's words: 'A firm resolve and a spiritual and militant activity, which is prepared to overcome all difficulties and obstacles with revolutionary élan.' Like Soviet leaders, the Nazis coupled these appeals with threats of executions for 'shirkers and war profiteers'. With respect to front-line soldiers, Goebbels sought to instil in

---

102 Walb, *Ich, die Alte – ich, die Junge*, p. 248.
103 Richard J. Evans, *The Third Reich at War* (New York: Penguin, 2009), p. 484. For an audio recording of the speech, see http://archive.org/details/JosephGoebbels-Sport-palastrede/.

them ideals of heroic self-sacrifice, as had long been in circulation in the Soviet Union. Specifically, he planned the publication of a 'heroic song' of soldiers' letters from Stalingrad that would conclude with an ode to Germany as eternal inspiration of their fighting. Goebbels's aide for the project was given bags of soldiers' letters that had been airlifted out of Stalingrad in late January 1943, but their wording proved too defeatist and the project was halted.[104] German soldiers, it appeared, were not attuned to the extreme self-abnegating heroism that coloured many Red Army soldiers' letters.[105]

The response from most Germans to Goebbels's total war campaign was muted. Some stalwart regime supporters welcomed the measures, noting they were long overdue. The only other positive response came from workers who voiced satisfaction that the better off now had to do their share. Yet this satisfaction was more indicative of class rifts in German society than of a working *Volksgemeinschaft*. Indeed, many party leaders were able to prevent their wives from being drafted, prompting further popular grumbling. Non-working German women, many of them wives of soldiers and as such recipients of generous family allowances, were reluctant to enrol in the war industry. While 3,048,000 women registered with labour offices by June 1943, following the government's conscription measures, by December 1943 only 500,000 were still doing war-relevant work. The rest had resigned or shifted to cushier office jobs. Overall, fewer German women worked in the war industry than did British women, not to mention women in the Soviet Union.[106] In her diary, Lore Walb followed total war measures

---

104 Jens Ebert, *Feldpostbriefe aus Stalingrad. November 1942 bis Februar 1943* (Göttingen: Wallstein, 2006), pp. 362–8.

105 For an apparently unedited collection of Red Army soldiers' last letters that emphasize the heroic, see G. A. Stefanovskii, P. R. Kotenok and N. Shakhmagonov, *Poslednie pis'ma s fronta* (5 vols., Moscow: Voennoe izd-vo, 1990–95). The different tonalities in Soviet and German soldier letters from the war were also a function of the different workings of military censorship in the Red Army and the Wehrmacht. Soviet censors read every individual letter circulating from front lines; German military censors only took samples. German soldiers and their correspondents could thus reasonably expect that their letters would not be read and they expressed themselves more freely than Red Army soldiers. In addition, Nazi officials tolerated a degree of 'grumbling', and they distinguished between superficial moods (*Stimmungen*) and basic comportment (*Haltung*). No such distinction obtained in the Soviet case. See Jochen Hellbeck, '"The Diaries of Fritzes and the Letters of Gretchens": Personal Writings from the German–Soviet War and Their Readers', *Kritika: Explorations in Russian and Eurasian History* 10:3 (2009), 571–606.

106 Noakes, 'Germany', p. 43. German women's participation in the war economy remains a subject of debate. While some scholars note that a higher proportion of German women worked during the war than in Britain, the fact remains that German women were reluctant to enter the war industry, to the chagrin of many Nazi German officials. See Noakes, 'Germany', pp. 41–3 and Adam Tooze, *The Wages of*

introduced by the government attentively, hoping she would not be called up and could complete her university degree the following year, which she in fact did in spring 1944.

The government's total war measures failed to uplift morale in the Reich. A military report from June 1943 voiced concern that many soldiers returned from their home leaves in a 'depressed' state. The soldiers were 'bitter about the prevailing defeatist mood, voiced in all spheres, by all sectors of the population at home'. The report particularly blamed 'the constant interception of enemy broadcasts by an unfortunately large share of the population'.[107] The despondent *Heimat* was a far cry from the home front Goebbels envisioned.

Later in 1943, the German government went further in emulating Soviet war culture. Clearly recognizing Soviet soldiers' fighting strength (and just short of openly admiring it), Nazi leaders began moulding the Wehrmacht in the Red Army's image. Already in July 1941, German General Staff officers called for increased ideological work among their troops to anchor them firmly in the 'national socialist worldview', since 'a German force without such a solid foundation would hardly be able to emerge victorious from a global political battle in which worldview confronts worldview'. Anyone who failed to recognize this showed a 'fundamental misconception of the task of total war, especially in the current situation'.[108] As this document made clear, only the war against the Soviet Union brought widespread German recognition that they were now steeped in an ideological war. It was ideological in part, they believed, because of the overt ideological nature of their opponent.[109] The calls for increased political education for Wehrmacht soldiers were renewed during the winter crisis of 1941 and again in the wake of Stalingrad. In December 1943, Hitler introduced the National Socialist Morale Officer (*Nationalsozialistischer Führungsoffizier*, NSFO), whose

---

Destruction: The Making and Breaking of the Nazi Economy (London: Allen Lane, 2006), p. 359.

107 Ortwin Buchbender and Horst Schuh, *Heil Beil! Flugbattpropaganda im Zweiten Welt Krieg, Dokumentation und Analyse* (Stuttgart: Seewald Verlag), p. 53. With the outbreak of war, the German government banned listening to foreign broadcasts and made 'defeatism' a capital offence. Executions for defeatism rose steadily throughout the war, reaching 5,764 in 1944. See Noakes, 'Germany', p. 54.

108 Volker R. Berghahn, 'NSDAP und "Geistige Führung" der Wehrmacht 1939–1943', *Vierteljahrshefte für Zeitgeschichte* 17:1 (1969), 17–71 (p. 31).

109 The commissar order, issued in March 1941, already indicated the ideological stakes of the coming war, but a larger awareness of the ideological standoff, made evident by the fierce resistance German soldiers met in the Soviet Union, did not arise until after June 1941. A retrospective 1944 document confirms this conclusion, see Berghahn, 'NSDAP und "Geistige Führung"', p. 28.

task was to 'thoroughly knead National Socialist ideology into the very fibre of the Wehrmacht'. The NSFO did not correspond exactly to the Soviet political commissar since he was chosen from army personnel. However, the Nazi party vetted all NSFO appointments. In practice, however, the morale officer was widely scorned; soldiers called him 'NSF-Zero'. Wehrmacht generals who had arrived at a modus vivendi with the Nazi Party, did not welcome this new politicization of the rank and file.[110]

Civilian Germans shared the scepticism toward 'Bolshevik' methods, which they saw their regime implementing as the war dragged on. A surveillance report from December 1943 summarized:

> In almost all parts of the population the opinion frequently was repeated that the Bolsheviks were far superior to us in implementing total war. The Soviets understood it in an exemplary fashion, developing truly total methods. On the other hand, some insightful compatriots stressed that the Russian authorities could well demand it from their primitive population, but such methods could not be applied to the German situation.[111]

The report indicated significant popular interest in Soviet war culture, but also consensus that Stalin's methods of mobilization worked only with 'primitive' people and could not be imposed on Germans. In spite of rising dissatisfaction with the Nazi regime's performance, most Germans agreed with the regime about the racial barriers separating Germans from Russians.

Ultimately, the Nazi regime was most successful in highlighting fundamental differences with the Soviet Union for the purpose of mobilizing Germans. 'Victory or Bolshevism', was the slogan on a poster mass-produced starting in 1943. A variation on the phrase, 'Victory or Downfall', used by Hitler in January 1943, the poster featured the established technique of racial contrasting, juxtaposing an image of a blonde young mother and her cheerful child with a nightmarish scene of corpses and grieving survivors, behind which loomed a menacing gangster type with Jewish traits (see Illustration 18).

Many Germans at the time felt the fear of Bolshevism that the poster sounded. The SPD reported that people spoke of the last bullet, which they would save for themselves once 'everything' was over. In Oldenburg in February 1943 a story circulated about a Russian girl working for a local

110 Ibid., pp. 34 and 45; Jürgen Förster, 'Geistige Kriegführung in Deutschland 1919–1945', in Jörg Echternkamp, ed., *Die deutsche Kriegsgesellschaft 1939–1945. Erster Halbband: Politisierung, Vernichtung, Überleben* (= *Das Deutsche Reich und der Zweite Weltkrieg*) (Munich: Deutsche-Verlags-Anstalt, 2004), pp. 469–640.
111 Boberach, ed., *Meldungen aus dem Reich*, vol. XV, p. 6135.

family who ostensibly said: 'Well Mistress. When the Russians come, I will make sure that they immediately shoot to kill and do not torture first.'[112] Fear also underlay the upsurge in German diary writing in 1943. These journals began sounding a new historical subjectivity, yet one where authors did not see themselves as dedicated fighters on the home front, but as victims of a calamity of historic proportions.[113] In the wake of Stalingrad, the people's community became recast as a community of fate (*Schicksalsgemeinschaft*).[114] German soldiers in Russia had been the first to describe themselves in these terms in winter 1941, following the Soviet counter-offensive that broke their sense of invincibility and made them fight even harder for sheer survival.[115] After Stalingrad, combat on the Eastern Front grew more violent, with German soldiers dying in increasing numbers. Here, too, the propaganda of fear worked, driving soldiers to fight to the finish, lest they endure unspeakable horrors at the hands of Soviet captors.[116]

In late May 1943, the SD noted 'the beginnings of a crisis of confidence' in the Nazi regime.[117] Goebbels received reports that Germans would not enter cinemas until the war newsreel, which they had so eagerly watched until 1942, concluded. Goebbels responded by locking all cinemas for entire shows, so that spectators who wanted to see the feature film had to watch the *Wochenschau*. The feature films meanwhile changed in character, as the German film industry shifted production from aggressively militarist films to escapist fare.[118] One month later, Goebbels ordered a decrease in production and the circulation of SD reports, charging reporters – rather than the people on whom they reported – with 'defeatism'. Yet the modified reports still irritated government readers and were halted after D-Day in June 1944.[119] The end of the surveillance project, which had served as much as a record of

---

112 Staatsarchiv Oldenburg, Best. 297E. No. 58 (23 February 1943). This story was also reported in the surveillance report of the Security Police; Tjaden may have been its source. See Boberach, ed., *Meldungen aus dem Reich*, vol. XIII, p. 4870.

113 zur Nieden, 'Umsonst geopfert?', p. 40.

114 Michael Geyer, '"Endkampf" 1918 and 1945: German Nationalism, Annihilation, and Self-Destruction', in Alf Lüdtke and Bernd Weisbrod, eds., *No Man's Land of Violence: Extreme Wars in the 20th Century* (Göttingen: Wallstein, 2006), pp. 37–67 (pp. 52–30); Noakes, 'Germany', p. 55.

115 Edele and Geyer, 'States of Exception', p. 374.

116 Omer Bartov, *Hitler's Army: Soldiers, Nazis, and War in the Third Reich* (Oxford University Press, 1991); Overmans, 'Menschenverluste der Wehrmacht', pp. 3–4 and 6.

117 David Welch, *The Third Reich: Politics and Propaganda* (2nd edn, London: Routledge, 2002), p. 142.

118 Ibid., p. 151.

119 Boberach, ed., *Meldungen aus dem Reich*, vol. I, pp. 36–7. After this, only a few reports on individuals appeared – the last of them in late March 1945.

what people thought as an intervention and attempt to transform them, expressed Nazi leaders' tacit recognition that the larger project of racially regenerating Germany had failed. Hitler expressed as much in March 1945, icily remarking that 'the [German] nation has proved to be the weaker and the future belongs solely to the stronger eastern nation. In any case only those who are inferior will remain after this struggle, for the good have already been killed.'[120] The same month, Goebbels leafed through a dossier with biographies and portraits of Soviet generals and marshals, commenting admiringly on their youth, energy and dedication to Bolshevism.[121] The biological pessimism, which Lore Walb sounded on the occasion of her soldier-cousin's death in 1941, had become a full-blown reality by 1945.

Lore Walb, meanwhile, remained fiercely attached to the German *völkisch* ideal. In March 1945, she wrote: 'But we *cannot* lose the war, what threatens us thereafter!'[122] Her words evinced no bad conscience about German war crimes, but rather a fear of total annihilation, which Goebbels and Hitler had prophesized should Germany lose the war. With its insistent denial, lack of reasoning and a larger aim, the entry (or for that matter Walb's entire diary) exemplified the mobilizing power as well as the limits of the strikingly particularistic project of national regeneration that had animated her and millions of Germans throughout the war.

Conclusion

This chapter has explored, in comparison and interaction, how the governments of Germany, Great Britain and the Soviet Union sought to mobilize their populations for total war. What it has revealed is the centrality of the Soviet war effort in the larger European setting, and its formative influence on the other war cultures. The comparison with Great Britain and Nazi Germany makes clear how totalizing the Soviet war effort was from the start, how much the regime expected of its population, and how exacting many Soviet citizens were toward themselves and others. The German attack in June 1941 surprised political and military leaders, but Soviet society and the economy quickly adapted to the demands of war since they had been placed

---

120 Albert Speer, *Inside the Third Reich* (New York: Macmillan, 1970), p. 440.
121 M. Jerin, 'Das Bild der militärischen und politischen Nazi-Eliten von der Sowjetunion während des Zweiten Weltkriegs', in Jochen Hellbeck, Alexander Vatlin and Lars Peter Schmidt, eds., *Russen und Deutsche in der Epoche der Katastrophen* (Moscow: ROSSPEN, 2012), pp. 242–3.
122 Walb, *Ich, die Alte – ich, die Junge*, p. 301.

on a war footing long beforehand. Throughout the war, Soviet leaders relied on a long-established and trusted mobilization model, notably the revolutionary concept of political education, which found wide application in the wartime Red Army, the civilian war industry and Soviet schools. All Soviet citizens were lectured on the war's meaning for their country and for them personally. In labouring or fighting for such high aims, they were expected to release an inner heroic potential. Underwritten by a comprehensive surveillance network and threats of dire sanctions, this mobilizing strategy indeed produced a widely visible disposition toward heroism, reflected not only in government posters and in the writings of military correspondents but also in the voices and actions of ordinary Soviet citizens. Soviet state mobilization during the war proved so effective because it utilized appeals that resonated broadly – the defence of homeland and the fight against the 'fascist barbarians'. This Soviet war culture operated in equal fashion at the military 'front' and in the civilian 'rear'; it was telling that on the same day that Order 227 ('Not a Step Back') was issued a similarly worded order was passed for civilian workers that punished small labour infractions as acts of desertion.[123]

Great Britain in 1939 was ill-prepared for the exigencies of war, partly because the British Empire had wagered on the preservation of peace, and partly because British leaders found it difficult in a democracy to deploy effective mobilization tools, such as a propaganda ministry or agencies of surveillance. France's defeat and Churchill's simultaneous appointment as prime minister changed this. Churchill's embrace of dire realism proved highly effective for mobilization purposes. How he and others portrayed the plight of Britain 'fighting it alone' catalyzed feelings of strength and determination that resonated with much of Britain's population. Mass-Observation, the most influential non-government polling institute, propagated the strength of British morale under German attack during the summer and autumn of 1940, and the government followed by instituting a 'morale chart' of its own.[124] In the process a British 'home front' was constituted; both martial and feminine, it adopted key features from Britain's First World War soldierly culture. That culture significantly did not attach itself to Britain's soldiers in the Second World War. In between stood two decades of pacifism, which in the eyes of many had made Britain's soldiers soft and unable to fight. Britain's military losses in the Pacific and in Africa underscored the spectre of its imperial decline. The British Army's weakness in

123 Barber and Harrison, *Soviet Home Front*, p. 63.
124 McLaine, *Ministry of Morale*, p. 217.

1941 and 1942 was accentuated by the strong performance of the Red Army, which riveted British audiences and boosted morale. Many Britons over the course of the war became fascinated with the Soviet style of war, recognizing its particular effectiveness. Vere Hodgson and many other British women came to embrace their heroic 'Russian sisters' as a gender ideal. Most Britons, in tune with what British media reported, believed that their Soviet Allies were in reality Russians, animated by Russian patriotism. This was a deliberate move on the part of the British government, which feared the spread of communist propaganda at home.

In even more powerful ways the Soviet war culture impressed Germans, who confronted it in much more direct ways. In contrast to British government leaders, the Nazis advertised the enemy's ideological nature, since ideology was at the essence of their war against the Soviet Union. They understood the significance of the Red Army's political commissars and ordered them shot. Yet over time, they and scores of German soldiers fighting on the Eastern Front realized that the commissars were not the sole carriers of Soviet ideology; the politicized fighting spirit was dispersed among the Red Army troops and the Soviet population. Many German observers began subliminally admiring the Red Army soldier, and some Nazi leaders sought to emulate Soviet war culture. But such efforts, which started as early as summer 1941, were ultimately rejected. For one, the increasingly unpopular Nazi apparatchiks had little appeal in the fighting Wehrmacht. Second, while acknowledging the superiority of the Bolshevik total mobilization, many Germans emphatically rejected 'Bolshevik methods' as *artfremd* – hostile to Germany's racial nature.

The relationship between civilians and the armed forces in wartime Germany was a mirror image of the British case. There was no home front to speak of throughout the war, in great part because Nazi leaders remembered acutely the course of the First World War and distrusted civilians' ability to shoulder the burdens of war. During the first years of war, the German government sought to ease the civilian population's plight, lest their bickering undermine the fighting spirit of front-line soldiers. These soldiers – hyper-masculine and emphatically presented as the 'best soldiers in the world' – embodied Nazi warrior culture. Throughout the war, Nazi leaders cast German civilians and 'the homeland' in a dependent role – at best an auxiliary to the military and at worst an 'anaemic' patient, feminine and weak. When the tide of war turned and Goebbels appealed for total war in February 1943, the rifts in the *Volksgemeinschaft* and popular disenchantment with the regime had become too large to overcome.

Germany, as is often argued, mobilized too late for total war. Germany, indeed, failed to mobilize its civilian workers during the early war years in a manner approximating the Soviet Union or Great Britain. Nazi propagandists did little to invoke a 'home front', as British officials and the media had done since summer 1940. But focusing on Germans alone cannot capture the total war waged by Germany, one more ruthlessly pursued than any other European wartime regime. Five million *Ostarbeiter* and 2 million Soviet POWs, in addition to millions of forced labourers in the coal-mines of Donbass and elsewhere in occupied Soviet territory, bore the brunt of this total war effort; the terms of their exploitation grew harsher as the war progressed. In November 1943 the minimum age for East European forced labourers in Germany was lowered to ten years of age. Naturally, Goebbels made no appeal to these armies of wretched workers during his Sports Palace speech.[125]

The oft-stated point that the Second World War was much more total than the previous Great War, in that it involved civilian populations of belligerent powers to a much greater extent and as a result claimed many more civilian than soldiers' lives is true, but it may obscure more than it reveals.[126] The overwhelming majority of civilians who lost their lives in the European theatre were Soviet or Polish citizens. They were killed not as an effect of some generic blurring of the lines between soldiers and civilians, but rather because they figured as prime targets in the Nazi ideological war of extermination. A study of total war in Europe 1939–1945 remains woefully incomplete if it fails to engage the qualitatively different ways in which the war was fought in the east on the territory of the Soviet Union. Nazi propagandists, for instance, poured ample resources into radio propaganda aimed at British listeners but made almost no effort to persuade Soviet audiences.[127] The reason was that Goebbels and other Germans regarded the British as racial kindred, and therefore receptive to sophisticated German propaganda techniques, unlike the 'primitive' peoples. Soviet intelligence officers in turn invested considerable care in reading and reforming the thoughts of their opponents. The Eastern Front took the shape of a steep

---

125 See Ulrich Herbert, 'Forced Laborers in the Third Reich: An Overview', *International Labor and Working Class History* 58 (2000), 192–218.

126 See, for instance, introduction to Jeremy Noakes, ed., *The Civilian in War: The Home Front in Europe, Japan and the USA in World War II* (University of Exeter Press, 1992), p. 2.

127 Gerwin Strobl, *The Germanic Isle: Nazi Perceptions of Britain* (Cambridge University Press, 2000); for Goebbels's short-lived idea in July 1941, nipped in the bud by Hitler, to employ radio propaganda toward people of the Soviet Union, see Welch, *Third Reich*, pp. 131–2.

cultural gradient. The Germans fought the Soviet Union with methods and concepts that differed vastly from those employed against other nations. In turn, the brutality with which Germans treated countless Soviet soldiers and civilians who fell into their hands, quickly became widely known in Soviet society thanks to Ilya Ehrenburg and other propagandists. Their writings about German atrocities became integral parts of Soviet hatred campaigns against the 'fascist conquerors', rendering fighting on the Eastern Front even more lethal.[128]

A comparative study of total war cultures reveals two dimensions that elude accounts of individual nations at war. It establishes how the term total war masks different degrees and forms of mobilization and different understandings of war aims for which individuals and groups can or should fight. In addition, the comparison brings to the fore a great deal of interaction and transfer between war cultures. Some of these entanglements were evident to wartime observers; others were not, because they failed to make an impression or had to be repressed. A case in point is the link between the Nazi enslavement of Soviet civilians and increased Soviet hatred of Germans; this connection eluded most Germans because of the racial blinders on their minds. Explorations of war cultures in interaction thus need to pay attention to what wartime actors saw and said, as well as exploring connections that remained unacknowledged or denied because they violated the boundaries of what could be said or thought at the time.

---

128 See, in particular, Edele and Geyer, 'States of Exception' and Catherine Evtuhov and Stephen Kotkin, eds., *The Cultural Gradient: The Transmission of Ideas in Europe, 1789–1991* (Lanham, Md: Rowman & Littlefield, 2003). The present perspective differs from Timothy Snyder's neo-totalitarian reading of the Eastern Front that makes no qualitative distinction between the Nazi and the Stalinist regimes. See Timothy Snyder, *Bloodlands: Europe between Hitler and Stalin* (New York: Basic Books, 2010).

13

Hors de combat

Mobilization and immobilization in total war

GEOFFREY COCKS

The combatant nations over the course of the Second World War could not and did not mobilize their populaces in their entirety. The sheer scale and complexity of industrialized society and the total war programme based on it created many spaces for 'inliers' who avoided complete mobilization. Total war by definition and aspiration is in any case a zero-sum operation. Those who are not available to the war effort are a loss in place of a gain. Thus mobilization for total war was dialectical since mobilization of entire nations for purposes of sustained warfare against other nations necessarily entailed many who on the basis of ordained predispositions or incapacities were immobilized. These included the young, the old, the sick, the disabled, the insane, the criminal and, to a considerable extent, women as well as the otherwise unavailable, unreliable or unsuitable such as vagabonds, clergy, pacifists, conscientious objectors and subversives, however defined. The Nazis for racial reasons also 'exterminated' millions of people, mostly Jews. This further reduced the number of Germans and others whom the Nazis could mobilize. It also cost the Nazis the military and industrial service of the many perpetrators of this crime against humanity. Moreover, not all of the millions upon millions of those mobilized for total war between 1939 and 1945 would remain mobilized. Total war itself, as war, immobilized millions of German civilians as well as soldiers as the dead, wounded or disabled. At the same time, the mounting losses of a losing war compelled the Nazis to try to ease the dialectic of mobilization and immobilization by shading incapacity into exploitable predisposition. Among other recourses, by 1943 completely disposable Jews were increasingly being used – up – as slave labour; by 1945 children, the elderly and even some women were fighting – or not – as soldiers.

The dynamics of Nazi total war

The relationship between mobilization and immobilization in Nazi total war was dynamic rather than static over time, space and circumstance. The boundaries between those mobilized and those not were often mobile rather than fixed and often porous rather than impermeable. This was because, as we have noted, state policy with regard to mobilization for total war had to change in response to wartime conditions. This was especially true in Nazi Germany given the peculiarly desperate circumstances the Third Reich faced in the end. Many who were 'out of combat' were liable to be back 'in combat' since often those who had been immobilized or demobilized had to be remobilized as civilians or even as soldiers. But such reorganization too diverted personnel, time and money from more permanently mobilized sectors of the war economy. And even, or especially, the Nazi wartime state also had to contend with instances and degrees of agency, contingency and conflict that could obstruct mobilization. In Germany most people, after all, were 'racial comrades' who had to be cultivated as well as coerced. This became ever more difficult given the disordering effects of the war, principally mounting sanguinary defeats at the front and devastating air attacks on the homeland. Mobilization efforts were also compromised by competition, duplication, infighting and organizational territorialism in a 'polycratic' Nazi state, all of which created some space for individual avoidance and even opposition. And while many self-mobilized as well in effective support of the war effort out of individual need, there were instances of counter-mobilization among the immobilized. This transpired underground in the dictatorships and openly in the democratic states. Sometimes membership in more than one immobilized group could reinforce such counter-mobilization, as in the case of pacifists, women and clergy in Great Britain. By the same token, however, most of those few in Nazi Germany who immobilized themselves as underground opponents to the regime were at the same time mobilized in support of the war effort. These people too had jobs that in one way or another contributed to the mobilization of the human resources to fight a total war. Thus there was always an unstable balance of costs and benefits to the nation at war in the maintenance of a dialectical and dynamic system of mobilization and immobilization.

As a racist totalitarian dictatorship, Nazi Germany counted large and numerous groups designated as politically or racially undesirable and thereby excluded from wartime mobilization. This elimination of civic space and civil society was a consequence of the Nazi regime's brutal will and wherewithal to impose and enforce its vision on German and eventually most of mid-century

European society. That this will and this vision were accepted and even embraced by a majority of Germans made exclusion of the Other from the *Volksgemeinschaft*, or racial community, all the more definitive and effective. Communists were the first to be excluded from the public spaces of Hitler's Germany, and absolutely, by the end of 1933. Then the Jews, more gradually but no less certainly, over the first few years of the regime; through official and public opprobrium, legal restriction and exclusion from 1935 onward; a brief burst of nationwide terror in 1938; and increasing segregation and emigration until the outbreak of war in 1939. And so on until the final catastrophe of the Holocaust, or Shoah, most of whose victims, however, were not German. This was the single most extreme – and unique – instance of the war against civilians that was part and parcel of the total war that was the Second World War. The Nazis also broadened criminality to include 'habitual criminals' suffering from 'hereditary' illnesses; they targeted the 'incurably insane' in German asylums and German homes for sterilization before the war as well as murder during it. More generally, Nazi leaders thought even more during the war of an ever larger category of 'asocials' (*Gemeinschaftsfremde*) who like 'Gypsies' were in one way or another to be eliminated from the Master Race following final victory (*Endsieg*). As early as 1933 Nazi Minister of the Interior Wilhelm Frick opined that fully 20 per cent of the German population *in toto* should not be permitted to reproduce.

The war radicalized the Nazi racial war against the Jews and other Others. It gave the regime the opportunity it needed to conduct mass murder on an unprecedented industrial scale. Hitler also waited for the cover of war to implement the killing of the handicapped, antedating the decision to 1 September 1939 to make clear the wartime 'necessity' – however hidden from the German public – for 'euthanasia'. The success of German arms during the first two years of the war brought millions of Jews under the murderous disposition of the Nazi regime. The looming final defeat that overshadowed Germany during the last two years of the war increased the desire of the Nazi regime to kill Jews in particular while they still could. In the long view the Nazis could regard human and material resources devoted to the total destruction of 'racial inferiors' as part of a broader total war. At the same time this exertion represented considerable costs at the expense of the total war against the nation states fighting Nazi Germany, though the wartime increase in mobilization of prison and camp labour compensated for this.

The war also complicated as well as occasioned mobilization and immobilization. Even in Nazi Germany, the boundaries between mobilized and immobilized before and during the Second World War changed with time and circumstance. First, the war created not only unprecedented millions of dead but also millions of wounded, injured, sick, and otherwise physically and mentally disabled soldiers and civilians as well as their dependants. Most of these not only were unavailable for mobilization, their care too, however minimal, came at a cost to the Nazi total war effort. Caring for the families of 'the fallen' – very often by women – was also something the Nazi regime had to do – or be seen to be doing – as part of another aspect of total war: the maintenance of public morale and support for the war from both mobilized and immobilized 'Aryans'. Second, the lengthening and worsening of the war required the regime to mobilize or remobilize increasing numbers of soldiers and workers from among those previously regarded as unfit for service. The very fact that total war required not only combat but labour and administration meant that there were many civilian jobs that had to be filled with the otherwise militarily immobilized. This occasioned increasingly ruthless wartime utilitarianism – what Winfried Süss has documented as heartlessly militarized social-utilitarian triage – that complemented but also compromised the wartime radicalization of the campaign against those the Nazis regarded as weak and useless. Over time and with the turn of the tide of the war against Germany, the question for the Nazis became not *too* young, not *too* old, not *too* sick, or not *too* disabled for whatever purpose the regime needed to mobilize these human resources. By the end of the war many of the much too young, much too old, much too sick, and much too disabled were being mobilized, hopelessly and fruitlessly, by a desperate regime in final eclipse. Even Jews from all over Europe, targeted for total extermination by the Nazi regime, were increasingly resorted to as mobilized slave labour from 1943 on. This, however, melded with the policy of extermination since Jews, like more than 2 million Russian prisoners, were to be worked to death (*Vernichtung durch Arbeit*). At the same time, the deterioration of Germany's military position meant the demobilizing extension of radical violence onto both old and newly mobilized cohorts in the form of shooting and hanging thousands of deserters and shirkers.[1] In this way as in others in Nazi Germany total war was both more total as well as less total due to the dynamic, dialectical relationship between mobilization and immobilization.

---

1 Nicole Kramer, *Volksgenossinen an der Heimatfront. Mobilisierung, Verhalten, Erinnerung* (Göttingen: Vandenhoeck & Ruprecht, 2011), pp. 207–44; Adam Tooze, *The Wages of Destruction: The Making and Breaking of the Nazi Economy* (London: Allen Lane, 2006), pp. 530–8; Winfried Süss, *Der 'Volkskörper' im Krieg. Gesundheitsverhältnisse und Krankenmord im nationalsozialistischen Deutschland* (Munich: Oldenbourg, 2003), pp. 32–40, 69, 213, 405–16.

Such dynamics were not exclusive to Nazi Germany during the Second World War, although the extent and nature of both adherence to and departure from ideology were at their extremities in Hitler's wartime Reich. The use of slave labour in wartime as well as peacetime was of course much easier for a police state, as the example of Stalin's Russia also shows. Both the Germans and the Japanese also mobilized the immobilized through their use of prisoners – including prisoners of war (mostly Russians and Chinese, respectively) – in human experiments. The Second World War made such recourses more necessary than ever, given the unprecedented scale of mobilization required not only in terms of soldiers but of factory and farm labour ever more essential to a war of attrition (*Materialschlacht*) of likewise unprecedented scale. In the USA, segregation of African-Americans was maintained in the military, both through the common labour jobs to which the men were assigned and, in a few instances of combat assignment, deployment as soldiers under Caucasian command. By intent and by effect, African-Americans were undermobilized in the USA. The war's voracious demand for human resources also contributed to the also political American decision to mobilize a regiment of Japanese Americans out of the internment camps to fight in Europe in 1944. Prison – i.e. criminal – labour too was common in the Western democracies as a means to free up more men for conscription. So was that of prisoners of war, mobilized universally under widely differing conditions, the exploitation of whose labour was codified in the Geneva Convention of 1929.[2]

The war Nazi Germany fought from 1939 to 1945 was, however, unique in being total in three dimensions. First, in the generic sense of the quantitative mobilization of workers broadly and diversely defined as well as soldiers that also characterized the industrialized total war fought by the other major warring nations. Total war between 1939 and 1945 was not *sui generis*. It was an outgrowth of the First World War, modern industrialism and the 'post-liberal' nation state. Even the Nazi extermination of the Jews represented an extreme manifestation of the nature of modern nation states which by national, ethnic, religious and cultural inclusiveness thereby excludes others. Germany already in the nineteenth century was paradigmatic for post-liberal capitalist modernization in the course of the twentieth century by virtue of its early coordination of economy and governance. The First World War too

---

2 Bob Moore and Kent Fedorowich, 'Prisoners of War in the Second World War: An Overview', in Moore and Fedorowich, eds., *Prisoners of War and their Captors in World War II* (Oxford: Berg, 1996), pp. 1–17 (p. 10).

was part of this process, accelerating state management of the economy not only in Germany but across Europe. The trend was continued after 1918 in liberal capitalist states in order to promote social and political stability. But the Nazis also fought a total war in two uniquely qualitative senses. One was war as an end in itself to prove the racial mettle of a warrior people destined to conquer, rule and populate the earth. As or more important was the total war of extermination against the weak at home and abroad that was 'a violent fantasy of racial mastery'.[3] By these two means the Nazis problematically magnified the dialectic of total war for themselves through the exclusion or marginalization of the less fit among both 'Aryans' and 'non-Aryans'.

German society offered the Nazi dictatorship a ready resource for quantitative mobilization. The German people by and large were disposed to support or at least follow the Nazi version of national recovery and resurgence in the largely disastrous wake of defeat in the First World War. Widespread resentment over the Versailles settlement was particularly fertile ground for Nazi political harrowing. Moreover, younger generations of bourgeois males in Germany were especially susceptible to appeals, through highly mobilized Nazi propaganda and otherwise, to national community as a response to the tensions, anxieties and conflicts that had accompanied the nation's recent rather precipitous industrialization and commercialization. The Nazi 'negative mobilization' of victims itself encouraged the 'positive mobilization' of Germans as perpetrators. A 'benefit' to this was the strengthening of the commitment of thousands upon thousands of Germans to fight for Hitler, Germany, and the ideal of a 'Master Race'. This racial-national ideal was a major theme of a pervasive and effective Nazi mass media dissemination of the illusion of what Linda Schulte-Sasse calls a fantasy of physical wholeness in place of the disruptive discontinuities of modern life. This fantasy, central to Nazi anti-Semitism, built upon common human fears of illness and death that were aggravated by Nazi insistence on 'health' as well as avalanching wartime threats to physical and mental well-being. Emblematic of such propaganda was the slickly produced feature film *Jud Süss* (1940), a vile anti-Semitic historical melodrama that did well at the wartime box office and was shown to SS guards at Auschwitz and to members of SS killing squads (*Einsatzgruppen*) in Russia.[4]

---

3 Mark Mazower, *Hitler's Empire: How the Nazis Ruled Europe* (New York: Penguin, 2008), p. 2.
4 Eric Rentschler, *The Ministry of Illusion: Nazi Cinema and its Afterlife* (Cambridge, Mass.: Harvard University Press, 1996), pp. 149–50, 154, 165; Linda Schulte-Sasse, *Entertaining the Third Reich: Illusions of Wholeness in Nazi Cinema* (Durham, NC: Duke University Press, 1996).

The three Nazi total wars complicated as well as complemented each other, however. The great majority of German men and a sizeable minority of German women were directly involved in the total war effort either as soldiers or as civilian workers. And they managed, out of a combination of effort, compulsion and circumstance to help keep Nazi Germany at war against most of the rest of the world for almost six years. But the Nazi mobilization of the Aryan population was also not without considerable limitations. The very act and fact of mobilization required significant concessions in time and effort just to maintain the status mobilized quo. There were the literal limits of what otherwise dutiful, disciplined and/or tractable Germans could or would take on. Mobilized Germans also could not remain mobilized all the time. On a regular basis they fell into the ranks of the immobilized due to inherent limitations of body and mind. These human frailties were aggravated by shrill and often stress-inducing Nazi insistence on health and productivity. One Nazi expert recommended that medicine should cease being 'defensive' and place strengthening of the healthy alongside or even ahead of curing of the sick.[5] This racist and Social Darwinist view in and of itself risked immobilization of many 'sick' in mobilization of fewer 'well'. Moreover, such insistence and concomitant propaganda, along with the network of controls and sanctions, might have encouraged workers and soldiers during the war but it also contributed to stress that itself could lead to physical or mental breakdown. The results took two basic forms. One was actual illness, disability or death. The other consisted of strategies of individual coping that involved manipulation of the pervasive Nazi medical control system put in place to monitor and maintain productivity. In terms of total war, such coping – ironically and tragically – constituted more lubrication than friction in the gears of the Reich's industrial and military machinery. For even though concern for individual health and well-being eroded or interrupted service to the total war effort, in so doing it created space to recuperate from the demands of the war state so as to continue to meet those demands.

These stratagems were both aided and inhibited by the severe shortage of doctors on the German home front, a shortage that led even to 'death deferments' for Jewish doctors in Germany and occupied Europe. German doctors had to deal with a rise in illness that pushed the work absenteeism rate during the war from 2–3 per cent to 13 per cent for wage earners and

---

5 Geoffrey Campbell Cocks, *The State of Health: Illness in Nazi Germany* (Oxford University Press, 2012), p. 189.

9 per cent for salaried employees. The regime and industry responded by attempting to impose stricter medical control over the civilian population. As one resident of Berlin observed in the case of a colleague who tried using caffeine to get her pulse racing before a medical examination, '[d]octors nowadays are usually very severe'.[6] Another way the Nazis tried to reduce the resort to illness, whether real or feigned, was to make doctors less accessible since a certification for illness was required to miss work. Naturally, those further up the social and professional scale were in a better position to exploit the situation. One state film bureaucrat complained that studio employees unwilling to work in Berlin were able to 'supply notes from prominent doctors . . . so that it usually proves impossible to attribute [their 'illness'] to fear of bombs'.[7] One staff member with the Foreign Ministry, when faced with a ban on voluntary resignations, decided that the 'only solution, I conclude, is another illness'.[8] The SS inveighed darkly against 'the flu' becoming a fashionable – and, because of its ubiquity – easily manipulable disease that just everyone had to have instead of just a manageable cold. The SS Security Service (SD) in one of its secret reports on the public mood asserted that 30–40 per cent of those reporting sick in Stuttgart were fit to work; in Munich a police sting operation resulted in 44 per cent of those reported sick suddenly getting well. The same evasions and opportunisms applied to the widespread demand for a wide variety of prescription drugs touted by the regime as a means of making the Nazi working and fighting worlds more productive through stimulants and more bearable through sedatives and analgesics.[9] The net effect of these popular coping strategies was short-term disruption but long-term – though again costly – sustainment of total war mobilization.

Qualitative total war as proof of racial superiority too was fraught for the Nazis. In February 1944 Reich Health Leader Conti in a secret speech in Breslau observed that 'war and health are opposites'. From the Nazi perspective, war itself was dysgenic since the racially fittest men were dying in battle while the less fit and unfit survived at home. Nazi racial ideology also decreed that mothers, children and infants join soldiers and armaments

---

6 Marie Vassiltchikov, *Berlin Diaries, 1940–1945* (New York: Vintage, 1987), p. 181; Cocks, *State of Health*, p. 191; Esther Gitman, 'The Rescue of Jewish Physicians in the Independent State of Croatia', *Holocaust and Genocide Studies* 23:1 (2009), 76–91.
7 Jo Fox, *Film Propaganda in Britain and Nazi Germany* (Oxford: Berg, 2007), p. 259.
8 Vassiltchikov, *Berlin Diaries*, p. 230.
9 'Mit der Grippe ist nicht zu spassen', *Stuttgarter NS-Kurier*, 31 January 1941, PC 5, Reel 106, Press Archives, Wiener Library, London; Cocks, *State of Health*, pp. 142–71, 195.

workers at the top of the list for wartime rations. One woman in Dresden observed in 1943 that 'the very little ones are blooming [since] children's food and ... full cream milk are provided ... up to the age of six'.[10] This long-term racial priority brought no benefits to the regime at the time – or ever – since all it did was clash with the immediate need to increase war production. The dialectic of total war also forced the Nazis to mortgage even their hallowed racial future by sending ever younger soldiers to the front as cannon fodder for the present. At the very end, a churlish Hitler even concluded that the German people by losing his war had failed the test of racial superiority.

The Nazi war against its racial enemies too came at considerable cost for the regime. First were the many thousands of skilled human resources driven into exile or killed. Second were the material and human resources the Nazi regime mobilized for the wartime extermination of the Jews. This ideologically central project cost the Germans in military and transport resources. Not least were the many Germans who sought or received deferments from military service to undertake the much less dangerous campaign against defenceless men, women and children. Third were significant costs to the perpetrators themselves. Many soldiers and police serving with killing squads in Russia and Poland suffered from a variety of physical and mental ailments due to the strain of mass shootings. Regular recourse to alcohol, 'refinements' to the method of execution, psychotherapy, and even reassignment and transfer were among the means used to deal with this problem. These costs were part of the reason the Nazis moved the mass killing out of the fields and forests and into gas chambers in extermination camps. Even there, however, the perpetrators were not immune to the physical and mental effects of their grisly labour. For all such human resource and maintenance reasons, the Nazis 'outsourced' as much of the murderous work in the death camps as they could to auxiliaries from occupied countries and to *Sonderkommandos* comprised of Jews in the crematoria.[11]

10 Victor Klemperer, *I Will Bear Witness: A Diary of the Nazi Years, 1942–1945*, trans. David Cameron Palastanga (New York: Random House, 1999), p. 190; Reg. Aachen 16486, 4, Nordrhein-Westfälisches Hauptstaatsarchiv, Düsseldorf; Süss, '*Volkskörper*', pp. 32–40; Lisa Pine, *Nazi Family Policy, 1933–1945* (Oxford: Berg, 1997), pp. 28–31, 184–7.

11 Gerhard L. Weinberg, *A World at Arms: A Global History of World War II* (2nd edn, Cambridge University Press, 2005), p. 477; Christopher R. Browning, *Ordinary Men: Reserve Police Battalion 101 and the Final Solution in Poland* (2nd edn, New York: HarperCollins, 1998), pp. 61, 66, 74–6, 85, 86, 103, 114–20, 122; Johannes Lang, 'Questioning Dehumanization: Intersubjective Dimensions of Violence in the Nazi Concentration and Extermination Camps', *Holocaust and Genocide Studies* 24 (2010), 225–46.

The brutal synergy between Einsatzgruppen and Wehrmacht in Russia 'immobilized' millions more victims of Nazi barbarism. Here as well there were costs to the Nazis. What Omer Bartov has termed the 'demodernization' of combat on the Eastern Front encouraged German troops to vent their anger on all the 'Others' who had always been portrayed as the source of German suffering. The degeneration of the war in the east from a series of heady Blitzkrieg victories into a grinding, losing war of attrition tore at traditional military discipline. Unit cohesion won by recruitment and replacement from the same home region broke down under the tremendous losses on the Eastern Front. Now units were increasingly heterogeneous, having in common only suffering and exposure to ongoing Nazi propaganda concerning the necessity of merciless racial-political warfare against communists, Slavs and Jews.[12] Such freshly augmented German fury against 'subhumans' led to greater German losses as well. And when final defeat loomed, fanaticism would contribute to even more self-destructive combat driven in part by fears of fantasized and factual revenge for German crimes and atrocities.

Racial warfare did bring in its train the 'bonus' of millions of slave labourers to free up German workers to fight. This 'free' labour joined criminals in German jails and prisons who also laboured for the war effort. Imprisonment and military recruitment had thinned criminals' ranks, though Nazi concentration on political and racial enemies had given 'normal' crime some social space. There were costs to keeping and mobilizing criminals. German jails suffered from high rates of execution, overcrowding, malnutrition, disease and death. The death rate among prisoners from the state penal system deployed to defuse unexploded bombs was 50 per cent. Foreign slave labourers were even less willing, less able and less healthy. Late in the war the Nazis increased productivity through 'performance feeding' (that is, a 'normal' ration) to the most productive even among labourers provided by the SS from the concentration camps. In 1943 the Propaganda Ministry funded research into the psyche of even hated and feared workers from Eastern Europe as another possible means of raising productivity.[13] Among

---

12 Omer Bartov, *Hitler's Army: Soldiers, Nazis, and War in the Third Reich* (Oxford University Press, 1991).

13 Ulrich Herbert, *Fremdarbeiter. Politik und Praxis des 'Ausländer-Einsatzes' in der Kriegswirtschaft des Dritten Reiches* (Berlin: Dietz, 1986), pp. 148–9, 351; Tooze, *Wages of Destruction*, pp. 530–8; [Günther] Lehmann, 'Zusammenhänge von Ernährung und Leistungssteigerung', September 1944, FD 545/46, 5243, Osenberg 'Recherche Nr. 31', Speer Collection, Imperial War Museum, London; Reichsministerium für Volksaufklärung und Propaganda to Hermann Göring, 22 April 1943, RFR 204, 107/12850,

slave labourers there were costly instances of individual and collective resistance to mobilization. Polish or Russian female slave labourers would become pregnant in order to be sent home by a regime unwilling to bear the cost or the existence of an unwanted child. Others placed irritating substances onto or into their bodies to simulate disease so as to be sent home by Nazi authorities fearful of epidemics. Shortage of transport and of Nazi patience as well as the ever greater need for labour eventually kept such women in Germany. Any offspring were adopted, institutionalized or killed, the cost to the war effort once more coming in the form of more German supervisory personnel. There was also widespread and persistent sabotage of munitions by slave labourers. In the last months of the war foreign workers from Western Europe slowed their work rate, regularly reported sick, and even absconded or went underground.[14] At the end of the war, the disruption – as well as the obscenely wasteful nature – of the labour camp system left hundreds of thousands of the starving, dead and dying.

The social economy of total war

There were several categories of Germans wholly or partially immobilized – by age, by mental or physical condition, by disposition, or by gender. Women occupied their own place in Nazi ideology as bearers and caretakers of children, racist long-term 'human rearmament' impinging on the immediate demands of total war. War benefits for soldiers' wives remained high while wages for women remained low. Fearing husbands at the front would worry about their wives working too hard outside the home, the regime relied for that reason as well mostly on slave and forced labour from abroad to work in munitions plants as well as alongside women (including girls drafted for work service in the countryside) and undrafted men on German farms. Late in the war an increasingly desperate regime also discovered it could not pay women enough to work outside the home and so Labour Front leader Robert Ley and Total War administrator Albert Speer developed the idea of having women do war work such as the packaging of pharmaceuticals at home. At Rheinmetall-Borsig between 1940 and 1943 the percentage of male German workers went from 84 per cent to

Reichsforschungsrat, Library of Congress, Washington, DC; Richard J. Evans, *The Third Reich at War* (New York: Penguin, 2009), pp. 454, 515–21.

14 Cocks, *State of Health*, pp. 120–1; Ulrich Herbert, 'Labor as Spoils of Conquest, 1933–1945', in David F. Crew, ed., *Nazism and German Society, 1933–1945* (London: Routledge, 1994), pp. 219–73 (pp. 248–9); Evans, *Third Reich at War*, pp. 704–6.

47 per cent, female German workers only from 11 per cent to 16 per cent, but foreign workers from 1 per cent to 35 per cent.[15]

Total war did bring women into the fray. Even the super-sexist SS had to alter its preconceptions; its journal *Das Schwarze Korps* now included coverage of women as munitions workers, army nurses and agricultural labourers. The traditionally female field of nursing had been augmented even before 1939 in anticipation of war. After 1939 as well female physicians just about made up for the Jewish doctors banned from practising in 1938; by 1943 women comprised around half of all medical students and about 17 per cent of all doctors between 1936 and 1945. The war also swept many German women into the military and even into the SS as auxiliaries. Demand from the armed forces came at some expense to the civilian sector. In late 1944 the Sickness Funds in Strassburg complained that the army was calling up women between the ages of twenty-four and twenty-nine, which was seriously depleting the office's workforce.[16] As early as 1942 the Supreme Command of the Wehrmacht (OKW) was constrained to remind all three branches of the armed services that even with all the women being employed by the military there was no such thing as a 'female soldier'. By the end of 1943 there were approximately 300,000 women serving with the Army Reserves, 130,000 female auxiliaries in the Luftwaffe, and 20,000 in the Kriegsmarine. In March 1945 the OKW called for the arming of women with pistols and anti-tank weapons while others served during the flagging weeks of the war as flak gunners.[17]

The experience of German women with total war was more similar than dissimilar to that of women in the other major warring nations. The modern

---

15 Cocks, *State of Health*, p. 187; 'Kriegsheimarbeitstagung', 28 July 1944, T78, Roll 189, Frames 926–34, National Archives, Suitland, Maryland; J. G. Schurig to Oberversicherungsamt Dresden-Bautzen, 24 January 1944, R 89, 22685, Bundesarchiv Koblenz; Tooze, *Wages of Destruction*, p. 359.

16 Birthe Kundrus, *Kriegerfrauen. Familienpolitik und Geschlechterverhältnisse im Ersten und Zweiten Weltkrieg* (Hamburg: Wallstein, 1995), pp. 341–6; Bernhard R. Kroener, 'Massnahmen zur Mobilisierung von Leistungsreserven im deutschen Machtbereich', in Militärgeschichtliches Forschungsamt, ed., *Das Deutsche Reich und der Zweite Weltkrieg* (Munich: DVA, 1999), vol. II, pp. 917–43 (p. 935); Evans, *Third Reich at War*, pp. 358–62, 595; Michael Burleigh and Wolfgang Wippermann, *The Racial State: Germany 1933–1945* (Cambridge University Press, 1991), pp. 250, 260; Cocks, *State of Health*, p. 111.

17 OKW to OKH, OKM and RdL, 22 June 1942, RL 4, II/285, Bundesarchiv-Militärarchiv, Freiburg im Breisgau; Birthe Kundrus, 'Nur die halbe Geschichte. Frauen im Umfeld der Wehrmacht zwischen 1939 and 1945 – Ein Forschungsbericht', in Rolf-Dieter Müller and Hans-Erich Volkmann, eds., *Die Wehrmacht. Mythos und Realität* (Munich: Oldenbourg, 1999), pp. 719–36 (p. 721); Ian Kershaw, *The End: The Defiance and Destruction of Hitler's Germany* (London: Penguin, 2011), p. 310.

bourgeois gender order ensured that wartime employment of women in the West was at most around 50 per cent. As elsewhere in the industrialized world, though, in Germany single women, especially working-class ones, had always had to work. In the 1920s more and more young women were taking jobs in a growing retail sector. In 1938 the Nazis themselves created more single women through a liberalized divorce law designed to promote remarriage and procreation that left many women unmarried and unsupported. The war forced not only the Nazi state to face the need for women to work but so too thousands of individual German women. This self-mobilization was a widespread but indirect contribution to the war effort, representing both degrees of agency and of constraint and placing many women between mobilization and immobilization. But it also constituted qualitative immobilization since these women rarely took on more dangerous and wearing jobs in munitions and weapons factories. Still, such women often suffered from increased illness and stress, reducing the value of their labour and laying claim to doctors and drugs also needed for war workers and soldiers. In 1943, a doctor in Darmstadt wrote to the Reich Health Office to complain about planned discontinuation of the sedative Dibrophen. A specialist in nervous disorders, he had found that Dibrophen had a considerable calming effect on women new to the workforce. One woman, who works both day and night as a conductor on a tram, is much less anxious and overwhelmed since she has been taking Dibrophen on a daily basis. The drug is also helpful for wives and mothers who have to worry as well as work. One patient agonizes over signing anything that might get her husband, who is at the front, in trouble. Another has a son who is missing in action. A third has to run a grocery by herself and has recently had her apartment building damaged in an air raid. Psychotherapy, the doctor says, might be safer and surer, but takes weeks while the drug works safely and right away. All of these women function quite well now as a result of taking Dibrophen. Similar drugs are available, but he worries about higher dosages and the long-term effects on patients of a drug with which he is not familiar.[18]

Only the Soviet Union mobilized women above the norm. This was in line with communist practice since 1917, although women in the Soviet Union before, during and after the Second World War suffered as well from paternalistic prejudices and practices. Soviet women were, out of military necessity, mobilized for combat to a degree far beyond that of any other

---

18 Cocks, *State of Health*, pp. 160–1; Pine, *Nazi Family Policy*, p. 18.

combatant state. By 1944 Russian women were serving in large numbers as combat aviators; there was even the exclusively female 46th Guards Women's Night Light-Bomber Regiment. By 1945 there were 246,000 women serving on the front lines. Great Britain, with its smaller population, addeded proportionally more women to the workforce during the war, but had always had many fewer women working in agriculture than did Germany with its many small family farms. In the USA, in spite of a great deal of propaganda about 'Rosie the Riveter', only 16 per cent of American women worked in war industries and represented a mere 2 per cent of all military personnel. The USA was also the only nation not to allow servicewomen in combat zones while women in the factories and in the military faced condescension or worse. Among the major industrialized nations, Japan did the least in mobilizing women. But even here total war demanded labour from women, particularly since the Japanese homeland did not enjoy the Nazis' much more readily accessible supply of continental slave labour. After the start of the war in China in 1937 women began taking unskilled jobs in heavy industry; by February 1944 there were 13,246,000 women out of 31,657,000 in the civilian labour force. Japan's relative reluctance to employ women was due to the belief of a militaristic government in the social and political stability provided by cultural preservation of the traditional family. This standard was a stronger motivation with greater effect than the Nazi reliance on a fully illusory racial standard in upholding the family as a biological unit. The Nazis introduced labour conscription of women in January 1943. Only in August 1944 did the Japanese government begin conscripting widows and unmarried women for work in the munitions industry; a Women's Volunteer Corps had recruited 201,487 women by March 1944, and 472,000 by August 1945.[19]

Age too played a dynamic role in Germany's total war. The elderly, generally defined by the Nazis as those over sixty years of age, were by and large immobilized. National Socialism had always regarded itself as a movement of youth and in power had tried to raise the German birth rate – with limited success – for racial and rearmament reasons. Its emphasis on and

---

19 Richard Overy, *Russia's War: Blood upon the Snow* (New York: Penguin, 1997), pp. 241–2; Michael C. C. Adams, *The Best War Ever: America and World War II* (Baltimore: Johns Hopkins University Press, 1994), pp. 12, 70, 85–6, 123–4, 132–5, 144–5; Yoshiko Miyake, 'Doubling Expectations: Motherhood and Women's Factory Work Under State Management in Japan in the 1930s and 1940s', in Gail Lee Bernstein, ed., *Recreating Japanese Women, 1600–1945* (Berkeley: University of California Press, 1991), pp. 267–95 (pp. 267–8, 281, 282, 290); Pine, *Nazi Family Policy*, p. 184; Tooze, *Wages of Destruction*, pp. 358–9, 513, 515.

increasing need for youthful energy and strength in first subduing and then fending off its many enemies made older Germans superfluous and unwanted. Together with Jews, mental patients and labourers from Eastern Europe, older patients with severe chronic illnesses were at the end of the Nazi wartime health care queue. In 1944 the SS was recommending with cold ice-floe logic that old people should try to live out 'natural' lives of fresh air and exercise. Still, many older Germans were compelled out of their own and the regime's necessity to work during the war. At the same time, the Nazis gave up on their dreams for youth as the guarantee of the future. Young boys as well as older men often assumed guard duties over prisoners of war in order to free up more able men for military service or jobs in industry. In 1945 older men were scraped together into the *Volkssturm*, the Nazis' last desperate attempt to stave off final defeat by means of a militia of those aged sixteen to sixty. In the course of the first four months of 1945, 27,000 Hitler Youth alone were killed in action. On the home front, retirees were mobilized as judges, but most commonly as doctors. So many young and middle-aged doctors had been drafted into the armed services that in December 1941 Health Leader Conti was already complaining to the Wehrmacht Medical Service it was 'grotesque' that there should be such an oversupply of physicians in the armed services that they had to work only a few hours a day.[20] So the Nazis were forced to man the home front with a high proportion of superannuated and overworked physicians in whom patients had little confidence.

Approximately 8.3 million German soldiers were killed, wounded or went missing in action during the Second World War. While the dead represented an absolute manpower loss, generation of wounded had long been a method of modern military strategy. The care of wounded in a modern medical regime requires many more human and material resources than do the dead, thereby producing and multiplying the effect of attrition that progressively wore down military fighting-power. To this must be added the millions of casualties due to illness. While most of these were temporary, by 1943 the number of permanent losses in personnel to injuries and illnesses was 41,792. For tuberculosis the annual figures ranged from 4,000 to 8,000, for blood disorders 3,500 to 4,000, and digestive problems 3,000 to 5,000. Special

---

20 Cocks, *State of Health*, pp. 189–90; 'Die über 60', *Das Schwarze Korps*, 30 March 1944, 5; Süss, '*Volkskörper*', p. 303; Burleigh and Wippermann, *Racial State*, p. 250; Evans, *Third Reich at War*, p. 517; Nicholas Stargardt, *Witnesses of War: Children's Lives under the Nazis* (London: Jonathan Cape, 2005), p. 316.

'stomach battalions' had to be organized for soldiers suffering from ulcers. A study in September 1943 of those judged unfit for service over the past year reported 11,000 soldiers had been rejected or released due to mental illness. It was only in the course of 1943 that permanent losses to illness and injury combined began to surpass nervous casualties by a wide margin. Cascading casualties by the last year of the conflict forced the German armed services to trawl sick bays for sick and wounded soldiers to send back into battle. Military medical practice was stood on its head, triage now meaning treatment only of those who could be patched up, with those seriously wounded, especially those with stomach wounds, left to die.[21]

This immobilization was met with a costly and labour-intensive Nazi campaign to integrate disabled soldiers into the war economy. The term *Kriegsversehrte* was introduced into common wartime parlance, which conflated heroism with utility and cowardice with disability. Disabled veterans (including thousands of *Kriegsbeschädigte* from the First World War) were not to be honoured, pitied or pensioned, they were to be put to work. By 1944 there were 8,500 widely feared stations for 'restorative therapy' of the disabled, sick and malingering staffed by 8,000 German and 1,500 foreign doctors. This effort, while uniform across the regime, was not unified. The SS sought to put its own war wounded to work but jealously guarded control over its men. And while the Reich Labour Minister was given authority over disabled veterans in 1944 in order to effect and propagandize the productive employment of these men, this did not include professional soldiers.[22]

Armaments Minister Speer complained that field hospitals were understating the severity of patients' wounds in order to retain them for possible deployment. A consulting army psychiatrist argued that too many men with head injuries were being declared unfit for military service and released to war work. He claimed that these men were now sitting at home doing nothing or occupied only with sweeping floors and peeling potatoes. And while there were glowing reports in the press and in self-congratulatory memoranda among the ministries and industries, many of the disabled remained immobilized. In 1943 it was claimed that 36,000 *Kriegsversehrte* were

21 Cocks, *State of Health*, p. 208; Antony Beevor, *The Fall of Berlin 1945* (New York: Penguin, 2002), p. 234; Martin K. Sorge, *The Other Price of Hitler's War: German Military and Civilian Losses from World War II* (New York: Greenwood Press, 1986), pp. 61–71.
22 Cocks, *State of Health*, p. 245; Karl H. Karbe, 'Enstehung und Ausbau des faschistischen Betriebsarztsystems und dessen Funktion bei der Ausbeutung der deutschen Arbeiter und ausländischen Zwangsarbeiter', in Achim Thom and Genadij Ivanovič Caregorodcev, eds., *Medizin unterm Hakenkreuz* (Berlin: Volk und Gesundheit, 1989), pp. 205–50 (p. 215).

working inside Germany. Even if accurate, this was a very small number given spiralling casualty rates; from August to December 1944 the number of soldiers killed, wounded or captured would exceed 1 million. Another 1943 report on the rehabilitation programme in an SS Convalescent Battalion in Austria said conditions were terrible with the men just sitting around doing nothing; in 1944 in Alsace some of the instructors were so debilitated they could not teach anymore. Demand for war wounded workers was also uneven, often because of ongoing medical problems that required treatment on the job. As former soldiers for a regime that exalted soldierly qualities, the expectations of *Kriegsversehrte* were also often disappointed by their treatment by employers. These disabled were paid less than other workers who had been mustered out of the Wehrmacht earlier in the war. Younger men in particular were already embittered as a result of having been disabled and so they often conducted themselves in an agitated or even aggressive way toward their fellow employees. The multiplying presence of these men also had a depressing effect on the German populace's confidence in victory. Such distress was magnified by shrill Nazi insistence since 1933 on health and condemnation of the unfit that filled the media with images of disability and illness. The approaching end of the war had an effect on the disabled as well. The Armaments Ministry complained in September 1944 that many of the disabled veterans were seeking desk jobs with a future and not the industrial labour jobs needed at the moment.[23]

The mass murder of the insane in the Third Reich was a function of Nazi racial theory in combination with the strong somatic tradition in German psychiatry. This unholy alliance of the scientific and the scatterbrained held that the insane were incurably inferior members of the race who must be eliminated. The war provided both cover and resource justification for a campaign that claimed 200,000 victims from 1939 right through to (and, in a few places, even beyond) the end of the war. A Nazi elaboration on the ad hoc starvation of mental patients in blockaded Germany during the First World War, the so-called T4 programme was part of the negative triage of the German racial body (*Volkskörper*) at war. T4 began with the murder of children by means of starvation or fatal injection and swiftly evolved into

23 Cocks, *State of Health*, pp. 245–7, 249–51; Kroener, 'Massnahmen zur Mobilisierung von Leistungsreserven im deutschen Machtbereich'; Carol Poore, 'Who Belongs? Disability and the German Nation in Postwar Literature and Film', *German Studies Review* 26:1 (2003), 21–42 (p. 22); Evans, *Third Reich at War*, p. 656.

systematic gassing of the adult insane. Only a very few patients in German asylums survived, either by luck or ties to Nazi officials.[24] Here too there were costs to the war effort. The German public upon which total war depended was uncomfortable with the 'secret' programme. Outcry in 1941 even prompted Hitler to suspend T4 although killing continued on local initiative. Such popular concern was due not only to some moral outrage but also to considerable mortal fear. Compulsory sterilization before the war of those with 'hereditary defects' had in theory and in practice reached deep into German society and Nazi party ranks. This, and the regime's utilitarian concern with mobilization of Germans for work and for war, had led to a reduction in the number of 'congenital' conditions (such as alcoholism and also clubfoot, from which Propaganda Minister Goebbels suffered) subject to sterilization. But now wartime families worried about wounded and disabled soldiers being subject to 'euthanasia'. So in 1941 the SD had to report that the policy of placing soldiers with brain injuries in mental asylums 'was not well understood' among the populace.[25] Also, while some already emptied asylums were converted to care for wounded soldiers, this required the cross-mobilization of both old staff and new. These too were human resources that could not be used for other war purposes.

Many Nazis and psychiatrists included homosexuals among those as suffering from congenital and incurable mental illness. Around 5,000 homosexuals (of perhaps 15,000 imprisoned) in Nazi concentration camps were exterminated. This by Nazi measure small number consisted mostly of male prostitutes and other adult homosexuals the regime designated as predatory. There was disagreement among German physicians and Nazi officials concerning the possibility of treatment for homosexuality. The SS of course occupied the extreme, calling for the death penalty. In 1943 Hitler did decree the death penalty for homosexuality, but – and here was the rub – for members of the SS. Clearly homosexuality was a problem the regime could not kill its way out of, as it was committed to do with Jews. Even the SS in its own barbaric way undertook to find a physical 'cure' for homosexuality through deadly human experiments on concentration camp prisoners. But there were also those who argued that homosexuality was a psychological illness that could be treated. This school of thought was backed by a doctor

24 Henry Friedlander, *The Origins of Nazi Genocide: From Euthanasia to the Final Solution* (Chapel Hill: University of North Carolina Press, 1995), pp. 164, 168–9, 176–7, 182–3; Süss, 'Volkskörper', pp. 127–51, 311–69.
25 Cocks, *State of Health*, p. 250.

related to Hermann Göring as head of a well-funded institute for psychotherapy in Berlin. While most of the treatments there were professionally prosaic, at least one SS officer threatened with execution was sent to the so-called Göring Institute where, as baroque proof he had been cured, he performed a sex act with a female prostitute before a panel of doctors.

While most homosexuals remained – undetected – part of the Nazi war effort, the debate over their nature and utility is an instance in the realm of science and medicine of the dynamics of mobilization and immobilization. For the masculinist SS, homosexuality was an especially threatening racial issue, just as mental illness in general was. Reichsführer-SS Himmler felt compelled in 1943 to write to Hitler's headquarters that men discharged from the SS for 'abnormal personality development' were not suffering from an 'organic' mental illness for which Nazi law mandated sterilization or death.[26] In the German military, homosexuality was a question of both race and resource. The Luftwaffe and the army took opposing positions on the issue, a division that both mobilized and immobilized homosexuals in the armed services. The psychotherapists had entrée into the Luftwaffe due to the Göring family and the Luftwaffe was the newest of the military branches and thus did not have the long association with traditional psychiatry that the army medical services had. It was also the case that airmen came to a much greater extent than the army from the middle classes, among whom psychological treatment was more normal and expected. The Luftwaffe recommended psychotherapeutic treatment for homosexual 'disorders' while army psychiatrists mandated a range of treatments and punishments for homosexual activity, including death.[27] Once again, immobilization required significant resources to manage, in this case medical specialists as well as the range of civilian and military administrators to supervise the punishment, treatment and work of another group variously designated by the Nazi regime as dangerous but also perhaps useful in the short run.

More straightforward was the case of those in Nazi Germany who in one way or another counter-mobilized against the regime. The Nazis had long before the war destroyed any organized political opposition. Yet there were still those in Hitler's Germany who exercised degrees of oppositional behaviour that ranged from the personal to the political. The Wehrmacht ended up sentencing more than 30,000 of its own soldiers to death, while many more

26 Ibid., p. 212.
27 Geoffrey Cocks, *Psychotherapy in the Third Reich: The Göring Institute* (2nd rev. edn, New Brunswick, NJ: Transaction, 1997), pp. 286–8, 294–300, 309.

on the home front were imprisoned or executed for subversion under a 1938 law against undermining the nation's military strength (*Zersetzung der Wehrkraft*). Throughout the war there were youths in German cities who adopted lifestyles that represented rejection of Nazi values. Some were from working-class backgrounds whose protests against the regime fell well short of organized resistance activity. There were also youths from the upper middle class who embraced jazz and swing music condemned by the Nazis as the nefarious product of Africans and Jews. From 1942 on hundreds of these youths were arrested and sent to labour or concentration camps, all at some cost to the war effort.[28] Individuals like Elise and Otto Hampl, who protested against the war because of the loss of a family member, also cost the Nazis time and effort in detection, imprisonment, arrest and execution. At the same time, both Hampls were employed, she as a domestic and he as a factory worker, jobs that, however indirectly and minimally, kept the German home front in the war. The same was true of the university students in Munich who made up the White Rose, which advocated an end to a war of conquest and extermination. The most prominent – and perhaps most promising – of the resistance groups in wartime Nazi Germany were members of the High Command who opposed Hitler as a gambler with Germany's existence as a nation and its reputation as a civilized people. These military officers exercised direct and powerful prosecution of the German war effort while at the same time seeking to end Hitler's life and thereby – they hoped – the war short of unconditional surrender. Their own mobilization and attempt at total immobilization of the German war effort underline the paradox of resistance in a modern authoritarian system. Out-liers in Nazi Germany were in little or no position to resist the regime since they were already immobilized through imprisonment or death. Only those within the system of rule and war were in a position to do anything about a system their own positions supported. Short of suicide in the face of a country mobilized materially and spiritually for national survival in war, more than ever in order to make a stand, one needed a place to stand.[29]

---

28 Detlev J. K. Peukert, *Inside Nazi Germany: Conformity, Opposition, and Racism in Everyday Life*, trans. Richard Deveson (New Haven: Yale University Press, 1987), pp. 78, 165–9, 206; Michael H. Kater, *Different Drummers: Jazz in the Culture of Nazi Germany* (Oxford University Press, 2003), pp. 153–61; Manfred Messerschmidt, 'German Military Law in the Second World War', in Wilhelm Deist, ed., *The German Military in the Age of Total War* (Leamington Spa: Berg, 1985), pp. 323–35.

29 Michael Geyer and John W. Boyer, eds., *Resistance against the Third Reich, 1933–1990* (University of Chicago Press, 1994).

The legacy of total war mobilization and immobilization

The experience and memory of the Second World War as the culmination of a century or more of 'nationalizing ... private pain'[30] inoculated millions of Germans and their political leaders against the ambitions and attractions of modern total warfare. This – as elsewhere around the world – was general cultural immobilization after the fact. Total war also brought areas of discrimination, contestation and persecution to greater individual, social and national consciousness. The result was that those immobilized – ethnic and religious minorities, women, homosexuals, the disabled, even the young and elderly – would often enough determine post-war generational spaces in which modern social conflict and challenge could be contested, confronted or resolved. In Great Britain, the efforts of pacifists like Vera Brittain to raise wartime consciousness of the 'obliteration bombing' of German cities contributed to significant public unease that long after the war fed reluctance to extend the honoured recognition to Bomber Command lavished upon other branches of the armed services. Among young Japanese, the experience of mobilization and immobilization reinforced pacifist sentiments suppressed in the 1930s and 1940s that after the war resurfaced in opposition to ongoing nationalist and militarist allegiances in the country.[31] Akira Kurosawa's film *No Regrets for Our Youth* (1946) is one early eloquent expression of this response to total war.

There are as well generalizable cautionary elements to the legacy of mobilization during the Second World War. In Germany as in other nations at war, the immobilized had been loss and burden in mobilization for total war. But where there is life – as often there was not in total war – there is both resource and recourse. Within qualitative and quantitative limits, the immobilized were mobilized and the mobilized immobilized. Those by degrees in or out of the war at any given time – due to gender, age, condition, disposition or choice – occupied dynamic spaces of constraint, agency, loss or gain for both themselves and for the state. This demonstrates how total the Second World War was in that its commands and constraints also created space for agency, opposition and – mostly – change over time that enhanced as well as compromised the state's capacity to respond to the war's challenges. The only

---

30 John Bodnar, '*Saving Private Ryan* and Postwar Memory in America', *American Historical Review* 106:3 (2001), 805–17 (p. 807).

31 Vera Brittain, *One Voice: Pacifist Writings from the Second World War* (London: Continuum, 2005), pp. 93–181; Saburō Ienaga, *The Pacific War: A Critical Perspective on Japan's Role in World War II*, trans. Frank Baldwin (New York: Pantheon Books, 1978), pp. 16, 18, 109, 113, 120, 215, 244–5, 251.

thing that was fully unique in the Nazi approach to total war was mass extermination as war aim in and of itself. Even here, though, total war against civilians and not just soldiers everywhere further mobilized nationalist and/or ethnic hatred against enemies as 'Others' while immobilizing countervailing empathy for these others' suffering. Modern institutions and instruments of coercion, seduction, distraction and instigation against fearful enemies powerfully real and powerfully imagined too were magnified in their effects by the total war environment of damage and threat to individual well-being. Both dictatorships and democracies also exploited modern internalized values of discipline, work and nationalized identity in their total war efforts. Even the 'peculiar' German tradition of coordination of governance and economy was paradigmatic for post-liberal Western capitalist nation states and central to the total wars they waged.

All such realities of late modern industrialized, commercialized and medicalized societies at war underscore the importance in several dimensions of the experiences of the observers as well as the servants and victims of total war. As historical subjects, the immobilized of the Second World War render the last line of John Milton's 'On His Blindness' (1655) apposite to one dynamic and dialectical wartime phenomenon of the late modern era: 'They also serve who only stand and waite'.

14

The war of the villages

The interwar agrarian crisis and the Second World War

ADAM TOOZE

Five years on from VE day and VJ day the United Nation's first estimates of global population showed 71 per cent of the world's population in 1950 as rural dwellers. The share in Asia and Africa was 83–85 per cent, 49 per cent in Europe and 36 per cent even in North America.[1] The Second World War was fought in an agrarian world. Of the major combatants only one, the United Kingdom, could be described as a fully urbanized society. Even in the USA, the industrial arsenal of democracy, in 1940, 43 per cent of the population lived in communities with fewer than 2,500 residents. The proportion in Hitler's Germany was similar.

There are arenas of conflict in the Second World War that seem very remote from this rural world. The strategic air war waged by Britain and America against the cities of Germany and Japan was in many respects the quintessential urban-industrial war. If they were not able to identify a legitimate urban target, the bomber crews were instructed to empty their payload over the countryside as though it were nothing but a blank void. From the point of view of 1940s strategic bombing, it might as well have been. But even the air war was not completely urban. Airbases were, as far as possible, sited in rural areas. Buildings and trees were perilous for air crews during take-off and landing. The term airfield should be taken literally. It was only from 1939 onwards that most runways were paved. The air war had a staggering appetite for land. By 1945, the American Army Air Force had spent $3 billion converting 19.7 million acres of US territory, an area the size of the state of New Hampshire into airbases, bombing ranges and other facilities.[2] Laid end to end the runways bulldozed out of the British countryside

---

1 *United Nations Demographic Yearbook* (New York: United Nations 1952).
2 Wesley Frank Craven and James Lea Gate, eds., *The Army Air Forces in World War II*, vol. VI: *Men and Planes* (University of Chicago Press, 1955), pp. 119–70.

between 1939 and 1945 would have made a 10 metre-wide road, 16,000 km long.[3] As a factor in landscape transformation the land hunger of the air war was several times larger than the post-war motorway system, which in Britain currently extends to no more than 3,500 km.

But the World War was not just sited in the landscape. Nor did it explode into an agrarian world from the outside, or strike it accidentally like a ruinous hailstorm. Many of the parties to the conflict emerged from a rural world. They were motivated by its problems. And their struggle in every arena of the war drew directly on the resources of the countryside, its people and its animals. As a result of this mobilization in many parts of the world the war unleashed more profound change in the social order of the agrarian world than in any other area of society.

Agrarian society under pressure

To generalize about this vast slice of humanity is dangerous of course. Agrarian systems were minutely differentiated by region, climate and type of crop. Rural society was riven with social cleavages. The gap between the landlord, the middling peasant and the precarious landless labourer was vast. But between nations the differences in the early decades of the twentieth century were nowhere near as large as they were to become. In the 1940s only the agriculture of North America and Australasia had begun seriously to mechanize. And even in the USA whereas there were in 1940 two horses, mules or oxen for every farm, there was only one tractor for every four farms and one truck for every six.[4] The basic equipment of agriculture was still common to farms across the world. The images of rural life in America captured in the photographs of Walker Evans in the 1930s would have been recognizable to many hundreds of millions of people across the world. Farming and farm incomes remained tied to the same somatic energy regime that had determined their development for millennia. And as we have come to appreciate, this was true also of most of the armies that fought the war. At the outbreak of the war, the US and British armies were exceptional precisely for the absence of horses from their ranks. When the Wehrmacht opened a new chapter in the history of modern warfare with its devastating lightning

3 C. M. Kohan, *Works and Buildings* (London: HMSO 1952); Bob Clarke, *The Archaeology of Airfields* (Chalford: The History Press, 2008).
4 Hans Binswanger, 'Agricultural Mechanization: A Comparative Historical Perspective', *World Bank Research Observer* 1:1 (1986), 27–56.

victory over France in May 1940, the vast majority of its traction outside the cluster of motorized Panzer divisions was provided by a cavalcade of over half a million horses.

If, to set the stage for an agrarian history of the Second World War, we are forced to choose a single common denominator of global agriculture in the 1920s and 1930s, it would be that of a crisis of modernization. Across the world the common experience was one of disequilibrium between bulging populations, increasingly disappointing progress in productivity and a diminishing margin of new land, which could easily be brought into production. The most dramatic way in which these tensions manifested themselves were in the common risks to which societies around the world were exposed. Western Europe last suffered outright starvation in the 1840s. But as the twentieth century began, the memory of famine or near famine conditions was common across Eastern Europe. Absolute poverty and chronic malnutrition were an everyday reality among millions of rural dwellers in Southern and Eastern Europe, as they were among rural populations across Asia. The fact that richer societies were by the late nineteenth century able to escape the spectre of outright famine, had less to do with the productivity of their agricultural systems, which was far outstripped by population growth, than with their ability to access international markets at times of stress. The blockade of the First World War brought hunger back to the cities of Central Europe.[5]

Meanwhile, the countryside was stirred by dramatic cultural change. Most importantly, mass literacy had spread to most of rural Europe in East and West by the early twentieth century. Famously, as recently as 1914 many of the peasant conscripts in the armies of Imperial Russia, Austro-Hungary and Italy had little idea of the nation that they were called upon to fight for. The experience of the First World War served as a nationalizing mechanism for all of the combatants, but outside Europe and North America, even in the 1930s this process was far from complete. It was the Second World War that would turn hundreds of millions of peasants into Chinese, Indians, Pakistanis, Vietnamese and Malayans.

At a time when the rural world was experiencing acute population pressure, land hunger was a common predicament across Eurasia. Throughout the nineteenth century, as transport costs fell, migration and new colonization had provided an escape valve. The closing of the USA to migration in the 1920s compounded fears of 'overpopulation' across Central,

---

5 Avner Offer, *The First World War: An Agrarian Interpretation* (Oxford: Clarendon Press 1989).

Southern and Eastern Europe.[6] In the 'empty spaces' of Manchuria, Chinese, Japanese and Korean migrants jostled for space.

If population pressure could not be vented by migration, this raised the prospect that a solution would be found through more or less violent redistribution of land at home. In Europe by the late nineteenth century land hunger was so severe that it repeatedly flared into 'land wars', first in Ireland, then in Russia in 1905, and then across the latifundia of Romania in 1907. The Italian countryside was in uproar after the First World War as was the territory of the Tsarist Empire after 1917. Lenin's turn to the market-based New Economic Policy in the spring of 1921 confirmed the verdict of the Russian Civil War. Russia could not be ruled against the peasants. The Communists endorsed the great peasant land grab of 1917 and suspended any hasty push toward the imposition of Soviet collectivization. Across much of Eastern Europe the stabilization of the 1920s was accompanied by large-scale land redistribution. In the 1930s the land question was once again to the fore in Spain, where the land hunger of the braceros fuelled the violence of the civil war in Andalusia and Extremadura.

None of these pressures would have been so acute if economic growth outside agriculture had been rapid. But, instead, the decades after the First World War saw slowing industrial growth. Ever since the global integration of markets had connected the populations of Europe, the Americas and Australasia through a series of commodity chains, agricultural producers had found themselves subjected to competitive pressure, commodity gluts and credit crises. But the economic switchback in the decades before and after the First World War was unprecedentedly violent. Between 1910 and 1920 agrarian prices surged across the world to levels never seen before, only to collapse between 1920 and 1921 and then to plunge again in the depression that hit commodity markets in 1928. Gloomy prognosticators had long diagnosed a contradiction between world markets and the survival of the small-scale, family farm. In the 1930s that contradiction appeared to have become absolute.

Since the mid-nineteenth century, despite protectionist pressures, the agricultural economy had been one of the main engines of globalization. In the First World War the idea of government control of the countryside had been so alien that it took even the most vulnerable combatants until 1916 to impose effective centralized purchasing and rationing. After the war the shock of near starvation suffered by many of the combatants gave a new

---

6 Adam McKeown, 'Global Migration 1846–1940', *Journal of World History* 15:2 (2004), 155–89.

strategic importance not so much to farmers as to food as an object of government policy. But it was the depression of the 1930s that led the developed world – the USA, Europe and Japan – to terminate the experiment with a globally integrated market for agriculture.[7] In the decade before the outbreak of the Second World War all the most sophisticated states in the world were engaged in systematically reshaping their agricultural sectors into national farm economies insulated from the world market. To address the 'problem of the villages' by the early 1930s the Japanese government had put in place price stabilization policies for rice, wheat and silk.[8] After 1932 even the British Empire resorted to agricultural tariffs for the first time in peacetime. Nazi Germany was the most comprehensive example of national protectionism, shutting its food market completely and minimizing imports of food, fertilizer and animal feed. In Germany, amidst Hitler's 'economic miracle' surreptitious rationing of the most import-dependent foodstuffs such as meat and milk began already in 1935.

It is a testament to the hybridity of Nazi ideology and to the transformative quality of the interwar crisis that this unprecedented system of delivery quotas, price controls and rationing was imposed on the rural world by a regime that more than any other in German history celebrated the freestanding peasant as the bedrock of the nation and that drew a large part of its electoral support from millions of agitated peasant voters.[9] At the same time in the East, the Soviet Union demonstrated the radical consistency of a different model. In 1928, Stalin resumed the struggle for control of the Soviet countryside that had been suspended by Lenin in 1921. Between 1928 and 1933, to build 'socialism in one country' and to lay the foundations for forced industrialization, two-thirds of Russia's 25 million independent land holdings and 83 per cent of its farm land were collectivized. At a stroke the Soviet regime centralized control of land, livestock and the harvest. In the process millions of farmers died of starvation. Millions more were targeted for execution and deportation as 'kulak' class enemies of the regime.[10]

7 Michael Tracy, *Government and Agriculture in Western Europe, 1880–1988* (London Harvester Wheatsheaf, 1989).
8 Kerry Smith, *Time of Crisis: Japan, The Great Depression, and Rural Revitalization* (Cambridge, Mass.: Harvard University Press, 2003); Penelope Francks, *Rural Economic Development in Japan: From the Nineteenth Century to the Pacific War* (London: Routledge, 2006).
9 Gustavo Corni, *Hitler and the Peasants: Agrarian Policy of the Third Reich, 1930–1939*, trans. David Kerr (New York and Oxford: Berg, 1990).
10 R. W. Davies and Stephen G. Wheatcroft, *Years of Hunger: Soviet Agriculture, 1931–1933* (Basingstoke: Palgrave Macmillan, 2004).

In the early 1930s the rural population collectivized in the Soviet Union came to perhaps 120 million souls. Another 140 million lived on the land across Western Europe. Japan's farm population came to 32 million with many more living in rural villages. Large as these farm populations were, they were overshadowed by the even larger populations of Asia, above all of China and India. Here land was even scarcer than it was in Western and Eastern Europe. Opportunities for political mobilization were far less. But among the jute farmers of Bengal or the rice paddies of the Mekong exposure to the vagaries of international markets was already considerable. Long treated as a quiescent mass, one of the great questions of the early twentieth century was whether the peasant masses, the 'toilers of the East' as communist propaganda liked to call them, would rise. If they rose up would they set their own course, or would they follow a leader? What would be the cause for which they fought? Would they fight for a new social order, for the nation, or for more parochial interests? Or, would they become the passive victims of a last round of imperialist land grabs, condemning them to exploitation, forced labour, land clearance and ethnic cleansing?

To construct a frame to encompass this variegated but interconnected agrarian history of the Second World War, four dimensions suggest themselves. First, the agrarian world was the source of the food, raw materials, human and animal labour power for all of the combatant countries and their populations, whether civilian or military. Second, given its essential role both as a productive resource and as the foundation of rural life, land was a key target of conquest. Third, the countryside was the stage on which much of the war was fought out. We should take the notion of the battlefield more literally than we sometimes do. Fourth, in many theatres the peasants who populated this battlefield, were not passive objects of conquest, nor were they merely bystanders or victims of collateral damage; in several major arenas in Europe and Asia, the peasants, as peasants, were strategic actors in the war.

Abundance: the agrarian war in the West

At one extreme of agrarian experience in the Second World War were the USA and the White Dominions of the British Empire – Canada, Australia and New Zealand. As surplus regions they served as they had done in the First World War, as a great strategic reserve of the Allied war effort. Provided the sea lanes could be held open they guaranteed that the Allied war effort would be better provided with food than its enemies. To save space, food was shipped above all in processed form. Exports of manufactured foodstuffs from the USA increased tenfold between 1940 and 1944, to no less than 1.6 billion dollars, a level at which they would remain until the European crisis began to recede in 1949. Even though they were not directly in the firing line, the impact of the Second World War on these highly productive agrarian systems was dramatic. In the wake of the crisis of the 1930s, the war further concentrated and intensified the reach of national farm policy. Agro-corporatist networks took shape that would endure down to the end of the twentieth century.

Whereas in the 1930s the problem of underemployed and surplus labour had hung over the depression-ridden farm economy of North America, wartime mobilization sucked workers off the land. Altogether 6 million people drained out of the US rural economy between 1940 and 1945.[11] The war had a particularly dramatic impact on the racialized sharecropping system of the South. Black labour left the cotton fields en masse to be replaced by new-fangled farm machinery. After slowing in the 1930s, the introduction of tractors accelerated to reach saturation levels by the early 1950s. US wheat- and corn-farming had long been pioneers of labour-saving technologies. But in cotton the 1940s marked a turning point with government agencies encouraging the larger plantations to adopt mechanization on an unprecedented scale. Meanwhile, for those wedded to the old labour-intensive methods there was the Emergency Farm Labor Supply Program initiated in August 1942.[12] Also known as the Barcero Program it would eventually draw hundreds of thousands of Mexicans as guestworkers to the USA. It was not terminated until 1962. Alongside the Mexicans, from 1943 onwards many thousands of Italian and German POWs mainly from Rommel's Afrika Corps found themselves hoeing cotton in the fields of Louisiana, Mississippi and Arkansas.[13]

In Europe too, low labour productivity was the curse of the farm economy. As Hitler's Germany reached full employment in 1936 it began to suffer from an acute shortage of affordable labour. At harvest time the Hitler Youth

11 Pete Daniel, 'Going among Strangers: Southern Reactions to World War II', *Journal of American History* 77:3 (1990), 886–911; Nan Elizabeth Woodruff, 'Mississippi Delta Planters and Debates over Mechanization, Labor, and Civil Rights in the 1940s', *Journal of Southern History* 60:2 (1994), 263–84.

12 Nan Elizabeth Woodruff, 'Pick or Fight: The Emergency Farm Labor Program in the Arkansas and Mississippi Deltas during World War II', *Agricultural History* 64:2 (1990), 74–85.

13 Jason Morgan Ward, 'Nazis Hoe Cotton: Planters, POWs, and the Future of Farm Labor in the Deep South', *Agricultural History* 81:4 (2007), 471–92.

was drafted en masse. Mechanization was much discussed, but there was not enough foreign exchange to afford the petrol or the large pneumatic tyres for modern tractors. The result was an impasse of strategic dimensions. Throughout the Second World War an agricultural economy that fell well short of supplying Germany's basic needs tied down more than 11 million adult workers, more than were employed either in industry or in the Wehrmacht. After 1942 the Third Reich's notorious slave labour programme was used to supply labour power to the armaments factories. But the forced foreign labour programme had its origin in agriculture. The mobilization call up in the autumn of 1939 created an immediate crisis on Germany's inefficient farms. The gaps were first filled with Polish prisoners of war and then with Frenchmen and Belgians. By 1944 POW and foreign labour made up 41 per cent of the workforce in German agriculture, the highest share of any sector.

Of course it was not just labour that Germany conquered. After its extraordinary run of victories between 1939 and 1942, one thing was clear. In the Second World War, unlike in the First World War, it would not be the Germans but the rest of Europe that would go short of food. As the Wehrmacht advanced there was much pillaging of livestock and grain stores. In Eastern Europe the Wehrmacht had instructions to feed itself from the land.[14] The result behind the lines in the first year of the occupation was chaos and starvation. Having established themselves in control, the Germans then moved to a system of more sophisticated exploitation that relied on large-scale purchasing operations. For Western European farmers this created a booming market. Highly efficient Dutch and Danish producers found that the Third Reich was willing to pay premium prices for butter. Farm earnings soared. After 1945 when Danish farmers returned to their normal trade patterns, the prices on offer from cash-strapped post-war Britain came as a rude awakening. The difference was that Germany as the occupying power did not pay for its food imports with its own export earnings, but from a bottomless credit line charged to the account of the Danish, French and Dutch central banks. Farm suppliers favoured by the Germans got paid, but at the price of increasingly disorderly inflation. It was the city population of German-occupied Europe that was left struggling to cope with starvation rations and rocketing black market prices. Tellingly, when peace came, the authorities in Denmark and the Netherlands sought to restore the

---

14 G. Aly, *Hitler's Beneficiaries: How the Nazis Bought the German People* (London: Verso, 2006).

distributive balance through currency reforms and special taxes designed to claw back the huge profits made by farmers on their edible assets.[15]

The basic constraint on the European farm economy in the Second World War as in the First World War was the blockade.[16] Along with oil and industrial raw materials this cut off the high-energy and high-protein feeds that European farmers had become used to sourcing from tropical suppliers. The effect was to reduce yields across Europe. Thought was given in Britain to a more direct attack on the Axis food supply. In 1942 Churchill considered plans to dust Germany's fields with a new generation of herbicidal chemicals that had been developed by Imperial Chemical Industries. The idea was rejected only because the RAF at the time was struggling to assemble a bomber fleet large enough to target Germany's cities, let alone its wheat fields. But the Anglo-American research effort continued at full speed and herbicidal chemicals were to have formed a major element in America's air war plan for the final destruction of Japan in 1946, Operation Downfall. As it turned out it was the British who became the pioneers of large-scale herbicidal attacks on the countryside. During their comprehensive agrarian counter-insurgency campaign in Malaya between 1952 and 1960, the British made heavy use of the chemical that would soon become notorious as Agent Orange to clear security perimeters and destroy 'bandit crops'.[17]

For much of the Second World War, in large parts of Western Europe the countryside was a place of relative safety, a place of evacuation for children, a place where one could hide from totalitarian persecution or retreat into 'inner emigration'. It was not until 1943 in Italy and then from June 1944 in France, Belgium and the Netherlands that the rural population once more witnessed the spectacle of modern war fought over the fields, hedgerows and dykes of the classic battlefields of Europe. The final campaigns of the war saw a vast escalation of firepower and the Allied advance through Italy and France was more ponderous and more deliberately prepared than the German assault had been in 1940 and 1941. As a result, when fighting bogged down for weeks on end, as it did around Monte Cassino or in Normandy, the destruction was vast. Most damaging of all was the defensive measures of last resort – inundation. In 1943 the Germans flooded the Pontine Marshes to

15 Paul Brassley, Yves Segers and Leen Van Molle, eds., *War, Agriculture and Food: Rural Europe from the 1930s to the 1950s* (New York: Routledge, 2012).

16 Karl Brandt, Otto Schiller and Franz Ahlgrimm, *Management of Agriculture and Food in the German-Occupied and Other Areas of Fortress Europe* (Stanford Food Research Institute 1953).

17 Peter Hough, *The Global Politics of Pesticides* (London: Earthscan, 1998), p. 61.

form a defensive belt south of Rome, unleashing a devastating return of malaria.[18] In the autumn of 1944 the Allies attempted to flood the Germans off the strategic Walcheren Island which threatened the approaches to the strategic port of Antwerp. As we shall see, these measures were dwarfed by truly massive acts of landscape destruction in the Asian war. But even without such desperate measures, the rural landscape could present a serious obstacle to modern, fast-moving warfare. For tank warfare the undulating, empty desert or the steppe was the ideal terrain. By contrast, the dense hedgerows of Normandy, the famous bocage, provided the defenders with ready-made fortifications on which to base a static defence. In the end, thousands of tanks had to be fitted with improvised hedge-cutting equipment to bulldoze their way through the French field system.

The image of an American-made Sherman tank with its steel bocage cutters smashing through the legacy of hundreds of years of French peasant labour is a fitting one to characterize the experience of West European farming either side of the Second World War. Technological 'catch-up' was one of the defining concepts of post-war economic growth. If there was one sector where this had real force it was in West European agriculture. By the interwar period a huge technological gap had opened up between peasant Europe and the urban, industrial, modern economy. After 1945 with an unprecedented investment in mechanization and fertilizer inputs, the European countryside rebuilt and mechanized even more rapidly than the ruined urban areas. In West Germany where there had been 30,000 tractors before the war, by 1955 there were 462,000.

The war for land

The mechanization and intensification of the post-war period enabled a much smaller farm population in Europe to achieve a standard of living unimagined before 1939. By the same token it made real the nightmare of the early twentieth-century agrarian ideologues, for whom a post-agrarian future promised national ruin. Confronted with the problems of the interwar agrarian economy their favoured strategy was simple: conquer more land. The European search for Lebensraum, of course had a long history. But by the late nineteenth century the main axis of imperialist competition had shifted. If the First World War was an imperialist war, it was about more

18 Frank M. Snowden, *The Conquest of Malaria: Italy, 1900–1962* (New Haven, Conn.: Yale University Press, 2006).

abstract concepts such as spheres of interest, or control of industrial raw materials and markets, not farmland. The revival of large-scale, state-organized programmes of conquest, land occupation and agrarian colonization, was one of the striking and apparently anachronistic features of the 1930s. The three most aggressive powers – Imperial Japan, fascist Italy and Nazi Germany – were unprecedentedly explicit and unabashed about the way in which they linked war and imperial conquest to the resolution of problems of the domestic social order.

Abyssinia was Mussolini's most violent and spectacular land grab, justified explicitly in terms of the need to secure living space. But the most sustained programme of fascist colonization was directed at Libya. 'Liberal' Italy had acquired the territory in its opportunistic war of 1911 but no sustained programme of settlement had followed.[19] It was fascism's boast that it would make good that neglect. In October 1938 Governor Italo Balbo personally commanded a fleet of sixteen ships carrying 20,000 Italian peasants destined for Tripoli, where they were to form the avant-garde of a new settler generation. By the time Italy entered the war in 1940, these agriculturalists had doubled in number, making up 40 per cent of the colonial Italian population. By the 1950s Balbo hoped to establish a population of 500,000 Italians in Libya, drawn from the overcrowded regions of Veneto and Emilia.

There is a striking similarity between Balbo's project in Libya and Japan's programme of settlement in Manchukuo in the 1930s. The coincidence of the Great Depression with the Japanese army's aggression in Manchuria after 1931 created a new fusion between external aggression and schemes for agrarian improvement.[20] Hitherto, in Japan's colonies in Taiwan and Korea imperial settlement had been confined to the cities. The main function of colonial agriculture was to provide cheap rice imports for Japan's urban population.[21] The new conception of settlement that took shape in Manchuria from the 1930s onwards reversed these priorities. The aim was not to import food, but to export Japan's surplus agrarian population. This culminated in the 1936 'Millions to Manchuria' programme that proposed to move 1 million peasant households to Manchuria. Given the scarcity of good land in Japan, experts calculated that fully 31 per cent of all existing family farms

19 Claudio G. Segre, 'Italo Balbo and the Colonization of Libya', *Journal of Contemporary History* 7:3/4 (1972), 141–55.
20 Louise Young, *Japan's Total Empire: Manchuria and the Culture of Wartime Imperialism* (Berkeley, Calif.: University of California Press, 1999).
21 Mitushiko Kimura, 'The Economics of Japanese Imperialism in Korea, 1910–1939', *Economic History Review* 48:3 (1995), 555–74.

were non-viable. Resettlement would both secure Japan's grip on Manchuria and allow the consolidation within Japan of a 'chuno' class of middle-sized farmers. By the early 1940s almost a third of a million Japanese had been lured to Manchuria by the promise of generous allocations of land. It was by far the largest settlement project realized by any of the Axis powers.[22]

Both the Italian colonization of Libya and Japan's emplacement in Manchuria were extremely violent, 'warlike' processes. The path for Balbo's colonization was cleared by a violent pacification campaign against the Libyan Bedouin, which culminated in herding tens of thousands of men, women and children into desert concentration camps where they died along with their livestock. In Manchukuo the Japanese settlers found themselves occupying what amounted to a guerrilla war zone. The land allocated to the incomers was extracted from existing Chinese colonists at gun-point. To the north the Japanese homesteaders were menaced by the Red Army. After the Kwantung Army's shocking defeats in the border battles of 1939, the Japanese settlers found themselves designated as 'human pillboxes' reinforcing the exposed northern flank. In both cases violence and settlement were integrally linked, but to the degree that both the Italian and Japanese projects originated as a strategic response to the crises of the early 1930s, they shared an oblique relationship to the new vectors of violence unleashed by Hitler's aggression after 1939. The vast cost of his African ambitions left Mussolini struggling to keep up with the pace of the main arms race in Europe. Though Italo Balbo's track record as a man of fascist violence was impeccable, his commitment to colonization in Libya made him one of the leading opponents of Mussolini's decision to join Hitler's war.[23] Likewise, the strategic direction of Japan's expansion into Manchuria was northwards against the Soviet Union. What soon became clear, however, was that on this axis of advance Japan would never find an answer to its basic dilemma of dependence on imported oil. By contrast, after 1940 the humiliation of Britain, France and the Netherlands at the hands of the Wehrmacht opened more promising avenues of advance to the south. Japan's fateful decision in the summer of 1941 to push towards the oil of Dutch Indonesia, combined with the decision not to join the Germans in the attack on the Soviet Union and instead to launch the assault on Pearl Harbor, had the effect of reducing

---

22 Sandra Wilson, 'The "New Paradise": Japanese Emigration to Manchuria in the 1930s and 1940s', *International History Review* 17:2 (1995), 249–86.
23 Nir Arielli, 'Beyond "Mare Nostrum":. Ambition and Limitations in Fascist Italy's Middle Eastern Policy', *Geschichte und Gesellschaft* 37:3 (2011), 385–407.

Japan's settlement project in Manchuria to a regional sideshow in what was now a far-flung battle for hegemony in the Pacific and Indian Ocean. It would not be until the final collapse of 1945, the communist upsurge across northern China and Stalin's decision to declare war on Japan that Manchuria re-emerged as what it had been in the 1930s, as a central arena of global conflict.

It would be wrong to suggest that by its comparatively late start on its career of open aggression Hitler's regime escaped these basic strategic dilemmas. Like Italy and Japan, the Third Reich too struggled to reconcile its ambitions for Eurasian conquest and settlement with the demands of a global air and naval war against the Western powers. But what set Nazi Germany apart was the way in which the main thrust of its campaign of colonial settlement was aligned with what emerged as the most intense military theatre of the war, the Eastern Front. This was not intended. When the Germans began planning for Eastern colonization in the form of the Generalplan Ost in 1940–41, they assumed that this huge programme of ethnic cleansing would be set in motion after the destruction of the Red Army.[24] Continuing resistance by Soviet guerrilla bands was welcomed as a source of renewal and hardening for future generations of German frontiersmen. By the autumn of 1941 it was clear that things were unlikely to go according to plan. But whereas in Manchuria and in Italy's African empire the unpredictable flux of the war led away from the original axis of colonial settlement, on the Ostfront the effect was the reverse. The most savage fighting of the war, the programmes of colonial conquest, the Judeocide and a draconian regime of extraction and ultra-violent counter-insurgency all intermingled in a nightmarish maelstrom.[25]

In this struggle the agrarian expanse of Ukraine played a particularly pivotal role. It was regarded as the bread basket of the German empire that would extend from the Baltic to the Black Sea. It was one of the most dreadful killing fields of the Holocaust. Added to which Ukraine had been a key battleground in the Russian revolution and the subsequent civil war and famine of the early 1920s.[26] And for some of the same reasons it was also the greatest arena for Stalin's struggle with the peasantry. Not for nothing the experience of Ukraine has come to be seen as paradigmatic of the gigantic ethnic cleansing and agrarian restructuring programmes that swept over the

24 Mark Mazower, *Hitler's Empire: Nazi Rule in Occupied Europe* (London: Penguin, 2009).
25 Christian Gerlach, *Kalkulierte Morde. Die deutsche Wirtschafts-und Vernichtungspolitik in Weissrussland 1941 bis 1944* (Hamburg: Hamburger Edition, 1999).
26 Timothy Snyder, *Bloodlands: Europe between Hitler and Stalin* (New York: Basic Books, 2010).

'bloodlands' of Eastern Europe between 1928 and 1945. One of the striking features of such accounts is the passivity of the victim populations that they describe. But what is not often recognized are the peculiar conditions that created this effect in Ukraine. The flat, unforested expanses that made the Ukraine prime farmland, were particularly unpromising territory from which to mount any kind of resistance. Pursued by roving aerial reconnaissance and highly mobile armoured columns, despite repeated efforts on the Soviet side, their partisans could find no footing.[27] As a result, unlike in other arenas of massive violence in the Second World War, in Ukraine the escalatory dynamic of insurgency and counter-insurgency was comparatively muted. The violence was top-down.

Not that terrain was the only factor in play. Given the years of violent hostility toward the Soviet regime, going back to 1918, it was not surprising that the invading Wehrmacht was initially welcomed in at least some parts of Ukraine with open arms. Both during and after the war there was much speculation as to the possibility that Germany might have mobilized the grievances of the victims of collectivization to unleash a peasant war against Stalin's regime. After 1945 in the first phase of the Cold War, ex officials in the German occupation regime working in collaboration with émigré agronomists and Sovietologists in the USA made much of the idea that the Third Reich had 'lost Ukraine' in the same way that botched American policy was to blame for 'losing China' to communism.[28] If only Germany had systematically enlisted the subordinate populations of the Soviet Union, the Soviets could have been defeated. In this counterfactual the possibility of exploiting peasant resentment at Soviet collectivization was an idée fixe. Nor should the scale of collaboration across the rural hinterland of the Ostfront be underestimated. By 1943 there were 600,000 Soviet men doing armed patrol duty in German police battalions and auxiliary units. Specific ethnic groups with a grudge were easily mobilized. And beginning in the Tartar regions of the south the agrarian administrators of the Wehrmacht did make an effort to institute large-scale land reform and to win the Soviet peasant for Hitler. But even if we abstract from the deeply imbued racial ideology of the Nazi regime, it is more than questionable whether there was any real prospect of establishing a viable anti-Soviet force between the Red Army and the Wehrmacht. And this applies in equal measure to the idea of an anti-communist

27 Matthew Cooper, *Phantom War: The German Struggle against Soviet Partisans, 1941–1944* (London: Macdonald and Janes, 1979).
28 Alexander Dallin, *German Rule in Russia, 1941–1945* (New York, St. Martin's Press, 1957).

agrarian front.[29] To assume that the peasants could have been bought simply by land redistribution implies that they failed to grasp the wider stakes in the war. In particular it imputes to them a remarkably unrealistic assessment of their likely future prospects in a Nazi order. When the Nazi occupiers in the Soviet Union extended their more 'liberal' agrarian system to the central and northern sectors of the Eastern Front, zones where the terrain was more amenable to partisan activity, it had none of the pacifying effect claimed for it in the south. In the swamps and forests of Belorussia, for all the appeal of their anti-Stalinist slogans among the remnant of the 'kulak' population, the Germans faced persistent resistance.

The first cadres of the partisans were recruited from dispersed elements of the Red Army, who themselves more often than not were conscripts from the countryside.[30] Roaming the rear areas, they had little option but to join up. As outsiders, without village attachment their chances of survival behind German lines were slim. Best of all they could form a relationship with a farm woman and seek to blend in. But in the Russian countryside there was little space for 'opting out' of the war. After starving to death most of the Russian POWs they had taken during the BARBAROSSA offensive, in the spring of 1942 the Germans began drafting millions of Eastern men and women for factory work. The Red Army for its part issued a compulsory order requiring all male villagers of fighting-age to join their local resistance centre. The result, behind most of the frontline of Army Group Centre and North, was a murderous three-year struggle. Anyone collaborating with the Germans faced terrifying reprisals by the partisans. The Soviet commissars that emerged from the forest whenever the Wehrmacht withdrew were a constant reminder that Stalin's regime was not dead. The Germans for their part punished resistance with mass executions and the destruction of thousands of villages. Against the major areas of resistance the SS and their auxiliaries mounted large-scale sweeps that resulted in destruction on a genocidal scale. But once the Red Army began its unrelenting rollback, no amount of reprisals could hold the balance. Between January 1943 and January 1944 the fighting strength of the partisans surged from 103,000 to 181,000. Fittingly, in the summer of 1944 it was the partisans that ushered in the final collapse of Army Group Centre. In preparation for the third

29 Christian Gerlach, 'Die deutsche Agrarreform und die Bevölkerungspolitik in den besetztensowjetischen Gebieten', in Christian Gerlach et al., *Besatzung und Bündnis: Deutsche Herrschaftsstrategien in Ost- und Südosteuropa* (Berlin: Verlag der Buchläden, 1995), pp. 9–60.
30 Kenneth Slepyan, *Stalin's Guerrillas: Soviet Partisans in World War II* (Lexington, Ky.: University of Kentucky Press, 2006).

anniversary of the German assault they mounted the largest guerrilla operation of the war. Fourteen thousand explosive charges severed the railway lines feeding the 3rd Panzer Army, the first German unit to face the devastating onslaught of Soviet offensive BAGRATION on 22 June 1944.

Peasant fighters

Substantial though the partisan movement on the Eastern Front may have been, it was never more than auxiliary to the Red Army. This contrasted with two arenas of the war in which the mobilized peasantry acted not as an auxiliary to the military campaign but as a decisive variable in their own right not just in the war, but in shaping the post-war order – Yugoslavia and China.

To a twenty-first century audience this juxtaposition of a now defunct Balkan state with the colossus of East Asia may seem peculiar. The two seem worlds apart. But in the history of early twentieth-century insurgencies the juxtaposition has an unexpected significance. Already in the 1920s after the disappointment of the urban revolutions of 1919–23, when the Comintern first turned its mind seriously toward the problem of peasant revolution, East Asia and the Balkans were conjoined.[31] And for a brief period after 1945, it was commonplace to mention the Yugoslav partisan leader Josip Broz Tito and Mao Zedong in a single breath. What they had in common was that both were leaders of autonomous agrarian resistance movements that turned victory in the war into a platform for social revolution. It was also this that made both of them into awkward allies for Stalin in the emerging global Cold War. As late as the early 1960s the American political scientist Chalmers Johnson would base his field-defining study of peasant nationalism on a close comparison of the Chinese and Yugoslav cases and he did so for pointed political and intellectual reasons.[32] After 1949 much American analysis of China, in the spirit of the McCarthy era tended to explain Mao's triumph in terms of 'America's political and military failures, Soviet empire building and elite conspiracies'.[33] By contrast, as Chalmers Johnson remarked, Tito's

---

31 George D. Jackson, *Comintern and the Peasant in East Europe, 1919–1930* (New York: Columbia University Press, 1966).

32 Chalmers Johnson, *Peasant Nationalism and Communist Power: The Emergence of Revolutionary China, 1937–1945* (Stanford University Press, 1962).

33 Suzanne Pepper, 'The Political Odyssey of an Intellectual Construct: Peasant Nationalism and the Study of China's Revolutionary History: A Review Essay', *Journal of Asian Studies* 63:1 (2004), 105–25 (p. 106). Chalmers Johnson, 'Peasant Nationalism Revisited: The Biography of a Book', *China Quarterly* 72 (1977), 766–85.

movement in Yugoslavia was more easily recognized for what it was: the triumph of a communist-led, peasant-based, patriotic resistance movement.

Neither in Yugoslavia nor in China was the Communist Party the obvious ally of the peasantry. In both the Chinese and Yugoslav communist parties there were loud voices who demanded slavish adherence to the maxims of Stalinist Communism, which was hardly a formula designed to endear them to the most influential voices in the rural community. It was the resistance struggle of the war that forged a new alliance between the communists and the peasants. The savage occupation regimes imposed by the Japanese and the Germans antagonized vast swaths of the population. Of course, the communists were not the only possible leaders of the resistance. But, Chalmers Johnson asserted, the more conservative resistance forces discredited themselves by vacillating between opposition to the occupiers and ill-calculated efforts to suppress their communist rivals. This opened the door for the communist guerrillas to claim for themselves the role of the undisputed champions of national resistance. Both the Yugoslav and Chinese communist parties showed remarkable flexibility in abandoning radical policies of land redistribution and collectivization so as to avoid antagonizing the richer peasants, whose collaboration was crucial to sustaining a successful guerrilla war. In his effort to challenge the McCarthyite consensus of the early Cold War, Johnson gave too much credence to the patriotic credentials of the communist parties. The details of the argument have been modified by generations of in-depth historical research. In China there has been a substantial re-evaluation of the significance of non-communist nationalist resistance. But this has not called into question the fundamental significance of the peasant mobilization brought about by the war.

Though the rise of the Chinese Communist Party would prove to be of far vaster consequence, the proportional level of mobilization achieved by Tito and the Yugoslav partisans was truly spectacular. In 1945 both Mao and Tito commanded armies of 800,000 fighters, though Yugoslavia's population was less than one-thirtieth the size of China's. This was all the more striking considering the unpromising beginnings of the communist-led resistance in Yugoslavia.[34] Even in the face of the German invasion in the spring of 1941, the Yugoslav party had remained true to the collaborationist line dictated by the Hitler–Stalin Pact of 1939. It was not until the summer of 1941 that the party went over to resistance, rapidly establishing several mountain

---

34 Melissa K. Bokovoy, *Peasants and Communists: Politics and Ideology in the Yugoslav Countryside, 1941–1953* (University of Pittsburgh Press, 1998), pp. 9–13.

bases. But it promptly squandered what little peasant support it enjoyed. The Užice Republic set up in western Serbia and Montenegro was an uncompromising Stalinist regime headed by the radical student leader Milovan Djilas. In a nation that was 75 per cent peasant, its aggressive drive against 'kulaks' was a PR disaster handing the initiative to the Serbian Chetniks and Bosnian Muslim groups who presented themselves as protectors of private property.

What gave the Yugoslav party a second chance was the spectacular brutality of the occupation. Faced with the scorched earth programme of the Germans and the Croatian Ustasha, the Serb and Bosnian peasants were left with little option but to fight for their survival. Initially, the Serb peasantry did so by rallying around the Chetniks, who formulated their own version of peasant nationalism. But the Chetniks limited their appeal by throwing themselves into a nightmarish whirlwind of inter-ethnic conflict. The internationalism of the communists immunized them against this temptation. Nevertheless, the communists would have been in no position to take advantage, if there had not been a decisive change in party line in the spring of 1942. At their new redoubt in Foča in eastern Bosnia the party activists reluctantly agreed to abandon immediate revolution. The crucial issue, as Tito proclaimed, was the attitude of the peasantry and 'the peasant follows whoever is strongest'. A strict code of conduct helped to establish the moral legitimacy of the partisans. Plundering would cease. In February 1943 the Communist Party announced that it respected the 'inviolability of private property and the full possibility for self-initiative in industry, trade and agriculture'. Land confiscations were codified in 1944 under a law that limited expropriations to collaborators and ethnic Germans. By May 1945 the land fund disposed of 1.6 million hectares out of a national total of 10 million. To further appeal to the peasantry, the Party adopted a productivist agenda focusing on harvest assistance and protection. 'Not a kernel of grain to the occupier' was their creed. The cooperative farms of Croatia soon established themselves as the granary of the partisan movement.

After 1945 the triumph of the Yugoslav peasant partisans culminated in a land reform that distributed 1.61 million hectares among 250,000 families. This secured for Tito the legitimacy he needed to assert himself against the overweening power of the Stalinist Soviet Union. In 1948 it was precisely for his failure to take action against the kulaks that Tito was expelled from the Cominform. When the Yugoslav regime, driven by the imperative to achieve its own brand of socialism in one country, attempted its own collectivization drive, this did not last. In 1953 under the pressure of its peasant base, socialist

Yugoslavia became the first post-war communist regime to reverse collectivization in favour of tolerating the continuation of small-scale farming.[35]

Agrarian war in Asia

The founders of the Chinese Communist Party did not come naturally to the task of peasant mobilization any more than did their Yugoslav counterparts. But by the mid-1920s, operating initially from the Guomindang's main base in southern Guandong, driven by the orders of the Comintern and the circumstances on the ground they found themselves as organizers of a peasant revolution. It was as such that they survived Chiang Kai-shek's onslaught in 1927, the nationalist attacks of the early 1930s and the Long March, to establish their new base in remote northern China. In the face of violent hostility with local warlords, feuding with the nationalist forces and the counter-insurgency operations of the Japanese the CCP would by 1945 ultimately establish nineteen distinct base areas spread across northern and central China. The largest of these base areas, notably Jinjiluyu with a population of 29 million and 7 million hectares of land, were as large as European countries. Since the 1970s a dense and controversial historical literature has dedicated itself to exploring the particular conditions and politics of each of these base areas. But two things at least are uncontroversial.

Economic historians may not be able to agree on whether or not the Chinese economy was improving in the interwar period. But it is undeniable that the Chinese peasantry was among the hardest pressed in the world. Population was so numerous and investment so minimal that even China's famously intense farming techniques were not enough to secure a standard of living much above subsistence. The depredations of the warlords and the shocks of the recession of the early 1930s, on top of periodic droughts and flooding were enough to push millions over the edge into abject penury and debt slavery. Furthermore, amidst this general sea of rural poverty, the area where the communists established their northern home base in Yan'an was among the very poorest.

Secondly, China's agrarian poverty was understood as a political issue. It was associated since the nineteenth century with national weakness, the threat of foreign intervention and the demand for patriotic resistance. Nationalism existed by the late nineteenth century both in the city and the

---

35 Catherine Lutard, 'La Question Paysanne Yougoslave: La Trahison des Communistes', *Cahiers Internationaux de Sociologie*, Nouvelle Série, 102 (1997), 107–38.

countryside.[36] But after 1937 Japan's full-scale territorial invasion provoked an unprecedented widening of nationalist sentiment and activism. In particular, the northern Chinese peasant population, who had hitherto been notable for their relative lack of interest in modern politics, found themselves facing an existential threat. Politicization of the Chinese countryside in the course of the struggle with Japan was a double-sided process. China's rural population was redefined as a national peasantry.[37] And the prevalent image of the Chinese nation was recast around the village.[38]

Over the following ten years, all of the political forces in China, the communists, the nationalists, the collaborationist governments and the satellites operating on behalf of the Japanese sought to respond to China's triple predicament of poverty, internal disorder and external threat. The collaborationist regimes had their own vision of stabilization. And when they got the balance of repressive violence and hands-off administration right, the Japanese and their allies were able to establish effective zones of pacification anchored by the so-called 'mutual guarantee system' or Pao Chia, under which village leaders took collective responsibility for excluding communist and other resistance elements. The drive to create Model Peace Zones was initiated in the summer of 1941 in the Yangzi delta region and achieved considerable success in the Shanghai and Hangchow areas. In 1944 the rich agricultural region between Kiangsu, Anhwei and Shantung was designated as a model province for a New China. But the balance of coercion, cooperation and inducement necessary to preserve these model zones was delicate at the best of times. In Northern China the Japanese too often resorted to the scorched earth policies of the 'Three Alls' – kill all, take all, burn all. Though many peasants were tempted to seek a quiet life of collaboration and acquiescence, after 1943 the threat of conscription into Japanese labour service left little option but to join the resistance.

The nationalist forces did not vacate the ground without a struggle. The National Republican Army is now generally acknowledged as having mounted far more serious military resistance than the communist guerrillas.[39] It was the KMT who from 1937 to 1944 took the risk and paid the

36 Henrietta Harrison, 'Newspapers and Nationalism in Rural China, 1890-1929', *Past & Present* 166 (2000), 181–204.

37 Xiaorong Han, *Chinese Discourses on the Peasant, 1900–1949* (Albany, NY: SUNY Press, 2005).

38 Margherita Zanasi, 'Far from the Treaty Ports: Fang Xianting and the Idea of Rural Modernity in 1930s China', *Modern China* 30:1 (2004), 113–46.

39 Mark Peattie, Edward Drea and Hans van de Ven, eds., *The Battle for China: Essays on the Military History of the Sino-Japanese War of 1937–1945* (Stanford University Press, 2011).

price of confronting the Japanese with a modern-style military resistance. But they did so without the infrastructure of legitimacy and domestic support that a modern war effort would have required. The results for the Chinese countryside were drastic. Though the nationalists had nominally committed themselves in 1937 to rent reduction and land reform, the nationalist war effort raised the depredations of warlordism to a new pitch. Press-gangs roamed the countryside drafting young men, tax rates escalated, inflation ran out of control and further devastation followed as the front line moved inland. Most spectacularly in Henan province on 8 June 1938 the retreating NRA blasted the dikes of the Yellow River unleashing a gigantic man-made flood that drowned at least 500,000 peasants and made perhaps as many as 5 million homeless.[40] By 1944, when the nationalists sought to reconquer the region, the local population needed no encouragement from the communists to chase them out.

The wasteland left by the retreating nationalist and rampaging Japanese was the space occupied by the communists. Though they would later proclaim themselves the heroes of the resistance, their main strategy was not actually war-fighting but the establishment of base areas, areas of pacification and state-building from which radiated tendrils of influence, in the form of militia and guerrilla networks. The communists never abandoned their radical vision for the transformation of China, but through bitter experience in the early 1930s they had learned the cost of pushing the collectivization line too hard too fast.[41] After 1935, given the tenuousness of their grip anywhere outside Yan'an the communists did not dare advocate a radical land reform, let alone Soviet-style collective farms. Mao's preferred mode of land reform involved not the annihilation of the rich peasants but the redistribution and levelling out of property within the village. The effect was to integrate the landless and to widen the base of the middle peasantry. In less consolidated bases the communists stuck to the line agreed with the nationalists as the basis for the United Front of 1937, prioritizing rent and debt reduction, combined with progressive taxation and minimum wages. More aggressive steps that risked reopening the question of class antagonism were only approved for those base areas that were firmly under communist control. In the Great Production Movement of 1944 they began

40 Diana Lary, 'Drowned Earth: The Strategic Breaching of the Yellow River Dyke, 1938', *War in History* 8 (2001), 191–207.
41 Mark Selden, *China in Revolution: The Yenan Way Revisited* (Armonk: M. E. Sharpe, 1995).

to experiment with the large-scale organization of mutual-aid production teams, a first step towards cooperative farming.

This flexible system of policy anchored on a small number of secure bases allowed the communists to survive repeated Japanese efforts to wipe them out. When in 1944 the Japanese lunged once more across central China in a desperate effort to open a land corridor to Burma, the result was to deal a further devastating blow to the nationalists, while opening the door to further communist expansion. By the time of the Japanese surrender in 1945 the communists commanded a 'liberated zone' consisting of one-quarter of the territory of China and one-third of its population. It was now poised to launch the transformation of the Chinese countryside. On 4 May 1946, the anniversary of the day of national humiliation in 1919, the Communist Party was given a new watchword: 'land to the tiller'. In 1942 and 1943 the Yan'an base area had experienced the violence and intimidation of a massive rectification campaign as the base was brought into ideological line. Now the party's energy was directed outwards in a violent campaign of coercive land redistribution. By September 1948 even Mao had to intervene to bridle the enthusiasm of local level cadres. Ideological rectification, land redistribution and military mobilization were fused together. Within two years 1.6 million peasants were drawn into the Red Army raising its strength from 1.2 to 2.8 million men. Whereas in Western Europe the mechanized armies of the Allies were frustrated by an immobile countryside, in China the countryside itself mobilized against the nationalists. As Fairbank and Goldman describe it: 'in 1949 in the climactic battle of the Huai-Hai region north of Nanjing, the Nationalist armored corps, which had been held in reserve as a final arbiter of warfare, found itself encircled by tank traps dug by millions of peasants mobilized by party leaders like Deng Xiaoping'.[42] But only once the nationalists had been driven back to Taiwan would the full force of the communist programme make itself felt across all of China, including the south where landlordism and nationalist sympathies were most deeply rooted. Between 1950 and 1952 with the Communist Party tightening its grip and a mass campaign against counter-revolutionaries in full swing, 47.8 million hectares, 43 per cent of Chinese agricultural land changed hands. The violence of the land reform movement and the suppression of the resistance that followed set the stage for the introduction of a nationwide compulsory grain delivery system and the dramatic push for full collectivization in the first half of 1956,

---

42 John King Fairbank and Merle Goldman, *China: A New History* (Cambridge, Mass: The Belknap Press of Harvard University Press, 1998), p. 336.

which on Mao's orders raised the share of collective farms from 4 to 63 per cent in six months.[43] By 1957 109 million peasant households, the largest nation of peasants in the world, once famed for their independence and resistance to central power had been integrated into a collectivized communist system.

India in war and revolution

The promise of collectivization was that it would enable Mao's regime to triple China's investment rate and break out of decades of economic stagnation.[44] But after 1945 the communists had no monopoly on land reform policy. The message that a new land settlement was the answer to the developmental impasse of the interwar period was driven home no less emphatically by the great capitalist success story of post-war Asia, Japan. Plans for the redistribution of 2 million hectares of land had already been prepared during the war by the Japanese Ministry of Agriculture. This was part of a piece with the Manchurian settlement planning of the 1930s. In 1945 with the energetic backing both of the US occupation authorities and the reformist Japanese socialist party, land reform was put back on the agenda. By 1950 the government had acquired and transferred 1.742 million hectares, a third of Japan's farm land. With 30 million parcels of land changing hands, less than 7.5 per cent of Japanese farmers were left without land of their own. In Japan, and then in Taiwan too, land reform was credited with stimulating investment and helping to raise growth rates to unprecedented levels.[45]

Japan's extraordinary growth and China's revolutionary transformation threw into question the experience of the other great peasant population of Asia, in India. On the face of it, the political facts seemed straightforward enough. Following the war, the British retreat was forced by the mobilization of a mass movement of huge proportions enrolling millions of Indian peasants in the nationalist Indian National Congress and the Muslim League. Not surprisingly, following independence in August 1947 land reform was announced as a matter of national priority in both India and Pakistan. In India responsibility was handed down to the state level to be decided on a decentralized basis. What ensued was what one authority has described as

43 Yu Liu, 'Why Did It Go so High? Political Mobilization and Agricultural Collectiviza-
    tion in China', *China Quarterly* 187 (2006), 732–42.
44 Mark Selden, *Political Economy of Chinese Development* (Armonk: M. E. Sharpe, 1992).
45 R. P. Dore, *Land Reform in Japan* (London: Athlone Press, 1984).

the most ambitious programme of land legislation in history, a veritable avalanche of statutes. And there were real improvements in the conditions in India's 600,000 villages. In particular, the abolition of the intermediary layer of zamindar tax farmers established more secure tenancy and a direct relation with the new Indian state for 20 million peasant households. However, as the enthusiasm of independence wore off, a more sober assessment set in. Despite copious land reform legislation, by the end of 1970 no more than 1.2 million acres had been distributed to landless farmers, a derisory one-third of one per cent of India's agricultural land.[46] In Pakistan the results of land reform efforts in the 1950s and 1970s were similarly modest. The mid-century crisis had brought independence to the subcontinent, but unlike in China or even in Japan, it had not brought about a radical transformation of society.

The explanation for the absence of social revolution in South Asia that was most readily to hand was cultural. The American social scientist Barrington Moore argued that India's conservative stability was due to caste and Hinduism.[47] And it is undeniably true that the cultural conditions for revolution were very different across much of India than they were in China. Furthermore, since class differences often ran along religious lines the effect of the immiseration of the countryside in the 1930s was to exacerbate intercommunal tension and reinforce religious identities. Economic tension produced not so much an impulse toward social revolution as toward communal partition. But to argue in reductive cultural terms that the mass of the Indian population was incapable of mounting resistance simply flies in the face of the evidence. Between 1919 and 1922, in the early 1930s and then again between 1937 and 1942, large masses of the population proved themselves capable of political mobilization and resistance to the British Raj. That resistance continued after 1945 in the southern region of Telengana and among Bengali sharecroppers in the so-called Tebhaga struggle. In the late 1960s peasant unrest resumed once again, this time against the postcolonial Indian state, with the neo-Marxist Naxalist movement spreading from West Bengal to dozens of provinces. Growing out of this revived radicalism, from the 1980s onwards historians associated with the so-called Subaltern School offered a new narrative of India's trajectory to independence.[48] What undercut the prospects of revolution was not religion or caste, they argued, but the

---

46 Wolf Ladejinsky, 'Land Ceilings and Land Reform', *Economic and Political Weekly* 7:5/7 (1972), 401–8.

47 J. Barrington Moore, Jr, *Social Origins of Democracy and Dictatorship: Lord and Peasant in the Making of the Modern World* (Boston: Beacon Press, 1966).

48 Ranajit Guha, ed., *Subaltern Studies I* (Oxford University Press, 1982).

narrow class limits of nationalist politics. The bitter truth revealed by the impasse of agrarian reform was that neither the nationalist leadership of Congress nor the Muslim League ever had any interest in unleashing the full force of a peasant revolution.[49]

Radically opposed though both these interpretations – culturalist and subaltern – are, what they have in common is that they downplay the effects of the historical conjuncture that concerns us most in this chapter, namely the war.[50] If we compare India with Yugoslavia and China, what is most striking is that in India the war had the effect of splintering the alliance between radical rural organizers, the nationalist movement and the peasantry on which a revolution driven by peasant nationalism depended. It was not that the war did not produce a political reaction in India. When Britain on 3 September 1939 pitched India into the war without even a perfunctory political consultation, the Muslim League went along, as did the Sikhs of the Punjab. But from the Congress party came a dramatic demonstration of nationalist resistance. Unlike in China, in India popular, anti-imperial nationalism was above all an anti-war movement. And at first it was both a wide-ranging and surprisingly unified force. In 1937, as international tensions mounted, Congress ministries had taken charge of numerous Indian provinces. In an effort to pressure them into protective legislation on debt relief and land tenure, the years after 1936 had seen an unprecedented mobilization of Indian peasants in the so-called kisan movement. Energized by activists from both the socialist wing of Congress and the Indian Communist Party they formed an assembly that came to be known as the All-India Kisan Sabha. In 1939 they came out vigorously against the war. In Punjab and the northern provinces, the British continued to recruit soldiers for the 2.5 million strong Indian army. Peasant producers made handsome profits. But the majority of India was clearly in opposition to Churchill's war.

But if the war mobilized and unified the anti-British forces, it could also tear them apart. In June 1941, Hitler's invasion of the Soviet Union changed the politics of India. By the end of 1941 the Indian Communists had been ordered by Moscow to throw their weight behind the Allied war effort. The left-wing activists who since the 1930s had championed the mobilization of the peasants found themselves in opposition to the mainstream of nationalist

49 Partha Chatterjee, 'For an Indian History of Peasant Struggle', *Social Scientist* 16:11 (1988), 3–17.
50 For a compelling narrative see Sumit Sarkar, *Modern India, 1885–1947* (Basingstoke: Macmillan, 1989).

sentiment. True to the line dictated to them by Moscow, the leading voices of the radical left in India were forced to proclaim that the Empire's war was a people's war. In so doing they flew in the face of public opinion and splintered the anti-British movement. With London failing to offer an acceptable path to independence and the defeat of the British Empire seemingly inevitable, on 8 August 1942 Gandhi declared that the time had come to 'do or die'. The British must quit India. He along with the rest of the Congress establishment were promptly arrested.[51]

As the storm of protest unleashed in the Quit India campaign spread to the countryside, the British faced their most dramatic challenge since the mutiny in 1857. Police reports for August and September 1942 read as though they were coming from behind the German lines in the Soviet Union, or from the Japanese in northern China. Over 200 police stations, 332 railway stations and 954 post offices were attacked. Thousands of telegraph lines were cut. Plundered from official stores and armouries, tens of thousands of rifles fell into the hands of Congress militants. In much of India the British lost control for weeks on end. In the Midnapur district of Bengal and in Satara in Maharashtra parallel administrations analogous to the communist bases in Yugoslavia and northern China emerged. In Bihar province Indian guerrilla bands, known as azad dastas, self-consciously modelling themselves on the anti-Nazi partisan movement, sustained an insurgency that lasted until the end of the war.[52]

The British reacted with massive force. Fifty-seven battalions were mobilized to repress the movement. At least 1,285 protesters were killed, 3,125 were wounded. But even this was not enough to quell the violence. By the middle of August the Viceroy was reduced to authorizing the RAF to strafe crowds of protesters. In total 91,836 people were arrested, 18,000 detained. India would fight its 'people's war' under the smothering repression of martial law. When the Viceroy made his usual procession to Calcutta in December 1942 he did so as if through hostile territory in an armoured convoy with guards posted at every railway crossing en route. An army of 3 million men was stationed in Bengal and Bihar provinces. They saw to it that the more than 2 million victims of the Bengal famine in 1943 died largely in silence. But even a smothering blanket of press censorship could not hide the collapse of

51 Francis G. Hutchins, *India's Revolution: Gandhi and the Quit India Movement* (Cambridge, Mass: Harvard University Press, 1973).
52 Vinita Damodaran, 'Azad Dastas and Dacoit Gangs: The Congress and Underground Activity in Bihar, 1942–44', *Modern Asian Studies* 26:3 (1992), 417–50.

the Raj's political legitimacy. There was no longer any doubt that once the war was over independence would come. But the disunity provoked by the war had disrupted the wide-ranging radical mobilization that up to the summer of 1941 had promised to tilt the balance within the nationalist movement decisively to the left. Quite unlike in Yugoslavia or China, in India it was the right-wing of the National Congress that emerged strengthened from the war. The Muslim League, for its part, had played a tactical game of wait and see. In the war's aftermath the Raj was primed for communal partition, not social revolution.

New divisions

The juxtaposition between the Chinese, Japanese and Indian agrarian systems was one glaring example in a world of new contrasts that emerged from the Second World War. Up to the late 1920s the agricultural systems of the world differed in many ways, but they were integrated more or less indirectly by far-flung commodity markets and relatively open routes of migration. The agrarian world that emerged from the crises of the 1930s and 1940s was partitioned, first into national systems by the Great Depression, then along the complex frontlines of the Second World War and finally into the ideological camps of the Cold War. In one world were the cosseted and protected agricultural systems of the rich industrialized nations, politically integrated, mechanized, with all surplus labour drained into the cities, insulated from world market pressures by impenetrable walls of protectionism. The second world of collectivized socialist agriculture was anchored in Europe on the coercive power of the Soviet state and in Asia on Mao's China with its North Korean and North Vietnamese imitators. Finally, across the rest of post-war Asia the peasant came to stand both as the new symbol of the impoverished Third World and as a strategic actor in a new arena of revolutionary and counter-insurgency warfare.

THE MORAL ECONOMY OF
WAR AND PEACE

Introduction to Part III

MICHAEL GEYER AND ADAM TOOZE

If the totalizing dynamic of violence of peoples' wars was the horizon of experience in the First World War and if this dynamic was debated at length in the interwar years, it was the basic reality of the Second World War. This was not only a matter of a more encompassing and exhausting effort on all sides that focused on the mobilization of natural and human resources as the first two sections of this volume suggest. Rather in the transition from the first to the second war the practices of mobilization came into consciousness of themselves as it were. That is to say, 'mobilization' and 'totality' moved from the realm of anticipated and much-debated practice into the realm of theoretical reflection, political ambition and artistic creation. They became part and parcel of an ultra-nationalist and racist discourse about the survival of nations that looked down upon old-fashioned imperialism and militarism and circled around the imperative that 'society must be defended'.[1] The more radical advocates, everywhere, argued that the war of the future would be 'existential', a struggle for survival, rather than merely 'instrumental', a war for (imperialist) gain. Some of these initiatives attached themselves to the grand ideologies of the time and carried along utopias of a new society, a 'new man' and a 'new woman' and, above all, of a new political compact based on mass participation. But total mobilization reached beyond rigid ideological dogma to become part of the consciousness of the age. It is this consciousness in all its ramifications that we try to capture with the notion of a 'moral economy' of war. We are interested here in the interplay of cultural norms and ways of thinking and the pursuit of war. The strongest claim is that both the means and the ends of violence are in need of justification in a people's war – and that all belligerents not only engaged in this kind of

---

1 Michel Foucault, *Society Must Be Defended: Lectures at the Collège de France, 1975–76*, ed. Mauro Bertani and Alessandro Fontana, trans. David Macey (New York: Picador, 2003).

'moral' discourse, but made it an integral part of what Clausewitz called the 'war plan' the purpose of war.

From the 1930s onwards, these modes of totalizing war became central stakes in the antagonism over the future of social order. Hellbeck's chapter in the preceding section on social mobilization explores the contemporary and competitive discussion of relative models of mobilization with an eye on Europe. Work on Japan and, for that matter, China would reinforce this point.[2] India's record in turn would highlight the very tension between the mass mobilization necessary and considered 'right' for totalizing war on the one hand and the quest for participation and self-determination on the other.[3] This tension between mobilization and the potential of empowerment was pervasive and not exclusively an effect of colonialism as the case of the USA would amply prove.[4] Populist (self-) empowerment was an intrinsic dimension of mass mobilization.

The bottom line is that the totalizing logic of people's war became a political, social and cultural 'project' and quite literally over-wrote military exigencies. The Second World War was a war of 'bellicist' societies. This was no longer quite 'war culture' as it is debated among historians of the First World War. Rather, mutually exclusive war 'projects' gave the dynamic of military violence their respective spin – 'spin' in the sense of a rhetoric of (just vs. unjust) war and in the sense of a drive toward a renovated and transformed society as an effect of the war; and 'spin' not least in the debates over military necessity and the limits of violence. This is the reason why a war-centric history of the Second World War cannot but engage in an enquiry into the culture of war.

But how should we approach 'war culture' in bellicist societies? The ideological stakes and the propaganda that mediated these stakes are

---

2 Michael A. Barnhart, *Japan Prepares for Total War: The Search for Economic Security, 1919–1941* (Ithaca: Cornell University Press, 1987); Louise Young, *Japan's Total Empire: Manchuria and the Culture of Wartime Imperialism* (Berkeley: University of California Press, 1998); Rana Mitter, *Forgotten Ally: China's World War II, 1937–1945* (London: Allen Lane, 2013).

3 Christopher Bayly and Tim Harper, *Forgotten Armies: The Fall of British Asia, 1941–1945* (London: Allen Lane, 2004); Christopher Bayly and Tim Harper, *Forgotten Wars: Freedom and Revolution in Southeast Asia* (Cambridge, Mass.: The Belknap Press of Harvard University Press, 2007).

4 Wendy Wall, *Inventing the American Way: The Politics of Consensus from the New Deal to the Civil Rights Movement* (Oxford University Press, 2008); John Morton Blum, *V Was for Victory: Politics and American Culture during World War II* (New York: Harcourt Brace Jovanovich, 1976); Kevin Michael Kruse and Stephen G. N. Tuck, eds., *Fog of War: The Second World War and the Civil Rights Movement* (Oxford University Press, 2012).

discussed in some detail in the second volume of the *Cambridge History of the Second World War* and so are the more formal legal efforts to contain violence. This still leaves a huge terrain to be covered, if we only think of the role of the media or the arts as agents in a people's war or the entire complex of physical and psychological war trauma that plays such an important role in the study of the First World War. But we concluded that despite an immense historiography on these subjects for some of the combatant nations, the very difference of the war 'projects' and, not to be underestimated, the global nature of belligerency throws up immense problems even within the framework of the exemplary and often 'Western'-biased treatment that we chose. It is one thing to compare First World War trauma culture in Germany and France; it is a quite different thing to compare SS soldiers, GI Joes and the Ivans of the Red Army – forget German, US American and Soviet society and culture – and then to compare any one of them with the soldiers of the 8th Route Army in China or the Indian soldiers fighting in Burma against the Japanese. The task is not impossible, but it does require the recognition that soldiering and war-making cannot be separated out from the moral economies that inform them wittingly or unwittingly and that the Second World War was mortal combat between mutually exclusive war projects – and indeed that there was right and wrong in this war. Suffice it to say, there is enough material to suggest that there are entire worlds yet to be explored and thorny issues yet to be resolved.

Then again, we set the goal to demonstrate society and culture as forces of war and it seemed to us that one way to do this is to explore the moral economy of war and peace. The starting point for this exploration was the historical observation that in the First World War the drive to totalization, though novel and radical, was profoundly frustrated. It was frustrated by the frictions of poorer and less easily organized societies, but also by the persistence in all the combatant states of a deeply entrenched civil society. In part this was institutionally anchored, in the institutions of parliaments for instance, which continued between 1914 and 1918 as they did not in Germany, Italy, Japan, the Soviet Union or Vichy France in the Second World War. In part the incompleteness of totalization was due to social formations such as the trade unions whose power was enhanced almost everywhere in the First World War. But above all this resistance against the totalizing dynamic of war also had a solid moral foundation. Almost from the outset, the First World War provoked resistance, opposition and criticism, which by 1917 and 1918 mounted to revolutionary scale. Everywhere it generated an intense debate about the rights and wrongs of war-fighting and everywhere it created a visceral debate over the representation of the war experience. Where in the Second World War was there space for such deep controversy; where were the space and the place for an anti-war movement?

The starting point for this kind of enquiry is the exploration of what may seem marginal concerns and marginal actors. They are marginal because the combatants in the Second World War presented themselves as monolithic politico-military-moral blocs the likes of which had not been seen since the wars of religion. But even their totalitarian impetus was in need of justification, and nowhere was this production of rationalizations more evident than in the treatment of enemy civilians and of mortal enemies. We now know that existential enemies did not simply exist, but were actively produced.[5] We also know that seemingly atavistic military practices (rape, sexual slavery, pillage, scorched earth) were anything but hidden manifestations of evil.[6] They were loudly articulated, proudly defended, and timidly challenged. Not least we know that a great reckoning was expected in case of defeat, which only hardened the stance of the defeated. Frühstück's essay and others in this section explore these transcripts for what they are – not only the (much disputed and denied) facts of an ugly war, but (im-)moral debates about what is right and wrong, what makes peoples and nations proud and what sullies their honour. This is the cultural reality of the Second World War as a peoples' war.

But this moral culture of war does not end with the totalitarian nations. For the Western democracies the totalizing and brutalizing dynamic of violence in the Second World War posed deep contradictions, even if they did not listen to the likes of Goebbels who accused them of terrorism and extermination. How were they to reconcile freedom, liberty and pluralism with the imperatives of totalizing war? And if they waged war against civilians how were they to justify their action in contradistinction to the Axis powers in Europe and Asia and in weary distance to Soviet or Chinese practices of war? Not least, what stance should the critical historian take in these swirling debates to remain truthful in the face of the historical evidence without embracing moral agnosticism on the one hand or moral hyperbole on the other. Again, Frühstück's essay demonstrates that especially a war-centric

---

5 Jeffrey Herf, *The Jewish Enemy: Nazi Propaganda during World War II and the Holocaust* (Cambridge, Mass.: The Belknap Press of Harvard University Press, 2006).

6 R Felix Römer, *Kameraden. Die Wehrmacht von Innen* (Munich: Piper, 2012); Jochen Hellbeck, *Die Stalingrad-Protokolle. Sowjetische Augenzeugen berichten aus der Schlacht* (Frankfurt am Main: S. Fischer, 2012); John W. Dower, *War Without Mercy: Race and Power in the Pacific War* (New York: Pantheon, 1986).

history of the Second World War must also be a moral history – and the less moralizing it is, the better it will get to the core issue of what is evil and what is good about the Second World War and the generation that fought it.

Defeating a terrifying enemy was a powerful answer to the question of right and wrong. But was every means justified, including domestic coercion in pursuit of mobilization? This question and its tantalizing possibilities give the issue of conscientious objection raised by both Pendas and Kessler its strategic significance. As Kessler shows in his chapter it was essential for the British Empire and the USA to be seen to be addressing the problem consistently in their own terms, in other words through the processes of the law. He thus shows how in this key area the democratic powers answered the strategic question of how to engage in totalizing mobilization without undermining liberty. In managing conscientious objection within the frame of the law, the Anglophone societies instituted in their war-fighting the basic concepts of the 'war and society' framework that would frame their victory. Counterfactually they reaffirmed that they were law-bound civil societies, whose structures had 'adjusted' to the unnatural impact of a war imposed on them by their enemies. War was postulated as an eruption into a static social and economic scene. In fact, as work like that of Kessler shows, the model of a pre-existing static scene of peace was itself ideological. Under the wrenching impact of the crises of the interwar period, the legal and administrative orders of both the British and American states were undergoing a process of dynamic and crisis-ridden change already in the 1930s. Through their ability to accommodate conscientious objectors (even if they shut them away in internment camps), the war enabled this transformation to be cast not as a challenge but as confirmation of their inalienable grasp of the freedoms they now made into their war 'project'.

Still, the power of conformity has to be reckoned with. As Pendas makes clear, the pacifist movement which in 1914 had never abandoned its running critique of war was largely silenced after 1939 and suppressed by 1941 among Western powers. Also, given the political stakes in a peoples' war it proved far harder to maintain a principled pacifist position. In the Soviet Union, Nazi Germany and Imperial Japan dissent was brutally destroyed.[7] The sole exception to this rule was British India, where a huge anti-war Quit India campaign mobilized a large fraction of the Hindu population and set the stage for independence and partition in 1947. Pacifism with its proud European

---

7 For Japan see Brian Daizen Victoria, *Zen War Stories* (London and New York: Routledge Curzon, 2002).

tradition had been thoroughly marginalized by 1941; it came back as 'non-violence' on the Indian subcontinent in the service of self-determination. 'Non-violence' was a peculiar instrument of conflict and confrontation, but it was an effective one, even if, like war itself, it had no future.

Was there a more durable way to master the tensions to which a totalizing people's war subjected the democracies? Welfare states provided one solution, as Smith suggests in his chapter. He focuses on the Western Allies. But the logic extended across the front line to the Nazi *Volksgemeinschaft* and Italian fascism too. Pendas, Porter and Bradley argue that beyond welfare there were the practices of humanitarianism, which expanded during the Second World War into a central function and purpose of liberal internationalism, entrenched in the United Nations Relief and Rehabilitation Administration (UNRRA) and subsequently in the United Nations. The ability of the USA in particular to seize the humanitarian high-ground, enabled of course by their far greater resources and the far less destructive effects of the war on their home economies, went a long way to foreclosing any more searching discussion of the consistency of the means and ends of their war efforts. Nonetheless, the universalism espoused by Roosevelt and Churchill as leaders of the United Nations was, as Porter and Bradley make clear, a genuine investment of their respective nations. The international relief organization UNRRA and its descendants have saved millions of lives. The cause of human rights remains for many the enduring legacy of the Second World War and, as Bradley emphasizes, a way out of the conundrums of an all-encompassing war. If we are still in search of a truly comprehensive system of international justice with which to contain the threat of aggressive war, there is no doubt that Nuremberg and Tokyo set the vital precedent. It should not surprise us that faced with our current disorder in the early twenty-first century, the moment of the 1940s continues to serve as a point of historical inspiration.

As the contributions to this volume have made clear, however, a truly global narrative is bound to destabilize the self-satisfaction of the Western victors. As Rana Mitter shows in the concluding essay of this section, the universalist desire to generalize sovereignty clashed with the imperial pretensions of the Europeans in Asia at least as dramatically as it had done with the overweening ambition of Japan. The violent attempt by the Europeans to reassert imperial power reached its embarrassing climax in 1956 in Suez. The promise of self-determination was intoxicating, all the more so when it was combined with the kinds of visions of modernity and progress. These, as Engerman and Smith show, were spelled out in glowing colours in the promises of a new era of social welfare, planned economic advance and global development, with the Soviet Union emerging as a competitive force in shaping the post-colonial world.

Whether or not we regard the universalism of the 1940s as the benchmark of twentieth-century progress, or as a pale shroud with which to veil the demise of stronger visions of self-determination, one thing that 1945 did not deliver was an age after war, a true post-war. To talk in those terms in Asia, the Middle East or Africa is simply to defy the evident fact of ongoing and nearly continuous military activity right the way down to the present day. But even in Europe though the peace has proven to be more durable than that in 1918, it was a more militarized peace than the world had ever seen. It was based on the threat of a totalized war, more radical than that imagined by even the most apocalyptic thinkers of the interwar era, a strategy whose logic only became evident in the wake of the violence of 1944–45. Perversely it was precisely that ultimate threat that enabled the disentangling of the mesh between militarism, culture, society and economy that was such a characteristic feature of the totalizing peoples' war that we map in this volume.

15

Sexuality and sexual violence

SABINE FRÜHSTÜCK

On 7 September 1940, sixteen-year-old Joan Wyndham noted in her diary, 'The bombs are lovely, I think it is all thrilling. Nevertheless, as the opposite of death is life, I think I shall get seduced by Rupert tomorrow. Rowena has promised to go to a chemist's with me and ask for Volpar Gels, just in case the French thingummy isn't foolproof.'[1] Joan was one of many for whom the war represented a time of excitement, romantic freedom and sexual transgression. For a privileged few, Lara Feigel has recently shown, the constant threat of death fuelled apocalyptic hedonism, romance between unlikely partners, and artistic and literary inspiration.[2] Similarly, wartime writings of infantrymen spoke of a 'hunger born of the hovering presence of death and the wild desire not to die unsatisfied, with a body still fierce and full and unused'.[3] Yet, from what we know today, the Second World War also constituted an unprecedented, vast web of sexual incitement, suppression and violence, much of which was organized and systematic and most of which victimized women rather than men.

Yet, for decades after the end of the Second World War, the historiography of war and military violence, on the one hand, and that of gender and sexuality, on the other, remained disconnected.[4] It seems as if the gendered nature of sexual violence during and after the Second World War cast a shadow far beyond the (mostly) men who inflicted it and the (mostly) women

---

1 Laurel Holliday, *Children in the Holocaust and World War II: Their Secret Diaries* (New York: Simon & Schuster, 1995), p. 283.
2 Lara Feigel, *The Love-Charm of Bombs: Restless Lives in the Second World War* (London and New York: Bloomsbury, 2013).
3 Mary Louise Roberts, *What Soldiers Do: Sex and the American GI in World War II France* (University of Chicago Press, 2013), p. 157.
4 For their comments on an earlier version of this chapter I am very grateful to Aaron Belkin, Joshua A. Fogel, Wendy J. Gertjejanssen, Dagmar Herzog, Or Porath, Nicholas Stargardt and Kirsten Ziomek.

who suffered it, down to the present writing of the history of war and the military by (mostly) men and the writing of the history of gender and sexuality by (mostly) women. Historians have produced impressive tomes of war and military history, but until recently their works have remained remarkably gender- and sexuality-free.[5] This blind spot is puzzling, for wartime soldiers were mostly young men, separated from their partners and freed from many social constraints. When stationed in occupied areas, they were given the sort of individual power they never had enjoyed in civilian society. Besides, 'masculine camaraderie, including bragging about sexual prowess, was a normal part of their everyday communication'.[6] Furthermore, the need to overcome fear went hand-in-hand with drinking and drunkenness, which contributed to rape, murder and other brutalities both at the front lines and in occupied territories.[7] Speaking from the perspective of America's war involvement, Mary Louise Roberts even makes a case for sex and romance standing at the centre of how the war was waged. After all, military commanders around the world believed that 'male sexual activity was healthy for battle'. Or, as General George Patton, best known for his command of the Seventh US Army and later the Third US Army in the European theatre, most famously explained, 'If they don't fuck, they don't fight.'[8]

Prior to the inroads made by scholars of gender and sexuality, particularly since the 1990s, historians noted a wartime taboo on talk about sexuality, in general, and sexual violence in particular. As if in mute echo of that silence, feminist scholarship for decades shied away from situating the discussion of gender and sexuality within the context of war. For example, despite a vast literature documenting nearly all aspects of the Holocaust and helping establish oral history as a respectable historiographical method, the subject of gender and sexuality in the Third Reich has been the object of study for only a little more than a couple of decades. Studies of gender and sexuality in the Third Reich never quite reached the recognition level of a public debate,

---

5 *The Cambridge History of Warfare* (Cambridge University Press, 2005) edited by Geoffrey Parker does not even include 'gender', 'rape', 'sexuality' or 'sexual violence' in the index.

6 Sönke Neitzel and Harald Welzer, *Soldaten: On Fighting, Killing and Dying – The Secret World War II Transcripts of German POWs*, trans. Jefferson Chase (New York: Alfred A. Knopf, 2012), p. 165.

7 Katarzyna J. Cwiertka, 'Alcohol and the Asia-Pacific War (1937–1945)', in *The Proceedings of the 12th Symposium on Chinese Dietary Culture* (Taipei: Foundation of Chinese Dietary Culture, 2011), pp. 253–67.

8 Roberts, *What Soldiers Do*, pp. 160, 258.

a point I will take up again below.[9] The situation is much different in Asia. There, in the wake of the demand for an apology from the Japanese government by a handful of former Korean sex slaves in 1992, a global public debate ensued about the Japanese wartime system of sexual slavery and the Nanjing rape–massacre of 1937. Yet despite this frequently reigniting public debate about these instances of systematic, organized sexual violence, we still know very little about other sites and forms of sex and sexuality during the Asia-Pacific war.

As the following pages elaborate, violence and sex have been relentlessly linked in wartime in manifold and sometimes contradictory ways. This chapter explores this linkage by focusing on two major sites of the Second World War, Japan's clash with the rest of Asia and Germany's aggression toward most of Europe. This double focus on two of the primary aggressors will allow me to describe the historical, ideological and cultural aspects of sex and sexuality in two regions that, for a short while, connected politically but remained culturally dramatically different.

The greater Japanese empire

There are a number of accounts of how Yayutz Bleyh, an Atayal woman in Taiwan, met her future Japanese husband. According to one, she had been born in a settlement and upon saving a Japanese settler's life, fell in love with him even as Taiwan 'was at war with the Japanese' and 'while fire was being exchanged'. Subsequently, she broke with her family to marry Nakano Chuzo, the Japanese man, and accompanied him to Taipei.[10] Whether this particular account is fact or fiction, we know from a handful of historiographies that empire-building and war-making in Asia did not eliminate unlikely romantic liaisons such as the one experienced by young Yayutz.[11] When parents failed to approve of such liaisons, young people left in search of new freedoms elsewhere, often in the colonies. Some female nurses, entertainers

9 Nomi Levenkron, 'Death and the Maidens: "Prostitution", Rape, and Sexual Slavery during World War II', in Sonja M. Hedgepeth and Rochelle G. Saidel, eds., *Sexual Violence against Jewish Women during the Holocaust* (Waltham: Brandeis University Press, 2010), pp. 13–28 (pp. 13–15).

10 Kirsten Ziomek, 'Subaltern Speak: Imperial Multiplicities in Japan's Empire and Post-War Colonialisms' (PhD dissertation, University of California at Santa Barbara, 2011), p. 211.

11 Paul D. Barclay, 'Cultural Brokerage and Interethnic Marriage in Colonial Taiwan: Japanese Subalterns and their Aborigine Wives, 1895–1930', *Journal of Asian Studies* 64:2 (2005), 323–60.

and sex labourers found love at the front lines while pursuing what was hailed as a patriotic duty of service second only to that of the soldiers. Yet, the historiography of sex and sexuality during the Second World War in Asia has focused on sexual violence rather than romance.

In contrast to Europe, where the Second World War began on 1 September 1939 with Germany's invasion of Poland and subsequent declarations of war on Germany by France and Britain, Japan had been engaged in imperialism and empire-building for decades. Prior to the 'official' beginning of the war – which some scholars identify with Japan's invasion of Manchuria on 8 September 1931, others with the Second Sino-Japanese War beginning on 7 July 1937, and yet others with Japan's attack on Pearl Harbor on 7 December 1941 and the subsequent declarations of war – Japan had pursued a multidirectional expansion for decades. Indeed the expansion began even before the Treaty of Shimonoseki of 17 April 1895 that sealed the end of the first Sino-Japanese War and left Japan victorious over China and in possession of Taiwan. The expansionist phase of modern Japan's history ended only on 14 August 1945, when Emperor Hirohito appealed to the Japanese people 'to bear the unbearable' – defeat.

Throughout this period, conscripts and soldiers were of principal concern to the accountants of sexuality within the Japanese defence elite, the public health bureaucracy, and academe alike. From 1940 onward, a modern health and defence regime was built that became articulated as the Greater East Asia Co-Prosperity Sphere. It unfolded as an empire that intimately tied its population's individual bodies to its defence capabilities. Japanese administrators of health and empire perceived healthy bodies to be the basis of the nation's military potency.

It is important to note that against the backdrop of a long-standing and elaborate male–male sexual culture among the samurai, Japan's feudal warrior class, and Buddhist monasteries alike, homosexuality did not become a medical or a moral concern of substance within the ranks of the Japanese Imperial Army nor beyond, as it would be in official Germany. No law prohibited or regulated same-sex relations; nor did military medical reports address the subject. As for women, their sexual desires were largely of no interest to the military or medical authorities. Women were to be good wives and wise mothers, and as such their primary role was to give birth. Hence, the first architects of this health and defence regime targeted the health and hygiene of male subjects and more specifically soldiers' sexual desires.

Official thinking on this subject is reflected in the Japanese treatment of prostitution. Unlike Germany, whose stance I consider later, Japan was unburdened by a Judeo-Christian sexual moral code and had a centuries-long history of prostitution embedded in a rich culture of the idealization of courtesans as entertainers whose skills included, but were by no means limited to, sexual services. Consequently, the emerging nation state attempted to centralize and formalize the control and management of prostitution without seriously contemplating its prohibition until after the Second World War. Historically, sex, at least for men, had been seen as one of the joys of life together with other forms of entertainment and comfort and even as a means of extending one's healthy lifespan.[12] Modern medicalized notions of a 'sexual instinct' or 'sex drive' only deepened the assumption of the inevitability of male sexual desire, which, in turn, easily translated into the wartime understanding that soldiers' sexual needs were to be managed but could not and should not be suppressed or completely controlled. It seemed only 'natural' to one soldier in 1937 Nanjing, for instance, that 'the men's fleshly desires, exacerbated by tedium, needed to be relieved'.[13] Such a view was widespread far beyond the military brass. Even after the war, Anzai Sadako, previously a Japanese field nurse employed by the Japanese Imperial Army on the Chinese front, recalled that she found it 'hard to think poorly of soldiers who frequented the military brothels' established by the military administration.[14]

As in National Socialist Germany and other regimes around the world, the control of soldiers' access to commercial sex was guided predominantly by concerns about protecting the men's physical and mental health while preventing infection of their innocent wives and children. Accordingly, venereal diseases were first systematically researched in military hospitals. Antibiotics such as Salvarsan, for the treatment of these diseases were first introduced in the military. Japan's first National Eugenics Law of 1941 – a mere shadow of Nazi racist eugenic laws, which were grounded in the idea of a 'racial restructuring of Europe' – aimed primarily at preventing individuals with inheritable diseases from reproducing.[15]

---

12 Janet R. Goodwin, *Selling Songs and Smiles: The Sex Trade in Heian and Kamakura Japan* (Honolulu: University of Hawai'i Press, 2007); Amy Stanley, *Selling Women: Prostitution, Markets, and the Household in Early Modern Japan* (Berkeley: University of California Press, 2012); Sabine Frühstück, 'Sex zwischen Wissenschaft und Politik', *Nachrichten der Gesellschaft für Natur-und Völkerkunde Ostasiens* 155–156 (1996), 11–41.

13 Ishikawa Tatsuzô, *Soldiers Alive*, trans. Zeljko Cipris (Honolulu: University of Hawai'i Press, 2003).

14 Anzai Sadako, *Yasen kangofu* (Tokyo: Fuji shobôsha, 1953), pp. 158–9.

15 For Japan's policies on Jewish refugees, see Martin Kaneko, *Die Judenpolitik der japanischen Kriegsregierung* (Berlin: Metropol, 2008).

Health examinations carried out by military hospitals and academies confirmed that one in ten recruits, or several tens of thousand men, suffered from at least one of several kinds of venereal disease. As in all fighting armies at the time, the most common were gonorrhoea, cancroid and syphilis. And as elsewhere until effective medication was developed, the diseases were treated with various baths, painful injections and treatments with special grasses and tinctures.[16] The authors of army and navy hygiene manuals claimed that a combination of condoms and creams applied to the genitals before and after sexual intercourse was the most effective means of preventing sexually transmitted diseases. More often, however, venereal diseases such as syphilis remained untreated, caused repeated skin eruptions and ulcers, brought about hair loss and the deterioration of the nose, and eventually affected the brain, turning the sufferer into a cripple. As Japanese field nurse Anzai Sadako reported, patients inevitably suffered from the loss of motor control, spinal cord phthisis, progressive paralysis and mental illnesses.

Only between the implementation of the General Mobilization Law in 1938 (Kokka Sôdôinhô) and the Law for the Strengthening of the National Body (Kokumin Tairyokuhô) in 1941 did legislation for the prevention of venereal diseases undergo a significant shift – from focusing on prostitutes to the entire population. Then, the largely preventive policies of the late nineteenth century were gradually replaced by proscriptive legislation, culminating in the implementation of the National Eugenics Law.

Long-term documentation of cases in military hospitals revealed that venereal diseases increased especially during times of war. The army addressed this by ordering weekly medical examinations of thousands of men and severely punishing those found to be diseased. During the 1894–95 Sino-Japanese War, military medical staff issued warnings that the Chinese were a promiscuous race and the country rife with syphilis.[17]

As military health education and punishment of infected soldiers by degradation or beating proved only partly effective, the authorities introduced more practical measures and began distributing condoms to soldiers.[18]

---

16 Kariya Haruo, *Edo no seibyô* (Tokyo: Sanichi shobô, 1993), pp. 22–3; Regina Mühlhauser, *Eroberungen, sexuelle Gewalttaten und intime Beziehungen deutscher Soldaten in der Sowjetunion, 1941–1945* (Hamburg: Hamburger Edition, 2010), p. 186.

17 Kaigunshô imukyoku, *Nisshin senyaku kaigun eiseishi* (Tokyo: Kaigunshô imukyoku, 1900).

18 Jûgun ianfu 110-ban henshû iinkai, ed., *Jûgun ianfu 110-ban: Denwa no mukô kara rekishi no koe ga* (Tokyo: Akashi shoten, 1992), p. 104.

Japanese condoms first came into widespread use at the beginning of Japan's aggression against China in 1931. Soldiers who left their bases were instructed to carry 'hygiene matches', small boxes containing two condoms. From 1938 until the end of the Second World War, rubber factories were put under the jurisdiction of the military, and condoms were formally classified as 'war munitions' (*gunjuhin*). The Imperial Army Ministry's Bureau of Supplies accounted for and distributed condoms, creatively named Attack Number One and Attack Champion for the Imperial Japanese Army or Iron Cap for the Imperial Japanese Navy.[19] Regimental commanders distributed them at 'comfort stations' (*ianjo*). Ways to enforce the use of a condom, however, remained limited, and practices varied from camp to camp. In 1942, for example, 32 million condoms were distributed to the Japanese military, roughly the equivalent of a ration of twenty condoms per man each year. In some comfort stations, condoms could be bought locally from the comfort station manager. In others condoms were either unavailable for long stretches of time or soldiers washed and reused them several times.[20]

The governing principle of male sexuality in Japan and the Japanese empire mirrored that of military establishments in Germany and elsewhere around the world: sex within and outside the military was organized in order to secure male access to female bodies while maximizing the maintenance of soldiers' health. Subsequently, this essentially militarist and masculinist logic permeated Japanese imperialist policies and practices in the broadest terms, reproducing on every level the dramatically unequal power relations between the male members of the imperial armed forces and the typically civilian female objects of their sexual desire.

During the Russo-Japanese War in 1904–5, the army attempted controlling soldiers' sexual activities by authorizing certain existing brothels for military-only use and building new ones exclusively for Japanese soldiers. These brothels became the site of military physicians' direct control over troops and prostitutes. In 1931, when the Japanese Imperial Army marched into China, the first brothels for exclusive military use were established in Shanghai. After 1937, military brothels were installed throughout China. Military administrators strove to avoid and suppress criticism of imperial troops' behaviour outside bases, at the front, or elsewhere in Japan's colonial

---

19 Ibid., p. 74; Chin Sung Chung, 'The Origin and Development of the Military Sexual Slavery Problem in Imperial Japan', *Positions: East Asian Cultures Critique* 5:1 (1997), 219–53 (p. 229).

20 Jûgun ianfu 110-ban henshû iinkai, ed., *Jûgun ianfu 110-ban*, p. 74.

empire. At the same time, they were primarily interested in protecting the designated protectors of the Japanese nation from unlicensed and thus presumably diseased prostitutes. By the end of the 1930s, when Japan entered all-out war with China, military-administered brothels were well entrenched.

After 1940 as large parts of the Pacific came under Japanese rule, including Burma, the Andaman-Nikobar Islands, the Indian territories in the west, Indonesia, and the Solomon and Marshall Islands, military brothels were established across the Japanese empire. When Japan began preparing for the offensive by the Allied forces, military brothels were also installed in Okinawa and other, mostly urban, parts of Japan.[21]

Initially, only Japanese prostitutes and other desperately poor and under-educated Japanese women were recruited for these establishments. Japan's Patriotic Women's Association, key members of which had long championed prostitution's eradication, eventually adopted as one of their duties on the home front the recruitment of prostitutes from the prostitution quarters of Japan's cities. Many of these women, to ease economic hardship, had been sold by their own families to the brothels. Others were recruited from the poorest towns and villages of rural Japan under the false pretence that they would work as maids or textile factory workers.

Not everyone agreed with such arrangements. One woman, the wife of a parliamentarian and mother of a young man, wrote to the abolitionist movement's journal, *Purity* (*Kakusei*), stating she would 'rather help her son dodge the draft than expose him to prostitution while serving in the military'.[22] This mother's concern with her son's morals and perhaps health had its counterpart within the military medical elite. As Japanese colonial rule expanded and military doctors believed that prostitutes infected soldiers with venereal diseases, Chinese, Korean, Dutch and other girls and women under Japanese colonial rule were forced into military-controlled sexual slavery, an operation that was euphemistically referred to as the 'comfort women system' (*ianfu seido*).

While the military brothels were established for soldiers and other military employees, civilian traders also were given access so long as their activities did not interfere with military needs. The 'recreation of military personnel' and civilian military employees was not to be disrupted. A number of rules

---

21 Hayashi Hirofumi, 'Die Verwicklung der japanischen kaiserlichen Regierung in das System der Militärbordelle ("Troststationen")', in Barbara Drinck and Chung-Noh Gross, eds., *Erzwungene Prostitution in Kriegs-und Friedenszeiten. Sexuelle Gewalt gegen Frauen und Mädchen* (Bielefeld: Kleine Verlag, 2006), pp. 106–18 (p. 108).
22 Hinata Daigishi Fujin, 'Fujin shakai to geishôgi mondai', *Kakusei* 1:3 (1911), 40–3.

needed to be observed and public morals upheld. A reservation before arrival was prohibited. The fee was the same as for officers. Anyone who violated any of these rules was denied further access to the facilities.[23]

By the early 1940s, even crusaders against prostitution were suggesting that sacrificing a small number of women for the health and moral benefit of the innocent majority was justifiable. Licensed prostitution was widely considered necessary, and thus the step to military-use-only brothels appeared only a minor variation. Simply put, men had sexual needs, and they had to be catered to. That said, not all men thought or acted in line with such views. To some military 'comfort stations' seemed grotesque. One officer gave the following description of an establishment in Nha-trang, Vietnam:

> The none-too-simple reality of it was that, rather than being stimulated, I felt I had been exposed to some grotesque world. Standing in line in broad daylight, doing it right under the nose of the people waiting for their turn, and the vivid image of men coming out one after another with their pants still half open. This ritual proceeded in conveyer-belt fashion in an atmosphere of a particular sort of tension, and rather than raising my spirits, made me, who knew nothing of the forbidden fruit of the tree of knowledge, flinch.[24]

When another Japanese soldier elsewhere was asked about how his encounter with an inmate of such a comfort station went, he replied, 'Dull.' A fellow solder inquired, 'Why is that?' The first responded, 'There is just no passion', to which the other replied, 'Idiot! What the hell did you expect!?'[25]

No matter what Japanese soldiers' expectations may have been, recruiters for the military and police lured girls and women into these comfort stations through false promises of work, coercion and even abduction. These methods reflected the techniques of civilian recruiters operating before the war and outside military camps during the war. One Korean woman named Mun, who was sixteen at the time of her abduction, described the experience as follows:

> One day, I went over to Haruko's house to visit. As the sun was going down, I left her house and headed home. Before I'd walked very far, a Japanese

23 Hirofumi, 'Die Verwicklung der japanischen kaiserlichen Regierung', p. 120; Won-Sang Han, 'Das japanische Militär im Krieg und sein System der Sexsklaverei', in Drinck and Gross, eds., *Erzwungene Prostitution in Kriegs-und Friedenszeiten*, pp. 169–82 (p. 170).
24 Yoshimi Yoshiaki, *Comfort Women: Sexual Slavery in the Japanese Military During World War II*, trans. Suzanne O'Brien (New York: Columbia University Press, 2000 [1995]), p. 140.
25 Ishikawa, *Soldiers Alive*, pp. 173–4.

man in a military uniform approached me. Suddenly, he grabbed my arm and pulled me, saying something to me in Japanese. That was a time when even hearing the word 'policeman' was a scary thing, so I was led off without saying a word ... I thought I was being taken to the military police.[26]

Instead, Mun was taken to a military comfort station in northeastern China. Another Korean woman, Kim Hak-sun, never forgot her first night at the comfort station she was taken to in 1941, when she was seventeen:

An officer came into the room and led me into the room next door, separated from the first by a cloth curtain ... I struggled against him, but he dragged me into the neighboring room by force. The officer tried to undress me while he was hugging me. I resisted, but my clothes were eventually all torn off. In the end, he took my virginity.[27]

Tens or hundreds of thousands of girls and women were enslaved in this manner, abused by imperial forces and held in the comfort stations. The Police Bureau ordered prefectural governments to name suitable recruiters and support them. Each prefecture chose one administrator, responsible for selecting women to be sent to China. Hence, the recruitment of these women was in the hands not only of the military leadership in Tokyo but also of other agencies of the state, particularly the police, the Ministry of Foreign Affairs, the government in Taiwan, and semi-governmental bodies. This also applied to the governor of Taiwan, who was asked to provide similar services to the Japanese military.[28]

These girls and women were forced to work as nurses, cooks, waitresses and seamstresses during the day, while at night they were regularly raped, beaten or seriously injured. One woman, who survived military sexual slavery, reported:

We never forgot to disinfect ourselves when the man was done. Near the bed in the corner of the room was a basin filled with a red disinfectant solution. Each time we finished we would carefully wash both the man's and the woman's private parts and wipe them with tissue paper. Because this solution chilled us inside, we prostitutes hardly ever got pregnant. They said it was to see if we had contracted a disease, but every seven days, without fail, we had to go to the hospital for an examination. Syphilis – if you had that, you know, your body would rot. Your whole body would be covered

26 Yoshiaki, *Comfort Women*, p. 107.
27 Ibid., p. 139.
28 Hirofumi, 'Die Verwicklung der japanischen kaiserlichen Regierung', p. 112.

with pustules and you would die a terrible death, or else you would go mad. We never missed an examination, because we didn't want that to happen to us.[29]

Military physicians examined soldiers and sex slaves for venereal diseases, albeit with different degrees of rigour. Despite the frequently proclaimed necessity of containing the overflow of men's sexual desires and needs, prostitutes were the declared source of disease. As a health hazard to men and their innocent wives and children, they were thought of as the latrine of the modern state. Thus their health was not considered worthy of protection, preservation or improvement for its own sake. Whereas the health of soldiers was maintained because they symbolically represented the 'national body', the health of women engaged in sex work – often as a last resort or because they were sold by their families, or enslaved by the military – was controlled and managed not for their sake but to protect the 'national body' from them and their diseases. Hence, health checks among the enslaved women mainly were carried out to prevent soldiers' infection with venereal diseases. Women were injected with so many drugs that they had miscarriages. No preventive measures were taken to safeguard them from disease, nor were their venereal diseases treated. Little or no notice was taken of cigarette burns, bruises, bayonet stabs, or even broken bones inflicted by soldiers.[30] Many of the women were simply abandoned or killed.

Comfort stations were most common in areas where Japanese military rule was secured and acknowledged by the local population. In such areas, raping local women was strictly forbidden so as to gain or maintain the local population's support.[31] The military establishment in Japan and elsewhere justified this policy as an antidote to civilian rape, a serious problem in war zones everywhere, but particularly toward the end of 1937 during the occupation of Nanjing and the massacre that occurred there.[32]

29 Yamazaki Tomoko, *Sandakan Brothel No. 8: An Episode in the History of Lower-Class Japanese Women*, trans. Karen Colligan-Taylor (New York: M. E. Sharpe, 1999 [1972]), p. 69.
30 The Jûgun Ianfu 110-ban Iinkai was formed in 1991 to interview former 'comfort women' and members of the Imperial Army about 'comfort stations' during the Second World War. Because of difficulties identifying and contacting people, the group established a phone hotline, Number 101, and later published the recorded calls; see Yamasaki Hiromi, 'Jûgun ianfu 110-ban' kaisetsu no keika', in Jûgun ianfu 110-ban henshû iinkaied, *Jûgun ianfu 110-ban*, pp. 11–16.
31 Hirofumi, 'Die Verwicklung der japanischen kaiserlichen Regierung', pp. 108–9.
32 Chung, 'Origin and Development of the Military Sexual Slavery Problem', p. 223; Joshua A. Fogel, ed., *The Nanjing Massacre in History and Historiography* (Berkeley: University of California Press, 2010) and 'The Nanking Atrocity and Chinese Historical

The Japanese also established military brothels in rural Chinese locales, where the local population strongly resisted Japanese rule or was suspected of doing so. In such areas, massacres and abuses of the local population, including the rape of local women, went unpunished. Japanese soldiers kidnapped, incarcerated and repeatedly raped local girls and women. In reality, these two types of 'comfort stations' mixed. When deployed on so-called punishment operations to areas that resisted Japanese rule, soldiers, who frequented military brothels in quiet urban areas, committed massacres and mass rapes.[33] The systematic nature of both types of sexual violence makes clear that most instances were not the crimes of a handful of men acting outside the control of the Japanese state and military administration.

Meanwhile, the Third Reich, encumbered by its own sexual fantasies, had emerged. The 1936 Anti-Comintern Pact sealed Japan's alliance with National Socialist Germany and Fascist Italy. This alliance crowned, at least for a while, Japan's long-standing infatuation with what had been a rather different Germany, which in decades past had substantially impacted the modernization of Japanese institutions. Yet despite this alliance, persistent ideological and political differences informed each country's sexual attitudes, experiences, practices and policies. The Second World War history of sexuality and sexual violence under Japanese imperialism in Asia in many ways echoed how sex and war intersected in Europe while substantially differing in others.

The Third Reich

I'm very fond of you and I want to be with you, but I'll never marry you. I'm married to my husband.
> Maria Braun to her American GI lover in *The Marriage of Maria Braun*,
> a film by Rainer Werner Fassbinder, 1979

Rainer Werner Fassbinder's film *The Marriage of Maria Braun* is the story of a young German wife who trades on the black market and works in a hostess bar to keep herself and her mother alive. An African-American soldier, whom she meets in the bar, becomes her lover. She kills him when her husband unexpectedly returns from a Soviet prison. Questioned in a court of law

Memory', in Bob Tadashi Wakabayashi, ed., *The Nanking Atrocity, 1937–38: Complicating the Picture* (New York: Berghahn Books, 2007), pp. 267–84.
33 Hirofumi, 'Die Verwicklung der japanischen kaiserlichen Regierung', pp. 109–10.

433

about her lover's death, she explains that she 'was very fond of him' but 'loved' only her husband. The liaison with the ill-fated soldier was just one of various romantic and sexual relations marking her will to live and which in the film represented the complexity of emerging post-war sexual relations.

For Fassbinder, Maria Braun's employment of sex also serves as an allegory of the reconsolidation of social and political authoritarianism in West Germany between 1945 and 1954. Significantly, the film says nothing about how under the National Socialist regime women's (and men's) bodies were abused or appropriated; how women (and many men), including German-Jewish and German Roma and Sinti were victimized during their pursuit and in the concentration camps; or how women and men in territories occupied by National Socialists suffered. In a sense, Braun's sexuality speaks at once of desperation *and* independence, but also of the silence bestowed on sexuality during the Second World War, a silence that Monika Hauser and other historians have begun to break.[34]

The boundaries between various kinds of consensual sex and sexual violence in the European theatre of war were porous and constantly shifting. From utilizing sex in search of intimacy and romance to disorderly conduct behind the front lines and in occupied territories, to organized centres of sexual violence such as military brothels, virtually no sexual encounter remained untouched by the war.

From early on, soldiers' sexuality was on Wehrmacht command's agenda.[35] The high rate of venereal diseases among First World War soldiers was one consideration; another concerned preventing homosexual relations among troops.[36] However, as Dagmar Herzog demonstrated, the sexual ideology of the National Socialist regime was not designed for the sole purpose of repressing sexuality. Instead, it combined strategies directed at controlling sexual desire with others meant to incite it. The brutal aspects of National Socialist sexual politics 'coexisted with injunctions and encouragement to the majority of Germans to seek and experience sexual pleasure'.[37] Nazi ideologues employed sexual politics 'as a device for reworking moral

34 Monika Hauser, 'Kriegsvergewaltigung – Ein beschwiegenes Kapitel der deutschen Geschichte', in Drinck and Gross, eds., *Erzwungene Prostitution in Kriegs- und Friedens-zeiten*, pp. 86–90 (pp. 88–9).

35 Dagmar Herzog, *Sex After Fascism: Memory and Morality in Twentieth-Century Germany* (Princeton University Press, 2005), p. 3.

36 Birgit Beck, *Wehrmacht und sexuelle Gewalt. Sexualverbrechen vor deutschen Militärger-ichten, 1939–1945* (Paderborn: Ferdinand Schöningh, 2004), p. 229.

37 Herzog, *Sex After Fascism*, p. 11.

1 *Eight Views of the World* by Richard Edes Harrison, USA, 1944.

It is through the widely popular medium of cartography that Americans came to understand the Second World War as a distinctly 'global' war. R. E. Harrison, at the time a freelancer for *Time/Fortune*, was one of the most artistic and creative propagators of this global imagination.

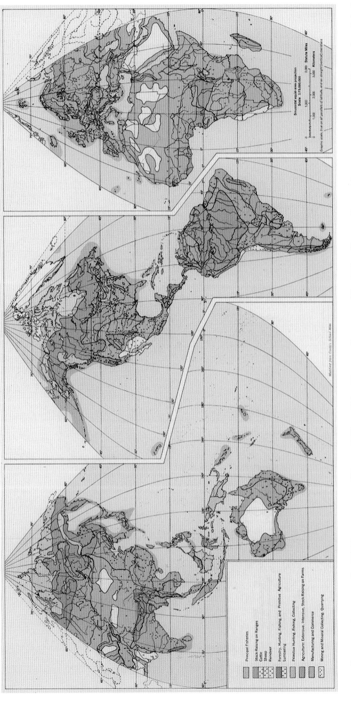

2 *Predominant Economies* by US Department of State, Office of the Geographer, 1943. The US military advanced programmes in visualizing the global dimensions of war. The map of predominant types of economies highlights the concentration of industrial power in an overwhelmingly agricultural world.

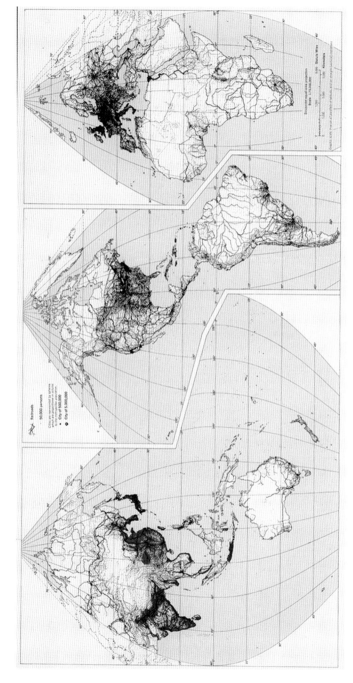

3 *The World: Populations and Railroads* by US Department of State, Office of the Geographer, 1943. It is not population as such that matters in war, but the ability to move people and, hence, to mobilize force.

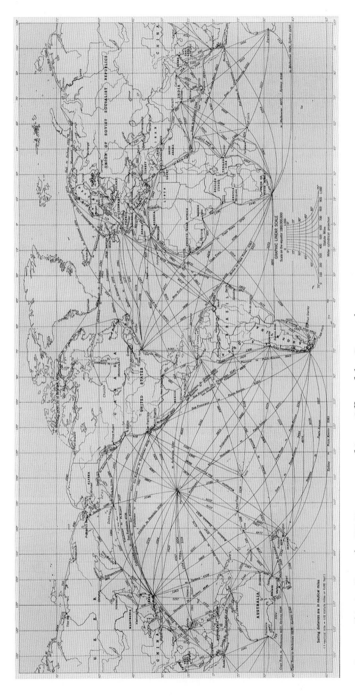

4 *Overseas Shipping Routes* by US Department of State, Office of the Geographer, 1943.

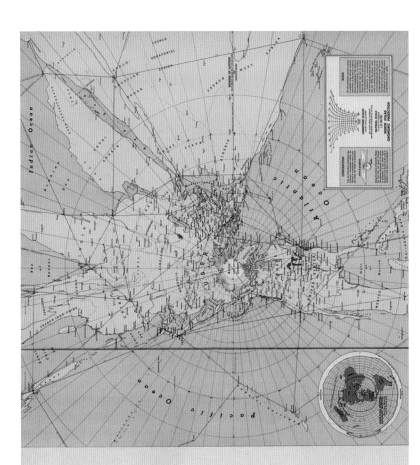

5 *Great Circle Airways* by Richard Edes Harrison, USA, 1944. The Great Circle Airways map with its natural scale at point of tangency 1:81,000,000. Its North Polar Gnomonic Projection was a subject of great fascination.

One World, One War

THE north polar sea is essentially the center of our world. To one side is North America, to the other Asia and—in different, Europe—triangular continental masses pointing south toward distant seas and toward barren Antarctica. But in the north, the bases of the two triangles almost touch. Bering Strait, the point of separation in the Pacific, is only fifty-odd miles wide, and it is difficult to judge whether Iceland, the stepping-stone in the Atlantic, belongs truly to the new or the old hemisphere.

Indeed, without a polar sea center, there might be one globe; but there would hardly be one world. If the continents were equidistantly separated, it would be very possible to have six wars and very difficult to make a single one out of them. In such case, almost all areas of the globe would have equal strategic value, and there would be no single trade routes of outstanding importance. It is the nearness of the northern continents that makes certain areas vital to world trade and to world security. Furthermore, there is a very close relationship between the geographical proximity of the various land masses and their population density. Over 90 per cent of the world's people live in lands north of the equator, essentially because it has always been shorter to travel close to the polar sea than to travel around the southern oceans.

The map to the left is in part a war map. It shows the World War II line-up of nations, and it traces the battle fronts and supply lines of the various areas. It is a map of the problems and the opportunities of fighting all over the world at once. While it includes obvious distortions, which increase toward the south, it serves as an excellent all-over strategy map. It is a continuous map that shows the world in one unbroken piece. Furthermore, it is centered within the great triangle formed by the world's power centers. This map deals always with a minimum of distortion. The map, therefore, is an index of the atlas that it introduces.

The maps that follow describe in greater detail various facets of the Northern Hemisphere world. They do not attempt more than a passing view of Africa, South America, and Australia, they do not aim to unstagle the plate names of such spots as Cyprus. They are a practical lesson map; they do not seek to be encyclopedic or to present the globe as a subject of abstract study. Rather they emphasize the too-long-forgotten realities of world geography.

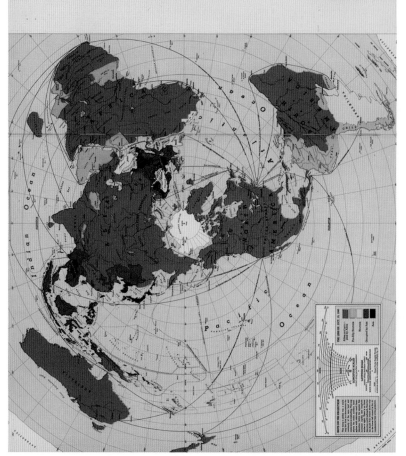

Centered on North Pole   *Centered on South Pole*

COMPLETE AZIMUTHAL EQUIDISTANT PROJECTIONS

6 *One World, One War* by Richard Edes Harrison, USA, 1944. This is the most famous of Harrison's maps. The first, 1941 edition had Germany and Japan occupying the entire space of the Soviet Union. The 1943/44 map shows the rather more desperate strategic predicament of the two aggressors.

8 *Nesh tysianchnii udar* [Our One-Thousandth Blow].
P. Sokolov-Skalia and N. Denisovskii, text by
V. Lebedev-Kumach. Stencilled posters were placed
in the windows of the TASS News Agency in
Moscow. Produced in 1944, this was the 1000th
poster. Under the main caption is a quote from
V. Maiakovskii: 'I want the pen to be on a par with
the bayonet . . .'.

7 *Smiling Through News and Pictures: 'First it was War Reporters.
Now It's Official Artists'* by Joseph [Joe] Lee, Great Britain, 1943.

9 *Production: America's answer!* by Jean Carlu, US Office of Emergency Management, Information Division, 1942. Jean Carlu (1900–97), a modernist French graphic designer, worked for the wartime production campaign. His expressive designs reflected a European aesthetic that reshaped American advertising.

10 *Rosie the Riveter* by Norman Rockwell, USA, 1943. Norman Rockwell's (1894–1978) 'Rosie the Riveter' became the icon for the American production drive during the Second World War.

11 *Ruby Loftus Screwing a Breech Ring* by Laura Knight, Great Britain, 1943. Laura Knight's (1877–1970) 'Ruby Loftus' gained a similar status in Great Britain, albeit in an altogether 'academic' oil painting, whose frisson consisted in the attention to the machinery, a Bofors gun block, and the stylized physical attractiveness of the model.

12 新女性美：螺線を切る [*Shinjoseibi: rasen wo kiru* – Modern Girls' Beauty: Spiral Cutting], by Shimano Shigeyuki. © Photo of destroyed work in: Hariu, Ichirō, Noi Sawaragi, et al., eds., *Senso to bijutsu 1937–1945* = Art in Wartime Japan 1937–1945. Tokyo: Kokusho Kankōkai Inc., 2007, p. 137.

13 *Frauen schaffen für Euch: Im Flugzeugbau* [Women Work for You: In Aeroplane Production] by Gert Gagelmann (?), Germany, 1943. The postcards of eighteen hyper-glamorized Fräuleins-at-work were a commercial venture that was extremely successful among soldiers.

15 *Zamenim.* [Let us replace them] by Vladimir Aleksandrovich Serov, Soviet Union, 1941. V. A. Serov (1910–1968) specialized in revolutionary historical paintings; he organized artistic work (camouflage, posters) during the siege of Leningrad.

14 *La Mujer tambien quiere ganar la guerra. Ayudemos la!* [She also wants to win the war. Help Her!] by unknown artist associated with the Partido Comunista de España, Spain, 1937. This poster articulates the distinct style of Mediterranean modernism, boldly inserts women into the industrial labour force, and manages to maintain a masculine gaze. It stands in for hundreds of similar posters around the world.

17 *Europas Sieg – Dein Wohlstand* [Europe's Victory – Your Prosperity], Germany, 1943. The linkage of victory and prosperity may come as a surprise.

16 *Avec l'ouvrier soldat pour le socialisme* [With the Worker Soldier for Socialism], Belgium, 1942. The politics of this French-language poster is peculiar to Nazi-occupied Belgium, but the design and iconography are not.

18 *Sieg oder Bolschewismus* [Victory or Bolshevism] by Mjölnir aka Hans Schweitzer, Germany, 1943. Hans Schweitzer (1901–80) had been the foremost Nazi propagandist since the 1920s. He deployed a distinctly graphic style, based on pencil or charcoal drawings, in his many propaganda posters.

19 *Tania* [The Heroic Feat of Zoia Kosmodemianskaia] by 'Kukryniksy': Porfirii Krylov, Nikolai Sokolov and Mikhail Kuprianov, Soviet Union, 1942–47, oil on canvas, 159 cm × 241 cm. Zoia Kosmodemianskaia (1925–41) was one of the most highly touted war heroines of the Soviet Union. The Kukryniksy collective were famous for their caricatures, but they also painted in oil. This painting draws on captured German photographs. Note the German photographers in the foreground.

20 *Ukraine 1942 – Judenaktion in Iwangorod* [Ukraine 1942, Jewish Action, Ivangorod] by unknown photographer, Poland/Ukraine, 1942. The photograph was mailed from the Eastern Front to Germany and intercepted at a Warsaw post office by members of the Polish Resistance. When the photo was published in 1959, it unleashed a controversy over its authenticity. Scholarship suggests that the small photo is an original print.

21 *Devastation of Bombed Nagasaki*, photograph by Yosuke Yamahata, Japan, 1945/1952. The photos by Yosuke Yamahata, a Japanese military photographer, were taken on 10 August 1945, a day after an atom bomb was dropped on Nagasaki. He took approximately 100 exposures, the only extensive record of the immediate aftermath of the bombing.

22 *Visitors view a photomural of corpses piled on the ground at Bergen-Belsen concentration camp,* photograph in 'Lest We Forget' exhibition at the Library of Congress, 30 June, 1945. 'Lest We Forget' was a two-week exhibition of 'life-size' photomurals depicting the horrors of the Nazi concentration camps that was displayed at the Library of Congress from 30 June through 14 July 1945. The exhibition was sponsored by two newspapers, the *St. Louis Post-Dispatch* and the *Washington Star*. It was visited by more than 80,000 people.

23 *Visitors view a photomural of survivors in their barracks in Buchenwald*, photograph in 'Lest We Forget' exhibition at the Library of Congress, 30 June, 1945.

24 꼴려감 [*Kkŭlyŏgam* – Stolen Away] by Soon-Duk Kim, South Korea, 1995, acrylic on canvas, 154 cm × 114.5 cm. Soon-Duk Kim's painting served therapeutic purposes, but was included in an exhibition and has since been selected by the Korean National Archives for preservation.

25 *Oborona Sevastopolia* [The Defence of Sevastopol] by Aleksandr Aleksandrovich Deineka, Soviet Union, 1942. Soviet war art is the quintessential war art of the Second World War. Aleksandr Deineka (1899–1969), one of the most important figurative modernists in the Soviet Union, holds a special place in this field and his allegorical painting about the defence of Sevastopol figures centrally in his oeuvre.

26 *Okraina Moskvy. Noiabr' 1941 goda* [The Outskirts of Moscow, November 1941] by Aleksandr Aleksandrovich Deineka, Soviet Union, 1942. Sombre paintings of urban scenes permeated by the violence of war were quite frequent in Soviet war art and form a contrast with the prevailing bombast of oil paintings and the heroic realism of posters.

27 *Sbityi as* [An Ace Shot Down] by Aleksandr Aleksandrovich Deineka, Soviet Union, 1943, oil on canvas, 283 cm × 188 cm. The evocative portrait of a shot down, German fighter pilot reinforces Deineka's image as a daring war artist.

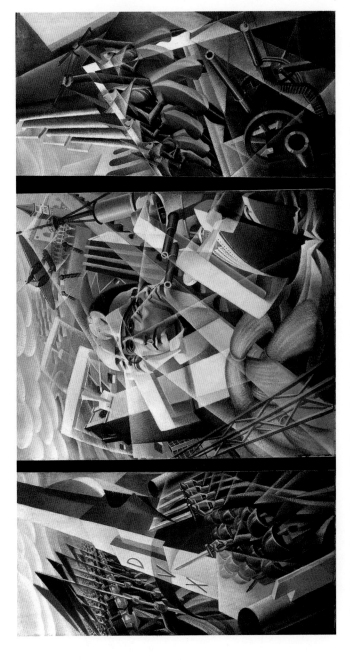

28 *Sintesi Fascista* [Fascist Synthesis] by Alessandro Bruschetti, Italy, 1935. Alessandro Bruschetti (1910–80), futurist painter and dedicated fascist, imagined war as a dynamic way of life for Italy.

29 *Guernica* by Pablo Picasso, Spain/France, 1937. Picasso (1881–1973) created this most iconic of all war paintings for the Spanish (Republican) Pavilion at the 1937 World's Fair in Paris.

30 *Le Charnier* [Charnel House] by Pablo Picasso, France, 1944/45, oil and charcoal on canvas. 199.8 cm × 250.1 cm. After *Guernica*, Picasso returned to the theme of war only once, in this never completed work.

31 *Totes Meer (Dead Sea)* by Paul Nash, Great Britain 1940/41. Paul Nash (1989–1946), the eminent British war artist of the First World War, is often criticized for aestheticizing war in his paintings as war artist in the Second World War.

32　アッツ島玉砕 [*Attsutōgyokusai* – Shattered Pearls (Honourable Death) on Attu Island]
by Fujita Tsuguharu. Fujita Tsuguharu (藤田嗣治, 1886–1968) is best known as a
Paris-based painter of beautiful women and cats and as an advocate for world peace,
but emerged as a brilliant and militarist war artist upon returning to Japan in 1933.
The image depicts the final 'Banzai' charge in the Battle of Attu on 29 May 1943, as a
result of which the Japanese garrison wiped itself out.

33　*Liberation* by Henry Carr, Great Britain/Italy, 1944. Henry Carr (1894–1970) was a war
artist with the British forces in Italy. This painting depicts a liberated Italian village in
ruins, its disoriented inhabitants, and the orderly routines of soldiers.

34 原爆の図 [*Genbaku no zu* – Hiroshima Panels] I: 幽霊 [*Yūrei* – Ghosts] by Toshi and Iri Maruki, Japan, 1950. Toshi (1912–2000) and Iri (1901–1995) Maruki (丸木俊 丸木位) were artists and anti-nuclear activists who struggled in their Hiroshima art to rescue formal beauty in order to better capture utter pain.

35 Majdanek Mausoleum, designed by architect Wiktor Tolkin (1922–2013), Poland, 1969. The Majdanek memorial consists of a mausoleum that now holds victims' ashes and a large abstract stone monument (not shown).

36 Mulackstrasse 37: Slide Projection of Former Jewish Residents (c.1932) by Shimon Attie, USA/Germany, 1991. The image by Shimon Attie (*1957) is part of the Writing on the Wall Series, 1991–93, in which he projected photographs from the pre-war era (1920–30) onto walls of an old East Berlin neighbourhood.

37 *'Rodina Mat' Zovet!'* [The Motherland Calls!] Mamayev Kurgan Memorial Complex, designed by sculptor Evgenii Vuchetich (1908–74), Soviet Union, 1959–67. The Mamayev Kurgan Memorial Complex with its monumental statue of Mother Russia as postcard.

38 RAF Bomber Command Memorial, designed by Liam O'Connor, Great Britain, 2012.

39 *Polenfeldzug, bei Danzig, Strasse Zoppot-Gdingen: Schlagbaum an der polnischer. Grenze wird beseitigt* [The Polish Campaign near Danzig, Road from Sopot to Gdańsk: The Barrier on the Polish Border Removed] by Hans Sönnke, Germany, 1939. Sönnke was a professional photographer in Danzig/Gdańsk. This photo was staged for propaganda purposes and dated 1 September 1939. This caption is the 1939 text. Both image and text have been widely used without further comment. Illustrations 39–44 are discussed in Chapter 27, 'Landscapes of destruction', by Dorothee Brantz.

40 *Murmansk* by Evgenii Khaldei, Soviet Union, 1942. The woman in the picture berated Evgennyi Khaldei (1917–97) for having nothing better to do than take her picture.

41 *Three Dead Americans on the Beach at Buna* [New Guinea] by George Strock, USA, 1942/43. This image by photojournalist George Strock (1911–77) was the subject of considerable controversy as to whether to publish it. Publication was authorized by President Roosevelt.

42 *Brama w Birkenau* [Entrance Gate to Auschwitz-Birkenau] by Stanisław Mucha, Poland, 1945. Mucha (1895–1976) took this photo after the liberation of Auschwitz.

43 *Blick vom Rathausturmnach Süden* [View from City Hall to the South]. Photograph of Dresden in 1945, taken by press photographer and photojournalist Richard Peter (1895–1977).

44 *Hiroshima, 6 August 1945,* photo taken from aboard the *Enola Gay* by George Caron, USA, 1945. The photo by the tail gunner of the B-29, George 'Bob' Carron (1919–95), became the official still photograph of the explosion. It was dropped as a leaflet over Japan the day after.

languages' – for instance, to control homosexuality and sex in individuals deemed racially inferior. They simultaneously 'attack[ed] Christian values *and* appropriate[d] them' by 'speaking constantly of the "sanctity" of racial purity, the "salvation" of Germany, and "guilt" and "sin" against the race or the *Volk*'.[38]

For all their rhetoric condemning Christian morals, Nazi ideologues upheld a conservative gender order. Women's task was to protect the German *Volkskörper*.[39] Every 12 August since 1934, the National Socialist state honoured prolific mothers with the Mother's Cross – bronze for mothers of four children, silver for mothers of six, and gold for mothers of eight or more children. Before the award ceremony, the mothers were examined with regard to their racial, eugenic and ideological health. As an extension of such pronatalist policies, the organization *Lebensborn* was founded in 1935 under the personal direction of Reichsführer and SS Chief, Heinrich Himmler. This project aimed at raising the birth rate of so-called Aryan children by promoting extramarital relations, particularly by SS members classified as racially pure. Subsequently it was expanded into several occupied European countries with populations deemed Aryan.[40]

Similarly, Gabriele Czarnowski demonstrated, marriage loans for genetically 'fit' couples originally were introduced as a labour policy aimed at decreasing male unemployment by removing women from the workforce. While initially a reactionary effort to re-domesticate women, after 1936 the law primarily served as a means of placing a growing share of married couples under eugenic surveillance, since racial and eugenic criteria were stipulations for eligibility. By 1937, the racial hygienic criteria dominated, and by 1939 one in three couples had been scrutinized. Hence, 'the public health examinations for marriage loans proved themselves to be one of the most important turning points between "supportive" and "eliminationist" reproductive policies'.[41] In dramatic contrast, German women in relationships with Jews, foreign men or forced labourers were prosecuted under 'race legislation', incarcerated in concentration camps, and their male partners were hung.[42]

---

38 Ibid., p. 10.
39 Beck, *Wehrmacht und sexuelle Gewalt*, p. 230.
40 Stefan Maiwald and Gerd Mischler, *Sexualität unter dem Hakenkreuz. Manipulation und Vernichtung der Intimsphäre im NS-Staat* (Hamburg: Europa-Verlag, 1999), pp. 117–18.
41 Gabriele Czarnowski, *Das kontrollierte Paar. Ehe-und Sexualpolitik im Nationalsozialismus* (Weinheim: Deutscher Studien Verlag, 1991), p. 105.
42 Christa Paul, 'Zwangsprostitution von Mädchen und Frauen im Nationalsozialismus', in Drinck and Gross, eds., *Erzwungene Prostitution in Kriegs- und Friedenszeiten*, pp. 91–104 (p. 101).

According to the ideal, the 'racially aware Aryan man' should not desire women deemed 'racially inferior'. Here, ideology intersected with more mundane considerations. The Wehrmacht aimed at controlling such consensual relationships, so as to prevent enemy espionage, an increase in venereal diseases, damage to alleged German superiority, harm to the Wehrmacht's reputation, and potential emotional conflicts of such relationships.[43] Nevertheless, the large number of venereal disease case studies in German-occupied territories reveals a picture of casual sexual encounters by Wehrmacht members, presumably with local women and girls (but which might also have been male–male encounters). This picture stood in surreal contrast to the rules of conduct that prescribed severe penalties for sex with women deemed racially inferior. From such records, it becomes clear that Wehrmacht and SS members had unprotected extramarital sex with forbidden women and girls; did not sanitize themselves; did not always report if they became sick; and did not always cooperate with the search for their recent sexual partners.[44]

In the eyes of the regime, homosexuality represented another form of undesirable sexual relationship. Here, too, women and men received different treatment. National Socialists assumed a natural sexual passivity and dependence upon men on the part of women. Thus, they considered female same-sex desire 'pseudo-homosexuality' and in itself not a basis for legal sanction. Unless denounced as 'asocials' or as regime opponents, lesbian women in Germany were more likely to be sent to labour camps or psychiatric hospitals than concentration camps.[45] In contrast, male same-sex desire earned a wide range of punishments – marginalization and discrimination, prison sentences, institutionalization in psychiatric hospitals, re-education, castration, imprisonment, and often death in concentration camps.[46]

The Third Reich significantly expanded the infamous Paragraph 175 (dating back to the German Criminal Code of 1871 and only completely

---

43 Regina Mühlhauser, 'Between "Racial Awareness" and Fantasies of Potency: Nazi Sexual Politics in the Occupied Territories of the Soviet Union, 1942–1945', in Dagmar Herzog, ed., *Brutality and Desire: War and Sexuality in Europe's Twentieth Century* (New York: Palgrave Macmillan, 2009), pp. 197–220 (p. 209).

44 Wendy Jo Gertjejanssen, 'Victims, Heroes, Survivors: Sexual Violence on the Eastern Front During World War II' (PhD dissertation, University of Minnesota, 2004), p. 87.

45 Maiwald and Mischler, *Sexualität unter dem Hakenkreuz*, p. 184. In Austria, by contrast, same-sex sexuality among women was regulated by paragraph 1291 of the criminal law and since 1852 was punishable by up to five years in prison; see Claudia Schoppmann *Verbotene Verhältnisse. Frauenliebe, 1938–1945* (Berlin: Querverlag, 1999).

46 Franz X. Eder, *Homosexualitäten. Diskurse und Lebenswelten, 1870–1970* (Weitra: Bibliothek der Prozinz, 2010), p. 68.

revoked in 1994), establishing new criteria for the prosecution of homosexuals. Homosexuals became public enemies, and Nazi leaders proclaimed the extermination of these 'genetic contagions' (*Volksseuche*) a national priority. David Raub Snyder noted that Hitler and Himmler classified gays along with criminals as 'asocials', and Jews as 'deviant subhumans' and vowed to eradicate these 'cosmic lice'.[47] 'A confused mix of traditional stereotypes, clichés, and pseudoscientific racial theories', to use David Raub Snyder's characterization, Nazi homophobia did not smoothly and coherently translate into court practice. Jurisprudence and sentencing practices when prosecuting individuals accused of homosexual offences ranged from indifference and traditional homophobia and stereotyping to, in a few cases, obvious outrage. Furthermore, while civilian authorities after 1940 automatically transferred individuals violating Paragraph 175 to concentration camps after they had completed their judicially imposed punishment, the Wehrmacht reintegrated most offenders.[48]

This incoherence in addressing homosexuality corresponded with Hitler's perspective on the subject. Hitler left untouched homosexuals among the National Socialist elite who unconditionally subordinated themselves to him. However, a homosexual who became a political burden to him was dropped, accused of the crime of pederasty, expelled from the party, or even executed. The so-called Röhm putsch of 1934 is perhaps the most prominent case in point.[49]

Similar punishment practices existed in camps, where some soldiers had sexual relationships with boys, usually referred to as 'doll boys' or 'dolly boys' (*Puppenjungen*). According to one former doll boy, the SS and others knew about these sexual relationships but did nothing unless a specific couple's relationship became publicly known. Outside Wehrmacht brothels, same-sex behaviour between two 'normal' men was considered 'an emergency outlet', while sexual relations between two 'men who both feel deeply for one another, was considered something filthy and repulsive'. Regardless of the nature of the relationship, however, when men were caught, they were tortured horrendously merely for being homosexual.[50]

---

47 David Raub Snyder, *Sex Crimes Under the Wehrmacht* (Lincoln: University of Nebraska Press, 2007), p. 103.
48 Ibid., pp. 105–7.
49 Franz Seidler, *Prostitution, Homosexualität, Selbstverstümmelung. Probleme der deutschen Sanitätsführung 1939–1945* (Neckarmünd: Kurt Vowinkel Verlag, 1977), p. 201. On Hitler's personal authorization of the murder of Ernst Röhm, the openly homosexual leader of the SA as well as other political rivals on 30 June 1934, see Eder, *Homosexualitäten*, p. 70; Maiwald and Mischler, *Sexualität unter dem Hakenkreuz*, pp. 46–91.
50 Gertjejanssen,'Victims, Heroes, Survivors', p. 113.

Preoccupation with non-normative sexual desires was by no means exclusive to the military elite of Germany. In the USA, for instance, the 1943 book *Psychology for the Fighting Man*, published by a committee of the National Research Council in collaboration with the Science Service, was directed to American enlistees. For the 'vigorously exercised body in the army', it claimed, sleep, food and sex 'become matters of primary urgency and concern'.[51] The book suggested that it was 'not easy for a man to get his sexual life into wise and proper adjustment', even though the military provided him with information on the psychological side of sex, the dangers of venereal disease, and the way prostitutes 'can contribute to the defeat of an army'.[52] Accordingly, the authors tried persuading individual soldiers that seeking sexual satisfaction with women other than their wives would not come 'without conflict with conscience and feelings of guilt which lower his efficiency and morale as a soldier'. At the same time, the authors expressed considerable tolerance for 'promiscuous sexual activity' on the part of a soldier 'whose standards are such that he can indulge without disgust and feeling of guilt' and still 'have a good fighting spirit'. The authors classified homosexual men as sexually abnormal and referred to homosexuality as a perversion, but they did not see it as an impediment to being excellent soldiers as long as they had 'no feelings of inferiority or shame, no mental conflict, over their homosexuality', readily applied 'their interest and energy to the tasks of army life', and quietly sought 'the satisfaction of their sexual needs with others of their own kind'.[53]

Hence, in the USA, as in Germany, discussions about the sexuality of soldiers during wartime were marked by ambivalence and contradictions. This incoherence highlighted tensions between two core concerns. First, was sex good for soldiers' performance as combatants and for military units' cohesion, and, if so, what kinds of sex and with what partners? Second, should the sexual ideology prescribed for members of the military cohere with that more broadly prescribed for the nation at war?

In the case of Germany, as the war dragged on, the widening gap between publicly proclaimed standards and actual policies and practices on the battleground, behind the front lines, and on the home front, particularly with regards to compensated sex and sexual slavery became an additional concern. Although in *Mein Kampf* (1924) Adolf Hitler had advocated the 'final

---

51 Committee of the National Research Council with the Collaboration of Social Service as a Contribution to the War Effort, *Psychology for the Fighting Man Prepared for the Fighting Man Himself* (Washington, DC: Infantry Journal and Penguin, 1943), p. 275.
52 Ibid., p. 277.
53 Ibid., p. 280.

extermination' of prostitution, declaring it a 'disgrace to humanity',[54] with the onset of war in 1939 his goal shifted from prostitution's eradication to its total control. All prostitutes in Germany and the occupied territories had to register and work in brothels supervised by the German police and the health authorities. They had to undergo examinations for sexually transmitted diseases twice a week.[55] They were deprived of their rights, criminalized, hunted and punished. Their criminalization, however, did not aim at eradicating prostitution, only rendering it invisible. In wartime, Hitler believed, prostitution was necessary in order to strengthen soldiers' fighting resolve.[56]

Accordingly in 1941, Himmler urged the establishment of brothels for use by members of the Wehrmacht and SS, as well as the most diligent foreign and forced workers in concentration camps. Failing to provide these facilities would be 'unworldly', for soldiers simply could not be 'denied their basic sexual needs'.[57] The establishment of Wehrmacht brothels was also justified as a means of preventing soldiers' infection with venereal diseases. Ultimately different brothels were established for different Wehrmacht ranks; the Wehrmacht high command was responsible for equipping these brothels.[58]

In 1942, Himmler excluded prostitutes from earlier prohibitions concerning sex with women of a cultural, religious or national group deemed inferior under National Socialist race laws. A twenty- to thirty-minute visit to a brothel, the new policy affirmed, was not a social relationship but a material and economic one.[59] Hence, no damage to the *Volkskörper* by 'mixed children' would result from sex with prostitutes.[60]

Under the new rubric, prostitution was broadly defined and the forcible detainment of prostitutes in brothels institutionalized. The SS selected women mainly from the Ravensbrück and Auschwitz-Birkenau camps, promising them freedom after half a year. The majority of those sex labourers who have been identified by name were German women classified as 'asocials'. Others were Polish, Ukrainian or Belorussian.[61] Those who 'volunteered' imagined that six months in a brothel would be preferable to

---

54 Adolf Hitler, *Mein Kampf*, ed. John Chamberlain et al. (New York: Reynal & Hitchcock, 1939 [1925]), p. 217.
55 Robert Sommer, 'Camp Brothels: Forced Sex Labour in Nazi Concentration Camps', in Herzog, ed., *Brutality and Desire*, pp. 168–96 (p. 180).
56 Herzog, *Sex After Fascism*, p. 51.
57 Paul, 'Zwangsprostitution von Mädchen und Frauen', p. 94.
58 Ibid., pp. 99–100.
59 Gertjejanssen, 'Victims, Heroes, Survivors', p. 189.
60 Beck, *Wehrmacht und sexuelle Gewalt*, p. 230.
61 Sommer, 'Camp Brothels', p. 175.

six months in a concentration camp. In reality, however, they were sent back to the camp, often infected with venereal diseases, or to the gas chambers.[62] As the war dragged on and more women learned that the promise of release after a few months was a hoax, fewer 'volunteered'. The daughter of one Auschwitz survivor recalled the following thoughts when she finally found her biological mother:

> I told her that I wanted to see what my real mother looked like and learn why she had given me away. She looked at me calmly and said, 'Child, I was in Auschwitz for five years.' That was it! She said it with such a sense of calm, so matter-of-factly. At that moment everything became clear, just – clear.[63]

In some territories under Wehrmacht control, civilian brothels were re-designated as exclusively Wehrmacht houses. Alternatively, new brothels were established. In the east, independent or unregulated prostitution flourished under German occupation. There, the Wehrmacht typically adopted existing brothels. Where no brothels had previously existed, the medical units that were in charge of establishing them forcefully recruited sex labourers.

According to the account of one SS man, in Warsaw's military brothels 'every woman had 14–15 men an hour. They changed the women every two days. We buried a lot of women there.'[64] In France, according to Insa Meinen, Wehrmacht brothels were established primarily to undercut fraternization between Wehrmacht soldiers and French women, and for 'racial' and defence reasons.[65] French women who had been interned because of their relations with Wehrmacht soldiers were also brought to these brothels.[66]

The sexual slavery within the Wehrmacht, SS and camp brothels was a form of serial rape even if it was not treated as such by the law. Beyond this organized sexual labour, the maintenance of military discipline was also at the core of how the law treated rape at and around the front lines and in the occupied territories. German men exercised sexual violence in the combat zone, but rape was also a form of aggression that structured the everyday life of occupation.[67] Members of the Wehrmacht, the SS and the police raped

---

62 Gertjejanssen, 'Victims, Heroes, Survivors', p. 234.
63 Wendy Jo Gertjejanssen, 'Victims, Heroes, Survivors: Sexual Violence on the Eastern Front during World War II' (PhD dissertation, University of Minnesota, 2004), p. 248.
64 Neitzel and Welzer, *Soldaten*, p. 168.
65 Insa Meinen, *Wehrmacht und Prostitution während des Zweiten Weltkrieges im besetzten Frankreich* (Bremen: Edition Temmen, 2002).
66 Paul, 'Zwangsprostitution von Mädchen und Frauen', p. 100.
67 Mühlhauser, 'Between "Racial Awareness" and Fantasies of Potency', p. 201.

women during battles and massacres, in the military rear and in the everyday situation of occupation. They exercised sexual torture as a means to terrorize their enemies and as an instrument in interrogation. Generally, Nazi authorities tolerated these forms of violence as normal aspects or products of warfare.[68]

Nevertheless, according to the law articulated in the *Reichstrafgesetzbuch*, rape during the Second World War was illegal and could be punished with incarceration and theoretically even the death penalty. However, rape was viewed by many as a minor offence in line with the idealized notions of masculinity nurtured in the almost exclusively male Wehrmacht and SS. Besides, as they did with homosexual offenders, the military judicial authorities generally evaluated servicemen convicted of rape on the basis of their ability and willingness to carry a weapon in good faith.[69] Punishment in the east was more lenient than in France, for instance, partly as a consequence of the Barbarossa Decree of 1941 that prescribed that crimes of Wehrmacht members were to be pursued only if the 'discipline and order of the military unit' was at stake. The death penalty, established in 1941, was considered only if the *Volksgemeinschaft* was at stake or if it was 'based on the necessity of righteous atonement'.[70] From a National Socialist perspective, the death penalty was neither desirable nor useful when punishing the rape of non-Aryan women. Judges typically punished sexual violence lightly because women in Eastern Europe were deemed racially inferior. Besides, sexual crimes could be pursued by a court of law only when a request was filed. Unsurprisingly, the number of documented cases is small. Many women must have refrained from coming forward to request the pursuit of the case.

Legacies and contexts

As we have seen in the examples of Imperial Japan and National Socialist Germany during the Second World War, many expressions of sexuality and especially instances of sexual mass violence emerged from a widely shared ideology about male sexual desire, the impossibility of completely controlling it, and the use-value of manipulating it. In many ways, the numerous instances of controlled, long-term, systematic and meticulously organized

68 Ibid., p. 203.
69 Snyder, *Sex Crimes*, p. 133.
70 Beck, *Wehrmacht und sexuelle Gewalt*, pp. 226–8.

sexual violence, whether in Japanese sexual slavery stations or in Wehrmacht and concentration camp brothels, reflected a normative notion of male sexuality even as it represented a sexual normativity gone horrifically wild. More specifically, numerous instances of such sexual violence were the result of a persistent and frequently reproduced notion of male sexuality as something that could and should be productively incited during war. In many places it appears that sexual violence occurred because of the very lack or insufficiency of control over men's behaviour or perhaps a disinterest in or inability enforcing it. The mass rapes by the Imperial Japanese Army in Nanjing and by the Wehrmacht and SS in Eastern Europe were only the two most notorious examples. At the same time, this sexual ideology fuelled and permeated a wide range of sexual and romantic encounters and relationships, and frequently cut across national and cultural boundaries, ranging from Joan's romance at the beginning of this chapter to the GIs in post-liberation France, one of whom recalled that even 'the few moments a man could snatch with a woman seemed somehow islands of sanity in a world gone mad. Or maybe sometimes bizarre and desperate sex were only an extension of that madness.'[71]

The story told in this chapter did not end in 1945. Rather, during the occupation era that lasted until 1952 in Japan and until 1955 in West and East Germany, sexual relations between members of the victorious occupying forces and the occupied populations were widespread. Allied forces in occupied areas from northern Africa to southern Japan established military brothels while also committing hundreds of thousands of rapes.[72] The conduct of Russian troops in occupied Europe, suggested Norman M. Naimark, might have been triggered in part by hate propaganda, by what had been done to the Soviet Union, by Germans' wartime claims of superiority and their continued

---

71 Roberts, *What Soldiers Do*, p. 157.
72 Gaby Zipfel, 'Ausnahmezustand Krieg? Anmerkungen zu soldatischer Männlichkeit, sexueller Gewalt und militärischer Einhegung', in Insa Eschebach and Regina Mühlhauser, eds., *Krieg und Geschlecht. Sexuelle Gewalt im Krieg und Sex-Zwangsarbeit in NS-Konzentrationslagern* (Berlin: Metropol Verlag, 2008), pp. 55–74 (p. 74); J. Robert Lilly, *Taken by Force: Rape and American GIs in Europe during WWII* (New York: Palgrave Macmillan, 2007); Roberts, *What Soldiers Do*; Norman M. Naimark, *The Russians in Germany: A History of the Soviet Zone of Occupation, 1945–1949* (Cambridge, Mass.: The Belknap Press of Harvard University Press, 1997); Harold Zink, *The United States in Germany, 1944–1955* (Princeton: Van Nostrand Company, 1957), p. 137; Judith Byfield, Carolyn Brown, Timothy Parsons and Ahmad Sikainga, eds., *Africa and World War II* (Cambridge University Press, 2015); Tanaka Yuki, *Japan's Comfort Women: Sexual Slavery and Prostitution During World War II and the US Occupation* (London: Routledge, 2002).

arrogance in spite of fearing the occupiers, and by resentment toward the strange, rich world of the West.[73] For Timothy Snyder, the rampage of rape and pillage was enabled by the failure to organize systematic evacuations. In the last few weeks of the war, 'German troops were racing west to surrender to the British or the Americans rather than the Soviets; civilians often lacked such options.' Consequently, 'German women often committed suicide, or tried to kill themselves to prevent rape.'[74]

While defeat constituted an important rupture in the political trajectory of both nations, the populations of Japan as well as Germany and large parts of Europe emerged from the interrogatory 1960s and 1970s with pronounced anti-war sentiments, an increasingly complicated relationship to patriotism and nationalism, and military establishments under strict civilian control. Today, Japan maintains its armed forces in spite of a constitution that prohibits the nation from ever possessing such forces or waging war again. That constitutional pacifism in Japan also continues to be undermined by a bilateral security agreement with the USA and a strong US military presence in Japan, primarily in Okinawa. Japan began sending soldiers abroad in 1992 and has continued doing so frequently for disaster relief and peacekeeping missions under strictly limited conditions but never for combat. In Germany, popular anti-war sentiment coexists uncomfortably with both a considerable weapons industry and military power that has been utilized in a variety of international missions, ranging from humanitarian and peacekeeping operations to combat under NATO tutelage. The military establishments of both Japan and Germany carefully train and closely monitor service members' conduct domestically and abroad in silent acknowledgement of the Second World War's legacy, including its variations on sexuality and sexual violence. Yet, at least for Japanese camps abroad we know that condoms are available and information about where sex can be safely bought circulates among service members.[75]

In Japan, where the post-war constitution stipulates a commitment to 'international peace based on justice and order', renounces 'war as a sovereign right of the nation and the threat or use of force as means of settling international disputes', and negates the 'right of belligerency of the state', the

---

73 Naimark, *The Russians in Germany*, pp. 69, 71–6, 114.

74 Timothy Snyder, *Bloodlands: Europe Between Hitler and Stalin* (New York: Basic Books, 2010).

75 Sabine Frühstück, 'After Heroism: Must Real Soldiers Die?' in Sabine Frühstück and Anne Walthall, eds., *Recreating Japanese Men* (Berkeley: University of California Press, 2011), pp. 91–111.

conservative political and educational elite worries about the negative impact that truthful history education about the Second World War – and the sexual slavery system in particular – might have on the patriotism of younger generations.[76] In Germany, public schools, media, museums and a variety of other institutions and events continue to educate citizens about the history of National Socialism and the Second World War, although the tone and depth of these efforts vary across the country and the breadth of sexual violence discussed above has never found a public place equal to other National Socialist horrors.

Since the Second World War, we have gained a better understanding of how the militarization of sexuality in wartime and beyond continues to sustain hegemonic masculinity. Officially, at least, nations pledge to punish sexual violence during war. The Tokyo War Crimes Tribunal addressed military sexual slavery and sexual violence, and carried out prosecutions.[77] But only at the Women's International War Crimes Tribunal on Japan's Military Sexual Slavery, held in Tokyo, 7–12 December 2000, was the Japanese emperor, wartime commander-in-chief, pronounced guilty of crimes against humanity, including sexual slavery. Even now some remain resistant to such judgements. Despite the public formal acknowledgement of and apologies for Japan's imperialist role in the Asia-Pacific war by former Prime Minister Miyazawa Kiichi and others, including current Emperor Akihito, the debate about the sexual slavery system has been repeatedly reignited by such conservative and right-wing politicians as former governor of Tokyo Ishihara Shintarô, mayor of Osaka Hashimoto Tôru, and current Prime Minister Abe Shinzô.[78]

In part as a result of the Nuremberg and Tokyo trials, among other events, in legal terms, at least, sexual violence against combatants and civilians no longer passes as an unfortunate but inevitable component of war but is firmly understood as a war crime. Wartime rape, including forced prostitution, has become illegal under international law, specifically the 1949 Geneva Conventions and the 1977 Protocols. Since the 1990s, 'sexual violence has drawn international attention as particularly gruesome, atrocious, widespread, and systematic in many conflicts', such as in the former Yugoslavia, Rwanda,

76 Sabine Frühstück, *Uneasy Warriors: Gender, Memory, and Popular Culture in the Japanese Army* (Berkeley: University of California Press, 2007).
77 Yuma Totani, *The Tokyo War Crimes Trial: The Pursuit of Justice in the Wake of World War II* (Cambridge, Mass.: Harvard University Asia Center, 2008).
78 For a list of such apologies, see http://en.wikipedia.org/wiki/List_of_war_apology_statements_issued_by_Japan.

Sierra Leone, Haiti, Liberia, Peru, Guatemala, and more recently the Democratic Republic of Congo, the Central African Republic and Uganda.[79] As Carol Gluck has recently pointed out, the International Criminal Court in Rome signed a statute in 1998 that named rape, sexual slavery and enforced prostitution both as war crimes (Article 8) and as crimes against humanity (Article 7) and thus put gender violence in the same category as torture and genocide. Most recently, the redefinition of rape as 'violation of innate human rights' instead of the original notion of the violation of 'honour' and 'dignity', resulted in the indictment – and conviction – for rape as a crime against humanity in the Yugoslav tribunal in The Hague in 2001.[80]

Despite these epoch-making legal developments, the sexual ideology that governed much sexual violence during the Second World War has proven quite durable beyond that war. At least some military cultures continuously reinforce a specific form of military masculinity and continue to sustain the far reach of militaristic ideals more generally. The sexualization of military aggression in military training, the militarization of sexuality during wartime, and specific local conditions continue to play a role in the occurrence of sexual violence in wars and other military contexts to this day. This is so in part because aggression training continues to be intensely gendered and sexualized in order to condition soldiers to individualize and internalize otherwise impersonal and abstract territorial conquest. The ongoing problem of sexual assaults in the US military, whether within its military academies or on the front lines, is a related case in point. A 2007 survey of women soldiers' experience in the Iraq War, for instance, showed significant post-traumatic stress syndrome resulting from the combination of combat stress and sexual assault.[81] Almost one-third of a nationwide sample of female veterans seeking health care through the Veterans Administration reported that they were raped or exposed to attempted rape during their service; 37 per cent of that

---

79 Rhonda Copelon, 'Toward Accountability for Violence against Women in War: Progress and Challenges', in Elizabeth D. Heineman, ed., *Sexual Violence in Conflict Zones: From the Ancient World to the Era of Human Rights* (Philadelphia: University of Pennsylvania Press, 2011), pp. 232–56 (p. 232).

80 Carol Gluck, 'Operations of Memory: "Comfort Women" and the World', in Sheila Miyoshi Jager and Rana Mitter, eds., *Ruptured Histories: War, Memory, and the Post-Cold War in Asia* (Cambridge, Mass.: Harvard University Press, 2007), pp. 47–77 (pp. 74–5).

81 Sara Corbett, 'The Women's War', *New York Times Magazine*, 18 March 2007. Prior to the most recent reports of numerous rape incidents of female service members in Iraq and Afghanistan, the 2003 sexual assault scandal at the United States Air Force Academy prompted a 96-page *Report of the Defense Task Force on Sexual Harassment & Violence at the Military Service Academies*, submitted to then Secretary of Defense Donald H. Rumsfeld, 30 June 2005.

group reported having experienced multiple rapes; and 14 per cent said that they were gang-raped.[82] Furthermore, America's strategic shift to the Middle East and Central Asia, Maria Höhn and Seungsook Moon have pointed out, means that the US military to an increasing degree relies on and helps sustain the global sex industry, just as in post-war Germany, France, Okinawa and South Korea.[83]

82 Steven Myers, 'Another Peril in War Zones: Sexual Abuse by Fellow GIs', *New York Times*, 28 December 2009.
83 Maria Höhn and Seungsook Moon, 'Empire at the Crossroads?', in Höhn and Moon, eds., *Over There: Living with the U.S. Military Empire from World War Two to the Present* (Durham, NC: Duke University Press, 2010), pp. 397–408 (p. 402).

16

A war for liberty

On the law of conscientious objection

JEREMY K. KESSLER

Introduction

One common understanding of the Second World War is that it was a contest between liberty and tyranny. For many at the time – and for still more today – 'liberty' meant the rule of law: government constrained by principle, procedure, and most of all, individual rights. For those states that claimed to represent this rule-of-law tradition, total war presented enormous challenges, even outright contradictions. How would these states manage to square the governmental imperatives of military emergency with the legal protections and procedures essential to preserving the ancient 'liberty of the subject'? This question could be and was asked with regard to many areas of law. The traditional order of property rights, for instance, was already in disarray thanks to the shocks of monopoly capitalism, labour militancy, the First World War, and the profound crisis of the Great Depression. Yet few rights would more directly test a wartime government's conception of the rule of law than the right of conscientious objection. The refusal of alleged pacifists to participate in the often lawless violence of the Second World War posed fundamental practical and normative challenges for all combatants – but especially for those who understood themselves to be fighting for individual liberty.

Of course, conscientious objection did not emerge as a problem for liberal governance in 1939. New governmental efforts to regulate civilian and military manpower in the late nineteenth century first raised the possibility – even the necessity – of accommodating individuals on the basis of their moral and religious beliefs. And the years preceding the First World War saw the institution of the first formal systems of military conscientious objection. During the interwar period, however, the virtue of maintaining, let alone extending, such individual rights protection was cast into doubt. By the early

1930s, for instance, Hitler and Stalin had parted ways with any liberal notion of legal culture, and launched breakneck programmes of centralization and collectivization. As a consequence, Russian and German pacifists would fare far worse in the Second World War than they had in the First World War, when their treatment was not so different from that of pacifists in the Entente. But even within the liberal nations, most interwar leaders felt that a radical transformation of the rule of law was necessary to create more secure and just democratic societies. By studying the development of the law of conscientious objection from the First World War through the Second World War, we can track both the growing separation between liberal and totalitarian governance and the internal crisis that wracked liberalism in these years.

During the Second World War, all of the major belligerents fought with conscript armies, but only a few created a formal legal process to accommodate pacifist citizens swept up in the draft – Great Britain, some of its Dominions, and the USA. Historians and legal scholars generally attribute the exceptional character of American, British and Commonwealth conscientious objector policy to long-term patterns in Anglo-American legal and political development.[1] These scholars emphasize a shared encounter with religious pluralism, a shared tradition of military voluntarism, and above all, a shared commitment to individual rights against state interference. Such explanations from the persistence of classical liberalism fit neatly within the ideology of the Anglo-American war effort itself, an ideology that framed the war as a struggle 'to establish, on impregnable rocks, the rights of the individual'[2] and to preserve 'that conception of liberty ... which we have all inherited'.[3] But this contrast between totalitarian lawlessness and the traditional liberties preserved by the Western powers is too static: the 'conception of liberty' for which the Anglo-Americans fought was in a state of flux during the 1930s and 1940s.

---

1 See, for example, Martin Ceadal, *Pacifism in Britain, 1914–1945: The Defining of a Faith* (Oxford: Clarendon Press, 1980); George Flynn, *Conscription and Democracy: The Draft in France, Great Britain, and the United States* (Westport, Conn.: Greenwood Press, 2002), 189–206; Edward P. Cain, 'Conscientious Objection in France, Britain and the United States', *Comparative Politics* 2:2 (1970), 275–307; John Whiteclay Chambers II, 'Conscientious Objectors and the American State from Colonial Times to the Present', in Charles Moskos and John Whiteclay Chambers II, eds., *The New Conscientious Objection: From Sacred to Secular Resistance* (Oxford University Press, 1993), pp. 23–47.

2 Winston Churchill, 'War Speech', 3 September 1939, in *Winston S. Churchill: His Complete Speeches, 1897–1963*, ed. Robert Rhodes James (New York: Bowker, 1974), vol. VI.

3 President Franklin D. Roosevelt, Proclamation 2425, Selective Service Registration, 16 September 1940 (www.presidency.ucsb.edu/ws/index.php?pid=15858).

The Second World War did not so much interrupt as continue by other means a decades-long, transatlantic debate about the proper relationship between personal liberty and state power. For many – perhaps most – participants in the debate, the task at hand was to shuck off traditional conceptions of liberty as much as to preserve them, to forge a third way between classical liberalism and the totalitarian alternatives. For dogged defenders of the old liberal line, however, the choice remained stark. Conscription – and the treatment of those who opposed it – became one important site for this larger contest. The law of conscientious objection developed by the Anglo-American combatants reflected less the liberal inheritance for which they claimed to fight than their ongoing search for novel forms of governance, a search that would continue in the post-war years.

This chapter describes the American, British and Commonwealth approaches to conscientious objection during the Second World War and contrasts them with how other belligerents treated those who refused to fight. In doing so, it reveals unexpected similarities between Anglo-American and alternative approaches, and important differences within the Anglo-American world. Taken together, these comparisons and contrasts situate Second World War conscientious objection within a larger legal struggle over the structure and limits of state power. This legal struggle shaped how the war was fought, even as its final resolution depended on the outcome of the war itself.

Conscientious objection before the Second World War

The problem of individual conscientious objection was first recognized by modern states in the last third of the nineteenth century. In the thirty years following the Franco-Prussian War, the Prussian model of universal military training and service swept the globe. Earlier forms of conscription had included broad regional, socio-economic, and sectarian carve-outs: urban populations, for instance, were often exempted; the wealthy could almost always buy their way out; and provisions were at times made for historically recognized pacifist religious sects. The Prussian model, on the other hand, was aimed at militarizing a far greater proportion of the population. This development in military affairs accompanied a more general expansion of state capacity, as governments around the world struggled to contour and control industrial revolution and global integration. In response, dissident social groups sought at times to restrain, at times to commandeer the increasingly powerful and pervasive military and administrative apparatus of the modern state.

The legal practice of conscientious objection – by which individuals seek to prove the sincerity of their non-violent convictions to government officials and thereby receive some form of individualized accommodation – emerged from this struggle over growing administrative power. Yet even as administrative power was itself a source of concern for anti-militarists, the practice of conscientious objection tended to take on administrative form, as executive officials – rather than courts – became responsible for adjudicating the sincerity of the individual conscience. This approach to the problem of conscience accompanied a more general turn to administrative decision-making in the late nineteenth and early twentieth centuries, as an increasingly interconnected world demanded expert, adaptive management of workers, owners, immigrants and soldiers.

The phrase 'conscientious objection' actually entered the English language in the 1850s, when a movement arose in England to oppose novel legislation mandating compulsory smallpox vaccination of children.[4] Eventually, the British Parliament responded to this campaign, instituting a system of 'conscientious objection' with the Vaccination Act of 1898. The Act's conscience clause required parents to satisfy a justice of the peace that they 'conscientiously believe[d] that vaccination would be prejudicial to the health of the child'.[5] Many anti-vaccinationists and their Liberal supporters in Parliament objected to this juridical procedure, arguing that conscience could simply not be judged.[6] They got their way in 1907 when the new Liberal government passed an Act allowing for a simple declaration of conscientious objection, without further judicial or administrative inquiry. The rate of objection nearly doubled after the passage of the Act.

Contemporaneously with Britain's smallpox regime, a few countries implemented formal protections for the individual conscience within their military manpower systems. The first to do so was Norway. In response to a peace movement backed by Quakers and socialists, the Norwegian Department of Defence issued a series of administrative orders between 1900 and 1902, first recommending that conscientious objectors be assigned to non-combatant duty and then exempting all sincere religious pacifists from

---

4 Nadja Durbach, *Bodily Matters: The Anti-Vaccination Movement in England, 1853–1907* (Durham, NC: Duke University Press, 2005), pp. 172–3; cf. Michel Foucault, *Security, Territory, Population: Lectures at the Collège de France, 1977–1978*, ed. Michel Senellart, trans. Graham Burchell (Basingstoke: Palgrave Macmillan, 2005), pp. 85–91.
5 Durbach, *Bodily Matters*, p. 180.
6 John Rae, *Conscience and Politics: The British Government and the Conscientious Objector to Military Service, 1916–1919* (London: Oxford University Press, 1970), pp. 43–4.

the draft.[7] A year later, the Australian Defence Act – which made all male citizens between the ages of 18 and 60 liable for compulsory service in time of 'emergency' – directed administrators to design procedures to accommodate religious pacifists in the event of conscription.[8] When compulsory military training was finally introduced in 1910, the procedures were as follows: if a man could prove the sincerity of his objections to war – whether religious or non-religious – in a common law court, he would then be entitled to non-combatant duties, generally in the armed forces. In New Zealand, which also established compulsory military training in 1910, military authorities rather than courts were left to make the determination of sincerity, and only religious objectors were recognized as legitimate.[9] In Australia and New Zealand, as in Norway, a coalition of religious and secular, socialist peace activists extracted these concessions to the anti-war conscience.

When the debate over military conscription came to Britain in 1916, Parliament adopted the language of 'conscientious objection' from the anti-vaccination context. It did not, however, adopt either the 1907 or the 1898 models for accommodating the anti-vaccination conscience, or the Australian model for dealing with military training objectors. Neither a simple affirmation nor appearance in a common law court sufficed to secure conscientious objector status. Instead, alleged conscientious objectors had to prove their sincerity before administrative tribunals established to determine each and every registrant's draft status.[10] During the First World War, the USA, Canada and New Zealand similarly assigned the task of determining the sincerity of objectors to administrative decision-making bodies. Australia would remain the exception in both the First and the Second World Wars, leaving this determination to common law courts. Elsewhere, expanding administrative states would both pose the primary threat to conscience and provide the primary arena for its accommodation.

While Denmark remained neutral during the First World War, it did mobilize its citizenry and – in response to forceful opposition from the Danish Socialist Party – passed a law providing for conscientious objection

---

7 Peter Brock, *Against the Draft: Essays on Conscientious Objection from the Radical Reformation to the Second World War* (University of Toronto Press, 2006), pp. 133–4.

8 Hugh Smith, 'Conscience, Law and the State: Australia's Approach to Conscientious Objection Since 1901', *Australian Journal of Politics and History* 35 (1989), 13–28 (p. 15).

9 R. L. Weitzel, 'Pacifists and Anti-Militarists in New Zealand, 1909–1914', *New Zealand Journal of History* 7:2 (1973), 123–47 (pp. 136–7).

10 James McDermott, *British Military Service Tribunals, 1916–1918* (Manchester University Press, 2011), pp. 36–58.

in 1917.[11] Mirroring the majority approach in Anglo-American nations, this law delegated the details of accommodation to administrators. Neutral Holland also mobilized during the First World War and, in response to draft resistance and lobbying from 'progressive clergy', implemented a system of conscientious objection in November 1917.[12] Whereas Denmark first established a right of conscientious objection by legislative act, conscientious objection in the Netherlands, as in Norway, was initially a matter of purely administrative regulation. The minister of war convened a 'secret advisory commission' to which draftees could appeal for conscientious objection recognition; if the commission found a man sincere, he would be assigned to non-combatant duty in the military.

Across the rest of the Continent during the First World War, the ability of pacifists to avoid punishment for refusing to fight depended on long-standing customs and informal practices. These norms and practices generally applied only to members of certain well-pedigreed pacifist religious sects; secular and heterodox pacifists were out of luck. In Russia, for instance, a host of non-violent Christian groups – including 'the Molokans, Dukhobors, Baptists, Evangelical Christians, Mennonites, and Tolstoians' – protested against the universalization of conscription in 1874.[13] But only the Mennonites – exempted from military service since their immigration under Catherine the Great – received formal accommodation. Other sectarians who refused to serve were tried by military courts and suffered incarceration and torture. The number of objectors and the severity of punishments both increased dramatically during the First World War. As will be discussed below, the situation changed dramatically after the Bolsheviks seized power.

Germany tended to be more accommodating than Imperial Russia, though mostly through informal means. Following the introduction of universal military service in 1867, Mennonite conscripts were permitted, 'if they so wished, to serve in the army in noncombatant capacity'.[14] While most Mennonites gave up their pacifist commitments in response to national emergency, about a third of the West Prussian Mennonites requested and received non-combatant duties during the First World War. Army officers

11 Henning Sørensen, 'Denmark: The Vanguard of Conscientious Objection', in Moskos and Chambers, eds., *The New Conscientious Objection*, pp. 106–13 (pp. 106–7).
12 J. G. van de Vijver, 'Appendix E: The Netherlands', in Moskos and Chambers, eds., *The New Conscientious Objection*, pp. 220–5 (p. 221).
13 Joshua A. Sanborn, *Drafting the Russian Nation: Military Conscription, Total War, and Mass Politics, 1905–1925* (Dekalb: Northern Illinois University Press, 2003), pp. 183–4.
14 Brock, *Against the Draft*, p. 282.

arrived at similar arrangements with Bible Students (Jehovah's Witnesses) and Seventh-Day Adventists, most of whom served in the medical corps. The military code made clear the informality of these accommodations, explicitly rejecting religious conscience as a legitimate ground of disobedience. Those men who refused orders to perform either non-combatant or combatant duty on conscientious grounds were, however, usually sent to psychiatric clinics for medical rather than military discipline.

In France, there is no record of even informal accommodation of pacifists during the First World War. Would-be conscientious objectors 'were treated as common deserters and given harsh sentences', generally one year in prison – with or without hard labour – for a first refusal to serve, followed by two-year stints after each subsequent refusal.[15] Scholars have attributed the French refusal to accommodate even the religious pacifist at times to the cultural dominance of just-war Catholicism, at times to the cultural dominance of republicanism or civic nationalism.[16] Both of these explanations are, however, troubled by the fact that between 1793 and 1815, 'all citizens whose denomination and moral beliefs forbid the bearing of arms' were able either to pay their way out of service or request non-combatant duty.[17] In any event, France may well have been the least accommodating of all belligerent nations during the First World War.

As this brief survey of First World War practice shows, accommodation of the anti-war conscience was – with the sole exception of Australia – managed by administrative decision-makers. National practices differed in four major respects: the range of anti-war beliefs accommodated; the range of accommodations offered; the civilian or military character of the decision-making process; and the formality of the decision-making process. German and Russian practices involved a relatively informal, military-run administrative process that recognized a narrower range of sectarian reasons for objecting. Anglo-American and Danish practices involved a relatively formalized, civilian-run administrative process that recognized a wider range of religious – and in some cases secular – reasons for objecting to combat service.

---

15 Michel L. Martin, 'France: A Statute but No Objectors,' in Moskos and Chambers, eds., *The New Conscientious Objection*, pp. 80–97 (p. 83).

16 See, for example, Margaret Levi, *Consent, Dissent, and Patriotism* (Cambridge University Press, 1997), pp. 185–6.

17 Flynn, *Conscription and Democracy*, pp. 200–1; Michel Martin, *Warriors to Managers: The French Military Establishment since 1945* (Chapel Hill: University of North Carolina Press, 1981), p. 167 n. 28.

Even in more accommodating countries, however, advocates for conscientious objectors argued that the administrative process was far too severe. In the USA, for instance, a new generation of civil libertarians assailed as tyrannical the administrative resolution of conscience claims.[18] Similar dissatisfaction with the administration of conscientious objection arose in Britain, where military service tribunals became an exemplary case of the danger of having administrators adjudicate individual rights.[19] In general, the debate over conscientious objection during the First World War foregrounded a larger debate about the increasing power administrators wielded over individual citizens in modern nation states, and about the relative independence of those administrators from judicial and legislative oversight. Although this debate had been well under way before the war, the unavoidable primacy of executive decision-making in wartime kicked it into a higher gear.[20]

The interwar debate over administrative governance

In the aftermath of the First World War, Britain and the USA dismantled most of their draft apparatus and many other wartime agencies. Yet their administrative states continued to grow in the 1920s, rapidly expanding during the 1930s in response to economic crisis. This growth occasioned a heated debate over the legitimacy of administrative governance – policy-making and adjudication by executive officials rather than legislatures and courts. While anxiety about administrative governance was particularly acute in Britain and the USA, '[e]ven in countries with well-established bureaucratic traditions, the emergence of the welfare state entailed a significant diffusion of normative power away from elected legislatures into an often fragmented and complex executive and administrative sphere'.[21] This section focuses on the Anglo-American debate, as it was mainly in this context that conscientious objection found a legitimate home during the Second World War. Nevertheless, continental developments – particularly the nightmarish

---

18 See, for example, John Nevin Sayre, 'Political Prisoners in America', *The Dial* (28 December 1918), 623–4.
19 See, for example, Robert S. W. Pollard, *Conscience and Liberty* (London: Allen & Unwin, 1940).
20 Daniel Ernst, 'Ernst Freund, Felix Frankfurter and the American Rechtsstaat: A Transatlantic Shipwreck, 1894–1932', *Studies in American Political Development* 23 (October 2009), 171–88 (p. 174).
21 Peter L. Lindseth, 'The Paradox of Parliamentary Supremacy: Delegation, Democracy, and Dictatorship in Germany and France, 1920s–1950s', *Yale Law Journal* (2004), 1341–415 (p. 1343).

picture of administrative governance that rose from the ruins of Weimar – would haunt the Anglo-American debate and the administration of conscientious objectors that it produced. Across the globe, administrative governance provided the framework within which the Second World War belligerents would sustain, transform or abandon the legal protection of individual liberty.

At the heart of the interwar debate over administrative governance were three interrelated questions about the proper relationship between agencies, courts and legislatures. The first question was to what extent administrative agencies should make policy. The classic nineteenth-century understanding of the function of administrators was to execute policies designed by legislatures, not to design their own. But in the early twentieth century, as social and economic conflict intensified, legislatures became increasingly keen to delegate policy-making authority to administrative experts. And even in the absence of such explicit delegation, the line between making and simply implementing policy tended to blur, worrying those committed to a classical liberal conception of the separation of powers.

The second question also concerned a blurring of the separation of powers – the increasing use of administrative bodies to adjudicate disputes involving individual rights. Here, it seemed, the legislature and executive were usurping the authority of common law courts, while imposing a mode of adjudication stripped of traditional procedural protections.[22]

Finally, the third question concerned the extent to which common law courts could review administrative decisions. This question tended to piggy-back on the first two, because judicial review, if available, might obviate many of the dangers of administrative policy-making and adjudication. If, on the other hand, the administrative state continued to take on legislative and judicial functions while escaping judicial review, a 'New Despotism' would be at hand – or so argued an influential 1929 manifesto

---

22 There was one basic difference between British and American anxieties about the erosion of the separation of powers. In the USA, legislative delegation of policy-making or adjudicative power to the executive branch was considered presumptively *unconstitutional*, the legislature, executive and judiciary being co-equal branches of government. In English law, on the other hand, there was no strictly 'constitutional' impediment to the delegation of legislative and judicial powers to the Executive', given 'the legal omnipotence of the King in Parliament'. Nonetheless, such delegations were seen as undermining prudential and customary norms. See Stanley A. de Smith, 'Delegated Legislation in England', *Western Political Quarterly* 2:4 (1949), 514–26; Michael Taggert, 'From "Parliamentary Powers" to Privatization: The Chequered History of Delegated Legislation in the Twentieth Century', *University of Toronto Law Journal* 55:3 (2005), 575–627 (pp. 595–6).

written by the Lord Chief Justice of England, Lord Hewart.[23] The goal of the new despots of the civil service, according to Lord Hewart, was 'to subordinate Parliament, to evade the Courts, and to render the will, or the caprice, of the Executive unfettered and supreme'.[24] At stake was not just the place of judicial and legislative bodies in the constitutional order, but their practical ability to check the executive's disregard for individual rights.

Critics of administrative governance on both sides of the Atlantic trumpeted the warnings of Lord Hewart, but he also had many detractors. One of the most important American opponents of the Hewart line happened to be the man who had written the blueprint for the USA's system of conscientious objection during the First World War – Felix Frankfurter. As an assistant in Woodrow Wilson's War Department, Frankfurter sketched the centralized administrative process that the government used to accommodate a wide range of anti-war belief within the draft apparatus.[25] This system exhibited many of the features of administrative governance considered so problematic by critics – policy-making powers unrestrained by legislative guidance, informal adjudicatory procedure, limited judicial review. During the inter-war period, Frankfurter would play a key role in extending these features of administrative governance to other areas of the American state.

Frankfurter and his allies objected to the conventional mode of evaluating administrative action, which asked 'whether private interests [were] adequately safeguarded' by a given administrative scheme.[26] For them, the task of administration was the expert balancing of public and private interests, not the sacrifice of the former to the latter: 'we can't consider whether private interests are safeguarded without equally considering the public interests that are asserted against them.'[27] As Frankfurter put it in a landmark 1927 article, the ultimate task of administrative law was to 'fashion ... instruments and processes at once adequate for social needs and the protection of individual freedom'.[28] If the priority of the classical view was the 'constraint of administrative discretion, Frankfurter thought it [should be] the freeing of administrators from the oversight of common-law courts'.[29]

23 Lord Hewart of Bury, *The New Despotism* (London: Ernest Benn, 1929).
24 Ibid., p. 17.
25 Jeremy K. Kessler, 'The Administrative Origins of Modern Civil Liberties Law', *Columbia Law Review* 114 (June 2014).
26 Ernst, 'American Rechtsstaat', p. 180.
27 Ibid. (quoting Frankfurter).
28 Felix Frankfurter, 'The Task of Administrative Law', *University of Pennsylvania Law Review* 75 (1927), 614–21 (p. 617).
29 Ernst, 'American Rechtsstaat', p. 173.

Frankfurter was not blind to the risk of abuse, even constitutional abuse, from unchecked administrators. But, he argued, such risk did not merit the imposition of legalistic constraints by courts of law: '[u]ltimate protection' against constitutional abuses by administrators was 'to be found in the people themselves, their zeal for liberty, their respect for one another and for the common good'.[30] In addition to this external, political check, he also recommended internal, administrative safeguards: 'a highly professionalized civil service, an adequate technique of administrative application of legal standards, a flexible, appropriate and economical procedure ... easy access to public scrutiny, and a constant play of criticism by an informed and spirited bar'.[31] This vision of a democratic and professional civil service free from judicial second-guessing inspired the generation of bureaucrats that built and manned the American state during the New Deal and the Second World War.

Frankfurter's influence also extended across the Atlantic. It was under his supervision that the legal scholar John Willis wrote the leading English response to Lord Hewart's assault on administrative governance – *The Parliamentary Powers of English Government Departments*.[32] At the heart of the book was a workmanlike review of English legal history, demonstrating that the parliamentary delegation of '"extraordinary" powers' to administrative officials had a long pedigree – a point that no less an authority than F. W. Maitland had made fifty years earlier.[33] Those like Lord Hewart who sought to instigate a moral panic over the 'new despotism' were engaged, Willis contended, in politically motivated scaremongering; they sought not to save the rule of law but to use a cramped interpretation of it to derail social and economic reform. In applying doctrines such as the 'strict interpretation' of statutes and the 'presumption in favour of the liberty of the subject', judges were simply imposing their 'personal preferences', preferences hostile to the egalitarian work of the bureaucracy.[34]

---

30 Frankfurter, 'Task of Administrative Law', p. 618.
31 Ibid.
32 John Willis, *The Parliamentary Powers of English Government Departments* (Cambridge, Mass.: Harvard University Press, 1933); see also Taggert, 'From "Parliamentary Powers" to Privatization', pp. 581–2.
33 Taggert, 'From "Parliamentary Powers" to Privatization', pp. 585–6; see also Peter L. Lindseth, 'Reconciling with the Past: John Willis and the Question of Judicial Review in Interwar and Postwar England', *University of Toronto Law Journal* 55 (2005), 657–89 (p. 664).
34 Willis, *Parliamentary Powers*, pp. 51, 80.

In an era in which some of the sharpest legal minds in Germany dedicated themselves to overthrowing the Weimar Republic and Stalin launched his collectivization drive and staged his show trials, Anglo-American debates about judicial review of administrative decision-making may look like a sideshow. But these debates were themselves occasioned by the same rolling political and economic crisis that toppled Weimar and entrenched Stalin's rule. How would liberal democracy survive in this world of class conflict, ethnic violence and 'Leviathan-states'?[35] For defenders of the classical interpretation of liberal democracy, the only hope was the preservation of an independent judiciary capable of preventing a tyrannical executive from suppressing both individual freedom and parliamentary decision-making. For the new guard, led by the likes of Frankfurter and Willis, the survival of both individual and parliamentary autonomy depended on the ability of expert administrators to solve social and economic problems.

While in Britain, the Liberal and Labour partisans of government intervention lost control of Parliament in 1931, the Democratic Party's electoral victories in 1932 and 1936 marked the closest the USA ever came to a labour government, dedicated to public regulation in the interest of the working man. This New Deal regime went on to create vast new administrative bodies, including the National Industrial Recovery Administration and the National Labor Relations Board, agencies empowered to manage the growing struggle between labour and capital and the inefficiencies of market competition. By standing in the way of these efforts, courts only escalated the social and economic crisis that threatened to overwhelm all branches of government – or so the advocates of administrative governance argued. On the other side, critics of the New Deal assailed the administrative state's expanding control of economy and society as a surrender to – rather than a stopgap against – totalitarian rule.

Frustrated by the courts' continuing resistance to New Deal administration, President Roosevelt used the momentum of his landslide re-election in 1936 to try to end the logjam once and for all. During the campaign, Roosevelt had characterized his political opponents as 'economic royalists' and the courts as the seat of oligarchy.[36] Flush with victory in the early

---

35 The term *l'état-Leviathan* was French jurist René Cassin's. See Jay Winter and Antoine Prost, *René Cassin and Human Rights: From the Great War to the Universal Declaration* (Cambridge University Press, 2013), pp. 84–5.

36 Jared A. Goldstein, 'The American Liberty League and the Rise of Constitutional Nationalism' (8 August 2012) (http://papers.ssrn.com/sol3/papers.cfm?abstract_id=2126811).

months of 1937, the President announced his plan to pack the Supreme Court – to force the retirement of some Justices and to expand the number of Justices he himself could appoint. He also pushed for an executive reorganization plan that would heighten presidential control over the administrative state. Although intended to marginalize New Deal critics, these initiatives actually gave new ammunition to the partisans of judicial review and a more restrained administrative state.

In the context of the Nazi government's escalating domestic and international aggression, the American President's efforts to consolidate power were especially vulnerable to charges of 'administrative absolutism'.[37] Many lawyers, including many former supporters, saw Roosevelt's move against the Supreme Court as an assault on the very foundations of the rule of law. Indeed, one of the leading opponents of court-packing, the New York corporate lawyer Grenville Clark, had voted for Roosevelt twice and supported many aspects of the New Deal. But in response to Roosevelt's attack on judicial autonomy, Clark launched a campaign to recover the prestige of the courts. Central to this campaign was his identification of judicial review with the protection of non-economic individual rights – civil liberties or '"personal" liberties'.[38]

While earlier British and American critics had focused on the threat that administrative governance posed to property rights, Clark and his ideological allies developed a new language that drew morally charged parallels between fascist and communist oppression of ethnic and religious minorities abroad and big government at home. They framed their challenge to the New Deal state as a defence of the rights of freedom of speech and religion, the rights of minorities, and the right to a fair trial. This framing enabled Clark and his elite legal allies at the American Bar Association (ABA) to co-opt a set of issues that had long been the concern of left-wing groups such as the American Civil Liberties Union (ACLU). But whereas these groups had often welcomed New Deal administrators as effective enforcers of the rights of workers, minorities and dissenters against the tyranny of wealthy

---

37 *Annual Report of the American Bar Association* 63 (1938), 331–68 (p. 343).
38 For the following discussion of Clark's advocacy, see Gerald T. Dunne, *Grenville Clark: Public Citizen* (New York: Farrar, Straus & Giroux, 1986); Jeremy K. Kessler, 'First Amendment Challenges to Economic Regulation in the Jehovah's Witness Cases' (paper presented at Freedom of Expression Scholars Conference, Yale Law School, 4 May 2014); Laura Weinrib, 'The Liberal Compromise: Civil Liberties, Labor, and the Limits of State Power, 1917–1940' (PhD dissertation, Princeton University, May 2011), pp. 412–29.

interests and jingoistic mobs, Clark and the ABA identified the courts as the bulwark of civil libertarianism.

Felix Frankfurter, himself a co-founder of the ACLU, was left to insist that Clark's 'view of the Supreme Court, as the great safe-guard of those democratic institutions that you and I so passionately care about, is much too romantic and too simplified'.[39] For Frankfurter, the first decades of the twentieth century had shown that the best checks on administrative decision-making were democratic politics and professional expertise, not the courts. Frankfurter himself had helped to design an administrative system protecting the rights of conscience during the last war. Unsurprisingly then, when Roosevelt appointed him to the Supreme Court in 1939, Frankfurter attempted to hold the line against the new vogue for judicial supremacy in the name of civil liberty. At that moment, however, the outbreak of the war in Europe reframed this domestic struggle over the American legal order.

One of the first cases that Grenville Clark and his newly formed Bill of Rights Committee championed involved the refusal of Jehovah's Witness children to participate in public-school flag salute ceremonies. In 1935, the Witnesses had begun to object to these ceremonies in response to the suffering of their German brethren, who were being imprisoned and shot for refusing to salute the Führer and to serve in the recently reinstituted system of German conscription.[40] Insensitive to this dynamic, American public schools began expelling recalcitrant Witness children. By the time the dispute reached the Supreme Court in 1940, Europe was in flames.

Indeed, Felix Frankfurter's majority opinion in *Minersville School District* v. *Gobitis*[41] became known as 'Felix's Fall of France opinion', as the Justice wrote it while the Wehrmacht marched toward Paris.[42] In it, Frankfurter reasoned that legislators and administrators were best suited to resolve the 'clash of rights' that arose between democratic majorities and dissenters, and that in such a time of international crisis, it was reasonable for political

39 Felix Frankfurter to Grenville Clark (1 July 1937), Grenville Clark Papers, Series VI, Box 1, Dartmouth College.
40 Shawn Francis Peters, *Judging Jehovah's Witnesses: Religious Persecution and the Dawn of the Rights Revolution* (Lawrence: University Press of Kansas, 2000), pp. 24–8; Peter Brock, 'Conscientious Objectors in Nazi Germany', in Peter Brock and Thomas P. Socknat, eds., *Challenge to Mars: Essays on Pacifism from 1918 to 1945* (University of Toronto Press, 1999), pp. 370–9 (pp. 370–1).
41 310 US 586 (1940).
42 Mary Dudziak, *War Time: An Idea, Its History, Its Consequences* (Oxford University Press, 2012), p. 59.

decision-makers to value national solidarity over individual difference.[43] Justice Harlan Fiske Stone, the lone dissenter in the case, Grenville Clark, and much of the legal press reached the opposite conclusion. As Nazi tyranny ran wild, they argued, it was all the more important to maintain – even expand – Anglo-American traditions of civil liberty and judicial power.

As this example suggests, the onset of war in Europe intensified the debate over administrative governance and its relationship to individual liberty. But war also scrambled that debate's battle-lines. While *Gobitis* appeared to pit partisans of political autonomy and state power against partisans of judicial review and civil liberties, many of those who celebrated the Jehovah's Witnesses' cause also wholeheartedly supported a contemporaneous push for peacetime conscription – an expansion of state control unprecedented in the nation's history. Indeed, at the same moment that he assailed the power of school boards to compel Witnesses to salute the flag, Grenville Clark was working *with* Felix Frankfurter to convince President Roosevelt to support a new draft law. And in writing that law, Clark would make sure to insulate the draft apparatus from judicial review.[44]

Just as earlier civil libertarians had argued that administrative agencies were often themselves the fairest and most efficient defenders of individual freedom, Clark saw the peacetime draft as a civil libertarian institution, uniquely capable of fairly and efficiently managing the manpower necessary to oppose totalitarianism. His preamble to the Selective Training and Service bill stressed both the libertarian and egalitarian character of the draft, explaining that its purpose was 'to insure the independence and freedom of the people of the United States', and that 'in a free society it is just and right that the obligations and risks of military training and service be shared by all'.[45] Given this framing, the more autonomy for draft administrators the better.

Clark's advocacy *for* the draft and *against* compulsory flag salutes in the spring of 1940 exemplified the legal and ideological challenge that the Second World War posed to its liberal belligerents. On the one hand, they were fighting a war for liberty, and as such needed to uphold and even extend their commitment to the personal freedoms that totalitarian regimes distinctively

---

43 Letter from Felix Frankfurter to Harlan Fiske Stone (27 May 1940), 4, Container 65, Harlan Fiske Stone Papers, Library of Congress.

44 A Bill to Protect the Integrity and Institutions of the United States Through a System of Selective Compulsory Military Training and Service, S. 4164 (20 June 1940), 12, Series IXA, Box 8, GCP.

45 Ibid., 1.

opposed. On the other hand, to contend with totalitarian mobilization, these nations would have to expand their administrative capacity, further eroding traditional notions of individual rights against state interference. Conscientious objectors stood at the intersection of these two wartime trajectories; it would largely fall to draft administrators to resolve the contradictions of a total yet ostensibly libertarian war.

Conscription and conscientious objection in the Second World War

The interwar debate over administrative governance had been structured by an overly-simplistic contrast between classical liberal and totalitarian approaches to the rule of law. Yet, as the war years would demonstrate in terrifying detail, this distinction captured a real truth. Whereas the states that fought the First World War had been broadly convergent in their legal systems, they drifted further and further apart during the interwar years. When it came to the recognition of individual rights and other legal constraints on executive decision-making, the conduct of the totalitarian nations departed markedly from both their more liberal counterparts and their own predecessor regimes. Yet the conduct of the 'liberal' nations also differed from the classical liberal ideals that so much anti-totalitarian rhetoric invoked. As the war made clear, the outcome of the interwar debate over administration in the Anglo-American world had been a hybrid form of governance that sought a middle path between classical liberalism and totalitarianism. It was this new administered liberalism that would contend with the forces of fascism during the Second World War and – shortly after the war's end – with Soviet communism.

The treatment of conscientious objectors during the Second World War reflected this complex legal landscape. While there were significant continuities with the First World War when it came to which countries afforded formal recognition of the individual conscience, the actual experiences of conscientious objectors depended upon their nations' changing attitudes toward state power. Imperial Germany, for instance, had offered few if any formal protections during the First World War. Yet state authorities had not been absolutist in their treatment of pacifists. As discussed above, military officers frequently assigned such men to the medical corps, and those who refused or did not receive this offer of alternative service were usually sent to psychiatric hospitals, not prisons. With Hitler's rise to power, however, Germany became a regime of total mobilization, in which a collective notion of civic identity went hand-in-hand with unfettered administrative authority. This legal and ideological transformation pervaded the military, eroding informal mores that had once created space, however narrow, for pacifist dissent.

By the time Germany reinstituted conscription in 1935, Hitler had already arrested many of the leaders of the interwar peace movement.[46] The 1935 draft law made no provision for conscientious objectors, and those who refused to serve altogether or sought non-combatant duty generally found themselves before a military court.[47] Military judges could offer defendants non-combatant duty in lieu of a conviction for disobedience, but they rarely did so, and a few Protestant sectarians who specifically requested medical duty during the war were executed. Scholars know of at least 280 trials of objectors, the majority of which involved Jehovah's Witnesses.[48] Before the outbreak of war, conviction for refusal to perform military service – whether combatant or non-combatant – meant a prison sentence, often followed by confinement in a concentration camp. Beginning in September 1939, however, execution became the norm.[49]

If anything, the Soviet Union was even more oppressive than Germany when it came to the treatment of pacifists during the Second World War. Yet the Revolution itself had not assured this outcome. As in other areas of Russian law, including the law of divorce and abortion, the early years of the Bolshevik regime witnessed significant liberalization in conscientious objection policy. In 1918, when Lenin reinstituted conscription, he reached a deal with Vladimir Chertkov, the leader of the Tolstoyans and founder of the United Council of Religious Communities (UCRC).[50] Codified in a January 1919 decree, the deal provided for alternative civilian service or unconditional exemptions for anyone with sincere religious objections to war.[51] The decree also authorized Chertkov's UCRC to 'offer expert testimony on the applications of conscientious objectors before people's courts', which would then select the appropriate form of accommodation.[52] Although 'extremely liberal' in form, this system was undermined from the start by 'militant atheists in

---

46 Brock, 'Conscientious Objectors in Nazi Germany', p. 370.
47 Ibid., pp. 371–5.
48 Karsten Bredemeier, *Kriegsdienstverweigerung im Dritten Reich* (Baden-Baden: Nomos, 1991).
49 Brock, *Against the Draft*, p. 427.
50 Ibid., p. 329.
51 Paul D. Steeves, ed., *The Modern Encyclopedia of Religions in Russia and the Soviet Union* (Gulf Breeze, Fla.: Academic International Press, 1993), vol. V, pp. 223–5.
52 Sanborn, *Drafting the Russian Nation*, p. 193.

the Commissariat of Justice', and by provincial officials during the Civil War, who frequently shot religious pacifists in contravention of superior orders.[53] The end of the Civil War halted these executions, but by 1923 the Commissariat of Justice had severely restricted the possible grounds of objection, and by 1929 only the long-recognized Mennonites could rely on accommodation. Even this carve-out for Mennonites was eliminated in 1935; imprisonment or forced labour was a pacifist's likely fate. By the time war broke out, 'most pacifists were either dead or dispersed and forced into silence'.[54] While details are sketchy, it appears that the few pacifists who continued to resist military service during the Second World War died by firing squad.[55]

Like the totalitarian powers to its west, Imperial Japan had no provision for conscientious objection in its draft law. Yet it also had few conscientious objectors. An upper-class strain of Japanese pacifism influenced by Tolstoyan and Quaker ideas generally did not advocate for conscientious objection at all, recommending a sacrificial death on the battlefield.[56] Those pacifists who more actively resisted the wartime state generally came from poorer backgrounds, and were affiliated with millenarian sects such as the Jehovah's Witnesses.[57] Authorities suppressed these groups after 1928, and many were imprisoned during the war.

France was the outlier in being a liberal democratic belligerent without formal protections for conscientious objection.[58] Like Russia, though for quite different reasons, the Third Republic had briefly flirted with liberalization but then retreated. Confronted with the horrors of the First World War, France had seen a surge of interest in conscientious objection in the 1920s: the Committee for the Defence of Conscientious Objection formed in 1920, followed by the League for Legal Recognition of Conscientious Objection in

---

53 Brock, *Against the Draft*, p. 330.
54 Sanborn, *Drafting the Russian Nation*, p. 199.
55 William Edgerton, *Memoirs of Peasant Tolstoyans in Soviet Russia* (Bloomington: Indiana University Press, 1993), pp. 106–7.
56 Brock, *Against the Draft*, pp. 190–1.
57 Cyril Powles, 'Pacifism in Japan, 1918–1945', in Brock and Socknat, eds., *Challenge to Mars*, pp. 427–39 (pp. 435–6).
58 Denmark, the Netherlands and Norway all had conscientious objector provisions on the books during the Second World War, though conscription was suspended in the Netherlands and Norway during the war, so conscientious objection was not an issue in these countries. Neutral Denmark maintained a system of conscientious objection throughout the period of German occupation, carrying forward the system it had first implemented in 1917. See Nils Petter Gleditsch and Nils Ivar Agøy, 'Norway: Toward Full Freedom of Choice?', in Moskos and Chambers, eds., *The New Conscientious Objection*, pp. 114–26 (pp. 114–15); Sørensen, 'Denmark', p. 108; van de Vijver, 'Appendix E: The Netherlands', p. 221.

1924.[59] In the early 1930s, however, the Ministries of War and the Interior took pains to clamp down on pro-conscientious objection propaganda, enlisting religious leaders to associate it with communism.[60] These efforts were largely successful. In 1931, a lone proposal to legalize conscientious objection was introduced in the National Assembly, but it went nowhere, and in 1934 the government actually dissolved the League for Legal Recognition.[61] Prior to the fall of France, the French military prosecuted and imprisoned those men who refused to serve; conscription was suspended under the Vichy regime. In the wake of the Second World War, a coalition of socialists, communists, Christian Democrats and Protestant ministers sought a legislative amnesty for pacifists imprisoned during the war. The Senate defeated their bill in 1953, however, and it would be another decade before France legalized conscientious objection.

With Russia, Germany and Japan all narrowing earlier protections for pacifists, and France maintaining its First World War policies, it is a striking fact that the other liberal democratic belligerents – all English-speaking – expanded their recognition of conscientious objection during the Second World War. In the USA, which instituted peacetime conscription for the first time in 1940, the draft was itself billed as a civil libertarian institution, a shield against totalitarian threats to individual freedom. The initial peacetime draft bill was written by a prominent civil libertarian, Grenville Clark, and he enlisted the help of another civil libertarian hero, Judge William Clark, in urging Congress to pass it. Two years earlier, Judge Clark had issued a landmark ruling striking down municipal restrictions on labour rallies[62] and, drawing on this pedigree, he assured the House Military Affairs Committee that there was nothing totalitarian about conscription:

> There are worse things than laying down ... life in the cause of freedom and justice ... [W]e see no analogy between selective compulsory military service and totalitarianism or any other 'ism.' Such an argument might be as logically applied to taxation. Our government must be defended as it is supported – by all of its citizens.[63]

---

59 Martin, 'France: A Statute but No Objectors', pp. 83–4.
60 Norman Ingram, 'The Circulaire Chautemps, 1933: The Third Republic Discovers Conscientious Objection', *French Historical Studies* 17 (1991), 387–409.
61 Flynn, *Conscription and Democracy*, p. 201.
62 *Hague* v. *CIO*, 25 F.Supp. 127 (D.NJ 1938), aff'd 307 US 496 (1939). *Hague* was the first case in which Grenville Clark's Special Committee on the Bill of Rights participated.
63 House Military Affairs Committee, Selective Compulsory Military Training and Service, Hearings Before the House Committee on Military Affairs, H.R. 10132 (1940), 20.

Most other civil libertarians and peace activists agreed with – or didn't think it worth resisting – the Clarks' egalitarian and libertarian arguments for the draft. Instead, these activists focused their energies on expanding accommodations for conscientious objectors. In the summer of 1940, the American Civil Liberties Union worked with the American Friends Service Committee (AFSC), a Quaker group, to lobby for a bill more respectful of draftees' civil liberties.[64] Three major changes emerged from their efforts. First, the definition of legitimate conscientious objector was expanded from any official member of a pacifist religious sect to any person who objected to all wars on the basis of his 'religious training and belief'. Second, designated conscientious objectors would have a choice of non-combatant service in the military *or* alternative service under civilian command. Finally, the Department of Justice, not local draft boards, would determine in the first instance who was a legitimate conscientious objector.

The third change was probably the most radical, as it removed the initial determination of conscientious objector status both from local control and from the federal agency whose primary responsibility was furnishing sufficient manpower for the war effort (the Selective Service System). As we will see, English advocates had also sought to centralize decision-making about conscientious objection and to insulate such decision-making from general manpower planning. The move against local control is particularly striking as it was at odds with a contemporaneous critique of administrative governance that associated centralization with the suppression of civil liberty. When it came to protecting unpopular and marginal groups, advocates were quite certain that national bureaucrats were preferable to local dignitaries.

The Department of Justice itself, however, blanched at the enormous increase in workload that conscientious objector determinations would entail.[65] If later intra-departmental debates are any indication, the Department was also likely concerned that the taking on of such a seemingly adjudicative task by a prosecutorial body would itself threaten the separation of powers.[66] In the end, Quaker lobbyists convinced the bill's conference committee to endorse a compromise whereby local draft boards would make

---

64 E. Raymond Wilson, 'Evolution of the Conscientious Objector Provisions in the 1940 Conscription Bill', *Quaker History* 64 (Spring 1975), 3–15 (p. 7).

65 J. Garry Clifford and Samuel R. Spencer, Jr., *The First Peacetime Draft* (Lawrence: University Press of Kansas, 1986), pp. 221–3. Wilson, 'Evolution of the Conscientious Objector Provisions', p. 10.

66 See, for example, Assistant to the Attorney General Matthew McGuire to Attorney General Robert Jackson (10 October 1940), 1, Container 93, Robert H. Jackson Papers, Library of Congress.

the initial determinations of whether an individual qualified as a conscientious objector and, if so, what kind of alternative service he should perform – non-combatant duty in the military or work under civilian command. If the man appealed this initial classification, however, the Department of Justice would review his file and make a recommendation to the relevant appeals board. A final appeal could be made to the Presidential Appeals Board.[67]

Throughout the back-room negotiations over administrative responsibility for determination of conscientious objector status, there was never any disagreement that the conclusions reached by the administrative process would be final. Many of the civil libertarians who composed and supported the draft law – civil libertarians such as Grenville Clark and William Clark – had fought, and would continue to fight, for expanded judicial review of administrative decision-making in other contexts, especially when civil libertarian rights were at stake. But, in their eyes, the draft law's administrative resolution of conscience claims served another kind of civil libertarian end – the defeat of totalitarianism. This administrative approach to the problem of conscientious objection was the norm across the English-speaking world, though the types of accommodation provided and the variety of procedural protections afforded to would-be objectors differed from country to country.

British political and military leaders had been reluctant to bring back conscription at all, given the bloody cost of the First World War. In the wake of Hitler's 1933 rise to power, the military focused on strengthening air defence, a strategic vision that aligned with the government's fiscal concerns. Both the Americans and the French, however, pleaded with the British leadership to reinstitute conscription and commit to continental defence. Eventually, the Chamberlain government did so – in response to Hitler's April 1939 abrogation of the Munich accords. British anti-war groups were more critical of the move to conscription than their American counterparts would be in 1940, but the government dampened criticism by adopting a highly accommodating stance toward conscientious objectors.[68]

Such an accommodating approach was uncontroversial, motivated by a pervasive sense that the local military service tribunals had failed to adequately protect conscience in the last war.[69] Three First World War conscientious objectors served in the wartime government, and Lord

---

67 Julien Cornell, *The Conscientious Objector and the Law* (New York: John Day, 1944), pp. 25–6.
68 Flynn, *Conscription and Democracy*, p. 194.
69 Cain, 'Conscientious Objection', pp. 288–99.

Beveridge, Neville Chamberlain and Winston Churchill all spoke publicly in support of the lenient treatment of conscientious objectors. In 1940, for instance, Beveridge told an audience of radio listeners that 'admission of the right of conscientious objection to serve in war is the extreme case of British freedom. Nor have I any doubt that it makes Britain stronger in war rather than weaker.'[70]

In the First World War, general military service tribunals had heard conscientious objector claims alongside a host of other requests for deferment or exemption. But the National Service (Armed Forces) Act of 1939 established a semi-autonomous system of 'Conscientious Objectors' Tribunals' to be administered by the Minister of Labour and National Service.[71] Under this system, any man required to register by the Act could ask to be provisionally included on the register of conscientious objectors, indicating whether he sought a total exemption, non-combatant duty in the military, or alternative civilian work. One of nineteen Local Conscientious Objector Tribunals would then consider the application. Either the applicant or the Minister of Labour could appeal a local decision to one of six Appellate Tribunals. The Appellate Tribunal's decision was final, and the 1939 Act explicitly provided that 'no determination of a local tribunal or the Appellate Tribunal ... can be called into question in any court of law.'[72]

In many respects the British law was more accommodating than the American. First and foremost, it created an entire administrative apparatus devoted to the consideration of claims of conscience, an apparatus at least formally walled off from the general manpower concerns faced by the local military service tribunals. Second, it offered the possibility of an unconditional exemption from all forms of wartime service, though less than 5 per cent of conscientious objectors actually received this status.[73] Third, the British civilian service option involved far less coercion than the American version. In Britain, conscientious objectors offered alternative civilian service were simply directed to seek employment in a relatively undermanned industry – agriculture or forestry, for instance. In the USA, on the other hand, the main non-military service was labour in Civilian Public Service

---

70 Quoted in Denis Hayes, *Challenge of Conscience: The Story of the Conscientious Objectors, 1939–1949* (London: Allen & Unwin, 1949), p. 6.
71 Rachel Barker, *Conscience, Government, and War: Conscientious Objection in Great Britain, 1939–1945* (London: Routledge, 1982), p. 12.
72 Pollard, 'Conscientious Objectors', p. 74.
73 Roger Broad, *Conscription in Britain, 1939–1964: The Militarisation of a Generation* (London: Routledge, 2006), p. 188.

Camps, administered by the Selective Service System in conjunction with the non-governmental National Service Board of Religious Objectors. These camps were often de facto, if not de jure, under military command. Fourth, the law designated that the chairmen of local tribunals should be judicial officers – county court judges or sheriffs. While these tribunals were administrative bodies, not common law courts, it was thought that the participation of judicial officers would nonetheless lead to fairer treatment of objectors. In the USA, there was no such effort to judicialize the administration of the draft boards. Fifth and finally, the British law recognized both religious and secular beliefs as legitimate grounds for conscientious objection, while the American statute required that the would-be conscientious objector demonstrate 'religious training and belief'.[74] On the other hand, American administrators often waived this requirement in practice.

The American system did offer would-be conscientious objectors two major advantages over the British system – an additional layer of administrative appeal and a more centralized process of administrative oversight. First, the existence of a single Presidential Appeals Board, overseen by the Director of Selective Service himself, gave individuals a third shot at receiving some form of accommodation. Second, both the Selective Service Director's responsibility for this final appellate body and the statutorily mandated involvement of the Department of Justice in advising on conscientious objector claims meant that objector advocates could focus their lobbying on a single group of officials in Washington, DC. This group of officials tended to be much more sympathetic to alleged conscientious objectors than the volunteers who staffed the local draft boards; this group also possessed the power to overrule those boards' decisions.[75] In Britain, in contrast, conscientious objector advocates continually complained about the decentralized decision-making of the Local and Appellate Tribunals, and called in vain on the Ministry of Labour and National Service to step in to normalize the process.[76] Accordingly, while official and academic histories of the US

---

74 Selective Training and Service Act, 54 Stat. 885 (1940).
75 Mulford Sibley and Philip Jacob, *Conscription of Conscience: The American State and the Conscientious Objector, 1940–1947* (Ithaca: Cornell University Press, 1952), pp. 71–81.
76 Barker, *Conscience, Government, and War*, pp. 16–17, Flynn, *Conscription and Democracy*, pp. 195, 200; Cain, 'Conscientious Objection', p. 292; Robert S. W. Pollard, 'Tribunals for Conscientious Objectors', in Robert S. W. Pollard, ed., *Administrative Tribunals at Work* (London: Stevens & Sons, 1950), p. 8.

Selective Service System tend to trumpet its 'Jeffersonian' structure – a fair amount of decision-making being left in the hands of local volunteers – the US system was in fact highly centralized when it came to the administration of conscientious objectors.

By war's end, the USA had inducted 10 million men and heard about 75,000 claims of conscientious objection, assigning 25,000 conscientious objectors to non-combatant service in the military, and 12,000 to work in Civilian Public Service camps.[77] Another 12,000 men were initially assigned non-combatant or alternative service status on conscientious grounds, but were later reclassified (either because they withdrew their objections, or were deferred on other grounds, such as an occupational or dependency deferment). About 20,000 applications were rejected. Britain inducted about 8 million men and women through military and labour drafts, and considered approximately 60,000 claims of conscientious objection, 1,000 from women.[78] About 20,000 conscientious objectors served in a civilian capacity, 15,000 performed non-combatant duty in the military, and 3,000 received unconditional exemptions. A third of all applications were rejected

The Canadian system of conscientious objection was less accommodating than either the British or the American. The initial National Resources Mobilization Act of June 1940 and its attendant regulations offered conscientious objection only to members of pacifist religious sects.[79] Members of a few sects – such as the Dukhobors and Kanadier Mennonites – were entitled to an absolute exemption, while the rest would have to perform some form of alternative service. Over the first two years of the draft, authorities eliminated the absolute exemptions, while gradually expanding the acceptable grounds of objection, first to sincere pacifists of any religious denomination, and then to any sincere pacifist who based his objections on some religious training and belief – the American baseline. Uniquely in the Anglo-American world, Canadian law provided no appeal – not even an administrative appeal – from these Boards' decisions.[80] These decisions were absolutely final, and could not be attacked in any court – even by a writ of habeas corpus. By

---

77 Flynn, *Conscription and Democracy*, pp. 191–2; Nicholas A. Krehbiel, *General Lewis B. Hershey and Conscientious Objection during World War II* (Columbia: University of Missouri Press, 2011), p. 145.

78 Barker, *Conscience, Government and War*, Appendix 3; Broad, *Conscription in Britain*, p. 188; Flynn, *Conscription and Democracy*, pp. 167, 196.

79 Thomas P. Socknat, 'Conscientious Objection in Canada', in Brock and Socknat, eds., *Challenge to Mars*, pp. 256–71.

80 Pollard, 'Conscientious Objectors', p. 77.

December 1945, about 10,000 Canadian men had received conscientious objector status.[81]

In a 1943 report, New Zealand's National Service Department bemoaned the problem of conscientious objection: 'Though comparatively few in number, conscientious objectors have proved to be by far the most difficult section of the population to deal with in the matter of national service.'[82] Of about 300,000 men that New Zealand mobilized for war, 5,000 sought conscientious objector status.[83] About 2,000 were deferred on other grounds, about 1,800 were assigned to non-combatant duty or work of national importance, and about 1,200 appeals were rejected outright. The task of identifying genuine objectors fell to six Armed Service Appeals Boards established to hear the full range of deferment and exemption claims. These Boards operated under the authority of the Director of National Service, and only the Director could reopen cases to introduce new evidence, such as evidence of fraud. Otherwise, the Boards' decisions were final, and no administrative appeals process existed. Those objectors assigned to 'work of national importance' were supervised by an additional 'Special Tribunal' with the power to compel evidence, conduct inquiries, and issue orders to ensure that a conscientious objector's salary never exceeded that of a soldier's. This Special Tribunal was closed to the public and its decisions could also not be appealed. As Robert Pollard remarked a year after the end of the war: 'The Special Tribunal has an advantage from the Government's point of view because there is no right of appeal from its decisions and yet it appears to be a judicial body.'[84]

As in the First World War, Australia proved the exception to the Anglo-American rule of administrative adjudication of conscientious objector claims. By 1941, any registrant could apply to a local court of summary jurisdiction, seeking either non-combatant duty or alternative civilian service on grounds of his 'conscientious beliefs'.[85] And, beginning in 1939, the Australian government expanded the First World War definition of

---

81 John A. Toews, *Alternative Service in Canada during World War II* (Canadian Conference of the Mennonite Brethren Church, 1959), p. 61.
82 Quoted in Pollard, 'Conscientious Objectors', p. 81.
83 J. E. Cookson, 'Pacifism and Conscientious Objection in New Zealand', in Brock and Socknat eds., *Challenge to Mars*, pp. 292–311.
84 Pollard, 'Conscientious Objectors', p. 81.
85 Ibid., p. 75; Peter Brock and Malcolm Saunders, 'Pacifists as Conscientious Objectors in Australia', in Brock and Socknat, eds., *Challenge to Mars*, pp. 272–91; Smith, 'Conscience, State, and the Law'.

'conscientious beliefs' to cover both religious and secular objections, mirroring British practice. Either the government or the applicant could appeal a decision of the local court to a court of full jurisdiction in the same territory or commonwealth; this judicial check seems to have largely satisfied pacifist observers of the draft process. Of the approximately 2,700 conscientious objector applications considered during the war, about 1,000 men were assigned to non-combatant duty in the military, another 1,000 to alternative civilian service, and about 600 were rejected.[86] Forty men received unconditional exemptions and sixty applications were still pending at war's end. In contrast to New Zealand, which assigned nearly 600 would-be conscientious objectors to detention camps, it appears that fewer than 200 Australian pacifists were imprisoned.[87] Similarly, Australia rejected just over 20 per cent of conscientious objector applications, while New Zealand rejected 40 per cent. These rejection rates were the outliers in the Anglo-American world, with British and American rates clustered in the middle.

Conclusion

This survey of conscientious objector policies during the Second World War shows both a diversity of approaches within the Anglo-American world and a stark divergence between the Anglo-American powers and their more statist and collectivist enemies and allies. As in the First World War, two long-running factors help explain the divergence: relative strategic isolation and a legal tradition of individual rights protection. Yet interwar strategic and legal developments had dampened the significance of both of these factors. Advances in air and naval power and the emergence of an enormous Pacific theatre threw into question the free security once enjoyed by island nations. At the same time, economic and political upheaval during the interwar period had eroded the traditional practices of individual rights protection. By the early years of the Second World War, the Anglo-American belligerents had parted ways with the rigid enforcement of property and

---

86 Brock and Saunders, 'Pacifists as Conscientious Objectors in Australia', pp. 284, 290 n. 41.

87 Compare ibid., p. 284 with Cookson, 'Pacifism and Conscientious Objection in New Zealand', p. 301. The number of conscientious objection claims actually adjudicated by authorities was about the same in the two nations.

contract rights, and had consigned whole areas of individual rights protection to powerful and pervasive administrative agencies shielded from judicial review.

Given these strategic and legal transformations, it is all the more striking that the Anglo-American nations actually *strengthened* their protections for conscientious objectors during the Second World War. They were indeed fighting a war for liberty, and their treatment of conscientious objectors reflected this ideological critique of totalitarian power as a threat to individual expression and identity. Yet to secure liberty of conscience, Anglo-American nations used the tools of administrative governance that many considered to be a major domestic threat to liberty, even a capitulation to totalitarian rule. There is a striking parallel here with the trajectory of Anglo-American economic governance, in which the 1930s and 1940s saw an unprecedented expansion of state intervention in the interest of securing the market economy.

One takeaway from these wartime experiments might have been that there was in fact no fundamental tension between administrative governance and individual liberty. Some English and American appraisals of wartime and post-war administrative governance made just this point, citing the treatment of conscientious objectors as one example among many of the synthesis of efficiency, expertise and rights protection that administrative decision-making had provided.[88] Indeed, one could say that the administrative resolution of conscience claims helped to defeat the totalitarian enemy in two senses: first, by maintaining an efficient system of manpower management uninterrupted by slow and inexpert judicial review; second, by incorporating an anti-totalitarian norm of freedom of conscience within the draft apparatus.

Yet this was not the lesson that the Anglo-American and European legal communities generally took from the war. Rather, they gradually accepted the identification of totalitarian misrule with administrative autonomy, and imposed new judicial checks on administrative decision-making.[89] Some

---

88 See, for example, *United States* v. *Estep*, 327 US 114, 137 (1946) (Frankfurter, J., concurring); Pollard, 'Tribunals for Conscientious Objectors', p. 9; Note, 'Restrictions on Judicial Review of Administrative Agencies Exercising Emergency Powers – Duty to Obey Orders Prior to Determination of Invalidity', *Yale Law Journal* 56 (1947), 403, 407.

89 Lindseth, 'The Paradox of Parliamentary Supremacy', pp. 1385–415; Reuel Schiller, 'Reining in the Administrative State: World War II and the Decline of Expert Administration', in Daniel Ernst and Victor Jew, eds., *Total War and the Law: The American Home Front in World War II* (Westport, Conn.: Praeger, 2002), pp. 185–206 (p. 200).

of the earliest instances of this new vogue for the judicial enforcement of individual rights would occur in the draft law context.[90] In this regard, the 'civilianization'[91] of Western militaries and the judicialization of their administrative states would go hand-in-hand, twinned features of a new war for liberty – a Cold War increasingly defined by American commitments to nuclear superiority and lightly regulated markets.

90 See, for example, *Dickinson v. United States*, 346 US 389 (1953); Jürgen Kuhlmann and Ekkehard Lippert, 'The Federal Republic of Germany: Conscientious Objection as Social Welfare', in Moskos and Chambers, eds., *The New Conscientious Objection*, pp. 98–105.
91 Jacques van Doorn, *The Soldier and Social Change* (London: Sage, 1975); James J. Sheehan, *Where Have All the Soldiers Gone? The Transformation of Modern Europe* (New York: Houghton Mifflin, 2008).

17

Against war

Pacifism as collaboration and as resistance

DEVIN O. PENDAS

The Second World War was clearly one of the most extravagantly violent events in human history. Yet this extraordinary paroxysm of violence and destruction did not go unanswered. Critical responses included, on the pragmatic end, humanitarian efforts at amelioration, whether by older groups like the International Committee of the Red Cross (ICRC) and the national Red Cross Committee or the Friends Service Committee, or new creations like the United Nations Relief and Rehabilitation Administration (UNRRA). Some individuals also spoke out, often for partisan reasons, against specific forms of violence in the war, whether aerial bombardment or ethnic and racial genocide. But the most morally consistent and politically challenging response came from pacifists, who called into question the very basis of the war itself. Pacifists were the most consistent, reasoned, and above all, *radical* critics of the war. What did they do when confronted with arguably the greatest challenge to their beliefs in the history of the modern world? And what effect did their actions have on those around them? The argument here is that pacifists had a difficult time finding a path of consistent and politically relevant action, whether under the adverse conditions of occupation and authoritarianism or the more open conditions of the Western democracies. In response, pacifism evolved into a more *moral* and less *political* form of critique. During the course of the war, its place was ultimately taken by humanitarianism, which accepted the unavoidability of military violence, but sought to ameliorate its worst effects.

Pacifism had emerged from the First World War at the pinnacle of its global influence and prestige. The spectacular violence of that war, combined with its seeming futility and failure to achieve the grandiose political objectives articulated by wartime leaders, lent enormous credibility to pacifist arguments.[1] To this, one might add the impact of M. K. Gandhi's campaign of non-violent resistance to the British Raj, which began to take off in 1919 with the Rowlatt Satyagraha, an event which resonated strongly with at least some Western pacifists.[2] More fundamental, at this stage, were the tremendous hopes aroused by the new League of Nations for a practical alternative to war as a means of settling international disputes.[3] Pacifism, at least in the early interwar period, was respectable, an alliance between utopianism and pragmatism that made it safe for statesmen and radical activists alike.

Pacifism had long presented itself as an alternative to humanitarianism. Though both were originally rooted in Christian piety, pacifism had a perfectionist streak alien to the more pragmatic humanitarians. Above all, pacifism had its roots in the oppositional culture of dissenting Protestants, whereas humanitarians were always more intimately connected with the state. Even the International Committee of the Red Cross, which would adopt a strict neutralism, was closely bound up with the Swiss state, itself rigorously neutral in nineteenth- and twentieth-century European conflicts. As Louis Appia, one of the founders of the ICRC put it, 'To humanize war, if that is not a contradiction, is our mission . . . But once we have voiced our undisguised rejection of war, we must take it as it is, unite our efforts to alienate suffering.'[4] To that end, humanitarians, starting with the ICRC, had enlisted the aid of states, both to allow them to provide relief services to the wounded, to POWs and, eventually, to displaced civilians in wartime, and to begin crafting an international law of armed conflict that would regulate the degree and kind of violence permissible in war without seeking to prohibit war as such by means of the Geneva and Hague Conventions.[5]

---

1 For Britain, see Adam Hochschild, *To End All Wars: A Story of Loyalty and Rebellion, 1914–1918* (Boston: Houghton Mifflin Harcourt, 2011). For the USA, Charles Chatfield, *For Peace and Justice: Pacifism in America, 1914–1941* (Knoxville: University of Tennessee Press, 1971). For Gandhi's influence see James Finn, *Protest: Pacifism and Politics – Some Passionate Views on War and Nonviolence* (New York: Random House, 1967), p. 122 and Thomas Weber, 'Gandhi's "Living Wall" and Maude Royden's "Peace Army"', *Gandhi Marg* 10 (1988), 199–212.
2 R. Kumar, ed., *Essays on Gandhian Politics: The Rowlatt Satyagraha of 1919* (Oxford: Clarendon Press, 1971).
3 Mark Mazower, *Governing the World: The History of an Idea* (New York: Penguin, 2013), pp. 116–53.
4 Caroline Moorehead, *Dunant's Dream: War, Switzerland and the History of the Red Cross* (New York: Carroll & Graf, 1998), p. 22.
5 For the legal dimension, see Geoffrey Best, *Humanity in Warfare: The Modern History of the International Law of Armed Conflicts* (New York: Columbia University Press, 1980).

Although the ICRC had performed magnificently in the First World War, it emerged from the war internally divided, and in the shadow of more radical attempts to abolish war altogether, most notably of course in the so-called Kellogg-Briand Pact of 1928.[6] In the interwar period, pacifism, not humanitarianism, seemed to offer the best response – morally and politically – to the horrors of war. But the manifest failure of the League of Nations and the Kellogg-Briand Pact to so much as slow down, much less stop, the return of world war in the 1930s began decoupling pacifism from pragmatic politics. The horrors of the Second World War, and the challenges of occupation, would complete the process. Pacifism would be forced to retreat back into opposition, largely marginal to great power politics and – the Nuremberg interlude excepted – to the crafting of the post-war settlement. Where non-violence succeeded in the post-war world it was as a type of domestic reform activism, as in the American Civil Rights movement. The international arena after 1945 would be dominated by humanitarians, increasingly supplemented by human rights politics as a more encompassing moral frame for ameliorative projects.[7]

Because the Second World War was a deeply ideological conflict on all sides, there was a widespread perception among all participants that they were engaged in a great moral crusade to save the world from evil. Under these circumstances, opposition to the war was perceived, not as a perhaps naive but generally noble point of view. Rather, it was widely interpreted as support for the enemy, and hence as immoral. As George Orwell wrote in 1942 'Pacifism is objectively pro-fascist. This is elementary common sense. If you hamper the war effort of one side you automatically help that of the other. Nor is there any real way of remaining outside such a war as the present one.'[8] Similarly, Maude Royden, a personal friend of Gandhi's who had tried (and failed) to organize a 'peace army' in 1932 to prevent the Japanese assault on Manchuria by interposing itself between the two warring sides, turned against pacifism with the outbreak of war in Europe, writing in 1941 that 'the real emptiness of pacifism is shown by its absence of any constructive policy in the least equaling the heroism that is poured into the

6 H. Josephson, 'Outlawing War: Internationalism and the Pact of Paris', *Diplomatic History* 3 (1979), 377–90.

7 Jay Winter and Antoine Prost, *René Cassin and Human Rights: From the Great War to the Universal Declaration* (Cambridge University Press, 2013).

8 George Orwell, 'Pacifism and the War', in George Orwell, *The Collected Essays, Journalism, and Letters*, vol. II: *My Country Right or Left, 1940–1943* (New York: Harcourt, Brace, & World, 1968), pp. 220–9 (p. 226).

destructive necessities of war.'[9] In the authoritarian states – the Axis powers and the Soviet Union – opposition to pacifism was supplemented with often draconian state repression. But nowhere was the moral dilemma of pacifism in the face of total, ideological war more keenly apparent than in the occupied countries.

Pacifism under occupation

Pacifists in occupied countries faced particular challenges, since under occupation pacifism could function as either resistance or collaboration. In France, for instance, there was a notable strand of pacifism among French collaborationists, many of whom had been opponents of a French war against Germany in the first place.[10] Pacifism had been a prominent force in French political life in the run up to the war.[11] Indeed, the 'peace party' spanned the political spectrum in 1938–39, united around a shared commitment to 'anti-parliamentarianism, anti-communism, and pacifism'.[12]

Many of the representatives of this unofficial but influential peace party would become leading figures under Vichy. Pierre Laval, one of the architects of the Vichy regime and head of the government from 1942 to 1944, was only the most prominent of these. Laval, a pacifist already during the First World War, saw collaboration with the Germans as a means of preserving the peace, not as an end in itself.[13] Pacifism here meant preserving peace at almost any price, though Laval also saw it – as he had in the interwar period – as a precondition for domestic reform and rebirth. To be sure, Laval's anti-communism loomed large in his desire for collaboration with the Germans.[14] Yet, as he explained privately to the American ambassador to Vichy, Admiral Leahy, he believed that a German victory was preferable because 'he felt that an understanding could be reached [with Germany] which would result in a lasting peace in Europe.'[15]

---

9 Cited in Arthur Downing, 'Political Christianity in Action: The Crusades of Agnes Maude Royden', *The Journal of the Rutgers University Libraries* (http://reaper64.scc-net. rutgers.edu/journals/index.php/jrul/article/viewFile/1635/3075).

10 See, for example, for the French case, Jean Defrasne, *Le pacifism en France* (Paris: Presses Universitaires de France, 1994), p. 194.

11 Jean-Paul Cointet, *Histoire de Vichy* (Paris: Plon, 1996), p. 39.

12 Ibid., p. 43.

13 Cited in Desfrasne, *Le pacifism en France*, p. 196.

14 Fred Kupferman, *Laval* (Paris: Balland, 1987), p. 337.

15 Geoffrey Warner, *Pierre Laval and the Eclipse of France* (London: Eyre & Spottiswoode, 1968), p. 292.

Many in the non-communist French left had embraced pacifism in the 1930s, wishing to avoid another 'union sacrée' with conservatives on behalf of a war effort they feared would once again merely distract from the struggle on behalf of the working class. Moreover, the syndicalist left feared that another war would simply strengthen the Soviet Union, increasing the power of the communists in the unions, further weakening syndicalists within the working-class movement. Several of these syndicalist union leaders served in the Vichy government.[16] Pacifist intellectuals also migrated into the collaborationist camp during the war. Alain (the pen-name of the philosopher Émile Chartier), best known for his 1921 anti-war polemic *Mars ou la guerre jugée*, contributed articles to the collaborationist (and politically fascist) *Nouvelle revue française*, as did Jean Giono, the pacifist novelist and peasant populist.[17]

There was of course a deep ambiguity in the pacifism of collaboration, since, as Orwell pointed out, it amounted in practice to support for the German war effort. Laval's reluctant implementation of German compulsory labour recruitment policies is only the most glaring instance of this.[18] Unlike those who collaborated with the Germans out of fascist convictions, who often actively volunteered for military service on behalf of the Germans, pacifist collaborators tended to support the Germans because they viewed German victory as inevitable and felt that the sooner the war ended, the better for everybody. Indeed, as Laval put it in his post-war diary, written as self-justification during his treason trial, 'the real crime was not that of having been present when the humiliation of defeat was inflicted upon us. The real crime was to have launched France upon a war obviously lost in advance, since no preparation, either diplomatic or military, had been made to forestall defeat.'[19] Laval's expectation that German victory would mean lasting peace for Europe may have been naive, but it also reflected an understanding that peace on almost any terms ought to be the highest priority of French policy. 'What I wished above everything,' he said after the war, 'was a peace which would leave intact our territory and our colonial empire.'[20] Peace – even at the price of German victory, which Laval felt likely anyway – was the precondition, he felt, for the survival of both France and its empire. Here Laval's pacifist predilection for peace combined with

---

16 Ibid., p. 278.
17 Julian Jackson, *France: The Dark Years, 1940–1944* (Oxford University Press, 2001), pp. 87–8, 207–8.
18 Hubert Cole, *Laval: A Biography* (New York: Putnam, 1963), pp. 227–30.
19 Pierre Laval, *The Diary of Pierre Laval* (New York: Charles Scribner, 1948), p. 163.
20 Ibid., p. 167.

realpolitik and an erroneous assessment of Germany's military prospects to make German victory look preferable to active resistance.

Pacifists in occupied countries who were more committed to principle than pragmatism tended to respond rather differently. One can take as emblematic here, the Danish pacifist group, Aldrig mere Krig (No More War), the Danish chapter of War Resisters International. Committed to total pacifism – the opposition to all war under any circumstances – the membership aspired to an explicitly Ghandian vision of non-violence. For example, members were required to take a pledge promising that, 'since I regard war as a crime against humanity I will resist and refuse to participate in any form of war, whether for the sake of defense, civil war or aggression' and had to promise to be non-violent within the family as well as in the public sphere.[21] It should come as no surprise, then, that Aldrig mere Krig applauded the Danish government's decision not to resist the German invasion on 9 April 1940, lamenting only that it had not been taken sooner.[22]

Yet the Danish government, in some ways like its Vichy counterpart, also decided to pursue a policy of cooperation, which kept Danes in charge of their own politics until the end of August 1943, when the Germans imposed military rule. This policy of cooperation meant that the Danish government could not be seen as actively encouraging resistance to the Germans. This included pacifist agitation. The government banned all public meetings except church services on 12 April 1940, three days after the occupation. Aldrig mere Krig decided to comply, advising its members as well that 'every kind of public demonstration, either by speeches or by distribution of pamphlets etc., whether to civilians or to military personnel, must be avoided.'[23] Instead, Aldrig mere Krig decided to focus its attentions inward, seeking to preserve the organization by maintaining private contacts and arranging private meetings, urging its members to show the 'utmost caution and patience'.[24] In addition to simply trying to survive as an organization, Aldrig mere Krig tried to make preparations for relief work once the war was over. This allowed Danish pacifists to avoid mere passivity and to 'make a positive contribution in the future', as one member put it.[25]

21 Peter Kragh Hansen, 'Danish War Resisters under Nazi Occupation', in Peter Brock and Thomas P. Socknat, eds., *Challenge to Mars: Essays on Pacifism from 1918 to 1945* (University of Toronto Press, 1999), pp. 380–94 (p. 382).
22 Ibid., p. 385.
23 Ibid., p. 386.
24 Ibid., p. 387.
25 Ibid., p. 388.

When the Germans imposed military rule on Denmark at the end of August 1943, active resistance in the country increased, including a wave a strikes and sabotage, as well as sporadic acts of armed resistance. Aldrig mere Krig, however, decided against participating in active resistance, even of a non-militant kind. There was a great fear within the organization of the reprisals which they felt would inevitably follow systematic campaigns of sabotage. This would lead to countless deaths, and, perhaps worse, trauma-tize both the survivors and perpetrators. 'Such experiences will never be forgotten by the survivors or relatives – or by those ordered to carry out the executions.'[26] Consequently, Aldrig mere Krig ordered its members to 'have no truck with any kind of illegal activity'.[27] Pacifism here became passive, eschewing even those non-violent forms of political action Aldrig mere Krig had advocated before the war. There was little evidence here of the call to self-sacrifice characteristic of Gandhian Satyagraha.

Other committed pacifists, however, managed to find ways to resist the German occupation that were nevertheless compatible with their ideals of non-violence. In Norway, for instance, several prominent pacifist pastors and theologians participated in the civilian resistance, helping support even acts of sabotage, all the while still insisting that 'one's task as a Christian was to love one's enemies and conquer evil with good.'[28] Secular pacifists too took part in the Norwegian resistance. Yet many secular pacifists claimed after the war that the movement had been insufficiently prepared to mount a truly effective campaign of non-violent resistance, noting that, as one of them said, it 'requires training of an intensity equal to military preparation.'[29] So while individual Norwegian pacifists took part in underground resistance activities, circulating propaganda and supporting non-violent sabotage, there was no sustained campaign of non-violent non-cooperation.

The one partial exception to this was a campaign organized by Helga Stene, a Norwegian member of the Women's International League for Peace and Freedom, a women's pacifist group founded in the Hague in 1915. In 1942, the Nazis proposed to introduce compulsory ideological youth training and service for Norwegian youngsters. Stene organized a protest campaign by parents. According to the historian Torleiv Austad, 'in a letter to the Nazi authorities the parents had stated that they did not wish their children to

---

26 Ibid., p. 389.
27 Ibid., p. 390.
28 Torleiv Austad, 'Pacifists in Nazi-Occupied Norway', in Brock and Socknat, eds., *Challenge to Mars*, pp. 395–408 (p. 400).
29 Ibid., p. 404.

participate in the youth service because that would violate their con-sciences.'[30] The text of the letter was distributed by the Norwegian under-ground, and Austad estimates that as many as 70 per cent of parents participated. In the event, the letter campaign proved a success and plans to introduce compulsory Nazi ideological training were abandoned.

Much pacifist resistance in occupied Europe was of a 'spiritual' nature, trying to preserve ideals of non-violence and, frequently, Christian charity, in opposition to both Nazi ideology and the violence of the war more generally. The Dutch pacifist newspaper *Kerk en Vrede* (Church and Peace), a publica-tion of the Dutch Christian pacifist organization (also called Church and Peace) founded in 1924, published articles that preached the spirit of Christian love and explicated the theological basis of non-violence. *Kerk en Vrede* managed to also criticize Nazi ideology explicitly as well as implicitly, urging readers to distance themselves from 'the lies of our time, such as Folk and Race, Nationalism and Patriotism'.[31] After Church and Peace, along with all other Dutch peace organizations, was closed down by the Germans in March 1941, spiritual resistance continued, notably from prominent pastors, who preached anti-Nazi sermons, advocating pacifism and specifically criticizing the round-up of Jews then taking place in Holland.

Pacifists under authoritarian rule

If pacifists in occupied Europe faced few good choices, the paths available to pacifists in the authoritarian states involved in the war were even less palatable. Both the Axis powers and the Soviet Union outlawed pacifist activism and criminalized conscientious objection. At the same time, how-ever, the conditions under which opposition to war, or at least to the current war, could be and were expressed varied across these authoritarian regimes, as did the nature of the opposition. To start with the case of Japan, there was a small but meaningful pacifist movement, most strongly associated with the *mukyokai* (non-church Christianity) movement, which had been founded by Uchimura Kanzo in the nineteenth century, but which in the twentieth century evolved into a loose affiliation of like-minded Christians, mainly but not exclusively middle-class intellectuals.[32] The most prominent of these

---

30 Ibid., p. 405.
31 Henk van den Berg and Ton Coppes, 'For Church and Peace: Dutch Christian Pacifists under Nazi Occupation', in Brock and Socknat, eds., *Challenge to Mars*, pp. 409–24 (pp. 412–13).
32 Carlo Caldarola, *Christianity: The Japanese Way* (Leiden: Brill, 1989).

wartime members was Yanaihara Tadao. Yanaihara was a professor of colonial policy at Tokyo Imperial University, who became a pacifist in the wake of the Manchurian Incident.[33] Following his criticism of the invasion of China in 1937, Yanaihara was forced out of his academic post, and lived a precarious existence for the rest of the war as an independent evangelist, publishing a small Christian monthly, but instructing his disciples to stay quiet about his teachings, lest the police find out and arrest him.

Jehovah's Witnesses formed the other prominent strand of Christian pacifism in Japan. The Japanese branch was founded in 1926 by Akashi Junzo, himself converted while working in the USA. Akashi became a vocal critic of Japan's aggressive foreign policy in the 1930s. 'Japan's actions toward China are without doubt acts of aggression,' he wrote, 'whose result will be Japan's destruction. The Emperor (*tenno*) is only a solitary human being, not divine. Under the leadership of this man-Tenno, the plan to conquer all of Asia, nay all the world, is nothing but the megalomania of the militarists who are being manipulated by Satan.'[34] There was a strong millenarian streak to Jehovah's Witness pacifism, but also an element of Christian socialism. Akashi interpreted war, in keeping with his reading of American *Watchtower* publications, as being waged for the benefit of the wealthy at the expense of the downtrodden. 'Capitalists represent the main force in society and the national structure and are the ringleaders in war, our greatest evil.'[35]

These millenarian and socialist tendencies made the Jehovah's Witnesses a larger threat to the imperial regime than the more respectable academic pacifism of the *mukyokai* Protestants. Consequently, the Witnesses faced substantially greater police repression.[36] In 1942, the entire Japanese membership of the Jehovah's Witnesses were sentenced to prison terms of two to ten years, several of them dying in prison, before being released by the Americans in 1945.

If religious conviction – mainly Christian, though there were small numbers of syncretistic Buddhist pacifists as well – was the main source of strict pacifism in Japan during the war, many on the left, socialists and communists, came to oppose what they saw as Japan's aggressive war and embraced defeatism and anti-militarism. While perhaps not as uncompromising as total pacifism, this defeatist sentiment represented a far greater challenge to the Japanese war

---

33 Cited in Cyril H. Powles, 'Pacifism in Japan, 1918–1945', in Brock and Socknat, eds., *Challenge to Mars*, pp. 427–39 (p. 431).
34 Cited in ibid., p. 435.
35 Ibid.
36 Cyril H. Powles notes that this police repression was 'unsurprising'. Ibid.

effort than did the very small number of pacifists. Of the 67,422 individuals arrested under the 1925 Public Security Preservation Law between 1928 and 1943, only 1,780 were religious critics of the regime, while over 65,000 were leftists. Of those prosecuted, 5,447 were leftists versus 456 religious activists.[37] While communists in particular continued to advocate the revolutionary overthrow of the imperial system, and therefore cannot be considered pacifists in any sense, Japanese leftists nevertheless came to oppose what they saw as an unnecessary and unjust war.

As John Dower has demonstrated, this was not simply labour unrest, but rather reflected a fairly widespread sense of disillusionment with the Japanese war effort. As Dower summarizes the situation, 'to an increasing number of citizens, it appeared, defeat had come to seem no more onerous than protracted misery under war; for some it was actually preferable.'[38] Though most Japanese continued to support the emperor and probably even the war effort, such defeatism appears to have been widespread, and clearly worried the regime. In any event, the numbers of those who came to hope for Japanese defeat in *this* war clearly exceeded the relatively small number of pacifists who rejected *all* war. Defeatism, especially when it led to concrete actions, such as work slowdowns or strikes, could have a greater impact than a more thorough, but less active, pacifism. Rising defeatism in Japan indicates that opposition to the war tended to increase when prospects for victory seemed to diminish, and the justness of the cause for which the war was waged was called into question.

If the police in Japan harassed, arrested and imprisoned pacifists, repression in Nazi Germany was even more severe. Hitler viewed pacifism as among the gravest threats to Germany, linked in his mind to Germany's defeat in the First World War and to the arch-enemy, Judeo-Bolshevism. As he put it, in *Mein Kampf*, 'In actual fact the pacifist-humane idea is perfectly alright perhaps when the highest type of man has previously conquered and subjected the world to an extent that makes him the sole ruler of this earth. Then this idea lacks the power of producing evil effects in exact proportion as its practical application becomes rare and finally impossible. Therefore, first struggle and then we shall see what can be done.'[39] One German lexicon

---

37 All numbers are from John Dower, 'Sensational Rumors, Seditious Graffiti, and the Nightmares of the Thought Police', in John Dower, *Japan in War and Peace: Selected Essays* (New York: The New Press, 1993), pp. 101–54 (p. 111).
38 Ibid., p. 133.
39 Adolf Hitler, *Mein Kampf*, trans. Ralph Manheim (Boston: Houghton Miffflin, 1943), p. 288.

published during the Third Reich defined pacifism as 'fundamental opposition to war, which easily leads to treason, especially as a result of international cooperation; adherents of pacifism (pacifists) in Germany in particular were for the most part traitors. The liberal-democratic peace movement, with a strong Jewish influence, sought to resolve conflicts between states and peoples by excluding war ... The National Socialist revolution has struck a death blow to treasonous pacifism.'[40]

It is therefore hardly surprising that pacifists were among the first political opponents targeted by the Nazi regime in 1933.[41] On 28 February, the leading German peace organization, the Deutsche Friedensgesellschaft (DFG), was banned; its newspaper, *Das andere Deutschland* was prohibited a week later. Many prominent pacifists were among those arrested in the first wave of political terror in 1933 including perhaps most prominently Carl von Ossietzky. Ossietzky, who had already served time in 1931 for publishing details of the army's secret military preparations during the Weimar Republic, was rearrested by the Nazis after the Reichstag fire and was sent to a concentration camp. Awarded the Nobel Peace Prize in 1935, he died in May 1936 from tuberculosis contracted while in custody. Many other prominent pacifists went into exile, including Kurt Tucholsky, Helmut von Gerlach, Helene Stöcker and Harry Graf Kessler. Many exiled pacifists continued their political activities, most prominently in the exile sections of the German League for Human Rights, which had branches in Paris, Strasbourg, Prague and London. It was thanks to the efforts of Gerlach's Paris section that Ossietzky won the Nobel Peace Prize. Nonetheless, political and personal divisions among exile pacifists prevented the formation of a truly united German pacifist opposition in exile.

As elsewhere, many pacifists who remained in the Third Reich tended, when possible, to retreat into 'inner emigration', to oppose the regime more in their prayers than by engaging in dangerous acts of resistance. For religious pacifists, the relatively accommodating stances of the Evangelical and Catholic churches with the regime, especially in the early years, may have undermined any inclination to more open resistance.[42] Because organized pacifism was

---

40 From the 1940 edition of the Meyer Lexicon, cited in Karl Holl, 'Pazifismus', in Otto Brunner, Werner Conze and Reinhart Koselleck, *Geschichtliche Grundbegriffe: Historisches-Lexikon zur politisch-sozialen Sprache in Deutschland* (Stuttgart: Ernst Klett, 1978), vol. IV, p. 785.
41 For an overview, see Karl Holl, *Pazifismus in Deutschland* (Frankfurt: Suhrkamp, 1988), pp. 204–19.
42 The Evangelical bishops issued a declaration of loyalty on 27 January 1934, while Pope Pius XI agreed to a Concordat with the regime on 20 July 1933.

destroyed, and because organized opposition was difficult and dangerous, most pacifist resisters were what Klemens von Klemperer has called 'the solitary witness'.[43] Simply spreading information about the regime's atrocities can be seen in this context as an act of resistance. The most famous of these, Kurt Gerstein, who helped disseminate information about the Final Solution in 1942, was a devout Christian though not in any strict sense a pacifist.[44] Several prominent members of the resistance circle around Harro Schulze-Boysen (the so-called Red Orchestra) were avowed pacifists. They helped compose opposition circulars for underground distribution.

In one such letter, *Die Sorge um Deutschlands Zukunft geht durch das Volk* (1942), co-authored by Schulze-Boysen and John Rittmeister, they engaged in a type of active defeatism similar to what was then taking place in Japan. This appears to have been a compromise position between principled pacifism and pragmatic political resistance. 'If Germany could not win the war against England when superiority in armoured divisions and air forces, in trained personnel and technical surprises still lay on Germany's side, then it certainly will not be able to win the war in the future, since the ever increasing superiority of our opponents is becoming increasingly apparent.'[45] The solution to Germany's future lay in establishing a socialist government that would seek alliances abroad with 'progressive forces in Europe and in the USSR'.[46] This message was hardly surprising, given the contacts between the Red Orchestra and Soviet Intelligence. More surprising, perhaps, was the prescription they offered for individual resistance. 'Everyone must take care that – whenever he can – he does the opposite of what is asked of him by the current regime.' At its most basic, according to the authors, this meant speaking the truth. 'We must demand of ourselves and others that we extract ourselves from the swamp of lies and cowardly and calculated optimism into which the masters of the Third Reich have drawn us' and the letter called on Germans to 'turn against the continuation of a war that in the best case would reduce not just the Reich but the entire continent to ruins'.[47] The

43 Klemens von Klemperer, 'The Solitary Witness: No Mere Footnote to Resistance Studies', in David Clay Laarge, ed., *Contending with Hitler: Varieties of German Resistance in the Third Reich* (Cambridge University Press, 1991), pp. 129–40.

44 Saul Friedlander, *Kurt Gerstein: The Ambiguity of Good* (New York: Alfred A. Knopf, 1969).

45 Anonymous (Harro Shulze-Boysen and John Rittmeister), *Die Sorge um Deutschlands Zukunft geht durch das Volk* (n.p., 1942), p. 3 (www.gdw-berlin.de/fileadmin/themen/b17/bilder/3507.pdf).

46 Ibid., p. 4.

47 Ibid., p. 5.

power of the truth would be their weapon of resistance, and would lead to a swifter defeat, and hence bring peace more quickly.

Pacifists in the Third Reich faced their greatest challenge when called up for military service. As in Japan and Russia, there were no provisions for conscientious objection in the Third Reich; indeed, when the draft was reinstated in 1935, it was explicitly criminalized.[48] Under changes implemented by the Nazis to both ordinary criminal (§§ 140–143 RStGB) and military law (§§ 64, 69 MStGB) failure to fulfil a military service obligation (*Dienstpflicht*) was criminal. § 48 MStGB stipulated that acts of secular or religious conscience were not necessarily excused and could be punished. Punishment at this point (1935–38) was rather mild under both civilian and military law – as little as one month imprisonment under § 140 RStGB and two years under § 64 MStGB. The real threat to conscientious objectors came with the 1938 Kriegssonderstrafrechtsverordnung (KSSVO) or Special Military Criminal Ordinance. This was a highly unusual law, in that it extended the jurisdiction of military courts to civilians. § 5 KSSVO, regarding Subversion of the War Effort (*Zersetzung der Wehrkraft*) allowed the death penalty for anyone 'who openly advocates or induces a refusal of service in the German or an allied military, or otherwise seeks to openly hinder or subvert the will of the German or an allied people to defend and assert themselves [*zur wehrhaften Selbstbeauptung*]'.[49] Wilhelm Keitel, Chief of OKW, issued a clarifying memorandum in which he explained that § 5 KSSVO replaced the relevant paragraphs in both civilian and military law. This new law, he wrote, 'imposes sanctions on the mere attempt to evade military service. Moreover, it expands the circle of potential perpetrators ... It is intended to cover every possible form of evasion of military service', including those who acted on the basis of religious conviction.[50] As early as 1935, that is, even before the actual introduction of capital punishment, the Reich government could announce in the context of the reintroduction of compulsory service, that 'the death penalty will be invoked in Germany to exterminate pacifism in time of war or national emergency.'[51]

---

48 For a full discussion of the legal status of conscientious objectors in Nazi Germany, see Karsten Bredemeier, *Kriegsdienstverweigerung im Dritten Reich. Ausgewählte Beispiele* (Baden-Baden: Nomos, 1991), pp. 49–78.

49 § 5 KSSVO, *Reichsgesetzblatt*, Teil I (Berlin: Reichsverlagsamt, 1939), p. 1456.

50 Wilhelm Keitel, 'Einführung in die Verordnung überer das Sonderstrafrecht im Kriege vom 17.08.38', cited in Rudolf Absolon, *Das Wehrmachtsstrafrecht im 2. Weltkrieg* (Kornelimünster: Bundesarchiv Abt. Zentralnachweisstelle, 1958), p. 51.

51 Cited in M. James Penton, *Jehovah's Witnesses and the Third Reich* (University of Toronto Press, 2004), pp. 170–1.

The standard sentence for subversion of the war effort was death. Although § 5 KSSVO allowed for a milder sentence in the event of mitigating circumstances, in fact the Reich Military Court became increasingly reluctant to find such mitigating circumstances, and then usually only in cases where a defendant changed his mind and acquiesced to military service.[52] Altogether, of those convicted of subversion of the war effort for refusing military service, 80–90 per cent were sentenced to death, of which a similar percentage were actually executed.[53] The exact number of individuals willing to risk such draconian punishment is not known.[54] On the lower end of estimates, Franz Seidler has found 196 death sentences imposed by the Reich Military Court for conscientious objection, though this was based on the only partially preserved records of the court and fails to include death sentences imposed by other military courts.[55] Peter Brock indicates there are roughly 280 known cases of conscientious objection, of which just over 250 were Jehovah's Witnesses.[56] Between 200 and 250 or roughly 80 per cent of Jehovah's Witnesses convicted of subverting the war effort were executed.[57]

If Jehovah's Witnesses constituted the clear majority of conscientious objectors in Nazi Germany, virtually all of the other objectors were also religious.[58] Yet it would be wrong to see these religious objectors as utterly apolitical, at least in all cases. The Catholic priest Franz Reinisch, for instance, refused to take the mandatory loyalty oath when called to serve as a medic, and was convicted of subversion of the war effort and executed in 1942. Among the reasons Reinisch gave for his refusal was his contention that 'the current government is no divinely sanctioned authority, but rather a nihilistic regime that acquired power only through violence, lies, and deception ... The Nazi principle "Violence trumps Law [Recht]" forces me into this position of duress. There can be for me no possible oath of loyalty to such

---

52 Detlef Garbe, *Between Resistance and Martyrdom: Jehovah's Witnesses in the Third Reich*, trans. Dagmar G. Grimm (Madison: University of Wisconsin Press, 1993), p. 369.
53 Bredemeier, *Kriegsdienstverweigerung*, p. 84.
54 For the archival difficulties in researching conscientious objectors in Nazi Germany, see Albrecht and Heidi Hartmann, *Kriegsdienstverweigerung im Dritten Reich* (Frankfurt: Haag & Herchen, 1986), pp. 3–4.
55 Franz W. Seidler, *Fahnenflucht. Soldat zwischen Eid und Gewissen* (Munich: Herbig, 1993), pp. 128–9.
56 Peter Brock, 'Conscientious Objectors in Nazi Germany', in Brock and Socknat, eds., *Challenge to Mars*, pp. 370–9 (p. 371).
57 Bredemeier, *Kriegsdienstverweigerung*, p. 85 and Garbe, *Between Resistance and Martyrdom*, p. 367.
58 The Hartmanns list one Social Democrat conscientious objector, while Bredemeier does not discuss any non-religious conscientious objectors.

a government.'[59] For a regime like the Nazis, any refusal of its absolute authority was an act, not of private conscience but of political rebellion. There could be no appeal to a higher authority than that of the Führer without threatening the very foundations of the Nazi order.

The Soviet Union was no more tolerant of pacifism than the Third Reich. This is hardly surprising. After all, the necessity for violence had been part of Marxist revolutionary ideology since its inception. For Marxist-Leninists in the Soviet Union, principled revolutionary violence was seen as politically necessary and morally justified. Pacifism was at best wishful thinking, at worst a tool of reaction. It is therefore all the more surprising that in the very early years of the Soviet Union, the state was relatively tolerant of pacifists. Tatiana Pavlova explains this 'paradox' in terms of the 'instability of Soviet power as well as the definitely anti-Bolshevik position of the Russian Orthodox Church'.[60] In an effort to break the power of the Orthodox Church, the Soviet regime declared an official policy of religious tolerance, which encompassed Protestant sects and Tolstoyans. In 1918, these sectarians founded the United Council of Religious Communities and Groups (UCRCAG) in order to defend their new-found religious freedom, including the right to refuse military service.[61]

On 4 January 1919, the Soviet state promulgated a decree allowing for conscientious objection, formulated with the help of UCRCAG, which was in turn asked to provide commissions of experts to assess applications for conscientious objector status. But as early as December 1920, the state began to limit UCRCAG's role, and gradually started to take an ever more punitive approach to conscientious objection.[62] Mennonite applicants for conscientious objector status, for instance, increasingly found their applications rejected beginning in the mid-1920s.[63] Still, in 1930, there remained over 1,000 conscientious objectors working in alternative service for religious reasons. A new decree on 7 December 1931 sentenced such conscientious objectors to three years in a labour camp. Thereafter, refusal of military service meant a stint in the Gulag.[64]

---

59 Cited in Hartmann and Hartmann, *Kriegsdienstverweigerung*, p. 26.
60 Tatiana Pavlova, 'Hundred Years of Russian Pacifism', *Journal of Human Values* 5:2 (1999), 147–55 (p. 149).
61 Ibid., p. 150.
62 Ibid.
63 Jacob J. Neufeld, *Path of Thorns: Soviet Mennonite Life under Communist and Nazi Rule* (University of Toronto Press, 2014), p. 24.
64 Pavlova, 'Hundred Years', p. 150.

Even before the outbreak of the Second World War, therefore, pacifism in the USSR had become a tiny, persecuted movement. As a consequence, its further development was more mystical than political, as perhaps befits the legacy of Tolstoy.[65] This is best exemplified by Daniil Andreev's *The Rose of the World*, mostly written in the Gulag immediately after the war and only circulated in samizdat form until 1991. Andreev offered an eschatological vision of a united world, pacified and living in spiritual unity under God's guidance.[66] Drawing on Tolstoy's mystical tradition, Andreev's vision was largely apolitical, a metaphysical account of the layers of spiritual existence. Andreev's views were decidedly ecumenical, indeed eclectic, rather than Orthodox, involving notions of reincarnation, demons, and multiple dimensions or elemental planes. Embedded in this hallucinatory architecture was a call for the creation of a League for the Transformation of the State, 'an international organization, both political and cultural in nature', designed to lead to the eventual creation of a Global Federation of Independent States.[67] Gandhi was named as a clear precursor for his 'saintly' politics, and the League was to be explicitly religious in orientation.[68] At the root of the project was to be religious revival, the practical difficulties resolved by the transformative power of God.

Pacifism in the liberal democracies

The situation confronting pacifists in the unconquered Western democracies, Britain and the USA, was quite different. To be sure, pacifists were subject to a fair amount of political pressure and police harassment, but for the most part they were allowed to propagate their beliefs and to engage in political agitation as long as it did not directly interfere with the war effort. Provisions were made for conscientious objectors, even if some chose for reasons of principle or politics to go to prison instead of rendering alternative service.[69] In no instances were pacifists executed for their activities. Yet despite this

---

65 Tolstoy's major statement of pacifist principle was as much a work of mysticism as anything. Lev N. Tolstoy, *The Kingdom of God is Within You, in The Complete Works of Count Tolstoy* (Boston: Dana Estes, 1905), vol. XX.
66 Daniil Andreev, *The Rose of the World* (Hudson, NY: Lindisfarne Books, 1997).
67 Ibid., p. 12.
68 Ibid., p. 15.
69 For a fuller treatment of conscientious objectors, see the chapter by Jeremy Kessler in the present volume.

much more open and safe environment, pacifism was a marginal political force, becoming less significant as the war progressed.

The wartime insignificance of pacifism was particularly striking in Britain, where pacifism and conscientious objection had been an especially brisant issue during the First World War.[70] As a consequence of the controversies of the First World War, pacifism emerged as a potent political force in interwar Britain, arguably stronger than in any other country. Indeed, A. J. P. Taylor maintained that, 'for a little while, [anti-war views] were the accepted orthodox view of the decade [the 1920s]'.[71] To be sure, Martin Ceadel is right to distinguish between what he terms pacificism and pacifism, that is, between pragmatic efforts to avoid war as 'irrational and inhumane', even if accepting that it might under some rare circumstances be necessary, and pacifism, the belief that war is 'always wrong and should never be resorted to, whatever the consequences of abstaining from fighting'.[72] What is striking, however, is the strong alliance between the pragmatists and absolutists in interwar Britain. Even mainstream politicians, like the Labour Party chairman George Lansbury, could be strong advocates of a relatively absolutist pacifism.[73] But Lansbury and the Labour Party were hardly the only vectors for mass pacifism in interwar Britain.

The Peace Pledge Union (PPU), founded in 1934 by the canon of St Paul's Cathedral, Dick Sheppard, which reached a peak membership of over 118,000 in 1937, was the dominant pacifist organization in interwar Britain.[74] The Society of Friends (Quakers) and the Fellowship of Reconciliation were the other major pacifist groups, though much smaller in numbers than the PPU. Ecumenical in every sense of the term, the PPU served as an umbrella organization for secular and religious pacifists, pragmatists and absolutists, socialists and liberals. In 1937, it merged with the socialist No More War movement. In the optimism of the post-war moment, when there was broad consensus that 'war was wrong and there should be no more of it', the differences between the pragmatists and the absolutists could easily be papered over.[75]

---

70 Hochschild, *To End All Wars*.
71 A. J. P. Taylor, *English History, 1914–1945* (Oxford University Press, 1965), p. 289.
72 Martin Ceadel, *Pacifism in Britain, 1914–1945: The Defining of a Faith* (Oxford: Clarendon Press, 1980), p. 3.
73 Jonathan Schneer, *George Lansbury* (Manchester University Press, 1990).
74 Andrew Rigby, 'The Peace Pledge Union: From Peace to War, 1936–1945', in Brock and Socknat, eds., *Challenge to Mars*, pp. 169–85 (p. 169).
75 Caroline Moorehead, *Troublesome People: The Warriors of Pacifism* (Bethesda: Adler & Adler, 1987), p. 89.

Hitler's rise to power in 1933 began to challenge this consensus and the war in Spain exacerbated the difficulties. The core problem was that many pacifists, both religious and secular, were broadly 'on the left'. Consequently, they viewed fascism as a particularly grave threat, even if some of them had difficulty distinguishing it from capitalism. So the question was how to oppose fascism without supporting militarism.

The first cracks began to appear in the parliamentary political parties. Things came to a head for the Labour Party in 1935. Under Lansbury's leadership, the party had resolved in 1933 to support total multilateral disarmament and pledged to take no part in any war.[76] By 1935, with war impending in Abyssinia, Germany announcing the reintroduction of conscription, and the League of Nations in disarray over how to respond, many Labourites were disillusioned with this stance. At the 1935 Party Conference, a motion was made demanding sanctions on Italy, including potentially the use of force, for its aggression in Africa. Lansbury managed to get the motion to include calls for an international conference on 'economic equality of opportunity for all nations in the underdeveloped regions of the earth', which he felt might resolve the issue.[77] But he failed to have the mention of armed force removed and in the end found himself outvoted by a faction headed by his rivals in the party leadership, Ernest Bevin and Clement Attlee. Earlier at the Conference, Attlee had outlined the alternate position. 'We are in favour of the proper use of force for ensuring the rule of law. Non-resistance is not a political attitude, it is a personal attitude. I do not believe it is a possible policy for people with responsibility.'[78] The motion – including the reference to use of force – passed overwhelmingly, and Lansbury was forced to resign as party chairman.

In the event, the League's collective security arrangements proved incapable of deterring or halting Italian aggression in Abyssinia. Moreover, like Lansbury, many pacifists were appalled to discover that collective security might require armed intervention, not just diplomatic deterrence and therefore 'was virtually indistinguishable from conventional defence'.[79] Above all, collective security arrangements faced the 'basic problem' that 'containment

76 Rhiannon Vickers, *The Labour Party and the World*, vol. 1: *The Evolution of Labour's Foreign Policy, 1900–51* (Manchester University Press, 2003), pp. 109–10.
77 Schneer, *Lansbury*, p. 168.
78 Cited in John Shepherd, *George Lansbury: At the Heart of Old Labour* (Oxford University Press, 2002), p. 323.
79 Moorehead, *Troublesome People*, p. 129.

was the policy blamed for the First World War.'[80] Appeasement, on the other hand, seemed to promise a way to maintain the alliance of pragmatism and principle. After stepping down as chair of the Labour Party, Lansbury drafted a manifesto for the Peace Pledge Union. The PPU staked its hopes for war prevention on 'economic appeasement and reconciliation', along the lines of Lansbury's 1935 proposal for an international conference on economic redistribution.[81] Outside the PPU, other pacifists argued vociferously for Appeasement as well, including the pacifist remnant within the Labour Party. As Labour MP James Hudson wrote in the PPU's newspaper, *Peace News*, 'we must have truck with dictators, either on the battlefield or round the conference table – and I choose the conference table.'[82] The assumption was that Germany's demands were both reasonable and to a degree justified by the injustices of Versailles. Philip Snowden wrote in 1937, 'An intelligent population, like the Germans, could never have rallied to the call of a leader like Hitler if they had not felt he expressed the national indignation.'[83] While the PPU in particular was careful to distinguish its principled stance from the government's more pragmatic, not to say opportunistic, policy of Appeasement, they often amounted to much the same thing. At the time of the Munich crisis in 1938, PPU sponsors offered to send 5,000 volunteers to the Sudetenland as non-violent monitors.[84]

The strong support for Appeasement among British pacifists and PPU members led some, not just George Orwell, to wonder whether the pacifist movement might not have gone soft on fascism, or worse. Rose Macaulay, for instance, remarked that 'occasionally when reading *Peace News*, I (and others) half think we have got ahold of the *Blackshirt* by mistake.'[85] Contemporary historians might not go quite so far, but they do note a drift from support for negotiations with Germany to an over-eagerness to see things from the German point of view.[86] David Lukowitz has argued that, while the PPU was not in fact actively pro-Nazi, 'it is hard to escape the conclusion that

80 Martin Ceadel, 'The Peace Movement between the Wars: Problems of Definition', in Richard Taylor and Nigel Young, eds., *Campaigns for Peace: British Peace Movements in the Twentieth Century* (Manchester University Press, 1987), pp. 73–99 (p. 90).

81 Ceadel, *Pacifism in Britain*, p. 274.

82 Cited in Rigby, 'The Peace Pledge Union', p. 181.

83 Cited in Moorehead, *Troublesome People*, p. 146.

84 Ibid., p. 172.

85 Cited in Julie V. Gottlieb, *Feminine Fascism: Women in Britain's Fascist Movement, 1923–1945* (London: I. B. Tauris, 2003), pp. 236–7.

86 Mark Gilbert, 'Pacifist Attitudes to Nazi Germany, 1936–1946', *Journal of Contemporary History* 27:3 (July 1992), 493–511.

there was too much sympathy for the German position, often the product of ignorance or superficial thinking. There was also a complete failure to grasp the nature of the Hitlerian system.'[87] Of course, most pacifists rejected the comparison, even while recognizing its political potency. '[I]f I was to be called a Fascist,' Vera Brittain wrote, 'I must prepare to endure even this ... I am now aware that if it suits the warmongers to rechristen me a Fascist, not one of the names which I have been given as a feminist will rescue me from this totally incompatible accusation.'[88] In the event, the discrediting of Appeasement with the outbreak of the war went a long way toward undermining the credibility of pacifism as well.

The start of the war, and especially the early Nazi victories in 1939 and 1940 more or less fatally undermined the alliance of pacifism and pacificism.[89] Many prominent PPU sponsors resigned and renounced their prior pacifism, including, perhaps most importantly, Bertrand Russell.[90] Many of those who renounced pacifism now argued that the only alternative to war was surrender to Hitler. As Storm Johnson put it, reasoning with Hitler had proven impossible. 'What is open to us is submission, the concentration camp, the death of our humblest with our best, the forcing of our children's minds into an evil mould. If he [the pacifist] says "I would choose this rather than war", he is using the right accorded him by our civilization to make a moral choice. But he must choose, not evade the implications of his choice.'[91]

Needless to say, not all pacifists changed their minds, but those who remained committed to non-violence came increasingly to see it in moral, not political terms. Lansbury is said to have declared shortly before his death in May 1940 that 'it would be better to be over-run by the Germans than to fight.'[92] This conviction was no longer political. As Caroline Moorehead has argued, opposition to the war 'became a matter of pure faith, a hard kernel of conviction, if not religiously, then at least morally, held, and almost always in solitude'.[93] This more personalist, moral and spiritual understanding of pacifism that came to dominate British pacifism in the war years was perhaps best expressed by D. S. Savage in a bitter exchange with George

87 David C. Lukowitz, 'British Pacifists and Appeasement: The Peace Pledge Union', *Journal of Contemporary History* 9:1 (1974), 115–27 (p. 126).
88 Cited in Gottlieb, *Feminine Fascism*, p. 237.
89 Ceadel, *British Pacifism*, p. 296.
90 Richard A. Rempel, 'The Dilemmas of British Pacifists during WWII', *Journal of Modern History* 50:4, supplement (1978), D1213–D1229 (p. D1215).
91 Cited in Ceadel, *British Pacifism*, p. 297.
92 Ibid., p. 298.
93 Moorehead, *Troublesome People*, p. 147.

Orwell in the pages of the *Partisan Review*. Orwell, Savage maintained, 'sees pacifism primarily as a political pheonomenon. That is just what it isn't. Primarily it is a moral phenomenon ... Pacifism springs from conscience – i.e. from within the individual human being.'[94]

The British state's more lenient policy toward conscientious objectors in the Second World War, as compared to the First, helped to secure this transformation of pacifism from a political into a personal, moral position, since it was now possible to opt out of the war without having to challenge the power of the state as such. As a result, the radical implications of pacifism were actually undermined. It is one thing to decline to participate in a war as an individual, and quite another to have persons in positions of power advocate for mechanisms designed to eliminate war altogether. The crusading nature of the Second World War, together with the liberalism of the British state, boxed pacifists into a personalist corner from which they had trouble emerging after 1945.

The story in the USA is similar to that of Britain, in that pacifism was tolerated, if not encouraged. The policy toward conscientious objectors was less generous, though still a far cry from the authoritarian states. The major difference is that pacifism – as distinct from isolationism – was a far less potent or mainstream political force in the USA between the wars than it had been in Britain. The move from pragmatism to moralism that characterized British pacifism was thus less pronounced in the USA. At the same time, because in the USA, the war discredited not only pacifism, but also isolationism, pragmatic approaches to peace preservation – internationalist multilateralism and proposals for collective security arrangements and a strengthening of international law – actually gained considerable strength during the war. If in Britain the retreat from pacifism meant a declining faith in multilateral security arrangements, quite the opposite was the case in the USA.

The American branch of the Fellowship of Reconciliation, the leading Christian pacifist organization, had a membership of 4,271 in 1935, which grew to 12,426 in 1941, a far cry from the 118,000 members of the PPU.[95] The secular War Resisters League (WRL) was even smaller, with 896 active members in 1940, peaking in 1944 at around 2,500 active members.[96] What was lacking altogether was a unifying organization to bring religious pacifists,

94 D. S. Savage, 'Pacifism and the War', in Orwell, *Collected Essays*, vol. II, pp. 220–3.
95 Christine A. Lunardini, *The American Peace Movement in the Twentieth Century* (Santa Barbara: ABC-Clio, 1994), p. 82.
96 Scott H. Bennett, *Radical Pacifism: The War Resisters League and Gandhian Nonviolence in America, 1915–1963* (Syracuse University Press, 2003), p. 75.

mainly from the historic peace churches, and their secular counterparts together. Indeed, as the war years would show, tensions between religious and secular pacifists ran high in the USA, since the Civilian Public Service Camps set up for conscientious objectors were run by the National Council for Religious Conscientious Objectors, a fact some secular pacifists found galling. Even WRL chairman, Evan Thomas admitted, 'we are such a small group that we would kid ourselves if we think we are of any social import-ance.'[97] Whether religious or secular, American pacifists had long viewed pacifism as a matter of individual conscience, rather than as a broad political movement. At the outset of the war in Europe, before America's entry into the conflict, John Haynes Holmes of the WRL argued that pacifism consisted of three things: common sense, because war was irrational, morality, because war was evil, and 'an act of faith – faith in the sense of a spiritual reliance upon forces invisible, imponderable, and omnipotent'.[98] With explicit refer-ence to Gandhi's non-violent resistance, Holmes added that 'pacifism is a practical application of a spiritualistic philosophy of life, as militarism, by which I mean reliance upon war as a final means of adjudication between nations, is a practical application of a materialistic philosophy of life.'[99] Similarly, at the start of the war, the Society of Friends issued the following proclamation: 'The fact that our country may have left itself with no way to meet aggression but that of force, is no reason for those to forsake their faith who have consistently urged that evil cannot be cured by war . . . There is a way of God for every situation.'[100]

Perhaps the most articulate voice for spiritual pacifism in America during the war years was A. J. Muste, the former Dutch Reformed minister turned labour leader who, from 1940 to 1953, served as executive director of the Fellowship of Reconciliation. On the eve of America's entry into the war, Muste argued that a specifically Christian pacifism was the only hope for salvaging civilization. 'Religion, social progress, democracy depend for sur-vival and triumph upon the adoption of a thorough-going, deeply motivated, positive, realistic pacifism.'[101] Rejecting 'crisis theology', which held that whatever God's morality was, in this world, one had no choice but to

---

97 Ibid., p. 74.
98 James H. Holmes, *What Pacifism Is, and Is Not* (New York: The Community Church, 1939/40), p. 15.
99 Ibid., p. 16.
100 'A Message from the Society of Friends to our Fellow Christians – Meeting for Sufferings, 1939', in Ruth Freeman, *Quakers and Peace* (New York: The Pacifist Research Bureau, 1947), p. 49.
101 A. J. Muste, *Non-Violence in an Aggressive World* (New York: Harper, 1940), p. 10.

embrace 'non-moral or even immoral' means, Muste argued that this view misunderstood both the Bible and the world. It only made sense if one assumed that God had no plan for this world and no power to enforce such a plan. Crisis theology arose, he maintained, 'from a fundamentally non-religious, non-prophetic dualism which assumes that when Jesus talked about love and meekness, He was setting forth impractical ideals'.[102] Thus, according to Muste, to accept war was to abandon religion; 'it is to admit that in this world the real power is not the God and Father of our Lord Jesus Christ who meets sin with suffering love, but Satan.'[103] Muste argued that, if one was truly faithful and believed in the power of God, then one had to admit that Jesus's call to renounce violence – as he himself had done – was not mere idealism, but a form of spiritual pragmatism. 'The pacifist who believes the world is God's world and that only God's methods will work in it, also seems to me to be a realist, indeed the supreme realist.'[104] Muste's plan for a 'real peace and a stable one' involved arms reduction aimed at eventual elimination, 'equal access to raw materials' for all peoples by means of free trade and currency stability, and a 'genuine federal world-government' similar to the American system.[105]

Conclusion

Pacifism manifestly failed to prevent or stop the mass violence of the Second World War. Yet Second World War era pacifism was not without important legacies. To begin with, it inspired a new generation of domestic reformers, who would use non-violent direct action to substantial political effect in the post-war period. At the same time, its obvious failures and limitations would inspire more pragmatically minded politicians and activists to pursue alternative ways to reduce and control mass violence – multilateral institutionalism, on the one hand, and humanitarianism, on the other.

The most obvious legacy of wartime pacifism was the way it fed directly and influentially into the emergence of post-war reform movements, most obviously the Civil Rights movement. The Congress of Racial Equality was founded as an offshoot of Muste's Fellowship of Reconciliation.[106] Muste,

---

102 Ibid., p. 35.
103 Ibid., p. 36.
104 Ibid., p. 44.
105 Ibid., p. 142.
106 August Meier and Elliot Rudwick, *CORE: A Study in the Civil Rights Movement, 1942–1968* (Oxford University Press, 1973).

along with Gandhi, was a major intellectual inspiration for the early Civil Rights movement.[107] Bayard Rustin, chief organizer of the March on Washington and one of the founders of the Southern Christian Leadership Council (SCLC) – recalled that after he broke with the Communist Party for becoming a 'war party' after the German invasion of the Soviet Union, he turned to Muste for guidance.[108] Muste was also a decisive influence on Jim Lawson, who in turn ran the workshops on non-violence that led to the sit-ins and freedom rides that formed the core of non-violent direct action for the Civil Rights movement.[109] And of course it was no coincidence that the SCLC's fund-raising arm (aimed at wealthy, mainly white northerners) was called the Gandhi Society.[110]

Similarly, the nuclear disarmament and anti-war movements that flourished in various domestic contexts in the post-war period often traced their lineage to the Second World War era.[111] What is striking about post-war anti-war movements is the extent to which they took on the character of domestic pressure groups, less focused on international mediation or institution building, and more on changing the military policies of their own states.[112] This turn to non-violent direct action in domestic politics reflects a postcolonial 'Gandhian moment', in which tactics developed specifically to combat liberal colonialism by highlighting its hypocrisy could be successfully deployed as pressure politics by citizens of liberal states to challenge sovereign authority.[113]

The seeming moral clarity of the Second World War may have undermined the legitimacy of pacifism as a political project in the Western

---

107 Inge Powell Bell, *CORE and the Strategy of Nonviolence* (New York: Random House, 1968). For Gandhi's influence on Martin Luther King Jr., see Thomas Weber, *Gandhi as Disciple and Mentor* (Cambridge University Press, 2004), pp. 165–73.
108 Martin Mayer, 'The Lone Wolf of Civil Rights [1964]', in *Reporting Civil Rights: Part Two, American Journalism, 1963–1973* (New York: Library of America, 2003), p. 134.
109 David Halberstam, *The Children* (New York: Random House, 1998), pp. 37–8.
110 Adam Fairclough, *To Redeem the Soul of America: The Southern Christian Leadership Conference and Martin Luther King, Jr.* (Athens, Ga.: University of Georgia Press, 1987), pp. 97–8.
111 Holger Nehring, *Politics of Security: British and West German Peace Movements and the Early Cold War, 1945–1970* (Oxford University Press, 2013); Doug Rossinow, *The Politics of Authenticity: Liberalism, Christianity, and the New Left in America* (New York: Columbia University Press, 1998); Lawrence S. Wittner, *The Struggle against the Bomb* (3 vols., Stanford University Press, 1995–2003).
112 Jeffrey Herf, *War by Other Means: Soviet Power, West German Resistance, and the Battle of the Euromissiles* (New York: Free Press, 1991) and Steve Breyman, *Why Movements Matter: The West German Peace Movement and U.S. Arms Control Policy* (Syracuse University Press, 2001).
113 Ramin Jahanbegloo, *The Gandhian Moment* (Cambridge, Mass.: Harvard University Press, 2013).

democracies, but in the USA it also did much to discredit American isolation-ism as well.[114] The moral clarity and the universalism proclaimed by the Allies made it imperative in the minds of many to revive the project of multilateral collective security. Across the American political spectrum during the war, there were attempts to formulate plans for a lasting peace based on multilateral institutions.[115]

What is striking is the degree of consensus that emerged during the war among American political leaders on the need for a multilateral approach to securing peace in the post-war period. Figures as diverse as Wendell Willkie, the 1940 Republican presidential nominee, Herbert Hoover, Roosevelt's Republican predecessor in the White House, Sumner Wells, FDR's foreign policy advisor, and Henry Wallace, Roosevelt's left-liberal Vice-President for most of the war called for major international institution building to provide a foundation for a durable peace.[116] America's leading statesmen agreed that there had been a failure to adequately plan for the peace during the last war, and the result was a turn to isolationism that they generally agreed had wrecked the post-war settlement. This in turn meant, as Henry Wallace put it, that there must be some 'machinery which can disarm and keep disarmed those parts of the world which would break the peace . . . Probably there will have to be an international court to make decisions in cases of dispute. And an international court presupposes some kind of world council.'[117] In short, then, they all pointed toward the United Nations.

Clearly, the United Nations that came into existence was more limited in scope and intent than the United Nations imagined in the fever dreams of wartime statesmen. Although more robust than the League of Nations that preceded it, the UN was from the outset a divided institution. The tensions within the Charter between the ambition to 'maintain or restore inter-national peace and security' and the guarantee of non-interference in domes-tic matters, together with the veto power of the five permanent members of the Security Council, means that the peacekeeping, and even more the peacemaking, function of the UN has been observed far more in the breach,

---

114 Susan Dunn, *1940: FDR, Willkie, Lindbergh, Hitler – the Election amid the Storm* (New Haven: Yale University Press, 2013), pp. 309–17.

115 Elisabeth Borgwardt, *A New Deal for the World: America's Vision for Human Rights* (Cambridge, Mass.: The Belknap Press of Harvard University Press, 2005).

116 See Wendell L. Willkie, *One World*, Herbert Hoover and Hugh Gibson, *The Problems of a Lasting Peace*, Henry A. Wallace, *The Century of the Common Man* and Sumner Welles, *The World of the Four Freedoms*, collected in *Prefaces to Peace: A Symposium* (New York: Simon & Schuster, 1943).

117 Wallace, *Century of the Common Man* in *Prefaces to Peace*, p. 384.

than in practice.[118] Similarly, attempts to criminalize aggressive war – as in the charge before both the Nuremberg and Tokyo war crimes tribunals of 'crimes against peace' – proved to be largely stillborn.[119] In the end, the most lasting legacy of Second World War era pacifism may have been to salvage humanitarianism as an alternative. Despite winning the 1944 Nobel Peace Prize, the International Committee of the Red Cross emerged from the war with its legacy severely tarnished by its failure to adequately address the Holocaust.[120] Its principle of neutralism and amelioration might easily have been dismissed as inadequate to the challenges posed by modern, ideological, crusading wars.[121] Yet the inability to craft a coherent and efficacious pacifist alternative actually opened a space for the ICRC to reclaim its role in international politics. This can be seen most explicitly in the crafting and widespread acceptance of the 1949 Geneva Conventions.[122] These offered a clear alternative to the Nuremberg attempt to criminalize aggressive war and returned to the decidedly nineteenth-century view that war was a necessary evil, whose horrors could be mitigated by careful legislation.[123] By seeking to define and protect non-combatants and to articulate a principle of proportionality in violence, the Geneva Conventions ran counter to the absolutism of both pacifism and total war.

The other dimension of humanitarianism – relief aid for victims of war – likewise came out of the war with enhanced status. While pacifists had been reduced to quietism and the politics of personal protest, humanitarian activists, whether in the ICRC, the various national Red Cross organizations, or new international organizations like UNRRA could be seen in a more heroic mould, as taking action and making a difference. UNRRA, for instance, proudly proclaimed in its official history that 'by mobilizing effectively the resources of many nations it was ready to act when the time for action arrived, and it was able to sustain a program of united action through

118 Charter of the United Nations (www.un.org/en/documents/charter.)

119 Devin O. Pendas, 'Toward World Law? Human Rights and the Failure of the Legalist Paradigm of War', in Stefan-Ludwig Hoffmann, ed., *Human Rights in the Twentieth Century* (Cambridge University Press, 2011), pp. 215–36.

120 Jean-Claude Favez, *The Red Cross and the Holocaust* (Cambridge University Press, 1999) and Arieh Ben-Tov, *Facing the Holocaust in Budapest: The International Committee of the Red Cross and the Jews of Hungary, 1943–1945* (Geneva: Henry Dunant Institute, 1988).

121 David P. Forsythe, *The Humanitarians: The International Committee of the Red Cross* (Cambridge University Press, 2005), p. 52.

122 Geoffrey Best, *War and Law since 1945* (Oxford: Clarendon Press, 1994), pp. 80–114.

123 See, for example, John Fabian Witt, *Lincoln's Code: The Laws of War in American History* (New York: Free Press, 2012).

the period of greatest emergency.'[124] Humanitarian relief work also drew on the spirit of good will which animated many pacifists. Indeed, many UNRRA workers were pacifists, but chose to act in a war zone to help, rather than protest. Isabel Needham, for instance, was an American Quaker pacifist who joined UNRRA because she 'believ[ed] in any undertaking, large or small, which offers help where help is needed' and, because, as a pacifist, she was 'deeply convinced . . . of the imperative need of international cooperation in constructive directions'.[125] Or, as another volunteer put it, 'we have carried out the plan drawn up by economists and drafted by lawyers, but we did it in the spirit of the Sermon on the Mount.'[126] In the end, the spirit of non-violence survived the horrors of the Second World War, but it did so in ways that left the politics of pacifism decisively transformed and in some ways diminished.

---

124 George Woodbridge, *UNRRA: The History of the United Nations Relief and Rehabilitation Administration* (3 vols., New York: Columbia University Press, 1950), vol. II, p. 552.
125 Ibid., p. 224.
126 Cited in Sharif Gemie, Fiona Reid, and Laure Humbert, *Outcast Europe: Refugees and Relief Workers in an Era of Total War, 1936–1948* (London: Continuum, 2012), p. 161.

18

Humanitarian politics and governance

International responses to the civilian toll in the Second World War

STEPHEN PORTER

The human toll of the Second World War dwarfed the combined efforts of states and civil society entities to ameliorate that suffering. Over 60 million people died, with scores of millions more left wounded, starving, sick and displaced from their homes. Most were civilians, with a younger and shakier suite of legal and institutional protections than those developed for prisoners of war. Across multiple continents, economies, social welfare networks and state governments were either in tatters or at least significantly disrupted, unable or unwilling to address the profound needs of the populations in their midst. The politics and technologies behind the most devastating war machinery the world had ever built left a civilizational void that no humanitarian commitment would, or could, possibly fill.[1]

And yet, the humanitarian efforts that arose to address this maelstrom ultimately proved proportional, if hardly equal, to the scale of destruction they emerged to address. The war created not only a high-water mark for human devastation but also for organized initiatives to assuage the effects of man-made catastrophes. Whether facilitating the needs of the displaced or civilians languishing in their homes and homelands, the scope of humanitarian aid during the era was almost unimaginably immense. Dotting and sometimes dominating the landscapes of North Africa, the Middle East, Asia and, especially, Europe were vast networks of refugee camps, hospitals, orphanages, soup kitchens, job and language training centres, and agricultural and industrial supply warehouses. As territories were claimed by Allied forces, and hostilities waned, the oceans carried many thousands of ships loaded with aid supplies and relief personnel across hemispheres and into ports where trains and trucks facilitated the journeys across land. Many

---

1 Keith Lowe, *Savage Continent: Europe in the Aftermath of World War II* (New York: St. Martin's Press, 2012), pp. 3–74.

millions of refugees took some of these same locomotives and vessels in other directions. Most were repatriated quickly, with a million others eventually resettled in new homelands where, in theory if not always in practice, they would be free from persecution and destitution.[2] While the needs of displaced refugees required some additional types of assistance beyond those demanded by the diverse groups of civilians languishing in their homes and homelands, humanitarian aid personnel of the era used 'relief' as a loose umbrella term to refer to the wide range of war-related humanitarian activities deployed on behalf of refugees and non-refugees alike. 'Relief' was additionally meant to convey the more temporary nature of assistance programmes – also sometimes more an ideal than a reality – over longer-term projects of economic, infrastructural and political 'rehabilitation', a term that in the post-war era would increasingly morph into programmes of international 'development'.[3]

Internationally organized aid during the era of the Second World War dwarfed anything before it, but it built on nearly a century of experience that made the robust humanitarian response to the Second World War appear as a just, strategically necessary, and even natural approach to many statesmen and civil society leaders in the victorious Allied countries. Since the formation of the International Committee of the Red Cross and first Geneva Convention in the 1860s, members of the international community – especially Western states – had embraced an expanding array of expectations for addressing the needs of the victims of warfare and related upheavals, whether in the form of law, non-binding norms or on-the-ground relief programmes. While legal developments over the decades remained mostly concerned with combatants, the devastation of the First World War and its aftermath sparked utterly unprecedented energies to alleviate the suffering of civilians. The wide array of institutions engaging in civilian assistance included the Red Cross, myriad civil society organizations (typically religiously oriented), the aid enterprises directed by Herbert Hoover, and, to a

---

2 United Nations Department of Public Information, Research Section, 'Refugees', Background Paper No. 78, 29 December 1953, Records of the United Service for New Americans, RG 246, F 597, YIVO Archives, Center for Jewish History, New York; Mark Wyman, *DP: Europe's Displaced Persons, 1945–1951* (Philadelphia: Balch Institute Press, 1989), pp. 15–37; Anna Holian, *Between National Socialism and Soviet Communism: Displaced Persons in Postwar Germany* (Ann Arbor: University of Michigan Press, 2011), pp. 1–3; R. M. Douglas, *Orderly and Humane: The Expulsion of Germans after the First World War* (New Haven: Yale University Press, 2012).

3 David Ekbladh, *The Great American Mission: Modernization and the Construction of a World Order* (Princeton University Press, 2011); Amanda McVety, *Enlightened Aid: U.S. Development as Foreign Policy in Ethiopia* (Oxford University Press, 2012).

significant but inconsistent degree, national governments and intergovern-mental bodies. The war's peace agreements produced and advanced a constellation of agreements and institutions designed to safeguard vulnerable populations, most prominently, the minority treaties and the League of Nations. Charged with the protection of various groups of political refugees over the 1920s and 1930s were the League-affiliated High Commission for Refugees, Nansen International Office for Refugees, and the International Labour Organization. These developments transformed an inchoate and sporadic range of responses to warfare and dispossession into a more ration-alized and persistent field of humanitarian assistance by the eve of the Second World War, albeit one that proved woefully inadequate to the humanitarian needs of the interwar years, much less to what followed.[4]

Expansive as they were, the aid endeavours of the Second World War proved far from perfect. The era's humanitarian projects – whether spon-sored by Allied militaries, civilian state entities or civil society organizations – were often marked by inefficient bumbling and, at times, a callous indiffer-ence or outright hostility toward the most vulnerable. Many of the refugees repatriated back to their countries of origin, for instance, went unwillingly, fearing persecution and hardship, and at times, returning to a country that had disappeared from the map. Of the 12 million ethnic German *Volksdeutsche* who were forced to 'return' to Germany after the war, many had never set foot in their supposed 'homeland', having been jarringly uprooted from communities to the east that some had known for generations.[5] Even when eligible for aid under a particular programme, people in need of assistance were too often neglected, pawns in larger contests between political and military factions.[6]

Starving and sick civilian citizens of the defeated Axis countries were at times either refused aid by occupying Allied militaries and, operating on a much smaller scale, civilian relief organizations or else granted only a fraction

---

4 Geoffrey Best, *Humanity in Warfare: The Modern History of International Law of Armed Conflicts* (London: Methuen, 1983); Michael N. Barnett, *Empire of Humanity: A History of Humanitarianism* (Ithaca: Cornell University Press, 2011), pp. 76–94; Johannes Paulmann, 'The Dilemmas of International Humanitarian Aid in the Twentieth Century', *Bulletin of the German Historical Institute* 34:1 (2012), 143–59; Claudena M. Skran, *Refugees in Inter-War Europe: The Emergence of a Regime* (Oxford: Clarendon Press, 1995); Michael R. Marrus, *The Unwanted: European Refugees in the Twentieth Century* (Oxford University Press, 1985), pp. 51–295; Mark Mazower, *Dark Continent: Europe's Twentieth Century* (London: Allen Lane, 1998), pp. 41–75, 138–81.

5 See *supra* note 2.

6 See, for example, William I. Hitchcock, *The Bitter Road to Freedom: A New History of the Liberation of Europe* (New York: The Free Press, 2008).

of the assistance offered to civilians from liberated countries. War relief was furthermore an overwhelmingly Western-led enterprise, though not exclusively so, with humanitarian efforts disproportionately directed toward Europe while massive suffering sometimes continued elsewhere with relatively little international attention paid. For instance, as meagre as the conditions could be for Germans – whose sustenance was largely provided for by the militaries of the four Allied occupiers – matters were far worse in the war's immediate aftermath in US-occupied Japan, where families were occasionally encouraged by authorities to mix sawdust into flour to stretch the scarce supply of food.[7] Similarly, while robust international refugee programmes helped to care for and dramatically reduce the number of European refugees produced through the war by the early 1950s, nothing approaching such international attention was directed toward the refugees produced by the Japanese defeat in Manchuria in 1945 or the Indo-Pakistani War of 1947.[8] Refugees from the Palestine War of 1948 faced a different fate altogether, becoming a population displaced in perpetuity, materially dependent on international aid but without a viable plan for civil incorporation into a traditional nation state.[9] And as large Anglo-American food programmes prepared to launch during the middle of the war for civilians in liberated European countries, over 7 million people – a conservative estimate – died of starvation and attendant diseases in India, China and Vietnam during the second half of the Second World War with relatively little attention from the Western Allies.[10]

The decade nevertheless witnessed the development of a staggeringly large and complex web of social welfare provision that affected, often

---

7 On the military occupations of Eastern and Central Europe, see Hitchcock, *Bitter Road*, pp. 125–208. On the occupation of Japan, see John W. Dower, *Embracing Defeat: Japan in the Wake of World War II* (New York: W. W. Norton, 2000), pp. 90–1 on sawdust; Kazuo Kawai, *Japan's American Interlude* (University of Chicago Press, 1960), pp. 16–33, 133–59.

8 Louise W. Holborn, *The International Refugee Organization: A Specialized Agency of the United Nations, Its History and Work, 1946–1952* (Oxford University Press, 1956); Jacques Vernant, *The Refugee in the Post-War World* (New Haven: Yale University Press, 1953); Gerard Daniel Cohen, *In War's Wake: Europe's Displaced Persons in the Postwar Order* (Oxford University Press, 2011), pp. 30–4, 61–7; Peter Gatrell and Nick Baron, *Population Resettlement and State Reconstruction in the Soviet–East European Borderlands, 1945–1950* (New York: Palgrave Macmillan, 2009), pp. 1–2; Dower, *Embracing Defeat*, pp. 48–58; Vazira Fazila and Yacoobali Zamindar, *The Long Partition and the Making of Modern South Asia: Refugees, Boundaries, Histories* (New York: Columbia University Press, 2007).

9 Benny Morris, *The Birth of the Palestinian Refugee Problem, 1947–1949* (Cambridge University Press, 1989).

10 Lance Brennan, 'Government Famine Relief in Bengal, 1943', *Journal of Asian Studies* 47:3 (1988), 541–66.

profoundly, the lives of scores of millions of people on a scale not seen before or since. The most important of these projects, in terms of its scope of operations, geopolitical innovation and the profound mark it left on humanitarian management was the behemoth intergovernmental aid institution at the heart of this chapter, the United Nations Relief and Rehabilitation Administration, commonly known as UNRRA to its many contemporary advocates and critics alike. Established in late 1943, the 'United Nations' in the organization's name had been coined by Franklin Roosevelt in late 1941 to refer to the Allied and Associated countries. UNRRA hardly comprised the entirety of the era's humanitarian initiatives. For instance, the military-led Allied occupations of Germany and Japan – the latter of which was predominantly an American endeavour – were outside of UNRRA's purview with the important exception of displaced persons operations in Germany. Nevertheless, UNRRA is generally regarded by its observers as far and away the largest and most important internationally organized humanitarian endeavour of the period, or arguably of any time previously or since. It eventually boasted forty-eight member states representing 80 per cent of the world's population. Its 20,000 employees hailed from fifty countries. The organization spent nearly $4 billion (unadjusted) between 1944 and 1947 to provide aid to 20 million war victims in sixteen formerly Axis-controlled countries in East Asia, Africa and across much of Europe. Enormous as this budget was for a civilian aid organization, it undersells the actual breadth of UNRRA's reach. Countless other people offered 'immeasurable assistance', in the words of one official, to UNRRA programmes through civil society organizations working alongside or underneath the institution's umbrella, dramatically expanding its operational scale. Civil society 'voluntary agencies' provided most of the personnel and much of the material aid, for instance, to UNRRA's 'Displaced Persons' camps, permitting much more ambitious operations than could have otherwise materialized. The three Western zones of occupied Germany alone housed 715,000 people at a single time, with scores of thousands more residing in similar camps in China, North Africa, the Levant, Austria, Italy and beyond. Setting aside the institution's considerable limitations for the moment, UNRRA operations often made the difference between destitution and relative comfort for the recipients of their aid, and for many, between life and death.[11]

---

11 George Woodbridge, *UNRRA: The History of the United Nations Relief and Rehabilitation Administration* (3 vols., New York: Columbia University Press, 1950). Quote from 'History – UNNRA, U.S. Zone, Germany, Report no. 24 – Annex (b)', September

Beyond the organization's vast operations, the mere establishment of UNRRA represented a remarkable diplomatic feat, achieved by state officials with often widely divergent positions on what post-conflict aid operations should look like. With the Allied liberation of Axis-controlled territories beginning well before the end of the war, the field of humanitarian assistance emerged as an early testing ground – an early hope – for the proponents of a post-war world where norms of social security would find a more global footing and international cooperation would trump violent conflict. Though often relatively overlooked in the subsequent historical record, UNRRA might indeed be considered a progenitor of the better-known international organizations and other systems of international collaboration that it pre-dated, not the least of which was the United Nations organization founded in San Francisco in 1945. In the words of one contemporary, UNRRA held the potential to offer 'the first blueprint of the post-war order'.[12]

Great-power designs for international humanitarianism

Post-conflict relief planning began audaciously early, and from the outset betrayed a belief that strategically deployed humanitarian aid could be motivated simultaneously by benevolence and the raw military and geopolitical imperatives of winning the war and controlling the terms of an eventual peace. In the summer of 1940, as Britons braced for what many assumed would be an imminent German invasion, Winston Churchill confidently promised the House of Commons that Britain would 'arrange in advance for the speedy entry of food into any part of the enslaved area' currently held by Germany upon liberation. After defending Britain's controversial naval blockade of critically needed civilian provisions to these same territories while they were still occupied by Axis powers, the Prime Minister announced that he would enlist the support of other countries in 'the building up of reserves of food' so that the conquered populations and Germans and Austrians alike would understand that 'the shattering of the Nazi power will bring to them all immediate food, freedom and peace.'[13] It was a bold proclamation given the current status of the war, one fuelled by

1947, p. 9, F Monographs – Displaced Persons – U.S. Zone – History of Employment Division, Office of the Historian, UNRRA Germany Mission fonds, S-1021-0080-10, UN Archives.

12 Grace Fox, 'The Origins of UNRRA', *Political Science Quarterly* 65:4 (1950), 561–84 (p. 561).

13 'A Year of War: Mr. Churchill's Survey', *The Times (London)*, 21 August 1940.

a vocal desire on the part of former Western aid workers from the First World War to be better prepared for the humanitarian crisis at the cessation of the current hostilities than many believed had occurred at the end of the previous conflict. These voices were echoed by intellectual and political elites who merged a desire to help war victims with a faith in modern techniques of population management. The Prime Minister additionally understood that well-planned relief operations could offer an outlet for the great food surpluses that had already begun to amass for Britain, the USA, Canada, Argentina and other major food-producing countries largely as a result of the blockade and naval warfare.[14]

The British viewed the USA as easily the most important of these potential partners in supplying aid provisions. Diplomats from the two countries would work closely with one another in the several-year relief planning period that culminated in the establishment of UNRRA. Soon after the Prime Minister's speech before the House of Commons – a full year before the USA entered the war – British officials approached their American counterparts about earmarking American wheat and other food surpluses for war relief needs. At about the same time, Britain began hosting a series of meetings at St James's Palace in London with representatives from the various European governments-in-exile to predict their country's respective humanitarian needs during the first half-year after liberation so that foodstuffs could be procured, stored and earmarked for eventual distribution. The meetings were chaired by chief British economic advisor Frederick Leith-Ross, a key proponent of post-war relief efforts for Britain and a vociferous diplomatic advocate for Allied-sponsored intergovernmental relief. John Maynard Keynes, renowned economist and another important British supporter of advance relief planning through multilateral arrangements, made an unofficial trip to Washington, DC in the spring of 1941 to persuade the USA to join the surpluses plans being formulated by Leith-Ross's committee in London. In July, representatives from the food-producing countries of Britain, the USA, Canada, Australia and Argentina met in Washington to form the International Wheat Council, one of a number of cooperatives that would emerge to pool needed resources for humanitarian planning.[15] A contemporary observer opined of the new council that 'here was the first

---

14 Ben Shephard, '"Becoming Planning Minded": The Theory and Practice of Relief, 1940–1945', *Journal of Contemporary History* 43:3 (2008), 405–19.
15 Woodbridge, *UNRRA*, vol. 1, pp. 7–9; Fox, 'Origins of UNRRA', pp. 562–4.

official international effort to implement freedom from want and a forecast of an intergovernmental relief organization.'[16]

Meanwhile, Leith-Ross's group was given official sanction in September 1941 as the Inter-Allied Post-War Requirements Committee, and continued commissioning investigations into projected relief needs. In the same month, the USA initiated similar studies within a new Special Research Division in the State Department. These various efforts helped to establish war relief bureaux within the respective foreign ministries of the two countries to respond to the humanitarian crisis that American and British forces faced upon the liberation of North Africa over the summer and autumn of 1942: the Middle East Relief and Refugee Administration (MERRA) for Britain and the Office of Foreign Relief and Rehabilitation Operations (OFRRO) for the USA. The organizations ran refugee centres in North Africa, Palestine and Syria mostly for dozens of thousands of Greeks, Dodecanesians, Poles and Yugoslavs driven from their homes by various belligerent forces. (These two regional entities would get subsumed by the much more expansive UNRRA after its establishment the following November.)[17] Such developments led Leith-Ross to predict that 'coordination after this war will have had no parallel since the Thirty Years' War.'[18]

The American interest in early multilateral planning for post-war relief needs was informed by a broader commitment by the Roosevelt administration, inaugurated and tested through domestic New Deal programmes, to organizing large-scale, multi-agency state solutions for massive social and economic problems. The bold intergovernmental vision for humanitarian aid that would materialize with UNRRA in late 1943 occupied the same frame

---

16 Fox, 'Origins of UNRRA', p. 564.
17 Woodbridge, *UNRRA*, vol. II, pp. 81–9; US Bureau of the Budget, *The United States at War: Development and Administration of the War Program by the Federal Government* (Washington: GPO, 1946), 409–28; US Department of State, *Foreign Relief and Rehabilitation Operations* (Washington: GPO, 1943); Elizabeth Clark Reiss, *The American Council of Voluntary Agencies for Foreign Service, ACVAFS: Four Monographs* (New York: The Council, 1985), 6; Division of Public Information, OFRRO, 'The Office of Foreign Relief and Rehabilitation Operations, Department of State' (Washington: GPO, 1943); *U.S. Senate Hearings on H.J. Res. 192, UNRRA Participation*, February 1944 (Washington: GPO, 1944), 30; *U.S. House Hearings on UNRRA Participation*, December 1943 to January 1944 (Washington, GPO, 1944); 'Planning for Peace Seen Gaining in U.S.', *New York Times*, 28 February 1943. On an important precedent of Western aid to refugees in the region, see Keith David Watenpaugh, 'The League of Nations' Rescue of Armenian Genocide Survivors and the Making of Modern Humanitarianism, 1920–1927', *American Historical Review* 115:5 (2010), 1315–39.
18 Francesca Wilson, *Advice to Relief Workers: Based on Personal Experiences in the Field* (London: John Murray & Friends Relief Service, 1945), p. 5.

as such other US-propelled multilateral endeavours as the Atlantic Charter of 1941 and various projects affiliated with the formation of the United Nations organization in San Francisco in 1945. The Roosevelt administration's proclivity to deploy its geopolitical goals for the post-war order through the form of the international institution represented a desire to offer, as one historian has phrased it, 'A New Deal for the world'. This philosophy roughly coalesced with an ascendant economic Keynesianism in Britain and Soviet socialism to make the internationalization of 'social security' – an international 'welfare state', as UNRRA was called by another historian – a highly valued goal among the Allies for a more prosperous, stable and peaceful post-war world.[19]

Looming perhaps even larger over these early approaches to wartime and post-war relief planning was the spectre of humanitarian aid initiatives in the era of the Great War. By the outbreak of the Second World War, the massive humanitarian operations directed by Herbert Hoover during the First World War and its aftermath had become mythologized in large reservoirs of popular memory. Already a renowned international mining engineer by the time that hostilities began in 1914, Hoover's first relief endeavour, the Commission for Relief in (German-occupied) Belgium (CRB), demonstrated his stunning diplomatic and administrative ability to manage vast and complex systems of food procurement and distribution amidst the fighting. Emerging in the wake of the CRB were several other Hoover-led civilian relief organizations, the last of which, the American Relief Administration for a Russian famine, operated until 1923. Each entity relied on varying degrees of support from the American state, governments allied with the USA and civil society organizations. Hoover's organizations and various other operations affiliated with them collectively covered a 7,000-mile expanse across Europe, parts of the Near East and North Asia. These activities represented major breakthroughs in international humanitarianism, whether in times of war or otherwise.[20]

---

19 Elizabeth Borgwardt, *A New Deal for the World: America's Vision for Human Rights* (Cambridge, Mass.: The Belknap Press of Harvard University Press, 2005); Jessica Reinisch, 'Introduction: Relief in the Aftermath of War' and Gerard Daniel Cohen, 'Between Relief and Politics: Refugee Humanitarianism in Occupied Germany', both in *Journal of Contemporary History* 43:3 (2008), 371–404 (pp. 365–6, 388) and 437–49.

20 See, for example, George H. Nash, *The Life of Herbert Hoover: The Humanitarian, 1914–1917* (New York: W. W. Norton, 1988), pp. 362–5; George H. Nash, *The Life of Herbert Hoover: Master of Emergencies, 1918–1919* (New York: W. W. Norton, 1996); Frank M. Surface and Raymond L. Bland, *American Food in the World War and Reconstruction Period: Operations under the Direction of Herbert Hoover, 1914 to 1924* (Stanford University Press, 1931); Suda Lorena Bane and Ralph Haswell Lutz, eds., *Organization of American*

Impressive as these feats were, however, Allied officials interested in developing a humanitarian response to the Second World War saw the Great War experience as something to avoid as much as emulate. Even while admiring Hoover's efforts, a consensus emerged that in the Great War's immediate aftermath, relief efforts often came too late, with insufficient resource support from participating states, and an insistence by the largest contributor, the USA, on keeping firm control over what were supposed to be internationally collaborative ventures. A similar faction in the US Congress that ultimately thwarted President Woodrow Wilson's plans for US involvement in the League of Nations dragged its feet in approving American contributions for post-war relief projects that demanded immediate, not delayed, attention. When funds from the US Treasury were approved, relief advocates complained that they were tied to so many stipulations that America's role in post-war aid operations often seemed more unilateral than part of the multinational entities that the USA had nominally joined.[21] Especially tarnishing the legacy of the Great War-era relief efforts was Hoover's insistence that recipient nations either pay for the supplies – mostly drawn from enormous US food surpluses amassed during the war – or take on debts that would later contribute to caustic environments of economic and political instability. In the assessment of some, then, the relief efforts of the Great War era sowed the seeds for future conflict even while ameliorating the suffering of millions.[22] Tainting the historical record further, the minority treaties emerging from the First World War's peace agreements along with the refugee aid offices directed by Fridtjof Nansen had both proven woefully inadequate in protecting the victims of state persecution. The League of Nations had similarly failed its charge to mediate international disputes through law and diplomacy rather than unilateralism and violence.[23]

For Soviet officials during the Second World War, the Great War's aid operations served as an especially potent cautionary tale for letting one country dominate the Soviets, namely, the USA. Hoover's Eastern operations

---

Relief in Europe, 1918–1919 (Stanford University Press, 1943); Merle Curti, *American Philanthropy Abroad: A History* (New Brunswick, NJ: Rutgers University Press, 1963), pp. 244–300.

21 Royal Institute of International Affairs, *Relief and Reconstruction in Europe, the First Steps: An Interim Report by a Chatham House Study Group* (London: Royal Institute of International Affairs, 1942); Shephard, '"Becoming Planning Minded"', pp. 407–8.

22 Susan Armstrong-Reid and David Murray, *Armies of Peace: Canada and the UNRRA Years* (University of Toronto Press, 2008), pp. 17–18, 39; Shephard, '"Becoming Planning Minded"', pp. 409–10.

23 Skran, *Refugees in Inter-War Europe*; Marrus, *Unwanted*, pp. 51–295; Mazower, *Dark Continent*, pp. 41–75, 138–81.

and those of other American-dominated relief efforts had often deliberately steered food and other resources away from Soviet factions during the Russian civil war and toward the White Russians, using aid as a political weapon to sap Russian support for Bolshevism.[24] As Soviet officials contemplated the prospect of humanitarian initiatives for the Second World War, they were confronted with a number of competing factors. On the one hand, the massive and vicious German advance eastward left little doubt that the countries of Eastern Europe and the western regions of the Soviet Union would require tremendous amounts of aid upon the war's cessation. And yet, the memory remained fresh of the American-dominated relief efforts of the First World War, posing, in the assessment of Soviet officials, a continued threat to their country's sovereign integrity during the anticipated relief stages of the current war and, especially, its aftermath.[25]

In the nearly two-year period between the Soviets' first proposed alternative to Leith-Ross's Committee in January 1942 and the establishment of UNRRA in November 1943, Soviet Foreign Minister Vyacheslav Molotov and his diplomatic corps pushed for an intergovernmental relief organization that would avoid US domination while helping the Soviets to achieve a stronger sphere of influence over neighbouring Eastern European states. Whereas the British-led Inter-Allied Committee envisioned a relief apparatus run through traditional political negotiations between state diplomats – one where the British held considerable leverage – the Soviets wanted relief to run through a highly centralized bureaucracy controlled largely by themselves and the British, a more efficient design, they argued. Other proposals by the Soviets were more explicit in their intentions to limit the institution's multilateral heft and defend national sovereignty. For one, the initial Soviet plan of January 1942 outlined an exclusively European entity, with no representation from the western hemisphere, Asia or the Middle East. The absence of the USA in the Soviet plan was particularly glaring, as the new Western belligerent was expected to be the major donor of relief provisions.

24 Bertrand M. Patenaude, *The Big Show in Bololand: The American Relief Expedition to Soviet Russia in the Famine of 1921* (Stanford University Press, 2002); Surface and Bland, *American Food in the World War*; Bane and Lutz, *Organization of American Relief in Europe*; Curti, *American Philanthropy Abroad*, pp. 244–300.
25 US Department of State, *Foreign Relations of the United States: Diplomatic Papers* [hereafter *FRUS*], *1942. General: Political and Economic Matters. Participation by the United States in the Work of the United Nations Relief and Rehabilitation Administration (UNRRA)* (Washington: GPO, 1943), pp. 89–162, especially pp. 159–62; Ben Shephard, *The Long Road Home: The Aftermath of the Second World War* (London: The Bodley Head, 2010), pp. 409–10.

Also conspicuously missing was the final member of the so-called Big Four powers, the Republic of China, whose ongoing war with Japan had amassed tremendous civilian and military casualties. Though Chinese diplomats ultimately played a less conspicuous role in the broader designs of the nascent relief organization than those of the other major powers, there was no doubt that the country's humanitarian needs would prove staggering. Soviet ambassador to the USA Maxim Litvinov additionally insisted to his Western counterparts that the governments of recipient countries control all aspects of relief distribution within their borders, essentially making the proposed international organization an acquisition and wholesale supply centre, and little else. Molotov, Litvinov and the rest of the Soviet diplomatic corps operated with the presumption that whoever controlled the final provisioning of international aid could achieve significant influence over the shape of the post-war governments in Eastern Europe, transforming relief provisioning into a sort of patronage politics on a truly massive scale for the Soviets.[26] Finally, Soviet officials regularly insisted that the proposed aid organization, along with the occupying militaries, automatically repatriate all refugees back to their places of origin rather than offer extended asylum or permanent resettlement for those deemed to be at risk of persecution upon return.[27]

The British and Americans had, needless to say, significant reservations about a vision for organized relief wherein the USA was assumed to become a major donor without administrative representation; the Chinese and other non-European war victims were omitted as aid recipients; and the Soviets possessed extensive authority to distribute, and potentially withhold, aid within Soviet borders and, presumably, parts of Eastern Europe as well. After digesting one of the Soviet proposals, Leith-Ross concluded that the Soviets sought to unilaterally determine the 'final form [of] inter-allied control' over relief operations. The American ambassador to Britain John Winant agreed, opining that the proposal 'would give undue influence to Russia through military-geographical factors which might result in pressure on refugee governments' exiled in the West from Central and Eastern

---

26 *FRUS, 1942, UNRRA Participation*, pp. 89–162, especially p. 155; Agreement for the United Nations Relief and Rehabilitation Administration (hereafter UNRRA Agreement), 9 November 1943, in Woodbridge, *UNRRA*, vol. III, Appendix III; Fox, 'Origins of UNRRA', pp. 562–4; Armstrong-Reid and Murray, *Armies of Peace*, pp. 18–19. On the role of China, also see Dean Acheson, *Present at the Creation: My Years in the State Department* (New York: W. W. Norton, 1969), p. 68; UNRRA, *UNRRA in China: 1945–1947* (New York: UNRRA, 1948).

27 UNRRA Agreement; Holian, *Between National Socialism and Soviet Communism*, pp. 81–119; Wyman, *DP*, pp. 61–85; Marrus, *Unwanted*, pp. 313–23.

Europe. The Soviet approach absurdly minimized, in Winant's assessment, the projected relief needs not just of war-torn areas outside of Europe, but also of Western Europe, Britain, the neutral powers and the enemy states, leaving the vast majority of the aid for the Soviet Union and its sphere of influence in Eastern Europe.[28] And though US and British officials were more reticent about Soviet demands that reluctant refugees from the East be forcibly repatriated after the liberation of German-occupied territories, both governments were well aware that this policy would run counter to the international legal principle of *non-refoulement*, a norm codified in several international agreements as recently as the 1930s. British and American officials additionally answered to increasingly vocal domestic constituencies who advocated on behalf of refugee groups and would undoubtedly oppose a policy of automatic repatriation.[29]

Yet beyond these differences between the diplomats were critical overlapping strategic interests which ultimately allowed sufficient room for compromise to bring the nascent UNRRA into existence. Confronting a world on the verge of destroying itself, officials from the Big Four as well as the other forty founding members of UNRRA, found a common desire amidst their myriad differences to secure a more stable, peaceful and prosperous future, one in which widespread war relief seemed a critical prerequisite. Significant differences between member states on the operations of international relief would remain, but through months of painstaking negotiations, UNRRA's members agreed to pursue their respective national interests on this matter multilaterally, namely through an intergovernmental aid institution of unprecedented size and scope.[30]

Dean Acheson credited some of this accomplishment to a fruitful diplomatic environment that emerged between representatives of the Big Four in

---

28 Thomas G. Paterson, *Soviet–American Confrontation: Postwar Reconstruction and the Origins of the Cold War* (Baltimore: Johns Hopkins University Press, 1973), pp. 75–98; *FRUS, 1942, UNRRA Participation*, pp. 89–92 (quotes from pp. 91–2).

29 Skran, *Refugees in Inter-War Europe*; Erika Mann and Eric Estorick, 'Private and Governmental Aid to Refugees', *Annals for the American Academy of Political and Social Sciences* 203 (1939), 142–54; Henry L. Feingold, *The Politics of Rescue: The Roosevelt Administration and the Holocaust, 1938–1945* (New Brunswick, NJ: Rutgers University Press, 1970); Malcolm J. Proudfoot, *European Refugees: A Study in Forced Population Movement* (Evanston, Ill.: Northwestern University Press, 1956), pp. 30–1; Marrus, *Unwanted*, pp. 170–2. Opposition would also eventually mount against the forcible movement of 12 million ethnic German *Volksdeutsche* to Germany after the war. Douglas, *Orderly and Humane*.

30 Executive Order 9453, Providing for the Participation of the U.S. in the Work of UNRRA; President Roosevelt, *First Report to Congress on U.S. Participation in Operations of UNRRA, as of September 30, 1944* (Washington: GPO, 1945), pp. 14–15.

the two years of negotiations. Initially, the Anglo-American alliance kept the most substantive meetings to themselves, typically led by Leith-Ross and Britain's ambassador to Washington Lord Halifax, Acheson, US Secretary of State Cordell Hull and New York governor and future UNRRA director Herbert Lehman. Over the course of 1942, especially, representatives from the two nations developed something of a united front over the shape of the future organization, one that balanced the presumed demands of the other Allies – most importantly, the Soviet Union and, to a lesser extent, China – with their own desires to maintain considerable control over relief. Attempts were made to mollify concerns by Chinese and Soviet officials that the Westerners intended to hijack the process, as when Hull assured Litvinov and the Chinese ambassador to the USA, Hu Shih, that recent US–British discussions, 'had kept them in mind from the beginning' and 'that no definite plans had yet been reached for a program'. The Secretary promised that the USA and Britain 'would let them see every tentative suggestion we reduced to writing and keep them advised of any phase of the conversations'.[31] As diplomats from the East began to join the negotiating meetings more regularly from later 1942 through 1943, Acheson recalled the 'congenial' atmosphere that developed. He fondly referred to the 'roly-poly' and 'voluble' Litvinov as 'an old-school Russian' who 'understood the forms and uses of courtesy' and 'presented an amusing antithesis' to the more reserved Lord Halifax. The working relations between the men crossed into social affairs that included dinner with the diplomats' families and regular painting sessions between the wives of Litvinov and Acheson, the former being English-born. When negotiations stalled over controversial details, the small group learned to step back to ruminate on broader issues of consensus: on, in Acheson's words, 'the world which was to be'.[32] By the time that UNRRA's draft agreement was sent to officials in the other 'United Nations' governments at the beginning of 1943, the blueprint for the institution had been already largely set through the negotiations by the Big Four. They were joined occasionally by Canada, whose officials regularly jockeyed for a degree of political and administrative influence over the organization more commensurate with their country's large contribution of foodstuffs.[33]

31 *FRUS, UNRRA Participation*, all quotes from pp. 115–16.
32 Acheson, *Present at the Creation*, p. 68.
33 'War Victim Relief Setup is Drafted', *Washington Post*, 11 January 1943. On Canada's involvement, see Armstrong-Reid and Murray, *Armies of Peace*.

Making UNRRA run

It was formalized at the November 1943 conference establishing UNRRA in Atlantic City, New Jersey that its forty-four member states would each be represented on a policy-making Council. The actual management of UNRRA, however, proved largely to be a great-power affair. Making policy decisions between the infrequent meetings of the Council was a powerful Central Committee comprised of the Big Four powers. The four also exerted prodigious influence on the European and Asian regional committees along with another bureau charged with procuring and providing supplies. Boasting one-half of the world's industrial output at the end of the war, the USA was slated to be the largest financial and material contributor. As such, it was agreed that the Americans would possess the most authority over UNRRA's operations among the great powers. President Roosevelt tapped Lehman to be the institution's first director general. With the 'full power and authority to carry out the operations contemplated by the Agreement', the director general was far and away the most powerful office in the organization. Lehman was followed in 1946 and 1947 by two other Americans, former New York City mayor Fiorello La Guardia and Major General Lowell Ward Rooks.[34]

The final revisions to UNRRA's constitution occurred at least as much through negotiations within relevant sectors of the US government as between the charter states. UNRRA advocates within the Roosevelt administration remained wary of the precedent set after the First World War with Congress's refusal to sign onto President Woodrow Wilson's proposal for the League, another intergovernmental civilian enterprise of unprecedented ambition. With rare exception, administration officials worked diligently to avoid the mistakes of the past by keeping Congressmen – especially key members of the opposition Republican Party – involved in the late planning stages for UNRRA. Michigan Republican Senator Arthur Vandenberg praised the US State Department for its outreach efforts, calling it 'amazingly cooperative, almost without precedent'. As an influential Republican member of the Senate Foreign Relations Committee and fresh convert to vibrant American multilateralism, Vandenberg's endorsement signalled a critically stronger American embrace of international collaboration than

34 Woodbridge, *UNRRA*, vol. I, pp. 4–7 (p. 5 for quote), and vol. III, Appendix III. On US industrial production, see Richard N. Gardner, *Sterling–Dollar Diplomacy: The Origins and the Prospects of our International Economic Order* (New York: McGraw-Hill, 1969), p. 178.

witnessed after the Great War.[35] Congress passed seven funding laws for the organization between March 1944 and July 1946 to the tune of more than $2.6 billion. This represented the lion's share of UNRRA's total budget, over two-thirds of the total contributions received from states and, much less significantly, non-governmental sources.[36]

The sales pitch extended beyond Congress to the American public. Herbert Hoover was conspicuously brought in as a consultant on UNRRA planning and operations as part of a broader message that the organization refused to play the part of an American 'Santa Claus' to the world. Like their counterparts in Britain, Americans were assured that UNRRA would not be permitted to engage in long-term rehabilitation projects – despite the second 'R' – only emergency relief that would presumably give recipient countries the footing to begin 'helping themselves'. Relief operations were discursively linked to the patriotic fervour behind the war effort. Hull, Acheson and Lehman publicly insisted time and again that America's contributions to the new organization could be used for both humanitarian good and for the strategic interests of the country.[37] As Lehman put it, since 'shattered economies, pestilence, starvation and death breed riot and anarchy', the USA 'must use food, clothing, shelter and the necessities of life as a real weapon to win complete and overwhelming victory and to secure the peace which must follow'.[38] The promotion of UNRRA to Congress and the American people echoed the rationales for the law that created the Government and Relief in Occupied Areas programme to provide food and other emergency needs to the citizens of Japan, Germany and Austria who were generally not eligible for UNRRA aid. A project run unilaterally by the US government, its supporters argued that a modicum of support for the defeated civilians, mostly food aid, was important not only on humanitarian grounds, but to prevent forms of social unrest that would endanger the work of American occupying forces.[39]

---

35 *Senate Hearings on UNRRA Participation*, February 1944, pp. 11–13 (p. 13 for quote).
36 Woodbridge, *UNRRA*, vol. i, pp. 105, 112–18, and vol. iii, p. 500.
37 For example, 'The Lehman OFRRO Blueprints its Task', *New York Times*, 7 January 1943.
38 'Lehman Discusses Food as a Weapon', *New York Times*, 1 February 1943.
39 *FRUS: Vol. ix, Foreign Economic Policy of the Historian, 1961–1963*, sec. 4 (Washington, GPO, 1964); US Senate Committee on Appropriations, *European Interim Aid and Government and Relief in Occupied Areas: Hearings Before the Committee on Appropriations, United States Senate, Eightieth Congress, First Session* (Washington: GPO, 1947); *FRUS, 1946. The Far East Volume viii* (Washington: GPO, 1946), pp. 85–604; Eiji Takemae, *The Allied Occupation of Japan and its Legacy*, trans. Robert Ricketts and Sebastian Swann (New York: Continuum, 2002); Nicholas Balabkins, *Germany under Direct Controls: Economic Aspects of Industrial Disarmament, 1945–1948* (Rutgers, NJ: Rutgers University Press, 1964).

Such messages found purchase. In an instance of hyperbole that nonetheless flirted with a practical truth, Dean Acheson opined in late 1944 that 'the Congress of the United States and the people of the United States are unreservedly behind this Administration' with regards to UNRRA.[40] Even though UNRRA had its persistent detractors, a poll of 1,260 Americans conducted in the autumn of 1945 found a full 82 per cent of respondents approved of Congress committing additional funds to the organization.[41]

In what would prove a more trudging campaign, advocates for UNRRA similarly worked to win over their Allied military leaders leery of what they perceived as the organization's intervention into the domain of civilian relief traditionally left to occupying military forces. Part of the resistance stemmed from a belief among the military authorities that they had taken greater strides in this war than ever before to looking after the needs of liberated civilians, and perhaps with good reason. William Hitchcock notes that 'Within months after the end of the war, British and American armies of occupation [in Germany] had transformed themselves into massive social and humanitarian agencies.' By the autumn of 1945, military authorities were even 'rejecting the idea that they were occupiers', instead championing the 'goal of winning "the battle of winter"'.[42] Something similar occurred in Japan, occupied predominantly by the USA, though it took longer to materialize, and with tragic consequences for a starving and sick population.[43] The military suspicion of UNRRA eventually dissipated though never vanished. As Supreme Commander of the Anglo-US-controlled Allied Expeditionary Force, General Dwight Eisenhower finally signed a working agreement with UNRRA officials in late 1944, a year after the organization's establishment and several months after the invasion of Normandy. The terms required that in the initial stages of territorial occupation much of the civilian relief effort would be handled by Allied forces. More aid operations would be transferred to the new civilian relief entity in time, but even then, UNRRA would remain under the ultimate authority of the military commanders.[44]

---

40 UNRRA, *Report of the Director General*, September 1944.
41 National Opinion Research Center, University of Chicago, October 1945, USNORC.450135.R18A.
42 Hitchcock, *Bitter Road*, p. 4.
43 Dower, *Embracing Defeat*, pp. 54–6; Kawai, *Japan's American Interlude*, pp. 133–5.
44 'Agreement to Regularize Relations between UNRRA and Supreme Commander, Allied Expeditionary Force, during the Military Period', Archives Nationales du Luxembourg, Luxembourg. Relations internationales. UNRRA, AE 8088 (www.ena.lu/mce.cfm).

The practical effects on the civilian relief institution were not as dramatic as such an agreement might suggest. Over its first year and a half of existence, bureaucratic growing pains, funding delays and a dearth of available personnel meant that UNRRA was scarcely prepared anyway to take on most of the large-scale tasks its advocates had envisioned for the enterprise. Once UNRRA operations were brought up to speed, its officials and personnel often developed relatively functional working relationships with members of the occupying militaries.[45]

Despite the tremendous amount of vital assistance that UNRRA provided to so many millions of war victims across such vast territory, the unprecedented relief organization came in for a range of criticisms: some well earned, some less so; some consistent, others contradictory. Despite early planning, UNRRA got off to a lumbering start. As Allied militaries conquered increasing swathes of territory from later 1943 through 1945, initial funding for relief operations arrived much more slowly than the humanitarian demands mounted. The sheer enormity of the enterprise exacerbated matters, prompting a Conservative Member of the British Parliament to call UNRRA 'a Colossus on so vast a scale that it has been, from the outset, muscle-bound, paralyzed by its own weight'. Officials additionally found it difficult in the early stages to recruit enough personnel with so much of the able-bodied population from the potential pool of employees serving in the military or performing important functions for the war cause at home. UNRRA consequently became staffed by relatively large numbers of older workers, women, conscientious objectors and others who couldn't or wouldn't engage in other areas of war work. Sceptics of the organization used the demographic composition of its workforce as a point of criticism, claiming that recruiters were 'scraping the bottom of the barrel'. Though some invoked the feminized monikers 'Mother UNRRA' and 'Auntie UNRRA' endearingly, for others the terms were deployed as part of a larger project of stigmatizing the institution with negative associations of femininity. This occurred despite the fact that in the middle of its operational tenure, two-thirds of UNRRA employees were men. A great many of them, in fact, were Americans, accused by other critics of over-masculinized behaviours including womanizing, drunkenness and displaying a brash, triumphalist

---

45 Sharif Gemie, Fiona Reid and Laure Humbert, *Outcast Europe: Refugees and Relief Workers in an Era of Total War, 1936–1948* (London: Continuum, 2012), pp. 357, 362–3, 424; Johannes-Deiter Steinert, 'British Humanitarian Assistance: Wartime Planning and Postwar Realities', *Journal of Contemporary History* 43:3 (2008), 421–35; Shephard, '"Becoming Planning Minded"'.

attitude. Some of the organization's opponents accused UNRRA of being dominated by Jews, which, depending on the perspective, might lead to charges of either using the organization to promote global communism or capitalist profiteering. A British Foreign Office official admitted that seeing Jewish businessmen in key leadership roles (Lehman, for instance, hailed from a prominent Jewish-American banking family) gave him 'the creeps'. The composition of its leadership and workforce, in these renderings, helped to explain why UNRRA was inefficiently run (which for a diversity of other reasons, in fact, it often was), hiding nefarious aims, or otherwise not in step with the harder-edge imperatives of military strategy, geopolitical gamesmanship or economic reconstruction.[46]

Perhaps the most ethically damning and empirically justified critiques pertained to the organization's propensity to favour nationalist parochialism and cultural prejudices in the provision of aid rather than neutral humanitarianism based primarily on need. The relief organization that emerged from so many domestic and international negotiations represented a set of genuine compromises. This was arguably UNRRA's great diplomatic achievement, but it could also prove harmful both to those war victims falling under UNRRA's mandate and those who were left outside of it.

UNRRA ultimately boasted vast distribution operations, in opposition to early Soviet preferences, but in line with Soviet designs, recipient states could exert considerable authority over operations within their sovereign borders. UNRRA officials were required to negotiate the terms of distribution with the sixteen recipient states. This not only made some aid operations especially bureaucratically cumbersome and kept aid from getting to those in need but offered critical points of leverage for certain states to use the delivery of supplies to their political and, at times, military advantage.[47] UNRRA operations in the Soviet Union and the emerging Soviet bloc in Eastern Europe drew charges, especially from some American opponents of UNRRA in the USA, of aid being distributed only where and how it would win the Soviets political advantage.[48] The Republic of China also anticipated

---

46 Gemie et al., *Outcast Europe*, pp. 321–3, 327, 332, 424, 488; Jessica Reinisch, '"Auntie UNRRA" at the Crossroads', *Past & Present* 218, supplement 8 (2013), 70–97; Reinisch, 'Introduction: Relief in the Aftermath of War', p. 386. All quotes from Gemie et al., *Outcast Europe*, pp. 321–3. For charges of inefficiency, see Shephard, '"Becoming Planning Minded"'. On the sometimes distasteful behaviour of American liberating forces and other organizations, see Hitchcock, *Bitter Road to Freedom*.

47 Woodbridge, *UNRRA*, vol. III, Appendix VII, pp. 238–349.

48 While there was much evidence for this phenomenon, UNRRA rank and file workers – many from the West – often maintained a strong commitment to the principle of

both the humanitarian and political advantages that UNRRA aid could have, in its ongoing civil war with the Chinese communists. Chinese officials employed the diplomatic skill of Chinese legal scholar Wei Tao-Ming to lobby for both copious UNRRA supplies and near total autonomy in their distribution. The Guomindang got its wish with the establishment of the Chinese National Relief and Rehabilitation Administration (CNRRA). While CNRRA offered critical assistance to millions of desperate Chinese civilians from 1945 to 1947, it also earned a reputation for using its $500 million in UNRRA food, medical supplies and other aid to advance the nationalist military agenda in the civil war.[49] Such practices extended to smaller nations as well, with UNRRA aid used to prop up right-leaning governments in Italy and Greece at the expense of political factions on the left and the populations associated with them.[50]

Even when UNRRA officials did control more of the channels of relief distribution, the organization's own rules sometimes prioritized geopolitics and an Allied desire for retribution over human need. This phenomenon was especially pronounced in refugee affairs, with the bulk of UNRRA's operations occurring in Europe. On a scale nearly impossible to fathom, an estimated 55 million Europeans were forcibly moved from their homes from the beginning of hostilities in 1939 through to the end of UNRRA's operations in 1947. By the end of the war, 11 million Europeans remained outside of their countries of original residence. The large majority of them resided in Germany, usually brought there as forced labourers or concentration camp inmates (the latter, numbering 700,000 survivors). Most of the remainder were scattered elsewhere in Europe and the eastern Mediterranean, usually having fled the advances of various belligerent ground forces. UNRRA officials and military authorities coined the term 'displaced persons' to categorize these 11 million refugees, a definition mainly limited to civilians outside of their countries of origin at the end of the hostilities. Most of the

---

letting need dictate the dispensation of relief. Andrew Harder, 'The Politics of Impartiality: The United Nations Relief and Rehabilitation Administration in the Soviet Union, 1946–7', *Journal of Contemporary History* 47:2 (2012), 347–69.

49 Rana Mitter, 'Imperialism, Transnationalism, and the Reconstruction of Postwar China, 1944–7', *Past & Present* 218, supplement 8 (2013), 51–69; Elizabeth Collingham, *The Taste of War: World War II and the Battle for Food* (London: Allen Lane, 2011), pp. 248–72; George H. Kerr, *Formosa Betrayed* (New York: Houghton Mifflin, 1965), pp. 158–87; UNRRA, *UNRRA in China: 1945–1947* (New York: UNRRA, 1948). On Wei Tao-Ming, see Acheson, *Present at the Creation*, p. 68.

50 Katerina Gardikas, 'Relief Work and Malaria in Greece', and Frank Snowden, 'Latina Province, 1944–1950', both in *Journal of Contemporary History* 43:3 (2008), 493–508 and 509–26.

hundreds of refugee camps and related support centres supervised by UNRRA were located in Germany. The organization, however, also boasted significant refugee aid operations in Austria, Italy, North Africa (especially Egypt), the Levant (especially Palestine and Syria) and China, where 1 million internally displaced Chinese, though not officially 'displaced persons', were given transportation assistance by CNRRA, paid for with UNRRA funds.[51]

Expansive as its presence was, though, a great many needy refugees fell outside of UNRRA's protective umbrella. These included huge numbers of European refugees displaced within their countries of origin.[52] Also remaining ineligible for UNRRA aid were the 12 million ethnic German *Volksdeutsche* who, as part of the war's peace agreements, were expelled from their homes in Central and Eastern Europe to Germany, a country where many, in fact, had never lived. The conditions under which they travelled were often horrific, replete with starvation, disease and abusive vengeance at the hands of local populations who had suffered under Nazi occupation. Though some UNRRA officials and personnel chafed at the policy, the organization was forbidden from offering the *Volksdeutsche* expellees material support, even when it was readily available.[53] The logic behind forbidding UNRRA assistance to the *Volksdeutche* echoed the rules that forbade UNRRA support to enemy civilians in Germany and Japan, vast populations who were also in desperate conditions after the war.[54] Added to this was the fact that, even for the displaced persons who did fall under its jurisdiction, UNRRA was forbidden in its constitution from offering them either significant aid provisions or resettlement assistance for those resisting repatriation. In the middle and later months of 1945, in particular, UNRRA refugee aid personnel often facilitated Allied militaries' efforts to repatriate 10 million displaced persons eastward at a remarkable pace of 33,000 per day. Some went willingly, but large numbers of those slated to return to the

51 Woodbridge, *UNRRA*, vol. II, pp. 469–96; Cohen, *In War's Wake*, pp. 35–57; Holian, *Between National Socialism and Soviet Communism*, pp. 3–4; Jessica Reinisch and Elizabeth White, eds., *The Disentanglement of Populations: Migration, Expulsion and Displacement in Postwar Europe, 1944–1949* (New York: Palgrave Macmillan, 2011).

52 In his official history of UNRRA (*UNRRA*, vol. II, p. 469), George Woodbridge estimates the number of internal refugees in the middle of the war to have been 8 million.

53 Douglas, *Orderly and Humane*, pp. 78, 187, 240, 243, 296; Rainer Schulze, 'Forced Migration of German Populations During and After the Second World War: History and Memory', in Reinisch and White, eds., *Disentanglement of Populations*, pp. 51–70.

54 UNRRA Agreement; Woodbridge, *UNRRA*. On the role of vengeance in the post-war period, see Lowe, *Savage Continent*, pp. 75–186. On Japan, see Dower, *Embracing Defeat*; Kawai, *Japan's American Interlude*; Takemae, *Allied Occupation of Japan*.

Soviet East did not. Though most had been forced by the Nazis into Germany and other formerly Reich-occupied territories to labour for the German war enterprise, they feared, often legitimately, political persecution upon their return for being accused of aiding the enemy.[55]

While in time, the Western militaries and UNRRA personnel worked to stay the practice of forced repatriation for over a million remaining displaced persons, the initial policy proved damning for many others. The issue of forced repatriation became a major source of criticism of UNRRA, and ultimately played a role in convincing a majority in the US Congress to stop funding the relief organization in 1946, forcing it to enter a wind-down phase beginning especially in 1947. In its place arose another largely US-funded humanitarian entity, the International Refugee Organization (IRO), which, without the membership of an emerging Eastern bloc, was more overtly controlled by its American benefactor. Chief among the differences between UNRRA and the successor IRO, the latter was tasked with resettling the 1 million refugees, largely hailing from the Soviet sphere, residing in the Western Allied zones of occupation in Germany and elsewhere, a development marking one of the early major battles of the Cold War.[56]

Legacies

The transition of international refugee management responsibilities to the IRO opens a window onto some wider geopolitical and institutional legacies that UNRRA bequeathed to the post-war international order. UNRRA's work on behalf of displaced persons dramatically advanced the field of internationally organized refugee protection and assistance beyond the interwar efforts of the League of Nations, various High Commissions and Nansen offices for Refugees, the International Labour Organization, and a range of civil society organizations based mostly in the West. The experience in refugee management acquired by so many personnel during UNRRA's tenure was passed further along to the UN High Commissioner for Refugees (1951–present) upon the dissolution of the IRO in 1952. Despite their own limitations, these latter two refugee aid entities, along with attendant international agreements and related organizations, built upon the legacies of UNRRA's massive

55 Holian, *Between National Socialism and Soviet Communism*, pp. 81–119; Wyman, *DP*, pp. 15–37; Cohen, *In War's Wake*, pp. 4–5, 18, 104; Andrew Janco, 'Soviet "Displaced Persons" in Europe, 1941–1951' (PhD dissertation, University of Chicago, 2012).
56 Holborn, *International Refugee Organization*; Vernant, *Refugee*; Cohen, *In War's Wake*, pp. 30–4, 61–7.

displaced persons operations to ensure that the protections afforded to refugees in the post-war world would remain, by and large, much stronger than during the interwar period.[57]

UNRRA's legacy can be measured in a variety of areas beyond refugee affairs, including the short-term stability that the enterprise created in dangerously unstable environments. UNRRA's emergency relief operations helped to provide space for longer-term projects of economic 'development', political rejuvenation and diplomatic engagement. Not unlike the Allied military occupations of the former Axis countries, UNRRA's more successful operations helped fragile governments concentrate on rebuilding their economies, infrastructures and political systems rather than the immediate pressure of keeping their populations alive and healthy. This was true not only for Western Europe, where the resources of the Marshall Plan, the European Coal and Steel Community, and other transnational projects would find solid enough terrain for rebuilding, and not just sustaining, that region of the continent. It also applied, if more equivocally, to the Soviet-occupied East and to China.[58] And with the exception of UN aid to refugees, while it was not the UN but the International Committee of the Red Cross and a host of international civil society organizations that assumed much of the international responsibility for war relief and related forms of emergency assistance during the Cold War and beyond, a number of international governmental organizations emerged or reconstituted themselves in UNRRA's wake to address more perpetual issues of social security for populations in need. The most direct of these was the World Health Organization, which, alongside the IRO, was the chief beneficiary of much of UNRRA's remaining staff, administrative architecture and material resources. The experience of UNRRA and related contemporary relief

---

57 Cohen, In War's Wake, pp. 30–4, 61–7; Holborn, International Refugee Organization; Proudfoot, European Refugees; Vernant, Refugee; Marrus, Unwanted. Particular mention should be made of the UN Relief and Works Agency for Palestinian Refugees in the Near East. Created in 1949, UNRWA has operated on a mostly parallel basis with the UNHCR, with the former charged with overseeing a particular refugee population on a perpetual, multi-generational basis. Kjersti G. Berg, 'Gendering Refugees: The United Nations Relief and Works Agency (UNRWA) and the Politics of Relief', in Nefissa Naguib and Inter Marie Okkenhaug, eds., Interpreting Welfare and Relief in the Middle East (Boston: Brill, 2008), pp. 149–74.

58 Ekbladh, Great American Mission; McVety, Enlightened Aid; Woodbridge, UNRRA, vol. II, pp. 81–256, 361–453, 469–532 (on 'DP' camp numbers, p. 502); Nicolaus Mills, Winning the Peace: The Marshall Plan and America's Coming of Age as a Superpower (New York: John Wiley, 2008); Gatrell and Baron, Population Resettlement; Paterson, Soviet–American Confrontation, pp. 75–98; Mitter, 'Imperialism, Transnationalism, and the Reconstruction of Postwar China'; Collingham, Taste of War, pp. 248–72.

initiatives were also instrumental in the creation or further development of such other UN entities as the International Labour Organization, the Food and Agriculture Organization and the Children's Fund.[59]

The organization also made a major impact on a wide host of civil society organizations engaged in humanitarian endeavours. In an acknowledgement that the contributions of member states would fall far short of predicted needs, UNRRA planners early on arranged for the significant involvement of non-state voluntary agencies in the organization's operations. One hundred and twenty-five voluntary agencies from some twenty countries formally helped to implement a variety of UNRRA programmes, exercising near complete administrative control over many displaced persons camps.[60] These philanthropies organized themselves into powerful national and international federations, not only of their own volition, but often at the urging of UNRRA officials and those of its member states, most importantly, the USA and Britain.[61] These federations, in turn, entered into formal working relationships with UNRRA as well as the occupying Allied military authorities that ran aid operations separate from UNRRA in Germany, Japan and elsewhere. A nearly endless stream of the rapidly popularized CARE packages, for instance, were sent as a result of such arrangements to countries throughout war-torn Asia and Europe courtesy of a conglomeration of American voluntary agencies.[62]

The massive state-directed aid programmes of the Second World War, in other words, created unprecedentedly vast opportunities for civil society organizations to engage in international humanitarian endeavours, even as the nature of those opportunities were regulated by governments. Over the ensuing years and decades, these developments allowed later incarnations of these non-governmental organizations to become more capable of running increasingly robust humanitarian missions across the globe, contributing to

---

59 Gemie et al., *Outcast Europe*, p. 334.

60 Woodbridge, *UNRRA*, vol. II, pp. 67–78.

61 The US State Department prompted American voluntary agency officials to organize their largest and most professional organizations into an umbrella federation known as the American Council of Voluntary Agencies for Foreign Assistance. Reiss, *American Council*, pp. 1–41. The British analogue, forged with the pressure of the British state, was the Council of British Societies for Relief Abroad. Gatrell and Baron, *Population Resettlement*, p. 71.

62 Aid to Germans, largely ineligible for UNRRA assistance, was offered by the Council of Relief Agencies Licensed to Operate in Germany (CRALOG). Licensed Agencies for Relief in Asia (LARA) emerged in the spring of 1946 to operate in Japan. Reiss, *American Council*; Elizabeth Clark Reiss and Eileen Egan, *Transfigured Night: The CRALOG Experience* (Philadelpia: Livingston, 1964); Dower, *Embracing Defeat*, p. 575.

what has been called an 'NGO revolution'. Some of these organizations have additionally built a degree of political heft and independence that has allowed them, frequently through discourses of human rights, to challenge the very nation states that had helped to nurture their maturation in the era of the Second World War. In this sense, one of UNRRA's more intriguing legacies may be that an interstate venture the likes of which the world had never or has since known played a seminal role in the unprecedented growth of today's thriving global civil society.[63]

The issue of human rights and its ideological cousin, humanitarianism, invites a concluding reflection on that blend of compassion and cold calculation that produced the moral economy of the Second World War. Never before had a coalition of powerful states made such a political and material commitment to ameliorate the harsh consequences of violent conflict. And while in many ways it would never again do so to such an extent, the impetus of humanitarianism remained a regular feature in the governing architecture of many states after the war, albeit one commonly dwarfed by other imperatives. And though leaders in the Allied militaries commonly resented what they perceived as the intrusion of relief workers from voluntary agencies and civilian government into territories that their forces had recently taken, in the assessment of one study, 'UNRRA established relief work as an essential part of all future military planning.'[64]

While humanitarianism clearly became more firmly embedded after the war in the operating logics of certain state and civil society institutions, the role of human rights was arguably weaker and certainly less overt. Unlike such documents as the 1941 Atlantic Charter, 1945 UN Charter and 1948 Universal Declaration of Human Rights that explicitly spoke in terms of the rights of individual human beings to certain protections and entitlements regardless of group status, UNRRA's operating documents laid more emphasis on various obligations of the international community to secure for particular groups of civilian war victims a certain level of humanitarian treatment. The era's human rights documents and attendant discourses furthermore emphasized timeless rights, whereas UNRRA was explicitly designed as a temporary response to crises that were deemed momentary.

---

63 There is a long history to the collaboration between state and voluntary associations in the name of humanitarianism, dating especially from the early nineteenth century. For a good overview of this phenomenon, see Barnett, *Empire of Humanity*. These issues are elaborated in Stephen Porter, *Benevolent Empire? Refugees, NGOs, and the American State* (forthcoming).

64 Gemie et al., *Outcast Europe*, p. 425.

Nevertheless, UNRRA should be seen, in part anyway, as a more pragmatically oriented, on-the-ground analogue to – a nascent test case for – the grand declarations and agreements of the era that communicated more directly and elegantly about the right of individuals to claim a measure of protection from the international community. Key UNRRA advocates and officials were, in fact, also involved in the formulation of the UN Charter and the Universal Declaration. Some saw their work as an application of the emerging principles of human rights to the actual lives of vulnerable people. This was especially true among Western UNRRA personnel who increasingly refused to forcibly repatriate displaced persons on the basis that some refugees were individuals with a genuine fear of persecution. If the frenetic demands of the work done by the relief workers of the Second World War resisted the measured consideration of well-articulated ideologies, we should nevertheless acknowledge those people's roles in promoting an ascendant vision of a liberal international order where collective social security might yield a more peaceful and prosperous world for the future.[65]

65 Cohen, *In War's Wake*, pp. 79–99. These issues are also elaborated in Porter, *Benevolent Empire*.

19

Making peace as a project of moral reconstruction

MARK PHILIP BRADLEY

On 1 October 1949 at the Musée Galliéra in Paris, the United Nations Educational Social and Cultural Organization (UNESCO) opened a massive public exhibition to celebrate 'mankind's age-old fight for freedom' to honour the adoption of the United Nations Universal Declaration of Human Rights just one year earlier. The exhibition's primary purpose was a didactic one, making visible 'the universal nature of the responsibility for achieving and defending human rights'. Visitors first encountered a planetarium. Through its windows they saw Earth turning in space, political divisions symbolically left unmarked, and heard a recorded voice repeating the first three articles of the Universal Declaration with their promises that 'everyone has the right to life, liberty and the security of person'. From there they strolled through a hallway of illustrated panels and panoramas that depicted 'man's slow emancipation' from prehistoric times to the present to 'illustrate the contribution of all peoples, nations and civilizations to the sum total of Human Rights'. The *Rights of Man Through the Ages* panels included elaborately presented versions of the Magna Charta, the American Declaration of Independence, the French Declaration of the Rights of Man and the Emancipation Proclamation while *Fighters for Freedom* featured a multicultural panoply of leaders from Europe, the Americas and Asia in the struggle for human rights, among them Montesquieu, Abraham Lincoln, Emmeline Pankhurst and Gandhi.

Visitors next encountered a pictorial 'history book' of the previous two decades. It demonstrated 'how rights were abused and violated by totalitarian states', a state of affairs the exhibit argued had led to the outbreak of the Second World War, and then showed how 'democratic states' worked 'to re-assert the rights' through the establishment of the United Nations. As one caption next to a photograph of a Nazi rally suggested, '[w]e must never forget recent scenes such as these if we wish the Declaration . . . to be anything but an expression of good intentions which again pave the way to the hells of concentration camps.' Visitors passed into a hall in which a dozen pillars devoted to the thirty articles of the Universal Declaration illustrated past examples of their protections and violations and reminded viewers of the centrality of the Declaration in the 'struggle for human rights'. A final part of the exhibition was 'devoted to the duties each person must fulfill if Human Rights are to become and remain a reality for all'. That pressing task, organizers told visitors as they were leaving the exhibition 'will only be complete when the Universal Declaration of Human Rights has been converted into fact'.[1]

The UNESCO exhibition captured the conscious and sustained efforts in the aftermath of the Second World War to put human rights at the centre of projects of moral reconstruction. Upon its adoption in 1948 by the United Nations General Assembly, the Universal Declaration of Human Rights was the first international instrument to articulate the global protection of individual human rights. The Declaration, as Jay Winter and Antoine Prost have written, 'was the final political and moral act agreed to by the alliance that won the Second World War'.[2] Human rights and their entanglements with the making of a moral peace were also at the centre of the 1945 United Nations Charter. Its Preamble proclaimed: 'We the peoples of the United Nations, determined to save succeeding generations from the scourge of war, which twice in our lifetime has brought untold sorrow to mankind ... reaffirm faith in fundamental human rights, in the dignity and worth of the human person, in the equal rights of men and women of all nations large and small.'[3]

The contrast with peacemaking just a quarter of a century earlier as the First World War came to a close was striking. The League of Nations Covenant, which established the precursor to the United Nations, made no mention of human rights nor did it accord attention to the individual person as the subject of peacemaking and international law. Most lexical measures of the printed usage of 'human rights' suggest it was virtually absent from international politics in the first half of the twentieth century. With the coming of the Second World War, its presence spiked upward

---

1 'Universal Rights: UNESCO Exhibition Open in Paris', *UNESCO Courier*, 2:9 (1 October 1949), 5, 7.

2 Jay Winter and Antoine Prost, *René Cassin and Human Rights: From the Great War to the Universal Declaration* (Cambridge University Press, 2013), p. 239.

3 Preamble, Charter of the United Nations (www.un.org/en/documents/charter/).

reflecting the increasing employment of a human rights frame to articulate the purposes of the war.[4]

The new moral vocabulary of individual human rights that drove the UN Charter and Universal Declaration propelled various regional and international bodies to produce an unparalleled series of declarations, covenants and conventions in the immediate post-war period. Among them were the Nuremberg Principles (1946), the American Declaration of the Rights and Duties of Man (1948), the Convention on the Prevention and Punishment of the Crime of Genocide (1948), the Fourth Geneva Convention Relative to the Protection of Civilian Persons in Time of War (1949), the European Convention on Human Rights (1950), the United Nations Conventions Relating to the Status of Refugees (1951) and Stateless Persons (1954), and the drafting of what would eventually become the International Covenants on Political and Civil Rights (1966) and Economic, Social and Cultural Rights (1966).

Historians until recently have largely ignored these developments, and renewed efforts to recapture their contemporary meaning and significance have sometimes been greeted sceptically. The presence of human rights in the UN Charter, some historians argue, was little more than oratorical 'ornamentalism', a kind of sop to pesky if well-intentioned internationalist do-gooders that most state policy-makers were quite certain would never disturb the smooth operation of realist great power politics. Moreover they question whether much came of the Charter's human rights promises, suggesting the aspirational quality of the Universal Declaration lacked any kind of legal grounding. In their view, the presence of human rights in the 1940s moral imagination was little more than 'death in birth'.[5]

Few contemporaries in fact saw human rights in isolation but rather as part of a constellation of sometimes inchoate but always interlocking post-war internationalist sentiments – among them calls for multilateralism, global justice, international policing and humanitarian intervention – that lay in tension with more nationally bounded and traditional conceptions of unilateral state sovereignty. In this liminal post-war moment when articulations of rights and sovereignty were both in play at the intersection of the domestic and the transnational, a variety of actors pushed on what were seen as the era's elastic conditions of possibility. Some operated in the top-down

---

4 A search of the *New York Times* electronic database for the term 'human rights' indicates a dramatic increase in wartime usage, as does a Google Ngram graphing of its use between 1900 and 1945.
5 Samuel Moyn, *The Last Utopia: Human Rights in History* (Cambridge, Mass.: Harvard University Press), p. 44.

elite sphere of the United Nations, but others emerged in more quotidian, bottom-up and local spaces as well. Their efforts reveal the contested imaginative terrain that made up the reach and limits of post-Second World War reconstruction.

Wartime morality and rights talk

The centrality of human rights in the moral language of post-war reconstruction emerged out of sustained efforts during the war itself to frame its very purpose as a struggle for human rights against totalitarianism. Franklin Roosevelt's Four Freedoms address, the Atlantic Charter and the United Nations Declaration came to represent an almost sacred trinity that expressed what the Allied powers fought to protect and preserve in the war again Germany, Italy and Japan. In his January 1941 Four Freedoms address, President Franklin Roosevelt told Congress that '[f]reedom means the supremacy of human rights everywhere.' The August 1941 Atlantic Charter promised the 'right of all peoples to choose the government under which they will live' and in victory offered 'the assurance that the men in all lands may live out their lives in freedom from fear and want'. If the words 'human rights' were absent from it, wartime policy-makers made clear their sensibilities were a palpable presence. 'There must be no swerving', Under-Secretary of State Sumner Welles told one wartime audience, 'from the great human rights and liberties established by the Atlantic Charter'. The United Nations Declaration in January 1942 proclaimed, 'complete victory over their enemies is essential to defend life, liberty, independence and religious freedom and to preserve human rights and justice in their own lands as well as in other lands'. British Prime Minister Winston Churchill promised the 'enthronement of human rights' when the war was won. In speech after speech in the early years of the war, statesmen and diplomats pointed to what they termed the 'concepts and spirit of human rights and human freedom' as a primary aim of the war.[6]

---

6 Franklin D. Roosevelt, Annual Message to the Congress, 6 January 1941 in Louise W. Holborn and Hajo Holborn, eds., *War and Peace Aims of the United Nations* (Boston: World Peace Foundation, 1943), pp. 33–4; *Atlantic Charter*, 14 August 1941 (http://avalon. law.yale.edu/wwii/atlantic.asp); Sumner Welles, 'Requirements for the Four Freedoms: Address before the New York Herald-Tribune Forum, New York City, 17 November 1942', in *Vital Speeches of the Day*, vol. IX (1942), pp. 114–16; Declaration by the United Nations, 1 January 1942, *Department of State Bulletin* 5 (1942), 3; Winston Churchill, Speech Before the World Jewish Congress, *Times* (London), 30 October 1942.

The rise of Hitler and Mussolini in the 1930s had been increasingly seen through the prism of totalitarianism and fascism, themselves new and sometimes opaque conceptual terms. They loosely conveyed a sense of powerful states whose policies collapsed distinctions between the public and the private, and imposed radical state-defined projects of collective action hostile to individual identities, liberties and freedom of action. By the late 1930s there was a growing sense of a wider world confronted by a stark choice between the antithetical demands of democracy and a militant dictatorial totalitarianism. As war intensified, a looser rhetoric of freedom and democracy became encapsulated in the language of human rights to capture the dangers posed by totalitarianism and fascism. In what was a searching and almost entirely novel set of wartime conversations about international guarantees of rights and their protections, human rights came to shape the imagined contours of the post-war peace. 'The relationship between human rights and a just peace', international rights advocates argued, 'is close and interlocking'.[7]

Wartime deliberations over the creation of an international bill of rights sought to identify the rights of individuals that transcended the nation state and how best those rights might be protected and enforced in a transnational space beyond the nation. Vigorous debate rather than easy consensus over the scope of what could be considered global human rights and their means of protection frequently marked these discussions. At their centre, however, was a shared certainty that a viable post-war order demanded unprecedented attention be given to human rights, a willingness to entertain a vastly expanded catalogue of protected rights and an inclination to radically rethink the relationships between individuals, the state and a new international order in which more traditional notions of inviolable state sovereignty might become considerably diminished. Their deliberations and the provisional international bills of rights they produced foreshadowed the centrality of human rights in the making of the post-war moral imagination.

Wartime rights talk emerged in a variety of state and non-state spaces. US State Department planners began constructing an international bill of rights in 1942 as well as a draft United Nations charter that envisioned including such a bill in it. At the same time, the American Law Institute initiated a similar project bringing together experts from Canada, China, France, pre-Nazi Germany, India, Italy, Panama, Poland, the Soviet Union, Spain, Syria, Great Britain and the USA who over two years would eventually produce the

---

7 Commission to Study the Organization of the Peace, *Fourth Report: Part III*, International Safeguard of Human Rights (May 1944), p. 6.

'Statement of Essential Human Rights by Representatives of the Principal Cultures of the World'. In 1942 the American Jewish Committee invited the renowned British international legal scholar Hersch Lauterpacht to draft an 'International Bill of Rights of Man', which when completed offered the most rigorous and thoughtful account of the potentialities of international human rights law in the wartime period. In the Americas, Mexico and Cuba began to prepare elaborate human rights declarations for presentation at a Pan-American conference in Mexico City in early 1945 that helped produce the Inter-American Juridical Committee's 'Draft Declaration of the International Rights and Duties of Man' later that year.

Strong transnational forces influenced these deliberations. If American constitutionalism and its bill of rights tradition was a starting point for many conversations, interest in economic and social rights and in past models for enforcement drew upon what advocates came to learn about social welfare provisions in European and Latin American constitutions and earlier international mechanisms aimed at protecting minority rights. The cosmopolitan quality of wartime rights talk was also reflected by the geographic diversity of those engaged in it many of whom were émigrés and exiles, often international lawyers, displaced by the war. The American Law Institute and Inter-American projects were most self-consciously global, but American, Canadian, European and Latin American jurists were a part of almost all of these discussions.

Guarantees of civil and political rights were largely uncontroversial among the drafters of wartime bills of rights. Freedom of religion and speech, in particular, were accorded a 'foremost place' as their violations by the 'fascist-ruled countries' were viewed as 'in part responsible for the recent war'.[8] Discussions over the inclusion of economic and social rights, on the other hand, could be heated. Most acknowledged in the wake of the international depression of the 1930s that these concerns were properly thought of in the framework of global security. New Deal social welfare legislation began to concretize economic rights claims in an American context, with Roosevelt's Four Freedoms address one early manifestation of their salience in wartime America. The release in Great Britain of what was popularly known as the Beveridge report, which would form the basis of the post-war British welfare

8 Hersch Lauterpacht, *An International Bill of Rights of Man* (New York: Columbia University Press, 1945), p. 106; Inter-American Juridical Committee, 'Draft Declaration of the International Rights and Duties of Man and Accompanying Report', 31 December 1945 (Washington, DC: Pan-American Union, 1946), p. 27.

state, was another wartime manifestation of these increasingly palpable concerns. The International Labour Organization adopted a charter of economic and social rights in 1944 that further equated individual well-being with global security. But others were less sure that such rights could be subject to international guarantees. Hans Kelsen, a towering figure in mid-twentieth-century international law, was deeply sceptical of international protections for economic and social rights, asking with some incredulity that proponents imagine 'the situation of an international court, when an individual says, "My right of social security is violated by my own State, because I have no job. I have a right to work, and now I am without a job."'[9]

The question of minority rights prompted even more extended discussion. Minority rather than individual rights had been the focus of international concern in the wake of the First World War, producing a set of minority treaties that required some but far from all post-war European nation states to provide linguistic, educational and religious autonomy to the more than 25 million minority peoples who lived in their borders. The treaties provided mechanisms for minorities to petition bodies within the League of Nations if these guarantees were violated and for some international juridical and administrative supervision of state policy. With the Nazi rise to power and German withdrawal from the League, the system fell apart in the 1930s.

Most wartime advocates of international bills of rights, even many of those most deeply concerned with what was becoming known about wartime Nazi death camps, argued the patchwork system of the minority rights treaties had not been effective in practice. An exclusive focus on minorities, they believed, could not provide the kinds of protections offered by a universalizing individual human rights regime in which all states were required to protect the ethnic, religious or linguistic minorities within their borders. A few dissented. Raphael Lemkin, at the margins of these discussions but who would emerge as the leading proponent of the Genocide Convention in the post-war period, called for the development of 'adequate machinery for the international protection of national and ethnic groups against extermination attempts and oppression in time of peace' in his 1944 study of *Axis Rule in Occupied Europe*.[10] But the broader wartime inclination was to push

---

9 Hans Kelsen, *The World's Destiny and the United States* (Chicago: World Citizens Association, 1941), p. 119.
10 Raphael Lemkin, *Axis Rule in Occupied Europe* (Washington, DC: Carnegie Endowment for the International Peace, 1944), p. xiv.

minority rights to the margins of discussions about an international bill of rights. Questions of race and gender were also treated in a minor key.

Even more significant than the range of rights articulated in the wartime period was the reach of discussions about enforcement that challenged traditional notions of state sovereignty. Almost without exception, those engaged in wartime human rights talk advocated an elastic notion of sovereignty in which states would no longer be the sole arbiter for the protection of individual human rights. An international bill of rights, most of its proponents acknowledged, was a 'radical innovation' that required a 'revolutionary' rethinking of the place of international law in the relationship between the individual and the nation. As Hersch Lauterpacht pointed out, international protection of human rights 'implies a more drastic interference with the sovereignty of the State than the renunciation of war . . . touching as it does intimately upon the relations of the State and the individual'.[11]

At issue in legal terms was the question of whether individuals could be the subject rather than the object of international law. Wartime rights advocates believed they could. Their assertions met with considerable support within the larger community of international legal scholars. The American and Canadian Bar Associations undertook a project focused on the international law of the future involving a veritable who's who of international lawyers in a two-year wartime study that sought to articulate how law could lay 'the bases of a just and enduring world peace'. Among their recommendations was the principle that '[e]ach state has a legal duty to see that conditions prevailing within its own population in a way which will not violate the dictates of humanity and justice or shock the conscience of mankind.'[12]

If a more supple conception of sovereignty was widely shared, wartime rights advocates offered a range of mechanisms through which international guarantees of individual human rights might be structured. At one end of the spectrum were minimalist calls for an aspirational bill of rights without any specific enforcement procedures beyond urging that its provisions be incorporated into the domestic law of individual states. At the other end of the spectrum were proposals for individual petition to an international court of human rights raising the possibility that new transnational juridical forms could trump state sovereignty. Most wartime rights advocates took a middle

---

11 Lauterpacht, *International Bill*, pp. vi, 82.
12 'Principles for the International Law of the Future', *American Journal of International Law* 38:2 (April 1944), 74, 76.

ground, though one it should be emphasized embodied a potentially trans-formative departure from past practices. This consensus incorporated the idea that there was a place for national enforcement and included provisions for making the international bill of rights a part of municipal law. At the same time, it embraced the idea that an international bill should contain language making it part of international law and emphasizing its protections of the individual were now a matter of world concern. The wartime rights consensus went even further, calling for the establishment of an international human rights commission that would have educative, supervisory and investigative powers and to which individuals and non-state actors along with states would have the right to petition.

Taken together what is most striking about the international bills of rights drafted in the wartime period is the expansive catalogue of individual civil, economic, social and political rights they put on the table and the growing certainty that post-war moral reconstruction required their trans-national protection. Wartime rights talk came to have a scale and scope that went far beyond the promises of the Four Freedoms, the Atlantic Charter and the UN Declaration that had first situated the language of human rights at the centre of Allied war aims. It provided a critical connective tissue grounding the lofty rhetoric of the early war years with the presence of human rights language in the United Nations Charter at war's end. Along with the 'affirmation of human rights' in its Preamble, the Charter's purposes and principles called on member states of the United Nations to promote 'universal respect for ... human rights and fundamental freedoms for all without distinction as to race, sex, language or religion'. The kind of work human rights might do in the post-war world emerged most clearly in Articles 55 and 56 of the UN Charter calling on all member states 'to take joint and separate action in cooperation with the organization' to promote the observance of human rights. The Charter also brought into being a human rights commission that contemporaries rightly anticipated would draft the Universal Declaration.[13]

If the UN Charter's Preamble and its more specialized provisions on human rights infused the aims and purposes of the post-war peace, other dimensions of the Charter posed potential obstacles to the realization of this new moral order. Worries in the USA about the conservative and racialist backlash the Charter's human rights provisions might produce and

---

13 UN Charter, Articles 1, 13, 55, 56, 60, 62, 68.

fears by the European imperial powers that human rights guarantees could be employed against them by anti-colonial movements to hasten the end of empire produced alarm among the great powers about the potentially revolutionary impact of the Charter's rights language. These concerns prompted the introduction of Article 2.7, better known as the domestic jurisdiction clause, that promised 'nothing in the Charter should authorize ... intervention in matters that are *essentially* [emphasis added] within the domestic jurisdiction of any state.'[14] What 'essentially' would come to mean after the war would powerfully shape the contours of the post-war moral imagination.

Conditions of possibility

At the close of the Second World War, the Charter's insistence that its member states protect the individual rights of all their citizens offered up the possibility of remaking the bounds of sovereignty and of a revolutionary transformation in the relationships between individuals, states and the international. These elastic conditions of post-war possibility were first manifested in a 1946 campaign for Indian rights in South Africa led by the Indian delegation to the United Nations. They sought to win majority support in the General Assembly for a resolution that criticized the South African government's passage of the Asiatic Land Tenure and Indian Representation Act for its discriminatory treatment of the country's Indian population. The ironies here ran especially deep. The South African Premier Field Marshal Jan Smuts, who had helped to draft the human rights language in the Preamble of the UN Charter apparently never dreaming it would have any substantive implications for his own apartheid government, insisted that the domestic jurisdiction clause prevented UN discussion of or action on the treatment of Indians in South Africa. But in the event after tense and sustained debate, India's argument that the General Assembly could hear and rule on cases like this one that violated Charter human rights language won the day by a two-thirds majority of Assembly members. 'The treatment of Indians in South Africa', the Assembly ruled, 'shall be in conformity with international obligations under the agreements concluded between the two Governments and the relevant provisions of the Charter'.[15]

---

14 UN Charter, Article 2.7.
15 *First United Nations General Assembly*, 2nd Part, No. 75: 831; Official Records of the General Assembly, *Plenary Meeting of the General Assembly Verbatim Records, 23 October–16 December 1946*: 1006–61; and Official Records of the General Assembly, *Jt. Committee of the First and Sixth Committees Summary Record of Meetings, 21–30 November 1946*.

The South African case offered evidence to some contemporary observers that the Charter provided considerably more than a statement of principles and spoke not only to the promotion but also the protection of individual human rights. The well-respected international lawyer Hersch Lauterpacht, who had written one of the wartime international bills of rights, argued that UN member states were 'under a legal' and 'not merely a moral obligation' to 'respect human rights and fundamental freedoms as repeatedly reaffirmed in the Charter'. Lauterpacht believed 'the tendency to question or ignore' its 'binding character' was rooted in a 'somewhat alarmist interpretation given' to the Charter's domestic jurisdiction clause. Quite the opposite, Lauterpacht argued, individual human rights were 'essentially of international concern'. This was not only the case in situations of 'systemic and flagrant violation of human rights on a scale likely to affect international peace and security' such as those of Nazi Germany. He drew attention to the General Assembly debates in the South African case and its affirmation that questions relating to human rights are not among those covered by the domestic jurisdiction clause.

Other non-state actors took notice, including the National Association for the Advancement of Colored People (NAACP) which submitted a petition to the UN in 1947 exposing racist practices in the USA and their violations of Charter norms. In what became An Appeal to the World!, the NAACP acknowledged such matters had been seen as 'a domestic question which is purely a matter of internal concern'. But under the UN Charter, the Appeal claimed, it 'becomes inevitably an international question and will in the future become more and more international, as the nations draw together'.[16]

The most dramatic instantiation of the post-war moral imagination was the Universal Declaration of Human Rights. The thirty articles making up the Universal Declaration were hammered out over a period of two years in committees that brought together such leading international figures as Eleanor Roosevelt, René Cassin of France, Charles Malik of Lebanon and P. C. Chang of China along with the active participation of representatives from a variety of Latin American states, the Soviet Union and India. The final document sought to protect not only individual civil and political rights, but economic and social rights as well. The rights to life, liberty, freedom of

---

16 National Association for the Advancement of Colored People, *An Appeal to the World! A Statement on the Denial of Human Rights to Minorities in the Case of Citizens of Negro Descent in the United States of America and an Appeal to the United Nations for Redress* (New York: NAACP, 1947).

expression and religion along with freedom of movement and freedom from slavery and torture were now articulated as international rather than solely national guarantees. The Declaration's enumeration of economic and social rights was especially striking as it linked post-war global security with individual rights to an adequate standard of living, to work and equal pay, to education and to cultural well-being. The Declaration's sweeping guarantees of their protections were as expansive as its catalogue of rights. 'Everyone is entitled to all the rights and freedoms set forth in the Declaration', its authors promised, 'without distinction of any kind'. Nothing, seemingly not even state sovereignty, was to trump the individual rights enumerated in the document. As one contemporary observer noted, the Declaration asserted 'that just as the real purpose of a State's government is to ensure the welfare of the individual human being, so the real concern of international law is with the welfare of individuals'. It had, in the words of Charles Malik as he introduced the Declaration to the General Assembly in 1948, 'the moral authority of the world'.[17]

The Universal Declaration was in fact aspirational, as critics were quick to point out, without the legal teeth of an international covenant or convention in what was a pragmatic bow to the possible in a moment when Cold War tensions between the USA and the Soviet Union and the broader struggle in the global South for postcolonial independence were beginning to escalate. News of the drafting and adoption of the Declaration vied with events such as the Berlin blockade, the establishment of the State of Israel and war with its Arab neighbours, the communist seizure of power in Czechoslovakia and the assassination of Gandhi. But in the Universal Declaration's concern with the individual, its capacious sensibility about what constituted human rights and its global aspirations for their protection, it revealed the lingering potency and expansiveness of wartime rights talk.

At the same time, these wartime convictions also animated a broader post-war turn to the language of human rights as the building blocks for post-war moral reconstruction. In Latin America, delegates at several Pan-American congresses during the war adopted a regional human rights vocabulary that anticipated the Universal Declaration and culminated in the adoption of the

---

17 United Nations Universal Declaration of Human Rights, 10 December 1948, Article 2 (www.un.org/en/documents/udhr/); New Zealand Department of External Affairs, 'Memorandum: Human Rights, 13 March 1947', cited in Paul Gordon Lauren, *The Evolution of International Human Rights: Visions Seen* (Philadelphia: University of Pennsylvania Press, 2011), p. 217; Malik cited in Mary Ann Glendon, *A World Made New* (New York: Random House, 2001), p. 164.

1948 American Declaration of the Rights and Duties of Man. Western European states began to draft their own rights lexicon in the post-war moment, producing the European Convention on Human Rights in 1950. Discussions at the United Nations in the late 1940s centred on a convention to outlaw genocide, a global freedom of information covenant, protective rights of asylum for refugees and the stateless and the drafting of legally binding guarantees of the political, economic and social rights enshrined in the Universal Declaration.

Post-war efforts at revising the Geneva Conventions and the International Military Tribunals at Nuremberg and Tokyo illustrate how deeply wartime rights talk infused post-war concerns with international morality. In Geneva member societies of the International Committee of the Red Cross (ICRC) began discussions in 1946 to craft new protections for soldiers and civilians in wartime. A series of Geneva Conventions from 1859 to 1929 had gradually expanded the rights of soldiers to medical treatment and the rights of prisoners of war. The pattern in each successive agreement had been reactive, meeting the deficiencies that had become apparent in the Convention after a just-concluded war. In 1946, however, the corrective was seen as potentially more far-reaching given the impact of total war on civilian populations whether it be forced transfers of population, extrajudicial killings, death camps or genocide. The ICRC, drawing on the moral vocabularies of the post-war moment, hoped to 'guarantee in all circumstances the essential rights of the individual, as well as the respect of the human dignity for all persons who, for any reason whatever, are in the hands of the enemy'. ICRC-led negotiations between 1946 and 1949 produced not only expanded protections for prisoners of war but also the entirely novel Fourth Convention that outlined protections for civilians in times of war and the obligations of all parties to protect their well-being. In another innovation that pushed hard against traditions of national sovereignty, the new Common Article Three asserted that some principles of the Geneva Conventions that had originally been designed to regulate war between states should now also apply in cases of internal conflict or civil war. As one ICRC official noted, 'it was an almost un-hoped for extension' of human rights protections into the legal charter of the laws of war.[18]

---

18 Jean S. Pictet, *Commentary on the Geneva Convention Relative to the Protection of Civilian Person in Time of War* (Geneva: International Committee of the Red Cross, 1958), pp. 12, 26; cited in William A. Hitchcock, 'Human Rights and the Laws of War: The Geneva Conventions of 1949', in Akira Iriye, Petra Goedde and William I. Hitchcock, eds., *The Human Rights Revolution* (Oxford University Press, 2012), pp. 93–112 (pp. 97, 103).

Meanwhile the Nuremberg and Tokyo trials drew on the human rights inflected post-war moral imagination to develop new concepts of universal justice. The International Military Tribunal at Nuremberg operated between November 1945 and October 1946 and brought twenty-four individual defendants, mainly high-level figures in the Nazi regime, before British, American, French and Soviet judges. The Allied powers did not initially support the idea of trial. British Prime Minister Winston Churchill believed the Nazi leadership should be taken out and shot. Some of President Franklin D. Roosevelt's closest advisors agreed, hoping also to strip Germany of its industrial potential to ensure it would never again become a world power. But ultimately arguments for due process and the pedagogic value of public trials prevailed. US Supreme Court Justice Robert Jackson, who became the chief prosecutor at Nuremberg, put the defendants up on three major charges all of which involved novel departures from past international practices: crimes against the peace, war crimes and crimes against humanity. Charges of crimes against the peace accused the Nazis of waging an illegal aggressive war and looked back to the Kellogg-Briand Pact of 1928 and efforts to outlaw war in the interwar period to stake their claims. War crimes were parsed as violations of laws of war codified in the existing Hague and Geneva Conventions (the 1949 Fourth Convention on the rights of non-combatants was not yet a part of international law). In what was the most innovative charge at Nuremberg, crimes against humanity were defined as 'murder, extermination, enslavement, deportation, and other inhumane acts against any civilian population, before or during the war, or persecutions on political, racial or religious grounds ... in connection with any crime within the jurisdiction of the tribunal, whether or not in violation of domestic law of the country where perpetrated'.[19] Its sensibility would become embedded in the language of the 1948 Genocide Convention.

If the concept of crimes against humanity has come to shape contemporary human rights law and practice, it did not receive full attention at Nuremberg where the trial began with a focus on aggressive war and shifted increasingly to the massive reality of war crimes, slave labour, plunder and spoliation. More immediately it was Nuremberg's insistence on holding individuals responsible for violations of emerging international norms that contributed to what in 1947 came to be called Nuremberg Principles. It was

---

19 International Military Tribunal, *Trial of Major War Criminals Before the International Military Tribunal, Nuremberg, 14 November 1945 – October 1946* [*TWC*] (Buffalo: Hein &Co. 2001), 1: 57.

no longer, as it had been in the past, acceptable to say, 'I was just following orders.' In what was perhaps the most substantial push against national sovereignty and for the individual as the subject of international law in the immediate post-war period, the judgments at Nuremberg argued 'individuals have international duties that transcend the national obligations of obedience imposed by the individual state.'[20] There were, however, differences around whether international law could retrospectively be applied in these cases. Justices at Nuremberg largely believed the Nazis could not be tried for crimes committed before the war began, but they did affirm that defendants could be charged for war crimes even if Nazi Germany was not a signatory to the full array of Hague and Geneva Conventions.

The cases that came before the Tokyo-based International Military Tribunal for the Far East between April 1946 and November 1948 largely followed the precedents set by Nuremberg in their focus on crimes against the peace, war crimes and individual accountability. War crimes charges focused on mass atrocities committed by Japanese troops in Nanjing in 1937 and the gross mistreatment of prisoners of war, most notably in what was termed the Burma-Siam Death Railway and the Bataan Death March. The Tokyo trials were later criticized for giving almost no attention to the operation of the Japanese wartime 'comfort woman' system, the human medical experimentation in bacteriological warfare that was part of the notorious Japanese Unit 731 in Manchuria or more generally gross violations of civilian human rights. In fact as recent studies of the trials have shown, a wider array of war crimes and crimes against humanity did come before the Tokyo tribunal, including charges of sexual slavery and medical experimentation, and the final judgments referenced not only war crimes against prisoners of war but also massacres, rape and torture of civilians.

Hovering over the Tokyo tribunal, as it did over Nuremberg, were accusations of victor's justice. It was the Allied powers that sat in judgment over their now-vanquished enemies, and there was little question of putting the USA on trial for firebombing Tokyo or dropping atomic weapons on Hiroshima and Nagasaki or for the sustained British wartime bombing of German cities. The problem of victor's justice was more acute in Tokyo given the remarkable dissent of Justice Rahabinod Pal, the Indian justice on the tribunal. In what was almost a book-length dissent, Pal disagreed with virtually the entire majority opinion of the tribunal. Much of Pal's argument

20 *TWC*, 11: 941.

went to his opposition to retroactive applications of international law but he also launched a broader attack on the assumption that international law promoted peace and human well-being. In reality, Pal argued, the great powers like the USA used law to advance their own expansionist aims against weaker powers in the international system. The exclusion of Western colonialism and the use of the atomic bomb from the formal counts of war crimes along with the absence of judges from the defeated powers on the tribunal, he argued, revealed that 'the one thing the victor cannot give to the vanquished is justice.'[21]

Pal's charges of victor's justice gained little traction among those who advocated the Allied cause as a project of post-war moral reconstruction. Telford Taylor, one of the chief prosecutors at Nuremberg, argued that German attacks on Allied cities were not a war crime as both Allied and Axis powers shared an understanding that 'aerial bombardment of cities and factories has become a recognized part of modern warfare as carried out by all nations.' In another instance at the Nuremberg trials, justices normalized the use of atomic weapons under the practices of aerial bombardment, arguing there 'is no doubt that the invention of the atomic bomb, when used, was not aimed at non-combatants ... but dropped to overcome military resistance'. The judges at Nuremberg did acknowledge the partiality of immunities granted to Allied war criminals, but noted the 'enforcement of international law has traditionally been subject to practical limitations' and excused the one-sidedness of the tribunals as the result of 'the extraordinary ... situation in Germany'.[22] Jackson explicitly stated that if the new norms of international justice were to acquire legitimacy they must in future apply to all states, including those sitting in judgment at Nuremberg.

It was not only elite international lawyers or cosmopolitan norm-makers at the United Nations who sought to take advantage of the expansive conditions of possibility in the early post-war period. Initiative also emerged from the bottom-up, entangling local moral entrepreneurship with efforts to recast global norms and practices. A series of cases made their way through US

---

21 *The Tokyo Judgment, The International Military Tribunal for the Far East: 29 April 1946–12 November 1948*, ed. B. V. A. Rölling and C. F. Ruter (Amsterdam: APA-University Press, 1977), p. 1232.

22 *TWC*, 3: 970, 4: 467; and Telford Taylor, *Final Report to the Secretary of the Army on the Nuremberg War Crimes Trials* (Buffalo: Hein & Co, 1997), p. 65 cited in Yuma Totani, *The Tokyo War Crimes Trial: The Pursuit of Justice in the Wake of World War II* (Cambridge, Mass.: Harvard University Press, 2008), pp. 251, 252.

courts in the late 1940s which employed what for Americans was the novel legal argument that the controlling authority of international human rights norms across national borders in the United Nations Charter and Universal Declaration trumped existing federal and state laws and claims of national sovereignty. Brought by Japanese American, African-American and Native American plaintiffs, these cases used a transnational frame to approach a variety of instances of domestic racial discrimination: in housing, in land and fishing rights, in public accommodation, in education and in marriage.

One such illustrative example, *Rice v. Sioux City Memorial Cemetery, Inc.* emerged in the wake of the death of Sergeant John Rice in the Korean War. Rice's widow had entered into a contract with the Sioux City cemetery for his burial. At the graveside services, several cemetery officials noted a number of Native American mourners and suspected Rice himself might have been Native American. They visited his widow who told them their assumption was correct. The cemetery, which enforced a 'Caucasians only' burial policy, ordered her husband's body removed. The action drew immediate and national attention, prompting President Truman to arrange for Rice to be buried at Arlington National Cemetery. Not placated by the President's symbolic gesture, Rice's widow sued in Iowa courts invoking the human rights enunciated by the UN.[23] When the Iowa Supreme Court dismissed the case, she took it to the US Supreme Court. In their brief for the Supreme Court, Rice and her lawyers dwelt at some length on Charter-inspired claims arguing that the Iowa court had 'violated the basic and very fundamental concepts of equality not only announced but also pledged by the United Nations Charter and all of the member nations of which the United States is one'.[24]

The petitioners in the Rice case and other global rights cases in this period, along with the judges who looked favourably on their arguments, acted to harness the potentialities of international human rights guarantees and more relaxed conceptions of national sovereignty to combat racial discrimination in the USA. For them, the Universal Declaration was believable on local ground. It would, for instance, allow a California court in a Japanese land rights case to argue in a 1950 opinion:

> [D]iscrimination against a people of one race is contrary to both the letter and to the spirit of the [UN] Charter which, as a treaty, is paramount to

---

23 *Rice v. Sioux City Memorial Park Cemetery, Inc.*, 60 N.W. 2d 116–17 (1953).
24 Brief in support of petition for writ of *certiorari* to the United States Supreme Court at 18–19.

every law of every state in conflict with it. [Californian] law must therefore yield to the treaty as the superior authority.[25]

The California court provided perhaps the most muscular assertion of the domestic reach of global rights norms in the American context. Nonetheless, a substantial number of state and federal courts, and several Supreme Court justices, proved receptive to these claims. Their responses, like those of the UN General Assembly in 1946 to the Indian case against South Africa, reveal the horizons of possibility unleashed by the rights-based post-war moral imagination.

So too do new histories of displaced persons (DPs) in 1940s Europe. They point to the ways in which the practices of post-war moral reconstruction and the quotidian experiences of rights were mutually constituting. As Daniel Cohen has argued, the crisis posed by the presence of millions of DPs in post-war Europe transformed definitions of statelessness from negative constructions of the pre-war stateless as individuals deprived of citizenship to the post-war 'political refugee' who was 'positively branded as a victim of human rights violations entitled to international protection'. Cohen also suggests that local representatives of the vast machinery established by the United Nations to manage displacement in Europe directly and decisively contributed to the making of human rights law, most notably the 1949 Fourth Geneva Convention and the 1951 Refugee Convention.[26]

Localized perspectives could also complicate aspects of the post-war moral imagination when individualist, familial and nationalist rhetoric clashed with European humanitarian and human rights activism. Tara Zahra has explored the ways in which the lens of the family and the nation came to overwhelm the internationalist values of social workers employed by the United Nations Relief and Rehabilitation Administration, and its successor the International Refugee Organization, in dealing with the hundreds of thousands of lost children in Europe after 1945. Here the experiences of stateless children were shaped less by human rights imperatives and norms from above than local and nationalist pressures from below.[27] Similarly Atina Grossman has examined how the putative right to be free from hunger, so much a part of the Four Freedoms wartime discourse of freedom from want and later enshrined

25 *Sei Fuji* v. *California*, Superior Court of Los Angles County, 24 April 1950 at 21; California State Archives.

26 Gerald Daniel Cohen, *In War's Wake: Europe's Displaced Persons in the Postwar Order* (Oxford University Press, 2012), pp. 79–99 (p. 83).

27 Tara Zahra, 'Lost Children: Displacement, Family and Nation in Postwar Europe', *Journal of Modern History* 81:1 (March 2009), 45–86.

in the Universal Declaration, was 'severely tested on the ground' in conflicts over food rations and entitlements in occupied Germany.[28]

The situation in what would become post-war West Germany was also deeply embedded in the post-war moral imagination of human rights, one that saw Germany during the war as a rights-abusing totalitarian state. West Germany was the first state to introduce phrases from the Universal Declaration of Human Rights directly into its constitution and was a vigorous proponent of the right to individual petition in the European Convention on Human Rights. Emergent global rights norms framed conceptions of domestic civil liberties along with more critical examinations of the crimes of the Nazi past. But as Lora Wildenthal and Pertti Ahonen have shown, the language of human rights also shaped appeals on behalf of Germans who were not Jewish or targeted by the Nazis but saw themselves as victims of the Allies and had fled or were expelled from their homes in Czechoslovakia, Poland and elsewhere in Europe during the war. Conservative German legal experts and expellee organizations sought international redress in the immediate post-war period, arguing their forced expulsions were violations of global human rights norms. So too, some argued, were Allied policies of aerial bombardment during the war and the forced retention of prisoners of war during occupation. If these claims produced little political traction as the enormity of Nazi crimes became apparent, they nonetheless built on the larger wartime and post-war sensibilities about the individual as the subject of international law and the relaxation of national sovereignty to adjudicate rights disputes.[29]

European conservative political and religious figures put the moral language of human rights to their own purposes in post-war state-led projects of reconstruction. During the war the itinerant French Catholic publicist Jacques Maritian praised the 'concept of, and devotion to, the rights of the human person' as 'the most significant political improvement of modern times', employing rights talk in a deliberately communitarian vein to lift up the moral 'human person' against what he saw as the dangers of the atomistic individual of liberal capitalism. When European conservatives found their way to human rights in the post-war period, they came to articulate a third

---

28 Atina Grossman, 'Grams, Calories and Food: Languages of Victimization, Entitlement, and Human Rights in Occupied Germany, 1945–49', in Iriye et al., eds., *Human Rights Revolution*, pp. 113–32 (p. 114).

29 Lora Wildenthal, *The Language of Human Rights in West Germany* (Philadelphia: University of Pennsylvania Press, 2012); Pertti Ahonen, *After the Expulsion: West Germany and Eastern Europe, 1945–1990* (Oxford University Press, 2004).

way between liberal atomism and materialist communism in what was an avowedly anti-secularist agenda. For these figures, human rights were 'the essential hallmark of Western civilization in contrast to "totalitarian" state slavery'. Among the main advocates for the European Convention on Human Rights, Samuel Moyn and Marco Duranti have argued, were Christian personalists whose interest in defining European civilization in terms of human rights and claims for a 'spiritual union' of Western European states 'consecrated the basic values of the Western side in Cold War politics'.[30]

The limits of post-war moral reconstruction

If the moral vocabularies of post-war reconstruction and human rights could be put to a range of purposes in the post-war era, they contained their own contradictions and fragilities. A universalizing impulse in post-war rights-based morality sometimes erased the particularities of the claims made in its name. Not only was this so at the Nuremberg trials where the murder of Jews was subsumed under the label of 'crimes against humanity', but moral universalism resonated even more broadly at the level of popular culture. This was most dramatically so as the war came to a close in representations of Nazi genocide against European Jews in which a particular Jewish fate came to be represented as universal human suffering.

Within a three-week period in April and May 1945 global publics were exposed to a barrage of horrific images of mass death in newspapers and pictorial magazines. The atrocity images reached viewers in other ways too. Film taken by the US Army Signal Corps during the liberation of the camps was shown in newsreel form at movie theatres in Great Britain, Western Europe and the USA. The St. Louis Post-Dispatch in cooperation with the federal government organized an exhibition of twenty-five 'life size atrocity photographs', many of which had already been circulated in newspapers and magazines, titled 'Lest We Forget'. Opening in early May, the photomural exhibition brought more than 80,000 spectators to St. Louis before it moved to the Library of Congress in June. (See Plate Section, Illustrations 22 and 23.)

If the almost unimaginable horrors depicted in the photographs were clear, their meanings were far from stable. They are not, as some historians mistakenly believe, evidence that the Holocaust was the driving force of wartime and immediate post-war moral concerns. The atrocity photographs

---

30 Moyn, *Last Utopia*, pp. 54, 76, 79.

were seldom contextualized in such a way that viewers would know that vast numbers of victims were Jewish, murdered by the Nazis because they were Jews. As Barbie Zelizer, the leading interpreter of the atrocity photographs suggests, individual photographs were usually employed to illustrate the broader 'Nazi horror' with little attention to specific place and circumstances. In the commentary that accompanied the photos, their subjects were 'political prisoners', 'military prisoners', 'slave laborers' or 'civilians of many nationalities' and only occasionally 'Jews'.[31] Such universalism lingered in popular perceptions throughout the immediate post-war period. As several scholars have recently noted, the presentation and reception of Anne Frank's diary in the 1950s, when it first became an international bestseller as well as a popular stage play and film, downplayed the centrality of the Jewish dimension of the story and the vividness of Anne's multi-faceted personality. In their place, the lives of the Franks were rendered as an uplifting symbol of humanity and Anne a clichéd figure 'who possessed a seemingly never-ending optimism and hope for mankind'.[32]

The problems of a rights-based moral universalism did not go unnoticed by contemporary observers. The American Anthropological Association's 1947 'Statement on Human Rights', prepared at the invitation of those drafting the Universal Declaration, rejected the notion of universal human rights altogether, emphasizing the plurality of cultural references and authorities for conceptions of rights.[33] Similarly UNESCO director Julian Huxley's efforts in 1947 to find a common philosophical basis for human rights floundered, with some interlocutors such as Gandhi questioning the whole enterprise of universal rights-making.[34] The 1949 UNESCO exhibit that had exhorted viewers to make the Universal Declaration of Human Rights their own operated as an über case of post-war high moral universalism.

---

31 Barbie Zelizer, *Remembering to Forget: Holocaust Memory Through the Camera Eye* (University of Chicago Press, 1998), pp. 86–140, *passim*.

32 Tony Kushner, '"I Want to go on Living after my Death": The Memory of Anne Frank', in Martin Evans and Ken Lunn, eds., *War and Memory in the Twentieth Century* (Oxford: Berg, 1997), pp. 3–25 (p. 17); and Allen H. Rosenfeld, 'Popularization and Memory: The Case of Anne Frank', in Peter Hayes, ed., *Lessons and Legacies: The Meanings of the Holocaust in a Changing World* (Evanston, Ill.: Northwestern University Press, 1991), pp. 243–78.

33 Executive Board, American Anthropological Association, 'Statement on Human Rights', *American Anthropologist* 49:4 (October–December 1947), 539–43.

34 Records of the Comité sur le principes philosophiques des droits d'home, 1947–52, Secretariat, UNESCO. For the published volume that emerged out of this project, see UNESCO, *Human Rights: Comments and Interpretations* (New York: Columbia University Press, 1949).

The timeless and teleological unfolding of human rights from prehistoric times to the present in the exhibition consciously worked to erase particularities, for instance locating Gandhi in the pantheon of human rights heroes despite his qualms over collapsing a new post-war moral order into the rubric of human rights.

When the UNESCO exhibit closed in Paris it travelled elsewhere in Europe and to Asia and Latin America in the early 1950s. As it did so, the post-war project of moral reconstruction had begun to wane. In the USA the global rights cases of the late 1940s so alarmed American conservatives that they sought to severely limit US participation in the post-war global human rights order. The American Bar Association began to wage a very public campaign against United Nations human rights norms as 'revolutionary and dangerous', targeting the Universal Declaration of Human Rights and the Genocide Convention as offering a 'blank check' to undermine 'our whole concept and theory of government'. Employing just a bit of red baiting in an article titled 'Human Rights on Pink Paper', ABA president Frank Holman warned that 'by a few pages of treaty language' the economic and social rights provisions of the Universal Declaration 'have transformed the government of the United States into a socialist state'.[35] In 1951, Senator John Bricker (Republican, Ohio) introduced a resolution opposing the draft UN International Covenant on Human Rights, a draft that was part of ongoing efforts to give the aspirational Universal Declaration legal standing. The Covenant, Bricker argued, 'would be more appropriately entitled as a Covenant on Human Slavery or subservience to government . . . [T]hose who drafted the Covenant on Human Rights repudiated the underlying theory of the Bill of Rights – freedom to be let alone.'[36] In early 1952, Bricker and his allies decided the grave peril that global human rights presented to American sovereignty and values required recourse to a constitutional amendment that severely constrained the treaty-making power of the President.

The voluminous hearings held on the Bricker amendment in 1952 and 1953 capture the nature of growing American opposition to wartime notions of relaxed sovereignty that had been an essential dimension of the post-war moral imagination. Laced throughout these discussions and debates, Senator Bricker – along with his allies in the Republican Party, the ABA and a host

---

35 Frank E. Holman, 'An "International Bill of Rights": Proposals Have Dangerous Implications for U.S.', *American Bar Association Journal* 34 (November 1948), 984, 986; Frank E. Holman, 'Human Rights on Pink Paper', *American Affairs* 11 (January 1949), 18–24.
36 *Congressional Record*, Senate, 1951: 8255.

of conservative organizations – made frequent reference to the use of the Charter in the American global rights cases as emblematic of the transnational assault on 'existing laws which are in our Bill of Rights and our Constitution, thereby forcing unacceptable theories and practices upon the citizens of the United States of America'. The draft covenant on human rights was denounced in testimony as 'utter nonsense', 'a blueprint for tyranny' and the 'greatest threat to American sovereignty'.[37] In these hearings, the postwar moral concern with human rights emerged as a marker and accelerator of more deeply rooted conservative suspicions of the 'international' and 'big government statism' and a worrying obstacle to their own efforts to preserve the practices of Jim Crow segregation at home. The political pressure was enough to prompt the Eisenhower administration to voluntarily withdraw from UN human rights efforts, telling Congress that international treaties were no longer 'the proper way to spread throughout the world the goals of human liberty' and welcoming 'a reversal of the trend toward using treaty-making power to effect internal social changes'.[38] The American state, which had been at the centre of the moral project of reconstruction immediately after the war, had now decisively stepped aside.

In part the Cold War pushed the human rights talk that guided post-war reconstruction to the edges of international politics except as an extension of the Cold War polemics between the USA and the Soviet Union. But the relationship of the Cold War to human rights in the 1940s was often messier and more diffuse. As Daniel Cohen argues, American and Soviet battles over the fate of displaced persons in post-war Europe, many of whom were later termed political dissidents, in fact helped set the Cold War in motion.[39] But what eventually put the breaks on a broader post-war constellation of internationalist-humanitarian-human rights sensibilities was more than simply the coming of the Cold War. For their part, imperial powers in Western Europe, most notably Great Britain and France, remained wary of advancing a transnational human rights agenda that potentially undermined efforts to maintain control over their colonial territories. At the same time, the attention of most states and peoples in the global South was increasingly

---

37 US Congress, Senate, Committee on the Judiciary, Treaties and Executive Agreements, *Hearings*, 82nd Congress, 2nd session, 1952. See also US Congress, Senate, Committee on the Judiciary, Treaties and Executive Agreements, *Hearings*, 83rd Congress, 1st session, 1953.
38 US Congress, Senate, Committee on the Judiciary, Treaties and Executive Agreements, *Hearings*, 83rd Congress, 1st session, 1953: 124.
39 Cohen, *In War's Wake*, p. 19.

focused on collective self-determination in the decolonization struggles of the 1950s and 1960s rather than the individual rights claims so central to the post-war moral visions of reconstruction.

If the post-war effort to put human rights at the centre of projects of moral reconstruction had reached its end times, its legacies for more contemporary expressions of global morality continue to run very deep. The 1970s brought the return of a renewed appreciation of the political work a commitment to individual protections of human rights in a space beyond the nation might do. The commitment to prisoners of conscience by the growing membership of Amnesty International and its Nobel Prize in 1977, claims for UN protections of political and civil rights among dissidents in the Soviet Union, the 1975 Helsinki accords, the Charter 77 movement in Eastern Europe, the international women's conference in Mexico City in 1975 and transnational campaigns against human rights abuses in Latin America and South Korea and apartheid in South Africa, to name just a few, were all products of a redeployment and reworking of post-war moral sentiment. The principles of individual responsibility for crimes of war that emerged at the Nuremberg and Tokyo trials have become basic principles of international law and the conceptual expression of crimes against humanity at the trials has driven campaigns for global justice, most notably the establishment of the International Criminal Court in 2002. At the same time, the post-war tendency toward absolutism in defining the contours of a universal moral order, and the reticence to linger on political, social and cultural particularities, inflected human rights politics in the 1970s and beyond. If its presence in the moment was fleeting, the power of the post-war imagination continues to shape contemporary human rights thought and practice as the central moral language through which we articulate our common humanity.

20

Renegotiating the social contract

Western Europe, Great Britain, Europe and North America

TIMOTHY B. SMITH

the circumstances of the war created an unprecedented sense of social solidarity among the British people, which made them willing to accept a great increase of egalitarian policies and collective state intervention.

Professor Richard Titmuss, London School of Economics 1950

Today the mines belong to the people.

British government statement, 1 January 1947, Quoted in Kenneth O. Morgan, *The People's Peace* (Oxford University Press, 1990), p. 35

Tous les pays du monde, aujourd'hui, s'efforcent de concevoir et de réaliser des plans de sécurité sociale ... La France est sortie de la guerre particulièrement meurtrie. Les vieux cadres sont brises, il faut reconstruire, il faut faire du neuf sous l'angle social, comme sous l'angle économique. Et c'est dans le cadre d'un effort d'ensemble pour l'edification d'un ordre social nouveau que se situe notre plan de sécurité sociale.

Pierre Laroque, 'Le plan français de Sécurité sociale', in the inaugural edition of the *Revue française du travail* 1 (April 1946), p. 9

The Nation shall ensure to the individual and family the conditions necessary to their development. It shall guarantee to all, especially to the child, the mother, and aged workers, the protections of their health, material security, rest and leisure.

Preamble to the Constitution of France, 1946

Tear down the old. Build up the new. Down with rotten, antiquated rat holes. Down with hovels. Down with disease. Down with crime. Let in the sun. Let in the sky. A new day is dawning. A new life. A new America!

Fiorello La Guardia, 1944, speaking of his plans for public housing in New York City. Quoted in Nicholas Dagen Bloom, *Public Housing that Worked: New York in the Twentieth Century* (Philadelphia: University of Pennsylvania Press, 2008), p. 13

Isn't it wonderful that in the midst of a total war, such a destructive war, we have seen the gestation of a vast social movement whose first buds had only to wait for the Armistice to open? France, England, the United States of America, various European nations and others are all witnessing the birth of plans for Social Security ... which will, one by one, color the map of the world.
    Dr Pierre Theil, *Les Annales de la médicine sociale* (January 1947). An entire edition of the journal devoted to a discussion of the Beveridge report

Promise of a new day

In December 1939, the Conservative British Cabinet minister Anthony Eden predicted: 'the war will bring about changes which may be fundamental and revolutionary in the economic and social life of the country.'[1] Reconstruction committees were struck up in Britain and in Canada in 1940. Concrete reconstruction goals were seen as crucial to maintaining high wartime morale. The promise of a pot of gold at the end of the war could serve as a powerful incentive to keep up the good fight. Indeed this was precisely what William Beveridge wrote in his famous 1942 report to the British government on the future of the nation's social welfare system calling for a comprehensive, cradle-to-grave welfare state:

the purpose of victory is to live into a better world than the old world; that each individual citizen is more likely to concentrate upon his war effort if he feels that his Government will be ready in time with plans for that better world; that, if these plans are to be ready in time, they must be made now.[2]

And so James Griffiths, a Labour stalwart and Minister of National Insurance in a wartime coalition government, did not exaggerate when he proclaimed: 'In one of the darkest hours of the war', at the end of 1942, the Beveridge report 'fell like manna from heaven'.[3] Indeed, quite literally: while dropping bombs on Germany, parts of the Low Countries and occupied France, the Royal Air Force also dropped 'millions of leaflets extolling the principles of the Beveridge Report, as Britain's master contribution to a better world'.[4]

---

1 Quoted in W. H. Greenleaf, *The Rise of Collectivism* (3 vols., London: Methuen, 1983), vol. I, p. 70.
2 Cmd 6404, William Beveridge, *Social Insurance and Allied Services* (London: HMSO), p. 171. Hereafter referred to as the Beveridge report.
3 Quoted in Peter Baldwin, *The Politics of Social Solidarity: Class Bases of the European Welfare State, 1875–1975* (Cambridge University Press, 1990), p. 116.
4 Kenneth O. Morgan, *The People's Peace: British History, 1945–1990* (Oxford University Press, 1990), p. 37.

In the USA too, the war gave energy to a new wave of ambitious programmes. In 1943 in his State of the Union address, Franklin D. Roosevelt (FDR) called for an *economic and social* 'second Bill of Rights under which a new basis of security and prosperity can be established for all'. FDR continued: 'after this war is won we must be *prepared* to move *forward*, in the implementation of these rights, to new goals of happiness and well-being.'[5]

The notion of the welfare state had originally been coined as an antithesis to the warfare state. In the war-making of the Allied powers they became entwined as a common promise of the United Nations in their struggle with Nazi Germany, fascist Italy and Imperial Japan. Within the Allied coalition it was a period of intense interaction and mutual observation and learning. But from this melting pot emerged not one single model of the 'Keynesian welfare state', but distinct European and North American models embedded in complex networks of economic, political and class relations. These post-war orders proved remarkably resilient persisting down to the 1970s. The arguments of the last generation over the neoliberal restructuring of the welfare state were arguments about structures established in the post-war period. Though the connection is undeniable, we must guard against these present-day concerns from overshadowing the history of the 1940s.

The Beveridge model

Britain's role in the Second World War was unique: it was bombed, but not invaded. It held out against the Axis powers longer than any other democracy and provided a safe haven for the exiled governments of occupied Europe. Britain's war experience came to serve as a core element of the national identity. As Baldwin writes: 'the bombing raids' indiscriminate destruction, blighting Bloomsbury as thoroughly as Brixton, prepared the ground psychologically for a wider sharing of risks.'[6] The national sacrifice, most people believed, would have to lead to a better world after the war. Otherwise, what was the point in fighting? Repelling Nazi barbarism was not enough. In Britain, the era of prolonged Depression and Appeasement in the 1930s were seen as an indictment of the old order. Building up the welfare state was one key way to refashion the social order,

---

5 Quoted in John Morton Blum, *V was for Victory* (New York: Harcourt, Brace, Jovanovich, 1976), p. 249. Emphasis in Roosevelt's original speech.
6 Baldwin, *Politics of Social Solidarity*, pp. 108–9.

to make good the damage done during the 'devil's decade' of the 1930s and to relegitimize the state.

It was no coincidence therefore that the most influential model of wartime social policy was the 'Beveridge plan' outlined in the report of 1942 and elaborated in his 1944 book, *Full Employment in a Free Society*. The Beveridge agenda mapped a comprehensive programme of economic and social policy including:

(1) full employment to be guaranteed by the state; the national budget as a macroeconomic tool; deficit spending as social policy
(2) a national health care system provided on free and equal terms to everyone
(3) free and equal access to education
(4) a new and key role for the central state in the provision and administration of a wide array of social services . . .
(5) . . . which implied the displacement or eclipse of charity and mutual aid
(6) universal old age pensions
(7) family allowances . . . as well as strengthened unemployment insurance, sickness and disability insurance, maternity benefits, funeral benefits and many more.

This truly comprehensive list of benefits was to provide insurance against major risks from cradle to grave. In monetary terms it was based on the promise of universal, flat-rate benefits in return for flat-rate contributions.

From a political and intellectual point of view, Beveridge's most long-lasting contribution was to argue that most of these benefits listed above ought to be provided as a right of citizenship, or a right acquired through contributions (payroll taxes) free of stigma. Charity was, by implication, declared passé. It was an intoxicating message that captured the egalitarian *zeitgeist*. It was the key theme of the 1945 election in Britain. The party most closely associated with the report, the Labour Party, won a resounding majority of seats in Parliament. With a record 47 per cent of the popular vote it was the welfare state that enabled the Labour Party to definitively displace the Liberal Party as the alternative to the Tories.

Not surprisingly, the welfare state came to be associated with social democracy and as such became the object of savage critique from the new right from the 1970s onwards. But this is misleading. In much of Europe welfare spending was as much a Christian Democratic as a Social Democratic preoccupation. And Beveridge was no advocate of dependency culture. He was a figure of transition, whose formative years dated to the era of new liberalism and the Lib–Lab pact. The aim of his programme was to strengthen, not diminish or undermine, individual responsibility. He wished to abolish poverty, yes, but not to discourage people from working, saving and fending for themselves. Universal and equal contributions would make the plan sound like a great national insurance policy, which, in a sense, it was. Fixing benefits at subsistence level left plenty of scope to the individual to improve on that level. The programme balanced redistributive elements, such as tax-funded universal health care, with regressive flat-rate contributions levied on all incomes and universal benefits provided to the wealthy and the middle class as well as the most needy. This was universalism, but of the lowest common denominator. But no matter. The lofty rhetoric carried the day.[7]

Beveridge's prose combined bullet point accuracy with high ambition:

> The scheme embodies six fundamental principles; flat rate of subsistence benefit; flat rate of contribution; unification of administrative responsibility; adequacy of benefit; comprehensiveness; and classification . . . the aim of the Plan for Social Security is to make want under any circumstances unnecessary . . . [These proposals] are a sign of the belief that the object of government in peace and in war is not the glory of rulers or of races, but the happiness of the common man . . . War breeds national unity. It may be possible, through sense of national unity and readiness to sacrifice personal interests to the common cause, to bring about changes which, when they are made, will be accepted on all hands as advances, but which it might be difficult to make at other times. Democracies . . . make war, today more consciously than ever, not for the sake of war, not for dominion or revenge, but war for peace.

The international impact of the Beveridge report

The Beveridge report was to social policy in the 1940s, what the Atlantic Charter of 1941, or the United Nations Declaration of Human Rights were to international affairs. Beveridge was read all around the world, from London to Bombay, from Canada to the USA, to France to Italy, to Australia and New Zealand, to Germany and South America. The report sold over 635,000 copies in the UK and another 150,000 outside Britain. It inspired politicians around the world, even in Washington, DC, the new centre of global power.

7 Jose Harris, *William Beveridge: A Biography* (rev. edn, Oxford: Clarendon Press, 1997).

According to Prime Minister Mackenzie King of Canada, he had a lengthy discussion of the report with FDR. The Conseil national de la Résistance (CNR) of France had taken refuge in London during the war, where its members imbibed strong doses of Beveridge. Several other wartime councils, from the Netherlands to Belgium, Canada, France and Australia were profoundly influenced by Beveridge, and by the war's seeming vindication of Keynesian economics and planning in general.

In the aftermath of the war Beveridge's influence was all-pervasive. One study of the history of social welfare in the Western world found that by 1950, the Beveridge report had been cited by over twenty countries when they introduced important social welfare programmes in the 1940s and 1950s. Australia's 1945 White Paper on Full Employment paraphrases entire passages of Beveridge's 1944 book, *Full Employment in a Free Society*. A Dutch study of the 1947 citizenship-based pension plan acknowledged the influence of Beveridge's report on the Dutch government in exile in London. The Van Rhijn Commission appointed to set general guidelines for the future development of the social security system in the Netherlands followed the Beveridge example closely.[8] The pension plan that grew from the report was accepted by every Dutch political party.

The message was the same among the French Resistance. Its national council, the CNR, called for a universal, comprehensive package of health, pension, maternal benefits and unemployment coverage. Planning for postwar social and economic reform would not be an afterthought. Both Vichy France and the Resistance brimmed with plans to remake the social order and many Resistance leaders would go on to become key social reformers during the 1940s and 1950s. The Parodi–Croizat–Laroque social security proposals of 1946 were written by men who had been in exile with de Gaulle in London and were influenced by British discussions.

In Canada, the Marsh, Cassidy, and Scott reports were all steeped in Beveridgean principles. Liberal Prime Minister William Lyon Mackenzie King, who in the 1930s had adopted a stern stance against federal assistance for the unemployed, fought the election of 1945 on a slogan promising 'A New Social Order for Canada'.[9] Back in Europe, the future serial Prime

---

8 For the Netherlands, see Ilona Dorrestijn and Vibeke Kingma, 'The AOW Scheme: History and Predecessors', in Marjolein van Everdingen and Gijsbert Vonk, eds., *The Dutch State Pension: Past, Present and Future* (Amstelveen: Sociale Verzekeringsbank, 2008), pp. 14–31.

9 See Dennis Guest, *The Emergence of Social Security in Canada* (3rd edn, Vancouver: University of British Columbia Press, 1997), p. 119.

Minister Achille van Acker put forth Beveridge-style proposals in Belgium. In Norway, during the 1945 election all political parties emerged from the German occupation supporting a joint political programme that highlighted the expansion of the social security system. The influence of Beveridge was strong as was the Swedish example. And finally, there was the abortive D'Aragona Commission in Italy, which urged the adoption of a unified system of health insurance funds.

Beveridge's influence even crossed the battle lines of the war. Hitler's Germany had inherited the world's most advanced welfare state from the Weimar Republic. In 1940 it embarked on a major redesign of its social insurance system, spearheaded by the German Labour Front (*Deutsche Arbeitsfront*, DAF) that envisioned abolishing the distinctions between blue- and white-collar insurance that had been fundamental to the system's design since the days of Bismarck. But after 1942 Robert Ley, the head of the Labour Front, found himself warding off comparisons with Beveridge, insisting that the Third Reich offered not merely better benefits but a genuine guarantee of full employment.[10]

Labour in power, 1945–1951

After the dramatic wartime fanfare, Attlee's post-war government did not disappoint. With the first-past-the-post, winner-takes-all electoral system providing a huge majority, the Labour government passed a remarkable seventy-five pieces of significant legislation, including almost all of Beveridge's proposals:[11]

- 1944 Education Act (passed by the Coalition government during the war, but expanded upon by Labour): opens up universities somewhat to the popular classes; extends school leaving age for high school.
- 1945 Family Allowance Act.
- 1946 National Insurance Bill: compulsory, universal, entire population is covered for sickness, unemployment, retirement, widows' pensions, maternity benefits.
- 1948 National Assistance Act: covers most who fell through the cracks of the above laws.

10 Shelly Baranowski, *Strength Through Joy: Consumerism and Mass Tourism in the Third Reich* (Cambridge University Press, 2007), pp. 223–4.
11 Kenneth O. Morgan, *Labour in Power, 1945–1951* (Oxford University Press, 1984), Preface.

- The above laws cover 25 million people. They all had to be classified and numbered. It was a massive exercise in social activism.
- Housing: a renewed commitment to building public housing for the working class. Between 1945 and 1951, around 80 per cent of the 1 million new permanent housing units built in Britain were publicly owned.[12]
- The nationalization of several industries, including gas, coal, steel, railways and air transportation. The nationalization of the Bank of England.
- 1948: National Health Service: free medical aid for all. A model for nations around the world – either to be embraced or, as in the USA, abhorred. Hospitals nationalized and put under control of twenty-eight regional hospital boards, whose members were appointed by the Minister of Health. All fees abolished; a few introduced in 1950–51 (eyeglasses, prescriptions, etc.)

Not all of these measures were revolutionary. In areas such as national insurance the effect of these reforms was to consolidate and centralize the results of an expansion in social spending that had begun already in the 1920s and 1930s. The First World War like the Second had an expansive impact on the welfare state. But in many areas the impact of the Second World War was obvious and undeniable. In particular, the Second World War pushed Britain in the direction of universalism.

The National Health Service was the most radical of the universal measures launched by the war. It had its origins in the Emergency Medical Service (EMS) that by the midpoint of the war was providing free medical care for twenty-six categories of civilians. Under conditions of a totalizing war, medical care could not be exclusively reserved for soldiers and sailors, as in the past, but had to be extended to include civilians as well – to those injured in the munitions factories and by German bombing raids, for instance. The EMS exposed the deficiencies in Britain's hotchpotch 'system' of health care. In place of a complicated patchwork of agencies, charities and independent hospitals, people at the highest levels of government began to envision the opposite – a single, universal, unitary, centralized health care system. And this is exactly what a White Paper published under the direction of a Conservative member of the Coalition government recommended in 1944 and what Britons got in 1948.

---

12 Edwin Amenta and Theda Skocpol, 'Redefining the New Deal: World War II and the Development of Social Provision in the United States', in Margaret Weir, Ann Shola Orloff and Theda Skocpol, eds., *The Politics of Social Policy in the United States* (Princeton University Press, 1988), pp. 81–122 (p. 98).

To a large extent, this all-embracing, universalistic social policy, freed from the shadow of the poorhouse and the haunting stigma of the means test, was a delayed reaction against the humiliating nineteenth-century style poor laws that had overshadowed working-class lives in Britain at the beginning of the twentieth century. As Aneurin Bevan, the Health Minister, declared: 'At last we have buried the Poor Law.' Symbolically, the 1946 National Assistance Act stated: 'the existing Poor Law shall cease to have effect'.[13] Here was a deliberately worded death certificate for the *ancien régime charitable*.

But the same universalism that abolished means-tested poor relief also had the effect of extending expensive welfare benefits to millions of new middle-class recipients. This reversed the trend of the interwar period. As social spending expanded in the interwar period the benefits had been highly concentrated. One half of all working-class families in Britain had some form of state assistance by the 1930s, and the figure for France was at least 30 per cent, but very, very few middle-class families received anything at all. Universalism, therefore, appears decidedly less redistributive and progressive upon closer examination. And yet that may miss the point, for without universalism, it might not have been possible in political terms to do so much for the poor. Paying the prince a pension was the cost of reducing pauperism.

The deans of British social policy history, Rodney Lowe and Howard Glennerster, have reminded us that despite expanding welfare and widening access to secondary education Labour failed to attack the fundamental class cleavages of British society. The fee-paying private schools survived, thanks to being granted tax exempt charitable status. Britain remained a class-ridden, unequal society. But cutting the rich down to size was never Beveridge's goal. The Labour government welfare policy was concerned primarily with poverty eradication, not the reduction of inequality. As the rise of inequality began to command public attention from the 1980s onwards, there has been a tendency to re-evaluate the welfare state of the 1940s through the lenses of today. But this is to misread the central thrust of the Beveridge design, which was above all directed toward establishing a robust safety net.

That is not to say that there was not a redistributive element in the mid-century moment. But this came as much through taxes as through the new system of welfare benefits. What is undeniable is the combined effect of taxes

---

13 Quoted in Derek Fraser, *The Evolution of the British Welfare State* (2nd edn, London, 1984), pp. 229–30.

Table 20.1 *Inequality before and after taxes and benefits, 1937–1977 (Gini coefficients)*

	Original income	Income after benefits	Cash income after taxes	Final income with services	Reduction in inequality (absolute)	Reduction in inequality (%)
1937	37	33	29	28	9	24
1949	26	21	16	14	12	46
1977	43	30	29	23	20	47

Source: 'Why did the post-war welfare state fail to prevent the growth of inequality?' (www.history.ac.uk/ihr/Focus/welfare/articles/glennersterh.html).

and benefits. As Glennerster himself notes, in 1949 taxes and transfers led to a 46 per cent reduction in inequality – double the level of the 1930s (Table 20.1).[14]

Faced with this redistributive push, the transformation in the political rhetoric in the British two-party system was dramatic. The Conservative Party (UK) election manifestos in 1945 and 1951 were replete with self-praise regarding the Conservatives' role in building up the welfare state in the interwar period and with promises to be a trustworthy steward of the programmes that Labour had introduced between 1945 and 1951. As Labour's successors, the Conservative administration headed by Winston Churchill boasted of its achievements in raising public housing construction to 300,000 new units in 1951–52.

The European welfare state

In virtually every rich or middling income nation, on the Allied side, there is a clear sense of demarcation: the welfare state before the war, and after the war. Existing programmes were made more generous and older provisions limiting coverage to the indigent or to industrial workers were generally removed. The common denominator was that after the war, social umbrellas opened up, sheltering the middle classes as well as the working classes.

When social insurance was introduced by Bismarck late in the nineteenth century, it was designed to 'sidetrack the process of [working class]

---

14 'Why did the post-war welfare state fail to prevent the growth of inequality?' (www.history.ac.uk/ihr/Focus/welfare/articles/glennersterh.html).

emancipation'. The new welfare policies of the post-war era were designed to *complete* that process. 'Poverty and need were no longer to exclude from full membership in the community ... Where social policy had earlier sprung from the hopes of society's elites for stability ... there now appeared to develop a broad consensus behind the welfare state.'[15] According to Peter Baldwin, when the middle class jumped aboard the train, the welfare state was irrevocably changed. When wartime conditions exposed tens of millions of middle-class Europeans to the hardships and risks so commonplace among the working class, the welfare state acquired a new anchoring in society, economy and polity by including the wealthy and the middle classes.

The Social Democratic Party had been actively developing the Swedish social model from the 1930s onwards. But the big change brought on by the war was that 'the bourgeois parties in the immediate postwar era also developed pressing reasons of direct and positive self-interest for their support of reform.' Those 'who had traditionally been excluded from welfare ... now saw their chance to be among the beneficiaries'.[16] It was in reaction to this transparently self-serving espousal of universalism that the Socialist parties of Sweden and Denmark acquired the dubious honour of being the only left-wing parties to have *opposed* universal social welfare programmes after 1945, favouring instead programmes that targeted their core constituents: the working class.

In the UK and much of Scandinavia the result of this inclusionary logic was a thoroughgoing universalism. Although most larger rich nations would by the end of the 1940s provide a full basket of social insurance to 75–90 per cent of their citizens, this was not always structured in a universalist fashion. In Germany and France, though the tendency toward greater social spending was irresistible, the spending tended to be channelled into corporatist arrangements, or separate and unequal pension and health funds linked to one's occupation, but underwritten and in some cases subsidized by the central state.

On the side of the victorious powers, France's post-war welfare system was a strange amalgam of post-war liberation ambition, with impulses from the interwar and the Vichy era. Vichy claimed to loathe the decadence of the Third Republic but in practice it expanded every social policy it inherited. It made particularly great strides in opening up the hospitals to all citizens, no matter their wealth (previously they had been limited to the indigent and

---

15 Baldwin, *Politics of Social Solidarity*, pp. 108–9.
16 Ibid., pp. 111, 112.

those who benefited from the 1928 law providing for limited health insurance). A decree of December 1941 signalled the end of hospitals as dumping grounds for the poor and transformed them into institutions open to all French citizens. Hospital commissions were brought under the tutelage of the prefects and the Minister of Health. Regional hospital centres were established, foreshadowing yet another post-war development. From this state of affairs, it was not a great leap toward national health insurance, which emerged less than a year after the war's end. An *ordonnance* of 15 June 1945 confirmed all Vichy social legislation and all edicts governing hospitals and health care.[17] The chief law governing public pensions in post-war France took until May 1946 to be passed. Most private sector industrial and commercial workers were included. Universalism failed in France as various occupational groups jockeyed for control over the new insurance funds they knew would emerge. But the state was invested with the duty of supervising and in many cases subsidizing the plethora of occupation-based pension regimes that had emerged by 1951.

The story of welfare expansion was not uniform. And recently some have challenged the idea of the Second World War representing a watershed, arguing that there is no significant bump in spending during the 1940s.[18] But this revisionist view is tenable only if one gives disproportionate weight to the authoritarian regimes of Spain and Portugal and several smaller European nations that did not possess the wealth necessary to build big welfare states during the 1940s. The larger states of Europe – UK, France, Germany and Italy – as well as the Scandinavian states all increased their spending. In 1938 France devoted 5 per cent of its GDP to social spending; by 1949, when industrial production had not caught up to 1938 levels, France devoted 8.2 per cent of its GDP to things social, or, an increase of 64 per cent. Whereas roughly 48–50 per cent of the population had health and pension coverage before the war, over 80 per cent did by 1950, and their benefits were now more generous. In Britain, the rise was more dramatic: by 1949, roughly 17 per cent of public expenditures were devoted to the social services, a 50 per cent increase over 1938, when Britain had already been a world leader

---

17 J. Deprun, 'Comment est née la nouvelle "charte hospitalière"', *Revue des établissements de bienfaisance* (November 1943), 245–8 and Timothy B. Smith, 'The Social Transformation of Hospitals and the Rise of Medical Insurance in France, 1914–1943', *The Historical Journal* 41:4 (1998), 1055–87 (pp. 1086–7).
18 Franz Nullmeier and Franz-Xaver Kaufmann, 'Post-War Welfare State Development', in Francis G. Castles, Stephan Leibfried, Jane Lewis, Herbert Obinger and Christopher Pierson, eds., *The Oxford Handbook of the Welfare State* (Oxford University Press, 2010), pp. 81–101.

in social spending along with Germany. Relatively poor Italy, too, in 1949 devoted 5.2 per cent of GDP to social spending, up from 3.3 per cent in 1938.[19]

Furthermore, these increases in spending on new programmes were all the more significant because there was a significant reduction after 1945 in spending on unemployment. As full employment became the norm, monies formerly tied up assisting the unemployed were rechannelled to new programmes. It was at this time, in 1945–49, that enormous blank cheques were written to future retirees. Largely unfunded pension promises were made during the 1940s and early 1950s. These did not show up on the accounts immediately, but nevertheless constituted a major new promise, a social right, a guarantee of a reasonably comfortable retirement and therefore an encouragement to consume and spend in the here and now. However one chooses to categorize it, the pension promises made in the UK and France in 1946, and Germany in 1957 represent a watershed indeed.

At first glance, it might appear foolhardy to have spent so liberally after the war, at a time when rationing of basic foodstuffs continued in several nations. But that was the very point: it was precisely *because* of the hardships of war and the Depression that preceded it, and because of the strains of post-war rationing, that politicians believed they must devote more of the nation's wealth to things social. A peoples' war must produce a peoples' peace. This is a point lost on critics like Corelli Barnett, who has charged that Britain spent recklessly on things social when it ought to have devoted its energies elsewhere – industrial infrastructure, education, etc. In fact Britain's spending on social welfare paled in comparison to its military spending during the 1940s. So why single it out, especially as Britain's European competitors were poorer, were in some cases more affected by the war, and yet increased their social spending at an even greater rate? As Tony Judt concluded in his sweeping survey of post-war Europe, 'far from dividing the social classes against each other, the European welfare state bound them closer together than ever before.'[20]

As Judt observed in 2005:

> in the aftermath of depression, occupation and civil war, the state – as an agent of welfare, security and fairness – was a vital source of community and social cohesion. Many commentators today are disposed to see state-ownership and state-dependency as the European problem, and salvation-from-above as the

19 Tony Judt, *Postwar: A History of Europe since 1945* (London: Heinemann, 2005), p. 76.
20 Ibid.

illusion of the age. But for the generation of 1945 some workable balance between political freedoms and the rational, equitable distributive function of the administrative state seemed the only sensible route out of the abyss.[21]

Judt's general point is well taken, but it could hardly be said that the distribution of social benefits in complex corporatist welfare states like those of France and Italy could be characterized as 'rational and equitable'. For all the talk of the post-war 'model', one should not overstate the rationalism of welfare policy formation.

These caveats aside, Judt's general point stands: today, parts of Europe where spending is inefficient might be damned with the big welfare state, but in 1945 all of Western Europe would have been damned *without* it. As Herbert Morrison argued in 1943 in defence of the Labour Party's ambitious social insurance plans:

> I have no doubt that it is the duty of this, or any other Government, to make provision for a minimum standard of life that will keep our population, without exception, decently fed, and properly looked after in illness, misfortune and old age. It may be asked, can we afford to do this? I would say – can we afford *not* to do it? The mere instinct of self preservation warns us not to allow in our midst the continued existence of a depressed, insufficiently fed minority . . . But if it did not, the instincts of common humanity would prompt us not to leave our brothers and sisters in fear and in need, while our national family has the means to lift them up to decent living. Once a community has reached a point of enlightenment and education where it is aware of the plight of its old, sick, out of work and unfortunate citizens, there is an imperative moral obligation upon it to care for them. This must be done.[22]

To fully comprehend the forces that led nations drained by war nevertheless to commit themselves to unprecedentedly expensive social schemes, we have to appreciate this sense that Morrison conveys that the welfare state was seen as the only possible model – other than communism – for a well-ordered future.

North America

If one wishes to confirm the significance of the shift wrought by the war, it is instructive to compare the politics of social welfare in Europe in the 1940s

---

21 Ibid., p. 77.
22 Herbert Morrison, *Prospects and Policies: Five Speeches on Post-War Subjects* (Cambridge University Press, 1943), pp. 5–6.

and 1950s with those of North America. There, the shock of the war was far more muted. Most notably, mid-century Canada and the USA stand out as the two rich nations that entered the second half of the twentieth century without providing health insurance for all. In both cases the resistance to public provision of basic services was deeply rooted. But this status quo had been challenged in the 1930s and 1940s, by the Great Depression and the activism of the New Deal. Unlike in Europe, however, this dynamic of change was not driven home by a traumatic war experience. Whereas over 60,000 British civilians were killed during the war by German bombs, North America was spared. Nor was there a 'Hunger Winter' as the Nether-lands would suffer in 1944–45 or Germany in 1946–47. The unscathed home front meant there was less of a need to rebuild a tattered social order after the war.[23]

It is not that North America was not profoundly affected by the crises of the 1930s and 1940s. As Keith Banting notes, of Canada, 'the hopeless inadequacy of welfare provision during the depression had convinced an entire generation of legal scholars and social welfare professionals that strong leadership from Ottawa was the key to ... a modern, coordinated social security system.' Efforts to centralize in the federal government a range of social benefits including unemployment relief had been struck down in 1937 as unconstitutional, violating the British North America Act's provision that welfare was a provincial matter. But 'after the Second World War, constitutional roadblocks that had seemed insurmountable during the 1930s proved much less formidable.'[24] In fact, even during the war, the pressure for centralization was powerful, as a parliamentary commission of 1940 success-fully pushed through a national unemployment system. During the latter stages of the war, in 1944, a national family allowance system was introduced, which might add 30–40 per cent to the take-home pay of a male breadwinner with two children. This was a remarkable change for a country that, in 1939, had no welfare state to speak of, ranking dead last in any league table of social spending among rich nations. Canada's new unemployment insurance plan was very generous by the standards of the day and it is inconceivable without the war's role in raising awareness of the truly national nature of the economy. In 1951, in a final echo of wartime solidarity, a national Old Age

---

23 A point made by Alan Brinkley for the USA: *The End of Reform: New Deal Liberalism in Recession and War* (New York: Alfred A. Knopf, 1995).
24 Keith Banting, *The Welfare State and Canadian Federalism* (2nd edn, Montreal and Kingston: McGill-Queen's University Press, 1987), p. 59.

Security (pension) plan was introduced, providing a national minimum in a highly fragmented, loose federation of ten provinces. Benefit levels in the national scheme were up to three times more generous than the provincial plans it replaced.[25]

Whereas the impact on Canada of the war was to allow it to 'make good' the deficits it had accumulated relative to other rich societies in the interwar period, in the USA the impact of the war was more ambiguous. In the 1930s the USA had already experienced a 'big bang' of social policy under the New Deal, including the advent of Social Security (pensions, which began paying out in 1940), a national minimum wage, support for the mortgage industry, the passage of the Wagner Act giving more power to unions, unemployment insurance, ADC (as 'welfare' was then called), and a whole host of regulatory measures which hemmed in Wall Street. By 1940 the USA's welfare state was one of the most advanced in the world, and America's reformist energies were, in comparison with Canada and much of Western Europe, spent. Over the following decade further social legislation fell victim to the division of powers and the executive's weak control of Congress. By 1945 with the economy booming few people were drawing benefits. There was no appetite for more taxes and spending. Whereas Truman's Health Care Act failed in 1948, the boldest post-war measures in the USA were the passage of the GI Bill in 1944 and the 1946 Employment Act, which committed the federal government to full employment and a dramatic extension of pension entitlements in 1950.

Despite the relative lack of policy innovation the effect of the Great Depression and the war was to produce an unprecedented compression in relative incomes and inequality. Between the 1930s and 1950s virtually every rich nation – from the USA and UK to Canada, Spain, Italy, Australia, Denmark and Sweden – witnessed a sudden drop in the fortunes of the top 10 per cent of the income ladder starting roughly in 1940.[26] The destruction of the value of capital, the decline of the stock market, robust inflation and above all steep new taxes had taken their toll on the wealthy. In the USA, as in Great Britain and Canada the new tax policies of the 1940s would have profound consequences on the future development of the class structure, taxing down the super-wealthy, and preventing higher incomes from pulling

25 Gerard William Boychuk, *Patchworks of Purpose: The Development of Provincial Social Assistance Regimes in Canada* (Montreal and Kingston: McGill-Queen's University Press, 1998), pp. 42–3.
26 Thomas Piketty, *Capital in the Twenty-First Century*, trans. Arthur Goldhammer (Cambridge, Mass.: The Belknap Press of Harvard University Press, 2014), pp. 318–19.

ahead of others during the boom years of Western capitalism. It is difficult to see how such a sudden introduction of steep income taxes could have come about without war. But, as Monica Prasad has argued so convincingly, this 'big bang' of progressive income taxes did not emerge from consensual politics or gradualistic policy. Rather, in the eyes of its opponents, wartime and post-war tax policy verged on the punitive. It emerged from an adversarial, first-past-the-post political culture in which the winner takes all. Though the right wing protested, it would be thirty years before the post-war settlement was overturned. It was not until the 1970s that the anti-tax movement regained its strength, and when the USA's and UK's 'adversarial' tax systems with their highly visible progressive tax rates, began to catch a majority of the population in their net, and a new anti-statist coalition was born.[27] In both Great Britain and North America what has been at stake in the advance of the new right has been the overturning of a distributional model established during the Second World War.

In the USA, the 1942 Revenue Act set the tone for a new era of high taxation. It increased corporate tax rates, pushing the top rate from 31 to 40 per cent. Various surtaxes were introduced. Personal income taxes rose substantially. Someone making under $2000 per year would pay 19 per cent; someone making over $200,000 would pay a top rate of 82 per cent in addition to the basic rate of 6 per cent. A typical wage earner might pay an effective income tax rate (the overall rate they paid on all their income) of 10–20 per cent; a high earner would pay as much as 60–80 per cent. The net effect of the 1942 Act was to increase the federal government's total tax intake by 50 per cent. Just three years earlier, only 5 per cent of Americans had paid income tax. By 1942, the 'Victory Tax' enshrined in the Revenue Act meant that 75 per cent of workers paid income tax. This was a time when a US President could proclaim that at a time of 'grave national danger, when all excess income should go to win the war ... no American citizen ought to have a net income, after he has paid his taxes, of more than $25,000'.[28] In today's money Roosevelt was calling for a *maximum* wage ceiling of $345,000. But Congress opposed him and his proposal went nowhere. Nevertheless, the high taxes introduced during the 1940s persisted for a quarter of a century, with top rates ranging from 65 to 90 per cent.

27 Monica Prasad, *The Politics of Free Markets* (University of Chicago Press, 2006), p. 280. See also Mark Blyth, *Great Transformations: Economic Ideas and Institutional Change in the Twentieth Century* (Cambridge University Press, 2002).
28 Quoted in Timothy Noah, *The Great Divergence* (New York: Bloomsbury, 2012), p. 18.

One of the effects of progressive income taxes at these high marginal rates was to place a de facto cap on the salaries of high earners in the corporate world, thus leaving a larger slice of the pie for the rest of the income distribution. The 'great compression' of the mid-century involved reducing the share of income going to upper management, CEOs and shareholders, to the benefit of workers. Once war debts were paid, a burden substantially alleviated by post-war inflation and 'financial repression', high taxes provided a large flow of funds to finance the massive infrastructure projects that were launched in all rich nations during the twenty-five years following the war. To the extent that much of this spending could be considered 'social' in nature – schools, universities, hospitals, cultural and recreational facilities – it constituted a considerable material extension of the welfare state.

At the heart of the post-war capitalist system in the USA, there may not have been a dramatic extension of the welfare state, but organized labour seized the opportunity presented by the Second World War to increase its influence. The pressure from the shop-floor was vigorous. During 1945–47, the USA averaged 4,750–4,950 strikes per year. Never before or since has the US federal government been so open to the influence of organized labour. Today it takes a giant leap of the historical imagination to remember a time when business and labour leaders could convene at the White House, as they did in November 1945, to attempt to chart a future for US labour relations. Nor is it easy to imagine a President of the US Chamber of Commerce saying, as Eric Johnson did in 1946, that 'Labor unions are woven into our economic pattern of American life, and collective bargaining is a part of the democratic process.'[29] Organized labour was a key part of the New Deal coalition that sustained the Democratic Party down to the era of civil rights. As Timothy Noah reminds us, 'between 1948 and 1964, every Democratic presidential nominee began his election campaign on Labor Day in Detroit's Cadillac Square.'[30]

Arguably, the fact that organized labour had a seat at the table in Washington from the 1940s through the mid-1960s was the most important post-war development for the average working man in the USA. Throughout the 1940s, 1950s and into the 1960s, federal and state politicians saw to it that the minimum wage grew in line with overall growth. Not that big business and the right wing of the Republican Party accepted this power shift passively. The backlash on the part of the Republican-controlled Congress

29 Quoted in ibid., p. 129.
30 Ibid., p. 135.

began in 1947 and was led by Senator Robert Taft. Its first success was the defeat of Truman's Fair Deal, which would have included health care insurance.

Given this precarious balance, the so-called Treaty of Detroit of 1950 between the United Auto Workers and General Motors is often portrayed as a great victory for the organized working class but in several ways it symbolized the abandonment of the quest for more generous publicly provided social services, health care in particular. After Truman's health care bill failed in 1948, American workers had to settle for a 1949 court ruling that required companies to bargain over health and pension benefits. The following year the Treaty of Detroit limited strikes in exchange for health, unemployment, vacation and other benefits. Ford and Chrysler followed suit with similar deals. In addition, cost-of-living increases to wages became the cornerstone of collective bargaining insulating the core workforce against any rise in inflation. As the economy boomed, more and more American companies sought to recruit scarce labour with enticements such as pensions, health insurance, paid vacations, and even educational funds for the children of employees. Fringe benefits, as they were known, were not considered wages, so companies were able to circumvent wage controls.

These wartime and post-war developments led directly toward the emergence of America's 'divided welfare state', as Jacob Hacker calls it, with a large private insurance sector supported, as of a 1949 law, by the tax-free status of the benefits provided. The result was, inevitably, a private, hidden welfare state, upheld by legislation and tax breaks that tended to reward those in the upper half of the income ladder. 'The public–private divided welfare state, born during the 1930s and 1940s, would prove nearly impossible to change in subsequent decades.'[31] The number of people covered by private pension and health plans *doubled between 1947 and 1949 alone*, as workers took advantage of their right to bargain collectively (thanks to the 1935 Wagner Act) and as companies continued the wartime trend of offering the promise of future fringe benefits in lieu of higher wages in the here and now.[32] By 1950, 60 per cent of the US public had basic hospitalization coverage. There is a tendency today to romanticize this period of labour

---

31 Jacob Hacker, *The Divided Welfare State: The Battle over Public and Private Social Benefits in the United States* (Cambridge University Press, 2002), pp. 169, 39.

32 Jennifer Klein, *For All These Rights: Business, Labor, and the Shaping of America's Public-Private Welfare State* (Princeton University Press, 2003).

strength and welfare capitalism but at the time these advances were seen as a defeat: organized labour had wanted a public system, European style.

It's the economy stupid

In the wake of the defeat of FDR and Truman's ambitious post-war social reform agenda in the USA, American progressives largely focused on the goal of higher economic growth, the spread (and government underwriting) of home ownership, the spread of private insurance propped up with tax breaks, and mass consumption. And the results were spectacular. Throughout the post-war decades the world capitalist economy with the USA at its heart grew faster than at any previous point in history. The result was to swamp the institutional differences and political struggles that had seemed so dramatic in the 1940s in a general sea of affluence. In a world in which the fear of 'globalization' did not exist, in which over 95 per cent of all manufactured goods imported by rich nations came from other rich nations, the prospect of freer trade seemed like a win–win opportunity to increase growth and thus to provide further revenue with which to support the maturing welfare state.

The favourable economic climate allowed the European welfare state to be entrenched in a new vision of the social order.[33] The expansion of social insurance figured at the centre of efforts to rebuild the social and political order. The post-war settlement was designed, among other things, to prevent a return of the bitter class antagonisms of the interwar years. Workers' rights, the rights to family support, leisure and pensions were enshrined in the new French constitution and in the German Basic Law. Workers would be welcomed as partners of the state – no longer would they be treated as enemies within. Though bitterly contested at the time, and denounced by the left as a sell-out, the Works Constitution Law of 1952 in West Germany established the right of workers in large companies to have representation on supervisory boards. In Germany's export champions the German worker would be integrated into the very heart of major firms' decision-making processes. This built up trust between workers and management and it also constituted an implicit promise that management would keep workers in the loop.[34]

---

33 The idea is Mark Mazower's, *Dark Continent: Europe's Twentieth Century* (London: Allen Lane, 1998).
34 A. J. Nicholls, *The Bonn Republic: West German Democracy, 1945–1990* (London: Longman, 1997), p. 99.

'In Austria, an analogous system of co-determination prevailed in nationalized industries, which accounted for perhaps 20 percent of employment, and was eventually extended to the rest of the economy.'[35] In the Netherlands, business, labor, government leaders worked on the PBOs (Publiekrechtelijke Bedrijfsorganisatie), which set employment levels and investment targets.

In Norway, the government set up planning councils and production committees. In Sweden, the 'Thursday Club' was founded, which brought together business, labour and government to exchange information. The Rehn-Meidner model (named after the Swedish trade union economists) blended a commitment to full employment with tax breaks for corporations willing to invest in job creation and productivity. At the same time the shop-floor wage structure was compressed by trade union bargaining and high marginal tax rates held the incomes of the wealthy elite within reasonable bounds. With these measures of 'predistribution' in place and growth booming, the welfare state was relieved of making good on excessively expensive commitments.

In a manner that is staggering to recall today, welfare and wage bargaining were directly integrated in the post-war social model. In Belgium, a 1944 social contract limited wage increases in return for a new social security system.[36] In Canada, family allowances, introduced in 1944, had the same purpose – they were meant to keep wages down by helping the truly needy, those with young families.[37] In Norway, workers received paid vacations and a shorter work-week as recompense for wage restraint in the immediate post-war years. The Dutch government offered unemployment insurance and pensions 'as a quid pro quo for wage moderation'.[38] The 1955 agreement in Sweden extending health and disability insurance plus active labour market policies (adult education, training) was counterbalanced by an agreement to limit wage increases. On several occasions during the 1940s and 1950s the Swedish, Austrian, German and Danish

---

35 Barry J. Eichengreen, *The European Economy since 1945: Coordinated Capitalism and Beyond* (Princton University Press, 2007), pp. 32–3.
36 Martin Conway, *The Sorrows of Belgium: Liberation and Political Reconstruction, 1944–1947* (Oxford University Press, 2012), p. 266.
37 Allan Moscovitch and Glenn Drover, 'Social Expenditures and the Welfare State: The Canadian Experience in Historical Perspective', in Allan Moscovitch and Jim Albert, eds., *The Benevolent State: The Growth of Welfare in Canada* (Toronto: Garamond Press, 1987), pp. 13–43 (p. 28).
38 Eichengreen, *European Economy*, p. 34.

governments expanded social policies in return for a commitment by organized labour to moderate their wage demands.

These trade-offs were supportable for both sides given the prospect of unprecedented rapid growth in GDP, which would enable future governments to continue to open the social spending spigots. After the period of depression in the 1930s and acute shortage and rationing in the 1940s the post-war world was now animated by a dream of never-ending prosperity. By the late 1950s and 1960s annual increases in social spending of 10 per cent were not unheard of, as a new programme was put into place, or as a major increase in benefits was rolled out, as with the massive increase to pension benefits in Germany in 1957 and in the UK and France the very next year.

The footprint of the post-war welfare state was not limited to financial transfers. In the cities of Europe damaged heavily in the war, the new welfare regime supported a vast programme of urban restructuring. In West Germany at least 9.5 million refugees and resettled people (expellees) from Central and Eastern Europe had to be rehoused. Where would they live? Forty per cent of Germany's entire housing stock was destroyed by the bombing. The state would have no choice but to play a large role in the answer to that question. Through a pragmatic mix of tax concessions to private builders and direct state funding, the Germans solved their housing crisis by the late 1950s. In the London metropolitan region over 3.5 million houses or apartments were destroyed or damaged by the Luftwaffe; 30 per cent of Britain's national stock was severely damaged or destroyed. In France the damage ran to 20 per cent. In Italy 1.2 million homes had been destroyed. The need to rebuild Europe's housing stock in a short time-frame dragged the state into a prominent role in the provision of housing.

End of the dream

In the aftermath of the Second World War the welfare state came to seem to many as an end of history. And this vision was only confirmed by the decades that followed in which welfare spending rose and unemployment was close to zero. In the early post-war period this was accompanied by the violent ideological clashes of the early Cold War. But by the 1960s even those had attenuated. There was an end of ideology. And it even seemed as though across the Iron Curtain capitalist and state socialist societies were converged on a similar model of industrial urban modernity. A generation after the war, however, this sense of stability fragmented from within giving way to a new era of crisis. The sudden breakdown in the Western capitalist model in the early 1970s, and the advent of stagflation and deindustrialization ripped aside the optimism of economic control. But it did so precisely at the moment at which the limits of the post-war welfare state were being questioned in an expansive direction.

We look back on this period with rose-tinted glasses but it is worth recalling that even as economies were growing at unprecedented rates, and even as the skilled and organized blue-collar male worker was generally thriving, many groups were almost completely ignored by social policy, and others were deprived of social and legal rights which were taken for granted by the 1970s. The 1940s and 1950s were no golden age for most women, for most immigrants, for the disabled, for low-income workers, for most elderly people, for tenants of ramshackle housing and for the consumers of unsafe goods. Many of the social 'rights' we value today in mature welfare states emerged during the late 1960s and 1970s, not during the immediate post-war era. Although wages were rising for most workers in rich nations during the post-war era, basic standards of workplace safety, and job security (rules governing dismissal, etc.) and the like were much lower by the standards of the 1970s. The 'right' of labour not to be dismissed summarily, so prized today, was generally not introduced until the late 1960s to mid 1970s, precisely when the economic miracle started running out of steam.

Viewed in retrospect we thus gain a new perspective on the wartime welfare state. What was particularly impressive about it was not so much its generosity as the rare coincidence between aspirations to social reform, the politics of inclusive mobilization, and the economic means to ratify them. Broad-based tax systems (sometimes based on income taxes and truly progressive, sometimes based on sales and payroll taxes and therefore regressive) were equally important. But this model could not continue in its expansionary mode indefinitely. Social spending could outstrip economic growth rates for perhaps two or three decades but eventually the party was over. The moment growth slowed down and inflation rose dramatically, mature welfare states that consumed over one-half of all state spending would have to adjust. Who would pay? Pensioners? Young workers and taxpayers? The wealthy? The middle class? The poor? Different nations found different answers to these questions. The burden of dealing with rising expectations, rising spending but falling growth, placed great strains on European and North American society only thirty years after war's end. The wartime welfare state was at the root of the distributional struggles that began during the 1970s and that are still with us.

21

The rise and fall of central planning

DAVID C. ENGERMAN

The Second World War came during the era that historian Dirk van Laak called 'planning euphoria', so it is hardly surprising that most Second World War combatants have ubiquitous myths about the power of central economic planning.[1] Those myths explained their nation's high levels of armament production under difficult if not desperate circumstances. Such 'miracles of production', the narratives typically have it, were made possible by a unity of national effort, in which political disputes over the economy were set aside in the national interest. Miracles required miracle-men like Germany's Albert Speer or the USSR's A. N. Voznesenskii, each widely praised for spearheading their nations' economic mobilization. And in many of these mythical versions, it was the dedication to central economic planning that brought forth the massive production and embodied the spirit of the national unity.

Promising to impose rational control on the world, planners set themselves up for disappointment, especially but not only in wartime. Nevertheless, at least until the 1970s, the vision of rational planning – no matter how often and how profoundly frustrated – inspired scholars, bureaucrats and politicians around the world. One reason that enthusiasm for planning continued in spite of mounting evidence of its failures was that planning had a certain imprecision to it. Even narrowing planning to mean centralized economic planning, the term still encompassed a wide range of missions. Some of those marching under the banner of central planning sought to increase production while others saw planning as a means of reducing consumption. Some celebrated charismatic miracle-men, while others praised scientific rationality. Some sought planning as a counterweight to market

---

1 Dirk van Laak, 'Planung, Planbarkeit, und Planungseuphorie', Docupedia-Zeitgeschichte (http://docupedia.de/zg/Planung%5Bdocupedia.de%5D), accessed 17 December 2014.

mechanisms while others wanted planning to ensure the survival of the market system. What politicians talked about when they talked about planning, then, was rarely clear.

Yet for all of these different purposes, some common threads emerge. First, the very fuzziness of what planning actually was facilitated widespread support for it even among groups with divergent visions and interests. Planning might seem at first glance an escape from politics. Yet a second common thread among many planning episodes in the twentieth century was planning's role in both reflecting and even occasioning disputes over both the goals and the mechanisms of economic activity. Planning was a means of shaping economic priorities and policies; since such policies had winners and losers, it should be no surprise that planning was a form of contention, not an escape from it.

While planning's vagueness facilitated wide support over the middle decades of the twentieth century, not all observers fell under its sway. A kind of planning phobia, a set of arguments against planning, emerged alongside planning euphoria. But planning's opponents mirrored its adherents, at least insofar as there was no unified anti-planning argument, only divergent and incompatible arguments. Broadly speaking, opponents of central planning fell into two camps: those attuned to its political dangers (that planning would encroach upon individual freedom), and those focused on economic results (planning would not improve overall economic performance). The latter line, in particular, grew in significance over the twentieth century. New generations of economists and economic historians developed increasingly sophisticated quantitative measures to determine whether planning had made an impact on national income. Yet planning's critics face the same pitfalls as its proponents. Those worried that planning put societies at risk of despotism greatly exaggerated the transformative possibilities of central planning. Those focused on economic performance, meanwhile, failed to recognize the divergent purposes of planning, which were just as often about shifting priorities and reducing consumption as about achieving optimal efficiency, or maximizing welfare.

From planning euphoria to actually existing planning

While there were utopian calls for centrally planned economic activity in the early twentieth century (or even earlier, in the case of Edward Bellamy's widely admired *Looking Backward, 2000 to 1887*, published in 1888), the first serious efforts to put planning in practice came not in a moment of high hopes but desperate straits: the crisis of world war.

What is widely considered the first planning agency of the twentieth century emerged in Germany in 1914. Facing an acute shortage of raw materials the electrical engineering industrialist Walter Rathenau cobbled together the *Kriegsrohstaffamt* (War Materials Office) in the Prussian War Ministry. In October 1916, following the further shocks to the German war effort of the battles at Verdun and on the Somme, Rathenau's efforts were displaced by a new phase of mobilization initiated by generals Paul von Hindenburg and Erich Ludendorff. Desiring a dramatic increase in ammunition and artillery production, the generals sought unprecedented control over all aspects of the German economy. Total mobilization, in short, required total control – not just over military production and strategic materials, but also over labour. Though Ludendorff celebrated this broad mobilization as an expression of national unity, the fierce everyday politics of economic policy told a different story. Most notable here were new efforts to control labour as simply one more economic resource to be put at the disposal of the army. Not surprisingly, however, workers – unlike raw materials – resisted such commands. Proposed regulations limited workers' mobility, ultimately treating them as soldiers without uniforms, subject to military command, to military discipline, and to meagre military wages. Labour leaders took this as a major challenge to the principle of *Burgfrieden* (literally peace within the castle; metaphorically, wartime Germany itself was the castle).[2] After heated parliamentary debate, labour leaders succeeded in getting a place at the table; the *Kriegsamt*'s draconian decrees on labour mobilization came at the price of conceding the presence of union representatives on every district committee.[3]

The totalizing aspirations of the *Kriegsamt*, born of severe shortages of raw materials and labour, never came close to fruition. The more severe labour regime could not create new workers, but could only shuffle them between various high-priority needs: from the front to the home front and back again. And having wrested responsibility for raw materials provisioning from Rathenau's War Materials Section (*Kriegsrohstoffabteilung*), the *Kriegsamt* could only play similar shell games with crucial war goods like coal. A central

---

2 Roger Chickering, *Imperial Germany and the Great War, 1914–1918* (Cambridge University Press, 1998), ch. 3.

3 The inclusion of labour representatives in corporatist economic arrangements is described exhaustively in Gerald D. Feldman, *Army, Industry, and Labor in Germany, 1914–1918* (Princeton University Press, 1966), part 3.

allocating organ like the *Kriegsamt* could not solve the problem of shortages through reallocation; even more efficient allocation could not create more coal or more workers. Germany's economic deficiencies ultimately spelled its defeat.

Despite this outcome, the *Kriegsamt* found many admirers. Bolshevik leaders like Lenin looked excitedly at the German efforts at the centralized management of an entire economy as a demonstration of the advantages of economic centralization for building state power. The Bolsheviks had not come to power with a specific economic programme. As Lenin later conceded, 'We have knowledge of socialism, but as for knowledge ... of organization and distribution of products, etc., that we do not have.'[4] Leading Bolshevik economists introduced the concept of planning in their classic *ABC of Communism* (1920): 'details must be thought out beforehand ...; and the work must be guided in uniformity with our calculations ... Without a general plan ... there can be no organization. But in the communist social order there is such a plan.'[5] That the Bolsheviks were facing an economy and society devastated first by the prosecution of the Great War and then by a multifront civil war (lasting until 1921) made Germany's wartime experience an all the more compelling example. The Bolsheviks' measures of 'War Communism' (especially *razverstka*, or reallotment) during the Russian Civil War – crop requisitions, labour restrictions, and so on – were responses to increasingly desperate economic conditions – much like the efforts of the *Kriegsamt* a few years earlier.[6]

A longer-term vision found its most famous expression in February 1920 in the GOELRO, or State Commission for Electrification of Russia. A year later, in February 1921, this planning mission was expanded in the State General Planning Commission, commonly known as Gosplan. Gosplan's origins were exceedingly modest; its staff numbered only thirty-four, focused exclusively on solving immediate local or sectoral problems like poor harvests, emigration and the like.[7] But by the late 1920s, Gosplan had become the leading economic institution within the Soviet Union, and an object of admiration

4 Lenin (1918), quoted in Michael Ellman, 'The Rise and Fall of Socialist Planning', in Saul Estrin, Grzegorz W. Kolodko and Milica Uvalic, eds., *Transition and Beyond: Essays in Honour of Mario Nuti* (New York: Palgrave Macmillan, 2007), pp. 17–34 (p. 18).
5 Bukharin and Preobrazhenskii (1920), quoted in ibid.
6 Lars T. Lih, *Bread and Authority in Russia, 1914–1921* (Berkeley: University of California Press, 1990).
7 E. H. Carr, *The Bolshevik Revolution, 1917–1923* (3 vols., New York: Macmillan, 1950), vol. II, p. 374; Eugène Zaleski, *Planning for Economic Growth in the Soviet Union, 1918–1932* (Chapel Hill: University of North Carolina Press, 1971), pp. 40–1.

among the increasing number of politicians and social scientists captivated by economic planning for its application of scientific analysis to economic problems. Gosplan itself expanded dramatically in size and scope, approaching a staff of 1,000 by 1926. Gosplan was not just growing rapidly but became an instrument for rapid economic growth; early plan goals called for doubling Soviet economic production over the life of the plan – and subsequent goals increased from there.[8] By early 1929, Gosplan published, to great fanfare, 2,000 pages comprising the first Soviet Five-Year Plan. Like many of the planning documents that followed, the Five-Year Plan focused on 'maximum industrialization of the country', and saw agriculture as merely providing resources for this goal. The determination to industrialize rapidly also dictated stringent foreign trade controls, increasing import of machinery and metals while drastically curtailing the import of consumer goods.[9] This, again, would appear in many national economic plans in later decades.[10]

Many in the capitalist world – few of them active in radical politics, even fewer card-carrying Communists – shared Gosplan's enthusiasm for a scientifically determined path to rapid economic growth. The American journalist Stuart Chase, who would later coin the term 'New Deal', gave the clear advantage to the Soviet system: 'it is clean cut, straightforward, and logical' unlike the 'industrial anarchy' of capitalism. Gosplan, situated 'at the border-line of the capacity of the human intellect', signalled the future.[11] Similar praise for Gosplan could be heard in Britain and continental Europe.[12] Planning, to these observers, offered a form of economic utopia, in which prosperity was guaranteed by subjecting previously untamed economic processes to human control. This version of 'planning euphoria' was especially prevalent in the 1920s, as social scientists celebrated technical expertise as a way to avoid deep-seated ideological conflict.[13]

8 E. H. Carr and R. W. Davies, *A History of Soviet Russia*, vol. 1: *Foundations of a Planned Economy, 1926–1929* (London: Macmillan, 1969), pp. 852–77.
9 Zaleski, *Planning for Economic Growth*, pp. 40, n. 118, 48–59, 71–2, 146.
10 V. G. Groman (June 1927), quoted in Carr and Davies, *Foundations of a Planned Economy*, p. 815.
11 Quoted in David C. Engerman, *Modernization from the Other Shore: American Intellectuals and the Romance of Russian Development* (Cambridge, Mass.: Harvard University Press, 2003), p. 161.
12 Gerd-Rainer Horn, *European Socialists Respond to Fascism: Ideology, Activism, and Contingency in the 1930s* (Oxford University Press, 1996), ch. 5.
13 Dirk van Laak, 'Planung. Geschichte und Gegenwart des Vorgriffs auf die Zukunft', *Geschichte und Gesellschaft* 34:3 (2008), 305–26; John M. Jordan, *Machine-Age Ideology: Social Engineering and American Liberalism, 1911–1939* (Chapel Hill: University of North Carolina Press, 1994).

Yet this view of Gosplan as an expression of human reason underestimated the extent to which it, like War Communism before it, reflected political imperatives and urgent economic crises. In the 1920s, before the creation of the first comprehensive, five-year plans, Gosplan was a key mechanism for state control and eventually state ownership of key industries. The plan grew with the state's involvement in the economy. And the announcement of the first Five-Year Plan in 1928 was less an effort to instantiate a utopia of scientific rationality on earth than a response to the Soviet Union's increasingly precarious economic circumstances: its increasing isolation from European trade, its ongoing problems obtaining sufficient food supplies from the agricultural sector, and its stagnating industrial growth.[14] The first Soviet Five-Year Plan celebrated rapid growth but was born of economic crisis.

Second, the supposedly technical and apolitical workings of Gosplan were belied by two forms of political dispute: among various economic organs vying for primacy, and between government organizations on the one hand and the Communist Party on the other. The people's commissariats did not readily relinquish control over their respective industries, leading to constant battles between Gosplan and aggrieved economic organs. These conflicts in turn provided occasions for Party involvement in the plans through what became an unending process of plan revision. No less an authority than Stalin declared that such corrections were an essential part of the plan, which 'cannot be eternal, permanent and unalterable'.[15] Leading Bolsheviks railed at Gosplan's supposed overreliance on 'professional statisticians and engineers' and its lack of attention to 'Party economic thought'.[16] For their part, Gosplan statisticians rued that 'the more corrections we make, the less realizable' the Plan becomes.[17] The first Five-Year Plan was born of politics, not technical rationality.

The first Soviet plan thus set the pattern for planning experiences later in the twentieth century. Far from being isolated from politics, planning became both an occasion for and an arena of dispute, a potent mixture of ideological differences and battles over turf. Second, the turn to planning was accompanied by significant new controls over foreign trade, efforts to

---

14 On agriculture, see Carr and Davies, *Foundations of a Planned Economy*, chs. 1–3; on trade, see Oscar Sánchez-Sibony, 'Red Globalization: The Political Economy of Soviet Foreign Relations in the 1950s and 60s' (PhD dissertation, University of Chicago, 2009), ch. 1.

15 Stalin (June 1930), quoted in Zaleski, *Planning for Economic Growth*, p. 73, n. 212.

16 Iu A. Larin (April 1929), quoted in Carr and Davies, *Foundations of a Planned Economy*, p. 801.

17 I. A. Kallinkov (1928), quoted in Zaleski, *Planning for Economic Growth*, p. 68.

suppress consumption, and a drive toward rapid industrialization. Finally, any shortcomings in Soviet planning were attributed to problems in execution, rather than formulation, suggesting that the only solution to planning problems was more planning.

Planning in the West

The Soviet experiment created an awed reaction across much of the world, including in 'liberal' Britain. In 1925 the dashing young Labour MP and future fascist leader Oswald Mosley issued his pamphlet 'Revolution by Reason', which envisioned a National Planning and Wage Commission that would have formal control over wages, investment and production.[18] By 1932, John Maynard Keynes overcame his earlier doubts about planning to acknowledge that state economic planning was a 'new conception . . . something for which we had no accustomed English word even five years ago'.[19] Meanwhile, after the fiasco of Ramsay MacDonald's second government, the Labour Party having lurched to the left espoused 'Socialist Planning'. For their part, business leaders in the early 1930s rallied behind a self-government for industry bill that would provide for government enforcement of cartel arrangements. Conservative enthusiasts such as future Prime Minister Harold Macmillan were first attracted to planning as a means of reducing overproduction and increasing profitability.

In the machinery of government itself, change lagged far behind this public debate. The Cabinet's Economic Advisory Council formed in the aftermath of the international economic shocks of 1931 was touted as an 'economic general staff' where, as Keynes put it, an 'expert analysis' based 'solely on scientific and technical grounds' might shape official policy. Yet the Council ultimately included only three economists, and played little role in policy formation.[20]

The Economic Advisory Council may not have amounted to much in Britain, but it reverberated through the Empire. In India, the Member for Finance in the Viceroy's Council wanted to create an Indian version of the Economic Advisory Council as the local 'expression of a very general and

---

18 Daniel Ritschel, *The Politics of Planning* (Oxford: Clarendon Press, 1997), pp. 58–61.
19 Richard Toye, *The Labour Party and the Planned Economy, 1931–1951* (Woodbridge: Royal Historical Society, 2003), p. 3.
20 Susan Howson and Donald Winch, *The Economic Advisory Council, 1930–1939: A Study in Economic Advice during Depression and Recovery* (Cambridge University Press, 1977), ch. 1 (esp. pp. 21, 24).

world-wide tendency'.[21] On the part of the nationalists the leading advocate of planning was none other than Jawaharlal Nehru, who chaired the Indian National Congress's National Planning Committee (NPC). For Nehru and his team of scientists and economists, national planning served as 'an exercise in the anticipation of power'.[22] The planning efforts drew on long-standing Indian themes as well as on broader international currents. The NPC's goal of economic self-sufficiency had long been a cornerstone of nationalist thought, dating back especially to the Swadeshi movement of 1905–11. The Soviet example of rapid industrialization through central economic planning enthralled Nehru and, even more, committee secretary K. T. Shah. Other NPC members preferred Britain's gradualist brand of Fabian socialism.[23] As independence drew near, industrialist G. L. Birla noted that his country had been 'seized with the fever of planning'. Though Nehru was jailed during the British repression of the Quit India campaign, plans abounded: the Indian Federation of Labour produced its 'People's Plan'; the industrialists produced their own plan; and even the Gandhians, no fans of centralization or industrialization, produced a plan.[24]

Rhetorical enthusiasm for planning was also surprisingly strong in the USA, led at first by American social scientists who saw Gosplan as a cure for capitalism's ills. These technocrats often drew inspiration from the War Industry Board and other First World War agencies. In the words of critic Randolph Bourne, the war had 'revealed a younger intelligentsia ... immensely ready for the executive ordering of events'.[25] Technocratic planning, they thought, could resolve, even prevent, conflicts; as one enthusiast wrote: 'We are so used to fighting that we cannot see that there is a better way – the way of planning.'[26] The most optimistic of the technocrats saw the administration of President Franklin D. Roosevelt (1932–44) as the best hope for technocratic planning. Roosevelt established the National Planning Board, chaired by his own uncle, to advise the Public Works Administration

21 Raghabendra Chattopadhyay, 'The Idea of Planning in India, 1930–1953' (PhD dissertation, Australian National University, 1985), pp. 35–6, 46.

22 Nehru quoted in Chattopadhyay, 'Idea of Planning in India', p. 105.

23 Benjamin Zachariah, *Developing India: An Intellectual and Social History, c.1930–50* (Delhi: Oxford University Press, 2005), ch. 5; Chattopadhyay, 'Idea of Planning in India', ch. 3.

24 'Preliminaries for Planning' (1945), in G. D. Birla, *The Path to Prosperity: A Collection of the Speeches & Writings of G. D. Birla* (Allahabad: Leader Press, 1950), p. 45; Chattopadhyay, 'Idea of Planning in India', ch. 4.

25 Bourne (1917), quoted in Guy Alchon, *The Invisible Hand of Planning: Capitalism, Social Science, and the State in the 1920s* (Princeton University Press, 1985), p. 21.

26 Ben Kizer, 'The Need for Planning', in *National Planning Round Table* (Minneapolis: National Conference on Planning, 1938), p. 2.

about which projects merited funding. Planners' hopes ran far ahead of the Planning Board's actual scope: optimistic board members hoped to develop 'a plan for national planning'.[27] American planning proponents often looked abroad, noting in particular that they 'could make ... use of the Russian experience'.[28] Eventually reconstituted as the National Resources Planning Board (NRPB), the board issued steady calls for centralized economic planning as the best means to achieve full employment.

The NRPB and predecessor agencies were more effective at engendering opposition than in influencing policy. The quintessential progressive journalist Walter Lippmann, for instance, cited the NRPB in his criticisms of planning and what he called 'collectivism'. Responding to the NRPB's lofty aspirations rather than its meagre accomplishments, he insisted that planners had no place setting their own goals. Such decisions rested with 'sovereign authority'. In times of war, this authority was clear – the 'general staff of the army' – but the problem of sovereign authority made planning ill-suited for democracies in peacetime.

Lippmann's critique of planning and 'collectivism' was an important source in what became the seminal critique of planning: Friedrich von Hayek's *Road to Serfdom*. That book, Hayek later recalled, had been 'stimulated' reading Lippmann's *Good Society*, which the author had sent him prior to publication. Hayek shared Lippmann's emphasis on the political (rather than economic) dangers of planning. Hayek insisted that peacetime planning for 'general prosperity' merely begged the question of broader economic goals, but he too conceded that things would be different in war, when economic goals would be clear and widely agreed upon.[29] Hayek also promoted those making a different argument against planning, most notably by resurrecting a brief against planning by fellow Austrian economist Ludwig von Mises. In the aftermath of the First World War, as a revolutionary enthusiasm for planning swept Central Europe, von Mises made the economic case against central planning. His essay 'Economic Calculation in the Socialist Commonwealth' (1920) emphasized the role of prices in the efficient functioning of the economy. Socialist planning, by rejecting market prices, could not be justified on economic grounds.[30]

27 Charles Merriam (1935), quoted in Alan Brinkley, *The End of Reform: New Deal Liberalism in Recession and War* (New York: Vintage, 1996), p. 246.
28 George Soule (1932), quoted in Engerman, *Modernization from the Other Shore*, p. 163.
29 Ben Jackson, 'Freedom, the Common Good, and the Rule of Law: Lippmann and Hayek on Economic Planning', *Journal of the History of Ideas* 73:1 (2012), 47–68.
30 Ludwig von Mises, 'Economic Calculation in the Socialist Commonwealth (1920)', in Friedrich A. von Hayek, ed., *Collectivist Economic Planning: Critical Studies on the Possibilities of Socialism* (London: Routledge & Sons, 1935), pp. 87–131.

Planning for war

Both the planning euphoria and the planning phobia of the 1930s would soon enough face the test of war, with Nazi Germany leading the way. When Hitler took office in 1933 he asked the German people to give him four years to fulfil his vision of national reconstruction. Behind the scenes military planners envisioned rearmament as two consecutive four-year plans. But the first plan actually to be announced by the regime, the New Plan initiated by Hitler's Central Banker and Economics Minister Hjalmar Schacht in 1934 was a product of circumstance. The New Plan drastically restricted imports, reconfigured trade mechanisms to encourage exports, and clamped down on domestic consumption, all so as to enable rapid economic recovery and rearmament to be squared with Germany's crippling shortage of foreign exchange.[31]

In 1936 Schacht's organization was supplemented by a new phase of Nazi economic measures, justified explicitly in terms of the Soviet comparison. In a secret memo to Göring drafted in September 1936 Hitler laid down a challenge: 'The German economy will either grasp the new economic tasks or else it will prove itself quite incompetent to survive in this modern age when a Soviet State is setting up a gigantic plan.' By 1940 he demanded, the German economy must be ready for war.[32] Already from 1933 onwards the War Ministry's economic staff, the *Wehrwirtschaftstab* (War Economy Headquarters) led by Colonel (later General) Georg Thomas had been preparing plans for the subordination of the entire national economy to military purposes in case of mobilization.[33] Now his military organization was overlaid by Göring's Four-Year Plan Organization, which neither replaced other economic organs nor sat squarely above them. As a result, sorting out clear lines of command became increasingly difficult. In addition, the planning agencies had to balance the military's immediate demand for armaments against the longer-term goal of augmenting industrial capacity. Nor could the planning agencies forget the consumers, whose demands needed to be 'guided' toward appropriate ends.[34] Furthermore, periodic

---

31 Adam Tooze, *The Wages of Destruction: The Making and Breaking of the Nazi Economy* (London: Allen Lane, 2006), pp. 91–5.
32 US Department of State, *Documents on German Foreign Policy, 1918–1945* (Washington: GPO, 1949), 5: 836–52.
33 Thomas (1935–36), in Berenice A. Carroll, *Design for Total War: Arms and Economics in the Third Reich* (The Hague: Mouton de Gruyter, 1968), pp. 41–2.
34 Avraham Barkai, *Nazi Economics: Ideology, Theory, and Policy* (New Haven: Yale University Press, 1990), p. 233.

foreign exchange crises demanded a renewed focus on foreign trade balances. Even in 1939, faced with a surging arms race, Hitler was forced to announce the slogan 'export or die'.[35] The result was not a centrally planned war economy, in General Thomas's assessment, but 'a war of all against all', as various ministries and military organizations fought for access to raw materials and industrial products.[36]

Planning in war

The exigencies of war brought some of the common aspects of national economic planning into clear relief. In spite of the combatants' vast differences in political organization and ideology, wartime economic policy placed a high rhetorical premium on central planning. Chief planners were celebrated as 'miracle-men' for their ability to mobilize all available human and material resources to fight total war. Such mobilizations, the choruses of praise ran, were possible only because of the single-minded devotion of economists able to create a unified economic effort. Yet these celebrations obscured the ways in which planning organs became arenas for intense politicking. Invocations of a single national purpose and of rationally organized economic decisions aside, conflict dominated economic planning endeavours among the war's combatants. These disputes were in part over resources, in part over who got to allocate resources, and in part over the very purposes of planning.

In Germany, first Fritz Todt and then from February 1942 Albert Speer served as the charismatic head of Munitions Production.[37] Albert Speer was also the leading figure in the grandly named *Zentrale Planung*, the Central Planning Committee, from where he orchested the self-declared 'armaments miracle'. Speer fashioned himself as an apolitical official leading a technical process.[38] But rather than opting for a button-downed, bureaucratic vision of technical efficiency, he cultivated a charismatic interventionist, troubleshooting style. Within the German war economy this produced tensions between Speer and the head of the *Planungsamt* (a staff office created to

---

35 Hitler (January 1939), quoted in Tooze, *Wages of Destruction*, p. 301.
36 General Georg Thomas (1939), quoted in Alan S. Milward, *The German Economy at War* (London: Athlone Press, 1965), p. 23.
37 Alan S. Milward, *War, Economy, and Society, 1939–1945* (London: Allen Lane, 1977), p. 114.
38 Tooze, *Wages of Destruction*, pp. 553, 558–60; Adam J. Tooze, *Statistics and the German State, 1900–1945: The Making of Modern Economic Knowledge* (Cambridge University Press, 2001), p. 273.

organize the flow of data to *Zentrale Planung*), the local economic advisor, businessman-turned-economic official Hans Kehrl. In the aftermath of an Allied attack on Berlin that reduced the *Planungsamt* offices to rubble and its statistical paperwork to ashes, Kehrl was distraught, concerned not just for his own organization but also for the future of the Nazi war effort without it. Speer, on the other hand, saw the destruction of the ministerial offices as a chance to liberate economic policy from the 'bureaucratic treatment of problems' that he thought had plagued the war effort. Kehrl's memoirs, written three decades later, still suggest his deep anger at Speer's incomprehension of real economic planning.[39]

Planning in wartime Japan had important similarities with the German variant. Japanese planning was closely tied to military aims while giving new form to old debates over basic questions of economic aims and organization. The Japanese creation of the state of Manchukuo in 1932 empowered the group of economic technocrats who came to dominate decision-making there. These technocrats, like those in Europe and the USA, supported a 'Third Way' between market liberalism on the one hand and communism on the other. Moving from the occupied territories to Tokyo in the late 1930s, these officials came to lead the New Order movement of the early 1940s. Under the leadership of the technocrat Kishi Nobusuke, a network of reform bureaucrats sketched out a comprehensive restructuring of Japan's wartime economy. Written before the Pacific War, these plans for a 'New Order' covered all aspects of Imperial Japan, from land reforms to finance. At the core of the plans was a proposal to separate ownership and management by creating industry associations that would make production decisions. The technocrats envisioned themselves as responsible for these associations from their hoped-for perches in the government economic bureaucracy. They expected that this arrangement would eliminate the conflicts that had riven Japanese economic life in the preceding decades.[40]

This abstract vision of rational and technocratic control, though, had little bearing on the political arrangements of Imperial Japan. Starting in the late 1930s, the Japanese Diet passed a number of measures that asserted government control over key economic processes with an aim to increased self-sufficiency. As usual, the planning began with an effort to allocate foreign

---

39 Hans Kehrl, *Krisenmanager im Dritten Reich. 6 Jahre Frieden, 6 Jahre Krieg: Erinnerungen* (Düsseldorf: Droste, 1973), p. 329.

40 Janice Mimura, *Planning for Empire: Reform Bureaucrats and the Japanese Wartime State* (Ithaca: Cornell University Press, 2011), ch. 5.

exchange, with import restrictions put in place in 1937. That same year, the Diet declared that the government 'had the right to exert direct control' over commodities, a right exercised in the first materials mobilization plan of 1938, which included a list of over 100 commodities. The Planning Board, also established in 1938, shifted to a focus on war mobilization, formulating a Four-Year Plan that received Cabinet approval only in January 1939 – long after its supposed 1938 start.[41]

The buildup for the broader Pacific War, which began with the surprise attack on the US naval base at Pearl Harbor in December 1941, offered the promise of industrial peace but in practice just shifted the venue for industrial conflict. The New Order reformers won a seeming victory with the Planning Board's creation of almost two dozen industrial control associations (*kogyo tosei kai*) in autumn 1941. Yet from the start they were led by private-sector managers, not New Order technocrats. Jurisdictional disputes, furthermore, broke out between the ministries that were supposed to supervise the associations. A bigger problem was that the consumers of products for mobilization – the army and the navy – had no direct input into industrial production decisions. The navy simply ignored this civilian production planning process, while the army set up its own cooperative associations (*kyoryokukai*) as a competing structure for supplies.[42]

By 1942, with the Pacific War in full swing, the production planning apparatus was just as dispersed as it ever had been. The Cabinet proved ineffective at reining in the various economic ministries that zealously guarded their independence, and a Ministerial Coordinating Committee added a new layer of bureaucracy that did little to bring mobilization under central control. Even Marshal Tojo's quasi-dictatorial powers over the whole war economy came with serious concessions to the *zaibatsu* (industrial conglomerates).[43] In late 1943 – almost two years after Pearl Harbor – most of the major policy organs were subsumed under a sprawling new Ministry of Munitions, which immediately set about formulating a materials mobilization plan. The serious efforts to fulfil the plan lasted about three months in early 1944 before that plan too went by the wayside.[44] Even with

41 Akira Hara, 'Japan: Guns before Rice', in Mark Harrison, ed., *The Economics of World War II: Six Great Powers in International Comparison* (Cambridge University Press, 1998), pp. 224–67 (pp. 231–8).

42 Richard Rice, 'Economic Mobilization in Wartime Japan: Business, Bureaucracy, and Military in Conflict', *Journal of Asian Studies* 38:4 (1979), 689–706.

43 Milward, *War, Economy, and Society*, pp. 117–18.

44 Hara, 'Japan: Guns before Rice', pp. 247–9.

preparations that went back to the 1920s, and a war that expanded according to its own timetable, then, Japan had a war planning apparatus that served above all as an arena for conflict between various government organs, as well as between bureaucrats and powerful industrial concerns.

Soviet wartime planning was at least spared the Japanese Planning Board's need to deal with private-sector enterprises. But that did not transform Gosplan into a paragon of rationality and central organization. Gosplan, like most Soviet institutions, had been badly shaken during Stalin's purges, so N. A. Voznesenskii's first task when he took the helm in 1938 was to stabilize it. He then sought to expand Gosplan's ambit to include not just formulating the plans but monitoring their fulfilment. He aimed, in the long run, to shift economic policy-making away from personal decrees and toward rationalized decision-making.[45] The impulse toward increased rationalization might have served the USSR well in peace, but was no match for the grim challenges occasioned by Operation BARBAROSSA in June 1941. Gosplan dramatically expanded its compass to incorporate numerous military tasks while at the same time it shifted its aims from economic growth to wartime mobilization. A new set of military departments within Gosplan were designed to wrest responsibility for production decisions away from the various economic ministries. Its assertion of direct control did not mean that it ceded any ground in planning: it still organized quarterly and annual plans and conducted fulfilment checks on some 30,000 indicators each month.[46]

Yet this intricate formal system of planning had little traction amid the chaos of massive losses of territory and population in the early stages of the war. Instead, the eighteen months after BARBAROSSA saw the emergence of what historians John Barber and Mark Harrison generously termed the 'informal system of high-level improvisation and individual initiative'. As in Japan and Germany, the emergency prompted the multiplication of new agencies that only muddied lines of reporting and responsibility. The weeks after BARBAROSSA, for instance, saw the creation of a wartime Cabinet, a first round of temporary commissions, and new commissariats for war supply – but no clear sense of how these new organs would relate to the existing apparatus or to each other. Plans to evacuate civilians and the bulk of the Soviet industrial base took place through a series of ad hoc measures that

45 Mark Harrison, *Soviet Planning in Peace and War, 1938–1945* (Cambridge University Press, 1985), pp. 18–37.
46 Ibid., p. 98.

themselves were frequently at odds with the fluid situation on the ground.[47] The desperate effort to relocate Soviet industry beyond the Ural Mountains while at the same time waging battles against an encroaching German Army made advance planning for production an impossible task.

By early 1943, after the worst of the emergency had passed, the informal system slowly gave way to the return of formal planning. Gosplan took responsibility for the crucial resources essential for Soviet victory: steel, electricity and food. And it gained official responsibility for the most important limiting factor for the Soviet war effort: labour.[48]

The return of the planning apparatus contributed, as Barber and Harrison comment, simultaneously to the centralization and decentralization of the Soviet economy:

> By a variety of measures, the wartime economy was more centralized than before or after the war. There was a big increase in the number of centrally planned commodities and plan indicators. Planning of high-priority industrial goods became more comprehensive and detailed ... At the same time, there were clearly limits to the centralization process ... In some areas of life the center interfered less, and left producers more to their own devices.[49]

At the same time, there had never been such a glaring discrepancy between circulating plan documents and actually planning the economy. After asserting more control over economic mobilization in 1943, Gosplan and other government organs produced a surfeit of plans that disguised the absence of real planning. A remarkable nine-page inventory compiled by the economist Eugène Zaleski lists well over 100 plans promulgated between 1941 and 1945. Most had a narrow scope: constructing a road on Lake Lagoda, for instance; strengthening the coal industry in Donbass (the subject of at least three plans); or rebuilding housing on Belorussian collective farms. Yet mixed among these were quarterly and annual plans for the national economy and a Five-Year Plan for post-war reconstruction.[50] Based on this list, and on the broader Soviet planning experience, Zaleski concluded that Voznesenskii and Gosplan did not so much *plan* the Soviet economy as *manage* it. The neatly arranged tables of planned production never reflected

---

47 John Barber and Mark Harrison, *The Soviet Home Front, 1941–1945: A Social and Economic History of the USSR in World War II* (London: Longman, 1991), pp. 197–9.

48 Ibid., pp. 201–3.

49 Ibid., p. 205.

50 Eugène Zaleski, *Stalinist Planning for Economic Growth, 1933–1952* (Chapel Hill: University of North Carolina Press, 1980), pp. 727–35.

or determined economic realities, but the process of circulating such plans served as a way to shape economic policy.[51]

If German mobilization had its 'miracle-man' in Speer and the USSR in Voznesenskii, there were many candidates for the laurels of planner-in-chief for the American 'miracle of production': Robert Nathan, Chair of the Planning Committee of the War Production Board (WPB); Robert Patterson, Under-Secretary of War; Brigadier General Albert Wedemeyer, head of the War Plans Division of the Department of War; Donald Nelson, chairman of the WPB; and Ferdinand Eberstadt, chairman of the Army-Navy Munitions Board. Yet the mere fact of so many candidates suggests the dispersion of authority for economic mobilization. There were many Americans charged with planning the impressive American mobilization, and many plans for it – but little coordinated planning.

The American mobilization, of course, took place in a very different political context than the Soviet, German or Japanese ones. By the time American mobilization planning began in earnest in 1939, the most radical elements of the New Deal had already given way to a 'Keynesian', growth-oriented strategy using fiscal and monetary techniques for macroeconomic stabilization. Outside the increasingly isolated group of planners housed at the NRPB, there was little official interest in transforming American economic organization.[52] Even so, from the late 1930s onwards, new agencies proliferated, some fifty-seven of which were engaged in one or another aspect of wartime mobilization. Most of these dealt with strategic raw materials, but others set prices and production priorities across the economy. These agencies bolstered the employment of economists in the federal government, with roughly 5,000 by the time of Pearl Harbor – up from one lonely 'economic ornithologist' a half-century earlier.[53]

This burgeoning staff was not a sign of unified national purpose but the opposite. As the USA geared up for war in early 1942, civilian agencies faced serious, even overwhelming competition from the military services themselves. Created by statute (unlike Roosevelt's alphabet soup of agencies, most of which were created by executive order), permanent, and with decades of experience in procurement, the Army-Navy Munitions Board was not interested in sharing power with fledgling civilian agencies.

---

51 This terminology comes from John Munro in his foreword to ibid., p. xxix.
52 Brinkley, *The End of Reform*, chs. 7–8.
53 Herbert Stein, 'The Washington Economics Industry', *American Economic Review* 76:2 (1986), 1–10 (p. 2).

The military–civilian conflict came to a head in 1942 in what one sardonic analyst called the 'Battle of the Potomac'.[54] The conflict began when the War Production Board that had been set up in January 1942 announced mandatory adherence to its Production Requirements Plan, which allocated supplies of dozens of scarce raw materials among industrial enterprises. Opposition came from all sides – but especially from the services, who feared that they would lose control over weapons supply chains. The overarching Production Requirements Plan even faced significant opposition within the WPB itself, from its sub-divisions that had earlier been responsible for allocating raw materials. The 'Battle of the Potomac' raged on for well over a year, after which the WPB proudly announced a new effort: the Controlled Materials Plan (CMP).

After the war, many observers heaped praise upon the CMP for organizing the 'miracle of production' that had turned the USA into an arsenal of democracy. Yet, from an institutional perspective, the CMP marked a serious retreat from the Production Requirements Plan. Rather than controlling a wide range of industrial output, the CMP focused on only three key inputs: steel, copper and aluminium. Rather than allocate the materials to the specific factory that would use it, furthermore, the CMP allocated the supplies to a government agency, which allocated to a contractor, which might in turn reallocate to a subcontractor. The CMP thus worked, as did the central planning system overseen by Albert Speer, through the military procurement apparatus – ultimately at the expense of the authority of the WPB itself. Military procurers soon joined with their industrial suppliers to the lasting benefit of both. Calling this approach 'planning by contract' conceals the fact that it was hardly centrally planned production; it involved only one sector of production and was not aimed at maximizing the efficiency or productivity of the economy as a whole. Indeed, the CMP came into effect in mid-1943 after the huge surge in US armaments production had been achieved. It was not proof of planning's success, but a concession that detailed production planning was unworkable.[55]

Even if the wartime planners in the USA faced different challenges than their counterparts in other nations, their work fit into the same general pattern. Wartime planning was, across the board, a series of ad hoc

54 Samuel P. Huntington, *The Soldier and the State: The Theory and Politics of Civil–Military Relations* (Cambridge: The Belknap Press of Harvard University Press, 1957), p. 338.
55 Hugh Rockoff, *America's Economic Way of War: War and the US Economy from the Spanish–American War to the First Gulf War* (Cambridge University Press, 2012), p. 188; Simon Kuznets, *National Product in Wartime* (New York: NBER, 1945), p. 90.

arrangements. It became an arena for additional conflict, not a means of resolving conflict; indeed, the impulse to plan led to new agencies and new layers of administration that expanded the number of actors and perhaps the intensity of conflict. These plans, furthermore, had different aims – some focused on increasing production, others on allocating scarce resources. The Second World War, in short, had a surplus of plans but a deficit of planning.

Talk of miracles of production, 'miracle-men', and the like – which was visible in most of the major combatants during and immediately after the war – suggests yet another tension particularly evident in wartime. Planners like Kehrl in Germany and Nathan in the USA saw themselves as techno-cratic professionals interested in applying modern organizational techniques to problems of government. The tools of their trade were input–output tables, production schedules and assessments of labour needs – not miracles or charismatic exhortations about national purpose. They aimed for max-imum efficiency and worried not just about headline-grabbing production records, but also about the wider ramifications, the potential for disruptive inflation and government deficits. Invocations of the miraculous, in contrast, tend to focus strictly on levels of production, especially the production of military materiel. Those hailing the production miracle worried less about the consequences, such as inflation, government deficits or other macroeco-nomic imbalances because they reduced the economic imperatives of fight-ing a war to the simple goal of production. Yet the claims to miracles of production tend to fall short even on their own terms. As economist Raymond Goldsmith noted shortly after the war:

> The munitions production of the major belligerents at full mobilization was roughly proportional to the size of their prewar industrial labor force combined with the prewar level of productivity in industry. This is hardly an astonishing result, but one which confirms the belief that basic economic factors rather than accidental developments or sudden changes in elemen-tary economic relationships – more familiar under the names of 'secret weapons' and 'miracles of production' – have determined the course of munitions production.[56]

It was the size and productivity of the respective economies, not different nations' 'miracle-men', that accounted for wartime production.

More recent sceptics of wartime planning, particularly in the USA, have followed Goldsmith and even harkened back to earlier critics of First World

---

56 Raymond W. Goldsmith, 'The Power of Victory: Munitions Output in World War II', *Military Affairs* 10:1 (1946), 69–80 (p. 79).

War planning like von Mises did. So economic historian Hugh Rockoff questioned the miraculousness of American economic performance in the Second World War by calling attention to divergence between a war economy and microeconomic efficiency. Rockoff, like von Mises, focused on planners' disruptions of microeconomic mechanisms rather than their planners' broader economic aims of macroeconomic stability.

But if the Second World War experience undercut planning euphoria, it also refuted, ironically, the concerns of planning phobia. Anti-planners like Lippmann, Hayek and others criticized the notion of planning for prosperity on the grounds that central economic planning was suitable only for nations at war. They were willing to concede the utility of planning during war, when (they argued) government authority necessarily expanded over many aspects of economic life, and when there would likely be a consensus among government officials and the general population on the need for sacrifices in order to win the war. Even the fiercest critics of central planning, in other words, overestimated the possibility of effective planning during wartime.

The post-war planning boom

Such scepticism was in short supply, however, in the 1940s. Encomiums for planning and planners appeared across Europe and around the world – in former Axis powers as well as Allies, in European colonial bureaucracies and among anti-colonial nationalists, and across a wide political spectrum. Even in the USA, leading Keynesian economist Seymour Harris proclaimed that the planning experience of the recent war provided essential lessons for American policy.[57] Yet this post-war stage of planning euphoria was not joined to the widespread institutionalization of economic planning; once again, planning talk ran far ahead of actual planning. Planning might have been, as historian Tony Judt had it, a political religion, but (perhaps like many religions) it gave rise to fundamental disagreements over the purposes and appropriate forms of worship. In Western Europe the profile of post-war planning was a mirror image of the pre-war situation. The states that had remained most firmly attached to liberalism in the 1930s, Britain and France, experimented after the war most aggressively with planning, whereas in those countries that had experienced more intrusive economic policies, most

---

57 Seymour Edwin Harris, *Economic Planning: The Plans of Fourteen Countries with Analyses of the Plans* (New York: Alfred A. Knopf, 1949).

notably Germany and Italy, the sympathies of policy-makers was closer to neoliberalism.

Nowhere had planning been more doggedly resisted in the 1930s than in France, but nowhere was it more enthusiastically espoused after the war. Leading the way within France was Jean Monnet. In both the First World War and the Second World War Monnet represented France in inter-allied economic missions, helping coordinate transport and munitions supplies. American insiders called him the 'unsung hero' of the war for helping turn the USA into an 'arsenal of democracy', a term which Monnet himself coined.[58] He took two lessons from his wartime experience. First, France needed to modernize industrially to compete in the post-war world economy. And second, the way to modernize was through an apparatus of economic planning. By the time the Fourth Republic was formed in 1946, the mechanisms for economic planning were in place.

Later that year, the new Commissariat général du Plan (CGP) announced its first 'indicative' plan under the name, 'Plan de modernization et d'Equipement'. Covering the period until 1950, it had two quite specific aims: first, to ensure access to German raw materials (which would both benefit French industry and weaken Germany's); and second, to increase the competitiveness of French industry in international markets.[59] It also became the chief conduit of information and funds for US Marshall Plan support for France. If Monnet's plan aims were straightforward, his proposed process was not. The first step was the creation of Modernization Commissions for six different sectors of the economy; each included what Monnet called 'all the vital elements of the nation'. Each commission would produce a draft plan for its sector of the economy, which would be passed along to a High Commissioner for Planning. This Commissioner, a technocratic expert, would then assemble a full plan and submit it to the Planning Council, a smaller body that included experts in the ministries and representatives from the private sector. The Council would then rework the plan and propose it to the government.[60]

In keeping with earlier patterns of planning, this process emphasized the apolitical and impartial nature of economic decision-making; the planning

58 Jim Lacey, *Keep from All Thoughtful Men How U.S. Economists Won World War II* (Annapolis: Naval Institute Press, 2011), pp. 27–8.

59 Alan S. Milward, *The Reconstruction of Western Europe, 1945–51* (Berkeley: University of California Press, 1984), pp. 128–30.

60 Richard F. Kuisel, *Capitalism and the State in Modern France: Renovation and Economic Management in the Twentieth Century* (Cambridge University Press, 1981), pp. 222–3.

apparatus included public input but had no contact with elected officials until presenting the final version. Monnet, indeed, insisted that the task of the planner-in-chief was merely to collate the recommendations of the Modernization Commissions. Despite its impressive name, the CGP had only a fifty-person staff that occupied a small Paris building, far from the grand façades of the ministries.[61] Its main task was 'collective problem solving', offering advice but not instructions; as Monnet promised one official, 'we will prepare the plan without imposing on anyone.' Or, as he later reassured an interlocutor, 'I am not capable of giving an order to anyone.'[62] This modesty undoubtedly helped Monnet win approval for the planning process. If the chief planner asserted so little authority, how could his agency threaten the prerogatives of the private sector, or the responsibilities of government agencies that dwarfed it in size? The process engaged a broad section of the population, yet it was narrower in aims and methods. It was essentially a set of cartel plans designed to spur the modernization and expansion of French industry in response to foreign economic threats.

French plans soon outgrew their modest origins. Even in the CGP's infancy, as France faced inflation and a poor harvest, it did not resist the temptation to expand beyond 'collective problem solving'. By the middle of 1947, the CGP aimed to implement wage and price controls as well as foreign trade restrictions. These controls were effective at holding down wages at large enterprises, but not prices of consumer goods, leading to a strike wave in autumn 1947. In response to such crises, French planners implemented a wider range of economic controls in order to meet ever-expanding aims.

The French experience of indicative planning, even if it differed markedly from Gosplan and wartime agencies, ultimately shared many key features of more stringent planning programmes. As originally conceptualized by Monnet, *planification* was not so much a response to a foreign trade crisis as an effort to avoid such a crisis once wartime exchange controls were removed. That said, its policy prescriptions, especially as planners expanded their horizons, looked familiar: industrial expansion in order to improve foreign trade possibilities while suppressing consumption in favour of investment.

Finally, French planning – in spite of Monnet's aims – became a new arena for political conflict rather than an exercise in technical rationality. The CGP's ultimate role was that of mobilizer: not so much the mobilization of

---

61 Peter A. Hall, *Governing the Economy: The Politics of State Intervention in Britain and France* (Oxford University Press, 1986), p. 141.
62 Kuisel, *Capitalism and the State in Modern France*, pp. 246–7.

resources, but the mobilization of the population in order to win its support (or at least reduce its resistance) to its vision of a modern French economy. In the caustic phrase of economist Charles Kindleberger: French planning was 'exhortatory rather than regulatory', at its best when it 'had a faint resemblance to a revivalist prayer meeting'.[63]

British economic policy went through similar peregrinations over the dozen years after the war – but with less formal celebration of planning per se. Clement Attlee's Labour government of 1945–51 picked up where the Labour Party of the pre-war years left off; it offered tremendous rhetorical support for planning while embarking on economic policies that had little room for actual planning. The pre-war divisions over economic policy were revivified after the war. Planning talk began as a response to scarcity, a means to maintain wartime rationing schemes in peacetime. Soon enough, planning talk shifted to provide the resources for the ambitious social welfare programmes outlined in the Beveridge report, published during the war. One faction within Labour proposed nationalization of industry, successfully pushing through government ownership of the Bank of England and of major infrastructure, including railways, road transport, civil aviation and utilities. These won relatively wide support from Conservatives who justified the reorganization in terms of economic efficiency. While French policymakers used planning to shape limited government intervention in the economy, British counterparts undertook more extensive intervention but without serious reference to the virtues of central planning.[64]

Elsewhere in Europe, planning received even less rhetorical support. The reconstruction of the West German economy, under the sign of neoliberalism and the social market economy, was officially set against any resumption of Nazi-era *dirigisme*. In practice, however, this dogmatic anti-plan stance was subverted by the vicissitudes of post-war reconstruction, including fuel shortages and the temporary balance of payments problems triggered by the Korean War crisis. Likewise in Italy, strong institutions of state intervention inherited from the fascist era, notably the industrial holding companies such as IRI, coexisted with government policies that

---

63 Charles Kindleberger, 'The Postwar Resurgence of the French Economy', in Stanley Hoffmann, ed., *In Search of France* (Cambridge, Mass.: Harvard University Press, 1963), pp. 118–58 (p. 155).
64 Alec Cairncross, *Years of Recovery: British Economic Policy, 1945–51* (New York: Methuen, 1985), chs. 11, 18; Andrew Shonfield, *Modern Capitalism: The Changing Balance of Public and Private Power* (Oxford University Press, 1965), chs. 6, 8; Hall, *Governing the Economy*, chs. 2–3.

resisted any return to the muscular planning euphoria of the Mussolini era. A strong central bank headed by Luigi Einaudi promoted a liberal line – so much so that American officials responsible for Marshall Plan aid to Western Europe complained that what Italy needed was 'more and better coordinated plans'.[65]

Yet just as central planning – as opposed to rhetorical planning euphoria – receded in Western Europe, it found a new home and a new set of adherents in the growing ranks of Europe's former colonies. Planning became a core element of economic policy in the newly independent nations, serving both economic and political goals. On the one hand, postcolonial leaders saw planning in much the same way as other peacetime planners: they were interested in rapid economic growth with increased self-sufficiency. Yet these plans for economic development also had crucial political goals: national plans could help weave together a nation out of the disparate and often divided entities bequeathed by the departing colonial powers. Nowhere was this truer than in Indonesia, which produced an Eight-Year Plan of eight volumes, seventeen chapters, and 1,945 paragraphs – connoting Indonesia's declaration of independence from Dutch rule on 17 August 1945; economic plans were symbols of national independence as well as national unity.[66]

In India Prime Minister Jawaharlal Nehru served as the founding chair of the Planning Commission (PC). But despite this high-level endorsement the Commission faced resistance from within the ministries of the new state and when it finally opened its doors in early 1950, the PC had the authority only to formulate plans and to offer recommendations to the Cabinet; plan formulation, furthermore, would take place 'in close understanding and consultations with the Ministries'. Yet even these arrangements were too much for India's first Finance Minister, who blasted the PC as a 'super-cabinet' that impinged on the authority of the ministries and resigned in a huff.[67] Such fears were much overblown; the Planning Commission had little institutional authority, and soon faced still more constraints. Since the Commission had been established within the Union (central) government, leaders of India's states felt shut out of the planning process. Nehru's solution

65 Shonfield, *Modern Capitalism*, chs. 9, 11–12; Paul Hoffman (1949), quoted in Milward, *Reconstruction of Western Europe*, p. 198.
66 David C. Engerman, 'The Romance of Economic Development and New Histories of the Cold War', *Diplomatic History* 28:1 (2004), 23–54.
67 Vivek Chibber, *Locked in Place: State-Building and Late Industrialization in India* (Princeton University Press, 2003), pp. 150–1.

was to create the National Development Council, further diluting the power of the PC in shaping policy.

Conclusion

In times of war or peace, whether aiming for victory or for prosperity, whether seeking to promote self-sufficiency or industrial production, economic planning was more likely to expand the range of political conflict rather than reduce it. At stake here was control over resources as well as the very purpose of planning. The actual experience of planning during the Second World War – replicated in later exercises – offered continual challenges to the resilient planning euphoria. The millenarian hopes of planners that planning would be an escape from ideological dispute were repeatedly dashed by political conflict, not to mention poor results. But this same experience also offers a corrective to the planning phobia that first emerged in the late 1930s. Simply put, planning was not a 'road to serfdom'. Democracies like France and India that experimented with planning in the post-war years put up mixed economic results but their democratic systems remained intact. Planning was a mechanism for control, in wartime as in peacetime. But it was not, in and of itself, a threat to democratic stability. Planning's opponents and proponents, both during and after the Second World War, shared an overestimation of the power of planning. Because it delivered no escape from politics, it was no harbinger of a totalitarian future. And because its purposes could be so varied, planning was never even a singular approach in theory, let alone in practice. If planning rarely realized the hopes of its enthusiasts, nor did it realize the fears of its critics.

22

Nationalism, decolonization, geopolitics and the Asian post-war

RANA MITTER

The aftermath

In November 1943, at the Allied conference in Cairo, the Chinese leader Chiang Kai-shek had private conversations with US president Franklin D. Roosevelt. Chiang's comments were aimed at the third Allied leader at the conference, British Prime Minister Winston Churchill. 'I praised Roosevelt's policy with regard to communism,' Chiang later wrote in his diary, 'but I hope his policy toward British imperialism can also be successful, to liberate those in the world who are oppressed.'[1] While Japan's aggression was the primary target of the Allies in Asia after 1941, both the USA and China were concerned to make sure that the European empires had had their day in the region. By 1945, there were a whole variety of expectations about the probable appearance of post-war Asia. The continent would be under the strong influence of the USA. China, one of the wartime victors, would exercise its role as one of the 'four policemen' that Roosevelt had hoped to define for the post-war world. Japan would be under US domination, as would large parts of Northeast Asia. British colonialism would take up where it left off in certain parts of Southeast Asia, including Malaya. India would achieve its long sought-for independence.

Some of this happened; a very great deal of it did not. The dynamics that created a new Asia as it emerged from the war between the Allies and Japan were a product of one particular force above all: anti-imperialist nationalism. In Europe, there were grand plans for reconstruction and nation-building, symbolized most strongly by the Marshall Plan. In Asia, there was little such forward planning. The defeat of Japan had come relatively early because of

---

1 Rana Mitter, *China's War with Japan, 1937–1945: The Struggle for Survival* (London: Allen Lane, 2013), p. 311.

the atomic bombings of Japan, and there had been little time to think of how the region would be defined in the post-war era. 'National liberation' filled a vacuum created by the lack of planning by the great powers.

One of the reasons for the messiness of the post-1945 settlement in Asia was the ambiguity of the great powers over the fate of empire. In Europe, the question was clearer: formal empire, in the style of the Nazi Reich, was to be consigned to history (even while the USSR and the USA established empires of varying informality). In Asia, while the USA had made anti-imperialism as a whole a significant part of its wartime mission, Britain, France and the Netherlands were not inclined to give up territories which they considered to have been seized by Japanese force. However, the European nations found themselves reconstituting empire in often hurried and difficult circumstances.

This chapter will examine four major regions of Asia and the way that they were shaped by the immediate post-war aftermath: China, India, Southeast Asia and Japan/Korea. All had participated in the war, albeit India as a less direct actor than the other three. The politics and societies of all of them were changed beyond alteration because of those wartime experiences.

A changing China

China was the key to the changes that affected East Asia in the immediate post-war. The assumption of all the Allies during the war was that Nationalist China would continue to play a major and essentially pro-American role in the post-war order. The fact that it did not do so, and was replaced by a powerful communist state, was the most important event in reshaping Asian order during those years. The reason that the Nationalists fell was, above all, because of the country's disastrous experience during the Second World War and the effects the conflict had on destroying any prospect of their state succeeding.

In 1945, Nationalist China was in a position that made it essentially unique among the wartime Allies. It was both a victor in war, with the responsibilities that came with such a role, and a deeply riven country with inadequate resources to take such a role up. China was simultaneously in the most powerful position that it had been in since the mid-nineteenth century, and more vulnerable than it had been since that same disastrous period.

The war against Japan had earned China the right to help shape the post-war world. Some 14 million Chinese had died during the war, and some 80–100 million had become refugees. The country had continued to resist

Japan essentially alone between 1937 and 1941, before the Allied entry into the war after Pearl Harbor. After 1941, many of the international developments during the war had taken place on the basis of a new post-imperialist world in which China would be an important actor in Asia. The British were always more sceptical than the Americans about the power of China to be a genuinely influential actor: Churchill spoke of China as a 'faggot vote' (that is, a puppet vote) for the USA in the new United Nations.[2]

However, the war marked a rapid leap in China's position globally. In 1937, there were still substantial extraterritorial rights on Chinese territory, with foreign-controlled enclaves within the major treaty port city of Shanghai. In 1943, the USA and Britain agreed on a new set of treaties, a century and a year after the establishment of the 'unequal treaties' that followed the Opium Wars. These ended extraterritorial rights on Chinese territory, thereby formally bringing to an end China's history as a country with sovereignty compromised by Western imperialism.

However, the relationship with the USA was compromised by the increasingly toxic relationship between the Americans and Nationalist Chinese. This was expressed most strongly in the disputes between the American Chief of Staff of the Chinese Army, General Joseph W. Stilwell, and Chiang Kai-shek. Stilwell became increasingly adamant that Chiang was refusing to contribute substantively to the war effort; Chiang was ever-more convinced that Stilwell was incompetent and much more tied to his own plans for glory than to China's needs.[3] Stilwell was eventually recalled in 1944, but the price to Chiang was high. Roosevelt, and Truman after him, knew that the war in Asia would be won in the Pacific, not on the Chinese mainland, and became further convinced that China was a fickle ally which should be placed at the back of the queue for assistance. China's contributions over four years included resisting Japan with difficulty between 1937 and 1941, but by the end of the war and the alliance with the USA, the two countries were extremely wary partners, each mistrustful of the political intentions of the other.

Assistance was particularly necessary because China's internal systems were shattered by the war. From 1944, areas under nationalist control were supported by the newly-created UNRRA (United Nations Relief and

2 Christopher Thorne, *Allies of a Kind: The United States, Britain and the War against Japan, 1941–1945* (Oxford University Press, 1978).
3 The classic revisionist account of this conflict is Hans J. van de Ven, *War and Nationalism in China, 1925–1945* (London: Routledge, 2003).

Rehabilitation Administration), which was tasked with providing relief in Europe and China. The need in China was desperate; reports detailed disease and starvation throughout the provinces that had been reclaimed from the Japanese.[4] The destruction was so serious that there was little prospect that the Nationalist government could exercise its new sovereign authority without significant external assistance. Much historiography has rightly paid attention to the dire state of the Nationalist government at the end of the war, encumbered with a corrupt bureaucracy, high inflation and a military that was on the verge of collapse. Relatively less attention has been paid to the circumstances in which this situation arose: the effort of continuing to resist against Japan had done immense damage to the Nationalist state.

One of the other effects of the war was to give much greater credibility to the Nationalists' great rivals, the communists, with their very different model of anti-imperialist resistance. During the initial phase of the war, the Chinese Communist Party (CCP) did tie themselves more explicitly to a 'united front' against Japan, but from 1943, there was much more concentration on the radicalization of policy, including major reforms on taxation and the establishment of a largely self-sufficient economic model. By the end of the war, the areas of communist control included much of North China and a population that was close to 100 million people.

The end of the war came very suddenly for China. The atomic bombings ended the conflict in the summer of 1945, when there had been widespread expectation that the war might go on well into 1946 and beyond. The sudden ending of the war meant that in China conflict now emerged between two different models of anti-imperialist nationalism. The Nationalist version of the ideology was based on an engagement with Western-dominated international society, but was being developed in conditions of extreme economic and military hardship that were debased by incompetent governance and corruption. The communist alternative, in contrast, was dynamic and growing. It was based on a very different model of China's place in the world. Rather than engaging with a Western-dominated world, it was driven by two factors: the influence of the Soviet Union of Lenin and Stalin, and the emergence of an indigenous revolution based on the peasantry.

The Chinese communist formula was a product of the war. The communists had been forced into the countryside by the mid-1930s, and their position was weak. The war with Japan gave them a formal role for the first time in

---

4 Rana Mitter, 'Imperialism, Transnationalism, and the Reconstruction of Post-War China: UNRRA in China, 1944–7', *Past & Present 218, supplement* **8** (2013), 51–69.

the united front against the invaders, and allowed them a great deal of space to develop. Development was by no means smooth: Japanese attacks as well as party infighting meant that many of the 'base areas' were eliminated or subjected to attrition. But the key base area of ShaanGanNing (that is, within the provinces of Shaanxi, Gansu, and Ningxia) in northwest China, with its base area at Yan'an, remained coherent and allowed Mao Zedong to consolidate his control over the Party through a series of 'Rectification' campaigns of ideological purity.[5]

In some respects, the two sides had similar goals in terms of their post-war aims. Both the Nationalists and the communists realized that there must be a new domestic social order, in which the state played a greater role in the ordering of society, whether in military matters or in the provision of social welfare. In addition, the framework within which they chose to remodel society was shaped significantly by international and transnational influences. The presence of UNRRA, one of the most important new international agencies of the era, gave particular impetus to this mode of thinking. While the relationship between UNRRA and the Chinese authorities was fraught with difficulties, the interaction between the international agency and the government was one of the first examples of the way in which high modernist developmental agencies would act in tandem with developmental states in the newly independent non-European world, with varying degrees of smoothness.[6] Discussions took place about the establishment of systems of health care and social services, some of which had been developed during the refugee crisis that had overtaken the wartime capital of Chongqing.[7]

As in other post-war societies in Europe and Asia, China had to consider how it could best deal with the fact that much of China had been under regimes that collaborated with the Japanese during the war. The most prominent of these collaborators, Wang Jingwei, had 'returned' to the Nationalist capital, Nanjing, and established a Japanese-sponsored

5 Important work on this period includes Lyman P. Van Slyke, *Enemies and Friends: The United Front in Chinese Communist History* (Stanford University Press, 1967); Mark Selden, *The Yenan Way in Revolutionary China* (Cambridge, Mass.: Harvard University Press, 1971); and Michael M. Sheng, *Battling Western Imperialism: Mao, Stalin, and the United States* (Princeton University Press, 1997).

6 James Scott, *Seeing Like a State: How Certain Schemes to Improve the Human Condition Have Failed* (New Haven: Yale University Press, 1999); Odd Arne Westad, *The Global Cold War: Third World Interventions and the Making of Our Times* (Cambridge University Press, 2006).

7 See, for example, Nicole Barnes, 'Disease in the Capital: Nationalist Health Services and the "Sick (Wo)man of East Asia" in Wartime Chongqing', *European Journal of East Asian Studies* 11:2 (2012), 283–303.

government in 1940. Wang himself had died in 1944, but various members of his government were placed on trial as was his wife, Chen Bijun, herself an influential figure in the regime. Chen made a powerful case at her trial that her husband's collaboration had actually helped to protect the lives of millions of Chinese who might otherwise have been attacked by the Japanese. The relatively lenient sentence she received suggested that the Nationalist authorities saw the point and realized that mass persecution of those who had worked with the Japanese might be unwise.[8] This caution was magnified by the fact that Chiang's government had cooperated closely with the former Japanese enemy after their surrender, instructing them to hold cities where they were garrisoned and surrender only to Nationalist, rather than communist commanders.[9]

However, any prospect of the Nationalists being able to rebuild the post-war state fell victim to two factors. First, the state had been hollowed out by the effects of war and was associated with corruption and incompetence, meaning that it had little popular credibility. Then, reconstruction dissolved in the face of an imminent civil war. In the aftermath of the war against Japan, there had appeared to be a brief period when the two sides might compromise and agree a coalition government, the preference of American negotiators at the time. However, the ideological position of the two sides, nationalists and communists, made it almost impossible to reconcile the two.

The Chinese Civil War resolved questions that had been opened up during the war against Japan. That war had been fought not only on the issue of Japanese domination of the region, but also the nature of the Chinese state. The experience of attack and occupation by Japan made it near-inevitable that the post-war state would be anti-imperialist in its nature. However, there was still no clarity about how far social transformation would go and how radical it would be. The war ended up a battle between the partial, flawed and ill-funded Nationalist vision of slow post-war reform of state–society relations, and the communist vision, radical in its desire to mobilize all society. The communist model also proposed a much more thorough reshaping of traditional property regimes. Some aspects of this change had emerged in the war: the Nationalists had centralized aspects of industrial production for military purposes, and communist base areas had

---

8 Charles Musgrove, 'Cheering the Traitor: The Post-War Trial of Chen Bijun, April 1946', *Twentieth-Century China* 30:2 (2005), 3–27.
9 Barak Kushner, *Men to Devils, Devils to Men: Japanese War Crimes and Chinese Justice* (Cambridge, Mass.: Harvard University Press, 2014).

seen a variety of economic experiments. By the time the Civil War ended, the momentum was entirely on the side of the communists. When Mao Zedong declared the establishment of the People's Republic of China on 1 October 1949, the state he ruled was the inheritor of the debates about anti-imperialism and social welfare that had been central to the war against Japan.[10]

India

The war had also changed India in highly significant ways. While India was not, for the most part, in the direct line of fire that marked China, the demands of the war had hugely changed the relationship between the colonial state and the colonized. Over 2.5 million troops had been mobilized in India. On the other hand, the declaration of war on behalf of India by the viceroy, Lord Linlithgow, had led to a heightening of tensions within the nationalist movement, as the Congress party objected to war being declared without their having been consulted first. By the end of the war, it was clear that India would take a very different path from what seemed likely in 1939.

The effects of the war on India were different from those on China. Apart from the bombing of some cities such as Calcutta in 1942–43, and the occupation of parts of the northeast, India's territory was not directly affected. Yet as well as supplying troops, India played a vital role in the supply of Allied troops and shipping in Asia as a whole. And the involvement of India in the war heightened tensions between the British and the nationalist movement as the latter became more active in its demands for independence. The Quit India movement of 1942 saw the end of cooperation between the Congress leaders and the British authorities, and led to the mass imprisonment of nationalist activists. The imprisonment of the Congress leaders gave an opportunity for the Muslim League, under Muhammad Ali Jinnah, to stand neutral but not express open hostility to the British position; as a result, the League's hold on authority in large parts of India grew, and the prospect of a separate Muslim state also became much greater.

When the leaders of the Congress, including Nehru and J. P. Narayan were released in March 1945, the political temperature was immensely high. By the end of the year, the major Congress leaders made it clear that they

10 Odd Arne Westad, *Decisive Encounters: The Chinese Civil War, 1946–1950* (Stanford University Press, 2003).

wanted independence as swiftly as possible.[11] One indicative element that showed the power of anti-imperialist rhetoric was the treatment of former fighters in the Indian National Army (INA) assembled by the nationalist Subhas Chandra Bose. The army had been set up by Bose, originally drawing on Indian prisoners of war in Singapore and Malaya, with Japanese sponsorship to create a force that would attack the British and free India. However, by the end of the war, it was clear that Japan was losing and that the INA would not be in a position to be part of a Japanese-dominated Asia. In August 1945, Bose attempted to leave Taiwan for the USSR, which he thought might provide a base for further anti-British activities. However, the aircraft crashed and Bose was badly burned and died shortly afterward. Although Bose was no longer present to put on trial, the British authorities held a series of trials in 1945–46 in which high-profile members of the INA were prosecuted for cooperating with the enemy. However, there was widespread anger within Indian nationalist opinion about the trials. The Congress leaders had not been supporters of Japan, but they found it hard to accept that cooperation with the Japanese in the pursuit of Indian independence could be considered treason. In practice, the British authorities reduced or commuted the long sentences for some defendants. It became eminently clear that public opinion in India, ahead of independence, would not permit the outright condemnation of the INA. Unlike Wang Jingwei in China, who was portrayed as a simple traitor by his Chinese opponents, Chiang and Mao, Bose was (and is) regarded as a patriot who sought a different path for India's freedom.[12] Wang and Bose had both been major nationalist leaders before the war, both collaborated with the Japanese, but their post-war reputations have been entirely different.

Britain too recognized that the independence struggles during the war had eaten away at the legitimacy of imperial rule. Before the war it might have been plausible to move more slowly toward independence, but after the war, it was clearly impossible. Although Winston Churchill claimed that he had not become the King's first minister to preside over the dissolution of the British Empire, the war had essentially bankrupted Britain and there was little enthusiasm to put in resources to hold an India which would clearly

11 Christopher Bayly and Tim Harper, *Forgotten Wars: The End of Britain's Asian Empire* (London: Allen Lane, 2007), p. 77.
12 Leonard A. Gordon, *Brothers against the Raj: A Biography of Indian Nationalists Sarat and Subhas Chandra Bose* (New York: Columbia University Press, 1990); Sugata Bose, *His Majesty's Opponent: Subhas Chandra Bose and India's Struggle against Empire* (Cambridge, Mass.: Harvard University Press, 2011).

soon end its colonial relationship with Britain. The Labour government elected in 1945 recognized this change and with the appointment of Lord Mountbatten as the final viceroy in 1946, acknowledged the need for swift withdrawal from India.

Southeast Asia

Southeast Asia was the most ambiguous area in the clash between different types of nationalism in wartime Asia. Although there was a significant collaborationist movement in China under Wang Jingwei, which claimed to be the natural successor to Sun Yixian's nationalist movement, it rendered itself ultimately implausible because of the sheer brutality of Japanese rule and its implacable opposition to Chinese nationalism as expressed either by Chiang Kai-shek or by Mao's communists. In India, the fears of Japanese invasion were never fulfilled in practice, and Japanese rule was never actually experienced by the indigenous population. In Southeast Asia, by contrast, while Japanese rule was generally brutal, local independence movements frequently took advantage of the forcible ousting of European rule to solidify their own positions.

The experience of Southeast Asia sat at the opposite end of a spectrum from China and India. There was no doubt that China, recognized as a full Ally of the Western powers, would be granted full sovereignty and a global role at the UN in the post-war settlement. Until quite late in the war, British Conservatives still remained doubtful as to whether India would be granted independence, but by the end of the war, independence was fairly assured. But Southeast Asia was in a very different position. Britain, France and the Netherlands, having been driven from the region in the most humiliating fashion, were now determined to regain the territories they had lost. However, the powers had failed to understand the profound change that had taken place in the region as a result of the Japanese occupation. The peoples of Southeast Asia were no longer willing to allow the defeated imperialists simply to take up rule where they had left off. The immediate aftermath of war saw a whole range of nationalist movements in the region attempting to find a new settlement. This meant that in a swathe of countries in the region, the end of the Second World War led not to peace, but the extension of war.

In Malaya, the Malayan People's Anti-Japanese Army took a leading role in resisting the Japanese. This grouping, which was led by the ethnic-Chinese dominated communists, was instrumental in fighting against the occupation of the peninsula. By spring 1945, British intelligence officers had given the

Malaysian communists reason to believe that their reward for cooperation would be the recognition of the communists as a legal force after the Japanese had been defeated.[13] At the end of the war, the communists and the Chinese nationalists, through their connections with the Southeast Asian Chinese diaspora network, were united in their opposition both to the Japanese and to the re-establishment of Western rule. These groups were the wartime seed at the heart of the independence movement in post-war Malaya.

The establishment of the British Administration of Malaya (BMA) in 1945–46 in some way echoed the measures taken in war-torn China during the same period.[14] Malaya had been devastated by the war, and there was insufficient food for the population. The BMA placed large numbers of people onto its books as employees in an attempt to create employment. Yet the returning British administration failed to realize that it could not simply take up the reins of rule where they had been dropped in 1942. Pre-war colonial attitudes continued to colour British rule, further fuelling nationalist resentment. Both the United Malays National Organization (UMNO), constituted in 1946, and the Malaysian Communist Party (with significant Chinese support) agitated for independence. The declaration of an Emergency in 1948 (which would not end officially until 1960) enabled the British authorities to separate the communists from the wider nationalist movement, but the path toward independence was clear, and it was achieved in 1957.

Burma was another location where there was an uneasy triangle between the British, the Japanese and the nationalists as the war ended. In Burma, the war had provided an opportunity for 'Bogyoke' (the general), the nationalist leader Aung San, to use his Burmese National Army to take up arms against the Japanese in March 1945. However, after the war was over, relationships with the British became fraught, as Aung San staked his claim to national leadership against the attempts of the British governor, Reginald Dorman-Smith. To make things worse, Churchill's government gave no indication that they thought any timetable was necessary for Burmese independence.

The other European powers that had had their Southeast Asian possessions snatched away now also moved to seize back their colonies. For France and the Netherlands, the desire to regain their empires was motivated by their realization that unlike Britain, their metropoles had been conquered

---

13 Bayly and Harper, *Forgotten Wars*, p. 32.
14 Ibid., p. 104.

and occupied by Germany. National humiliation was to be soothed by the act of recolonization. Yet here also the would-be conquerors failed to understand that the region had changed hugely. The communist movement in Vietnam, the Viet Minh, had established its credentials and position during the last years of the anti-Japanese war. The French moved back in and re-established their rule with remarkable brutality. The Viet Minh made it clear that they did not oppose the arrival of British and American troops to liberate the region but were wholly against the return of the French. However, the Allies supported the re-establishment of French rule, sending the Viet Minh underground by early 1946. The stage was set for the Indochina wars that would dominate the next few decades.[15]

In Indonesia, the Allies struggled to recapture the former Dutch possession. In the early twentieth century, different strands of Southeast Asian nationalism had come to the fore in the Dutch East Indies, including Islamic revivalism and communism. The dominant figure was the leftist secular nationalist, Soekarno (Sukarno). The Dutch had been obdurate in the pre-war period in refusing to engage with the aspirations of the Indonesians, and the invasion and occupation by Japan appeared a major turning point.[16] During the war, the Japanese and the Indonesian nationalists, including Soekarno, were in an uneasy alliance in which nonetheless Soekarno managed to project himself as the embodiment of the nation. In the final months of the war in 1945, Soekarno declared the Indonesian republic. By the time the Allies arrived on the islands in the autumn, it was clear that the Indonesians were in no mood for the resumption of Dutch rule.

The story of what happened to the Southeast Asian colonies belongs to the history of decolonization and the Cold War as much as it does to that of a longer Second World War. Many of the wars lasted for years. Burma gained its independence in 1948. However, the Malayan 'Emergency' dragged on for years, with the communist insurgency under Chin Peng continuing even after Malaysia's independence in 1957. The wars in Indochina would continue even longer, with the French war that ended in 1954, succeeded by an American war, and finally by a brief one with China (1979). These wars were all shaped by the rising nationalism that was a product

15 Mark Philip Bradley, *Imagining Vietnam and America: The Making of Postcolonial Vietnam, 1919–1950* (Chapel Hill: University of North Carolina Press, 2000).
16 Jean Gelman Taylor, *Indonesia: Peoples and Histories* (New Haven: Yale University Press, 2004), ch. 11.

of the turmoil created by the swift replacement of Western imperialism with its Japanese counterpart in 1941–42.

Shifting geopolitics

The three regions described above had their own individual histories. They also exist as part of a changing post-war regional order. Superficially, there was a similarity with Europe. The effects of the Potsdam conference of July–August 1945 were to divide up Europe into two blocs, an American-sponsored one in the west of the continent and a Soviet-dominated one in the East. Although the two blocs were in opposition to one another, there was a relatively swift recognition of the demarcation of each bloc's territory. (Exceptions, such as Stalin's attempts to blockade West Berlin in 1948, and the 1961 Berlin Wall crisis, proved the rule: overall, the Cold War divisions in Europe remained remarkably stable and recognized until 1989.)

The settlement in Asia was far less certain. It had been widely expected that the war would continue well into 1946 and beyond. The sudden ending of the war in 1945 meant that an only half-formed set of ideas for a post-war East Asia were ready. The factor that made the greatest difference was, ultimately, China. The United Nations structure was set up in the expectation that Nationalist China would be an important actor in the post-war era. But the communist victory banished the Nationalists to Taiwan.

The mere fact of China having become a communist state did not preclude it playing a role in the new regional order. The USSR, after all, now played a full role in the United Nations. However, both the USA and China took steps that made it immensely difficult to reintroduce China to international society. The domestic climate in the USA was consumed by an argument over 'Who Lost China?', the accusation made against the State Department and other officials that they had actively assisted the communists to gain power in China. The failure to understand that the communist revolution had come about in large part because of military and political successes that had no connection with the American presence in the country meant that it became impossible to suggest that diplomatic relations should be opened with the new government in Nanjing. (Until 1978, the US embassy in China would be maintained in Taipei.) However, the nascent People's Republic of China made its own contribution to the split between the two sides. In June 1950, Kim Il Sung, the North Korean leader, indicated his intention to launch an assault on the US-oriented South. Anxious to measure up to Stalin's expectations, Mao took the decision to send forces (officially as volunteers) to support the North Koreans.[17] There is no doubt that the proximate origin of the Korean War was provocation by the communist bloc. The combination of actions by the USA and China led to a situation where, by the time the Korean War was a reality, there was no meaningful way for the two countries to communicate.

The separation between the two states proved highly damaging for the post-war order. In Europe, the balance of power was clearly divided between the USA and the Soviets. In Asia, the division was not so clear. While the USSR and China were allied, the Soviets were not proxies for the Chinese, and there was no sense in which the Soviets could represent or make geostrategic decisions on behalf of China. This created a fundamental problem for the reconstitution of order in post-war Asia. Up to 1949, it was clear that a reconciliation between China and Japan, under American sponsorship, was possible. Chiang Kai-shek was criticized for his seeming leniency toward the Japanese invaders.[18] However, a glance at his wartime diaries confirms that Chiang's feelings of anger toward Japan were deep and genuine. Instead, he had adapted rather swiftly to the post-war world in which China now had a position of geopolitical superiority toward Japan, and where the communists, not the Japanese, were the primary enemy. Chiang had been using China's status as one of the victorious Allied powers to do what the USA, Britain and other victors had done: he made allies of former enemies.

Chiang's own views of the post-war settlement drew on an understanding that Asia would be largely dominated by the USA. At the same time, anti-imperialism and an independent Asia was a high priority. During the war, Chiang had mused on the possibility of a Chinese role in keeping Korea independent, along with gaining independence for Vietnam (in Chiang's mind, the latter would have come under joint Sino-American tutelage).[19] In contrast, Mao's policy was clearly oriented toward the socialist bloc and an alliance with the USSR. This did not necessarily mean slavish devotion to Moscow on all issues, but there is little doubt that from the middle of the Chinese Civil War (1946–49), Mao's vision of the People's Republic was as a

---

17 Sheila Miyoshi Jager, *Brothers at War: The Unending Conflict in Korea* (New York: W. W. Norton, 2013); Chen Jian, *China's Road to the Korean War* (New York: Columbia University Press, 1994).

18 Barak Kushner, 'Ghosts of the Japanese Imperial Army: The "White Group" (Baituan) and Early Post-War Sino-Japanese Relations', *Past & Present* **218**, supplement 8 (2013), 117–50.

19 Mitter, *China's War*, p. 311.

state that firmly 'leaned to one side'.[20] Chiang and Mao both had anti-imperialism as an indelible part of their vision of post-war Asia; but they intended to articulate it in the very different contexts of the two emergent Cold War blocs.

Of course, Chiang's vision of a new Asia was rendered pointless by his loss of the mainland to the communists. By the mid-1950s, there were essentially two separate orders within East Asia. The first was an American-dominated order which was symbolized by the 'final' peace treaty signed at San Francisco in 1951 and ratified in 1952. Japan's signature of the treaty restored it to sovereignty, although its defence policy remained under US control. However, there was no Chinese endorsement of the treaty. The USA had wanted to invite the Republic of China (on Taiwan), which it recognized as the legitimate government, to San Francisco; the UK wished to invite the PRC, which it had recognized in 1950. (In 1952, there was a separate treaty between the Nationalist government and Japan signed at Taipei.) While the defeated power, Japan, did ultimately recognize its defeat, the enemy against whom it had first launched its original assault did not agree to be part of the resolution of the war. The PRC actually denounced the treaty, not least because it failed to declare that certain Pacific islands including the Paracels and Spratlys were in fact Chinese territory. The lack of ultimate resolution of the Second World War in East Asia, and the failure to include China in the final settlement, led to an unevenness that would make the creation of solid multilateral relationships in the region a chimera.

The effects of isolation on China (and North Korea) mark one of the most important, if negative, legacies from the post-war period. One of the most important factors that had led to war between China and Japan in 1937 was the failure to contain either country successfully within an international system which could arbitrate disputes and constrain aggressive actors. In the post-war era, even though Europe was split, both the western and eastern halves operated within a new international system in which the USA and the USSR were represented in the UN and through other organizations. In contrast, the isolation of post-war China from the wider international system had effects both domestic and international. At home, policies such as the Anti-Rightist Campaign (1957) and the Great Leap Forward (1958–62) became even more shrill in the context of China's relatively limited international

---

20 Chen Jian, *Mao's China and the Cold War* (Chapel Hill: University of North Carolina Press, 2001), pp. 46–8.

exposure. Abroad, there was little opportunity for China to be socialized into the existing international system.

One effect of China's isolation from the USA and the relative separation of India from the wider Cold War blocs was the emergence of a new discourse of African–Asian solidarity. In a sense, this was a natural product of the discourse of national liberation that was so active in Asia during the war. Before 1937, the region had been a patchwork of colonial and semi-colonial regimes. By 1942, the only parts of East and Southeast Asia that were neither occupied by Japan nor effectively under its control were the ramshackle Nationalist Chinese state and its uneasy communist allies in their base areas. The increasingly stark divisions of the Cold War concealed an important similarity in the states that emerged in post-war Asia, that they were all inheritors of the anti-imperialist thread that was at the centre of both resistance and collaboration during the war years. The Bandung Conference, held in Indonesia in 1955, symbolized the emergence of an anti-imperialist discourse of liberation that brought together actors who had previously had only very limited opportunities to create a political language of their own. The conference became the point of origin for a new language of non-alignment toward the blocs, as well as a rivalry between China and India for leadership of the new grouping. However, the rivalries marked both a legacy of nationalism during the war as well as a further complexity in the emerging Cold War.

Japan and Korea

The emergence of a new order that might be shaped by the newly emergent nationalists of China, India and Southeast Asia could only happen because of the hole left by the sudden disappearance of the alternative order that had been so prominent until 1945: imperial domination of Asia by Japan. In August 1945, Japan's leaders were still debating whether they might carry on fighting, and only the Soviet entry into the war and the atomic bombings finally brought the conflict to an end.[21] Less than four years earlier, the prospect of a new order in Asia seemed realistic; by autumn 1945, the Japanese dream of empire had faded away. The term 'decolonization' has not been used as frequently for the ending of Japan's empire as it has been for that of Britain and France. However, the sudden end of Japan's empire forced

---

21 Richard Frank, *Downfall: The End of the Imperial Japanese Empire* (New York: Random House, 1999).

societies in the region to make choices about how they would cope with the postcolonial world. For countries such as China or the former Western colonies in Southeast Asia, the question was a different one; these areas had not been colonies in the classic sense so much as invaded and occupied territories where governance had been thrown together in the pressured circumstances of war. Japan's formal colonies in Asia had rather different histories: Taiwan had become a Japanese possession in 1895, and Korea in 1910 (after a long period of strong Japanese influence). The client state of Manchukuo was, technically, not a colony, but in fact operated as one from 1932.

The defeat of Japan meant the return of Taiwan to China. This should have been a liberation, but in practice, the returning Nationalist government treated Taiwan almost like a new colonial possession. Over the years, Japan had been tolerated, if not exactly welcomed, as colonial overlords, and much of the island's elite had received their education in Japanese. However, the closeness of the elites to their former colonial overlords, along with the fact that during the war many Taiwanese fought on the Japanese side, meant that there was huge mutual suspicion between them and the incoming Nationalists. The installation of Chen Yi as governor of the province in 1945 exacerbated affairs: he refused to speak Japanese, insisting that the island's elites must speak Mandarin when talking to him, even though few of them had ever learned the dialect. Chen also made it clear that the islanders' history of colonial subjugation by Japan meant that he was unwilling to allow them much leeway in their own governance. Tensions between the two sides finally exploded in February 1947, when a crackdown on illegal tobacco sales led to an all-out rebellion by the indigenous population against the nationalist administration of the government. The rebellion was put down with great brutality, with some 10,000 or more Taiwanese being killed, many of whom were the island's best-educated elites. In 1949, Taiwan became the seat of the rump Republic of China after the loss of the mainland to the communists. However, the 1947 'incident' shaped relations between the Taiwanese and the mainlanders for half a century afterward.[22]

Manchukuo was a fiction that came into being only because of the increasing scepticism about colonies that marked the post-First World War era. The Japanese occupation of the northeastern region of China (Manchuria) began with a staged attack on the railway near Shenyang (Mukden) on

---

22 Lai Tse-han, Ramon H. Myers and Wei Wou, *A Tragic Beginning: The Taiwan Uprising of February 28, 1947* (Stanford University Press, 1991).

18 September 1931, and within a few months, a supposedly autonomous and independent state known as Manchukuo ('Land of the Manchus') was established. In practice, the region was entirely subject to Japanese political and economic demands, with local collaborators providing a thin veil of autonomy to a colonial enterprise. By late 1945, however, the increasing desperation of the Japanese army along with the prospect of Soviet entry into the war in Asia made it clear that Manchukuo would not long survive. Like Taiwan, there was little question that the territory would be returned to China. However, the fate of Manchuria became dependent on the machinations of the great powers. Along with the cession of the Kurile Islands, at Yalta, Roosevelt agreed that in return for Soviet entry into the war in Asia, the USSR would gain special rights in Manchuria.[23]

On 9 August 1945, Soviet troops began to move across the border into Manchukuo. Within just a few days they had subjugated the region as the formerly feared Kwantung Army retreated, in some cases fleeing so fast that they left civilians behind. For the next few months, the Soviet Union would occupy the region, seizing large parts of its industrial infrastructure and taking it back across the border. One result was a crisis in the winter of 1945–46, which led to a severe shortage of electric power, preventing factories and power plants operating and creating a deep anger among the region's residents (both the indigenous Chinese and the Japanese waiting to be repatriated). However, from March to May 1946, Stalin did order the withdrawal of Soviet troops from the region, fulfilling his agreement to cooperate with the government of Chiang Kai-shek.

Yet Taiwan and Manchukuo shared one thing in common: they would be incorporated into an existing country, the Republic of China. Very different ideas had to be proposed for the other great colonial possession of Japan's empire: Korea.

Korea had first fallen under Japanese influence following the Sino-Japanese War of 1894–95, and had become a full colony of Japan in 1910. Japanese rule was deeply unpopular in Korea, but the peninsula played an important role in Japan's wartime effort, with over 5 million Koreans conscripted as forced labourers. More controversially, significant numbers of Koreans served in the Japanese armed forces, particularly after conscription was stepped up in 1944.

---

23 Jager, *Brothers at War*, p. 17.

The question of Korea's post-war fate had been discussed during the Cairo Conference of November 1943. Roosevelt's preference was that Korea should be subjected to some form of trusteeship, a development of the idea of mandates that had been promoted by the League of Nations after the Great War. Stalin was supportive of the idea, although he felt that the period of trusteeship should be short, and Churchill was won round to it after it was made clear that it had no direct implications for Britain's colonial holdings in the region.[24] Yet the sudden ending of the war once again proved the most important element in shaping the fate of the Korean peninsula. Knowing of the atomic bomb, Stalin moved fast to send troops into Manchuria on 9 August 1945, hoping to make a Soviet conquest of the region a fait accompli by the time the war ended. Japan's speedy defeat left the Americans concerned that the USSR might conquer all of Korea, and the new Truman administration recommended a division of the country into two halves, one under American control, the other under the Soviets, with the aim of creating a united state at some future date. Stalin agreed to the division of the country, which would take place at the 38th parallel.

Two very different models emerged in the two parts of the peninsula. In the North, the Soviets started by inviting in large numbers of Korean citizens of the USSR (many of them internal deportees during the Stalinist purges), but then moved to find a figure who would be able to combine Korean nationalism with acquiescence with Soviet demands. Their eventual choice was the little-known guerrilla fighter Kim Il Sung. The regime imposed on the region clamped down on organizations which might seem subversive or pro-American. Within the next few years, some 2 million refugees had fled from the northern zone of Korea to the South.[25]

However, in the North, the old Japanese colonial regime was at least rooted out, even if it was replaced by a regime of equal brutality. In the American-controlled South, there was surprise among the Korean population when it became apparent that the USA intended to maintain Japanese colonial commanders in the country for some time to come. US troops under Lieutenant General John R. Hodge would not provide administration for the southern zone; that would come from Abe Nobuyuki, the Japanese Governor General. A communist movement, the Korean People's Republic, became increasingly powerful. Korean nationalist feeling became

24 Ibid., pp. 16–17.
25 Ibid., p. 26.

increasingly outraged, as the feeling grew that the Americans might be tempted to restore the kind of authoritarian rule that had been seen under Japanese colonialism. Leftist and nationalist groups became ever more vocal about the failures of an American occupation which seemed to be able to do little to provide the basic needs, including food and fuel, needed by the Koreans.

Korea was at a distinct disadvantage in carving out a post-war role because so few of its population had been involved directly in wartime nationalism. The resistance of the Chinese and the wary combination of collaboration and resistance that marked much of Southeast Asia provided a platform for a programme of post-war national liberation in those two regions. In Korea, in contrast, the liberation had taken place almost entirely because of the actions of the great powers. And it was the great powers that continued to shape Korea in the immediate post-war period. Continuing tensions between the two sides gave way to outright hostility by 1950. Kim Il Sung was eager to launch an invasion of the South, an aim in which he was supported by Stalin. The People's Republic had been established only a few months previously, yet Mao felt that he had to prove the PRC's worth in the face of the challenge from fellow socialist states. On 25 June 1950, the first shots of the Korean War rang out.

The emergence of conflict in Korea illuminated some of the continuing crises that had been triggered by the Second World War in Asia but had not been resolved in 1945. The war itself showed that the peace was highly contingent and that the possibility of conflict breaking out again in Asia was real. It also demonstrated for China in particular that the danger of attack from the east, and from the sea, remained a real possibility. While Japan could not attack China again in its own right, the Pacific region still contained a power hostile to the regime, the USA. This made it imperative for China to avoid conflict on its western borders (and Mao's falling-out with the USSR in the 1960s would open the way for the breach to be healed with the Americans in the 1970s). Finally, one of the most important consequences of the war in China, the struggle over property regimes, became relevant for the rest of the region too. The war had seen changing views of traditional property regimes across the region, including greater central control of labour, capital and industrial production in China and India. These divisions would also become central to the ongoing conflicts in Korea, divided between an industrializing state-capitalist model in the South and a collectivist authoritarian state in the North. Vietnam and Taiwan too would be part of that wider regional struggle.

Unfinished business

In Asia, and not just Korea, world war turned into Cold War with barely a break in the fighting in some parts of the region. While many legacies of the wartime period remained, the Cold War dynamics took over and shaped many of the developments of the next few decades. Overall, American dominance remained strong, with a major Pacific naval presence and allies in Japan, Taiwan and South Korea. The Soviet influence was more marginal though always threatening, as with its ally North Korea, and it made gains in the region, including a unified Vietnam. However, the biggest ideological shift was to the Americans' advantage: the Sino-Soviet split of 1960 which led ultimately to the opening to the USA in 1971–72.

But as late as the turn of the millennium, it would still have been possible to argue that the post-war US-driven settlement in Asia had essentially held good. The legacy of 1945 had not been laid to rest as it had in Europe, but it was no longer a direct issue in terms of regional hegemony.

A turbulent first decade of the new century exposed how much of the 'unfinished business' of 1945 remained ripe for resolution. In particular, the rise of China during the presidency of Hu Jintao (2002–12) showed that there were plenty of areas in which the 1945 settlement in Asia had been essentially inadequate. After the end of the Second World War, Western Europe worked together to write the history of the recent past. Most importantly, the key belligerents, Britain, France and Germany, developed (under American sponsorship) a broadly equivalent post-war history of fascism faced and overcome. The fall of the communist bloc in 1989 removed the most obvious alternative narrative of the Second World War from the continent. In general, today the North Atlantic speaks with one voice on the meaning of the war, even if the voice has different emphases in different parts of the continent.

No such consensus has ever formed in Northeast Asia. As a consequence, in the mid-2010s, China and Japan, the two powers in the region with the most unreconciled view of their mutual conflict, drew on clashing interpretations of their Second World War experience. Japanese right-wingers spoke in ever-louder tones about a revisionist view of Tokyo's imperial wars in Asia in the 1930s and 1940s. The Japanese revisionist view is only shared by one section of the Japanese public, although that grouping does include prominent politicians in the ruling Liberal Democratic Party. It is almost entirely domestically directed, and is vigorously opposed by liberal elements within Japan itself. There is no significant external constituency that is supportive of the idea that Japan's aggression in Asia prior to 1945 should be reassessed in overall positive terms.

China, in turn, produced a revisionist argument about its role during the war: the promotion of China as a country that played a highly significant international role in the ultimate defeat of the Japanese empire in 1945, and now deserved to reap the benefits of its sacrifices. There is a significant domestic audience in China for the idea that China should be given more credit for its contribution to the defeat of Japan in 1945 and that this acknowledgement of China's wartime sacrifice should help bolster contemporary ideas of Chinese identity. But unlike the revisionist Japanese discourse, the Chinese rediscovery of their wartime history is intended to have an internationalist element. However, it shares a problematic element with the Japanese discourse: it is based on political rather than historical assumptions. The Chinese desire to recast their wartime contribution in the eyes of the world goes against the grain of the politics of the Mao era, as it makes some attempt to restore the reputation of the Chinese Nationalists under Chiang Kai-shek, and acknowledges that without the efforts of (mostly Nationalist) armies to hold down some 750,000 or more Japanese troops, the history of East Asia might have been very different. But it is only in recent years that the Nationalist contribution has been given due credit on the Chinese mainland.[26]

The rehabilitation of the Nationalists is not a product of a desire for historical accuracy, however. The current Chinese regime is keen to take the more positive elements of Nationalist resistance to Japan (previously rarely mentioned) during the war and draw on it for current geopolitical needs. Most of the Western world paid little attention to the seventieth anniversary of the Cairo Conference, which fell in November 2013. But in China and Taiwan, it was noted with interest. The 1943 Cairo Conference was the only conference of the Second World War where China was treated as an equal Allied power with the USA and Britain (not the USSR, which was neutral in the war against Japan). For decades, this was not mentioned in Chinese textbooks because of the unfortunate historical reality that the Chinese leader who represented China at Cairo was not Mao Zedong but Chiang Kai-shek. But the new, grudging tolerance of Chiang on the mainland

---

26 On revisionist views on history in the Asia-Pacific region since the end of the Cold War, see the essays in Sheila Miyoshi Jager and Rana Mitter, eds., *Ruptured Histories: War, Memory, and the Post-Cold War in Asia* (Cambridge, Mass.: Harvard University Press, 2007).

means that it is now possible to use Cairo to demonstrate a wider point, that China was on the side of the Allies at the most crucial moment for civilization in the past century.

However, it is also clear that the 'meaning' of Cairo is being heavily oriented toward contemporary Chinese views of the Asia-Pacific settlement. The Cairo Declaration stated that 'It is their purpose that Japan shall be stripped of all the islands in the Pacific which she has seized or occupied since the beginning of the first World War in 1914, and that all the territories Japan has stolen from the Chinese, such as Manchuria, Formosa, and The Pescadores, shall be restored to the Republic of China.' It also added the statement that Japan should 'be expelled from all other territories which she has taken by violence and greed'.[27]

Chinese news media reported extensively that this formulation gave the authority of international law to Chinese claims over the Diaoyu/Senkaku Islands. In the early 2010s, disputes had arisen over these eight small uninhabited rocks in the East China Sea. To the Japanese, they were known as the Senkaku; the Chinese referred to them as the Diaoyu (in Taiwan, the Diaoyutai). However, the Chinese interpretation showed the fluid nature of the way in which they used the legacy of the Second World War in pressing their claims. The first part of the Cairo Declaration does not name the Diaoyu Islands explicitly, and since they were designated as Japanese in 1895, they do not fall under the 'since 1914' clause.

To add to the complexity, the Ma Ying-jeou administration on Taiwan has made it clear that it supports the idea that the islands should return to Chinese sovereignty. But since the Cairo Declaration explicitly demands that the territory should return to 'the Republic of China', this opens up a new area of confusion in which the Taipei government, not Beijing, might be considered the rightful inheritor of the Chiang regime on the mainland. In addition, in Taiwan there has been lively debate over the validity of the Cairo Declaration as a legal document, as opposed to a statement of intent. Taiwan's public sphere is much freer than China's, and there have been significant voices that have doubted President Ma's reading of sovereignty over the islands.

The eruption of this dispute in the present era shows how the freezing of the Cold War in post-war Asia prevented the creation of multilateral organizations and treaties that might have created a stable framework in the

---

27 Cairo Communiqué: the text and a reproduction of the original document can be found at: www.ndl.go.jp/constitution/e/shiryo/01/002_46/002_46tx.html.

region. China notes, correctly, that the 1952 San Francisco Treaty, which was supposed to mark the final settlement of the war in Asia, excluded the People's Republic. But the reasons for this exclusion draw blame onto both actors in the dispute. The USA refused to recognize Mao's regime, excluding an emergent power from helping define an overall settlement in the region. And China, with Stalin's support, backed up North Korea in its attack on South Korea, making a settlement with the USA close to impossible.

Elsewhere in the region, the essential instability of the 1945 settlement also threatens to reshape the region. The failure to create an agreed peace treaty across the region suggests that the legacy of 1945 in the region will take many years to resolve. In the Cold War, the legacy of the war was subsumed under the superpower conflict that dominated the globe. But the early twenty-first century has seen the rise of China as a key regional actor with geopolitical ambitions, as well as a more powerful role for India and various of the countries of Southeast Asia. Ironically, as we move further away from any living memory of the Second World War in the region, its political significance is rising, not waning.

PART IV

*

IN THE AFTERMATH OF CATASTROPHIC DESTRUCTION

Introduction to Part IV

MICHAEL GEYER AND ADAM TOOZE

In one of his curiously looping essays, the German film-maker and public intellectual Alexander Kluge conjures up the story of Max Horkheimer, one of the founders of the Frankfurt School of Critical Theory, working all night in Los Angeles during the days of the blackout in 1941–42. Horkheimer could not fall asleep, because he doubted he would wake up again, a case of relayed terror. Nightly he worked toward what would become the *Dialectic of Enlightenment*, one of the classics of twentieth-century thought.[1] Kluge was struck by a startling observation that Horkheimer felt compelled to repeat over and over again: You must not be *wahrheitssadistisch* – sadistic in the name of truth. Horkheimer meant to say according to Kluge:

> that there are realities which, if they were reported realistically, would cause such deep injuries that we have to decelerate information about them, so that experience can catch up with them. With this notion he described what a metaphor does, what poetry produces. In the face of unbearable experience, poetry shapes the vessels, labyrinths, threads, in which terror decelerates enough so that our sense experience can deal with it without being injured.[2]

In this final section we present a series of essays that explore in an exemplary fashion the ways in which individuals, peoples and indeed a global community, itself a product of the war, comes to grip with man-made mass destruction.

Horkheimer was right. Poetry proved to be a remarkable vessel in the age of world wars for giving terror language and thus making unspeakable pain

---

1 Max Horkheimer and Theodor W. Adorno, *Dialectic of Enlightenment: Philosophical Fragments* (London: Verso, 1997 [1944]).
2 Alexander Kluge, 'The Moment of Tragic Recognition with a Happy Ending', in Michael Geyer, ed., *The Power of Intellectuals in Contemporary Germany* (University of Chicago Press, 2001), pp. 381–93 (pp. 389–90).

bearable. But it is equally true that the idea of deceleration is very German indeed and has remained suspect not least for that reason. A telling counter-example would be Zbigniew Herbert's poem 'Dwie krople' ('Two Drops'), whose formal beauty only intensifies the searing pain of death and destruction.[3] Herbert had been active in the Polish Resistance, the Home Army, and emerged as one of Poland's supreme poets and moralists. His poem sharpens the dramatic recognition of the pity of war, whereas Horkheimer appeals to the power of language to capture experience without having to repeat it. We find the antidote to both in a movie by an American film-maker whose films have become global commodities, though this one is rather the exception. The 1979 satire *1941* by Steven Spielberg with Dan Aykroyd and John Belushi about the fabled Great Los Angeles Air Raid in the night of 24–25 February 1942 skewers the hysteria of Los Angelenos in the face of what proved not to be a Japanese attack.[4] The hysteria about a bombing raid that was not happening is one side of the story. The ease with which moving images could capture the terror of war and make it palatable to mass audiences is the other. And, perhaps, the altogether negative response to a satire about the Second World War and the American way of 'getting off' on it, is the third. The three examples – Horkheimer, Herbert and Spielberg – point in very different directions. They have in common the realization that the creative faculties of language and image make war 'real' even for those who have been there and have been part of it and make the repercussions of violence tolerable. In this sense 'culture' is a force of war.

The sheer angularity of apperceptions of violence suggests that the possibilities within this universe of a culture of war are seemingly endless. There is not just the diversity of attitudes and opinions or the multitude of media and platforms to communicate them. There are also civilizational frameworks that guide them, allow for certain expressions while eliding or ostracizing others.[5] A rich, if occasionally somewhat self-satisfied literature has emerged to explore the range of cultural productions that have shaped the experience of war.[6] Lately, this literature has recaptured what Horkheimer had

---

3 Zbigniew Herbert, *Selected Poems*, trans. Czesław Miłosz and Peter Dale Scott (Harmondsworth: Penguin, 1968), p. 21, with the famous caption: 'No time to grieve for roses, if the forests are burning'.

4 Steven Spielberg, *1941*, 113 min, colour (United States: Universal Pictures, 1979).

5 Julia Thomas, 'Photography, National Identity, and the "Cataract of Times": Wartime Images and the Case of Japan', *American Historical Review* 103:5 (1998), 1475–501.

6 The range of possibilities is covered by one of the foremost authors on the theme of war and culture. John W. Dower, *Ways of Forgetting, Ways of Remembering: Japan in the Modern World* (New York: The New Press, 2012) and *Cultures of War: Pearl Harbor, Hiroshima, 9–11, Iraq* (New York: W. W. Norton, 2010).

known in 1941 and many others had picked up as a key insight about the First World War. It took an extraordinary creative effort, cultural, religious and scientific, to reclaim the security of the senses that was so radically wrecked by the war's mighty destruction.[7] The term 'trauma' has become the universal currency for this affliction of war, but apart from being an anachronism it rather hides than exposes the disorientation that war engenders.[8] It is only surpassed by the uses and misuses of 'memory' as the omnibus term to capture the fact that war retains a presence long after the killing has come to an end.[9] Obviously, this is not a good reason to give this entire realm of cultural production short shrift, as we did in this volume. But we faced once more the problem that the phenomenal clarity that the symmetry of (military) destruction in the First World War on the Western Front generated is entirely absent in the Second World War and that the material for civilizational comparisons is remarkably slim despite the evident world-wide nature of the conflict. Suffice it to say that Jie-Hyun Lim's and Monica Black's thought provoking contributions should be ample evidence for the potential of this kind of transnational history of memory. They make clear how fruitful it is to focus on the shock waves that the destructive force of the Second World War generated.

As if picking up on Max Horkheimer, the eminent international relations theorist Quincy Wright opined in 1942 that in the face of the 'revolutionary outbreak against [the] basic laws' of the international order peace would be quite different. There would be no '"back to normalcy" without delay', but much as in the aftermath of the American Civil War, it would take time and it would be 'necessary to establish an order more adequate than the "peace" which preceded and produced the hostility'.[10] There was only a way forward and no way back. This war was too deep a break. Quincy Wright, of course,

---

7 Jay M. Winter, *Sites of Memory, Sites of Mourning: The Great War in European Cultural History* (Cambridge University Press, 1995); Peter D. Tame, Dominique Jeannerod and Manuel Bragança, eds., *Mnemosyne and Mars: Artistic and Cultural Representations of Twentieth-Century Europe at War* (Newcastle upon Tyne: Cambridge Scholars Publishing, 2013); Paul Cornish and Nicholas J. Saunders, eds., *Bodies in Conflict: Corporeality, Materiality, and Transformation* (Abingdon: Routledge, 2014).
8 Svenja Goltermann, *Die Gesellschaft der Überlebenden. Deutsche Kriegsheimkehrer und ihre Gewalterfahrungen im Zweiten Weltkrieg* (Munich: Deutsche Verlags-Anstalt, 2009).
9 However, there are also new departures: Mary Fulbrook, *Dissonant Lives: Generations and Violence through the German Dictatorships* (Oxford University Press, 2011); Tessa Morris-Suzuki, ed., *East Asia beyond the History Wars: Confronting the Ghosts of Violence* (Abingdon and New York: Routledge, 2013).
10 Quincy Wright, 'Political Conditions of the Period of Transition', *International Conciliation* 379 (1942), 264–79 (pp. 264–6).

thought of ways to construct a new international order, but on a more profound level the challenge consisted in growing a new civilizational order, in which the dead were buried so that the living could live and remember. This proved to be not only a difficult and long-lasting challenge, but also a treacherous one as Peter Gordon demonstrates. It is for good reasons that German thought is so much at the centre of this entire enterprise and that German-Jewish émigrés and exiles were the ones who had a lasting effect. It took this particular group – so deeply German and so violently alienated from their culture – to face up to the challenge of mass death and mass murder. This does not mean that one must endorse the particulars of their diagnosis, but they were in the first line of thinkers who faced up to the unbearable experience of man-made mass death and mass murder. The combination of rootedness and alienation is less unique than the essays in this section might suggest, but this is for a future history (of East Central Europe, the Soviet Union, Japan, China) to figure out – and this would still leave open the questions of when and where an Anglo-American literature would find its Archimedean point.[11]

It must be said though that, however profoundly philosophers and theologians thought about mass death and however affecting the poetry of war, occupation, annihilation and, above all, of the Holocaust has been, these were not the main modes of cultural engagement with the experience of the war. The preferred medium of war memory was film and television, as Lucy Noakes explains. These are not exactly media of deceleration, in Horkheimer's sense, but media of normalization and repetition that cast the extraordinary violence of the war in familiar narratives, images and soundtracks. The Western victors certainly had the upper hand in this respect, although the Soviet Union generated its own, exceedingly popular mass culture of war commemoration. In this case, it is the film-makers (and writers) in Japan – Akira Kurosawa may stand in for an older generation and Isao Takahata and his animated film *Hotaru no haka* ('Grave of the Fireflies') for a younger one – who were the exception, perhaps because the mainstream culture of Japan was so solidly in denial.

They know well and their films show that '[i]t is a mistake to think that the dead are dead.'[12] Neither mass cultural memory nor the good fortune of

11 Campbell Craig, *Glimmer of a New Leviathan: Total War in the Realism of Niebuhr, Morgenthau, and Waltz* (New York: Columbia University Press, 2003).
12 Alexander Kluge, 'It is a Mistake to Think that the Dead Are Dead: Obituary for Heiner Müller', in Geyer, ed., *The Power of Intellectuals*, pp. 212–17.

economic growth and prosperity could hold back the dead and the murdered. We might think of their ghostly presence as a belated recognition of the surfeit of violent death. But their persistence rather seems to be a reminder, as Monica Black suggests, of the violent energies that societies are capable of generating. They are with us not because of 'them' but because of 'us'. In any case, their unquiet makes clear that the labour of recognition that mass death engenders is not a past that will go away.

How do we write history in the aftermath of total destruction? How do we write history if both victory and defeat defy world historic redemption? Ultimately, it is these two questions that the essays in the final section struggle with from a diverse range of angles, cultural, historical, geographical and philosophical. It is these questions that create the problem of perspective that is at the root of the transnational 'historians debates' that Lim traces out in such an original fashion in his contribution. What would it mean to write a critical history of the Second World War? Given our own imbrication in this history, is a critical history even desirable? After the liberation of Auschwitz? And if Auschwitz, what about Hiroshima? And what about the everyday pain of violation? The unquiet memory of the comfort women continues to overshadow Japan's relations with its neighbours and seems capable, as Lim shows, of ever more elaborate transnational evocation. Meanwhile, as Noakes describes, even in the most self-satisfied media spheres, in Britain and the USA, and under the censorship of the Soviet regime, the memory of the war refused to settle.

Dorothee Brantz discusses how iconic images are capable of reproducing this unquiet. Richard Peters's heart-breaking vista of Dresden, 'Blick vom Rathausturm nach Süden' hardly needs amplification as an indictment of the ruination left in the wake of progress. Between the archaic *Time Life* image of American warriors sprawled dead on a beach in 1943, lapped by the Pacific, with their landing-craft burned in the background, the brutal scorching of the other city of Angels, Archangelsk, and the image two years later of the Hiroshima blast, one can see compressed Adorno's famously dystopian history from the slingshot to the atom bomb. Indeed, if we adopt a global perspective on the Second World War, the fracture of time and space is so extreme that Horkheimer's and Adorno's sketch, in *The Dialectic of Enlightenment*, of a malign progression in military technology appears unduly linear. As the global struggles of the Cold War would confirm, the atomic bomb would not displace the slingshot. The two would coexist in lethal juxtaposition and continue to coexist to this very day.

23

Interpretations of catastrophe

German intellectuals on Nazism, genocide and mass destruction

PETER E. GORDON

'It was as if an abyss had opened.' This was the response of the political theorist Hannah Arendt when she first heard the reports about Auschwitz in 1943. '*This ought not to have happened,*' she added. 'Something happened to which we cannot reconcile ourselves. None of us ever can.'[1] The story of how intellectuals sought to reckon with catastrophe in the aftermath of the Second World War is rich with ambivalence. Perhaps inevitably, it is a story of diminishing confidence in the powers of the intellect itself. Both by training and by habitus intellectuals may seem uniquely ill-equipped to comprehend historical events where brutality and violence have altogether vanquished the fragile constructs of the mind. It is therefore unsurprising that many of the most significant post-war interpretations of genocide and civilizational collapse have fastened on the theme of unintelligibility itself. This chapter addresses the various strategies by which European intellectuals, both secular and religious, sought to understand the catastrophic events of mid-twentieth-century Europe. It does not offer a synopsis, as this would surely be impossible within the bounds of a single essay. Instead it explores only a small set of representative cases, most of them from the period immediately following the armistice, and all of them devoted only to the case of Germany, chiefly because it became for many intellectuals the paradigm for reflections concerning civilizational collapse. Divided into four sections the chapter addresses four distinctive genres in the history of thinking about catastrophe: historical, philosophical, literary and theological.

Before turning to the substance of the analysis it may seem fitting to offer some preliminary explanation as to why intellectual responses to the war would merit the historian's attention. 'After all' (so might run the objection)

---

1 Hannah Arendt, *Essays in Understanding* (New York: Schocken Books, 2005), pp. 13–14.

'intellectuals lock themselves away in the cabinet of consciousness and worry themselves with conceptual abstractions that have little bearing upon the actual course of historical events.' Confronted with such scepticism, the intellectual can only offer a modest reminder that historical interpretation is already the work of conceptual abstraction and the very idea of a *non-interpreted* past, though perhaps a postulate, is not itself an object of historical knowledge. Interpretation without history is empty; but history without interpretation is blind. This may be true a fortiori for the interpretation of catastrophe, which places a special burden on the mind, either to find some significance in the wreckage of human affairs or to surrender to the nominalist's fatalistic conclusion that catastrophe cannot be understood at all.

Friedrich Meinecke and the German catastrophe

The distinguished German historian Friedrich Meinecke (1862–1954) was born in 1862, nearly a decade before the founding of the Wilhelmine Reich, and he died in 1954, nearly a decade after the Third Reich's defeat. Although in his early career he had enjoyed a high profile and considerable authority as the editor of the distinguished journal, the *Historische Zeitschrift*, during the Nazi era his influence diminished considerably and he became (as he wrote to his Austrian colleague Heinrich von Srbik) 'the most private of private individuals'.[2] He expressed his 'despair' to his daughter Sabine Rabl that the 'old great culture' of his beloved homeland was giving way to 'a terrible [sic] new and rootless religion'.[3] In 1946, after a lifetime of historical scholarship that he had devoted primarily to themes in eighteenth- and nineteenth-century German intellectual and political history, the octogenarian authored a brief summary of his reflections on the most recent events of his country in a book entitled *Die deutsche Katastrophe* (later translated into English in 1950 as *The German Catastrophe*).[4]

Meinecke's historiographical legacy has not weathered well the ravages of time. Throughout his career he stood as the proud representative of a strain of liberal nationalism that fell into sharp disrepute after the Second World War. Especially social historians of a Marxist orientation were inclined to

2 Quoted from the informative study by Mark W. Clark, *Beyond Catastrophe: German Intellectuals and Cultural Renewal after World War II, 1945–1955* (Lanham, MD: Lexington Books, 2006), p. 26.

3 Quoted from ibid., p. 25.

4 Friedrich Meinecke, *Die deutsche Katastrophe* (Wiesbaden: Eberhard-Brockhaus-Verlag, 1946).

dismiss him for his Olympian devotion to a culture of German classical erudition and his seeming indifference to the explanatory significance of economics and social power. Eckart Kehr saw Meinecke as an historian of the 'intellectually disoriented bourgeoisie' to whom he offered the solace and exaltation of a 'high mountain' perspective. His vision of history had little to do with 'practical' affairs and he had no concern whatsoever for the daily struggles of the 'mob' that lives in the confinement of a 'squalid valley' and 'cannot see the light beyond'.[5] It is true that Meinecke was chiefly concerned with ideas on a rarefied plane. His major works address topics such as the era of political reform and German nationalist awakening during the Napoleonic wars (*Das Zeitalter der deutschen Erhebung, 1795–1815*, 1913); the transformation from cosmopolitanism to nationalism in German political thought (*Weltbürgertum und Nationalstaat*, 1908); and the rise of a distinctively German tradition of historicism from Herder to Ranke (*Die Entstehung des Historismus*, 1936).[6] But it is arguably this rarefied species of national-liberal ideology that makes Meinecke such a fascinating specimen of his time. Both his enquiry into the causes of the 'German catastrophe' and the remedies he proffers are revealing precisely because they typify a *Denkstil* (thinking style) that would become increasingly antiquated within the post-war guild of professional historians.

In the preface to *The German Catastrophe* the octogenarian explains that while composing the book he confronted serious difficulties with his vision and except for a few notes he had to depend 'almost wholly upon my memory'. His efforts are remarkable for the simple reason that it was written amidst the rubble and ashes: Meinecke and his wife had fled Berlin in 1945 and they witnessed the end of the Third Reich from Franconia; after a brief stay in Göttingen they returned to Berlin, where Meinecke was appointed the first honorary rector of the newly founded Free University.[7] *The German Catastrophe* is thus among the very first works by a German

---

5 Eckhart Kehr, 'Modern German Historians', in Kehr, *Economic Interest, Militarism, and Foreign Policy: Essays on German History*, ed. Gordon Craig (Berkeley and Los Angeles: University of California Press, 1977) (pp. 181–2).

6 Friedrich Meinecke, *Die Entstehung des Historismus* (Munich: R. Oldenbourg Verlag, 1936); Meinecke, *Das Zeitalter der deutschen Erhebung, 1795–1815* (Bielefeld and Leipzig: Velhagen & Klasing, 1913). For an overall assessment, see *Friedrich Meinecke heute: Bericht über ein Gedenk-Colloquium zu seinem 25. Todestag am 5. und 6. April 1979*, ed. Michael Erbe, with contributions from C. Brands et al. (Berlin: Colloquium Verlag, 1981).

7 Peter Th. Walter, *Emigrierte Historiker in den Vereinigten Staaten 1945–1950. Blick oder Sprung über den Grossen Teich?* in Christoph Cobet, ed., *Einführung in Fragen an die Geschichtswissenschaft in Deutschland nach Hitler* (Frankfurt am Main: Ch. Cobet, 1986), pp. 41–50 (p. 46).

historian to undertake the difficult task of explaining the causes of his country's disaster. 'All Hitler's political successes ... have all vanished away into nothingness,' Meinecke observed. 'The riddle that confronts us today and the catastrophe through which we are now living surpass all previous occurrences of similar kind.'[8]

According to Meinecke Nazism exemplified a 'degeneration' of the German tradition, and was the outgrowth of two major trends of the nineteenth century – socialism and nationalism – that in Germany had a 'wholly peculiar character'.[9] From the time of the War of Liberation, however, the German people had developed a new 'realism' that took possession of its spiritual life. By the middle of the nineteenth century the culture was bent upon realizing 'a synthesis of intellectual and force' although with a 'preponderance on the side of the new ideas of power and nationalism'. For Meinecke the decisive fact in German history was that nationalist feeling set in earlier and deeper than the socialist movement, and as a consequence the German revolutions of 1848 were less 'a cry for greater freedom' and in larger part 'a cry for power'.[10] This thirst for power found in Bismarck its greatest hero, and unification was thus achieved under the aegis of a Prussian militarism that abandoned the values of classical liberalism – values which Meinecke associated most of all with Goethe and the so-called 'golden age' of Germany's national liberation.

By the 1880s a new strain of populist anti-Semitism had achieved political organization. The Jews, Meinecke writes, were 'inclined to enjoy indiscreetly' their new-found economic freedom. However, notwithstanding their 'negative and disintegrating influence' the Jews 'also achieved a great deal that was positive in the cultural and economic life of Germany', although this contribution was forgotten by the new anti-liberal movement that took 'the first steps toward National Socialism'. With the coming of the First World War Germany reached a turning point. Although the bourgeoisie and the working class were momentarily unified in the war effort, this partnership was soon broken: the 'supposedly educated bourgeoisie' was now afflicted with not only 'reckless national egoism' and 'indifference to the requirements of Europe's vital existence', but also 'an uncritical overestimate of German political strength'. The conflict over war aims carried over into the post-war

---

8 Meinecke, *Die deutsche Katastrophe*, author's preface, p. xi.
9 Ibid., p. 7.
10 Ibid., p. 9.

era, when right-wing nationalists blamed socialists for Germany's defeat and this stab-in-the-back legend nourished an enduring hatred for the new republic.

According to Meinecke all modern civilization requires the 'harmonious relationship between the rational and irrational forces of life'.[11] But in the climate of military humiliation and economic disarray that engulfed German society in the years following the First World War the older classical-liberal synthesis of 'power and spirit' began to lose its hold. A 'mechanistic' or technological approach to life gained a disproportionate prestige and the 'spiritual' element of German liberalism declined. The new democracy drew much of its support from technicians and engineers whose approach to life was primarily 'utilitarian' and 'calculating' but who nevertheless felt a 'suppressed metaphysical desire' that yearned for expression. They eventually found their leader in the 'petty painter and aquarellist Hitler' who had once earned a living 'in construction work' and during those impecunious years 'whipped up his hatred of the Jews into a general *Weltanschauung*'.[12] Hitler appealed to all of those classes who felt discontent with the Weimar Republic although according to Meinecke there lurked in his persona 'some element that was "foreign" to us Germans and difficult to understand'. His ultimate seizure of power was due not merely to personal factors but to a confluence of long-term historical trends and political contingencies – especially the fall of Brüning and von Papen's appointment to the presidential cabinet, and, finally, the decision by Reichspräsident Hindenburg to appoint Hitler as chancellor on 30 January 1933.

For Meinecke the Third Reich was 'not only the greatest misfortune that the German people have suffered in their existence, but also their greatest shame'.[13] But he took comfort in the thought that it was aberrant rather than a genuine outgrowth of German history:

> However crushing and shameful the fact is that a band of criminals could succeed for twelve years in forcing the German people under its leadership and in bringing a great part of the people to believe that they were following a great ideal – this very fact nevertheless has a calming and comforting aspect. The German people were not fundamentally diseased with criminal sentiments but were only suffering for a while with a severe infection from poison administered to it.[14]

11 Ibid., p. 34.
12 Ibid., p. 37.
13 Ibid., p. 86; quoted in the review in *Die Zeit*.
14 Ibid., p. 95.

In the wake of the Second World War Meinecke counselled acceptance and a recognition that 'the divine and the demonic' in humanity are 'indissolubly linked'.[15] He specifically believed that the German people could welcome its compulsory demilitarization, since it would permit a return to those spiritual values that had always remained at the core of the German character. 'The desire to become a world power', he wrote, 'has proved to be a false idol.' For the future it remained the task for the German people to establish themselves in the twin pillars of their spiritual tradition, cultural and religious. After the debased syncretism of the 'German Christian' movement that had been introduced under the Nazi regime, Germany would now rediscover its moral compass by returning to its common heritage in Protestantism and Catholicism. But the German people would also need to return to the culture of the *Goethezeit*, the era of a 'genuinely German spiritual production' that had also contributed to the entire 'cosmopolitan cultural community of the Christian Occident'. For there was in Meinecke's opinion perhaps no artefact that was 'more German than Goethe's *Faust*'. Meinecke therefore proposed that 'in every German city and larger village' there should be established 'Goethe-Communities' to which would be assigned the task of 'conveying to the heart of the listeners through sound the most vital evidences of the great German spirit, always offering the noblest music and poetry together'. Each week, perhaps on a late Sunday, the German people would find edification and spiritual nourishment in the poetry of Goethe and Schiller and the music of great German composers such as Bach, Mozart and Beethoven.

For the reader today it is easy to fault Meinecke's study of the German catastrophe for its naivety and antiquated trust in a depoliticized conception of historical phenomena, a trust which Wolf Lepenies has diagnosed as a susceptibility for 'the seduction of culture'.[16] As Eric Michaud has explained, the great irony of this liberal conception of aesthetic ennoblement is that the cult of art would remain an inspiration to the Nazi regime itself, which through the theatricality of its mass rallies, its architecture and museums,

15 Ibid., p. 108.
16 Wolf Lepenies, *The Seduction of Culture in German History* (Princeton University Press, 2006). For the canonical literature on the vicissitudes of German liberalism see especially James J. Sheehan, *German Liberalism in the Nineteenth Century* (University of Chicago Press, 1978); and Lothar Gall, *Der Liberalismus als regierende Partei. Das Grossherzogtum Baden zwischen Restauration und Reichsgründung* (Wiesbaden: F. Steiner, 1968); and Gall, 'Liberalismus und bürgerliche Gesellschaft. Zur Charakter und Entwicklung der liberalen Bewegung in Deutschland', *Historische Zeitschrift* 220 (1975), 324–56.

sought to realize an 'aestheticization of politics'.[17] Although this is a charge Meinecke would not have accepted, his book drew much criticism especially from scholars in the USA. Already in 1950, the sociologist Paul Massing, a left-Marxian affiliate of the Institute for Social Research, dismissed Meinecke for embracing a distinctively German *Weltanschauung* that ignored the principles of social equality and remained 'steeped in authoritarian thinking'.[18] The historian Gordon Craig was no more charitable. He found *The German Catastrophe* 'a disappointing book' especially because its abstract musings implied a 'fatalism' that 'can be used to exculpate . . . peoples of all responsibility for their actions'. Craig hastened to add that Meinecke had again betrayed this fatalism in a recent (October 1949) issue of the German journal *Der Monat*, in which he referred to 'an inner destiny which works by and large in all human life and brings forth good and evil, blessings and misfortunes intertwined'.[19] But verdicts such as these should not blind us to the historical significance of Meinecke's book. It remains of interest chiefly because it is the valedictory statement of a German liberal who still, even after his country's defeat, clung to an unlikely species of cultural nationalism: he still cherished the consoling thought that his nation could turn back for spiritual and depoliticized guidance to the redemptive treasures of the *Goethezeit*. Others were less sanguine and they sought the roots of the historical catastrophe in culture itself.

Music, madness, catastrophe: Mann's *Doctor Faustus*

Thomas Mann ranks among the most esteemed German novelists of the twentieth century. Born in 1875 in the Hanseatic port city of Lübeck he was the child of a successful grain merchant whose respectable career in business furnished much of the factual detail for his first major novel, *Buddenbrooks*, which was published in 1901. Over the next two decades his fame grew, thanks to both short stories and novellas such as the 1912 *Death in Venice*, which portrays the spiritual and moral dissolution of an ageing and repressed author, epic novels such as *The Magic Mountain*, which explores similar

---

17 Eric Michaud, *The Cult of Art in Nazi Germany* (Stanford University Press, 2004).
18 Paul W. Massing, review of Friedrich Meinecke, *The German Catastrophe: Reflections and Recollections*, trans. Sidney B. Fay (Cambridge, Mass.: Harvard University Press) in *The New Republic* (10 April 1950), 20–1. Paul W. Massing (1902–1979) was an affiliate of the Institute for Social Research and the author of *Rehearsal for Destruction: A Study of Political Anti-Semitism in Imperial Germany* (1949).
19 Gordon A. Craig, review of Meinecke, *The German Catastrophe* in *American Political Science Review* 44:4 (1950), 1029–31 (p. 1031).

themes of illness and intellectual disorientation in a Swiss sanatorium for tuberculosis patients (1924), the massive, biblical tetrology *Joseph and his Brothers* (1933–42), and the late, unfinished novel, *Confessions of Felix Krull, Confidence Man* (1954). His political orientation was idiosyncratic. In his early years Mann had cleaved to a highly self-reflective species of ironic conservatism (the mood which pervades his 1918 essay *Betrachtungen eines Unpolitischen*, or, *Reflections of an Unpolitical Man*) but eventually he came to support the Weimar Republic as the only reasonable course for Germany. Although he was awarded the Nobel Prize for literature in 1929 his political statements in favour of democracy earned him the antipathy of the Nazi regime, which revoked his citizenship in 1936. He spent the duration of the Second World War in Los Angeles, where he lived not far from other German émigrés in exile such as Theodor Adorno and Arnold Schoenberg, and where he wrote his great novel of personal and political crisis, *Doctor Faustus: The Life of the German Composer Adrian Leverkühn as Told by a Friend*. Mann only returned to Europe in 1952 and died in Switzerland in 1955.

Doctor Faustus is a multi-faceted book that interlaces an enquiry into the demonic nature of artistic genius with a political allegory about Germany's descent into dictatorship and war. The novel is written as if it were the biography of the composer (or *Tonsetzer*, Mann's archaic term) Adrian Leverkühn as narrated by Serenus Zeitblom, a childhood friend who is apparently recalling the details of Leverkühn's tragic life during the later phase of the Second World War: Zeitblom begins writing the biography on 23 May 1943, and he concludes his story as the last bombs have fallen on Germany and the devastated nation has been 'razed to the ground'. The composer's pact with the devil is presented as an implicit reprisal of the tragedy told by Goethe in his celebrated drama *Faust* (which is often characterized as the single most consequential work in the German literary canon), but it is also meant to serve as an allegory for the downfall of the soul of the German nation, which has achieved its greatness only through a poisonous alchemical experiment that binds cultural genius to the demonic.

Subtle gestures of allusion identify Adrian Leverkühn as a latter-day Doctor Faustus, in whom we see an embodiment of the German soul. Born in the later nineteenth century, Leverkühn pursues a variety of studies (like Goethe's restless hero): first theology, then philosophy, and then music, to which he devotes himself with single-minded passion, seeking instruction from his old teacher, Wendell Kretzschmar, and he then blazes an independent trail as an avant-garde composer of radical and terrifying works that shatter the rules of traditional tonality. The culminating work of his musical career is the *Apocalipsis cum figuris*, an 'apocalyptic oratorio' which Zeitblom describes as a 'a formal utopia of terrifying ingenuity' and 'a single immense variation on lamentation' that offers a violent retort to the jubilant conclusion of Beethoven's ninth symphony.[20] The dark secret in Leverkühn's genius is the 'compact' he has made with demonic madness: he wilfully contracts syphilis from a prostitute who is identified in the novel by the name of an exotic butterfly, *Hetaera Esmerelda*. In the centre of the narrative we read the 'dreadful treasure' that Zeitblom has inherited from his friend, the transcript in which the half-mad composer records his dialogue with Satan and the fatal bargain the devil offers:

> We pledge to you the vital efficacy needed for what you will accomplish with our help. You will lead, you will set the march for the future, lads will swear by your name, who thanks to your madness will no longer need to be mad. In their health they will gnaw at your madness, and you will become healthy in them. Do you understand? It is not merely that you will break through the laming difficulties of the age – you will break through the age itself, the cultural epoch, which is to say, the epoch of this culture and its cult, and dare a barbarism, a double barbarism, because it comes after humanitarianism, after every conceivable root-canal work and bourgeois refinement.

Like the encounter with Satan in Dostoyevsky's *The Brothers Karamazov* (which clearly served as Mann's novel), the reader does not learn if the dialogue is real or merely the fantastical consequence of the composer's delirium. But the question does not require a solution: Zeitblom narrates the entirety of the novel in an allegorical mode that inhibits realism; its personalities speak and act with studied exoticism, appearing less as individuals than as cultural types. This is true most of all of the composer himself, whose artistic achievements symbolize the fusion of genius with madness which remained a perennial obsession throughout Mann's oeuvre. But it is also true for the host of friends and acquaintances who pass through Leverkühn's life and are witnesses to his downfall.

Perhaps most troubling of all is Mann's representation of Jewish characters in the novel. There is Saul Fitelberg, the Polish-Jewish impresario with 'almond-shaped eyes full of Mediterranean merriment' who speaks a mixture of German and French and declares himself 'a respected champion of avant-garde culture'. To this character Mann assigns the task of a rambling

---

20 Thomas Mann, *Doctor Faustus*, trans. John Woods (New York: Alfred A. Knopf, 1997), p. 511.

discourse on the troubled alliance of Germans and Jews: 'We Jews have everything to fear from the German character,' Fitelberg says, *'qui est essentiellement anti-sémitique.'* And yet 'as a Jew one is basically skeptical of the world and inclined toward Germanness', for 'in reality there are only two nationalisms, the German and the Jewish, and the rest is child's play.' The Germans, he concludes, 'with their nationalism, their arrogance, their fondness for their own incomparability … the Germans will bring about their own misfortune, a truly Jewish misfortune, *je vous le jure.* The Germans should allow the Jew to play the *médiateur* between them and society, to be the manager, the impresario, the agent of Germanness – the Jew is definitely the man for the job, he should not be sent packing, he is international, and he is pro-German.'[21]

The rhapsodic speculations of characters such as Fitelberg are little more than occasions for Mann to expatiate upon his own opinions (a strategy that he pursued even further in his other great novel of ideas, *The Magic Mountain*). It is well known that Mann consulted Theodor Adorno for the musicological portions of the book in which Leverkühn effects the breakthrough to the system of twelve-tone or serial composition (a method which was in fact developed by Arnold Schoenberg, a teacher to Alban Berg, who had tutored Adorno himself). Adorno's contribution to the novel – especially in Kretzschmar's lectures on Beethoven's 'late style' and in the account of serial composition – has been debated at length. Although the philosopher is not directly acknowledged in the novel, the libretto to Leverkühn's *Apocalypse* contains the word 'Wiesengrund' (Adorno's middle name, taken from his father). That Mann felt his debt to Schoenberg and his circle is clear from the author's note that appears at the book's close, where Mann states that the serial method described in chapter 22 is 'in the truth the intellectual property of a contemporary composer and theoretician Arnold Schoenberg'.

The question of creative debt is significant insofar as Mann makes Leverkühn into a symbol for the German national condition. That Leverkühn is a Protestant Christian (like Mann himself) while Schoenberg himself was Jewish gives this symbolism a double edge: Mann could be seen as encoding his novel with an ironic and unstated homage to a Jewish 'genius' even while the novel also celebrates (and damns) its German hero for his 'demonic' character. These complications of identity are not incidental insofar as Mann uses the novel to speculate on the origins of the German catastrophe.

---

21 Ibid., pp. 427–8.

Most disquieting, however, is the character of Dr Chaim Breisacher, who expatiates on the civilizational decline of Judaism when it transforms its 'national god' into 'an abstract and generally humane God in heaven'. Breisacher is presented as an 'arch conservative' who longs for a religion of the 'genuine *Volk*' rather than one that is 'merely ethical'. In the chapter devoted to Breisacher's rhapsodies the closing remark comes from Zeitblom, who admits that despite his 'pro-Jewish sympathies' Breisacher is among the 'quite annoying specimens of the race'. Zeitblom ends with a question: 'Can one hold it against Jewish sagacity if its keen-eared sensitivity for what is new and yet to come, proves itself in aberrant situations as well, where the avant-garde and the reactionary coincide?'[22]

Mann's novel only gestures toward without answering its manifold speculations on the causes of Germany's downfall. It is too much to say that Breisacher (who was modelled after the real but no-less bizarre intellectual Oskar Goldberg) is the most blameworthy harbinger of Nazi ideology, though he surely contributes to the poisonous brew that is said to have engulfed Germany. Zeitblom's allusion to the fusion of avant-gardism with political reaction as distinctively Jewish thereby raises the ugly theme of the 'Jewish fascist'. Whether Mann intended to blame the victims for their own persecution remains open to debate.

The broader question about Mann's novel is whether it does not indulge in the romantic equation between artistic greatness and demonic possession, as if Germany's downfall were the final manifestation of a grandeur that – like Nietzsche's *Übermensch* – lies beyond moral categories of good and evil. Mann did not intend this: in *The Story of a Novel*, which records the author's own reflections on writing *Doctor Faustus*, Mann expressed his fear that the book might help to inspire 'a new German myth, flattering the Germans with their demonism [*Dämonie*]'. The fact remains, however, that the novel invites confusion insofar as it often seems ready to sift through aesthetic terrain to discover the actual sources of political catastrophe. Walter Benjamin characterized fascism as the aestheticization of politics, but he meant that this was an ideological *effect* rather than a cause: he did not wish to imply that the political origins of fascism were themselves traceable to aesthetics. Some have gone even further to suggest that the Nazis embraced a redemptive 'cult of art' which furnished ideological motivation for the doctrine of

---

22 Ibid., p. 300.

racial supremacy.[23] But the persona of Adrian Leverkühn serves as an unlikely vehicle for the exploration of such themes. Although *Doctor Faustus* remains of great significance especially for its poetic speculations concerning a subterranean link between avant-garde genius and disease, it is difficult to avoid the conclusion that such analogies only conspire to obscure real questions of political culpability in the Second World War. Thomas Mann nonetheless ranks among the very first of the novelists and poets who braved the difficult task of laying bare the horrors of the war with the tools of the imagination. Others would follow, and to each of them the sheer impossibility and the necessity of the task would present itself anew.[24]

Enlightenment and catastrophe: the Frankfurt School

'Enlightenment,' wrote Max Horkheimer and Theodor Adorno, 'understood in the most embracing sense of the progression of thought, has always committed itself to the task of liberating human beings from fear and establishing them as masters. But the wholly enlightened earth is radiant with triumphant calamity [*Unheils*].'[25] This historical and philosophical paradox serves as the central insight around which Horkheimer and Adorno organized the masterpiece they entitled *Dialectic of Enlightenment: Philosophical Fragments*. Composed jointly by the two authors between 1939 and 1944 from the safety of exile in Los Angeles, the text was first circulated in replicated typescript in a limited edition among members of the Institute for Social Research and was officially published in Amsterdam in 1947. In the original 1944 preface the authors wrote that their purpose was 'to explain why humanity, instead of entering a truly human state, is sinking into a new kind of barbarism [*Barbarei*]'. Although the ambition to achieve rational mastery of the world as institutionalized in the modern sciences was supposed to further the cause of freedom and human betterment, human reason had devolved into an uncritical and unreflective instrument of destruction. This catastrophic dénouement was due in part to what the Marxist theorist George Lukács had identified in the 1920s as the *reification* (the loss of agency

---

23 Michaud, *Cult of Art*.

24 For a reflection on the difficulty of this task and an analysis of major exemplars, see James E. Young, *Writing and Rewriting the Holocaust: Narrative and the Consequences of Interpretation* (Bloomington: Indiana University Press, 1988).

25 Max Horkeimer and Theodor W. Adorno, *Dialectic of Enlightenment: Philosophical Fragments*, trans. Edmund Jephcott (Stanford University Press, 2002), p. 1. Hereafter identified as *DE*. All quotations from this edition but with my own occasional modifications of the translation based upon consultation of the original.

and reduction to objecthood) afflicting social consciousness under modern capitalism. But Horkheimer and Adorno went even further. Insofar as the logic of exchange value had reduced all intrinsic difference to a generalized fungibility, the individual was being gradually absorbed into the culture industry. Thought itself, the authors wrote, 'is being turned into a commodity'. The problem was not unique to capitalism. For Horkheimer and Adorno the broader purpose of their book was to explain nothing less than 'the present collapse of bourgeois civilization [*Zusammenbruch der bürgerlichen Zivilisation*]'.[26]

While it would be facile to read *Dialectic of Enlightenment* exclusively as a commentary on the significance of the Second World War it was clearly that too. The book is permeated from beginning to end with the anti-utopian view that contemporary society had entered a final stage in the dialectic of reason and barbarism. Although they still clung to remnants of the Marxist critique of capitalist society, Horkheimer and Adorno could no longer endorse the more orthodox thesis (articulated by, inter alia, their colleagues Franz Neumann and Otto Kirchheimer) that saw in fascism an outgrowth of monopoly capitalism. Following their colleague Friedrich Pollock, Horkheimer and Adorno instead subscribed to a modified Marxist view of fascism as a radically anti-traditional system of 'state capitalism' in which the expected primacy of economic factors no longer obtained and politics had gained an unprecedented independence in the steering of the totalitarian project.[27] This view permitted them to develop a more extensive genealogy that sought the roots of fascism not in the contradictions of capitalist modernity but rather much further back in the prehistory of human reason itself.

The central argument of *Dialectic of Enlightenment* is that the modern world has reached an end-phase of catastrophic unfreedom that only brings to completion the contradictions that were already latent at the birth of human subjectivity. At the conjectural origins of human life, the individual subject felt himself overwhelmed with fear in the face of his natural surroundings and therefore gradually developed the rational instruments by which to overcome his fear and master his environment. Reason was therefore born of the drive for self-preservation and was perfected as a tool for world domination. At the earliest stages humanity had developed myths as rudimentary explanatory schemes for natural phenomena that were otherwise unintelligible, and in this sense myth already anticipated the more sophisticated

---

26 *DE*, 'Preface', p. xiv.
27 See Freidrich Pollock, 'Is National Socialism a New Order?', *Zeitschrift für Sozialforschung/Studies in Philosophy and Social Science* 9 (1941), 200–25.

schema of rational enlightenment and natural-scientific explanation. But as humanity advanced, it eventually sought to disenchant nature even of these anthropomorphizing myths until eventually nature was little more than a meaningless and undifferentiated substrate. The exchange principle of modern capitalism merely formalizes the view that nature consists in an infinitely fungible mass. Meanwhile, the mathematical reasoning that supports natural-scientific and technological understanding reinforces a positivistic affirmation of the merely given. Reason loses any critical or self-reflexive capacity and becomes nothing more than the validation of what exists. But this means that the history of rational self-liberation culminates in fatalism; the bid for freedom ends in unfreedom and enlightenment reverts to myth.

Horkheimer and Adorno illustrate this ironic outcome through an ingenious reading of Homer's *Odyssey* in which Odysseus figures as the prototype of bourgeois man who exercises his cunning so as to emancipate himself from his mythical surroundings. But his adventures demonstrate the bad dialectic of instrumental reason insofar as with the ever apparent advance in his mastery of nature Odysseus also suffers a negation of his own human nature: he must disfigure himself in order to survive. Although enlightenment promises an authentic liberation of the human being for a higher realization of his humanity, the trial of rational self-liberation requires not only the domination of external nature but also the domination of one's own subjectivity. The nightmares of domination as described by de Sade merely dramatize the mutual entwinement of sadism and masochism in the pleasureless pleasure of fully rationalized society. The history of civilization is therefore the history of 'the introversion of sacrifice'. Pleasure must yield to the ethos of secular asceticism, while the happiness which was supposed to stand as the ideal for human freedom dissolves into the grim affirmation of the world as it is. Ultimately this means that the subject's bid for survival and domination concludes with the subject's entrapment and the loss of critical reflection. 'What appears as the triumph of subjectivity, the subjection of all existing things to logical formalism, is bought with the obedient subordination of reason to what is immediately at hand.' Human experience loses the prospect of any genuine satisfaction beyond the commodified pleasures that are manufactured by the culture industry: 'The actual is validated, knowledge confines itself to repeating it, thought makes itself mere tautology.'[28] The emancipatory and critical faculty in human consciousness is thereby dissolved.

---

28 *DE*, p. 20.

Much of the argumentation of *Dialectic of Enlightenment* antedates the time when the full extent of Nazi atrocities had been revealed. The authors found an important source of inspiration in the 'Theses on the Philosophy of History', a manuscript which their colleague Walter Benjamin had entrusted to Hannah Arendt in 1941 and which she had then passed on to Adorno. Infamous for its perplexing syncretism of Marxist and messianic imagery, the manuscript portrayed the 'angel of history' as a figure who is turned toward the past and sees the endless chain of historical events as 'one single catastrophe, which keeps piling wreckage upon wreckage and hurls it at his feet'. Although the angel would like to restore unity to the historical continuum, a storm blows the angel backwards into the future while 'the pile of debris before him grows toward the sky. What we call progress is *this* storm.'[29] In a letter to Horkheimer that accompanied the manuscript Adorno explained: 'It contains Benjamin's final concepts ... none of [his] works shows him closer to our intentions than this. This relates above all to the conception of history as permanent catastrophe.'[30]

Dialectic of Enlightenment is a work of seemingly relentless philosophical pessimism. Even today much of the critical literature on the book remains preoccupied with the question as to whether it permits any warrant for hope that the history of entanglement of reason and barbarism might be undone. In the summer of 1942 Horkheimer wrote to the theologian Paul Tillich that 'We can hope for no more than that, would day ever break, our writings will be recognized as a very little star that had shown, though barely perceptible, in the horrible night of the present.'[31] But this is merely a subjective expression of a wish that their book not be forgotten and it does nothing to explain the apparent paradox that afflicted their argument: how can a critique of reason retain its validity if its genealogical unmasking of reason as domination is exhaustive? How can one issue a wholesale indictment of human reason if reason is to retain at least the force that is a prerequisite for critique? The second-generation critical theorist Jürgen Habermas has argued that Horkheimer and Adorno remained caught in this paradox and did not succeed in showing the way out. They 'surrendered themselves to an

29 Walter Benjamin, 'On the Concept of History', in Benjamin, *Selected Writings*, ed. Howard Eiland and Michael Jennings (Cambridge, Mass.: Harvard University Press, 2006), vol. IV, pp. 389–400 (p. 392).
30 Quoted in Rolf Wiggershaus, *The Frankfurt School: Its History, Theories, and Political Significance*, trans. Michael Robertson (Cambridge, Mass.: MIT Press, 1995), p. 311.
31 Letter of 12 August 1942, quoted from the Pollock Archive in Helmut Dubiel, *Theory and Politics: Studies in the Development of Critical Theory*, trans. Benjamin Gregg (Cambridge, Mass.: MIT Press, 1985), p. 84.

uninhibited skepticism regarding reason, instead of weighing the grounds that cast doubt on this skepticism itself'. Had they recognized the genuinely redemptive significance of rational communication rather than identifying reason only with instrumental reason they 'could not have been disturbed by the decomposition of bourgeois culture that was then being enacted in Germany for all to see'.[32] Habermas is perhaps right that the authors failed to circumvent the paradox of a totalizing critique of reason. But it is perhaps unfair to expect philosophical restraint and rational justification from authors who were still struggling to comprehend the immediate fact of unrestrained brutality. In 1968, just a year before his death, Adorno delivered a radio address on the Hessischen Rundfunk on the theme of 'Education after Auschwitz' in which he declared that *'the premier demand upon all education is that Auschwitz not happen again. Its priority before any other requirement is such that I believe I need not and should not justify it.'*[33]

The concept of God after Auschwitz

Born in 1903, Hans Jonas was one of the large number of students, many of them Jewish, who studied philosophy under the direction of Martin Heidegger at the Philipps-Universität in Marburg. Among his colleagues were Karl Löwith, Hannah Arendt and Emmanuel Levinas. A gifted historian of religion, between 1934 and 1954 Jonas published a two-volume study of the Gnostic religious cult of late antiquity, a work which appeared in English in 1958 as *The Gnostic Religion*.[34] His experiences in Germany left a devastating imprint: upon learning that his teacher Heidegger had joined the Nazi party, Jonas left Germany for England, and from there went to Palestine, only to return to Europe as a member of the British Army. He returned to his family home in Mönchen-Gladbach on Germany's western edge only to learn that his mother had been among the millions who had been murdered in Auschwitz. Vowing never to live in Germany again, Jonas eventually found a teaching post at the New School for Social Research in New York where his

---

32 Jürgen Habermas, 'The Entwinement of Myth and Enlightenment: Max Horkheimer and Theodor Adorno', in Habermas, *The Philosophical Discourse of Modernity: Twelve Lectures*, trans. Frederick G. Lawrence (Cambridge, Mass.: MIT Press, 1990), pp. 106–30.

33 Theodor W. Adorno, 'Education after Auschwitz', in Adorno, *Can One Live after Auschwitz? A Philosophical Reader*, ed. Rolf Tiedemann (Stanford University Press, 2003), pp. 19–33 (p. 19, my emphasis).

34 Originally published as *Gnosis und spätantiker Geist* (2 vols., 1934–54), available in English as Hans Jonas, *The Gnostic Religion: The Message of the Alien God & the Beginnings of Christianity* (Boston: Beacon Press, 1958).

old friend Hannah Arendt numbered among his colleagues. He authored major works of environmentalist philosophy that helped to inspire the German Greens, including *The Phenomenon of Life* and *The Imperative of Responsibility*.[35] Among his major awards was the Peace Prize of the German Booksellers' Association, which he received in 1987. One of his most memorable works is a 1984 lecture that he delivered at Tübingen University upon receiving the Dr Leopold Lucas Prize. It is entitled 'The Concept of God after Auschwitz: A Jewish Voice'.[36]

In this brief survey of various interpretations of the mid-century catastrophe Jonas's lecture is distinguished by its startling, even extravagant suggestion that the horror of the Nazi extermination camps forces us to reconsider not only our categories of moral and political judgement but also our understanding of the divine. According to Jonas this task is specifically urgent for the Jew rather than the Christian, since for Christianity 'the world is anyway largely of the devil and always an object of suspicion' given the doctrine of original sin. For the Jew, however, God is the 'Lord of *history*' and precisely for this reason the Nazi genocide must call into question – at least for the Jewish believer – 'the whole traditional concept of God'.[37] With this preliminary explanation Jonas proposes something very strange – a speculative and imaginative experiment that verges on heresy: he asks that his audience indulge him as he entertains a '*myth* of my own invention', which is supposed to motivate the new conception of God for the post-Auschwitz era.

'In the beginning,' Jonas writes, 'for unknowable reasons':

> the ground of being, or the Divine, chose to give itself over to the chance and risk and endless variety of becoming. And wholly so: entering in the adventure of space and time, the deity held back nothing of itself: no uncommitted or unimpaired part remained to direct, correct, and ultimately guarantee the devious working-out of its destiny in creation.[38]

---

35 Hans Jonas, *Das Prinzip Verantwortung. Versuch einer Ethik für die technologische Zivilisation* (Frankfurt am Main: Suhrkamp, 1979); Jonas, *The Phenomenon of Life: Toward a Philosophical Biology* (New York: Harper & Row, 1966).

36 Hans Jonas, 'Der Gottesbegriff nach Auschwitz'. First published in Fritz Stern and Hans Jonas, *Reflexionen finsterer Zeit* (Tübingen: J. C. B. Mohr, 1984); in English as 'The Concept of God after Auschwitz: A Jewish Voice', in Hans Jonas, *Mortality and Morality: A Search for the Good after Auschwitz*, ed. Lawrence Vogel (Evanston, Ill.: Northwestern University Press, 1996), 131–43. For this chapter I have consulted both the English translation and the German reprint: *Der Gottesbegriff nach Auschwitz. Eine jüdische Stimme* (Frankfurt am Main: Suhrkamp, 1987).

37 Jonas, 'The Concept of God', p. 133.

38 Ibid., p. 134.

In this myth God is said to have 'renounced his being' for the sake of the world, but then hoped to receive his divinity 'back from the odyssey of time'. The process has no teleological guarantee because the unfolding of history will grant only the 'chance harvest of unforeseeable temporal experience'. The act of divine 'self-forfeiture' yields to nothing more than an open plane of possibility which includes not only the risk of self-transfiguration but self-disfigurement as well. The creation of humanity presents God with the ultimate promise and danger. 'The advent of man means the advent of knowledge and freedom, and with this supremely double-edged gift the innocence of the mere subject of self-fulfilling life has given way to the charge of responsibility under the disjunction of good and evil.' Because God has surrendered its atemporal being to the chance of time human history is the ultimate field of uncertainty. The divine waits 'with the bated breath of suspense, hoping and beckoning, rejoicing and grieving, approving and frowning', since even if God lacks the transcendent power to intervene, the divine recognizes 'the reflections of his own state as it wavers in the record of man'.[39]

This is not the concept of God that is found in traditional Judaism. The God of the Hebrew Bible is sovereign over history and conspires with occasionally grandiose gestures (as in the Exodus from Egypt) to guide his beloved people forward through time and onward to redemption. In classical philosophical statements such as those by Maimonides, God is all-powerful and wholly sovereign over creation even though the divine essence is said to transcend human knowledge. The new post-Auschwitz divinity that Jonas entertains no longer enjoys sovereign *control* over history but has surrendered itself to it. More striking still, however, it lacks the attribute of transcendence, the separation of the divine from its mundane creation, which remains a cardinal theme in Jewish tradition. Jonas insists that the Jewish God is not the *deus absconditus* (the hidden God) as theorized by Aquinas and radicalized by the theologians of the Protestant Reformation, especially because the Jewish God has revealed himself through principles of justice. The God of Jewish tradition is therefore both all-powerful and his actions on behalf of humanity are intelligible at least in some measure. Jonas's conception of God remains faithful to tradition by insisting that the divine is still intelligible and still benevolent. But Jonas tests the boundaries of Jewish tradition by imagining that the divine no longer enjoys any transmundane

---

39 Ibid., p. 136.

power that would distinguish his essence from creation. In this respect Jonas parts company from other contributors to the conversation about post-Holocaust Jewish thought such as Richard Rubinstein, Eliezer Berkowitz and Emil Fackenheim.[40] According to Jonas, a radical revision is crucial if we are not willing to surrender the concept of God entirely: 'After Auschwitz, we can assert with greater force than ever before that an omnipotent deity would have to be either not good or . . . totally unintelligible.'[41]

For Jonas, then, any conception of God that would be compatible with the horrors of the extermination camp would have to undergo a dramatic revision. We can and must retain the expectation that the Jewish God is benevolent and intelligible. But we must surrender the notion that God is all-powerful. Unless one takes the fateful step beyond the threshold of belief itself, this is the only solution to the painful fact that throughout the catastrophic events of the war God did not intervene:

> in view of the enormity of what, among the bearers of his image in creation, some of them time and again, and wholly unilaterally, inflict on innocent others, one would expect the good God at times to break his own, however stringent, rule of restraint and intervene with a saving miracle. But no saving miracle occurred. Through the years that 'Auschwitz' raged God remained silent. The miracles that did occur came from man alone: the deeds of those solitary, mostly unknown 'just of the nations' who did not shrink from utter sacrifice in order to help, to save, to mitigate – even, when nothing else was left, unto sharing Israel's lot . . . But God was silent.[42]

According to Jonas, when we consider the horrifying fact of human brutality in the death camps and the equally horrifying fact that God did not demonstrate his sovereign power by intervening to prevent the slaughter of innocents, our only recourse is the radical conception of a God who lacks the attribute of omnipotence. This 'suffering God' is not the same as the Christological doctrine according to which the divine invested himself in

---

40 Richard Rubinstein, *After Auschwitz: Radical Theology and Contemporary Judaism* (Indianapolis: Bobbs-Merrill, 1966); Eliezer Berkowitz, *Faith after the Holocaust* (New York: Ktav, 1973); Emil Fackenheim, *God's Presence in History: Jewish Affirmations and Philosophical Reflections* (New York University Press, 1970). A survey of the problem is provided in Zachary Braiterman, *(God) after Auschwitz: Tradition and Change in Post-Holocaust Jewish Thought* (Princeton University Press, 1998). Also see Michael Wyschogrod, 'Some Theological Reflections on the Holocaust', *Response* 9:1 (1975), 65–8; Amos Funkenstein, 'Theological Interpretations of the Holocaust', in François Furet, ed., *Unanswered Questions: Nazi Germany and the Genocide of the Jews* (New York: Schocken Books, 1989), pp. 275–303.
41 Jonas, 'The Concept of God', p. 140.
42 Ibid.

finite form at one discrete point in time so as to redeem all creation. Jonas conceives of a divine cosmogony that undoes omnipotence from the very beginning for the sake of human freedom. This conception actually accords with the anthropomorphic image of God in the Hebrew Bible who is portrayed as a personality who constantly suffers and grieves with humanity. For Jonas this is 'the becoming God' who is utterly vulnerable to history and who is especially vulnerable to historical evil, an evil that is introduced into the world not from God but from the hearts and acts of human beings.

Jonas proposed this radical conception of God in part as a rejoinder to the Gnostic teachings to which he devoted the earlier part of his scholarly career. The God of Judaism does not allow for Manichaean dualism: there is no evil demi-urge that governs the mundane realm. But this resistance to the idea of metaphysical evil only intensifies the need in Judaism for some explanation as to why God did not act to counter human evil. The only explanation is that God *could not act* because the cosmogonic creation of the world also involved the self-abnegation of divine power. According to Jonas this idea is not as exotic to Jewish tradition as it might at first appear, since the esoteric teachings of Jewish mysticism or Kabbalah (as reconstructed by the great Jewish historian Gershom Scholem) actually promote the idea that the world began with a mighty act of divine contraction or withdrawal. Jonas claims that his own myth extends this idea, such that God's self-limitation is now understood to be a total limitation of divine power.[43]

This self-limitation by the divine has an important moral-political lesson, since it hands over to humanity the ultimate responsibility for the outcome of divine history: 'Having given himself whole to the becoming of the world, God has no more to give: it is man's now to give to him.' For Jonas this means that humanity is burdened with an unqualified responsibility. In supplanting the idea of divine omnipotence with the idea of a suffering God, the responsibility for the fate of the world passes irrevocably from divine to human hands. Only this cosmogonic revision permits us to recognize that what happened in the death camps was not the consequence of natural catastrophe or the visitation of some demonic power: Auschwitz is not the Lisbon earthquake. Because the course of history is the responsibility of human beings alone we can understand that the Nazi genocide emerged neither from the upsurge of a 'blind, natural causality' nor from the designs of a satanic, non-natural evil. In this respect Jonas may offer a helpful

---

43 Ibid., p. 142.

corrective to the poetic imaginings of Thomas Mann, whose *Doctor Faustus* entertains questionable analogies likening the Nazi catastrophe to both naturalistic disease and demonic power. Needless to say, Jonas does not permit himself to entertain the obvious alternative to his radical cosmogony, which is that culpability and responsibility rest with human beings alone for the simple reason that the God who might have relieved them of their responsibility or shared it with them does not exist. But this catastrophic solution to the question of the Nazi catastrophe is one Jonas does not openly consider, perhaps because it would award to the perpetrators a kind of metaphysical efficacy, as if in committing themselves to the erasure of one sector of humanity they achieved the erasure of God as well. The irony of Jonas's argument, however, is that by logical implication it allows for this unspoken possibility: a divinity who has given itself over without qualification to the uncertainties of history is infinitely vulnerable to human action even to the point of death. If we accept Jonas's radical cosmogony we cannot prohibit the thought that the catastrophe of the camps was also a catastrophe for the possibility of any future theology.[44]

Concluding remarks

The idea that the Second World War and the Holocaust confront the human understanding with a special challenge to received categories of epistemology as well as historical and moral judgement has become a truism of our time.[45] The very notion of a catastrophe is suggestive of a rupture or discontinuity with tradition. But the soundness of such a truism deserves reconsideration. Among the many difficulties with the notion of a radical break in history is the fact that the Nazi genocide was only one case – though it was indeed an especially egregious case – of the many genocides that human beings have visited upon each other in modern history: valid

---

44 In this respect Jonas's argument may be construed as a rejoinder to 'death-of-God' theology. For an important collection on this theme, see Bernard Murchland, ed., *The Meaning of the Death of God* (New York: Vintage, 1967). Needless to say, most theologians in the Christian and Jewish traditions continue to believe in the possibility of religion after Auschwitz. See, for example, David Tracy, 'Religious Values after the Holocaust: A Catholic View', in Abraham Peck, ed., *Jews and Christians after the Holocaust* (Philadelphia: Fortress Press, 1982), pp. 87–107; and Johann Baptist Metz, 'Christians and Jews after Auschwitz', in Metz, *The Emergent Church: The Future of Christianity in a Postbourgeois World* (New York: Crossroad, 1981), pp. 17–33.

45 For a powerful exploration of this theme see Saul Friedländer, ed., *Probing the Limits of Representation: Nazism and the 'Final Solution'* (Cambridge, Mass.: Harvard University Press, 1992).

comparisons can be made to the Armenian genocide, the mass murder of Bosnian Muslims in the former Yugoslavia, and, with due recognition of the difference between ethno-racial and class violence, to the horrors of Stalinist collectivization. Nor is the phenomenon confined to Europe: an especially striking case is the mass murder of the Herero and Namaqua peoples in Southwest Africa at the beginning of the twentieth century. The notion that the murder of the Jews in Europe signifies a genuine discontinuity to all of human history is therefore an overstatement, although this qualification surely does not diminish one's horror at the Nazis' crimes nor does it allow for a disburdening of empathy for the suffering of the victims.

No less catastrophic was the USA's use of the atomic bomb, first dropped on Hiroshima (5 August 1945) and then on Nagasaki (9 August 1945). Immediate death tolls in the first bombing climbed as high as 70,000 civilians, but an estimated 70,000 additional individuals died from radiation over the next five years; the death toll in Nagasaki reached as high as 70,000.[46] Already on 8 August, the French writer Albert Camus published an untitled editorial in the Resistance journal, *Combat*, where he wrote that 'technological civilization has just reached its final degree of savagery [*la civilisation mécanique vient de parvenir à son dernier degré de sauvagerie*].'[47] This was most likely the very first comment by a public intellectual on the devastation of the nuclear age.[48] But of course Camus's moral outrage – which concluded with the stark statement that humanity must 'choose definitively between hell and reason [*choisir définitivement entre l'enfer et la raison*]' was without effect: Nagasaki was bombed the next day. Two months later, Camus's colleague Jean-Paul Sartre published an essay entitled 'The End of the War' in his newly-founded journal, *Les Temps modernes* (October 1945) in which he suggested that the bomb had dramatically changed the relationship between humanity and nature: 'No longer is there a human species,' Sartre wrote. 'The community which has made itself the guardian of the atomic bomb is above the natural kingdom, since it is responsible for its life and its death.'[49]

46 On the aftermath, see Robert Jay Lifton, *Death in Life: Survivors of Hiroshima* (New York: Random House, 1967).

47 Albert Camus, an untitled editorial, originally published in *Combat* (8 August 1945), translated by Ronald Santoni and reprinted with the title, 'After Hiroshima: Between Hell and Reason', *Philosophy Today* 32:1 (1988), 77–8.

48 Camus's statement was followed by Bertrand Russell, whose essay, 'The Bomb and Civilization' was published in the *Forward*, a Glasgow newspaper, on 18 August 1945 (39:33), pp. 1 and 3.

49 Jean-Paul Sartre, 'La fin de la guerre', in Sartre, *Situations III: Les lendemains de guerre* (Paris: Gallimard, 1949), pp. 63–71. Reprinted in English as 'The End of the War', in Sartre, *The Aftermath of War*, trans. Chris Turner (New York: Seagull Books, 2008).

In the immediate aftermath of war, the perception of a violent rupture with the past was a great temptation. It was perhaps most tempting within the European theatre itself, where Allied forces did not use the atomic bomb but where traditional bombs (used not only on Dresden, Leipzig and other major cities, but also on provincial towns with little or no strategic importance) resulted in even higher rates of civilian death. An estimated total of 600,000 German civilians died from Allied bombing. In his 1999 lectures, 'Air War and Literature', the novelist W. G. Sebald calls this scale of destruction 'unprecedented'.[50] This violence only added to the widespread impression on all sides of a truly global catastrophe. That violence on such orders of magnitude could occur, especially at the heart of European civilization itself, confronted European intellectuals with a genuine affront to their confidence in patterns of sociability and erudition to which they had committed their lives. This hyperbolic verdict on the very idea of historical meaning would later become a constant preoccupation for theorists such as Maurice Blanchot, who observed in 1980 that 'the disaster does not put me in question, but annuls the question, makes it disappear – as if along with the question, "I" too disappeared in the disaster.'[51] Other philosophers claimed that the very search for meaning in history betrayed an illicit attempt to smuggle theological concepts into human events: it was this confusion between 'redemptive history' and 'world history' that, according to Karl Löwith, had spawned the 'eschatological' evils of the twentieth century.[52]

The most discerning and courageous of Europe's intellectuals resisted the urge to see in the European catastrophe a radical departure from patterns of civilization, and they tried instead to recognize the strong lines of cultural and social continuity that connected the catastrophe to the deeper past. Despite his traditionalist attachment to German culture, Friedrich Meinecke took tentative steps in this direction that challenged his own long-enduring pride in the distinctiveness and superiority of his national tradition. Thomas Mann, too, notwithstanding his personal preoccupations with themes of disease and demonic genius, wrestled with the question of whether Nazism was somehow an expression of the German soul. Mann

---

50 W. G. Sebald, 'Air War and Literature' (Zürich Lectures), in Sebald, *On the Natural History of Destruction*, trans. Anthea Bell (New York: Modern Library, 2004), pp. 1–104 (p. 4).

51 Maurice Blanchot, *The Writing of the Disaster*, trans. Ann Smock (University of Nebraska Press, 1995), p. 28.

52 Karl Löwith, *Meaning in History: The Theological Implications of the Philosophy of History* (University of Chicago Press, 1957), p. 203.

went further than Meinecke by detecting the causes of the Nazi affliction in the very resources of spiritual 'greatness' that Meinecke believed immune: Faust's own soul became the staging ground for the battle between good and evil. But neither Meinecke nor Mann could break free of their cultural nationalism to consider the possibility that the so-called German catastrophe might not have been distinctively German at all.

Max Horkheimer and Theodor Adorno were better prepared to treat the catastrophe in a fashion unconstrained by such categories. This was due in part to their neo-Marxian view that saw in fascism a radicalization of tendencies prevalent throughout bourgeois modernity. But it was also due to their controversial and pan-historical interpretation of Nazism as the culminating catastrophe in a dialectic of enlightenment that stretched backward to the origins of human reason itself. This interpretation – more recently adopted in a less ambitious mode by the sociologist Zygmunt Bauman among others – has the great advantage of permitting comparison across a broad range of historical and social phenomena. From the historian's point of view, it has the disadvantage of suppressing historical detail to such an extent that all of modernity looks as if it were in a condition of generalized catastrophe. Radical critics of bourgeois society may find this portrait appealing even if it leaves them in the paradoxical position of condemning modernity without differentiating between its manifest failures and its unredeemed ideals. It is one of the ironies of this tale that an indiscriminate condemnation of modernity as wholesale catastrophe bears a certain resemblance to the Gnostic nightmare of a fallen world. Horkheimer and Adorno themselves always resisted this Gnostic alternative: like Hans Jonas, they recognized that even in the midst of catastrophe the idea of a benevolent God remains enormously important if only because it serves as the historical analogue to our own secular confidence in the redemptive powers of criticism. Unlike Jonas they did not believe that the catastrophe should compromise the enduring significance of utopia: if there is a concept of God after Auschwitz, perhaps its true value, even for the non-believer, lies not in the solace it may provide the anguished soul, but rather in its contrastive function as an undamaged standard by which one can measure the full extent of catastrophe.[53]

---

53 See, for example, Max Horkheimer, 'Theism and Atheism', in Eduardo Mendieta, ed., *The Frankfurt School on Religion: Key Writings by the Major Thinkers* (New York: Routledge, 2005), pp. 213–24.

24

The ghosts of war

MONICA BLACK

When we think about our relationship in the present to the past that is the Second World War, we often describe that relationship in terms of history and memory – not of haunting, and not of ghosts. What are the ghosts of war, after all, but metaphors for memories? We certainly do not give historical agency to ghosts; they do not 'really' haunt the living in an unrestful afterlife. History gets written in books, produced in films, taught in classrooms. Memories we represent in concrete, in marble and granite; we design the memorials, maintain the camps, renovate the monuments, organize and build the museums. It is we who exercise agency over history and over memories – over what gets written and remembered, and over what floats away from us – or at least, we think we do. Over ghosts we have no power to command, only to deny. Reinhart Koselleck's work on war memorials is, in a certain sense, emblematic of this attitude. For Koselleck, such memorials are built less from any compunction the dead might impose on us than they are constructed by and for the living – to meet the demands of identity and serve the evolving political exigencies of the nation state. Jean-Claude Schmitt probably sums up the sentiment of most historians when he writes that 'The dead have no existence other than that which the living imagine for them.'[1]

Not everyone is so certain. Heonik Kwon has written about the ghosts of the Vietnam War (or, as it is called in Vietnam, the American War). He describes Vietnamese society as one that regularly encounters the ghosts of war, and where such ghosts are 'very much public figures'. In the

---

[1] Jean-Claude Schmitt, *Ghosts in the Middle Ages: The Living and the Dead in Medieval Society*, trans. Teresa Lavender Fagan (University of Chicago Press, 1998); Reinhart Koselleck, 'Kriegerdenkmale als Identitätsstiftungen der Überlebenden', in Odo Marquard and Karlheinz Stierle, eds., *Identität* (Munich: Wilhelm Fink Verlag, 1979), pp. 255–76.

Vietnamese state's official ideology of heroic martyrdom and revolutionary struggle, war death tends to mean soldierly death. But in the southern and central parts of the country – where the battle lines of the Vietnam/ American War were so indistinct – the category of 'war dead' can refer to almost anyone: soldier and civilian, women and men, the very old and the very young, communists and anti-communists and people who were neither (or both). The dead of that conflict were victims of what was fought, sometimes all at once, as civil war, anti-imperialist war, anti-communist war, revolutionary war, and peoples' war – and the dead of those simultaneous conflicts were often hastily and improperly buried, sometimes in mass graves. As a result, their ghosts have become 'ontological refugees ... who are uprooted from home' and whose memory therefore remains unsettled. People in Vietnam undertake various ritual practices to acknowledge these ghosts, who, perhaps more than anything else, want to be remembered by the living and have their difficult deaths and their suffering recognized. What becomes clear in Kwon's brilliant study is how central ghosts are to local communal relationships in today's Vietnam. People seek intimacy and sympathetic relations with the displaced and wandering spirits of the dead through ritual practice, which is at the centre of religious morality and the 'ethics of memory'.[2]

The themes of Kwon's work – the long-term social consequences of violent, mass death and improperly buried dead; displaced spirits trying to finish business they cannot seem to complete without the help of the living; the rupture and disorder that war death unleashes, which may be not merely social, but indeed cosmological – these themes have been pursued by surprisingly few historians of the Second World War. Yet all of them are fundamental to the social history of that conflict. Jay Winter understood this very well with respect to the First World War. There was an explosion of interest, he showed, in spiritualism during and after the First World War, precisely because so many were missing, their fates unknown, and so many were never decently buried. People keen to communicate with the dead held séances or engaged in spirit photography. The living tirelessly sought out the dead, and contrived various means through which to learn their fates.[3]

---

2 Heonik Kwon, *Ghosts of War in Vietnam* (Cambridge University Press, 2008), pp. 17, 16, 163.
3 Jay Winter, *Sites of Memory, Sites of Mourning: The Great War in European Cultural History* (Cambridge University Press, 1995).

As powerful an impact as Winter's work has had on the cultural history of the First World War, a corresponding impact has not been felt in the historiography of the Second World War. We know very little about the ghosts of that war. It is true, of course, that we talk about 'the ghosts of war' – but in that case ghosts are a powerful metaphor for the past in the present, or death-in-life – one that conveys a sense of the enduring grief of that conflict and the seeming incompleteness of any remedy for it. To my knowledge, no historian has yet tried to unearth the ghost stories of the Second World War and explain their historical significance. Yet whether one affirms or rejects the notion of ghosts, or the idea that they have business here among us, many who survived the Second World War told afterward of being visited by the dead, who 'spoke in many voices and took many forms'.[4] The living encountered ghosts who shamed them, plagued their consciences, appeared in their dreams and their nightmares. Those who survived the war also report ghosts who reached out to save them from harm or carried out deeds of retribution on their behalf.

In southern and central Vietnam, coexisting with the ghosts of war, given their material and historical displacement and the violence of their deaths, requires the living to practise various rites of accommodation. The rituals of burial can be understood as one such rite, and in Vietnam, living with ghosts often means formally reburying the neglected remains of the dead of war who were laid to rest unfittingly or in the wrong places. Across time and in many parts of the world, rituals of proper burial have been intended precisely to keep the dead at bay, to prevent them from revisiting the living. Orthodox Christians have held that the soul's ability to proceed to heaven or hell depends on the body being laid to rest properly.[5] In Russian tradition, one might carry a dead body out through a window, rather than through a familiar door, to confuse the spirit and prevent the dead from returning.[6] In Germany, one said that windows had to be left open to allow the soul of the dead to escape to its ultimate fate; mirrors and shiny surfaces were often veiled to prevent them from seeing their reflection and compelling the living to follow them in death. Many communities have also recognized what they

---

4 Svenja Goltermann, 'The Imagination of Disaster: Death and Survival in Postwar West Germany', in Alon Confino, Paul Betts and Dirk Schumann, eds., *Between Mass Death and Individual Loss: The Place of the Dead in Twentieth-Century Germany* (New York: Berghahn, 2008), pp. 261–74 (p. 265).

5 Maria Bucur, *Heroes and Victims: Remembering War in Twentieth-Century Romania* (Bloomington: Indiana University Press, 2009), p. 54.

6 Catherine Merridale, *Night of Stone: Death and Memory in Twentieth-Century Russia* (New York: Penguin, 2000), p. 39.

see as a fitting time-line for a human life, and accepted certain kinds of death as natural and appropriate, others as unnatural and wrong. In various places and moments in time, it has been precisely when these time-lines and rules of appropriate death and leave-taking and propitiation are violated that ghosts appear.

In the Second World War, millions died 'before their time' and untold scores were committed to the earth in graves so vast and so packed with bodies – as at Babi Yar – that the earth rumbled and tried to belch them forth as they decayed. The bones of the dead were left bleaching in the sun on the vast steppes of Russia, abandoned in the rubble of bomb-collapsed buildings, vanished at the bottom of the sea, or were obliterated altogether by atomic bombs and in crematoria. When so many died so early, so violently, and when the bodies of so many millions of dead were lost forever and never buried, we would indeed have to wonder if there were no ghosts of the Second World War. But how human beings choose to engage with the dead changes over time, and so do the ghosts of war. Whether or not ghosts are 'real' in some naturalistic sense, they are 'part of social action and take on the structuring force of the patterns of social life'.[7] As the structures of social life change, so too do ghosts. Ghosts, in other words, are historical entities. What the living take to be their significance, and the ways in which ghosts are permitted (or not) to participate in social life in the ways Kwon describes – these are also historical matters. The ghosts of the Second World War were different from their earlier, First World War counterparts; they did different things, related differently to the living, and seem to have had different social purposes. In order to appreciate these differences, and the arguably still-unresolved historical consequences of the ghosts of the Second World War, we must begin not in 1945 or even 1939, but with the First World War.

★ ★ ★

[T]he drift of modern history domesticates the fantastic and normalizes the unspeakable. And the catastrophe that begins it is the Great War.[8]

In the area around Auschwitz, ghosts abounded long before the Second World War. 'For centuries, Poles, Germans, and Jews came from all over, bringing their tales and their ghosts to the marshy, birch-covered hill country at the upper reaches of the Vistula River.' There was always talk of various

---

7 Kwon, *Ghosts of War*, p. 19.
8 Paul Fussell, *The Great War and Modern Memory* (Oxford University Press, 2000), p. 74.

spectres, revenants and poltergeists; of will-o'-the-wisps that lured people into the forests; of sprites and spooky lights that materialized in the marshes foretelling death. 'Late in the evening, the maids from the Anhalt parsonage would see a pastor in his cassock – he had died long before – sitting in front of the house, reading.'[9] Silesian folk-tales described the spirit of a child, barefoot and dressed only in a white shirt, who would return once every fifty years to try and find someone with the mettle to speak to him and discover where he lay buried in unhallowed ground. The ghosts of war also haunted the landscape of Central Europe long before the catastrophes of the twentieth century. In the early 1920s, folk stories from the Thirty Years War were still told about the restless spirits of Swedish soldiers from the armies of Gustavus Adolphus who had died far from their native soil, and of how they tried to get home.[10]

What finally began to supplant stories like these, perhaps for all time, was the First World War, and even twenty years after the Great War's end, on the eve of Hitler's invasion of Poland, its spectres had not yet been dispelled. But if ghosts lingered in all the combatant countries, their significance was interpreted differently in varying contexts. In victorious Britain and France and in America, despite profound ambivalence about the human costs of the war, dead soldiers could – if nothing else – be lauded as fallen heroes who had successfully restrained tyranny, aggression and expansionism. Yet in those lands whose soldiers' deaths appeared unredeemed, and where the war's sacrifices proved far more difficult to justify, war's revenants gained a variety of new meanings. In Italy, the fascists drew 'from blood already spilled the mandate to spill new blood'. The experience of the trenches, of death, of violence, of unpredictable loss, provided the foundation for a new political religion, one which drew on a lineage of '*Calvary, resurrection, holocaust*, and *transcendence*'. This lent an aura of ancient sacredness to a thoroughly modern politics and cult of political violence.[11] George Mosse famously called the post-First World War tendency to sacralize the war – to look back on it not only as a meaningful but also hallowed event – 'the myth of the war experience'. 'The cult of the fallen soldier became a centerpiece of the religion of nationalism after the war', Mosse wrote.[12]

---

9 Stephan Wackwitz, *An Invisible Country*, trans. Stephen Lehmann (Philadelphia: Paul Dry, 2005), pp. 3–4.

10 Will-Erich Peuckert, *Schlesische Sagen* (Munich: Eugen Diederichs, 1924), pp. 133, 163.

11 Sergio Luzzatto, *The Body of Il Duce: Mussolini's Corpse and the Fortunes of Italy*, trans. Frederika Randall (New York: Metropolitan Books, 2005), pp. 3–4.

12 George Mosse, *Fallen Soldiers: Reshaping the Memory of the World Wars* (Oxford University Press, 1990), p. 7.

This was also quite true in Germany, to be sure. But there, the effects of unredeemed death would prove catastrophic. Already in the midst of the First World War, a German soldier's brief autobiographical novel had popularized the idea that the war dead were 'wanderers between two worlds'. The author, Walter Flex, insisted that death flowed easily and indissolubly together with life. Death was in this sense never final, and no more 'real' a state of existence than life. When the war ended, ruinously, in 1918, Germany found itself in the throes of revolution. Though the Kaiser abdicated, bringing an abrupt end to the imperial past, and a republic was born, this brought forth no dominant political force, let alone a single galvanizing idea or course of redemptive action, as would take shape to the east, in revolutionary Russia. In Germany, the national trauma of loss remained unredressed and it transformed society. Dealing with death on such a scale – death uncompensated by national victory – was a shattering experience that provoked anomie and nihilistic responses. Citizens across a broad political spectrum came to see themselves as a community of fate with the fallen, and the fallen as not really all that dead. Life and death were a continuity, many concluded, inseparable and equal stages of existence. The dead were not mere ghosts, confined only to a grey, twilight existence. They lived on, more alive than the living, their existence more justified, more noble, more real.

Surely these beliefs were inspired in part by the violence of First World War deaths, the lingering and unbearable horror of mechanized war at the Western Front, and the paralyzing sense of absurd futility, in the war that unfolded in Eastern Europe, of gaining territory only to lose it again almost immediately. Surely these and the desire for a better future for the dead contributed to speculations about ghosts, which abounded not only in Germany but in many parts of Europe. Unmitigated grief yielded a powerful desire for contact with the dead. Käthe Kollwitz, the German sculptor and printmaker, whose son Peter's death in battle in 1914 moved her to create some of her most searing work, never said she saw her dead son's ghost, but she did report receiving signs from him and said she could 'feel [his] being', which she said consoled her and helped her in her work. She wondered what might happen if she met Peter in the afterlife – would they recognize each other? – and wrote about the possibility of 'establishing a connection' with the dead, 'here, in this life of the senses . . . I don't care whether that is called theosophy or spiritism or mysticism', she wrote.[13] In France, Britain and

---

13 Käthe Kollwitz, *The Diary and Letters of Käthe Kollwitz*, trans. Richard Winston (Evanston, Ill.: Northwestern University Press, 1988), p. 76.

Germany – across all classes and among men and women alike – those who remained behind tried through various means to make contact with their departed loved ones.

In the post-First World War, post-civil war Soviet Union, there was a rather different story to tell. Officially, society and state abandoned the dead of the First World War, even going so far as to castigate them as soldiers of imperialism, as they turned to the millennial project of constructing the world's first socialist society. But those dead continued to irk the living with their undeniable presence, compelling communist officials to expend considerable energy trying to make people stop telling stories about ghosts and indulging other 'superstitions'. (Of course, lest we forget, the Soviet state's legitimizing symbol was the incorruptible corpse of Lenin. Legends arose early in Soviet history that Lenin would leave the mausoleum where he had been laid to rest to check on the progress of socialism. Such legends were also tinged with the anxiety that if that progress was insufficient, Lenin's unhappy ghost might take its revenge.)[14]

The ghosts of the First World War do not often seem to have intended harm, much less vengeance. In fact, some generously lent their assistance to the living. British soldiers recalled witnessing their dead comrades' ghosts; one insisted that a ghostly stretcher bearer had conveyed him to safety.[15] Wilfred Owen, the great British war poet, wrote 'Strange Meeting' about the ghost of a German soldier whom he, Owen, had killed, and who materializes and leads him down to hell – but even then, the two former enemies faced eternity together.[16] If the ghosts of the First World War dead did not intend harm, they were teachers of lessons nevertheless. In Abel Gance's film *J'accuse*, the mad soldier Jean Diaz sees members of a ghostly army who arise from their graves to learn whether the living have been worthy of their terrible sacrifices. Similar was the case of Roland Dorgelès's 1923 novel *Le Reveil des morts* (*The Awakening of the Dead*), in which 'the fallen rise again in order to bring justice and morality back into Frenchman's lives.'[17] The living dead stalked German post-war cinema as well, if in different forms and with varying meanings, in films like *Nosferatu* and *Metropolis*. Yet the French, German and Russian stories of the dead and ways of relating to their ghosts

14 Karen Petrone, *The Great War in Russian Memory* (Bloomington: Indiana University Press, 2011), pp. 42, 59.
15 Owen Davies, *The Haunted: A Social History of Ghosts* (Basingstoke: Palgrave Macmillan, 2007), p. 55.
16 Winter, *Sites of Memory*, p. 212.
17 Mosse, *Fallen Soldiers*, p. 105.

were distinctive. In Germany, the idea that the dead walked among the living was not limited to society's fringe but embraced by people in many walks of life and across the political spectrum. This formed a dramatic contrast to the French idea of soldier-survivors who are haunted by armies of spectral comrades.[18] In Russia, the dead of the First World War, whose deaths could not be redeemed, ceded space in national memory, ultimately, to those whose could: the revolutionary dead.[19]

But in many places, the problem of haunting after the First World War was almost undeniably compounded by the powerlessness of the vast majority of the bereaved to recover the bodies of their dead. How people deal with the dead is crucial to the reproduction of culture, and often to the ways societies order themselves. Rules about how to bury, when to bury and where, are saturated with condensed historical meanings, even if they are enshrined in the most banal public ordinances. After the First World War, so many were missing, never to return – their bones abandoned on the battlefield or in mine craters. The living faced difficult and disturbing questions. Who would wash the corpse and sew the shroud? How would the dead be asked for forgiveness?[20] Where was one to mourn without a grave? How could one be sure that those who perished had been buried – that is, laid to rest – at all? In springtime in the Carpathians, it became a tradition to send out parties to search for bones revealed by melting snows.[21] But questions plagued the living nonetheless: what would the dead find to eat and drink? Would they hear the lamentations made for them? Would God hear the lamentations?[22]

★ ★ ★

Then came the National Socialists. When they beat the drums of war, they claimed in part to do so on behalf of the dead. Understanding the power of political liturgy, they idealized dead soldiers as martyrs for a glorious cause of

18 Michael Geyer, 'Insurrectionary Warfare: The German Debate about a Levée en Masse in October 1918', *Journal of Modern History* 73:3 (2001), 459–527 (p. 509).
19 Petrone, *The Great War*, p. 71.
20 These are just two of the myriad Russian-Jewish customs of death described in Nathaniel Deutsch, *The Jewish Dark Continent: Life and Death in the Russian Pale of Settlement* (Cambridge, Mass.: Harvard University Press, 2011), pp. 272, 278.
21 Bucur, *Heroes and Victims*, p. 57.
22 The centrality of lamenting to interactions between the living and the dead in Transylvanian village communities is described in Gail Kligman, *The Wedding of the Dead: Ritual, Poetics, and Popular Culture in Transylvania* (Berkeley and Los Angeles: University of California Press, 1988), pp. 153, 157.

national rebirth and purification. They declared the right to speak for the dead, and claimed to appreciate better than anyone the value of their precious sacrifice. They invented and staged elaborate rituals, in part based on an imagined Germanic warrior past, to impart the solemnity and pomp deemed necessary to honour the martyrs of their own cause alongside those of Tannenberg and Langemarck. Redeeming the dead through victory in war would give meaning to their sacrifice; perhaps this would dispatch those unhappy spectres once and for all. But the ever-present dead of the First World War would also guide the hand of the living, allowing the armies of 1939 to reclaim the territories stripped from the German empire when it collapsed under the pressure of defeat in 1918 – and with those territories the neglected graves of the First World War.

In the years between 1939 and 1943, Germany's great losses in the Great War were suddenly being redeemed; the nation was powerful again, taking back through force of arms what many Germans felt had been so ignominiously and illegitimately lost more than two decades before. Hitler gave a speech in 1942 in which he 'announced that "1918" was overcome'.[23] In a spirit of triumphal megalomania, regime-approved poets wrote extravagant verse about the blood of the dead soaking eastern battlefields and transforming the soil of a new empire. Germany's artists and architects, intoxicated by this idea, made plans to build monumental temples for the fallen called *Totenburgen* – vast, fortress-like structures under which the dead were to be buried in massive crypts. *Totenburgen* were designed very purposefully to be placed at the borders of the Reich, from Norway to North Africa, where they would mark out the territory of a new Germany with the nation's dead, thus reinforcing a perceived connection between German blood and German soil.[24] *Totenburgen* were intended not only to spell out the boundaries of a new German empire within a new Europe, but to reconfigure space itself. They became a symbolic instrument of colonization, redrawing the maps as Germany's armies advanced across Eastern Europe.

This reconstruction of space and reclaiming of the past had its counterpart in the massive killing and ethnic cleansing operations in Poland, the Soviet Union and Yugoslavia, as German forces set out to 'purify' newly conquered territory by extinguishing the lives of those who had no place in their new

---

23 Thomas Kühne, 'Todesraum: War, Peace, and the Experience of Mass Death, 1914–1945', in Helmut Walser Smith, ed., *The Oxford Handbook of Modern German History* (Oxford University Press, 2011), pp. 527–47 (p. 528).

24 Wolfgang Schäche, 'Die Totenburgen des Nationalsozialismus', *Arch+71* (October 1983), 72–5 (p. 72).

order. The blood of the war dead, the Nazis held, would remake the territories conquered in the east as *Heimat*, or homeland, a culturally and even spiritually defined space. But this reconfiguration of space could not be imagined without the simultaneous elimination of 'dangers' – pre-eminently the Jews.

Nazi mass murder did not stop even when the tide turned against Germany. In fact, in the regime's twilight, as the front shifted back toward the west, the killing became more frenzied, more nihilistic, more desperate. Jews, along with victims of dozens of other communities, nationalities, ethnicities and religions, political prisoners, homosexuals, disabled persons and many others, were massacred, gassed in huge groups, forced without mercy on to the road in death marches. At this point in the war, the killing was no longer 'racial' or 'ethnic' in nature, but the furious response of a system in its own death throes, enduring its own catastrophic implosion, and consuming whatever lay in its wake.[25]

Driven out or forced otherwise to abandon their villages and towns in eastern Prussia, Silesia, the Sudetenland and elsewhere in Eastern Europe at the end of the war, Germans left behind their homes and their shops, and they left behind their cemeteries. The loss of territory in Eastern Europe meant losing German dead yet again, and no war would redeem the losses this time. The cult of the living dead that had so animated German politics and culture died, like Nazism, an ignominious death. In what would become the Federal Republic of Germany, the war dead would no longer be publicly lionized, though private organizations formed to care for their graves continued to write and speak of their precious and 'holy' sacrifice throughout the 1950s. Young West German pupils continued to be taken on organized trips to visit war memorials and care for war graves – mostly those from the First World War in Belgium and France, since these could still be reached despite the Cold War division of Germany and of Europe. In the Federal Republic, there was a legal mandate to maintain 'war graves' in perpetuity. But after a war waged almost equally against armies and civilians – what was a war grave? A 1952 law – the Law for the Maintenance of the Graves of Victims of War and Tyranny – protected the graves not only of victims of the Holocaust, the civilian dead of the bombing war, and soldiers, but even members of the SS, as the world learned when US President Ronald Reagan visited a Bitburg cemetery in 1985.

---

25 Daniel Blatman, *The Death Marches: The Final Phase of Nazi Genocide* (Cambridge, Mass.: Harvard University Press, 2011).

In East Germany, the picture was similar and very different. In the communist state, public ceremonial and remembrance focused not on German dead – who could not be mourned publicly, certainly not as heroes. Such energies were instead directed toward glorifying the dead of East Germany's great benefactor and liberator from fascism, the Soviet Union. Under communism, German war cemeteries and war graves, as sites of public commemoration, were anathema. But privately, around the Seelow Heights or the village of Halbe, where the battle had been brought to the very doorsteps of local inhabitants, families buried their dead at home, and kept their graves, quietly, as personal memorials.[26]

* * *

The very circumstances of Second World War deaths – which, in many cases, were utterly unprecedented in the whole of human experience – shaped new relationships between the living and the dead after 1945. Seventy years later, we still grope in the dark to imagine death that comes accompanied by a 'noiseless flash' – 'whiter than any white' – and an explosion that levels everything in sight and has the power to vaporize a human body.[27] We write books and deliver academic lectures and yet remain speechless, unable still fully to fathom or explain camps designed for the sole purpose of murder, a 'world of death and phantoms', as Primo Levi wrote.[28] Hiroshima and the Holocaust are events of such singularity that they are difficult to compare to anything else, including one another, certainly. But perhaps they were united in one respect: that they involved unprecedented forms of killing and dying that fused death and life in ways that may be novel in all of human history.

One survivor of the USA's atomic bombing of Japan recalled seeing people 'blackened by burns', with no hair left and their skin hanging off their bodies. '[W]herever I walked I met these people ... I can still picture them in my mind – like walking ghosts ... They didn't look like people of this world.'[29] An aspect of the 'special lexicon of the bombs', John Dower writes, was the

---

26 Alf Lüdtke, 'Histories of Mourning: Flowers and Stones for the War Dead, Confusion for the Living – Vignettes from East and West Germany', in Gerald Sider and Gavin Smith, eds., *Between History and Histories: The Making of Silences and Commemorations* (University of Toronto Press, 1997), pp. 149–79.

27 John Hersey, *Hiroshima* (New York: Vintage, 1989), pp. 8, 10.

28 Primo Levi, *Survival in Auschwitz* (New York: Touchstone, 1996), p. 171.

29 Cited in Robert Jay Lifton, 'On Death and Death Symbolism: The Hiroshima Disaster', *The American Scholar* 34:2 (1965), 257–72 (p. 259).

'procession of ghosts': when the bombs exploded, people put their hands and forearms up over their faces in an instinctively protective gesture. This burned their arms terribly; in order to prevent their burned and exposed flesh from sticking and thus damaging it further, they walked along with their hands and arms stretched out before them. They became, in the words of one contemporary, the '"living dead" – humans . . . made monstrous'.[30]

In the middle of the 1960s, Robert Jay Lifton wrote of the 'enduring taint' of death among these survivors, who developed a unique identity as *hibakusha*. This taint was felt to have attached itself not only to *hibakusha* themselves, but even to their unborn children: it extended 'not only to one's entire psychobiological organism, but to one's posterity'. In this sense, *hibakusha* felt that their encounter with death was permanent, 'epidemic-like', and 'infinitely transmissible'. They carried death within them. *Hibakusha* not only lived metaphorically 'in the shadow of death', but symbolically took on the 'identity of the dead', relating to them so completely that they 'incorporated [them] into their own beings'.[31]

Some of those who survived the Holocaust also lived what has been characterized as a 'suspended existence', hovering somewhere between death and life, or felt that they had died but 'no one [could] see it'.[32] The Yiddish poet Kadya Molodowsky wrote of 'Shadows com[ing] at night to invite me to Dead Sabbath / Their hands pressed, / Folded on spines – / In order not to touch the impure world, / In order to observe the dead Sabbath / That has burned up the week, / This life, / And all the holidays.'[33]

Survivors of the Shoah described feeling that 'they carr[ied] the dead within them, an unbearable burden of guilt and remembrance'.[34] That burden also included the intensely wounding knowledge that there was no grave to keep. Ruth Klüger, who survived Auschwitz and other camps, but whose father and brother did not, writes, 'Where there is no grave, we are condemned to go on mourning.'[35] This is not 'just' a problem of memory or grief. It is arguably similar to the idea that Kwon expresses about the ghosts

---

30 John Dower, 'Ground Zero 1945: Pictures by Atomic Bomb Survivors' (http://ocw.mit.edu/ans7870/21f/21f.027/groundzero1945/gz_essay01.html).

31 Lifton, 'On Death', pp. 264–5.

32 Colin Davis, *Haunted Subjects: Deconstruction, Psychoanalysis, and the Return of the Dead* (Basingstoke: Palgrave Macmillan, 2007), p. 101.

33 Kadya Molodowsky, 'Dead Sabbath', in *Paper Bridges: Selected Poems of Kadya Molodowsky*, trans. Kathryn Hellerstein (Detroit: Wayne State University Press, 1999), p. 397.

34 Christopher Clausen, 'Dialogues with the Dead', *The American Scholar* 61:2 (1992), 177–84 (p. 183).

35 Ruth Klüger, *Still Alive: A Holocaust Girlhood Remembered* (New York: Feminist Press, 2001), p. 80.

of war in Vietnam: that the very displacement of the dead, the horrific circumstances of their deaths, and the forever unresolved question of the fate of their bodies make it impossible to settle their memory, to settle their ghosts. The unresolved or unredeemed ghost has featured in literary tradition since antiquity, its appearance serving as 'the sign of a disturbance in the symbolic, moral, or epistemological order'.[36] Ghosts are very much present in Klüger's work; she in fact writes that ghosts might be the only way to describe the Jewish catastrophe, because 'a ghost is something unresolved, particularly a violated taboo, an unremedied crime.'[37] Perhaps it was in part for just such reasons that the *landsmanshaftn*, Jewish associations of survivors from various localities, published memorial books after the war that were meant implicitly to act as gravestones.[38] Molodowsky, too, referred to her 1946 book *Only King David Remained* as a book of '*khurbm-lider* (holocaust/destruction poems)' – a 'tombstone for a life that had vanished'.[39]

★ ★ ★

Among Germans, the taint of death clung to those who survived the war in a very different way. It is true that this taint remained long unacknowledged by some, who largely focused on their own misery, and their own losses, rather than on the lives brutally terminated by Germany's war machine and in its death camps. Many Germans felt their own victimization first and last. But others who came of age in the shadow of Auschwitz responded differently, feeling powerfully the existential curse of genocide.[40]

There were certainly also those Germans who retained powerful traditions of dealing with ghosts – particularly vengeful ghosts, as it happens – after 1945. We know about them because Germans told about them, repeated rumours about their activities, and passed those rumours from person to person. Later, the rumours were transcribed by a folklorist, and made their way into an archive in Freiburg where they sit uneasily today, in boxes and folders and on bookshelves. The Germans who told these ghost stories were

36 Davis, *Haunted Subjects*, p. 2.
37 This is my translation of the German original, quoted in Catherine Smale, '"Ungelöste Gespenster?" Ghosts in Ruth Klüger's Autobiographical Project', *Modern Language Review* 104:3 (2009), 777–89 (p. 778).
38 Gabriel N. Finder, 'Yizkor! Commemoration of the Dead by Jewish Displaced Persons in Postwar Germany', in Confino, Betts, and Schumann, eds., *Between Mass Death*, pp. 232–57 (p. 244).
39 Molodowsky quoted in Kathryn Hellerstein, 'Introduction', in *Paper Bridges*, p. 42.
40 A. Dirk Moses, *German Intellectuals and the Nazi Past* (Cambridge University Press, 2009).

the former inhabitants of various centuries-old German-speaking enclaves across the map of Eastern Europe, many of them expelled from those communities after the war. They described leaving the ghosts of war behind, but not in the sense of forgetting them. Instead, they said, they had sought to stir the ghosts of war to plague those who now took up residence in their former homes and who came to settle in their former towns. Germans driven out of their communities in the Bohemian Forest left salt in the form of crosses on the floorboards of their deserted homes to summon spirits to vex the new settlers. Forced to abandon the graves of their long-dead kin, expelled Germans told stories of 'Czechs' haunted by their deceased families' spirits. These Czechs became so fearful of vengeful German ghosts, expellees said, that they refused to be buried anywhere but their 'own' homelands. A story went around among former Sudeten Germans that no Czech would live in their now-haunted villages. Constantly harassed by ghosts, the new settlers were said to have fled to the country's interior, forcing the Czechoslovak government to raze the Germans' former villages.[41] Expellees also claimed to receive intelligence that their former Czech neighbours had abandoned misappropriated German homes for fear they were bewitched. 'Czechs' reported seeing 'figures moving' in their gardens, which they 'believed to be [dead] Germans'.[42]

A story told by an erstwhile trackman on the Katowice railway named Josef K., suggested that the living feared the tales the dead might tell. Women raped and killed by Red Army soldiers ('*Bolschewiki*') had their 'tongues cut out', Josef K. reported, 'so that they could not tell, at the Last Judgment, who had murdered them'. Anticipating this, it was said, one fourteen-year old victim made a 'red Soviet star' in the snow beside where she lay dying. Even without this sign in blood, Josef K. said, 'everyone would have known that the murderers were soldiers. But, the people said, even the blood of the dead shows it. And the Lord God marks it.'[43]

Sources like these, at least in the German context, have remained largely untouched by historians until quite recently. Yet we are beginning to look, in creative ways, for the traces of unquiet spirits. On the basis of post-war West German medical files, Svenja Goltermann has written about how the dead haunted the dreams and waking lives of those who had experienced and

41 These and many similar stories can be located in the archives of the Johannes-Künzig-Institut für ostdeutsche Volkskunde (JKI), Karasek Collection (SK), in the files labelled 'Neue Sagenbildung' (NS).
42 JKI/SK/NS, 04/01–20.
43 JKI/SK/NS, 04/03–142.

committed acts of wartime violence.[44] In the archives of the Institute for the Frontier Areas of Psychology and Mental Health (IGPP) in Freiburg, there is an extraordinary trove of letters describing many kinds of uncanny experiences, including ghost stories and accounts of dreams in which the dead appeared to the living. In one such letter, Ilse Fucke-Michels, one of the sisters of Eva Braun, described a dream she had on the night of 29 April 1945. She attended a dinner in fancy dress; across the table, under the lamplight, sat Adolf Hitler and her sister Eva, who said, 'Don't be angry, this is my last party, everything is going to be fine!' As Ilse later learned, it was on that night that the pair had committed suicide.[45] Other spectres appeared in broad daylight. A man described trimming hedges one morning in his Upper Bavarian village when he was alerted by his dog to a figure standing amidst some trees. It was the man's old friend, Peter, in full-dress officer's uniform. He seemed relaxed and cheerful. The man stuck out his hand and called to Peter; but as he went to touch him, he grasped nothing but air. Bitterly disappointed, the man noted the precise time and date, only to learn later that it was just then that his friend had died.[46]

According to various folkloric traditions, such figures are not, properly speaking, ghosts, but wraiths: that is, they are apparitions of persons who have only very recently died or are on the verge of death.[47] One woman in Britain reported that a friend had lost his mother during the war. Shortly after, he had been evacuated to the countryside and billeted in a farmhouse. After dozing off one night, he awakened to see a 'phosphorescent glow beside his bed. This gradually materialized in the form of his mother, bending over him, smiling.' By the time he lit a candle, she was gone. This story comes from a report on 'Death and the Supernatural' from the Mass-Observation project, whose volunteers collected information on every aspect of daily life in Britain from the late 1930s through the mid-1960s. The volunteer who wrote the report noted that the story of the glow that turned into the man's dead mother was the most frequent kind of ghost people reported seeing:

---

44 Svenja Goltermann, *Die Gesellschaft der Überlebenden. Deutsche Kriegsheimkehrer und ihre Gewalterfahrungen im Zweiten Weltkrieg* (Munich: Deutsche Verlags-Anstalt, 2009).
45 IGPP, Sannwald Sammlung, F.-J. Letter from Ilse F.-M., undated.
46 Hans Bender, *Verborgene Wirklichkeit. Parapsychologie und Grenzgebiete der Psychologie* (2nd edn, Freiburg: Walter-Verlag Olten, 1973), pp. 61–2.
47 Linda-May Ballard, 'Before Death and Beyond: Death and Ghost Traditions with Particular Reference to Ulster', in Hilda R. Ellis Davidson and W. M. S. Russell, eds., *The Folklore of Ghosts* (Cambridge: The Folklore Society, 1980), p. 32.

This type of apparition, usually causing no fear and appearing in a quite normal form is the sort of 'ghost' in which people seem to place the most credence. There are practically no accounts of ghosts in terrifying circumstances, head in hands or with clanking chains. The floating white apparition is described quite frequently ... but it is the apparition or presence in a normal form, appearing or making itself felt at or not long after the person's death which is both the most frequent and the least suspect to those giving the accounts.[48]

Ghosts also appeared to people years after the war in a variety of forms. A German woman recalled walking down a city street in 1947 and encountering a blind man, possibly a war veteran, whose hands were both missing, accompanied by a woman. Sometime after passing the pair, she felt what she described as a 'light blow', after which she realized that the whole street she was walking on was suddenly 'animated by shadowy human forms moving about individually and in clusters About half as high as the buildings,' this woman recalled, 'floated human-sized beings with great grey wings.' Later, she felt such a pair of wings above her, quite close by. This experience, she felt, had given her 'a glimpse into an otherwise unseeable world', and she wondered whether somehow what she had experienced had been 'transmitted' to her by the blind man.[49]

Stories about ghost encounters among Germans and Britons after the Second World War often feature ghosts who appeared once and then departed; sometimes, they disclosed a message, and then left, not to return again. As the Mass-Observation reporter noted, these spirits looked like the people they had been in life, and were not generally terrifying or even alarming to the living. In fact, they may have been a source of comfort. In these stories, the dead take their leave of this world in peace. To be sure, there are other, quite different, examples – those from Silesia or the Sudetenland for example – in which ghosts were presumed to be doing their disruptive work on behalf of communities to which they had belonged in life, even in the absence of those communities. In the psychiatric files Goltermann has worked with, the living sometimes had the sense that the dead pursued them, shaming them, terrorizing them, denouncing them. But it is not altogether clear that in the years after 1945 people saw ghosts as being in need of something that the living could supply. A number of the examples

---

48 Mass-Observation Archive, University of Sussex, FR 1315, 'Death and the Supernatural', June 1942, p. 30.
49 IGPP Sannwald Sammlung, F.-J. Letter from Lotte F., 7 July 1954.

considered here suggest that the ghosts of the Second World War appeared to the living in order to depart – precisely not to remain ghosts. This seems rather a striking difference from the situation after the First World War, when whole societies became obsessed with the living dead and how to propitiate them and to make themselves worthy of their mortal sacrifices.

Not only do the ghosts of the Second World War not seem to have come back to judge the living *en masse* the way First World War ghosts did, survivors after 1945 also do not seem to have encountered ghosts who wanted to stick around and take up a particular local role, as Kwon describes in today's Vietnam. Different times and places call for different ghosts. Alexander Etkind offers a very memorable example of this when he describes a 500-rouble banknote in today's Russia. It bears an image of Solovetsky Monastery with wooden pyramids rather than onion domes on top. The pyramids were built when the monastery was a camp, and the camp a part of the Gulag, by its prisoners. 'Probably the most realistic, down-to-earth way to understand this amazing banknote is to see it as a ghostly apparition', he writes, one that Russians carry in their wallets and use to buy things, pay bills. 'The picture on the banknote,' he continues, 'reminds those who are in the know about a hidden secret of the past – a specialty of ghosts. This is probably how ghosts come to us these days, to haunt the public sphere and marketplace rather than aristocratic manors and deserted graveyards.'[50]

If we do not see, after the Second World War, the same widespread efflorescence of spiritualism that Winter described after the First World War – an active seeking out of the dead that transcended social status, gender and nationality – this should not be taken as 'evidence' that people after the Second World War did not live with or communicate with ghosts. Spiritualism as a method may not have had the same currency after 1945 that it had before, but we do know that clairvoyants were extremely popular in the years after the Second World War as sources of knowledge about the fate of the dead. And clearly – as in the instance of the man trimming his hedges, the man who saw his dead mother in the farmhouse, or the woman who saw a whole street filled with great-winged ghosts – people took care to remember their encounters, to write them down, to tell them to others, and to try and understand what they meant. To understand the ghosts of the Second World War, and their social purpose and meaning better, we need actively to seek out more stories like these. But we need also to look in

50 Alexander Etkind, *Warped Mourning: Stories of the Undead in the Land of the Unburied* (Stanford University Press, 2013), pp. 5–7.

different places. Rather than searching for Victorian ghosts in haunted houses with clanking chains, we need to scour novels, art, the internet, banknotes.

* * *

Since the Second World War, there have been a variety of attempts to understand the impact of death on contemporary societies in the broadest (and often rather universalizing) sense. This was even true in the 1950s and 1960s – an era long held to be marked by a generalized 'denial of death'. In 1965, Briton Geoffrey Gorer argued that death had become as unspeakable in polite company as pornography; French historian Philippe Ariès, following Gorer, rejected a modernity in which mourning had been declared indecent. Yet this same moment, just a generation removed from the killing fields of the Second World War, saw the rise of thanatology, following on the heels of such publications as the American Herman Feifel's *The Meaning of Death* in 1959 and, ten years later, the Swiss Elizabeth Kübler-Ross's book, *On Death and Dying*. Ghosts – among other phenomena often classified as 'paranormal' – became the subject of considerable scientific research in West Germany and elsewhere in this same period. In the Federal Republic and in Western Europe generally, the doyen of parapsychology was psychologist Hans Bender (1907–1991). Bender, who held the chair in parapsychology at the Albert-Ludwigs University in Freiburg – the first of its kind in any German academic institution – was instrumental in establishing the aforementioned Institute for the Frontier Areas of Psychology and Mental Health and was also to have an enormously successful media career in the Federal Republic.[51] In the late 1960s, in a series of articles in the tabloid *BILD* on such topics as dream interpretation, precognition, clairvoyance, astrology, telepathy and encounters with ghosts, Bender solicited stories from the public about their own experiences of such phenomena. Some of the ghost encounters described above came from those thousands of letters that deluged Bender's offices in the 1950s and 1960s and after.

We might ask ourselves why this generation of scholars in a variety of fields, who lived as mature adults through the Second World War era – Ariès, Bender, Feifel and Gorer were all born between 1905 and 1916; Kübler-Ross is a bit of an outlier, having been born in 1926 – suddenly became interested in the midst of their own middle age in the question of what it

---

51 Anna Lux, 'On All Channels: Hans Bender, the Supernatural, and the Mass Media', in Monica Black and Eric Kurlander, eds., *Revisiting the 'Nazi Occult': Histories, Realities, Legacies* (forthcoming).

means to die, how we die, what afterlife might be like, and in the history of death. Some theorized at the time that the increasing medicalization and technologization of death or the ecological crises that increasingly engulfed the planet were responsible for this apparently new interest. Others looked to World War Three, which loomed large in the Cold War imagination with the threat of erasing humanity altogether. Ghosts may proliferate 'in response to the catastrophes of the past', or 'in anticipation of the catastrophes of the future'.[52]

And certainly, the ghosts of war continue to flourish in popular culture. In 2012, under the headline 'Does This Image Show the Ghosts of WWII Prisoners on Their Death March?', the Daily Mail published a picture taken by a retired army officer along the route of the 1945 Sandakan death marches. In it, the figures of ghostly soldiers seemed to appear.[53] An online archive of British Second World War memories sponsored by the BBC contains accounts of wartime ghosts.[54] Readers have posted numerous ghost stories of the 'I have heard tell' variety to the online Axis History Forum.[55] In 2012, Igor Ostachowicz's widely discussed novel, Noc żywych żydów ('Night of the Living Jews') was published, which imagines Warsaw as a giant graveyard with Jewish zombies emerging from the sewers. A recent episode of a Polish ghost-hunter television show was called 'Przeklęte rewiry Tajemnice Muranowa' ('Cursed Districts, the Secrets of Muranów'). Muranów district was the location of the Warsaw Ghetto and is the home of the new Museum of the History of Polish Jews.[56]

Katherine Verdery has explained the critical political role played by the dead of the Second World War in Yugoslavia and its successor states – 'corpses without number, lying in limestone caves, mass graves, and other sites all across the landscape'. These dead, she explains, were mobilized in an effort to rewrite the history of the Second World War during the wars that broke Yugoslavia apart. Under the Tito regime, all public memory of the specific circumstances of Second World War deaths – massacres committed

52 Etkind, Warped Mourning, p. 217.
53 Tony Whitfield, 'Does This Image Show the Ghosts of WWII Prisoners on Their Death March?' Daily Mail, online edition, 27 September 2012 (www.dailymail.co.uk/news/article-2209468/Does-image-ghosts-WWII-prisoners-death-march-Former-Army-Officer-takes-haunting-image-route-took.html).
54 Alan French, 'The White Figure: A True Wartime Ghost Story', BBC People's War Campaign, Remembering World War Two, 14 October 2004 (www.bbc.co.uk/history/ww2peopleswar/stories/71/a3972071.shtml).
55 Axis History Forum discussion, 'Ghost Stories from WWII' (http://forum.axishistory.com/viewtopic.php%3Ff=34&t=75365).
56 Personal communication, Dan Magilow.

by various groups, but the central perpetrators of which were often the Croatian Ustaša – had been erased. Nor was any mention made of the killings perpetrated by communist partisans. But people in Yugoslavia remembered: they remembered the massacres, who did them, and where the dead lay buried. Verdery writes, 'The silencing of this grim subject [of wartime atrocities and massacres] meant that none of the murders could be avenged (very important, in this area), and so neither the souls of these dead nor the minds of those close to them could rest in peace.' In the 1980s, nationalists found that they could inflame ethnic tensions to powerful political effect, and broadcast pictures on television of bodies and bones being recovered from mass graves where they had been so dishonourably dumped in the darkest days of the 1940s.[57] The reburial of these dead in one's 'own' soil after months-long exhumations became part of establishing the distinct territories of new Bosnian, Croatian and Serbian states.

Today, the politics of Second World War death and memory continue to have dramatically different valences all over the world. In Germany, the 'graves law' (*Gräbergesetz*), as it is colloquially known, is if anything even more capacious than in 1952. It now protects the graves of those who died as victims of communist tyranny and the Germans expelled from Eastern Europe in 1945 and after. Yet while those graves are maintained in perpetuity, in most cemeteries, they occupy the outermost edges, physically and symbolically. It is not on the memory of 'German war dead' that contemporary German identity and democracy are built. Opinions may differ about what Peter Eisenman's Memorial to the Murdered Jews of Europe is asking us to remember (or forget), but it is this highly stylized, nearly five-acre cemetery of undulating slate-grey concrete coffins that stands at the centre of Berlin's bustling life. Meanwhile, Russians, whose own memorial culture permits little open mourning for the dead of Stalin's tyranny and the Gulag, can and do commune with the graves of Soviet Second World War dead in Germany, in Berlin, where they died and were buried in enormous numbers. Russian families gather today in Treptow Park, on the grounds of the enormous and imposing war memorial there, for reunions, even weddings. In Japan, the war dead remain central to public life, and the struggle over their memory and meaning continues – particularly with respect to Yasukuni Shrine, where the spirits of the war dead, including war criminals, are enshrined. While the Japanese government has 'embraced the politics of apology' – a ritual that has

---

57 Katherine Verdery, *The Political Lives of Dead Bodies: Reburial and Postsocialist Change* (New York: Columbia University Press, 1999), pp. 99–100.

become central to democracies around the globe over the decades since 1945 – conflicting experiences and memories of the war and wartime death, represented, often, by a great variety of political interest groups, complicate official recognition of Japanese responsibility for wartime atrocities.[58] At a more local and less politicized level, family members continue to care for the souls of their dead, and to 'visit and talk' with their spirits, at Yasukuni. They donate cherry trees, whose blossoms have multi-layered meanings 'embedded ... in the processes of life, death, and rebirth' to commemorate their dead loved ones.[59]

Surely we do not imagine that we undertake the commemoration and burial and remembrance of the dead of war solely for ourselves, as Koselleck would have it; it is clear that we need the dead, but perhaps some of the dead also have a need to remain with us and under our care. The ghosts of some wars appear to be needier than others, for reasons that remain unclear and require further contemplation. Avery Gordon writes about the 'seething presence' in contemporary society of the inexplicable yet undeniable traces that past violence has left on this world – producing what Toni Morrison calls 'invisible things that are not necessarily not-there'.[60] For Gordon, leaving ghosts out of the story of the modern world – as many scholars would insist we do – makes it hard to make sense of some things. 'We do not usually experience things, nor are affects produced, in the rational and objective ways our terms tend to portray them.' To claim that ghosts have no life other than the ones we give them is a 'representational mistake' that endangers an accurate retelling of the past and our relationship to and embeddedness in it.[61] Recognizing the presence of ghosts in our time, in our world, in the variety of forms they take must remain an open-ended process. Even if we could bury them all properly, with the greatest respect and care, performing all the rituals of propitiation we can imagine, we could never lay the ghosts of war 'to rest'. Perhaps instead we might learn to acknowledge and live with them, productively, imaginatively, unpredictably.[62]

58 Franziska Seraphim, *War Memory and Social Politics in Japan, 1945–2005* (Cambridge, Mass.: Harvard University Press, 2006), pp. 322–3.
59 Emiko Ohnuki-Tierney, *Kamikaze, Cherry Blossoms, and Nationalisms: The Militarization of Aesthetics in Japanese History* (University of Chicago Press, 2002), pp. 185, 301.
60 Toni Morrison quoted in Avery Gordon, *Ghostly Matters: Haunting and the Sociological Imagination* (Minneapolis and London: University of Minnesota Press, 2008), p. 17.
61 Gordon, *Ghostly Matters*, p. 22.
62 Etkind, *Warped Mourning*, p. 219.

25

Popular memory, popular culture

The war in the post-war world

LUCY NOAKES

On 7 July 2005 suicide bombers exploded four bombs across the London transport network, killing fifty-two and injuring many more. That day fell just before a long Bank Holiday weekend, designed by the British government to act as a commemoration of the sixtieth anniversary of the end of the Second World War. This confluence of dates was not lost on the British press, nor indeed on the many public figures who rushed to compare the bombings of 2005 with the Second World War bombing of London. Sir Ian Blair, Metropolitan Police Commissioner, commented that 'if London can survive the Blitz, then it can survive four miserable events like this' while the *Daily Mirror* exhorted its readers to 'adopt the famous Blitz spirit'.[1] Britain was not alone in drawing on the Second World War to frame the contemporary. In his speech marking the sixtieth anniversary of the Japanese assault on Pearl Harbor, President George W. Bush linked the 'good' war of the mid-twentieth century with the 'war on terror' of the twenty-first, noting that America's wartime role as 'freedom's defender ... continues to this hour'.[2] Similarly, de Gaulle drew on the cultural memory of the Free French, in support of the French forces during the Algerian War of Independence (1954–62), while British politicians invoked the memory of the Second World War as being fought against oppression and for the rights of small nations, in support of the Falklands/Malvinas War of 1982, and the first Gulf War of 1991.[3] Speaking at a military parade in Moscow celebrating the sixty-seventh anniversary of the defeat of Nazi Germany, President Putin claimed that Russia has 'a great moral right' to 'strengthen security' in the contemporary

---

1 *Daily Express*, 9 July 2005; *Daily Mirror*, 9 July 2005.
2 Transcript of remarks by President Bush on USS *Enterprise*, 7 December 2001 (www. freerepublic.com/focus/fr/585968/posts).
3 Lucy Noakes, *War and the British: Gender and National Identity, 1939–1991*. (London: I. B. Tauris, 1998), pp. 108–15.

world as 'it was our country that bore the brunt of the Nazi attack . . . routed the enemy and liberated the world's peoples.'[4] In Germany memories of the Allied bombing of German cities have been mobilized by both the far right and by peace protesters.[5] These multivalent mobilizations of the Second World War as a means of framing more recent conflicts, grow out of the widespread and deep-rooted nature of cultural memories of the war. This chapter explores just some of the ways in which the war continues to be visible both transnationally and in different national communities, all of which have drawn on wartime memories in the construction and contest-ation of post-war identities.

Of course no two nations 'remember' the war in the same way; while some may have widespread agreement about the meaning and memory of the war years, in others 'memory wars' have replaced the war itself as a site of conflict. The German *Historikerstreit* (historians' quarrel) of the 1980s is perhaps the best-known example of these memory wars, but one could also consider the problematic memory of the wartime Vichy state in post-war France, or the protests of ethnic Russians when the Estonian government removed a memorial to the Red Army in 2007.[6] Similarly, the 2014 uprising in the Ukraine was marked by accusations of 'fascism' as the ultra-nationalist minority celebrated the memory of the Nazi collaborator Stepan Bandera and Putin cast himself as the defender of the nation's Jewish community.[7] Conflicts over the memory of the war are not restricted to Europe: the annual visit of Japanese Prime Minister Koizumi to the Yasukuni Shrine, dedicated to all Japanese war dead, including convicted war criminals, between 2001 and 2006 strengthened the belief among many that Japan has not fully acknowledged its wartime history.[8] Tensions over the contested Diaoyu/Senkaku Islands have reinvigorated a sense in China that Japan has never atoned for war crimes, in turn reminding us that the European periodization of the war excludes the actions of the Japanese, and the death of many thousands of Chinese, between 1937 and 1939.[9] Even where there is

---

4 President Putin, Moscow speech, 9 May 2012 (http://eng.kremlin.ru/transcripts/3780).
5 Andreas Huyssen, 'Air War Legacies: From Dresden to Baghdad', *New German Critique* 90 (2003), 163–76.
6 Richard Evans, *In Hitler's Shadow: West German Historians and the Attempt to Escape from the Nazi Past* (London: I. B. Tauris, 1989); Henri Rousso, *The Vichy Syndrome: History and Memory in France since 1944*, trans. Arthur Goldhammer (Cambridge, Mass.: Harvard University Press, 1991); http://news.bbc.co.uk/1/hi/world/europe/6599937.stm.
7 *The Guardian*, 8 March 2014.
8 Philip Seaton, *Japan's Contested War Memories: The 'Memory Rifts' in Historical Conscious-ness of World War II* (Abingdon: Routledge, 2007), p. 82.
9 *Daily Telegraph*, 28 February 2014.

widespread agreement about the meaning and memory of the war, forms of commemoration and remembrance can be controversial. The 2004 dedication of the National World War II Memorial in Washington, DC was seen by its supporters as 'an important symbol of national unity' and by its detractors as 'a triumphal act of hubris in stone and bronze', indicating more about early twenty-first century 'American imperialism' than it did about the 'greatest generation' and the 'good war'.[10]

It is, however, in Europe that the historical memory of the Second World War provided the most powerful 'foundational myths' for the post-war period. As satellite states of the USSR 'agreed' that their populations had united under the leadership of communist partisans during the war years, welcoming the Soviet Union as a liberator, Western Europe reimagined West Germany as an essential ally in the Cold War, a process of revisionism that entailed the final abandonment of any large-scale process of de-Nazification. With the end of the Cold War these foundational myths came under pressure and the decades since have seen the 'unravelling' of many 'official' memories of the war in Europe.[11] This destabilization opened up space for marginalized and oppositional memories of the conflict to find a wider audience. In Germany and Britain memories of the Allied area bombing campaign became increasingly visible. The Holocaust found a new centrality in both East and West Europe as the foundations of existing narratives of the war, and the power alliances of the post-war period, began to crumble in the new world order. In Judt's striking phrase, the Holocaust became the 'entry ticket' to Europe, enshrined in numerous sites of memory, symbolizing the centrality of the post-war discourse of human rights to the contemporary European Union.[12] Holocaust memories, themselves contested, became preserved in European national and international histories in these years in a manner that bears comparison with the creation of Yad Vashem in 1953 Israel, where it functioned as both a memorial and as a focus for a shared national identity in a nation under construction. Although the end of the Cold War was by no means the only cause of these memory shifts, the swift collapse of Soviet communism, the re-emergence of old nationalisms, and the reunification of Germany

---

10 Elizabeth Doss, 'War, Memory and the Public Mediation of Affect: The National World War II Memorial and American Imperialism', *Memory Studies* 1:2 (2008), 227–50.

11 Tony Judt, 'The Past is Another Country: Myth and Memory in Post-War Europe', *Daedalus* 121:4 (1992), 83–118 (p. 85).

12 Tony Judt, *Postwar: A History of Europe since 1945* (London: Heinemann, 2005), p. 803.

provided both the spark and the context for shifting paradigms of memory at the end of the twentieth century.

These memories of the Second World War have to be both transmitted and agreed at a cultural, as well as a political, level. The 'official memories' that Judt outlines, seen in national ceremonies of commemoration, national museums and officially authorized histories have to be widely agreed; their narratives have to be recognizable to the wider community. This process is, of course, more apparent in 'open', pluralistic societies than in 'closed', 'totalitarian' states, but even in societies such as the USSR, official memories can only muffle oppositional ones, never completely silence them. Popular culture provides a site for the articulation, circulation and reception of memory, acting as a space where memories can be made visible, agreed, opposed and contested. This space, however, is not neutral. The processes by which memories become visible in popular culture are shaped by their political context and by wider power relations. In Britain, for example, a battle for the memory of the Second World War took place in the 1980s, with popular culture forming much of the terrain that was battled over by the new right in its claim to a narrative of the war which mobilized a pugnacious Churchillian rhetoric over and above a 'peoples' war' narrative that emphasized the creation of an egalitarian wartime society.[13] This reconception of the war years made sense in a society that was moving to the right, beginning the long process of dismantling the welfare state, discarding collectivism and drawing on this narrative to emphasize the 'new threat' to sovereignty some believed was posed by the European Union.

Cultural memory is formed in the interstices between memories of lived experience and the range of cultural forms that represent a shared past to the wider group. Quite simply, representations of the past on the public stage that do not accord with the sense of the past found among enough of that public will struggle to reach a wide audience. They need to 'ring true' in order to be considered authentic. At the same time, individual memories of the past, and the cultural memories that circulate among particular interest, community and family groups that do not fit with the representations found on this public stage will struggle to find a wider audience. While recognizing the social relations of power that act to give precedence to, or to marginalize, particular experiences, this hegemonic approach nonetheless insists that marginalized memories always retain the potential to find a space on the

---

13 E. P. Thompson, *Writing by Candlelight* (London: Merlin, 1980), p. 130.

public stage and to become a part of the dominant cultural memory. It is this understanding of cultural memory as never fixed and always open to contestation that this chapter takes in its discussion of three 'sites of memory' of the Second World War: war films of the 1950s, televisual representations of the war in the 1960s and 1970s, and the wave of anniversary commemorations since the 1980s.

War films of the 1950s

The decades immediately following the Second World War saw a widespread reimagining of the war years, as post-war societies attempted to come to terms with the past by remembering the war in a way that both justified the sacrifices of wartime and enabled governments and states to present *their* vision of the present by reference to the war years: either as a reaction against wartime policies, as in Germany, Japan and Italy, or as a continuation of such, as in Britain, the USSR and the USA. The war appeared in a variety of forms in its immediate aftermath: novels, memorials, photographs and landscapes being just a few of the 'sites of memory' through which the war remained visible, but war films, perhaps the pre-eminent means by which the conflict was represented during the war itself, remained a key site for the circulation of cultural memories of the war in the 1940s and 1950s. Hollywood, the pre-eminent site for film production in the mid-twentieth century, produced films such as *Battleground* (1949) and *The Sands of Iwo Jima* (1949), which, while they showed the horrors of combat and war's impact on the individual, also emphasized the values for which the 'good war' had been fought, now being mobilized again in the Cold War.[14] The genre of the war film proved, however, at least until the 1960s, to be one aspect of film production in many countries that was resistant to the 'Americanization' of national cultures. Italian neo-realist films of the 1940s serve to illustrate the strength of national war experiences in cultural memory, and the relationship between the post-war state, its citizens, and the films being produced. In the immediate aftermath of war, as Italy reconstructed itself as a European democracy, neo-realist cinema provided a 'powerful and populist counter-argument to the coercive and homogenizing vision of nationalism under Fascism', representing a nation deeply divided by class, region, politics and

---

14 John Bodnar, *The 'Good War' in American Memory* (Baltimore: Johns Hopkins University Press, 2010).

poverty.[15] Films such as *Rome: Open City* (Rossellini, 1945) and *Bicycle Thieves* (di Sica, 1948) 'eschewed the monumental and epic dimensions' of Italian film-making under Mussolini, focusing instead on social injustice, represented cinematically through the conventions of documentary realism.[16] Neo-realism thrived in the political turmoil of the post-war years, as political parties that had been banned in Fascist Italy fought to mobilize support and establish parliamentary dominance. Following the electoral success of the Christian Democrats in the 1948 elections, and the establishment of the new Italian constitution in the same year, neo-realism declined, its representation of deeply ingrained divisions and social injustices appearing increasingly irrelevant to a nation that saw itself as modernizing, democratic and prosperous. The war films produced in the 1950s in Britain and the USSR are no less firmly linked to the political and cultural landscapes in which they were produced and consumed. Representing the war years to audiences who would often have their own memories of the conflict, they were shaped by the needs of the nation state to produce a particular understanding of the war, and by the desire of members of that nation state to see representations that accorded with their own experiences.

British cinema-goers in the 1950s were, it would appear, mildly obsessed with the war years. Although the national habit of cinema-going was in decline from its height in the 1930s British cinemas still had weekly ticket sales of 14.5 million in 1959.[17] According to the annual survey of box office returns conducted for *Kinematograph Weekly*, British war films were the highest or second highest grossing films for seven of the years between 1950 and 1960, when sixty-four British war films were released.[18] These films were a part of what Graham Dawson has identified as a wider 'pleasure culture of war', sitting alongside novels, autobiographies and comics which retold wartime stories, providing a popular cultural accompaniment to the geographical landscape of bomb-sites in many cities and towns.[19] In this pleasure culture, war was imagined as an almost entirely male adventure, a gendered experience through which boys could become

---

15 Brent J. Piepergerdes, 'Re-envisaging the Nation: Film Neorealism and the Post-War Italian Condition', *ACME: An International E-Journal for Critical Geographies* 6:2 (2007), 231–57 (p. 233).

16 Marcia Landy, *Italian Film* (Cambridge University Press, 2000), p. 17.

17 John Ramsden, 'Refocusing the "People's War": British War Films of the 1950s', *Journal of Contemporary History* 33:1 (1998), 35–63 (p. 36).

18 Ramsden, 'Refocusing the "People's War"', p. 41.

19 Graham Dawson, *Soldier Heroes: British Adventure, Empire and the Imagining of Masculinity* (London: Routledge, 1994), p. 233.

men in a military rite of passage, and in which the 'peoples' war' was recast as a male, military endeavour. While the war films of the 1950s were more nuanced than the comic book stories for boys being published simultaneously, they did nonetheless represent the war years largely in terms of the military experience, privileging the viewpoint of the middle- and upper-class officer while relegating women and the working class to a supporting role. Central to films made during 'the peoples' war', most of 'the people' were invisible in the films of the 1950s.

Many of the most popular war films of the 1950s drew on true stories and the wartime experiences of particularly 'heroic' men. Not all of these were combatants; of the most popular films, only *The Dam Busters* (1955) and *Reach for the Sky* (1956) could claim conventional 'soldier heroes' as leading characters, while *The Cruel Sea* (1953) examined the role of the 'isolated and morally troubled leader' through the figure of Captain Ericson, a trope that was to be deployed to great effect five years later in the character of Lieutenant Colonel Nicholson in *Bridge Over the River Kwai* (1958).[20] Although social tensions sometimes become apparent in these films, they are unerringly resolved in favour of the social order, and although the male middle-class heroes sometimes struggled with the demands of wartime service, they nonetheless rose to the occasion, sublimating individual desires to collective war aims. As Penny Summerfield has argued, the popular war films of the 1950s 'depicted a just war' won by 'self-controlled upper and middle-class officers in charge of well disciplined and loyal lower-class servicemen'.[21]

What, though, do these films tell us about British society in the 1950s? Even at the time, they were often unpopular with film critics. The film journal *Films and Filming* described *The Dam Busters* (1956) as 'an average film' which publicists had turned into 'the most successful film of the year' while *The Battle of the River Plate* (1956) had 'such a stiff upper lip that it is almost expressionless'.[22] They were popular, however, with audiences, many of whom had personal memories of wartime, and who were understandably keen to see (some of) their experiences recreated in a heroic light on the big screen while their children, who experienced the war through family stories

20 Christine Geraghty, *British Cinema in the 1950s: Gender, Genre and the 'New Look'* (London: Routledge, 2000), p. 187.

21 Penny Summerfield, 'Film and the Popular Memory of the Second World War in Britain 1950–1959', in Philippa Levine and Susan R. Grayzel, eds., *Gender, Labour, War and Empire: Essays on Modern Britain* (Basingstoke: Palgrave Macmillan, 2009), pp. 157–76 (p. 172).

22 *Films and Filming* (January 1956), cited in Ramsden, 'Refocusing the "People's War"', pp. 41–2.

and wider popular culture, also formed a key part of the audience. According to Neil Rattigan, they were 'the last ditch effort by the dominant class to maintain its hegemony by rewriting the history of the celluloid war in its own favour', but although the egalitarianism of the war years was marginalized in these films, they were nonetheless often more nuanced in their depiction of the war years than Rattigan suggests.[23] War itself often appears in the films as an obscenity; a horror expressed in *The Cruel Sea* through Ericson's response when his attempts to destroy a U-boat result in the deaths of Allied sailors: 'No one murdered them. It's the war. The whole bloody war. We've just got to do these things and say our prayers at the end.'[24] Men like Ericson displayed the stoicism so central to the British popular memory of the war, but they also struggled with this, providing glimpses of the emotional turmoil beneath the repressed public face of masculinity. The social and cultural shifts of the decade, with its gradual loss of deference, new models of masculinity and withdrawal from empire, were reflected in the war films, which while they often produced a more conservative narrative of wartime than the films made during the war years, nonetheless provided a space for reflection on post-war British society.[25] As Britain struggled to adjust to both a new world order and to significant domestic changes, war films, while reassuring the British that the war had indeed been their 'finest hour', also provided a space for reflection on Britain's role in this changing world.

Given the centrality of film to Soviet culture it is unsurprising that film provided a key means through which the story of the war years was conveyed to the Russian people. Unlike Britain or Italy, film-makers in the Soviet Union worked under direct state control, but like Britain and Italy the films produced after the war differed markedly from those produced during the war years. During the war years, the majority of films produced focused on the conflict, with forty-nine of the seventy titles produced between 1941 and 1945 sitting comfortably within the war film genre.[26] Unlike most

23 Neil Rattigan, 'The Last Gasp of the Middle Class: British War Films of the 1950s', in W. W. Dixon, ed., *Re-Viewing British Cinema, 1900–1992: Essays and Interviews* (New York: SUNY Press, 1994), pp. 143–53 (p. 150).

24 *The Cruel Sea* (Frend, 1953).

25 Martin Francis, 'Remembering War, Forgetting Empire? Representations of the North African Campaign in 1950s British Cinema', in Lucy Noakes and Juliette Pattinson, eds., *British Cultural Memory and the Second World War* (London: Bloomsbury, 2013), pp. 111–32.

26 Peter Kenez, 'Black and White: The War on Film', in Richard Stites, ed., *Culture and Entertainment in Wartime Russia* (Bloomington: Indiana University Press, 1995), pp. 157–75 (p. 166).

British and American wartime films, however, the films made in the Soviet Union in this period did not divide into 'home front' and 'war front' films: for many, there was no division between home front and war front. The Nazi invasion of 1941 meant that much of the most densely populated areas of the western Soviet Union was occupied, under siege or the site of intensive fighting. While US citizens avoided the worst of the attacks on civilians that so marked the Second World War, and inhabitants of mainland Britain underwent sporadic, sometimes intensive, aerial bombardment but never invasion, the people of the Soviet Union were besieged and attacked by air and by land, making the home front/war front dichotomy meaningless for many. Wartime films such as *She Defends Her Motherland* (1943) reflected this experience, representing civilians as partisans, unified, resolute and merciless in their opposition to the Wehrmacht. In these films, women often symbolized 'mother Russia': *Prisoner No. 217* (1945) and *Zoya* (1944) both had as their heroes young women who displayed the determination, courage and fortitude being urged on the Soviet people during the war, while the hero of *The Rainbow* (1944) was the partisan mother of a new-born baby.[27] Representing the moral strength and physical courage the audiences were expected to display, the Soviet wartime film, like those produced in other combatant nations, displayed an image of a unified nation in which everyone played their part; united both behind its leaders and in its determination to rout the enemy.

However, following the war, the heroic defenders of the Soviet Union became embodied in one, solitary, figure: that of Stalin. Key examples of this include *The Fall of Berlin* and the two-part *The Battle of Stalingrad* (both 1949), which the viewer might expect to focus on the actions of the Red Army and the civilian population of the city but which, like Chiaureli's *The Fall of Berlin*, instead emphasizes Stalin's apparent strategic genius and inspiring leadership. The Stalinist cult of personality, marginalized somewhat during the war years as propaganda focused on the heroic Soviet people, returned with a vengeance after 1945. Rather than the united, heroic people of the wartime films, 'the viewer gets the impression that in winning the war what mattered was not the heroism of the simple soldier, who remains faceless, but brilliant leadership': the leadership of Stalin, the embodiment of the Soviet Union.[28]

---

27 Lynne Attwood, 'Sex and the Cinema', in Igor Kon and James Riorda, eds., *Sex and Russian Society* (Bloomington: Indiana University Press, 1993), pp. 64–88 (p. 70).
28 Peter Kenez, *Cinema and Soviet Society: From the Revolution to the Death of Stalin* (London: I. B. Tauris, 2007).

After Stalin's death in 1953, Soviet society experienced 'the thaw', as political restrictions on what could and couldn't be said and represented were loosened. Popular culture began to reflect this partial loosening of restrictions, and war films produced during this period were sometimes critical of Soviet and military leadership, and occasionally cynical about the motivations of the people in wartime. In these films, the war was a tragedy as well as a victory.

Among these were *The Cranes are Flying*, released early on in the period of de-Stalinization, in 1957, and *Ivan's Childhood* (1962), made toward the end of this period, as 'Kruschev began to tighten cultural controls once again.'[29] These films are complex in their representation of the war years, shaped as much by the emerging cultural memory of Stalinism as by the experience of conflict. In Russian culture, cranes symbolize heroic death on the battlefield and Boris, one of the three main characters in *Cranes*, indeed dies a heroic death, shot by a sniper as he rescues a wounded comrade from battle.[30] However, there the similarities between this and earlier Soviet war films end. A focus on the experience and motivation of individuals, rather than leaders or a collective people, recognition of the war as a calamity, not just a victory, and an understanding of the conflict as a rupture, were key features of films of this period. In these films, the victory over Germany was won, at great cost, by the Soviet peoples, not just the Kremlin leadership, as in *The Fall of Berlin*, or by idealized types, as in wartime films like *She Defends Her Motherland*.

Both *The Cranes are Flying* and *Ivan's Childhood* place this wartime heroism firmly within an exploration of the traumatic impact of the conflict. In *Cranes*, the heroine, Veronika, suffering the strain of the death of her parents in a bombing raid and the loss of her fiancé at the front, is raped by his cousin. Traumatized by these events, she marries her rapist, whom she later leaves, facing life alone once she has confirmed her fiancé died on the battlefield. Veronika 'hardly resembles traditional Soviet female paradigms': she doesn't wait for her fiancé to return, nor does she embody the heroic, sacrificial spirit of the wartime USSR.[31] Instead, she is recognizably human, her experiences and her responses providing a more nuanced exploration of the war's impact

29 Denise J. Youngblood, 'A War Remembered: Soviet Films of the Great Patriotic War', *American Historical Review* 106:3 (2001), 839–56 (p. 845).

30 *The Cranes are Flying* (Kalatozov, 1957).

31 Josephine Woll, *Real Images: Soviet Cinema and the Thaw* (London: I. B. Tauris, 2000), p. 74.

than earlier films. Tarkovsky's *Ivan's Childhood* was even more ambiguous in its portrayal of the wartime Soviet Union: the destruction of the Russian countryside mirroring the destruction of childhood innocence, the film's opening moments contrasting a prelapsarian, pre-war idyll with the blasted landscape and shattered childhood of Ivan, the young protagonist, drawn into the conflict and motivated by a determination to avenge the death of his mother and obliteration of his pre-war life. *Ivan's Childhood* has no moment of redemption, nothing to indicate that the sacrifices of war were worthwhile; like Veronika in *Cranes*, Ivan is indifferent to his fate, his childhood 'blasted into smithereens by the Nazis', but unlike Veronika, he doesn't survive the war; there is no potential for a new life here.[32] Ivan is caught and hanged, but in contrast to the young heroes of wartime films, his death is not atoned for by victory; although the penultimate scenes of the film take place in Soviet-occupied Berlin, Ivan's death is an individual tragedy, not part of a collective wartime sacrifice.

Although very different in both cinematic technique and historical contexts, the Soviet films of 'the thaw', like the British films of the 1950s, can be seen as indicative of a shifting popular memory of the war years. While the British films portrayed a unified wartime nation, embodied in the figures of male officers, rather than 'the people' of the wartime films, these men were often complex figures, riven by doubt and sometimes guilt, serving as an index of changing configurations of both class and gender, and, occasionally, providing a space for exploration of Britain's changing relationship with empire.[33] The films of the Soviet thaw likewise reflected a shifting memory of the war, increasingly seen as a time of suffering rather than a collective national victory under Stalin. They can be seen as an early indicator of the 'transition from triumph to trauma' which has marked the popular memory of the war years in post-Soviet cultures.[34] While the Second World War was still a lived experience and personal memory for many millions of Europeans in the 1950s, this brief examination of some films of the period demonstrates the reimagining of the war in popular culture, a process which has continued in the often-contested representations of the war years since.

---

32 Ibid., p. 139.
33 Francis, 'Remembering War, Forgetting Empire'.
34 Tatiana Zhurzenkho, 'Heroes into Victims: The Second World War in Post-Soviet Memory Politics', *Eurozine* (2012) (www.eurozine.com/articles/2012-10-31-zhurz-henko-en.html).

Televising the war in the 1960s and 1970s

The 1960s and 1970s saw some of the most powerful myths of wartime begin to unravel. Coverage of the Eichmann trial in 1961 increased global awareness of crimes committed between 1940 and 1944, while in France Ophuls's majestic documentary *The Sorrow and the Pity* (1969) laid bare the complexities of life in occupied and Vichy France, confronting viewers with the anti-Semitism, animosities and ambitions that informed the actions of many members of de Gaulle's 'eternal France'. Generational, racial, classed and gendered divisions in the USA, made visible by the Civil Rights movement and the country's ever more unpopular entanglement in Vietnam meant its self-image as a selfless moral and political leader, arguably the key ideological legacy of the war in the USA, became harder to maintain. Roosevelt's 'Four Freedoms' had not been realized and, indeed, the USA's covert support of murder squads in South and Central America 'reproduced crimes for which the Nazis had been tried'.[35] The patriotic war films of the 1940s and 1950s were displaced by more cynical representations of wartime, John Wayne's self-sacrificing Marines of *The Sands of Iwo Jima* (1949) making space for the killers of *The Dirty Dozen* (1967) and the comically amoral bank robbers of *Kelly's Heroes* (1970). Against such a background, an unquestioning belief in the 'good war' of the 1940s became increasingly difficult to preserve unscathed.

The generational ruptures of the 1960s that became so visible in May 1968 in France and in the anti-Vietnam War movement in the USA had an even more profound effect in West Germany. Since 1945 a dominant memory had developed which both deplored the cruelties of the Nazi regime and saw this regime as the product of a particular set of historical circumstances of which the German people were victims, not active agents. Although divergent views and expressions of guilt were articulated, these were marginal to most accounts of the war found in historical studies and popular representations alike, such as the popular 1959 television series *So Weit die Füsse Tragen*, which traced the escape of a German POW from a Siberian labour camp, thus reproducing the notion of the soldiers of the Wehrmacht as victims, not perpetrators, and neatly avoiding issues of guilt and responsibility. The ruptures of the 1960s and 1970s challenged this hegemony, and prefigured the academic divisions of the *Historikerstreit* in

---

35 Michael C. Adams, *The Best War Ever: America and World War II* (Baltimore: Johns Hopkins University Press, 1994), p. 139.

the 1980s. If 'post-war prosperity was the key factor in creating the conditions for an international wave of protests', these nonetheless took place within local contexts, and responded to local histories.[36] In Germany, the context was the failure of the post-war de-Nazification process, and the 'legacy of silence' surrounding the Nazi period in an era of social, cultural and political conservatism.[37]

This silence, while never total, was certainly apparent in popular culture of the period. Television had replaced film as the key medium of entertainment by the early 1960s and by the mid 1970s, 95 per cent of the West German public had access to a television at home.[38] Until 1984, German television had just two national channels: ARD, which began broadcasting in 1954, and ZDF, in 1963. This second channel, ZDF, broadcast many documentary histories of Nazism between 1963 and 1971, and again from 1978 to 1986. The first wave of programming was made for and by the generation who had personal experience of Nazism, and while the programmes took a 'decidedly anti-Nazi stance', they also employed a 'range of strategies designed to strengthen the audience's loyalty to the new state and lift the moral burden of Nazism from its shoulders'.[39] The Holocaust, and Jewish and other victims of the Nazi regime, remained marginal to these programmes. Unsurprisingly, this began to change from the late 1960s onwards. As Michael Schneider has argued: 'Since the fathers failed to indict themselves for their monstrous pasts, they were put on trial by proxy by the radicalized sons and daughters in 1968.'[40]

The generational divisions and critiques of 1968 had a particular significance in West Germany. While the radicalized youth of the era were always in a minority, they nonetheless articulated a wider sense of dissatisfaction with the ways in which Germany had 'come to terms' with the Nazi past. After all, in 1968, ex-Nazis were still very present in German public life: Edda Göring, daughter of Hermann, was in court trying to keep possession of a sixteenth-century painting her father had 'acquired' from the city of Cologne;

36 Nick Thomas, *Protest Movements in 1960s West Germany: A Social History of Dissent and Democracy* (Oxford: Berg, 2003), p. 18.
37 Dan Bar-On, *Legacy of Silence: Encounters with Children of the Third Reich* (Cambridge, Mass.: Harvard University Press, 1991).
38 Wulf Kansteiner, 'Nazis, Viewers and Statistics: Television History, Television Audience Research and Collective Memory in West Germany', *Journal of Contemporary History* 39:4 (2004), 575–98 (p. 577).
39 Ibid., p. 582.
40 Michael Schneider, 'Fathers and Sons, Retrospectively: The Damaged Relationship between Two Generations', *New German Critique* 31 (1984), 3–51 (pp. 11–12).

Heinrich Lübke, president of the FRG, was revealed to have helped plan and build concentration camps, and the rapidly terminated post-war policy of de-Nazification had left local bureaucrats and civil servants who had worked under the Nazi regime in positions of power and influence. Both the 1961 Eichmann trial and the trials of twenty-three former SS members between 1963 and 1968 had seen the use of 'Befehlsnotstand' (just following orders) as a defence strategy, raising issues of collective guilt and responsibility that had previously been marginal to West German perceptions of the Nazi period. It was against this more turbulent background that the US 'miniseries' *Holocaust* was broadcast in 1979.

One response to the heightened presence of the Nazi period in West German national consciousness was seen in the 'Hitler wave', the reactionary resurgence of interest in National Socialism and in particular in the figure of Hitler that appeared in the mid-1970s, part of a conservative reaction against both the critiques of post-war Germany emerging out of the challenges of 1968, and as a response to the perceived threat to the established social and political hegemony from far left groups like the Red Army Faction.[41] However, the 'Hitler wave' had far less impact on the popular memory of the Nazi period in the FRG than the broadcasting of *Holocaust* over one week in January 1979. Shown on the small 'third channel' WDR, the American dramatization of the events of the Holocaust, traced through the stories of two German families in the 1930s and 1940s, nonetheless drew large and attentive audiences. Over 40 per cent of West German television viewers watched the programme every night and the government was swamped by 255,000 requests for the 20,000 booklets it had prepared to accompany the series.[42] The televised debates that followed each episode were overwhelmed with telephone calls from viewers wanting to discuss the programme, and ask why and how a German regime had attempted to carry out genocide in mid-twentieth-century Europe. *Der Spiegel*, which had published articles before the series broadcast decrying it as a crass 'Americanization' of European history, ran a cover story immediately after its broadcasts entitled 'Holocaust: The Past Returns', and subtitled 'Murder of the Jews Moves the Germans'.[43] It was surely this emotional impact of the dramatization that

---

41 Andrei S. Markovits and Beth Simone Noveck, 'West Germany', in David S. Wyman, ed., *The World Reacts to the Holocaust* (Baltimore: Johns Hopkins University Press, 1996), pp. 391–446 (p. 428).

42 Ibid., p. 429.

43 Tom Dreisbach, 'Transatlantic Broadcasts: "Holocaust" in America and West Germany', *Penn History Review* 16:2 (2009), 76–97 (p. 86).

largely accounts for its influence; the events it recounted were well known, if not foregrounded, in West German culture and society. Americanized, sentimental and melodramatic it may well have been, but the pleasures of narrative and representation, and the personalization of some of the most traumatic events in European history served to move the Holocaust, and questions of German guilt and responsibility, to the centre of West German cultural and political life. After *Holocaust*, atonement for the crimes of the Nazi past became a central, though always controversial, element of West German political discourse; as Habermas argued, the 'traumatic refusal to pass away of a moral imperfect past tense ... burned into our national history'.[44]

While post-*Holocaust* West Germany struggled with 'the past that will not pass', British popular cultural representations of the war were largely affectionate, nostalgic and self-referential. Even television programming which examined lesser-known events of the war years, such as the 1974 television play *It's a Lovely Day Tomorrow*, a dramatization of the 1943 tragedy at Bethnal Green Underground Station, where 173 people were crushed to death, emphasized the collective and communal spirit of the British at war. The Second World War permeated the British television schedules. Not only were the war films of the 1940s and 1950s staples of daytime scheduling, but numerous drama series and television plays, comedy and documentaries revisited the war years, drawing on the tropes of camaraderie, stoicism and unity seen in the earlier war films in their representations of wartime Britain.

Graham Dawson and Bob West's 1984 article 'Our Finest Hour?' set the scene for much of the subsequent research into the popular memory of the Second World War in post-war Britain. Arguing that the popular memory of the war that had become dominant in the 1980s had seen a partial erasure of the more radical aspects of the 'peoples' war', Dawson and West examined the 'complex and contradictory' field of popular memory to find that any 'sense of struggle and contestation has been erased' in a Thatcherite reappropriation of the war as a Churchillian adventure.[45] These conflicts over the popular memory of the war were played out in culture, in

44 Jürgen Habermas, 'On the Public Use of History', in Neil Levi and Michael Rothberg, eds., *The Holocaust: Theoretical Readings* (Edinburgh University Press, 2003), pp. 63–8 (p. 63).

45 Graham Dawson and Bob West, 'Our Finest Hour? The Popular Memory of World War II and the Struggle over National Identity', in Geoff Hurd, ed., *National Fictions: World War Two in British Films and Television* (London: BFI Publishing, 1984), pp. 8–13 (pp. 10, 12).

historical writing and in political debate. While it could be expected that television would provide a key battleground for these struggles, in fact the representations of the war that were broadcast were remarkably homogeneous.

Although some televised British dramatizations of the war, such as *Licking Hitler* (1978) and *The Imitation Game* (1980) did explicitly engage in the struggles over the memory of the war that were taking place, the majority of televised representations continued to sit fairly comfortably within the consensus that the Second World War had indeed been Britain's 'finest hour'. While there was disagreement over *why* this was the case – whether it was a celebration of Churchillian leadership and patriotic rhetoric, or a celebration of wartime collectivism and the creation of the welfare state – the British still largely agreed that the Second World War had been a high point in national history. Television represented the war years in ways that ensured their ongoing appeal to large audiences, and their continued, if increasingly contested, place at the heart of British national identity. The pleasures of nostalgia and the representation of the war as, ultimately, a moment of unity in which the nation somehow 'found itself', continued to shape narratives and to attract a viewing audience. The attractions of this narrative are fairly obvious: in a period when social and political consensus was breaking down, when widely shared cultural customs were looking increasingly fragile and when Britain's self-image as a world leader was self-evidently delusional, a nostalgic return to an imagined national past offered comfort and stability. In popular television representations of the war years, such as *A Family at War* (1970–72), *Colditz* (1972–74) and most famously *Dad's Army* (1968–77), a unified national past provided reassurance in a time of rapid social, political, cultural and economic change.

Cultures of commemoration: the war in the late twentieth and early twenty-first centuries

As the Second World War receded further into history, a desire to commemorate those years became more pronounced. From the 1980s onwards, a series of commemorative events and ceremonies grew up around key dates of the Second World War. Beachfront and battlefield acts of commemoration vied with parades, street parties and religious services to mark the final days of the war. Of course, the war had been marked in national commemorative cultures before, perhaps most notably in the growth of the 'cult' of the Great

Patriotic War as a foundational myth of the USSR in the 1970s.[46] From the 1980s, this 'cult' spread to the West, as the increasing age of veterans combined with shifts in international relations and politics to produce an atmosphere conducive to the growth of both formalized and more informal acts of commemoration and war remembrance. Veterans and their families around the world often took part in the formal commemorations, as well as participating in informal 'pilgrimages' to scenes of battle and internment, such as the D-Day landing beaches of Normandy, and the sites of the Kokoda Track and the 'Burma railway' in Southeast Asia.[47] The formal commemorative events were often transnational, designed to bring nations together in a shared agreement about the legacy of the war for the post-war world. What this legacy was, however, was determined as much by the time of the commemoration, as it was by the acts being commemorated. At a point of increased Cold War tensions and British 'Euroscepticism', *The Times* took the opportunity in 1984 to note that the D-Day landings were not only the 'zenith of achievement for the Anglo-American partnership', they were evidence of a still substantial 'cultural and historical bond' which must 'strike deeper into the national imagination than anything formulated in the chancelleries of Europe'.[48] However, shifts in popular memory, which were to become more apparent in the post-Cold War ceremonies, were already being vocalized, seen, for example, when US journalist Harry Smith, covering the beachside ceremonies for *This Morning*, commented wryly that the USSR might have 'gotten a little more credit here today for having decimated the Germans so much to maybe open the door on this front a little bit'.[49] Ten years later, President Clinton may have emphasized the independent spirit and self reliance of US troops 'driven by the voice of free will and responsibility nurtured in Sunday schools, town halls and sandlot ballgames' in his speech at the American cemetery of Colleville-sur-Mer but he did so to an audience that included the Presidents of Poland and Slovakia, satellite states of the USSR in 1984.[50] By 2005, the 'memory wars' in Eastern Europe had spilled

---

46 Roger Markwick, 'The Great Patriotic War in Soviet and Post-Soviet Collective Memory', in Dan Stone, ed., *The Oxford Handbook of Post-War European History* (Oxford University Press, 2012), pp. 692–713.

47 Bruce Scates, *Anzac Journeys: Returning to the Battlefields of World War Two* (Cambridge University Press, 2013).

48 *The Times*, 6 June 1984.

49 Cited in Jean Pickering, 'Remembering D-Day: An Exercise in Nostalgia', in Jean Pickering and Suzanne Kehde, eds., *Narratives of Nostalgia, Gender and Nationalism* (New York University Press, 1997), pp. 182–210 (p. 204).

50 *Los Angeles Times*, 7 June 1994.

over into transnational commemorations, President Bush fanning the flames in his open letter to the Latvian President, which noted that while 'in Western Europe, the end of World War Two meant liberation', in Eastern Europe it 'marked the Soviet occupation ... and the imposition of Communism'.[51] The commemorative activities of the late twentieth and early twenty-first centuries thus reflected the shifting geopolitical landscape: the end of Soviet communism, the expansion of the European Union, the growth of transnational discourses of human rights, the apparent 'triumph' of the USA and liberal democracy, and subsequent challenges to this new world order.

Set within this changing topography was a renewed interest in memorializing the victims of the war. While the collapse of Soviet hegemony saw the widespread removal of memorials that had legitimized the post-1945 political regimes as anti-fascist, the period since 1989 has seen the creation of numerous new memorials. In Europe and the USA, much of this wave of memorialization has centred on the Holocaust: the United States Holocaust Memorial Museum in Washington, DC (1993), the London Imperial War Museum Holocaust Exhibition (2000) and the Jewish Museum of Berlin (2001) are all part of the same wave of remembrance that saw the creation of the Memorial to the Murdered Jews of Europe in central Berlin and the adoption of International Holocaust Memorial Day by the European Union in 2005. While not without their critics, these state-sanctioned 'sites of memory' were generally received very positively, as a part of the 'memory boom' identified by Winter which, in their command to remember, both situated the Second World War as the 'good war' and placed contemporary nation states as its inheritors, acting to legitimize the 'humanitarian' military interventions of the period as a continuation of the West's commitment to human rights.[52] Far more controversial were two other nationally specific memorial projects that were also part of the 'memory boom': the National World War II Memorial in Washington, DC (2004) and the RAF Bomber Command Memorial in London (2012). (See Plate Section, Illustration 38.)

Memorials can be understood as material products of popular memory: physical sites of memory created in the intersections between (usually) national identity creation and the desire of the bereaved to have both

---

51 Cited in Martin Evans, 'Memories, Monuments, Histories: The Re-thinking of the Second World War since 1989', *National Identities* 8:4 (2006), 317–48 (p. 333).

52 Jay Winter, *Remembering War: The Great War between Memory and History in the Twentieth Century* (New Haven: Yale University Press, 2006); Mark Mazower, 'The Strange Triumph of Human Rights', *Historical Journal* 47:2 (2004), 379–98.

recognition of their loss and a site at which to mourn. Although usually created to memorialize the dead of a particular conflict, their meanings are shaped by the politics of the present. For example, while the Soviet Treptow Monument in Berlin had particular, temporally specific, meanings when it was unveiled in 1949, including acting as a site of pilgrimage for the bereaved and as a reminder of Soviet hegemony in post-war East Germany, its primary function now is as a stop on the Berlin tourist trail, a material mnemonic of the Cold War in Central Europe. The US National World War II Memorial and the British Bomber Command Memorial, both built long after the events they commemorate, act less as sites of personal pilgrimage for the bereaved, and more as statements about the meanings of the war in the early twenty-first century.

The origins of the National World War II Memorial can be found in the historical conditions of the late twentieth and early twenty-first centuries, which saw a desire to 'say thank you' to 'the greatest generation' combined with a renewed interest in the values that the popular memory of the Second World War in the USA emphasized in the aftermath of 9/11. Unlike the 'living memorials' which dominated the commemorative landscape in the immediate post-war period, this new memorial was uncompromising in its traditional physical form and function.[53] This was to be a memorial whose meaning could not be mistaken: a material assertion of the sacrifice of the USA during the war and of the gratitude the post-war nation felt for this sacrifice. The use of Tom Hanks, star of *Saving Private Ryan* (1998), as the public face of the fund-raising campaign, strengthened these meanings: Hanks informed his audience that this 'greatest generation . . . did nothing less than save the world', and that 'it is time to say thank you'.[54] Drawing on a popular memory of the war as a war for freedom, and a popular representation of the conflict that emphasized personal sacrifice, Hanks's involvement both fed into the 'memory boom' of the period and shaped it in particular, temporally and culturally specific, ways. Situated in the centre of Washington, DC on The Mall, close to the White House and Capitol Hill, this was to be a memorial whose significance to the nation was unmistakable. However, this positioning, together with its design, also lay at the heart of much subsequent criticism.

53 Andrew M. Shanken, 'Planning Memory: Living Memorials in the United States during World War II', *The Art Bulletin* 84:1 (2002), 130–47.
54 www.wwiimemorial.com/archives/newsreleases/bm15_30.avi. Originally broadcast 1999.

In a highly critical reading of the memorial Elizabeth Doss has argued that its neoclassical style and monumental scale act as symbolic reminders of American imperial power, appropriating the collectivist values articulated during the Second World War for contemporary political ends.[55] Placed at the geographic centre of American power the memorial is the creation of a particular time and place: a physical reminder that America fought 'for freedom' in the Second World War and, by implication, continues to do so. Fighting against fascism in the 1940s, communism during the Cold War and Islamic radicalism in the 'war on terror', the memorial aids a particular narrative of modern American history: one that positions America on the side of 'freedom' in a range of conflicts. At the same time, it elides both the internal divisions of the war years, in particular the festering inheritance of slavery and the Jim Crow laws that saw segregation in the US Army and race riots in Detroit, and the rather mixed history of America's various Cold War interventions. In its monumental scale it acts to marginalize alternative memories, such as those of the historian and veteran Howard Zinn, who argued in 2004 that he refused 'to be corralled into justifying the wars of today' by 'drawing on the emotional and moral capital of World War II'.[56]

If Zinn and other veterans felt that 'their war' was being marginalized in this triumphant and imperialist memorial, a group of British veterans, those who had served with Bomber Command, were arguing at the same time that 'their war' had never been recognized. The 'air war', of which these men were a part, has long proved to be a particularly unstable and divisive aspect of the cultural memory of the war years. Although the Blitz on London and other cities has long been central to British popular memory of the war, acting as a shorthand for British stoicism and unity, the Allied area bombing of German towns and cities has been marked by its absence in dominant British memory cultures, while its post-war significance to German popular memories of the war, at the familial, local and national level, is contested, and its meaning was at the heart of the *Historikerstreit*.[57] The air war in the Pacific has been no less divisive: the USA experiencing its own *Historikerstreit* in the arguments over the planned 'Enola Gay' exhibition at the Smithsonian Museum in 1994–95.[58] The memorial campaign by the group of British

55 Doss, 'War, Memory and the Public Mediation of Affect'.
56 Howard Zinn, 'Dissent at the War Memorial', *The Progressive*, 8 August 2004 (www.progressive.org/august04/zinn0804.html).
57 Jörg Arnold, *The Allied Air War and Urban Memory* (Cambridge University Press, 2011).
58 David Thelen, 'History after the Enola Gay Controversy: An Introduction', *Journal of American History* 82:3 (2005), 1029–35.

veterans and their supporters was one aspect of this much wider contestation over the memory of the bombing war.

Following a long campaign a memorial was unveiled in Green Park, London, in 2012. Commemorating the over 55,000 servicemen who died while serving with Bomber Command (an attrition rate of approximately 45 per cent), the memorial attempts to incorporate the problematic memory of Bomber Command into the dominant British popular memory of the Second World War. The activities of Bomber Command have long been marginal to this popular memory; the aerial bombing of Germany, and the resulting deaths of approximately 600,000 civilians, have proved difficult to fit within a dominant memory that emphasizes British stoicism, unity and essential decency.[59] When a memorial to Arthur 'Bomber' Harris, the commander-in-chief of Bomber Command, was erected in London in 1992 the opening ceremony was disrupted and the memorial was subsequently and repeatedly vandalized.[60] As debates about the military necessity and moral legitimacy of the bombing campaign continued, the wartime role of Bomber Command has proved somewhat difficult to fully locate within the 'finest hour' mythology with which British cultural remembrance of the Second World War remains so heavily invested.[61]

Like the National World War II Memorial, the Bomber Command Memorial sought to emphasize national triumph, incorporating individual service and sacrifice into a unifying national narrative. However, unlike the Washington memorial, where gold stars represent individual lives collectively, it does so figuratively, literally containing the brass figures of seven exhausted airmen within the dominant memory of the war. Placed within a stone pavilion inscribed with quotes from Churchill, the figures are doubly integrated into national history, standing on a plinth that states 'H.M. Queen Elizabeth unveiled this memorial 18 June in the year of her Diamond Jubilee 2012'. In the centre of the capital, unveiled by the Queen, surrounded by quotations from Churchill, the Bomber Command Memorial would appear to be a recognition by the state that the wartime sacrifice of members of

---

59 Hew Strachan, 'Strategic Bombing and the Question of Civilian Casualties up to 1945', in Paul Addison and Jeremy Crang, eds., *Firestorm: The Bombing of Dresden, 1945* (London: Pimlico, 2006), pp. 1–17 (p. 16).

60 Mark Connelly, *Reaching for the Stars: A New History of Bomber Command in World War II* (London: I. B. Tauris, 2001), p. 2.

61 Frances Houghton, 'The "Missing Chapter": Bomber Command Aircrew memoirs in the 1990s and 2000s', in Noakes and Pattinson, eds., *British Cultural Memory*, pp. 155–74 (p. 162).

Bomber Command stood alongside that of other members of the nation, a belated repayment of a national debt.

However, the controversial nature of aerial bombing has made the political nature of war memorials highly visible. Objections from the Mayor of Dresden were only allayed after it was agreed to include an inscription that commemorated the victims of the bombing. In the context of debates about Britain's role in the 'war on terror', a memorial to British attacks on civilians gained a new resonance. Like Harris's statue, the memorial has been vandalized, first with the word 'Islam' and, once that was removed, with the phrase 'Lee Rigby's killers shud hang', in reference to the murder of an off-duty soldier in 2013. Thus a memorial that was meant to belatedly recognize the service of members of Bomber Command, writing them into the popular memory of the war in Britain, has instead become a focus for both debate about the aerial bombing campaign, and for controversy about the 'war on terror'. The plural meanings of war memorials which are created socially, and often differ from the intended meanings underpinning their creation, are clearly evident in the Bomber Command Memorial: acknowledgement of sacrifice and the repayment of a national debt are countered by concerns about the destruction caused by aerial bombing and contemporary tensions around British identity in the 'war on terror'. The hegemonic and contested nature of the popular memory of the Second World War has rarely been so visible as it is in the current wave of memorialization.

Conclusion

This chapter traced some of the changing meanings of the Second World War through a consideration of particular, geographically and temporally situated examples of popular cultural representations, and popular memory, of the war. For Europe in particular, the memory of the war has been a site of struggle and contestation, both within national contexts, where nation states have drawn on particular elements of the past in the construction of a national history, and in the transnational context, seen in the distinct narratives of the war on either side of the Iron Curtain, and the negotiations over those narratives in the years since 1989. In the constant construction of popular memory, forgetting is as important as remembering. While the British of the 1950s remembered collective service and sacrifice through the war films of that decade, they 'forgot' the subsequent decline of British power and the rise of US hegemony. In the Soviet Union, war films of the same period began by placing Stalin at the centre of the Great Patriotic War but ended the decade with more critical reflections on the conflict, critiques of Stalinism as well as representations of war's barbarity. Television drama in the 1960s and 1970s provided a means for German audiences to personally engage with the Holocaust, while contemporary British audiences enjoyed nostalgic representations of the war that enabled a temporary escape from the increasing social and political divisions that marked the beginning of the end of the post-war consensus. The wave of commemoration and memorialization of the late twentieth and early twenty-first centuries demonstrated the political nature of cultural remembering, as memorials erected some seven decades after the war's end proved unexpectedly controversial. Popular memory, and the popular and official cultures through which this circulates on the public stage, are shaped as much by the politics of the present as by the events of the past.

As Jameson argued, the omnipresence of the past in the contemporary world reflects an anxiety about the instabilities of modernity, providing a sense of continuity in a rapidly changing world.[62] However, this promise of stability is itself a chimera, as popular memory shifts in accordance with the contemporary. The nature of the events being remembered, the barbarity and scale of the war, make this a difficult memory, one in which traumatic and disturbing memories keep obstinately pushing through to the surface. Mark Mazower's salutary reminder that the legacy of the twentieth century for modern Europe is as much of death and destruction as it is of progress and prosperity should be borne in mind when considering the popular memory of the war which attempts to 'forget' at least as much as it remembers.[63]

62 Fredric Jameson, *Postmodernism, or the Logic of Late Capitalism* (Durham, NC: Duke University Press, 1991).
63 Mark Mazower, *Dark Continent: Europe's Twentieth Century* (London: Allen Lane, 1998).

26

The Second World War in global memory space

JIE-HYUN LIM

Holocaust meets the postcolonial

It was on 8 March, International Women's Day, in 2013 that a monument to Korean 'comfort women' was unveiled in front of the Bergen County courthouse in New Jersey. Alongside four other monuments, commemorating the victims of African-American slavery, the Holocaust, the Armenian genocide, and the Irish potato famine, a new memorial stone to Korean comfort women took its place in the county's 'ring of honour' outside the courthouse as part of a memory island. This was not an unprecedented event. The memory of Korean comfort women (the euphemism used by the Japanese military for sexual slaves) began migrating to the USA early in the twenty-first century. Korean American Civic Empowerment (KACE) was one of the main promoters of the transpacific migration of the comfort women's memory to the USA. KACE sponsored two comfort women monuments in Palisades Park and in Bergen County, New Jersey and lobbied successfully for House Resolution 121 (2007) asking the Japanese government for an official apology. KACE's memory activity included the 2011 art exhibition, *Come from the Shadows: The Comfort Women*, in New York City.

What attracts one's attention in this transpacific memory campaign is the collaboration between KACE and the Kupferberg Holocaust Center of Queensborough Community College. The two jointly organized a meeting of Korean comfort women and Holocaust survivors in the auditorium of Queensborough Community College on 13 December 2011; the meeting received broad media coverage in Korea. Subsequently, they launched the North Asian History Internship, a jointly operated programme designed to teach American college students about atrocities committed by Japanese imperial armed forces. The programme has focused on the violation of women's rights by highlighting the experiences of the comfort women.[1] The Holocaust and comfort women are encountered mnemonically a posteriori in transnational memory space, though no de facto entangled history exists. The mnemonic confluence of the Holocaust and the comfort women, facilitated by the transatlantic and transpacific migration of memory, epitomizes the extraterritoriality of the global memory of the Second World War. The performativity of wartime memory is shifting from the national to the transnational.

About a year after the Queensborough meeting of comfort women and Holocaust survivors, a parallel transnational memory performance took place on 6 December 2012 in Melbourne, Australia. In front of the German consulate, eighty-four-year-old Alf Turner read out an Australian Aborigine petition protesting against Nazi persecution of the Jewish people. Then he handed over the document to a German consul, watched by 200 supporters, among whom were Holocaust survivors and members of the Jewish community. The ceremony was a re-enactment of William Cooper's 1938 anti-Nazi protest action, made only weeks after Kristallnacht. William Cooper, the seventy-seven-year-old secretary of the Australian Aboriginal League, an Aboriginal elder of the Yorta Yorta tribe and Alf Turner's grandfather, had led a delegation to deliver a petition condemning the Nazi persecution of the Jews to the German consulate in Melbourne.[2] Cooper's show of solidarity with German Jews in 1938 is in stark contrast with the post-war 'White Australia' policy that denied entry visas to Oriental Jews. Cooper's unique protest against the Nazis has only come to prominence in the twenty-first century, reflecting the confluence of postcolonial and Holocaust memory in the global memory space.

The mnemonic solidarity between Holocaust survivors, comfort women and Australian Aborigines across the globe is truly remarkable. It is even more remarkable given that their stories were unconnected throughout the course of the Second World War. Entangled is the memory, not the history. What is no less extraordinary from a different angle is the global connectivity

---

1 news.chosun.com/site/data/html_dir/2013/03/09/2013030900651.html; KACE, 'Compilation of Korean News Articles on Comfort Women Survivors and Holocaust Survivors' Meetings', 21 December 2011 (http://us.kace.org/?s=meeting+with+comfort+women+and+Holocaust+survivors).

2 Dan Goldberg, 'An Aboriginal Protest against the Nazis, Finally Delivered', *Haaretz*, 10 October 2012 (www.haaretz.com/jewish-world/jewish-world-features/an-aboriginal-protest-against-the-nazis-finally-delivered.premium-1.483806).

of denial discourses and apologetic memories. Martin Krygier, son of a Polish-Jewish refugee and law professor in Australia, drew attention persuasively to the parallels between the nationalist denial of the Jedwabne massacre in Poland and the racist defence of the forced removal of Aboriginal children (the lost generation) from their families in Australia.[3] Krygier's catalogue could also be applied to the deniers of comfort women, the Nanjing massacre, the Wehrmacht atrocities, apartheid, military massacres at My Lai and No Gun Ri, not to mention Holocaust deniers. It is not certain whether all these denials are interconnected and cross-referential. However, personal connectivity in apologetic memory, though not a pure denial, in the case of the Jedwabne massacre and Wehrmacht actions at least seems evident.[4]

These scenes of mnemonic connectivity across the globe represent the clash of two opposing performativities – critical and apologetic memory. The remembrance of the Second World War has been shaped by varied and often conflicting perspectives and positionalities – the memories of victims and perpetrators, passive victimhood and agency, bystanders and accomplices, victory and defeat, resistance and collaboration, empires and colonies, occupation and liberation, dictatorship and democracy, coercion and consent, heroes and villains, men and women, captors and prisoners, soldiers and civilians and other sets of contestants. Contested memories in this binary setting were mostly fixated within national borders. Thus, coming to terms with the Second World War remained largely a national project in the last century, often leading to a national apologetic memory: 'The result was a memory of a *world* war with the *world* left out.'[5] This chapter tries to rescue the memory of the Second World War from 'la tyrannie du national'. This endeavour demands more than a compilation of national memories. Rescuing memory from the nation is a 'moral business' requiring the articulation of global performativity in remembering the Second World War, which links fragmented memories of war, dictatorship, colonialism and genocide through cross-referencing it with a global critical memory.

---

3 Martin Krygier, 'Neighbours: Poles, Jews and the Aboriginal Question', *East Central Europe* 29 (2002), 297–309.
4 Piotr Forecki, *Od Shoah do Strachu: spory o polsko-żydowską przeszłość i pamięć w debatach publicznych* (Poznań: Wydawnictwo Poznańskie, 2010), p. 309.
5 Carol Gluck, 'Operations of Memory: "Comfort Women" and the World', in S. M. Jager and R. Mitter, eds., *Ruptured Histories: War, Memory, and the Post-Cold War in Asia* (Cambridge, Mass.: Harvard University Press, 2007), pp. 47–77 (p. 48).

Nationalization of memory

Naoki Sakai tells a story about the Japanese translation of the German word *Nationalsozialismus* in the early 1990s. At the request of the *Asahi Journal*, Naoki submitted an essay to the journal, but his manuscript was turned down repeatedly. The problem was that Sakai translated 'Nationalsozialismus' as *kokumin shakaishugi* (socialism of the nation) instead of *kokka shakaishugi* (socialism of the state). Sakai's term, *kokumin shakaishugi*, was unacceptable to the left-wing editor of the *Asahi Journal*. Yet, the English word for 'nation' is not singularly definable, as it has different meanings in varying contexts. It has been rendered most frequently in Japanese as *kokumin* (nation) or *minzoku* (ethnicity or ethnic nation). 'Nation' was also translated as *kokka* (state), though rarely. However, many Japanese left-wing intellectuals believed that the word 'nation' in 'Nationalsozialismus' signified *kokka* (state). By using the term *kokka shakaishugi* (state socialism) they could rescue *kokumin* (nation) from Nazism. *Showa-shi* (the Showa history) debate in 1955 confirms the sacralization of *kokumin* again. The nation-centred dichotomy of *kokumin* (nation) and *hi-kokumin* (non/anti-nation) in the *Showa-shi* debate foreclosed the possibility of a *hi-kokumin* asking about the *kokumin*'s historical responsibility.[6] Post-war democracy in Japan was inclined to democratize, rather than problematize, the nation.

Interrogating Japan's responsibility for war remained a solely national business. The *kokumin*'s ethnocentric worldview is closely connected with the distorted memory of the Japanese empire as the colonized, not the colonizer. This inverted memory of empire allowed the Japanese to adopt a postcolonial rather than post-imperial positionality. The history of modern Japan, from 1853 when Perry's American ships landed in the bay of Uraga to 1952 when American occupation forces left the country, was periodized as the 'Hundred Years War' against the West. The Second World War was just one episode in the century-long epic struggle between Asia and the West, between the colonized and colonizers.[7] While the Japanese nation metamorphosed into the colonized, the colonized Koreans, Taiwanese and

---

6 Naoki Sakai, 'History and Responsibility: On the Debates on the Showa History', in Jie-Hyun Lim, Barbara Walker and Peter Lambert, eds., *Mass Dictatorship and Memory as Ever Present Past* (Basingstoke: Palgrave Macmillan, 2014), pp. 120–38 (pp. 120–1). Stalin banned the term 'National Socialism' in 1931–32 perhaps because of the ideological ventriloquism of Stalinism and Nazism. The GDR leaders seemed to prefer the term 'German fascism' to Nazism too.

7 Sebastian Conrad, 'The Dialectics of Remembrance: Memories of Empire in Cold War Japan', *Comparative Studies in Society and History* 56:1 (2014), 4–33 (pp. 13, 17–18).

Chinese, as 'third country nationals', were consigned to oblivion. This metamorphosis of the colonizers into the colonized is key to understanding why *kokumin* (nation) has been so cherished in the memory of colonialism and war in Japan.

To Sukarno, a self-identified left nationalist, National Socialism was perceived as *kokumin shakaishugi* (nation-socialism) and therefore good. When he received an honorary degree from the University of Indonesia on 2 February 1963, Sukarno delivered a speech on nationalism and leadership. Benedict Anderson remembered vividly Sukarno's address in praise of Hitler on that day: 'wah, Hitler was extraordinarily clever really ... this Third Reich would really and truly bring happiness to the people of Germany'.[8] On other occasions, Sukarno frequently described Sun Yixian (Sun Yat-sen), Kemal Atatürk, Gandhi and Ho Chi Minh on a par with Hitler. When Dutch colonizers compared Sukarno's government with the pro-Nazi Quisling regime, and the young Indonesian independence fighters with the Hitler Youth and the SS, it was not that much more obscene. The problem was that they failed to remember Anton Mussert, the Führer of the Dutch National Socialist Movement, who argued for Dutch access to German *Lebensraum* in the Slavic east, where they could bring to bear their colonial experience in Java and Sumatra.

But there are individual memories that defy the *kokumin*-(nation-) centred remembrance. Upon the unconditional surrender of Japan, about 600 Japanese soldiers continued to fight the 'Hundred Years War' against the 'West' by joining Sukarno's Indonesian independence fighters. Those who fell in the fight were buried in the national heroes' cemetery and remembered as Indonesian national heroes. Chil-Sung Yang, a Korean soldier who contracted with the Japanese army to guard the Allied POW camp, was one of those fallen heroes. He was captured in the Garut basin in November 1948 and executed as a war criminal on 10 August 1949 for having fought against Dutch colonialism alongside Indonesian fighters. Though he has been remembered as a national hero in Indonesia and buried in the national heroes' cemetery in Garut, his personal history sank into oblivion in postcolonial Korea because of his collaboration with the Japanese army. Yet, the plurality of memories across half the globe with reference to Chil-Sung Yang is too complex to be captured by any one national memory: Dutch war criminal, Indonesian

---

8 Benedict Anderson, *The Spectre of Comparisons: Nationalism, Southeast Asia and the World* (London: Verso, 1998), pp. 1–2.

national hero, Japanese colonial collaborator, Korean national traitor, and innocent colonial victim by his fate.[9]

Europeans also spared no effort in nationalizing war memory. The widespread silence about non-national victims was most prominent in the first decade of the post-war period. First of all, Jews were ousted from the national memory of war across Europe. The Jewish persecution and Holocaust had to be either nationalized or excluded from patriotic memory. Various instances are notable in this regard. The Gendarmerie Nationale reported on a demonstration of about 300 people shouting 'France to the French' in the fourth *arrondissement* of Paris on 19 April 1945. The demonstration was triggered by the expulsion of a person occupying the apartment of a Jew, who had returned to Paris. When Netty Rosenfeld applied for a job at Radio Herrijzend Nederland run by the Dutch Resistance after liberation in 1944, she was told that Rosenfeld was not a suitable name for public broadcasting. A reader's letter to *De Patriot*, a former Dutch Resistance paper, insisted on the Jews' duty to thank those who fell victim on the Jews' behalf. In Belgium, the 'patriotic clause', initiated by the Catholic opposition, claimed to exclude Jews from national compensation because they had been deported for being Jews, not for being Resistance fighters.[10]

Jewish survivors were excluded from the national memory of war in Germany too. While many Germans were forced to acknowledge Nazi atrocities under Allied occupation, repentance could not be made compulsory. A survey in November 1946 showed that 37 per cent of Germans thought 'the extermination of Jews and Poles and other non-Aryans was necessary for the security of Germans.' Almost the same ratio of Germans agreed to the proposition that 'Jews should not have the same rights as those belonging to the Aryan race.' In a 1952 poll, 37 per cent of West Germans affirmed that it was better for Germany not to have Jews on its territory. Adenauer's reparations plan faced opposition. The Christian Democratic Union (CDU) opposed payments to Jewish victims, claiming it would only fuel anti-Semitism among those who objected to preferential treatment for Jews. The Communist Party (KPD) also opposed the reparations plan, but for a different reason; they claimed that only capitalists and financiers in Israel

---

9 Utsumi Aiko, *Chosenjin BCkyū senpanno kiroku* (Tokyo: Keisoshobo, 1982); Utsumi Aiko and Murai Yoshinori, *Sekidoka'no Chosenjin hanran* (Tokyo: Keisoshobo, 1980).

10 Pieter Lagrou, 'Victims of Genocide and National Memory: Belgium, France and the Netherlands 1945–1965', *Past & Present* 154 (1997), 181–222 (pp. 182, 193, 198–9); Ian Buruma, *Year Zero: A History of 1945* (New York: Penguin, 2013), pp. 134–35.

would benefit.[11] The collective memory in Germany and in many other West European countries was imbued with a national bigotry that was reminiscent of the division between *kokumin* and *hi-kokumin* in Japanese memory.

A series of *Kameradenschinder* (comrade abuse) trials between the late 1940s and early 1960s in West Germany is most telling.[12] Some returned POWs were criminally charged for denouncing and abusing their 'comrades' while in Soviet POW camps. Unlike the leniency shown toward Nazi criminals in the 1950s, the West German judiciary eagerly prosecuted German POWs who had collaborated with their Soviet captors. These collaborators were accused of victimizing fellow Germans. While West German public opinion tended to exonerate convicted Nazi war criminals because they were simply following orders, the same leniency did not apply to POWs accused of Soviet collaboration. Aiding Soviet authorities was viewed as a more serious crime than being a Nazi. Some verdicts maintained that defendants had violated the bonds of 'comradeship' and the soldierly ideal of masculine virtue – the very ideals that had facilitated German soldiers' participation in genocidal warfare. West German courts were more keen to punish a 'crime against nation' than a 'crime against humanity'.

The memory of Jewish suffering also was repressed and marginalized in communist Eastern Europe. It simply did not fit into the Soviet narratives of the workers' anti-fascist front and the 'Great Patriotic War'. If Western Marxists disregarded Jewish suffering under the banner of socialist universalism, East European communists openly gave voice to their anti-Semitism through the use of the label 'rootless cosmopolitanism'. In the GDR, the Communist Party launched an anti-Semitic campaign, purging 'cosmopolitans' alongside 'German fascists' and capitalists as traitors to the nation. The Party rejected Jewish restitution for the same reason as the Belgian Catholic party. Władysław Gomułka in 'People's Poland' resolutely fought against national nihilism and proclaimed the mono-ethnic nation state as the goal. Similarly, in North Korea in his anti-revisionist campaign in 1956–58, Kim Il Sung defended his dictatorship by criticizing 'national nihilism'. Kim was as proud of being a nationalist as he was of being a communist.

---

11 Robert G. Moeller, *War Stories: The Search for a Usable Past in the Federal Republic of Germany* (Berkeley: University of California Press, 2001), pp. 26–7; Tony Judt, *Postwar: A History of Europe since 1945* (London: Heinemann, 2005), pp. 58–9.

12 Frank Biess, 'Between Amnesty and Anti-Communism: The West German Kameradenschinder Trials, 1948–1960', in Omer Bartov, Atina Grossmann and Mary Nolan, eds., *Crimes of War: Guilt and Denial in the Twentieth Century* (New York: The New Press, 2002), pp. 138–60.

The legitimacy of his *Chu-che* (collective subjectivity/sovereignty) dictator-ship derived from the public memory of Kim's anti-Japanese partisan struggle.[13]

The communist regime itself was a hotbed for the memory of the nationalist episteme. The socialist ideal of the ethical and political unity of society reinforced the primordial concept of nation as an organic community. No wonder the grassroots memory of anti-Semitism in the interwar period continued under the regime of 'People's Democracy'. Top-down orders for the fair treatment of Jewish citizens often were blocked by prejudiced low-ranking local bureaucrats. For instance, the Polish Communist Party's (PPR) central committee instructors were at a loss when they realized that workers were unwilling publicly to condemn perpetrators of the 1946 Kielce pogrom. Many factory workers and organized peasants opposed a resolution condemning the pogrom and began to perceive the PPR as 'Jewish' in opposition to native workers. An anonymous reporter submitted an account of a meeting of Stanisław Mikołajczyk's opposition activists: 'the third speaker ... put out a resolution that Jews should also be expelled from Poland, and he also remarked that Hitler ought to be thanked for destroying the Jews (tumultuous ovation and applause).'[14]

However, the banal stereotype of an anti-Semitic Poland explains nothing. Vichy's responsibility for the extermination of Jews in France, as well as the Netherlands' extraordinary rate of Jewish exterminations (approximately 80 per cent), were not significantly better than the record in Poland, where Nazi occupation policy was incomparably harsher. One encounters here a puzzling Polish paradox, namely that the very absence of a Quisling-like regime proved to be disastrous. Unlike anti-Semitic collaborationists in other countries, Polish anti-Semitic nationalists were never compromised. They fought against the Nazis and even risked their lives to rescue Jews by joining the *Żegota*, the underground organization to save Jews. Thus, a patriotic Pole could be a hero of the Resistance, a saviour of Jews, and an anti-Semite. Those

---

13 Jeffrey Herf, *Divided Memory: The Nazi Past in the Two Germanys* (Cambridge, Mass.; Harvard University Press, 1997), pp. 33–6; Robert Cherry, 'Holocaust Historiography: The Role of the Cold War', *Science & Society* 63:4 (Winter, 1999–2000), 459–77 (pp. 459–60); Norman Geras, 'Marxists before the Holocaust', *New Left Review* 224 (1997), 19–38 (pp. 37–8); Jie-Hyun Lim, 'The Nationalist Message in Socialist Code: On the Court Historiography in People's Poland and North Korea', in S. Sogner, ed., *Making Sense of Global History: The 19th International Congress of Historical Sciences Commemorative Volume* (Oslo: Universitetsforlaget, 2001), pp. 373–88.

14 Jan T. Gross, *Fear: Anti-Semitism in Poland after Auschwitz* (New York: Random House, 2006), pp. 98, 120–2, 225–6.

anti-Semitic saviours of Jews saved Jews so as to save the honour of the Polish nation. The nation was deified in this way, and the memory of anti-Semitism remained a part of patriotic memory in post-war Poland.

Jews could be Poles posthumously because 'dead Jews make good Poles'. Jews were integrated into the Polish national memory only through the politics of numbering. With the rise of the national communist faction, the genocide of Polish Jews was made an integral part of the ethnic Polish tragedy. The Holocaust had been interpreted as a German-Jewish conspiracy against Poles to maximize Polish wartime martyrdom and suffering. It was against this background that 'partisans' led by Mieczysław Moczar launched an attack on the *Wielka Encyklopedia Powszechna* (*WEP*; Great Universal Encyclopaedia) in 1967. The distinction drawn between 'concentration camps' (*obozy koncentracyjne*) and 'extermination camps' (*obozy zagłady*) in the *WEP* was criticized for prejudicially favouring Jewish suffering over Polish martyrdom. In the public memory fabricated by the Communist Party, it was the Poles who were sentenced to annihilation by the Nazis while the Jews were subject to forced resettlement. The Warsaw Ghetto Uprising was seen as 'a specific kind of fighting of the Polish underground'.[15]

Across Europe, Jews were not the only ones alienated from patriotic memory. Foreign slave workers were excluded from the German compensation scheme until 2 August 2000, when the Bundestag passed a law to recompense foreign slave workers. POW returnees were greeted with silent disdain in all warring countries. Their capture signified cowardice, rather than brave resistance; thus they had to bear the burden of national defeat and responsibility for the calamitous war. Some of them were suspected of national treason. Sinti and Roma were stigmatized under laws permitting their surveillance and incarceration as justified measures for preserving public order. As supporters of another totalitarian regime, communists were also ineligible for individual compensation. The West German judiciary found it necessary for the maintenance of social order to place asocials in protective custody and imprison them. Discriminatory compensation practices, based on ethnicity, race, ideology and sexuality, went along with the nationalization of memory.

---

15 Michael Steinlauf, 'Teaching the Holocaust in Poland', in Joshua D. Zimmerman, ed., *Contested Memories: Poles and Jews during the Holocaust and Its Aftermath* (New Brunswick, NJ: Rutgers University Press, 2003), pp. 262–70 (pp. 265–6).

Gender was another important factor affecting the nationalization of memory. Paragraph 175 of the Nazi criminal code, which punished male homosexuality, was deemed compatible with the West German democratic constitution and remained part of the criminal code. 'Aryans' punished for violating Nazi racial codes for sex, especially women punished for having sexual relations with foreign POWs, did not qualify as victims.[16] Until the early 1990s, the memory of comfort women was erased from the national memory in postcolonial Korea. Though the Batavian court convicted the Japanese for forcing Dutch women POWs into prostitution, the issue was more about racial transgression than sexual exploitation. Even when the suppressed memory surfaced in the early 1990s, it remained a matter of the 'sexualized nation' or 'nationalized sexuality'.[17] Memory activists for the comfort women proposed building a monument to comfort women at Independence Hall in Korea in 1991, but in vain. Comfort women did not fit the heroic narrative of Independence Hall. Only when the nationalist narrative in the global memory space transformed victimhood into the sublime could the memory of comfort women be highlighted as a way of nationalizing sexuality.

Sublime victimhood

A bitter irony of war memory across the globe initially was that perpetrators of the Axis crimes became self-proclaimed victims. Paradoxically, victimizers had a more urgent need to explore the experience of being victimized, as if mimicking victims could exonerate their own war atrocities, massacres and genocidal crimes. Given the substantial degree of popular backing, voluntary self-mobilization, and the high level of plebiscitary acclamation for the Nazi regime, the *kleine Leute* ('ordinary people') in the Axis powers were more likely 'willing victims' than innocent ones. The mnemonic magic of turning petty perpetrators or accomplices into innocent victims was possible because perpetration and victimhood are played out within the national collective – between evil Nazis and good Germans, between *hi-kokumin* and *kokumin*, between Resistance fighters and collaborators. Thus, it excludes the memory

---

16 Moeller, *War Stories*, pp. 28–9.
17 Hyunah Yang, 'Hankookin gunwuianburŭl giŏkhandanŭngeot' [Remembering Korean Comfort Women], in Elaine H. Kim and Chungmoo Choi, eds., *Dangerous Women* (Korean translation, Seoul: Samin, 2000), pp. 157–76 (p. 175).

of suffering by non-national others, such as Jews, foreign slave workers, comfort women, alien Slavic communists and homosexuals.

Japan as 'the only nation ever to have been atom-bombed' could enjoy a privileged position in the competition for victimhood. Hiroshima as an absolute evil was often compared with the Holocaust. Auschwitz and Hiroshima were often named as terrible twin symbols of man-made mass death and even singled out as two archetypical examples of white racism.[18] No wonder that the word Holocaust, in translated form, was used as early as 1949 in Japan. Takashi Nagai, a Catholic medical doctor known as the saint of Urakami church, addressed Nagasaki victims as 'lambs without blemish, slain as a whole-burnt offering on an altar of sacrifice, atoning for the sins of all the nations during World War II'. Nagai picked out the word *hansai* (燔祭), the Japanese translation of 'Holocaust' from chapter 22 of Genesis to explicate the sublime world-redemptive suffering of the Japanese *hibakusha*, A-bomb victims.[19] Nagai's speech is one of the earliest recorded public uses of 'Holocaust' in the post-war world.

With its biblical semiotics, *hansai* facilitated the nationalist sublimation of victims (*higaisha*) into sacrifices (*giseisha*). Victimhood nationalism, as a political religion, comes into being in the sublime transition from victims to sacrifices. By transposing *pro domino mori* into *pro patria mori*, it could sacralize fallen soldiers and national suffering.[20] For those victims, however, sublimation was nothing other than humiliation. Disregarding their will, abstract ideas instrumentalized and thus re-victimized victims. One A-bomb survivor wrote bluntly that people in Hiroshima did not like to be treated as 'data' in the political movement that utilized their misery. The suicide of Kikuya Haraguchi, a poet and A-bomb victim, remains a poignant memory in this regard. He chose to die by his own hand instead of dying from

---

18 Ian Buruma, *The Wages of Guilt: Memories of War in Germany and Japan* (Korean translation, Seoul: Hangyŏreh Shinmusa, 2002), pp. 119–26; John W. Dower, 'An Aptitude for Being Unloved: War and Memory in Japan', in Omer Bartov et al., eds., *Crimes of War*, pp. 217–41 (p. 226).

19 Tetsuya Takashi, *Kokka to Gisei* [State and Sacrifice] (Korean translation, Seoul: Chaikgwahamke, 2008), pp. 72–83; John W. Dower, 'The Bombed: Hiroshimas and Nagasakis in Japanese Memory', *Diplomatic History* 19:2 (1995), 275–95 (p. 285).

20 For victimhood nationalism, see Jie-Hyun Lim, 'Victimhood Nationalism in Contested Memories: National Mourning and Global Accountability', in Aleida Assmann and Sebstian Conrad, eds., *Memory in a Global Age: Discourses, Practices and Trajectories* (Basingstoke: Palgrave Macmillan, 2010), pp. 138–62. It is difficult to catch this semantic sublimation in the German '*Opfer*' and the Polish '*ofiara*', signifying victim and sacrifice simultaneously, but the division between victim and sacrifice is rather clear in English and East Asian languages.

A-bomb radiation exposure. Committing suicide was his last resort to save his individual subjectivity and human dignity.[21] With his death, Haraguchi protested against the victimhood narrative that instrumentalized A-bomb survivors. The story did not end here, however.

Fire bombings, *hikiage* – the repatriation of Japanese civilians – the suffering of the Japanese POWs, and the wartime misery of hunger and military oppression also have been emphasized in order to vindicate Japanese victimhood. By projecting guilt and responsibility onto the evil militarists as *hi-kokumin* (anti/non-national) perpetrators, ordinary Japanese could remain *kokumin* (national) victims. If Japanese military leaders, as *hi-kokumin* victim-izers, were totally responsible, then ordinary Japanese, as *kokumin* victims, were exempt from war accountability. Thus, 'it became commonplace to speak of the war dead themselves – and indeed, of virtually all ordinary Japanese – as being victims and sacrifices.'[22] The public memory of Japanese victimhood was not only self-generated; the Supreme Commander of the Allied Powers (SCAP) assumed that the Japanese people had been slaves of feudal habits of subservience to authority. SCAP's Orientalist view exempted poor, ordinary Japanese from war culpability and guilt. Passive victims cannot be held accountable for the misuse of power. Deprived of agency, ordinary Japanese were innocent of the nation's various transgressions done in their names and with their participation.

Remembering Hiroshima and Nagasaki easily became a way of forgetting the Nanjing massacre, comfort women, the maltreatment of POWs and countless other war atrocities. The striking parallels between the imperial 'commemorative building project for the construction of Greater East Asia' (*daitoa kensetsu kinen eizo keikaku*) of 1940 and the Hiroshima Peace Memorial Park of 1949 – both projects of the world-renowned architect Tange Kenzo – are symptomatic of the Japanese apologetic memory.[23] Conventional war atrocities also seemed insignificant compared to the apocalyptic hell of Hiroshima and Nagasaki. The term 'Pacific War', imposed by SCAP, was another deliberate conceptual tool, allowing the Japanese to avoid taking responsibility for war crimes committed against their Asian neighbours. With its focus on bilateral conflict between America and Japan, the term 'Pacific War' downplayed Japanese military aggression. That partly explains why

21 Kenzaburo Oe, *Hiroshima Noto* [Hiroshima Notes] (Tokyo: Iwanamishoten, 1965), pp. 6, 8.
22 Dower, 'Aptitude for Being Unloved', p. 228.
23 Lisa Yoneyama, *Hiroshima Traces: Time, Space, and the Dialectics of Memory* (Berkeley: University of California Press, 1999), pp. 1–3.

'the Japanese people don't have much consciousness of having invaded China and have a tendency to emphasize only the sufferings they bore in the Pacific War.'[24]

Iris Chang's tactic in naming the Nanjing massacre the 'forgotten Holocaust' and 'pacific Holocaust' is thought to be a deliberate response to the nuclear universal victimology of Hiroshima and Nagasaki. By claiming that the Japanese in Nanjing outdid 'the Romans of Carthage (*only* 150,000 died in that slaughter)' in her bestselling book, Chang made a diachronic hierarchy of victims based on world history.[25] It is interesting to note that 'forgotten Holocaust' and 'Poland's Holocaust' have been used in Polish historiography in defence of the apologetic memory. In this historiography, the Ukrainian, Belorussian, Lithuanian, German and Jewish nationalists in interwar Poland had constituted a grave danger to the survival of Poland and a barrier to nation-building. As a result, interwar Poland remained a 'state of nationalities' (*państwo narodowościowe*) instead of a nation state. What is unforgettable and unforgivable was that many of these ethnic minorities sided with either the Soviet Union or Nazi Germany and collaborated in killing and oppressing ethnic Poles. Poles became 'the first people in Europe to experience the Holocaust' and 'the treatment of Poles by the Germans was even worse than that of Jews' in the Polish apologetic memory of war.[26]

Apologetic memory in conjunction with victimhood nationalism in Japan raises a serious epistemological question concerning the decontextualization of history. Shoichi Watanabe, a right-wing philologist, is a walking conjunction of victimhood nationalism and apologetic memory, when he says that the 'atomic bombings of Japan – for which the US never apologized – constitute a human rights issue in comparison to which the problem of comfort women could be defined as only a commercial act'.[27] Albeit far from Watanabe's malignant intentions, Yoko Kawashima Watkins's *hikiage-mono* (repatriation story) is another example. The novella tells how the narrator, an eleven-year-old Japanese girl, and her family faced threats to their lives, hunger, and fear

24 James Orr, *The Victim as Hero: Ideologies of Peace and National Identity in Postwar Japan* (Honolulu: University of Hawai'i Press, 2001), p. 32.
25 Iris Chang, *The Rape of Nanking: The Forgotten Holocaust of World War II* (New York: Basic Books, 1997), pp. 5–6.
26 Tadeusz Piotrowski, *Poland's Holocaust: Ethnic Strife, Collaboration with Occupying Forces and Genocide in the Second Republic, 1918–1947* (Jefferson, NC: McFarland & Company, 1998); Richard C. Lukas, *Forgotten Holocaust: The Poles under German Occupation* (revised edn, New York: Hippocrene Books, 2005).
27 Karoline Postel-Vinay with Mark Selden, 'History on Trial: French Nippon Foundation Sues Scholar for Libel to Protect the Honor of Sasakawa Ryoichi' (www.japanfocus. org/-Karoline-Postel_Vinay/3349).

of sexual assault on their way home to Japan from Nanam, a northern Korean town. Upon Japan's defeat in the Second World War some 2 million Japanese expellees from Manchuria and northern Korea encountered a similar fate, an East Asian version of the European *wypędzenie/Vertreibung* (expulsion). But Watkins's story is detached from Japanese colonialism; thus, Western readers ignorant of East Asian history may read grassroots revenge or retribution by colonized Koreans as wanton disregard for human dignity and life. Consequently, Watkins's novella contrasts Koreans as evil perpetrators with Japanese as innocent victims.[28] This naive decontextualization of history could have been counterbalanced by entangled memories of war and colonialism in the trans-Asian/Pacific space.

Günther Grass's *Im Krebsgang* (Crabwalk) is quite a contrast to Watkins's naive saga that is decontextualized from history. While *Im Krebsgang* focuses on the tragic fate of 8,000 German civilian refugees on the *Wilhelm Gustloff*, which was torpedoed and sunk by a Soviet submarine, it never fails to contextualize the disaster by alluding to the history of the ship in the service of the Nazis' 'Strength through Joy' campaign, the Nazi career of its dedicatee – Wihelm Gustloff – and the history of shipping murderers of the Condor Legion in Guernica. This novella makes clear that thousands of German victims on board the *Wilhelm Gustloff* could have been Nazi collaborators/victimizers. The historical meandering implied in the title 'crabwalk' cautions against the use of a naive dichotomy of victimizers and victims in absolute terms. Its political implication was to criticize revisionist historiography in the 1990s that essentialized German suffering through the decontextualization of history. Indeed, Grass's cautious handling of contextualization seems distinct from Jörg Friedrich's account of the Allied bombing, which equated the suffering of German civilians with the suffering of European Jews through linguistic associations of *Einsatzgruppe*, *Gaskeller*, *vernichtet* and *Zivilisationsbruch*.[29]

To criticize Friedrich's narrative for decontextualizing history does not mean justifying Allied bombings as a punishment for historical culprits, rather it means locating German suffering in its historical context. For example, Friedrich insists that Luftwaffe records regarding the 'Battle of Britain' provide no indication that the Germans had a deliberate plan to

---

28 Yoko Kawashima Watkins, *So Far from the Bamboo Grove* (New York: Beech Tree, 1994), Korean translation: *Yoko-Iyagi* (Seoul: Munhakdongne, 2005).

29 Jörg Friedrich, *Der Brand. Deutschland im Bombenkrieg, 1940–1945* (Munich: Propyläen Verlag, 2002).

bomb civilian targets. But the Luftwaffe's air raid on Wieluń, a small Polish town in the morning of 1 September 1939, was outside his perspective. The command word for this air raid, which marked the beginning of the Second World War, was 'direkt auf den Marktplatz!' The air bombing of the market square killed an estimated 1,200 Polish civilians and destroyed roughly 70 per cent of the town. It was no coincidence that the air commandant in charge of the air raid on Wieluń was Major General Wolfram Freiherr von Richthofen – the same officer who had ordered the Condor Legion to bomb Guernica during the Spanish Civil War on 26 April 1937. Indeed Wieluń was Poland's Guernica.[30] Friedrich's story of bombing included Nagasaki, but excluded Guernica and Wieluń.

In West Germany, the suffering of expellees from Eastern Europe and German POWs in the Soviet Union was collectively mourned. Their private memories structured the public memory of communist brutality and the loss of the German east. Politicians in West Germany often compared what Germans had suffered under the communists to what Jews had suffered under the Nazis. The argument that German expellees were driven from their historic homelands because of their ethnicity reminded one of Nazi racist crimes. Germans subject to brutal retaliation in internment camps modelled on the Nazi concentration camps were regarded as victims of 'a crime against humanity'. German POWs in Soviet camps were claimed as the victims of the ethnic hatred and racial prejudices of the Russians. Discursively it was a continuation of Goebbels's attempts to orientalize Russians as subhuman Asian hordes.[31] Although the worst offenders were soldiers from Belorussia and the Ukraine who were thirsty for revenge, the rumour of the Asian-Tatar soldiers as sexual predators circulated widely.

The Cold War divided the memory of victimhood in the two Germanys. In the GDR, the expulsion of Germans from brotherly communist countries was hardly questioned. It was not *Vertreibung* (expulsion), but *Umsiedlung* (resettlement). Mention of the rape of German women by Red Army soldiers was taboo. Instead the Allied bombing of East German cities was emphasized and interpreted as a devious plan to sabotage the building of socialism. GDR citizens had been primarily the victims of criminal Allied bombings. At times

---

30 Tadeusz Olejnek, *Wieluń: Polska Guernika* (Wieluń: BWTN, 2004). That famously arrogant Richthofen later led the Luftwaffe to invade Greece, Yugoslavia and Russia. His bombers carpet-bombed Stalingrad; as his diary remarks: 'my two-day major assault on Stalingrad with good incendiary effects right from the start'; Antony Beevor, *The Second World War* (New York: Little, Brown and Company, 2012), p. 337.

31 Moeller, *War Stories*, pp. 78–82.

the suffering of bombing victims in the GDR area was equated with the suffering of the Jews in the Holocaust. Ultimately Walter Ulbricht posed as the leader of a future-oriented, German anti-colonial revolt against American imperialism. Just as the Japanese nation metamorphosed into the colonized in the Pacific War structure, East Germans could occupy the morally comfortable position of the colonized with reference to American imperialism in the Cold War setting. It found an echo in the German extreme leftist claim that Germans were now victims of the manipulations and interests of others – American occupiers, multinational corporations and the international capitalist order.[32]

In the post-Cold War era, the German victimhood narrative exceeded all limits. Erika Steinbach, the former president of Der Bund der Vertriebenen (BdV, Federation of Expellees), never hesitated to describe the suffering of German expellees by using the terms 'forced labor, extermination camp and genocide'. While she equated the misery of German expellees with the suffering of Jews in the Holocaust, the Poles and Czechs who victimized these expellees were equated with the Nazi perpetrators of the Holocaust.[33] In Steinbach's decontextualized world of victims, it did not matter if these German expellees bore some responsibility for Nazism or not. Just like the apologetic memory in Japan, Steinbach seemed to stick to 'an age-old strategy of self-exculpation, one guilt is set against the other and thereby reduced to zero'.[34] That strategy of self-exculpation in the victimhood narrative in Germany and Japan gave rise to a furious response from the people victimized by Nazism and Japanese colonialism, which in turn served only to strengthen victimhood nationalism in those nations.

Compared to the decontextualized memories of victimhood in Germany and Japan, victims of Nazi and Japanese aggression responded by over-contextualizing history. On the flipside, over-contextualized memories exonerated individual perpetrators from legal culpability and moral sins. It was within this framework of over-contextualized memories that the Laudański brothers claimed their innocence. As the only living Poles convicted for killing Jewish neighbours in Jedwabne, they defined themselves in the era of People's Poland as the 'victims of fascism, of capitalism, of the *Sanacja* regime'. After the 'Fall', capitalism and the *Sanacja* regime were replaced by socialism

---

32 Herf, *Divided Memory*, p. 110; Judt, *Postwar*, p. 471.
33 Jan Piskorski, *Vertreibung und Deutsch-Polnische Geschichte* (Osnabrück: fibre Verlag, 2005), pp. 37, 42ff.
34 Aleida Assmann, 'On the (In)Compatibility of Guilt and Suffering in German Memory', *German Life and Letters* 59:2 (2006), 187–200 (p. 194).

and People's Poland in the Laudański brothers' memories. The perpetrators changed, but the Laudański brothers' position as collective victims remained intact: 'like the whole nation we suffered under the Germans, the Soviets, and the People's Republic of Poland.'[35] Individual victimizers became collective victims by covering themselves with the umbrella of victimhood nationalism.

The Korean public's fury at Watkins's novella was a response to its inverted portrayal of the Japanese as victims and Koreans as victimizers. In the schematic dichotomy of collective guilt and innocence rooted in the vernacular memory among Koreans, the Japanese can be nothing other than a uniform mass of victimizers. The bitter experience of individual Japanese expellees cannot be real under the abstract category of the Japanese as perpetrators. That explains why their criticism of Watkins's novella was framed in positivistic terms such as 'distortion of truth', 'fabrication of facts' and 'historical lies'. What is truly interesting is that Korean critics use the historical parallelism of the victimhood between Jews and Koreans to convince Western readers. The Holocaust is appropriated as a way of selling their victimhood to a global audience and thus a metonymic weapon of reterritorializing memory. One Amazon reader's book review claimed: 'this book is akin to an escape narrative of an SS officer's family running away from Birkenau Auschwitz concentration camp while the heroin [sic] daughter of the Nazi officer is running away from cruel and dangerous Jews freed from concentration camps and Poles.'[36]

It is amazing to find a parallel from the apologetic memory in Poland, which took the form of the critical response to Jan Gross's *Neighbours*. Positivistic terms like 'a novel with footnotes', 'lacking objectivity', 'undocumented facts', 'made-up lies' and 'gross misinterpretation' dominated the immediate response. One Amazon book reviewer was frightened by the fact that Gross's book was placed in the non-fiction category of books instead of fiction.[37] The Polish self-portrait of the 'crucified nation' as the eternal victim of neighbours to the East and West cannot accept the image of themselves as bystanders,

---

35 Anna Bikont, 'We of Jedwabne', in Antony Polonsky and Joanna Michlic, eds., *The Neighbors Responded: The Controversy over the Jedwabne Massacre in Poland* (Princeton University Press, 2004), p. 294.

36 ML (New York), Amazon reader review, 16 January 2007 (www.amazon.com/review/product/0844668109/ref=cm_cr_dp_all_helpful?%5Fencoding=UTF8&coliid=&showViewpoints=1&colid=&sortBy=bySubmissionDateDescending).

37 See Amazon reader reviews (www.amazon.com/Neighbors-Destruction-Jewish-Community-Jedwabne/product-reviews/0142002402/ref=cm_cr_pr_viewpnt_sr_1?ie=UTF8&showViewpoints=0&filterBy=addOneStar).

let alone victimizers. If over-contextualization negates the coexistence of perpetrators and victims, and perhaps bystanders within the same nation, decontextualization conceals the past of perpetrators who became victims under certain circumstances such as when their former victims sought revenge. Thus nations are increasingly engaged in 'a distasteful competition over who suffered most', which provides an appropriate historical-political setting for the antagonistic complicity of nationalisms between perpetrators and victims.

Historikerstreit globally

The year 2000 was indelibly imprinted in global memory space. Transnational, self-reflexive, critical, alien- and gender-sensitive memories came up simultaneously. On 27–29 January 2000, twenty-three heads of state, fourteen deputy prime ministers and other representatives from forty-six countries gathered in Stockholm to discuss Holocaust education, remembrance and research. At the end of this history-summit meeting, all attendees signed the 'Stockholm Declaration', which proposed remembering the Holocaust as a transnational civic virtue. In May 2000, the publication of Jan Gross's book *Sąsiedzi* (*Neighbours*) triggered a *Historikerstreit po polsku* (Polish historians' quarrel). As the Poles greeted Leszek Kołakowski's warnings about an incipient, painful *Historikerstreit* in Eastern Europe, the heated controversy over the Jedwabne massacre brought 'a genuine moral revolution' to post-communist Poland and awakened the sleeping complicity of the region. On 2 August 2000, the Bundestag passed a law to recompense foreign slave workers for their wartime labour. Last but not least, the Women's International War Crimes Tribunal on Japan's Military Sexual Slavery was convened in Tokyo in December 2000. Transnational memory activists for comfort women convicted the dead Emperor Hirohito of a 'crime against humanity'.

From the viewpoint of transnational memory, all *Historikerstreite* in the post-war era incubated the conflict between critical and apologetic memory. Compared to the 1950s and the 1960s, the global memory landscape in 2000 obviously represented a sea change. Indeed, the 'past is more difficult to be predicted than the future'. *Der Spiegel*'s recent article on the Fritz Fischer controversy (the *Historikerstreit* on the First World War), described apologetic memory as the *Zeitgeist* in 1960s Germany. When Fischer's thesis on German culpability for war was made public in 1961, the conservatives in the Bundestag were resolved 'to combat and eradicate the habitual, negligent and deliberate distortions of German history and Germany's image today, distortions that are sometimes made with the intention of dissolving the Western community'.[38] The German Foreign Ministry tried to prevent Fritz Fischer from travelling to the USA for a series of lectures in 1964. The change is all the more dramatic when compared with the German public's enthusiastic reception of Daniel Goldhagen in 1996, despite his essentialist interpretation of German anti-Semitism.

The Eichmann trial and the Frankfurt Auschwitz trial in the early 1960s were moments of awakening for the repressed memories of war, genocide, dictatorship and colonialism. Politically correct history is impossible, because one cannot turn the clock back. But politically correct memory is possible, because memory is in the making now. That explains why the generation of 1968 launched the memory war against apologetic memory. The Vietnam War detonated the bomb of critical memory globally. Bertrand Russell used his citizen's tribunal as a variant of the Nuremburg tribunal to accuse the USA of genocide. Telford Taylor, the American prosecutor in Nuremburg, expressed his agreement with his publication of *Nuremburg and Vietnam: An American Tragedy*. Jean-Paul Sartre added a colonial dimension by associating the American genocide in Vietnam with the French colonialists' bloody war against Algerian anti-colonial fighters. The anti-racism in the Vietnam–genocide discourse was reinforced by Holocaust analogies to which many Jewish student activists contributed. The Vietnam War prompted young revisionist historians in Greece to see the UK and USA, not as saviours of Greece from communist tyranny, but as imperialists that strangled a genuinely popular radical movement.[39]

American atrocities in Vietnam also fuelled the Japanese interest in exposing Japanese atrocities in the 'Fifteen Years War' (1931–45). After chronicling American war atrocities in Vietnam as a journalist for *Asahi shinbun*, Honda Katsuichi came to reflect on this matter. In the summer of 1971, Honda spent forty days travelling along the route of Japanese military aggression in China to collect

---

38 Dick Kurbjuweit, 'World War I Guilt: Culpability Question Divides Historians Today', *Der Spiegel*, 14 February 2014 (www.spiegel.de/international/world/questions-of-culpability-in-wwi-still-divide-german-historians-a-953173.html).

39 Berthold Molden, 'Vietnam, the New Left and the Holocaust: How the Cold War Changed Discourse on Genocide', in Assmann and Conrad, eds., *Memory in a Global Age*, pp. 79–96; Mark Mazower, 'The Cold War and the Appropriation of Memory: Greece after Liberation', in István Deák, Jan T. Gross and Tony Judt, eds., *The Politics of Retribution in Europe: World War II and Its Aftermath* (Princeton University Press, 2000), pp. 212–32 (pp. 224–5).

eyewitness accounts and other evidence. He published a series of travel reports in the *Asahi* newspaper, which later were published in book form as *Chugoku no tabi* (Journey to China). Honda's book on the Nanjing massacre met with angry criticism from the conservatives, who denied and minimized the massacre by naming it the 'Nanjing *incident*'. Maoist China has been rather indifferent to the Nanjing massacre per se because its 'present significance' was to stop American imperialists' remilitarization of Japan. It was much later on 15 August 1985 that the 'memorial for the compatriot victims in the Nanjing massacre by the Japanese invading troops' was completed. It was renovated and expanded again in 1997, the same year Iris Chang's *Rape of Nanking* was published.[40]

Epistemologically a shift from documents to testimonies underlies the emergence of critical memory globally. If Nuremburg is marked as 'the victory of the written over the oral', the Eichmann trial freed victims to speak and opened the era of witnesses. Raul Hilberg's thorny question of 'is it not equally barbaric to write footnotes after Auschwitz?' epitomizes that shift. Hilberg's question reads as a warning signal to pompous historians of the positivistic truth.[41] The dilemma was that perpetrators and rulers monopolize a narrative and history while victims have only experiences and voices. Testimonies are important and sometimes the only sources, but victims' memories are incomplete, imbalanced and often incorrect. However, conventional historians interrogate and interpret witnesses and dismiss testimony for its inaccuracy, as if memory is a truth game. As the Eichmann trial showed, the 'KZ' witnesses did not endeavour to prove factually, but rather to transmit affectively. How to transmit intransmissible experiences was the challenge they confronted.

In his convincing psychoanalysis of a survivor's memory of 'four chimneys blown up', when only one chimney at Auschwitz actually blew up, Dori Laub pointed to the gap between intellectual memory and deep memory. The survivor-witness's deep memory of four chimneys reflects the reality of the unimaginable occurrence of a Jewish armed revolt, but it is irreconcilable with the historical fact of one chimney. Both are right in 'the aporia of Auschwitz', bearing the 'non-coincidence between facts and truth, between

---

40 Daqing Yang, 'The Malleable and the Contested: The Nanjing Massacre in Postwar China and Japan', in T. Fujitani, Geoffrey M. White and Lisa Yoneyama, eds., *Perilous Memories: The Asia-Pacific War(s)* (Durham, NC: Duke University Press, 2001), pp. 50–86.
41 Raul Hilberg, 'I Was Not There', in Berel Lang, ed., *Writing and the Holocaust* (New York: Holmes & Meier, 1988), pp. 17–25 (pp. 17, 20, 25).

verification and comprehension'.[42] Nonetheless, historians of denial are insistent. They never comprehend the aporia of Auschwitz and keep interrogating so as to disprove witness testimonies. It is not difficult for deniers to find inconsistencies in logic, factual inaccuracies, and petty textual faults in meandering testimonies. Then they ask 'why weren't we told before if it were true?' But the truth is they didn't listen. The right question should be 'why weren't we listening before?'[43] One should note that it took four years for Jan Gross to acknowledge the testimony of Szmuel Waszerstajn as a source for his book on Jedwabne.

However, the task of transmitting the intransmissible risks the sacralization of memory. A certain degree of sacralization of memories is inevitable for individuals, as it makes one's past something unique, incommensurable with others' experiences. On the national level, however, collective memory comes into being through communication, education, commemoration, rituals and ceremonies among the masses. By nature, such a collective memory cannot be sacralized. Rather it is an arena of political contestation. But the generic Historikerstreit shows that sacralization of traumatic memory has been the epistemological mainstay of apologetic memory, because it can effectively block the critical gaze of outsiders upon 'our own unique past'. By not allowing outsiders any chance to understand 'our own unique past', sacralized memories preserve a monopoly on understanding the past. The uniqueness discourse of the Holocaust, the colloquial thesis of 'you foreigners can never ever understand our own tragic national past' in the generic Historikerstreit, justifies apologetic memory globally. Beyond any doubt, the Holocaust is in many crucial aspects an unparalleled or singular event. But this does not mean it is unique and cannot be subject to comparative analysis.

Thematically the topic of 'complicity/collaboration' is the most salient and globally shared issues in the Historikerstreit on war, genocide, dictatorship and colonialism. Once liberated from the Manichaean Cold War demonism of a few bad victimizers and many innocent victims, the complicity/collaboration issue became vibrant. Postcolonial criticism, the political project of democratizing democracy in the post-dictatorial regimes, and Vergangenheitsbewältigung (coming to terms with the past) in post-communist Eastern

42 Marianne Hirsch and Leo Spitzer, 'The Witness in the Archive: Holocaust Studies/Memory Studies', Memory Studies 2:2 (2009), 151–70 (pp. 156, 159, 161).
43 Krygier, 'Neighbours: Poles, Jews and the Aboriginal Question', p. 300.

Europe accelerated the debate in three dimensions: (post-)colonial guilt, genocidal complicity and agency and responsibility.

First, postcolonial criticism broke the repressive connection between history and the nation, and thus shook the binaries of national resistance and colonial collaboration and of colonial continuity and postcolonial discontinuity. In the East Asian memory space, Manchukuo, the Japanese puppet state in Manchuria, is a good example. Though it is a key to understanding postcolonial East Asia, Manchukuo belonged nowhere in the East Asian memory space after 1945. There was something suspicious in this long total silence. In fact, both the rightist and leftist dictatorship in the two Koreas inherited historical legacies of the defence state, military mobilization, national ceremonies, big sports festivals, and Confucianism as the official ideology, from Manchukuo. The strange amalgam of the American Taylor system, social engineering, mobilization in the total war system of interwar Germany and Japan, and the planned economy and industrial warriors of the Soviet Union flowed to the developmental dictatorship in South Korea through Manchukuo.[44] Manchukuo, as a memory of colonial guilt, had no place in the postcolonial nationalist narrative.

Postcolonial criticism pays attention also to the continuity of guilt between colonial genocide and the Holocaust. Viewed from the postcolonial perspective, the colonial (dis-)continuity between German colonialists' genocide in the Herero and Nama wars in 1904–7 and the Holocaust could be better explained in the memory of Euro-colonialism. As a group of black radical intellectuals pointed out sharply, Western European colonialism, fascism and Nazism shared the same practices, methods and objects.[45] The Nazi utopia of a racially purified German empire mimicked Western colonialism, 'turning imperialism on its head and treating Europeans as Africans'. Nazi Germans

---

44 Suk-Jung Han, 'The Suppression and Recall of Colonial Memory: Manchukuo and the Cold War in the Two Koreas', in Lim, Walker and Lambert, eds., *Mass Dictatorship and Memory*, 165–79 (pp. 172–4).

45 Cedric J. Robinson, 'Fascism and the Intersection of Capitalism, Racialism and Historical Consciousness', *Humanities in Society* 3 (1983), 325–49; Jürgen Zimmerer, 'Die Geburt des Ostlandes aus dem Geiste des Kolonialismus. Die nationalsozialistische Eroberungs- und Beherrschungspolitik in (post-)kolonialer Perspektive', *Sozial Geschichte* 19:1 (2004), 10–43; Benjamin Madley, 'From Africa to Auschwitz: How German South West Africa Incubated Ideas and Methods Adopted and Developed by the Nazis in Eastern Europe', *European History Quarterly* 35:3 (2005), 429–64; Enzo Traverso, *The Origins of Nazi Violence* (New York: The New Press, 2003); Robert Gerwarth and Stephan Malinowski, 'Der Holocaust als kolonialer Genozid? Europaeische Kolonialgewalt und nationalsozialistischer Vernichtungskrieg', *Geschichte und Gesellschaft* 33 (2007), 439–66.

must have felt a kind of 'white man's burden' vis-à-vis Slavic people as 'white negroes'. And 'the Slavs would be the German equivalent of the conquered native populations of India and Africa in the British empire.'[46] Indeed, 'Western' colonialism provided an important historical precedent for the Nazis' genocidal thinking. A historical connection between colonial genocide and Nazi crimes is undeniable.

The second issue is genocidal complicity. The memory of the genocide at the individual level reflects the dictum that 'structure does not kill but individuals do'. The mass killing had been continuously implemented and supplemented by ordinary men who made improvisatory and face-to-face decisions in local conditions. Murderers were flesh-and-blood human beings just like us. We should consider the existential-ethical question posed by Christopher Browning: 'If the men of Reserve Police Battalion 101 could become killers under such circumstances, what group of men cannot?' In other words, 'placed in comparable situations and similar social constituencies, you or I might also commit murderous ethnic cleansing.'[47] Noda Masaaki's psychoanalysis of Japanese veteran perpetrators leaves a poignant memory in this regard. Despite their acknowledgement of wrongdoing, most of these perpetrators could not remember the faces of their victims. As the interview progressed, however, the face of the victim returned to one veteran soldier's memory in an instant of genuine repentance.[48] Masaaki's finding echoes Zygmunt Bauman's reflection on 'the emancipatory role of the feeling of shame' in the Historikerstreit in Poland.

On the macro level, genocidal complicity resonates with the denationalization of memory. For example, deconstructing the patriotic memory of resistance revealed the collaboration and genocidal complicity in the wartime history of the Vichy regime. Paradoxically speaking, the 'de-Resistantialization' made it possible to criticize collaboration and complicity in deporting Jewish neighbours. But the critical engagement with the memory of genocidal complicity did not stop at the 'Vichy syndrome'. Soon the 'Algerian syndrome' followed. Maurice Papon on trial personified the twin genocidal complicity: the round-up and deportation of the Jews from Bordeaux in

---

46 Mark Mazower, *Dark Continent: Europe's Twentieth Century* (London: Allen Lane, 1998), p. xiii; Ian Kershaw, *Hitler, 1936–45: Nemesis* (New York: W. W. Norton, 2001), pp. 400, 405.

47 Christopher Browning, *Ordinary Men: Reserve Police Battalion 101 and the Final Solution in Poland* (New York: HarperCollins, 1992), p. 189; Michael Mann, *The Dark Side of Democracy: Explaining Ethnic Cleansing* (Cambridge University Press, 2005), p. 9.

48 Noda Masaaki, *Senso to Zaiseki* [War and Guilt] (Tokyo: Iwanamishoten, 1998).

Vichy France and the bloody killing of Algerian immigrant-demonstrators on 17 October 1961. Nevertheless, he was convicted and sentenced only for the crime committed against Jews.[49] The memory of genocidal complicity in France and other European countries was certainly denationalized, but not yet de-Europeanized.

The third issue of 'agency and responsibility' overlaps with issues of colonial continuity and genocidal complicity. Terminological debutants – 'mass dictatorship', 'Fürsorgediktatur', 'Konzensdiktatur', 'everyday fascism' and 'palingenetic consensus' – in the 1990s indicate the shift from coercion to consent in studies of dictatorships. Paradoxically, that shift promoted the critical memory of dictatorship by focusing on the agency of *kleine Leute* who can no longer remain passive victims. Once historical actors are reinstated, they cannot be exonerated from responsibility and culpability. As Václav Havel constantly stressed, the line did not run clearly between victimizers and victims. Rather, it ran through each individual. Not everyone was an accomplice but everyone was in some measure co-responsible for what had been done. The Japanese historians' debate on the total war system, in which voluntary participation and self-mobilization were discussed, can be put in the same context. The change from the apologetic memory of *kokumin* victims to the critical memory of self-mobilized historical actors made it impossible for ordinary Japanese to be exempt from war accountability.[50]

Like the *Historikerstreit* in Eastern Europe, the Korean *Historikerstreit* on 'mass dictatorship' glossed over the responsibility and complicity of the masses in submitting to dictatorship. The political experience of democratization in South Korea shows that the fascist habitus still reigns in everyday practices and influences people's way of thinking, even though the developmental dictatorship as a political regime is long gone. The point of the debate was how to explain the obstinate fascist habitus and the strong nostalgia for the developmental dictatorship among democratic citizens and how to democratize the democracy haunted by the legacy of the dictatorship. Though the thesis of mass dictatorship has been caught in the cross-fire of leftist-liberal historians and sociologists, the moral implication of 'mass

---

49 Joan B. Wolf, *Harnessing the Holocaust: The Politics of Memory in France* (Stanford University Press, 2004), pp. 189–98.
50 See the five volumes of the 'Mass Dictatorship in the Twentieth Century' series published by Palgrave Macmillan (2011–14). See also Konrad H. Jarausch, ed., *Dictatorship as Experience: Towards a Socio-Cultural History of the GDR* (New York: Berghan Books, 1999). For the Japanese case, see Yasushi Yamanouchi, J. Victor Koschmann and Ryūichi Narita, eds., *Total War and Modernization* (Ithaca: Cornell University East Asian Series, 1998).

dictatorship' is far from the apologetic memory. On the contrary, the myth of the working masses as resistance fighters and innocent victims in the old anti-fascist demonology justified self-exculpation and apologetic memory. Adam Michnik's self-reflection of 'whether we are not all children of totalitarian communism, whether we do not all carry inside ourselves the habits, the customs, and the flaws of that system' stands on the same terrain.[51]

Multidirectional memory

The Museum of Occupations in Tallinn, Estonia installed two massive mock-up trains at the gateway into the back half of the exhibition, one bearing the Nazi swastika, the other the Soviet red star. Two locomotives in the centre stage of the museum represent the political symmetry between two totalitarian regimes – Nazism and Stalinism. It reminds one of Andrzej Wajda's film, *Katyń*, which begins with scenes of the dramatic encounter between two streams of Polish refugees in the middle of the bridge near Kraków. Nazi Germans are chasing the one group fleeing to the east, while the Red Army is hunting the other group to the west. The Prague Declaration on European Conscience and Communism signed on 3 June 2008 reflects this bitter wartime memory of 'nowhere to go' among East Europeans. The Prague Declaration calls for 'the equal treatment of and non-discrimination against victims of all the totalitarian regimes' based on the recognition of both the Nazi and communist crimes as crimes against humanity. Then, the Declaration suggests the day of the signing of the Molotov–Ribbentrop Pact on 23 August as 'a day of remembrance of the victims of both Nazi and communist totalitarian regimes'.

The Prague Declaration soon encountered opposition. The 'seventy years declaration' signed on 20 January 2012, the seventieth anniversary of the Wannsee Conference of 1942, criticized the Prague Declaration's 'attempts to obfuscate the Holocaust by diminishing its uniqueness and deeming it to be equal, similar or equivalent to communism'. The clash between the two declarations reflects differences in historical experiences during and after the Second World War. If East Europeans tend to emphasize the similarities

---

51 Jie-Hyun Lim and Yong-woo Kim, eds., *Daejŭngdŏkje II* [Mass Dictatorship, vol. 2] (Seoul: Chaeksesang, 2005), pp. 401–615; Adam Michnik, *Letters from Freedom: Post-Cold War Realities and Perspectives*, ed. Irena Grudzińska Gross (Berkeley: University of California Press, 1998), p. 152. When the late dictator Park's daughter was elected to the presidency in December 2012, criticism of mass dictatorship evaporated into thin air.

of communism and Nazism as totalitarian regimes, West Europeans maintain the uniqueness of the Holocaust. I do agree with the principle of 'agree
to disagree', which promotes multiple memories, the recognition of cultural
difference and empathy with others. However, what is to be problematized
here is the essentialist perception of the Holocaust. Uniqueness and compar-
ability are not either/or questions, but bound to the specific historical
context. If the relativization of the Holocaust contributed to the apologetic
memory in the German *Historikerstreit*, the discourse of Holocaust uniqueness chokes critical memory in Israel. The so-called new historians' criticism
of the Zionist appropriation of the Holocaust in Israel was never meant
to endorse necessarily the apologetic memory in Germany or Holocaust
denial in Iran. Whether to be critical or apologetic depends on the discursive
loci of the uniqueness and relativism of the Holocaust in specific historical
contexts.

As Michael Rothberg points out, memory is not a zero-sum game of
competition. The recognition of one suffering does not deny the other
suffering. On the contrary, the interaction, negotiation, confluence, cross-
references and conjunction of different historical memories across the globe
empower the performativities of critical memory vis-à-vis apologetic
memory. The Australian Aborigine leader William Cooper's protest action
against the Nazi persecution of Jews in 1938 is a good example. The swift
response by African-Americans to the 1948 'Genocide Convention' is another
landmark of global critical memory. In the petition delivered to the UN –*We
Charge Genocide* – in 1951, American black radicals pinpointed parallels
between Nazi perpetrators and racist perpetrators in the USA. The General
Assembly did not adopt their petition. However, the UN's official denial and
Raphael Lemkin's accusation could not stop W. E. B. Dubois from recalling
'the scream and shots of a race riot in Atlanta and the marching of the Ku
Klux Klan' during his visit to the ruins of the Warsaw ghetto in 1949. Dubois
confessed he could get a 'more complete understanding of the Negro
problem' through a 'clearer understanding of the Jewish problem in the
world'.[52]

The 'migrant archive' of the Holocaust in today's Germany inspires multidirectional memory[53] too: the Kurdish-German staging of an adaptation of

---

52 Eric J. Sundquist, *The Oxford W. E. B. Dubois Reader* (Oxford University Press, 1996),
   p. 471.
53 I borrow this term from Michael Rothberg, *Multidirectional Memory: Remembering the
   Holocaust in the Age of Decolonization* (Stanford University Press, 2009).

Holocaust survivor Edgar Hilsenrath's novel about the Armenian genocide, Şęnocak's novel which places the Holocaust into contact with the Armenian genocide and dislocates ethnicity radically in the person of its German-Turkish-Muslim narrator, and the engagement of a multiethnic collective with the Holocaust through the *Stadtteilmütter* project. All this experimental memory activism in the migrant archive deconstructs the Holocaust uniqueness discourse, increasingly used to discipline non-Jewish minorities.[54] The mnemonic confluence of the Holocaust and comfort women seems to signify the extraterritoriality of global memory and the potentiality of post-nationalist, solidaristic memory communities. However, 'cosmopolitan memory' does not necessarily guarantee the deterritorialization of memory. The Holocaust, as cosmopolitan memory, can be appropriated for the purpose of appealing to a global audience in order to persuade that audience of national suffering and thus serve as a weapon of reterritorializing memory.

From the viewpoint of multidirectional memory, problematizing today's East European memory would not mean criticizing the deconstruction of Holocaust uniqueness, but rather the sublimation of national victimhood. The East European *Historikerstreit*, including the Jedwabne controversy and *Vergangenheitsbewältigung* in Baltic countries, shows that the obsession with national victimhood blinds Eastern Europeans to their complicity in perpetrating the Holocaust. What is no less problematic in the East European *Historikerstreit* is that it never confronted postcolonial criticism. Wojciech Roszkowski, a popular anti-communist Polish historian in samizdat under martial law and a co-signatory of the Prague Declaration, writes in his bestselling 2004 history textbook for high school students that the nineteenth century is characterized by the expansion of European civilization to the rest of the world and thus that Eurocentrism is inevitable to some degree.[55] In order to develop global critical memory, the East European *Historikerstreit* should provincialize European memory through the multidirectional negotiation of the memories of the Holocaust, the two totalitarian regimes of Nazism and Stalinism, and the postcolonial criticism.

---

54 Michael Rothberg and Yasemin Yildiz, 'Memory Citizenship: Migrant Archives of Holocaust Remembrance in Contemporary Germany', *Parallax* 17 (2011), 37–41.
55 Anna Radziwiłł and Wojciech Roszkowski, *Historia dla Maturzysty. Wiek XIX* (Warsaw: PWN, 2004), p. 7.

27

Landscapes of destruction

Capturing images and creating memory through photography

DOROTHEE BRANTZ

The Second World War culminated in unprecedented violence and the massive destruction of landscapes across the globe. The invention of new technologies played a decisive role in this proliferation of violence, but also in the documentation and especially visualization of destruction. One of the most instrumental technologies to plan and later document this destruction was photography. In the words of historian Gerhard Paul, photographs were increasingly operationalized as multifunctional weapons that served a broad range of political ideologies.[1]

War and photography have been tightly intertwined since the mid-nineteenth century. Indeed, technological innovation in one field frequently also promoted the advance of the other, which became especially apparent with aerial photography.[2] Documenting the totality of war, photography increasingly became a tool of mass destruction and a means for representing the ideology of warfare and its aftermath. Moreover, photographs not only illustrated the war as an event; they themselves gave rise to an iconography that reached far into the post-war world capturing the historical imaginations of future generations. Emerging as a new type of witness to the traumata of the twentieth century, some photographs even generated their own historical narratives and became instrumental in the construction of memories, both personal and collective.[3] Photographs visualize cultural norms. Iconic images, in particular, document what a society considers worth depicting.

1 Gerhard Paul, *Bilder Macht. Studien zur 'Visual History' des 20. und 21. Jahrhunderts* (Göttingen: Wallstein, 2013), p. 8.
2 Sonja Dümpelmann, *Flights of Imagination: Aviation, Landscape, Design* (Charlottesville: University of Virginia Press, 2014); Jeanne Haffner, *The View from Above: The Science of Social Space* (Cambridge, Mass.: MIT Press, 2012).
3 Aleida Assmann, *Erinnerungsräume. Formen und Wandlungen des kulturellen Gedächtnisses* (Munich: C. H. Beck, 2006).

They provide us with powerful sources to unearth such cultural norms, how they were linked to distinct national contexts, and how their meaning has changed over time.

Asking more concretely about the role of landscapes in the visualization of violence in times of war might enable us to recognize these multiple levels of meaning because landscapes unite physical spaces and visual representations. Generally speaking, a landscape is a more or less natural terrain (that can include forests, fields, mountains, towns, cities) inscribed with cultural representations of nature. Underscoring their close association with the modern emphasis on the visual as primary mode of perception, landscapes require an observer who reflects on the scenery or who actively creates them through the cultivation of land.[4] This cultivation of nature in thought was always tightly linked to different forms of visual representations, especially painting, but also photography. According to W. J. T. Mitchell landscape functions as a medium.[5] Through it cultural constructions of nature are operationalized to serve processes of identity formation, which can further be instrumentalized for ideological purposes. Consequently, landscapes are also politicized spaces. They are inscribed with ideas of nation and national identity.[6] The rise of photography in the nineteenth century and its popularization in the twentieth century has pushed this association to a new level because it provided a means to record and infinitely reproduce particular images of (nationalized) landscapes. As such, landscapes are characterized by much more than their aesthetic or ecological qualities, which becomes particularly manifest in times of war. Landscapes of belligerence attest to the cultivation of warfare in space.[7] In times of total war, landscapes are not just turned into battlefields, they are themselves mobilized in the production of violence and its representation. Landscapes of destruction have become emblematic for the twentieth-century imaginaire of warfare.

---

4 Denis Cosgrove, 'Landscape as Cultural Product', in Simon Swaffield, ed., *Theory in Landscape Architecture: A Reader* (Philadelphia: University of Pennsylvania Press, 2002), pp. 165–6; John Brinckerhoff Jackson, *Discovering the Vernacular Landscape* (New Haven: Yale University Press, 1984).

5 W. J. T. Mitchell, ed., *Landscape and Power* (University of Chicago Press, 1994), p. 5.

6 Peter Burke, *Eyewitnessing: The Use of Images as Historical Evidence* (Ithaca: Cornell University Press, 2001), p. 43; and Jens Jäger, 'Picturing Nations: Landscape Photography and National Identity in Britain and Germany in the Mid-Nineteenth Century', in Joan M. Schwartz and James R. Ryan, eds., *Picturing Place: Photography and the Geographical Imagination* (London: I. B. Tauris, 2003), pp. 117–40.

7 Dorothee Brantz, 'Environments of Death: Trench Warfare on the Western Front, 1914–1918', in Charles Closmann, ed., *War and the Environment: Military Destruction in the Modern Age* (College Station: Texas A&M University Press, 2009), pp. 68–91; Kurt Lewin, 'Kriegslandschaft', *Zeitschrift für angewandte Psychologie* 12 (1916), 440–7.

Examining six iconic images of the Second World War, this chapter seeks to question the relationship between landscapes of destruction, their photographic representation, and the creation of historical narratives. Covering different types of landscapes in Europe and the Pacific, these images span the duration of the war from September 1939 to August 1945. Of course, six photos can only offer a glimpse and there are surely many other pictures worth considering. All of these photographs are official images that were published in popular media. Each of them reveals a specific relationship to distinct landscapes of war and modes of destruction as well as to their subsequent historicization, which was, as we will see, frequently tied to conflicting notions of ideology and commemoration. At first glance, images readily reveal their meaning, making them easily accessible to large audiences, but upon closer inspection they open up multiple levels of meaning and interpretation that expose much more complex notions of visuality and memory formation, which also raises a number of questions regarding the usability of photographs as historical records. As Bernd Boll has rightly questioned: do National Socialist propaganda pictures unfold their ideological intentions for a second time when they are displayed as illustrations of historical events?[8] Surely, we cannot take photographs as straightforward depictions of reality, rather we need to view them as already carefully staged visualizations of a photographer's aims or even orders by a third party (by ministries of propaganda). Hence, if we want to use such photographs as historical records, we must carefully question the intentions connected to them, starting with the conditions under which they were produced (including by whom), how they were presented to the public, and how they have been received and reproduced over time. In addition to looking at what is depicted in a photograph, one must ask what was (intentionally) left out because these absences might also reveal a great deal about the broader cultural context in which a picture operates and which cultural norms it expresses, particularly when it comes to the destructive capacities of total war.

Photography as a means to capture landscapes of destruction

The visual depiction of warfare has a long tradition. Large paintings of brightly coloured battle scenes have long highlighted the heroic aspects of

---

8 Bernd Boll, 'Das Bild als Waffe: Quellenkritische Anmerkungen zum Foto-und Film-material der deutschen Propagandatruppen 1938–1945', *Zeitschrift für Geschichtswissenschaft* 54 (2006), 974–98.

fighting and dying for crown or nation.[9] The emergence of photography as a medium to depict violent conflicts dates to the Crimean War of the 1850s.[10] Just a decade later, the US Civil War already generated tens of thousands of images. At first, due to technological limitations, the photography of warfare presented rather static impressions featuring weapons, portraits of soldiers, or battlefields once the fighting had stopped. By the First World War, photography had not only become a widespread means to document war, it had turned into an integral part of military action. Aerial photography, for example, opened up new perspectives for military reconnaissance and the understanding of battlefields just as soldiers increasingly dug underground in the trenches on the Western Front.[11] Photographic images from above created a new horizontality that laid the groundwork for future air wars. On the ground, new hand-held cameras made it possible to capture the war in action and in almost any location as long as lighting conditions were sufficient. First World War photography contributed to the totalizing nature of machine warfare by expanding the visual repertoire of documentation and hence also communication between the front lines and the home fronts.

Such new dimensions of visualization were made possible by the new technological means to create images, but over time they also gave rise to a distinct historical record about the changing attitudes toward what ought to be depicted about warfare and how. For one, new ways of seeing were tied to new visualizations of time. Most classical battle paintings treated time amorphously because they often depicted collages of entire battles in one image. In other words, paintings often transported meaning by eliminating the sequence of events through collapsing historical time on a two-dimensional canvas. Photographs operate very differently even though they function on the same two-dimensional plane. A photograph cannot collapse a sequence of events (except perhaps in a montage). Instead it cuts out a particular moment in time (that might be staged or not). Powerful photographs are able to depict a highly expressive moment, but they also transcend the instant of the image itself. They bridge the gap between a moment that is ripped from the flow of time and the historical narrative that weaves together a sequence of events.

9 Burke, *Eyewitnessing*, pp. 146–54.
10 Bernd Hüppauf, 'The Emergence of Modern War Imagery in Early Photography', *History and Memory* 5 (1993), 130–51.
11 Anton Holzer, *Die andere Front: Fotografie und Propaganda im Ersten Weltkrieg* (Darmstadt: Primus, 2007); Bernd Hüppauf, 'Kriegsfotografie', in Wolfgang Michalka, ed., *Der Erste Weltkrieg. Wirkung, Wahrnehmung, Analyse* (Munich: Seehammer, 2000), pp. 875–909. See also the recent issue of the journal *Fotogeschichte* (33, 2013), which is devoted to 'Der Weltkrieg der Bilder: Fotoreportage und Kriegspropaganda in der illustrierten Presse, 1914–1918'.

A photograph usually communicates its message in one image, which makes it especially vulnerable to manipulation and staging. Such staging could take place at the time the picture was taken, in the darkroom or at the cutting table where cropping and retouching offered additional venues to manipulate a shot. Finally, the way in which such images were presented in the media – alongside other images or in conjunction with written texts – provided a third site to stage photographs and hence suggest a particular meaning. As such, photographs are highly susceptible to propaganda, a well-known and frequently exploited fact not only in times of war, but especially then. During the Second World War all sides employed special corps of photographers who were an official part of the military, not just in Nazi Germany. For instance, France's Service Cinématographique des Armées was established in 1939; Britain's Army Film and Photographic Unit in 1941; and the Army Pictorial Service in the US Signal Corps as well as the Office of War Information were established in 1942. In the Soviet Union, photographers were even uniformed soldiers and a regular part of the armed forces. They produced millions of photographs meant to inform those at home (both governmental agencies and the public) about the events on the front lines. Capturing an immediacy (that we should not confuse with authenticity), they presented the official record, which often stood in stark contrast to the photographs shot by civilians or privately taken by soldiers and other military officials. As such they fulfilled an immediate purpose, but many photographs were also taken to create a historical record for future generations. Photographs immortalized the violence of warfare and how this violence was inscribed in the destruction of landscapes.

The symbolism of territorial annihilation: the invasion of Poland
(Plate Section, Illustration 39: *Polenfeldzug, bei Danzig, Strasse Zoppot-Gdingen* by Hans Sönnke)

In the early morning hours of 1 September 1939, fifty-four divisions of the German Wehrmacht invaded Poland. One of the most symbolic territorial breaches occurred the border between Danzig and the Polish Corridor. During the mid-morning, the Danzig State Police, which had already been infiltrated by German soldiers during the summer, crossed into the Polish Corridor. Since the Versailles Treaty had granted Danzig the status of a military free zone, they did not encounter any resistance and basically just walked in. This fateful, even if rather unspectacular event, was not really documented.

The few photographs that were taken created the impression of a leisurely horseback ride through the countryside rather than a military invasion. In the afternoon, infantry troops of the 4th Army arrived accompanied by the PK 689, a propaganda company of photographers and camera crews.[12] Given the special significance of this particular border, which in National Socialist ideology embodied the 'shame of Versailles', some photographers suggested to stage a more picturesque invasion scenery in order to appropriately document this historic event for posterity.

One of those photographers was a civilian named Hans Sönnke, a professional local photographer who took pictures all over Danzig that day to document the outbreak of war. Illustration 39 shows thirteen men removing the wooden barrier that marked the border between Danzig and Poland. They were members of the Danzig state police, soldiers of the Wehrmacht's 4th Army Group North, and two border reinforcement patrols. To facilitate this removal and to give the picture a more dramatic touch, the barrier had already been sawed. A sign of the Polish coat of arms that had already been removed was demonstratively held in the picture to add to the symbolism of the scene. The picture is taken from the Polish side in the direction of Danzig. Smiling soldiers add to the impression that this was a friendly invasion and generally joyful event without any intervention from the Polish side. The picture presents the invasion of Poland as an easy conquest where an unwanted border was simply removed in an act of rightful territorial return. But this invasion was neither rightful nor easy. Only a few hundred kilometres to the north at Westerplatte, for example, there was heavy fighting. According to Gerhard Paul, this scene should be understood as a symbolic staging for the photographers and camera crews who were present.[13] Even to those who were present at the scene, the artificiality of the event was blatantly obvious. Werner Thimm, one of the participating soldiers, later recalled this event as a totally ridiculous affair.[14]

Asking about the role of landscape in this scene, one might say that there is no particular landscape here; and indeed, the image is cropped in a way that any vista disappeared. This is no classical landscape; instead what we have is a very special type of symbolic space – a territorial border. The fact that the coat of arms is placed in such a central position underscores that the

12 Miriam Y. Arani, 'Die Fotografien der Propagandakompanien der deutschen Wehrmacht als Quellen zu den Ereignissen im besetzten Polen, 1939–1945', *Zeitschrift für Ostmitteleuropa-Forschung* 60:1 (2011), 1–49.

13 Paul, *BilderMacht*, p. 139.

14 Guido Knopp, *100 Jahre. Die Bilder des Jahrhunderts* (Munich: Econ, 1999), p. 148.

special significance of this space was well known to everyone present. The image presents landscape as a territorial space linked to the idea of nation, an idea that is undergirded by constant contestations over the legitimacy of national boundaries. This image in particular depicts the grave violation of such a territorial space, and in conjunction with it, the Treaty of Versailles.

Does this seemingly joyful image depict violence? Perhaps not in a conventional sense because no one is getting physically hurt; indeed, there is no visible conflict and no enemy. Yet, this image depicts a clear violation of territorial sovereignty. As Charles Maier has argued, up to 1945 we lived in an era of 'territorial modernity', where the political loyalties of most people were mapped onto the national territories that also provided the locus of resources for assuring their physical and economic security.[15] Hence, any violation of territorial borders was not just an affront to the sovereignty of a nation but to the collective identity of its population. In violating the national sovereignty of Poland, the Wehrmacht robbed its population of this territorial identification, which as we know was just a precursor to the actual extermination of millions of Poles and Polish Jews. This image also marked an end point in a quite different vein because it was one of the last times where German civilian photographers were allowed to capture a theatre of war. On 7 September, the German Ministry of Propaganda issued a directive that forbade civilians to photograph military activities.[16] Hence this image also bore witness to the forthcoming militarization of photography in an era of total war.

Today, this photograph is considered as one of the most iconic pictures of the outbreak of the Second World War; however, at the time, it hardly received any press at all. Sönnke had sent the image to the German Press Agency in Berlin right away, but it was not cleared by the agency's censorship bureau until 5 September. Given the quick turn of events in the early days of the war, the image was already too dated by then to receive broad media coverage. Only a few illustrated weekly magazines like the *Berliner Illustrierte* actually printed versions of the picture. Hans Sönnke also published a postcard series to document 'the liberation of Danzig'. After the war, the image was occasionally distributed by Ullstein Bilderdienst (often with wrong captions), but its actual canonization came only in the 1990s when a German televised history programme about the images that made history

---

15 Charles S. Maier, 'Transformations of Territoriality 1600–2000', in Gunilla Budde, Sebastian Conrad and Oliver Janz, eds., *Transnationale Geschichte. Themen, Tendenzen und Theorien* (Göttingen: Vandenhoeck & Ruprecht, 2006), pp. 32–55 (p. 48).
16 Paul, *BilderMacht*, p. 142.

prominently featured this picture.[17] Since then it has appeared in countless schoolbooks and other popular media. In recent years it frequently appears as an 'eye catcher' without any textual explanation.[18] Since 2008 its status was further valorized when it emerged in permanent exhibition displays like the German Historical Museum in Berlin. Moreover, the availability of this image on the website of the Bundesarchiv, which owns this picture, has added further legitimacy to the image. In Poland, this image is known but not widely disseminated because it highlights the September trauma of invasion rather than documenting Poland's resistance as much more widely circulated images of the fight at Westerplatte do.[19] This photograph underscores how the status of an image can be elevated long after the journalistic moment of the picture has passed. In other words, the historical narrative that surrounds an image and ultimately lends it its meaning can change over time, making it difficult to discuss photographs in relation to notions of authenticity. Its power does not lie in its immediacy or authenticity, but rather in its symbolism, both with regard to the depiction of military violence and the subsequent power of commemoration.

The manipulation of landscape in total war: Murmansk 1942 (Plate Section, Illustration 40: *Murmansk* by Evgennyi Khaldei)

The Russian port city of Murmansk, located on Kola Bay near the Arctic Circle, held special significance for the Soviet Union during the Second World War because it was an essential link to Western Ally support lines. The city served as a landing port for the Allies' Arctic convoys that supplied vital materials to be transported to the Russian mainland via the Murman train line. Just days after the invasion of the Soviet Union on 21 June 1941, the Wehrmacht launched Operation SILVER FOX, a three-staged joint German–Finnish military operation which aimed to conquer Murmansk and cut these Allied supply lines.[20] Intended as a Blitzkrieg, the operation quickly revealed

---

17 The programme *Bilder, die Geschichte machten* aired on the second German television station (ZDF) between 1991 and 1994 under the direction of Guido Knopp who subsequently also published the book *100 Jahre. Die Bilder des Jahrhunderts.*
18 Paul, *BilderMacht*, p. 148.
19 Beate Kosmala, 'Lange Schatten der Erinnerung. Der Zweite Weltkrieg im kollektiven Gedächtnis', in Monika Flacke, ed., *Mythen der Nationen – 1945. Arena der Erinnerungen, Exhibition Catalogue of the Deutsche Historische Museum* (Mainz: von Zabern, 2004), vol. II, p. 517.
20 Chris Mann and Christer Jörgensen, *Hitler's Arctic War* (Hersham: Ian Allan Publishing, 2002).

the German miscalculations when it came to fighting that far north. The Wehrmacht's support structure was badly organized, maps were insufficient, and the troops were ill-prepared to fight in these environmental conditions. By the end of September, the failure of this operation had become apparent and for the rest of the war, the Germans were unable to occupy Murmansk. For the Red Army, the defence of Murmansk was one of the few successes during the early months of the war, which was not just strategically, but also morally significant.

Since conquest proved impossible, Hitler ordered the total destruction of the city in June 1942. Repeated aerial attacks with incendiary bombs during the following days destroyed most of the city. Illustration 40, taken by Evgennyi Khaldei, depicts this utter devastation, which proportionally equalled that of St Petersburg and Stalingrad.

Since most of the city was constructed of wood, most buildings had burned in the firestorms. There were virtually no reminders of human settlement except for the chimneys that stuck out of the ground like crosses signifying the tremendous loss this city and its population had endured. This image depicts a cityscape that has been reverted to a landscape where human construction has been all but eliminated. The landscape looks empty and abandoned. This sense of abandonment is further intensified by the old woman walking in the foreground. Shouldering a heavy suitcase, she is carrying off some belongings, perhaps all that she has left. In this scene, abandonment seems to be the only option.

The damage was not collateral. Indeed, the destruction of Murmansk can be viewed as part of the scorched-earth tactic that was employed by the Germans and the Russians during the Second World War. As the term indicates, the practice of scorched earth entails the total destruction (usually burning) of an environment in order to prevent an enemy from taking advantage of vital natural resources (plants and animals) as well as infrastructures (rail lines, bridges, etc.). Since this practice tends to harm local populations much more than enemy armies, it was outlawed in the 1907 Hague Convention, which, however, did not hinder Hitler or Stalin employing it during the Second World War. In a radio broadcast on 3 July 1941, Stalin had called for the complete destruction of all agricultural land and infrastructures as the Red Army was retreating. The Germans were not supposed to find anything that might aid their fight against the Soviet Union. During the following four years, much of the western and some of the northern parts of the Soviet Union fell victim to this tactic of totally destroying the environment and hence the basis for human survival. This image of Murmansk offers a powerful visualization of such environmental devastation. The ground looks burned and clouded in a haze of smoke. The black cloud above lends the image additional drama. At first sight it looks like a huge black cloud hovering above the scorched ground. Upon closer examination, however, it becomes clear that this 'cloud' is the result of retouching in the dark room. Such stylistic retouching was a common practice in Soviet war photography. Through the manipulation of photographs, landscapes of destruction were enhanced, which intensified their narrative.

But this image was also quite atypical for Soviet war photography because it does not emphasize the heroic aspects of war. Most Soviet official photography focused on war heroes and their selfless fight for the survival of the nation. Depictions of suffering were usually suppressed because they supposedly diminished the country's resolve. Perhaps Soviet officials derived a different narrative from this image, but to those involved, it certainly represented suffering. According to Khaldei's own diary entry, the old woman in the picture was appalled that someone photographed this scenery. While passing him, she cried: 'Are you not ashamed to expose our misfortune?'[21] Khaldei was not thrilled by suffering. War had become Khaldei's primary motive out of necessity and historical circumstance rather than choice. By focusing on the victims of war rather than the heroic aspects of fighting, he tried to expose the human tragedy inherent in war.

Like all Russian front-line photographers, Khaldei was an official uniformed member of the Red Army. At the time he primarily worked for the Soviet news agency TASS. After leaving Murmansk, he went on to photograph the war in Sebastopol, Bucharest, Budapest, Vienna and finally Berlin where he shot his most well-known picture of the raising of the Soviet flag on the Reichstag. Regarded as one of the Soviet Union's most valuable war photographers, he was even sent to Nuremberg to cover the war crimes trials.

After the war, Chaldej himself fell victim to abandonment. Despite being one of the most renowned photographers of the war, he was dismissed from TASS in 1948 because he was Jewish. Later he worked for *Prawda*, but was fired for the same reason in 1972 when anti-Semitism was once again on the rise in the Soviet Union. His pictures continued to be used in the press, in schoolbooks, and for other propaganda purposes, but Khaldei was all but forgotten. Only after the Cold War ended was he rediscovered, primarily in

---

21 Jewgeni Chaldej, *Kriegstagebuch* (Berlin: Das Neue Berlin, 2011), p. 186.

the West, where exhibitions of his work were shown in Vienna, Paris, Lausanne, Verona, New York, Los Angeles, San Francisco and Berlin.

The Murmansk photograph stands as testimony to the power of manipulation. War itself hinges on the violent manipulation of landscapes. Indeed, as long as wars were territorial, the conquest of land and its transformation stood at the centre of military action. The tactic of scorched earth functioned as the ultimate expression of the environmental manipulation inherent in total war.

Natural beauty as human tragedy: dead soldiers on Buna Beach (Plate Section, Illustration 41: *Three Dead Americans on the Beach at Buna* by George Strock)

In January 1942, Japanese forces invaded the Australian-administrated territories of New Guinea. During the following three years, a fierce campaign ensued that included prolonged fighting at Buna Beach where the Japanese were especially well fortified in camouflaged bunkers. The Allied forces under the command of Douglas MacArthur had underestimated the Japanese resolve to hold this territory, which was strategically important for securing landing points to support other military campaigns in the region. Moreover, American troops were ill-prepared to fight in unfamiliar swamp and jungle environments. The death toll was unusually high, outnumbering the Allied casualties of the more famous campaign at Guadalcanal by three to one. By the end, nearly 8,000 Japanese (over 90 per cent), 2,000 Australians and 2,400 Americans had been killed either in combat or by diseases like malaria, dengue fever, bush typhus and tropical dysentery.[22] Among the Allied casualties were the three soldiers shown in illustration 41 taken by George Strock. Entitled 'Three Dead Americans on the Beach at Buna', it showed three dead soldiers who take up the foreground and middle-ground of the picture.

Interestingly, the centre of the picture is just sand. The soldiers appear in a curve-like formation that draws the eye along their dead bodies to the sunken landing craft that sticks out of the water splashing the beach. In the background, palm trees provide the horizontal frame and place this scene in the Pacific War. These soldiers were probably killed by machine-gun fire. The tide has come in at least once to cover their bodies with sand. The body in front is already covered in maggots signalling its state of decomposition.

22 Harry Gailey, *MacArthur Strikes Back: Decision at Buna, New Guinea, 1942–1943* (New York: Ballantine Books, 2000).

Originally, the picture was taken on 31 December 1942, but due to censorship, it was not published until 20 September 1943. It was shown as part of a trio of photos depicting the stump of a soldier's amputated leg taken in a hospital, a picture of paratroopers in Sicily, and the photograph of the three dead soldiers on Buna Beach. This picture broke an important taboo. Although the men were not identifiable, they were the first undraped and uncoffined dead Americans to appear in the US popular press during the Second World War. Already in early August *Life* had shown a picture of a dead soldier covered by a blanket, showing only his right boot and left elbow. *Life* ran this stark, haunting photograph alongside a full-page editorial entitled 'Why print this picture, anyway, of three American boys dead upon an alien shore?' The editorial stated that: 'words are never enough . . . words do not exist to make us see, or know, or feel what it is like, what actually happens.' This image offered a more immediate impression of the cruelty of war. Invoking all sorts of stereotypes about America, such as women baking apple pie, man harvesting an orchard, and boys going to play baseball, the editorial insisted that this beach did not show America, but that it signified American pride and its resolve to win this battle for freedom. These dead soldiers supposedly symbolized 'three units of freedom' that needed to be defended at all costs.

This photograph, which has become one of the most well-known images of American death in the Second World War II, marked a significant shift in US policy regarding the presentation of the war on the home front. Until 1943, the protection of public sentiments had been the guiding principle when it came to presenting the war in the media. Consequently, there were no images of dead US soldiers. However, by summer 1943, President Roosevelt and the War Department were increasingly concerned that Americans were becoming too complacent about the war. Thinking that the American public needed to be confronted with the reality of battle and the presence of death in fighting in order to strengthen support for the war, they lifted the ban on images depicting US casualties. Strock's picture and others that followed in *Life* and elsewhere had the desired effect. The sale of war bonds rose again.

This new policy was highly controversial. Some considered it voyeuristic and unnecessarily stark while others appreciated the honesty. The *Washington Post*, for one, celebrated the new policy. In an editorial, it stated that:

> An overdose of such photographs would be unhealthy. But in proper proportion they can help us to understand something of what has been sacrificed for the victories we have won. Against a tough and resourceful enemy, every gain entails a cost. To gloss over this grim fact is to blur our

vision. If we are to behave as adults in meeting our civilian responsibilities, we must be treated as adults. This means simply that we must be given the truth without regard to fears about how we may react to it.[23]

Many soldiers, too, praised the photograph and the accompanying editorial. One lieutenant wrote: 'Your Picture of the Week is a terrible thing, but I'm glad that there is one American magazine which had the courage to print it.' A private wrote: 'This editorial is the first thing I have read that gives real meaning to our struggle.'[24]

Despite this new policy of realism, images of war were never authentic. For one, the bodies of American soldiers were never shown mutilated or bloody. Instead, wounded soldiers were usually shown as they were receiving help, suggesting that everyone was well cared for. Death was presented as heroic, but also as depersonalized. Facing down, these three dead soldiers were reduced to their bodily existence, a bodily existence that faded away with every new wave that spread more sand over them. This image is highly aestheticized in the way it presents death in conjunction with the surrounding landscape. At first sight, this landscape might appear very picturesque, but if one looks more closely, this environment is itself a destructive force. While the landscape might look beautiful, the actual environment turned out to be treacherous and threatening, not just because of the Japanese soldiers who lay camouflaged in the jungle, but also due to the impassability of the swamps and the inherent threat of jungle diseases. The maggots that were eating away at the soldiers' bodies demonstrated that landscapes of destruction were filled with all sorts of destructive forces in addition to human technologies and the seeming beauty of nature led to a false aestheticization of death.

The illusion of perspective: the gatehouse at Auschwitz-Birkenau (Plate Section, Illustration 42: *Brama w Birkenau* by Stanisław Mucha)

The entrance gate to Auschwitz-Birkenau stands as the physical reminder for the mass murder committed during the Holocaust. Over 1.3 million people were deported to Auschwitz and over a million of them died there. Close to 900,000 were gassed soon after passing through this gate. The gatehouse was

23 Editorial, *The Washington Post*, 21 September 1943, reprinted in Paul Lester, *Photojournalism: An Ethical Approach* (Hillsdale, NJ: Lawrence Erlbaum, 1991).
24 Susan D. Moeller, *Shooting War: Photography and the American Experience of Combat* (New York: Basic Books 1989), p. 207.

built in 1943, originally consisting of the middle tract and an entrance for trucks on the right side of the building. Shortly before the deportation of Hungarian Jews commenced in April 1944, train tracks and a ramp were added as well as a second wing to the left side of the building itself. Between late April 1944 and January 1945, 438,000 Jews from Hungary and thousands more from all over Europe passed through this gate. Only a few survived.

When the Polish photographer Stanisław Mucha arrived at Auschwitz-Birkenau in February 1945, the camp had ceased to exist as a killing factory. Bowls, buckets and canisters were among the only remnants that hinted at the presence of people just a few weeks before. Mucha was part of a Polish-Soviet investigative commission that was supposed to document the physical remains and technical infrastructures of this extermination camp. Mucha took thirty-eight photographs of the camp, one of them depicting the entrance gate and train tracks, which has become one of the most well-known images of concentration camps (illustration 42).

This picture works with one of the most powerful concepts in landscape – perspective. Since the Renaissance, perspective has served as a visual means to accentuate specific aspects in relation to size and position vis-à-vis a particular foreground and background. With regard to the depiction of landscapes, perspective is often related to linearity. Stanisław Mucha's image employs perspective in order to guide the viewer's eye along two dominating lines – diagonally along the train tracks toward the gateway and then horizontally along its walls. These two perspectives link the foreground and background leading the viewer toward the gateway and into the depth on the other side of the gate.[25] Mucha's emphasis on such clear lines makes the picture appealing and horrifying at once because through its almost geometric arrangement, the image encapsulates the technocratic sense of rationalization that characterized this locale of mass murder. This impression is further emphasized by the bleak appearance of the winter landscape that amplifies the black and white contrasts. The straight lines of the image suggest distance. The absence of people, indeed anything living, heightens that impression. In itself this photograph tells more about lines and the ability of architecture and infrastructures to fill space and create an energizing dynamic.[26] It is precisely the absence of people that makes this image so

25 See the essay by Christoph Hamann, 'Fluchtpunkt Birkenau: Stanisław Muchas Foto vom Torhaus Auschwitz-Birkenau (1945)', in Gerhard Paul, ed., *Visual History: Ein Studienbuch* (Göttingen: Vandenhoeck & Rupprecht, 2006), pp. 283–302.
26 Ibid., p. 292.

powerful and ultimately useful as a source to approach the history of the Holocaust. As Susan Crane has argued, images of Holocaust atrocities are highly problematic.[27] For one, they were taken without the consent of those who are depicted, hence furthering their exploitation. Moreover, overexposure to images of atrocity, she argues, may harm rather than enable an open engagement with the history of genocide. This picture of the Auschwitz entrance, rather than exposing atrocity, operates through the power of suggestion.

The gateway looks like an entrance, like the final destination of all of the rail lines that seemingly come from everywhere (suggestively from all over Europe). Moreover, the gateway appears to offer a glimpse of the other side of the building, allowing a cautious look inside the camp. Despite their appeal, the stark lines created by the building function as a clear separation between the inside and outside of the camp. But this sense of inside and outside is shockingly false. Contrary to the widespread use of this image, the perspective is not leading into the camp, but out. Hence, viewers are not catching a glimpse of the world inside the camp, but they are caught right in the middle of it. As soon as one realizes this reversed position, one is caught up in a sense of disorientation, and this disorientation coupled with the absence of human beings lends the image a strong sense of desolation and incomprehensibility.

In this image the Holocaust is present and absent at the same time. Since this image does not expose any actual acts of murder, it is broadly usable in the media to signify the unspeakability of the Holocaust without necessarily raising difficult questions about guilt and responsibility. The picture has been used countless times, either in reference to Auschwitz itself or as a signifier for the Holocaust more generally. The gate has been used as a stylistic device to raise questions about the historical significance of the Holocaust and its centrality in (German) constructions of memory and identity at the turn of the millennium. For example, in 1998, the German weekly *Der Spiegel* placed this image at the centre of a cover that presented a collage of significant events and iconic images of the twentieth century.[28] The gate is only shown in black with a mushroom cloud overhead. In other media, the image has been demonstratively depicted out of focus to sound a warning that the memory of the Holocaust might be fading from the public's conscience.[29]

---

27 Susan A. Crane, 'Choosing Not to Look: Representation, Repatriation, and Holocaust Atrocity Photography', *History and Theory* 47:3 (2008), 309–30.
28 Cover of *Der Spiegel*, 2 November 1998.
29 *Tageszeitung*, 27 January 2005.

This photograph has certainly become a document to the unspeakable and a testament to the haunting power of absence. With its emptiness and lack of life, this seemingly calm landscape hinted at the daunting void that mass murder has left behind.

The resilience of trauma: Dresden 1945
(Plate Section, Illustration 43: *Blick vom Rathausturmn ach Süden* by Richard Peter)

The air war on cities started in September 1939 with the Wehrmacht's bombing of Warsaw, Coventry, Rotterdam and London and ended with the US Air Force's dropping of the atomic bomb in August 1945. The Second World War elevated air war to a strategic method of mass destruction, especially when it came to targeting civilian populations in urban centres. Aerial photography served as a crucial tool to plan, conduct and later assess this destruction. On 13 and 14 February 1945, the city of Dresden was the target of extensive Allied bombing.[30] Up to that point, the city, which was famous for its Italianate Baroque architecture and rich cultural life, had been spared from aerial attacks, but at the Yalta Conference in February 1945, the Allied powers had identified Dresden as a potential target because the city had become a central base camp for moving German military forces to the Eastern Front. At the same time, Dresden was a major locale for the growing number of refugees from the east who were fleeing the advance of the Red Army.

Shortly after 10 p.m. on 13 February, the British Royal Air Force opened the two-day bombing raids with 244 planes carrying 900 tons of bombs. Just three hours later a second squadron delivered twice that tonnage, igniting a huge conflagration that incinerated most of the central city. The following day, American planes continued the bombardment. At the end of those two days, half the city lay in ruins, about 25,000 people were dead and many more wounded.[31]

---

30 The literature on the bombing of Dresden is vast; see, for example, Paul Addison and Jeremy Crang, eds., *Firestorm: The Bombing of Dresden, 1945* (Chicago: Dee, 2006); Frederick Taylor, *Dresden: Tuesday February 13, 1945* (New York: HarperCollins, 2004); and Tami Davis Biddle, 'Dresden 1945: Reality, History, and Memory', *Journal of Military History* 72:2 (2008), 413–49.

31 There has been much controversy over the number of people who were killed during these air raids. According to a 2008 expert commission, about 25,000 people died whereas right-wing apologists elevate the number to 250,000. Rolf-Dieter Müller, ed., *Historikerkommission zu den Luftangriffen auf Dresden zwischen dem 13. und 15. Februar 1945* (Dresden: Rat der Stadt, 2008).

One of the most iconic images of the destruction of Dresden is the photograph 'Blick vom Rathausturm nach Süden'(The View from City Hall to the South) by Richard Peter (illustration 43). The image first appeared in a book of photographs published in 1949 under the title *Dresden: Eine Kamera klagt an* (A Camera Accuses).[32] Already the title was highly suggestive since it foregrounded the camera as author, which somewhat objectified the accusation and simultaneously eradicated question of guilt. In the book, 104 images were laid out on 86 pages. The first edition of 50,000 copies sold out the first year. The book consisted of eight chapters, each depicting a specific era or theme in Dresden's pre- and immediate post-war period. Notably, the Nazi period did not appear in any of the images, further underscoring the unwillingness to critically engage with questions of responsibility or guilt. Instead, the focus of the book centred on the socialist reconstruction of Dresden, which was underscored by Max Zimmering's poem that accompanied the photographs. As the only text in the book, it condemned war, blamed the destruction of the city on Western imperialism, and celebrated the city's liberation by the Red Army and its subsequent socialist reconstruction. Dresden's city hall is a recurrent motif in the book. Six different images are devoted to it, ranging from pristine pre-war pictures to several photographs showing its destruction (including the one shown here) and finally its reconstruction in the post-war era.

The picture opened the book's gallery of ruinscapes (*Ruinenlandschaft*). Actually, this photo shows a landscape of rubble (*Trümmerlandschaft*) marked by utter destruction. Everything except one building in the upper left corner is destroyed. There are no trees and no people – only the skeletons of buildings remain. All of the windows and roofs are gone. To put it in military parlance, the buildings have been 'opened to the sky'. Air war required new ways of seeing. In order to make sense of this kind of urbicide, which constituted a new dimension of total warfare where the urban environment and its civilian populations had become a primary target of military operations, viewers had to develop a new appreciation for the non-figurative in landscape. At first sight, this landscape of rubble makes the city unrecognizable. The only identifiable figure is the statue of benevolence (symbolizing good government) that looks down on the city. With her crouched posture and outreached hand pointing toward the destruction below, she appears to ask –why did this happen? As some authors have suggested, this figure looks

---

32 Richard Peter, *Dresden. Eine Kamera klagt an* (Dresden: Dresdener Verlagsgesellschaft, 1949).

like the angle of history who lost the wind under her wings and is forced to look back upon the destruction wondering how a future is possible.[33] Functioning as the only recognizable feature to enable viewers to see the resemblance between the pre- and post-war city of Dresden, the statue also lends an aesthetic quality to the picture. Through this aestheticization of destruction, the landscape of rubble is turned into a ruinscape. The appreciation of ruins has a long tradition, but the urban air war of the Second World War added a new dimension to the notion of ruinscapes because these ruins were not simply landmarks, they were the forced living environments for thousands of people.[34]

Belonging to the distinct iconography of rubble photography, this picture of Dresden has become one the most famous images of the destruction of Germany in 1945. Right after the war, countless photographers had documented the aftermath of Nazi Germany, which was nowhere as visible as in bombed cities. Such images were readily available in the early post-war years, but with the growing focus on reconstruction and the establishment of post-war societies, most of them disappeared. Only in the 1980s, alongside a general new engagement with Germany's Nazi past, did they re-emerge. Since German unification and the revitalization of the urban and urban memory spaces, these images have enjoyed a remarkable comeback, appearing in books and on postcards everywhere. Richard Peter's book was also reissued in several editions in 1980, 1982 and 1995.

For Germans the images of the ruins of German cities serve as visual markers for the end of the war and the immediate post-war era. For some, it underscored, as Jens Jäger put it, the 'victimization of survivors', which led to a narrowed focus on the local implications of the war while making it possible to ignore the destruction caused elsewhere.[35] Of course, such images carry a different meaning for the former Allies or for Jews and others who had fled the Nazi regime. Especially for the latter groups, such photographs are probably highly ambivalent because they depict their destroyed home cities, but they also attest to the defeat of the regime that had destroyed their sense of home in the first place. In general, such photographs are quite

---

33 Wolfgang Hesse, 'Der glücklose Engel. Das zerstörte Dresden in einer Fotografie von Richard Peter', *Forum Wissenschaft* 22 (2005), 30–5.

34 Julia Hell and Andreas Schönle, eds., *Ruins of Modernity* (Durham, NC: Duke University Press, 2010).

35 Jens Jäger, '1945: Die Trümmeridentität deutscher Städte', in Daniela Kneissel, ed., *Fotografie als Quelle der Zeitgeschichte: Kategorien, Schauplätze, Akteure* (Munich: Martin Meidenbauer, 2010), p. 106.

malleable for different users across the political spectrum. The Dresden photograph is a perfect example for that malleability. In 2005, anti-fascist activists used this image to call for a silent candle-light memorial to commemorate the bombing of the city and to send a clear signal against the neo-Nazi misuse of this date for their own purposes.[36] In the USA, too, the example of Dresden was repeatedly invoked to question the practice of bombing cities during the Iraq War.[37] But this photograph has also been used by apologists of the Nazi period who want to emphasize the victimization of Germans during the Second World War. For example, in 2009, neo-Nazis used this image on a widely discussed poster to announce a 'grief march (*Trauermarsch*) for the German victims of the Allied terror bombing'.[38] Despite their radically different intentions, all sides invoked the trauma of air war.[39] According to Paul Lerner and Mark S. Micale, trauma is not an event per se, rather it entails experiencing or remembering an event in the mind of an individual or the life of a community.[40] As such it is open to a wide range of interpretations. Photographs play a central role in this type of memory because they create meaning through representation. Iconic images replace actual experience. They embody trauma as representation.

The threat of total annihilation: the mushroom cloud over Hiroshima
(Plate Section, Illustration 44: *Hiroshima, 6 August 1945* by George Caron)

Monday, 6 August 1945 started as a beautiful summer day. The skies were blue with no clouds in sight. Around 8 a.m., a plane appeared on the horizon. Inhabitants of Hiroshima saw the plane but thought it must be a weather plane because air raids consisted of a squadron of planes not a single aircraft. For the pilots of the B-29 *Enola Gay*, these beautiful skies also offered perfect conditions because this mission required good visibility. The chosen target

---

36 Steven Hoelscher, 'Dresden, a Camera Accuses: Rubble Photography and the Politics of Memory in a Divided Germany', *History of Photography* 36:3 (August 2012), 288–305.

37 Andreas Huyssen, 'Air War Legacies: From Dresden to Baghdad', *New German Critique* 90 (2003), 163–76.

38 Hoelscher, 'Dresden, a Camera Accuses', p. 290.

39 Davide Deriu, 'Picturing Ruinscapes: The Aerial Photograph as Image of Historical Trauma', in Frances Guerin and Roger Hallas, eds., *The Image and the Witness: Trauma, Memory and Visual Culture* (London: Wallflower Press, 2007), pp. 189–203.

40 Mark S. Micale and Paul Lerner, 'Trauma, Psychiatry, and History: A Conceptual and Historiographical Introduction', in Mark S. Micale and Paul Lerner, eds., *Traumatic Pasts: History, Psychiatry, and Trauma in the Modern Age, 1870–1930* (Cambridge University Press, 2001), pp. 1–28 (p. 20).

was the easily identifiable T-shaped Aioi Bridge in the centre of the city. At 8:15, 'Little Boy'detonated only a few feet off target. It only took forty-three seconds from the release to the detonation of this bomb, but these few seconds changed the world, not just in Hiroshima.

Up to this point, the city had been spared by US air attacks, which had focused on Tokyo, Osaka and Nagoya. The harbour city of Hiroshima was still a pristine site. Since the Sino-Japanese War in 1894, Hiroshima had been an important military base, but 85 per cent of the city's 350,000 inhabitants were civilians, 30,000 of whom were forced workers from Korea and China. About 70,000 people – one-fifth of the city's population – were killed instantly by the thermal flash that extinguished everything within a 250-metre radius of the detonation site. All that remained were atomic shadows. The shock wave that followed created a firestorm that radiated outward 5 kilometres in each direction of ground zero. As the smoke of the bomb rose to form what has become known as a mushroom cloud, gamma rays spread at the speed of light injuring thousands more immediately and leading to radiation sickness and genetic defects for generations to come. Soon the cloud had disappeared and with it the city of Hiroshima. Never before had a single bomb killed that many people and caused such massive destruction. Given that the majority of the city had been built of wood, most of it was burned to the ground leaving basically no infrastructure for recovery. For instance, out of forty-five hospitals only three remained operational. From the perspective of the American military, this mission was a success far exceeding the expectations about the destructive potential of the bomb. When the crew of the *Enola Gay* returned to its base on Tinian Island, they were celebrated as heroes. For them this had been a truly awe-inspiring experience, and not only for them, but for many generations who have since come into contact with images of the bomb.

When President Truman had ordered the dropping of the bomb, neither he nor the military commanders and scientists who had been working at Los Alamos for years to develop the atom bomb had a clear understanding of the destructive potential of this weapon. Only in hindsight and through the visual documentation of the event and its aftermath did the devastating dimensions of this military technology become apparent.

The photograph of the mushroom cloud (illustration 44) was taken by the tail gunner of the *Enola Gay*, George Caron, with a small hand-held camera. In itself, the image of the mushroom cloud depicts nothing of the destruction it caused; nevertheless it is one of the most powerful pictures of the Second World War and surely it is also one of its most haunting images. The ten-mile-high cloud exposed the new verticality of warfare that extended the environment of war high above the clouds. This image served as the ultimate expression of how warfare no longer centred on the devastation of land-scapes, but on the creation of new skyscapes. Whereas the destruction of landscapes on the ground unearthed the violent transformation of living spaces, these new skyscapes depicted the atomic cloud perpendicular to the regular clouds and hence in an even more radical opposition to the natural environment that surrounded it. There simply was nothing natural about the atom bomb.

The power of this image lies in its ability to uncover another dimension of the totality of warfare. The photograph encapsulates the most radical and powerful amalgamation of science, technology and the politics of warfare; an amalgamation that not only created new vertical environments but that also caused a hitherto unseen extent of destruction and loss of human life. Beyond this actual destruction, the mushroom cloud signified the potential for final annihilation.

This image captures everything and nothing. It is, at once, overwhelming and sublime. It depicts at once the potential for the total extermination of human existence and it does so without showing any destruction at all. Replacing the human face of war with the abstraction of a skyscape, this image literally clouded and displaced questions of morality and guilt. The mushroom cloud has turned the reality of destruction into a non-figurative display of light and dark. In not depicting anything that our eyes can translate into (imagined or real) experiences, this image is open to a wide range of interpretations. The photograph is deeply tied to specific national contexts and the collective memories that shape particular notions of national identity. To some this is an image of victory and heroism, while for others it serves as a visualization of nuclear annihilation. Indeed, there probably is not another image that has been construed in such different ways and placed in so many political and cultural contexts since its first appearance in 1945.

In the USA, a small version of the image was first shown in the *New York Times* on 15 August, just a few days after the Japanese offer to surrender. The broader public probably saw this picture for the first time in the weekly illustrated *Life* on 20 August.[41] Instantly, it became an icon of the American victory over Japan and the techno-scientific prowess of the USA more broadly. The crew of this mission were viewed as heroes who had saved thousands of other American soldiers from having to fight against the

---

41 'War's Ending', *Life*, 20 August 1945, p. 26.

Japanese. For a long time, this picture of the mushroom cloud was one of the few images shown about Hiroshima. At first no pictures of the destruction on the ground were published. The first black and white photographs of Japanese victims were released in 1952 in *Life* magazine. The first film footage appeared in the early 1970s, and the first colour photographs only in the 1980s.[42] The dearth of pictures about Hiroshima was juxtaposed by the widespread exploitation of images of the mushroom cloud in advertising and pop culture. Examining the cultural meaning of and fascination with the mushroom cloud in American society, Peggy Rosenthal identified ten main metaphors ranging from the bomb as a procreational symbol of the nuclear age to the bomb as proof of the political and military dominance of the USA in the world. She also registered a deep fascination with the aesthetics of the bomb.[43]

A telling example of how closely the Hiroshima bomb was tied to the USA's national identity and the politicized construction of a collective memory was the controversy over a planned Smithsonian National Air and Space Museum exhibition to commemorate the fiftieth anniversary of the end of the Second World War and the dropping of the atom bomb. Originally, museum curators wanted to give a voice to the American and Japanese sides, but they were so severely criticized by veterans and politicians who felt that their 'sacrifice and valor was being downgraded' that the exhibition was cancelled and the museum's director Martin Harwit resigned.[44] Of course this is not to say that the American public were not interested in the Japanese perspective. John Hersey's essay 'Hiroshima' based on eyewitness accounts of survivors, which was published in *The New Yorker* in August 1946, was sold out within hours. The subsequent book has been read by many generations since and in 1999, it was voted as the most important piece of journalism in the past 100 years.[45]

The Japanese engagement with the atomic bomb was understandably different. The same year that the Smithsonian was supposed to show the 'Enola Gay' exhibit, the Yokohama Museum of Art staged an exhibition

---

42 Paul, *BilderMacht*, p. 249.
43 Peggy Rosenthal, 'The Nuclear Cloud as Cultural Image', *American Literary History* 3:1 (1991), 63–92.
44 Michael J. Hogan, 'The Enola Gay Controversy: History, Memory, and the Politics of Presentation', in Michael J. Hogan, ed., *Hiroshima in History and Memory* (Cambridge University Press, 1996), pp. 200–32.
45 John Hersey, *Hiroshima* (New York: Vintage, 1946). The list of the 100 most influential works of American journalism was generated by a panel of journalists and the New York University journalism faculty in 1999.

about photography in 1940s Japan. While there were many pictures of landscapes and Japanese culture, there were no pictures about the war, the atom bomb, or its consequences. This notable absence, as Julia Thomas has pointed out, was indicative of Japan's amnesia in relation to its wartime past.[46] Linking Japanese national identity to ahistorical conceptions of an essentialized culture, there was no room for depictions of destruction or for its victims.[47] As survivors of the atom bomb, the Hibakusha were important carriers of memory, but their stories were largely ignored in a society exposed to US censorship and focused on post-war recovery not memory.[48] Still in 2011, in an exhibit about Japanese post-war photography in the Helmut Newton Museum of Photography in Berlin, images of the destruction of Hiroshima and Nagasaki were literally black-boxed in a separate section of the exhibition.

But the image of the mushroom cloud is nevertheless an important part of our pictorial memory when it comes to wartime destruction. It illustrates not only national differences in the interpretation of imagery, but also underscores the necessity to recognize our shared history and responsibility when it comes to dealing with this kind of total destruction. After all, the atomic bomb did not just affect Japan and the USA but more or less the entire world. For one, 10 per cent of Hibakusha were Korean. Moreover, since 1945 more than 2,000 atomic tests have been conducted in many parts of the world. Indeed, over the years, derivatives of this photograph have appeared in numerous contexts, especially in anti-nuclear war campaigns that link this destructive past to the potential for future annihilation.

Conclusion

The mushroom cloud has become the iconic image of the nuclear age. Even though it carries quite different connotations in different societies, it has also created a common link between the end of the Second World War and the global power struggles that followed. To some extent that is true for all of the images discussed here. Surely, they are just six pictures out of millions

---

46 Julia A. Thomas, 'Photography, National Identity, and the "Cataract of Times"': Wartime Images and the Case of Japan', *American Historical Review* 103:5 (1998), 1475–501.

47 Julia A. Thomas, 'Landscape's Mediation between History and Memory: A Revisualization of Japan's (War-Time) Past', *East Asian History* 36 (2008), 55–71 (p. 56).

48 Yuki Miyamoto, *Beyond the Mushroom Cloud: Commemoration, Religion, and Responsibility after Hiroshima* (New York: Fordham University Press, 2012).

of photographs that were shot during the Second World War. Each high-lighted a key event, and each contributed to distinct aspects of the war's visual commemoration. All of them have several things in common. For one, none show actual acts of violence. Indeed, none of these pictures show what we might expect from images of warfare – fighting. In none of them do we see an enemy, there is no combat, at least not in the conventional sense. But it is precisely that absence of fighting that might be so illustrative of the totality of the Second World War. This war did not just centre on conventional battles (even though there were plenty of them). It led to unspeakable violence, massive destruction and mass death on many levels beyond the face-to-face encounter of soldiers. In total war, enemies do not have to face each other in order to kill and destroy. Moreover, the destructive power of this war continued far into the post-war world, all the way to the present. Photography and the media more generally played a decisive role in this perpetuation of ubiquitous violence. The fact that the six images discussed in this chapter do not depict actual acts of violence certainly has advantages and disadvantages. By not showing mutilated bodies and dead people, this essay purposefully abstains from depicting the suffering of others.[49] Through photographs, violence receives a social purpose because the depicted act has been witnessed by (at least) a photographer and received by an audience. The photographed victims of such acts of violence have no chance to add their consent to the particular use of the picture, hence they might be victimized again. Moreover, as studies have shown, the educational impact of graphic images is rather questionable.[50] In general, we have to ask if a photograph has to explicitly show violence in order to be considered an image of aggression.[51] Or is it maybe precisely the absence of readily visible violence that forces us to engage with an image and the history behind it? Perhaps war photographs are particularly powerful if they not only depict what is present, but also manage to capture implied absences in landscapes of destruction because this forces us to think about the deeper implications of violence on physical environments as well as landscapes of the memory.

49 Susan Sontag, *Regarding the Pain of Others* (New York: Farrar, Straus & Giroux, 2003).
50 Cornelia Brink, *Ikonen der Vernichtung. Öffentlicher Gebrauch von Fotografien aus natio-nalsozialistischen Konzentrationslagern nach 1945* (Berlin: Akademie Verlag, 1998).
51 Cornelia Brink and Jonas Wegerer, 'Wie kommt die Gewalt ins Bild? Über den Zusammenhang von Gewaltakt, fotografischer Aufnahme und Bildwirkung', *Foto-geschichte* 125 (2012), 5–14.

Bibliographical essays

1 The economics of the war with Nazi Germany
Adam Tooze and Jamie Martin

The defining modern contribution on the economic dimensions of the Second World War is Mark Harrison, ed., *The Economics of World War II* (Cambridge University Press, 1998), which brings the massive database of GDP figures compiled by Angus Maddison for the OECD to bear on the epoch of the war. An updated version of Maddison's database is available at www.ggdc.net/maddison/maddison-project/home.htm.

This macroeconomic approach displaces Alan S. Milward's earlier classic *War, Economy and Society, 1939–1945* (London: Allen Lane, 1977), which offered an incisive interpretation of the wartime intertwining of politics, military strategy and economics.

The background to the interwar crisis was the failed attempts to restore the international economy after the First World War; see Robert Boyce, *The Great Interwar Crisis and the Collapse of Globalization* (Basingstoke: Palgrave Macmillan, 2009) and *British Capitalism at the Crossroads, 1919–1932* (Cambridge University Press, 1987), Anne Orde, *British Policy and European Reconstruction after the First World War* (Cambridge University Press, 1990) and Adam Tooze, *The Deluge: The Great War and the Remaking of Global Order, 1916–1931* (London: Penguin, 2014).

For two classic, and conflicting, interpretations of the course of the Great Depression and the breakdown of the gold standard regime, see Charles Kindleberger's *The World in Depression, 1929–1939* (Berkeley: University of California Press, 1973) and Barry Eichengreen's *Golden Fetters: The Gold Standard and the Great Depression, 1919–1939* (Oxford University Press, 1992).

Monographs on national economic policies during the 1930s abound. On France, key contributions include Robert Frankenstein, *Le Prix du Réarmement*

Français (Paris: Publications de la Sorbonne, 1982), Kenneth Mouré, *Managing the Franc Poincaré* (Cambridge University Press, 1991) and Michel Margairaz, *L'État, les finances et l'économie: histoire d'une conversion, 1932–1952* (Paris: Comité pour l'histoire économique et financière de la France, 1991). Adam Tooze, *The Wages of Destruction: The Making and Breaking of the Nazi Economy* (London: Allen Lane, 2006) reconsiders the economic decision-making of the Nazi regime and its relation to the Reich's larger strategic aims. For obvious reasons, military-strategic concerns bulk less large in the history of the New Deal, but David M. Kennedy, *Freedom from Fear: The American People in Depression and War* (Oxford University Press, 1999) offers key insights. Alan Brinkley, *The End of Reform: New Deal Liberalism in Recession and War* (New York: Knopf, 1995) sketches the transitions in economic thinking in the USA. Key contributions to a rich literature on Britain in the 1930s include G. C. Peden, *British Rearmament and the Treasury, 1932–1939* (Edinburgh University Press, 1979) and David Edgerton's *Warfare State: Britain, 1920–1970* (Cambridge University Press, 2005). Talbot Imlay's *Facing the Second World War: Strategy, Politics, and Economics in Britain and France, 1938–1940* (Oxford University Press, 2003) offers a comprehensive assessment of the political-economic aspects of British and French strategic decision-making in the 1930s. On the Soviet Union the indispensable collection is Robert William Davies, Mark Harrison and S. G. Wheatcroft, eds., *The Economic Transformation of the Soviet Union, 1913–1945* (Cambridge University Press, 1994).

Tooze's *Wages of Destruction* covers the war effort in Germany. A key earlier work in German is Ludolf Herbst, *Der totale Krieg und die Ordnung der Wirtschaft* (Stuttgart: Deutsche Verlags Anstalt, 1982). On the occupied economies of Europe, the most recent survey is Hein A. M. Klemann and Sergei Kudryashov, *Occupied Economies: An Economic History of Nazi-Occupied Europe, 1939–1945* (Oxford: Berg, 2012).

A bracing revisionist perspective on the UK war economy, which meshes with Tooze's interpretation of the Nazi war effort is provided by David Edgerton, *Britain's War Machine: Weapons, Resources, and Experts in the Second World War* (London: Allen Lane, 2011). For the Soviet Union the essential reference is John Barber and Mark Harrison, *The Soviet Home Front, 1941–1945: A Social and Economic History of the USSR in World War II* (London: Longman, 1991).

The extraordinary story of US wartime mobilization still lacks the blockbuster account that it so richly deserves. The leading survey of US war economics is Hugh Rockoff, *America's Economic Way of War: War and the US Economy from the Spanish–American War to the Persian Gulf War* (Cambridge University Press, 2012). More popular accounts include A. J. Baime, *The Arsenal of Democracy: FDR, Detroit, and an Epic Quest to Arm an America at War* (New York: Houghton Mifflin, 2014) and Arthur Herman, *Freedom's Forge: How American Business Produced Victory in World War II* (New York: Random House, 2012).

The interwar and wartime origins of the Bretton Woods international monetary regime are traced in Richard Gardner, *Sterling-Dollar Diplomacy: The Origins and the Prospects of Our International Economic Order* (New York: McGraw-Hill, 1969) and Alfred E. Eckes, *A Search for Solvency: Bretton Woods and the International Monetary System, 1941–1971* (Austin: University of Texas Press, 1975). Benn Steil provides a dramatic account of *The Battle of Bretton Woods: John Maynard Keynes, Harry Dexter White, and the Making of a New World Order* (Princeton University Press, 2013). Harold James, *International Monetary Cooperation since Bretton Woods* (Oxford University Press, 1996) follows the evolution of the Bretton Woods system from its origins at the end of the war to its disintegration in the 1970s.

On post-war reconstruction the key accounts are still Alan S. Milward, *The Reconstruction of Western Europe, 1945–51* (London: Methuen, 1984) and Michael J. Hogan, *The Marshall Plan: America, Britain and the Reconstruction of Western Europe, 1947–1952* (Cambridge University Press, 1987).

Integrating the history of grand strategy and armaments expenditure with economic and financial history for the period after 1945 in the way that it has been done for the period 1929–45 remains a challenge. The argument made here that the period through to the late 1950s was characterized not by a post-war rupture but by a continuity with the high armaments spending of the 1930s is derived from David Edgerton's path-breaking *Warfare State*. A wide arc is traced by G. C. Peden, *Arms, Economics and British Strategy: From Dreadnoughts to Hydrogen Bombs* (Cambridge University Press, 2007). The argument was anticipated by Michael Geyer in *Deutsche Rüstungspolitik* (Frankfurt: Suhrkamp, 1984). We still lack a comprehensive history of the period from the Great Depression to the late 1950s that questions conventional assumptions about the rise of the welfare state and the end of militarism.

2 Finance for war in Asia and its aftermath
Gregg Huff

China

There is no previous study of war finance in Asia as a whole between 1937 and 1945 or of the post-war financial aftermath of wartime financial policies. Of the various country studies, China is by far the best served with three major books: Arthur N. Young, *China's Wartime Finance and Inflation, 1937–1945* (Cambridge, Mass.: Harvard University Press, 1965), Chang Kia-Ngau, *The Inflationary Spiral: The Experience of China, 1939–1950* (New York: John Wiley, 1958) and Shun-Hsin Chou, *The Chinese Inflation, 1937–1949* (New York: Columbia University Press, 1963). Together, they provide a good picture of Chinese finance, inflation and the issues surrounding both. Arthur Young was financial advisor to the Chinese government during the war and provides useful information from his own recollections and diaries. His *China and the Helping Hand, 1937–1945* (Cambridge, Mass.: Harvard University Press, 1963) has a wider focus than finance but includes much material on it, some of which also appears in his later book. Hara Akira, although writing extensively on the war, has given little attention to finance. For some of his findings, see 'L'économie Japonaise pendant la deuxième guerre mondiale', *Revue d'histoire de la Deuxième Guerre Mondiale*, 23e Année, no. 89, *La guerre en asie* (January 1973), 33–56 and 'Japan: Guns before Rice', in Mark Harrison, ed., *The Economics of World War II: Six Great Powers in International Comparison* (Cambridge University Press, 1998), pp. 224–67.

Economists will particularly appreciate specialist journal articles, and these are essential to understand fully Chinese inflation and its causes. Especially readable is Colin D. Campbell and Gordon C. Tullock, 'Hyperinflation in China, 1937–49', *Journal of Political Economy* 62:3 (1954), 236–45 while Andrew Chung Huang, 'The Inflation in China', *Quarterly Journal of Economics* 62:4 (1948), 562–75 provides a valuable account of inflation just as hyperinflation was unfolding. For part of the story of public finance from the perspective of nationalist China's finance minister for much of the war, see H. H. Kung, 'China's Financial Problems', *Foreign Affairs* 23:1 (1944), 222–32. A technical article, written to show the relationship between monetary expansion and hyperinflation, is Teh-wei Hu, 'Hyperinflation and the Dynamics of the Demand for Money in China, 1945–1949', *Journal of Political Economy* 79:1 (1971), 186–95.

Good summaries and useful analysis, although without full referencing, of war finance and inflation and some of the associated political issues, were put together by John G. Greenwood and Christopher J. R. Wood in a series of three articles in the Hong Kong journal *Asian Monetary Monitor*. The articles are: 'The Chinese Hyperinflation. Part 1: Monetary and Fiscal Origins of the Inflation, 1932–1945', *Asian Monetary Monitor* 1:1 (1977), 25–39, 'The Chinese Hyperinflation. Part 2: The Crisis of Hyperinflation, *Asian Monetary Monitor* 1:2 (1977), 32–45 and 'The Chinese Hyperinflation. Part 3: Price Stabilisation after the 1949 Revolution', *Asian Monetary Monitor* 2:1 (1978), 27–34.

Limited published material exists on either Japanese wartime finance in China or on communist monetary systems. Young, *China's Wartime Finance* has some useful data on both. Peter Schran, *Guerrilla Economy: The Development of the Shensi-Kansu-Ninghsia Border Region, 1937–1945* (Albany: State University of New York Press, 1976) includes an analysis of fiscal systems and inflation, although this suffers from a lack of reliable data. A study, of that part of Shandong controlled by the communists is Sherman Xiaogang Lai, *A Springboard to Victory: Shandong Province and Chinese Communist Military and Financial Strength, 1937–1945* (Leiden: Brill, 2011).

Japan

Japanese economists have devoted relatively little time to analysing wartime finance and post-war inflation, perhaps in part because the absence of reliable official price statistics for 1937 to 1950 make this difficult. The most satisfactory analytical account of Japanese finance between 1937 and 1950 is Raymond W. Goldsmith, *The Financial Development of Japan, 1868–1977* (Princeton University Press, 1983). Jerome B. Cohen, *Japan's Economy in War and Reconstruction* (Minneapolis: University of Minnesota Press, 1949) is a classic study that, drawing on the large volume of reports of the USA's Strategic Bombing Survey, supplies many of the details omitted from Goldsmith's account. A subsequent volume by Cohen contains material on Japan's early post-war reconstruction and high inflation but focuses more on the 1950s: Jerome B. Cohen, *Japan's Postwar Economy* (Bloomington: Indiana University Press, 1960). Three edited collections contain a number of essays that deal usefully with post-war Japanese policies toward economic reconstruction and inflation: Juro Teranishi and Yutaka Kosai, eds., *The Japanese Experience of Economic Reforms* (Basingstoke: Macmillan, 1993), Erich Pauer, ed., *Japan's War Economy* (London: Routledge, 1999) and Tetsuji Okazaki and Masahiro Okuno-Fujiwara, eds., *The Japanese Economic System and its Historical Origins* (Oxford University Press, 1999).

Southeast Asia

The principal source on Southeast Asia is Gregg Huff and Shinobu Majima 'Financing Japan's World War II Occupation of Southeast Asia', *Journal of Economic History* 73:4 (2013), 937–77. Indonesia is discussed in Shibata Yoshimasa, 'The Monetary Policy in the Netherlands East Indies under the Japanese Administration', *Bijdragen Tot de Taal-, Land-en Volkenkunde* 152:4 (1996), 699–724. Professor Shibata also has a valuable book-length study of

Japanese monetary policy in occupied areas: Shibata Yoshimasa, *Senryochi Tsuka Kinnyu Seisaku no Tenkai (Japan's Monetary Policy in the Occupied Territories)* (Tokyo: Nihon Keizai Shinbun Sha, 1999). Robert Cribb, 'Political Dimensions of the Currency Question 1945–1947', *Indonesia* 31 (1981), 113–36 is a fascinating study of the post-Second World War currency situation in Indonesia, while a chapter in Paul Kratoska's classic study of the Japanese occupation of Malaya deals with wartime finance and banking organized by the Japanese: Paul H. Kratoska, *The Japanese Occupation of Malaya* (London: Hurst & Company, 1998). The same author analyses post-war Malaya in detail in 'Banana Money: Consequences of the Demonetization of Wartime Japanese Currency in British Malaya', *Journal of Southeast Asian Studies* 23:1 (1992), 322–45. Data for money and inflation in the Philippines can be found in Eduardo Z. Romualdez, 'Financial Problems Created by the War', *Journal of the Philippine National Historical Society* 10:4 (1962), 448–518.

3 War of the factories
Jeffrey Fear

Essential global/comparative starting points are Alan S. Milward, *War, Economy and Society, 1939–1945* (London: Allen Lane, 1977), Richard Overy, *Why the Allies Won* (New York: W. W. Norton, 1995) and Mark Harrison, ed., *The Economics of World War II: Six Great Powers in International Comparison* (Cambridge University Press, 1998). Overviews of the economic contributions of the occupied colonies for Germany are Hein Klemann and Sergei Kudryashov, *Occupied Economies: An Economic History of Nazi-Occupied Europe, 1939–1945* (London: Berg, 2012) and Mark Mazower, *Hitler's Empire: How the Nazis Ruled Europe* (London: Penguin Books, 2009); for Japan: Peter Duus, Ramon H. Myers and Mark R. Peattie, eds., *The Japanese Wartime Empire, 1931–1945* (Princeton University Press, 1996) and Louise Young, *Japan's Total Empire: Manchuria and the Culture of Wartime Imperialism* (Berkeley: University of California Press, 1998).

Most historiography tends to be written through national lenses with decidedly different points of emphasis. For Russia, debates about the effectiveness of planning, the role of Stalin, and the role of Lend-Lease are highlighted. Mark Harrison's works are central: Mark Harrison and Paul R. Gregory, *Guns and Rubles: The Defense Industry in the Stalinist State* (New Haven: Yale University Press, 2008) and Mark Harrison, *Soviet Planning in Peace and War, 1938–1945* (Cambridge University Press, 1985); also Lennart

Samuelson, *Plans for Stalin's War Machine* (Basingstoke: Macmillan, 2000) and Paul R. Gregory, ed., *Behind the Façade of Stalin's Command Economy: Evidence from the Soviet State and Party Archives* (Stanford: Hoover Institution Press, 2001).

Japanese historiography focuses on the origins of post-war institutions such as the rise of the developmental state and growth of a dual structure: Hironori Sasada, *The Evolution of the Japanese Developmental State: Institutions Locked in by Ideas* (London: Routledge, 2013); Takafusa Nakamura and Kônosuke Odaka, eds., *The Economic History of Japan, 1600–1990*, vol. III: *Economic History of Japan, 1914–1955: A Dual Structure* (Oxford University Press, 1999). The United States Strategic Bombing Survey, *The Effects of Strategic Bombing on Japan's War Economy* (Washington, DC: US Government, December 1946) and Jerome B. Cohen, *Japan's Economy in War and Reconstruction* (Minneapolis: University of Minnesota Press, 1949) are still invaluable.

German historiography used to be based on the Blitzkrieg concept or 'peace economy in wartime'; see the United States Strategic Bombing Survey, *The Effects of Strategic Bombing on the German War Economy* (Washington, DC: Government Printing Office, 1945) or Alan S. Milward, *The German Economy at War, 1939–1945* (London: Athlone Press, 1965). Adam Tooze and Jonas Scherner have re-characterized it more as a wartime economy in peacetime; see Adam Tooze, *The Wages of Destruction: The Making and Breaking of the Nazi Economy* (London: Allen Lane, 2006), Jonas Scherner, 'Nazi Germany's Preparation for War: Evidence from Revised Industrial Investment Series', *European Review of Economic History* 14 (2010), 433–68 and Jonas Scherner, '"Armament in Depth" or "Armament in Breadth"? German Investment Pattern and Rearmament during the Nazi Period', *Economic History Review* 66:2 (2013), 497–517. For a particularly sharp debate about corporate complicity and industrialists' 'room to manoeuvre' or degree of 'voluntarism' in the Nazi state, see Christoph Buchheim and Jonas Scherner, 'The Role of Private Property in the Nazi Economy: The Case of Industry', *Journal of Economic History* 66 (2006): 390–418 in contrast to Peter Hayes, 'Corporate Freedom of Action in Nazi Germany', *Bulletin of the German Historical Institute* 45 (Fall 2009), 29–42.

'Declinism' and Dunkirk have influenced the British interpretation of its wartime effort. The strongest argument about Britain's unpreparedness and backwardness is Corelli Barnett, *Audit of War: The Illusion and Reality of Britain as a Great Nation* (London: Macmillan, 1986). David Edgerton's works stress Britain's military preparedness and its connections to its Empire; see

David Edgerton, *Warfare State: Britain, 1920–1970* (Cambridge University Press, 2005) and *Britain's War Machine: Weapons, Resources, and Experts in the Second World War* (London: Allen Lane, 2011). Also in this vein, G. C. Peden, *Arms, Economics and British Strategy: From Dreadnoughts to Hydrogen Bombs* (Cambridge University Press, 2007).

US historiography tends to be written in the heroic mode; see Francis Walton, *The Miracle of World War II: How American Industry Made Victory Possible* (New York: Macmillan, 1956) and Arthur Herman, *Freedom's Forge: How American Business Produced Victory in World War II* (New York: Random House, 2012). But many interpret it as the end of New Deal progressivism with the rise of the military-industrial complex and big business capturing a disproportionate share of military contracts: David Kennedy, *Freedom from Fear: The American People in Depression and War, 1929–1945* (Oxford University Press, 1999) or Paul A. C. Koistinen, *Arsenal of World War II: The Political Economy of American Warfare, 1940–1945* (Wichita: University Press of Kansas, 2004). Recently Maury Klein, *A Call to Arms: Mobilizing America for World War II* (New York: Bloomsbury, 2013) stresses the hardships and political dissension in the mobilization process. Mark R. Wilson, *Destructive Creation: American Business and the Winning of World War II* (Philadelphia: University of Pennsylvania Press, forthcoming) pushes the American mobilization effort back to 1938 and argues that the war undermined corporate concentration as midsize manufacturers were also important.

4 Controlling resources
Coal, iron ore and oil in the Second World War
David Edgerton

There are no general works focusing on raw materials and their control in the Second World War but Ian O. Lesser, *Resources and Strategy: Vital Materials in International Conflict, 1600–Present Day* (London: Macmillan, 1989) has a good general chapter on it. The main focus on raw materials has come in the course of studies of war by economic historians. Alan Milward's *War, Economy and Society, 1939–1945* (London: Allen Lane, 1977) remains an outstanding and unsurpassed survey, with much to say on raw materials. Other notable studies by British historians all, like Milward, with special interests in Germany include Paul Kennedy, *The Rise and Fall of the Great Powers: Economic Change and Military Conflict from 1500 to 2000* (New York: Vintage, 1987), Richard Overy,

Why the Allies Won (New York: W. W. Norton, 1995) and Adam Tooze, *The Wages of Destruction: The Making and Breaking of the Nazi Economy* (London: Allen Lane, 2006). Indeed recent years have seen many works refreshing our understanding of the economics of war and raw materials specifically in the Second World War. In addition to Tooze we may note Talbot C. Imlay, *Facing the Second World War: Strategy, Politics, and Economics in Britain and France, 1938–1940* (Oxford University Press, 2003), David Edgerton, *Britain's War Machine: Weapons, Resources, and Experts in the Second World War* (London: Allen Lane, 2011) and the fifth volume of Bernhard R. Kroener, Rolf-Dieter Muller and Hans Umbreit, *Germany and the Second World War: Organization and Mobilization of the German Sphere of Power* which consists of two huge parts: *Wartime Administration, Economy, and Manpower Resources, 1939–1941* (Oxford University Press, 2000) and *Wartime Administration, Economy, and Manpower Resources, 1942–1944/5* (Oxford University Press, 2003). Mark Harrison, ed., *The Economics of World War II: Six Great Powers in International Comparison* (Cambridge University Press, 1998) is a series of national studies, focusing on macroeconomic measures. The issue of occupation is an important one in relation to raw materials, and has been treated most recently in Hein Klemann and Sergei Kuryashov, *Occupied Economies: An Economic History of Nazi-Occupied Europe, 1939–1945* (London: Berg, 2012). Peter Liberman, *Does Conquest Pay? The Exploitation of Occupied Industrial Societies* (Princeton University Press, 1996) is an excellent work by a political scientist, with two chapters on the Second World War. His answer is yes.

For particular raw materials, official histories and reports are still required, such as United States Strategic Bombing Survey reports for Germany and Japan (some of which are available online), for example, USSBS, *Coals and Metals in Japan's War Economy* (Volume no. 36) (1947) or USSBS, *The War against Japanese Transportation, 1941–1945* (Volume no. 54), and the British official histories, such as W. H. B Court, *Coal* (London: HMSO, 1951), J. Hurstfield, *The Control of Raw Materials* (London: HMSO, 1953) and D. J. Payton-Smith, *Oil: A Study of War-Time Policy and Administration* (London: HMSO, 1971). On oil, see also John W. Frey and H. Chandler Ide, eds., *A History of the Petroleum Administration for War, 1941–1945* (1946), reprinted by the University Press of the Pacific, Hawai'i, 2005. There is now also interest from environmental historians, particularly in the case of raw materials. See Matthew Evenden, 'Aluminum, Commodity Chains, and the Environmental History of the Second World War', *Environmental History* 16 (2011), 69–93.

There are no general treatments of iron ore or coal in the Second World War, though the case of oil is better served by virtue of the interest the industry attracts and its multinational nature. See especially Robert Goralski and Russell Freeburg, *Oil and War: How the Deadly Struggle for Fuel in WWII meant Victory or Defeat* (New York: Morrow, 1987), Daniel Yergin, *The Prize: The Epic Quest for Oil, Money, and Power* (New York: Free Press, 1990) and much more critical Timothy Mitchell, *Carbon Democracy: Political Power in the Age of Oil* (London: Verso, 2012). Major oil companies have relevant histories including J. H. Bamberg, *The History of the British Petroleum Company*, vol. II: *The Anglo-Iranian Years, 1928–1954* (Cambridge University Press, 1994) and Jan Luiten van Zanden, Joost Jonker, Stephen Howarth and Keetie Sluyterman, *A History of Royal Dutch Shell*, vol. II: *Powering the Hydrocarbon Revolution, 1939–1973* (Oxford University Press, 2007). For bauxite, see Robin S. Gendron, Mats Ingulstad and Espen Storli, *Aluminum Ore: The Political Economy of the Global Bauxite Industry* (Vancouver: University of British Columbia Press, 2013); for tin, see Mats Ingulstad, Andrew Perchard and Espen Storli, eds., *History of the Global Tin Industry: The Devil's Metal* (London: Routledge, 2014). The sea is receiving increasing attention – a good and relevant case is Michael B. Miller, *Europe and the Maritime World: A Twentieth-Century History* (Cambridge University Press, 2012).

5 The human fuel
Food as global commodity and local scarcity
Lizzie Collingham

The Stanford University series published in the 1950s is an invaluable source of information. Notable volumes are: Karl Brandt in collaboration with Otto Schiller and Franz Ahlgrimm, *Management of Agriculture and Food in the German-Occupied and Other Areas of Fortress Europe: A Study in Military Government* (Stanford University Press, 1953), R. J. Hammond, *Food and Agriculture in Britain, 1939–45: Aspects of Wartime Control* (Stanford University Press, 1954), B. F. Johnston with Mosaburo Hosoda and Yoshio Kusumi, *Japanese Food Management in World War II* (Stanford University Press, 1953), E. M. H. Lloyd, *Food and Inflation in the Middle East, 1940–1945* (Stanford University Press, 1956) and Eric Roll, *The Combined Food Board: A Study in Wartime International Planning* (Stanford University Press, 1956). For collections of essays covering a wide geographical area, see Paul H. Kratoska, ed., *Food Supplies and the Japanese Occupation in South-East Asia* (Basingstoke: Macmillan, 1998), Bernd Martin and Alan S. Milward, eds., *Agriculture and Food Supply in the Second*

World War. Landwirtschaft und Versorgung im Zweiten Weltkrieg (Ostfildern: Scripta Mercaturae Verlag, 1985), Brian Short, Charles Watkins and John Martin, eds., *The Front Line of Freedom. British Farming in the Second World War* (Exeter: British Agricultural Society, 2006) and Frank Trentmann and Flemming Just, eds., *Food and Conflict in Europe in the Age of the Two World Wars* (Basingstoke: Palgrave Macmillan, 2006). Gustavo Corni and Horst Gies, *Brot, Butter, Kanonen. Die Ernährungswirtschaft in Deutschland unter der Diktatur Hitlers* (Berlin: Akademie Verlag, 1997) is very detailed and Christian Gerlach, *Krieg, Ernährung, Völkermord. Forschungen zur deutschen Vernichtungs-politik im Zweiten Weltkrieg* (Hamburg: Hamburger Edition, 1998) makes the connection between food and the Holocaust. The USA is covered by Joachim Bengelsdorf, *Die Landwirtschaft der Vereinigten Staaten von Amerika im Zweiten Weltkrieg* (St Katharinen: Scripta Mercaturae Verlag, 1997) and Amy Bentley, *Eating For Victory: Food Rationing and the Politics of Domesticity* (Chicago: University of Illinois Press, 1998) while William Moskoff, *The Bread of Afflic-tion: The Food Supply in the USSR during World War II* (Cambridge University Press, 1990) is essential to understanding the food situation in the Soviet Union. The nationalist perspective on China's food situation is given by Tsung-han Shen, 'Food Production and Distribution for Civilian and Mili-tary Needs in Wartime China, 1937–1945', in Paul Sih, ed., *Nationalist China During the Sino-Japanese War, 1937–1945* (New York: Exposition Press, 1977), pp. 167–93 and Jin Pusen, 'To Feed a Country at War: China's Supply and Consumption of Grain during the War of Resistance', in David P. Barrett and Larry N. Shyu, eds., *China in the Anti-Japanese War, 1937–1945: Politics, Culture and Society* (Oxford: Peter Lang, 2001), pp. 157–69. My own book, Lizzie Collingham, *The Taste of War: World War II and the Battle for Food* (London: Allen Lane, 2011) explores the issues touched in this chapter in greater depth.

6 Sea transport
Michael Miller

British and American official histories, if often ponderous in detail, provide the most comprehensive review of Allied transportation services in the Second World War. For Britain the starting point is C. B. A. Behrens's magisterial *Merchant Shipping and the Demands of War* (London: HMSO, 1954). S. W. Roskill's multi-volume *The War at Sea, 1939–1945* (London: HMSO, 1954, 1956, 1960, 1961) although primarily a naval history, is indispensable for the broader shipping context. See also W. N. Medlicott, *The Economic Blockade* (2 vols., London: HMSO, 1952, 1959) and, although limited in analytical value, from The Second World War 1939–1945 Army series: R. Micklem, *Transportation* (London: The War Office, 1950), J. B. Higham and E. A. Knighton, *Movements* (London: The War Office, 1955) and D. W. Boileau, *Supplies and Transport*, vol. 1 (London: The War Office 1954). There are also superb historical records at the United Kingdom's National Archives (Ministry of Transport series). Useful too is the report of the Liverpool Port Emergency Committee in the files of the Mersey Docks and Harbour Board at the Merseyside Maritime Museum in Liverpool. For the USA, see the United States Army in World War II series, especially the two volumes by Richard M. Leighton and Robert W. Coakley, *Global Logistics and Strategy, 1940–1943* (Washington, DC: Center of Military History United States Army, 1995) and *Global Logistics and Strategy 1943–1945* (Washington, DC: Office of the Chief of Military History, 1968), as well as three volumes on the Technical Services: Chester Wardlow, *The Transportation Corps: Responsibilities, Organization, and Operations* (Washington, DC: Office of the Chief of Military History, 1951), Chester Wardlow, *The Transportation Corps: Movements, Training, and Supply* (Washington, DC: Center of Military History, 1956) and Joseph Bykofsky and Harold Larson, *The Transportation Corps: Operations Overseas* (Washington, DC: Center of Military History, 1957).

For works in English on Japanese shipping, see the United States Strategic Bombing Survey, *The War against Japanese Transportation, 1941–1945* (Washington, DC, 1947) and Mark P. Parillo, *The Japanese Merchant Marine in World War II* (Annapolis: Naval Institute Press, 1993). The fate of the German merchant marine can be followed in the Medlicott volumes and Günther Steinweg, *Die Deutsche Handelsflotte im Zweiten Weltkrieg. Aufgaben und Schicksal* (Göttingen: Otto Schwartz, 1954) and Susanne Wiborg and Klaus Wiborg, *1847–1997. Unser Feld ist die Welt. 150 Jahre Hapag-Lloyd* (Hamburg: Hapag-Lloyd AG, 1997). French shipping history in the war is best followed in the TT series of the Service historique de la marine at Vincennes. See also Marthe Barbance, *Histoire de la Compagnie Générale Transatlantique: Un siècle d'exploitation maritime* (Paris: Arts et Métiers Graphiques, 1955). On the Netherlands, see L. L. von Münching, *De Nederlandsche koopvaardijvloot in de tweede wereldoorloog. De lotgevallen van Nederlandse koopvaardijschepen en hun bemanning* (Bussum: De Boer Maritiem, 1978) and H. Th. Bakker, *De K.P.M. in oorlogstijd. Een overzicht van de verrichtingen van de Koninklijke Paketvaart-Maatschappij en haar personeel gedurende de wereldoorlog 1939–1945* (Amsterdam: N. V. Koninklijke Paketvaart-Maatschappij, 1950). On Norway, see Kaare

Petersen, *The Saga of Norwegian Shipping: An Outline of the History, Growth and Development of a Modern Merchant Marine* (Oslo: Dreyers, 1955).

For First World War comparisons, see C. Ernest Fayle's *Seaborne Trade* (3 vols., New York: Longman's Green & Co., 1920–24) and his *The War and the Shipping Industry* (London: Humphrey Milford / Oxford University Press, 1927). Equally valuable are J. A. Salter, *Allied Shipping Control: An Experiment in International Administration* (Oxford: Clarendon Press 1921), Louis Guichard, *Histoire du blocus naval (1914–1918)* (Paris: Payot, 1929) and Henri Cangardel, *La marine marchande française et la guerre* (Paris: Les Presses Universitaires de France 1927). On the broader history of twentieth-century ocean transport, see Michael B. Miller, *Europe and the Maritime World: A Twentieth-Century History* (Cambridge University Press, 2012).

7 Knowledge economies
Toward a new technological age
Cathryn Carson

An excellent introduction to Second World War R&D is given in Walter E. Grunden, Yutaka Kawamura, Eduard Kolchinsky, Helmut Maier and Masakatsu Yamazaki, 'Laying the Foundation for Wartime Research: A Comparative Overview of Science Mobilization in National Socialist Germany, Japan, and the Soviet Union', in Carola Sachse and Mark Walker, eds., *Politics and Science in Wartime* (University of Chicago Press, 2005), pp. 79–106. Guy Hartcup, *The Effect of Science on the Second World War* (New York: St. Martin's Press, 2000) is a popular account from a somewhat older perspective. Specific aspects are taken up in, for example, Roy M. MacLeod, *Science and the Pacific War* (Dordrecht: Kluwer, 2000), Peter Galison, 'Physics between War and Peace', in Steven A. Walton, ed., *Instrumental in War: Science, Research, and Instruments Between Knowledge and the World* (Leiden: Brill, 2005), pp. 363–403.

The scholarly literature is largely organized by national frames. For the US case, Daniel J. Kevles, *The Physicists: A History of a Scientific Community in Modern America* (New York, Knopf, 1977) is still the easiest entry point, supported by scholarship on aeronautics, radar and the Manhattan Project. Technical histories written after the war are still valuable sources, including the OSRD series *Science in World War II*. The official Manhattan Project report of 1945, Henry De Wolf Smyth, *Atomic Energy for Military Purposes*

(Princeton University Press, 1945), remains a classic source. Work on Britain is well-developed. David Edgerton, *Britain's War Machine: Weapons, Resources, and Experts in the Second World War* (London: Allen Lane, 2011) is a sharply argued synthesis that engages much previous scholarship. On France, the histories of science, military technology and industry have largely remained distinct literatures. Some beginnings for a synthetic story can be found in Amy Dahan and Dominique Pestre, *Les sciences pour la guerre, 1940–1960* (Paris: Éditions de l'École des Hautes Études en Sciences Sociales, 2004) and Dominique Pestre, ed., *Deux siècles d'histoire de l'armement en France* (Paris: CNRS, 2005).

The German case is exceptionally well researched. In English good overviews are Susanne Heim, Carola Sachse and Mark Walker, eds., *The Kaiser Wilhelm Society under National Socialism* (Cambridge University Press, 2009) and Monika Renneberg and Mark Walker, eds., *Science, Technology, and National Socialism* (Cambridge University Press, 1994). Of the volumes in the series *Geschichte der Kaiser-Wilhelm-Gesellschaft im Nationalsozialismus*, Helmuth Maier's *Forschung als Waffe* (Göttingen: Wallstein, 2007) and several edited volumes on armaments research are particularly rich. Important on related topics are Sören Flachowsky, *Von der Notgemeinschaft zum Reichsforschungsrat. Wissenschaftspolitik im Kontext von Autarkie, Aufrüstung und Krieg* (Stuttgart: Steiner, 2008), Matthias Berg, Jens Thiel and Peter T. Walter, eds., *Mit Feder und Schwert. Militär und Wissenschaft – Wissenschaftler und Krieg* (Stuttgart: Steiner, 2009) and Günter Nagel, *Wissenschaft für den Krieg. Die geheimen Arbeiten der Abteilung Forschung des Heereswaffenamtes* (Stuttgart: Steiner, 2012).

For the Soviet Union, with the exception of studies on nuclear weapons (David Holloway, *Stalin and the Bomb: The Soviet Union and Atomic Energy, 1939–1956* (New Haven: Yale University Press, 1994)) and rocketry (Asif A. Siddiqi, *The Red Rockets' Glare: Spaceflight and the Soviet Imagination, 1857–1957* (Cambridge University Press, 2010)) and overviews such as Loren R. Graham, *Science in Russia and the Soviet Union* (Cambridge University Press, 1993), the best entry is through the defence industry, beginning with Mark Harrison, ed., *Guns and Rubles: The Defense Industry in the Stalinist State* (New Haven: Yale University Press, 2008). Ronald Amann and Julian Cooper, eds., *Industrial Innovation in the Soviet Union* (New Haven: Yale University Press, 1982) gives a still-valuable overview, particularly the chapters by David Holloway. For Japan, Walter E. Grunden, *Secret Weapons & World War II: Japan in the Shadow of Big Science* (Lawrence: University Press of Kansas, 2005) is comprehensive and helpfully comparative. Other sources include Morris Low, *Science and the Building of a New Japan* (New York: Palgrave Macmillan, 2005) and Hiromi Mizuno, *Science for the Empire: Scientific Nationalism in Modern Japan* (Stanford University Press, 2009).

There is a large literature on wartime nuclear projects. In addition to the works cited in the chapter, the following selections on the Manhattan Project are informative: Robert Serber, *The Los Alamos Primer: The First Lectures on How to Build an Atomic Bomb* (Berkeley: University of California Press, 1992), Robert S. Norriss, *Racing for the Bomb: General Leslie R. Groves, the Manhattan Project's Indispensable Man* (South Royalton, Vt.: Steerforth Press, 2002) and Michael D. Gordin, *Five Days in August: How World War II Became a Nuclear War* (Princeton University Press, 2007). On the German fission project, *Operation Epsilon: The Farm Hall Transcripts* (Berkeley: University of California Press, 1993) reproduces the conversations of ten interned German scientific leaders in 1945; along with Mark Walker, *German National Socialism and the Quest for Nuclear Power* (Cambridge University Press, 1989), the best entry point is David C. Cassidy, *Uncertainty: The Life and Science of Werner Heisenberg* (New York: W. H. Freeman, 1992). There are continued suggestions that the German project proceeded further than has been discovered, but in a careful weighing, the evidence remains sketchy.

Resources for the general history of science abound. An entry-level text is Peter J. Bowler and Iwan Rhys Morus, *Making Modern Science: A Historical Survey* (University of Chicago Press, 2005). Good overviews are provided by R. C. Olby, G. N. Cantor, J. R. R. Christie and M. J. S. Hodge, eds., *Companion to the History of Modern Science* (London: Routledge, 1996), John Krige and Dominque Pestre, eds., *Science in the Twentieth Century* (Amsterdam: Harwood Academic, 1997) and Arne Hessenbruch, ed., *Reader's Guide to the HIstory of Science* (Chicago: Fitzroy Dearborn, 2000).

8 Environments, states and societies at war
Chris Pearson

This chapter aims to contribute to the burgeoning field of research into the environmental history of war. Edmund P. Russell's book *War and Nature: Fighting Humans and Insects with Chemicals from World War 1 to Silent Spring* (Cambridge University Press, 2001) served as a catalyst for work in this area. Since then, several edited volumes have introduced a range of case studies: Charles E. Closmann, ed., *War and the Environment: Military Destruction in the*

Modern Age (College Station, Tex.: Texas A&M University Press, 2009); Chris Pearson, Peter Coates and Tim Cole, eds., *Militarized Landscapes: From Gettysburg to Salisbury Plain* (London: Continuum, 2010) and Richard P. Tucker and Edmund P. Russell, eds., *Natural Enemy, Natural Ally: Toward an Environmental History of Warfare* (Corvallis: Oregon State University Press, 2004). Numerous articles in journals such as *Environmental History* and *Environment and History* have added further case studies. They vary from focused research on individual cities (Rauno Lahtinen and Timo Vuorisalo, '"It's war and everyone can do as they please!": An Environmental History of a Finnish City in Wartime', *Environmental History* 9 [2004], 679–700) to global overviews of war and resource use (John R. McNeill, 'Woods and Warfare in World History', *Environmental History* 9 [2004], 388–410).

Some environmental histories of war have focused on the relationship between militaries and the environment, such as Lisa M. Brady, *War Upon the Land: Military Strategy and the Transformation of Southern Landscapes during the American Civil War* (Athens, Ga.: University of Georgia Press, 2012) and Chris Pearson, *Mobilizing Nature: The Environmental History of War and Militarization in Modern France* (Manchester University Press, 2012). This work has added to, and at times challenged, military histories on the relationship between terrain and tactics, such as Harold Winters, *Battling the Elements: Weather and Terrain in the Conduct of War* (Baltimore and London: Johns Hopkins University Press, 1998). Other environmental histories explore the political, cultural and social dimensions of war. See Chris Pearson, *Scarred Landscapes: War and Nature in Vichy France* (Basingstoke: Palgrave Macmillan, 2008).

Environmental historians have uncovered various environmental dimensions of the Second World War, including natural resource use (Richard Tucker, 'The World Wars and the Globalization of Timber Cutting', in Tucker and Russell, *Natural Enemy, Natural Ally*, pp. 110–41), civilian recycling programmes (Tim Cooper, 'Challenging the "Refuse Revolution": War, Waste and the Rediscovery of Recycling, 1900–50', *Historical Research* 81 (2007), 710–30), militarization (Judith A. Bennett, *Natives and Exotics: World War II and Environment in the Southern Pacific* [Honolulu: University of Hawai'i Press, 2009]) and the political mobilization of nature (Pearson, *Scarred Landscapes*). However, they have not yet produced a global overview of the war's environmental history. Certain areas also require more attention, such as the role of animals, which forms part of the wider history of animals in war. John Sheail, 'Wartime Rodent-Control in England and

Wales', in Brian Short, Charles Watkins and John Martin, eds., *The Front Line of Freedom: British Farming in the Second World War* (Exeter: British Agricultural History Society, 2006), pp. 55–66 and Marcus Hall, 'World War II and the Axis of Disease: Battling Malaria in Twentieth-Century Italy', in Closmann, *War and the Environment*, pp. 112–31 point the way for further research. Another area that requires further research and reflection is the social experience of wartime environments. This was extremely diverse, from British child evacuees experiencing country life for the first time to Japanese Americans interned in desert camps in the western USA (for the latter, see Connie Y. Chiang, 'Imprisoned Nature: Toward an Environmental History of the World War II Japanese American Incarceration', *Environmental History* 15 [2010], 236–67). More attention also needs to be paid to the relationship between wartime and post-war militarization (which is broached in Marianna Dudley, *An Environmental History of the UK Defence Estate, 1945 to Present* [London: Bloomsbury, 2012]) and the environmental dimensions of the transition to the Cold War.

9 Death and survival in the Second World War
Richard Bessel

The subject of death and survival in the Second World War is vast, and the literature that it has generated or that touches upon it is correspondingly huge. Enormous effort has been made to describe, tabulate and document the human cost of the Second World War. Nevertheless, overall statistics of the dead that arose from the war necessarily are somewhat inexact; the reporting and recording of the dead was not always carried out precisely, and in many cases not at all; numbers of dead often have been the subject of political debate, with some parties seeking to maximize the totals while others seek to minimize them; and it is not completely clear whether some deaths that occurred during the Second World War really can be attributed to the war. Approximate overall totals can be found in I. C. B. Dear and M. R. D. Foot, eds., *The Oxford Companion to World War II* (Oxford University Press, 1995). Such figures are still often taken from the earlier calculations of Gregory Frumkin, *Population Changes in Europe since 1939* (London: Allen & Unwin, 1951), Boris Urlanis, *Wars and Population* (Moscow: Progress Publishers, 1971), and David Singer and Melvin Small, *The Wages of War, 1816–1965: A Statistical Handbook* (New York: John Wiley, 1972). Considerable insight into the scale of military losses across the world may be found in the more recent volume by Williamson Murray and Allan Millett, *A War to Be Won: Fighting the Second*

World War (Cambridge, Mass.: Harvard University Press, 2000). For detailed analysis of German military losses, see Rüdiger Overmans, *Deutsche militärische Verluste im Zweiten Weltkrieg* (Munich: R. Oldenbourg, 1999). On Soviet war dead, see Michael Ellman and S. Maksudov, 'Soviet Deaths in the Great Patriotic War: A Note', *Europe-Asia Studies* 46:4 (1994), 671–80.

The fate of prisoners of war is discussed in S. P. MacKenzie, 'The Treatment of Prisoners in World War II', *Journal of Modern History* 66:3 (1994), 487–520, and in the relevant articles in Rüdiger Overmans, ed., *In der Hand des Feindes. Kriegsgefangenschaft von der Antike bis zum Zweiten Weltkrieg* (Cologne: Böhlau, 1999). Given the scale of the mass murder committed against Soviet soldiers in German captivity, it is understandable that this has generated a substantial literature, following the pioneering monograph by Christian Streit, *Keine Kameraden. Die Wehrmacht und die sowjetischen Kriegsgefangenen 1941–1945* (3rd edn, Bonn: Dietz, 1991).

For the effects of Japan's Pacific War, the definitive texts remain those by John Dower: *War without Mercy: Race and Power in the Pacific War* (New York: Pantheon, 1986), and *Embracing Defeat: Japan in the Wake of World War II* (New York: W. W. Norton, 2000). Also, Alvin D. Cox, 'The Pacific War', in Peter Duus, ed., *The Cambridge History of Japan*, vol. VI: *The Twentieth Century* (Cambridge University Press, 1988), pp. 315–82. For China, see Lloyd Eastman's contribution, 'Nationalist China during the Sino-Japanese War, 1939–1945', in John K. Fairbank and Albert Feuerwerker, eds., *The Cambridge History of China*, vol. XIII, part 2: *Republican China, 1912–1949* (Cambridge University Press, 1986), pp. 547–608. On Japanese army atrocities, see Jean-Louis Margolin, *L'armée de l'empereur: Violence et crimes du Japon en guerre, 1937–1945* (Paris: Colin, 2007).

For Russia, Catherine Merridale's sensitive discussion in *Night of Stone: Death and Memory in Twentieth Century Russia* (London: Granta, 2000) contains much insight about the consequences of the enormous casualties suffered by the Soviet Union during the 'Great Patriotic War'. On the effects specifically on the Red Army, see Merridale's *Ivan's War: Life and Death in the Red Army, 1939–1945* (New York: Picador, 2007). In recent years, in the wake of the opening of archival sources following the collapse of the Soviet bloc, detailed monographs have been published giving a far more detailed and accurate understanding of the terrible scale of the suffering and death across Eastern Europe. Among the most important are those by Karel Berkhoff, *Harvest of Despair: Life and Death in Ukraine Under Nazi Rule* (Cambridge, Mass.: Harvard University Press, 2004), Christian Gerlach, *Kalkulierte Morde. Die deutsche Wirtschafts-und Vernichtungspolitik in Weissrussland 1941 bis 1944*

(Hamburg: Hamburger Edition, 1999) and Dieter Pohl, *Nationalsozialistische Judenverfolgung in Ostgalizien 1941–1944. Organisation und Durchführung eines staatlichen Massenverbrechens* (Munich: Oldenbourg, 1994). On the German army's role in the occupation of the USSR generally, see Dieter Pohl, *Die Herrschaft der Wehrmacht. Deutsche Militärbesatzung und einheimische Bevölkerung in der Sowjetunion 1941–1944* (Munich: Oldenbourg, 2008).

On the human toll of the bombing in Europe, the authoritative work now is Richard Overy, *The Bombing War: Europe, 1939–1945* (London: Allen Lane, 2013). Also Claudia Baldoli, Andrew Knapp and Richard Overy, eds., *Bombing, States and Peoples in Western Europe, 1940–1945* (London: Continuum, 2011). For the effects of the bombing in Britain and Germany, reference also should be made to the recent study by Dietmar Süss, *Tod aus der Luft. Kriegsgesellschaft und Luftkrieg in Deutschland* (Munich: Siedler Verlag, 2011).

The campaigns of mass murder and genocide in German-occupied Europe have generated an enormous literature. Here only a couple of the most important and insightful attempts at a comprehensive account of the murder of Europe's Jewish population can be mentioned: Saul Friedländer's magisterial *The Years of Extermination: Nazi Germany and the Jews, 1939–1945* (London: Weidenfeld & Nicolson, 2007) and Peter Longerich's *Holocaust: The Nazi Persecution and Murder of the Jews* (Oxford University Press, 2010). Insight into the difficulties involved in attempting to pin down the precise numbers of victims may be gained from Dieter Pohl's essay in the catalogue for the exhibition underneath the Memorial to the Murdered Jews of Europe in Berlin: Dieter Pohl, 'Menschenleben und Statistik', in Stiftung Denkmal für die ermordeten Juden Europas, ed., *Materialien zum Denkmal für die ermordeten Juden Europas* (Berlin: Nicolai, 2005), pp. 72–77. The key text on the National Socialist campaign to murder Europe's Sinti and Roma population remains Michael Zimmermann, *Rassenutopie und Genozid. Die nationalsozialistische 'Lösung der Zigeunerfrage'* (Hamburg: Christians, 1996).

With regard to famine in Europe, what happened in Greece under German occupation occupies a prominent position, and good accounts may be found in Mark Mazower, *Inside Hitler's Greece: The Experience of Occupation, 1941–44* (New Haven and London: Yale University Press, 1993) and Violetta Hionidou, *Famine and Death in Occupied Greece, 1941–1944* (Cambridge University Press, 2006). The horrors experienced by the inhabitants of Leningrad during the wartime siege are discussed in John Barber and Andrei Dzeniskevich, eds., *Life and Death in Besieged Leningrad, 1941–44* (Basingstoke: Palgrave Macmillan, 2005). On the causes and extent of famine in Bengal, debate was sparked by the Nobel Prize winner Amartya Sen, *Poverty and Famines: An Essay on Entitlement and Deprivation*

(Oxford: Clarendon Press, 1981); see also Paul Greenough, *Prosperity and Misery in Modern Bengal: The Famine of 1943–1944* (Oxford University Press, 1982), as well as the discussions in the general text by Cormac Ó Gráda, *Famine: A Short History* (Princeton University Press, 2009). A comparative discussion of the major wartime famines in Asia may be found in Sugata Bose, 'Starvation amidst Plenty: The Making of Famine in Bengal, Honan and Tonkin, 1942–45', *Modern Asian Studies* 24:4 (1990), 699–727.

For accounts of German and Japanese campaigns of biological warfare and their effects, see Friedrich Hansen, *Biologische Kriegsführung im Dritten Reich* (Frankfurt am Main and New York: Campus Verlag, 1993) and Sheldon H. Harris, *Factories of Death: Japanese Biological Warfare 1932–45 and the American Cover-up* (London and New York: Routledge, 1994). On disease and epidemics in Eastern Europe during the war, refer to Paul Julian Weindling, *Epidemics and Genocide in Eastern Europe, 1890–1945* (Oxford University Press, 2000).

The themes of survival, the emergence from mass violence and the subsequent effects of wartime death on a mass scale form an important theme running through many studies of the aftermath of the Second World War. A good starting point is provided by the collection edited by Richard Bessel and Dirk Schumann, *Life after Death: Approaches to a Cultural and Social History of Europe during the 1940s and 1950s* (Cambridge University Press, 2003). Tony Judt has important things to say about this theme in his magnum opus *Postwar: A History of Europe since 1945* (London: Heinemann, 2005). For a panoramic account of the painful legacy of the war and post-war violence, see Keith Lowe, *Savage Continent: Europe in the Aftermath of World War II* (London: Viking, 2012). An account of the dreadful story of post-war ethnic violence in Europe is presented in Norman M. Naimark, *Fires of Hatred: Ethnic Cleansing in Twentieth-Century Europe* (Cambridge, Mass.: Harvard University Press, 2001). The theme of death and survival comprises an important element of many sensitive local and regional studies of the aftermath of the war. Noteworthy examples for Germany include Neil Gregor, *Haunted City: Nuremberg and the Nazi Past* (New Haven and London: Yale University Press, 2008) and Monica Black, *Death in Berlin: From Weimar to Divided Germany* (Cambridge University Press, 2010). On Germany generally, see Richard Bessel, *Germany 1945: From War to Peace* (London and New York: HarperCollins, 2009). For Japan, see John Dower, *Embracing Defeat: Japan in the Wake of World War II* (New York: W. W. Norton, 2000). For Russia, see Catherine Merridale, *Night of Stone: Death and Memory in Twentieth Century Russia* (London: Granta, 2000).

The literature on the effects of the Shoah on Jewish consciousness among survivors and their co-religionists after 1945 is substantial. On the Jews in post-war Germany, see above all Michael Brenner, *After the Holocaust: Rebuilding Jewish Lives in Postwar Germany* (Princeton University Press, 1997) and Eva Kolinsky, *After the Holocaust: Jewish Survivors in Germany after 1945* (London: Pimlico, 2004). For Israel, see Tom Segev, *The Seventh Million: The Israelis and the Holocaust* (New York: Hill & Wang, 1993). Reference also may be made to the recent collection edited by David Cesarani and Eric J. Sundquist, *After the Holocaust: Challenging the Myth of Silence* (Abingdon: Routledge, 2012).

10 Wars of displacement
Exile and uprooting in the 1940s
Yasmin Khan

Histories of wartime displacement are but one chapter in the histories of refugee movements, migrations and the creation of diasporas around the world in the twentieth century. For overviews, see Robin Cohen, *The Cambridge Survey of World Migration* (Cambridge University Press, 2010) and Peter Gatrell, *The Making of the Modern Refugee* (Oxford University Press, 2013).

There are some powerful general narratives of refugee upheaval and displacements during and after the war. Classic accounts include Timothy Snyder, *Bloodlands: Europe between Hitler and Stalin* (New York: Basic Books, 2012) and Mark Mazower, *Dark Continent: Europe's Twentieth Century* (London: Allen Lane, 1998). See also Ben Shephard, *The Long Road Home: The Aftermath of the Second World War* (London: Bodley Head, 2010). The European story dominates the histories of Displaced Persons in Europe, the focus of a number of other narratives and edited volumes. See Mark Wyman, *DPs: Europe's Displaced Persons, 1945–1951* (Ithaca: Cornell University Press, 1998), Jessica Reinisch and Elizabeth White, eds., *The Disentanglement of Populations: Migration, Expulsion and Displacement in Post-War Europe, 1944–49* (Basingstoke: Palgrave Macmillan, 2011) and Gerard Daniel Cohen, *In War's Wake: Europe's Displaced Persons in the Postwar Order* (Oxford University Press, 2012). A number of specific histories of Jewish, Ukrainian and Polish experiences are available, for instance, Debórah Dwork and Robert Jan van Pelt, *Flight from the Reich: Refugee Jews, 1933–1946* (New York: W. W. Norton, 2012). There's also an increasing interest in Europeans who took refuge in Asia, for example, Bei Gao, *Shanghai Sanctuary: Chinese and*

Japanese Policy toward European Jewish Refugees during World War II (Oxford University Press, 2013).

Until recently, the German dimension to this history, and the experience of the expellees had not been fully integrated into this scholarship despite an extensive literature available in German. Useful accounts in English include, R. M. Douglas, *Orderly and Humane: The Expulsion of the Germans after the Second World War* (New Haven: Yale University Press, 2012) and Mathias Schulze, ed., *German Diasporic Experiences: Identity, Migration, and Loss* (Waterloo: Wilfrid Laurier University Press, 2008). Tara Zahra, *The Lost Children: Reconstructing Europe's Families after World War II* (Cambridge, Mass.: Harvard University Press, 2011) and Jessica Reinisch, *The Perils of Peace: The Public Health Crisis in Occupied Germany* (Oxford University Press, 2013) both address specific aspects of public health and family life.

Integrated or comparative analysis of the global population upheaval of the 1940s is less common. More recently, some edited collections have sought to place the refugee movements of the 1940s in an international framework. For instance, Panikos Panayi and Pippa Virdee, *Refugees and the End of Empire: Imperial Collapse and Forced Migration in the Twentieth Century* (New York: Palgrave Macmillan, 2011) and Mark Mazower, Jessica Reinisch and David Feldman, eds., *Post-War Reconstruction in Europe: International Perspectives, 1945–1949* (Oxford University Press, 2011). Peter Gatrell has also emphasized the comparative dimensions in his own work. Regional and area studies fill in the picture for different parts of the world, particularly for China, for Palestine and for India. On China's wartime and some of the effects on civilian displacement, see Stephen R. MacKinnon, *Wuhan, 1938: War, Refugees, and the Making of Modern China* (Berkeley: University of California Press, 2008) and for a more panoramic overview, Rana Mitter, *China's War with Japan, 1937–1945: The Struggle for Survival* (London: Allen Lane, 2013).

On India, Burma and Southeast Asia's social transformations during the war, the most reliable syntheses are by Christopher Bayly and Tim Harper, *Forgotten Armies: Britain's Asian Empire & the War with Japan* (London: Penguin, 2005) and Christopher Bayly and Tim Harper, *The End of Britain's Asian Empire* (London: Penguin, 2008). Sunil Amrith has pioneered analysis of the Bay of Bengal as an interconnected region of migration and has much to say about wartime disruptions: Sunil Amrith, *Migration and Diaspora in Modern Asia* (Cambridge University Press, 2011) and *Crossing the Bay of Bengal: The Furies of Nature and the Fortunes of Migrants* (Boston: Harvard University Press, 2013). On India's Partition, there is much detailed scholarship but again this is rarely placed in a global or comparative framework: Ian Talbot and Gurharpal Singh, *The Partition of India* (Cambridge University Press, 2009) and Yasmin Khan, *The Great Partition: The Making of India and Pakistan* (New Haven: Yale University Press, 2007) are starting places. Partition studies reveal the complex identities of refugees and their struggle in the face of bureaucratic nation states, in particular, Vazira Fazila-Yacoobali Zaminder, *The Long Partition and the Making of Modern South Asia: Refugees, Boundaries, Histories* (New York: Columbia University Press, 2010).

The scholarship about Palestine in 1948 has stimulated lengthy debates although many of these debates take contemporary politics and struggles as a point of reference. The 'New Historians' have generated much controversy. Benny Morris's key work *The Birth of the Palestinian Refugee Problem, 1947–1949* (Cambridge University Press, 1989) was revised by the same author in *The Birth of the Palestinian Refugee Problem Revisited* (Cambridge University Press, 2004). For a different take, see Ilan Pappé, *The Ethnic Cleansing of Palestine* (Oxford: Oneworld, 2007). On the difficulties of reprising this history, see Eugene L. Rogan and Avi Shlaim, *The War for Palestine: Rewriting the History of 1948* (Cambridge University Press, 2007).

On the ideologies of expulsion and population exchange, there is still much scope for new research. One case study is Matthew James Frank, *Expelling the Germans: British Opinion and Post-1945 Population Transfer in Context* (Oxford University Press, 2007). Around the world there are a great number of personal accounts and memoirs by those who were displaced in the 1940s reliving their experiences and memories. Many of these are published but many remain as raw accounts in archives or recorded by oral history projects, awaiting assimilation into their proper place in the historical record.

11 The war of the cities
Industrial labouring forces
Rüdiger Hachtmann

The industrial labouring forces, i.e. the history of the organization of work and of industrial production; the composition of the workforce; the mobilization of additional human resources; labour law and organized labour movements; as well as the mentalities of the industrial working class, are all aspects of the history of the war economies of the six primary belligerents from 1939 to 1945. They are also aspects of each nation's social history. Yet, no comparative or even a transnational survey of the topic exists. Moreover, national historiography on these different aspects of industrial labouring forces has taken very different forms in the respective nations. At first glance, this may seem surprising; however, the last decade has witnessed a decline in scholarly interest in the history of industrial work, and an even greater decrease in interest in the history of labour movements, the mentalities of workers and working-class society.

Nevertheless, Second World War anthologies are available that include contributions on the labouring forces of the primary belligerents. See, for example, Mark Harrison, ed., *The Economics of World War II: Six Great Powers in International Comparison* (Cambridge University Press, 1998) and Jeremy Noakes, ed., *The Civilian in War: The Home Front in Europe, Japan and the USA in World War II* (University of Exeter Press, 1992). For a transnational overview on the social and economic development of the primary belligerents, see in particular Richard Overy, *Why the Allies Won* (New York: W. W. Norton, 1995).

On individual and collective changes in labour law between 1939 and 1945, as well as restrictions on workers' movement related to the war economy, national surveys on war mobilization constitute a good starting point, provided that they situate it within a broader timespan. On the USA, see Alan Gropman, *Mobilizing U.S. Industry in World War II: Myth and Reality* (Washington, DC: Institute for National Strategic Studies, 1996). German labour law, in particular, has developed into an independent research field. Because of its already bellicose orientation in 1933, it experienced more fundamental changes when compared with the USA or Great Britain. On Germany, see Andreas Kranig's classic and still relevant work, *Lockung und Zwang. Zur Arbeitsverfassung im Dritten Reich* (Stuttgart: Deutsche-Verlag-Anstalt, 1983). Yet, little research to date has been done on the numerous exemptions and special provisions for foreign workers under Nazi labour law after 1941.

On German industries' use of foreign workers, see Ulrich Herbert's path-breaking study: *Hitler's Foreign Workers: Enforced Foreign Labor in Germany under the Third Reich*, trans. William Templer (Cambridge University Press, 1997). Since its publication, countless local and regional studies have expanded empirically on this study; yet, the recruitment of foreign workers in occupied countries has not received significant coverage; important information on this topic can be found, above all, in Karsten Linne and Florian Dierl, eds., *Arbeitskräfte als Kriegsbeute. Der Fall Ost-und Südosteuropa 1939–1945* (Berlin: Metropol, 2011).

Studies on POWs and their economic mobilization exist for many nations. See, for example, the definitive work on Soviet POWs in Germany: Christian Streit, *Keine Kameraden. Die Wehrmacht und die sowjetischen Kriegsgefangenen 1941–1945* (Bonn: Deutsche-Verlag-Anstalt, 1978); for German POWs in the USA, see Antonio Thompson, *Men in German Uniform: POWs in America during World War II* (Knoxville: University of Tennessee Press, 2010); on the mobilization of the Soviet Gulag system for the war effort, see Paul Gregory and Valery Lazarev, eds., *The Economics of Forced Labor: The Soviet Gulag* (Stanford: Hoover Institution Press, 2003). On women's mobilization, see the classic work of Leila J. Rupp, *Mobilizing Women for War: German and American Propaganda, 1939–1945* (Princeton University Press, 1978).

While the organizational history of unions during the Second World War has received little attention in the last decade, one can find important information on the topic in more generalized studies on unions. For Great Britain, see Chris Wrigley, *British Trade Unions since 1933* (Cambridge University Press, 2002). The history of unions in wartime Japan and Germany constitutes something of an exception to the above rule. Numerous biographies exist on the leaders of the German Labour Front (DAF) that provide valuable empirical information on the DAF – the Nazi labour organization which, however, bore little resemblance to unions. See Ronald Smelser, *Robert Ley: Hitler's Labor Front Leader* (New York: Berg, 1988). See also Michael Schneider, *Unterm Hakenkreuz. Arbeiter und Arbeiterbewegung 1933 bis 1939* (Bonn: Dietz, 1993) as well as the work by the same author, *In der Kriegsgesellschaft. Arbeiter und Arbeiterbewegung 1939 bis 1945* (Bonn: Dietz, 2014). Additionally, see the introduction in Rüdiger Hachtmann, ed., *Ein Koloss auf tönernen Füssen. Das Gutachten des Wirtschaftsprüfers Karl Eicke über die Deutsche Arbeitsfront vom 31. Juli 1936* (Munich: Oldenbourg, 2006), 7–94 and Rüdiger Hachtmann, *Das Wirtschaftsimperium der Deutschen Arbeitsfront* (Göttingen: Wallstein, 2012). On the Japanese workers' association Sanpo and its discussion councils after 1939, both modelled on the DAF, see Stephen S. Lange, *Organized Workers and Social Politics in Interwar Japan* (Cambridge University Press, 1981), Sheldon Garon, *The State and Labor in Modern Japan* (Berkeley: University of California Press 1987), Andrew Gordon, *The Evolution of Labor Relations in Japan: Heavy Industry, 1853–1955* (Cambridge, Mass.: Council on East Asian Studies/Harvard University Press, 1988) and Janis Mimura, *Planning for Empire: Reform Bureaucrats and the Japanese Wartime State* (Ithaca: Cornell University Press, 2011).

While the expansion of Fordism as a production regime in the war context has received little scholarly attention, broader studies include information on this topic. See, in particular, Mansel G. Blackford, *The Rise of Modern Business: Great Britain, the United States, Germany, Japan and China* (3rd edn, Chapel Hill: University of North Carolina Press, 2008). On the relationship between forced labour and the Ford production regime, see Rüdiger Hachtmann, 'Fordism and Unfree Labor: Aspects of the Work Deployment of Concentration Camp Prisoners in German Industry between 1941 and 1944', *International Review of Social History* 55:3 (2010), 485–513. On the concept of Fordism, see Rüdiger Hachtmann, 'Fordismus', Docupedia-Zeitgeschichte: Begriffe, Methoden und Debatten der zeithistorischen Forschung, docupedia. de / zg / Fordismus?oldid=84605.

12 Battles for morale
An entangled history of total war in Europe, 1939–1945
Jochen Hellbeck

Since Erich Ludendorff first popularized the term 'total war' in 1935, numerous historians have utilized it to describe the Second World War as a new type of war – one with vaster aims, more fatalities, and a nebulous boundary between front and rear, soldiers and civilians, combatants and non-combatants. Yet most studies remain locked in single national perspectives. One exception is the recent wave of scholarship revisiting the comparison between Nazi Germany and the Soviet Union: Michael Geyer and Sheila Fitzpatrick, eds., *Beyond Totalitarianism: Stalinism and Nazism Compared* (Cambridge University Press, 2009), Michael David-Fox, Peter Holquist and Alexander M. Martin, eds., *Fascination and Enmity: Russia and Germany as Entangled Histories, 1914–1945* (University of Pittsburgh Press, 2012), Gerd Koenen, *Der Russland-Komplex. Die Deutschen und der Osten, 1900–1945* (Munich: Beck, 2005) and Karl Eimermacher and Astrid Volpert, eds., *Verführungen der Gewalt. Russen und Deutsche im Ersten und Zweiten Weltkrieg* (Munich: Fink, 2005). With respect to the war, these studies elucidate the increasing entanglement and brutality of the fighting styles of the Wehrmacht and the Red Army, as well as shed light on the different principles animating the two political regimes – racial modelling in the Nazi case and political universalization on the Soviet side. They also provide valuable insights into the differing prisms through which Germans and Soviet citizens viewed and engaged one another. Still, few studies venture beyond the objects of traditional totalitarian analysis or bring other actors into the comparison. Notable exceptions include Detlef Vogel and Wolfram Wette, eds., *Andere Helme – andere Menschen? Heimaterfahrung und Frontalltag im Zweiten Weltkrieg. Ein internationaler Vergleich* (Essen: Klartext, 1985), Lizzie Collingham, *The Taste of War: World War II and the Battle for Food* (London: Allen Lane, 2011) and Stephen Kotkin, 'World War Two and Labor: A Lost Cause?' *International Labor and Working-Class History* 58 (Fall, 2000), 181–91.

Given how rarely national historiographies on total war engage one another, the numerous similarities in concepts, methodologies and evolution appear particularly striking. Historians of Great Britain, Germany and the Soviet Union and Russia are steeped in similar discussions on popular involvement in the war effort. The term that surfaces with slight variations in each case is the 'people's war'; at issue is whether the term expresses a wartime social reality, a chimera of regime propagandists, or a post-war invention.

Britain ended the war victoriously and the Labour Party reaped the popular benefits of the social compact prepared during the war; consequently, many post-war memoirists and historians unquestioningly accepted the official narrative of wartime unity between British citizens and their government. Angus Calder first called this narrative into question in *The People's War: Britain, 1939–1945* (New York: Pantheon Books, 1969). The government, he argued, did little to prepare its citizenry for war. Under German air attack, ordinary Britons took the initiative, asserting a new, radical popular populist agenda. The post-war government hijacked these populist policies for the purposes of self-legitimation and national consolidation. Following Calder's publication, social historians continued challenging what they believed were overly glossy representations of British society in the Second World War: Nick Tiratsoo, *From Blitz to Blair: A New History of Britain since 1939* (London: Pluto Press, 1997) and Sonya Rose, *Which People's War? National Identity and Citizenship in Wartime Britain, 1939–1945* (Oxford University Press, 2003). Still other scholars turned a critical eye to the claim that most Britons remained apathetic to the war effort. Working in the repertoires of cultural and micro-history, these scholars identify the wartime politics of mobilization as a socially transformative practice. In their view, individual agency and state ideology are mutually constitutive; thus, they locate the generation of popular morale within public and state institutions created to measure and mould it: Robert Mackay, *Half the Battle: Civilian Morale in Britain during the Second World War* (Manchester University Press, 2002) and James Hinton, *The Mass Observers: A History, 1937–1949* (Oxford University Press, 2013).

In Soviet scholarship, wartime unity remained the mantra until the communist regime's collapse. Nikita Khrushchev's 1956 'secret speech', aimed at exposing Stalin as a weak leader, if anything only reinforced the myth of a peoples' war directed by the Communist Party. In the 1990s this myth came under massive attack. Historians flocked to the hitherto closed archives and published countless sources contradicting the traditional Soviet tale of collective mass heroism and selfless devotion. Two particularly impressive documentary collections are V. A. Zolotarev and A. S. Emelin, eds., *Velikaia Otechestvennaia* (Moscow: TERRA, 1993–2002) and I. A. Ioffe and Nina Petrova, eds., *'Molodaia gvardiia' (g. Krasnodon). Khudozhestvennyi obraz i istoricheskaia real'nost'. Sbornik dokumentov i materialov* (Moscow: Veche, 2003). Based primarily on these documentary findings, some revisionist works, such as Catherine Merridale *Ivan's War: Life and Death in the Red Army, 1939–1945* (New York: Metropolitan Books, 2006) have highlighted the Soviet government's use of violence against its citizenry in order to discredit the Soviet narrative as pure propaganda. Yet, in making this claim, these historians lose sight of the fact that the documents of the 'archival revolution' were themselves products of their political time and should not be mistaken for the full historical record. Echoing Calder's populist claims, other historians locate the spirit of a Soviet 'peoples' war' in resistance to the Stalinist government: Robert W. Thurston and Bernd Bonwetsch, eds., *The People's War: Responses to World War II in the Soviet Union* (Urbana: University of Illinois Press, 2000). But, these studies rely largely on sources from the post-Stalin period, and thus may transmit retrospective projections. Like its British counterpart, Russian historiography recently witnessed a counter-revisionist trend; this trend treats ideology as a socially creative force and details how the state and Soviet citizenry jointly elaborated a myth of the 'Great Patriotic War': Lisa A. Kirschenbaum, *The Legacy of the Siege of Leningrad, 1941–1995: Myth, Memories, and Monuments* (Cambridge University Press, 2006), Amir Weiner, *Making Sense of War: The Second World War and the Fate of the Bolshevik Revolution* (Princeton University Press, 2002) and Jochen Hellbeck, *Stalingrad: The City that Defeated the Third Reich* (New York: Public Affairs, 2015).

The experience of total defeat resulted in German scholarship on the Second World War developing a unique slant. As elsewhere, German historiography in the 1960s and 1970s shifted from political to social history. However, the first generation of social historians in Germany, wary of lingering German nostalgia for the Nazi era, avoided engaging the Nazi movement's social and national ideals, preferring to view them as propaganda constructs divorced from reality. More recently, along with a shifting popular perspective on ordinary Germans as perpetrators rather than victims of Nazi rule, a new wave of scholarship has begun investigating the Nazis' popular claims, particularly the concept of *Volksgemeinschaft* (people's community), which connotes unity, consensus and considerable agency. Like British and Russian historiography, these studies eschew distinguishing between state and society and between regime ideology and social reality. Instead, they underscore the degree to which politics, and with it, the materialization of ideological claims, took place as social practice. A notable example is Frank Bajohr and Michael Wildt, eds., *Volksgemeinschaft. Neue Forschungen zur Gesellschaft des Nationalsozialismus* (Frankfurt: Fischer, 2009). Janosch Steuwer reviews this historiographical development in 'Was meint und nützt das Sprechen von der "Volksgemeinschaft"? Neuere Literatur zur Gesellschaftsgeschichte des Nationalsozialismus', *Archiv für Sozialgeschichte* 53 (2013), 487–534. Interestingly, the interpretive weight of this more recent work rests on the early, pre-war years of Nazi rule. How the war – as the final aim of Nazi politics – remade German citizens is broached in Peter Fritzsche, *Life and Death in the Third Reich* (Cambridge, Mass.: The Belknap Press of Harvard University Press, 2008). However, the topic requires further exploration.

The three historiographies would benefit from more engagement with one another, as well as with the historiographies of other belligerent nations. One issue awaiting scrutiny involves techniques for measuring and heightening morale in 'totalitarian' and 'non-totalitarian' states: How did techniques of Mass-Observation compare with those of the *Sicherheitsdienst* and the NKVD? How did they interact? Apart from some suggestive points made in a comparative essay on First World War surveillance – Peter Holquist, '"Information is the Alpha and Omega of Our Work": Bolshevik Surveillance in Its Pan-European Context', *Journal of Modern History* 69:3 (1997), 415–60 – no work exists on the subject. Another question concerns the regimes' imperial realms and the war's global scope. Future studies should address Indian troops and civilian subjects as objects and subjects of British morale campaigns. Additionally, they should compare the imperial practices of the different regimes: How did British policy toward imperial subjects compare with that of Russian leaders toward various groups of non-Russian Soviet citizens? How did it compare with Nazi policy concerning *Gemeinschaftsfremde* in the German context? How did the respective regimes, as well as people on the ground, reach out to colonized people on the other side to legitimize their own war effort and to demoralize their opponents? Ultimately, the history of the Second World War as a total war can only be gauged as a global and entangled history.

13 Hors de combat
Mobilization and immobilization in total war
Geoffrey Cocks

There is no dedicated historical literature per se on those not mobilized in Germany between 1939 and 1945. Major works on the dynamic and dialectical realities of Nazi mobilization of the German populace for war include the ten volumes published by the Militärgeschichtliches Forschungsamt, ed., *Das Deutsche Reich und der Zweite Weltkrieg* (Munich: DVA, 1984–2008) and Adam Tooze, *The Wages of Destruction: The Making and Breaking of the Nazi Economy* (London: Allen Lane, 2006). An exhaustive focus on the extent of and limits to exploitation of foreign labour may be found in Ulrich Herbert, *Fremdarbeiter. Politik und Praxis des 'Ausländer-Einsatzes' in der Kriegswirtschaft des Dritten Reiches* (Berlin: Dietz, 1986).

The role played by health, medicine and illness in mobilization and immobilization is documented in Winfried Süss, *Der 'Volkskörper' im Krieg. Gesundheitsverhältnisse und Krankenmord im nationalsozialistischen Deutschland 1939–1945* (Munich: Oldenbourg, 2003). Geoffrey Campbell Cocks, *The State of Health: Illness in Nazi Germany* (Oxford University Press, 2012) details the policy, practice and experience of health, illness, and medicine as both Nazi resource and individual recourse. Martin K. Sorge, *The Other Price of Hitler's War: German Military and Civilian Losses from World War II* (New York: Greenwood, 1986) provides comprehensive coverage of German war casualties.

Detlev J. K. Peukert, *Volksgenossen und Gemeinschaftsfremde. Anpassung, Ausmerze und Aufbeghren unter dem Nationalsozialismus* (Cologne: Bund Verlag, 1982) considers the extent and limits in everyday life of conformity and exclusion as well as the wide spectrum of nonconformity, refusal, protest, resistance and opposition. The following address specific groups as subjects in and out of German mobilization for total war. Nicole Kramer, *Volksgenossinnen an der Heimatfront. Mobilisierung, Verhalten, Erinnerung* (Göttingen: Vandenhoeck & Ruprecht, 2013) explores the environment and experience of women on the home front. Nicholas Stargardt's *Witnesses of War: Children's Lives under the Nazis* (London: Jonathan Cape, 2005) studies the impact of total war on German children. Christopher Browning, *Ordinary Men: Reserve Police Battalion 101 and the Final Solution in Poland* (2nd edn, New York: HarperCollins, 1998) offers a case study of mobilization of

Holocaust perpetrators that includes the losses in personnel due to physical and mental complaints.

14 The war of the villages
The interwar agrarian crisis and the Second World War
Adam Tooze

For a hugely influential reading of modern history in terms of the agrarian dynamic, see J. Barrington Moore Jr, *Social Origins of Democracy and Dictatorship: Lord and Peasant in the Making of the Modern World* (Boston: Beacon Press, 1966).

On the long-run development of European agricultural protection, see Michael Tracy, *Government and Agriculture in Western Europe, 1880–1988* (London: Harvester Wheatsheaf, 1989) and Niek Koning, *The Failure of Agrarian Capitalism: Agrarian Politics in the United Kingdom, Germany, the Netherlands and the USA, 1846–1919* (London: Routledge, 1994).

On the crisis of the First World War, see Avner Offer, *The First World War: An Agrarian Interpretation* (Oxford: Clarendon Press 1989).

On the land wars that followed the First World War, see David Mitrany, *The Land and the Peasant in Romania: The War and Agrarian Reform, 1917–1921* (Oxford University Press, 1930), Eric R. Wolf, *Peasant Wars of the Twentieth Century* (New York: Harper & Row 1969), Max Sering, ed., *Die agrarischen Umwälzungen im ausserrussischen Osteuropa* (Berlin and Leipzig: Walter de Gruyter, 1930), G. Brenan, *The Spanish Labyrinth* (Cambridge University Press, 1978) and Paul Preston, ed., *Revolution and War in Spain, 1931–1939* (London: Methuen, 1984).

For examples of the interwar economic crisis of global agriculture from either end of Eurasia, see Tirthanakar Roy, 'Roots of Agrarian Crisis in Interwar India: Retrieving a Narrative', *Economic and Political Weekly* 41:52 (2006/7), 5389–400 and Martin Ivanov and Adam Tooze, 'Convergence or Decline on Europe's Southeastern Periphery? Agriculture, Population, and GNP in Bulgaria, 1892–1945', *Journal of Economic History* 67:3 (2007), 672–704.

For accounts of Nazi agricultural policy in the 1930s and 1940, see Adam Tooze, *The Wages of Destruction: The Making and Breaking of the Nazi Economy* (London: Allen Lane, 2006) and Gustavo Corni, *Hitler and the Peasants: Agrarian Policy of the Third Reich, 1930–1939*, trans. David Kerr (New York and Oxford: Berg, 1990).

On Japan, see Kerry Smith, *Time of Crisis: Japan, the Great Depression, and Rural Revitalization* (Cambridge, Mass.: Harvard University Press, 2003) and Penelope Francks, *Rural Economic Development in Japan: From the Nineteenth Century to the Pacific War* (London: Routledge 2006). On Japanese imperialism, Louise Young's *Japan's Total Empire: Manchuria and the Culture of Wartime Imperialism* (Berkeley: University of California Press, 1998) is indispensable. On the post-war period, R. P. Dore's *Land Reform in Japan* (London: Athlone Press 1984) is unsurpassed.

On the Soviet Union, see R. W. Davies and Stephen G. Wheatcroft, *Years of Hunger: Soviet Agriculture, 1931–1933* (Basingstoke: Palgrave Macmillan, 2004) and Lynn Viola, *The Unknown Gulag: The Lost World of Stalin's Special Settlements* (Oxford University Press, 2007).

On the US farming economy during the Second World War, see Ronald E. Seavoy, *The American Peasantry: Southern Agricultural Labor and its Legacy, 1850–1995: A Study in Political Economy* (Westport, Conn.: Greenwood Press, 1999), Pete Daniel, *Breaking the Land: The Transformation of Cotton, Tobacco, and Rice Cultures since 1880* (Urbana: University of Illinois Press, 1985) and Sidney Baldwin, *Poverty and Politics: The Rise and Decline of the Farm Security Administration* (Chapel Hill: University of North Carolina Press, 1968).

On West European agriculture under Nazi occupation the classic reference is Karl Brandt, Otto Schiller and Franz Ahlgrimm, *Management of Agriculture and Food in the German-Occupied and other Areas of Fortress Europe* (Stanford, Calif.: Stanford Food Research Institute, 1953). The state of the art is summarized in Paul Brassley, Yves Segers and Leen Van Molle, eds., *War, Agriculture and Food: Rural Europe from the 1930s to the 1950s* (New York: Routledge, 2012).

The most important recent English-language contribution on the Yugoslav peasant partisans is Melissa K. Bokovoy, *Peasants and Communists: Politics and Ideology in the Yugoslav Countryside, 1941–1953* (University of Pittsburgh Press, 1998).

On China the initial answer to Chalmers Johnson's *Peasant Nationalism and Communist Power: The Emergence of Revolutionary China, 1937–1945* (Stanford University Press, 1962) came from Mark Selden, *China in Revolution: The Yenan Way Revisited* (Armonk: M. E. Sharpe, 1995). The base areas literature that followed was vast and is ably summarized by Suzanne Pepper in her review essay 'The Political Odyssey of an Intellectual Construct: Peasant Nationalism and the Study of China's Revolutionary History: A Review Essay', *Journal of Asian Studies* 63:1 (2004), 105–25.

Much of the recent literature on China in the 1930s and 1940s has shifted focus from the countryside and the communist narrative to focus on the urban spaces, nationalist China and themes of collaboration. An excellent overview is provided by Stephen R. MacKinnon, Diana Lary and Ezra F. Vogel, eds., *China at War: Regions of China, 1937–1945* (Stanford University Press, 2007). Among recent contributions that remain wedded to the classical questions of communism and rural revolution there has been a tendency to widen the focus. Particularly notable are: Dagfinn Gatu, *Village China at War: The Impact of Resistance to Japan, 1937–1945* (Vancouver: UBC Press, 2008), Yung-fa Chen, *Making Revolution: The Communist Movement in Eastern and Central China, 1937–1945* (Berkeley: University of California Press, 1986), David S. Goodman, *Social and Political Change in Revolutionary China: The Taihang Base Area in the War of Resistance to Japan, 1937–1945* (Lanham, Md.: Rowman & Littlefield, 2000) and Odoric Y. K. Wou, *Mobilizing the Masses: Building Revolution in Henan* (Stanford University Press, 1994).

The Indian literature though highly contentious is comparatively underdeveloped. The best overview which skilfully blends history from below with a political grand narrative is Sumit Sarkar, *Modern India, 1885–1947* (Basingstoke: Macmillan, 1989). Sugata Bose develops a distinctive social and economic approach in *Agrarian Bengal: Economy, Social Structure, and Politics, 1919–1947* (Cambridge University Press, 1986) and 'Starvation amidst Plenty: The Making of Famine in Bengal, Honan and Tonkin, 1942–45', *Modern Asian Studies* 24:4 (1990), 699–727.

For a sensible effort to square the circle in India, see Mridula Mukherjee, *Peasants in India's Non-Violent Revolution: Practice and Theory* (New Delhi: Sage, 2004).

On the politics of Quit India, see Francis G. Hutchins, *India's Revolution; Gandhi and the Quit India Movement* (Cambridge, Mass.: Harvard University Press, 1973).

15 Sexuality and sexual violence
Sabine Frühstück

Only since the 1990s has the research agenda of gender and sexuality studies begun to erode traditional historiographies of war, finding that rape in wartime is neither always nor exclusively an act of violence (as opposed to an act of desire). Rather, wartime rape occurs in a number of contexts and often has contradictory motivations and goals. Moreover in order to more fully understand wartime sexual experiences, it is important to broaden the study of sexuality during war beyond analyses of sexual violence and instead examine the full range of wartime sexual relations.

Dagmar Herzog in *Sex After Fascism: Memory and Morality in Twentieth-Century Germany* (Princeton University Press, 2005) proposed the latter. A number of meticulous and powerful studies focus on the former. See, for instance, Birgit Beck's *Wehrmacht und sexuelle Gewalt. Sexualverbrechen vor deutschen Militärgerichten, 1939–1945* (Paderborn: Ferdinand Schöningh, 2004). For close examinations of sexual slavery in concentration camps and beyond, see Barbara Drinck and Chung-Noh Gross, eds., *Erzwungene Prostitution in Kriegs-und Friedenszeiten. Sexuelle Gewalt gegen Frauen und Mädchen* (Bielefeld: Kleine, 2006), Insa Eschebach and Regina Mühlhauser, eds., *Krieg und Geschlecht. Sexuelle Gewalt im Krieg und Sex-Zwangsarbeit in NS-Konzentrationslagern* (Berlin: Metropol, 2008), Sonja M. Hedgepeth and Rochelle G. Saidel, eds., *Sexual Violence against Jewish Women during the Holocaust* (Waltham: Brandeis University Press, 2010) and Dagmar Herzog, ed., *Brutality and Desire: War and Sexuality in Europe's Twentieth Century* (New York: Palgrave Macmillan, 2008).

The Eastern Front, notoriously understudied, received thorough treatment in Wendy J. Gertjejanssen, 'Victims, Heroes, Survivors: Sexual Violence on the Eastern Front During World War II' (PhD dissertation, University of Minnesota, 2004), and in individual chapters of the edited volumes noted above. The Western Front received close attention in Insa Meinen, *Wehrmacht und Prostitution während des Zweiten Weltkrieges im besetzten Frankreich* (Bremen: Edition Temmen, 2002), in several chapters in the previously noted volume by Drinck and Gross, and in Mary Louise Roberts, *What Soldiers Do: Sex and the American GI in World War II France* (Chicago University Press, 2013).

A number of works have brought new light on the war history of homosexuality, including William J. Spurlin, *Lost Intimacies: Rethinking Homosexuality under National Socialism* (New York: Peter Lang, 2009), Leisa D. Meyer, 'The Lesbian Threat: Within the World War II Women's Army Corps', in Nicole Ann Dombrowski, ed., *Women and War in the Twentieth Century: Enlisted with or without Consent* (New York: Garland Publishing, 2004), Allan Bérubé, *Coming Out Under Fire: The History of Gay Men and Women in World War Two* (Chapel Hill: University of North Carolina Press, 2010), Burkhard Jellonnek and Rüdiger Lautmann, eds., *Nationalsozialistischer Terror gegen Homosexuelle: Verdrängt und ungesühnt* (Paderborn: Ferdinand

Schöningh, 2002), Claudia Schoppmann, *Verbotene Verhältnisse. Frauenliebe, 1938–1945* (Berlin: Querverlag, 1999) and the relevant chapters in Franz X. Eder, *Homosexualitäten. Diskurse und Lebenswelten, 1870–1970* (Weitra: Bibliothek der Provinz, 2010). Aaron Belkin's *Bring Me Men: Military Masculinity and the Benign Façade of American Empire, 1898–2001* (Oxford University Press, 2012) weaves these threads together with other sexual issues that have emerged within the US armed forces and beyond. Anson Rabinbach and Sander L. Gilman, eds., *The Third Reich Sourcebook* (Berkeley: University of California Press, 2013) contains numerous relevant primary documents.

The historiography of sex and sexuality in twentieth-century East Asia has yielded a substantial body of scholarship since the early 1990s, including Sabine Frühstück, *Colonizing Sex: Sexuality and Social Control in Modern Japan* (Berkeley: University of California Press, 2003) and Gregory M. Pflugfelder, *Cartographies of Desire: Male–Male Sexuality in Japanese Discourse, 1600–1950* (Berkeley: University of California Press, 1999). The study of wartime sexuality, however, remains heavily focused on the sexual slavery system of the Imperial Japanese Army, ranging from Yūko Suzuki, *Sensōsekinin to jendā: 'Jiyūshugi shikan' to Nihongun 'ianfu' mondai* (Tokyo: Miraisha, 1997), Yoshimi Yoshiaki, *Comfort Women: Sexual Slavery in the Japanese Military during World War II*, trans. Suzanne O'Brien (New York: Columbia University Press, 1995) and Song Yŏn-ok and Kim Yŏng, *Guntai to seibōryoku: Chōsen Hantō no 20-seiki* (Tokyo: Gendai Shiryō Shuppan, 2010) to George Hicks, *The Comfort Women: Japan's Brutal Regime of Enforced Prostitution in the Second World War* (New York: W. W. Norton, 1994), among many other publications. The Nanjing massacre has been assessed, rather controversially, by Iris Chang, *The Rape of Nanking: The Forgotten Holocaust of World War II* (New York: Basic Books, 1997), followed by a flood of works that nuanced or utterly refuted her assertions, most prominently Joshua A. Fogel, *The Nanjing Massacre in History and Historiography* (Berkeley: University of California Press, 2000).

A growing literature tackles various forms of sexual labour during the occupation by US armed forces and beyond. See, for instance, Robert J. Lilly, *Taken by Force: Rape and American GIs in Europe During World War II* (New York: Palgrave Macmillan, 2007) and Maria Höhn and Seungsook Moon, eds., *Over There: Living With the U.S. Military Empire from World War Two to the Present* (Durham, NC: Duke University Press, 2010). For Japan, Yuki Fujime, *Joseishi kara mita Iwakuni Beigun kichi: Hiroshimawan no gunjika to seibōryoku* (Hiroshima: Hiroshima Joseigaku Kenkyujo, 2010) and Sarah

Kovner, *Occupying Power: Sex Workers and Servicemen in Postwar Japan* (Stanford University Press, 2011) represent pioneering works.

16   A war for liberty
On the law of conscientious objection
Jeremy K. Kessler

There is no single, comparative survey of conscientious objection across all Second World War belligerents. The general picture can be reconstructed from three volumes: Peter Brock, *Against the Draft: Essays on Conscientious Objection from the Radical Reformation to the Second World War* (University of Toronto Press, 2006), Peter Brock and Thomas P. Socknat, eds., *Challenge to Mars: Essays on Pacifism from 1918 to 1945* (University of Toronto Press, 1999) and Charles Moskos and John Whiteclay Chambers II, eds., *The New Conscientious Objection: From Sacred to Secular Resistance* (Oxford University Press, 1993).

For comparisons of the law of conscientious objection across the democratic belligerents, see George Flynn, *Conscription & Democracy: The Draft in France, Great Britain, and the United States* (Westport, Conn.: Greenwood Press, 2002), Margaret Levi, *Consent, Dissent, and Patriotism* (Cambridge University Press, 1997), Edward P. Cain, 'Conscientious Objection in France, Britain and the United States', *Comparative Politics* 2:2 (1970), 275–307, Robert S. W. Pollard, 'Conscientious Objection in Great Britain and the Dominions', *Journal of Comparative Legislation and International Law* 28 (1946), 72–82, and Elliot Feldman, 'An Illusion of Power: Military Conscription as a Dilemma of Liberal Democracy in G.B., the U.S., and France' (3 vols., PhD dissertation, Massachusetts Institute of Technology, 1972).

In addition to the material found in the above volumes, the following works provide useful single-country background information.

Australia: J. W. Main, *Conscription: The Australian Debate, 1901–1970* (Melbourne: Cassell, 1970) and Hugh Smith, 'Conscience, Law and the State: Australia's Approach to Conscientious Objection since 1901', *Australian Journal of Politics and History* 35:1 (1989), 13–28.

Great Britain: Rachel Barker, *Conscience, Government, and War: Conscientious Objection in Great Britain, 1939–1945* (London: Routledge, 1982), Brian Bond, *British Military Policy between the Two World Wars* (Oxford: Clarendon Press, 1980), Roger Broad, *Conscription in Britain, 1939–1964: The Militarisation of a Generation* (London: Routledge, 2006), Martin Ceadal, *Pacifism in Britain,*

1914–1945: The Defining of a Faith (Oxford: Clarendon Press, 1980), David Edgerton, *Warfare State: Britain, 1920–1970* (Cambridge University Press, 2005), James McDermott, *British Military Service Tribunals, 1916–1918* (Manchester University Press, 2011) and John Rae, *Conscience and Politics: The British Government and the Conscientious Objector to Military Service, 1916–1919* (Oxford University Press, 1970).

Canada: J. L. Granatstein and J. M. Hitsman, *Broken Promises: A History of Conscription in Canada* (Oxford University Press, 1977), Amy Shaw, *Crisis of Conscience: Conscientious Objection in Canada during the First World War* (Vancouver: University of British Columbia Press, 2009), Thomas P. Socknat, *Witness against War: Pacifism in Canada, 1900–1945* (University of Toronto Press, 1987) and John A. Toews, *Alternative Service in Canada during World War II* (Canadian Conference of the Mennonite Brethren Church, 1959).

France: Anthony Adamthwaite, *France and the Coming of the Second World War, 1936–1939* (London: Frank Cass, 1977), Bernard Boene and Michel L. Martin, eds., *Conscription et armée de métier* (Paris: FEDN, 1991), Alistair Horne, *The French Army and Politics, 1870–1970* (London: Macmillan, 1984), Eugenia C. Kiesling, *Arming against Hitler: France and the Limits of Military Planning* (Lawrence: University Press of Kansas, 1996), Michel Martin, *Warriors to Managers: The French Military Establishment since 1945* (Chapel Hill: University of North Carolina Press, 1981), Eugen Weber, *The Hollow Years: France in the 1930s* (New York: W. W. Norton, 1994), Norman Ingram, 'The Circulaire Chautemps, 1933: The Third Republic Discovers Conscientious Objection', *French Historical Studies* 17 (1991), 387–409 and Michel L. Martin, 'Raison de conscience et raison d'état: L'Objection au service militaire en France', *Annales de l'Université de Toulouse* 31 (1991), 5–23.

Germany: Karsten Bredemeier, *Kriegsdienstverweigerung im Dritten Reich* (Baden-Baden: GRIN Verlag, 1991), Ute Frevert, *A Nation in Barracks: Modern Germany, Military Conscription, and Civil Society* (Oxford: Berg, 2004), Detlef Garbe, *Zwischen Widerstand und Martyrium. Das Zeugen Jehovas im Dritten Reich* (4th edn, Munich: Oldenbourg Verlag, 1999), Albrecht Hartmann and Heidi Hartmann, *Kriegsdienstverweigerung im Dritten Reich* (Frankfurt am Main: Haag & Herchen, 1986) and Adam Tooze, *The Wages of Destruction: The Making and Breaking of the Nazi Economy* (London: Allen Lane, 2006).

New Zealand: Paul Baker, *King and Country Call: New Zealanders, Conscription, and the Great War* (University of Auckland Press, 1988), John Crawford, *Kia Kaha: New Zealand in the Second World War* (Oxford University Press, 2000) and R. L. Weitzel, 'Pacifists and Anti-Militarists in New Zealand, 1909–1914', *New Zealand Journal of History* 7:2 (1973), 128–47.

Russia: Maya Eichler, *Militarizing Men: Gender, Conscription, and War in Post-Soviet Russia* (Stanford University Press, 2012), William Edgerton, *Memoirs of Peasant Tolstoyans in Soviet Russia* (Bloomington: Indiana University Press, 1993), Ellen Jones, *Red Army and Society: A Sociology of the Soviet Military* (Boston: Allen & Unwin, 1985), Joshua A. Sanborn, *Drafting the Russian Nation: Military Conscription, Total War, and Mass Politics, 1905–1925* (Dekalb: Northern Illinois University Press, 2003) and Timothy J. Colton, 'The Impact of the Military on Soviet Society', in Seweryn Bialer, ed., *The Domestic Context of Soviet Foreign Policy* (Boulder: Westview, 1981), pp. 119–38.

USA: Christopher Capozzola, *Uncle Sam Wants You: World War I and the Making of the Modern American Citizen* (Oxford University Press, 2008), John Whiteclay Chambers II, *To Raise an Army: The Draft Comes to America* (New York: Free Press, 1987), J. Garry Clifford and Samuel R. Spencer, Jr, *The First Peacetime Draft* (Lawrence: University Press of Kansas, 1986), Julien Cornell, *The Conscientious Objector and the Law* (New York: John Day, 1944), Cynthia Eller, *Conscientious Objectors and the Second World War* (New York: Praeger, 1991), George Flynn, *The Draft, 1940–1973* (Lawrence: University Press of Kansas, 1993), Joseph Kip Kosek, *Acts of Conscience: Christian Nonviolence and Modern American Democracy* (New York: Columbia University Press, 2011), Nicholas A. Krehbiel, *General Lewis B. Hershey and Conscientious Objection during World War II* (Columbia: University of Missouri Press, 2011), Daniel Kryder, *Divided Arsenal: Race and the American State during World War II* (Cambridge University Press, 2001), Kimberley Phillips, *War! What Is It Good For? Black Freedom Struggles and the U.S. Military from World War II to Iraq* (Chapel Hill: University of North Carolina Press, 2012), Mulford Sibley and Philip Jacob, *Conscription of Conscience: The American State and the Conscientious Objector, 1940–1947* (Ithaca: Cornell University Press, 1952) and James T. Sparrow, *Warfare State: World War II Americans and the Age of Big Government* (Oxford University Press, 2011).

Some of the works cited above cover the First World War period, the crucial precedent for Second World War conscientious objector policies. For an overview of conscientious objection during the First World War, see Martin Ceadel, 'Pacifism', in Jay Winter, ed., *The Cambridge History of World War I*, VOL. II: *The State* (Cambridge University Press, 2014), pp. 576–605. For the international law of conscientious objection that emerged in the wake of the Second World War, see Jeremy K. Kessler, 'The Invention of a Human Right: Conscientious Objection at the United Nations, 1947–2011', *Columbia Human Rights Law Review* 44:3 (2013), 753–91.

For overviews of the draft as a historically specific form of military manpower policy, see Eliot A. Cohen, *Citizens and Soldiers: The Dilemmas of Military Service* (Ithaca: Cornell University Press, 1985) and Daniel Moran and Arthur Waldron, *The People in Arms: Military Myth and National Mobilization since the French Revolution* (Cambridge University Press, 2003). For the decline of the draft, see James J. Sheehan, *Where Have All the Soldiers Gone? The Transformation of Modern Europe* (New York: Houghton Mifflin, 2008).

For the larger debate about administrative governance that framed draft law and policy in the first half of the twentieth century, see Peter Caldwell and William Scheuerman, eds., *From Liberal Democracy to Fascism: Legal and Political Thought in the Weimar Republic* (Boston: Humanities Press, 2000), Daniel R. Ernst, *Tocqueville's Nightmare: The Administrative State Emerges in America, 1900–1940* (Oxford University Press, 2014), Aaron L. Friedberg, *In the Shadow of the Garrison State: America's Anti-Statism and Its Cold War Grand Strategy* (Princeton University Press, 2000), Joanna Grisinger, *The Unwieldy American State: Administrative Politics since the New Deal* (Oxford University Press, 2012), Ira Katznelson, *Fear Itself: The New Deal and the Origins of Our Time* (New York: Liveright, 2013), Marc Stears, *Progressives, Pluralists, and the Problems of the State: Ideologies of Reform in the United States and Britain, 1906–1926* (Oxford University Press, 2002), G. Edward White, *The Constitution and the New Deal* (Cambridge, Mass.: Harvard University Press, 2000), Jay Winter, *Socialism and the Challenge of War: Ideas and Politics in Britain, 1912–18* (London: Routledge, 2014), Jay Winter and Antoine Prost, *René Cassin and Human Rights: From the Great War to the Universal Declaration* (Cambridge University Press, 2013), Peter L. Lindseth, 'Reconciling with the Past: John Willis and the Question of Judicial Review in Interwar and Postwar England', *University of Toronto Law Journal* 55:3 (2005), 657–89, Peter L. Lindseth, 'The Paradox of Parliamentary Supremacy: Delegation, Democracy, and Dictatorship in Germany and France, 1920s–1950s', *Yale Law Journal* 113:7 (2004), 1341–415, Charles C. Maier, 'Leviathan 2.0: Inventing Modern Statehood', in Emily S. Rosenberg, ed., *A World Connecting, 1870–1945* (Cambridge, Mass.: Harvard University Press, 2012), pp. 29–282, Reuel Schiller, 'Reining in the Administrative State: World War II and the Decline of Expert Administration', in Daniel Ernst and Victor Jew, eds., *Total War and the Law: The American Home Front in World War II* (Westport, Conn.: Praeger, 2002), pp. 185–206, Bernardo Sordi, 'Révolution, Rechtsstatt, and the Rule of Law: Historical Reflections on the Emergence of Administrative Law in Europe', in Susan Rose-Ackerman and Peter L. Lindseth, eds., *Comparative Administrative Law* (Northampton, Mass.: Edward Elgar, 2010), pp. 23–36 and Michael

Taggart, 'From "Parliamentary Powers" to Privatization: the Chequered History of Delegated Legislation in the Twentieth Century', University of Toronto Law Journal 55 (2005), 575–627.

17 Against war
Pacifism as collaboration and as resistance
Devin O. Pendas

The historiography of pacifism during the Second World War is surprisingly spotty. Some countries – Great Britain and the USA – are well covered, while others – Russia springs to mind – have barely any coverage at all. Most of the literature covers the longer history of modern pacifism, treating the Second World War as but one, often rather modest, episode outside the main lines of development that connect the vibrant pacifism of the First World War to the Cold War peace movements. Explicit comparisons, much less analyses of transnational networks, are few and far between when it comes to the Second World War era. Above all, what is missing in the historiography is any general treatment of the global history of pacifism during the Second World War.

The geographical disparity of interest can be explained in part by the substantial differences in the political strength of pacifism in various national contexts. The historiography is much better developed for places where pacifists could operate with relative freedom, as compared to the authoritarian countries where pacifism was a repressed, underground activity. The lack of transnational historiography in this field can be explained in part – but only in part – by the fact that the war disrupted and in many cases destroyed existing transnational networks and organizations, such as War Resisters International. Yet the ideas and practices of pacifism remained strikingly transnational in character, even if the ability to maintain contacts across borders was interrupted by the war. Obviously, because pacifism addressed itself primarily to state practices of violence, national context matters, but because the war, by its very nature, was global and destructive of national boundaries, the history of pacifism during the Second World War needs fundamentally to be understood in a transnational and comparative context.

In that regard, the fundamental starting place for the historiography of pacifism is Peter Brock and Thomas P. Socknat, eds., *Challenge to Mars: Essays on Pacifism from 1918 to 1945* (University of Toronto Press, 1999). Though the essays collected here are formulated as national cases studies, and explicit comparisons between the cases are for the most part absent, the volume nevertheless covers the widest range of pacifist activities, and importantly includes many of the minor combatants otherwise overlooked, as well as covering Germany and Japan.

Aside from this volume, the historiography of pacifism remains strikingly bound by national borders. General histories of modern pacifism have been written for many of the major combatant nations involved in the Second World War. For France, see Jean Defrasne, *Le pacifism en France* (Paris: Presses Universitaires de France, 1994) and for Germany, see Karl Holl, *Pazifismus in Deutschland* (Frankfurt: Suhrkamp, 1988). Perhaps unsurprisingly, given the relative prominence of pacifist activity in these countries, Great Britain and the USA have received the greatest coverage. For modern British pacifism, the premier study is Martin Ceadel, *Pacifism in Britain, 1914–1945: The Defining of a Faith* (Oxford: Clarendon Press, 1980). This can be usefully supplemented by Caroline Moorehead's *Troublesome People: The Warriors of Pacifism* (Bethesda: Adler & Adler, 1987). Richard Taylor and Nigel Young, eds, *Campaigns for Peace: British Peace Movements in the Twentieth Century* (Manchester University Press, 1987) collects some useful essays as well, though most do not focus on the Second World War era. For the USA, the equivalent of Ceadel's study is Charles Chatfield, *For Peace and Justice: Pacifism in America, 1914–1941* (Knoxville: University of Tennessee Press, 1971). Christine A. Lunardini's *The American Peace Movement in the Twentieth Century* (Santa Barbara: ABC-Clio, 1994) is also worthwhile. Charles F. Howlett and Robbie Liberman provide a more comprehensive overview in *A History of the American Peace Movement from Colonial Times to the Present* (Lewiston, NY: Edwin Mellen Press, 2008). Japan and Russia, as well as the various smaller powers generally lack these sorts of general histories of pacifism, at least in English, German or French.

These general histories can be usefully supplemented by more specific studies of individuals and organizations. Scott H. Bennett's *Radical Pacifism: The War Resister's League and Gandhian Nonviolence in America, 1915–1963* (Syracuse University Press, 2003) is an excellent institutional history of an important pacifist group. For specific issues, there are some important articles, especially on British pacifism, such as Mark Gilbert's 'Pacifist Attitudes to Nazi Germany, 1936–1946', *Journal of Contemporary History* 27:3 (1992), 493–511 and David C. Luukowitz's 'British Pacifists and Appeasement: The Peace Pledge Union', *Journal of Contemporary History* 9:1 (1974), 115–27. Alongside these specific studies, one might place biographies of various prominent pacifists, whether statesmen such as George Lansbury, or activists such as A. J. Muste. Lansbury has two excellent biographies: Jonathan Schneer,

George Lansbury (Manchester University Press, 1990) and John Shepherd, *George Lansbury: At the Heart of Old Labour* (Oxford University Press, 2002). For Muste, Nat Hentoff's older *Peace Agitator: The Story of A. J. Muste* (New York: Macmillan, 1963) remains useful, but may be complemented by the more recent book by Leilah Danielson, *American Gandhi: A. J. Muste and the History of Radicalism in the Twentieth Century* (Philadelphia: University of Pennsylvania Press, 2014).

Because the historiography of Second World War era pacifism remains so nationally oriented, there are a number of areas where further research would be extremely valuable. Surprisingly, there is no general history of the influence of Gandhi on Western pacifism. Thomas Weber's *Gandhi as Disciple and Mentor* (Cambridge University Press, 2004) has some useful case studies, though these focus on the post-war period when it comes to Western thinkers. It would be also worthwhile to know more about any efforts that were made – at least on a transatlantic basis – to maintain the pre-war networks of pacifist activism. Finally, the connections and disjunctures between First and Second World War era pacifism have been studied for individual countries, especially Great Britain, but a comprehensive history of twentieth-century pacifism remains much to be desired.

18 Humanitarian politics and governance
International responses to the civilian toll in the Second World War
Stephen R. Porter

The historiography of organized civilian relief efforts in the era of the Second World War has been, until recently, relatively thin, with chronology offering a partial explanation. As Jessica Reinisch explains in her introduction to a special issue on the subject in the *Journal of Contemporary History* (43:3, 2008), relief work has been overlooked either as 'a postscript to military encounters or a simple stepping stone to subsequent Cold War clashes' (372). That entire journal issue has been joined by other recent collections in reversing the trend, including, Sharif Gemie, Fiona Reid and Laure Humbert, *Outcast Europe: Refugees and Relief Workers in an Era of Total War, 1936–1948* (London: Continuum, 2012) and *Past & Present* 218:8 (2013). Susan Armstrong-Reid and David Murray, *Armies of Peace: Canada and the UNRRA Years* (University of Toronto Press, 2008) represents one of a handful of useful studies offering a national or regional frame on war relief.

A handful of recent monographs explore the war's aftermath more generally, including Keith Lowe, *Savage Continent: Europe in the Aftermath of World War II* (New York: St. Martin's Press, 2012), Ben Shephard, *The Long Road Home: The Aftermath of the Second World War* (London: Bodley Head, 2010) and William I. Hitchcock, *The Bitter Road to Freedom: A New History of the Liberation of Europe* (New York: Free Press, 2008). On post-war transformations in international institution building, international law and reconstruction, see Elizabeth Borgwardt, *A New Deal for the World: America's Vision for Human Rights* (Cambridge, Mass.: The Belknap Press of Harvard University Press, 2005), Mark Mazower, *No Enchanted Palace: The End of Empire and the Ideological Origins of the United Nations* (Princeton University Press, 2009), Benn Steil, *The Battle of Bretton Woods: John Maynard Keynes, Harry Dexter White, and the Making of a New World* (Princeton University Press, 2013) and Nicolaus Mills, *Winning the Peace: The Marshall Plan and America's Coming of Age as a Superpower* (New York: John Wiley, 2008).

The historiography on the era's refugee affairs boasts a long and impressive lineage. Notable texts include R. M. Douglas, *Orderly and Humane: The Expulsion of Germans after the First World War* (New Haven: Yale University Press, 2012), Jessica Reinisch and Elizabeth White, eds., *The Disentanglement of Populations: Migration, Expulsion and Displacement in Postwar Europe, 1944–1949* (New York: Palgrave Macmillan, 2011), Anna Holian, *Between National Socialism and Soviet Communism: Displaced Persons in Postwar Germany* (Ann Arbor: University of Michigan Press, 2011) and Gerard Daniel Cohen, *In War's Wake: Europe's Displaced Persons in the Postwar Order* (Oxford University Press, 2011). Among some excellent older texts on the issue, see Jacques Vernant, *The Refugee in the Post-War World* (New Haven: Yale University Press, 1953).

The starting point for contemporary texts on UNRRA is George Woodbridge, *UNRRA: The History of the United Nations Relief and Rehabilitation Administration* (3 vols., New York: Columbia University Press, 1950). There exists a wealth of available publications on UNRRA both by the organization itself and member states. The same holds for first-hand accounts by aid workers. Anticipated biases aside, Dean Acheson's *Present at the Creation: My Years in the State Department* (New York: W. W. Norton, 1969) offers an indispensable record of the diplomacy that produced UNRRA.

Until recently, studies of voluntary agencies in the era have been written from 'within the church'. Some offer excellent references for the scholar. As a whole, however, the field evokes the observation by political scientist Michael Barnett that 'all communities get their histories wrong, and the humanitarian community is no exception'. Barnett's *Empire of Humanity: A History of Humanitarianism* (Ithaca: Cornell University Press, 2011), however, is an exceptionally strong piece of scholarship on aid initiatives during the era of the Second World War.

19 Making peace as a project of moral reconstruction
Mark Philip Bradley

On wartime articulations of the project of moral reconstruction, the essential works include Glenda Sluga, *Internationalism in the Age of Nationalism* (Philadelphia: University of Pennsylvania Press, 2013), Elizabeth Borgwardt, *A New Deal for the World: America's Vision for Human Rights* (Cambridge, Mass.: The Belknap Press of Harvard University Press, 2005) and Robert Latham, *The Liberal Moment: Modernity, Security and the Making of Postwar International Order* (New York: Columbia University Press, 1997). For interwar legacies, see Eric D. Weitz, 'From the Vienna to the Paris System: International Politics and the Entangled Histories of Human Rights, Forced Deportations and Civilizing Missions', *American Historical Review* 113:5 (2008), 1313–43, Susan Pedersen, 'Review Essay: Back to the League of Nations', *American Historical Review* 112:4 (2007), 1099–103 and Carole Fink, *Defending the Rights of Others: The Great Power, the Jews and International Minority Protection* (Cambridge University Press 2004). On the American place in the moral reconstruction projects of the 1940s, see Carol Anderson, Eyes *Off the Prize: The United Nations and the African American Struggle for Human Rights, 1944–1955* (Cambridge University Press, 2003) and Mark Philip Bradley, *The United States and the Global Human Rights Imagination* (Cambridge University Press, 2015).

For the history of the Universal Declaration of Human Rights, Mary Ann Glendon, *A World Made New* (New York: Random House, 2001) remains the starting point but is now usefully supplemented by Jay Winter and Antoine Prost, *René Cassin and Human Rights: From the Great War to the Universal Declaration* (Cambridge University Press, 2013). For two contrasting approaches to the making of the European Convention on Human Rights, see A. W. Brian Simpson, *Human Rights and the End of Empire: Britain and the Genesis of the European Convention* (Oxford University Press, 2001) and Marco Duranti, *Human Rights and Conservative Politics in Postwar Europe* (Oxford University Press, 2014). On the Genocide Convention, see Samantha Power, *'A Problem from Hell': America and the Age of Genocide* (New York: Basic Books, 2002) and John Cooper, *Raphael Lemkin and the Struggle for the Genocide*

Convention (Basingstoke: Palgrave Macmillan, 2008). For the freedom of information covenant, see Kenneth Cmiel, 'Human Rights, Freedom of Information, and the Origins of Third-World Solidarity', in Mark Philip Bradley and Patrice Petro eds., *Truth Claims: Representation and Human Rights* (New Brunswick, NJ: Rutgers University Press, 2002), pp. 107–30. The Fourth Geneva Convention and Common Article Three are treated in William A. Hitchcock, 'Human Rights and the Laws of War: The Geneva Convention tions of 1949', in Akira Iriye, Petra Goedde and William I. Hitchcock, eds., *The Human Rights Revolution* (Oxford University Press, 2012), pp. 93–112 and the problem of statelessness is nicely articulated in Linda K. Kerber, 'The Stateless as the Citizen's Other: A View from the United States', *American Historical Review* 112:1 (2007), 1–34. On Nuremberg, Elizabeth Borgwardt's much anticipated book will be transformative but Telford Taylor's first-person account *The Anatomy of the Nuremberg Trials* (New York: Alfred A. Knopf, 1992) remains important as does Geoffrey Robinson's *Crimes Against Humanity: The Struggle for Global Justice* (New York: New Press, 2000) and Arieh Kochavi's *Prelude to Nuremberg: Allied War Crimes Policy and the Questions of Punishment* (Chapel Hill: University of North Carolina Press, 1998). On the Tokyo trials, see Yuma Totani, *The Tokyo War Crimes Trial: The Pursuit of Justice in the Wake of World War II* (Cambridge, Mass.: Harvard University Press, 2008) and Timothy Brook, 'The Tokyo Judgment and the Rape of Nanking', *Journal of Asian Studies* 60:3 (2001), 673–700.

The quotidian dimensions of the post-war project of moral reconstruction emerge in Gerald Daniel Cohen, *In War's Wake: Europe's Displaced Persons in the Postwar Order* (Oxford University Press, 2012), Tara Zahra, *The Lost Children: Reconstituting Europe's Families after World War II* (Cambridge, Mass.: Harvard University Press, 2011), Atina Grossman, *Jews, Germans and Allies: Close Encounters in Occupied Germany* (Princeton University Press, 2009), Pertti Ahonen, *After the Expulsion: West Germany and Eastern Europe 1945–1990* (Oxford University Press, 2004) and Lora Wildenthal, *The Language of Human Rights in West Germany* (Philadelphia: University of Pennsylvania Press, 2013). On the post-war universalization of the Holocaust, see Barbie Zelizer, *Remembering to Forget: Holocaust Memory Through the Camera Eye* (University of Chicago Press, 1998) and G. Daniel Cohen, 'The Holocaust and the "Human Rights Revolution": A Reassessment', in Iriye et al., eds., *The Human Rights Revolution*, pp. 53–72. Growing Cold War inflections in the Soviet use of human rights discourse in the 1940s emerges in Francine Hirsch, 'The Soviets at Nuremberg: International Law, Propaganda and the Making of the Post War Order', *American Historical Review* 113:3 (2008), 701–30 and Jennifer Amos, 'Embracing and Contesting: The Soviet Union and the Universal Declaration of Human Rights, 1948–1958', in Stefan Ludwig-Hoffmann, ed., *Human Rights in the Twentieth Century* (Cambridge University Press, 2010), 147–65. Thoughtful discussions of the broader problems of universalism in this period emerge in Sunil Amrith and Glenda Sluga, 'New Histories of the United Nations', *Journal of World History* 19:3 (2008), 251–74 and Samuel Moyn, 'The First Historian of Human Rights', *American Historical Review* 116:1(2011), 58–79.

For a range of competing interpretative perspectives on decolonization and politics of post-war reconstruction within the global South, see Bradley Simpson, *The First Right: Self-Determination and the Transformation of Post-1941 International Relations* (Oxford University Press, 2015), Roland Burke, *Decolonization and the Evolution of International Human Rights* (Philadelphia: University of Pennsylvania Press, 2010), Jan Eckel, 'Human Rights and Decolonization: New Perspectives and Open Questions', *Humanity* 1.1 (2010), 111–35 and Manu Bhagavan, 'A New Hope: India, the United Nations and the Making of the Universal Declaration of Human Rights', *Modern Asian Studies* 44:2 (2010), 311–47. A very different account of the wider significance of post-war moral reconstruction than the one presented here emerges in Samuel Moyn, *The Last Utopia* (Cambridge, Mass.: Harvard University Press, 2010) and Mark Mazower, *No Enchanted Palace: The End of Empire and the Ideological Origins of the United Nations* (Princeton University Press, 2009).

20 Renegotiating the social contract
Western Europe, Great Britain, Europe and North America
Timothy B. Smith

For roughly twenty years following the end of the Second World War, discussion of the social impact of the conflict was dominated by British observers such as T. H. Marshall and Richard Titmuss. These London School of Economics professors portrayed mid-century Britain in 'end of history' terms – all was best in the best of all possible worlds. The class conflict had been 'abated'. History had reached its end point as the 'social rights' of the twentieth century completed the process of political emancipation begun during the Glorious Revolution. Marshall's 1949 speech-turned-article, 'Citizenship and Social Class', was printed in his 1950 book *Citizenship and Social*

Class and Other Essays (Cambridge University Press, 1950) and reprinted in several collected volumes to this very day. Since the 1950s it has been impossible to write broadly about the Western welfare state without mentioning Marshall. Titmuss's book, *Essays on the Welfare State* (London: George Allen & Unwin, 1951) was also very influential into the 1970s. The classic statement of a wartime and post-war 'consensus' in favour of a larger welfare state was Paul Addison's *The Road to 1945* (London: Jonathan Cape, 1975).

Consensus or not, by the 1960s, it became apparent to a majority of Britons that the war had not, after all, erased class distinctions nor had the post-war welfare state eliminated poverty. As the sociologist Peter Townsend reminded Britons in books and government reports, no amount of 'social rights' could negate the hard reality of economic inequality and limited social mobility. Most damningly, the 1940s welfare state provided 'citizenship' rights, perhaps, but to men not women. Therefore just how 'universal' was the post-war welfare state?, asked Carole Pateman, Jane Lewis and many other scholars. More people started to question the very idea of wartime solidarity and consensus. The issue was debated at length in an entire 1992 edition of the journal *Twentieth Century British History*. Other relevant books include Stephen Brooke, *Labour's War: The Labour Party and the Second World War* (Oxford University Press, 1992) and Stephen Brooke, ed., *Reform and Reconstruction: Britain after the War, 1945–1951* (Manchester University Press, 1995). For a history of post-war welfare reform from a highly sympathetic viewpoint, see the work of Kenneth O. Morgan, including *Labour in Power, 1945–1951* (Oxford University Press, 1984) and *The People's Peace: British History, 1945–1990* (Oxford University Press, 1990). More objective work can be found in the various writings of Rodney Lowe, including 'The Second World War, Consensus and the Foundation of the Welfare State', *Twentieth Century British History* 1:2 (1990), 152–82.

The degree to which Britain changed during the Second World War was a highly politicized question as the country descended into labour unrest, inflation and political impotency during the 1970s. Conservatives rewrote history, suggesting that the war had indeed changed everything, but for the worse. The post-war welfare 'consensus' had been the root of Britain's post-war problems, charged Margaret Thatcher. And court historians like Correlli Barnett supplied the intellectual cover. See Barnett's trilogy, all published by Macmillan: *The Audit of War* (1986), *The Lost Victory* (1995) and *The Verdict of Peace* (2001). More nuanced accounts can be found in the work of Derek Fraser, *The Evolution of the British Welfare State* (3rd edn, Basingstoke: Palgrave Macmillan, 2006), Howard Glennerster, *British Social Policy: 1945 to the Present*

(3rd edn, Oxford University Press, 2007), Rodney Lowe, *The Welfare State in Britain since 1945* (Basingstoke: Palgrave Macmillan, 2005) and Nicholas Timmins, *The Five Giants: A Biography of the Welfare State* (London: HarperCollins, 1995). The best general, comparative study remains Peter Baldwin's *The Politics of Social Solidarity: Class Bases of the European Welfare State, 1875–1975* (Cambridge University Press, 1990).

For the USA, two books are crucial: Jennifer Klein's *For All These Rights: Business, Labor, and the Shaping of America's Public-Private Welfare State* (Princeton University Press, 2003) and Jacob Hacker's *The Divided Welfare State: The Battle over Public and Private Social Benefits in the United States* (Cambridge University Press, 2002). Both books emphasize the degree to which government-underwritten private insurance helped to squeeze out the possibility of universal social programmes and, ultimately, to cement class inequalities.

The various books of Suzanne Mettler, including the widely acclaimed *Soldiers to Citizens: The G.I. Bill and the Making of the Greatest Generation* (Oxford University Press, 2007), are important. A good comparative study is Peter Swenson, *Capitalists against Markets: The Making of Labor Markets and Welfare States in the United States and Sweden* (Oxford University Press, 2002).

Andrew Shennan's *Rethinking France: Plans for Renewal, 1940–1946* (Oxford: Clarendon Press, 1989) is the key text for France. Also useful are Eric Jabbari, *Pierre Laroque and the Welfare State in Postwar France* (Oxford University Press, 2012) and Philippe-Jean Hesse and Jean-Pierre Le Crom, eds., *La protection sociale sous le régime de Vichy* (Presses Universitaires de Rennes, 2001). On Germany, Robert Moeller's *Protecting Motherhood: Women and the Family in the Politics of Postwar West Germany* (Berkeley: University of California Press, 1996) is fascinating. There is also the monumental three-volume study by Johannes Frerich and Martin Frey, *Handbuch der Geschichte der Sozialpolitik in Deutschland* (Munich: Oldenbourg, 1993) and the standard textbook by Heinz Lampert, *Lehrbuch der Sozialpolitik* (7th edn, Berlin: Springer, 2004). For Italy see Maurizio Ferrera, *Il welfare state in Italia* (Bologna: Il Mulino, 1984). On the issue of women during the war and immediate post-war era see Margaret Randolph Higonnet, Jane Jenson, Sonia Michel and Margaret Collins Weitz, eds., *Behind the Lines: Gender and the Two World Wars* (New Haven: Yale University Press, 1989). For Canada see Dennis Guest, *The Emergence of Social Security in Canada* (3rd edn, Vancouver: University of British Columbia Press, 1997) and Dominique Marshall, *The Social Origins of the Welfare State: Quebec Families, Compulsory Education, and Family Allowances, 1940–1945* (Waterloo, Ont.: Wilfrid Laurier University Press, 2006).

21 The rise and fall of central planning
David C. Engerman

There is a large scholarly literature (and even larger polemical one) on central planning, almost all of it organized around national case studies. What follows is a brief overview of relevant literature for the cases examined in this chapter. In the interests of space, these indispensable works are not included in the notes except in reference to specific quotations.

For details on the formation of the Soviet planning apparatus, see the exhaustive works by E. H. Carr (later joined by R. W. Davies) and published by Macmillan, including *The Bolshevik Revolution, 1917–1923* and *Foundations of a Planned Economy, 1926–1929*. The most thorough analysis of Soviet planning over the life of the USSR is a trio of books by Eugène Zaleski, all published by the University of North Carolina Press: *Planning for Economic Growth in the Soviet Union* (1971), *Stalinist Planning for Economic Growth* (1980) and *Planning Reforms in the Soviet Union* (1967). See also Michael Ellman, 'The Rise and Fall of Socialist Planning', in Saul Estrin, Grzegorz W. Kolodko and Milica Uvalic, eds., *Transition and Beyond* (New York: Palgrave Macmillan, 2007), pp. 17–34 and Peter Rutland, *The Myth of the Plan* (London: Hutchinson, 1985).

On France, see Richard Kuisel, *Capitalism and the State in Modern France* (Cambridge University Press, 1981), Stephen Cohen, *Modern Capitalist Planning* (Cambridge, Mass.: Harvard University Press, 1969) and Peter Hall, *Governing the Economy* (Oxford University Press, 1986).

On India, for an overall picture of Indian economic policy, see Francine Frankel, *India's Political Economy* (Princeton University Press, 1977). For incisive accounts on the travails of Indian planning in the 1950s and 1960s, see Vivek Chibber, *Locked in Place* (Princeton University Press, 2003) and two articles by Medha Kudaisya: 'Reforms by Stealth', *South Asia* 25:2 (2002), 216–20 and 'A Mighty Adventure', *Modern Asian Studies* 43:4 (2009), 939–78. On planning's origins in India, see Raghabendra Chattopadhyay, 'The Idea of Planning in India' (PhD dissertation, Australian National University, 1985).

On American planning conceptions before the Second World War, see Guy Alchon, *The Invisible Hand of Planning* (Princeton University Press, 1985) and John Jordan, *Machine-Age Ideology* (Chapel Hill: University of North Carolina Press, 1994).

Scholarship on Second World War economic mobilization is huge – more than can be covered comprehensively here. For overviews, see Alan S. Milward, *War, Economy and Society, 1939–1945* (London: Allen Lane, 1977) and the nation-by-nation essays in Mark Harrison, ed., *The Economics of World War II* (Cambridge University Press, 1998).

Histories of individual national mobilization are impressive in both depth and insight. On the Soviet Union in wartime, see Mark Harrison, *Soviet Planning in Peace and War* (Cambridge University Press, 1985) and John Barber and Mark Harrison, *The Soviet Home Front* (London: Longman, 1991). On the USA, see Alan Brinkley, *The End of Reform* (New York: Vintage, 1996) and Hugh Rockoff, *America's Economic Way of War: War and the US Economy from the Spanish–American War to the Persian Gulf War* (Cambridge University Press, 2012). Two other accounts of American economic mobilization stand above the many others: Paul A. C. Koistinen, *Arsenal of World War II: The Political Economy of American Warfare 1940–1945* (Lawrence: University Press of Kansas, 2004) and Maury Klein, *A Call to Arms: Mobilizing America for World War II* (New York: Bloomsbury, 2013). On Japan, see Janice Mimura, *Planning for Empire: Reform Bureaucrats and the Japanese Wartime State* (Ithaca: Cornell University Press, 2011) and Richard Rice, 'Economic Mobilization in Wartime Japan: Business, Bureaucracy, and Military in Conflict', *Journal of Asian Studies* 38:4 (1979), 689–94. On Germany, see among many excellent works, Adam Tooze, *The Wages of Destruction: The Making and Breaking of the Nazi Economy* (London: Allen Lane, 2006), Avraham Barkai, *Nazi Economics* (New Haven: Yale University Press, 1990) and Alan S. Milward, *The German Economy at War* (London: Athlone Press, 1965).

For ideas of planning – as apart from actual plans – see Daniel Ritschel, *The Politics of Planning* (Oxford: Clarendon Press, 1997), Johanna Bockmann, *Markets in the Name of Socialism* (Stanford University Press, 2011) and Dirk van Laak, 'Planung. Geschichte und Gegenwart des Vorgriffs auf die Zukunft', *Geschichte und Gesellschaft* 34:3 (2008), 305–26.

22 Nationalism, decolonization, geopolitics and the Asian post-war
Rana Mitter

Writing on the post-1945 world tends, for understandable reasons, to concentrate on the emergence of the Cold War. This set of readings tries to identify work that deals more specifically with the legacy of the Second World War as it is reflected in the years immediately after 1945; a related but distinct area. The legacy of the war in Asia is not as well covered in the Anglophone literature as it might be, simply because the field has started to develop in recent years as new sources become available. There is, however, a growing literature on the aftermath of the Japanese empire in Asia. On repatriation of the Japanese who were left behind, see Lori Watt, *When Empire Comes Home: Repatriation and Reintegration in Postwar Japan* (Cambridge, Mass.: Harvard University Asia Center, 2009) and Mariko Asano Tamanoi, *Memory Maps: The State and Manchuria in Postwar Japan* (Honolulu: University of Hawai'i Press, 2009).

The reckoning for the Japanese role in the war is also a growing field. Barak Kushner's *Men to Devils, Devils to Men: Japanese War Crimes and Chinese Justice* is one important new work (Cambridge, Mass.: Harvard University Press, 2014), and a useful collection of essays is Harald Fuess, ed., *The Japanese Empire in East Asia and its Postwar Legacy* (Munich: Iudicium, 1998). The aftermath of the war in Korea is addressed in Sheila Miyoshi Jager, *Brothers at War: The Unending Conflict in Korea* (New York: W. W. Norton, 2013).

Much of the scholarship relating to Mao's China treats the revolution of 1949 as the 'zero hour' of a new Chinese political and social settlement. However, there are fine works on the Chinese civil war, including Odd Arne Westad, *Decisive Encounters: The Chinese Civil War, 1946–1950* (Stanford University Press, 2003) and Suzanne Pepper, *Civil War in China: The Political Struggle 1945–1949* (Lanham, Md.: Rowman & Littlefield, 1999).

On Southeast Asia, Christopher Bayly and Tim Harper's *Forgotten Armies: The End of Britain's Asian Empire* (London: Allen Lane, 2007) gives a compelling account of the emergence of nationalism in British Southeast Asia in the immediate post-war. Vietnam's post-war nationalism is examined in Mark Philip Bradley,*Vietnam at War: The Search for Meaning* (Oxford University Press, 2009) and *Imagining Vietnam and America: The Making of Postcolonial Vietnam, 1919–1950* (Chapel Hill: University of North Carolina Press, 2000). The literature on the aftermath of war in India is also growing. Ramachandra Guha, *India after Gandhi: The History of the World's Largest Democracy* (New York: Harper, 2007), is a comprehensive and thoughtful account of post-war India, and Yasmin Khan's *The Raj at War: India, 1939–1945* (London: Random House, 2015) examines the way in which the war and post-war shaped India.

There is a growing recognition of a transnational element in the politics of post-war Asia. Some of these themes are explored in the essays in Matthew Hilton and Rana Mitter, eds., *Transnational History* (special issue of *Past & Present* 218:8, 2013).

23 Interpretations of catastrophe
German intellectuals on Nazism, genocide and mass destruction
Peter E. Gordon

The idea of the Second World War as an historical catastrophe is sufficiently labile as to rear its head in nearly every genre of history, philosophy, literature and political thought in the latter half of the twentieth century. Inspired in part by Walter Benjamin's essay, 'On the Concept of History', available in English in Walter Benjamin, *Selected Writings*, ed. Howard Eiland and Michael Jennings (Cambridge, Mass.: Harvard University Press, 2006), vol. iv, pp. 389–400, the view that bourgeois society represents the culmination of a millennium-long ascent of instrumental reason uncontrolled by any moral-political commitment became a central theme for Benjamin's colleagues Theodor W. Adorno and Max Horkheimer in their book *Dialectic of Enlightenment: Philosophical Fragments*, ed. Gunzelin Schmid Noerr, trans. Edmund Jephcott (Stanford University Press, 2007). Adorno developed related themes in his own post-war writings, recently collected as Theodor W. Adorno, *Can One Live After Auschwitz? A Philosophical Reader*, ed. Rolf Tiedemann (Stanford University Press, 2003). For the larger history of the Frankfurt School the classic study is Martin Jay, *The Dialectical Imagination: A History of the Frankfurt School and the Institute of Social Research, 1923–1950* (Berkeley: University of California Press, 1996); a more recent study that includes discussion of Jürgen Habermas, the 'second generation' theorist, is Rolf Wiggershaus, *The Frankfurt School: Its History, Theories, and Political Significance*, trans. Michael Robertson (Cambridge, Mass.: MIT Press, 1995).

For an historical overview of how post-war intellectuals in the German Federal Republic coped with the problem of Nazism, see Dirk Moses, *German Intellectuals and the Nazi Past* (Cambridge University Press, 2009). For a cultural historian's view of German intellectual life in Berlin immediately after the defeat of the Third Reich, see Wolfgang Schivelbusch, *In a Cold Crater: Cultural and Intellectual Life in Berlin, 1945–1948* (Berkeley: University of California Press, 1998). A serviceable overview is Mark W. Clark, *Beyond Catastrophe: German Intellectuals and Cultural Renewal after World War II, 1945–1955* (Lanham, Md.: Lexington Books, 2006). Until quite recently, German intellectuals were reluctant to address their own catastrophic experiences during the Allied bombing; this theme received its canonical treatment with the publication of the book by W. G. Sebald, *A Natural History of Destruction*, trans. Anthea Bell (New York: Modern Library, 2004).

A deservedly famous account of what it was like to experience the bombing of Hiroshima is by John Hersey, first published in *The New Yorker* magazine in 1946; later published as *Hiroshima* (New York: Random House, 1989); for a recent attempt to place the events of Hiroshima into a global history of catastrophe and commemoration see Ran Zwigenberg, *Hiroshima: The Origins of Global Memory Culture* (Cambridge University Press, 2014).

Karl Löwith's argument that the 'evils' of the twentieth century are the result of a misapplication of theological and eschatological themes of progress to human affairs can be found in his classic book, *Meaning in History: The Theological Implications of the Philosophy of History* (University of Chicago Press, 1957). A more historical account of 'absolute evil' appears in the third and culminating volume of the classic study by Hannah Arendt, *The Origins of Totalitarianism* (new edn, New York: Harcourt, Brace, Jovanovich, 1973). It has been a topic of much discussion that Arendt later characterized evil not as 'absolute' but as 'banal'. See her famous and controversial book, *Eichmann in Jerusalem: A Report on the Banality of Evil* (London: Penguin, 2006). An illuminating discussion of the apparent change is Richard J. Bernstein, 'Did Hannah Arendt Change Her Mind? From Radical Evil to the Banality of Evil', in Larry May and Jerome Kohn, eds., *Hannah Arendt: Twenty Years Later* (Cambridge, Mass.: MIT Press, 1997), 127–46; for a broader account of the theme of radical evil in modern philosophy, see Richard J. Bernstein, *Radical Evil: A Philosophical Interrogation* (Cambridge: Polity Press, 2002); the classic biographical study is Elisabeth Young-Bruehl, *Hannah Arendt: For Love of the World* (2nd edn, New Haven Yale University Press, 2004). Alongside Arendt's famous and much-contested idea of the 'banality of evil' one should also consult the theme of a 'grey zone' in victims' behaviour in extreme situations, a term coined by survivor Primo Levi in his classic study, *The Drowned and the Saved* (New York: Simon & Shuster, 1988 [1986]). The degradation of the victim in the camps is made into an organizing philosophical and political theme in the work of Giorgio Agamben, for whom the figure of the 'Musselmann'(as described by Primo Levi) becomes the paradigm of modern subjectivity; see Agamben, *Homo Sacer: Sovereign Power and Bare Life* (Stanford University Press, 1998) and *Remnants of Auschwitz: The Witness and the Archive*, trans. Daniel Heller-Roazen (New York: Zone, 2002).

The catastrophes of the Second World War have also inspired metaphysical and theological speculation, where catastrophe and evil are often closely intertwined. See, for example, the collection of essays on this theme by Hans

Jonas, *Mortality and Morality: A Search for Good After Auschwitz*, ed. Lawrence Vogel (Evanston, Ill.: Northwestern University Press, 1996); a different perspective can be found in Richard Rubinstein, *After Auschwitz: History, Theology, and Contemporary Judaism* (2nd edn, Baltimore: Johns Hopkins University Press, 1992) and Eliezer Berkovits, *Faith After the Holocaust* (New York: Ktav, 1997); for a general study of Jewish theology after the Holocaust, see Zachary Braiterman, *(God) After Auschwitz* (Princeton University Press, 1998); a fine anthology on the topic is Steven T. Katz, ed., *The Impact of the Holocaust on Jewish Theology* (New York University Press, 2007). The catastrophic violence visited upon European Jewry has also played a crucial role in the reorientation of Christian theology, and it influenced the profound changes in Catholic doctrine leading up to the reforms of Vatican II. On this topic see John Connelly *From Enemy to Brother: The Revolution in Catholic Teaching on the Jews, 1933–1965* (Cambridge, Mass.: Harvard University Press, 2012). In a post-theological mode, the catastrophes of the twentieth century have also played a major role in recent French philosophy; see, for example, Maurice Blanchot, *The Writing of the Disaster*, trans. Ann Smock (orig. *L'Ecriture du désastre*, 1980; in English, University of Nebraska Press, 1995); and also see Jean-François Lyotard, *The Différend: Phrases in Dispute*, trans. Georges Van Den Abbeele (Minneapolis: University of Minnesota Press, 1988). In such texts the very idea of a specific historical catastrophe threatens to dissolve into generalized themes of sublimity and unintelligibility. This trend, an ambivalent conclusion to the secularization of the idea of evil, culminates in an unworkable paradox: in a misplaced attempt to assign catastrophe a universal significance, the interpretation of human events is wholly disabled.

24 The ghosts of war
Monica Black

Literature on the ghosts of the Second World War is virtually non-existent. Luckily, we do have a small number of excellent examples of such literature from other modern wars. Heonik Kwon, *Ghosts of War in Vietnam* (Cambridge University Press, 2008) is an outstanding, profound, methodologically rich study of this topic. Jay Winter's *Sites of Memory, Sites of Mourning: The Great War in European Cultural History* (Cambridge University Press, 1995), is a landmark in the literature on the social impact of death in France, Britain and Germany after the First World War, and traces, among many other things, survivors' attempts to contact the spirit world.

If little work has been done on interactions between the living and the ghosts of the dead of war, there are a number of crucial works that deal with military death in the World Wars, its social and cultural repercussions, and attempts to memorialize it. On Germany specifically, see Utz Jeggle, 'In stolzer Trauer. Umgangsformen mit dem Kriegstod während des 2. Weltkriegs', *Tübinger Beiträge zur Volkskultur* (September 1986), 242–59, and the always-evocative essays of Michael Geyer, especially: 'The Place of the Second World War in German History and Memory', *New German Critique* 71 (1997), 5–40, 'Insurrectionary Warfare: The German Debate about a *Levée en Masse* in October 1918', *Journal of Modern History* 73 (2001), 459–527 and 'Vom Fortleben der Toten: Überlegungen zu einer Geschichte der Kriegstoten', in Belinda Davis, Thomas Lindenberger and Michael Wildt, eds., *Alltag, Erfahrung, Eigensinn. Historisch-anthropologische Erkundungen* (Frankfurt am Main: Campus, 2008). Alf Lüdtke, 'Histories of Mourning: Flowers and Stones for the War Dead, Confusion for the Living – Vignettes from East and West Germany', in Gerald Sider and Gavin Smith, eds., *Between History and Histories: The Making of Silences and Commemorations* (University of Toronto Press, 1997), pp. 149–79, deals with the uneasy (and fascinating) issue of commemorating Second World War deaths in East and West Germany.

For a wide-ranging treatment of attempts to lend meaning to soldiers' deaths after the World Wars, see George Mosse's now-classic *Fallen Soldiers: Reshaping the Memory of the World Wars* (Oxford University Press, 1990). Mosse focuses on Germany but also makes excursions into Italy, France and England. How Romanians dealt with war death from the eve of the First World War to the post-communist period is taken up by Maria Bucur, *Heroes and Victims: Remembering War in Twentieth-Century Romania* (Bloomington: Indiana University Press, 2009). Why dead bodies – many of them corpses linked to the World Wars – became central to politics in the post-socialist Balkans is the theme of Katherine Verdery, *The Political Lives of Dead Bodies: Reburial and Postsocialist Change* (New York: Columbia University Press, 1999).

On the connection between commemorations of war death and national identity, see Reinhart Koselleck, 'Kriegerdenkmale als Identitätsstiftungen der Überlebenden', in Odo Marquard and Karlheinz Stierle, eds., *Identität* (Munich: Wilhelm Fink Verlag, 1979), pp. 255–76. Benedict Anderson, *Imagined Communities* (London: Verso, 1983) discusses the centrality for nationalism of the cult of the unknown soldier.

For a longer-term look at how Europeans have perceived war death, see Klaus Latzel, *Vom Sterben im Krieg. Wandlungen in der Einstellung zum Soldatentod vom Siebenjährigen Krieg bis zum II. Weltkrieg* (Warendorf: Verlag Fahlbusch & Co., 1988). Luc Capdevila and Danièle Voldman, *War Dead: Western Societies and the Casualties of War* (Edinburgh University Press, 2006) examines how societies in Europe, the USA and South America have dealt with the dead of war in a great variety of conflicts, including the World Wars.

We do not yet have a study that seeks to analyse or interpret – from an anthropological-historical perspective – the rituals or practices of death in Nazi camps during the Holocaust. However, parts of Inga Clendinnen, *Reading the Holocaust* (Cambridge University Press, 1999) are highly suggestive in this regard. Gabriel Finder writes about early forms of memorialization of Jewish dead by survivors. See 'Yizkor! Commemoration of the Dead by Jewish Displaced Persons in Postwar Germany', in Alon Confino, Paul Betts and Dirk Schumann, eds., *Between Mass Death and Individual Loss: The Place of the Dead in Twentieth-Century Germany* (New York: Berghahn Books, 2008), pp. 232–58.

Concerning various rites of death and burial in Germany from the First World War to the post-1945 period – not only where soldiers but also civilians were concerned – see Monica Black, *Death in Berlin: From Weimar to Divided Germany* (Cambridge University Press, 2010) and many of the essays in Confino et al., eds. *Between Mass Death and Individual Loss*. For a wonderfully wide-ranging and poetically conceived examination of the meaning and practices of death – and not infrequently, mass death – in Russia and the Soviet Union over the entirety of the twentieth century, see Catherine Merridale, *Night of Stone: Death and Memory in Twentieth-Century Russia* (New York: Penguin, 2000). Alexander Etkind, *Warped Mourning: Stories of the Undead in the Land of the Unburied* (Stanford University Press, 2013), explores the distinctive memorial practices Russians have devised to deal with the haunting presence of Stalinist terror and mass death in post-Soviet life.

Though this chapter has focused largely on Germany and Europe, the material discussed suggests the possibility of doing similar kinds of work in other parts of the world. As Kwon argues, 'War in my home and war in their home seem to be two quite different historical grounds for ... the cultural production of ghosts' (*Ghosts of War*, p. 14). When war was nearly everywhere, we may find the ghosts of war almost anywhere we look.

25 Popular memory, popular culture
The war in the post-war world
Lucy Noakes

Geoff Eley's work provides a considered overview of the shifts in the popular memory of the war. 'The Past under Erasure? History, Memory and the Contemporary', *Journal of Contemporary History* 46:3 (2011), 555–73, considers the complex relationship between memory and history with regard to post-war Germany, while 'Finding the People's War: Film, British Collective Memories and World War II', *American Historical Review* 106:3 (2001), 818–38, remains an invaluable text. Eley has written the foreword to Lucy Noakes and Juliette Pattinson, eds., *British Cultural Memory and the Second World War* (London: Bloomsbury, 2013) and to Martin Evans and Kenn Lunn, eds., *War and Memory in the 20th Century* (Oxford: Berg, 1997). For memory of the war in France, see Henri Rousso, *The Vichy Syndrome: History and Memory in France Since 1944* (Cambridge, Mass.: Harvard University Press, 1991); for the USA, see John Bodnar, *The 'Good War' in American History* (Baltimore: Johns Hopkins University Press, 2010) and Michael C. Adams, *The Best War Ever: America and World War II* (Baltimore: Johns Hopkins University Press, 1994); for Japan, see Philip Seaton, *Japan's Contested War Memories: The 'Memory Rifts' in Historical Consciousness of World War II* (Abingdon: Routledge, 2007), and for Russia and Germany see Arja Rosenholm and Withold Bonner, eds., *Recalling the Past: (Re)constructing the Past. Collective and Individual Memory of World War II in Russia and Germany* (Helsinki: Aleksanteri Institute, 2008). Tony Judt's 'The Past is Another Country: Myth and Memory in Post-War Europe', *Daedalus* 121:4 (1992), 83–118, is a thoughtful early reflection on changes to European memories of the war during and after the Cold War, brought up to date by Dan Stone's 'Memory Wars in the "New Europe"', in D. Stone, ed., *The Oxford Handbook of Postwar European History* (Oxford University Press, 2012), pp. 714–32.

For overviews of memory theory see Susannah Radstone and Bill Schwarz, eds., *Memory: Histories, Theories, Debates* (New York: Fordham University Press, 2010) and the journal *History and Memory* (Indiana University Press). The original and most detailed exposition of popular memory theory, one of many competing approaches to memory in an ever-proliferating field is The Popular Memory Group, 'Popular Memory: Theory, Politics, Method', in Richard Johnson, Gregor McLennan, Bill Schwarz and David Sutton, eds., *Making Histories: Studies in History Writing and Politics* (London: Hutchinson, 1982), pp. 205–52.

26 The Second World War in global memory space
Jie-Hyun Lim

A synthetic overview of the Second World War in the global memory space is still to be found. There are some pioneering works of comparative studies of memories. See Ian Buruma, *The Wages of Guilt: Memories of War in Germany and Japan* (New York: Farrar, Straus & Giroux, 1994), Omer Bartov, Atina Grossmann and Mary Nolan, eds., *Crimes of War: Guilt and Denial in the Twentieth Century* (New York: New Press, 2002) and Ian Buruma, *Year Zero: A History of 1945* (New York: Penguin, 2013). Some articles in Aleida Assmann and Sebastian Conrad, eds., *Memory in a Global Age: Discourses, Practices and Trajectories* (Basingstoke: Palgrave Macmillan, 2010) are suggestive too. Jie-Hyun Lim, Barbara Walker and Peter Lambert, eds., *Mass Dictatorship and Memory as Ever Present Past* (Basingstoke: Palgrave Macmillan, 2014) focuses on memories of dictatorships across the globe.

For the cross-referencing of the Holocaust and postcolonial memory, Michael Rothberg's *Multidirectional Memory: Remembering the Holocaust in the Age of Decolonization* (Stanford University Press, 2009) is outstanding. His concept of multidirectional memory can be regarded as an alternative to the cosmopolitanization of memory by Daniel Levy and Natan Sznaider, *The Holocaust and Memory in the Global Age*, trans. Assenka Oksiloff (Philadelphia: Temple University Press, 2006). Peter Novick, *The Holocaust in American Life* (Boston: Houghton Mifflin, 1999) can be referred to also.

For comparative studies of memory in the Asia-Pacific region, see T. Fujitani, Geoffrey M. White and Lisa Yoneyama, eds., *Perilous Memories: The Asia-Pacific War(s)* (Durham, NC: Duke University Press, 2001) and S. M. Jager and R. Mitter, eds., *Ruptured Histories: War, Memory, and the Post-Cold War in Asia* (Cambridge, Mass.: Harvard University Press, 2007). Focused on Japanese memories within the transnational perspective are Lisa Yoneyama, *Hiroshima Traces: Time, Space, and the Dialectics of Memory* (Berkeley: University of California Press, 1999) and James Orr, *The Victim as Hero: Ideologies of Peace and National Identity in Postwar Japan* (Honolulu: University of Hawai'i Press, 2001). Tetsuya Takashi's *Kokka to Gisei* [State and Sacrifice] (Tokyo: Japan Broadcast Publishing Company, 2008) and *Yasukuni Mondai* [Yasukuni Question] (Tokyo: Chikuma Shobo, 2005) can be read together with George L. Mosse, *Fallen Soldiers: Reshaping the Memory of the World Wars* (Oxford University Press, 1990).

For European memories, Monika Flacke, *Mythen der Nationen: 1945–Arena der Erinnerungen* (2 vols., Berlin: Deutsches Historisches Museum, 2004), is most comprehensive, but a compilation of national memories. Pieter Lagrou,

The Legacy of Nazi Occupation: Patriotic Memory and National Recovery in Western Europe, 1945–1965 (Cambridge University Press, 2000) and Konrad H. Jarausch and Thomas Lindenberg, eds., *Conflicted Memories: Europeanizing Contemporary History* (New York: Berghahn Books, 2007) deal with West European memories. István Deák, Jan T. Gross and Tony Judt, eds., *The Politics of Retribution in Europe: World War II and Its Aftermath* (Princeton University Press, 2000) is more East European memory oriented. Robert G. Moeller, *War Stories: The Search for a Usable Past in the Federal Republic of Germany* (Berkeley: University of California Press, 2001), Jeffrey Herf, *Divided Memory: The Nazi Past in the Two Germanys* (Cambridge, Mass.: Harvard University Press, 1997) and Bill Niven, ed., *Germans as Victims: Remembering the Past in Contemporary Germany* (Basingstoke: Palgrave Macmillan, 2006) are highly suggestive for memory in Germany.

Michal Brumlik and Karol Sauerland, eds., *Umdeuten, verschweigen, erinnern. Die spaete Aufarbeitung des Holocaust in Osteuropa* (Frankfurt am Main: Campus Verlag, 2010) surveys rather comprehensively *Historikerstreit* in Eastern Europe. As for the Polish *Historikerstreit*, see Paweł Machcewicz and Krzysztof Persak, eds., *Wokół Jedwabnego: Studia* [About Jedwabne: Studies] (Warsaw: IPN, 2002), Antony Polonsky and Joanna B. Michlik, eds., *The Neighbors Respond: The Controversy over the Jedwabne Massacre in Poland* (Princeton University Press, 2004) and Mariusz Gądek, *Wokół Strach: Dyskusja o Książce Jana T. Grossa* [About Fear: Discussion of Jan Gross's Book] (Kraków: Znak, 2008). Piotr Forecki, *Od Shoah do Strachu: spory o polsko-zydowską przeszłość i pamięć w debatach publicznych* [From Shoa to Fear: Controversies on Polish-Jewish Past and Memory in Public Debates] (Poznań: Wydawnictwo Poznańskie, 2010) provides a balanced analysis.

27 Landscapes of destruction
Capturing images and creating memory through photography
Dorothee Brantz

Even though the rise of photography was tightly linked to warfare from the beginning, research into the history of wartime photography is still scarce. Valuable overviews are given by Gerhard Paul, *Bilder des Krieges, Krieg der Bilder. Die Visualisierung des mordernen Krieges* (Paderborn: Schöningh, 2004), Gerhard Paul, ed., *Das Jahrhundert der Bilder: 1900–1949* (Göttingen: Vandenhoeck & Ruprecht, 2009), Anton Holzer, ed., *Mit der Kamera bewaffnet. Krieg und Fotografie* (Marburg: Jonas Verlag, 2003) and Anne Wiles Tucker and Will Michels, eds., *War/Photography: Images of Armed Conflict and its Aftermath* (New Haven: Yale University Press, 2012). One can also find a number of relevant articles in the journals *History of Photography* and *Fotogeschichte* (especially in the special issue *Krieg und Fotografie* 85 (2002). An important essay that initially opened up this field is Bernd Hüppauf's 'The Emergence of Modern War Imagery in Early Photography', *History and Memory* 5:1 (1993), 30–51. Susan Sonntag's *Regarding the Pain of Others* (New York: Farrar, Straus & Giroux, 2003) is a key text for understanding the troubled relationship between human suffering and its visual representations.

Books about or by wartime correspondents are of course a rich source of information; see among others Margaret Bourke-White, *Moments in History* (New York: DAP, 2013), Rémy Desquesnes, *Witness: Magnum Photographs from the Front Line of World War II* (Paris: Flammarion, 2009), Jean Lacouture, *Robert Capa, 1913–1954* (New York: Thames & Hudson, 2008) and Antony Penrose, ed., *Lee Miller's War: Photographer and Correspondent with the Allies in Europe, 1944–1945* (London: Thames & Hudson, 2005). The German-Russian Museum in Berlin Karlshorst has published a series of works by Russian Second World War photographers, among them Museum Berlin-Karlshorst, ed., *Das mitfühlende Objektiv. Michail Sawin, Kriegsfotografie 1941–1945* (Berlin: Elefanten Press, 1998), Margot Blank, ed., *Michail Trachman: Kriegsfotografie 1941–1945* (Berlin: Espresso Verlag, 2002) and Museum Berlin-Karlshorst, ed., *Nach Berlin! Timofej Melnik, Kriegsfotografie 1941–1945* (Berlin: Elefanten Press, 1998). Books on photographers who documented the destruction of German cities include Marc Barbey, ed., *Hommage à Berlin. Hein Gorny, Adolph C. Byers, Friedrich Seidenstücker, Photographien 1945–1946* (Berlin: Collection Regard, 2011), Klaus Honnef and Walter Müller, eds., *Hermann Claasen, Nie wieder Krieg!: Bilder aus dem zerstörten Köln* (Cologne: Wienand, 1994) and Richard Peter, *Dresden: Eine Kamera klagt an* (Dresden: Dresdener Verlagsgesellschaft, 1949).

For the history of wartime photography in the USA and Great Britain, see Peter Maslowski, *Armed with Cameras: The American Military Photographers of World War II* (New York: Free Press, 1993), Susan D. Moeller, *Shooting War: Photography and the American Experience of Combat* (New York: Basic Books, 1989) and Fred McGlade, *The History of the British Army Film & Photographic Unit in the Second World War* (Solihull: Helion & Co., 2010). On Japan, see especially Julia A. Thomas, 'Landscape's Mediation between History and Memory: A Revisualization of Japan's (War-Time) Past', *East Asian History*

36 (2008) and Julia A. Thomas, 'Photography, National Identity, and the "Cataract of Times": Wartime Images and the Case of Japan', *American Historical Review* 103 (1998), 1475–501.

One crucial issue in the history of war photography is the reception and use of images. In relation to the Holocaust, this has been discussed by Susan A. Crane, 'Choosing Not to Look: Representation, Repatriation, and Holocaust Atrocity Photography', *History and Theory* 47 (2008), 309–30, Habo Knoch, *Die Tat als Bild. Fotografien des Holocaust in der deutschen Erinnerungskultur* (Hamburg: Hamburger Edition, 2001) and Janina Struk, *Photographing the Holocaust: Interpretations of the Evidence* (London: I. B. Tauris, 2004). The role of visual images in post-war reconstruction is examined in Dagmar Barnouw, *Germany 1945: Views of War and Violence* (Bloomington: Indiana University Press, 1996), Davide Deriu, 'Picturing Ruinscapes: The Aerial Photograph as Image of Historical Trauma', in Frances Guerin and Roger Hallas, eds., *The Image and the Witness: Trauma, Memory and Visual Culture* (London: Wallflower Press, 2007), pp. 189–203, Steven Hoelscher, '"Dresden, a Camera Accuses": Rubble Photography and the Politics of Memory in a Divided Germany', *History of Photography* 36 (2012), 288–305 and Yohikuni Igarashi, *Bodies of Memory: Narratives of War in Postwar Japanese Culture, 1945–1970* (Princeton University Press, 2000).

Up to now, there are no works that focus on war and landscape photography, but Sonja Dümpelmann's *Flights of Imagination: Aviation, Landscape, Design* (Charlottesville: University of Virginia Press, 2014) and Jeanne Haffner's *The View from Above: The Science of Social Space* (Cambridge, Mass.: MIT Press, 2013) discuss the relevance of wartime aerial photography for the study of landscapes. On the environmental history of the Second World War, more generally, see the bibliographical essay by Chris Pearson in this volume.

Overall, the conceptual and empirical interrelationships among photography, war and landscape offer a rich, yet underdeveloped, arena for investigation into the transnational history of the role of the environment in visual representations and in the history and memory of warfare.

Index